THE GOSPEL ACCORDI

# LUKE

## VOLUME 4

# THE
# PREACHER'S
# OUTLINE & SERMON
# BIBLE™

THE GOSPEL ACCORDING TO

# LUKE

VOLUME 4

# THE
# PREACHER'S
# OUTLINE & SERMON
# BIBLE®

NEW TESTAMENT

KING JAMES VERSION

Leadership Ministries Worldwide
Chattanooga, TN

*The Preacher's Outline & Sermon Bible*® is written for God's people to use in their preparation for preaching and teaching.  Leadership Ministries Worldwide wants God's people to use *The Preacher's Outline & Sermon Bible*®.  The purpose of the copyright is to prevent the reproduction, misuse, and abuse of the material.

May our Lord bless us all as we preach, teach, and write for Him, fulfilling His great commission to make disciples of all nations.

Please address all requests for information or permission to:
Leadership Ministries Worldwide
PO Box 21310
Chattanooga, TN  37424-0310
Ph.# (423) 855-2181   FAX (423) 855-8616   E-Mail info@outlinebible.org
http://www.outlinebible.org

Library of Congress Catalog Card Number: 96-75921
International Standard Book Number: 1-57407-004-5

Printed in the United States of America

3   4   5               00   01   02

Publisher &
Distributer

## DEDICATED:

To all the men and women of the world
who preach and teach the Gospel of our
Lord Jesus Christ
and
To the Mercy and Grace of God.

————————— & —————————

- Demonstrated to us in Christ Jesus our Lord.

  "In whom we have redemption through His
  blood, the forgiveness of sins, according to the
  riches of His grace." (Eph. 1:7)

- Out of the mercy and grace of God His Word has
  flowed. Let every person know that God will have
  mercy upon him, forgiving and using him to fulfill
  His glorious plan of salvation.

  "For God so loved the world, that he gave his only
  begotten Son, that whosoever believeth in him should
  not perish, but have everlasting life. For God sent not
  his Son into the world to condemn the world; but that
  the world through him might be saved." (Jn 3:16-17)

  "For this is good and acceptable in the sight of God
  our Saviour; who will have all men to be saved, and to
  come unto the knowledge of the truth." (I Tim. 2:3-4)

————————— & —————————

**The Preacher's Outline and Study Bible®**
is written for God's people to use
in their study and teaching of God's Holy Word.

9/98

# OUTLINE BIBLE RESOURCES

This material, like similar works, has come from imperfect man and is thus susceptible to human error. We are nevertheless grateful to God for both calling us and empowering us through His Holy Spirit to undertake this task. Because of His goodness and grace **The Preacher's Outline & Sermon Bible®** - New Testament is complete in 14 volumes, and the Old Testament volumes release periodically. **The Minister's Handbook** is available and *OUTLINE* Bible materials are releasing electonically on **POSB-CD** and our **Web site**.

God has given the strength and stamina to bring us this far. Our confidence is that, as we keep our eyes on Him and grounded in the undeniable truths of the Word, we will continue working through the Old Testament volumes and the second series known as **The Teacher's Outline & Study Bible.** The future includes helpful *Outline Bible* books and **Handbook** materials for God's dear servants.

To everyone everywhere who preaches and teaches the Word, we offer this material firstly to Him in whose name we labor and serve, and for whose glory it has been produced.

Our daily prayer is that each volume will lead thousands, millions, yes even billions, into a better understanding of the Holy Scriptures and a fuller knowledge of Jesus Christ the incarnate Word, of whom the Scriptures so faithfully testify.

> As you have purchased this volume, you will be pleased to know that a small portion of the price you have paid has gone to underwrite and provide similar volumes in other languages (Russian, Korean, Spanish and others yet to come) — To a preacher, pastor, lay leader, or Bible student somewhere around the world, who will present God's message with clarity, authority, and understanding beyond their own. *Amen*.

For information and prices, kindly contact your *OUTLINE* Bible bookseller or:

*LEADERSHIP*
*MINISTRIES*
*WORLDWIDE*

P.O. Box 21310, 515 Airport Road, Suite 107
Chattanooga, TN 37424-0310
(423) 855-2181 FAX (423) 855-8616
E-Mail - outlinebible@compuserve.com
www.outlinebible.org — *FREE* download materials          9/98

**PUBLISHER & DISTRIBUTOR OF OUTLINE BIBLE MATERIALS**

## Currently Available Materials, with New Volumes Releasing Regularly

- **THE PREACHER'S OUTLINE & SERMON BIBLE®** — DELUXE EDITION

- **THE PREACHER'S OUTLINE & SERMON BIBLE®** —  OLD TESTAMENT

- **THE PREACHER'S OUTLINE & SERMON BIBLE®** — SOFTBOUND EDITION
  Identical content as Deluxe above. Lightweight, compact, and affordable for overseas & traveling

- **THE PREACHER'S OUTLINE & SERMON BIBLE®** — 3 VOL HARDCOVER w/CD

- **THE PREACHER'S OUTLINE & SERMON BIBLE®** — NIV SOFTBOUND EDITION

- **The Minister's Personal Handbook - What the Bible Says...to the Minister**
  12 Chapters - 127 Subjects - 400 Verses *OUTLINED* - Paperback, Leatherette, 3-ring

- **THE TEACHER'S OUTLINE & STUDY BIBLE™ • New Testament Books •**
  Complete 45 minute lessons - 4 months of studies/book; 200± pages - Student Journal Guides

- **OUTLINE Bible Studies series: 10 Commandments - The Tabernacle**

- **Practical Word Studies: New Testament - 2,000 Key Words Made Easy**

- **CD-ROM: Preacher, Teacher, and Handbook-** (Windows/STEP) - **WORD**Search

- **Translations of Preacher, Teacher, and Minister's Handbook:** Limited Quantities
  *Russian — Spanish — Korean* Future: French, Portuguese, Hindi, Chinese
  — *Contact us for Specific Language Availability and Prices* —

## For quantity orders and information, please contact either:

LEADERSHIP MINISTRIES WORLDWIDE            *Your OUTLINE Bible Bookseller*
PO Box 21310
Chattanooga, TN  37424-0310
(423) 855-2181  (9am - 5pm Eastern) • FAX  (423) 855-8616 (24 hours)
E•Mail - outlinebible@compuserve.com.
➥  FREE Download Sample Pages — www.outlinebible.org

• *Equipping God's Servants Worldwide with OUTLINE Bible Materials* •
LMW is a nonprofit, international, nondenominational mission agency    9/98

# ACKNOWLEDGMENTS

Every child of God is precious to the Lord and deeply loved. And every child as a servant of the Lord touches the lives of those who come in contact with him or his ministry. The writing ministry of the following servants have touched this work, and we are grateful that God brought their writings our way. We hereby acknowledge their ministry to us, being fully aware that there are so many others down through the years whose writings have touched our lives and who deserve mention, but the weaknesses of our minds have caused them to fade from memory. May our wonderful Lord continue to bless the ministry of these dear servants, and the ministry of us all as we diligently labor to reach the world for Christ and to meet the desperate needs of those who suffer so much.

## THE GREEK SOURCES

1       Expositor's Greek Testament, Edited by W. Robertson Nicoll. Grand Rapids, MI: Eerdmans Publishing Co., 1970

2.      Robertson, A.T. Word Pictures in the New Testament. Nashville, TN: Broadman Press, 1930.

3.      Thayer, Joseph Henry. Greek-English Lexicon of the New Testament. New York: American Book Co, No date listed.

4.      Vincent, Marvin R. Word Studies in the New Testament. Grand Rapids, MI: Eerdmans Publishing Co., 1969.

5.      Vine, W.E. Expository Dictionary of New Testament Words. Old Tappan, NJ: Fleming H. Revell Co. No date listed.

6.      Wuest, Kenneth S. Word Studies in the Greek New Testament. Grand Rapids, MI: Eerdmans Publishing Co., 1966.

## THE REFERENCE WORKS

7.      Cruden's Complete Concordance of the Old & New Testament. Philadelphia, PA: The John C. Winston Co., 1930.

8.      Josephus' Complete Works. Grand Rapids, MI: Kregel Publications, 1981.

9.      Lockyer, Herbert. Series of Books, including his Books on All the Men, Women, Miracles, and Parables of the Bible. Grand Rapids, MI: Zondervan Publishing House, 1958-1967.

10.     Nave's Topical Bible. Nashville, TN: The Southwestern Co., No date listed.

11.     The Amplified New Testament. (Scripture Quotations are from the Amplified New Testament, Copyright 1954, 1958, 1987 by the Lockman Foundation. Used by permission.)

12.     The Four Translation New Testament (Including King James, New American Standard, Williams - New Testament In the Language of the People, Beck - New Testament In the Language of Today.) Minneapolis, MN: World Wide Publications.

13.     The New Compact Bible Dictionary, Edited by T. Alton Bryant. Grand Rapids, MI: Zondervan Publishing House, 1967.

14.     The New Thompson Chain Reference Bible. Indianapolis, IN: B.B. Kirkbride Bible Co., 1964,

## THE COMMENTARIES

15.     Barclay, William. Daily Study Bible Series. Philadelphia, PA: Westminster Press, Began in 1953.

16.     Bruce, F.F. The Epistle to the Ephesians. Westwood, NJ: Fleming H. Revell Co., 1968.

17.     Bruce, F.F. Epistle to the Hebrews. Grand Rapids, MI: Eerdmans Publishing Co., 1964.

18.     Bruce, F.F. The Epistles of John. Old Tappan, NJ: Fleming H. Revell Co., 1970.

19. Criswell, W.A. <u>Expository Sermons on Revelation</u>. Grand Rapids, MI: Zondervan Publishing House, 1962-66.

20. Greene, Oliver. <u>The Epistles of John</u>. Greenville, SC: The Gospel Hour, Inc., 1966.

21. Greene, Oliver. <u>The Epistles of Paul the Apostle to the Hebrews</u>. Greenville, SC: The Gospel Hour, Inc., 1965.

22. Greene, Oliver. <u>The Epistles of Paul the Apostle to Timothy & Titus</u>. Greenville, SC: The Gospel Hour, Inc., 1964.

23. Greene, Oliver. <u>The Revelation Verse by Verse Study</u>. Greenville, SC: The Gospel Hour, Inc., 1963.

24. Henry, Matthew. <u>Commentary on the Whole Bible</u>. Old Tappan, NJ: Fleming H. Revell Co.

25. Hodge, Charles. <u>Exposition on Romans & on Corinthians</u>. Grand Rapids, MI: Eerdmans Publishing Co., 1972-1973.

26. Ladd, George Eldon. <u>A Commentary On the Revelation of John</u>. Grand Rapids, MI: Eerdmans Publishing Co., 1972-1973.

27. Leupold, H.C. <u>Exposition of Daniel</u>. Grand Rapids, MI: Baker Book House, 1969.

28. Morris, Leon. <u>The Gospel According to John</u>. Grand Rapids, MI: Eerdmans Publishing Co., 1971.

29. Newell, William R. <u>Hebrews, Verse by Verse</u>. Chicago, IL: Moody Press, 1947.

30. Strauss, Lehman. <u>Devotional Studies in Galatians & Ephesians</u>. Neptune, NJ: Loizeaux Brothers, 1957.

31. Strauss, Lehman. <u>Devotional Studies in Philippians</u>. Neptune, NJ: Loizeaux Brothers, 1959.

32. Strauss, Lehman. <u>James, Your Brother</u>. Neptune, NJ: Loizeaux Brothers, 1956.

33. Strauss, Lehman. <u>The Book of the Revelation</u>. Neptune, NJ: Loizeaux Brothers, 1964.

34. <u>The New Testament & Wycliffe Bible Commentary</u>, Edited by Charles F. Pfeiffer & Everett F. Harrison. New York: The Iverson Associates, 1971. Produced for Moody Monthly. Chicago Moody Press, 1962.

35. <u>The Pulpit Commentary</u>, Edited by H.D.M. Spence & Joseph S. Exell. Grand Rapids, MI: Eerdmans Publishing Co., 1950.

36. Thomas, W.H. Griffith. <u>Hebrews, A Devotional Commentary</u>. Grand Rapids, MI: Eerdmans Publishing Co., 1970.

37. Thomas, W.H. Griffith. <u>Outline Studies in the Acts of the Apostles</u>. Grand Rapids, MI: Eerdmans Publishing Co., 1956.

38. Thomas, W.H. Griffith. <u>St. Paul's Epistle to the Romans</u>. Grand Rapids, MI: Eerdmans Publishing Co., 1946.

39. Thomas, W.H. Griffith. <u>Studies in Colossians & Philemon</u>. Grand Rapids, MI: Baker Book House, 1973.

40. <u>Tyndale New Testament Commentaries</u>. Grand Rapids, MI: Eerdmans Publishing Co., Began in 1958.

41. Walker, Thomas. <u>Acts of the Apostles</u>. Chicago, IL: Moody Press, 1965.

42. Walvoord, John. <u>The Thessalonian Epistles</u>. Grand Rapids, MI: Zondervan Publishing House, 1973.

# MISCELLANEOUS ABBREVIATIONS

| | | |
|---|---|---|
| & | = | And |
| Arg. | = | Argument |
| Bckgrd. | = | Background |
| Bc. | = | Because |
| Circ. | = | Circumstance |
| Concl. | = | Conclusion |
| Cp. | = | Compare |
| Ct. | = | Contrast |
| Dif. | = | Different |
| e.g. | = | For example |
| Et. | = | Eternal |
| Govt. | = | Government |
| Id. | = | Identity or Identification |
| Illust. | = | Illustration |
| K. | = | Kingdom, K. of God, K. of Heaven, etc. |
| No. | = | Number |
| N.T. | = | New Testament |
| O.T. | = | Old Testament |
| Pt. | = | Point |
| Quest. | = | Question |
| Rel. | = | Religion |
| Resp. | = | Responsibility |
| Rev. | = | Revelation |
| Rgt. | = | Righteousness |
| Thru | = | Through |
| V. | = | Verse |
| Vs. | = | Verses |
| Vs. | = | Versus |

| **A** Your *Scripture Passage* always printed out | *First*: Glance at the **Subject Heading**. Think about it for a moment. *Then*: Glance at the **Subject Heading** & the **Major Points** together. |
| --- | --- |
| **B** Your *Sermon Outline* located next to each verse | *Now*: Glance at both the **Major Points & Subpoints** while reading the Scripture. Note how the points are beside the applicable verse—simply stating what the Scripture is saying—in Outline form. |
| **C** A Wealth of *Practical Commentary* Material | |
| **D** *Illustrations* and *Applications* for every audience | *Finally*: Read the **Commentary**. KEY: Note that the *major point numbers* in the *outline* match those in the *commentary*. |
| **E** *Support Scripture* thoroughly researched & written out | |

## MATTHEW 6:1-4

**CHAPTER 6**

**K. The Right Motive for Giving,**[DS1] **6:1-4**

1. **Alms—doing good & giving**
   a. Warning: Do not seek recognition
   b. The reason: God will not reward

2. **The wrong motive**
   a. Giving for recognition
   b. Characteristic of

Take heed that ye do not your alms before men, to be seen of them: otherwise ye have no reward of your Father which is in heaven.

2 Therefore when thou doest thine alms, do not sound a trumpet before thee, as the hypocrites do in the synagogues and in the streets, that they may have glory of men. Verily I say unto you, They have their reward.

3 But when thou doest alms, let not thy left hand know what thy right hand doeth:

4 That thine alms may be in secret: and thy Father which seeth in secret himself shall reward thee openly.

hypocrites
   c. Reward: Recognition by men only

3. **The right motive**
   a. Giving unconsciously
   b. Giving quietly— privately—secretly

4. **The reasons**
   a. Father sees in secret
   b. Father rewards openly

## DIVISION IV

### THE TEACHINGS OF THE MESSIAH TO HIS DISCIPLES: THE GREAT SERMON ON THE MOUNT, 5:1-7:29

### K. The Right Motive for Giving, 6:1-4

(6:1-4) **Introduction—Motive**: what a man does matters greatly to God. God expects men to be kind and to do good in the world: to help others both through personal involvement and through giving generously and sacrificially.

But there is something else that God expects, something of critical importance: God expects a man to have *the right motive*. Just why a man does good and shows kindness matters greatly to God. It matters so much that a person's eternal fate is determined by his motive. Because of this, Christ warns us about right and wrong motives.

1. Alms—doing good and giving (v.1).
2. The wrong motive (v.2).
3. The right motive (v.3-4).
4. The reason (v.4).

1 (6:1) **Alms—Service—Giving**: there is the giving of alms—doing good and giving to others. The word "alms" means righteous acts; giving in order to meet the needs of the poor. To the Jew, giving alms and righteousness meant the same thing. Giving alms was the greatest thing a Jew could do; it was the first act of religion. It was considered to be the very embodiment of righteousness, so much so that the two words began to be used synonymously. Giving alms merited and assured one of righteousness and salvation. (See note 5—Mt.5:6.) Christ warned there is great danger in giving and doing alms. Take heed and guard yourself. Do not give for recognition, or you will lose your reward.

**Thought 1.** There are two important lessons in this verse.
1) Man must guard and be alert to the deception of giving and doing good before men. A person's heart can be deceived. The sin creeps up on man; it is insidious and subtle. It will keep a person from receiving anything from God.
2) A person must give alms and do good. It is a duty of the Christian. In this passage alone Christ says four times, "Do alms."

**"But all their works they do for to be seen of men" (Mt.23:5).**
**"Beware of the scribes, which desire to walk in long robes, and love greetings in the markets, and the highest seats in the synagogues, and the chief rooms at feasts" (Lk.20:46).**

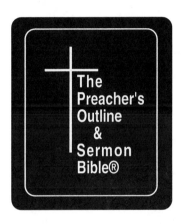

The
Preacher's
Outline
&
Sermon
Bible®

---

"

*Woe is unto me, if I*
*preach not the gospel*

"
*(I Cor. 9:16).*

---

# THE GOSPEL ACCORDING TO

# LUKE

## INTRODUCTION

**AUTHOR**: Luke (1:3). Luke is also the author of Acts.

The early church fathers held Luke to be the author of both the Gospel of Luke and Acts: Irenaeus (about A.D. 130-200); Clement of Alexandria (about A.D. 150-215); Origen (about A.D. 185-254); and Tertullian (about A.D. 160-200). (See *The Pulpit Commentary*, Vol.16. Grand Rapids, MI: Eerdmans, 1950, p.1f, for an excellent discussion on the introductory material on Luke.)

A study of both books bears evidence that Luke is the author. The writer was evidently a physician. Greek medical terms are used. An analysis of the Gospel and Acts together shows the same style and language. There is also a clear understanding of the Roman and Greek world of the first century. The content of the two books shows a strong unity. There is a stress upon the resurrection, the Holy Spirit, the person of Christ, and the ministry to the Gentiles.

There is also enormous evidence that the writer of Acts was an acquaintance of Paul. This is clearly seen in the "we" section of Acts. In three sections of Acts, there is a remarkable switch from "they" and "he" to "we." The "we" sections give a first-hand account (Acts 16:10-17; 20:5-21:18; 27:1-28:16).

1.    Luke is first seen with Paul at Troas. He switches from using "he" and "they" to "we." Luke joined Paul on his journey to Philippi and evidently remained in Philippi until Paul returned from Jerusalem (Acts 16:10).

2.    Luke later went to Jerusalem with Paul when Paul was arrested (Acts 20:5-21:15).

3.    Luke is seen with Paul again while Paul was a prisoner in Caesarea. He also accompanied Paul the prisoner to Rome (Acts 27:1-28:15).

4.    Paul calls Luke "the beloved physician" (Col.4:14; Phile.24).

5.    Luke is the last one to remain with Paul in his imprisonment (2 Tim.2:11).

**DATE**: uncertain. Probably A.D. 58-62.

The author ends Acts abruptly with Paul's two-year imprisonment at Rome, so the writing would have been done some time after Jesus' ascension, just prior to the end of Acts. Another factor is that Luke says nothing about the Fall of Jerusalem. The fall of the city was prophesied by Jesus, and it actually took place in A.D. 70; therefore, the writing took place before A.D. 70. Considering these two factors, Luke must have written the Gospel sometime between A.D. 58-62.

**TO WHOM WRITTEN**: to "the most excellent Theophilus," a Gentile convert (Lk.1:3; Acts 1:1). The words "most excellent" indicate that he was a high official in the Roman government. The book of Acts is also addressed to him personally. (See note, *Theophilus*--Acts 1:1 for more discussion.)

**PURPOSE**: to set forth an eyewitness account of Jesus, the Son of Man, the Savior of the world.

Luke wished Theophilus to know the certainty of those things which he had believed. Thus Luke sets out to write an orderly and accurate account of the whole life of Jesus (Lk.1:1-4).

**SPECIAL FEATURES**:

1.    Luke is "The Gospel for Man" or "The Gospel for Gentiles." Luke shows that God is interested in all men everywhere, not just in the Jews (Lk.2:14, 32; 3:38; 4:25-27; 7:2-10; 9:51-54; 10:30-37; 13:29; 17:16; 24:47).

2.    Luke is "The Gospel of Individuals." Luke shows that Jesus was deeply interested in individuals. He tells of Zechariah and Elizabeth, the parents of John the Baptist (Lk.1:5-25, 39-45; 67-79); of Mary and Martha (Lk.10:38-42); of Zacchaeus (Lk.19:2-10); of Cleopas and his companion (Lk.24:18); and of the woman who anointed Jesus' feet in the home of Simon the Pharisee (Lk.7:36f). The parables in Luke also tend to stress individuals, whereas in Matthew they stress the Kingdom.

3.    Luke is "The Gospel of Salvation." Luke uses the words "salvation" and "Savior" or their various forms many more times than any of the other Gospel writers.

4.    Luke is "The Gospel of the Outcasts and Sinners." Luke tells of the feast Matthew held for tax collectors and sinners (Lk.5:30); of the woman anointing Jesus' feet with her tears and wiping them with her hair (Lk.7:36-50); of tax collectors and sinners drawing near to hear Jesus teach (Lk.15:1). He alone tells of the Prodigal Son (Lk.15:11-32); of the Pharisee and tax collector (Lk.18:9-14); of Zacchaeus, the tax collecting "sinner" (Lk.19:1-10). Many of his parables center around the outcasts (Lk.7:41f; 12:13-21; 16:1-12, 19-31; 18:1-8, 9-14).

5.    Luke is "The Gospel of the Poor." Luke tells of the shepherds who were of a poor class (Lk.2:8f); of Mary, who made the purification offering of the poor (Lk.2:24; cp. Lev.12:8). He says that Jesus came to preach the Gospel to the poor (Lk.4:18-6:20), and the poor have the Gospel preached to them (Lk.7:22).

6.    Luke is "The Gospel of Women." Luke's world was a world that treated women only as things, as little more than chattel property, knowing nothing of women's rights. But Luke gives them a special place. He shows how God honored Elizabeth, Mary, and Anna (Lk.1:5f; 2:25f). He tells about the widow of Nain (Lk.7:11-18); the sinful woman who anointed Jesus' feet (Lk.7:36-50); and the three women who were healed of evil spirits including Mary Magdalene, Joanna, and Susanna (Lk.8:2-3). He writes about the sisters Mary and Martha (Lk.10:38-42); the bent-over lady (Lk.13:11-13); the widow who gave all to God (Lk.21:1-4); and the women who lined the road and wept as Jesus sagged under the weight and burden of the cross (Lk.23:27-31). He also includes women in some of his parables (Lk.15:8-10; 18:1-8).

7.  Luke is "The Gospel of Children." The birth of Jesus and John the Baptist are given in detail (Lk.1-2). Luke's point is to show that God was at work even in the infant stages of the Savior. Luke alone gives the story of Jesus' boyhood (Lk.2:41-52). He alone emphasizes Jesus' ministry to the "only son" and "only daughter" of a desperate parent (Lk.7:12; 8:42; 9:38).

8.  Luke is "The Gospel of Prayer" or "The Gospel of Devotion." Prayer is often emphasized.
    a.  There are the prayers of Jesus: at His baptism (Lk.3:21); in the wilderness (Lk.5:16); before choosing the disciples (Lk.6:12); immediately prior to predicting His death (Lk.9:18); at the transfiguration (Lk.9:28f); when the seventy returned (Lk.10:17-24, esp. 21-22); before giving the Lord's Prayer (Lk.11:1); for Peter (Lk.22:32); in the Garden of Gethsemane (Lk.22:39-46); for His enemies (Lk.23:34); and on the cross (Lk.23:46). Most of these are recorded by Luke alone. They show Jesus' facing every crisis of life by prayer.
    b.  There are the parables of Jesus that deal with prayer: the friend at midnight (Lk.11:5-8); the unjust judge (Lk.18:1-8); the Pharisee and Publican (Lk.18:9-14).
    c.  There are the exhortations and warnings about prayer (Lk.6:28; 11:2; 10:47; 22:40, 46).

9.  Luke is "The Gospel of Praise." He uses the phrase "praising God" more than all the rest of the New Testament combined.
    a.  Some of the great Christian hymns are taken from Luke. The "Ava Maria" from the words of the angel to Mary (Lk.1:28-33); "The Magnificat" from Mary's song (Lk.1:46-55); "The Benedictus" from Zacharias (Lk.1:68-79); the "Gloria in Excelsis" from the song of the heavenly angels (Lk.2:13-14); and "The Nunc Dimittis" from the rejoicing of Simeon (Lk.2:29-32).
    b.  People are seen praising God when helped (Lk.2:20; 5:25-26; 7:16; 13:13; 17:15; 18:43).
    c.  The words "joy" and "rejoicing" are used time and time again (for example Lk.1:14, 44, 47; 10:21).
    d.  There are references to laughter (Lk.6:21) and merriment (Lk.15:23, 32) and to joy (Lk.15:6, 9; 19:6).
    e.  The Gospel ends with joy (Lk.24:52) even as it began with joy (Lk.1:14).

10. Luke is "The Gospel of Christ's Passion." This is seen in three significant emphases.
    a.  There are the many references to His death. Moses and Elijah discuss Jesus' death at His transfiguration (Lk.9:31). Luke says the time for Jesus to be received up has arrived (Lk.9:51); therefore, Jesus sets His face to go up to Jerusalem (Lk.9:51). Jesus refers to His death as a baptism and stresses a constraint to accomplish it (Lk.12:50). Jesus sends a message to Herod that after His ministry He will finish His course on the third day (Lk.13:32). He then continues to speak of perishing in Jerusalem (Lk.13:33-35). And Jesus foretells His passion in a statement that is unique to Luke (Lk.17:25).
    b.  There is the long space given over to the passion narrative.
    c.  There are the times that Scripture is said to be fulfilled by Jesus death (Lk.9:22; 13:33; 17:25; 18:31; 20:17; 22:37; 24:7, 26f, 44, 46).

11. Luke is "The Gospel of the Holy Spirit."
    a.  The persons involved in the preparation for the Savior's coming are said to be Spirit filled and Spirit led: John the Baptist (Lk.1:15); Elizabeth and Zechariah (Lk.1:41, 67); and Simeon (Lk.2:25-27).
    b.  The Holy Spirit is said to be active in the life and ministry of Jesus. Mary was told that the Holy Spirit would come upon her (Lk.1:35). John the Baptist predicted Jesus would be baptized with the Holy Spirit and fire (Lk.3:16). The Holy Spirit came upon Jesus after His baptism "in a bodily shape, like a dove" (Lk.3:22). The Holy Spirit filled and led Him into the wilderness to be tempted of the devil (Lk.4:1). Jesus returned from His temptations to begin His ministry in Galilee "in the power of the Spirit" (Lk.4:14). While preaching, He claimed "the Spirit of the Lord is upon me" (Lk.4:18). He rejoiced in the Spirit when the seventy returned and gave a good report (Lk.10:21); He told His disciples that the Father would give the Spirit to those who asked (Lk.11:13). He said that blasphemy against the Holy Spirit is an unforgivable sin (Lk.12:10). He told His disciples that the Holy Spirit would tell them what to say in emergencies (Lk.12:12). He closed His ministry by assuring His disciples, "Behold, I send the promise of my Father upon you...." (Lk.24:49).

# OUTLINE OF LUKE

**THE PREACHER'S OUTLINE & SERMON BIBLE**™ is *unique*. It differs from all other Study Bibles & Sermon Resource Materials in that every Passage and Subject is outlined right beside the Scripture. When you choose any *Subject* below and turn to the reference, you have not only the Scripture, but you discover the Scripture and Subject *already outlined for you—verse by verse.*

*For a quick example*, choose one of the subjects below and turn to the Scripture, and you will find this marvelous help for faster, easier, and more accurate use.

*In addition, every point* of the Scripture and Subject is *fully developed in a Commentary with supporting Scripture* at the bottom of the page. Again, this arrangement makes sermon preparation much easier and faster.

*Note something else*: The Subjects of Luke's Gospel have Biblical titles, but they have also been given *practical titles or titles of application* which sometimes have more appeal to people. This *benefit* is clearly seen for use on billboards, bulletins, church newsletters, etc.

*A suggestion*: For the quickest overview of Luke, first read *all the major titles* (I, II, III, etc.), then come back and read the subtitles.

---

## OUTLINE OF LUKE

**I. THE ANNOUNCEMENT OF THE COMING OF JESUS, THE SON OF MAN, 1:1-2:52**

    A. Luke's Gospel Account: The Truth of the Word, 1:1-4
    B. Zacharias and Elisabeth, The Parents of John the Baptist: Godly Parents, 1:5-25
    C. Mary, the Mother of Jesus: Submission to God's Will, 1:26-38
       (cp. Matthew 1:18-25)
    D. Elisabeth's Supernatural Proclamation: A Very Unusual Testimony, 1:39-45
    E. Mary's Magnificent Song About God: God's Glorious Mercy and Deliverance, 1:46-56
    F. John's Birth and Naming: An Event for All Generations, 1:57-66
    G. Zacharias' Inspired Prophecy: God's Savior and His Forerunner, 1:67-80
    H. Jesus' Birth: Its Unusual Events, 2:1-24
       (Matthew 1:18-25; 2:1; cp. John 1:14)
    I. Simeon's Prophecy: Jesus' Life and Fate Foretold, 2:25-35
    J. Anna's Praise: The Child Jesus is Praised by a Prophetess, 2:36-38
    K. Jesus' Growth as a Child, 2:39-40
    L. Jesus as a Young Boy in the Temple: Jesus' First Recognition of Messiahship, 2:41-52

**II. THE SON OF MAN'S APPEARANCE, 3:1-4:15**

    A. The Forerunner, John the Baptist: The Pivotal Point of History, 3:1-6
       (Matthew 3:1-6; Mark 1:2-6; John 1:19-28)
    B. The Plain Message of John the Baptist: A Message for All Ages, 3:7-20
       (Matthew 3:7-12; Mark 1:7-8)
    C. The Baptism of Jesus: Obedience and God's Approval, 3:21-22
       (Matthew 3:13-17; Mark 1:9-11; John 1:29-34)
    D. The Genealogy of Jesus: The Roots of the Messiah, 3:23-38
       (Matthew 1:1-17)
    E. The Temptation of Jesus: Victory Over Temptation, 4:1-15
       (Matthew 4:1-11, 12-17; Mark 1:12-13, 14-15)

**III. THE SON OF MAN'S ANNOUNCED MISSION AND PUBLIC MINISTRY, 4:16-9:17**

    A. Jesus Announces His Mission: A Graphic Picture of Rejection, 4:16-30
       (cp. Matthew 13:53-58; Mark 6:1-6)
    B. Jesus Ministers and Makes an Amazing Impact: A Day in the Life of Jesus, 4:31-44
       (Matthew 8:14-17; Mark 1:21-39)
    C. Jesus Calls His First Disciples: Steps to Calling Men, 5:1-11
       (Matthew 4:18-22; Mark 1:16-20; John 1:35-51)
    D. Jesus Cleanses the Untouchable, 5:12-16
       (Matthew 8;1-4; Mark 1:40-45)
    E. Jesus Proves His Amazing Power to Forgive Sins, 5:17-26
       (Matthew 9:1-8; Mark 2:1-12)
    F. Jesus Reveals His Great Mission: The Greatest Mission of All, 5:27-39
       (Matthew 9:9-17; Mark 2:13-22)
    G. Jesus Teaches That Need Supersedes Religion, 6:1-11
       (Matthew 12:1-13; Mark 2:23-28; 3:1-6)

J.  The Great Proof that Jesus is the Messiah: The Resurrection, 11:29-36
    (Matthew 5:14-16; 12:38-42; Mark 4:21-22; cp. Luke 8:16)
K.  The Severe Charges Against Religionists, 11:37-54
    (cp. Matthew 23:13-36)
L.  The Things Men Should Fear, 12:1-12
M.  The Parable of the Rich Fool: The Man of Wealth and What He Should Fear, 12:13-21
N.  The Genuine Believer: Worry Not About Necessities, 12:22-34
    (Matthew 6:25-34)
O.  The Parable of the Faithful and Unfaithful Steward: A Strong Warning—Be Prepared, 12:35-48
    (Matthew 24:37-25:30)
P.  The Three Gross Misconceptions of Man, 12:49-59
Q.  The Truth About Suffering and Sin: The Great Need for All to Repent, 13:1-9
    (cp. Matthew 21:18-21; Mark 11:12-14, 20-26; Isaiah 5:1-7)
R.  People vs. Religion: Which is More Important? 13:10-17
S.  The Parables of the Mustard Seed and Leaven: The Kingdom of God, 13:18-21
    (Matthew 13:31-33; Mark 4:30-32)

VI.  **THE SON OF MAN'S GREAT JOURNEY TO JERUSALEM (STAGE II): HIS TEACHING AND PUBLIC CONFLICT, 13:22-17:10**

A.  The Saved Discussed, 13:22-30
B.  The Tragic Rejection of Jesus, 13:31-35
    (Matthew 23:37-39; cp. Luke 19:41-44)
C.  The Religionists and Their Error, 14:1-6
    (cp. Matthew 12:9-13)
D.  The Importance of Humility, 14:7-14
E.  The Parable of the Great Supper: The Invitation and Man's Excuses, 14:15-24
    (cp. Matthew 22:1-14)
F.  The Cost of Discipleship, 14:25-35
    (cp. Matthew 5:13; cp. Matthew 10:37-39; Mark 9:50)
G.  The Parable of the Lost Sheep: The Lost Sinner Out in the World, 15:1-7
    (cp. Matthew 18:11-14)
H.  The Parable of the Lost Coin: The Lost Sinner Within the Home, 15:8-10
I.  The Parable of the Prodigal Son: The Wayward Son, 15:11-24
J.  The Parable of the Elder Son: The Self-Righteous Religionist, 15:25-32
K.  The Parable of the Unjust Steward: Man and Money, 16:1-13
L.  The Misunderstanding About Wealth and God's Kingdom, 16:14-18
M.  The Rich Man and Lazarus: The Self-Indulgent vs. the Man of Faith, 16:19-31
N.  The Christian Disciple and Four Laws, 17:1-10
    (cp. Matthew 18:6; 17:20)

VII.  **THE SON OF MAN'S GREAT JOURNEY TO JERUSALEM (STAGE III): HIS LESSONS AND WARNINGS, 17:11-19:27**

A.  The Lesson on Need and Gratitude, 17:11-19
B.  The Coming Day of God's Kingdom and Jesus' Return, 17:20-37
    (cp. Matthew 24; Mark 13)
C.  The Parable of the Unjust Judge: The Secret of Prayer—Persistence, 18:1-8
D.  The Parable of the Pharisee and the Publican: The Spirit Needed for Prayer, 18:9-14
E.  The Little Children and Jesus, 18:15-17
    (Matthew 19:13-15; Mark 10:13-16)
F.  The Rich Young Ruler: The Cost of Eternal Life, 18:18-30
    (Matthew 19:16-30; Mark 10:17-31)
G.  The Prediction of the Cross, 18:31-34
    (Matthew 20:17-19; Mark 10:32-34)
H.  The Healing of Blind Bartimaeus: Steps to Getting Help from God, 18:35-43
    (cp. Matthew 20:29-34; Mark 10:46-52)
I.  The Conversion of Zaccheus: The Meaning of Conversion, 19:1-10
J.  The Parable of the Pounds: Every Man is Being Tested, 19:11-27

VIII.  **THE SON OF MAN'S DRAMATIC ENTRANCE INTO JERUSALEM: HIS CLAIM AND CONFLICT, 19:28-21:4**

A.  The Triumphal Entry: Jesus' Claim to be King, 19:28-40
    (Matthew 21:1-11; Mark 11:1-11; John 12:12-19)
B.  The Dramatic Prediction: Judgment Upon Jerusalem, 19:41-44
    (cp. Matthew 23:37-39; Luke 13:34-35)
C.  The Cleansing of the Temple: The Righteous Anger of Jesus, 19:45-48
    (Matthew 21:12-16; Mark 11:15-19; cp. John 2:13-16)

# THE GOSPEL ACCORDING TO

## LUKE

| | | CHAPTER 1 | believed among us,<br>2 Even as they delivered them unto us, which from the beginning were eyewitnesses, and ministers of the word; | **2** | **The gospel is a record of eyewitnesses & ministers of the Word** |
| | | **I. THE ANNOUNCEMENT OF THE COMING OF JESUS, THE SON OF MAN, 1:1-2:52** | 3 It seemed good to me also, having had perfect understanding of all things from the very first, to write unto thee in order, most excellent Theophilus, | **3** | **The gospel is a record of a man who was led to write** |
| | | **A. Luke's Gospel Account: The Truth of the Word, 1:1-4** | | | |
| **1** | **The gospel is a record of historical events** | Forasmuch as many have taken in hand to set forth in order a declaration of those things which are most surely | 4 That thou mightest know the certainty of those things, wherein thou hast been instructed. | **4** | **The gospel is a record to establish the truth** |

## DIVISION I

### THE ANNOUNCEMENT OF THE COMING OF JESUS, THE SON OF MAN, 1:1-2:52

### A.     Luke's Gospel Account: The Truth of the Word, 1:1-4

(1:1-4) **Introduction**: the Gospel of Luke is a written proclamation of the truth about Jesus Christ. This is the thrust of this first passage in Luke's gospel. Luke is writing to declare the glorious news that the Son of Man, God's Son, has come to earth to seek and to save all who are lost. Luke's gospel is an accurate, orderly account of the truth about Jesus Christ. Note: this introduction of Luke is the very form used by the historians of his day. This points strongly to the fact that Luke intended it to be circulated among churches and believers.

1.     The gospel is a record of historical events (v.1).
2.     The gospel is a record of eyewitnesses and ministers of the Word (v.2).
3.     The gospel is a record of a man who was led to write (v.3).
4.     The gospel is a record to establish the truth (v.4).

**1**  (1:1) **Scripture—Gospel**: Luke's gospel is a record of historical events. Note several facts.

1.     "Many...set forth" the events of Christ's life. Many had written about the life and work of Christ, but they were not as *complete* nor as *orderly* as Luke wished to record (cp. v.3). A quick comparison of the first two chapters of Luke with Mark and Matthew will show this. Luke includes many more events than the other two Synoptic Gospels, and the Gospel of John had not yet been written. The fact that *many* had written a record on the life of Christ is strong evidence that the events are true.

2.     The events or things of Christ's life were "most surely believed." The words for "most surely believed" (plerophoreo, peplero phoremenon) also mean things that were fulfilled, that were actually performed, or that had run their full course (cp. 2 Tim.4:5). Luke is saying that the *things of Christ* were not only believed, but they were also accomplished or fulfilled among the believers of that day. The *things* (events, matters) of Christ actually took place; they were purposeful; they were destined to be accomplished and fulfilled.

The point is this: the things of Christ are a record of historical events, things that actually happened and that actually fulfilled the purpose of God. Therefore, the things are "most surely believed among us [believers]." What are the *things* accomplished and believed? Both the things of the New Testament and of the Old Testament. The whole Bible is a record of "those things."

> "For God so loved the world, that he gave his only begotten Son, that whosoever believeth in him should not perish, but have everlasting life" (Jn.3:16).
> "For the Son of man is come to seek and to save that which was lost" (Lk.19:10).
> "Forasmuch then as the children are partakers of flesh and blood, he also himself likewise took part of the same; that through death he might destroy him that had the power of death, that is, the devil; and deliver them who through fear of death were all their lifetime subject to bondage. For verily he took not on him the nature of angels; but he took on him the seed of Abraham. Wherefore in all things it behoved him to be made like unto his brethren, that he might be a merciful and faithful high priest in things pertaining to God, to make reconciliation for the sins of the people. For in that he himself hath suffered being tempted, he is able to succour them that are tempted" (Heb.2:14-18).
> "[Christ Jesus] who, being in the form of God, thought it not robbery to be equal with God: but made himself of no reputation, and took upon him the form of a servant, and was made in the likeness of men: and being found in fashion as a man, he humbled himself, and became obedient unto death, even the death of the cross. Wherefore God also hath highly exalted him, and given

him a name which is above every name: that at the name of Jesus every knee should bow, of things in heaven, and things in earth, and things under the earth; and that every tongue should confess that Jesus Christ is Lord, to the glory of God the Father" (Ph.2:6-11).

"Who his own self bare our sins in his own body on the tree, that we, being dead to sins, should live unto righteousness: by whose stripes ye were healed" (1 Pt.2:24).

"[God] hath delivered us from the power of darkness, and hath translated us into the kingdom of his dear Son: in whom we have redemption through his blood, even the forgiveness of sins: who is the image of the invisible God, the first-born of every creature: for by him were all things created, that are in heaven, and that are in earth, visible and invisible, whether they be thrones, or dominions, or principalities, or powers: all things were created by him, and for him: and he is before all things, and by him all things consist. And he is the head of the body, the church: who is the beginning, the firstborn from the dead; that in all things he might have the preeminence. For it pleased the Father that in him should all fulness dwell; and, having made peace through the blood of his cross, by him to reconcile all things unto himself; by him, I say, whether they be things in earth, or things in heaven" (Col.1:13-20).

"For in him dwelleth all the fulness of the Godhead bodily. And ye are complete in him, which is the head of all principality and power" (Col.2:9-10).

"Therefore if any man be in Christ, he is a new creature: old things are passed away; behold, all things are become new" (2 Cor.5:17).

**Thought 1.** The early believers had no difficulty whatsoever believing the *things* of Christ.
1) The *things* were "most surely believed."
2) Many were writing an account of the events.

**Thought 2.** The "many" who wrote about the life of Jesus are not known by name. They are the silent and humble heroes of God, never known by the world, but well-known by God. Some of their writings served as a *source* for Luke (v.3). Note two things.
1) Their ministry of writing was used greatly by God. Some of what they wrote was either included in the Gospel of Luke or at least stirred thoughts in Luke's mind to record an event.
2) God's silent, quiet, and humble servants are always used by Him just as much as the ones out in the forefront. Their ministry is just as important, if not more so. Some that are last will most definitely be first.

> **"And, behold, there are last which shall be first, and there are first which shall be last" (Lk.13:30; cp. Mt.19:30; 20:16; Mk.10:31).**

**2** (1:2) **Ministers—The Word, Proof of:** Luke's gospel is both a record of *eyewitnesses* and a record of *ministers of the Word*. Luke himself was not an eyewitness of the day-to-day life of Christ. If he ever saw Christ personally, there is no mention of it. However, Luke was a constant and very dear companion of Paul (see Introduction—Luke; note—Acts 16:10). He also had contact with other apostles. What Luke says is that the sources of his writing were eyewitnesses of Christ and ministers of the Word of Christ. The apostles, of course, would be his prime sources. In addition, there were other disciples who followed Jesus either continuously or occasionally. Note these simple facts.

1. The ministers of the Word were eyewitnesses of both *The Word* (Christ Himself) and of the Word of Christ (His teaching, doctrine, and instructions).
2. The ministers of the Word were eyewitnesses "from the beginning," eyewitnesses of every event and word of Christ, eyewitnesses of His life day by day.
3. The ministers of the Word heard as well as saw Christ; some heard and saw Him day by day. Therefore, Luke's gospel is a true record of both the acts and words of Christ.
4. The ministers of the gospel set out immediately to *minister* the Word to others. The word was of critical importance to them. They gave their lives to the ministry of the Word.
5. The ministers of the gospel did not create the Word (message) themselves. They were not ministering their own ideas and thoughts; they were ministering "*The Word of God.*"
6. The ministers of the Word have given us a written gospel that is an eyewitness account. It agrees exactly with what was seen, heard, and proclaimed by Christ and preached to the people of His day and to the world since then.

> **"That which was from the beginning, which we have heard, which we have seen with our eyes, which we have looked upon, and our hands have handled, of the Word of life; (for the life was manifested, and we have seen it, and bear witness, and show unto you that eternal life, which was with the Father, and was manifested unto us;) that which we have seen and heard declare we unto you, that ye also may have fellowship with us: and truly our fellowship is with the Father, and with his Son Jesus Christ. And these things write we unto you, that your joy may be full" (1 Jn.1:1-4).**

**3** (1:3) **Gospel—Scripture:** Luke's gospel is the record of a man who was led to write. Four facts point out just how strongly Luke felt led to record the life of Christ.

1. Luke had "perfect understanding [parakoloutheo] of all things." The word "understanding" means to study, to follow up, to search out diligently, to investigate, to trace accurately, to become acquainted with. Luke says that having been acquainted with and having investigated *all things*, he was determined to record the facts himself.
2. Luke says he had perfect understanding (investigated all things) "from the very first." The word "first" (anothen) can and often does mean *from above*. Some understand Luke to be saying that he had investigated the things *from above*. Several things point to this translation.

a. If Luke meant *from the first or beginning,* why did he not use the same word (arches) which he used in verse 2? It seems to be much more accurate to say he chooses a different word (anothen) because he is saying something different, *from above.*

b. The prophets are said to have proclaimed things *from above.* They are said to "have enquired and searched diligently, who prophesied of the grace that should come unto you: searching what, or what manner of time the Spirit of Christ which was in them did signify, when it testified beforehand the sufferings of Christ, and the glory that should follow. Unto whom it was revealed, that not unto themselves, but unto us they did minister the things, which are now reported unto you by them that have preached the gospel unto you with the Holy Ghost sent down from heaven; which things the angels desire to look into" (1 Pt.1:10-12). Scripture also says, "For the prophecy came not in old time by the will of man: but holy men of God spake as they were moved by the Holy Ghost" (2 Pt.1:21).

c. Luke is certainly recording *all things from above,* investigating and searching diligently to write what "the Spirit of Christ which was in [him] did signify" (1 Pt.1:11). He is certainly speaking as a holy man of God "moved by the Holy Spirit" (2 Pt.1:21). He is certainly proclaiming the gospel of the Lord Jesus Christ, the good news of Him who came from above.

3. Luke says he is writing things "in order" (kathexes). Luke is the only writer in the New Testament to use this word. He uses it in the gospel only once and in Acts twice (Acts 11:4; 18:23). The question is, what does Luke mean by *orderly?* Consecutive or chronological arrangement? Logical arrangement? Subject arrangement? Inspired or Spirit-led arrangement? The meaning is not clear. Perhaps he is saying that he is writing a full account of the life of Christ and that his account is a *better arrangement,* that is, it has more order and is better arranged than those in existence.

4. Luke is writing to a man named "Theophilus." Who was he? We are not told. But note two facts.

a. He was called "most excellent Theophilus." "Most excellent" (kratistos) is a title of rank and honor. The same title is used of Felix and Festus (Acts 23:26; 24:3; 26:25).

b. He was a person who desired or needed to know about Jesus Christ. He was probably a convert for whom Luke deeply cared. Some feel he was a man investigating the validity of Christianity. Theophilus is the immediate reason Luke *felt led* to write. (See note, *Theophilus*—Acts 1:1 for more discussion.)

**Thought 1.** Note two critical points.

1) A person must be *prepared* to serve Christ. A person must study, investigate, search out, become acquainted with the truth of Christ.

> **"Study to show thyself approved unto God, a workman that needeth not to be ashamed, rightly dividing the word of truth" (2 Tim.2:15).**

2) A person must be led to serve Christ, no matter the task. He must be led by the Spirit of Christ.

> **"For as many as are led by the Spirit of God, they are the sons of God" (Ro.8:14).**
> **"Ye have not chosen me, but I have chosen you, and ordained you, that ye should go and bring forth fruit, and that your fruit should remain: that whatsoever ye shall ask of the Father in my name, he may give it you" (Jn.15:16).**

**Thought 2.** We can have great confidence in the truth and accuracy of the written record of Christ.

> **"All scripture is given by inspiration of God, and is profitable for doctrine, for reproof, for correction, for instruction in righteousness" (2 Tim.3:16).**

**Thought 3.** Note a tremendous challenge to us. Luke cared so much for one man that he dedicated himself to writing not a long letter, but a whole book in order to instruct the man. Imagine the dedication and the days and months required! All for one person (initially)!

> **"What man of you, having an hundred sheep, if he lose one of them, doth not leave the ninety and nine in the wilderness, and go after that which is lost, until he find it?" (Lk.15:4).**

**4** (1:4) **Gospel—Truth:** Luke's gospel is a record to establish the truth. Luke's purpose is clearly stated: "That thou might know the certainty of those things, wherein thou hast been instructed."

1. The man (Theophilus) *had already heard.*
2. The man *needed to know* the absolute truth of those things.

**Thought 1.** Luke's account of Christ is the absolute truth. We can *"know the certainty of those things."*

**Thought 2.** Hearing the things of Christ, even being instructed in them is not enough. We are to study and learn, to know the absolute certainty of them.

> **"For the prophecy came not in old time by the will of man: but holy men of God spake as they were moved by the Holy Ghost" (2 Pt.1:21; cp. Mk.13:31; Lk.21:33).**
> **"These were more noble than those in Thessalonica, in that they received the word with all readiness of mind, and searched the scriptures daily, whether those things were so" (Acts 17:11).**

**B. Zacharias and Elisabeth, The Parents of John the Baptist: Godly Parents, 1:5-25**

1 **The parents of John the Baptist**
  a. They lived in the days of Herod
  b. The father was a priest & the mother was of a priestly family

2 **They were parents who were righteous**

3 **They were parents with human problems**
  a. They had no child
  b. They were elderly

4 **They were parents who worshipped**

5 **They were parents who prayed & led others to pray**

6 **They were parents greatly favored by God**
  a. Their worship & prayers were favored by a visit from an angel

  b. Their prayers were answered: They received the promise of a son

  c. Their son was to be great

  d. Their son was to be a prophet

  e. Their son was to be the forerunner of the Messiah

7 **They were parents who found it difficult to believe the humanly impossible**[DS1]

8 **They were parents who had to be disciplined by God**

9 **They were parents who saw God fulfill His promise**

5 There was in the days of Herod, the king of Judaea, a certain priest named Zacharias, of the course of Abia: and his wife was of the daughters of Aaron, and her name was Elisabeth.
6 And they were both righteous before God, walking in all the commandments and ordinances of the Lord blameless.
7 And they had no child, because that Elisabeth was barren, and they both were now well stricken in years.
8 And it came to pass, that while he executed the priest's office before God in the order of his course,
9 According to the custom of the priest's office, his lot was to burn incense when he went into the temple of the Lord.
10 And the whole multitude of the people were praying without at the time of incense.
11 And there appeared unto him an angel of the Lord standing on the right side of the altar of incense.
12 And when Zacharias saw him, he was troubled, and fear fell upon him.
13 But the angel said unto him, Fear not, Zacharias: for thy prayer is heard; and thy wife Elisabeth shall bear thee a son, and thou shalt call his name John.
14 And thou shalt have joy and gladness; and many shall rejoice at his birth.
15 For he shall be great in the sight of the Lord, and shall drink neither wine nor strong drink; and he shall be filled with the Holy Ghost, even from his mother's womb.
16 And many of the children of Israel shall he turn to the Lord their God.
17 And he shall go before him in the spirit and power of Elias, to turn the hearts of the fathers to the children, and the disobedient to the wisdom of the just; to make ready a people prepared for the Lord.
18 And Zacharias said unto the angel, Whereby shall I know this? for I am an old man, and my wife well stricken in years.
19 And the angel answering said unto him, I am Gabriel, that stand in the presence of God; and am sent to speak unto thee, and to show thee these glad tidings.
20 And, behold, thou shalt be dumb, and not able to speak, until the day that these things shall be performed, because thou believest not my words, which shall be fulfilled in their season.
21 And the people waited for Zacharias, and marvelled that he tarried so long in the temple.
22 And when he came out, he could not speak unto them: and they perceived that he had seen a vision in the temple: for he beckoned unto them, and remained speechless.
23 And it came to pass, that, as soon as the days of his ministration were accomplished, he departed to his own house.
24 And after those days his wife Elisabeth conceived, and hid herself five months, saying,
25 Thus hath the Lord dealt with me in the days wherein he looked on me, to take away my reproach among men.

# DIVISION I

## THE ANNOUNCEMENT OF THE COMING OF JESUS, THE SON OF MAN, 1:1-2:52

**B.**     **Zacharias and Elisabeth, The Parents of John the Baptist: Godly Parents, 1:5-25**

(1:5-25) **Introduction**: every generation needs the example of godly parents. The parents of John the Baptist were godly, dynamic examples of what parents should be. They were human, showing some weaknesses, but they were striking examples for all.

1.    The parents of John the Baptist (v.5).
2.    They were parents who were righteous (v.6).
3.    They were parents with human problems (v.7).
4.    They were parents who worshipped (v.8-9).

5.  They were parents who prayed and led others to pray (v.10).
6.  They were parents greatly favored by God (v.11-17).
7.  They were parents who found it difficult to believe the humanly impossible (v.18-19).
8.  They were parents who had to be disciplined by God (v.20-22).
9.  They were parents who saw God fulfill His promise (v.23-25).

**1** (1:5) **John the Baptist, Family of**: the parents of John the Baptist. Note three facts.

1.  The baby John was promised to his parents during the reign of Herod the Great, right at the very end of his reign (B.C.37-4) (See DEEPER STUDY # 3—Mt.2:3-4.)
2.  John's father was Zacharias or Zecharias.
    a.  His name means *Remembered of Jehovah*.
    b.  He was from the country, a mountainous or hilly section.
    c.  He was of "the course of Abia [or Abijah]." This simply means a division of the priests. Remember that all the male descendants of Aaron were priests. There were over twenty thousand at this time and only one temple, so they had to be divided into groups (1 Chron.24:1-6). Zacharias served in the eighth group or division (1 Chron.24:10). There were twenty-four groups, and each group served in the temple for one week, twice a year.
3.  John's mother was Elisabeth, or Elizabeth.
    a.  Her name means *One whose oath is to God*.
    b.  She was the daughter of a priest.
    c.  She was a pure woman, a virgin at her marriage. A priest was required to marry a virgin (Lev.21:14).

**2** (1:6) **Righteousness—Family**: they were parents who were righteous. Note four facts.

1.  They "were *both* righteous." They were joined together and committed to each other, and they lived for God and for each other as husband and wife.
2.  They were "righteous *before God*." Together they came "before God" seeking Him, that is, seeking to please Him and to live as He said.
3.  They were "walking in *all* the commandments and ordinances of the Lord." They controlled their thoughts, minds, tongues, and behavior, diligently seeking to please the Lord in all they did.
4.  They were "blameless." This, of course, does not mean they were perfect. It means they were faithful, living in such a way that no one could charge them with open sin. They offended no one; they lived honestly before both God and men.

**3** (1:7) **Family—Parents**: they were parents with human problems. Being righteous did not free them from problems. They had to face the problems of this world just as all persons do. But there was a difference: they were righteous before God. Therefore, they had the presence of God to help them through the problems. They had two serious problems.

1.  They were childless. This was a terrible calamity to the people of that day. Children were considered a blessing from God, a great heritage of the Lord. In fact, a Jew whose wife could not bear children was thought to be cut off from God. He was expected to divorce his wife, remarry, and bear children. Therefore, being childless was a critical problem to Zacharias and Elizabeth, a problem that weighed ever so heavily upon their hearts and never left their minds. They felt disfavored and displeasing to God.
2.  They were elderly. All the problems that come with age either faced them or stood before them as a threat.

> "He maketh his sun to rise on the evil and on the good, and sendeth rain on the just and on the unjust" (Mt.5:45).
> "There hath no temptation [trial] taken you but such as is common to man: but God is faithful, who will not suffer you to be tempted above that ye are able; but will with the temptation also make a way to escape, that ye may be able to bear it" (1 Cor.10:13).
> "Reproach hath broken my heart; and I am full of heaviness: and I looked for some to take pity, but there was none; and for comforters, but I found none" (Ps.69:20).

**4** (1:8-9) **Parents—Worship**: they were parents who worshipped. Zacharias was faithful to his priesthood. He had been chosen and ordained by God to be a priest, and he was faithful to that call. He was faithful and steadfast in his duties despite the lack of blessings from God, that is, being childless. Remember that bearing a son in that day and time was considered one of the greatest blessings and signs of God's approval. Not having a son was thought to be an indication of God's disapproval.

What happened was this. In the temple's daily worship, incense was burned upon the altar by a priest before the morning sacrifice and after the evening sacrifice. The offering of incense symbolized that the sacrifices were being offered up to God in the sweetest and most prayerful of spirits. The aroma of the incense was just like prayer; it enveloped the sacrifice and carried it before the very throne of God.

The priests considered the burning of incense to be the highest privilege of the priestly functions. However, because of the large number of priests, some never had the opportunity to offer it up to God. Just who received this privilege was determined by drawing lots. On this particular day, Zacharias experienced one of the greatest days of his life. The lot fell upon him. He was the chosen priest to offer the incense.

The point is this: Zacharias was faithful to God's call. He had been chosen and ordained by God to be a priest, and he had accepted and given his life to that call. He was faithful in his worship despite his *problems and lack of blessings* from God (being childless).

"Blessed is the man that endureth temptation [trials]: for when he is tried, he shall receive the crown of life, which the Lord hath promised to them that love him" (Jas.1:12).

"Behold, we count them happy which endure. Ye have heard of the patience of Job, and have seen the end of the Lord; that the Lord is very pitiful, and of tender mercy" (Jas.5:11).

5 (1:10) **Father—Prayer**: they were parents who prayed. Zacharias was praying while he offered the incense up to God, and he had led the people to pray while he sought the Lord in their behalf (cp. v.13). He had led them to be a praying people. They were to be as involved in the prayer and worship as he was. (What a lesson for congregations!)

"Again I say unto you, That if two of you shall agree on earth as touching any thing that they shall ask, it shall be done for them of my Father which is in heaven" (Mt.18:19).

"Seek the LORD and his strength, seek his face continually" (1 Chron.16:11).

"He shall call upon me, and I will answer him: I will be with him in trouble; I will deliver him, and honour him" (Ps.91:15).

6 (1:11-17) **Parents—Blessings**: they were parents greatly favored by God. God is bound to bless and highly favor any parent...

- who is righteous.
- who worships.
- who prays.
- who leads others to worship and pray.

God favored Zacharias and Elizabeth in five ways.

1. Their need was met by God in a very personal way. God sent an angel to Zacharias. Note the angel appeared on the right side of the altar of incense, the very place of prayer. It was while he was praying, in the act of obedience, that God met his need in this special way.

2. Their prayers were answered. Note the exact words of the Scripture: "Thy prayer is heard." What prayer?

⇒ Was Zacharias pouring his heart out about being childless, despite his age?

⇒ Was Zacharias praying for the redemption of Israel, for the coming of the Messiah?

Scripture does not say. But *both* prayers were now being answered. Elizabeth was to bear a son, and the Messiah was to be born. Their son was to be named John which means *the grace of Jehovah*.

3. Their son was to be great.

a. He would cause his parents to rejoice because of his *life*. He was to be everything that parents could want in a child. He would not shame them, but he would bring joy to their hearts.

b. He would cause many to rejoice because of his *contribution* to society. He would bring joy to all their friends, and he would bring joy to the nation as a whole. Many would joy in such a commitment and contribution as his.

c. He would be great in the sight of God Himself, great because of his *faithfulness* (obedience). He would be like one of the great prophets of old.

d. He would live a *disciplined* and *controlled* life, abstaining from wine and strong drink and from the very appearance of evil.

e. He would be filled with the *Holy Spirit* from the very first, a vessel chosen by God for a very special service, *fitted* in a very special way.

**Thought 1.** Note the five traits that made John great. How desperately believers need the same traits in their own lives.

"I beseech you therefore, brethren, by the mercies of God, that ye present your bodies a living sacrifice, holy, acceptable unto God, which is your reasonable service. And be not conformed to this world: but be ye transformed by the renewing of your mind, that ye may prove what is that good, and acceptable, and perfect, will of God" (Ro.12:1-2).

"And I thank Christ Jesus our Lord, who hath enabled me, for that he counted me faithful, putting me into the ministry" (1 Tim.1:12).

**Thought 2.** The point to see about Zacharias and Elizabeth is that God did hear their prayer and bless them richly. He favored them because they were faithful to Him.

"If ye abide in me, and my words abide in you, ye shall ask what ye will, and it shall be done unto you" (Jn.15:7).

"And whatsoever we ask, we receive of him, because we keep his commandments, and do those things that are pleasing in his sight" (1 Jn.3:22).

4. Their son was to be a prophet, turning many to the Lord God.

5. Their son was to be the forerunner of the promised Messiah. His ministry was to be like that of Elijah, the greatest of the prophets (Mal.4:5; cp. Mt.17:10).

7 (1:18-19) **Parents—Promises—Faith, Weakness of**: they were parents who found it difficult to believe the humanly impossible. Note two things.

1.     Zacharias just could not believe the message and the promise of God. He had been praying, but apparently he had not thought God would answer, certainly not by doing the impossible—by overruling the laws of nature. Note that Zacharias' question was the question of unbelief. He asked the very same question asked by Abraham (Gen.15:8), but Zacharias asked the question in a spirit of unbelief. He informed the angel that he and Elizabeth were too old to have children.

2.     The very Word and promise of God should have been enough to convince Zacharias, but he was weak in faith. He had to ask for additional assurance. He asked for a sign—a sign other than *God's Word and promise* (see DEEPER STUDY # 1, *Gabriel*—Lk.1:19).

---

**DEEPER STUDY # 1**

(1:19) **Gabriel**: means the *man of God* or the *hero of God* or the *mighty one of God*. Note that Gabriel said two things about himself...
1.     He is the one who actually stands in the presence of God.
2.     He is the one who brings good news to men.
     ⇒ He shared the restoration of Israel with Daniel (Dan.8:16; 9:21f).
     ⇒ He shared the birth of the forerunner with Zacharias (Lk.1:13f).
     ⇒ He shared the birth of the Messiah with Mary (Lk.1:26f).

---

**8** (1:20-22) **Distrust—Unbelief—Discipline of God**: they were parents who had to be disciplined by God. Zacharias had failed to believe God; therefore, he had to be disciplined and taught to grow in trust more and more.

1.     Zacharias had asked for a sign. He had let his tongue speak instead of his heart. Therefore, God gave him a sign—the sign of stopping his tongue during the nine months before John was born.

2.     Zacharias had failed to receive the Word of God. Therefore, God took away his ability to share the Word to men.

3.     Zacharias had spoken words of distrust and unbelief; therefore, God saved him from speaking any more words of distrust and unbelief.

> **Thought 1.** Every true child of God knows the discipline of God's hand. His discipline differs with each of us, but each of us can recognize His discipline nevertheless (see outline and notes—Heb.12:5-13).

> > **"And ye have forgotten the exhortation which speaketh unto you as unto children, My son, despise not thou the chastening of the Lord, or faint when thou art rebuked of him: for whom the Lord loveth he chasteneth, and scourgeth every son whom he receiveth"** (Heb.12:5-6).
> > **"As many as I love, I rebuke and chasten: be zealous therefore, and repent"** (Rev.3:19).
> > **"Thou shalt also consider in thine heart, that, as a man chasteneth his son, so the LORD thy God chasteneth thee"** (Dt.8:5).
> > **"Blessed is the man whom thou chastenest, O LORD, and teachest him out of thy law"** (Ps.94:12).
> > **"My son, despise not the chastening of the LORD; neither be weary of his correction: for whom the LORD loveth he correcteth; even as a father the son in whom he delighteth"** (Pr.3:11-12).
> > **"O LORD, correct me, but with judgment; not in thine anger, lest thou bring me to nothing"** (Jer.10:24).

> **Thought 2.** God will not allow man to disbelieve and distrust forever. The day is coming when he will stop all disbelief and distrust just as He did with Zacharias.

Note that Zacharias tarried in the temple much longer than usual. The people became restless, wondering what had happened. When he came out, he was supposed to lead the people in a benediction, but he was unable to speak. All he could do was motion with his hand. Note a significant lesson: the people could tell Zacharias had been in the presence of God. They thought he had seen a vision. Despite Zacharias' unbelief, he had still lived a faithful life before God; therefore, God still met him and gave His promise to Zacharias and Elizabeth.

> **Thought 1.** What hope for us all, even when our faith is weak!

**9** (1:23-25) **Promises—Seeking God**: they were parents who saw God fulfill His promise. But note: these parents did two things that reveal why God was able to bless them.

1.     They were responsible. Zacharias was sick; he had lost his voice completely. Yet he fulfilled his duties despite being disciplined with the infirmity. He did what he could, responsibly and faithfully. What an example!

2.     They withdrew into the presence of God. After Zacharias completed his duties, he and his dear wife returned home. Of course, Zacharias would stick close to home, walking in meditation and prayer because of his experience and being unable to talk with others. But note especially Elizabeth's behavior. She hid herself for five months. Why? For the same reason any of us would withdraw after being visited by such an angelic being with so great a message. She needed time alone with God to absorb all that was happening and to prepare herself for the rearing of one who was destined to be so greatly used by God.

Note how the thought that she was hiding her pregnancy from the public is inaccurate. She hid herself only for the first five months of her pregnancy. She became public after the five months (cp. v.39-40, 57).

**Thought 1.** Note a crucial point. The call to special service necessitates a period of preparation, especially the preparation of oneself in the presence of God. Time alone with God for meditation and prayer over God's call is essential.

"Therefore also now, saith the LORD, turn ye even to me with all your heart, and with fasting, and with weeping, and with mourning: and rend your heart, and not your garments, and turn unto the LORD your God: for he is gracious and merciful, slow to anger, and of great kindness, and repenteth him of the evil" (Joel 2:12-13).

"Let us draw near with a true heart in full assurance of faith, having our hearts sprinkled from an evil conscience, and our bodies washed with pure water" (Heb.10:22).

"Draw nigh to God, and he will draw nigh to you. Cleanse your hands, ye sinners; and purify your hearts, ye double minded" (Jas.4:8).

"Is any among you afflicted? let him pray. Is any merry? let him sing psalms" (Jas.5:13).

"The LORD is nigh unto them that are of a broken heart; and saveth such as be of a contrite spirit" (Ps.34:18).

"Be merciful unto me, O God, be merciful unto me: for my soul trusteth in thee: yea, in the shadow of thy wings will I make my refuge, until these calamities be overpast" (Ps.57:1).

| | C. Mary, the Mother of Jesus: Submission to God's Will, 1:26-38 (cp. Mt.1:18-25) | be called the Son of the Highest: and the Lord God shall give unto him the throne of his father David: | 1) Son of the Highest |
|---|---|---|---|
| **1 The angel Gabriel** a. Was sent from God b. Was sent to the most obscure place | 26 And in the sixth month the angel Gabriel was sent from God unto a city of Galilee, named Nazareth, | 33 And he shall reign over the house of Jacob for ever; and of his kingdom there shall be no end. | 2) Son of David[DS3] c. His eternal kingdom |
| **2 Mary was pure, a virgin**[DS1] | 27 To a virgin espoused to a man whose name was Joseph, of the house of David; and the virgin's name was Mary. | 34 Then said Mary unto the angel, How shall this be, seeing I know not a man? | **6 Mary was expected to believe the miraculous** a. Her perplexity b. Her conception: By the Holy Spirit & the power of God |
| **3 Mary was highly favored by God** | 28 And the angel came in unto her, and said, Hail, thou that art highly favoured, the Lord is with thee: blessed art thou among women. | 35 And the angel answered and said unto her, The Holy Ghost shall come upon thee, and the power of the Highest shall overshadow thee: therefore also that holy thing which shall be born of thee shall be called the Son of God. | c. Her child: The Son of God |
| **4 Mary was very human** a. Greatly troubled b. Fearful | 29 And when she saw him, she was troubled at his saying, and cast in her mind what manner of salutation this should be. 30 And the angel said unto her, Fear not, Mary: for thou hast found favour with God. | 36 And, behold, thy cousin Elisabeth, she hath also conceived a son in her old age: and this is the sixth month with her, who was called barren. 37 For with God nothing shall be impossible. | **7 Mary was encouraged to believe: "With God nothing is impossible"** a. God's other miracle b. God's great power |
| **5 Mary was told she was to bear the Messiah** a. His name: Jesus[DS2] b. His great person | 31 And, behold, thou shalt conceive in thy womb, and shalt bring forth a son, and shalt call his name JESUS. 32 He shall be great, and shall | 38 And Mary said, Behold the handmaid of the Lord; be it unto me according to thy word. And the angel departed from her. | **8 Mary was submissive** |

# DIVISION I

## THE ANNOUNCEMENT OF THE COMING OF JESUS, THE SON OF MAN, 1:1-2:52

## C.     Mary, the Mother of Jesus: Submission to God's Will, 1:26-38

(1:26-38) **Introduction**: little information is given about Mary in the Bible. However, what is said is striking and sets before us a tremendous example of *submissiveness to God's will*. Submissiveness to God is an absolute essential for every believer.

    1.    The angel Gabriel (v.26).
    2.    Mary was pure, a virgin (v.27).
    3.    Mary was highly favored by God (v.28).
    4.    Mary was very human (v.29-30).
    5.    Mary was told she was to bear the Messiah (v.31-33).
    6.    Mary was expected to believe the miraculous (v.34-35).
    7.    Mary was encouraged to believe: "With God nothing is impossible" (v.36-37).
    8.    Mary was submissive (v.38).

**1** (1:26) **Nazareth—Gabriel**: the angel Gabriel was sent from God. This was Gabriel's second mission surrounding the birth of Jesus (see DEEPER STUDY # 1—Lk.1:19). Note the time is given. It was six months after Elizabeth's conception that Gabriel was sent to an obscure village, Nazareth of Galilee. Galilee bordered Gentile or heathen nations; therefore, it was sometimes called Galilee of the Gentiles. Nazareth was a despised city, considered inferior by the rest of Israel. The people were a conquered people especially despised by the Romans. The city and its citizens were the object of deep prejudice by Jews and Romans alike (cp. Jn.1:46). (See DEEPER STUDY # 4, *Nazareth*—Mt.2:23; 13:53-58.)

    **Thought 1.** God is no respecter of persons or places. He sends a message to Nazareth as readily as He does to Jerusalem (cp. Lk.1:5-25), to a believer in Nazareth (Mary) as quickly as he does to a believer in Jerusalem (Zacharias).

    **Thought 2.** A place, whether city or nation, is not judged by its institutions and advantages, but by the righteous people within its borders (cp. Gen.18:23f).

**2** (1:27) **Jesus Christ, Birth—Mary—Betrothed—Espoused—Purity**: Mary was pure, a virgin. She had never been touched by a man, not immorally. This is unmistakably and clearly stated. She confirmed the fact herself (cp. v.34).

15

1.     The argument that the Hebrew word "alma" means a young woman who could have a questionable character is weak (Is.7:14). When a Hebrew spoke of a young woman (alma) he meant virgin. This is clear when the word *alma* is studied. The word is used six times in the Bible, always referring to a young woman with pure character.

⇒ Rebekah, the young woman, was certainly a virgin (Gen.24:43). The whole context verifies the point.
⇒ Miriam, the young sister of Moses, was also pointed to as a virgin by the context (Ex.2:8).
⇒ Young women of pure character were those who were worthy to participate in the worship of God (Ps.68:25).
⇒ The young women who were worthy of Solomon's love were not of impure character (Song of Sol.1:3).
⇒ There were young women who were compared with queens and concubines (Song of Sol.6:8).
⇒ The maiden (young woman) of Proverbs was contrasted with the adulterous woman (Pr.30:19-20).

In view of the heavy weight of this argument, the logical translation of *alma* is virgin. Of course, the virgin birth does not rest on this argument. However, we need to realize that unbelief snatches at every little gnat, trying its best to add every thing it can to disprove the divinity of Christ.

**Thought 1.** Man desperately needs to turn from his unbelief and to trust Christ with all his heart. There is little time left for any of us.

"For God so loved the world, that he gave his only begotten Son, that whosoever believeth in him should not perish, but have everlasting life" (Jn.3:16).
"And as it is appointed unto men once to die, but after this the judgment" (Heb.9:27).

2.     Mary was espoused to Joseph. Being espoused was something like an engagement, except it was more binding. It lasted one year. Two matters are important in discussing Mary's virginity.
a.    In the espousal period sexual contact was adultery and resulted in stoning.
b.    The espousal was so serious a matter that if it were broken a divorce had to be secured.
3.     Mary and Joseph were both godly, so godly that God could choose them to be the parents of His Son. It was impossible that God would have chosen an immoral man and woman to bear and rear His Son, not when He had the power to control the events.

**Thought 1.** There are two striking lessons in the purity of Mary.
1)    God expects both women and men to be sexually pure, untouched by a man or woman until they are married.
2)    God is looking for pure women and men to use in the ministry of the gospel and in meeting the desperate needs of the world.

"For this is the will of God, even your sanctification, that ye should abstain from fornication: that every one of you should know how to possess his vessel in sanctification and honour....For God hath not called us unto uncleanness, but unto holiness" (1 Th.4:3-4, 7).
"Now concerning the things whereof ye wrote unto me: It is good for a man not to touch a woman. Nevertheless, to avoid fornication, let every man have his own wife, and let every woman have her own husband" (1 Cor.7:1-2).
"But fornication, and all uncleanness, or covetousness, let it not be once named among you, as becometh saints" (Eph.5:3).
"Lay hands suddenly on no man, neither be partaker of other men's sins: keep thyself pure" (1 Tim.5:22).
"The aged women likewise, that they be in behaviour as becometh holiness....that they may teach the young women to be sober, to love their husbands, to love their children, to be discreet, chaste, keepers at home, good, obedient to their own husbands, that the word of God be not blasphemed" (Tit.2:3-5).
"Ye have heard that it was said by them of old time, Thou shalt not commit adultery: but I say unto you, That whosoever looketh on a woman to lust after her hath committed adultery with her already in heart" (Mt.5:27-28).
"These are they which were not defiled with women; for they are virgins. These are they which follow the Lamb whithersoever he goeth. These were redeemed from among men, being the firstfruits unto God and to the Lamb" (Rev.14:4).
"Who shall ascend into the hill of the LORD? or who shall stand in his holy place? He that hath clean hands, and a pure heart; who hath not lifted up his soul unto vanity, nor sworn deceitfully" (Ps.24:3-4).

---

**DEEPER STUDY # 1**

(1:27) **Jesus Christ, Virgin Birth:** in looking at the virgin birth of Christ, man needs to think deeply and honestly. Both are necessary: man must be honest, and he must engage in concentrated thought. One question needs to be asked. Why would God's Son have to enter the world through a virgin? Or more simply put, why was Christ born of a virgin? Why was a virgin birth necessary? (Note: Mary confirmed that she was a virgin, v.34.)

1.     The birth of God's Son required a miracle. He could not be born through the natural process as other men are. If He had been born as other men, His very birth would indicate that He was no more than mere man. Very simply, any person who enters the world through a man and a woman is a mere man or a mere woman. He or she can be nothing more. But this is not so with Christ. Christ already existed. Therefore, if God willed to send His Son into the world, He would

have to choose another way. All Christ needed was a body. As He Himself said to God the Father: "A body hast thou prepared for me" (Heb.10:5).

2.     The birth of God's Son required a combined act on God's part and on woman's part. If God's Son were to become a man and identify with men, He had to come through the process of conception through a woman. Why? Because man can only come through the woman. Therefore, if God willed to send His Son into the world as a man, He would have to perform a miracle, causing Mary to conceive by an act of His divine power.

> **Thought 1.** A question needs to be asked. Why is it so hard to believe that God can cause Mary to miraculously conceive? Why is it so hard to believe that God exists and that "God so loved the world, that he gave his only begotten Son, that whosoever believeth in him should not perish, but have everlasting life" (Jn.3:16)?

> **Thought 2.** Just imagine what science can do in the fertilization of female eggs today. Is God not able to do so much more? How foolish our unbelief causes us to act. The problem is not God, but our faith: "With God nothing shall be impossible" (Lk.1:37; 18:27. Cp. Heb.11:6, which is a warning to all.)

3.     The birth of God's Son required a miraculous nature—both a divine nature and a human nature.
⇒   He had to be born of a woman to partake of human nature. (Cp. Heb.2:14-18.)
⇒   He had to be born by a miraculous act of God so as not to partake of man's corruption. This was critical if we are to escape corruption and live forever. Think about it. Our faith must be in an incorruptible Savior if we are to be covered by His incorruption. God had to identify with us by becoming one with us and by conquering our depraved and doomed nature. (See DEEPER STUDY # 3, *Jesus Christ, Birth*—Mt.1:16 for more discussion.)

4.     The birth of God's Son required the birth of a perfect nature. Why? Because a perfect life needed to be lived. Righteousness, that is, perfection, needed to be secured. An Ideal Life (that is, a perfect, righteous life) had to be lived so that it could stand for and cover all men in perfection and in righteousness. Honest thought confesses that no man has been or is perfect. Man comes short. His *coming short* of God's glory is tragically pictured in the ultimate fate of life: death.

But God acted. God did everything to secure righteousness and perfection for man. He took every step and performed every act necessary to *save His people* from their sins and from death. He did it from beginning to end, from birth to exaltation. God sent His Son into the world, not through a man and a woman but through a miraculous act of His own upon the virgin Mary. Jesus Christ was thereby the God-Man. This says at least four things. (See notes—Ro.5:1; DEEPER STUDY # 2—8:3 for more discussion.)

a.   As God-Man, Christ was able to consummate both the human and divine. He had the capacity and innate power not to sin (see DEEPER STUDY # 3—Mt.1:16). Therefore His Godly nature empowered Him to live righteously, never doing wrong and always choosing and doing right (Heb.5:8; 2 Cor.5:21). By living a sinless life, Christ was able to secure righteousness, the Ideal Righteousness, that will cover and stand for all men.

b.   As God-Man, Christ was also able to bear the sins and the judgment of sin for all men. When He died, He died as the Perfect and Ideal Man. Therefore, His death is able to cover and stand for all men.

c.   As God-Man, Christ was able to arise from the dead. Note the phenomenal words: "...His [God's] son Jesus Christ, our Lord, which was made of the seed of David according to the flesh [that is, made a man]; and declared to be the Son of God with power, according to *the spirit of holiness* by the resurrection from the dead" (Ro.1:3-4). He lived a perfect and holy life by which He became the Perfect and Ideal Man; therefore, His resurrection covers and stands for every man.

d.   As God-Man, Christ was exalted to sit at the right hand of the Father—to live eternally in the heavenly dimension of being, in God's very own presence. As the Perfect and Ideal Man, His exaltation into the heavenly or spiritual dimension is able to blaze the path into heaven for every man. He is the forerunner into heaven for every man (Heb.6:20). His exaltation as the Ideal Man covers and stands for the exaltation of every man.

5.     The birth of God's Son required the creative Word of God. God created the world by simply speaking the Word. God always creates by the power of His Word and the power of His Word alone. Therefore, when God chose...
•   to create a body for His Son, He created that body by simply speaking the Word (Heb.10:5).
•   to send His Son into the world, He sent His Son by simply speaking the Word.

It is the same with the new birth or the re-creation of man's spirit. It is by the Word of God, God's simply speaking the Word, that man is born again. The act of the spiritual birth, of the re-creation, is not seen, felt, or touched. Nothing physical happens, but the re-creation does occur. *It occurs by the Word of God* (cp. 1 Pt.1:23).

6.     The birth of God's Son required the virgin birth because Christ is the *only begotten* Son of God. He is God's only Son, who possesses all the nature and fulness of God Himself (Ph.2:6-7; Col.2:9). Therefore, His birth had to be different. He had to enter the world differently from others, for He is different by the very nature of His being. He had to enter the world in such a way as to proclaim His divine nature, yet in such a way that would allow Him to partake of human nature. This is critically important. His birth had to involve both the act of mankind and of God Himself. Why? Because the Son of God had to be proclaimed to be the Son of God.
⇒   There is no salvation apart from His *being* the Son of God.
⇒   There is no salvation apart from His being *proclaimed* to be the Son of God.

Man can be saved only if the Son of God *is*, only if He exists, and only if He is *proclaimed*. The Son of God must *exist*, and we must *hear* of Him if we are to be saved. He and His message are both essential. His virgin birth proclaims Him to be the *only begotten* Son of God, the only Son sent into the world by the direct and miraculous intervention of God.

7.     The birth of God's Son required a second Adam, a second man...
•   born just like the first Adam, by the Word of God using natural substance.
•   born to become what the first Adam failed to become: the Representative Man, the Ideal Man, the Pattern, the Perfect One in whom all men could find their Representative, their Ideal, their Pattern, their Perfection.

> - born to be what Adam failed to be: the Man who always chose to love and obey God in all things, thereby passing on the nature of the ideal righteousness and perfection that can stand for and cover all men.
> - born to become what the first Adam failed to pass on to man: the Way to God, the Truth of God, and the Life of God which all men can trust and follow (Jn.14:6).
> - born to offer what the first Adam failed to pass on to man: the nature of righteousness and life, both life abundant and life eternal (cp. Ro.5:15-19; Jn.10:10).
>
> 8. The birth of God's Son required an espoused state, and not a single or married state. Why?
> ⇒ Because a single woman would cause far more questioning and heap far more contempt upon Christ and His followers.
> ⇒ Because a married woman would not be a virgin and God's Son had to be born of a virgin as indicated by the points above.
>
> The espoused state provided the ideal marital relationship for God to use in sending His Son into the world (see note 2—Lk.1:27). The fact that Jewish society was using the espoused relationship as a preparation for marriage shows how God was preparing the world for the coming of His Son. (See Deeper Study # 1, *Fulness of Time*—Gal.4:4.)
>
> **"But when the fulness of the time was come, God sent forth his Son, made of a woman, made under the law" (Gal.4:4).**

**3** (1:28) **Grace—God, Call of—Favored by God**: Mary was highly favored by God. Three simple, yet meaningful, things were said to Mary.

1. She was to be highly favored by God. Note the angel did not immediately tell Mary how she was to be favored by God, that she was God's choice to bear and to be the mother of the Messiah. That came later in the conversation. The angel had to give her time to adjust to the shock of his spectacular appearance. For right now, he simply announced that she was to be highly favored by God—*a unique privilege*.

> **Thought 1.** Just think! God does *favor* us: He saves us, gifts us, uses us. We are favored by the God of the universe—a phenomenal privilege and an awesome responsibility to make ourselves available to receive His favors.

2. The Lord was also with Mary. She did not walk through life alone. God was with her. Mary's life had pleased God to the point that He could favor her and be with her. She allowed God to walk with her and look after her life, so God was able to be with her. This means that God...
- *had been* with her (past).
- *was* with her (present).
- *would be* with her (future).

No matter where Mary had to walk or what she had to do, God promised to be with her.

3. Mary was to be blessed among women. It should be noted that this clause is not in the oldest and best manuscripts. Nevertheless, the point is made in v.48. Mary was to be blessed and to be called blessed by men of all generations (cp. Judg.5:24 for a similar declaration by Deborah concerning Jael).

**4** (1:29-30) **Humility**: Mary was very human. She was both troubled and stricken with fear. The fear was understandable, for an angelic being from God stood before her. He stood in all the dazzling splendor that is necessary to reveal that he was truly from God. The fact that Mary was *troubled* needs to be briefly considered.

1. Mary was "troubled at his saying," at what the angel told her. It was the message that caused her to be troubled, the fact that...
- she was highly favored.
- the Lord was with her.
- she was blessed among women.

> **Thought 1.** Since Christ has come, every person can now...
> - be highly favored by God.
> - have the Lord's presence.
> - be blessed among all others.

2. Mary was troubled because she did not understand how God could so greatly favor a person like herself. She never expected to be greatly favored by Him. This was deep humility. Mary was not a proud, self-centered, flighty, or frivolous young lady who was conscious of herself or felt that she merited and deserved the attention of others. She was a young lady who loved God and had determined to live a pure and responsible life. Apparently, from her response throughout this passage, she had a sweet spirit that was full of softness, warmth, and tenderness, and was responsive and willing, subjective and giving, thoughtful and kind. However, Mary never dreamed she was anyone special. Therefore, when she heard that God was to favor her and use her in a very special way, she was troubled. How could she, so ordinary and humble, do anything special for God? What a striking example Mary was!

> **"But he giveth more grace. Wherefore he saith, God resisteth the proud, but giveth grace unto the humble" (Jas.4:6).**
> **"For all those things have been, saith the LORD: but to this man will I look, even to him that is poor and of a contrite spirit, and trembleth at my word" (Is.66:2).**
> **"Though the LORD be high, yet hath he respect unto the lowly: but the proud he knoweth afar off" (Ps.138:6).**

**5** (1:31-33) **Jesus Christ, Deity**: Mary was told by the angel how she was to be favored by God. She was to bear and be the mother of the Messiah. Note three startling and profound things about Mary's Son.
1.  *His name*. Mary was actually told what she was to name the Messiah: Jesus (see DEEPER STUDY # 2, *Jesus*—Lk.1:31).
2.  *His great person*.
    a.  He was to be called the Son of the Highest. The Highest, of course, is God. Therefore, Jesus is the Son of God, that is, of the very nature of God. He is "over all, God blessed for ever. Amen" (Ro.9:5).
    b.  He was to be the Son of David and was to receive the throne of David. He was of the line of David. This indicates that Mary was a descendant of David; therefore, Christ Himself would become a descendant of David (see DEEPER STUDY # 3—Lk.1:32-33).
3.  *His eternal kingdom*. Jesus was to teach that His kingdom would not be of this earth, for nothing on this earth lasts (Jn.19:36). Therefore, the kingdom was to be spiritual, by which it would be eternal (see DEEPER STUDY # 3—Mt.19:23-24).

---

**DEEPER STUDY # 2**
(1:31) **Jesus** (iesous): Savior; He will save. The Hebrew form is *Joshua* (yasha), meaning Jehovah is salvation or He is the Savior. The idea is that of deliverance, of being saved from some terrible disaster that leads to perishing (cp. Jn.3:16). (Cp. Lk.9:23; Ro.8:3; Gal.1:4; Heb.2:14-18; 7:25.)

---

**DEEPER STUDY # 3**
(1:32-33) **Jesus Christ, Names—Titles, Son of David**: Christ is the Son of David, a descendant of David. Note two things.
1.  Christ is to reign upon the throne of David. But it will not be the people who will give Him the throne. They will not allow Him to rule over them. The throne will be given to Him by God. God will be the One to place Him upon the throne and give Him the rule over the people (see note—Mt.1:1).
2.  The promise of ruling over the house of Jacob and of possessing a kingdom forever apparently has both a literal and a spiritual meaning, both a temporal and eternal meaning (see DEEPER STUDY # 3—Mt.19:23-24; note—Lk.3:24-31; DEEPER STUDY # 3—Jn.1:45; DEEPER STUDY # 4—1:49; note—Ro.11:1-36, esp. 11:25-36).

---

**6** (1:34-35) **Jesus Christ, Birth; Deity; Son of God—Faith**: Mary was expected to believe the miraculous, but she was puzzled. She was not doubting or distrusting the message. She was not asking for some sign or proof like Zacharias (v.18). She was simply asking for more information. She was single and had never known a man sexually. How could she possibly bear a child without knowing a man? Note exactly what is said about her conception.
1.  "The Holy Spirit shall *come upon thee*." The thought *is not after* the manner of men, but *after the manner* of God's Spirit. What is the manner or operation of God's Spirit? God's Spirit sets apart and activates, creates and re-creates by *the Word of God*. God's Spirit simply speaks and it is done (see DEEPER STUDY # 1, pt.5—Lk.1:27). There is no such idea as a *crude mating* between the Holy Spirit and Mary. God's Spirit simply speaks and it is done, no matter what is to be done. (How foolish are the *crude thoughts* and unbelief of men!)
2.  "The power of the Highest [God] shall *overshadow thee*." God Himself was going to look after the whole matter. The child's conception and growth during pregnancy and His birth and life were under the shadow and wing of Almighty God. It was God's power that saw to the whole operation, not the presence or power of an angel or of a man or of any other creature.
3.  The child born of Mary would *be holy*, "the Son of God." Note the most critical point: who "the Son of God" is.
    ⇒ He is "the holy One" born by the power and the Word and the will of God through the virgin Mary.
    ⇒ He is "the holy One" whom "God sent forth...made of a woman" by His power, Word, and will (Gal.4:4).

**Thought 1.** Believers are to believe the miraculous.

> "And Jesus said unto them, Because of your unbelief: for verily I say unto you, If ye have faith as a grain of mustard seed, ye shall say unto this mountain, Remove hence to yonder place; and it shall remove; and nothing shall be impossible unto you" (Mt.17:20).
> "Jesus said unto him, If thou canst believe, all things are possible to him that believeth" (Mk.9:23).
> "Commit thy way unto the LORD; trust also in him; and he shall bring it to pass" (Ps.37:5).
> "Trust in the LORD with all thine heart; and lean not unto thine own understanding" (Pr.3:5).

**7** (1:36-37) **Faith—God, Power of**: Mary was encouraged to believe that "with God nothing is impossible." God encouraged Mary with two *impossible* facts.
1.  The news that her sister Elizabeth, who was beyond child-bearing age, had conceived a son in her old age and was now six months pregnant. The fact that God could take her sister in her old age and cause her to conceive demonstrated God's power. Visiting Elizabeth would encourage Mary.
2.  With men much is impossible. To say that all things are possible with men is far from the truth. When Mary heard and meditated upon the simple statement, "With God all things are possible," she was bound to be encouraged. The statement was simple and striking. It could be easily remembered and understood.

**Thought 1.** God expects us to believe Him and His power, regardless of circumstances and our feelings of insignificance.

> "But Jesus beheld them, and said unto them, With men this is impossible; but with God all things are possible" (Mt.19:26).
> "I know that thou canst do every thing, and that no thought can be withholden from thee" (Job.42:2).
> "But our God is in the heavens: he hath done whatsoever he hath pleased" (Ps.115:3).

**8** (1:38) **Surrender**: Mary was submissive. Her response was immediate and brief, only one short sentence, yet it was striking and meaningful.

1. The word "handmaid" (doule) means slave-girl. Mary was saying that she was a bond-slave, willing to sell herself out completely to God. She would possess herself no longer but would give herself completely to God.

2. God's Word was her will. She surrendered totally to obey God. She would serve as He willed, being completely obedient and fulfilling His purpose entirely. She would act "according to *Thy Word*."

Imagine what Mary was saying, the enormous depth of her trust and dedication to God.

1. There was the idea of being an unwed mother (Lk.1:26f; Mt.1:18). Who of that day would ever believe Mary's story? Required was a willingness to be available to God regardless of the price.

2. There was Joseph's discovery of her pregnancy (Mt.1:19). The shock of broken trust and of personal embarrassment were more than a person could be expected to bear (Mt.1:20). Required was a willingness on Joseph's part to forget self completely.

3. There was the threat of being condemned to death because of adultery (Dt.22:23f). She had to face the possibility of being stoned because she would appear to be immoral (cp. Jn.8:5).

**Thought 1.** Surrender to God is an absolute essential both for salvation and service.

> "For whosoever shall do the will of my Father which is in heaven, the same is my brother, and sister, and mother" (Mt.12:50).
> "So likewise, whosoever he be of you that forsaketh not all he hath, he cannot be my disciple" (Lk.14:33).
> "And the world passeth away, and the lust thereof: but he that doeth the will of God abideth for ever" (1 Jn.2:17).
> "I delight to do thy will, O my God: yea, thy law is within my heart" (Ps.40:8).
> "Teach me to do thy will; for thou art my God: thy spirit is good; lead me into the land of uprightness" (Ps.143:10).
> "My son, give me thine heart, and let thine eyes observe my ways" (Pr.23:26).

| | D. Elizabeth's Supernatural Proclamation: A Very Unusual Testimony, 1:39-45 | Holy Ghost: | | with the Spirit |
|---|---|---|---|---|
| | | 42 And she spake out with a loud voice, and said, Blessed art thou among women, and blessed is the fruit of thy womb. | 2 | 4) Spoke loudly |
| 1 Mary visited Elizabeth | 39 And Mary arose in those days, and went into the hill country with haste, into a city of Juda; | 43 And whence is this to me, that the mother of my Lord should come to me? | 3 | She proclaimed a uniqueness about Mary & her child |
| a. Went with haste | | | | She proclaimed that Mary's child was her Lord |
| b. Went to the town of Juda | | | | |
| c. Entered Elizabeth's home & greeted her | 40 And entered into the house of Zacharias, and saluted Elisabeth. | 44 For, lo, as soon as the voice of thy salutation sounded in mine ears, the babe leaped in my womb for joy. | | a. The great confession |
| | | | | b. The clear sign |
| d. Was welcomed by Elizabeth's supernatural proclamation | 41 And it came to pass, that, when Elisabeth heard the salutation of Mary, the babe leaped in her womb; and Elisabeth was filled with the | 45 And blesssed is she that believed: for there shall be a performance of those things which were told her from the Lord. | 4 | She proclaimed that Mary's faith would receive the promise |
| 1) Heard Mary's greeting | | | | |
| 2) Felt the babe leap | | | | |
| 3) Was instantly filled | | | | |

# DIVISION I

## THE ANNOUNCEMENT OF THE COMING OF JESUS, THE SON OF MAN, 1:1-2:52

## D.     Elizabeth's Supernatural Proclamation: A Very Unusual Testimony, 1:39-45

(1:39-45) **Introduction**: whatever confession was borne about the Baby conceived in Mary was of critical importance. Why? Because the baby was...
- Jesus (v.31).
- The Son of the Highest (v.32).
- The Son of David (v.32).
- The Ruler over the house of Jacob forever (v.33).
- The Ruler whose kingdom has no end (v.33).
- The One born of the Holy Spirit (v.35).
- The Son of God Himself (v.35).

In this passage God sees to it that a supernatural confession is proclaimed, a crucial confession that needs to be studied in depth. Note that this is the very first testimony ever given by human lips about Jesus.
1.     Mary visited Elizabeth (v.39-42).
2.     Elizabeth proclaimed a uniqueness about Mary and her child (v.42).
3.     Elizabeth proclaimed the child to be her Lord (v.43-44).
4.     Elizabeth proclaimed that Mary's faith would receive the promise (v.45).

1    (1:39-42) **Encouragement—Comfort—Trials**: Mary visited Elizabeth, and her visit was memorable. She went "with haste" (spoudes). The word means speed, diligence, care, earnestness, zeal. The idea is that Mary went with purpose and earnestness. She was not going on a casual, friendly visit. She had a very specific reason for going, a meaningful purpose. She was going so that she and Elizabeth could encourage and share with each other. They both had similar situations. God had acted upon both their bodies, performing a miracle for both. Elizabeth's womb was made alive for the son of Zacharias to be conceived,  and Mary's womb had conceived as a virgin. Mary in particular could be encouraged, for Elizabeth was already six months pregnant. The six months' pregnancy was visible evidence that God had already acted upon her miraculously. It should be noted that Mary knew about Elizabeth's miraculous conception, but Elizabeth did not know about Mary's conception. Zacharias and Elizabeth lived in Juda. The town is unknown today, but most commentators think it was the same as Hebron. Hebron is said to be in the hill country of Juda and to belong to the priests (Josh. 21:10-11).

Mary entered Elizabeth's home and greeted her. It was at the *very moment* of Mary's greeting that Elizabeth's supernatural greeting began. Mary greeted Elizabeth, and three unusual things immediately happened.
1.     The babe leaped in Elizabeth's womb. The baby had leaped or kicked before, but this leap was different from all the others. It was a sign to Elizabeth that the Babe within Mary was someone very, very special, someone who was about to be revealed to her under the filling (influence) of the Holy Spirit.
2.     Elizabeth was instantly "filled with the Holy Spirit," and a very special spirit of prophecy was given her. The Holy Spirit seized her and led her to greet Mary as the mother of the Messiah, the coming Lord. Note: Elizabeth was living an obedient life before God. This was the reason God was able to use her and the Holy Spirit was able to infill her with His presence.
3.     Elizabeth spoke in a loud voice. She was full of joy and exaltation for the Messiah, full of unusual emotions. She was under the influence and impulse of the Spirit of God. She was being guided to proclaim that the Baby of Mary was "the Lord" (v.43, 45).

2    (1:42) **Jesus Christ, Honored—Mary, Blessed—Humility—Envy**: Elizabeth proclaimed a uniqueness about Mary and her child. Note three things.

1.    The very first act toward Christ was a *proclamation of praise*. Elizabeth was the *first* person to know about the birth of Christ other than Mary, and God saw to it that her first act was to honor His Son. God would have His Son to be honored on earth even as He is honored in heaven.

> "By him therefore let us offer the sacrifice of praise to God continually, that is, the fruit of our lips giving thanks to his name" (Heb.13:15).
> "But ye are a chosen generation, a royal priesthood, an holy nation, a peculiar people; that ye should show forth the praises of him who hath called you out of darkness into his marvellous light" (1 Pt.2:9).

2.    Mary was blessed, but she was blessed because "the fruit of her womb" was great.

3.    Elizabeth demonstrated a very sweet and humble spirit, a meekness and love that were so desperately needed by so many. She was older, and by being the wife of a priest, she was recognized by the world as being of a higher social class and more honorable. Yet Mary, poor and unrecognized by the world, had been chosen by God to serve in a more special way. Elizabeth showed no envy or jealousy, no hurt or withdrawal. Contrariwise, she rejoiced over Mary's call.

> "Let nothing be done through strife or vainglory; but in lowliness of mind let each esteem other better than themselves. Look not every man on his own things, but every man also on the things of others" (Ph.2:3-4).

**3**    (1:43-44) **Confession—Jesus Christ, Deity**: Elizabeth proclaimed the child to be her Lord.

1.    Note the great confession of Elizabeth. Elizabeth called Mary's Baby, "my Lord." In a moment of quickening power, the Holy Spirit revealed that the Babe was not only the promised Messiah, but He was the Son of the Highest, of God Himself (Lk.1:32, 35). There was no question that Elizabeth was using the term "Lord" in its highest sense. She was under the power of the Holy Spirit; therefore, she was confessing the truth under the influence of God. The truth was that the coming Child of Mary was the Messiah, the Son of the living God. She was also contrasting her son with the Son of Mary. Her own son was to be great, but the Son of Mary was greater. He was *her Lord*, the Lord God Himself, the Son of the Highest.

2.    Note the clear sign given to Elizabeth. The sign was unmistakable. Upon hearing the greeting of Mary as she entered the door, Elizabeth's heart leaped for joy and the babe in her womb leaped much more than usual. In Elizabeth's words, "The babe leaped in my womb *for joy* [exultation]." God caused the babe to leap (the word is strong, indicating a struggling leap) as a sign of great joy in the presence of One so great that Elizabeth would call Him "my Lord."

**Thought 1.** Elizabeth's confession of her Lord was a very personal thing. She apparently never shared it with John. John did not know Jesus was the Messiah until Jesus' baptism (Jn.1:31-34). John had to discover and confess Christ for himself. So do we all. It is a *personal* decision.

> "Whosoever therefore shall confess me before men, him will I confess also before my Father which is in heaven" (Mt.10:32).
> "He saith unto them, But whom say ye that I am? And Simon Peter answered and said, Thou art the Christ, the Son of the living God. And Jesus answered and said unto him, Blessed art thou, Simon Barjona: for flesh and blood hath not revealed it unto thee, but my Father which is in heaven" (Mt.16:15-17).
> "Whosoever shall confess that Jesus is the Son of God, God dwelleth in him, and he in God" (1 Jn.4:15).

**Thought 2.** Elizabeth's confession was bound to encourage Mary.

1)    *God sees to it that we are encouraged* when we need encouragement. Mary needed assurance, so God took her where she could be assured. But note: she obeyed God. She went where God led her. It was while she was obeying that God was able to encourage her.

> "But the very hairs of your head are all numbered. Fear ye not therefore, ye are of more value than many sparrows" (Mt.10:30-31).
> "For I the LORD thy God will hold thy right hand, saying unto thee, Fear not: I will help thee" (Is.41:13).
> "But now thus saith the LORD that created thee, O Jacob, and he that formed thee, O Israel, Fear not: for I have redeemed thee, I have called thee by thy name; thou art mine" (Is.43:1).

2)    Elizabeth willingly humbled herself to help Mary. She was older and held a higher position as the wife of a priest, yet she denied and surrendered herself to push Mary and her child forward.

> "I have showed you all things, how that so labouring ye ought to support the weak, and to remember the words of the Lord Jesus, how he said, It is more blessed to give than to receive" (Acts 20:35).
> "Rejoice with them that do rejoice, and weep with them that weep" (Ro.12:15).

"We then that are strong ought to bear the infirmities of the weak, and not to please ourselves" (Ro.15:1).

"Bear ye one another's burdens, and so fulfil the law of Christ" (Gal.6:2).

**4** (1:45) **Faith—Promise**: Elizabeth proclaimed that Mary's faith would receive the promise. Note two significanct points.

1. There are two reasons why Mary has been blessed by believers of every generation.
   a. Mary believed the Word of God sent to her (Lk.1:38). Contrast her belief with Zacharias' unbelief (Lk.1:20).
   b. Mary was related to Christ in a very, very special way.

**Thought 1.** The same two facts are essential for us if we wish to be blessed by God.
1) We must believe the Word of God sent to us.

"Blessed are they that hear the word of God, and keep it" (Lk.11:28).

"If a man love me, he will keep my words: and my Father will love him, and we will come unto him, and make our abode with him" (Jn.14:23).

"If ye abide in me, and my words abide in you, ye shall ask what ye will, and it shall be done unto you" (Jn.15:7).

"For this cause also thank we God without ceasing, because, when ye received the word of God which ye heard of us, ye received it not as the word of men, but as it is in truth, the word of God, which effectually worketh also in you that believe" (1 Th.2:13).

"Whosoever therefore shall be ashamed of me and of my words in this adulterous and sinful generation; of him also shall the Son of man be ashamed, when he cometh in the glory of his Father with the holy angels" (Mk.8:38).

2) We must become related to Christ by adoption. We must become the adopted children of God.

"But when the fulness of the time was come, God sent forth his Son, made of a woman, made under the law, to redeem them that were under the law, that we might receive the adoption of sons. And because ye are sons, God hath sent forth the Spirit of his Son into your hearts, crying, Abba, Father" (Gal.4:4-6).

2. The result of Mary's believing the Word of God was that she was to see the performance of God's promises, the things told her from the Lord.

"Whereby are given unto us exceeding great and precious promises: that by these ye might be partakers of the divine nature, having escaped the corruption that is in the world through lust" (2 Pt.1:4).

"Know therefore that the LORD thy God, he is God, the faithful God, which keepeth covenant and mercy with them that love him and keep his commandments to a thousand generations" (Dt.7:9).

"He hath remembered his covenant for ever, the word which he commanded to a thousand generations" (Ps.105:8).

| | E. Mary's Magnificent Song About God: God's Glorious Mercy & Deliverance, 1:46-56 | to generation.<br>51 He hath showed strength with his arm; he hath scattered the proud in the imagination of their hearts.<br>52 He hath put down the mighty from their seats, and exalted them of low degree.<br>53 He hath filled the hungry with good things; and the rich he hath sent empty away.<br>54 He hath holpen his servant Israel, in remembrance of his mercy;<br>55 As he spake to our fathers, to Abraham, and to his seed for ever.<br>56 And Mary abode with her about three months, and returned to her own house. | 4 God had reversed the order of things on earth<br>a. Had scattered the proud<br><br>b. Had dethroned the mighty & exalted the humble<br><br>c. Had filled the hungry & emptied the rich<br><br>5 God had helped His people<br>a. Remembered His mercy<br><br>b. Remembered promise to send the Messiah<br><br>6 Conclusion: Mary visited Elizabeth for about three months |
|---|---|---|---|
| 1 God was the subject of her song<br>2 God was her Savior<br><br>a. Had considered her low estate<br>b. Causes her to be remembered<br><br>3 God was to be proclaimed<br>a. His power<br>b. His holiness<br>c. His mercy | 46 And Mary said, My soul doth magnify the Lord,<br>47 And my spirit hath rejoiced in God my Saviour.<br>48 For he hath regarded the low estate of his handmaiden: for, behold, from henceforth all generations shall call me blessed.<br>49 For he that is mighty hath done to me great things; and holy is his name.<br>50 And his mercy is on them that fear him from generation | | |

# DIVISION I

## THE ANNOUNCEMENT OF THE COMING OF JESUS, THE SON OF MAN, 1:1-2:52

### E.    Mary's Magnificent Song About God: God's Glorious Mercy and Deliverance, 1:46-56

(1:46-56) **Introduction**: Mary's song is known as the *Magnificat*. It has some similarity to the Song of Hannah (1 Sam.2:1-10). However, there is a striking difference between the two songs. Hannah proclaimed a triumph over her enemies; Mary proclaimed God and His glorious mercy to man. Mary was proclaiming the salvation of God, a salvation wrought through the promised Messiah, her Savior. She predicted that the Savior would be welcomed by those who reverenced Him (v.50); but He would be rejected by the proud, the powerful, and the rich (v.51-53).

1.    God was the subject of her song (v.46).
2.    God was her Savior (v.47-48).
3.    God was to be proclaimed (v.49-50).
4.    God had reversed the order of things on earth (v.51-53).
5.    God had helped His people (v.54-55).
6.    Conclusion: Mary visited Elizabeth for about three months (v.56).

1 (1:46) **Praise of God**: God was the subject of Mary's song. Mary was not singing about herself; she was not praising herself. She was not thinking about things which she might accomplish. She said very definitely, "My soul doth magnify *the Lord*." The Lord was the subject of her song, the subject of her praise and rejoicing. Note two things.

1.    Mary was bound to be tired and exhausted. She had just arrived from a long trip and had not even had time to sit down. As soon as she walked in the door, Elizabeth began her proclamation of praise under the inspiration of the Holy Spirit. Mary's song followed right on the heels of Elizabeth's song. Mary forgot her tiredness, for her faith was being confirmed. She now knew that the angel who had come to her was not a figment of her imagination, not an illusion, not a false vision, not some dreamy state of mind (v.28). He was real; and his message that she, as a virgin, would bear the Son of God was true. Her faith was reassured and confirmed.

**Thought 1.** God assures and confirms the faith of us all. We believe and trust, and as the need arises, God steps in to confirm the reality of what we believe.

**"Know therefore that the LORD thy God, he is God, the faithful God, which keepeth covenant and mercy with them that love him and keep his commandments to a thousand generations" (Dt.7:9).**

**Thought 2.** The one thing that can overcome tiredness and exhaustion is an experience with God. More than anything else, the experience of *genuine* prayer and seeking God will cause a person to forget tiredness of body. How desperately we need to seek God!

**"Come unto me, all ye that labour and are heavy laden, and I will give you rest" (Mt.11:28).**

2.    The word "magnify" (megalunei) means to declare the greatness of. The idea is habitual; that is, it was the habit of Mary's soul to magnify the Lord. She kept on magnifying Him.

**Thought 1.** Mary was greatly blessed by God, yet she did not slip into the sin of pride, nor did she think that she was a favorite of God. The more we are blessed by God, the more dangerous the sin of pride becomes. We must learn to live praising God more and more. The more He blesses us, the more we must learn to praise Him.

"But ye are a chosen generation, a royal priesthood, an holy nation, a peculiar people; that ye should show forth the praises of him who hath called you out of darkness into his marvellous light" (1 Pt.2:9).
"Sing praises to the LORD, which dwelleth in Zion: declare among the people his doings" (Ps.9:11).
"Enter into his gates with thanksgiving, and into his courts with praise: be thankful unto him, and bless his name" (Ps.100:4).

**2** (1:47-48) **Humility**: God was Mary's Savior. Mary said three significant things.

1. God saw her need for a Savior. Mary recognized her need, that she was a sinner and needed a Savior just like everyone else. And, more importantly, she made a *personal confession*: "God is *my* Savior." She was proclaiming that God saw her need and saved her.
2. God saw her low estate. Mary recognized where she had come from, just how lowly a person she was. In the eyes of the world, she was a *nobody: poor, obscure, unknown, insignificant,* of *little purpose* and *meaning* in life. The very expression "the low estate of His handmaiden" suggests that Mary was even considered the least within her own household.

**Thought 1.** God usually chooses the least person to more clearly demonstrate His mercy and power (cp. Gideon, Judg.6:15; Leah, Gen.29:31; believers, 1 Cor.1:26-29).

**Thought 2.** We must all know where we have come from, just how far down we were when God saved us (Ro.3:23).

"But God commendeth his love toward us, in that, while we were yet sinners, Christ died for us" (Ro.5:8).
"This is a faithful saying, and worthy of all acceptation, that Christ Jesus came into the world to save sinners; of whom I am chief" (1 Tim.1:15).
"For Christ also hath once suffered for sins, the just for the unjust, that he might bring us to God, being put to death in the flesh, but quickened by the Spirit" (1 Pt.3:18).

**Thought 3.** No matter how *low*, how *nothing* we may be, God cares and will reach down and out to us. He will take us by the hand, lift us up, and give us purpose, meaning, and significance. God will make us somebody and use us, giving us a full and meaningful life (Jn.10:10).

"Humble yourselves in the sight of the Lord, and he shall lift you up" (Jas.4:10).
"For thus saith the high and lofty One that inhabiteth eternity, whose name is Holy; I dwell in the high and holy place, with him also that is of a contrite and humble spirit, to revive the spirit of the humble, and to revive the heart of the contrite ones" (Is.57:15).

3. God will cause her to be remembered. All believers will highly esteem her and her great dedication to God. But note what Christ said:

"And it came to pass, as he spake these things, a certain woman of the company lifted up her voice, and said unto him, Blessed is the womb that bare thee, and the paps which thou hast sucked. But he said, Yea rather, blessed are they that hear the word of God, and keep it" (Lk.11:27-28).

**3** (1:49-50) **God, Attributes**: God was to be proclaimed. Mary proclaimed three of the glorious attributes of God.

1. Mary proclaimed God's power. Two things in particular were in her mind, two phenomenal things.
   a. The promised Messiah was *now* to be born. The hope of the world was now to be fulfilled after so many generations of waiting. God's power was now to be demonstrated in a way never before witnessed.
   b. The promised Messiah was to be born of a virgin. It was to be an event and a method never before witnessed. A miracle was to be performed! The enormous power of God was to be demonstrated *even in the birth of the Messiah*! As Mary testified, "He that is mighty hath done *to me* great things."

"And when he was come nigh, even now at the descent of the mount of Olives, the whole multitude of the disciples began to rejoice and praise God with a loud voice for all the mighty works that they had seen" (Lk.19:37).
"O Lord, open thou my lips; and my mouth shall show forth thy praise" (Ps.51:15).
"And let them sacrifice the sacrifices of thanksgiving, and declare his works with rejoicing" (Ps.107:22).

2. Mary proclaimed God's holiness: "Holy is His name"; that is, God is to be set apart as different from all others (see note and DEEPER STUDY # 1—1 Pt.1:15-16). His very nature, His very being is different. God is both pure being and pure in being, both perfect being and perfect in being. God is holy in name and holy in being, set apart and different from all others.

"Who is like unto thee, O LORD, among the gods? Who is like thee, glorious in holiness, fearful in praises, doing wonders?" (Ex.15:11).

"Exalt the LORD our God, and worship at his holy hill; for the LORD our God is holy" (Ps.99:9).

3. Mary proclaimed God's mercy. There were at least two thoughts in Mary's mind.
   a. God's glorious mercy to her. He had proven to be her personal Savior (see note—Lk.1:47-48).

   "It is of the LORD's mercies that we are not consumed, because his compassions fail not. They are new every morning: great is thy faithfulness" (Lam.3:22-23).

   "Who is a God like unto thee, that pardoneth iniquity, and passeth by the transgression of the remnant of his heritage? he retaineth not his anger for ever, because he delighteth in mercy" (Mic.7:18).

   b. God's glorious mercy in finally sending the Messiah (Savior) to those who feared (reverenced) Him. Note that Mary saw God's mercy passing down from generation to generation.

   "Giving thanks unto the Father, which hath made us meet to be partakers of the inheritance of the saints in light: who hath delivered us from the power of darkness, and hath translated us into the kingdom of his dear Son" (Col.1:12-13).

   "In every thing give thanks: for this is the will of God in Christ Jesus concerning you" (1 Th.5:18).

   "By him therefore let us offer the sacrifice of praise to God continually, that is, the fruit of our lips giving thanks to his name" (Heb.13:15).

   "But the mercy of the LORD is from everlasting to everlasting upon them that fear him, and his righteousness unto children's children" (Ps.103:17).

   "For thy mercy is great above the heavens: and thy truth reacheth unto the clouds" (Ps.108:4).

**4** (1:51-53) **God, Sovereignty—Power:** God had reversed the order of things on earth. Mary proclaimed what the results of the Messiah's coming were to be. There were to be three results, and all three are given in the Greek aorist tense; that is, they are proclaimed as having already happened. Mary saw into the future, and standing there in the future, she proclaimed what the Messiah's coming had already done.

What Mary saw was that the Lord had reversed the order of things on earth. And note: He had done it with "the strength of His arm," that is, not by love but by power.

1. The Lord had scattered the proud. The proud are prideful in their thoughts, in "the imagination of their hearts." They think themselves better...

   * by looks
   * by person
   * by position
   * by wealth
   * by ability
   * by heritage
   * by achievement
   * by possessions

Mary predicted that at the end of time, the Lord will have scattered all such pride. The proud will have been scattered "in the imagination of their hearts."

2. The Lord had dethroned the mighty and exalted the humble. The mighty are those who sit in positions of power, authority, and influence over others. The picture concerns those who take their power and...

   * seek their own ends
   * fail to serve
   * deprive others
   * push others down
   * abuse others
   * enslave others
   * bypass others
   * misuse others

Mary predicted that at the end of time, the Lord will have dethroned the mighty and exalted them of low degree (see notes—Mt.19:28).

3. The Lord had filled the hungry and emptied the rich. Those who were rich only in this world's goods are seen stripped of all their earthly goods and sent away empty. And those who had nothing of this world, but who put their trust in God, are seen as having received all good things (see note—Eph.1:3 for discussion).

**5** (1:54-55) **God, the Savior; Love of:** God had helped His people. Two specific helps were proclaimed.

1. God had remembered His mercy. The people (Israel) desperately needed God's mercy and God's deliverance. They were enslaved by the Romans; therefore, they were frantic in their search for deliverance, so frantic many were turning to false messiahs and other answers to escape their plight. Some were even finding their security in the Roman state and in humanistic answers instead of God. If a people ever needed God to remember His mercy, it was then. Mary proclaimed that the Lord had remembered His mercy.

2. God had remembered His promise of the Messiah. He had promised the Messiah to the fathers of Israel, to Abraham and to Abraham's seed. And note: the promise had now been fulfilled. God had sent the Messiah, the Savior of the world. (See DEEPER STUDY # 1, *Abraham*—Jn.4:22; DEEPER STUDY # 1—Ro.4:1-25 for more discussion.)

   "Now to Abraham and his seed were the promises made. He saith not, And to seeds, as of many; but as of one, And to thy seed, which is Christ" (Gal.3:16).

   "If God were your Father, ye would love me: for I proceeded forth and came from God; neither came I of myself, but he sent me" (Jn.8:42).

"Then came the Jews round about him, and said unto him, How long dost thou make us to doubt? If thou be the Christ, tell us plainly. Jesus answered them, I told you, and ye believed not: the works that I do in my Father's name, they bear witness of me. But ye believe not, because ye are not of my sheep, as I said unto you. My sheep hear my voice, and I know them, and they follow me: and I give unto them eternal life; and they shall never perish, neither shall any man pluck them out of my hand. My Father, which gave them me, is greater than all; and no man is able to pluck them out of my Father's hand" (Jn.10:24-29).

**6** (1:56) **The Conclusion**: Mary remained with Elizabeth for about three months, the very time that was needed to make sure she was pregnant. She needed the encouragement of Elizabeth until the fact had actually happened and was proven. Note the simple childlikeness of Mary, her need for the support and encouragement of her older sister who was probably more spiritually mature.

"We then that are strong ought to bear the infirmities of the weak, and not to please ourselves" (Ro.15:1).
"Bear ye one another's burdens, and so fulfil the law of Christ" (Gal.6:2).

| | F. John's Birth and Naming: An Event for All Generations, 1:57-66 | that is called by this name.<br>62 And they made signs to his father, how he would have him called. | |
|---|---|---|---|
| **1 The child's birth**<br>a. Sealed God's power | 57 Now Elisabeth's full time came that she should be delivered; and she brought forth a son. | 63 And he asked for a writing table, and wrote, saying, His name is John. And they marvelled all. | c. The father confirmed the name John |
| b. Sealed God's mercy | 58 And her neighbours and her cousins heard how the Lord had showed great mercy upon her; and they rejoiced with her. | 64 And his mouth was opened immediately, and his tongue loosed, and he spake, and praised God. | **3 The child's birth caused several important results**<br>a. The father was miraculously healed and praised God |
| c. Caused all to rejoice | 59 And it came to pass, that on the eighth day they came to circumcise the child; and they called him Zacharias, after the name of his father. | 65 And fear came on all that dwelt round about them: and all these sayings were noised abroad throughout all the hill country of Judaea. | b. The people were awe-stricken<br>c. The events were spread abroad |
| **2 The child's name sealed a prophetic witness**<br>a. The child was circumcised: Given up to God | 60 And his mother answered and said, Not so; but he shall be called John. | 66 And all they that heard them laid them up in their hearts, saying, What manner of child shall this be! And the hand of the Lord was with him. | d. The sense of destiny surrounded the child |
| b. The name was disputed | 61 And they said unto her, There is none of thy kindred | | |

# DIVISION I

## THE ANNOUNCEMENT OF THE COMING OF JESUS, THE SON OF MAN, 1:1-2:52

## F. John's Birth and Naming: An Event for All Generations, 1:57-66

(1:57-66) **Introduction**: the birth of a child is a significant event for every parent. But the birth of John was a significant event for every generation, an event that says much to every man.
1. The child's birth (v.57-58).
   a. Sealed God's power.
   b. Sealed God's mercy
   c. Caused all to rejoice.
2. The child's name sealed a prophetic witness (v.59-63).
3. The child's birth caused several important results (v.64-66).

**1** (1:57-58) **God, Mercy of—Mercy**: the child's birth sealed God's power and mercy.
1. The child's birth sealed God's power. Note these facts.
   ⇒ Elizabeth had conceived when she was old, beyond child-bearing years (Lk.1:18, 36).
   ⇒ Zacharias had been visited by the angel of God and told exactly what would happen (Lk.1:11f).
   The fact that the child was born just as God had said is evidence of God's glorious power. God was able to control natural events and to send forth the forerunner of the Messiah *exactly* as He had promised.

> **"For with God nothing shall be impossible" (Lk.1:37).**
> **"But Jesus beheld them, and said unto them, With men this is impossible; but with God all things are possible" (Mt.19:26).**
> **"I know that thou canst do every thing, and that no thought can be withholden from thee" (Job 42:2).**
> **"But our God is in the heavens: he hath done whatsoever he hath pleased" (Ps.115:3).**

2. The child's birth sealed God's mercy, showed that God was merciful in two ways.
   a. The fact that John was born as a *baby of promise* demonstrated that God has mercy upon people, even upon an insignificant woman with a desperate need (see note—Lk.1:7).

> **"The LORD is merciful and gracious, slow to anger, and plenteous in mercy" (Ps.103:8; cp. v.1-8 for a description of God's mercy).**
> **"But the mercy of the LORD is from everlasting to everlasting upon them that fear him" (Ps.103:17).**
> **"Praise ye the LORD. O give thanks unto the LORD; for he is good: for his mercy endureth for ever" (Ps.106:1).**

   b. The fact that God used John in His plan of salvation demonstrated God's mercy. John was to be greatly involved with the Messiah. God allowed him the glorious privilege. Such a high privilege and call clearly demonstrated God's glorious mercy.

**Thought 1.** The very same privilege is given to us. God wants to use everyone of us in His plan of salvation, both to be saved and to bear witness of His salvation.

> **"For this is good and acceptable in the sight of God our Saviour; who will have all men to be saved, and to come unto the knowledge of the truth. For there is one God, and one mediator between God and men, the man Christ Jesus" (1 Tim.2:3-5).**

3. The child's birth caused all to rejoice. God's mercy upon a person's life was bound to make some rejoice. Elizabeth's neighbors and cousins rejoiced with her and all believers rejoice since her. God has had mercy upon the world, and John's birth was one of the significant proofs of His mercy. God sent the forerunner to proclaim the coming of the promised Messiah. The fact that John was born as Scripture predicted and as Zacharias witnessed is proof of God's mercy. God did exactly as He had said. He sent the forerunner to prepare the way for the coming Savior of the world.

**2** (1:59-63) **Prophecy, Fulfilled—Obedience:** the child's name sealed a prophetic witness. What happened is interesting. All Jewish males were circumcised on the eighth day after birth (see DEEPER STUDY # 1—Ph.3:3; cp. Gen.17:12; Lev.12:3). Circumcision was the Jewish ceremony where the child was offered up or dedicated to God. Circumcision was the rite or sign that the child was to be a follower of God, a true Jew. It was also the day on which the child was officially named.

Some of the neighbors and relatives wanted the child to be named after the father, Zacharias. However, Elizabeth objected, knowing that the angel had told Zacharias to name the child John. The relatives took the matter to Zacharias, asking him to write the name out for all to see. They, of course, were expecting Zacharias to be pleased with their suggestion that the child be called after him. But Zacharias shocked them. He confirmed that the child was to be named John. He dared not doubt and disobey God again. He was under the discipline of God for having disobeyed Him before.

The point is that the name John sealed the prophetic witness. The angel had told Zacharias what to name the child. His name was to be John, and Zacharias had borne witness to the angel's visit and promise, even to the angel revealing that the child was to be named John. John was the *prophetic name* given by God's messenger. Zacharias obeyed God and bore testimony to the prophecy; thus, Zacharias sealed the prophetic witness by confirming the name John.

**Thought 1.** The very fact that the child was named John adds proof to the whole event's being true, as having really happened.

**Thought 2.** The prophetic witness is true. Zacharias confirmed it by naming the child John.

> **"These [signs] are written, that ye might believe that Jesus is the Christ, the Son of God; and that believing ye might have life through his name" (Jn.20:31).**

**Thought 3.** Note that the obedience of Zacharias removed the discipline of God for his sin. Zacharias named the child John despite all the pressure from friends and the practice of the day to name the first son after the father. God had *told* Zacharias what to do in naming the child, and when he obeyed, the discipline of God was removed from his life.

**3** (1:64-66) **John the Baptist, Birth:** the child's birth caused several important results.

1. The father was miraculously healed; consequently, he began to praise God. The restraint upon Zacharias' tongue was removed. Note: he had been shut up with his own thoughts, deaf and dumb for nine months. God healed him, opened his ears and loosed his tongue and he began to do exactly what he should do: praise God. Note that his last spoken words had been words of questioning, distrust, and unbelief (Lk.1:18).
2. The people were awe-stricken. The word "fear" (phobos) does not mean terror and fright, but reverence. It means a reverential awe, a reverential fear of God. The people stood in reverence before the events, awe-stricken over what was happening and wondering what else was going to happen. God was working. His hand was evident.
3. The events were spread abroad. God's hand upon the child was the subject of the countryside. (Note. It *should* have been the subject of all. God's movement should always be at the very center of men's conversations.)
4. The sense of destiny surrounded the child. Note that the people kept the things "in their hearts." They did not forget what they were hearing. There was something unusual about the message surrounding the child. Expectations were running high, and many were holding the things in their memory waiting for the child to grow, to see what would happen.

**Thought 1.** All four results should take place in our lives. We should be praising God; we should be awe-stricken at the events; we should spread the events abroad; we should see the destiny surrounding John. We have the privilege of knowing just who John was, the forerunner of the Messiah Himself.

> **"And if ye call on the Father, who without respect of persons judgeth according to every man's work, *pass the time of your sojourning here in fear*: forasmuch as ye know that ye were not redeemed with corruptible things, as silver and gold, from your vain conversation received by tradition from your fathers; but with the precious blood of Christ, as of a lamb without blemish and without spot: who verily was foreordained before the foundation of the world, but was manifest in these last times for you" (1 Pt.1:17-20).**
>
> **"*He sent redemption unto his people*: he hath commanded his covenant for ever: holy and reverend is his name. The fear of the LORD is the beginning of wisdom: a good understanding have all they that do his commandments: his praise endureth for ever" (Ps.111:9-10).**
>
> **"God is greatly to be feared in the assembly of the saint, and to be had in reverence of all them that are about him" (Ps.89:7).**

| | G. Zacharias' Inspired Prophecy: God's Savior & His Forerunner, 1:67-80 | 74 That he would grant unto us, that we being delivered out of the hand of our enemies might serve him without fear, | 1) Enables us to serve God without fear |
|---|---|---|---|
| **1 Zacharias was filled with the Holy Spirit** | 67 And his father Zacharias was filled with the Holy Ghost, and prophesied, saying, | 75 In holiness and righteousness before him, all the days of our life. | 2) Enables us to live righteously & to serve God forever |
| **2 Part 1: God's Savior**<sup>DSI</sup> | 68 Blessed be the Lord God of Israel; for he hath visited and redeemed his people, | 76 And thou, child, shalt be called the prophet of the Highest: for thou shalt go before the face of the Lord to prepare his ways; | **3 Part 2: God's forerunner, John the Baptist** |
| a. The One through whom God visited & redeemed His people | 69 And hath raised up an horn of salvation for us in the house of his servant David; | 77 To give knowledge of salvation unto his people by the remission of their sins, | a. To be called the prophet of the Highest |
| b. The mighty Savior: Of David's house | 70 As he spake by the mouth of his holy prophets, which have been since the world began: | 78 Through the tender mercy of our God; whereby the dayspring from on high hath visited us, | b. To prepare Lord's way |
| c. The One prophesied | 71 That we should be saved from our enemies, and from the hand of all that hate us; | 79 To give light to them that sit in darkness and in the shadow of death, to guide our feet into the way of peace. | c. To proclaim salvation: Forgiveness of sins |
| 1) The time: Since the world began | 72 To perform the mercy promised to our fathers, and to remember his holy covenant; | 80 And the child grew, and waxed strong in spirit, and was in the deserts till the day of his showing unto Israel. | d. To proclaim the rise of the heavenly Son |
| 2) The prediction: He will save us from our enemies | 73 The oath which he sware to our father Abraham, | | 1) Thru God's mercy |
| d. The One who fulfilled the promised mercy & covenant, the oath made to Abraham | | | 2) To give light |
| | | | **4 Conclusion: John's childhood fulfills the prophecy** |

# DIVISION I

## THE ANNOUNCEMENT OF THE COMING OF JESUS, THE SON OF MAN, 1:1-2:52

### G.  Zacharias' Inspired Prophecy: God's Savior and His Forerunner, 1:67-80

(1:67-80) **Introduction**: Zacharias' song is known as the Benedictus to many worshippers. Benedictus is the opening word of the song in the Latin translation. It is sometimes recited in worship services. Note that it is a prophecy (v.67) about the coming Messiah (v.68-75) and His forerunner, John the Baptist (v.76-80). The person and ministry of both are predicted and proclaimed.

1.   Zacharias was filled with the Holy Spirit (v.67).
2.   Part 1: God's Savior (v.68-75).
3.   Part 2: God's forerunner, John the Baptist (v.76-79).
4.   Conclusion: John's childhood fulfills the prophecy (v.80).

**1**   (1:67) **Holy Spirit**: Zacharias was filled with the Holy Spirit. Once Zacharias obeyed God, God removed His discipline and healed him of his deafness and dumbness (v.62, 64). Immediately thereafter, God filled Zacharias with the Holy Spirit. The infilling with God's Spirit indicated two things.

1.   Zacharias was forgiven his sin of unbelief. It was his questioning of God, that is, his distrust and unbelief, that had caused his deafness and dumbness (Lk.1:20-22). As soon as Zacharias demonstrated faith in God's promise, he was healed and was forgiven his sin (cp. v.64-66).

2.   Zacharias' being filled with the Holy Spirit is a picture of what happens to us. We believe and obey God, then God immediately forgives our sins and fills us with His Spirit.

**"Then Peter said unto them, Repent, and be baptized every one of you in the name of Jesus Christ for the remission of sins, and ye shall receive the gift of the Holy Ghost" (Acts 2:38).**

**2**   (1:68-75) **Jesus Christ, Son of David—Covenant, Abrahamic—Salvation—Righteousness**: the first part of Zacharias' prophetic song concerned God's Savior. Four things were predicted about the Messiah. Note that Zacharias was standing in the future and looking back. The verbs are in the past tense. He was predicting how someone could stand in the future and proclaim *what the Messiah had done.*

1.   The Messiah was the One through whom God visited and redeemed His people. It was God Himself who visited the earth in the Person of the Messiah. He had not neglected nor left the world alone. In the past, God had been actively involved in the world's affairs. He had sent His Word and His messengers to the world, but now God was becoming *personally* involved in the world. He was visiting the world Himself.

Note the purpose for His visit. He came to redeem His people, to save and rescue them from sin and death and separation from God. It cost Him; He had to pay the enormous price of redemption—a life for a life (see note, *Redemption—* Eph.1:7).

2.     The Messiah was the mighty Savior of David's house. The phrase "horn of salvation" is a reference to Christ. The word "horn" throughout the Old Testament was a symbol of strength, power, and might. The Messiah is called the "horn" or the "mighty One of salvation" because He alone possesses the might, the strength, and the power to save.

But note where the horn or the Messiah was raised up: "in the house of His servant David." David was raised up by God to deliver and to rule over His people Israel. But Christ was raised up to deliver and to rule over God's people. There is one huge difference. Christ was sent to deliver and to rule over everyone, and His deliverance and rule were to be forever. The Messiah was the horn promised to David, the One who fulfilled the prophecies made concerning David (see note—Mt.1:1).

> **"There will I make the horn of David to bud: I have ordained a lamp for mine anointed" (Ps.132:17. Cp. Ps.89:24, 29.)**

3.     The Messiah was the One prophesied. The idea is that God was working out His plan for the world. He was on the throne bringing to pass all that He had promised.
  a.     The Messiah had been foretold since the world began. He was *the Seed of the woman* who was to break the serpent's head (Gen.3:15). He was the Seed promised to Abraham and his heirs (Gen.12:1-4. See Deeper Study # 1—Ro.4:1-25.)
  b.     The prediction of the Messiah dealt with salvation. The Messiah was to save believers from their enemies and from all who hated them. Carnal men (the Jews, the fleshly, the worldly-minded) think of salvation as material and physical deliverance; but God never meant salvation to last only for a few short years, the years of a man's life. He cares much more for man than that. By salvation God means spiritual and eternal salvation, a deliverance and life that will never end. He is interested in saving men from the enemies that wage an endless war against the spirit and enslave men both now and eternally: the enemies of sin, death, and condemnation.

4.     The Messiah was the One who fulfilled the promised mercy and covenant, the oath made to Abraham. God had promised Abraham both mercy and the covenant of faith. God promised Abraham that if he would get up and leave his old country to follow Him, then Abraham would receive both the mercy of God and the covenant of faith. The covenant was based upon "the promised seed," Christ Himself. Thus Zacharias, under the inspiration of the Holy Spirit, was proclaiming the Messiah to be the fulfillment of the promised mercy and covenant to Abraham. The Messiah was *the promised mercy and Seed to Abraham* (see Deeper Study # 1, *Abraham*—Ro.4:1-25 for detailed discussion. Cp. Dt.6:9, 12-13; 1 Ki.8:23; Neh.1:5; 9:32.)
  ⇒     The Messiah brings the mercy of God to man (the mercy promised to Abraham and his seed): the Messiah delivers man out of the hands of his enemies (cp. v.71, 74).
  ⇒     The Messiah establishes the covenant of faith with man (the covenant promised to Abraham and his seed): the Messiah saves all who believe the promises of God just as Abraham believed (cp. Ro.4:1-25).

> **"He [Abraham] staggered not at the promise of God through unbelief; but was strong in faith, giving glory to God; and being fully persuaded that, what he had promised, he was able also to perform. And therefore it [faith] was imputed [counted] to him for righteousness. Now it was not written for his sake alone, that it was imputed [counted] to him; but for us also, to whom it shall be imputed [counted], if we believe on him that raised up Jesus our Lord from the dead; who was delivered for our offences, and was raised again for our justification" (Ro.4:20-25).**

Now note: God has mercy and delivers man through faith for two very specific purposes.
1.     The first purpose is that men might serve Him without fear. God does not want men living in fear, fearing the future and the *imaginary gods and demons* of this world. He does not want men's fearing the pain of death and the coming judgment of hell. God wants men to have peace of mind and heart, to feel secure and to know meaning and purpose throughout all of life.

> **"Forasmuch then as the children are partakers of flesh and blood, he also himself likewise took part of the same; that through death he might destroy him that had the power of death, that is, the devil; and deliver them who through fear of death were all their lifetime subject to bondage" (Heb.2:14-15).**
> **"Behold, God is my salvation; I will trust, and not be afraid: for the LORD JEHOVAH is my strength and my song; he also is become my salvation" (Is.12:2).**

2.     The second purpose is that men might live righteously and serve God *forever*.

> **"But after that the kindness and love of God our Saviour toward man appeared, not by works of righteousness which we have done, but according to his mercy he saved us, by the washing of regeneration, and renewing of the Holy Ghost; which he shed on us abundantly through Jesus Christ our Saviour; that being justified by his grace, we should be made heirs according to the hope of eternal life" (Tit.3:4-7).**
> **"For he hath made him to be sin for us, who knew no sin; that we might be made the righteousness of God in him" (2 Cor.5:21).**
> **"And that ye put on the new man, which after God is created in righteousness and true holiness" (Eph.4:24).**

"Being filled with the fruits of righteousness, which are by Jesus Christ, unto the glory and praise of God" (Ph.1:11).

"Awake to righteousness, and sin not; for some have not the knowledge of God: I speak this to your shame" (1 Cor.15:34).

"Sow to yourselves in righteousness, reap in mercy; break up your fallow ground: for it is time to seek the LORD, till he come and rain righteousness upon you" (Hos.10:12).

---

**DEEPER STUDY # 1**

(1:68) **Israel**: Zacharias addressed God as "the Lord God of Israel." Why did he limit God to Israel? Why did he not address God as *the Lord God of the earth*? There are several reasons (see DEEPER STUDY # 1, *Israel*—Jn.4:22).

1. Israel was the chosen people of God, the people chosen to love, obey, and worship Him supremely.

2. As the *chosen* people of God, Israel had been given (entrusted with) both the Word and promises of God to a lost and dying world.

3. As the *recipient* of God's Word and promises, Israel was to be given the Messiah, His salvation and redemption.

4. As the *people* of salvation and redemption, Israel was given the task to make God known, to be the missionary force to reach a lost and dying world.

Zacharias was thinking of God's promise to Israel, of the glorious fact that the promise of the Messiah was now being fulfilled. He knew nothing of Israel's rejection of the Messiah, of God's turning to the Gentiles, of the birth of a new people (the church). Therefore, he did the natural thing: he praised the Lord God of Israel.

---

**3** (1:76-79) **John the Baptist—Jesus Christ, Purpose**: the second part of Zacharias' prophecy concerned John the Baptist. Four things were also predicted about John.

1. John was to be the prophet of the Highest. Note several facts.

   a. There had been no prophet in Israel for some four hundred years. John was to be the first since Malachi.

   b. Christ was called "the Highest," that is, the *Most High* which is a title for God. Thus the deity, the very Incarnation of God in Christ, was being proclaimed. He is "God blessed for ever" (Ro.9:5).

   c. John was called the prophet of the Highest, of Christ, or of God Himself.

2. John was to prepare the Lord's way. He was to be the forerunner of the Messiah, the one who was to prepare the people for the coming of the Lord (cp. Lk.3:3-6).

3. John was to proclaim salvation, even the forgiveness of sins. Note that salvation comes by the forgiveness of sin. Salvation is conditional. One's sins must be forgiven before he can be saved (Eph.1:7). John's purpose was to call men to salvation, to be forgiven of their sins.

4. John was to proclaim the heavenly Son's rise. Note that Christ, the Messiah, is called "the Son of righteousness" (Mal.4:2; 2 Pt.1:19; Rev.22:16). He is the "Dayspring from on High," the morning light, the rising sun who has "visited us." John was to proclaim the rise of the Messiah, and in particular two things about His rise.

   a. The Messiah was being sent through the tender mercy of God.

   "For God so loved the world, that he gave his only begotten Son, that whosoever believeth in him should not perish, but have everlasting life. For God sent not his Son into the world to condemn the world; but that the world through him might be saved" (Jn.3:16-17).

   "But God, who is rich in mercy, for his great love wherewith he loved us, even when we were dead in sins, hath quickened us together with Christ, (by grace ye are saved)" (Eph..2:4-5)

   b. The Messiah was being sent to give light...

   • to those who sit in darkness.

   "A light to lighten the Gentiles, and the glory of thy people Israel" (Lk.2:32).

   "In him was life; and the life was the light of men....That was the true Light, which lighteth every man that cometh into the world" (Jn.1:4, 9).

   "And this is the condemnation, that light is come into the world, and men loved darkness rather than light, because their deeds were evil. For every one that doeth evil hateth the light, neither cometh to the light, lest his deeds should be reproved. But he that doeth truth cometh to the light, that his deeds may be made manifest, that they are wrought in God" (Jn.3:19-21).

   "Then spake Jesus again unto them, saying, I am the light of the world: he that followeth me shall not walk in darkness, but shall have the light of life" (Jn.8:12).

   "I am come a light into the world, that whosoever believeth on me should not abide in darkness" (Jn.12:46).

   • to those who are in the shadow of death.

   "Verily, verily, I say unto you, He that heareth my word, and believeth on him that sent me, hath everlasting life, and shall not come into condemnation; but is passed from death unto life" (Jn.5:24).

   "Forasmuch then as the children are partakers of flesh and blood, he also himself likewise took part of the same; that through death he might destroy him that had the power of death, that is, the devil; and deliver them who through fear of death were all their lifetime subject to bondage" (Heb.2:14-15).

- to guide our feet into the way of peace.

> "Jesus saith unto him, I am the way, the truth, and the life: no man cometh unto the Father, but by me" (Jn.14:6).
> "Peace I leave with you, my peace I give unto you: not as the world giveth, give I unto you. Let not your heart be troubled, neither let it be afraid" (Jn.14:27).
> "These things I have spoken unto you, that in me ye might have peace. In the world ye shall have tribulation: but be of good cheer; I have overcome the world" (Jn.16:33).

**4** (1:80) **John the Baptist—Growth, Spiritual**: John's childhood is described only in this single verse. Nothing else is known. He grew as a normal boy physically, but three things are said about him that differ from the normal child.

1. He advanced far beyond other boys spiritually. He waxed (grew) strong in spirit. He was a boy of strong heart and commitment, of strong will and decisiveness, of strong conscience and conviction, of strong drive and initiative. He was God's servant, a young man who was committed to follow, obey, and serve God.

2. He was reared in a different environment than most boys—in the desert. The desert was an obscure place, a place of quietness, far from the worldliness of the cities and masses of men. The desert was made for meditation and thought, for seeking God.

3. He stayed at his desert home until God called him to launch his ministry to Israel. This points to a life of obedience both to parents and to God.

> **Thought 1.** The crying need of the hour is for believers to grow in the Lord Jesus Christ—to grow strong in the spirit.

> > "That we henceforth be no more children, tossed to and fro, and carried about with every wind of doctrine, by the sleight of men, and cunning craftiness, whereby they lie in wait to deceive; but speaking the truth in love, may grow up into him in all things, which is the head, even Christ" (Eph.4:14-15).
> > "But grow in grace, and in the knowledge of our Lord and Saviour Jesus Christ. To him be glory both now and for ever. Amen" (2 Pt.3:18).
> > "And now, brethren, I commend you to God, and to the word of his grace, which is able to build you up, and to give you an inheritance among all them which are sanctified" (Acts 20:32).

CHAPTER 2

**H. Jesus' Birth: Its Unusual Events, 2:1-24**
(Mt.1:18-25; 2:1; cp. Jn.1:14)

**1 The miraculous taxation**
a. An event of the world used by God to fulfill His plan

b. An event that forced Joseph to Bethlehem
1) From Galilee
2) Out of Nazareth
3) Into Judaea
4) To the city of David, Bethlehem
c. An event that led to the fulfillment of Scripture despite man's plans

**2 The shocking place of birth**

**3 The unbelievable appearance of a real angel to shepherds**

a. His appearance: Shone in the glory of the Lord

b. His message: Reassured—good news

1) A proclamation: The Messiah's birth[DS1,2]

2) A charge: Visit the child
3) A sign: The location

And it came to pass in those days, that there went out a decree from Caesar Augustus, that all the world should be taxed.
2 (And this taxing was first made when Cyrenius was governor of Syria.)
3 And all went to be taxed, every one into his own city.
4 And Joseph also went up from Galilee, out of the city of Nazareth, into Judaea, unto the city of David, which is called Bethlehem; (because he was of the house and lineage of David:)
5 To be taxed with Mary his espoused wife, being great with child.
6 And so it was, that, while they were there, the days were accomplished that she should be delivered.
7 And she brought forth her firstborn son, and wrapped him in swaddling clothes, and laid him in a manger; because there was no room for them in the inn.
8 And there were in the same country shepherds abiding in the field, keeping watch over their flock by night.
9 And, lo, the angel of the Lord came upon them, and the glory of the Lord shone round about them: and they were sore afraid.
10 And the angel said unto them, Fear not: for, behold, I bring you good tidings of great joy, which shall be to all people.
11 For unto you is born this day in the city of David a Saviour, which is Christ the Lord.
12 And this shall be a sign unto you; Ye shall find the babe wrapped in swaddling clothes, lying in a manger.
13 And suddenly there was with the angel a multitude of the heavenly host praising God, and saying,
14 Glory to God in the highest, and on earth peace, good will toward men.
15 And it came to pass, as the angels were gone away from them into heaven, the shepherds said one to another, Let us now go even unto Bethlehem, and see this thing which is come to pass, which the Lord hath made known unto us.
16 And they came with haste, and found Mary, and Joseph, and the babe lying in a manger.
17 And when they had seen it, they made known abroad the saying which was told them concerning this child.
18 And all they that heard it wondered at those things which were told them by the shepherds.
19 But Mary kept all these things, and pondered them in her heart.
20 And the shepherds returned, glorifying and praising God for all the things that they had heard and seen, as it was told unto them.
21 And when eight days were accomplished for the circumcision of the child, his name was called JESUS, which was so named of the angel before he was conceived in the womb.
22 And when the days of her purification according to the law of Moses were accomplished, they brought him to Jerusalem, to present him to the Lord;
23 (As it is written in the law of the Lord, Every male that openeth the womb shall be called holy to the Lord;)
24 And to offer a sacrifice according to that which is said in the law of the Lord, A pair of turtledoves, or two young pigeons.

& dress
**4 The spectacular appearance of the heavenly host**

**5 The excited shepherds seeking evidence**
a. They immediately decided to visit

b. They rushed to see

c. They excitedly shared the message

d. They caused a stir

**6 The awe-stricken, pondering mother**

**7 The common, non-religious shepherds worshipping God**

**8 The unusual naming of the child: Named by God Himself**

**9 The unexpected observance of the legal ceremonies**
a. Circumcision[DS3]
b. Purification after childbirth
c. Dedication to the Lord

**10 The deliberate choice of God to have a poor family bear His Son**

# DIVISION I

## THE ANNOUNCEMENT OF THE COMING OF JESUS, THE SON OF MAN, 1:1-2:52

**H.      Jesus' Birth: Its Unusual Events, 2:1-24**

(2:1-24) **Introduction**: the prophecy given by Jacob back in Genesis was now being fulfilled.

**"The scepter shall not depart from Judah, nor a lawgiver from between his feet, until Shiloh [the Messiah] come; and unto him shall the gathering of the people be" (Gen.49:10).**

1.     Note how the scepter of rule had departed from Judea. Judea was under the rule of Rome with Caesar Augustus reigning as emperor. Cyrenius was governor of Syria, and Judea was included in the province of Syria. Herod was now the *King of Judea*. A usurper, a foreign, alien power, now ruled over Judea.
⇒     Judea was no longer ruled by one of its own princes; it was ruled by an Idumean prince, a descendant of Esau, Herod the Great.
⇒     The promised land was no longer in the hands of Israel; it was in the hands of a heathen power.
⇒     The prince (ruler) was no longer appointed by God; he was empowered by Rome.
⇒     The temple was no longer cared for by the prince of God; it was (misused) under the authority of a usurper.
⇒     The priests of God were no longer the ministers of God; they were the servants of the secular world.
2.     Note how clearly and how dramatically the prophecy was fulfilled: the scepter had most definitely departed from Judea, and *now* it was time for Shiloh to come. And He would come. God destined His coming in the counsel and fore-knowledge of His will.

The prophecy of *Shiloh's coming* was fulfilled in Jesus Christ. Jesus Christ was Shiloh who was to come. His coming into the world was surrounded by the most unusual events.
1.     The miraculous taxation (v.1-6).
2.     The shocking place of birth (v.7).
3.     The unbelievable appearance of a real angel to shepherds (v.8-12).
4.     The spectacular appearance of the heavenly host (v.13-14).
5.     The excited shepherds seeking evidence (v.15-18).
6.     The awe-stricken, pondering mother (v.19).
7.     The common, non-religious shepherds worshipping God (v.20).
8.     The unusual naming of the child: named by God Himself (v.21).
9.     The unexpected observance of the legal ceremonies (v.22-23).
10.    The deliberate choice of God to have a poor family bear His Son (v.24).

[1]     (2:1-6) **Jesus Christ, Birth—Bethlehem—God, Providence**: there was the miraculous taxation. Three things should be noted.
1.     The taxation was used by God to fulfill His plan for the birth of the Messiah. It had been prophesied that the Messiah was to be born in Bethlehem, and Scripture had to be fulfilled. Joseph and Mary lived in Galilee, and Mary was now great with child. How was God going to make sure that the child was born in Bethlehem? The taxation happened just at the right time and in the right way; that is, everyone had to return to the city of his birth to pay his taxes. God was miraculously controlling the events of the world, working all things out for good so that He might fulfill His promise to send the Savior into the world.
2.     The taxation forced Joseph to Bethlehem. Everyone had to return to the city of his birth. Note the great detail given in describing the journey to Bethlehem. The point is that Bethlehem was the prophesied city of the Messiah's birth (Mic.5:2). The Scribes understood it (Mt.2:5-6) and so did the common people (Jn.7:42). The taxation was certainly an event wrought in the plan of God to fulfill Scripture.
3.     The taxation led to the fulfillment of Scripture, despite man's plans. Mary was about to deliver; she was "great with child" (v.5). Apparently, Joseph and Mary had planned for the child to be delivered in Nazareth; but God overruled. He either caused or used the taxation and saw to it that Joseph and Mary were forced to Bethlehem.
Now in summary, why was all this necessary? Why did Jesus have to be born in Bethlehem?
a.     The Messiah was the prophesied Son of David (see notes—Lk.3:24-31; Mt.1:1; DEEPER STUDY # 3—Jn.1:45; DEEPER STUDY # 4—1:49 for discussion).
b.     David had been born in Bethlehem; therefore, it was necessary for the Son of David to be born there.
c.     Scripture foretold that the Messiah would be born in Bethlehem (Mic.5:2).

[2]     (2:7) **Jesus Christ, Birth**: there was the shocking place of birth. Jesus was not born in comfortable surroundings. Shockingly, He was born in a stable and laid in a manger or feeding trough. The birth is covered in one simple verse, yet much can be gleaned from it.
1.     Jesus was born in a smelly stable. He was neglected and turned away by men from the very beginning. There was no room in the inn, and Mary was about to deliver. If someone had cared, room could have been made for her.
2.     Jesus was born in poverty. If Joseph had possessed the money, he could have bought a room.
3.     Jesus was born in obscurity and loneliness. The birth took place away from people, all alone. Note that Mary herself wrapped the child in swaddling clothes and laid Him in a manger.
4.     Jesus was born in humiliation. He did not enter the world...
• in a hospital,
• in a comfortable home,
• in the home of a friend or relative,
• under a doctor's care,
• under the stars of heaven, nor even out in the open,
• but in a smelly stable, the lowest imaginable place for a birth.
5.     Jesus was born into a corruptible world full of sin and selfishness, greed and unkindness. This is seen in that...
• the world (represented in the innkeeper) was so wrapped up in its affairs that it could not help a woman bearing a child.
• no one would make room for Mary in the inn. Money and personal comfort were more important to all who had become aware of the situation.

**Thought 1.** Note how so many missed the first coming of Christ. How many will miss the second coming of Christ?

> "And take heed to yourselves, lest at any time your hearts be overcharged with surfeiting, and drunkenness, and cares of this life, and so that day come upon you unawares" (Lk.21:34).
> "Teaching us that, denying ungodliness and worldly lusts, we should live soberly, righteously, and godly, in this present world; looking for that blessed hope, and the glorious appearing of the great God and our Saviour Jesus Christ" (Tit.2:12-13).

3 (2:8-12) **Shepherds:** there was the unbelievable appearance of a real angel to shepherds. In the eyes of many, an angel would never appear to a shepherd. Shepherds would seldom be found praising and worshipping God; as a result they were looked upon as anything but worshippers. Their reputation was lowly at best, and religious people snubbed and ignored them. They were despised because they were unable to attend services and to keep the ceremonial laws of washing and cleansing. Their flocks just kept them too busy. What a beautiful foretaste of the salvation to come: God gave the first message of His Son to common shepherds, those looked upon as sinners.

1. The angel's appearance was that of splendor and glory. This was the shekinah glory (see note—Mt.17:5-8).
2. The angel's message was one of reassurance and good news. He proclaimed the Messiah's birth and charged the shepherds to visit the child. He gave them a sign: they would find the babe lying in a manger.

**Thought 1.** The Savior was coming to call sinners to repentance; therefore, the first announcement of His coming was given to sinners.

> "And Jesus answering said unto them, They that are whole need not a physician; but they that are sick. I came not to call the righteous, but sinners to repentance" (Lk.5:31-32).
> "For ye see your calling, brethren, how that not many wise men after the flesh, not many mighty, not many noble, are called: but God hath chosen the foolish things of the world to confound the wise; and God hath chosen the weak things of the world to confound the things which are mighty; and base things of the world, and things which are despised, hath God chosen, yea, and things which are not, to bring to nought things that are: that no flesh should glory in his presence" (1 Cor.1:26-29).

---
**DEEPER STUDY # 1**
(2:11) **Jesus—Savior:** see DEEPER STUDY # 2—Lk.1:31; note—2:21.

---
**DEEPER STUDY # 2**
(2:11) **Christ—Messiah:** see DEEPER STUDY # 2—Mt.1:18; note—Lk.2:21.

---

4 (2:13-14) **Angels:** there was the spectacular appearance of the heavenly host. The word "host" means an army of angels, "ten thousand times ten thousand" (Dan.7:10; cp. Ps.68:17). God either gave the shepherds a special sight into the spiritual world and dimension or caused the spiritual dimension to appear to physical sight. Note: the angels did two things.
1. They cried out for glory to be lifted up to God...
   • who is the highest possible Being.
   • who dwells in the highest realm of being possible, in heaven itself.
2. They cried out for peace, for good will toward men. By peace is meant the peace of reconciliation, the good will between God and man. The alienation and separation, struggle and divisiveness, restlessness and fear caused by sin needed to be solved. The heavenly host was praising God that the alienation and separation were now being solved in the birth of the "Savior, which is Christ the Lord."

> "And, having made peace through the blood of his cross, by him to reconcile all things unto himself; by him, I say, whether they be things in earth, or things in heaven" (Col.1:20).

5 (2:15-18) **Shepherds:** there were the excited shepherds' seeking evidence. Note their excitement.
1. They decided immediately to visit. "They said one to another, let us now go...."
2. They *rushed* to see for themselves. There is a sense of extreme urgency in these words. They acted with haste, rushed, hurried. They felt an urgency to act and to act now. They wasted no time. Note: they found the babe just as the angel had said.
3. They shared the message. They first experienced seeing the child themselves, then they shared their experience wherever they went. They were the first to bear witness to the Savior of the world.
4. They caused a stir among the people. Note that nothing is said about these hearers' seeking out the child. They only wondered about what they heard; they never responded and never moved to find Him for themselves.

6 (2:19) **Mary—Humility—Trust:** there was the awe-stricken, pondering mother. This is a beautiful picture of a humble, trusting heart. Mary had been told that her child was of God, truly of God. Above all others she knew that the Messiah, the very Son of God, had now come. She had been through so much: pregnant, yet unmarried; the possibility of being found out and of rumors heaped upon rumors; the discussions with Joseph and with her parents; the long trip from Nazareth; the exhaustion of giving birth without help in a smelly stable; the visit of some rough-hewn shepherds with an amazing story of the heavenly host's proclaiming the praises of God. Mary was tired, as weary and exhausted as a person could be. So much had happened, and she was at the very center of it all. No one could even begin to know the thoughts that had filled her mind for nine months, nor could anyone know the feelings and emotions of the experience. The wonder, the amazement, the astounding reality was too much to talk about. All she could do was continue in the humble sweetness

that had so characterized her over the past months. She merely bowed once again in *humble adoration* to God and *quietly entrusted* all these things into God's keeping. She said nothing, only pondered in her heart what was happening.

**7** (2:20) **Shepherds**: there were the common, non-religious shepherds worshipping God.

1. The shepherds had spread the message, but note a shocking fact. The shepherds alone are seen praising God. No one else is seen seeking or praising the Savior.
2. The shepherds were praising God for what they had *heard* and *seen*. God had spoken to them and they had received the message. They obeyed God's instructions to seek out the Messiah; therefore, they had been privileged to see the Messiah. They had reason to praise God. (How many hear and see, yet never respond and never praise God?)

> "For I know the thoughts that I think toward you, saith the LORD, thoughts of peace, and not of evil, to give you an expected end. Then shall ye call upon me, and ye shall go and pray unto me, and I will hearken unto you. And ye shall seek me, and find me, when ye shall search for me with all your heart" (Jer.29:11-13).

**8** (2:21) **Jesus Christ, Name**: there was the unusual naming of the child. The child was named by God Himself.

1. The child Jesus was named by God before He was conceived in the womb (Lk.1:31).
2. The name Jesus (iesous) means Savior or He will save. The Hebrew form of the name is Joshua which means *Jehovah is salvation*.

> "For this is good and acceptable in the sight of God our Saviour; who will have all men to be saved, and to come unto the knowledge of the truth. For there is one God, and one mediator between God and men, the man Christ Jesus; who gave himself a ransom for all, to be testified in due time" (1 Tim.2:3-6).
>
> "But after that the kindness and love of God our Saviour toward man appeared, not by works of righteousness which we have done, but according to his mercy he saved us, by the washing of regeneration, and renewing of the Holy Ghost; which he shed on us abundantly through Jesus Christ our Saviour; that being justified by his grace, we should be made heirs according to the hope of eternal life" (Tit.3:4-7).

**9** (2:22-23) **Jesus Christ, Fulfills Law**: there was the unexpected observance of the legal ceremonies. There were three legal ceremonies which Jesus underwent.

1. There was the ceremony of circumcision (see DEEPER STUDY # 1—Ph.3:3).
2. There was the ceremony of purification. This was a ceremony Mary had to go through. After the birth of a boy child, a woman was considered unclean for forty days (eighty for a girl child). She could work around the home and engage in normal activities, but she could not take part in religious ceremonies. She was religiously, that is, ceremonially, unclean. After a woman's forty or eighty days were up, she was to make an offering in the temple (Lev.12:1-8).
3. There was the ceremony of dedication to the Lord (v.23; cp. Ex.13:2, 12, 15; Lev.27:6; Num.18:15-16). A male child was presented (dedicated) in the temple when the family was close to Jerusalem.

Why would Jesus, the Son of God, be subjected to the legal observances of the law? He was not a stranger to the covenants of God (circumcision). He had created the covenants Himself. He was not lacking in commitment (the Dedication Ceremony). He was God Himself, the One to whom all babies were dedicated, yet He was subjected to all the legal requirements. Why? Very simply...

> "[He was] made of a woman, made under the law, to redeem them that were under the law, that we might receive the adoption of sons" (Gal.4:4-5).
>
> "[He was] made like unto his brethren, that he might be a merciful and faithful high priest in things pertaining to God, to make reconciliation for the sins of the people. For in that he himself hath suffered being tempted, he is able to succour them that are tempted" (Heb.2:17-18).
>
> "Think not that I am come to destroy the law, or the prophets: I am not come to destroy, but to fulfil" (Mt.5:17; see note—Mt.5:17-18).

---

**DEEPER STUDY # 3**
(2:22) **Circumcision**: see DEEPER STUDY # 1—Ph.3:3.

---

**10** (2:24) **Offering of Poor**: there was the deliberate choice of God to have a poor family bear His Son. Note that Mary offered two pigeons. This was the offering of the poor. Rich people were required to offer a lamb and a pigeon. Therefore, God chose a poor family to rear His only Son in an ordinary home without any luxuries.

> **Thought 1.** No matter what we have to bear in life, Christ has already borne it—even poverty (see note 3—Lk.2:40 for discussion). He knows the suffering we undergo; therefore, He is able to strengthen and carry us through the suffering.

> "For we have not an high priest which cannot be touched with the feeling of our infirmities; but was in all points tempted like as we are, yet without sin. Let us therefore come boldly unto the throne of grace, that we may obtain mercy, and find grace to help in time of need" (Heb.4:15-16).

| | I. Simeon's Prophecy: Jesus' Life and Fate Foretold, 2:25-35 | | |
|---|---|---|---|
| 1 Simeon, a man who walked close to God<br>  a. A man who was just & devout<br>  b. A man who looked for the Messiah<br>  c. A man who was led by the Holy Spirit<br>  d. A man who was given an unusual promise<br><br>  e. A man who saw & held the Messiah<br><br><br><br>2 The child was God's salvation<br><br>  a. The source of peace | 25 And, behold, there was a man in Jerusalem, whose name was Simeon; and the same man was just and devout, waiting for the consolation of Israel: and the Holy Ghost was upon him.<br>26 And it was revealed unto him by the Holy Ghost, that he should not see death, before he had seen the Lord's Christ.<br>27 And he came by the Spirit into the temple: and when the parents brought in the child Jesus, to do for him after the custom of the law,<br>28 Then took he him up in his arms, and blessed God, and said,<br>29 Lord, now lettest thou | thy servant depart in peace, according to thy word:<br>30 For mine eyes have seen thy salvation,<br>31 Which thou hast prepared before the face of all people;<br>32 A light to lighten the Gentiles, and the glory of thy people Israel.<br>33 And Joseph and his mother marvelled at those things which were spoken of him.<br>34 And Simeon blessed them, and said unto Mary his mother, Behold, this child is set for the fall and rising again of many in Israel; and for a sign which shall be spoken against;<br>35 (Yea, a sword shall pierce through thy own soul also,) that the thoughts of many hearts may be revealed. | b. The One appointed to be God's salvation<br>c. The One prepared for all people<br><br>d. The light to unbelievers<br>e. The glory to believers<br><br>f. The parents marvelled at the predictions<br><br>3 The child was to cause the rise & fall of many<br><br>4 The child's fate was sealed<br>  a. His fate: To be opposed & put to death<br>  b. His purpose: To reveal the inner thoughts of man's heart |

# DIVISION I

## THE ANNOUNCEMENT OF THE COMING OF JESUS, THE SON OF MAN, 1:1-2:52

## I. Simeon's Prophecy: Jesus' Life and Fate Foretold, 2:25-35

(2:25-35) **Introduction**: it was time for the child to be dedicated and offered up for God's keeping and care. The parents took the child to the temple, and someplace in the temple, they came across a man named Simeon. Just who Simeon was is not known. Some think he was a priest, but Scripture does not say. All we know is what is recorded here. He was a man who loved God very much, so much that God was able to use him in a most magnificent way. He used Simeon to proclaim one of the greatest messages of all time: the events and fate of the child Messiah's life.

  1.    Simeon, a man who walked close to God (v.25-27).
  2.    The child was God's salvation (v.28-33).
  3.    The child was to cause the rise and fall of many (v.34).
  4.    The child's fate was sealed (v.34-35).

**1** (2:25-27) **Simeon—Dedication**: Simeon was a man who walked closely with God. He walked so closely that God was able to use him in a most magnificent way to encourage Joseph and Mary. Five things are said about him personally.

  1.    Simeon was a just and devout man. The word "just" (dikaios) means righteous, well-behaved, living as one should live. Simeon was a man who treated other people as he should: justly.

The word "devout" (eulabes) means cautious and careful in relation to God. It means reverence for God, being pious. Simeon was very careful in his relation toward God.

  2.    Simeon was a man who looked for the coming of the Messiah (see DEEPER STUDY # 2—Mt.1:18). This is what is meant by "the consolation of Israel." Faithful believers among the Jews felt that Israel could find consolation only in the Messiah. They longed and ached with all hope and patience for His coming. Joseph of Arimathaea was another example of one who "waited for the kingdom of God" (Mk.15:43).

> **Thought 1.** The world can find consolation only in the coming of Christ.

> **"For the grace of God that bringeth salvation hath appeared to all men, teaching us that, denying ungodliness and worldly lusts, we should live soberly, righteously, and godly, in this present world; looking for that blessed hope, and the glorious appearing of the great God and our Saviour Jesus Christ; who gave himself for us, that he might redeem us from all iniquity, and purify unto himself a peculiar people, zealous of good works" (Tit.2:11-14).**

> **Thought 2.** Believers must long for the Messiah, ache with all hope and patience for His return (cp. 2 Pt.3:3-18).

  3.    Simeon was a man led by the Holy Spirit. The idea seems to be that the Spirit was upon him continually. In most instances throughout the Old Testament the Spirit only came upon men for special service. It is not said that the Spirit abode upon them continually; however, the Spirit does seem to have rested upon Simeon continually. This shows just how closely Simeon was living to God. He must have been a very, very special man, a man who held God ever so dear to his heart and whom God held ever so close to His heart.

  4.    Simeon was a man who was given an unusual promise. Apparently, Simeon was constantly studying the Scriptures, in particular searching the prophecies concerning the coming salvation of the Messiah (1 Pt.1:10). At some point,

the Holy Spirit revealed to him that he would not die until he had seen the Messiah. Just think how closely Simeon must have lived to God! He was unquestionably a very special person to God.

5. Simeon was a man who saw and held the Messiah. Note that Simeon was again led by the Spirit; he was led into the temple. This was the day for which he had longed and ached, the day he was to see and embrace the Messiah. A first-born son was always taken to the temple to be dedicated to the Lord. Immediately, Simeon saw that this child was different from all the others; he recognized the child as the Christ-child. He took the child up into his arms and proclaimed Him to be the long-awaited Messiah.

**Thought 1.** The point to note about Simeon is his closeness to God. He was a man who stands as a dynamic example of *strong dedication*. Because of his *strong dedication*, God was able to bless Simeon beyond imagination.

> **"O love the LORD, all ye his saints: for the LORD preserveth the faithful, and plentifully rewardeth the proud doer" (Ps.31:23).**
> **"Whom having not seen, ye love; in whom, though now ye see him not, yet believing, ye rejoice with joy unspeakable and full of glory" (1 Pt.1:8).**
> **"Keep yourselves in the love of God, looking for the mercy of our Lord Jesus Christ unto eternal life" (Jude 21).**
> **"I know thy works, and charity, and service, and faith, and thy patience, and thy works; and the last to be more than the first" (Rev.2:19).**

**2** (2:28-33) **Salvation—Jesus Christ, Life and Fate**: the child was God's salvation. Once Simeon had embraced the Messiah, he broke out into song. The song is called the *Nunc Dimittis*, again being known by the opening words of the song in the Latin. Note several points.

1. The child was God's salvation; He was to be the source of peace for the world. Simeon had "seen and embraced" the Messiah, God's salvation. Therefore, he was now ready to die in peace. Note that He believed and trusted God—all of God's promises. He praised God for fulfilling His Word "according to thy word." It was because of God's faithfulness that he was ready to die. He knew that he would live on "with his fathers" forever. (See note—Jn.14:27.)

> **"Peace I leave with you, my peace I give unto you: not as the world giveth, give I unto you. Let not your heart be troubled, neither let it be afraid" (Jn.14:27).**
> **"These things I have spoken unto you, that in me ye might have peace. In the world ye shall have tribulation: but be of good cheer; I have overcome the world" (Jn.16:33).**

2. The child was the One appointed to be God's salvation. He was appointed and prepared in "the determinate counsel and foreknowledge of God" (Acts 2:23). Note also this was the confession of Simeon. He confessed that the child was God's salvation.

**Thought 1.** Everyone must confess that the child Jesus is God's salvation, through whom God saves the world.

> **"Whosoever therefore shall confess me before men, him will I confess also before my Father which is in heaven" (Mt.10:32).**
> **"Whosoever shall confess that Jesus is the Son of God, God dwelleth in him, and he in God" (1 Jn.4:15).**

3. The child, God's salvation, was prepared for all people. Simeon saw that God's salvation was not for any one people or nation or group. The Messiah had come to save all men. Anyone could now be saved, no matter who he was or what he had done. Prejudice and favoritism were unknown to God. He was not willing that any should perish.

> **"For I am not ashamed of the gospel of Christ: for it is the power of God unto salvation to every one that believeth; to the Jew first, and also to the Greek" (Ro.1:16).**
> **"The Lord is not slack concerning his promise, as some men count slackness; but is long-suffering to us-ward, not willing that any should perish, but that all should come to repentance" (2 Pt.3:9).**

4. The child, God's salvation, was to be a light to the Gentiles, to the unbelievers of the world. The child came to be the Light of the world. This simply means that He came to be the Revelation of God, to reveal the way, the truth, and the life to men (see note, pt.4—Lk.1:76-79).

> **"Jesus saith unto him, I am the way, the truth, and the life: no man cometh unto the Father, but by me" (Jn.14:6).**
> **"Then spake Jesus again unto them, saying, I am the light of the world: he that followeth me shall not walk in darkness, but shall have the light of life" (Jn.8:12).**

5. The child, God's salvation, was to be the glory of Israel, of true believers. The Messiah was to be the glory of all Israelites (Jews) who truly believed. In fact, He was to be the glory of all who believed, no matter what nationality. The reason is clearly given by Scripture.

a. The believer is justified.

> **"In the LORD shall all the seed of Israel be justified, and shall glory" (Is.45:25).**

b. The believer is saved to live with God eternally.

> **"Whereas thou hast been forsaken and hated, so that no man went through thee, I will make thee an eternal excellency, a joy of many generations....Violence shall no more be**

heard in the land, wasting nor destruction within thy borders; but thou shalt call thy walls Salvation, and thy gates Praise. The sun shall be no more thy light by day; neither for brightness shall the moon give light unto thee: but the LORD shall be unto thee an everlasting light, and thy God thy glory" (Is.60:15, 18-19).

6. The parents marvelled at the predictions. The predictions would amaze anyone, but they were given for an additional reason. Joseph and Mary needed to be assured and encouraged. Their need was only natural. Imagine what they had been through and were yet to go through because of the child (see note—Lk.2:7; 2:40; DEEPER STUDY # 1—Mt.1:18-25). God saw to it that they were strengthened in this experience.

**3** (2:34) **Jesus Christ, Person; Work—Decision**: the child was to cause the rise and fall of many. The child was to be what the Scripture calls the *stone of stumbling* and the *chief cornerstone*.

Many would stumble and fall over Him. They would not notice, look, study, prefer, choose, believe, or trust Him and the salvation He was to bring. They would simply choose another way other than God. Therefore, they would stumble and fall over Him just as they would stumble over a stone lying in their path.

Many would rise because of Him. They would take notice, choose, and believe Him and the salvation He was to bring. Therefore, He would become their foundation, their cornerstone.

**Thought 1.** Decisively, Jesus Christ causes every man to make a choice. A man either rejects the Messiah, God's salvation, and falls (eternally); or he accepts and he rises (eternally). (See DEEPER STUDY # 7, *Jesus Christ, the Stone*—Mt.21:42; DEEPER STUDY # 9—21:44 for more discussion.)

> "Sanctify the LORD of hosts himself; and let him be your fear, and let him be your dread. And he shall be for a sanctuary; but for a stone of stumbling and for a rock of offence to both the houses of Israel, for a gin and for a snare to the inhabitants of Jerusalem. And many among them shall stumble, and fall, and be broken, and be snared, and be taken" (Is.8:13-15).
> "Unto you therefore which believe he is precious: but unto them which be disobedient, the stone which the builders disallowed, the same is made the head of the corner, and a stone of stumbling, and a rock of offence, even to them which stumble at the word, being disobedient: whereunto also they were appointed" (1 Pt.2:7-8).

**4** (2:34-35) **Jesus Christ, Death—Humanism**: the child's fate was sealed. The child was to be opposed and eventually killed. He was the "sign which shall be spoken against."

**Thought 1.** Christ was a sign of both God's love and judgment. It is this that causes men to react. Men want a god that brings only enough law and morality to give order to society. They want a god that allows them to live as they desire, not a God who demands total self-denial and obedience (see note and DEEPER STUDY # 1—Lk.9:23). *They want a god of indulging love, not of sacrificial love; a god of license, not of demanding love.* Therefore, when Christ is set before men as the Messiah of self-denying love and obedience, they react. Why? Because if they disobey Him and fail to live sacrificial lives, they bring judgment upon themselves.

**Thought 2.** Within every society, Christ and His genuine followers are *spoken against* with varying degrees of reaction and persecution. The *speaking against* ranges all the way from simply ignoring believers to killing them (martyrdom). There is...

- ignoring
- ridiculing
- abusing
- hating
- imprisoning
- murdering
- persecuting
- slandering

Note the words spoken to Mary, "A sword shall pierce through thine own heart also." This is a reference to the sorrow she was to experience at the cross, seeing her Son, the only begotten Son of God, rejected and killed by men (cp. Jn.19:25-27).

Note also, the purpose for the child's death: to reveal the inner thoughts of man's heart.

**Thought 1.** Man either sees the love of God and surrenders to the saving grace of God, or else he looks upon the cross as a repulsive sight and rejects the saving grace of God. He either sees Christ's dying for his sins and receives the forgiveness of God offered by the cross, or else he recoils from the thought of sin within himself and turns from the forgiveness of the cross (see note, pts.2-4—Mt.16:21-23).

> "For the preaching of the cross is to them that perish foolishness; but unto us which are saved it is the power of God" (1 Cor.1:18).
> "Or despisest thou the riches of his goodness and forbearance and longsuffering; not knowing that the goodness of God leadeth thee to repentance?" (Ro.2:4).
> "They have cast away the law of the LORD of hosts, and despised the word of the Holy One of Israel" (Is.5:24).
> "To whom shall I speak, and give warning, that they may hear? behold, their ear is uncircumcised, and they cannot hearken: behold, the word of the LORD is unto them a reproach; they have no delight in it" (Jer.6:10).
> "The wise men are ashamed, they are dismayed and taken: lo, they have rejected the word of the LORD; and what wisdom is in them?" (Jer.8:9).
> "Yea, they made their hearts as an adamant stone, lest they should hear the law, and the words which the LORD of hosts hath sent in his spirit by the former prophets: therefore came a great wrath from the LORD of hosts" (Zech.7:12).

| | J. Anna's Praise: The Child Jesus is Praised by a Prophetess, 2:36-38 | 37 And she was a widow of about fourscore and four years, which departed not from the temple, but served God with fastings and prayers night and day. | 4 She never ceased to worship—night or day |
|---|---|---|---|
| 1 She was a prophetess | 36 And there was one Anna, a prophetess, the daughter of Phanuel, of the tribe of Aser: she was of a great age, and had lived with an husband seven years from her virginity; | 38 And she coming in that instant gave thanks likewise unto the Lord, and spake of him to all them that looked for redemption in Jerusalem. | 5 She knew the child instantly & gave thanks |
| 2 She never lost hope over many, many years | | | |
| 3 She never grew bitter in the face of sorrow | | | 6 She shared the message with all believers |

# DIVISION I

## THE ANNOUNCEMENT OF THE COMING OF JESUS, THE SON OF MAN, 1:1-2:52

### J. Anna's Praise: The Child Jesus is Praised by a Prophetess, 2:36-38

(2:36-38) **Introduction**: nothing is known about Anna except what is given here. She was the daughter of Phanuel. Apparently, her father's name had been taken from the place Phanuel, the place where Jacob wrestled with God face to face (Gen.32:24-30). Anna's name means *gracious*. She seems to have been a person of enormous devotion, one who lived as though face to face with God, ever receiving His grace and sharing His grace with others. She knew she had descended from the tribe of Aser.

A man, Simeon, had just borne witness that the child Jesus was the *Salvation of God*. Now a woman, Anna, bore the very same witness. Both men and women acknowledged the child to be the Messiah, the Salvation of God. Both men and women of every generation are urged to hope in Him for salvation. Jesus is our hope.

1. She was a prophetess (v.36).
2. She never lost hope over many, many years (v.36).
3. She never grew bitter in the face of sorrow (v.36).
4. She never ceased to worship—night or day (v.37).
5. She knew the child instantly and gave thanks (v.38).
6. She shared the message with all believers (v.38).

**1** (2:36) **Prophetess**: Anna was a prophetess. This was most unusual. There had not been a prophet in Israel for some three hundred years, yet God is seen as having raised up a prophet, and a woman at that. Women leaders were very rare in that day. She was apparently a very special person, one who loved God and hoped in God with all her being (cp. v.37). She was evidently on a spiritual par with other saintly women used by God throughout Scripture such as Miriam, Hannah, and Deborah. As a prophetess, she was constantly studying the Word of God that she might be approved of God and proclaim the unsearchable riches of His grace (cp. 2 Tim.2:15; 4:2). The point is, Anna's hope was in God; therefore, God blessed her greatly. God will always bless the person who hopes in Him.

"Be of good courage, and he shall strengthen your heart, all ye that hope in the LORD" (Ps.31:24).
"Behold, the eye of the LORD is upon them that fear him, upon them that hope in his mercy" (Ps.33:18).
"And now, Lord, what wait I for? my hope is in thee" (Ps.39:7).
"Hope thou in God: for I shall yet praise him, who is the health of my countenance, and my God" (Ps.42:11).
"For thou art my hope, O Lord GOD: thou art my trust from my youth" (Ps.71:5).
"Blessed is the man that trusteth in the LORD, and whose hope the LORD is" (Jer.17:7).

**2** (2:36) **Steadfastness—Perseverance**: Anna never lost hope over many, many years. She was about eighty-four years old (v.37), but she still believed and still looked for the Messiah. She still looked for the salvation that God was to send to the world. She never forsook her belief, but held fast, *enduring to the end*.

"And because iniquity shall abound, the love of many shall wax cold. But he that shall endure unto the end, the same shall be saved" (Mt.24:12-13).
"As the Father hath loved me, so have I loved you: continue ye in my love" (Jn.15:9).
"And let us not be weary in well doing: for in due season we shall reap, if we faint not" (Gal.6:9).
"Behold, we count them happy which endure. Ye have heard of the patience of Job, and have seen the end of the Lord; that the Lord is very pitiful, and of tender mercy" (Jas.5:11).
"Behold, I come quickly; hold that fast which thou hast, that no man take thy crown" (Rev.3:11).

**3** (2:36) **Dedication—Sorrow—Widow**: Anna never grew bitter in the face of sorrow. She had been married at an early age and had lived with her husband only seven years when he died. She remained a widow, but not out of bitterness or disappointment. She never remarried because of conviction—the conviction that her life belonged to God. Before her hus-

41

band died, she had been committed to her husband; and from what is recorded in this passage, she was bound to have been an ideal wife. When her husband died, she apparently understood this to be a sign that God wanted her life totally committed to Him. Therefore, she dedicated herself to serving Him and Him alone for the remainder of her life. She placed her hope in God and in God alone.

> "I say therefore to the unmarried and widows, It is good for them if they abide even as I" (1 Cor.7:8).
> "But this I say, brethren, the time is short: it remaineth, that both they that have wives be as though they had none; and they that weep, as though they wept not; and they that rejoice, as though they rejoiced not; and they that buy, as though they possessed not; and they that use this world, as not abusing it: for the fashion of this world passeth away. But I would have you without carefulness [anxiety]. He that is unmarried careth for the things that belong to the Lord, how he may please the Lord: but he that is married careth for the things that are of the world, how he may please his wife. There is difference also between a wife and a virgin. The unmarried woman careth for the things of the Lord, that she may be holy both in body and in spirit: but she that is married careth for the things of the world, how she may please her husband. And this I speak for your own profit; not that I may cast a snare upon you, but for that which is comely, and that ye may attend upon the Lord without distraction" (1 Cor.7:29-35).

Note in particular the words, "that ye may attend [concentrate] upon the Lord without distraction."

**4** (2:37) **Devotion—Worship**: Anna never ceased to worship, night or day. This is a phenomenal statement: she never left the temple, but "served God with fastings and prayers night and day." This either means that she had been given some kind of *room* at the temple or else she was at worship every day never missing a service (cp. Lk.24:53). Anna was a godly woman, a woman to whom God meant everything. She was totally devoted to God, sold out to Him completely, hoping in Him and in Him alone. Note two things.

1. The fastings and prayers indicate that she was extremely disciplined, possessing the consistency in devotions that so many lack.

2. She fasted and prayed night and day despite being elderly, eighty-four years old. She did not give herself to the flesh as she grew old: overeating, oversleeping, immoral gratification, or meaningless activities that waste time. She devoted herself to serving and hoping in God, praying and bearing witness as His servant.

> "Seek the LORD and his strength, seek his face continually" (1 Chron.16:11).
> "Men ought always to pray, and not to faint" (Lk.18:1; cp. Eph.6:18; 1 Th.5:17).
> "But sanctify the Lord God in your hearts: and be ready always to give an answer to every man that asketh you a reason of the hope that is in you with meekness and fear" (1 Pt.3:15).
> "Ye are my witnesses, saith the LORD, and my servant whom I have chosen: that ye may know and believe me, and understand that I am he: before me there was no God formed, neither shall there be after me" (Is.43:10).

**5** (2:38) **Jesus Christ, Savior—Redemption**: Anna knew the child instantly and gave thanks. She was the Lord's servant, so the Lord guided her life step by step. He took care of her, looking after her welfare. She belonged to God so much that God could guide her every step. He saw to it that her path crossed the path of the child Messiah. He fulfilled her hope. Note she came in at the very moment that Jesus was in the temple, and she immediately began giving thanks to God for the Christ-child. What is the message of her thanksgiving? *Redemption.* Redemption is that for which she praised God. The child was the Messiah who was to redeem all people (see note, pts. 1, 2, 3—Lk.2:28-33. See note—Eph.1:7.) Note the word "likewise." This refers back to what Simeon had prophesied. She prophesied and proclaimed the same message: the child Jesus is the glorious hope of man's redemption.

> "He sent redemption unto his people: he hath commanded his covenant forever: holy and reverend is his name" (Ps.111:9).
> "Let Israel hope in the LORD: for with the LORD there is mercy, and with him is plenteous redemption" (Ps.130:7).
> "Fear not: for I have redeemed thee, I have called thee by thy name; thou art mine" (Is.43:1).
> "Being justified freely by his grace through the redemption that is in Christ Jesus" (Ro.3:24).
> "But of him [of God] are ye in Christ Jesus, who of God is made unto us wisdom, and righteousness, and sanctification, and redemption" (1 Cor.1:30).
> "Christ hath redeemed us from the curse of the law, being made a curse for us: for it is written, Cursed is every one that hangeth on a tree" (Gal.3:13).
> "In whom we have redemption through his blood, the forgiveness of sins, according to the riches of his grace" (Eph.1:7; cp. Col.1:14).
> "Who gave himself for us, that he might redeem us from all iniquity, and purify unto himself a peculiar people, zealous of good works" (Tit.2:14).
> "Neither by the blood of goats and calves, but by his own blood he entered in once into the holy place, having obtained eternal redemption for us" (Heb.9:12).
> "Forasmuch as ye know that ye were not redeemed with corruptible things, as silver and gold, from your vain conversation received by tradition from your fathers" (1 Pt.1:18).

"And they sung a new song, saying, Thou art worthy to take the book, and to open the seals thereof: for thou wast slain, and hast redeemed us to God by thy blood out of every kindred, and tongue, and people, and nation" (Rev.5:9).

6 (2:38) **Witnessing:** Anna shared the message with all believers. She knew of others who were looking for the Messiah's coming, so she shared the glorious news with them (see DEEPER STUDY # 2—Mt.1:18). She had seen the child-Messiah, the salvation of God, the glorious hope of all men.

"Let the redeemed of the LORD say so, whom he hath redeemed from the hand of the enemy" (Ps.107:2).
"And the things that thou hast heard of me among many witnesses, the same commit thou to faithful men, who shall be able to teach others also" (2 Tim.2:2).
"Go ye therefore, and teach all nations, baptizing them in the name of the Father, and of the Son, and of the Holy Ghost: teaching them to observe all things whatsoever I have commanded you: and, lo, I am with you alway, even unto the end of the world" (Mt.28:19-20).

| | K. Jesus' Growth as a Child, 2:39-40 |
|---|---|
| 1 He was led by His parents to fulfill all the law<br>2 He was reared in Nazareth<sup>DS1</sup> | 39 And when they had performed all things according to the law of the Lord, they returned into Galilee, to their own city Nazareth. |
| 3 He grew as a child: Physically, spiritually, & mentally<br>4 He possessed God's grace | 40 And the child grew, and waxed strong in spirit, filled with wisdom: and the grace of God was upon him. |

# DIVISION I

## THE ANNOUNCEMENT OF THE COMING OF JESUS, THE SON OF MAN, 1:1-2:52

## K.  Jesus' Growth as a Child, 2:39-40

(2:39-40) **Introduction**: Jesus' growth as a child is simply stated. What is said is meaningful and applicable to the life of all thoughtful readers.

1. He was led by His parents to fulfill all the law (v.39).
2. He was reared in Nazareth (v.39).
3. He grew as a child: physically, spiritually, and mentally (v.40).
4. He possessed God's grace (v.40).

**1** (2:39) **Jesus Christ, Fulfilled Law**: Jesus was led by His parents to fulfill all the law. Note two significant facts.

1. God had sent His Son into the world to fulfill the law, not to destroy it. By keeping all the law, Jesus would be perfectly righteous and become the *Ideal Man*, the Man who would be the *Pattern* for all men to follow.

Another way to say the same thing is that God has given us a perfect life to follow, not just written letters and words. By fulfilling the law and by never failing in a single point, Jesus became the Perfect Man, the Ideal Life which men are to imitate. Men are now to look to Jesus and follow Him instead of following the law. Jesus has fulfilled the law; therefore, He embraces and includes all the law *and more* in His life (see notes—Mt.5:17-18; DEEPER STUDY # 2—Ro.8:3).

2. In order to fulfill the law, Jesus had to keep the law and every observance of it. He had to "fulfill all righteousness" (Mt.3:15). Now note: by keeping all of the law, Jesus was symbolically predicting what He was to do for sinful man. He was going to secure righteousness and perfection by fulfilling the law, and thereby He was to become the Ideal Man. As the Ideal Man, whatever He did would cover any man who followed Him. The man who followed Jesus would be covered by His righteousness (perfection), His death, His resurrection, and His ascension. The man who truly trusted Jesus Christ to cover him with His righteousness would be covered by His righteousness.

It is for these reasons that God led Mary and Joseph to fulfill all the law for the child Messiah (also see notes—Lk.2:22-23; DEEPER STUDY # 3—Mt.8:20 for more discussion).

> **"And Jesus answering said unto him, Suffer it to be so now: for thus it becometh us to fulfil all righteousness. Then he suffered him" (Mt.3:15).**
> **"Think not that I am come to destroy the law, or the prophets: I am not come to destroy, but to fulfil" (Mt.5:17).**
> **"For what the law could not do, in that it was weak through the flesh, God sending his own Son in the likeness of sinful flesh, and for sin, condemned sin in the flesh" (Ro.8:3).**
> **"For since by man came death, by man came also the resurrection of the dead" (1 Cor.15:21).**

**2** (2:39) **Jesus Christ, Childhood—Nazareth**: Jesus was reared in Nazareth.

1. Luke simply says that after Jesus' dedication in the temple, His parents returned to Nazareth. There is no mention of Matthew's account...
   - of their return to Bethlehem where the wise men visited them (Mt.2:1-12).
   - of their flight into Egypt (Mt.2:13-15).
   - of Herod's slaughter of the children (Mt.2:16-18).
   - of the threat of Archaleus (Mt.2:19-22).

2. Nazareth was an ideal place for the child Messiah to be brought up (see DEEPER STUDY # 1, *Nazareth*—Lk.2:39 for discussion). However, Nazareth was an obscure place, despised and reproached by other people (cp. Jn.1:46). It was a humiliating place to be reared. Therefore, as with Jesus' birth in a stable, which was the lowest of places, He continued to identify with people in the most severe circumstances. He, too, knew what it was to be born and brought up in a despicable place. From the very first, He *made Himself of no reputation* (Ph.2:7).

> **"But made himself of no reputation, and took upon him the form of a servant, and was made in the likeness of men" (Ph.2:7).**
> **"For ye know the grace of our Lord Jesus Christ, that, though he was rich, yet for your sakes he became poor, that ye through his poverty might be rich" (2 Cor.8:9).**

"For even Christ pleased not himself; but, as it is written, The reproaches of them that reproached thee fell on me" (Ro.15:3).

---

**DEEPER STUDY # 1**

**(2:39) Nazareth**: the hometown of Joseph and Mary and of Jesus Himself during His childhood and early manhood. There were at least two advantages to Jesus' being brought up in Nazareth.

1.    It was a quiet town, small and infamous, ready-made for a close community and for neighborliness and quiet contemplation.

2.    It was also a town in touch with the modern life and world events of that day. Two of the major roads in the ancient world passed within eyesight of the hills surrounding the city: the road stretching between the great cities of the North and South (from Rome to Africa), and the road stretching between the great cities of the East and West. Jesus can be imagined sitting and standing on the hills observing (perhaps even meeting) some of the travellers and caravans using the major routes as they crisscrossed the world. He had opportunity to observe and study the nature and dealings of all kinds of men and nationalities as they used the major routes. How often His heart must have ached and wept as a child over a world lost and needing to be found.

---

**3**    **(2:40) Jesus Christ, Childhood—Humiliation**: Jesus grew as a child—physically, spiritually, and mentally.

1.    The idea is that Jesus grew as a normal child. But note the added words: "*waxed strong* [ekrataiouto] in spirit" (a vigorous growth). He did not just grow in wisdom, He was "*filled* with wisdom" (pleroumenon sophiai). Simply stated, Jesus grew perfectly at every stage of life.

⇒ He grew physically as well as the human body could grow (perfectly well and healthy).

⇒ He "waxed strong in spirit," as strong as a child could grow.

⇒ He was "filled with wisdom," as much as a child could be filled.

No other child had ever been or ever will be perfect in growth at the various stages of childhood, but the Christ-child was. He grew as well as a child can grow: *filled* perfectly with all the qualities that fill a child.

2.    Why did Christ come into the world as a child and not as a full-grown man? The first man, Adam, stood at the head of the human race as the natural representative of man, and he had been created as a full-grown man. Why not Jesus Christ, the second Adam? He, too, was sent into the world to stand at the head of the human race as the spiritual representative of man. Going through the stages of growth as a baby, then as a child, and then as a teenager is a humbling experience. Why did God subject His Son to such humiliation? There are at least two reasons.

a.    Christ needed to set a striking example for every person, no matter the age, even for children. In *lowliness of mind*, He went through the experience of a helpless babe, then a dependent child, and then an independent and responsible man. The very fact that the Son of God stooped so low is shocking to any thoughtful person. It sets a striking example of *humility and lowliness of mind* for every man.

> "Let nothing be done through strife or vainglory; but in lowliness of mind let each esteem other better than themselves. Look not every man on his own things, but every man also on the things of others. Let this mind be in you, which was also in Christ Jesus: who, being in the form of God, thought it not robbery to be equal with God: but made himself of no reputation, and took upon him the form of a servant, and was made in the likeness of men: and being found in fashion as a man, he humbled himself, and became obedient unto death, even the death of the cross" (Ph.2:3-8).

b.    Christ needed to demonstrate a striking truth to all men: no person can enter heaven unless they first become as a little child. There was no better way to demonstrate the lesson than for the Son of God Himself to go through the humbling experience of becoming a child before becoming a man.

> "Verily I say unto you, Except ye be converted, and become as little children, ye shall not enter into the kingdom of heaven. Whosoever therefore shall humble himself as this little child, the same is greatest in the kingdom of heaven" (Mt.18:3-4).

c.    Christ needed to experience every situation, condition, and trial of man in order to become the *Perfect Sympathizer or Savior*. For this reason, He experienced the most humiliating experiences possible. He experienced...

- being born to an unwed mother (Mt.1:18-19).
- being born in a stable, the worst of conditions (Lk.2:7).
- being born to poor parents (Lk.2:24).
- having his life threatened as a baby (Mt.2:13f).
- being the cause of unimaginable sorrow (Mt.2:16f).
- having to be moved and shifted as a baby (Mt.2:13f).
- being reared in a despicable place, Nazareth (Lk.2:39).
- having His father die during His youth (see note, pt.3—Mt.13:53-58).
- having to support His mother and brothers and sisters (see note, pt.3—Mt.13:53-58).
- having no home, not even a place to lay His head (Mt.8:20; Lk.9:58).
- being hated and opposed by religionists (Mk.14:1-2).
- being charged with insanity (Mk.3:21).
- being charged with demon possession (Mk.3:22).

- being opposed by His own family (Mk.3:31-32).
- being rejected, hated, and opposed by listeners (Mt.13:53-58; Lk.4:28-29).
- being betrayed by a close friend (Mk.14:10-11, 18).
- being left alone, rejected, and forsaken by all of His friends (Mk.14:50).
- being tried before the high court of the land on the charge of treason (Jn.18:33).
- being executed by crucifixion, the worst possible death (Jn.19:16f).

Note that each of these experiences reaches the depth of humiliation. Christ stooped to the lowest point of human experience in every condition in order to become the *Perfect Sympathizer* (Savior). He can now identify with and feel for any person's circumstances.

> **"For verily he took not on him the nature of angels; but he took on him the seed of Abraham. Wherefore in all things it behoved him to be made like unto his brethren, that he might be a merciful and faithful high priest in things pertaining to God, to make reconciliation for the sins of the people. For in that he himself hath suffered being tempted, he is able to succour them that are tempted" (Heb.2:16-18).**

> **"For we have not an high priest which cannot be touched with the feeling of our infirmities; but was in all points tempted like as we are, yet without sin. Let us therefore come boldly unto the throne of grace, that we may obtain mercy, and find grace to help in time of need" (Heb.4:15-16).**

**4** (2:40) **Jesus Christ, Childhood—Fulness of God's Grace:** Jesus possessed God's grace (charis theou). The idea is that God's grace rested upon Jesus in *full measure*, without any lack or shortcoming whatsoever.

Jesus was choosing to grow perfectly, coming short in nothing. Therefore, God showered Him with His grace, His favor. God favored Him by looking after and taking care of Him perfectly.

> **"For he whom God hath sent speaketh the words of God: for God giveth not the Spirit by measure unto him" (Jn.3:34).**

> **"But of him are ye in Christ Jesus, who of God is made unto us wisdom, and righteousness, and sanctification, and redemption" (1 Cor.1:30).**

| | L. Jesus as a Young Boy in the Temple: Jesus' First Recognition of Messiahship, 2:41-52 | after three days they found him in the temple, sitting in the midst of the doctors, both hearing them, and asking them questions. | surprising<br><br>a. He listened to teachers<br>b. He asked questions |
|---|---|---|---|
| **1 His faithfulness in worship was noteworthy**<br>a. Parents' faithfulness<br>b. Parents taught Him<br>c. Jesus' special year: Became a man at age twelve | 41 Now his parents went to Jerusalem every year at the feast of the passover.<br>42 And when he was twelve years old, they went up to Jerusalem after the custom of the feast. | 47 And all that heard him were astonished at his understanding and answers.<br>48 And when they saw him, they were amazed: and his mother said unto him, Son, why hast thou thus dealt with us? behold, thy father and I have sought thee sorrowing. | **4 His mission was misunderstood by His parents** |
| **2 His social development was normal**<br>a. His parents left to return home<br>b. Jesus was missing from the caravan<br>c. His parents thought He was with others, playing and socializing | 43 And when they had fulfilled the days, as they returned, the child Jesus tarried behind in Jerusalem; and Joseph and his mother knew not of it.<br>44 But they, supposing him to have been in the company, went a day's journey; and they sought him among their kinsfolk and acquaintance. | 49 And he said unto them, How is it that ye sought me? wist ye not that I must be about my Father's business?<br>50 And they understood not the saying which he spake unto them. | **5 His first known recognition of Messiahship was at an early age** |
| d. His parents returned to find Him | 45 And when they found him not, they turned back again to Jerusalem, seeking him.<br>46 And it came to pass, that | 51 And he went down with them, and came to Nazareth, and was subject unto them: but his mother kept all these sayings in her heart.<br>52 And Jesus increased in wisdom and stature, and in favour with God and man. | **6 His obedience to His parents was striking**<br><br>**7 His growth was in favor with both God and man**[DS1] |
| **3 His knowledge was** | | | |

# DIVISION I

## THE ANNOUNCEMENT OF THE COMING OF JESUS, THE SON OF MAN, 1:1-2:52

**L.**     **Jesus as a Young Boy in the Temple: Jesus' First Recognition of Messiahship, 2:41-52**

(2:41-52) **Introduction**: this is an extremely important and interesting passage. It is the only passage that covers Jesus' childhood. It is important, for it gives us the first *known* time that Jesus claimed to be the Messiah. The lessons found within the passage are inexhaustable.

1. His faithfulness in worship was noteworthy (v.41-42).
2. His social development was normal (v.43-45).
3. His knowledge was surprising (v.46-47).
4. His mission was misunderstood by His parents (v.48).
5. His first known recognition of Messiahship was at an early age (v.49-50).
6. His obedience to His parents was striking (v.51).
7. His growth was in favor with both God and man (v.52).

**1**  (2:41-42) **Worship—Jesus Christ, Childhood**: Jesus' faithfulness in worship as a young boy was noteworthy. Note several things.

1. Jesus' parents were faithful in their worship. This fact is specifically stated. It was their *custom* to keep the feast of the Passover every year. All male Jews who lived within twenty miles of Jerusalem were required by law to attend the temple three times a year: at the Passover, Pentecost, and the Feast of Tabernacles (Ex.23:14-17). Women were exempt from the law, but they could attend if they wished. Note what Mary chose to do: both "parents went to Jerusalem every year." They were both faithful in their worship by choice, not by restraint.

2. Jesus' parents led and taught Him to be faithful in worship. It is not specifically said that Jesus went to Jerusalem with His parents every year, but the implication is that He did. Note the words "Now His parents went...every year at the...Passover." It was the custom for "all that could hear with understanding" to be present if at all possible (Neh.8:2).

Also note His knowledge and ability to discuss issues with religious authorities (v.46-47). This indicates that His parents continually taught Jesus, seeing to it that He was in the synagogue worshipping and learning at every opportunity. God had placed the child Jesus into their hands as a *bundle of trust*. The child belonged to God. He had only entrusted the child's keeping into their hands to see that He was looked after and taught. It was their responsibility to see that He grew physically, mentally, and spiritually and to see that He became all He could become. The parents were faithful to their duty.

> **Thought 1.** What an example for all parents. Children are but a *bundle of trust* placed into our hands by God. They belong to God, not us. Therefore, we are to train up a child in the way he should go (Pr.22:6).

3. This was a very special year for Jesus. He had just turned twelve years old. When a Jewish boy reached thirteen years of age, he became a *son of the law* which meant that he was now considered a man and was expected to keep all the

law. It was suggested that a boy be brought to the Passover Feast a year or two early so that he might become familiar with the Temple and the Feasts. When the eleven- and twelve-year old initiates arrived, they were naturally given a great deal of attention and special instruction (v.46-47).

**Thought 1.** Note two critical points.
1) Every child should be taught from the very first about God and worship, about the world and a person's responsibility in it.
2) Every child, when he comes of age, should be charged with becoming a "son of the law," a man *before God*, being responsible and making his contribution to the world—*all in the name of the Lord*.

> **"And thou shalt teach them [commandments] diligently unto thy children, and shalt talk of them when thou sittest in thine house, and when thou walkest by the way, and when thou liest down, and when thou risest up" (Dt.6:7).**
> **"Train up a child in the way he should go: and when he is old, he will not depart from it" (Pr.22:6).**
> **"Come, ye children, hearken unto me: I will teach you the fear of the LORD" (Ps.34:11).**

**2** (2:43-45) **Jesus Christ, Childhood:** Jesus' social development was normal. This is gleaned from what happened in these verses. The parents had finished their worship obligations and were returning home to Nazareth. Jesus had remained behind, but they did not know it. They thought He was off playing and socializing with some of the other families and children in the caravan. The caravans were large and the roads were packed with thousands of pilgrims leaving the Feast. We can glean from this that Jesus was sociable and fit right in with people. The very fact that His parents would think He was off socializing with others points to a normal social development. Note: they were so sure that He was socializing that they did not bother to look for Him until nightfall (v.44). When they did not find Him among their relatives and friends, they returned to Jerusalem to search for Him.

**Thought 1.** A child's social development is important. A child is to be helped and encouraged, led and directed to play with others. However, he must also be taught how to play and how to associate with others. He must be taught to be..
- patient
- giving
- joyful
- loving
- kind
- helpful
- peaceful
- loyal
- caring
- disciplined

...not bragging, revengeful, arrogant, jealous, selfish, or easily provoked.

**3** (2:46-47) **Jesus Christ, Knowledge of:** Jesus' knowledge was surprising. It took His parents three days to find Him. When they found Him, He was in the temple, in the very precinct or room where classes and discussion took place among the doctors of theology and religion. It was a prominent place, and it was a custom to hold open classes and discussions so that the public could listen and learn. The stress of Luke at this point is the surprising knowledge of Jesus. His knowledge and understanding were phenomenal.

1. Jesus was found "in the midst of the doctors." There were some very prominent *Doctors of Religion* in that day, men who were very capable theologically. There was...
- Gamaliel, the great teacher of Paul or Saul of Tarsus.
- Hillel, one of the most revered liberal teachers with a large school of followers (see DEEPER STUDY # 1—Mt.19:1-12).
- Shammai, one of the most revered conservative teachers who also had a school of followers (see DEEPER STUDY # 1—Mt.19:1-12).
- Jonathan, who paraphrased the sacred books.
- Simeon, who was to later succeed Hillel.
- Nicodemus, who was so revered by his peers that he was sent to interview Jesus alone.

Some of these scholars were probably engaged in the discussion with Jesus, for news of the young boy and his phenomenal understanding must have swept through the halls of the temple, arousing the curiosity of the *Doctors*. Remember, Jesus had been in the temple for at least three days. The point to note is how Jesus was making use of the opportunity He had. He was in Jerusalem exposed to these eminent scholars for only a few days, so He grasped the opportunity to learn and perhaps teach all He could.

2. Jesus was found thirsting for knowledge and understanding. Note exactly what is said.
   a. He was *"hearing"* (akouonta) what the teachers said. He listened closely, attentively, with rapt attention. He was "swift to hear" (Jas.1:19).
   b. He was "asking them questions" (eperotonta). He wanted answers, more understanding. He thirsted for truth and sought it.
   c. He answered (apokrisesin) their questions.

Note that His questions and answers revealed phenomenal knowledge and understanding, so much so that everyone was astonished, even the doctors. The word astonished (existanto de) means that all were amazed, overwhelmed, bewildered, and wondered at His understanding.

> **"I have more understanding than all my teachers: for thy testimonies are my meditation. I understand more than the ancients, because I keep thy precepts" (Ps.119:99-100).**

**Thought 1.** This is a striking lesson for both children and adults.
1) Every opportunity to learn the truth should be grasped.
2) We should *thirst* for knowledge and understanding.

> **"Then said Jesus to those Jews which believed on him, If ye continue in my word, then are ye my disciples indeed; and ye shall know the truth, and the truth shall make you free" (Jn.8:31-32).**
>
> **"And beside this, giving all diligence, add to your faith virtue; and to virtue knowledge" (2 Pt.1:5).**
>
> **"But let him that glorieth glory in this, that he understandeth and knoweth me, that I am the LORD which exercise lovingkindness, judgment, and righteousness, in the earth: for in these things I delight, saith the LORD" (Jer.9:24).**
>
> **"Yea, if thou criest after knowledge, and liftest up thy voice for understanding" (Pr.2:3).**
>
> **"Happy is the man that findeth wisdom, and the man that getteth understanding" (Pr.3:13).**
>
> **"Get wisdom, get understanding: forget it not" (Pr.4:5).**
>
> **"The heart of him that hath understanding seeketh knowledge: but the mouth of fools feedeth on foolishness" (Pr.15:14).**
>
> **"Buy the truth, and sell it not; also wisdom, and instruction, and understanding" (Pr.23:23).**
>
> **"Then shall we know, if we follow on to know the LORD: his going forth is prepared as the morning; and he shall come unto us as the rain, as the latter and former rain unto the earth" (Hos.6:3).**

**4** (2:48) **Jesus Christ, Mission—Forgetfulness:** Jesus' mission was misunderstood by His parents. This is seen in Mary's words to Jesus. She was rebuking Jesus rather sternly. In her disturbance and sorrow, she forgot who He was. It is not that she was not to teach and discipline or direct Him; she was. But He was now a young man by law, and He was where He should be, going about His Father's business.

**Thought 1.** There is warning here. Too often disturbance and sorrow cause us to *forget who Jesus is*. We allow circumstances to cloud our minds, to disturb us and bring sorrow into our lives. And we soon *forget Jesus*, His understanding of the situation and His business of ministering to our needs.

> **"Only take heed to thyself, and keep thy soul diligently, lest thou forget the things which thine eyes have seen, and lest they depart from thy heart all the days of thy life: but teach them thy sons, and thy sons' sons" (Dt.4:9).**

**5** (2:49-50) **Messiahship:** Jesus' first known recognition of Messiahship was at an early age. This is a very significant point. This is the first time that Jesus claimed to be the Son of God. Note two points.
1. He called God His Father. Joseph was standing there, so Jesus was gentle in the way He worded His statement, but He was clear and definite in referring to God as His Father. Just *when* He knew He was the Messiah, the Son of God, is not known; and frankly, all suggestions are pure speculation. But this fact is known. At age twelve, He was conscious of a *unique relationship with God*, a relationship unlike other children: God was His Father, and He was the Son of God, the *unique Son* in the sense that He alone had been begotten of the Father.
This is seen even more clearly when Jesus' answer is studied.
2. Jesus was saying to His mother that His Father (God) had been looking after Him. He had been about His Father's business, doing what His Father wanted Him to do; therefore, He was under His Father's care and watchful eye. There was no need for her, His mother, to be worrying.

**Thought 1.** Every man needs to *place himself under* God's care and watchful eye. A decision to follow Christ as Lord causes God to adopt a person as a child of His and places a person under the Father's care.

3. Jesus was saying that He had work to do for His Father (God) even if that work was not understood. He could not go home with them until He had finished His Father's work. He first had to do what His Father willed.

> **"But Jesus answered them, My Father worketh hitherto, and I work" (Jn.5:17).**
>
> **"I must work the works of him that sent me, while it is day: the night cometh, when no man can work" (Jn.9:4).**
>
> **"Jesus answered them, I told you, and ye believed not: the works that I do in my Father's name, they bear witness of me" (Jn.10:25).**
>
> **"I have glorified thee on the earth: I have finished the work which thou gavest me to do" (Jn.17:4).**

**Thought 1.** Christ is the Son of God, the only begotten Son of the Father (Jn.3:16f).

**Thought 2.** Every person is to serve God first, even if the work is not understood. And it is often not understood. We must be faithful to God and His call even if we are misunderstood and opposed.

"Remember now thy Creator in the days of thy youth, while the evil days come not, nor the years draw nigh, when thou shalt say, I have no pleasure in them" (Eccl.12:1).

**Thought 3**. Sometimes our families are the strongest opposition confronting our decision and work for God (cp. Mt.10:37).

**6** (2:51) **Children—Family—Obedience**: Jesus' obedience to His parents was striking. This is both a beautiful and striking picture. Jesus was *subject* to His parents; He obeyed them. As the Son of God, He set the perfect example of what a child should be to His parents. He obeyed His parents despite the fact...

- that Joseph was not His true father.
- that He was stronger in spirit.
- that He was filled with wisdom.
- that God was His Father.

"Children, obey your parents in the Lord: for this is right. Honour thy father and mother; (which is the first commandment with promise;) that it may be well with thee, and thou mayest live long on the earth" (Eph.6:1-3; cp. Col.3:20).

"But if any widow have children or nephews, let them learn first to show piety at home, and to requite [repay] their parents: for that is good and acceptable before God" (1 Tim.5:4).

"Even a child is known by his doings, whether his work be pure, and whether it be right" (Pr.20:11).

"Hearken unto thy father that begat thee, and despise not thy mother when she is old" (Pr.23:22).

Note that Mary again kept all these things in her heart. In humble faith she said nothing, not talking with relatives or neighbors nor boasting in her Son and His uniqueness. She was quiet, humbly waiting upon God to use Jesus as He so willed. In due time she knew that God would reveal Him and His salvation to the world.

**7** (2:52) **Jesus Christ, Childhood**: Jesus' growth was in favor with both God and man.

1. Mentally, Jesus was "filled with wisdom" (v.40). He learned from teachers and from personal study and thought just as all children learned. Yet He differed from other children in that He learned perfectly, coming short in nothing.

**Thought 1.** Note how few children follow the example of Jesus. Few really seek to learn. Most just take what is assigned and do the minimum that is required. Few pursue real excellence.

2. Physically, He grew in an orderly fashion just as all other children grow.

**Thought 1.** Some children do not develop physically, not like they should. Some are incapable due to deformity or abnormality. However, there are other children who fail to develop as they should because they do not get the physical exercise necessary to develop. They sit around instead of being outside playing and working.

3. Spiritually, He "waxed strong in spirit" (v.40) and "in favor with God" (v.52). He looked to God in perfect obedience, and God nurtured Him in His perfect favor.

**Thought 1.** Note how few children follow the example of Jesus. Few children really grow spiritually. Few are willing to buck the crowd, accepting the challenge of Jesus and standing up for Him.

4. Socially, He grew in favor with men. He was friendly, loving, caring, helpful, unselfish, pure, honest, and humble. He was welcomed by the other families in His community.

**Thought 1.** Note that some children do not follow Jesus' example in developing socially. Some children are not welcomed by other families.

---

**DEEPER STUDY # 1**
(2:52) **Increased** (proekorten): means to grow steadily, to keep advancing. The picture is that of Jesus' cutting His way through the advancing years just as a pioneer cuts through the wilderness to reach his destination.

| | CHAPTER 3 | of God came unto John the son of Zacharias in the wilderness. | |
|---|---|---|---|
| | II. THE SON OF MAN'S APPEARANCE, 3:1-4:15 | 3 And he came into all the country about Jordan, preaching the baptism of repentance for the remission of sins; | **3 He was a man who preached repentance & forgiveness of sin** |
| | A. The Forerunner, John the Baptist: The Pivotal Point of History, 3:1-6 (Mt.3:1-6; Mk.1:2-6; Jn.1:19-28) | 4 As it is written in the book of the words of Esaias the prophet, saying, The voice of one crying in the wilderness, Prepare ye the way of the Lord, make his paths straight. | **4 He was a man who cried out apocalyptically: Prepare, make the paths of God straight** |
| **1 He was a man who launched the most pivotal point of history** | Now in the fifteenth year of the reign of Tiberius Caesar, Pontius Pilate being governor of Judea, and Herod being tetrarch of Galilee, and his brother Philip tetrarch of Ituraea and of the region of Trachonitis, and Lysanias the tetrarch of Abilene, | 5 Every valley shall be filled, and every mountain and hill shall be brought low; and the crooked shall be made straight, and the rough | a. Humbled shall be exalted b. Proud shall be abased c. Crooked shall be straightened out d. Rough shall be smoothed |
| **2 He was a man called out of the wilderness** | 2 Annas and Caiaphas being the high priests, the word | ways shall be made smooth; 6 And all flesh shall see the salvation of God. | e. God's salvation shall be seen |

# DIVISION II

## THE SON OF MAN'S APPEARANCE, 3:1-4:15

## A.    The Forerunner, John the Baptist: The Pivotal Point of History, 3:1-6

(3:1-6) **Introduction—History, Pivotal Point of**: the coming of Jesus Christ was the pivotal point of human history. When He came to earth, earth saw the Son of God Himself (1 Jn.1:1-3). His impact upon the world can never be overstated. He changed the world so much that men measure their years by Him. Some may dispute His significance, but they are wrong. And their misjudgment will be confronted some day in the future. When? When Christ returns. Scripture declares that He is going to return to earth. He is going to return as a Judge, not as a Savior—the Judge who will prove that He is the King of kings and Lord of lords, the God of very God, the Messiah. He is going to prove that He is the Salvation of God Almighty.

A Person of such magnitude, the Person whose coming was to be the pivotal point of history, needed a forerunner. He needed someone who could run ahead of Him and arouse the people to prepare for His coming. That forerunner was John the Baptist, a man who is an example to us all.

1.    He was a man who launched the most pivotal point of history (v.1).
2.    He was a man called out of the wilderness (v.2).
3.    He was a man who preached repentance and forgiveness of sin (v.3).
4.    He was a man who cried out apocalyptically: prepare, make God's paths straight (v.4-6).

1  (3:1) **History, Pivotal Point—Jesus Christ—Fulness of Time**: John was a man who launched the most pivotal point of history—the coming of Christ. Some may dispute that the coming of Christ is the most significant event in history, but Scripture proclaims that God will someday reveal the fact to all. Luke points to the fact by dating the coming of Christ with significant events and historical rulers. The very first event was God's call of John. Therefore, the beginning of the greatest period in all history began with the call of John, the Lord's forerunner. Note several facts.

1.    Tiberius Caesar was in the fifteenth year of his reign when God called John. Tiberius was the second Roman Emporer, beginning his reign in A.D. 14. Therefore, the emergence of John took place between A.D. 28-29.

2.    Pontius Pilate was governor of Judea. He was both the civil ruler and a military commander. The situation had grown so bad in Judea that Rome had to remove Archelaus from civil control and move in a military commander. Therefore, Judea was ruled directly by Roman authority at this time. Pilate held office from A.D. 26-36.

3.    Herod Antipas was tetrarch of Galilee and Perea. Tetrarch simply means a ruler over a fourth part. Herod Antipas was the son of Herod the Great. He inherited his territory at his father's death and ruled from B.C. 4 to A.D. 39. Note that he was the ruler over Galilee where Jesus spent most of His time ministering. (See DEEPER STUDY # 1,2, *Herod*—Mt.14:1-14 for more discussion.)

4.    Philip was tetrarch of Ituraea and Trachonitis. He was a reputable leader, known as a fair and just ruler. Caesarea Philippi was built and named after him. Caesarea was where Peter made his great confession.

5.    Lysanius was tetrarch of Abilene. Nothing of importance is known about him.

6.    Annas and Caiaphas were High Priests. This statement throws a revealing light upon the high priesthood of Jesus' day. It shows just how political and corrupt the high priesthood had become. There was never to be more than one priest at any given time, for the priesthood was supposed to be for life and was supposed to be hereditary. But with the coming of Roman rule, the High Priest became a political power base. Rome used the position to secure power over Jewish life. They offered and gave the position to men who were cooperative and willing to let the people follow Roman rule. For example, between B.C. 37-A.D. 26 twenty-eight different men were installed and removed as High Priests.

The point Luke is making is just this: the High Priest's office had become corrupted, and religious positions had become politically motivated. Annas, who had served as High Priest between A.D. 7-14, was still the power behind the throne. Caiaphas was officially the High Priest in Rome's eyes, but Annas was still the one to whom most Jewish leaders looked. This is actually seen during the trials of Jesus. Jesus was taken first to Annas, despite the fact that he was not the official High Priest (Jn.18:13).

> **"Who gave himself for our sins, that he might deliver us from this present evil world, according to the will of God and our Father" (Gal.1:4).**
> **"The time is fulfilled, and the kingdom of God is at hand: repent ye, and believe the gospel" (Mk.1:15).**

**2** (3:2) **Minister, Call of—God, Call of—Institutional Religion**: John was a man called out of the wilderness. Note three points.

1. God's call came to John in the wilderness, in an obscure place. The place where John was reared was so slightly populated that it was known as a wilderness. The area consisted of only six small towns or villages scattered far apart. God found him in the most obscure place.

> **Thought 1.** The place where a person is does not matter; a person's heart is what matters. If a person's heart is right toward God, God will call him no matter where he is. No one is hidden from God, no matter how obscure his residence is. The Word of God is not limited; it reaches even to the wilderness.

2. God's call was a very personal matter. Note: John never revealed how God spoke to him. Did God call him through a vision, through the appearance of an angel, through an audible voice, or through an inner sense? We do not know. John kept the matter in his heart; it was just too intimate, too meaningful an experience. And his heart was genuine and pure. He was not willing to lower his intimacy with God by talking about it and boasting in it, that is, by acting super-spiritual.

3. God's call was for John to serve God rather than to serve institutional religion. John was somewhere around thirty years of age, the age when he was to become a full-fledged priest by descent. Remember, his father Zacharias was a priest, and the priesthood was by descent. He was supposed to have been in training for some five years, and when he reached age thirty he was to begin serving in the temple. But God's call to John was to a different ministry, a ministry that fitted into God's plans much more than institutional religion.

> **Thought 1.** It is God who calls a man, not institutional religion. A man's first loyalty is to God, not to institutional religion.

> **Thought 2.** God moves outside *institutional religion* as well as within institutional religion (cp. Simeon, probably a priest, and Anna, a prophetess within the temple). Note two things.
> 1) *Institutional religionists* often frown and oppose those ministering *outside* the institution. They feel threatened, as though the *outside minister* is against them. Sometimes they are right; the outsider is sometimes against them. But if the outside minister is truly ministering, there should be support and encouragement. However, too often cooperation is not given. The institutional religionist too often fears the loss of authority, position, and security; therefore, he opposes the *outside minister*. Such motives are corrupt and need to be corrected. Ministers, both within and without institutional religion, need to be about God's call and business. They should not be wasting time by struggling against each other. Time is too short, and God's call comes to men both within and without institutional religion. Each needs to support the other in God's calling.
> 2) A man must do and serve God as God calls and wills.

> > **"Ye have not chosen me, but I have chosen you, and ordained you, that ye should go and bring forth fruit, and that your fruit should remain: that whatsoever ye shall ask of the Father in my name, he may give it you" (Jn.15:16).**
> > **"And all things are of God, who hath reconciled us to himself by Jesus Christ, and hath given to us the ministry of reconciliation....Now then we are ambassadors for Christ, as though God did beseech you by us: we pray you in Christ's stead, be ye reconciled to God" (2 Cor.5:18, 20).**
> > **"Whereof I was made a minister, according to the gift of the grace of God given unto me by the effectual working of his power" (Eph.3:7).**
> > **"And I thank Christ Jesus our Lord, who hath enabled me, for that he counted me faithful, putting me into the ministry" (1 Tim.1:12).**
> > **"Whereunto [the gospel] I am appointed a preacher, and an apostle, and a teacher of the Gentiles" (2 Tim.1:11).**

**3** (3:3) **Repentance—Forgiveness—Baptism**: John was a man who preached repentance and forgiveness of sins. Note the exact wording: he preached "the baptism of repentance for the remission of sins." This simply means that if a man wished to be forgiven his sins, he repented. He turned from his sins, and changed his life; then he was baptized. Baptism was the sign to his neighbors and the world that he was changing his life (repenting) because he wanted God to forgive his sins. The order is this:
⇒ A man wanted God to forgive his sins.

⇒ The man therefore made a decision to repent, to turn from his sinful ways, and to change his life (see note and Deeper Study # 1, *Repentance*—Acts 17:29-30).
⇒ The man was immediately baptized.

Now note. It was baptism that proclaimed to everyone that the man wanted forgiveness and was turning from his sins (repenting). Baptism was the act, the sign, that said to the world that the man was thereafter going to live a changed life so that God would forgive his sins.

Two simple facts are being stated.

1.	Forgiveness of sins is conditional. A man must repent to be forgiven, and if he truly repents, he is baptized. Baptism is part of the act of repentance!

2.	Baptism is the immediate witness and sign that a man is repenting and changing his life. If a man is truly sincere in seeking forgiveness, he is baptized and does change his life, turning away from sin and turning to God (see Deeper Study # 2—Mt.3:11; notes—Mk.1:3-5; Jn.1:24-26 for more detailed discussion on John's baptism).

"Then Peter said unto them, Repent, and be baptized every one of you in the name of Jesus Christ for the remission of sins, and ye shall receive the gift of the Holy Ghost" (Acts 2:38).

"I indeed baptize you with water unto repentance: but he that cometh after me is mightier than I, whose shoes I am not worthy to bear: he shall baptize you with the Holy Ghost, and with fire" (Mt.3:11).

"I tell you, Nay: but, except ye repent, ye shall all likewise perish" (Lk.13:3).

"Repent ye therefore, and be converted, that your sins may be blotted out, when the times of refreshing shall come from the presence of the Lord" (Acts 3:19).

"Cast away from you all your transgressions, whereby ye have transgressed; and make you a new heart and a new spirit: for why will ye die?" (Ezk.18:31).

"Therefore also now, saith the LORD, turn ye even to me with all your heart, and with fasting, and with weeping, and with mourning" (Joel 2:12).

**4** (3:4-6) **Prepare**: John was a man who cried out apocalyptically: "Prepare ye the way of the Lord, make His paths straight" (see Deeper Study # 3, *Roads*—Mk.1:3). John warned the people and he quoted Isaiah 40:3-5 as his authority. He took the points Isaiah had made and proclaimed them to the people.

1.	Prepare, for the humbled shall be exalted. Every valley (the humble believers of the earth) shall be filled, that is, received, enriched, raised up, and exalted.

2.	Prepare, for the proud shall be abased. Every mountain and hill shall be brought low. The mountains and hills would be the great and the less great, the self-sufficient and the self-confident, the prideful and the boastful, the conceited and the arrogant. They shall lose everything they have and be brought low. They shall be made as the dust of the earth if they do not repent.

3.	Prepare, for the crooked shall be straightened. The crooked thief and businessman, the crooked husband and wife, the crooked student and professor—all the crooked sinners of the earth who are bent out of shape—all who repent shall be made straight by the Messiah.

4.	Prepare, for the rough ways shall be made smooth. All the rough ways of the earth—the ways of hopelessness, helplessness, loneliness, emptiness, insecurity, guilt, shame, sin, death, false religion, and empty worship—all shall be made smooth. The way to life and peace shall be planed, made level, and easy to reach.

5.	God's salvation shall be seen by all flesh. Not only the Jews, but all people shall see the Messiah, God's salvation to the world. When the way is prepared, the Savior will appear.

John's preaching aroused thousands. It woke them and stirred them to prepare and to look for the Messiah. Apparently, it was the multitude who listened to John who eventually became the followers of Christ. It was also the same multitude who created the excitement needed to spread the news of the Messiah's coming.

"Prepare to meet thy God, O Israel" (Amos 4:12).

"Sow to yourselves in righteousness, reap in mercy; break up your fallow ground: for it is time to seek the LORD, till he come and rain righteousness upon you" (Hos.10:12).

"Therefore also now, saith the LORD, turn ye even to me with all your heart, and with fasting, and with weeping, and with mourning: and rend your heart, and not your garments, and turn unto the LORD your God: for he is gracious and merciful, slow to anger, and of great kindness" (Joel 2:12-13).

"But in a great house there are not only vessels of gold and of silver, but also of wood and of earth; and some to honour, and some to dishonour. If a man therefore purge himself from these, he shall be a vessel unto honour, sanctified, and meet for the master's use, and prepared unto every good work" (2 Tim.2:20-21).

"Therefore be ye also ready: for in such an hour as ye think not the Son of man cometh" (Mt.24:44).

"Watch ye therefore: for ye know not when the master of the house cometh, at even, or at midnight, or at the cockcrowing, or in the morning" (Mk.13:35).

| | B. The Plain Message of John the Baptist: A Message for All Ages, 3:7-20 (Mt.3:7-12; Mk.1:7-8) | 13 And he said unto them, Exact no more than that which is appointed you. | people |
|---|---|---|---|
| 1 He preached condemnation | 7 Then said he to the multitude that came forth to be baptized of him, O generation of vipers, who hath warned you to flee from the wrath to come? | 14 And the soldiers likewise demanded of him, saying, And what shall we do? And he said unto them, Do violence to no man, neither accuse any falsely; and be content with your wages. | c. The soldiers: Were to love and care enough to provide security & service to the nation |
| 2 He preached repentance | 8 Bring forth therefore fruits worthy of repentance, and begin not to say within yourselves, We have Abraham to our father: for I say unto you, That God is able of these stones to raise up children unto Abraham. | 15 And as the people were in expectation, and all men mused in their hearts of John, whether he were the Christ, or not; | 6 He preached the Messiah's coming |
| 3 He preached against pride | | 16 John answered, saying unto them all, I indeed baptize you with water; but one mightier than I cometh, the latchet of whose shoes I am not worthy to unloose: he shall baptize you with the Holy Ghost and with fire: | a. The Messiah's person |
| 4 He preached judgment | 9 And now also the axe is laid unto the root of the trees: every tree therefore which bringeth not forth good fruit is hewn down, and cast into the fire. | | b. The Messiah's baptism[DS1] |
| | | 17 Whose fan is in his hand, and he will throughly purge his floor, and will gather the wheat into his garner; but the chaff he will burn with fire unquenchable. | c. The Messiah's judgment[DS2] |
| 5 He preached social justice | 10 And the people asked him, saying, What shall we do then? | | |
| a. The people: Were to love & care enough to share their material possessions | 11 He answereth and saith unto them, He that hath two coats, let him impart to him that hath none; and he that hath meat, let him do likewise. | 18 And many other things in his exhortation preached he unto the people. | 7 He preached many other things |
| | | 19 But Herod the tetrarch, being reproved by him for Herodias his brother Philip's wife, and for all the evils which Herod had done, | 8 He preached against sin in high places |
| | | | a. He preached against the governor's sin |
| b. The tax collectors: Were to love and care enough to stop exerting their authority & cheating | 12 Then came also publicans to be baptized, and said unto him, Master, what shall we do? | 20 Added yet this above all, that he shut up John in prison. | b. The result: He was arrested |

# DIVISION II

## THE SON OF MAN'S APPEARANCE, 3:1-4:15

**B.     The Plain Message of John the Baptist: A Message for All Ages, 3:7-20**

(3:7-20) **Introduction**: the message of John the Baptist was powerful, a message for all ages.
1.     He preached condemnation (v.7).
2.     He preached repentance (v.8).
3.     He preached against pride (v.8).
4.     He preached judgment (v.9).
5.     He preached social justice (v.10-14).
6.     He preached the Messiah's coming (v.15-17).
7.     He preached many other things (v.18).
8.     He preached against sin in high places (v.19-20).

**1**    (3:7) **Condemnation—Preaching**: John preached condemnation. Note two things.
1.     He preached the truth about men, what they *were* and *had become*. They were "vipers," poisonous. They had allowed themselves to be poisoned and were now poisonous to others. They were sick and doomed, and they were biting others, making them sick and dooming them.
2.     He preached the wrath to come (cp. v.8, 17).

**"He that believeth on the Son hath everlasting life: and he that believeth not the Son shall not see life; but the wrath of God abideth on him" (Jn.3:36).**
**"For this ye know, that no whoremonger, nor unclean person, nor covetous man, who is an idolater, hath any inheritance in the kingdom of Christ and of God. Let no man deceive you with vain words: for because of these things cometh the wrath of God upon the children of disobedience" (Eph.5:5-6).**

"Kiss the Son, lest he be angry, and ye perish from the way, when his wrath is kindled but a little. Blessed are all they that put their trust in him" (Ps.2:12).

2 (3:8) **Repentance**: John preached repentance. Note that a man must first repent, then bear fruit. And the fruit must be worthy (deserving), consistent with repentance—fruit that shows a changed heart and a turning away from sin. (See notes—Lk.3:3; note and DEEPER STUDY # 1—Acts 17:29-30).

"I tell you, Nay: but, except ye repent, ye shall all likewise perish" (Lk.13:3).
"Cast away from you all your transgressions, whereby ye have transgressed; and make you a new heart and a new spirit: for why will ye die?" (Ezk.18:31).
"Walk worthy of the Lord unto all pleasing, being fruitful in every good work, and increasing in the knowledge of God" (Col.1:10).

3 (3:8) **Pride—Preaching—Self-righteousness**: John preached against pride (see note—Ro.12:16. Cp. 1 Cor.4:10; 5:6.) Many of the people believed they were acceptable to God simply because they were Jews, that is, because they were children of Abraham and of godly forefathers. Many felt acceptable to God because they had undergone a religious ritual, that of circumcision. They felt the righteousness of their fathers had saved them. How they lived mattered little. They were saved because they were *special*—special enough to be acceptable to God (see DEEPER STUDY # 1—Ro.4:1-25).

**Thought 1.** Most people are prideful. They feel they are special enough to be acceptable to God, that God would never reject them. They feel acceptable because they...
- have godly parents
- have been baptized
- are not too bad
- are good enough
- are blessed with so much
- are somewhat religious
- are members of a church
- are regular worshippers

"And he spake this parable unto certain which trusted in themselves that they were righteous, and despised others" (Lk.18:9).
"The way of a fool is right in his own eyes: but he that hearkeneth unto counsel is wise" (Pr.12:15).
"All the ways of a man are clean in his own eyes; but the LORD weigheth the spirits" (Pr.16:2; cp. Pr.21:2).
"Most men will proclaim every one his own goodness: but a faithful man who can find?" (Pr.20:6).
"There is a generation that are pure in their own eyes, and yet is not washed from their filthiness" (Pr.30:12).
"Yet thou sayest, Because I am innocent, surely his anger shall turn from me. Behold, I will plead with thee, because thou sayest, I have not sinned" (Jer.2:35).

4 (3:9) **Judgment—Preaching**: John preached judgment. Note several things.
1. God is the Divine Woodman who cuts down the trees.
2. The axe is already lying at the roots of the trees.
3. The trees are *not yet* cut down, but all men are warned.
4. There are many trees: some lofty (the proud), some stately (leaders), some diseased, some bearing good fruit, some bearing bad fruit, and some bearing no fruit at all.
5. All trees that do not bear good fruit will be cut down and cast into the fire (see DEEPER STUDY # 4—Lk.16:24; DEEPER STUDY # 2—Mt.5:22).

"But that which beareth thorns and briers is rejected, and is nigh unto cursing: whose end is to be burned" (Heb.6:8).
"But now the righteousness of God without the law is manifested, being witnessed by the law and the prophets; even the righteousness of God which is by faith of Jesus Christ unto all and upon all them that believe: for there is no difference: for all have sinned, and come short of the glory of God" (Ro.3:21-23).
"For the time is come that judgment must begin at the house of God: and if it first begin at us, what shall the end be of them that obey not the gospel of God? And if the righteous scarcely be saved, where shall the ungodly and the sinner appear?" (1 Pt.4:17-18).
"But the fearful, and unbelieving, and the abominable, and murderers, and whoremongers, and sorcerers, and idolaters, and all liars, shall have their part in the lake which burneth with fire and brimstone: which is the second death" (Rev.21:8).

5 (3:10-14) **Justice—Preaching—Fruit—Repentance—Life, Changed**: John preached social justice. John stirred people. The people wanted to know how repentance would affect their lives, just what a changed life would mean. What kind of fruit should they bear? John answered in the most practical terms.
1. The average citizen was to love and care enough to share his material goods with those who were in need. John mentioned clothing and food, the basic necessities of life. But note: the giving was to be sacrificial. The *giver* was to give all but one coat and half a meal. The giver was to love and care so much that he would be gripped with mercy and unself-

ishness. He would give what he had. Such fruit would be evidence of repentance, of a life truly changed, of a man who was truly seeking God to forgive his sins (see note—Lk.3:3).

2.    The despised tax collectors were to love and care enough to stop exerting their authority and cheating people. Tax collectors in Jesus' day were literally despised because they represented the Roman government and levied more taxes than necessary, pocketing the excess. A tax collector who wanted God to forgive his sins had to change his life, becoming a man of justice and equitableness. He had to love and care for others enough to treat them fairly and respectfully and justly.

3.    The soldiers were to be respectful and loving, truthful and honest, contented and responsible. Note the three specific charges to soldiers.

      a.    They were to do violence to no man. The word "violence" (diaseisete) means to shake violently, agitate, terrify. The thought is that some extorted money by terrifying people. Roman soldiers were, of course, posted to protect the interests of Rome. It was common for soldiers to allow illegal things to go on for a bribe.

      b.    They were to charge no man falsely. If a man did not pay a bribe, he was often falsely accused by the soldier.

      c.    They were to be content with their wages. Dissatisfaction and grumbling over their wages was a common complaint of soldiers.

A soldier was to change his life completely: to respect and love people, be truthful and honest, contented and responsible.

Note that John's message demanded a changed life. What then were the fruits that demonstrated one was truly repenting and seeking forgiveness of sins? Very practically, *"the fruits of righteousness"* (cp. v.8).

> **"And this I pray, that your love may abound yet more and more in knowledge and in all judgment; that ye may approve things that are excellent; that ye may be sincere and without offence till the day of Christ; being filled with the *fruits of righteousness*, which are by Jesus Christ, unto the glory and praise of God" (Ph.1:9-11).**
> **"But the fruit of the Spirit is love, joy, peace, longsuffering, gentleness, goodness, faith, meekness, temperance: against such there is no law" (Gal.5:22-23).**
> **"For the fruit of the Spirit is in all goodness and righteousness and truth" (Eph.5:9).**
> **"But the wisdom that is from above is first pure, then peaceable, gentle, and easy to be intreated, full of mercy and good fruits, without partiality, and without hypocrisy" (Jas.3:17).**

**[6]**  (3:15-17) **Jesus Christ, Messiah—Preaching**: John preached the Messiah's coming. He stressed three points in particular.

1.    The Messiah's person. The Messiah was more "worthy" and "mightier" than he.

      a.    More worthy: John was not worth the rank of a slave before Christ. Slaves were the ones who loosed the sandals and washed the feet of guests. He was as *nothing* before the Lord. What an attitude of humility!

      b.    Mightier: Jesus was mightier in both person (as above) and work (baptism and judgment, v.16-17).

2.    The Messiah's baptism (see Deeper Study # 1—Lk.3:16 for discussion).

3.    The Messiah's judgment. Note these points.

      a.    The "fan" or winnowing fork (pluon) is the Messiah's power to pick up both the wheat and the chaff.

      b.    The "floor" is the earth which will be purged or cleansed of all chaff.

      c.    The "wheat" represents believers who truly repent and bring forth fruit. They will be gathered into His barn (His kingdom or the new heavens and earth).

      d.    The "chaff" represents those who only profess, who are counterfeit wheat. They lie on the floor (the earth) with the wheat, but they are not wheat. They shall be "burned with unquenchable fire." (See note—Lk.3:17 for discussion.)

---

**DEEPER STUDY # 1**

(3:16) **Baptism**: the word "baptism" (baptizein) means to dip, to immerse, to submerge, to place into. John's baptism was with water, but Jesus' baptism was "in [en] the Spirit and fire."

1.    John's baptism was both a preparation and a symbol of the spiritual baptism that Jesus was to bring. John's water baptism meant two things.

First, it symbolized cleansing from all sin. A person was being prepared for the cleansing that Christ would provide.

Second, it symbolized separation or dedication. A person was setting his life apart to God in a renewed spirit of dedication. He was committing himself to the Christ about whom John was preaching.

2.    Jesus' spiritual baptism is a double baptism. Only one preposition is used for "the Spirit and fire," the preposition "in."

First, Jesus baptizes the person *in the Spirit*. He dips, immerses, and places the person in the Spirit. A person may be carnal and materialistic, but once he has been baptized into the Spirit by Christ, he becomes spiritually minded (Ro.8:5-7). The Jews had longed and looked for the day when the Spirit would come. The prophets had predicted His coming time and again; therefore, the people knew exactly what John was predicting (cp. Ezk.36:26-27; 37:14; 39:29; Is.44:3; Joel 2:28). Note: John's baptism was called "the baptism of repentance"; that is, the person who repented was baptized. There could be no question; it was understood. If one repented and actually turned to the Lord, he was baptized.

Second, Jesus baptized the person *in fire*. Fire has several functions that graphically symbolize the work of Christ. It illuminates, warms, melts, burns, and utterly destroys. The difference between baptism with water and fire is the difference between an outward work and an inward work. Water only cleanses the outside; fire purifies within, that is, the heart. Jesus Christ separates a person from his former life and purifies him within by the fire of His Holy Spirit. It should be noted that in John's mind the "baptism of fire" meant that the Messiah was to destroy the enemies of Israel. It was "the messianic fire of judgment" that was to come from the throne of David (see Deeper Study # 2—Mt.1:18; notes—11:1-6; 11:2-3; Deeper Study # 1—11:5; Deeper Study # 2—11:6; note—Lk.7:21-23).

---

**DEEPER STUDY # 2**

(3:17) **Unquenchable Fire** (puri asbesto): this literally reads "with fire unquenchable." It is fire that cannot be quenched, snuffed out, extinguished. The idea is that the fire is everlasting, burning on and on and never ending (see Deeper Study # 3—Mt.25:41).

---

**7** (3:18) **Preaching**: John preached many other things. Note the word "exhortation" (parakalon). It means to admonish, urge, beseech, entreat. John pierced the ears and the hearts of the people; he pressed and pressed upon the people their need to prepare for the coming of the Lord.

> "But in a great house there are not only vessels of gold and of silver, but also of wood and of earth; and some to honour, and some to dishonour. If a man therefore purge himself from these, he shall be a vessel unto honour, sanctified, and meet for the master's use, and prepared unto every good work" (2 Tim.2:20-21).
> "Therefore also now, saith the LORD, turn ye even to me with all your heart, and with fasting, and with weeping, and with mourning: and rend your heart, and not your garments, and turn unto the LORD your God: for he is gracious and merciful, slow to anger, and of great kindness" (Joel 2:12-13).

**8** (3:19-20) **Preaching—Sin, Preaching Against**: John preached against sin in high places. He rebuked the ruler Herod for his evil life and carnal excess, for his terrible sin of adultery. (See Deeper Study # 1—Mt.14:1-14.)

> "Thus saith God, Why transgress ye the commandments of the LORD, that ye cannot prosper? because ye have forsaken the LORD, he hath also forsaken you" (2 Chron.24:20).
> "Now the works of the flesh are manifest, which are these; Adultery, fornication, uncleanness, lasciviousness, idolatry, witchcraft, hatred, variance, emulations, wrath, strife, seditions, heresies, envyings, murders, drunkenness, revellings, and such like: of the which I tell you before, as I have also told you in time past, that they which do such things shall not inherit the kingdom of God" (Gal.5:19-21).
> "Behold, the Lord cometh with ten thousands of his saints, to execute judgment upon all, and to convince all that are ungodly among them of all their ungodly deeds which they have ungodly committed, and of all their hard speeches which ungodly sinners have spoken against him" (Jude 14-15).

| | C. The Baptism of Jesus: Obedience and God's Approval, 3:21-22 (Mt.3:13-17; Mk.1:9-11; Jn.1:29-34) |
|---|---|
| **1 Jesus' obedience**<br>  a. Obedient along with the people<br>  b. Obedient in prayer | 21 Now when all the people were baptized, it came to pass, that Jesus also being baptized, and praying, the heaven was opened, |
| **2 God's signs of approval**<br>  a. The heavens were opened<br>  b. The Spirit descended<br>  c. The voice of God spoke | 22 And the Holy Ghost descended in a bodily shape like a dove upon him, and a voice came from heaven, which said, Thou art my beloved Son; in thee I am well pleased. |

# DIVISION II

## THE SON OF MAN'S APPEARANCE, 3:1-4:15

**C.    The Baptism of Jesus: Obedience and God's Approval, 3:21-22**

(3:21-22) **Introduction—Baptism**: baptism is both obeying God and securing God's approval. This is why Jesus was baptized, and it is why we are to be baptized.
1.    Jesus' obedience (v.21).
2.    God's signs of approval (v.22).

[1]    (3:21) **Baptism—Obedience—Prayer**: baptism is an act of obedience to God. Jesus was obeying God in being baptized. This is seen in two acts.
1.    Jesus obeyed God by being baptized with the people. Note the words, "When all the people were baptized." Some scholars say Jesus was baptized *after* all the people were baptized; others *while* they were being baptized. It does not matter which is factual. The point is this: Jesus was right in the midst of the people, *obeying* God with them. He was doing exactly what God wanted, identifying with the people.
One thing sets these people apart from the rest of the public. They heard John's message and responded, doing exactly what God wanted. They were obeying God's call, doing what was right, obeying righteousness. Now again, note that Jesus was baptized "when all the people were baptized," right along with them. He was doing at least two things. (see outline and notes—Mt.3:13; 3:15; Mk.1:9-11 for more discussion).
   a.    He was demonstrating that He, the Son of God, was *fulfilling all righteousness* (see note—Mt.5:17-18). He, too, was being obedient to God, *fulfilling every law* of God for man.
   b.    He was demonstrating His humiliation, that He was Man, fully Man. As Man He was required to live obediently to God just as other men were. There was one difference, however; Jesus lived a sinless life, and by such He became the Perfect and Ideal Man, the Pattern for all men (see DEEPER STUDY # 3—Mt.8:20).

**Thought 1.** Every man should respond to the gospel of God; that is, he should seek God to forgive his sins, repent, and be baptized. This is God's will for every man. Every man should obey God and fulfill all righteousness. Baptism is an act of obedience; it is obeying God right along with other believers.

> "Then cometh Jesus from Galilee to Jordan unto John, to be baptized of him. But John forbad him, saying, I have need to be baptized of thee, and comest thou to me? And Jesus answering said unto him, Suffer it to be so now: for thus it becometh us to fulfil all righteousness. Then he suffered him" (Mt.3:13-15).
> "He that believeth and is baptized shall be saved; but he that believeth not shall be damned" (Mk.16:16).
> "Jesus answered, Verily, verily, I say unto thee, Except a man be born of water and of the Spirit, he cannot enter into the kingdom of God" (Jn.3:5).

**Thought 2.** No man is above any other man, not in the eyes of God. God's own Son had to obey Him; He had to be baptized as a *sign of obedience* to God. We, too, have to be baptized if we are truly repenting and seeking God to forgive our sins. We are not above God's will and His instructions to "repent and be baptized" (Acts 2:38).

> "Then Peter said unto them, Repent, and be baptized every one of you in the name of Jesus Christ for the remission of sins, and ye shall receive the gift of the Holy Ghost" (Acts 2:38).
> "Go ye therefore, and teach all nations, baptizing them in the name of the Father, and of the Son, and of the Holy Ghost" (Mt.28:19).

**"And now why tarriest thou? arise, and be baptized, and wash away thy sins, calling on the name of the Lord"** (Acts 22:16).

2.  Jesus obeyed God in prayer. While Jesus was being baptized, He was praying. His mind and thoughts were upon God. He was in fellowship and communion with God. This is as it should be. Why would a person's mind be elsewhere while he is being baptized if he is sincere?
    ⇒ Baptism is an *outward* sign of God's working *within* the heart of a person. The *inward working* and *inward grace of God is sought by prayer*. Thus, *true* baptism is the first act whereby a man shows that he is in communion with God.
    ⇒ Baptism, the most significant act of discipleship, will be followed by a changed life. A changed life demonstrates that a person is repenting and seeking God to forgive his sins. Therefore, while a person is being baptized, he is in a spirit of prayer seeking God's grace and favor as he walks out into an alien and wicked world.
    ⇒ Baptism launches the new life of the believer. Baptism is to be the first act of the repenting believer, the first confession to the public that a person is going to change his life and live for God. (See DEEPER STUDY # 1, *Baptism*—Acts 2:38 for more discussion.) *Baptism is the first public confession of a person's inward prayer of confession to God.* Thus baptism, the outward public confession to man, should follow right upon the heels of the inward private confession to God. The spirit of prayer that started it all should be the same spirit of prayer that finishes it all. The prayer that confessed to God privately should continue right on through to the prayer that confesses to the public at large. In fact, from the very moment of the inward prayer of a person's confession to God, the heart should continue in a spirit of prayer right on through life. The believer's very spirit should be a spirit of continued prayer. Such was Jesus' obedience in prayer. Such is to be our obedience in prayer. An unbroken communion with God in prayer is the ache of God for us.

> **"Men ought always to pray, and not to faint"** (Lk.18:1).
> **"Continuing instant in prayer"** (Ro.12:12).
> **"Praying always with all prayer and supplication in the Spirit, and watching thereunto with all perseverance and supplication for all saints"** (Eph.6:18).
> **"Be careful for nothing; but in every thing by prayer and supplication with thanksgiving let your requests be made known unto God"** (Ph.4:6).
> **"We give thanks to God and the Father of our Lord Jesus Christ, praying always for you"** (Col.1:3).
> **"Continue in prayer, and watch in the same with thanksgiving"** (Col.4:2).
> **"Night and day praying exceedingly"** (1 Th.3:10).
> **"Pray without ceasing"** (1 Th.5:17).
> **"The effectual fervent prayer of a righteous man availeth much"** (Jas.5:16).
> **"But the end of all things is at hand: be ye therefore sober, and watch unto prayer"** (1 Pt.4:7).

**2** (3:22) **Baptism**: baptism secures God's approval. When a person is baptized, God is very pleased, for the person is *obeying* and *following* in the steps of Jesus. Jesus' baptism pleased God. God showed His approval in three ways.
1.  The heavens were opened (v.21). This was probably for two purposes.
    a.  To give Jesus a very special sight and sense of God's glory and presence. The Lord's baptism was the launch of His ministry to men. He needed a very special glimpse and sense of God's glory and presence. He needed the stamp of God's approval and power (cp. Acts 7:56; Ezk.1:1).
    b.  To reveal to John and perhaps to the others standing there (if the opening of heaven were visible to all) that Jesus was truly the Lamb of God who takes away the sin of the world (Jn.1:29).
2.  The Holy Spirit descended upon Jesus in "a bodily shape like a dove." The dove was a sacred bird to the Jews. It was a symbol of peace and gentleness, of purity and innocence, but even more significant it was often identified with the Spirit of God. When the dove descended upon Jesus, it symbolized the Spirit of God Himself descending upon Jesus. He was descending upon Jesus to identify Jesus as the Messiah and to endue Jesus with the power of God (see outline and notes—Mk.1:9-10). John went out of his way to stress that the Spirit's descent upon Jesus was unique: He abode (Jn.1:32) and He remained upon Jesus (Jn.1:33). The Holy Spirit entered the life of Jesus once for all, permanently and powerfully, in His full manifestation and unlimited power.
3.  The voice of God was heard (see note—Mt.3:16-17).

**Thought 1.** When we genuinely obey God and are baptized, God is pleased. We also secure His approval in the same three ways.
1)  God opens heaven up to us and gives us a very special sense of His presence, a sense of His approval, a sense that we are pleasing Him immensely.

> **"Blessed be the God and Father of our Lord Jesus Christ, who hath blessed us with all spiritual blessings in heavenly places in Christ"** (Eph.1:3).
> **"But God, who is rich in mercy, for his great love wherewith he loved us, even when we were dead in sins, hath quickened us together with Christ, (by grace ye are saved;) and hath raised us up together, and made us sit together in heavenly places in Christ Jesus"** (Eph.2:4-6).

2) God manifests and reveals His Spirit to us in a very special sense. We are obeying Him, and significant moments of obedience bring special manifestations of the Spirit (see note—Jn.14:21).

> **"He that hath my commandments, and keepeth them, he it is that loveth me: and he that loveth me shall be loved of my Father, and I will love him, and will manifest myself to him" (Jn.14:21).**
>
> **"But as it is written, Eye hath not seen, nor ear heard, neither have entered into the heart of man, the things which God hath prepared for them that love him. But God hath revealed them unto us by his Spirit: for the Spirit searcheth all things, yea, the deep things of God" (1 Cor.2:9-10).**
>
> **"In whom we have redemption through his blood, the forgiveness of sins, according to the riches of his grace; wherein he hath abounded toward us in all wisdom and prudence; having made known unto us the mystery of his will, according to his good pleasure which he hath purposed in himself: that in the dispensation of the fulness of times he might gather together in one all things in Christ, both which are in heaven, and which are on earth; even in him" (Eph.1:7-10).**
>
> **"The mystery which hath been hid from ages and from generations, but now is made manifest to his saints: to whom God would make known what is the riches of the glory of this mystery among the Gentiles; which is** *Christ in you, the hope of glory***" (Col.1:26-27).**

3) God's Word is heard. The fact that we are baptized is a sign that we have heard His command to be baptized, and because we are obeying Him, He continues to speak to us day by day as we seek His will in the Bible and prayer.

> **"Behold, I stand at the door, and knock: if any man hear my voice, and open the door, I will come in to him, and will sup with him, and he with me" (Rev.3:20).**
>
> **"That which we have seen and heard declare we unto you, that ye also may have fellowship with us: and truly our fellowship is with the Father, and with his Son Jesus Christ" (1 Jn.1:3).**

| | | | |
|---|---|---|---|
| | **D. The Genealogy of Jesus: The Roots of the Messiah,**[DS1] **3:23-38** (Mt.1:1-17) | of Joseph, which was the son of Jonan, which was the son of Eliakim, | |
| **1 Jesus was about thirty years of age** | 23 And Jesus himself began to be about thirty years of age, being (as was supposed) the son of Joseph, which was the son of Heli, | 31 Which was the son of Melea, which was the son of Menan, which was the son of Mattatha, which was the son of Nathan, which was the son of David, | |
| **2 Davidic heir: To be the Messianic King (v.24-31)** | 24 Which was the son of Matthat, which was the son of Levi, which was the son of Melchi, which was the son of Janna, which was the son of Joseph, | 32 Which was the son of Jesse, which was the son of Obed, which was the son of Booz, which was the son of Salmon, which was the son of Naasson, | **3 Adamic heir: To be Messianic High Priest (v.32-38)** |
| | 25 Which was the son of Mattathias, which was the son of Amos, which was the son of Naum, which was the son of Esli, which was the son of Nagge, | 33 Which was the son of Aminidab, which was the son of Aram, which was the son of Esrom, which was the son of Phares, which was the son of Juda, | |
| | 26 Which was the son of Maath, which was the son of Mattathias, which was the son of Semei, which was the son of Joseph, which was the son of Juda, | 34 Which was the son of Jacob, which was the son of Isaac, which was the son of Abraham, which was the son of Thara, which was the son of Nachor, | |
| | 27 Which was the son of Joanna, which was the son of Rhesa, which was the son of Zorobabel, which was the son of Salathiel, which was the son of Neri, | 35 Which was the son of Saruch, which was the son of Ragau, which was the son of Phalec, which was the son of Heber, which was the son of Sala, | |
| | 28 Which was the son of Melchi, which was the son of Addi. which was the son of Cosam, which was the son of Elmodam, which was the son of Er, | 36 Which was the son of Cainan, which was the son of Arphaxad, which was the son of Sem, which was the son of Noe, which was the son of Lamech, | |
| | 29 Which was the son of Jose, which was the son of Eliezer, which was the son of Jorim, which was the son of Matthat, which was the son of Levi, | 37 Which was the son of Mathusala, which was the son of Enoch, which was the son of Jared, which was the son of Maleleel, which was the son of Cainan, | |
| | 30 Which was the son of Simeon, which was the son of Juda, which was the son | 38 Which was the son of Enos, which was the son of Seth, which was the son of Adam, which was the son of God. | **4 Godly heir: To be Messianic Prophet of God** |

# DIVISION II

## THE SON OF MAN'S APPEARANCE, 3:1-4:15

### D.      The Genealogy of Jesus: The Roots of the Messiah, 3:23-38

(3:23-38) **Introduction**: Jesus was now ready to begin His ministry. But did He have the *right*? What proof was there that He was the Messiah, the Son of God? In this passage Luke makes a phenomenal point. He says that even the roots of Jesus, His genealogy, prove He is the Messiah. His roots give Him the right to claim Messiahship, to claim that He is the Savior, the Son of God.

1. Jesus was about thirty years of age (v.23).
2. He was Davidic heir: He was to be the Messianic King (v.24-31).
3. He was Adamic heir: He was to be the Messianic High Priest (v.32-38).
4. He was Godly heir: He was to be the Messianic Prophet of God (v.38).

---

**DEEPER STUDY # 1**

(3:23-38) **Jesus, Genealogy**: there are two significant facts here. First, Luke follows Mary's line (genealogy), the line of Jesus' mother. Second, he traces Mary's line all the way back to Adam. What he does is show that God's Son actually became a man. Jesus was the promised Messiah. Luke is writing to Gentiles who placed great emphasis on a transcendental God, a God way out in space someplace who was thought to be far removed from the day-to-day affairs of men. Luke had to show that Jesus was man, fully human. He was a man born of a woman, full of emotions and feelings and personal day-to-day experiences just like all other men.

Matthew's genealogy is different (Mt.1:1). Matthew was writing primarily to Jews who placed great emphasis on pure lineage. An impure lineage deprived a Jew of his nationality, of his right to be called a Jew; and tragically, this meant that he lost his right to be called a child of God. To combat this problem, Matthew traces Jospeh's line all the way back through King David and Abraham, the founding father of Israel. He does this to show that Jesus had the legal right to the throne of David and to the promises made to Abraham. This is not to say that Jesus was the actual physical son of Joseph, but rather as the Son of God, Jesus was sent into the family of Joseph. By such He became the legal heir of Joseph (see Deeper Study # 3—Mt.1:16; Deeper Study # 2—Jn.8:23). This meant two things. First, Jesus was legally of the pure line of the Jewish nation. He fulfilled the Old Testament prophecies that said the Messiah would be born of the Jewish nation. Second, as a Jew and as the Son of God, Jesus had the legal right to claim Messiahship. He had the legal right to the throne of David and to the promises made to Abraham (see Deeper Study # 1—Jn.4:22; Deeper Study # 1—Ro.4:1-25. Cp. Gen.12:1-3.)

---

**1** (3:23) **Jesus Christ, Age of**: Jesus was about thirty years of age when He launched His ministry. Why did He wait until He was thirty before beginning His ministry?
1. Thirty was the age when the Levites began their work (Num.4:47).
2. Thirty was also the age when a Scribe was allowed to begin his teaching ministry.
3. Thirty was the age whan a man was thought to reach full development and maturity.

Now, note a crucial point. Jesus needed to live thirty years as other men lived, learning and maturing in the day-to-day routine of life and responsibility (cp. Heb.5:8). Why?
1. Jesus needed to prove faithful, to secure righteousness right down where men live, right in the day-to-day duties...
   - of work (He was a carpenter by trade).
   - of family (He became the head of the house when Joseph died).
   - of physical growth (He grew and matured as all men do, day by day).
   - of mental growth (He studied and learned as all men do).
   - of spiritual growth (He sought God as all men should).

> **"Though he were a Son, yet learned he obedience by the things which he suffered" (Heb.5:8).**

2. Jesus needed to show (demonstrate, paint the picture of) how men should live in the routine of day-to-day living.
3. Jesus needed to learn from the day-to-day experiences of life (as Man)—learn so that He could teach men from experience exactly how they should live.
4. Jesus needed to learn from day-to-day experiences so He could better help and succor men throughout their lives. By ploughing through the experiences of life, He could better help men plough through their day-to-day experiences (see note—Lk.2:40 for detailed discussion).

---

**2** (3:24-31) **Jesus Christ, Davidic Heir—King**: Jesus was the Davidic heir—He was qualified to be the Messianic King. God had given to David and His seed (the Messiah) the promise of eternal government (2 Sam.7:12; Ps.39:3f; 132:11).

The Jews believed these promises of God. Therefore Jesus, "who is called Christ" (Mt.1:16), was the promised Son of Abraham, the promised Son of David (Mt.1:1).

Note how often Jesus was called the son of David. (Cp. Mt.12:23; 15:22; 20:30-31; 21:9, 15; Acts 2:29-36; Ro.1:3; 2 Tim.2:8; Rev.22:16.) It was the common title and popular concept of the Messiah. Generation after generation of Jews looked for the promised deliverer of Israel. The people expected Him to be a great general who would deliver and restore the nation to its greatness. In fact, they expected Him to make the nation the center of universal rule. He would, under God, conquer the world and center the glory and majesty of God Himself in Jerusalem. And from His throne, the throne of David, He would execute "the Messianic fire of judgment" upon the nations and peoples of the world (see Deeper Study # 2—Mt.1:18; Deeper Study # 3—3:11; notes—11:1-6; 11:2-3; Deeper Study # 1—11:5; Deeper Study # 2—11:6; Lk.7:21-23. Referring to these notes will show what the Jewish concept of the Messiah was.) If Luke can prove that Jesus' roots (genealogy) go all the way back to David and Adam, then he will have shown how seriously one must take the claims of Jesus to be the Messiah (see Deeper Study # 2—Mt.1:18).
1. The Messianic King was prophesied.

> **"He shall build a house for my name, and I will stablish the throne of his kingdom for ever" (2 Sam.7:13).**
> **"Thou hast delivered me from the strivings of the people; and thou hast made me the head of the heathen: a people whom I have not known shall serve me" (Ps.18:43).**
> **"He shall have dominion also from sea to sea, and from the river unto the ends of the earth....Yea, all kings shall fall down before him: all nations shall serve Him" (Ps.72:8, 11).**
> **"I have made a covenant with my chosen, I have sworn unto David my servant, Thy seed will I establish for ever, and build up thy throne to all generations" (Ps.89:3-4).**
> **"Thou spakest in vision to thy holy one, and saidst, I have laid help upon one that is mighty; I have exalted one chosen out of the people. I have found David my servant; with my holy oil have I**

anointed him: with whom my hand shall be established: mine arm also shall strengthen him....And I will beat down his foes before his face, and plague them that hate him" (Ps.89:19-21, 23).

"I will make him my firstborn, higher than the kings of the earth....His seed also will I make to endure for ever, and his throne as the days of heaven....His seed shall endure for ever, and his throne as the sun before me. It shall be established for ever as the moon, and as a faithful witness in heaven" (Ps.89:27, 29, 36-37).

"The LORD said unto my Lord, Sit thou at my right hand, until I make thine enemies thy footstool. The LORD shall send the rod of thy strength out of Zion: rule thou in the midst of thine enemies" (Ps.110:1-2).

"The LORD hath sworn in truth unto David; he will not turn from it; of the fruit of thy body will I set upon thy throne....There will make the horn of David to bud: I have ordained a lamp for mine anointed. His enemies will I clothe with shame: but upon himself shall his crown flourish" (Ps.132:11, 17-18).

"And he shall judge among the nations, and shall rebuke many people: and they shall beat their swords into plowshares, and their spears into pruninghooks: nation shall not lift up sword against nation, neither shall they learn war any more" (Is.2:4).

"I saw also the Lord sitting upon a throne, high and lifted up, and his train filled the temple" (Is.6:1).

"The government shall be upon his shoulder: and his name shall be called Wonderful, Counsellor, The mighty God, The everlasting Father, The Prince of Peace. Of the increase of his government and peace there shall be no end, upon the throne of David, and upon his kingdom, to order it, and to establish it with judgment and with justice from henceforth even for ever" (Is.9:6-7).

"And there shall come forth a rod out of the stem of Jesse, and a Branch shall grow out of his roots" (Is.11:1).

"In that day there shall be a root of Jesse, which shall stand for an ensign of the people; to it shall the Gentiles seek" (Is.11:10).

"Behold, a king shall reign in righteousness" (Is.32:1).

"Thine eyes shall see the king in his beauty" (Is.33:17).

"Behold, the Lord GOD will come with strong hand, and his arm shall rule for him: behold, his reward is with him, and his work before him" (Is.40:10).

"How beautiful upon the mountains are the feet of him that bringeth good tidings, that publisheth peace; that bringeth good tidings of good, that publisheth salvation; that saith unto Zion, Thy God reigneth!" (Is.52:7).

"Behold, my servant shall deal prudently, he shall be exalted and extolled, and be very high" (Is.52:13).

"Behold, the days come, saith the LORD, that I will raise unto David a righteous Branch, and a King shall reign and prosper, and shall execute judgment and justice in the earth. In his days Judah shall be saved, and Israel shall dwell safely: and this is his name whereby he shall be called, THE LORD OUR RIGHTEOUSNESS" (Jer.23:5-6).

"They shall serve the LORD their God, and David their king, whom I will raise up unto them" (Jer.30:9).

"For thus saith the LORD; David shall never want a man to sit upon the throne of the house of Israel" (Jer.33:17).

"Thus saith the Lord GOD; Remove the diadem, and take off the crown: this shall not be the same: exalt him that is low, and abase him that is high. I will overturn, overturn, overturn, it: and it shall be no more, until he come whose right it is; and I will give it him" (Ezk.21:26-27).

"And David my servant shall be king over them; and they all shall have one shepherd: they shall also walk in my judgments, and observe my statutes, and do them. And they shall dwell in the land that I have given unto Jacob my servant, wherein your fathers have dwelt; and they shall dwell therein, even they, and their children, and their children's children for ever: and my servant David shall be their prince for ever" (Ezk.37:24-25).

"The stone that smote the image became a great mountain, and filled the whole earth" (Dan.2:35).

"And in the days of these kings shall the God of heaven set up a kingdom, which shall never be destroyed: and the kingdom shall not be left to other people, but it shall break in pieces and consume all these kingdoms, and it shall stand for ever" (Dan.2:44).

"Behold, one like the Son of man came with the clouds of heaven, and came to the Ancient of days, and they brought him near before him. And there was given him dominion, and glory, and a kingdom, that all people, nations, and languages, should serve him: his dominion is an everlasting dominion, which shall not pass away, and his kingdom that which shall not be destroyed" (Dan.7:13-14).

"From the going forth of the commandment to restore and to build Jerusalem unto the Messiah the Prince shall be seven weeks, and threescore and two weeks" (Dan.9:25).

"Afterward shall the children of Israel return, and seek the LORD their God, and David their king; and shall fear the LORD and his goodness in the latter days" (Hos.3:5).

"The LORD also shall roar out of Zion, and utter his voice from Jerusalem; and the heavens and the earth shall shake: but the LORD will be the hope of his people, and the strength of the children of Israel. So shall ye know that I am the LORD your God dwelling in Zion, my holy mountain: then shall Jerusalem be holy, and there shall no strangers pass through her any more" (Joel 3:16-17).

"Out of thee shall he come forth unto me that is to be ruler in Israel; whose goings forth have been from of old, from everlasting....And he shall stand and feed in the strength of the LORD, in the majesty of the name of the LORD his God; and they shall abide: for now shall he be great unto the ends of the earth" (Mic.5:2, 4).

"In that day will I raise up the tabernacle of David that is fallen, and close up the breaches thereof; and I will raise up his ruins, and I will build it as in the days of old" (Amos 9:11).

"And he shall judge among many people, and rebuke strong nations afar off; and they shall beat their swords into plowshares, and their spears into pruninghooks: nations shall not lift up a sword against nation, neither shall they learn war any more" (Mic.4:3).

"The LORD hath taken away thy judgments, he hath cast out thine enemy: the king of Israel, even the LORD, is in the midst of thee: thou shalt not see evil any more" (Zeph.3:15).

"And speak unto him, saying, Thus speaketh the LORD of hosts, saying, Behold the man whose name is The BRANCH; and he shall grow up out of his place, and he shall build the temple of the LORD: even he shall build the temple of the LORD; and he shall bear the glory, and shall sit and rule upon his throne: and the counsel of peace shall be between them both" (Zech.6:12-13).

"Rejoice greatly, O daughter of Zion; shout, O daughter of Jerusalem: behold, thy King cometh unto thee: he is just and having salvation....And he shall speak peace unto the heathen: and his dominion shall be from sea even to sea, and from the river even to the ends of the earth" (Zech.9:9-10).

(Also see some Topical Bible or Reference Work: God and Jesus Christ, Kingdom of.)
2.    Jesus Christ was the Messianic King.

"Where is he that is born King of the Jews? for we have seen his star in the east, and are come to worship him....And thou Bethlehem, in the land of Juda, art not the least among the princes of Juda: for out of thee shall come a Governor, that shall rule my people Israel" (Mt.2:2, 6).

"The Son of man shall send forth his angels, and they shall gather out of his kingdom all things that offend, and them which do iniquity" (Mt.13:41).

"When the Son of man shall come in his glory, and all the holy angels with him, then shall he sit upon the throne of his glory" (Mt.25:31).

"And Jesus stood before the governor: and the governor asked him, saying, Art thou the King of the Jews? And Jesus said unto him, Thou sayest" (Mt.27:11).

"And Jesus came and spake unto them, saying, All power is given unto me in heaven and in earth" (Mt.28:18).

"He shall be great and shall be called the Son of the Highest: and the Lord God shall give unto him the throne of his father David: He shall reign over the house of Jacob for ever; and of his kingdom there shall be no end" (Lk.1:32-33).

"Nathanael answered and saith unto him, Rabbi, thou art the Son of God; thou art the King of Israel" (Jn.1:49).

"My kingdom is not of this world: if my kingdom were of this world, then would my servants fight, that I should not be delivered to the Jews: but now is my kingdom not from hence. Pilate therefore said unto him, Art thou a king then? Jesus answered, Thou sayest that I am a king. To this end was I born" (Jn.18:36-37).

"Pilate wrote a title, and put it on the cross. And the writing was, JESUS OF NAZARETH THE KING OF THE JEWS" (Jn.19:19).

"Him hath God exalted with his right hand to be a Prince and a Saviour" (Acts 5:31).

"To this end Christ both died, and rose, and revived, that he might be Lord both of the dead and living" (Ro.14:9).

"But every man in his own order: Christ the firstfruits; afterward they that are Christ's at his coming. Then cometh the end, when he shall have delivered up the kingdom to God, even the Father; when he shall have put down all rule and all authority and power. For he must reign, till he hath put all enemies under his feet. The last enemy that shall be destroyed is death" (1 Cor.15:23-26).

"Which he wrought in Christ, when he raised him from the dead, and set him at his own right hand in the heavenly places, far above all principality, and power, and might, and dominion, and every name that is named, not only in this world, but also in that which is to come: and hath put all things under his feet, and gave him to be the head over all things to the church" (Eph.1:20-22).

"God also hath highly exalted him, and given him a name which is above every name: that at the name of Jesus every knee should bow, of things in heaven, and things in earth, and things under the earth; and that every tongue should confess that Jesus Christ is Lord, to the glory of God the Father" (Ph.2:9-11).

"Who is the blessed and only Potentate, the King of kings, and Lord of lords; Who only hath immortality, dwelling in the light which no man can approach unto; whom no man hath seen, nor can see; to whom be honour and power everlasting" (1 Tim.6:15-16).

"But this man, after he had offered one sacrifice for sins for ever, sat down on the right hand of God; from henceforth expecting till his enemies be made his footstool" (Heb.10:12-13).

"[Christ] who is gone into heaven, and is on the right hand of God; angels and authorities and powers being made subject unto him" (1 Pt.3:22).

"Jesus Christ, who is the faithful witness, and the first begotten of the dead, and the prince of the kings of the earth. Unto him that loved us, and washed us from our sins in his own blood, and hath made us kings and priests unto God and his Father; to him be glory and dominion for ever and ever. Amen. Behold, he cometh with clouds; and every eye shall see him, and they also which pierced him: and all kindreds of the earth shall wail because of Him" (Rev.1:5-7).

"These things saith he that is holy, he that is true, he that hath the key of David, he that openeth, and no man shutteth; and shutteth, and no man openeth" (Rev.3:7).

"To him that overcometh will I grant to sit with me in my throne, even as I also overcame, and am set down with my Father in his throne" (Rev.3:21).

"And I saw, and behold a white horse: and he that sat on him had a bow; and a crown was given unto him: and he went forth conquering, and to conquer" (Rev.6:2).

"And the kings of the earth, and the great men, and the rich men, and the chief captains, and the mighty men, and every bondman, and every free man, hid themselves in the dens and in the rocks of the mountains; and said to the mountains and rocks, Fall on us, and hide us from the face of him that sitteth on the throne, and from the wrath of the Lamb: for the great day of his wrath is come; and who shall be able to stand?" (Rev.6:15-17).

"The kingdoms of this world are become the kingdoms of our Lord, and of his Christ; and he shall reign for ever and ever" (Rev.11:15).

"And I heard a loud voice saying in heaven, Now is come salvation, and strength, and the kingdom of our God, and the power of his Christ: for the accuser of our brethren is cast down, which accused them before our God day and night" (Rev.12:10).

"Behold a white cloud, and upon the cloud one sat like unto the Son of man, having on his head a golden crown, and in his hand a sharp sickle" (Rev.14:14).

"These shall make war with the Lamb, and the Lamb shall overcome them: for he is Lord of lords, and King of kings" (Rev.17:14).

"I saw heaven opened, and behold a white horse; and he that sat upon him was called Faithful and True, and in righteousness he doth judge and make war. His eyes were as a flame of fire, and on his head were many crowns; and he had a name written, that no man knew, but he himself....Out of his mouth goeth a sharp sword, that with it he should smite the nations: and he shall rule them with a rod of iron: and he treadeth the winepress of the fierceness and wrath of almighty God. He hath on his vesture and on his thigh a name written, KING OF KINGS, AND LORD OF LORDS" (Rev.19:11-12, 15-16).

"Blessed and holy is he that hath part in the first resurrection: on such the second death hath no power, but they shall be priests of God and of Christ, and shall reign with a thousand years" (Rev.20:6).

**3** (3:32-38) **Adamic Heir—Roots—Genealogy**: Jesus was the Adamic heir—He was qualified to be the Messianic High Priest, the Perfect High Priest who represents man before God and God before man. This was the very *function* of the High Priest: to represent men before God and God before men. The High Priest bore the name of God before men, and He carried the names of men before God (Ro.8:33-34; Heb.2:17; 9:24; 1 Jn.2:1-2; cp. Is.49:16). In relation to the Messiah, this meant two things.

1. The Messiah must *know man perfectly*, and He must *know God perfectly*. He must be the Perfect God-Man in Person, in Being, in Essence. He had to be Man, yes, but He also had to be God Incarnate in human flesh. He had to be born of Adam, that is, of Adam's seed, of human flesh; but He also had to possess the very nature of God. This was the only way man could ever have a Perfect High Priest. It was absolutely necessary—because of the very nature of a depraved world—that a Perfect High Priest be *Perfect God-Perfect Man*.

2. The Messiah must also *be able to represent God before man*, represent God perfectly; and He must *be able to represent man before God*, represent man perfectly. As Scripture says "[Messiah must] be faithful to God that appointed Him" (Heb.3:2).

The Messiah had to live as Perfect God in order to represent God to man. The Messiah also had to live as Perfect Man (never sinning) in order to represent man before God (if man was to be represented as perfect before God).

Scripture declares that Jesus did live a perfect life, that He never sinned (2 Cor.5:21; Heb.4:15; 9:28; 3:5).

1. The Messianic High Priest was typified by two men or priests in the Old Testament.
    a. By Melchizedek.

    "And Melchizedek king of Salem brought forth bread and wine: and he was the priest of the most high God. And he blessed him, and said, Blessed be Abram of the most high God, possessor of heaven and earth: and blessed be the most high God, which hath delivered thine enemies into thy hand. And he gave him tithes of all" (Gen.14:18-20).

    "The LORD hath sworn, and will not repent, Thou art a priest for ever after the order of Melchizedek" (Ps.110:4).

    b. By Aaron.

    "And thou shalt bring Aaron and his sons unto the door of the tabernacle of the congregation, and wash them with water. And thou shalt put upon Aaron the holy garments, and anoint him, and sanctify him; that he may minister unto me in the priest's office. And thou shalt bring his sons, and clothe them with coats: and thou shalt anoint them, as thou

**didst anoint their father, that they may minister unto me in the priest's office: for their anointing shall surely be an everlasting priesthood throughout their generations" (Ex.40:12-15).**

2.   The Messianic High Priest was prophesied.

**"And their nobles shall be of themselves, and their governor shall proceed from the midst of them; and I will cause him to draw near [as High Priest], and he shall approach unto me: for who is this that engaged his heart to approach unto me? saith the LORD. And ye shall be my people, and I will be your God" (Jer.30:21-22. Note how the governor draws near in High Priestly fashion.)**

**"And speak unto him, saying, Thus speaketh the LORD of hosts, saying, Behold the man whose name is The BRANCH; and he shall grow up out of his place, and he shall build the temple of the LORD: even he shall build the temple of the LORD; and he shall bear the glory, and shall sit and rule upon his throne; and he shall be a priest upon his throne: and the counsel of peace shall be between them both" (Zech.6:12-13).**

3.   Jesus Christ is the Messianic High Priest.

**"Wherefore, holy brethren, partakers of the heavenly calling, consider the Apostle and High Priest of our profession, Christ Jesus; Who was faithful to him that appointed him" (Heb.3:1-2).**

**"Seeing then that we have a great high priest, that is passed into the heavens, Jesus the Son of God, let us hold fast our profession. For we have not an high priest which cannot be touched with the feeling of our infirmities; but was in all points tempted like as we are, yet without sin. Let us therefore come boldly unto the throne of grace, that we may obtain mercy, and find grace to help in time of need" (Heb.4:14-16).**

**"And no man taketh this honour unto himself, but he that is called of God, as was Aaron. So also Christ glorified not himself to be made an high priest; but he that said unto him, Thou art my Son, to day have I begotten thee...though he were a Son, yet learned he obedience by the things which he suffered; and being made perfect, he became the author of eternal salvation unto all them that obey him" (Heb.5:4-5, 8-9). (See outline—Heb.4:14-5:10 for overview. See outlines—Heb.4:14-7:28 for full picture.)**

**4**   (3:38) **Jesus Christ, Prophet**: Jesus is the Godly heir—He was qualified to be the Messianic Prophet of God Himself. Jesus Christ Himself proclaimed what the Messianic Prophet of God was to do.

**"He came to Nazareth, where he had been brought up: and, as his custom was, he went into the synagogue on the sabbath day, and stood up for to read. And there was delivered unto him the book of the prophet Esaias. And when he had opened the book, he found the place where it was written, The Spirit of the Lord is upon me, because he hath anointed me to preach the gospel to the poor; he hath sent me to heal the brokenhearted, to preach deliverance to the captives, and recovering of sight to the blind, to set at liberty them that are bruised, To preach the acceptable year of the Lord. And he closed the book...and he began to say unto them, This day is this scripture fulfilled in your ears" (Lk.4:16-21).**

1.   The Messianic Prophet of God was prophesied.

**"The LORD thy God will raise up unto thee a Prophet from the midst of thee, of thy brethren, like unto me; unto him ye shall hearken" (Dt.18:15).**

**"The people that walked in darkness have seen a great light: they that dwell in the land of the shadow of death, upon them hath the light shined" (Is.9:2).**

**"And there shall come forth a rod out of the stem of Jesse, and a Branch shall grow out of his roots: and the spirit of the LORD shall rest upon him, the spirit of wisdom and understanding, the spirit of counsel and might, the spirit of knowledge and of the fear of the LORD; and shall make him of quick understanding in the fear of the LORD: and he shall not judge after the sight of his eyes, neither reprove after the hearing of his ears: but with righteousness shall he judge the poor, and reprove with equity for the meek of the earth: and he shall smite the earth with the rod of his mouth, and with the breath of his lips shall he slay the wicked" (Is.11:1-4).**

**"Behold my servant, whom I uphold; mine elect, in whom my soul delighteth; I have put my spirit upon him: he shall bring forth judgment to the Gentiles. He shall not cry, nor lift up, nor cause his voice to be heard in the street. A bruised reed shall he not break, and the smoking flax shall he not quench: he shall bring forth judgment unto truth. He shall not fail nor be discouraged, till he have set judgment in the earth: and the isles shall wait for his law" (Is.42:1-4).**

**"How beautiful upon the mountains are the feet of him that bringeth good tidings, that publisheth peace; that bringeth good tidings of good, that publisheth salvation; that saith unto Zion, Thy God reigneth!" (Is.52:7).**

**"Behold upon the mountains the feet of him that bringeth good tidings, that publisheth peace! O Judah, keep thy solemn feasts, perform thy vows: for the wicked shall no more pass through thee; he is utterly cut off" (Nah.1:15).**

2.   Jesus Christ was the Messianic Prophet of God (see above statement of Christ, Lk.4:16-21).

> "And the multitude said, This is Jesus the prophet of Nazareth of Galilee" (Mt.21:11).
>
> "And there came a fear on all: and they glorified God, saying, That a great prophet is risen up among us; and, That God hath visited his people" (Lk.7:16).
>
> "Nevertheless I must walk to day, and to morrow, and the day following: for it cannot be that a prophet perish out of Jerusalem" (Lk.13:33).
>
> "For he whom God hath sent speaketh the words of God: for God giveth not the Spirit by measure unto him" (Jn.3:34).
>
> "Then those men, when they had seen the miracle that Jesus did, said, This is of a truth that prophet that should come into the world" (Jn.6:14).
>
> "Many of the people therefore, when they heard this saying, said, Of a truth this is the Prophet" (Jn.7:40).
>
> "I have many things to say and to judge of you: but he that sent me is true; and I speak to the world those things which I have heard of him....Then said Jesus unto them, When ye have lifted up the Son of man, then shall ye know that I am he, and that I do nothing of myself; but as my Father hath taught me, I speak these things" (Jn.8:26, 28).
>
> "They say unto the blind man again, What sayest thou of him, that he hath opened thine eyes? He said, he is a prophet" (Jn.9:17).
>
> "For I have not spoken of myself; but the Father which sent me, he gave me a commandment, what I should say, and what I should speak. And I know that his commandment is life everlasting: whatsoever I speak therefore, even as the Father said unto me, so I speak" (Jn.12:49-50).
>
> "Believest thou not that I am in the Father, and the Father in me? the words that I speak unto you I speak not of myself: but the Father that dwelleth in me, he doeth the works....He that loveth me not keepeth not my sayings: and the word which ye hear is not mine, but the Father's which sent me" (Jn.14:10, 24).
>
> "Henceforth I call you not servants; for the servant knoweth not what his lord doeth: but I have called you friends; for all things that I have heard of my Father I have made known unto you" (Jn.15:15).
>
> "For I have given unto them the words which thou gavest me; and they have received them, and have known surely that I came out from thee, and they have believed that thou didst send me....And I have declared unto them thy name, and will declare it: that the love wherewith thou hast loved me may be in them, and I in them" (Jn.17:8, 26).

**CHAPTER 4**

**E. The Temptation of Jesus: Victory Over Temptation, 4:1-15**
(Mt.4:1-11, 12-17; Mk.1:12-13, 14-15)

**1 Being prepared to serve God**[DSI]
  a. By being filled with the Spirit
  b. By spending time alone with God
  c. By being tried & tested
  d. By fasting & praying

**2 Tempt. 1: To meet the necessities of life by His own power**
  a. Satan's temptation: To misuse His power
  b. Jesus' answer: Man needs more than bread—he needs God's life or spiritual food

**3 Tempt. 2: To seek His ambition by compromise**
  a. Satan's enticement: He shows the world's possessions & glory
  b. Satan's claim: He controls world & its glory
  c. Satan's offer: He will give the world to whomever he wills

And Jesus being full of the Holy Ghost returned from Jordan, and was led by the Spirit into the wilderness,
2 Being forty days tempted of the devil. And in those days he did eat nothing: and when they were ended, he afterward hungered.
3 And the devil said unto him, If thou be the Son of God, command this stone that it be made bread.
4 And Jesus answered him, saying, It is written, That man shall not live by bread alone, but by every word of God.
5 And the devil, taking him up into an high mountain, showed unto him all the kingdoms of the world in a moment of time.
6 And the devil said unto him, All this power will I give thee, and the glory of them: for that is delivered unto me; and to whomsoever I will I give it.
7 If thou therefore wilt worship me, all shall be thine.
8 And Jesus answered and said unto him, Get thee behind me, Satan: for it is written, Thou shalt worship the Lord thy God, and him only shalt thou serve.
9 And he brought him to Jerusalem, and set him on a pinnacle of the temple, and said unto him, If thou be the Son of God, cast thyself down from hence:
10 For it is written, He shall give his angels charge over thee, to keep thee:
11 And in their hands they shall bear thee up, lest at any time thou dash thy foot against a stone.
12 And Jesus answering said unto him, It is said, Thou shalt not tempt the Lord thy God.
13 And when the devil had ended all the temptation, he departed from him for a season.
14 And Jesus returned in the power of the Spirit into Galilee: and there went out a fame of him through all the region round about.
15 And he taught in their synagogues, being glorified of all.

  d. Satan's condition: A person must worship & follow him
  e. Jesus' answer: He must worship & follow God alone

**4 Tempt. 3: To prove Himself through sensationalism**
  a. Satan's temptation
    1) To choose another way
    2) To misuse & twist the Scripture to suit his own ends
    3) To give people sensations—a religion of feelings
  b. Jesus' answer: God is not to be tempted—God's way alone is to be followed

**5 Conclusion: Satan left Jesus for a while**

  a. Jesus' great power
  b. Jesus' great fame
  c. Jesus' great ministry

# DIVISION II

## THE SON OF MAN'S APPEARANCE, 3:1-4:15

## E.    The Temptation of Jesus: Victory Over Temptation, 4:1-15

(4:1-15) **Introduction**: victory over temptation is essential before we can live and minister for God. No temptation has ever confronted man that Jesus Christ has not confronted. This is seen in this passage. In His confrontation, Jesus reveals what lies behind each temptation and how to conquer it. Once it has been conquered, we can then live a victorious life and serve God effectively.

    1.    Being prepared to serve God (v.1-2).
    2.    Temptation 1: to meet the necessities of life by His own power (v.3-4).
    3.    Temptation 2: to seek His ambition through compromise (v.5-8).
    4.    Temptation 3: to prove Himself through sensationalism (v.9-12).
    5.    Conclusion: Satan left Jesus for a while (v. 13-15).

**1** (4:1-2) **Ministry, Preparation—Service**: Jesus was being prepared to serve God. He was about to launch the most important work ever performed by man. His work was to determine the eternal fate of the world and of every man in the world. Jesus had to be strengthened and prepared perfectly, without flaw. Two things were involved in His preparation.

First, there was God's plan. Jesus had to be totally committed to carry out God's plan no matter what happened. God's plan was the cross, the way of sacrifice and suffering in order to help others. Jesus would always be tempted to choose the easier course of self, power, and glory. He needed to gain the victory *once-for-all*. Not that He would not be tempted again; He would. But He needed a strong moment of victory to show that He could conquer the temptation.

Second, Jesus' preparation involved a personal need for strength and assurance. The only way Jesus could be strengthened and gain assurance was to be tempted. He had to struggle against temptation to become tough and strong, and to be assured that He could conquer and be victorious over the trials of life.

Now, note the first two verses. They give the four essentials necessary for preparation. Jesus had to be prepared to serve God. (How much more do we!)

    1.    Jesus was "full of the Holy Spirit." Note the emphasis upon the Holy Spirit. He is mentioned twice.

a.   Jesus had a dramatic experience with the Spirit at His baptism (Lk.3:21-22).

b.   Jesus was "led by the Spirit" (egeto en toi pneumati). Note the Greek word "en." It means *in*, which means that Jesus was not only "led by the Spirit" He was led "in the Spirit," step by step and day by day. A man must be *in the Spirit* to be led by the Spirit.

2.   Jesus was led to spend time alone with God. He was led to get all alone in the wilderness. Time alone with God is necessary for preparation.

3.   Jesus was led to be tried and tested. Trials toughen us, make us stronger, and give us greater assurance so that we can face whatever lies ahead.

4.   Jesus was led to fast and pray, two absolute essentials in one's preparation to do a great work for God.

---

**DEEPER STUDY # 1**

(4:1-2) **Temptation** (perirazo): the word temptation is used here in both a good and a bad sense. In the good sense it means to test, to try, to prove. It does not mean to seduce into sin. Its purpose is not to defeat or to destroy. The idea is not that one is tempted, seduced, enticed, and pulled into sin by the Holy Spirit (cp. Jas.1:13); but one is tested, proved, strengthened, reinforced, and purified through the trials of temptation.

In the bad sense, it means to tempt, to seduce, to entice, and to pull someone away from God into the way of sin, of self, and of Satan (Mt.4:1; 1 Cor.7:5; 1 Th.3:5; Gal.6:1; Jas.1:13-14).

Jesus was led into the wilderness by the Spirit *to be tested*. The Spirit did not seduce or entice Jesus to do evil, but He led Jesus into circumstances whereby He could learn obedience and discipline. Through such trials, Jesus was to be perfected and enabled to succor all those who suffer trials (Heb.4:15-16; 5:8). (See notes—Mt.4:2-4; 4:5-7; 4:8-10.)

Six things need to be said about overcoming temptation.

1.   Temptation has its bottom root in passion and appetite (Mk.7:20-23; Jas.1:14). It comes directly from within, from man's heart, not from without. And it does not come from God. "God cannot be tempted with evil; neither tempteth he any man" (Jas.1:3). God does not tempt any man in a bad sense. What He does is look upon His people as they endure temptation, and He strengthens them to bear the temptation. By such He teaches them discipline and obedience for a greater work (Ro.8:28; 2 Cor.1:3-4; Heb.5:8; 1 Pt.1:6-7).

2.   No man confronts any temptation that is not common to all men (1 Cor.10:13).

3.   God does not allow the believer to be tempted beyond what he is able to bear. There is always a way to escape (1 Cor.10:13).

4.   Jesus Christ understands temptation. He was tempted in all points just as all men are tempted, yet He never sinned (Heb.2:18; 4:15).

5.   Jesus Christ is a sympathetic High Priest in helping the believer through temptation (Heb.2:17-18; 4:15).

6.   Temptation is overcome (a) by submitting to God and resisting the devil (Jas.4:7-8; 1 Pt.5:8-9), and (b) by using and obeying Scripture to combat temptation (Lk.4:4; cp. Dt.4:8; 4:12; 6:13, 16; 8:3; 10:20).

---

2   (4:3-4) **Jesus Christ, Temptation—Self-Sufficient—Necessities**: the first temptation was for Jesus to meet the necessities of life by His own power. Note two things.

1.   Satan's temptation was for Jesus to misuse His power and His ability. (See note—Mt.4:2-4.) Jesus was very hungry. He had the power to create food and to meet His need, and the tempter tempted Him to use His power upon Himself. But note the wrong in this temptation. Jesus would have been misusing His power by using it in an illegitimate way. His power had not been given to use upon Himself, but to demonstrate His deity by showing men that He was the Son of God. Never once did He use His power upon Himself nor for His own ends—not even when He was hanging upon the cross (cp.Mt.26:42; Lk.23:35). He always used His power to help men, thereby demonstrating and giving evidence that what He was claiming was true: He is the Son of God sent to save the world.

The point is just this: Satan wanted Jesus to prove His Messiahship by *centering* His attention and power upon Himself. If Jesus had used His power upon Himself...

•   He would be trusting Himself and not the Father, acting completely independent of the Father and the Father's will.

•   He would be saying that men could use their abilities to center upon themselves instead of helping a world lost in need.

•   He would be teaching that men could use their abilities to build themselves up (pride) instead of honoring God and His will.

2.   Jesus' answer was that something more than physical food was needed. Man needs to be fed spiritually. He needs his spiritual needs met. The point is that Jesus alone can meet man's spiritual needs; therefore He, the Son of God, must use His power only as God wills. (See note—Mt.4:2-4 for detailed discussion.)

**Thought 1.** A man has needs, the very necessities of life. There are the necessities of...

| | | |
|---|---|---|
| • food | • friends | • self-esteem |
| • clothing | • acceptance | • work |
| • shelter | • recognition | • rest and recreation |

The necessities are legitimate. However, the problem arises when we are tempted...

•   to use our ability independent of God, forgetting His will and doing our own thing.

•   to focus our ability upon ourselves, getting and banking more and more instead of meeting the needs of a desperate world.

•   to use our abilities to build ourselves up instead of acknowledging God as the Source of our abilities. Too many seek fame, honor, and praise for selfish ends. Too many want to be recognized as superior and better, as having more position, authority, clothes, houses, cars, lands, and looks.

The great wrong with this is twofold.
1) We misuse our ability. Forgetting God and His will, we focus upon self.
2) We live for the physical and not for the spiritual, for receiving and not for giving. There is a spiritual hunger that just is not met by bread, that is, the physical and material. (See note—Eph.1:3 for detailed discussion.)

> "Ho, every one that thirsteth, come ye to the waters, and he that hath no money; come ye, buy, and eat; yea, come, buy wine and milk without money and without price. Wherefore do ye spend money for that which is not bread? and your labor for that which satisfieth not? hearken diligently unto me, and eat ye that which is good, and let your soul delight itself in fatness. Incline your ear, and come unto me: hear, and your soul shall live" (Is.55:1-3).

> "And Jesus said unto them, I am the bread of life: he that cometh to me shall never hunger; and he that believeth on me shall never thirst" (Jn.6:35).

> "This is the bread which cometh down from heaven, that a man may eat thereof, and not die. I am the living bread which came down from heaven: if any man eat of this bread, he shall live for ever: and the bread that I will give is my flesh, which I will give for the life of the world" (Jn.6:50-51).

> "Verily, verily, I say unto you, He that heareth my word, and believeth on him that sent me, hath everlasting life, and shall not come into condemnation; but is passed from death unto life" (Jn.5:24).

> "Neither have I gone back from the commandment of his lips; I have esteemed the words of his mouth more than my necessary food" (Job 23:12).

> "How sweet are thy words unto my taste! yea, sweeter than honey to my mouth" (Ps.119:103).

> "Thy words were found, and I did eat them; and thy word was unto me the joy and rejoicing of mine heart: for I am called by thy name, O LORD God of hosts" (Jer.15:16).

**3** (4:5-8) **Jesus Christ, Temptation—Compromise—Ambition:** the second temptation was for Jesus to seek His ambition (God's kingdom) through compromise. (See note—Mt.4:8-10.) Jesus had come to earth to seek and to save men *eternally*, to secure their loyalty for God, and to set up the Kingdom of God forever (see DEEPER STUDY # 3—Mt.19:23-24). This was the ambition of Jesus. The only way to fulfill His ambition was by the cross (freeing men from sin, death, and judgment). Note what happened in this temptation.
1. Satan enticed Jesus in a moment of time. Satan *flashed* across Jesus' mind all the kingdoms of the world in their enormous glory.
2. Satan claimed that he controlled the possessions and glory of the world. Sometime later, Jesus substantiated Satan's claim. Jesus said that Satan is "the prince of this world" (Jn.12:31; 14:30). Other Scriptures say that he is "the prince...the spirit that worketh in the children of disobedience" (Eph.2:2) and the "god of this world" (2 Cor.4:4).
3. Satan offered Jesus all the possessions and glory of the world. The world was under His influence and control; therefore, he could give it to anyone whom he wished.
4. Satan, however, had one condition. Jesus had to worship Satan, that is, follow and obey the way of Satan's world. Jesus had to compromise Himself...
   • by compromising His standards and behavior.
   • by compromising His loyalty and faithfulness to God.
   • by compromising His ministry and mission.

Note Jesus' answer: He was quick and decisive, totally dependent upon Scripture to conquer the temptation. "Thou shalt worship the Lord thy God, and him only shalt thou serve" (v.8). He must worship, follow, and serve God alone, not the way and standards and evil of the world. He would follow God even if it meant not realizing His ambition. There is a right way and a wrong way to achieve one's end and purpose; and He, the Son of God, would choose the right way.

**Thought 1.** The *power* and the *glory* of the world comes from many things. *Worldly power and glory* come from...

| | | | |
|---|---|---|---|
| • houses | • authority | • cars | • excitement |
| • lands | • influence | • possessions | • fame |
| • wealth | • success | • stimulation | • position |

A man is often taken up to a mountain by Satan and shown the power and glory of the world. The man is offered whatever he wants if he will do but one thing: worship Satan, that is, follow the path of *worldliness*. Man feels that if he compromises and goes along with the world (everyone else), he will get what he wants and move ahead much faster.

**Thought 2.** Note a significant point. There is nothing wrong with ambition and desiring to fulfill one's calling in life. There is nothing wrong with experiencing the power and the glory of whatever one's calling is. The wrong is found in following Satan (evil) when tempted to satisfy one's desires and ambitions instead of following God.

> "For what is a man profited, if he shall gain the whole world, and lose his own soul? or what shall a man give in exchange for his soul?" (Mt.16:26).

> "And be not conformed to this world: but be ye transformed by the renewing of your mind, that ye may prove what is that good, and acceptable, and perfect, will of God" (Ro.12:2).

> "Thou therefore endure hardness, as a good soldier of Jesus Christ. No man that warreth entangleth himself with the affairs of this life; that he may please him who hath chosen him to be a soldier" (2 Tim.2:3-4).

> "Love not the world, neither the things that are in the world. If any man love the world, the love of the Father is not in him. For all that is in the world, the lust of the flesh, and the lust of the eyes, and the pride of life, is not of the Father, but is of the world" (1 Jn.2:15-16).

"For the grace of God that bringeth salvation hath appeared to all men, teaching us that, denying ungodliness and worldly lusts, we should live soberly, righteously, and godly, in this present world" (Tit.2:11-12).

**4** (4:9-12) **Jesus Christ, Temptation—Sensationalism—Obedience**: this particular temptation was for Jesus to be sensational. The thought flashed across Jesus' mind that if He jumped off the pinnacle of the temple, God would cause angels to catch Him. God would never let Him be dashed to bits. Therefore, when the people saw the angels float Him to the ground, they would be stunned into belief and become His followers immediately. (Remember Jesus had not yet done a miracle. Satan had no idea of the miracles to come, nor that men would be slow to believe even with all the evidence of signs and wonders.) Note that Satan's temptation was threefold.

1. Satan tempted Jesus to choose some way other than God's way (see note and DEEPER STUDY # 1—Lk.9:23). God's way was the way of the cross and of identifying with man in his trials and sufferings (cp. Heb.4:15-16. Then cp. Heb.2:14-18 with Jn.3:16. Cp. also Heb.5:7-9.)

2. Satan tempted Jesus to misuse Scripture by twisting it to suit His purposes. Scripture did say that God would take care of His Son no matter what. The heavenly angels were given charge to help Him in everything.

3. Satan tempted Jesus to give people sensations, a religion of feelings. People do not want a life of self-denial and sacrifice, of too much discipline and control. They want the spectacular, something that will be a quick fix, something...

⇒ to stir their emotions and flesh.
⇒ to stimulate their feelings and give gratification.
⇒ to meet their needs with less and less effort.
⇒ to feed their body and soul without cost.

Jesus' answer was straightforward and decisive: "Thou shalt not tempt the Lord thy God." There is no way other than God's way; God's way alone is to be pursued and followed. And God's Word is not to be stretched or twisted (presumed upon) trying to make another way. Men must be taught the truth. The way to God is the way of the cross.

> **Thought 1.** All men are tempted to bypass God, to choose another way. The way of the cross is hard and difficult, yet it is the only way to God (see note and DEEPER STUDY # 1—Lk.9:23). Trying to devise another way to God only spells doom. (Cp. Jn.14:6; 1 Tim.1:15; 2:5-6; Tit.3:4-7).
>
> > "Much more then, being now justified by his blood, we shall be saved from wrath through him" (Ro.5:9).
> > "And, having made peace through the blood of his cross, by him to reconcile all things unto himself; by him, I say, whether they be things in earth, or things in heaven" (Col.1:20).
> > "For the preaching of the cross is to them that perish foolishness; but unto us which are saved it is the power of God. For it is written, I will destroy the wisdom of the wise, and will bring to nothing the understanding of the prudent" (1 Cor.1:18-19).
> > "How much more shall the blood of Christ, who through the eternal Spirit offered himself without spot to God, purge your conscience from dead works to serve the living God?" (Heb.9:14).
> > "Forasmuch as ye know that ye were not redeemed with corruptible things, as silver and gold, from your vain conversation received by tradition from your fathers" (1 Pt.1:18).
>
> **Thought 2.** Some try to twist or stretch Scripture...
> 1) To allow them to do what they want (sin).
> 2) To devise some way to God other than the cross.

**5** (4:13-15) **Ministry**: the conclusion to Jesus' temptations was striking. Satan *departed for a season.* He left Jesus alone for a while. The victory was won; the temptation was conquered, and Satan was routed for a while. He would be back, but for now there was peace and freedom to carry on the ministry. Note the immediate result of the Lord's victory.

1. Jesus' great power was demonstrated.
2. Jesus' great fame was spread abroad.
3. Jesus' great ministry in the synagogue was admired.

> **Thought 1.** Victory over temptation does not mean a person is freed forever from temptation. In this life temptation will always return. It did for Jesus; it will for us (see note and DEEPER STUDY # 1,3—Mt.4:1-11).
>
> > "Then said he unto the disciples, It is impossible but that offences will come: but woe unto him, through whom they come!" (Lk.17:1).
>
> **Thought 2.** Victory over temptation will lead to great results in a person's life. It will give more power, a greater testimony, and a greater ministry.
>
> > "Blessed is the man that endureth temptation: for when he is tried, he shall receive the crown of life, which the Lord hath promised to them that love him" (Jas.1:12).
> > "To him that overcometh will I grant to sit with me in my throne, even as I also overcame, and am set down with my Father in his throne" (Rev.3:21).
> > "Because thou hast kept the word of my patience, I also will keep thee from the hour of temptation, which shall come upon all the world, to try them that dwell upon the earth" (Rev.3:10).

| | III. THE SON OF MAN'S ANNOUNCED MISSION AND PUBLIC MINISTRY, 4:16-9:17 | 22 And all bare him witness, and wondered at the gracious words which proceeded out of his mouth. And they said, Is not this Joseph's son? | 4 Scene 3: The people's declining response |
|---|---|---|---|

**III. THE SON OF MAN'S ANNOUNCED MISSION AND PUBLIC MINISTRY, 4:16-9:17**

**A. Jesus Announces His Mission: A Graphic Picture of Rejection, 4:16-30** (cp. Mt.13:53-58; Mk.6:1-6)

**1 A dramatic scene**
a. Jesus visited His hometown
b. Jesus entered the synagogue—His custom on the Sabbath

**2 Scene 1: Jesus' dramatic reading from the prophet Isaiah—concerned the Messiah**
a. The Messiah is to be anointed by the Spirit
b. The Messiah is to preach the gospel
c. The Messiah is to minister

d. The Messiah is to preach the age of salvation

**3 Scene 2: Jesus' phenomenal claim**

a. The rapt attention of the people

b. The claim of Jesus to be the Messiah

16 And he came to Nazareth, where he had been brought up: and, as his custom was, he went into the synagogue on the sabbath day, and stood up for to read.
17 And there was delivered unto him the book of the prophet Esaias. And when he had opened the book, he found the place where it was written,
18 The Spirit of the Lord is upon me, because he hath anointed me to preach the gospel to the poor; he hath sent me to heal the brokenhearted, to preach deliverance to the captives, and recovering of sight to the blind, to set at liberty them that are bruised,
19 To preach the acceptable year of the Lord.
20 And he closed the book, and he gave it again to the minister, and sat down. And the eyes of all them that were in the synagogue were fastened on him.
21 And he began to say unto them, This day is this scripture fulfilled in your ears.

22 And all bare him witness, and wondered at the gracious words which proceeded out of his mouth. And they said, Is not this Joseph's son?
23 And he said unto them, Ye will surely say unto me this proverb, Physician, heal thyself: whatsoever we have heard done in Capernaum, do also here in thy country.
24 And he said, Verily I say unto you, No prophet is accepted in his own country.
25 But I tell you of a truth, many widows were in Israel in the days of Elias, when the heaven was shut up three years and six months, when great famine was throughout all the land;
26 But unto none of them was Elias sent, save unto Sarepta, a city of Sidon, unto a woman that was a widow.
27 And many lepers were in Israel in the time of Eliseus the prophet; and none of them was cleansed, saving Naaman the Syrian.
28 And all they in the synagogue, when they heard these things, were filled with wrath,
29 And rose up, and thrust him out of the city, and led him unto the brow of the hill whereon their city was built, that they might cast him down headlong.
30 But he passing through the midst of them went his way,

**4 Scene 3: The people's declining response**
a. First: They were impressed
b. Second: They questioned
c. Third: They demanded proof—insisted He heal (prove) Himself, that is, work miracles

**5 Scene 4: The people's painful rejection**

a. Illust. 1: Only one needy widow had her needs met in Elijah's day—because only one widow accepted Elijah

b. Illust. 2: Only one needy leper was cleansed in Elisha's day—because only one leper accepted Elisha

**6 Scene 5: The people's true spirit**
a. An insane wrath: A close-mindedness
b. An insane assault: To silence Jesus

c. The insane behavior of the people failed

# DIVISION III

## THE SON OF MAN'S ANNOUNCED MISSION AND PUBLIC MINISTRY, 4:16-9:17

## A.     Jesus Announces His Mission: A Graphic Picture of Rejection, 4:16-30

(4:16-30) **Introduction**: Jesus Christ claimed to be the Messiah, and His claim was rejected by the people of His day. His claim is still rejected by people today. A graphic picture of rejection is painted in the present passage.
1.     A dramatic scene (v.16).
2.     Scene 1: Jesus' dramatic reading from the prophet Isaiah—concerned the Messiah (v.17-19).
3.     Scene 2: Jesus' phenomenal claim (v.20-21).
4.     Scene 3: the people's declining response (v.22-23).
5.     Scene 4: the people's painful rejection (v.24-27).
6.     Scene 5: the people's true spirit (v.28-30).

**1** (4:16) **Jesus, Worship of**: this was a dramatic scene. Jesus visited His hometown of Nazareth where He had been reared (see DEEPER STUDY # 4, *Nazareth*—Mt.2:23). On the Sabbath He entered the synagogue for worship. Note it was His custom to worship on the Sabbath. He was faithful in His worship of God and faithful to the church. This was the very synagogue that Jesus had always attended as a child. It was a small community synagogue where everyone would know everyone else. Jesus and the congregation were neighbors; some were close to His family.

The synagogue had no preachers or ministers as we know them (see DEEPER STUDY # 2, *Synagogue*—Mt.4:23). The leaders would simply invite some person to read and preach. They had been hearing a good deal about their neighbor Jesus, so they invited Him to read and preach this Sabbath.

**2** (4:17-19) **Jesus Christ—Messiah, Ministry—Mission**: the first scene was Jesus' dramatic reading from the prophet Isaiah. The prophecy centered around the Messiah (cp. Is.61:1-2). Note six things.
1. Jesus stood to read the Scripture because of His reverence for the Scripture. (v.16).

   **Thought 1.** There should always be reverence for the Scripture, both in hearing and in reading it (cp. Neh.8:5).

2. The Messiah was to be anointed by the Spirit (v.18). The Messiah was to be both *called* and *equipped* by the Spirit (cp. Lk.3:21-22).

   **Thought 1.** When God calls, He anoints; He equips the messenger with His Spirit. The Holy Spirit goes with the messenger wherever God sends him.

3. The Messiah was to preach the gospel. The word "gospel" (evaggelizesthai) means to evangelize. Note the Messiah was to preach to two classes of people.
   a. He was to preach to the poor. The "poor" means not only poor in material possessions but also *poor in spirit* (see DEEPER STUDY # 2—Mt.5:3).
   b. He was to preach deliverance to the captives (aichmalotois). This is a picture of prisoners of war. (See note, *Redemption*—Eph.1:7.)
4. The Messiah was to minister. A threefold ministry was mentioned.
   a. He was to heal the *brokenhearted*. Note that He was not only to help the brokenhearted, He was to *heal* the brokenhearted, those who were...
   - crushed by grief
   - shattered
   - opposed
   - cut off
   - blemished by sin
   - violated by sin
   - infected
   - diseased
   - weakened
   - subdued
   - injured
   - bankrupt

   b. He was to give sight to the *blind*, not only to those who were spiritually blind, but to those who were blind physically.
   c. He was to set at liberty those who were *bruised*. He was to set free those who were physically, mentally, emotionally, psychologically, and spiritually bruised—those who were...
   - disabled
   - injured
   - wounded
   - hurting
   - afflicted
   - battered

5. The Messiah was to preach the age of salvation. The term "acceptable year" means the era, the age or day of salvation (cp. 2 Cor.6:2). It means that the age of the Messiah had come.
6. Note a significant point. Jesus was reading from Is.61:1-2, but He abruptly stopped in the middle of v.2. Why? Because the last part of the verse had to do with judgment and Jesus' present ministry was salvation, not judgment. His future ministry would be to judge the world (Is.61:2b). (Cp. Is.58:6.)

**3** (4:20-21) **Jesus Christ, Claims—Messiah**: the second scene was Jesus' phenomenal claim. The scene was one of eager expectation. Jesus closed the book, handed it to the minister, and sat down; sitting was the posture for preaching in the synagogue. All eyes "were fastened on Him" (esan atenizontes autoi), a descriptive phrase meaning fixed, gazing, spellbound. They stared at Him in rapt attention; their eyes were locked upon Him eagerly waiting to see what He had to say.

His voice pierced the air: "This day is this scripture fulfilled in your ears"—a phenomenal claim.

The word "today" is important. The people thought of the Messiah's coming and the Messianic age in terms of the future. Jesus proclaimed that He was the Messiah—that the Messianic Age was then and now—that all the Scripture of Isaiah was *fulfilled* in Him. He proclaimed...

- that He was the One upon whom the Spirit abode.
- that He was the One anointed to preach the gospel to the poor and captives.
- that He was the One who healed the brokenhearted.
- that He was the One who gave sight to the blind.
- that He was the One who freed the bruised.
- that He was the One who preached the acceptable year of the Lord, the age of salvation.

> "He saith unto them, But whom say ye that I am? And Simon Peter answered and said, Thou art the Christ, the Son of the living God. And Jesus answered and said unto him, Blessed art thou, Simon Barjona: for flesh and blood hath not revealed it unto thee, but my Father which is in heaven" (Mt.16:15-17).
>
> "But Jesus held his peace. And the high priest answered and said unto him, I adjure thee by the living God, that thou tell us whether thou be the Christ, the Son of God. Jesus saith unto him, Thou hast said: nevertheless I say unto you, Hereafter shall ye see the Son of man sitting on the right hand of power, and coming in the clouds of heaven" (Mt.26:63-64).
>
> "Then he said unto them, O fools, and slow of heart to believe all that the prophets have spoken: ought not Christ to have suffered these things, and to enter into his glory?" (Lk.24:25-26).

"The woman saith unto him, I know that Messias cometh, which is called Christ: when he is come, he will tell us all things. Jesus saith unto her, I that speak unto thee am he" (Jn.4:25-26).

"Then said Jesus unto them, When ye have lifted up the Son of man, then shall ye know that I am he, and that I do nothing of myself; but as my Father hath taught me, I speak these things. And he that sent me is with me: the Father hath not left me alone; for I do always those things that please him" (Jn.8:28-29).

"Jesus said unto her, I am the resurrection, and the life: he that believeth in me, though he were dead, yet shall he live: and whosoever liveth and believeth in me shall never die. Believest thou this? She saith unto him, Yea, Lord: I believe that thou art the Christ, the Son of God, which should come into the world" (Jn.11:25-27).

"Even as the Son of man came not to be ministered unto, but to minister, and to give his life a ransom for many" (Mt.20:28).

"For the Son of man is come to seek and to save that which was lost" (Lk.19:10).

"The thief cometh not, but for to steal, and to kill, and to destroy: I am come that they might have life, and that they might have it more abundantly" (Jn.10:10).

"This is a faithful saying, and worthy of all acceptation, that Christ Jesus came into the world to save sinners; of whom I am chief" (1 Tim.1:15).

**4** (4:22-23) **Jesus Christ, Response to—Signs**: the third scene was the people's declining response. Note how drastically the people's response declined.

1. First, they were impressed with His eloquence, His charm and winning words, and the power of His message. Note the word "wondered" (ethaumazon). It means they began to marvel and to be astonished at the gracious words flowing from His mouth. They were taking *pride* in one of their own neighbor's being so capable.

2. Second, they began to question. This was a quick reaction, a quick change. Sitting there listening, the questions began to arise in their thoughts: "Is this not Joseph's son?" Matthew is even more descriptive. The people were sitting there glancing around, asking in their minds, "Is not this...His mother...His brethren...His sisters. Are they not all with us?" (Mt.13:55-56). "And they were offended in Him" (Mt.13:57). The word "offended" means they stumbled over Him. They could not imagine that someone from their own town—someone whom they had known since a child—could be the Messiah, the Son of God.

3. Third, they demanded proof, insisted that He had to heal, that is, prove Himself by working miracles in their midst. Remember, all this was still thoughts in their minds. They were still sitting there listening to Him, but their thoughts were *stumbling* over His claim to be the Messiah. Jesus knew their thoughts, so He stopped His message and directed a statement to them: "You are thinking, saying to me, Physician, heal, prove yourself. Prove yourself by doing the miracles you did in Capernaum."

The point is this: the response of the people to Jesus' claim deteriorated from being *impressed* to being *offended* to *demanding proof*.

**Thought 1.** Many are impressed with Jesus Christ at first, but when they are presented with His claims and the cross, they become offended and demand proof. His claim to be the Incarnate God in human flesh—to be the virgin-born Son of God—who must die for man's sin by being crucified upon a vulgar cross, is offensive to some. Many refuse to accept such phenomenal claims and vulgar scenes. They want a religion of grand images, beautiful pictures, and soft words.

"Then said Jesus unto him, Except ye see signs and wonders, ye will not believe" (Jn.4:48).

"For the Jews require a sign, and the Greeks seek after wisdom: but we preach Christ crucified, unto the Jews a stumbling-block, and unto the Greeks foolishness" (1 Cor.1:22-23).

**5** (4:24-27) **Jesus Christ, Rejection of—Salvation**: the fourth scene was the people's painful rejection. Jesus continued to speak, directing His remarks toward His hometown audience. But note: Jesus knew they had already rejected Him. Therefore, He would not gratify their curiosity and demand for signs, nor would He continue to preach; but rather He would give a twofold warning.

1. "No prophet is *accepted* in His own country." They had rejected Him and He knew it. They could not hide the fact. They had (as is so often the case)...
   - allowed familiarity to breed contempt.
   - thought it farfetched that the claims of a hometown boy could be true.
   - given in to envy among neighbors.

Note the words "His own country." Jesus was bound to be thinking of all Israel as well as Nazareth. The Jewish nation would eventually reject Him, the true Messiah.

2. God would reject those who rejected His prophet, the Messiah. Jesus warned the people by recalling two well known stories in the history of Israel. The audience could not miss the point. In the past, God had not given His mercy to people who just *thought* they were "God's people" (the Jews), but God had given His mercy to those whose hearts were turned toward Him and who accepted Him.
   a. There was the one needy widow in Elijah's day. She was the only widow who had her need met by God in the day of famine. There were many without food, destitute and starving, yet God sent His prophet to help only this one person; and she was a despised Gentile. Why? When there were so many others who *professed to be God's chosen people*, why would God help only this one poor widow? Why would God turn away from

the Jews to another person? The point is clear. She was the only one whose heart was turned toward God and who accepted Him.

    b. There was also the one leper who had his leprosy cleansed by Elisha. When God sent Elisha to heal Naaman, Elisha passed by many Jewish lepers, many who thought they were the chosen people of God. But the prophet stopped to help none of these. He was sent to heal the Syrian Gentile, the one person whose heart accepted God.

**Thought 1.** Salvation requires more than mere profession, more than just thinking one is chosen of God and that one will never be rejected by God. A person's heart must be turned toward God (repentance) and must accept God (belief) in order to be saved.

> **"He that believeth on him is not condemned: but he that believeth not is condemned already, because he hath not believed in the name of the only begotten Son of God"** (Jn.3:18).
> **"He that believeth on the Son hath everlasting life: and he that believeth not the Son shall not see life; but the wrath of God abideth on him"** (Jn.3:36).
> **"I said therefore unto you, that ye shall die in your sins: for if ye believe not that I am he, ye shall die in your sins"** (Jn.8:24).
> **"Take heed, brethren, lest there be in any of you an evil heart of unbelief, in departing from the living God"** (Heb.3:12).

**6** (4:28-30) **Jesus Christ, Rejection of**: the fifth scene was the people's true spirit. Note what Jesus said to the people sitting before Him.

    1.   Jesus said (predicted) that God would turn and give His mercy to someone else if the people rejected Him. God would turn to those who were responsive to Him. He would not continue to appeal to those who were always rejecting and hardening their hearts.

    2.   Jesus also made a much broader statement. He said that God would turn from Israel ("His country," v.24) if Israel continued to reject Him.

As a result of these two statements, the people's reaction grew hostile and violent. They "rose up." Note three facts.
    1.   Their insane wrath: a close-mindedness.
    2.   Their insane assault: a violent attempt to silence Jesus.
    3.   Their insane behavior: a failure. Somehow Jesus was able to escape their assault. How? Perhaps the people were stricken with a moment of confusion, a moment of shock, or some temporary blindness which enabled Him to quickly escape.

**Thought 1.** The Lord will not continue to strive after a man, not forever. A person can go too far too often and face eternity without the presence of God. A person must surrender to the Spirit of God while there is still time.

> **"And the LORD said, My spirit shall not always strive with man"** (Gen.6:3).
> **"Happy is the man that feareth always: but he that hardeneth his heart shall fall into mischief"** (Pr.28:14).
> **"He, that being often reproved hardeneth his neck, shall suddenly be destroyed, and that without remedy"** (Pr.29:1).
> **"Or despisest thou the riches of his goodness and forbearance and longsuffering; not knowing that the goodness of God leadeth thee to repentance? But after thy hardness and impenitent heart treasurest up unto thyself wrath against the day of wrath and revelation of the righteous judgment of God"** (Ro.2:4-5).
> **"Take heed, brethren, lest there be in any of you an evil heart of unbelief, in departing from the living God. But exhort one another daily, while it is called To day; lest any of you be hardened through the deceitfulness of sin. For we are made partakers of Christ, if we hold the beginning of our confidence stedfast unto the end"** (Heb.3:12-14).

**Thought 2.** A person or a people may wish to silence Jesus and His followers, but their efforts will be to no avail. The message of the gospel will never be silenced.

> **"Thou art the Christ, the Son of the living God....upon this rock I will build my church; and the gates of hell shall not prevail against it"** (Mt.16:16, 18).
> **"Heaven and earth shall pass away: but my words shall not pass away"** (Lk.21:33; cp. Mt.5:18).
> **"Blessed be the LORD, that hath given rest unto his people...according to all that he promised"** (1 Ki.8:56).
> **"The works of his hands are verity and judgment; all his commandments are sure"** (Ps.111:7).

| | B. Jesus Ministers and Makes an Amazing Impact: A Day in the Life of Jesus, 4:31-44 (Mt.8:14-17; Mk.1:21-39) | country round about. | |
|---|---|---|---|
| 1 Jesus came down to Capernaum | 31 And came down to Capernaum, a city of Galilee, and taught them on the sabbath days. | 38 And he arose out of the synagogue, and entered into Simon's house. And Simon's wife's mother was taken with great fever; and they besought him for her. | 4 He cured the most needful<br>a. So needful, a great fever<br>b. So needful, could not speak or seek Jesus for herself<br>c. So needful, could not even come to Jesus<br>d. So needful, He came & healed her; she arose & ministered |
| 2 He taught in the morning service with authority<br>3 He delivered the most unclean<br>a. A man with an unclean spirit sat in worship | 32 And they were astonished at his doctrine: for his word was with power.<br>33 And in the synagogue there was a man, which had a spirit of an unclean devil, and cried out with a loud voice, | 39 And he stood over her, and rebuked the fever; and it left her: and immediately she arose and ministered unto them.<br>40 Now when the sun was setting, all they that had any sick with divers diseases brought them unto him; and he laid his hands on every one of them, and healed them. | 5 He healed the diseases of those who sought Him out |
| 1) Evil spirits acknowledged Jesus' deity | 34 Saying, Let us alone; what have we to do with thee, thou Jesus of Nazareth? art thou come to destroy us? I know thee who thou art; the Holy One of God. | 41 And devils also came out of many, crying out, and saying, Thou art Christ the Son of God. And he rebuking them suffered them not to speak: for they knew that he was Christ. | 6 He rebuked the evil spirits from making a false profession |
| 2) Jesus rebuked the evil acknowledgement<br>3) Jesus cast out the unclean spirit<br>b. The people were amazed | 35 And Jesus rebuked him, saying, Hold thy peace, and come out of him. And when the devil had thrown him in the midst, he came out of him, and hurt him not.<br>36 And they were all amazed, and spake among themselves, saying, What a word is this! for with authority and power he commandeth the unclean spirits, and they come out. | 42 And when it was day, he departed and went into a desert place: and the people sought him, and came unto him, and stayed him, that he should not depart from them.<br>43 And he said unto them, I must preach the kingdom of God to other cities also: for therefore am I sent. | 7 He sought to be alone, seeking the presence of God<br>a. He tried to get alone<br>b. He was sought out & was begged to stay<br>8 He persisted in His mission despite pressure to be sidetracked |
| c. The people spread His fame | 37 And the fame of him went out into every place of the | 44 And he preached in the synagogues of Galilee. | |

# DIVISION III

## THE SON OF MAN'S ANNOUNCED MISSION AND PUBLIC MINISTRY, 4:16-9:17

**B.     Jesus Ministers and Makes an Amazing Impact: A Day in the Life of Jesus, 4:31-44**

(4:31-44) **Introduction**: this is one of the most interesting passages in all of Scripture. This is the very beginning, the very launch of Jesus' ministry. What Luke does is paint the picture of a typical day so that the reader will have some idea of what a day was like in the life of Jesus. Note how busy and pressuring and tiring the day was, and note the powerful lessons applicable to our lives.

1.     Jesus came down to Capernaum (v.31).
2.     He taught in the morning service with authority (v.32).
3.     He delivered the most unclean (v.33-37).
4.     He cured the most needful (v.38-39).
5.     He healed the diseases of those who sought Him out (v.40).
6.     He rebuked the evil spirits from making a false profession (v.41).
7.     He sought to be alone, seeking the presence of God (v.42).
8.     He persisted in His mission despite pressure to be sidetracked (v.43-44).

**1**     (4:31) **Capernaum—Jesus' Headquarters**: Jesus came down to Capernaum, a city of Galilee. Note the exact wording and look at verse 44: "He preached in the synagogues of Galilee." Capernaum became the *headquarters* of Jesus. Nazareth was Jesus' hometown, but the city had rejected Him. He had to move elsewhere. The city He chose as the center of His operations was Capernaum. Capernaum was the manufacturing center of Palestine; therefore, it was strategically located, always flooded with travelling merchants. The major roads passed through its borders, roads which connected such metropolitan cities as Damascus, Jerusalem, and the great Syrian cities of Tyre and Sidon. The great caravan route leading to the Mediterranean Sea also ran through the city (cp. Is.9:1). It was an ideal location for the spread of the gospel, an ideal location for the Messiah to use as His base of operations. (See note, *Capernaum*—Mt.4:12-13.)

**2** (4:32) **Preaching—Jesus Christ, Teaching of**: Jesus taught in the morning worship service with authority. His teaching was not ordinary, not the kind of teaching the people were used to hearing. They were astonished at His doctrine. It was what He taught that astounded them: "His word was with power."

⇒ His Word had authority, the authority of God's Spirit.
⇒ His message had a commanding force to it.
⇒ His message had the power of God's Spirit upon it, *quickening* the Word to the hearts of the hearers. (See note—Mt.7:29.)

> "Jesus answered them, and said, My doctrine is not mine, but his that sent me. If any man will do his will, he shall know of the doctrine, whether it be of God, or whether I speak of myself. He that speaketh of himself seeketh his own glory: but he that seeketh his glory that sent him, the same is true, and no unrighteousness is in him" (Jn.7:16-18).
> "Believest thou not that I am in the Father, and the Father in me? the words that I speak unto you I speak not of myself: but the Father that dwelleth in me, he doeth the works" (Jn.14:10).

**3** (4:33-37) **Unclean—Evil Spirit—Sin—Resisting**: Jesus delivered the most unclean. Note several facts. (See outline and notes—Mk.1:23-28.)

1. The man was "in the synagogue," actually attending the worship service; yet he was desperately unclean, as dirty as could be.

2. The man had the spirit "of an unclean demon." "Unclean" (akathartou) means that the man was both morally and ceremonially unclean, dirty, dishevelled, filthy. He was worshipping, but he was morally unclean and corrupt; his life was all dishevelled.

3. The evil spirit *acknowledged* Jesus' deity. He knew three things. (See note, pt.2—Mk.1:23-24 for detailed discussion.)

    a. He had nothing to do with Jesus. He was unclean, dirty, and sinful in comparison with Jesus.

    b. He knew that he was to be destroyed by Jesus, that a day of judgment was coming.

> "For this purpose the Son of God was manifested, that he might destroy the works of the devil" (1 Jn.3:8).

    c. He knew that Jesus was "the Holy One of God." (Lk.4:34). He knew and proclaimed that he stood face to face with the true Messiah, the Son of the living God.

**Thought 1.** The person who is morally unclean and dirty is in desperate straits. He is gripped by an evil force that cries out in the very face of God...

- "Let us alone.
- What have we to do with thee, thou Jesus of Nazareth?
- Art thou come to destroy us—now?
- I know thee who thou art; the Holy One of God."

> "Ye stiffnecked and uncircumcised in heart and ears, ye do always resist the Holy Ghost: as your fathers did, so do ye" (Acts 7:51).
> "And they have turned unto me the back, and not the face: though I taught them, rising up early and teaching them, yet they have not hearkened to receive instruction" (Jer.32:33).
> "As for the word that thou hast spoken unto us in the name of the LORD, we will not hearken unto thee" (Jer.44:16).
> "But they refused to hearken, and pulled away the shoulder, and stopped their ears, that they should not hear" (Zech.7:11).

3. Jesus rebuked the evil spirit's acknowledgement. This is a critical point: Jesus stopped the acknowledgement, the proclamation of the evil spirit. Jesus would not have the evil spirit's witnessing to His deity. Why? Because it was a false witness, a profession only. The evil spirit was not confessing from the heart nor from the will to follow Jesus. He had not been born again. The *only confession* Jesus accepted was the confession of a man who made a deliberate decision to follow Him *as Lord*. (See note—Mk.1:25-26.)

> "That if thou shalt confess with thy mouth the Lord Jesus, and shalt believe in thine heart that God hath raised him from the dead, thou shalt be saved. For with the heart man believeth unto righteousness; and with the mouth confession is made unto salvation. For the scripture saith, Whosoever believeth on him shall not be ashamed. For there is no difference between the Jew and the Greek: for the same Lord over all is rich unto all that call upon him. For whosoever shall call upon the name of the Lord shall be saved" (Ro.10:9-13).

4. Jesus cast out the unclean spirit and saved the man. How? By His Word, by simply saying, "Hold thy peace, and come out of him." Note the great power of the Lord's Word.

> "And Jesus came and spake unto them, saying, All power is given unto me in heaven and in earth" (Mt.28:18).

"As thou hast given him power over all flesh, that he should give eternal life to as many as thou hast given him" (Jn.17:2).

5. The evil spirit threw the man down, but he came out of the man and did not hurt him. (See note, pt.2—Mk.1:25-26 for detailed discussion.)

6. The people were amazed, astonished, shocked, stunned. Note what amazed them: His Word—the authority and power of His Word to *cleanse* even the most unclean.

7. The people spread His fame everywhere, witnessing to His cleansing and healing power. They could do no other, for they were witnessing a power never before seen.

**Thought 1.** The Lord has the power to save and cleanse anyone who comes to Him, no matter how possessed by evil.

"As thou hast given him power over all flesh, that he should give eternal life to as many as thou hast given him" (Jn.17:2).

"That ye may know....what is the exceeding greatness of his power to usward who believe, according to the working of his mighty power" (Eph.1:18-19).

"I know that thou canst do every thing, and that no thought can be withholden from thee" (Job 42:2).

**4** (4:38-39) **Helpless, The—Needful, The—Ministering:** Jesus cured the most needful. After the worship service, Jesus went to Peter's home. Peter's mother-in-law was critically ill. Note these simple facts.

1. She was desperately needful, overtaken with a "great fever."

2. She was so helpless she could not even speak to ask Jesus for help.

3. She was so weakened she was unable to rise out of bed to seek the help of Jesus.

4. Jesus came to her and rebuked the fever by simply speaking the Word, and she arose and began to minister.

**Thought 1.** Jesus is the great hope of the most needful. No matter how *desperate or helpless or weakened*—Jesus will speak the Word of healing. All that is needed is a willing heart and mind.

Even if a person is so helpless that he is unable to speak verbally, that person can call upon the Lord by thought, and God will still save him.

"For whosoever shall call upon the name of the Lord shall be saved" (Ro.10:13).

"But that ye may know that the Son of man hath power on earth to forgive sins, (then saith he to the sick of the palsy,) Arise, take up thy bed, and go unto thine house" (Mt.9:6).

**5** (4:40) **Helpless, The—Ministering:** Jesus healed all the diseases of those who sought Him out. Again, note several simple facts. (See outline and notes—Mk.1:32-34 for detailed discussion.)

1. It was early evening and the sun was setting. Jesus had been ministering rather extensively all day and was tired, yet He was approachable. He could be approached at all hours. There was never a closed door into His presence.

2. The people who came to Him were totally helpless. Every one of them had to be brought, yet someone cared enough to bring them.

**Thought 1.** Note two challenging lessons.

1) The most helpless can come or be brought to Jesus. He is always available to help.

2) There is a strong challenge to us. We need to care enough to bring the helpless to Jesus.

3. Jesus did not bypass or overlook a single one. He touched every one and healed every one. No matter the disease, they were healed.

**Thought 1.** No one, no matter how helpless, ever comes to Jesus that He does not help. Rich or poor, strong or weak, the Lord forbids no one.

"When the even was come, they brought unto him many that were possessed with devils: and he cast out the spirits with his word, and healed all that were sick: that it might be fulfilled which was spoken by Esaias the prophet, saying, Himself took our infirmities, and bare our sicknesses" (Mt.8:16-17).

"They that are whole need not a physician; but they that are sick. I came not to call the righteous, but sinners to repentance" (Lk.5:31-32).

"How God anointed Jesus of Nazareth with the Holy Ghost and with power: who went about doing good, and healing all that were oppressed of the devil; for God was with him" (Acts 10:38).

"For thou hast been a strength to the poor, a strength to the needy in his distress, a refuge from the storm, a shadow from the heat, when the blast of the terrible ones is as a storm against the wall" (Is.25:4).

"Surely he hath borne our griefs, and carried our sorrows: yet we did esteem him stricken, smitten of God, and afflicted" (Is.53:4).

6 (4:41) **Evil Spirits**: Jesus rebuked the evil spirits from making false professions (see notes—Lk.4:33-37; Mk.1:25-26).

7 (4:42) **Jesus Christ, Prayer**: Jesus sought to be alone, seeking the presence of God. Jesus was exhausted and drained, spiritually as well as physically. Apparently, He had been ministering all day and night, that is, for almost twenty-four hours without a break.
1. He tried to get alone in a desert place. He needed to be refreshed and revived in body and spirit. He wanted time alone with God.
2. He was sought out by the people who begged Him to stay. They were desperate and helpless.

**Thought 1.** Note two great lessons.
1) We need to seek the renewal of our bodies and spirits in the Lord's presence—seek renewal much more than most of us do.
2) We need to seek Him out and beg for His help while He may be found. When Jesus was on the earth in the body, He could help only those who surrounded Him. Now that He is in the Spirit and able to minister everywhere at once, so few of us are seeking Him out. What an example these people were in seeking Him!

"**Seek the LORD and his strength, seek his face continually**" (1 Chron.16:11).
"**Seek ye the LORD while he may be found, call ye upon him while he is near**" (Is.55:6).
"**But it is good for me to draw near to God: I have put my trust in the Lord GOD, that I may declare all thy works**" (Ps.73:28).
"**The LORD is nigh unto all them that call upon him, to all that call upon him in truth**" (Ps.145:18).
"**Let us draw near with a true heart in full assurance of faith, having our hearts sprinkled from an evil conscience, and our bodies washed with pure water**" (Heb.10:22).

8 (4:43-44) **Jesus Christ, Mission**: Jesus persisted in His *mission* despite the pressure of some persons to sidetrack Him. Jesus had to preach in other cities as well, so He could not stay with those clamoring after Him. He had to fulfill His mission. He could not be sidetracked. Everyone had to hear the Gospel. He had to give others the opportunity as well. He knew that the more He could reach and disciple, the more others would hear and be reached. So He set His face like a flint and marched on despite all who "stayed Him" (kateichon): tried to prevent, hinder, stop, hold Him back.

"**For the Son of man is come to seek and to save that which was lost**" (Lk.19:10).
"**I must work the works of him that sent me, while it is day: the night cometh, when no man can work**" (Jn.9:4).

CHAPTER 5

C. Jesus Calls His First Disciples: Steps to Calling Men, 5:1-11
(Mt.4:18-22; Mk.1:16-20; Jn.1:35-51)

1 Lake Gennesaret
2 Step 1: Seeing a vision of people who need to hear the Word of God

3 Step 2: Seizing resources
   a. Seeing the resources available

   b. Seeing a man: Simon
   c. Leading the man to serve

4 Step 3: Removing reluctant obedience

And it came to pass, that, as the people pressed upon him to hear the word of God, he stood by the lake of Gennesaret,
2 And saw two ships standing by the lake: but the fishermen were gone out of them, and were washing their nets.
3 And he entered into one of the ships, which was Simon's, and prayed him that he would thrust out a little from the land. And he sat down, and taught the people out of the ship.
4 Now when he had left speaking, he said unto Simon, Launch out into the deep, and let down your nets for a draught.
5 And Simon answering said unto him, Master, we have toiled all the night, and have taken nothing: nevertheless at thy word I will let down the net.
6 And when they had this done, they inclosed a great multitude of fishes: and their net brake.
7 And they beckoned unto their partners, which were in the other ship, that they should come and help them. And they came, and filled both the ships, so that they began to sink.
8 When Simon Peter saw it, he fell down at Jesus' knees, saying, Depart from me; for I am a sinful man, O Lord.
9 For he was astonished, and all that were with him, at the draught of the fishes which they had taken:
10 And so was also James, and John, the sons of Zebedee, which were partners with Simon. And Jesus said unto Simon, Fear not; from henceforth thou shalt catch men.
11 And when they had brought their ships to land, they forsook all, and followed him.

5 Step 4: Demonstrating godly power
   a. A great catch made
   b. A catch so great the net breaks
   c. A catch so great other help is needed
   d. A catch so great both boats are filled
   e. A catch so great the boats began to sink

6 Step 5: Stirring a deep confession
   a. Of sin
   b. Of Christ as Lord
   c. Of awe—reverence—fear

7 Step 6: Challenging men to discipleship, that is, to catch other men[DS1,2]

8 Step 7: Watching for the decision to forsake all

# DIVISION III

## THE SON OF MAN'S ANNOUNCED MISSION AND PUBLIC MINISTRY, 4:16-9:17

## C.    Jesus Calls His First Disciples: Steps to Calling Men, 5:1-11

(5:1-11) **Introduction**: Jesus Christ set out to catch men, that is, to catch them for God. He desires to catch all men, but He is unable to catch everyone by Himself. He needs help, the help of all who will follow Him. The present passage is a descriptive picture of how Jesus goes about calling men to help Him in the enormous task of reaching the world.
1.    Lake Gennesaret (v.1).
2.    Step 1: seeing a vision of people who need to hear the Word of God (v.1).
3.    Step 2: seizing resources (v.2-3).
4.    Step 3: removing reluctant obedience (v.4-5).
5.    Step 4: demonstrating godly power (v.6-7).
6.    Step 5: stirring a deep confession (v.8-9).
7.    Step 6: challenging men to discipleship, that is, to catch other men (v.10).
8.    Step 7: watching for the decision to forsake all (v.11).

[1]    (5:1) **Lake Gennesaret**: the scene of this experience took place on Lake Gennesaret which was the same as the Sea of Galilee (see DEEPER STUDY # 1—Mk.1:16; Lk.8:22).

[2]    (5:1) **Word of God, Hunger for—Righteousness—Vision**: the first step to calling men is seeing a vision of people—people who need the Word of God. The people were actually "pressing" (epikeisthai) in upon Jesus. They gathered and crowded around Him. Note why: to hear the Word of God. They pressed to hear the Word of God. They had a craving, a *hunger and thirst* after righteousness. Note two things.
1.    Jesus met the hunger and thirst of people.

> "Blessed are they which do hunger and thirst after righteousness: for they shall be filled" (Mt.5:6).
> "Blessed are ye that hunger now: for ye shall be filled. Blessed are ye that weep now: for ye shall laugh" (Lk.6:21).
> "But whosoever drinketh of the water that I shall give him shall never thirst; but the water that I shall give him shall be in him a well of water springing up into everlasting life" (Jn.4:14).

"In the last day, that great day of the feast, Jesus stood and cried, saying, If any man thirst, let him come unto me, and drink" (Jn.7:37).

"As newborn babes, desire the sincere milk of the word, that ye may grow thereby: if so be ye have tasted that the Lord is gracious" (1 Pt.2:2-3).

"They shall hunger no more, neither thirst any more; neither shall the sun light on them, nor any heat" (Rev.7:16).

"And the Spirit and the bride say, Come. And let him that heareth say, Come. And let him that is athirst come. And whosoever will, let him take the water of life freely" (Rev.22:17).

"They shall be abundantly satisfied with the fatness of the house; and thou shalt make them drink of the river of thy pleasures" (Ps.36:8).

"For he satisfieth the longing soul, and filleth the hungry soul with goodness" (Ps.107:9).

"Ho, every one that thirsteth, come ye to the waters, and he that hath no money; come ye, buy, and eat; yea, come, buy wine and milk without money and without price" (Is.55:1).

"And the LORD shall guide thee continually, and satisfy thy soul in drought, and make fat thy bones: and thou shall be like a watered garden, and like a spring of water, whose waters fail not" (Is.58:11).

2.    Jesus saw that He could never meet the needs of all the people, not by Himself. He needed others to help.

"Therefore said he unto them, The harvest truly is great, but the labourers are few: pray ye therefore the Lord of the harvest, that he would send forth labourers into his harvest" (Lk.10:2).

**3** (5:2-3) **Resource—Opportunity, Serving**: the second step to calling men is seizing resources. Jesus had to find some way to handle the throng of people both then and later. The crowds were so large and their needs so many that He just could not handle their disorder. He could not meet the needs of everyone. Standing there and being confronted with the present problem, He scanned the horizon for some way to handle the matter.

As He looked around, He saw an opportunity and laid His plans. He saw a boat and a fisherman in the boat, and He needed both. The boat could be used as a pulpit, and the man could become a disciple. He asked the man to let Him use the boat as a pulpit and to steer the boat out from land a short distance. The point is this: Jesus seized and used the resources available. He had the vision of people's needing the Word of God, but He needed a pulpit and others to help, so He scanned the horizon and found both.

"Say not ye, There are yet four months, and then cometh harvest? behold, I say unto you, Lift up your eyes, and look to the fields; for they are white already to harvest. And he that reapeth receiveth wages, and gathereth fruit unto life eternal: that both he that soweth and he that reapeth may rejoice together" (Jn.4:35-36).

**4** (5:4-5) **Obedience—Reluctance**: the third step to calling men is the *removal of reluctant obedience*. As soon as Jesus finished His preaching, He decided to win Peter's loyalty and discipleship. But first, He had to humble Peter. He had to show Peter that He, the Messiah, could look after and take care of him. He told Peter to put out to sea and fish. Peter objected because he had fished all night and had caught nothing. However, he stopped right in the middle of his objection and obeyed Jesus. Note what had happened.

1.    Peter was reluctant to obey Jesus. He objected to what Jesus asked. He was thoroughly *exhausted*, for he had "toiled all night." He was *disappointed*, because he had caught nothing, and he had worked enough hours already. Despite needing to be home in bed, he had stayed to help the Lord in His preaching by loaning his boat to Him.

2.    Peter caught himself in the middle of his objection and obeyed. What caused the switch, the change from reluctance to willing obedience? Probably two things.

a.    Peter was pretty well convinced that Jesus was who He claimed to be, the Messiah.

b.    Peter was drawn somewhat to follow Jesus. Therefore, when he began to object to Jesus' will, there was a prick of conscience, and he obeyed his conscience. He followed his heart...

• not his *mind*, thinking there were no fish.
• not his *experience*, having already tried and failed to catch fish.
• not his *body*, being too tired and exhausted, just incapable of going on.

**Thought 1.** Reluctance should always give in to obedience. We need the spirit that will *try* for God, no matter what the obstacles or how hopeless a situation may seem.

**Thought 2.** When a man is drawn to Christ, he desperately needs to obey his heart and to obey it immediately.

"Not slothful in business; fervent in spirit; serving the Lord" (Ro.12:11).

"Therefore, my beloved brethren, be ye stedfast, unmoveable, always abounding in the work of the Lord, forasmuch as ye know that your labour is not in vain in the Lord" (1 Cor.15:58).

"That ye be not slothful, but followers of them who through faith and patience inherit the promises" (Heb.6:12).

**5** (5:6-7) **Jesus Christ, Power—Obedience, Results—Humility**: the fourth step to calling men is *demonstrating godly power*. Peter's obedience produced results; his obedience caught fish, and the catch was no ordinary catch. It was much more, so much more that there could be no question about Jesus. Jesus was behind the miracle; Jesus was demonstrating the power of God. (Remember this was the very purpose of Jesus, to win Peter's loyalty and willingness to become a disciple on a full-time basis.) What happened is a little humorous when we remember what Jesus was doing with Peter, and Peter's reluctance and objection, weariness and exhaustion. There was a sense in which the Lord was really laying it on Peter, really letting him have it. Peter thought he was tired, but he did not know what exhaustion was yet. The Lord must have stood to the side smiling to Himself. How our Lord loved this man Peter, even now! He was after Peter's loyalty, and He was going to get it even if He had to make Peter drop in his tracks (which was exactly what was to happen, v.8). At any rate, there was some humor in what began to happen to this man who was so reluctant, moaning and groaning about his tiredness. Just imagine Peter already bone weary, grumbling in his mind at this carpenter's telling him, the skilled fisherman, how to fish. Imagine Peter's exhaustion and weariness, reluctance and objection, moaning and groaning; and then all of a sudden a catch is made, a catch so great that he was going to have to work wearily along for hour upon hour.

⇒ Peter's net broke.
⇒ Peter had to call for another whole crew and boat to help.
⇒ Both boats were filled as full to capacity.
⇒ Then to top it off, both boats began to sink.

Jesus had His man! What else was Peter to do other than what followed? In all the humor of the situation, our Lord's heart was bound to be full of rejoicing because this big hunk of a fisherman, man though he was, was like a little child before the Lord. He was broken in humility before the Lord, and the experience was but the first of many experiences of brokenness yet to come.

> **"I know that thou canst do every thing, and that no thought can be withholden from thee" (Job 42:2).**
>
> **"Yea, before the day was I am he; and there is none that can deliver out of my hand: I will work, and who shall let [hinder, stop] it?" (Is.43:13).**

**6** (5:8-9) **Confession**: the fifth step to calling men is *stirring a deep confession*. Peter knew exactly what had happened. He had been reluctant and objected to the Lord's request, and he had not been too happy that the great catch had caused so much trouble. But he was a skilled fisherman, and he knew that the great catch was no ordinary catch; it was a miracle of the Lord, a miracle which the Lord was using to teach him that he was to obey without reluctance and objection.

Note exactly what happened. When Peter saw the boat's beginning to sink, he raced over to Jesus, fell upon his knees, and in a sense (continuing the humor) said, "Lord, I've had enough. Let me alone. I'll do anything." His confession was threefold.

1. He confessed his sin of disobedience and unbelief: of being reluctant to obey the Lord, of questioning the Lord's will and knowledge and power.

2. He confessed Jesus to be the *Lord*. Note that Peter had previously called Jesus "Master" (epistate, v.5), which is a word used to address anyone in authority. But Peter had learned better. He now called Jesus "Lord" (kurie). He is the Lord who is holy and convicting, who must be obeyed and followed.

3. He confessed a fear, a reverence, an awe for the Lord (cp. v.9-10).

> **"Then said I, Woe is me! for I am undone; because I am a man of unclean lips, and I dwell in the midst of a people of unclean lips: for mine eyes have seen the King, the LORD of hosts" (Is.6:5).**
>
> **"I have heard of thee by the hearing of the ear; but now mine eye seeth thee: wherefore I abhor myself, and repent in dust and ashes" (Job 42:5-6).**
>
> **"And Abraham answered and said, Behold now, I have taken upon me to speak unto the LORD, which am but dust and ashes" (Gen.18:27).**
>
> **"And, behold, one like the similitude of the sons of men touched my lips: then I opened my mouth, and spake, and said unto him that stood before me, O my lord, by the vision my sorrows are turned upon me, and I have retained no strength" (Dan.10:16).**
>
> **"That if thou shalt confess with thy mouth the Lord Jesus, and shalt believe in thine heart that God hath raised him from the dead, thou shalt be saved. For with the heart man believeth unto righteousness; and with the mouth confession is made unto salvation" (Ro.10:9-10).**
>
> **"If we confess our sins, he is faithful and just to forgive us our sins, and to cleanse us from all unrighteousness" (1 Jn.1:9).**
>
> **"Only acknowledge thine iniquity, that thou hast transgressed against the LORD thy God, and hast scattered thy ways to the strangers under every green tree, and ye have not obeyed my voice, saith the LORD" (Jer.3:13).**
>
> **"He that covereth his sins shall not prosper: but whoso confesseth and forsaketh them shall have mercy" (Pr.28:13).**
>
> **"Now therefore make confession unto the LORD God of your fathers, and do his pleasure: and separate yourselves from the people of the land, and from the strange wives" (Ezra 10:11).**

**7** (5:10) **Call—Discipleship—Mission**: the sixth step to calling men is *challenging men to discipleship*, that is, to *catch other men*. Note two significant facts.

1. The words "fear not" (me phobon) indicate that Peter was actually scared and frightened. Jesus was calming him, telling him to trust and stop fearing. He, the Lord, was in charge and looking after everything.

2. The call to Peter was to "catch men." The word "catch" (zogreo) means to *catch alive* or to *catch for life*. The idea is that Peter was no longer to catch (fish) for death, but he was to catch (men) for life.

> "And he saith unto them, Follow me, and I will make you fishers of men" (Mt.4:19).
> "And of some have compassion, making a difference: and others save with fear, pulling them out of the fire; hating even the garment spotted by the flesh" (Jude 22-23).
> "Ye have not chosen me, but I have chosen you, and ordained you, that ye should go and bring forth fruit [souls], and that your fruit should remain: that whatsoever ye shall ask of the Father in my name, he may give it you" (Jn.15:16).
> "He [Paul] is a chosen vessel unto me, to bear my name before the Gentiles, and kings, and the children of Israel" (Acts 9:15).
> "Also I heard the voice of the LORD, saying, Whom shall I send, and who will go for us? Then said I, Here am I; send me" (Is.6:8).
> "Then the word of the LORD came unto me, saying, Before I formed thee in the belly I knew thee and before thou camest forth out of the womb I sanctified thee, and I ordained thee a prophet unto the nations" (Jer.1:4-5).
> "The fruit of the righteous is a tree of life; and he that winneth souls is wise" (Pr.11:30).
> "And they that be wise shall shine as the brightness of the firmament; and they that turn many to righteousness as the stars for ever and ever" (Dan.12:3).

---

**DEEPER STUDY # 1**

(5:10) **James**: there were two disciples named James. (1) The James mentioned in this passage, the brother of John, was the son of Zebedee. He along with Peter and his brother John formed an inner circle around the Lord (Mt.17:1; Mk.5:37; 9:2; 14:33). He is never mentioned apart from John. He was killed with the sword by Herod (Acts 12:2). (2) James the less was the son of Alphaeus (Mt.10:3). He was called *the less* because he was shorter of stature.

It should be noted that two other men named James are mentioned in the New Testament. (1) There is James the Lord's half-brother (Mt.13:55; Mk.6:3; Gal.1:19). He and the Lord's other brothers and sisters did not believe Jesus to be the Messiah until after Jesus' resurrection (Jn.7:5; Acts 1:14). James, however, became a great leader and pastor in the early church. He pastored the Jerusalem Church (Acts 12:17; 15:13; 21:18; Gal.1:19; 2:9, 12), and he wrote the Epistle of James. (2) There is also James who was the father of Judas (Lk.6:16; Acts 1:13, ASV).

---

**DEEPER STUDY # 2**

(5:10) **Apostle—Witnessing**: see DEEPER STUDY # 5—Mt.10:2. Cp. 2 Cor.5:19-20; Jn.20:21; Acts 1:8.

---

**8** (5:11) **Decision—Dedication—Forsaking All**: the seventh step to calling men is *watching for the decision to forsake all*. Note three things.
1. The men responded immediately.
2. The men left all: their businesses, their professions, and the biggest catch they had ever seen.
3. The men followed Jesus. He was the Lord who had spoken, and they were to be His disciples who obeyed and followed.

> "And he said to them all, If any man will come after me, let him deny himself, and take up his cross daily, and follow me" (Lk.9:23).
> "If any man come to me, and hate not his father, and mother, and wife, and children, and brethren, and sisters, yea, and his own life also, he cannot be my disciple" (Lk.14:26).
> "So likewise, whosoever he be of you that forsaketh not all that he hath, he cannot be my disciple" (Lk.14:33).
> "If any man serve me, let him follow me; and where I am, there shall also my servant be: if any man serve me, him will my Father honour" (Jn.12:26).

| | D. Jesus Cleanses the Untouchable, 5:12-16 (Mt.8:1-4; Mk.1:40-45) | departed from him. | b. The leper was cleansed |
|---|---|---|---|
| **1 Jesus was confronted by a desperate man, an untouchable**<br>a. He was full of leprosy[DS1]<br>b. He saw Jesus: Fell on his face & called Jesus Lord; he begged for cleansing<br>**2 Jesus cleansed the untouchable**<br>a. Jesus touched him & said, "I will" | 12 And it came to pass, when he was in a certain city, behold a man full of leprosy: who seeing Jesus fell on his face, and besought him, saying, Lord if thou wilt, thou canst make me clean.<br>13 And he put forth his hand, and touched him, saying, I will: be thou clean. And immediately the leprosy | 14 And he charged him to tell no man: but go, and show thyself to the priest, and offer for thy cleansing, according as Moses commanded, for a testimony unto them.<br>15 But so much the more went there a fame abroad of him: and great multitudes came together to hear, and to be healed by him of their infirmities.<br>16 And he withdrew himself into the wilderness, and prayed. | **3 Jesus charged the newly cleansed man**<br>a. To tell no man: Boast not; watch being prideful[DS2]<br>b. To rush to obey God<br><br>**4 Jesus made an impact**<br>a. His fame spread rapidly<br>b. The crowds thronged to hear Him & to be healed by Him<br><br>c. He withdrew into the wilderness to pray |

# DIVISION III

## THE SON OF MAN'S ANNOUNCED MISSION AND PUBLIC MINISTRY, 4:16-9:17

### D.   Jesus Cleanses the Untouchable, 5:12-16

(5:12-16) **Introduction—Untouchable, The**: some persons are treated by society as though they are untouchable. Some persons are so gripped and enslaved, so depraved and destitute, so different and derelict, so down and out, so helpless and hopeless that they become untouchable to most people. But not to Jesus. And that is the whole thrust of this event. Jesus will touch the untouchable and He will cleanse the untouchable.

1.   Jesus was confronted by a desperate man, an untouchable (v.12).
2.   Jesus cleansed the untouchable (v.13).
3.   Jesus charged the newly cleansed man (v.14).
4.   Jesus made an impact (v.15-16).

1   (5:12) **Jesus Christ, Seeking—Sin, Terrible—Spiritual Cleansing**: Jesus was confronted by a desperate man, an untouchable.

1.   The man was full of leprosy. The man was evidently full of sores and extremely disfigured (see DEEPER STUDY # 1, *Leprosy*—Lk.5:12).
2.   The man saw Jesus. He forgot all else...
   • forgot all the people surrounding Jesus.
   • forgot the shame of his condition.
   • forgot the embarrassment.
   • forgot that he was not to approach within six feet of anyone.

Nothing mattered but the *hope* he felt within, the possibility that Jesus would help him in his desperate condition. He rushed up to Jesus while people were scattering about, fearing the contagion of the disease. He fell upon his face and cried out, "Lord, if thou wilt, thou canst make me clean." Note several things. (See outline and notes—Mt.8:1-4; Mk.1:40-45 for additional discussion.)

   a.   The man's determination to seek Jesus' help. Nothing and no one was going to stop him, not even the fear and threats of people whom he would be frightening with the contagiousness of his disease.
   b.   The man's humility. He actually prostrated himself, falling upon his face before Christ.
   c.   The man's confession of Christ. He called Jesus "Lord."
   d.   The man's request was to be cleansed, not healed. He was asking for both spiritual and physical cleansing. He knew he was dirty and defiled both within and without.

> "The LORD is nigh unto them that are of a broken heart; and saveth such as be of a contrite spirit" (Ps.34:18).
> "The sacrifices of God are a broken spirit: a broken and a contrite heart, O God, thou wilt not despise" (Ps.51:17).
> "And rend your heart, and not your garments, and turn unto the LORD your God: for he is gracious and merciful, slow to anger, and of great kindness" (Joel 2:13).
> "But I am poor and needy; yet the Lord thinketh upon me: thou art my help and my deliverer; make no tarrying, O my God" (Ps.40:17).
> "Wash me thoroughly from mine iniquity, and cleanse me from my sin" (Ps.51:2).
> "Help us, O God of our salvation, for the glory of thy name: and deliver us, and purge away our sins, for thy name's sake" (Ps.79:9).
> "When Jesus heard it, he saith unto them, They that are whole have no need of the physician, but they that are sick: I came not to call the righteous, but sinners to repentance" (Mk.2:17).
> "For we have not an high priest which cannot be touched with the feeling of our infirmities; but was in all points tempted like as we are, yet without sin" (Heb.4:15).

---

**DEEPER STUDY # 1**

(5:12) **Leprosy**: leprosy was the most terrible disease in the day of Jesus, and it was greatly feared. It was disfiguring and sometimes fatal. In the Bible leprosy is a type of sin.

1. The leper was considered *utterly unclean*—physically and spiritually. He could not approach within six feet of any person, including family members. "His clothes shall be rent, and his head bare, and he shall put a covering upon his upper lip, and shall cry, Unclean, unclean" (Lev.13:45).

2. He was judged as *dead—the living dead*. He had to wear a black garment so he could be recognized as from among the *dead*.

3. He was banished as an *outcast, totally ostracized* from society—considered without hope of going to heaven. "All the days wherein the plague shall be in him he shall be *defiled*; he is *unclean*; he shall *dwell alone*; *without the camp* shall his habitation be" (Lev.13:46). He could not live within the walls of any city; his dwelling had to be outside the city gates.

4. He was thought to be *polluted, incurable* by any human means whatsoever. Leprosy could be cured by God and His power alone. (Note how Christ proves His Messiahship and deity by healing the leper.)

Imagine the anguish and heartbreak of the leper's being completely cut off from family and friends and society. Imagine the emotional and mental pain. There are other recorded instances of lepers' being healed (cp. Mt.10:8; 11:5; Mk.1:40; Lk.7:22; 17:12; and perhaps Mt.26:6; cp. Mk.14:3).

---

**2** (5:13) **Jesus Christ, Power—Salvation—Spiritual Cleansing**: Jesus cleansed the untouchable. Note several things.

1. Jesus was *moved with compassion*, deeply moved (Mk.1:41). The sight gripped Jesus' heart. The man's condition was wretched. Just imagine…

- his body full of sores
- his flesh eaten away
- his loneliness
- his alienation

- his emptiness
- his hopelessness
- his helplessness
- his desperation

2. Jesus reached out and touched the man, an unheard of act. The man was an untouchable, a man full of leprosy, the most feared and dreaded and contagious disease known to the world of that day. Yet Jesus condescended, lowered Himself to touch the man. No other man would. The man had been a leper for years, so many years that he was now full of leprosy, a very advanced stage. During all those years no one could help him. He had not been touched by a human hand for so many years, he probably could not remember the softness of a tender touch.

3. Jesus said, "I *will*—I will make you clean."

**Thought 1.** Jesus wills for the untouchable to be cleansed and fully restored, restored within his own heart and restored within society. Jesus wishes to touch every man who has become untouchable.

"But when he saw the multitudes, he was moved with compassion on them, because they fainted, and were scattered abroad, as sheep having no shepherd" (Mt.9:36).
"And Jesus went forth, and saw a great multitude, and was moved with compassion toward them, and he healed their sick" (Mt.14:14).
"Like as a father pitieth his children, so the LORD pitieth them that fear him" (Ps.103:13).
"In all their affliction he was afflicted, and the angel of his presence saved them: in his love and in his pity he redeemed them; and he bare them" (Is.63:9).

4. Jesus spoke the word of cleansing, "Be thou clean." Jesus saved the man spiritually, physically, and socially. The man was fully cleansed. But note how: he was cleansed by the *Word* of Jesus.

**Thought 1.** The Lord's Word is sufficient, able to save and heal unto the uttermost (Heb.7:25).

"How God anointed Jesus of Nazareth with the Holy Ghost and with power: who went about doing good, and healing all that were oppressed of the devil; for God was with him" (Acts 10:38).
"Wherefore he is able also to save them to the uttermost that come unto God by him, seeing he ever liveth to make intercession for them" (Heb.7:25).
"For all those things hath mine hand made, and all those things have been, saith the LORD: but to this man will I look, even to him that is poor and of a contrite spirit, and trembleth at my word" (Is.66:2).

**3** (5:14) **Warning—Believers, Duty**: Jesus charged the newly cleansed man to do two things (see note and DEEPER STUDY # 4—Mt.8:4; note—Mk.1:44 for additional discussion).

1. Jesus demanded: tell no man. The man had been saved from the depths and pit of defilement. Few ever go that deep and become so full of leprosy (sin). He had been saved from so much, and he was now full of joy and rejoicing, bubbling over with happiness. He wanted to run all about telling the world, but there was a danger in this, the danger…

⇒ of pride and boasting within himself.
⇒ of jealousy and envy's arising within others toward him.

2. Jesus demanded: rush and obey God. The man first needed to worship and offer thanks to God and to learn to obey God's Word before doing anything else (see DEEPER STUDY # 2, *Leprosy*—Lk.5:14).

"As newborn babes, desire the sincere milk of the word, that ye may grow thereby: if so be ye have tasted that the Lord is gracious" (1 Pt.2:2-3).

"Study to show thyself approved unto God, a workman that needeth not to be ashamed, rightly dividing the word of truth" (2 Tim.2:15).

"Then they that gladly received his word were baptized: and the same day there were added unto them [the church] about three thousand souls. And they continued stedfastly in the apostles' doctrine and fellowship, and in breaking of bread, and in prayers" (Acts 2:41-42).

---

**DEEPER STUDY # 2**

(5:14) **Leprosy:** in the unlikely event a leper was ever cured, there was a detailed list of laws and rituals he had to go through. These rituals gave the priests time to confirm the cure and led the leper to make a thanksgiving offering to God (Lev.14:1-32; cp. 13:38-59). Jesus was charging the man to make his offering to God and to receive the certificate that he was cleansed.

---

**4** (5:15-16) **Jesus Christ, Response—Prayer:** Jesus' impact was enormous. Multitudes thronged to hear Him and to be healed of their infirmities.

1.  Jesus had both the message of salvation and the power to heal infirmities, but it was "by Him" and Him alone that both came.

2.  Jesus knew the source of His message and power: God and prayer. Therefore, He often withdrew to get alone with God and to seek His face and commune with Him.

| | | |
|---|---|---|
| **1 An investigative committee visited Jesus**<br>a. They were representatives from everywhere<br>b. They were to investigate Jesus' claims<br>c. Jesus' power was set to face the opposition<br><br>**2 The approach necessary for forgiveness of sins**<br>a. Must seek help from others<br>b. Must believe in Jesus' power.<br>c. Must persist[DS1]<br><br><br><br><br><br><br>d. Must seek forgiveness | **E. Jesus Proves His Amazing Power to Forgive Sins, 5:17-26**<br>(Mt.9:1-8; Mk.2:1-12)<br><br>17 And it came to pass on a certain day, as he was teaching, that there were Pharisees and doctors of the law sitting by, which were come out of every town of Galilee, and Judaea, and Jerusalem: and the power of the Lord was present to heal them.<br>18 And, behold, men brought in a bed a man which was taken with a palsy: and they sought means to bring him in, and to lay him before him.<br>19 And when they could not find by what way they might bring him in because of the multitude, they went upon the housetop, and let him down through the tiling with his couch into the midst before Jesus.<br>20 And when he saw their faith, he said unto him, Man, thy sins are forgiven thee. | 21 And the scribes and the Pharisees began to reason, saying, Who is this which speaketh blasphemies? Who can forgive sins, but God alone?<br>22 But when Jesus perceived their thoughts, he answering said unto them, What reason ye in your hearts?<br>23 Whether is easier, to say, Thy sins be forgiven thee; or to say, Rise up and walk?<br>24 But that ye may know that the Son of man hath power upon earth to forgive sins, (he said unto the sick of the palsy,) I say unto thee, Arise, and take up thy couch, and go into thine house.<br>25 And immediately he rose up before them, and took up that whereon he lay, and departed to his own house, glorifying God.<br>26 And they were all amazed, and they glorified God, and were filled with fear, saying, We have seen strange things to day. | **3 The power necessary to forgive sins: The power of God alone**<br><br>**4 The proof that Jesus can forgive sins, that He is the Son of Man[DS2]**<br><br><br><br>a. His Word: It works<br>b. His claim: He is God, the Son of Man[DS3]<br><br><br><br><br>c. His power: He saves & heals<br>d. His impact<br> 1) Upon the man: The man glorified God<br> 2) Upon the crowd: They were amazed & glorified God & feared |

# DIVISION III

## THE SON OF MAN'S ANNOUNCED MISSION AND PUBLIC MINISTRY, 4:16-9:17

## E. Jesus Proves His Amazing Power to Forgive Sins, 5:17-26

(5:17-26) **Introduction**: this is a critical passage of Scripture. It deals with forgiveness of sins—the most important issue that ever confronts man. Can a man's sins be forgiven, truly forgiven? If so, is Jesus Christ the One who has the power to forgive sins?
1.	An investigative committee visited Jesus (v.17).
2.	The approach necessary for forgiveness (v.18-20).
3.	The power necessary to forgive sins: the power of God alone (v.21).
4.	The proof that Jesus can forgive sins, that He is the Son of Man (v.22-26).

**1** (5:17) **Religionists—Criticism—Wayside—Commitment, Lack of**: an investigative committee of religionists visited Jesus. Note several facts.
1.	The committee was comprised of representatives from all over the country. Every major area was represented.
2.	The Pharisees and Scribes were the religious leaders of Israel (see DEEPER STUDY # 1—Lk.6:2; DEEPER STUDY # 2,3—Acts 23:8).
3.	The committee had come to *sit by* (v.17), to investigate, to observe Jesus, not to participate in the services and ministry. They were "sitting by," not sitting at His feet and learning from Him.
4.	Jesus' power was set to face the opposition. The power of God was upon Him, and He continued right on ministering. He did not let those who just *sat by* and were *critical* affect His preaching or ministry. He was immovable in His message and call.

> **Thought 1.** Note three critical points.
> 1)	There are always those who just *sit by*, who are just *spectators*, never really listening or learning, never becoming involved.
> 2)	There are always those who are critical, who set themselves up as knowing best, who are censors and judges of what the preacher or teacher does. They listen and watch to make sure nothing is too different. If it is, they begin to criticize and judge.
> 3)	The preacher or teacher must continue on in his call and ministry. "To his own Master he standeth or falleth" (Ro.14:4).

**2** (5:18-20) **Forgiveness—Jesus Christ, Seeking—Faith—Persistence**: the approach necessary for forgiveness was clearly demonstrated. These men took four steps in seeking forgiveness and healing from Jesus. The same four steps are necessary for anyone to receive forgiveness of sin.

1.    They *sought help*. The man had sought the help of his friends, and they were all seeking the help of Jesus. The man was unable to help himself, to secure forgiveness and wholeness by himself. He had to have help, the help of Jesus and of friends. The same was true of all the friends of the man. They were unable to provide forgiveness and wholeness to the sick man. They, too, knew that they needed the help of Jesus and of one another.

**Thought 1.** It is always necessary to seek Jesus' help. And it is often necessary to seek the help of friends as well.

2.    They *believed* and had confidence in Jesus' power to forgive sins and to heal. They believed that, if they came, Jesus had the power to help and that He loved and cared enough to help. Therefore, they came to Jesus. And note the inconvenience and difficulty they faced in coming. The man was bedridden. They would have to pick up his bed and carry it through the streets. Also, the crowds would be huge, perhaps making it impossible to get the bed through the throng of people. What belief! What desperation! The very kind of desperation and belief necessary to secure forgiveness and healing.

3.    They *persisted* despite enormous difficulty. Just as they had thought, the crowds were huge, much too large to get through to Jesus. But they did not give up. They went around to the side or back of the house and climbed up to the roof with the bed of the man. They removed some of the roof and used ropes to lower the man's bed below, right before the feet of Jesus. Of course sitting there, Jesus observed the whole scene, as surprised as everyone else that men would be so bold and persistent. But as with any of us, the spirit of their bold persistence and the reason for such a spirit made all the difference in the world. They were desperate; their need was great and they were helpless without Jesus' help. Such a spirit touched the Lord's heart and still touches His heart today.

4.    They *sought forgiveness*. The man was definitely seeking forgiveness of sins as well as healing of body. The whole scene points to this fact. The man was paralyzed. There was the possibility that he had been injured or become diseased because of some foolish sin in the past. It was also the common belief of that day that suffering was due to sin. The man's mind was upon his sin as the *cause* of his problem; therefore, he wanted Jesus to forgive his sin as well as heal him.

Note three things.

1.    Jesus saw "their faith," the faith of the friends as well as of the sick man. The faith of the friends had a large part in the man's sins being forgiven. What a lesson to us, for our families and friends!

> **"We then that are strong ought to bear the infirmities of the weak, and not to please ourselves" (Ro.15:1).**
> **"Bear ye one another's burdens, and so fulfil the law of Christ" (Gal.6:2).**
> **"And let us not be weary in well doing: for in due season we shall reap, if we faint not" (Gal.6:9).**
> **"I was eyes to the blind, and feet was I to the lame. I was a father to the poor: and the cause which I knew not I search out" (Job 29:15-16).**
> **"She stretcheth out her hand to the poor; yea, she reacheth forth her hands to the needy" (Pr.31:20).**
> **"But a certain Samaritan, as he journeyed, came where he was: and when he saw him, he had compassion on him, and went to him, and bound up his wounds, pouring in oil and wine, and set him on his own beast, and brought him to an inn, and took care of him" (Lk.10:33-34)**

2.    The faith Jesus saw was a faith that believed and persisted against all kinds of obstacles, a faith that really believed and persisted. This is crucial to remember in seeking forgiveness.

> **"And I say unto you, Ask, and it shall be given you; seek, and ye shall find; knock, and it shall be opened unto you. For every one that asketh receiveth; and he that seeketh findeth; and to him that knocketh it shall be opened" (Lk.11:9-10).**
> **"But without faith it is impossible to please him: for he that cometh to God must believe that he is, and that he is a rewarder of them that diligently seek him" (Heb.11:6).**
> **"But if from thence thou shalt seek the LORD thy God, thou shalt find him, if thou seek him with all thy heart and with all thy soul" (Dt.4:29).**
> **"Many are the afflictions of the righteous: but the LORD delivereth him out of them all. He keepeth all his bones: not one of them is broken" (Ps.34:19-20).**
> **"The LORD redeemeth the soul of his servants: and none of them that trust in him shall be desolate" (Ps.34:22).**
> **"Commit thy way unto the LORD; trust also in him; and he shall bring it to pass" (Ps.37:5).**
> **"Oh how great is thy goodness, which thou hast laid up for them that fear thee; which thou hast wrought for them that trust in thee before the sons of men!" (Ps.31:19).**
> **"Trust ye in the LORD for ever: for in the LORD JEHOVAH is everlasting strength" (Is.26:4).**
> **"And ye shall seek me, and find me, when ye shall search for me with all your heart" (Jer.29:13).**

3.    Jesus Himself forgave the man's sins. This is a critical fact to note. Jesus did not say, "Man, God forgives your sins." He said, "Man, I forgive your sins."

> **"Him hath God exalted with his right hand to be a Prince and a Saviour, for to give repentance to Israel, and forgiveness of sins" (Acts 5:31).**

"Be it known unto you therefore, men and brethren, that through this man is preached unto you the forgiveness of sins" (Acts 13:38).

"In whom we have redemption through his blood, the forgiveness of sins, according to the riches of his grace" (Eph.1:7).

---

**DEEPER STUDY # 1**

(5:19) **House**: many houses of Jesus' day had an outside stairway that climbed up to a second floor. The roof was easily reached from this stairway. The roof was flat and made of tile-like rocks matted together with a straw and clay-like substance. The roofs were sturdy enough for people to sit upon and carry on conversations and other activities (see note—Mt.24:17). These men dug and scooped out an opening through the roof. They were so sure of Jesus' power to help, nothing was going to prevent them from getting to Jesus—an unstoppable faith.

---

**3** (5:21) **Forgiveness—Belief**: the power necessary to forgive sins was clearly stated to be found in God alone. Only God has the power to truly forgive sins. The religionists knew this; but they failed to see that Jesus Christ was One with God, the Son of God Himself—that He was One with God in being and nature, in exaltation and dominion, in love and compassion, in authority and power—all of which necessitated His coming to earth as the Incarnate God in human flesh (see notes—Jn.1:1-2; note and DEEPER STUDY # 1—1:14; note—Ph.2:7). They were seen standing before Jesus thinking and reasoning, but not speaking aloud. In their minds they were saying He was guilty of blasphemy, but at this point they did not charge Him publicly.

**Thought 1.** This is the very point over which so many religionists stumble: that Jesus Christ is God incarnate in human flesh, the Son of God who has come to save the world.

"For God so loved the world, that he gave his only begotten Son, that whosoever believeth in him should not perish, but have everlasting life" (Jn.3:16).

"Say ye of him, whom the Father hath sanctified, and sent into the world, Thou blasphemest; because I said, I am the Son of God?" (Jn.10:36).

**4** (5:22-26) **Jesus Christ, Deity; Power; Impact—Forgiveness**: the proof that Jesus can forgive sins and is the Son of Man was clearly demonstrated. Jesus knew the thoughts of the religionists. He read their minds, giving evidence of His deity.

**Thought 1.** Jesus knows our thoughts, just what we are thinking, whether thoughts…
- of unbelief or belief
- of impurity or purity
- of selfishness or unselfishness
- of deception or truth
- of worldliness or godliness
- of wrong or right

"I know that thou canst do every thing, and that no thought can be withholden from thee" (Job 42:2).

Note how Jesus set out to prove His deity, His right and power to forgive sins.

1. His Word and the fact that it works proves His deity. He posed a test of God's power. He suggested that He merely *speak the Word*, "Rise up and walk." *If His Word worked to heal the man, then His Word to forgive sins must work also.*

2. His claim proved His deity. He is God, the Son of Man (see DEEPER STUDY # 3—Mt.8:20). He was not afraid to put Himself to the test. He wanted all men to know and believe. Therefore, that "ye may know that [I] the Son of Man hath power upon earth to forgive sins," I purpose to prove My power in the lives of those who seek forgiveness.

"Jesus heard that they had cast him out; and when he had found him, he said unto him, Dost thou believe on the Son of God? He answered and said, Who is he, Lord, that I might believe on him? And Jesus said unto him, Thou hast both seen him, and it is he that talketh with thee" (Jn.9:35-37).

"Jesus said unto her, I am the resurrection, and the life: he that believeth in me, though he were dead, yet shall he live: and whosoever liveth and believeth in me shall never die. Believest thou this? She saith unto him, Yea, Lord: I believe that thou art the Christ, the Son of God, which should come into the world" (Jn.11:25-27).

"And I saw, and bare record that this is the Son of God" (Jn.1:34).

3. His power proved His deity. Dramatically, Jesus spoke the Word, and the man arose. He was healed immediately. How? By the Word of the Lord. *God's Word* proved itself. When Jesus spoke the *Word of healing*, the man was healed; when Jesus spoke the *Word of forgiveness*, the man was forgiven.

"And Jesus came and spake unto them, saying, All power is given unto me in heaven and in earth" (Mt.28:18).

"How God anointed Jesus of Nazareth with the Holy Ghost and with power: who went about doing good, and healing all that were oppressed of the devil; for God was with him" (Acts 10:38).

4.    His impact proved His deity. The man glorified God. The people were amazed, and they glorified God and were stricken with fear (awe and reverence).

**Thought 1.** The proofs of Jesus' deity should be studied closely by all religionists and skeptics.

**Thought 2.** Note four critical points.
1)    Jesus is still *willing* to speak the Word of forgiveness and healing.
2)    Jesus is the Son of Man and *purposes* to forgive the sins of all who are willing (see DEEPER STUDY # 3—Mt.8:20).
3)    Jesus has both the power and will to speak the Word of forgiveness and healing to those who *seek* it.
4)    The impact of Jesus' life upon so many is evidence of His deity. The fact that some are genuinely glorifying God and serving Him in awe and reverence is *strong evidence* that Jesus has the power to forgive sins.

---

**DEEPER STUDY # 2**
(5:23) **Sins—Forgiven**: the common belief of that day was that suffering was due to sin. Jesus' healing of the man was the proof that the man's sins were truly forgiven and that He had the power to forgive sins. The religionists could not logically deny this (see DEEPER STUDY # 4—Mt.26:28).

---

**DEEPER STUDY # 3**
(5:24) **Son of Man**: see DEEPER STUDY # 3—Mt.8:20.

---

| | F. Jesus Reveals His Great Mission: The Greatest Mission of All, 5:27-39 (Mt.9:9-17; Mk.2:13-22) | ers, and likewise the disciples of the Pharisees; but thine eat and drink? | tioned Jesus' behavior |
|---|---|---|---|
| **1 The mission of calling outcasts**[DS1]<br>a. He went forth<br>b. He saw<br>c. He called<br>d. The outcast left all & followed Jesus<br>e. The outcast reached his friends | 27 And after these things he went forth, and saw a publican, named Levi, sitting at the receipt of custom: and he said unto him, Follow me.<br>28 And he left all, rose up, and followed him.<br>29 And Levi made him a great feast in his own house: and there was a great company of publicans and of others that sat down with them. | 34 And he said unto them, Can ye make the children of the bridechamber fast, while the bridegroom is with them?<br>35 But the days will come, when the bridegroom shall be taken away from them, and then shall they fast in those days. | b. Jesus' answer: His presence brings joy & vitality to life<br><br>**4 The mission of dying** |
| **2 The mission of calling sinners to repentance**<br>a. The religionists questioned Jesus' associations<br>b. Jesus' answer<br>  1) He illustrated His mission<br>  2) He stated His mission<br>**3 The mission of bringing real joy**<br>a. The religionists ques- | 30 But their scribes and Pharisees murmured against his disciples, saying, Why do ye eat and drink with publicans and sinners?<br>31 And Jesus answering said unto them, They that are whole need not a physician; but they that are sick.<br>32 I came not to call the righteous, but sinners to repentance.<br>33 And they said unto him, Why do the disciples of John fast often, and make pray- | 36 And he spake also a parable unto them; No man putteth a piece of a new garment upon an old; if otherwise, then both the new maketh a rent, and the piece that was taken out of the new agreeth not with the old.<br>37 And no man putteth new wine into old bottles; else the new wine will burst the bottles, and be spilled, and the bottles shall perish.<br>38 But new wine must be put into new bottles; and both are preserved.<br>39 No man also having drunk old wine straightway desireth new: for he saith, The old is better. | **5 The mission of launching a new life & spiritual movement**<br>a. Illust. 1: Not patching the old, but starting a new<br><br>b. Illust. 2: Not putting His teaching (wine) in old bottles, but in a new bottle<br><br>c. Illust. 3: The new is difficult to accept—it takes time |

# DIVISION III

## THE SON OF MAN'S ANNOUNCED MISSION AND PUBLIC MINISTRY, 4:16-9:17

**F.** **Jesus Reveals His Great Mission: The Greatest Mission of All, 5:27-39**

**(5:27-39) Introduction**: the greatest life ever lived on earth was the life of Jesus Christ. Therefore no mission can ever compare with the mission which He was sent to do. The great mission of Christ was…
- a quickening mission: to make people alive to God.
- an eternal mission: to give people life forever.
- a purposeful mission: to cause people to commit their lives to God unconditionally.

Luke's very purpose in this passage is to reveal the great mission of Christ. With the skillful mind of a man who knew the Lord intimately, he weaves several events together to spell out the great mission of the Lord.
1. The mission of calling outcasts (v.27-29).
2. The mission of calling sinners to repentance (v.30-32).
3. The mission of bringing real joy (v.33-34).
4. The mission of dying (v.35).
5. The mission of launching a new life and spiritual movement (v.36-39).

1 **(5:27-29) Jesus Christ, Mission—Ministers**: there was the mission of calling outcasts, those who are rejected by society. (See notes—Mt.9:9; note and DEEPER STUDY # 1—Mk.2:14 for additional discussion.)
    1. Jesus "went forth." There is deliberate purpose in this statement. Jesus got up and left either the house (Lk.5:19) or the city. He went forth for the specific purpose of seeking the outcast (cp. Lk.19:10; Jn.20:21).
    2. Jesus "saw a publican [tax collector] named Levi [Matthew]." He was an outcast, the most hated of men among the public (see DEEPER STUDY # 1, *Tax Collector*—Lk.5:27). Yet when Jesus saw him, He "saw a man named Levi [Matthew]," a sinner, a man who was hurting within, a man who needed a cause. (See note—Mt.9:9 for detailed discussion.)
    3. Jesus called the outcast. Very simply yet forcibly Jesus said , "Follow me." Note two facts.
      a. Note the great *love* and *compassion* of Jesus for the outcast. The man was despised. By associating with such an outcast, Jesus was exposing Himself to criticism and rejection by the *upper class*, the acceptable and social of society.
      b. Note the great humility of Christ. He stooped down to reach an outcast; but remember, He had come to earth to save sinners, those who were outcasts from heaven.

**Thought 1.** Jesus' call is issued to all men, for all men are outcasts, the outcasts of heaven. However, there is a condition to becoming an acceptable person to God. A person must humble himself before Jesus, just as Jesus humbled Himself before us.

"And said, Verily I say unto you, Except ye be converted, and become as little children, ye shall not enter into the kingdom of heaven" (Mt.18:3).

"For godly sorrow worketh repentance to salvation not to be repented of: but the sorrow of the world worketh death" (2 Cor.7:10).

"He humbled Himself, and became obedient unto death, even the death of the cross" (Ph.2:8. Cp. Ph.2:6-9.)

"The LORD is nigh unto them that are of a broken heart; and saveth such as be of a contrite spirit" (Ps.34:18).

"Therefore also now, saith the LORD, turn ye even to me with all your heart, and with fasting, and with weeping and with mourning" (Joel 2:12).

**Thought 2.** The person who is truly an outcast of society, who is rejected and despised by people, can be saved and delivered from emptiness and loneliness. Jesus Christ will save him. In fact, He longs to save and deliver the outcast, the empty and lonely of the earth.

"Come unto me, all ye that labour and are heavy laden, and I will give you rest. Take my yoke upon you, and learn of me; for I am meek and lowly in heart: and ye shall find rest unto your souls. For my yoke is easy, and my burden is light" (Mt.11:28-30).

"Ho, every one that thirsteth, come ye to the waters, and he that hath no money; come ye, buy, and eat; yea, come, buy wine and milk without money and without price" (Is.55:1).

"Come now, and let us reason together, saith the LORD: though your sins be as scarlet, they shall be as white as snow; though they be red like crimson, they shall be as wool" (Is.1:18).

"Say unto them, As I live, saith the Lord GOD, I have no pleasure in the death of the wicked; but that the wicked turn from his way and live: turn ye, turn ye from your evil ways; for why will ye die?" (Ezk.33:11).

"Come, and let us return unto the LORD: for he hath torn, and he will heal us; he hath smitten, and he will bind us up" (Hos.6:1).

4. The outcast left all and followed Jesus. Matthew was very wealthy. This is the emphasis of Lukes' words, "he left all." (Note also v.29 where Matthew made a "great feast" in his own house. The house itself must have been very large to hold so many people.)

This outcast "left all," responding to Jesus immediately. How could a man such as Matthew give up so much to follow Jesus? Because money cannot buy happiness, peace, security, completeness, satisfaction, fulfillment, confidence, or assurance. Money can only buy things. Matthew had, as so many do, plenty of things: houses, land, clothes, food, furnishings. But he was *empty and restless* in heart, *incomplete and insecure* in spirit, *unfulfilled and dissatisfied* in life. When he confronted Jesus, he saw the possibility that Jesus could meet all his needs, really meet them.

**Thought 1.** It is hard for rich men to enter heaven, for they are attached to this material world. Matthew was one of the few who was willing to give up all in order to follow Jesus. Thus, the Kingdom of Heaven shall be his.

"Then said Jesus unto his disciples, Verily I say unto you, That a rich man shall hardly enter into the kingdom of heaven. And again I say unto you, It is easier for a camel to go through the eye of a needle, than for a rich man to enter into the kingdom of God. When his disciples heard it, they were exceedingly amazed, saying, Who then can be saved? But Jesus beheld them, and said unto them, With men this is impossible; but with God all things are possible" (Mt.19:23-26; cp. Mt.19:16-26).

"So likewise, whosoever he be of you that forsaketh not all that he hath, he cannot be my disciple" (Lk.14:33).

"For whosoever will save his life shall lose it; but whosoever shall lose his life for my sake and the gospel's, the same shall save it. For what shall it profit a man, if he shall gain the whole world, and lose his own soul?" (Mk.8:35-36).

5. The outcast reached his friends. This is a beautiful picture of the kind of witness every believer should be. Matthew's heart was filled immediately with the genuine joy for which he had ached. There was so much difference, so much love, joy, and peace; he just could not contain it. It burst forth. He had to tell his friends, but it would take so long to visit each one separately; he had to figure out a way to reach them sooner. How could he do it quicker? Having a feast came to his mind. So he held a feast for his friends to meet Jesus.

Matthew was excited about his faith. He knew the depth of emptiness from which he had come, and he was ever so appreciative and thankful. (Remember: Matthew, the outcast, was the one who wrote the *Gospel of Matthew*.) He wanted his friends to meet Jesus personally and to come to know the salvation given by Christ.

"Then said Jesus to them again, Peace be unto you: as my Father hath sent me, even so send I you" (Jn.20:21).

"To wit, that God was in Christ, reconciling the world unto himself, not imputing their trespasses unto them; and hath committed unto us the word of reconciliation. Now then we are ambassadors for Christ, as though God did beseech you by us: we pray you in Christ's stead, be ye reconciled to God" (2 Cor.5:19-20).

"And the things that thou hast heard of me among many witnesses, the same commit thou to faithful men, who shall be able to teach others also" (2 Tim.2:2).

---

**DEEPER STUDY # 1**

(5:27) **Tax Collector**: a tax collector was bitterly hated by the people. There were three reasons.

1. Tax collectors served the Roman conquerors. Most tax collectors were Jews, but in the people's eyes they had denied their Jewish heritage and betrayed their country. They were thus ostracized, completely cut off from Jewish society and excommunicated from Jewish religion and privileges.

2. They were cheats, dishonest and unjust men. Most tax collectors were extremely wealthy. The Roman government compensated tax collectors by allowing them to collect more than the percentage required for taxes. Tax collectors greedily abused their right, adding whatever percent they wished and felt could be collected (see DEEPER STUDY # 1—Ro.13:6). They took bribes from the wealthy who wished to avoid taxes, fleeced the average citizen, and swindled the government when they could.

3. They were assuming rights that belonged only to God. God alone was King in the eyes of the Jews. This was a strong conviction of the Jews; therefore, God and the ruler appointed by God were considered to be the head of Jewish government. God was their God, and they were His people. Taxes were to be paid only to Him and His government, which was centered only in the temple of Judaism. To pay taxes to earthly rulers was an abuse and a denial of God's rights. Therefore, tax collectors were excommunicated from Jewish religion and privileges. They were accursed, anathema.

---

2 (5:30-32) **Jesus Christ, Mission**: there was the mission of calling sinners to repentance. Note two things.

1. The religionists questioned Jesus' association with the outcasts and sinners. They criticized and judged Him.
   a. He was associating with those who were not socially acceptable. Sinners and outcasts had rejected society. They had forsaken the ways of acceptability. Why would Jesus associate with such outcasts and sinners who so clearly rebelled against society and its approved behavior?
   b. He was associating with those who were religiously and ceremonially unclean. Many, if not all, had not sought religious and ceremonial cleansing. They were guilty of breaking every law of religion and decency. Their behavior and uncleanness were bound to rub off, contaminating and misleading anyone associating with them, including Jesus.
2. Jesus answered their question by illustrating and stating His mission.
   a. The sick (sinners) are the ones who need a physician (Him, the Savior). Note: a man may be sick...
      • and not know it; therefore his sickness is never cured.
      • and not call the physician; therefore, his sickness is never cured.
   b. The mission of Jesus was not to call the righteous but sinners to repentance.

**Thought 1.** The righteous either do not know or do not accept the fact that they need repentance. Sinners do know, but they may not accept the depth of their need nor turn from their sin in order to be saved by Jesus.

"For the Son of man is come to seek and to save that which was lost" (Lk.19:10).

"For God sent not his Son into the world to condemn the world; but that the world through him might be saved" (Jn.3:17).

"The thief cometh not, but for to steal, and to kill, and to destroy: I am come that they might have life, and that they might have it more abundantly" (Jn.10:10).

"And if any man hear my words, and believe not, I judge him not: for I came not to judge the world, but to save the world" (Jn.12:47).

"This is a faithful saying, and worthy of all acceptation, that Christ Jesus came into the world to save sinners; of whom I am chief" (1 Tim.1:15).

"Behold, I stand at the door, and knock: if any man hear my voice, and open the door, I will come in to him, and will sup with him, and he with me" (Rev.3:20).

3 (5:33-34) **Jesus Christ, Mission—Believer, Joy; Life—Fasting**: there was the mission of bringing real joy. The religionists questioned Jesus' loose behavior and the fact that He was teaching His disciples the same loose behavior. What is meant by *loose behavior*? Jesus' disciples were eating and drinking, actually feasting when they should have been fasting. By law religious Jews fasted twice a week, every Monday and Thursday (Lk.18:12). Jesus was not only religious, He was a religious teacher, and even more, He was claiming to be the Messiah Himself. Why was He not fasting? (See note—Mk.2:18-22 for detailed discussion.) Note something important. The religionists fasted as a ritual; their days for fasting were already determined. The ritual or the custom and tradition determined their fast. Their need for God, for a very special sense of God's presence, had nothing to do with fasting. Fasting was purely a matter of ritual and custom.

Jesus' answer was revealing and of utmost importance. He claimed that He was the *Bridegroom*, and as long as He was with them, there was no need for them to fast. Now note what Jesus was saying. (See note—Mt.9:15; Mk.2:19.)

1. His presence brought joy and vitality to life, not ritual and ceremonial demands.
2. There was no need to be fasting for a special sense of God's presence if the Bridegroom, the Son of God, was already present.

3.    His mission was that of a Bridegroom, to bring joy and vitality to life.

> "These things have I spoken unto you, that my joy might remain in you, and that your joy might be full" (Jn.15:11).
> "Hitherto have ye asked nothing in my name: ask, and ye shall receive, that your joy may be full" (Jn.16:24).
> "For the kingdom of God is not meat and drink; but righteousness, and peace, and joy in the Holy Ghost" (Ro.14:17).
> "As sorrowful, yet alway rejoicing; as poor, yet making many rich; as having nothing, and yet possessing all things" (2 Cor.6:10).
> "Rejoice in the Lord alway: and again I say, Rejoice" (Ph.4:4).
> "Whom having not seen, ye love; in whom, though now ye see him not, yet believing, ye rejoice with joy unspeakable and full of glory" (1 Pt.1:8).
> "Thou wilt show me the path of life: in thy presence is fulness of joy; at thy right hand there are pleasures for evermore" (Ps.16:11).
> "In thy name shall they rejoice all the day: and in thy righteousness shall they be exalted" (Ps.89:16).
> "Therefore with joy shall ye draw water out of the wells of salvation" (Is.12:3).
> "I will greatly rejoice in the LORD, my soul shall be joyful in my God; for he hath clothed me with the garments of salvation, he hath covered me with the robe of righteousness, as a bridegroom decketh himself with ornaments, and as a bride adorneth herself with her jewels" (Is.61:10).

**4**    (5:35) **Jesus Christ, Mission; Death**: there was the mission of dying. Note two points.
        Jesus said, "the Bridegroom shall be taken away." He meant that He was appointed to die. Dying upon the cross was His primary mission for coming to earth. Note three significant points.
1.    His death enables His Spirit to be present with all believers around the world (Jn.14:16-18, 26; 15:26; 16:7, 13).
2.    His death brings sorrow to the heart of any who see it and understand it. However, His death brings joy soon after, for there is the knowledge that Jesus lives forever (Jn.16:16-22; Heb.7:25; cp. Eph.1:19-23).
3.    His death and its cleansing power can be *forgotten* (2 Pt.1:9). The Lord's presence can fade from our consciousness. We can become so busy and preoccupied with the affairs of the world that we lose our sensitivity to the Lord's presence. At such times we need to get alone with God. Our concern for God's presence should be so great that neither food nor sleep matter. Nothing matters except regaining the consciousness of God's presence. We need to fast and pray, and pray and fast.

**Thought 1.** His death caused the first disciples to fast; it ought to cause us to fast...
•    when we first learn of His death and what it really means.

> "Thus it is written, and thus it behoved Christ to suffer, and to rise from the dead the third day" (Lk.24:46).
> "For God so loved the world, that he gave his only begotten Son, that whosoever believeth in him should not perish, but have everlasting life" (Jn.3:16).
> "But God commendeth his love toward us, in that, while we were yet sinners, Christ died for us" (Ro.5:8).
> "Who his own self bare our sins in his own body on the tree, that we, being dead to sins, should live unto righteousness: by whose stripes ye were healed" (1 Pt.2:24).
> "For Christ also hath once suffered for sins, the just for the unjust, that he might bring us to God, being put death in the flesh, but quickened by the Spirit" (1 Pt.3:18).

•    when we are reminded rather forcibly that He died for us. Such times should be heart-rending times, precious times of prayer and fasting.
•    when we allow His presence to slip out of our mind for some length of time. We need to get alone and meditate upon His death, allowing nothing to interfere, including food.

> "Watch and pray, that ye enter not into temptation: the spirit indeed is willing, but the flesh is weak" (Mt.26:41).
> "Seek the LORD and his strength, seek his face continually" (1 Chron.16:11).
> "And he spake a parable unto them to this end, that men ought always to pray, and not to faint" (Lk.18:1).
> "He shall call upon me, and I will answer him: I will be with him in trouble; I will deliver him, and honour him" (Ps.91:15).
> "Likewise the Spirit also helpeth our infirmities: for we know not what we should pray for as we ought: but the Spirit itself maketh intercession for us with groanings which cannot be uttered. And he that searcheth the hearts knoweth what is the mind of the Spirit, because he maketh intercession for the saints according to the will of God" (Ro.8:26-27).
> "The hand of our God is upon all them for good that seek him; but his power and his wrath is against all them that forsake him. So we fasted and besought our God for this: and he was entreated of us" (Ezra 8:22-23).

"If my people, which are called by my name, shall humble themselves, and pray, and seek my face, and turn from their wicked ways; then will I hear from heaven, and will forgive their sin, and will heal their land" (2 Chron.7:14).

**5** (5:36-39) **Jesus Christ, Mission**: there was the mission of a new life and a new spiritual movement. Jesus gave three points to illustrate what He meant.

Illustration 1: a piece of new cloth is not used to patch an old garment, for it fails to match the old garment. Jesus was saying that He was not patching up the old life, but starting a new life and a new movement (cp. v.36. See notes—Mt.9:16; Mk.2:21 for discussion.)

Illustration 2: the new wine is not put into old bottles, for the new wine would burst the old bottles. Jesus was saying that He was not putting His teaching into the old life and movement, but He was launching a new life and movement for God (cp. v.37. See notes—Mk.2:22.)

Illustration 3: the new wine is difficult to accept if one has been drinking old wine. Jesus was saying that His new life and spiritual movement would be difficult to accept; it would take time. Men were slow to give up the old, for they were too content with it (their religious ways and self-righteousness). Therefore, men would often refuse to even consider the new life and movement.

"Therefore if any man be in Christ, he is a new creature: old things are passed away; behold, all things are become new" (2 Cor.5:17).

"That ye put off concerning the former conversation the old man, which is corrupt according to the deceitful lusts; and be renewed in the spirit of your mind" (Eph.4:22-23).

"And have put on the new man, which is renewed in knowledge after the image of him that created him" (Col.3:10).

"Not by works of righteousness which we have done, but according to his mercy he saved us, by the washing of regeneration, and renewing of the Holy Ghost" (Tit.3:5).

"Being born again, not of corruptible seed, but of incorruptible, by the word of God, which liveth and abideth for ever" (1 Pt.1:23).

"Whosoever believeth that Jesus is the Christ is born of God: and every one that loveth him that begat loveth him also that is begotten of him" (1 Jn.5:1).

"Jesus answered and said unto him, Verily, verily, I say unto thee, Except a man be born again, he cannot see the kingdom of God" (Jn.3:3).

| | | |
|---|---|---|
| | **CHAPTER 6** | bath. |
| | | 6 And it came to pass also |
| | **G. Jesus Teaches that Need** | on another sabbath, that he |
| | **Supersedes Religion,** | entered into the synagogue |
| | **6:1-11** | and taught: and there was a |
| | (Mt.12:1-13; Mk. 2:23-28; | man whose right hand was |
| | 3:1-6) | withered. |
| **1 The Sabbath** | | 7 And the scribes and Phari- |
| **2 Fact 1: Meeting man's real** | And it came to pass on the | sees watched him, whether |
| **needs is more important** | second sabbath after the first, | he would heal on the |
| **than religion & ritual** | that he went through the corn | sabbath day; that they might |
| a. The need: The disci- | fields; and his disciples | find an accusation against |
| ples were hungry, so | plucked the ears of corn, and | him. |
| they plucked corn | did eat, rubbing them in their | 8 But he knew their |
| b. The opposition: The | hands. | thoughts, and said to the man |
| religionists became | 2 And certain of the Phari- | which had the withered hand, |
| upset because a religi- | sees said unto them, Why do | Rise up, and stand forth in |
| ous rule was broken[DS1] | ye that which is not lawful to | the midst. And he arose and |
| c. The answer of Jesus: | do on the sabbath days? | stood forth. |
| An illustration | 3 And Jesus answering them | 9 Then said Jesus unto |
| | said, Have ye not read so | them, I will ask you one |
| 1) David hungered | much as this, what David did, | thing; Is it lawful on the sab- |
| | when himself was an hun- | bath days to do good, or to |
| | gred, and they which were | do evil? to save life, or to |
| 2) David overrode the | with him; | destroy it? |
| religious rules to | 4 How he went into the | 10 And looking round about |
| meet a need[DS2] | house of God, and did take | upon them all, he said unto |
| | and eat the showbread, and | the man, Stretch forth thy |
| | gave also to them that were | hand. And he did so: and his |
| | with him; which it is not law- | hand was restored whole as |
| | ful to eat but for the priests | the other. |
| d. The point: The Son of | alone? | 11 And they were filled with |
| Man[DS3] is as great as | 5 And he said unto them, | madness; and communed one |
| David—He is the Lord | That the Son of man | with another what they might |
| | is Lord also of the sab- | do to Jesus. |

| |
|---|
| of the Sabbath |
| **3 Fact 2: Doing good & sav-** |
| **ing life are more impor-** |
| **tant than religion & ritual** |
| a. The need: A man's |
| right hand shriveled |
| |
| b. The opposition by the |
| religionists[DS4] |
| c. The question & challenge |
| of Jesus |
| |
| 1) He perceived their |
| thoughts |
| |
| |
| |
| 2) He challenged them |
| to think honestly |
| |
| |
| |
| |
| 3) He healed the man— |
| doing good |
| d. The point: To do good |
| and to save life super- |
| sedes rituals |
| |
| e. The religionists' |
| insane anger |

# DIVISION III

## THE SON OF MAN'S ANNOUNCED MISSION
### AND PUBLIC MINISTRY, 4:16-9:17

## G. Jesus Teaches That Need Supersedes Religion, 6:1-11

(6:1-11) **Introduction**: men have the tendency to institutionalize religion, to make it full of form and ritual, rules and regulations, ceremonies and services. Men, religionists and laymen alike, are too often guilty of "having a *form* of godliness, but denying the power thereof" (2 Tim.3:5). This is the very point Jesus is making in this passage. The power of godliness exists to meet the needs of man. Yet too often, religion is placed before man and his needs. Maintaining the religious organization and form, keeping things the way they have always been, is considered more important than meeting the needs of man.

1. The Sabbath (v.1).
2. Fact 1: meeting man's real needs is more important than religion and ritual (v.1-5).
3. Fact 2: doing good and saving life are more important than religion and ritual (v.6-11).

**1** (6:1) **Sabbath**: note that both of these events took place on the Sabbath (v.1, 6). This is the very thrust of Luke: to show that religion and ritual must never be put before the needs of man. (See DEEPER STUDY # 1, *Sabbath*—Mt.12:1 for discussion.)

**2** (6:1-5) **Necessities—Religion—Rituals—Jesus Christ, Deity**: first, *real needs* are more important than religion and rituals. The disciples had a real need: they were extremely hungry. They had not eaten since the day before (Mt.12:1; Mk.2:23). As they were passing by a corn field, they began to pluck and eat some corn. They were not stealing the corn, for a hungry traveller was permitted by law to eat a few ears of corn when passing by a field (Dt.23:25). The crime was that the disciples *worked* by plucking the ears of corn *on the Sabbath day*.

This was a serious offense to the orthodox Jew. Just how serious can be seen in the strict demands governing the Sabbath. Law after law was written to govern all activity on the Sabbath, laws which prohibited a person from contemplating any kind of work or activity. A good example of the legal restriction and the people's loyalty to it is seen in the women who witnessed Jesus' crucifixion. They would not even walk to His tomb to prepare the body for burial until the Sabbath was over (Mk.16:1f; Mt.28:1f).

It was a serious matter to break the Sabbath law. A person was condemned, and if the offence were serious enough, the person was to die.

This may seem harsh to some, but when dealing with the Jewish nation, one must remember that it was their religion that held them together as a nation through centuries and centuries of exile. Their religion (in particular their beliefs about

God's call to their nation), the temple, and the Sabbath became the *binding force* that kept Jews together and maintained their distinctiveness as a people. It protected them from alien beliefs and from being swallowed up by other people through intermarriage. No matter where they were, they met and associated together and held on to their beliefs. A picture of this can be seen in the experience of Nehemiah when he led some Jews back to Jerusalem (Neh.13:15-22; cp. Jer.17:19-27; Ezk.46:1-7).

All the above explains to some degree why the religionists opposed Jesus with such hostility. Their problem was that they had allowed religion and ritual, ceremony and liturgy, position and security, recognition and livelihood to become more important than the basic essentials of human life: personal need and compassion, and the true worship and mercy of God. (See note and DEEPER STUDY # 1—Mt.12:10. This is an important note for this point.)

Note several things.

1. Jesus used David's experience to illustrate His point. David had eaten the showbread in the tabernacle when he was hungry (see DEEPER STUDY # 2—Lk.6:4; Mk.2:25-27).

2. Jesus declared that "[He] the Son of Man is Lord also of the sabbath." This was His very point. He was as great as David, in fact, greater; for He was the Son of Man. Therefore He was the Lord over the Sabbath (see notes and thoughts—Mt.12:1-8; Mk.2:23-28 for detailed discussion).

> "Therefore let all the house of Israel know assuredly, that God hath made that same Jesus, whom ye have crucified, both Lord and Christ" (Acts 2:36).
>
> "Him hath God exalted with his right hand to be a Prince and a Saviour, for to give repentance to Israel, and forgiveness of sins" (Acts 5:31).
>
> "God is faithful, by whom ye were called unto the fellowship of his Son Jesus Christ our Lord" (1 Cor.1:9).
>
> "But to us there is but one God, the Father, of whom are all things, and we in him; and one Lord Jesus Christ, by whom are all things, and we by him" (1 Cor.8:6).
>
> "And Jesus came and spake unto them, saying, All power is given unto me in heaven and in earth" (Mt.28:18).
>
> "And hath put all things under his feet, and gave him to be the head over all things to the church" (Eph.1:22).
>
> "[Jesus Christ] who is gone into heaven, and is on the right hand of God; angels and authorities and powers being made subject unto him" (1 Pt.3:22).

**Thought 1.** Christ shows that human needs are far more important than religious rituals and rules. However, two things must always be kept in mind.

1) The need must be a *real need* before religious rituals and rules are to be superseded. We are not to abuse, neglect, or ignore religious worship and ceremonies. Sometimes, however, a real need does arise that has to be taken care of immediately.

2) Jesus Christ is the Lord of the Sabbath (Sunday); therefore, He should be the One who says when a need should supersede a religious ceremony. We must be living closely enough to Him in fellowship and worship, sacrifice and ministry to sense what should be done.

> "Even as the Son of man came not to be ministered unto, but to minister, and to give his life a ransom for many" (Mt.20:28).
>
> "Then said Jesus to them again, Peace be unto you: as my Father hath sent me, even so send I you" (Jn.20:21).
>
> "I have showed you all things, how that so labouring ye ought to support the weak, and to remember the words of the Lord Jesus, how he said, It is more blessed to give than to receive" (Acts 20:35).
>
> "We then that are strong ought to bear the infirmities of the weak, and not to please ourselves" (Ro.15:1).
>
> "Bear ye one another's burdens, and so fulfil the law of Christ" (Gal.6:2).

---

**DEEPER STUDY # 1**

(6:2) **Scribes—Scribal Law—Pharisees**: these Pharisees were probably Scribes. The Scribes were a profession of men sometimes called lawyers (see DEEPER STUDY # 1—Mt.22:35). They were some of the most devoted and committed men to religion in all of history and were of the sect known as the Pharisees. However, every Pharisee was not a Scribe. A Scribe was more of a scholar, more highly trained than the average Pharisee (see DEEPER STUDY # 3, *Pharisees*—Acts 23:8). They had two primary functions.

1. The Scribes copied the written law, the Old Testament Scriptures. In their copying function, they were strict copiers, meticulously keeping count of every letter in every word. This exactness was necessary, for God Himself had given the written law to the Jewish nation. Therefore, the law was not only the very Word of God, it was the greatest thing in the life of the Jewish nation. It was considered the most precious possession in all the world; consequently, the Jewish nation was committed to the preservation of the law (Neh.8:1-8). A young Jew could enter no greater profession than the profession of Scribes.

2. The Scribes studied, classified, and taught the moral law. This function brought about the Oral or Scribal Law that was so common in Jesus' day. It was the law of rules and regulations. There were, in fact, so many regulations that over fifty large volumes were required when they were finally put into writing. The great tragedy was that through the centuries, the Jews began to place the Oral law over the written law (see note—Mt.12:1-8; note and DEEPER STUDY # 1—12:10; note—15:1-20).

The Scribes felt that the law was God's final word. Everything God wanted man to do could be deduced from it; therefore, they drew out of the law every possible rule they could and insisted that life was to be lived in conformity to these rules. Rules were to be a way of life, the preoccupation of a man's thoughts. At first these rules and regulations were taught by word of mouth; however, in the third century after Christ, they were put into certain writings.

*The Halachoth*: rules that were to govern the ritual of worship.

*The Talmud*: made up of two parts.
  ⇒ The Mishnah: sixty-three discussions of various subjects of the law.
  ⇒ Germara: the sacred legends of the people.

*Midrashim*: the commentaries on the writings.

*Hagada*: thoughts on the commentaries.

---

**DEEPER STUDY # 2**

(6:4) **Showbread**: the word means *the bread of the face* or *the bread of the Presence*. It symbolized the *Presence of God* who is the Bread of Life. The showbread was twelve loaves of bread that were brought to the house of God as a symbolic offering to God. It was a thanksgiving offering expressing appreciation and praise to God for food. The loaves were to be taken to the Holy Place by the Priest and placed on the table before the Lord. The loaves symbolized an everlasting covenant between God and His people: He would always see to it that His people had whatever food was necessary to sustain them (see outline—Mt.6:25-34). The loaves were to be changed every week. The old loaves became food for the priests and were to be eaten by them alone.

---

**DEEPER STUDY # 3**

(6:5) **Son of Man**: see DEEPER STUDY # 3—Mt.8:20.

---

**3** (6:6-11) **Life, Saving—Needs—Jesus Christ, Deity; Power—Rituals**: second, doing good and saving life are more important than religious rituals.

1. The need was a man whose right hand was shriveled. The only thing we know about the man with the withered hand is just that: he had a withered hand. The gospels say nothing else about him. However, there is a dramatic background given by one of the books which was never accepted into the New Testament: *The Gospel According to the Hebrews*. This gospel says that the man was a carpenter who made his living with his hands. It adds that the man pleaded with Jesus to heal him that he might not have to beg for food in shame.

2. The religionists "watched" (pareterounto) Jesus. The meaning is that they watched closely just as an animal does its prey. Note their purpose was to accuse Him. (See note and DEEPER STUDY # 1—Mt.12:10. This is an important note for understanding why the religionists conflicted so much with Jesus.)

3. Jesus knew their thoughts, so He challenged them to think and contemplate the matter and to be honest in their conclusion. "Is it lawful on the sabbath to do good, or to do evil? to save life, or to destroy it?" Note several facts.
    a. He knew their thoughts. This was evidence of His deity.
    b. Jesus was claiming to be the *Lord of good and the Lord of salvation*, the One who does good and the One who saves life.
    c. Jesus' love reached out even to those who opposed Him so violently, at least for a while, as long as there was some hope to reach them. He appealed to them to be open and honest, to think and reason, and to be willing to confess the truth. What He was doing was good and did save life. He was the Lord of good and the Lord of salvation.

4. Jesus' point was clear: to do good and to save life always supersedes religion and rituals. Picture the scene. Jesus stood there looking around upon the religionists; there was stone silence while He scanned His audience. He was awaiting their answer to His question (v.9). He longed for them to answer honestly, to confess Him as the Lord of good and the Lord of salvation, but there was only stone silence. All of a sudden with a thunderous voice He commanded: "Stretch forth thy hand. And he [the man] did so: and his hand was restored whole."

**Thought 1.** The man's life had to be saved; his hand had to be restored. The man might never stand before the Lord again. Now was the day of salvation, not tomorrow.

> "For he saith, I have heard thee in a time accepted, and in the day of salvation have I succoured thee: behold, now is the accepted time; behold, now is the day of salvation" (2 Cor.6:2).

**Thought 2.** Doing good and saving life never abuses the Sabbath or Sunday. In fact, there is no better day to help and minister than on the Lord's day.

**Thought 3.** If we do not help people—no matter the day, even on the Sabbath—then we are *withholding good and doing evil to our neighbor.*

> "Master, which is the great commandment in the law? Jesus said unto him, Thou shalt love the Lord thy God with all thy heart, and with all thy soul, and with all thy mind. This is the first and great commandment. And the second is like unto it, Thou shalt love thy neighbour as thyself" (Mt.22:36-39).
> "Love worketh no ill to his neighbour: therefore love is the fulfilling of the law" (Ro.13:10).
> "Hereby perceive we the love of God, because he laid down his life for us: and we ought to lay down our lives for the brethren. But whoso hath this world's good, and seeth his brother

have need, and shutteth up his bowels of compassion from him, how dwelleth the love of God in him? My little children, let us not love in word, neither in tongue; but in deed and in truth. And hereby we know that we are of the truth, and shall assure our hearts before men" (1 Jn.3:16-19).

"He hath showed thee, O man, what is good; and what doth the LORD require of thee, but to do justly, and to love mercy, and to walk humbly with thy God?" (Mic.6:8).

5. The religionists became insanely mad. They were filled with madness (eplesthesan anoias) which means insane rage. According to Mark, they immediately stormed out of the synagogue and joined forces with the Herodians in plotting how to kill Jesus (see notes and thoughts—Mk.3:6).

---

**DEEPER STUDY # 4**

**(6:7) Israel, History—Law—Legalism—Scribes—Pharisees**: in understanding the Scribes and Pharisees it is helpful to understand that the Jews were above all else *a people of God's Law*. Their nation was based on the Ten Commandments and the first five books of the Old Testament, known as the Law or Pentateuch (Genesis, Exodus, Leviticus, Numbers, Deuteronomy). This fact alone, that the nation was based upon God's Law, makes Israel unique among surviving nations of the world.

There are several significant stages in Israel's history that show just how dominating a force the Law was in the nation's survival.

1. The Jews were a people created by God in one man, Abraham (Gen.12:1-3). Abraham believed he was called by God to be the father of a great nation, and he passed the belief down to his son, Isaac.

2. The Jewish population grew enormously during the four-hundred years of slavery in Egypt, originating from the twelve sons of Jacob. They had been led to Egypt by Joseph to save the family during a life-threatening famine. Again, the significant fact was that the fathers passed on to their children the faith of Abraham: that they were the people of God, chosen to become the greatest of all nations.

3. The nation itself was officially formed at Mt. Sinai when God gave the Law to Moses. The nation was appointed for a spiritual purpose: to be the guardian of God's law. This event was extremely significant, for Israel was being appointed as the messenger of God to the rest of the world, as the people who were to bear testimony to the only living and true God and to His Law. They were to be God's missionary force to the world.

4. The Jewish people had been conquered and scattered all over the world time after time. In Old Testament history they had been conquered and scattered by the Assyrians, Babylonians, and Persians; yet they had survived attempt after attempt to annihilate them as a people. The one thing that bound the people together, enabling them to survive was the Law of God and their belief and practice of it (see notes and DEEPER STUDY # 1—Mt.12:10; 12:1-8).

5. A small remnant of the Jewish people had been allowed to return to rebuild the capital, Jerusalem, and to start over again under the leadership of Nehemiah and Ezra.

It was at this point in Israel's history that the birth of the Scribes took place (about B.C. 450). In a most dramatic moment in the nation's history, Ezra the Scribe took the Law (Genesis-Deuteronomy) and read it aloud to the handful of people who had returned. He then led the people to rededicate themselves to being the people of God's Law (Neh.8:1-8). The rededication was strong and meaningful. It had to be, for the nation had almost been wiped out, and there were but a few who had returned to begin the nation anew.

Therefore, the law became the greatest thing in the people's lives; and the most honored profession became the Scribe who was made responsible to study, teach, and preserve the law (see DEEPER STUDY # 1—Lk.6:2). Through the years the Scribes took the law of God and attempted to define every key phrase and word of the law. By so doing, they ended up with thousands and thousands of rules and regulations to govern the lives of the people. The people would thereby become distinct from all other people and be protected from intermarriage and from being swallowed up by the cultures of other nations. These rules and regulations were called the Scribal Law. Interestingly, when the Scribal Law was finally compiled, it compiled more than fifty volumes.

The Pharisees were born as a group several hundred years later (about B.C. 175). Antiochus Epiphanes of Syria marched against Jerusalem and captured the nation and made a deliberate attempt to destroy the Jewish people. To prevent the annihilation of their life and nation as a people, a group of men dedicated themselves at all cost to keep every detail of the law (Scribal Law). The practice of the Scribal Law by these men soon became a profession, for working to keep thousands and thousands of laws just left no time for anything else. Very simply stated, the practice of the Scribal Law required more time than a man had; therefore, the profession of Pharisees was born—born to practice and preserve the law. A Pharisee genuinely believed that by obeying the law and imposing it upon the people, he was saving his people and their nation. It was the law that made the Jewish people, their religion, and their nation different from all other people. Therefore, the Pharisee had a consuming devotion to see that the law was taught and practiced among the people.

These two things, *extreme legalism and extreme devotion*, were the two major traits of the Pharisees. But the same two traits lying within a self-centered heart can lead to terrible abuse.

1. A man can become a stern legalist, laying burden after burden upon men. Such legalism knows little of the mercy and forgiveness of God.

2. A man can become monastic, separate from the people.

3. A man can become *super-religious*, or *super-spiritual*, with a *holier than thou* attitude and aire.

4. A man can become prideful because he belongs to a certain profession and holds a particular place or position or title or because he is more disciplined in keeping the rules. Thus, he feels more elevated than others, more honored, more religious, and more acceptable to God.

5. A man can become hypocritical. There is just no way to keep thousands and thousands of rules and regulations. Human nature militates against and prevents perfect obedience.

6. A man can become showy and ostentatious. Strict discipline and personal achievement put a desire within a person to show his achievements and to seek recognition.

7. A man can become hypocritical, publicly acting and preaching one thing, but privately practicing another.

| | H. Jesus Chooses His Men: Who Is Chosen & Why, 6:12-19 (Mk.3:13-19) | James the son of Alphaeus,and Simon called Zelotes, 16 And Judas the brother of James, and Judas Iscariot, which also was the traitor. 17 And he came down with them, and stood in the plain, and the company of his disciples, and a great multitude of people out of all Judaea and Jerusalem, and from the sea coast of Tyre and Sidon, which came to hear him, and to be healed of their diseases; 18 And they that were vexed with unclean spirits: and they were healed. 19 And the whole multitude sought to touch him: for there went virtue out of him, and healed them all. | 5 He chose them to minister with Him a. They ministered to two distinct groups 1) To followers 2) To the multitude b. They had a threefold ministry 1) To preach 2) To heal |
|---|---|---|---|
| 1 He chose them after prayerful consideration— after praying all night | 12 And it came to pass in those days, that he went out into a mountain to pray, and continued all night in prayer to God. | | |
| 2 He chose them from among His disciples 3 He chose them to be apostles | 13 And when it was day, he called unto him his disciples: and of them he chose twelve, whom also he named apostles; | | |
| 4 He chose diverse personalities | 14 Simon, (whom he also named Peter,) and Andrew his brother, James and John, Philip and Bartholomew. 15 Matthew and Thomas, | | 3) To lead people to touch Jesus |

# DIVISION III

## THE SON OF MAN'S ANNOUNCED MISSION AND PUBLIC MINISTRY, 4:16-9:17

## H.  Jesus Chooses His Men: Who Is Chosen and Why, 6:12-19

(6:12-19) **Introduction**: Jesus needs people. He needs men, women, boys, and girls who will carry His message of salvation to the world. This passage is a picture of how Jesus goes about choosing people to serve Him.
   1.   He chose them after prayerful consideration—after praying all night (v.12).
   2.   He chose them from among His disciples (v.13).
   3.   He chose them to be apostles (v.13).
   4.   He chose diverse personalities (v.14-16).
   5.   He chose them to minister with Him (v.17-19).

1 (6:12) **Prayer—Call**: Jesus chose His men after prayerful consideration. He had continued all night in prayer, discussing and sharing with God. It was a momentous decision. Think about it. The destiny of the world and the fate of mankind was to rest upon the shoulders of these men. They were to carry the message of salvation to the world. If they failed, the world would be lost and man would be eternally doomed. Jesus needed to know exactly who to choose. He needed to talk the matter over with His Father. He needed to be spiritually renewed; He needed His spirit and mind quick and sharp and full of God's presence as He made the *critical choices*. So He prayed, but He not *only* prayed, He wrestled with God *all night* in prayer. Note that He got all *alone* on top of a mountain where He would not be disturbed.

**Thought 1.** In all honesty, how many minutes do we spend in prayer a day? Some say they pray all day as they go about their affairs. Praying as we walk throughout the day is good and commendable. We should "pray without ceasing" (1 Th.5:17). Christ did. But praying throughout the day by flickering our minds over to God for a moment here and there is not *concentrated prayer*, not the kind of prayer that really moves and causes things to happen. Thinking and talking to God here and there is *fellowship prayer*. Fellowship prayer is easy. It is very common to share with God as we walk through the day. But what is needed and what the Bible means primarily by prayer is *concentrated prayer*, a time set aside when we get all alone with God and share specific matters with Him. Christ sets a dynamic example of *concentrated prayer* in this passage. (See notes—Mt.6:9-13.)

"**And in the morning, rising up a great while before day, he went out, and departed into a solitary place, and there prayed**" (Mk.1:35).
"**And when he had sent them away, he departed into a mountain to pray**" (Mk.6:46).
"**And he withdrew himself into the wilderness, and prayed**" (Lk.5:16).
"**And it came to pass, as he was alone praying, his disciples were with him: and he asked them, saying, Whom say the people that I am?**" (Lk.9:18).
"**And he was withdrawn from them about a stone's cast, and kneeled down, and prayed**" (Lk.22:41).

2 (6:13) **Disciple—Call**: Jesus chose His men from among His disciples. There were a large number of people following Jesus as disciples. A disciple was a learner. But a disciple in that day was much more than what we mean by a student who just studies a subject taught by a teacher. A disciple was a person who *attached* himself to his teacher and who followed his teacher wherever he went, studying and learning all he could from the teacher's life as well as from his word. (See note—Mt.28:19-20 for detailed discussion and application.)

Note that Jesus called His disciples to Him; He called all those who had attached themselves to Him. (It would be interesting to know who all these were.) Out of these disciples, Jesus chose twelve to serve as His apostles and to join Him in His great mission and ministry. They were to serve with Him in a very, very special way (cp. v.17-19. See outline—Lk.5:27-39.)

> **"And the things that thou hast heard of me among many witnesses, the same commit thou to faithful men, who shall be able to teach others also" (2 Tim.2:2).**

**3** (6:13) **Apostle—Ministry—Believers—Ambassador:** Jesus chose His men to be apostles (see DEEPER STUDY # 5, *Apostle*—Mt.10:2). Note three things.

1. The word "apostle" (apostolos) means to send out. An apostle is a man chosen directly by the Lord Himself or by the Holy Spirit (cp. Mt.10:1-2; Mk.3:13-14; Lk.6:13; Acts 9:6, 15; 13:2; 22:10, 14-15; Ro.1:1). He was a man who had either seen or been a companion of the Lord Jesus.

2. Jesus called Himself an apostle (apesteilos, Jn.17:3), and He is called the *Apostle* and High Priest of our profession (Heb.3:1).

3. Others were also called apostles (Acts 14:4, 14, 17; 1 Th.2:6; 2 Cor.8:23; Ph.2:25; Gal.1:19; Ro.16:7). However, there is a distinct difference between all these and the twelve whom Christ chose. The first twelve were...

- chosen by the Lord Himself while on earth.
- chosen to *be with Him* during His earthly ministry (Mk.3:14).
- chosen to be trained by Him alone, personally.
- chosen to be the eyewitnesses of His resurrection (Acts 1:22).
- chosen to be the ones who were to carry forth His message which had come from His very own mouth.

There is a sense in which the gift of apostleship is still given and used in the ministry today (see DEEPER STUDY # 5, *Apostle*—Mt.10:2).

**Thought 1.** The believer is the ambassador for Christ, one who goes forth representing Christ Himself both by life and word. The believer is to *reflect* the very life of Christ.

> **"To wit, that God was in Christ, reconciling the world unto himself, not imputing their trespasses unto them; and hath committed unto us the word of reconciliation. Now then we are ambassadors for Christ, as though God did beseech you by us: we pray you in Christ's stead, be ye reconciled to God" (2 Cor.5:19-20).**

**Thought 2.** The Lord does pick *a few* from among His followers (disciples) to serve Him in very special ways. Every church has to have its leaders; and every area, state, country, and generation has to have its leaders. God must have those who will go beyond in sacrificing and giving, serving and ministering in every place and generation.

> **"There was a man sent from God, whose name was John" (Jn.1:6).**
> **"And I will give you pastors according to mine heart, which shall feed you with knowledge and understanding" (Jer.3:15).**
> **"And I will set up shepherds over them which shall feed them: and they shall fear no more, nor be dismayed, neither shall they be lacking, saith the LORD" (Jer.23:4).**
> **"He saith unto him the third time, Simon, son of Jonas, lovest thou me? Peter was grieved because he said unto him the third time, Lovest thou me? And he said unto him, Lord, thou knowest all things; thou knowest that I love thee. Jesus saith unto him, Feed my sheep" (Jn.21:17).**
> **"Take heed therefore unto yourselves, and to all the flock, over the which the Holy Ghost hath made you overseers, to feed the church of God, which he hath purchased with his own blood" (Acts 20:28).**
> **"Feed the flock of God which is among you, taking the oversight thereof, not by constraint, but willingly; not for filthy lucre, but of a ready mind" (1 Pt.5:2).**
> **"Come ye near unto me, hear ye this; I have not spoken in secret from the beginning; from the time that it was, there am I: and now the Lord GOD, and his Spirit, hath sent me" (Is.48:16).**

**4** (6:14-16) **Apostles:** Jesus chose diverse personalities. There were at least three businessmen: Peter, James, and John. All three were fishermen with rather large businesses (Mk.1:19-20; Lk.5:2-3). One apostle was perhaps wealthy: Matthew, the tax collector. His house must have been an estate, for it was large enough to handle a huge crowd for a large feast (Lk.5:27-29). One was a political nationalist, an insurrectionist, Simon the Zealot. The Zealots were pledged to overthrow the Roman government and to assassinate as many Roman officials and Jewish cohorts as possible (Lk.6:15; Acts 1:13). One was evidently deeply religious: Nathanael (Jn.1:48). So far as is known, there was no outstanding official or famous citizen among the apostles.

Their personalities were a strange mixture. Matthew, being a tax collector and ostracized by the Jewish community, was bound to be a hard-crusted, non-religious individual (Mt.9:9). The fishermen James and John were of a rough breed with thundering personalities (Mk.3:17). Simon the Zealot was possessed with a fanatical, nationalistic spirit (Lk.6:15; Acts 1:13). Peter was apparently a rough fisherman with a loud, rough-hewn personality (Mk.14:71). The power of Christ to give purpose and meaning to life and to bring peace among men is clearly seen in His ability to bring so diverse a group together under one banner. (See DEEPER STUDY # 4-*15*—Mk.3:16-19 for a discussion on each of the apostles.)

> **"But God hath chosen the foolish things of the world to confound the wise; and God hath chosen the weak things of the world to confound the things which are mighty; and base things of the world, and things which are despised, hath God chosen, yea, and things which are not, to bring to nought things that are: that no flesh should glory in his presence" (1 Cor.1:27-29).**

**5** (6:17-19) **Mission—Call—Ministry:** Jesus chose His men to carry out His mission with Him. Note that the twelve were now *with Him in a very special relationship*. Jesus "came down with them, and stood in the plain." Standing there, He and the twelve were faced with a multitude of people. The twelve were now to learn what their mission was to be.

1.    Their mission was to learn to minister to two distinct groups: "the company of His disciples" and the multitude of people.

2.    Their mission was to learn to carry out a threefold ministry.

    a.    The ministry of preaching to those who "came to hear Jesus" (v.17).

**Thought 1.** The minister and teacher of God is to preach and teach. He is to share with all those who come to hear Jesus.

> **"Go ye therefore, and teach all nations, baptizing them in the name of the Father, and of the Son, and of the Holy Ghost: teaching them to observe all things whatsoever I have commanded you: and, lo, I am with you alway, even unto the end of the world" (Mt.28:19-20).**
> **"And he said unto them, Go ye into all the world, and preach the gospel to every creature" (Mk.16:15).**

    b.    The ministry of healing (v.17-18).

**Thought 1.** The minister and teacher of God is to minister to the diseased and brokenhearted of his community and world. In the name and power of Jesus, he is to heal the sick and mend the brokenhearted.

> **"How God anointed Jesus of Nazareth with the Holy Ghost and with power: who went about doing good, and healing all that were oppressed of the devil; for God was with him" (Acts 10:38).**
> **"He healeth the broken in heart, and bindeth up their wounds" (Ps.147:3).**
> **"Then said Jesus to them again, Peace be unto you: as my Father hath sent me, even so send I you" (Jn.20:21).**

    c.    The ministry of leading people to *touch Jesus* in order to receive His virtue (v.19). The Greek word "virtue" (dunamis) means power. The people were *touching Jesus* in order to receive His power.

**Thought 1.** The servant of God is to be an instrument of Jesus' power. Jesus' power is to flow through His servant and flow outward to men.

> **"And Jesus came and spake unto them, saying, All power is given unto me in heaven and in earth" (Mt.28:18).**
> **"But ye shall receive power, after that the Holy Ghost is come upon you: and ye shall be witnesses unto me both in Jerusalem, and in all Judaea, and in Samaria, and unto the uttermost part of the earth" (Acts 1:8).**
> **"Now unto him that is able to do exceeding abundantly above all that we ask or think, according to the power that worketh in us" (Eph.3:20).**
> **"Preach the word; be instant in season, out of season; reprove, rebuke, exhort with all longsuffering and doctrine" (2 Tim.4:2).**

| | I. Jesus Teaches the Perils of the Material World, 6:20-26 (Mt.5:3-12) | your name as evil, for the Son of man's sake. | reproached |
|---|---|---|---|
| | | 23 Rejoice ye in that day, and leap for joy: for, behold, your reward is great in heaven: for in the like manner did their fathers unto the prophets. | 2) The attitude to have while being perse-cuted: Rejoicing |
| | | | 3) Reward: To be great |
| 1 The promise to those who reject materialism | 20 And he lifted up his eyes on his disciples, and said, Blessed be ye poor: for yours is the kingdom of God. | | |
| a. The poor: Shall inherit the Kingdom of God | | 24 But woe unto you that are rich! for ye have received your consolation. | 2 The judgment of those who follow materialism |
| b. The hungry: Shall be filled | 21 Blessed are ye that hunger now: for ye shall be filled. Blessed are ye that weep now: for ye shall laugh. | | a. The rich: Shall want |
| | | 25 Woe unto you that are full! for ye shall hunger. Woe unto you that laugh now! for ye shall mourn and weep. | b. The full: Shall hunger |
| c. The sorrowful: Shall laugh | | | c. The merry: Shall weep |
| d. The persecuted for Jesus' sake | 22 Blessed are ye, when men shall hate you, and when they shall separate you from their company, and shall re-proach you, and cast out | | |
| 1) The persecuted de-scribed: The hated, the ostracized, & the | | 26 Woe unto you, when all men shall speak well of you! for so did their fathers to the false prophets. | d. The prideful & com-promising: Shall have earthly approval only |

# DIVISION III

## THE SON OF MAN'S ANNOUNCED MISSION AND PUBLIC MINISTRY, 4:16-9:17

## I.     Jesus Teaches the Perils of the Material World, 6:20-26

(6:20-26) **Introduction**: this is a shocking passage to the world, for Jesus switches the world's values completely around. He rejects entirely the *materialism* (things) of the world and warns the worldly and materialistic that severe judgment is coming.

1.     The promise to those who reject materialism (v.20-23).
2.     The judgment to those who follow materialism (v.24-26).

1  (6:20-23) **Materialism—Worldliness—Righteousness—Persecution**: the promise to those who reject materialism.

1.     Blessed are the poor. This does not mean that a man must be poverty-stricken and financially poor. Hunger, na-kedness, and slums are not pleasing to God, especially in a world of plenty. Jesus is not talking about material poverty. He means what he adds in Matthew: "poor in spirit" (cp. Mt.5:3). "Poor in spirit" means several things.

   a.   To acknowledge one's utter helplessness before God, one's spiritual poverty, one's spiritual need; acknowledging that one is solely dependent upon God to meet his need.
   b.   To acknowledge one's utter lack in facing life and eternity apart from God; to acknowledge that the real blessings of life and eternity come only from a right relationship with God (see note—Eph.1:3; cp. Jn.10:10; Gal.5:22-23).
   c.   To acknowledge one's utter lack of superiority before all others and one's spiritual deadness before God; to acknowledge that no matter what one has achieved in this world (fame, fortune, power), he is no better, no richer, no more superior than the next person. His attitude toward others is not proud and haughty, not superior and overbearing. To be "poor in spirit" means acknowledging that every human being is a real person just like everyone else—a person who has a significant contribution to make to society and to the world. The person who is "poor in spirit" approaches life in humility and appreciation, not as though life owes him, but as though he owes life. He has been given the privilege of living; thus, he journeys through life with a humble attitude, that is, with an attitude of being poor in spirit and contributing all he can out of a spirit of appreciation.

Two critical steps are taken by the person who truly acknowledges his spiritual poverty.
   a.   He turns his primary attention away from the things of this world, knowing things can never make him rich in spirit.
   b.   He turns his primary attention to God and His kingdom, knowing that God alone can make him rich in spirit (see note—Eph.1:3).
The opposite of being "poor in spirit" is having a spirit that is full of self. There is a world of difference between these two spirits. There is the difference of thinking one is righteous and acknowledging one has the need for righteousness. There is the difference of *having self-righteousness* and of having *another's righteousness*. Man must have *another's right-eousness*. Self-righteousness goes no farther than self, that is, no farther than death. *Another's righteousness*, that is, Christ's righteousness, lives forever (2 Cor.5:21; Ph.3:9. See note—Ro.3:21-22; note and DEEPER STUDY # 1—Gal.2:15-16. See outline and notes—Ro.10:4.)

The promise to the *poor* is phenomenal. Note the exact words: "yours is the kingdom of heaven." The promise is not "yours shall be," but "yours is." The poor in spirit receive the Kingdom of Heaven *now* (see DEEPER STUDY # 3—Mt.19:23-24).

2.     Blessed are the hungry. This is spiritual hunger, not physical hunger. Again, being physically hungry is not a blessing. It is often sad and tragic. Jesus is saying, "Blessed are they who hunger spiritually, who hunger after righteous-ness." It means to have a starving spirit, a spirit that craves righteousness.

In the Bible righteousness means two simple but profound things. It means both *to be right and to do right*. (See DEEPER STUDY # 5, *Righteousness*—Mt.5:6 for more discussion.)

    a.  There are those who stress *being righteous and neglect doing righteousness*. This leads to two serious errors.

        1)  False security. It causes a person to stress that he is saved and acceptable to God because he has *believed in* Jesus Christ. But he neglects doing good and living as he should. He neglects obeying God and serving man.

        2)  Loose living. It allows one to go out and do pretty much as he desires. He feels secure and comfortable in his *faith in Christ*. He knows that what he does may affect his fellowship with God and other believers, but he thinks his behavior will not affect his salvation. He thinks that no matter what he does he is still acceptable to God.

           The problem with this stress is that it is a false righteousness. Righteousness in the Bible means *being righteous* and *doing righteousness*. The Bible knows nothing about being righteous without living righteously.

    b.  There are those who stress *doing righteousness and neglect being righteous*. This also leads to two serious errors.

        1)  Self-righteousness and legalism. It causes a person to stress that he is saved and acceptable to God because he does good. He works and behaves morally and keeps certain rules and regulations. He does the things a Christian should do by obeying the main laws of God. But he neglects the basic law: the law of love and acceptance—that God loves him and accepts him not because he does good but because he loves and trusts the righteousness of Christ (see note and DEEPER STUDY # 5—Mt.5:6).

        2)  Being judgmental and censorious. A person who stresses that he is righteous (acceptable to God) because he keeps certain laws often judges and censors others. He feels that rules and regulations can be kept, for *He* keeps them. Therefore, anyone who fails to keep them is judged, criticized, and censored.

           The problem with this stress is that it, too, is a false righteousness. Again, righteousness in the Bible is both *being righteous and doing righteousness*. The Bible knows nothing of being acceptable to God without *being made righteous in Christ Jesus* (see notes and DEEPER STUDY # 5—Mt.5:6; Ro.5:1 for more discussion. Cp. 2 Cor.5:21.)

           Note that Jesus does not say, "Blessed are the righteous," for no one is righteous (Ro.3:10). He says, "Blessed are they who *hunger and thirst* after righteousness." Man is not righteous, not perfectly righteous. His chance to be righteous is gone. He has already come short and missed the mark. He is already imperfect. Man has but one hope: that God will love him so much that He will somehow *count* him righteous. That is just what God does. God takes a man's "hunger and thirst after righteousness" and counts that hunger and thirst as righteousness (see DEEPER STUDY # 2—Ro.4:22).

           The promise to those who hunger after righteousness is fulfilling. They will be filled with abundant life: love, joy, peace, longsuffering, gentleness, goodness, faith, meekness, temperance (Gal.5:22-23).

3.    Blessed are the sorrowful, the persons who weep and mourn. The idea is a broken heart, a desperate, helpless weeping. It is weeping over sin; it is a broken heart over evil and suffering; it is a brokenness of self that comes from seeing Jesus on the cross and realizing that one's own sins put Him there (cp. Jas.4:9).

Who are they who mourn? Who are they so full of grief and sorrow that they cry and weep and utter groanings deep from within? There are three persons who mourn and utter such groanings.

    a.  The person who is *desperately sorry* for his sin and unworthiness before God. He has such a sense of sin that his heart is just broken (Lk.18:13).

    b.  The person who really *feels* the desperate plight and terrible suffering of others. The tragedies, the problems, the sinful behavior of others; the state, the condition, the lostness of the world—all weigh ever so heavily upon the heart of the mourner.

    c.  The person who *experiences* personal tragedy and intense trauma.

The promise to the one who weeps is that he shall laugh (gelasete). The word means *loud laughter* that arises from a deep-seated joy and comfort. The laughter comes from two things.

    a.  It comes from seeing the end of sin and shame, sorrow and suffering, tragedy and trauma.

    b.  It comes from being comforted (paraclesia, see note—2 Cor.1:3). Note two glorious truths.

        1)  There is a present comfort.

          ⇒  A settled peace: a relief, a solace, a consolation within.

          ⇒  An assurance of forgiveness and acceptance by God.

          ⇒  A fullness of joy: a sense of God's presence, care and guidance (Jn.14:26); a sense of His sovereignty, of His working all things out for good to those who love Him (Ro.8:28; cp. Jn.10:10; 15:11; 2 Cor.6:10; Ps.16:11).

        2)  There is an eternal comfort.

          ⇒  A passing from death to life (Jn.3:16; Jn.5:24f).

          ⇒  A wiping away of all tears (Is.25:8; Rev.7:17; 21:4).

4.    Blessed are the persecuted, the persons who are persecuted for Jesus' sake. The persecuted are those who endure suffering *for Christ*. Jesus spelled out what He meant by persecution. He means being hated, ostracized, reproached, and having one's name spoken against.

Note the attitude a person is to have while being persecuted. The person is to "rejoice" and "leap for joy." How is such possible? By keeping one's eyes on the reward. Note the words, "Rejoice and leap for joy; for, behold, your reward is great in heaven."

Believers are forewarned: they shall suffer persecution (Jn.15:20; 16:4; Ph.1:29; 2 Tim.3:12; 1 Jn.3:13; 1 Pt.4:12f).

a. Believers suffer persecution because they *are not of this world*. They are called out of the world. They are *in the world*, but they are not *of the world*. They are separated from the behavior of the world; therefore, the world reacts against them (Jn.15:19).

b. Believers suffer persecution because they *strip away the world's cloak of sin*. They live and demonstrate a life of righteousness. Such exposes the sins of people (Jn.15:21, 24; cp. 15:18; 2 Tim.3:12).

c. Believers suffer persecution because the world does not know God or Christ. They want no God, no Lord other than themselves and their own imaginations. They want to do just what they want, to fulfill their own desires and not what another Lord wishes and demands (Jn.15:21; 16:3).

d. Believers suffer persecution because the world is deceived in its concept and belief of God. The world conceives God to be the Person who fulfills their earthly desires and lusts (Jn.16:2-3). Man's idea of God is that of a *Supreme Grandfather*. He protects, provides, and gives, no matter one's behavior, just so the behavior is not too far out. God (the Supreme Grandfather) will accept and work all things out in the final analysis. But the true believer teaches against this. God is love, but He is also just and demands righteousness. The world rebels against this concept of God (Jn.16:2-3).

The promise to the persecuted is twofold. Their reward is great in heaven, and they are following in the footsteps (testimony) of the great prophets of the past.

1. The persecuted receive a great reward now.
   a. They experience a special honor (Acts 5:41).
   b. They experience a special consolation (2 Cor.1:5).
   c. They are given a very special closeness, a glow of the Lord's presence (see note—1 Pt.4:14).
   d. They become a greater witness for Christ (2 Cor.1:4-6).
2. The persecuted will receive the Kingdom of Heaven eternally (Heb.11:35f; 1 Pt.4:12-13; see DEEPER STUDY # 3—Mt.19:23-24).

**2** (6:24-26) **Judgment—Materialism**: the judgment to those who follow materialism.

1. The warning is strong to the rich. Who are the rich? Realistically, in comparison to what the vast majority of the world has, a rich person is anyone who has anything to put back beyond meeting the true needs of his own family. This is exactly what Christ and the Bible say time and again (cp. also Mk.12:41-44; Lk.21:1-4; Acts 4:34-35).

Why are the rich warned? Because wealth pulls a person away from the Kingdom of Heaven. It is difficult for a rich person to enter heaven. Christ made this statement because of the things that *pulled* the rich young ruler away from heaven. There is a lure, an attraction, a force, a power, a pull that reaches out and draws any of us who look at or possess wealth. There are pulls so forceful that they will enslave and doom any rich person who fails to turn and embrace God.

   a. *Wealth creates the big "I."* The wealthy are usually esteemed, honored, and envied. Wealth brings position, power, and recognition. It boosts *ego*, making a person self-sufficient and independent in this world. As a result there is a tendency for the rich man to feel that he is truly independent and self-sufficient, that he needs nothing. And in such an atmosphere and world of thought, God is forgotten. The rich person forgets there are things that money cannot buy and events from which money cannot save. Peace, love, joy—all that really matter within the spirit of man—can never be bought. Neither can money save one from disaster, disease, accident, and death.

   b. *Wealth tends to make one hoard.* The Bible lays down the principle of handling money for all men, even for the poor:

> **"Let him labor...that he may have to give to him that needeth" (Eph.4:28).**
> **"Thou shalt love thy neighbor as thyself" (Mt.19:19; 22:39).**

The world reels in desperate need. People are starving, sick, unhoused, and unclothed by the millions; and teeming millions are spiritually lost and without God in this world and doomed to die without ever knowing Him. When any of us sit still and objectively look at the world in its desperate plight, how can we keep from asking: "How can any man hoard and not help—even to the last available penny? Why would any man keep more than what he needs for himself and his family?"

As God looks at the rich, He is bound to ask the same questions. In fact, His questions are bound to be more pointed and forceful. This is exactly what Christ said to the rich young ruler:

> **"Go and sell that thou hast; and give to the poor, and thou shalt have treasure in heaven: and come and follow me" (Mt.19:21).**

   c. *Riches tend to make a man selfish.* For some unexplainable reason, the more we get, the more we want. When we taste the things of this world and become comfortable, we tend to fear loosing our possessions. We struggle to keep what we have and to get more. True, many are willing to make contributions, but only a certain amount, an amount that will not lower their overall estate or standing or level of comfort and possessions. There are few who give all they are and have to Christ to meet the needs of the world.

As Jesus said, "It is difficult, very difficult for the rich [meaning those who have anything in comparison with most of the world] to enter heaven" (cp. Lk.18:24). If we do not have compassion and take care of our brothers (fellowman) when they are in desperate need, how can we expect God to have compassion and take care of us when we face the desperate need for heaven? It is foolish for us to think that a loving and just God will meet our need for eternal life when we would not meet the need of our fellowman for earthly life. The rich have the means to help and to save human life, *if they would*.

d. *Wealth attaches one to the world*. Wealth enables one to buy things that...

- make him comfortable
- please his taste
- expand his experience
- stir his ego
- challenge his mental pursuit
- stimulate his flesh
- stretch his self-image

If a man centers his life upon the things of the world, his attention is on the world not on God. He tends to become wrapped up in securing more and in protecting what he has. Too often, he gives little if any time and thought to heavenly matters. Wealth and the things it can provide usually consume the rich.

The judgment of the rich is their wealth on earth. The word received (apechete) means a receipt in full. Their only "consolation" (paraklesin, help, aid, encouragement) is to be on this earth—the wealth they have. There will be no consolation after this life—no help, no aid, no encouragement, no cheer. They are *paid in full*. They choose this life, so all the good they shall receive is the good they now experience.

"For we brought nothing into this world, and it is certain we can carry nothing out" (1 Tim.6:7).

"But they that will be rich fall into temptation and a snare, and into many foolish and hurtful lusts, which drown men in destruction and perdition" (1 Tim.6:9).

"Your gold and silver is cankered; and the rust of them shall be a witness against you, and shall eat your flesh as it were fire. Ye have heaped treasure together for the last days" (Jas.5:3).

"And when thy herds and thy flocks multiply, and thy silver and thy gold is multiplied, and all that thou hast is multiplied; then thine heart be lifted up, and thou forget the LORD thy God, which brought thee forth out of the land of Egypt, from the house of bondage" (Dt.8:13-14).

"The increase of his house shall depart, and his goods shall flow away in the day of his wrath" (Job 20:28).

"Though he heap up silver as the dust, and prepare raiment as the clay" (Job 27:16).

"Surely every man walketh in a vain show; surely they are disquieted in vain: he heapeth up riches, and knoweth not who shall gather them" (Ps.39:6).

"For he seeth that wise men die, likewise the fool and the brutish person perish, and leave their wealth to others" (Ps.49:10).

"Trust not in oppression, and become not vain in robbery: if riches increase, set not your heart upon them" (Ps.62:10).

"Wilt thou set thine eyes upon that which is not? For riches certainly make themselves wings; they fly away as an eagle toward heaven" (Pr.23:5).

"For riches are not for ever: and doth the crown endure to every generation?" (Pr.27:24).

"A faithful man shall abound with blessings: but he that maketh haste to be rich shall not be innocent" (Pr.28:20).

"Yea, I hated all my labor which I had taken under the sun: because I should leave it unto the man that be after me" (Eccl.2:18).

"As the partridge sitteth on eggs, and hatcheth them not; so he that getteth riches, and not by right, shall leave them in the midst of his days, and at his end shall be a fool" (Jer.17:11).

2. The warning is strong to the full. The full are the opposite of those who hunger for righteousness. The full are those who are filled with all that the world has to offer; in essence they are full of themselves, their own desires, urges, and cravings. They have no hunger for righteousness at all. Scripture identifies the full as those who...

- fill their bellies with the husks of the world (Lk.15:16).
- serve their own bellies and not the Lord Jesus Christ (Ro.16:18).
- indulge in the meats (things, sins) of the world (1 Cor.6:13; cp. 6:9-13).
- make their god their bellies (Ph.3:19).
- "[are] filled with all unrighteousness, [such as] fornication, wickedness, covetousness, maliciousness; full of envy, murder, debate, deceit, malignity; whisperers, backbiters, haters of God, despiteful, proud, boasters, inventors of evil things, disobedient to parents, without understanding, covenantbreakers, without natural affection, implacable, unmerciful: who knowing the judgment of God, that they which commit such things are worthy of death, not only do the same, but have pleasure in them that do them" (Ro.1:29-32).

The judgment of the full shall be hunger. This means they...

- shall leave all that filled them behind when they die (Lk.12:20; 16:25).
- shall have no desires filled after this life.
- shall have no delights fulfilled throughout eternity.
- shall hunger for good (righteousness) and for the good things throughout eternity.

"Because thou sayest, I am rich, and increased with goods, and have need of nothing; and knowest not that thou art wretched, and miserable, and poor, and blind, and naked" (Rev.3:17).

"They are enclosed in their own fat: with their mouth they speak proudly" (Ps.17:10)

"Behold, this was the iniquity of thy sister Sodom, pride, fullness of bread, and abundance of idleness was in her and in her daughters, neither did she strengthen the hand of the poor and needy" (Ezk.16:49).

3. The warning is strong to the merry, to those who laugh now. This means three things.

*Laughing now* refers to those who have no sense of sin, no sorrow or regret over evil and suffering, no brokenness over the cross and their own sin. Their joy is carnal and sensual.

Laughing now refers to those who are laughing it up *in the world* with all its comfort and ease, pleasures and stimulations, recreations and pastimes. Their joy is the indulgence and entertaining of their flesh.

Laughing now refers to those who pay little or no attention to the reality of the world, a world suffering under the weight of evil and disaster, greed and selfishness, sin and death. Their joy is found in denying and ignoring the truth of the world or in giving a pittance of time or money to help in order to ease their consciences.

The warning and judgment to the merry is mourning and weeping. They are doomed because they refused to face the reality of a world lost in sin and evil, a world that needed their attention and help. They refused to help the needy, those who suffered and wept so much in this world. Therefore, they shall be left alone in the next world to mourn and weep over their great loss.

"That the triumphing of the wicked is short, and the joy of the hypocrite but for a moment" (Job 20:5).

"Even in laughter the heart is sorrowful; and the end of that mirth is heaviness" (Pr.14:13).

"For as the crackling of thorns under a pot, so is the laughter of the fool: this also is vanity" (Eccl.7:6).

"And gladness is taken away, and joy out of the plentiful field; and in the vineyards there shall be no singing, neither shall there be shouting: the treaders shall tread out no wine in their presses; I have made their vintage shouting to cease" (Is.16:10).

"Cleanse your hands, ye sinners; and purify your hearts, ye double minded. Be afflicted, and mourn, and weep: let your laughter be turned to mourning, and your joy to heaviness. Humble yourselves in the sight of the Lord, and he shall lift you up" (Jas.4:8-10).

4. The warning is strong to the prideful and compromising. These are the opposite of those who are persecuted for Christ's sake. The worldly speak well of those who live worldly...

- who live as they live.
- who speak as they speak.
- who compromise.
- who seek their company and approval.
- who never point out the truth of sin and death, judgment and hell.

Worldly men want attention and esteem, position and place, honor and praise, recognition and applause. Men honor such ambitions and rewards. Therefore, they speak well of men who attain such. But note what Jesus said. He said that *false prophets* were those of whom the world spoke well, and this was their reward, all they would ever receive. They coveted worldly recognition and honor and they received it, but at the expense of heavenly recognition and honor.

**Thought 1.** We are not to be as false prophets, slapping men on the back, acknowledging and compromising with their worldliness. If we do, the world will speak well of us, but we shall lose our reward. What the believer must do is tell the truth to all men: all men need a Savior and their eternal fate depends upon their coming to Him for salvation, seeking His righteousness.

"Let me not, I pray you, accept any man's person; neither let me give flattering titles unto man" (Job 32:21).

"He that goeth about as a talebearer revealeth secrets: therefore meddle not with him that flattereth with his lips" (Pr.20:19).

"He that saith unto the wicked, Thou art righteous; him shall the people curse, nations shall abhor him" (Pr.24:24).

"A lying tongue hateth those that are afflicted by it; and a flattering mouth worketh ruin" (Pr.26:28).

"A man that flattereth his neighbor spreadeth a net for his feet" (Pr.29:5).

"The LORD shall cut off all flattering lips, and the tongue that speaketh proud things" (Ps.12:3).

"For the time will come when they will not endure sound doctrine; but after their own lusts shall they heap to themselves teachers, having itching ears" (2 Tim.4:3).

"Whose mouths [false teachers] must be stopped, who subvert whole houses, teaching things which they ought not, *for filthy lucre's* [gain] *sake*" (Tit.1:11).

"But there were false prophets also among the people, even as there shall be false teachers among you, who privily shall bring in damnable heresies, even denying the Lord that bought them, and bring upon themselves swift destruction. And many shall follow their pernicious ways; by reason of whom the way of truth shall be evil spoken of" (2 Pt.2:1-2).

|  | J. Jesus Teaches the New Principles of Life, 6:27-38 (Mt.5:39, 43-48; 7:12) | ners also do even the same. 34 And if ye lend to them of whom ye hope to receive, what thank have ye? for sinners also lend to sinners, to receive as much again. | c. In lending |
| --- | --- | --- | --- |
| 1 The principles of life a. Governing relationships 1) Love & do good 2) Bless & pray 3) Offer the other cheek b. Governing property 1) Deprive not 2) Give 3) Do not demand material goods c. Governing behavior[DS1] | 27 But I say unto you which hear, Love your enemies, do good to them which hate you, 28 Bless them that curse you, and pray for them which despitefully use you. 29 And unto him that smiteth thee on the one cheek offer also the other; and him that taketh away thy cloke forbid not to take thy coat also. 30 Give to every man that asketh of thee; and of him that taketh away thy goods ask them not again. 31 And as ye would that men should do to you, do ye also to them likewise. | 35 But love ye your enemies, and do good, and lend, hoping for nothing again; and your reward shall be great, and ye shall be the children of the Highest: for he is kind unto the unthankful and to the evil. 36 Be ye therefore merciful, as your Father also is merciful. 37 Judge not, and ye shall not be judged: condemn not, and ye shall not be condemned: forgive, and ye shall be forgiven: | 3 The reward for living right a. Shall be great b. Shall be the children of the Most High c. Shall be acting as God's children 4 The promise: Reciprocal behavior—you will receive what you give a. In relationships b. In property |
| 2 The argument: A disciple's behavior must surpass a sinner's a. In love b. In doing good | 32 For if ye love them which love you, what thank have ye? for sinners also love those that love them. 33 And if ye do good to them which do good to you, what thank have ye? for sin- | 38 Give, and it shall be given unto you; good measure, pressed down, and shaken together, and running over, shall men give into your bosom. For with the same measure that ye mete withal it shall be measured to you again. | c. The principle: A person receives what he gives |

# DIVISION III

## THE SON OF MAN'S ANNOUNCED MISSION AND PUBLIC MINISTRY, 4:16-9:17

## J.    Jesus Teaches the New Principles of Life, 6:27-38

(6:27-38) **Introduction**: the principles spelled out by Jesus are shocking. They go against every grain of society and every fiber of a man's being. Man rebels by nature against what Jesus is saying; however the new principles must be heeded, for they are the salvation of society and the hope of man for life.

1.    The principles of life (v.27-31).
2.    The argument: a disciple's behavior must surpass a sinner's (v.32-34).
3.    The reward for living right (v.35-36).
4.    The promise: reciprocal behavior—you will receive what you give (v.37-38).

[1]    (6:27-31) **Life, Principles of—Believers, Behavior of**: there are the new principles of life. Two things should be noted immediately. Jesus was speaking to his disciples (v.20) and to those who would hear (v.27). He knew that all would not hear. Even if they were disciples, some just closed their ears if they did not like what they heard. And what Jesus was about to preach was a complete switch from the way men and society lived. He was about to say some things men had never heard or thought about. He knew some were going to shut their ears, so He warned them and encouraged them to guard against not listening.

1.    There are the new principles governing human relationships. Jesus touched on five specific behaviors.
   a.    Love: "Love your enemies." Believers are to *love all men, even enemies*. They are to respect and honor all men (1 Pt.2:17). Every human being has something that is commendable, even if it is nothing but the fact that he is a fellow human being with a soul to be reached for God. Note two facts.
      First, loving one's enemies is against human nature. The behavior of human nature is to react: to hate, strike back, and wish hurt. At best, human nature treats enemies with coldness and distance. The root of human reaction against enemies is self and bitterness. (Self-preservation is not evil of itself. See note and DEEPER STUDY # 1, *Love*—Mt.5:44. The section on agape love points out that love is not complacent acceptance of wickedness and license.)
      Second, the one thing that a believer can have for enemies *is mercy and compassion*. Those who are enemies may choose to remain antagonistic, but the believer can still forgive in mercy and compassion. In fact, if the believer does not have compassion for those who hate him, he has gained nothing of the spirit of Christ (v.36).
   b.    Do good: "Do good to them which hate you." Imagine the impact of these words to the world of Jesus' day. They were an enslaved people conquered and hated by the Romans, yet Jesus was saying, "Do good to them." (See note, *Love—Enemies*—Mt.5:44 for more discussion.)

Note that *doing good* goes beyond words; it actually does things for the person who hates. It reaches out to him through his family and friends, employment and business. It searches for ways to do good to him, realizing that he needs to be reached for God. If no immediate way is found, then the Christian continues to bless him, ever waiting for the day when the hater will face one of the crises that comes to every human being. And then the believer goes and does good, ministering as Christ Himself ministered.

> **"Therefore if thine enemy hunger, feed him; if he thirst, give him drink: for in so doing thou shalt heap coals of fire on his head" (Ro.12:20).**
> **"See that none render evil for evil unto any man; but ever follow that which is good, both among yourselves, and to all men" (1 Th.5:15).**
> **"If thou see the ass of him that hateth thee lying under his burden, and wouldest forbear to help him, thou shalt surely help with him" (Ex.23:5).**
> **"If thine enemy be hungry, give him bread to eat; and if he be thirsty, give him water to drink" (Pr.25:21).**

c. Bless people: "Bless them that curse you." People do curse, and sometimes they curse other people. When someone curses a believer, the believer is to bless his curser, not rail back. He is to speak softly, to use kind and reconciling words.

> **"Bless them which persecute you: bless, and curse not" (Ro.12:14).**
> **"Not rendering evil for evil, or railing for railing: but contrariwise blessing; knowing that ye are thereunto called, that ye should inherit a blessing" (1 Pt.3:9).**
> **"A soft answer turneth away wrath: but grievous words stir up anger" (Prov.15:1).**

d. Pray for others: "Pray for them which despitefully use you." Note this refers not only to those who speak despitefully but those who *use us despitefully*. It is an attempt to shame and to hurt both our name and body. Someone tries to shame, dishonor, disgrace and reproach us. And they go even farther; they misuse, mistreat, abuse, attack, and persecute us. What are we to do? Christ says, "Pray for them. When they despitefully use you, pray for them." (a) Pray for God to forgive the persecutor. (b) Pray for peace between one's self and the persecutor. (c) Pray for the persecutor's salvation and correction.

> **"Then said Jesus, Father, forgive them; for they know not what they do. And they parted his raiment, and cast lots" (Lk.23:34).**
> **"And he [Stephen] kneeled down, and cried with a loud voice, Lord, lay not this sin to their charge. And when he had said this, he fell asleep" (Acts 7:60).**

Prayer for the persecutor will greatly benefit the believer. It will keep the believer from becoming bitter, hostile, and reactionary.

e. Offer the other cheek: "Unto him that smiteth thee on the one cheek offer also the other." The word for cheek (siagon) really means the jaw or jawbone. It is a strong blow, a punch and not just a slap of contempt. Of course, there is contempt and bitterness, but there is also physical injury. Christ is saying that the believer is not to strike back, not to retaliate against...

- bitter insults or contempt.
- bodily threats or injury.

When suffering *for the gospel's sake*, for his personal testimony for Christ, the believer is to respond to physical abuse just as his Lord did. He is to demonstrate *moral strength through a quiet and meek spirit*, trusting God to touch the heart of his persecutors. (See notes—Mt.5:38-39 for more discussion.)

> **"And they spit upon him, and took the reed, and smote him on the head" (Mt.27:30).**
> **"And when he had thus spoken, one of the officers which stood by struck Jesus with the palm of his hand, saying, Answerest thou the high priest so?" (Jn.18:22).**
> **"They have gaped upon me with their mouth; they have smitten me upon the cheek reproachfully; they have gathered themselves together against me" (Job 16:10).**
> **"But the fruit of the Spirit is love, joy, peace, longsuffering, gentleness, goodness, faith, meekness, temperance: against such there is no law" (Gal.5:22-23).**
> **"In meekness instructing those that oppose themselves; if God peradventure will give them repentance to the acknowledging of the truth" (2 Tim.2:25).**
> **"Recompense to no man evil for evil. Provide things honest in the sight of all men" (Ro.12:17).**
> **"Thou shalt not avenge, nor bear any grudge against the children of thy people, but thou shalt love thy neighbor as thyself: I am the LORD" (Lev.19:18).**
> **"Say not thou, I will recompense evil; but wait on the LORD, and he shall save thee" (Pr.20:22).**
> **"Say not, I will do so to him as he hath done to me: I will render to the man according to his work" (Pr.24:29).**
> **"Seek ye the LORD, all ye meek of the earth, which have wrought his judgment; seek righteousness, seek meekness: it may be ye shall be hid in the day of the LORD'S anger" (Zeph.2:3).**

2. There are the new principles governing property. Jesus touched upon two specific behaviors.

    a. Deprive not: "Him that taketh away thy cloke forbid not to take thy coat also." The Jews wore both an inner and an outer garment. If a man took the outer garment, the believer was to offer his inner garment as well. Jewish law allowed the inner garment to be taken as a debt or pledge, but never the outer garment. A man might have several underclothings, but only one outer garment (cp. Ex.22:26-27).

        Giving one's cloak is difficult. It means the believer does not defend, stand up, or dispute the taking of his property. He forgives, and he gives more to the person who takes. He even gives his coat (tunic) if necessary. A believer does not get tied up and consumed with his rights and privileges in or out of court. He has time only to go about his duty. He is tied up and consumed with living—living to the fullest for Christ and reaching out to a world lost and consumed with *disputes and needing the peace which only God can bring*. (See note and thoughts—Mt.5:39-41 for additional discussion.)

    b. Give: "Give to every man that asketh of thee." The believer is to help those who have need, and he is to readily help. Note that Christ allows no excuse. The picture is that the believer *gives and does not turn away* when a person asks. Note, however, the Bible does not say to give without discretion.

> **"A good man showeth favor, and lendeth: he will guide his affairs with discretion"**
> **(Ps.112:5).**

**Thought 1.** There are two significant attitudes to control the believer's giving.

    1) The believer is to live in readiness—a readiness to give and to lend (cp. 2 Cor.8:11-15, esp. 11). He does not live for this earth and world. He lives for God and for heaven. His citizenship is in heaven, from whence he looks for the Savior (Ph.3:20). Thus, his attachment to earthly things is only for meeting the necessities of life and for helping others. He exists to help and to give.

> **"Sell that ye have, and give alms; provide yourselves bags which wax not old, a treasure in the heavens that faileth not, where no thief approacheth, neither moth corrupteth"** (Lk.12:33).
>
> **"Distributing to the necessity of saints; given to hospitality"** (Ro.12:13).
>
> **"As we have therefore opportunity, let us do good unto all men, especially unto them who are of the household of faith"** (Gal.6:10).
>
> **"Charge them that are rich in this world, that they be not highminded, nor trust in uncertain riches, but in the living God, who giveth us richly all things to enjoy; that they do good, that they be rich in good works, ready to distribute, willing to communicate [give]"** (1 Tim.6:17-18).
>
> **"But to do good and to communicate [give] forget not: for with such sacrifices God is well pleased"** (Heb.13:16).
>
> **"Now therefore perform the doing of it [giving]; that as there was a readiness to will [to give], so there may be a performance also out of that which ye have. For if there be first a willing mind, it is accepted according to that a man hath, and not according to that he hath not. For I mean not that other men be eased, and ye burdened: but by an equality, that now at this time your abundance may be a supply for their want, that their abundance also may be a supply for your want: that there may be equality: as it is written, He that had gathered much had nothing over; and he that had gathered little had no lack"** (2 Cor.8:11-15).

    2) The believer is to work for two reasons: (1) to meet his own necessities; and (2) to have enough to help those in need.

> **"Let him that stole steal no more: but rather let him labour, working with his hands the thing which is good, that he may have to give to him that needeth"** (Eph.4:28).
>
> **"I have showed you all things, how that so labouring ye ought to support the weak, and to remember the words of the Lord Jesus, how he said, It is more blessed to give than to receive"** (Acts 20:35).

    c. Demand not: "Of him that taketh away thy goods ask them not again." Often a person fails to pay back what he borrowed. He takes and keeps what he borrowed, whether tools, clothing, food, or money. The believer is not to demand them back, not if the person *needs* them and is going to be deprived and hurt if they are taken back. The believer has to consider two facts: first, the person's need; second, if the person has no need, the sin of allowing license and irresponsibility versus alienating and turning the person away from one's testimony of Christ. The believer must not allow license and irresponsibility, but he must be careful not to lose his chance of winning the person to Christ. No item, no amount of money is worth his soul.

> **"Give to him that asketh thee, and from him that would borrow of thee turn not thou away"** (Mt.5:42).

3. There is the new principle which governs all behavior, the *Golden Rule* itself: "As ye would that men should do to you, do ye also to them." (See DEEPER STUDY # 1—Lk.6:31.)

**DEEPER STUDY # 1**

**(6:31) Golden Rule—Righteousness—Justice**: the golden rule is probably the most well-known thing Jesus ever said. It is the summit of ethics, of behavior, of righteousness, of godliness. It is a very practical statement of God's love; that is, God has done to us just as He wants us to do to Him. God has treated us just as He wants us to treat Him (and everyone else).

The golden rule reveals the heart of God. It shows us exactly how God's heart longs for us to live and act. It is a simple one-sentence statement revealing what love really is and what life in heaven (the perfect world) is to be like. It tells believers that, as citizens of both heaven and earth, they are to live as the golden rule dictates while still on the earth.

There are four significant facts that set the golden rule apart from all other teaching.

1. The golden rule is a simple one-sentence statement that embraces all human behavior. The fact that all law and all love can be stated in one simple sentence is amazing. The simple statement of the golden rule includes all "the law and the prophets" (Mt.7:12).

2. The golden rule *demands true law and justice*. Note the wording; it is not negative and passive, yet it tells man how not to behave. It restrains man. For example, the golden rule is teaching a man not to lie, steal, cheat, or injure; and it is teaching much more.

3. The golden rule is concerned with true love, that is, with positive, active behavior.
   a. It is more than not doing wrong (lying, stealing, cheating).
   b. It is more than just doing good (helping, caring, giving).
   c. It is *looking, searching, seeking for ways to do the good* that you want others to do to you; and then doing that good to others.

4. The golden rule teaches the whole law, for the whole law is contained in the words: "Thou shalt love thy neighbor as thyself" (Mt.22:39-40). Every human being would like to have all others treat him perfectly: to love and care for him to the ultimate degree and to express that love and care. The believer is to so love and care while still on earth. He is to give earth a taste of heaven before all things end. Men, being treated so supremely and getting a taste of heaven, might then turn to God.

---

**2** **(6:32-34) World, Behavior of—Self-Denial**: Jesus presented a logical argument for the believer to live as God says. The argument is strong: a believer's behavior must surpass a sinner's behavior.
   ⇒ Sinners love those who love them.
   ⇒ Sinners do good to those who do good to them.
   ⇒ Sinners lend to secure an interest or favor or some gain.

Note three points.
1. The shocking truth: believers who do not live as Christ says do no more than sinners.
2. The world sees virtue and goodness as love; they see doing good and lending as being neighborly. And it is good to love, to do good, and to lend.
3. But loving, doing good, and lending are not enough. It does not get a person into heaven. It is not what Christ did. Christ denied Himself in order to win the world. He loved His enemies and did good to those who hated Him. It might be said that He even loaned His life to the world.

> **"Christ died for the ungodly" (Ro.5:6).**
> **"While we were yet sinners, Christ died for us" (Ro.5:8).**
> **"When we were enemies, we were reconciled to God by the death of His Son" (Ro.5:10).**

The believer is to do the very same as Christ: deny and sacrifice himself to win the world and offer them the privilege of being saved to the utmost. It takes more than the virtue and goodness of love and doing good and lending among men to become a follower of Christ. It takes the denial and sacrifice of oneself for the sake of reaching the unlovely for Christ, those who are...

- enemies
- haters
- cursers
- borrowers
- persecutors
- thieves
- despiteful
- needful
- selfish

**3** **(6:35-36) Reward**: the reward for living as Jesus said is challenging. The obedient believer shall receive a threefold reward.

1. He shall receive a *great reward*. All that the believer suffers and loses on earth will be restored. But note: what he lost will not only be restored, he will *receive well beyond* what he has lost. He will receive an *enormous reward* for having obeyed the Lord and for having sacrificed in order to meet the needs of a dying world. What will the *great reward* be? It will be at least twofold: eternal life and inheriting all that God the Father has.

> **"Verily, verily, I say unto you, He that heareth my word, and believeth on him that sent me, hath everlasting life, and shall not come into condemnation; but is passed from death unto life" (Jn.5:24).**
>
> **"That being justified by his grace, we should be made heirs according to the hope of eternal life" (Tit.3:7).**
>
> **"Blessed be the God and Father of our Lord Jesus Christ, which according to his abundant mercy hath begotten us again unto a lively hope by the resurrection of Jesus Christ from the dead,**

to an inheritance incorruptible, and undefiled, and that fadeth not away, reserved in heaven for you" (1 Pt.1:3-4).

"Then shall the King say unto them on his right hand, Come, ye blessed of my Father, inherit the kingdom prepared for you from the foundation of the world" (Mt.25:34. See Deeper Study # 3— Mt.19:23-24.)

Simply stated, the believer shall receive both *eternal life* and *an inheritance* for having obeyed Christ and having served so sacrificially while on earth. The believer shall have part in the glorious work of God that will be performed in the new heavens and earth, a work that will go on from glory to glory.

2. He shall be the child of the Highest, of God Himself.

"But when the fulness of the time was come, God sent forth his Son, made of a woman, made under the law, to redeem them that were under the law, that we might receive the adoption of sons. And because ye are sons, God hath sent forth the Spirit of his Son into your hearts, crying, Abba, Father" (Gal.4:4-6).

"The Spirit itself beareth witness with out spirit, that we are the children of God: and if children, then heirs; heirs of God, and joint-heirs with Christ; if so be that we suffer with him, that we may be also glorified together" (Ro.8:16-17).

3. He shall be acting as God's child. What a privilege! The privilege of actually behaving as God behaves! The privilege of demonstrating and showing mercy! Acting as God acts, being merciful as God is merciful will do a great thing for us. It will stir great assurance and confidence within.

"Abide in him; that, when he shall appear, we may have confidence, and not be ashamed before him at his coming" (1 Jn.2:28).

**4** (6:37-38) **Reward—Justice:** Jesus made a phenomenal promise to the disciple who lives as He said—the promise of reciprocal behavior, of receiving back just what he gave.

1. Personal relationships are involved in reciprocal behavior. Three specific behaviors are covered: judging, condemning, and forgiving others. Jesus was saying two things.
   a. If we judge and condemn and are unforgiving of others, then both men and God will treat us the same. We shall be judged, condemned, and unforgiven both on earth and in heaven.
   b. If we do not judge and condemn men, but rather forgive them, then God and most men will not judge and condemn us; they will also be forgiving.
2. Property matters are involved in reciprocal behavior. The believer is to give and to possess a spirit of giving and not to be selfish and hoarding. If he gives, he shall receive back much more. In fact, his cup shall be *running over*. God will pour all the good things of this earth into his life (bosom).
3. The principle is clear and challenging: a person receives what he gives. This is definitely true of God and usually true of men. What a man puts into life is what he gets out of life.

"Is it [your purpose] not to deal thy bread to the hungry, and that thou bring the poor that are cast out to thy house when thou seest the naked, that thou cover him; and that thou hide not thyself from thine own flesh? Then shall thy light break forth as the morning and thine health shall spring forth speedily: and thy righteousness shall go before thee; the glory of the LORD shall be thy rereward [rear guard]" (Is.58:7-8).

| | K. Jesus Teaches His Rules for Discipleship: The Need to Watch, 6:39-45 (Mt.7:3-5, 17-18; 10:25; 12:35) | that is in thine own eye? Thou hypocrite, cast out first the beam out of thine own eye, and then shalt thou see clearly to pull out the mote that is in thy brother's eye. | c. The criticizer is a hypocrite d. Judging oneself enables one to see clearly & to see how to help others. |
|---|---|---|---|
| 1 **Watch blindness: One's leaders & how one leads** a. If both are in darkness b. Both stumble & fall | 39 And he spake a parable unto them, Can the blind lead the blind? shall they not both fall into the ditch? | 43 For a good tree bringeth not forth corrupt fruit; neither doth a corrupt tree bring forth good fruit. | 4 **Watch the fruit that a man brings forth** a. Every tree is known by its fruit b. Every tree reproduces after its nature or kind |
| 2 **Watch the Master (Lord)** a. The disciple must submit b. He shall be as his master | 40 The disciple is not above his master: but every one that is perfect shall be as his master. | 44 For every tree is known by his own fruit. For of thorns men do not gather figs, nor of a bramble bush gather they grapes. | |
| 3 **Watch hypocrisy & criticism of others** a. Both have a problem b. The criticizer has the biggest problem | 41 And why beholdest thou the mote that is in thy brother's eye, but perceivest not the beam that is in thine own eye? 42 Either how canst thou say to thy brother, Brother, let me pull out the mote that is in thine eye, when thou thyself beholdest not the beam | 45 A good man out of the good treasure of his heart bringeth forth that which is good; and an evil man out of the evil treasure of his heart bringeth forth that which is evil: for of the abundance of the heart his mouth speaketh. | c. Every man reproduces what is in his heart |

# DIVISION III

## THE SON OF MAN'S ANNOUNCED MISSION AND PUBLIC MINISTRY, 4:16-9:17

## K. Jesus Teaches His Rules for Discipleship: The Need to Watch, 6:39-45

(6:39-45) **Introduction**: man is to watch how he lives. Both the quality and fate of his life depend upon it.

⇒ God cares about the quality of a man's life. He wants every man to have the fullest life that he possibly can.
⇒ God cares about the destiny of a man, where a man will spend eternity. He wants every man to receive eternal life.

There are four rules, four warnings that must be watched if we are to live life to the fullest and be assured of eternal life.
1. Watch blindness: one's leaders and how one leads (v.39).
2. Watch the Master (the Lord Himself) (v.40).
3. Watch hypocrisy and the criticism of others (v.41-42).
4. Watch the fruit that a man brings forth (v.43-45).

[1] (6:39) **Spiritual Blindness—Darkness**: the first rule is to watch blindness; watch one's leaders and how one leads. "Can the blind lead the blind?" Note several things.

1. Note who the blind are. They are the leaders: the preachers, teachers, parents—anyone who has influence or responsibility for anyone else. In fact, any person can be blind and lead someone else down the same path of blindness. But observe a significant fact. Jesus also says that the blind are those who follow: the pupil, learner, listener, seeker, child—anyone who looks up to someone else for guidance.

2. Note why people are blind. There are several clear reasons.
   a. A person can be born blind. He can be handicapped, never having had the opportunity to see the *truth* of things, never having been exposed to the light.
   b. A person can be blind because of some injury. He used to be able to see and had every opportunity to see, but now he is blind, blind because...
      • he injured himself by some careless act. (He is guilty of blinding himself to the Light.)
      • he was blinded by someone else, either deliberately or carelessly. (Others led him astray, led him off into the darkness.)
      • he was blinded by nature. (Circumstances, heritage, location kept him from ever having the opportunity to escape the darkness.)
   c. A person can be blind because he wants and chooses to be in the dark. The dark is his choice; he finds the dark is enjoyable and comfortable; therefore, he refuses to come out into the light and to see the truth of things.
   d. A person can be blind because he closes his eyes or turns his head and looks away. He just refuses to see the light, the truth.

Jesus warned against being blind. He said blindness leads to two tragic results.
1. Both walk in darkness, both the leader and the follower. Being a leader does not guarantee that one walks in the light. A leader can be blind, and if the leader is blind, then the follower will remain blind. The leader must see and have his sight if the follower is to ever see. (Note the awesome responsibility upon leaders.)
2. Both stumble and fall "into the ditch." Being a leader does not guarantee that one will not fall. The blind person will stumble and fall no matter who he is, leader or not. And note, a leader will especially stumble about and fall if he is on strange or unfamiliar terrain. The truth of Christ is totally unknown terrain to the blind teacher, no matter his profession.

"Whosoever therefore shall break one of these least commandments, and shall teach men so, he shall be called the least in the kingdom of heaven: but whosoever shall do and teach them, the same shall be called great in the kingdom of heaven. For I say unto you, That except your righteousness shall exceed the righteousness of the scribes and Pharisees, ye shall in no case enter into the kingdom of heaven" (Mt.5:19-20).

"Desiring to be teachers of the law; understanding neither what they say, nor whereof they affirm" (1 Tim.1:7).

"If any man teach otherwise, and consent not to wholesome words, even the words of our Lord Jesus Christ, and to the doctrine which is according to godliness; he is proud, knowing nothing, but doting about questions and strifes of words, whereof cometh envy, strife, railings, evil surmisings, perverse disputings of men of corrupt minds, and destitute of the truth, supposing that gain is godliness: from such withdraw thyself" (1 Tim.6:3-5).

"For the time will come when they will not endure sound doctrine; but after their own lusts shall they heap to themselves teachers, having itching ears; and they shall turn away their ears from the truth, and shall be turned unto fables" (2 Tim.4:3-4).

"But there were false prophets also among the people, even as there shall be false teachers among you, who privily shall bring in damnable heresies, even denying the Lord that bought them, and bring upon themselves swift destruction" (2 Pt.2:1).

"And the light shineth in darkness; and the darkness comprehended it not" (Jn.1:5).

"And this is the condemnation, that light is come into the world, and men loved darkness rather than light, because their deeds were evil" (Jn.3:19).

"But if thine eye be evil, thy whole body shall be full of darkness. If therefore the light that is in thee be darkness, how great is that darkness?" (Mt.6:23).

"But if our gospel be hid, it is hid to them that are lost: in whom the god of this world hath blinded the minds of them which believe not, lest the light of the glorious gospel [the truth] of Christ, who is the image of God, should shine unto them" (2 Cor.4:3-4).

"This I say therefore, and testify in the Lord, that ye henceforth walk not as other Gentiles walk, in vanity of their mind, having the understanding darkened, being alienated from the life of God through the ignorance that is in them, because of the blindness of their heart" (Eph.4:17-18).

[2] (6:40) **Self-Denial—Dedication**: the second rule is to watch the life of the Master, of the Lord Jesus Christ Himself. "The disciple is not above his Lord: but...shall be as his Master." Note several points.

1. The word "perfect" (katertismenos) means to complete, render fit, mend. It is a common word often used for mending, repairing, or restoring broken things such as nets (Mt.4:21) or men (Gal.6:1).

2. The point is forceful: "the disciple is not above his Master" (see note, pt.1—Mt.10:24-25). The disciple is not better than his Lord; therefore, he cannot expect to be treated better, nor can he expect to receive more in this world than his Lord. The disciple cannot expect to be better by having more honor, praise, recognition, or esteem. He cannot expect to have more comfort, rest, or pleasure. The Lord suffered, humbled, and denied Himself for the sake of the world and its needs. The disciple, as a follower of the Lord, does the same; he denies himself in order to reach the world for his Lord (see note and DEEPER STUDY # 1—Lk.9:23).

"That whosoever believeth in him should not perish, but have eternal life" (Jn.3:15).

"Let this mind be in you, which was also in Christ Jesus: who, being in the form of God, thought it not robbery to be equal with God: but made himself of no reputation, and took upon him the form of a servant, and was made in the likeness of men: and being found in fashion as a man, he humbled himself, and became obedient unto death, even the death of the cross" (Ph.2:5-8).

"Then said Jesus to them again, Peace be unto you: as my Father hath sent me, even so send I you" (Jn.20:21).

"But ye shall receive power, after that the Holy Ghost is come upon you: and ye shall be witnesses unto me both in Jerusalem, and in all Judaea, and in Samaria, and unto the uttermost part of the earth" (Acts 1:8).

3. The goal of the disciple is to "be as his Master." The disciple seeks to be like his Master: conformed, mended, repaired, restored (perfected) into His very image.

"That I may know him, and the power of his resurrection, and the fellowship of his suffeings, *being made conformable* unto his death" (Ph.3:10).

"Ye are my witnesses, saith the LORD, and my servant whom I have chosen: that ye *may know and believe me, and understand* that I am he" (Is.43:10).

"But we all, with open face beholding as in a glass the glory of the Lord, are *changed into the same image* from glory to glory, even as by the Spirit of the Lord" (2 Cor.3:18).

[3] (6:41-42) **Criticism—Hypocrisy**: the third rule is to watch hypocrisy and criticism of others. Note a crucial fact: Jesus was speaking to everyone seated before Him. No matter how moral, decent, strong, religious, or free of visible sin, He was speaking to everyone seated in the audience. No one was exempt. Everyone was to watch out for hypocrisy and criticism of others. Why? Because whatever is in a person's eye, even if it is only a speck, is serious. Even a speck causes the eye to water, squint, blink, and close. The speck hinders a person's sight (life, walk), holding him back from full sight and service. Now note four points about the parable.

1. Both persons, the one being criticized and the criticizer, do have a problem. Both have a need to clean the dirt out of their eyes. Neither one is free of dirt. Not a single person serves in perfect obedience and ministry to the Lord. There is at least a speck in everyone's eye.

2. The criticizer has the biggest problem. This is usually overlooked. Criticism of others is a beam. If one has only a speck in his eye, when he begins to criticize others, he immediately catches a beam in his own eye. *Criticism is the tree that strikes the eye and blinds one* to his own need, his need for continued confession and repentance. The criticizer becomes blinded to his constant need for the righteousness of Jesus Christ.

"**But he that lacketh these things is blind, and cannot see afar off, and hath forgotten that he was purged from his old sins" (2 Pt.1:9).**

3. The criticizer is a hypocrite (see DEEPER STUDY # 2—Mt.23:13). He is but a man who is like all other men, full of ever so many faults and coming ever so short, yet he finds fault with others. He criticizes, grumbles, gripes, condemns, judges, and censors others while he too is guilty of so much in so many other areas. And note: his greatest fault is that he sets himself up as the *Judge*, as the one who has the right to judge men.

4. The disciple must examine himself first. Judging himself first will enable him to *see clearly* just how to help others. Rigid examination is required. Simple honesty and thought say that a man must clean the dirt out of his own eye before he can see clearly enough to help others clean their eyesight.

"**Judge not, that ye be not judged" (Mt.7:1).**
"**Who art thou that judgest another man's servant? to his own master he standeth or falleth. Yea, he shall be holden up: for God is able to make him stand" (Ro.14:4).**
"**Let us not therefore judge one another any more: but judge this rather, that no man put a stumblingblock or an occasion to fall in his brother's way" (Ro.14:13).**
"**Therefore judge nothing before the time, until the Lord come, who both will bring to light the hidden things of darkness, and will make manifest the counsels of the hearts: and then shall every man have praise of God" (1 Cor.4:5).**
"**There is one lawgiver, who is able to save and to destroy: who art thou that judgest another?" (Jas.4:12).**

**4** (6:43-45) **Fruit-Bearing—Words—Tongue:** watch the fruit that a man brings forth.

1. Every tree is known by its fruit, its nature. A good man is not judged by a bad piece of fruit here and there but by the good fruit he bears. Every tree produces some bad fruit, yet the tree is not cast away. A tree is not rejected unless it *leans toward* bad fruit. When testing and examining men, we must observe not single acts here and there; but the tenor, the lean, the whole behavior of their lives. How important! (See note—Mt.7:17 for detailed discussion.)

2. Every tree reproduces after its nature, after its kind. How can we tell if a man is false? There is one revealing mark: the fruit he gathers. A man is known by the fruit he feeds upon and the fruit he feeds to others (see outlines and notes—Jn.15:1-8). If he feeds himself on thorns and thistles and not on grapes and figs, that is one way to tell. If he feeds thorns and thistles to others instead of grapes and figs, that is another way to tell.

Thorns and thistles are false food, worldliness (see DEEPER STUDY # 3—Mt.13:7, 22). Grapes and figs are true food. There is only one true food for the soul of man: the Lord Jesus Christ and His Word. (See note—Jn.6:1-71; outlines and notes—Jn.6:30-36; 6:41-51. Cp. all outlines and notes 6:1-71; DEEPER STUDY # 4—Jn.17:17; cp. 5:24; 1 Pt.2:2-3.) A man must feed on and feed others the truth of the Lord and His Word. Any other source of food for the human soul is false food: it is thorn and thistle (worldliness). If eaten or served to others, it will choke the life out of the soul (Mt.13:7; cp. 1 Jn.2:15-16; 2 Cor.6:17-18; Ro.12:1-2).

3. Every man reproduces what is in his heart. Note that Jesus is dealing with a man's mouth, the *words* a man speaks. A man speaks what is in his heart. His words expose his heart, the kind of man he is. The idea is that words come out of an overflowing heart: "Out of the abundance [overflow] of the heart the mouth speaketh." A man's words expose five things about him.

⇒ A man's words expose his true nature: what he is really like beneath the surface.
⇒ A man's words expose what he is down deep within his heart: his motives, desires, ambitions, or the lack of initiative.
⇒ A man's words expose his true character: good or bad, kind or cruel.
⇒ A man's words expose his mind, what he thinks: pure or impure thoughts, dirty or clean thoughts.
⇒ A man's words expose his spirit, what he believes and pursues: the legitimate or illegitimate, the intelligent or ignorant, the true or false, the beneficial or wasteful.

"**Even so every good tree bringeth forth good fruit; but a corrupt tree bringeth forth evil fruit" (Mt.7:17).**
"**Even so faith, if it hath not works, is dead, being alone. Yea, a man may say, Thou hast faith, and I have works: show me thy faith without thy works, and I will show thee my faith by my works" (Jas.2:17-18).**
"**Having your conversation honest among the Gentiles: that, whereas they speak against you as evildoers, they may by your good works, which they shall behold, glorify God in the day of visitation" (1 Pt.2:12).**
"**Now the works of the flesh are manifest, which are these; Adultery, fornication, uncleanness, lasciviousness, idolatry, witchcraft, hatred, variance, emulations, wrath, strife, seditions, heresies, envyings, murders, drunkenness, revellings, and such like: of the which I tell you before, as I have also told you in time past, that they which do such things shall not inherit the kingdom of God. But the fruit of the Spirit is love, joy, peace, longsuffering, gentleness, goodness, faith, meekness, temperance: against such there is no law" (Gal.5:19-23).**

| | **L. Jesus Teaches Two Foundations of Life: Genuine vs. Counterfeit Discipleship, 6:46-49** (Mt.7:24-27) | built an house, and digged deep, and laid the foundation on a rock: and when the flood arose, the stream beat vehemently upon that house, and could not shake it: for it was founded upon a rock. | 1) He builds a house 2) He digs deep 3) He lays a rock foundation c. Result: It stands |
|---|---|---|---|
| **1 The foundation of discipleship is obedience** | 46 And why call ye me, Lord, Lord, and do not the things which I say? | 49 But he that heareth, and doeth not, is like a man that without a foundation built an house upon the earth; against which the stream did beat vehemently, and immediately it fell; and the ruin of that house was great. | **3 The false disciple: Lays no foundation** a. He hears, but does not obey b. He is like a builder 1) Builds a house 2) Does not dig 3) Lays no foundation c. Result: A great fall |
| **2 The true disciple: Lays a foundation** a. He comes & hears & does b. He is like a builder | 47 Whosoever cometh to me, and heareth my sayings, and doeth them, I will show you to whom he is like: 48 He is like a man which | | |

# DIVISION III

## THE SON OF MAN'S ANNOUNCED MISSION AND PUBLIC MINISTRY, 4:16-9:17

## L. Jesus Teaches Two Foundations of Life: Genuine vs. Counterfeit Discipleship, 6:46-49

(6:46-49) **Introduction—Life—Foundation—Profession, False vs. True:** Jesus Christ was a carpenter by trade and profession. He knew houses; He knew the building trade.

Several important matters about building a house need to be noted here.
1. Hearing instructions. This is critical. Knowing how to build is critical.
   a. One must hear and follow (obey) the instructions.
   b. One must hear and build upon what he hears for future building. Builders must always be "laying up on store for themselves a good foundation against the time to come...." (1 Tim.6:19).
2. Selecting the foundation. This, too, is critical. Selecting the site and material determine the future of the house.
   a. One must build upon a solid foundation. There is only one foundation upon which to build: the rock (1 Cor.3:11).
   b. One must make his call and choice to build sure (2 Pt.1:10).
   c. One must know that building upon rock takes time and skill.
3. Counting the cost. This also is critical. The fact is brought out by Christ in another passage. Beginning and not finishing the house brings mockery and shame (Lk.14:28-30).

Several introductory applications are clearly seen in this picture of house building.
1. Every person has a house, a life to build. How he builds his life determines his destiny, not just for this life, but for eternity. How he builds his life makes all the difference between...
   - success and failure
   - life and death
   - reward and loss
   - acceptance and rejection
   - standing and falling
2. There is only One foundation for every life: Jesus Christ (1 Cor.3:11). He is the Rock upon which both individuals and churches are to build (Mt.16:18).
3. Everyone either builds upon this world or upon Christ, heaven itself. Jesus teaches that there are two kinds of builders.
   a. A wise builder: hears and obeys (v.47-48).
   b. A foolish builder: hears and does not obey (v.49).

1. The foundation of discipleship is obedience (v.46).
2. The true disciple: lays a foundation (v.47-48).
3. The false disciple: lays no foundation (v.49).

**1** (6:46) **Profession—Foundation—Life:** the foundation of discipleship is *obedience, doing the things which Jesus says*. There is no substitute. If a person wishes to be a follower of Jesus Christ, that person has to do what Jesus says.
1. Both builders in this passage call Jesus "Lord." Both acknowledge Him as Lord. Both pray and call Him "Lord, Lord," and both witness before others that He is Lord. Both are known as followers of Jesus.
2. Jesus questions disobedience and disloyalty. He rebukes and warns anyone who calls Him Lord and does not do what He says. As Lord He is due allegiance and expects loyalty from all, especially those who call Him Lord.
3. A profession of words is not enough. Even repeating one's profession, "Lord, Lord," is not enough. One can cry before the world and still be questioned and warned by Christ: "Why do you not do the things which I say?"
4. A person is cheating himself to profess and not obey. Profession without obedience gives a false security; it makes one feel like he is acceptable to God when he is not. Christ says he is not, for the only foundation to discipleship, that is, the only way to be accepted by God, is to do the things which Christ says.

**2** (6:47-48) **Foundation—Disciple—Trials**: the true disciple *lays a foundation*. Note three points.

1. The true disciple comes to Christ, hears Christ and does what Christ says. All three steps are essential.
2. The true disciple is like a builder.
   a. The disciple builds a house. Every person has a house to build, a life to build. Once in the world, we cannot escape the fact. We are building our lives, and how we build our lives determines our eternal destiny.

   God's own Son instructs a man how to build. A man hears and follows (obeys) the instructions or hears and rejects (disobeys) the instructions and builds his own way. The instructions, the words of Christ, are the materials which determine the structure and fate of our lives. Our lives and our destiny depend upon how we respond to the sayings of Christ.
   b. The disciple digs deep to lay the foundation (footing). This is critical to note. The ground is not soil, it is rock. Great effort and energy are demanded. The most expensive and costly thing to a builder is *hitting rock*, yet rock is by far the best foundation.
      ⇒ This builder chooses the rock for his foundation. He did not just hit it while digging for his footing; he knew the rock was there and chose it as the right foundation for his house. He deliberately chose *the most sure and secure* foundation available.
      ⇒ This builder *dug deep*. He took no chances. He wanted to be absolutely sure and secure, as sure and secure as possible. So he *dug* as deep as possible.
      ⇒ This builder was willing to put both the *time and effort and cost* into digging rock. It was difficult, exhausting, and expensive; yet he did it. Why? Because it was *his house* and he wanted to be absolutely sure and secure.
   c. He lays the foundation upon the rock. Christ is the only foundation upon which we can build and structure our lives. "Other foundations can no man lay than that is laid, which is Jesus Christ" (1 Cor.3:11; cp. Eph.2:20; 1 Pt.2:4-5).

   **Thought 1.** The Lord is not a lifeless rock, but "a living stone" (1 Pt.2:4). When we come to Him "as a living stone," we are "built up a spiritual house" (1 Pt.2:5).

   > "As newborn babes, desire the sincere milk of the word, that ye may grow thereby: if so be ye have tasted that the Lord is gracious. To whom coming, as unto a living stone, disallowed indeed of men, but chosen of God, and precious, ye also, as lively stones, are built up a spiritual house, an holy priesthood, to offer up spiritual sacrifices, acceptable to God by Jesus Christ" (1 Pt.2:2-5).

3. The true disciple stands. The house (his life) he built stands against the storms of life and eternity. Now note: he is not exempt from the storms of life. Just because he built upon a rock does not mean storms will not come. In fact, it is because storms do come that he built upon the rock. This man (the true disciple) knows that it rains "on the just and on the unjust" (Mt.5:45). All kinds of storms will come, the storms of...

| | | | |
|---|---|---|---|
| • sickness | • suffering | • death | • mistreatments |
| • sin | • disappointment | • accidents | • abuse |
| • temptation | • tension | • complaints | • hospitalization |

**Thought 1.** A man must build upon Jesus Christ. There is no other foundation that can withstand the coming storms of trouble, problems, afflictions, evil, and death.

> "Jesus saith unto them, Did ye never read in the scriptures, The stone which the builders rejected, the same is become the head of the corner: this is the Lord's doing, and it is marvellous in our eyes?" (Mt.21:42).
> "For other foundation can no man lay than that is laid, which is Jesus Christ" (1 Cor.3:11).
> "And are built upon the foundation of the apostles and prophets, Jesus Christ himself being the chief corner stone" (Eph.2:20).
> "Wherefore also it is contained in the scripture, Behold, I lay in Sion a chief corner stone, elect, precious: and he that believeth on him shall not be confounded" (1 Pt.2:6).
> "This is the stone which was set at nought of you builders, which is become the head of the corner" (Acts 4:11).
> "Laying up in store for themselves a good foundation against the time to come, that they may lay hold on eternal life" (1 Tim.6:19).
> "Nevertheless the foundation of God standeth sure, having this seal, The Lord knoweth them that are his. And, Let every one that nameth the name of Christ depart from iniquity" (2 Tim.2:19).

**Thought 2.** When the storms come, no man falls if he has built his life upon Christ.
1) God accepts us in Christ; He adopts us as a child of His.

> "But when the fulness of the time was come, God sent forth his Son, made of a woman, made under the law, to redeem them that were under the law, that we might receive the adoption of sons. And because ye are sons, God hath sent forth the Spirit of his Son into your hearts, crying, Abba, Father" (Gal.4:4-6).

"Having predestinated us unto the adoption of children by Jesus Christ to himself, according to the good pleasure of his will, to the praise of the glory of his grace, wherein he hath made us accepted in the beloved" (Eph.1:5-6).

2) God promises to provide the necessities of life.

"But seek ye first the kingdom of God, and his righteousness; and all these things shall be added unto you" (Mt.6:33; cp. Mt.6:25-34).

3) God promises to work out all things (all storms) for good to those who build wisely.

"And we know that all things work together for good to them that love God, to them who are the called according to his purpose" (Ro.8:28).

4) God blesses those who "hear the Word of God, and keep it" (Lk.11:28).
5) Christ promises joy to those who hear and receive the things He said.

"These things have I spoken unto you, that my joy might remain in you, and that your joy might be full" (Jn.15:11; cp. Jn.13:17).

**3** (6:49) *Foundation—Disciple*: the false disciple *lays no foundation*. Note three points.

1. The false disciple hears Christ but *does not do* what Christ says.
   ⇒ He ignores what Christ says.     ⇒ He is too busy.
   ⇒ He applies himself elsewhere.    ⇒ He does not think about the consequences.
2. The false disciple is like a builder.
   a. He does build a house, but note a very critical point. He hears the instructions of the Master Builder (through church, parents, radio, book, friends, television). He has been told how to build, and he knows where to build; therefore, he is expected to build according to instructions. In fact, it is shocking if he does not build a solid house (note the question and shock of Christ in v.46).
   b. He does not dig. How foolish! Here is the depth of man's foolishness well illustrated. Why does he not dig?
      ⇒ The rock is too time-consuming and demanding.
      ⇒ He fails to look ahead, to consider the future.
      ⇒ He wants to be doing something else.
   c. He lays no foundation, no footing. What a tragedy! He knew better, but he ignored the Master Builder's instructions. The false disciple heard what the prophets and righteous men of old desired to hear (Mt.13:17; 1 Pt.1:10). What a privilege he had! And how he abused that privilege! Week after week, day after day, year after year he heard; yet, he never followed the instructions on how to build his life.
3. The false disciple *falls*. The house (his life) he built collapses against the storms of life and eternity.
   a. "The storm did burst against it." Floods of trials do come. They cannot be stopped; the house without a foundation cannot stand. Note: "Immediately it fell; and the *ruin of that house was great.*"
   b. Every man's work shall be made manifest. Our work is to be tested in this life through many, many trials, and in the next life by Christ. Great will be the fall of a life if it is not built upon Christ. The man who built his house upon sand *has to face* Christ in that day (1 Cor.3:13).

**Thought 1.** The person who builds upon sand clings to a *false trust*. His faith and trust are in the wrong thing.

"He that trusteth in his riches shall fall: but the righteous shall flourish as a branch" (Pr.11:28).
"He that trusteth in his own heart is a fool: but whoso walketh wisely, he shall be delivered" (Pr.28:26).
"For thou hast trusted in thy wickedness: thou hast said, None seeth me. Thy wisdom and thy knowledge, it hath perverted thee; and thou hast said in thine heart, I am, and none else beside me" (Is.47:10).
"Thus saith the LORD; Cursed be the man that trusteth in man, and maketh flesh his arm, and whose heart departeth from the LORD" (Jer.17:5).
"Say unto them which daub it with untempered mortar, that it shall fall: there shall be an overflowing shower; and ye, O great hailstones, shall fall; and a stormy wind shall rend it" (Ezk.13:11).
"And they come unto thee as the people cometh, and they sit before thee as my people, and they hear thy words, but they will not do them: for with their mouth they show much love, but their heart goeth after their covetousness" (Ezk.33:31).

**Thought 2.** The person who builds upon the sands of this world of sin shall fall.

"The righteousness of the perfect shall direct his way: but the wicked shall fall by his own wickedness" (Pr.11:5).

"Were they ashamed when they had committed abomination? nay, they were not at all ashamed, neither could they blush: therefore they shall fall among them that fall: at the time that I visit them they shall be cast down, saith the LORD" (Jer.6:15).

"Every man's work shall be made manifest: for the day shall declare it, because it shall be revealed by fire; and the fire shall try every man's work of what sort it is. If any man's work abide which he hath built thereupon, he shall receive a reward. If any man's work shall be burned, he shall suffer loss: but he himself shall be saved; yet so as by fire" (1 Cor.3:13-15).

"For yourselves know perfectly that the day of the Lord so cometh as a thief in the night. For when they shall say, Peace and safety; then sudden destruction cometh upon them, as travail upon a woman with child; and they shall not escape" (1 Th.5:2-3; cp. 2 Pt.3:4, 9-13).

"There are the workers of iniquity fallen: they are cast down, and shall not be able to rise" (Ps.36:12).

"Therefore shall his calamity come suddenly; suddenly shall he be broken without remedy" (Pr.6:15).

"How shall we escape, if we neglect so great salvation; which at the first began to be spoken by the Lord, and was confirmed unto us by them that heard him" (Heb.2:3).

| | **CHAPTER 7**<br><br>**M. Jesus Finds Great Faith in a Soldier: Great Faith, What It Is, 7:1-10**<br>(Mt.8:5-13) | them. And when he was now not far from the house, the centurion sent friends to him, saying unto him, Lord, trouble not thyself: for I am not worthy that thou shouldest enter under my roof: | **in Jesus Christ**<br><br>a. In Jesus as Sovereign Lord |
|---|---|---|---|
| 1 Jesus returned to Capernaum | Now when he had ended all his sayings in the audience of the people, he entered into Capernaum. | 7 Wherefore neither thought I myself worthy to come unto thee: but say in a word, and my servant shall be healed. | b. In Jesus' supreme power & Word |
| 2 Great faith cares deeply for people*DS1* | 2 And a certain centurion's servant, who was dear unto him, was sick, and ready to die. | 8 For I also am a man set under authority, having under me soldiers, and I say unto one, Go, and he goeth; and to another, Come, and he cometh; and to my servant, Do this, and he doeth it. | |
| 3 Great faith feels unworthy in approaching Jesus Christ | 3 And when he heard of Jesus, he sent unto him the elders of the Jews, beseeching him that he would come and heal his servant. | | |
| 4 Great faith seeks God | 4 And when they came to Jesus, they besought him instantly, saying, That he was worthy for whom he should do this: | 9 When Jesus heard these things, he marvelled at him, and turned him about, and said unto the people that followed him, I say unto you, I have not found so great faith, no, not in Israel. | 6 Great faith stirs the great power of Jesus Christ<br>a. Jesus marvelled<br>b. Jesus commended the soldier |
| | 5 For he loveth our nation, and he hath built us a synagogue. | 10 And they that were sent, returning to the house, found the servant whole that had been sick. | c. Jesus healed the servant |
| 5 Great faith is centered | 6 Then Jesus went with | | |

# DIVISION III

## THE SON OF MAN'S ANNOUNCED MISSION AND PUBLIC MINISTRY, 4:16-9:17

## M. Jesus Finds Great Faith in a Soldier: Great Faith, What It Is, 7:1-10

(7:1-10) **Introduction**: Jesus Christ meets the need of everyone—Gentile or Jew, rich or poor, leader or follower, ruler or slave. He bridges the gaps, prejudices, and divisions between men. The one essential for securing His help is faith. A person must have faith in Christ and His power. The fact is clearly demonstrated in what happened between this soldier and Jesus. Note that Jesus termed this man's faith "great faith."

1. Jesus returned to Capernaum (v.1).
2. Great faith cares deeply for people (v.2).
3. Great faith feels unworthy in approaching Jesus Christ (v.3).
4. Great faith seeks God (v.4-5).
5. Great faith is centered in Jesus Christ (v.6-8).
6. Great faith stirs the great power of Jesus Christ (v.9-10).

**1** (7:1) **Jesus Christ, Headquarters**: Jesus returned to Capernaum. Capernaum was His headquarters where He now lived (see note—Lk.4:31).

**2** (7:2) **Care**: great faith cares deeply for people. The soldier was a man who cared deeply for people. Note the word "dear" (entimos) meaning esteemed, honored, precious, prized. In the society of that day, a slave was nothing, only a tool or a thing to be used as the owner wished. He had no rights whatsoever, not even the right to live. An owner could mistreat and kill a slave without having to give an account. But this soldier loved his slave. This reveals a deep concern and care for people. It would have been much less bother to dispose of the slave or to ignore him and just let him die, but not this soldier. He cared. Note how he *personally* looked after the slave, a person who meant nothing to the rest of society. But his arms and love were wide open to do all he could to help this person who was helpless. This alone, helping a person who meant nothing to society, was bound to affect Christ dramatically.

> "Thou shalt love thy neighbour as thyself" (Mt.22:39).
> "This is my commandment, That ye love one another, as I have loved you" (Jn.15:12).
> "Let love be without dissimulation [hypocrisy]. Abhor that which is evil; cleave to that which is good" (Ro.12:9).
> "And the Lord make you to increase and abound in love one toward another, and toward all men, even as we do toward you" (1 Th.3:12).
> "If ye fulfil the royal law according to the scripture, Thou shalt love thy neighbour as thyself, ye do well" (Jas.2:8).

---

**DEEPER STUDY # 1**
(7:2) **Centurion:** see Deeper Study # 1—Acts 23:23.

---

**3** (7:3) **Rejection—Unworthiness:** great faith feels unworthy in approaching Jesus. The soldier was a man who had heard about Jesus and what he had heard made him feel unworthy. Note several things.

1.  Luke's account differs from Matthew's. Luke says the centurion sent some religious leaders to approach Jesus, whereas Matthew says that the centurion approached Jesus. What needs to be remembered is that in a dictatorial society, whatever a leader commands others to do is counted as his act, as he himself having done it. The leader's representatives act for him; thus, he is said to have done it.

2.  The centurion was in a place where he could hear about Jesus. He was where he could hear the message of hope, and when the news came, he did not close his mind or ignore it. He responded.

3.  The centurion, however, felt unworthy to approach Jesus himself. Why?
    ⇒ He was a soldier, trained to take life and probably guilty of having taken life. What he had heard about Christ was the message of love and brotherhood.
    ⇒ He was a sinner, a terrible sinner, a Roman heathen, *totally unworthy* and rejected in the eyes of most. He felt that Jesus, too, would count him unworthy and reject him.

4.  The centurion requested help from others. He asked them to intercede for him. Note: he did not allow his sense of unworthiness and rejection to defeat him; neither was he too proud to ask for help, despite his superior position.

> **Thought 1.** A man must expose himself to the gospel, be where the gospel is preached, and humble himself before the Lord if he wishes the blessings of God.

>> **"For I say, through the grace given unto me, to every man that is among you, not to think of himself more highly than he ought to think; but to think soberly" (Ro.12:3).**
>> **"But he giveth more grace. Wherefore he saith, God resisteth the proud, but giveth grace unto the humble" (Jas.4:6).**
>> **"Humble yourselves in the sight of the Lord, and he shall lift you up" (Jas.4:10).**
>> **"The LORD is nigh unto them that are of a broken heart; and saveth such as be of a contrite spirit" (Ps.34:18).**
>> **"Though the LORD be high, yet hath he respect unto the lowly: but the proud he knoweth afar off" (Ps.138:6).**
>> **"He hath showed thee, O man, what is good; and what doth the LORD require of thee, but to do justly, and to love mercy, and to walk humbly with thy God?" (Mic.6:8).**
>> **"For thus saith the high and lofty One that inhabiteth eternity, whose name is Holy; I dwell in the high and holy place, with him also that is of a contrite and humble spirit, to revive the spirit of the humble, and to revive the heart of the contrite ones" (Is.57:15).**

**4** (7:4-5) **Seeking God—Jew—Gentile—Rejected—Prejudice:** great faith seeks God. The soldier was a man who sought God.

1.  He was not a superficial religionist. He had heard about the God of Israel and accepted Him, rejecting the gods of Rome. This he did despite the hostility and rejection of the Jews. He was so drawn to God that he evidently was going to let nothing stop him from discovering the truth.

2.  He was a man of faith (v.9), a man who loved God. The very reason he would love the Jewish nation (a people who despised him) and build a synagogue was because of his love for God. His faith and love had to be genuine. It was most unusual for a Gentile, especially a Gentile official, to care for the Jews. Anti-semitism was the common thing. The Jew and Gentile had no dealings with one another. (See notes—Mt.15:26-27; Mk.7:25; Deeper Study # 1—7:27.) Note how far he went to serve God: he *loved* those who had formerly rejected and despised him, and he did what he could to edify and enhance the worship of God's people by building a synagogue. His love and faith were so strong and evident that those who had despised him now felt close to him—close enough to intercede for him.

>> **"But without faith it is impossible to please him: for he that cometh to God must believe that he is, and that he is a rewarder of them that diligently seek him" (Heb.11:6).**
>> **"They should seek the Lord, if haply they might feel after him, and find him, though he be not far from every one of us" (Acts 17:27).**
>> **"Seek the LORD, and his strength: seek his face evermore" (Ps.105:4).**

**5** (7:6-8) **Faith:** great faith is centered in Jesus Christ. The centurion was a man of faith. The centurion illustrated perfectly what faith is (Heb.11:6).

1.  It is believing that "Christ is": that He is sovereign Lord (Heb.11:6). All power is subject to Him.

2.  It is believing that "Christ is a rewarder of those that diligently seek Him" (Heb.11:6). He will use His power in behalf of those who do seek Him.

Note that the centurion had diligently sought Jesus, believing Jesus could meet his need. Many believers diligently seek the Lord, but the centurion's faith was so much greater than most believers. Why? Because he believed that *the Word of Christ was all that was needed.* Jesus did not have to be present for the need to be met. As a centurion, he had authority over men. All he had to do was issue an order and it was carried out, whether he was present or not. He was a sovereign commander. He was saying, "How much more are you, O' Lord. But speak the word only, and my need shall be met." What a forceful and powerful lesson on faith for all!

"And Jesus came and spake unto them, saying, All power is given unto me in heaven and in earth" (Mt.28:18).

"Commit thy way unto the LORD; trust also in him; and he shall bring it to pass" (Ps.37:5).

"It is better to trust in the LORD than to put confidence in man" (Ps.118:8).

"Trust ye in the LORD for ever: for in the LORD JEHOVAH is everlasting strength" (Is.26:4).

"Seek ye the LORD while he may be found, call ye upon him while he is near" (Is.55:6).

**6** (7:9-10) **Faith—Jesus Christ, Power of**: great faith stirs the great power of Jesus. The centurion was a man who stirred the great power of Jesus.

1. Jesus marvelled. Only twice is Jesus said to have marvelled at people: at the centurion, and at the people in Nazareth because of their unbelief (Mk.6:6). What an impact this man made upon Jesus!

2. Jesus embraced and commended the soldier. He embraced him for his faith, not for who he was or for what he had done as a soldier. *Believing*, that is, true faith, is a rare thing. Not many believe; yet belief in Christ is one of the greatest qualities of human life—a quality ignored, neglected, and in some cases denied.

He commended him before others. There are times when recognition and commendation are to be given, but again, note for what. It is for spiritual graces, for spiritual strength. However, caution should always be exercised lest the temptation of pride and self-importance set in.

3. Jesus healed the servant, and His power to meet the centurion's request proved His Messiahship—that He was truly the Son of God.

> **Thought 1.** Jesus Christ has the power to meet our needs; however, there is one prerequisite: faith. We must believe that Jesus Christ *can* meet our needs.
>
> "And Jesus answering saith unto them, Have faith in God. For verily I say unto you, That whosoever shall say unto this mountain, Be thou removed, and be thou cast into the sea; and shall not doubt in his heart, but shall believe that those things which he saith shall come to pass; he shall have whatsoever he saith. Therefore I say unto you, What things soever ye desire, when ye pray, believe that ye receive them, and ye shall have them" (Mk.11:22-24).
>
> "But I know, that even now, whatsoever thou wilt ask of God, God will give it thee" (Jn.11:22).
>
> "Wherefore he is able also to save them to the uttermost that come unto God by him, seeing he ever liveth to make intercession for them" (Heb.7:25).

| | | N. Jesus Raises a Widow's Son: Great Compassion & Power, 7:11-17 | 14 And he came and touched the bier: and they that bare him stood still. And he said, Young man, I say unto thee, Arise. | 3 | The great power of Jesus a. To bypass traditional beliefs b. To stop the death processional c. To raise the dead |
|---|---|---|---|---|---|
| 1 | Jesus entered Nain—many were present to witness the conquest of death | 11 And it came to pass the day after, that he went into a city called Nain; and many of his disciples went with him, and much people. | 15 And he that was dead sat up, and began to speak. And he delivered him to his mother. | | |
| 2 | The great compassion of Jesus: He was touched a. By death, a dead man b. By a broken heart c. By a loving, caring, beloved woman | 12 Now when he came nigh to the gate of the city, behold, there was a dead man carried out, the only son of his mother, and she was a widow: and much people of the city was with her. | 16 And there came a fear on all: and they glorified God, saying, That a great prophet is risen up among us; and, That God hath visited his people. | 4 | The great fear of the people a. They glorified God b. They believed Him to be a prophet c. They acknowledged God's dealing with them again |
| | d. The Lord saw: Had compassion[DS1] & spoke, giving assurance | 13 And when the Lord saw her, he had compassion on her, and said unto her, Weep not | 17 And this rumour of him went forth throughout all Judaea, and throughout all the region round about. | | d. They bore witness |

# DIVISION III

## THE SON OF MAN'S ANNOUNCED MISSION AND PUBLIC MINISTRY, 4:16-9:17

**N.    Jesus Raises a Widow's Son: Great Compassion and Power, 7:11-17**

(7:11-17) **Introduction—Resurrection, The**: the most phenomenal event in all history is the resurrection of the dead. It may be the fact of Jesus Himself being resurrected or the promise of believers' being raised someday or of Jesus raising the dead—some men just have enormous difficulty believing such claims. Luke knew this, so he wanted to help unbelieving minds. In this event Luke shared the great compassion and power of Jesus to raise the dead.

1.    Jesus entered Nain—many were present to witness the conquest of death (v.11).
2.    The great compassion of Jesus: He was touched (v.12-13).
3.    The great power of Jesus (v.14-15).
4.    The great fear of the people (v.16-17).

**1** (7:11) **Jesus Christ, Following—Seeking, Reasons**: Jesus entered Nain. This is the only time this city is named in the Bible. It was only about six miles from Nazareth and a day's journey from Capernaum. Note two facts.

1.    It is the same area where Elisha raised the son of the Shunammite woman (2 Kings 4:18-37). Therefore, it became an area where the great compassion and power of God had been manifested.

2.    Many were present to witness the great conquest of death. There were many of His disciples present, and there were multitudes of other people, those who did not believe. The unbelievers were following Him for any number of reasons:

⇒ curiosity
⇒ neighborly fellowship
⇒ a belief in His ethics
⇒ a need for help

⇒ admiration
⇒ a desire for something to do
⇒ being impressed with His teaching
⇒ thinking Him to be a great prophet

**2** (7:12-13) **Compassion**: the great compassion of Jesus is seen in that He was touched. Note four points.

1.    Jesus was touched by death. Apparently, the sight of death always touched Him. The fact that men die is what brought Him to earth. Probably the whole scene of sin and death flashed across His mind—the scene of...

⇒ man's sin and death (Ro.5:12; 6:23; Heb.9:27).
⇒ the great cost of sin and death, that is, His own death in bearing the sins and death of the world (1 Pt.2:24; 1 Jn.2:1-2).

**"For to this end Christ both died, and rose, and revived, that he might be Lord both of the dead and living" (Ro.14:9).**

2.    Jesus was touched by a broken heart, the broken heart of the mother. Note her situation. She was a widow, apparently somewhat up in years with only one child, a grown son. He had just died, and now she was all alone in the world—a world that was harsh and rough on women, offering them little chance for earning a living and little help on a permanent basis. Hereafter, the woman would be without any permanent companion, provider, or protector; and there was no one to carry on the family line. The family name would die out with her death. She was brokenhearted, full of hurt and pain, without understanding and hope. When Jesus saw all this, He was touched and moved with compassion.

3.    Jesus was touched by a loving and caring woman, a woman who was much beloved. Note that "many people of the city was with her." This indicates that she had been a woman who *loved and cared* for others throughout the years. Therefore, others loved and cared for her. She was a beloved person. Jesus is always touched and moved to help those who have helped others (Lk.6:38).

**"Blessed are the merciful: for they shall obtain mercy" (Mt.5:7).**

Now note a fact: in this particular need, no one asked Jesus for help. He initiated the help Himself, acted purely out of His own compassion. Why did He not always do this? The woman seemed to be the difference. Her life was apparently so filled with love and care for others that she just stood out as a glorious example of what love for God is all about (Mt.22:38-39; Jn.13:34-35; 1 Jn.4:7).

4. The Lord saw and, having compassion, assured the woman. Note three striking facts.
   a. It was "the Lord" who saw her. This is the first time Luke uses the title "the Lord" by itself, and it is striking. The point Luke is making is that "the Lord," the Sovereign Power of the universe, saw this woman who was utterly heartbroken. "The Lord" of all power actually saw her.
   b. It was "the Lord" who had compassion upon her. The fact is shocking, for the sovereign power of the universe actually felt compassion for a simple woman. He was not just the sovereign power of a vast universe who was *way off in outer space someplace*, unattached and disinterested in this earth and its inhabitants. Contrariwise, He was vitally interested, interested enough to be looking and seeing; and He was concerned about what He saw, full of compassion for the heartbroken (see note—Lk.7:13).
   c. It was "the Lord" who spoke and gave assurance. Again, the fact was shocking, for the sovereign power of the universe actually spoke and gave assurance to a simple woman. Luke is definitely stressing the staggering thought: "the Lord," the sovereign majesty of the universe, *speaks* to men; and *His Word* gives great assurance. The Lord is vitally interested in the affairs of men, even in the plight of a simple woman.

> "Who shall separate us from the love [compassion] of Christ? shall tribulation, or distress, or persecution, or famine, or nakedness, or peril, or sword?" (Ro.8:35).
> "For we have not an high priest which cannot be touched with the feeling of our infirmities; but was in all points tempted like as we are, yet without sin" (Heb.4:15).
> "Casting all your care upon him; for he careth for you" (1 Pt.5:7).
> "For he remembered that they were but flesh; a wind that passeth away, and cometh not again" (Ps.78:39).
> "Like as a father pitieth his children, so the LORD pitieth them that fear him" (Ps.103:13).
> "But the mercy of the LORD is from everlasting to everlasting upon them that fear him, and his righteousness unto children's children" (Ps.103:17).
> "In all their affliction he was afflicted, and the angel of his presence saved them: in his love and in his pity he redeemed them; and he bare them, and carried them all the days of old" (Is.63:9).
> "It is of the LORD'S mercies that we are not consumed, because his compassions fail not" (Lam.3:22).

---

**DEEPER STUDY # 1**

(7:13) **Compassion** (esplagchnisthe): to be moved inwardly, to yearn with tender mercy, affection, pity, empathy, compassion. It is the very seat of a man's affections. It is the deepest movement of emotions possible; being moved within the deepest part of one's being.

---

**3** (7:14-15) **Jesus Christ, Power—Resurrection, The:** the great power of Jesus. Three surprising acts are seen here.

1. The power of Jesus to bypass traditional beliefs. The people of that day believed that a person became polluted by touching a corpse. The person became ceremonially unclean, unacceptable to God. By touching the bier or body, Jesus was showing that He possessed the right and power to override religious laws and beliefs. He was the Sovereign Power even over religious beliefs and over death and life.

2. The power of Jesus to stop the death processional. Note the pallbearers stopped; they "stood still." They obeyed His touch.

> **Thought 1.** Willingness and obedience on the part of the pallbearers and the mother were essential for Jesus to raise the dead son. We, too, must be willing and obedient if we wish to be raised from the dead.

> "If by any means I might attain unto the resurrection of the dead" (Ph.3:11; cp. Ph.3:7-11).

3. The power of Jesus to raise the dead. It was the command, the simple yet powerful *Word* of Jesus, that raised the dead.

> "Verily, verily, I say unto you, He that heareth my word, and believeth on him that sent me, hath everlasting life, and shall not come into condemnation; but is passed from death unto life. Verily, verily, I say unto you, The hour is coming, and now is, when the dead shall hear the voice of the Son of God: and they that hear shall live. For as the Father hath life in himself; so hath he given to the Son to have life in himself; and hath given him authority to execute judgment also, because he is the Son of man. Marvel not at this: for the hour is coming, in the which all that are in

the graves shall hear his voice, and shall come forth; they that have done good, unto the resurrection of life; and they that have done evil, unto the resurrection of damnation" (Jn.5:24-29).

"Therefore doth my Father love me, because I lay down my life, that I might take it again. No man taketh it from me, but I lay it down of myself. I have power to lay it down, and I have power to take it again. This commandment have I received of my Father" (Jn.10:17-18).

"Jesus said unto her, I am the resurrection, and the life: he that believeth in me, though he were dead, yet shall he live: and whosoever liveth and believeth in me shall never die. Believest thou this? She saith unto him, Yea, Lord: I believe that thou art the Christ, the Son of God, which should come into the world" (Jn.11:25-27).

"For he must reign, till he hath put all enemies under his feet. The last enemy that shall be destroyed is death" (1 Cor.15:25-26).

"For the Lord himself shall descend from heaven with a shout, with the voice of the archangel, and the trump of God: and the dead in Christ shall rise first: then we which are alive and remain shall be caught up together with them in the clouds, to meet the Lord in the air: and so shall we ever be with the Lord. Wherefore comfort one another with these words" (1 Th.4:16-18).

"Fear not; I am the first and the last: I am he that liveth, and was dead; and, behold, I am alive for evermore, Amen; and have the keys of hell and of death" (Rev.1:17-18).

"He will swallow up death in victory; and the Lord GOD will wipe away tears from off all faces; and the rebuke of his people shall he take away from off all the earth: for the LORD hath spoken it" (Is.25:8).

**4** (7:16-17) **Jesus Christ, Response—God, Fear of**: the great fear of the people. The word "fear" (phobos) means a fear of reverence and of awe. Seeing the dead man sit up and speak struck the fear of God in their hearts.

1.    They glorified God (edoxazon ton theon). The tense is imperfect active, "they *began* to glorify God" and *continued* to glorify God.

2.    They believed Jesus to be a *great* prophet.

3.    They acknowledged that God was dealing with them. There was a widespread revival going on throughout all Israel. The message of John the Baptist had been heard by multitudes, and Jesus was affecting the lives of scores of people. The people felt that God was now visiting and dealing with Israel once again.

4.    They bore witness everywhere.

"Herein is my Father glorified, that ye bear much fruit [witness]; so shall ye be my disciples" (Jn.15:8).

"Giving thanks unto the Father, which hath made us meet [fit] to be partakers of the inheritance of the saints in light" (Col.1:12).

"By him therefore let us offer the sacrifice of praise to God continually, that is, the fruit of our lips giving thanks to his name" (Heb.13:15).

"But ye are a chosen generation, a royal priesthood, and holy nation, a peculiar people; that ye should show forth the praises of him who hath called you out of darkness into his marvellous light" (1 Pt.2:9).

"Ye that fear the LORD, praise him" (Ps.22:23).

"And my tongue shall speak of thy righteousness and of thy praise all the day long" (Ps.35:28).

"O Lord, open thou my lips; and my mouth shall show forth thy praise" (Ps.51:15).

"Enter into his gates with thanksgiving, and into his courts with praise: be thankful unto him, and bless his name" (Ps.100:4).

| | O. Jesus Answers The Question of John the Baptist: Is Jesus the Messiah? 7:18-28 (Mt.11:1-15) | is preached. 23 And blessed is he, whosoever shall not be offended in me. | of the Messiah d. He promised both the blessing & judgment of the Messiah |
|---|---|---|---|
| 1 John, in prison, heard of Jesus' loving works a. John was puzzled: Pictured a stern Messiah b. John sent two disciples to question Jesus' Messiahship | 18 And the disciples of John showed him of all these things. 19 And John calling unto him two of his disciples sent them to Jesus, saying, Art thou he that should come? or look we for another? 20 When the men were come unto him, they said, John Baptist hath sent us unto thee, saying, Art thou he that should come? or look we for another? | 24 And when the messengers of John were departed, he began to speak unto the people concerning John, What went ye out into the wilderness for to see? A reed shaken with the wind? 25 But what went ye out for to see? A man clothed in soft raiment? Behold, they which are gorgeously apparelled, and live delicately, are in kings' courts. 26 But what went ye out for to see? A prophet? Yea, I say unto you, and much more than a prophet. | 3 The forerunner, John himself, proved Jesus was the Messiah a. His conviction & staunchness b. His self-denial & discipline c. His prophetic mission |
| 2 The ministry & message of Jesus proved He was the Messiah a. He demonstrated the power & works of the Messiah b. He fulfilled the prophecies of the Messiah[DSI] c. He preached the gospel | 21 And in that same hour he cured many of their infirmities and plagues, and of evil spirits; and unto many that were blind he gave sight. 22 Then Jesus answering said unto them, Go your way, and tell John what things ye have seen and heard; how that the blind see, the lame walk, the lepers are cleansed, the deaf hear, the dead are raised, to the poor the gospel | 27 This is he, of whom it is written, Behold, I send my messenger before thy face, which shall prepare thy way before thee. 28 For I say unto you, among those that are born of women there is not a greater prophet than John the Baptist: but he that is least in the kingdom of God is greater than he. | d. His identity as the true forerunner 4 The Kingdom of God proved Jesus was the Messiah |

# DIVISION III

## THE SON OF MAN'S ANNOUNCED MISSION AND PUBLIC MINISTRY, 4:16-9:17

## O. Jesus Answers the Question of John the Baptist: Is Jesus the Messiah? 7:18-28

(7:18-28) **Introduction—Messiah**: some question the Messiahship of Jesus Christ. It may be out of rebellion or in moments of weakness and despair, but the questions arise. John the Baptist had a moment of wondering. What we need to remember is that *honest* questions never disappoint God; only rebellion is judged by Him. God will meet and answer any honest question posed by a hurting or needful person. This passage gives Jesus' answer to John's question; this is the final proof of Jesus' Messiahship.

1. John, in prison, heard of Jesus' loving works (v.18-20).
2. The ministry and message of Jesus proved He was the Messiah (v.21-23).
3. The forerunner, John himself, proved Jesus was the Messiah (v.24-27).
4. The Kingdom of God proved Jesus was the Messiah (v.28).

**1** (7:18-20) **Messiah, Misconceptions of—John the Baptist**: John was in prison (cp. Lk.3:19-20; 9:9). His disciples brought him word about Jesus' loving works. Apparently his disciples were allowed to visit him. He was anxious to hear about Jesus and the Messianic movement, so they related the wonderful miracles and teachings of Jesus. However, their report included nothing about eliminating the injustices of men nor freeing men from the tyranny and rule of others; nothing about fulfilling the hope of men for the great Messiah who was to take over the world and rule in righteousness, executing judgment upon all men and nations. In fact, the very opposite seemed to be taking place; for when the people were aroused to exalt Jesus as their King, He withdrew and discouraged their actions (Lk.5:16).

What John heard puzzled him, for Jesus seemed to be fulfilling only half of the prophecies concerning the Messiah, the half dealing with ministry. The prophecies dealing with righteousness and judgment were not being fulfilled (see notes—Mt.11:1-6; 11:2-3).

John needed assurance, so he sent two disciples to question Jesus' Messiahship: "Art thou He that should come: or look we for another?"

**2** (7:21-23) **Messiah—Messiahship—Jesus Christ, Deity**: the ministry and message of Jesus proved He was the Messiah. Jesus gave four assurances to John, assurances that proved His Messiahship beyond question.

1. Jesus demonstrated the power and works of the Messiah (v.21). Note what happened when John's disciples approached Jesus and told Him that John needed assurance. Jesus turned and gave the two disciples an example of what His ministry was. They had only heard about His ministry; now they were to see for themselves. He cured many and gave sight to many. Apparently, He ministered for about an hour (v.21).

The point was this. Jesus was telling John not only to hear what He claimed (the claims of Messiahship) but also to look at what He was doing and judge Him by what He did for people. He did not just profess to be the Messiah, He was proving it. He was proving it by ministering to people in *the power of God*. In particular, He demonstrated two glorious truths.

    a.   He demonstrated that God truly exists and that He is sovereign. He is above and beyond nature, and He has the power to override the laws of nature by miraculously healing the sick.

    b.   He demonstrated that God loves and cares for man and has planned a way for man to be saved and delivered forever.

2.    Jesus fulfilled the prophecies of the Messiah. After ministering to the people, Jesus turned to the two disciples of John and told them to go tell John what they had *seen* and *heard*. Note two things.

    a.   John was questioning Jesus' Messiahship. The reports he had heard said nothing about Jesus' mobilizing the people into a great army. Jesus was not plotting the strategy to free Israel from Roman domination and to set up the Kingdom of God. John had heard nothing about the Day of the Lord, about the Messianic fire of judgment, about cities' falling and sinners' being judged. And his time was running out. He would be tried and executed soon. The answer Jesus sent back to John was a totally new concept of Messiahship. It is God's idea of Messiahship, radically different from man's idea. It was a demonstration and proclamation of salvation, of God's care and love for persons. (See notes—Lk.3:24-31; DEEPER STUDY # 3—Jn.1:45 for discussion. Also see notes—Mt.1:1; DEEPER STUDY # 2—1:18; DEEPER STUDY # 3—3:11; notes—11:1-6; 11:2-3; DEEPER STUDY # 1—11:5; DEEPER STUDY # 2—11:6; DEEPER STUDY # 1—12:16; note—22:42.)

    b.   Jesus was saying that His power and concern (love) were the power and concern *predicted* for the Messiah, and both were unlimited (see DEEPER STUDY # 1—Lk.7:22. See note, pt.2—Mt.11:4-6 for detailed discussion.)

3.    Jesus preached the gospel of the Messiah. The "poor" represented those who were "poor in spirit," those who had need and acknowledged their need. God's heart and compassion reached out to any who came and brought their need to Him. It was these, the poor in spirit, to whom He preached the good news. (See note, pt.4—Mt.11:4-6 for more discussion.)

4.    Jesus promised both the blessing and judgment of the Messiah (see DEEPER STUDY # 2—Mt.11:6). Note the two facets of what Jesus promised—the two areas of work predicted about the Messiah.

    a.   The area of blessing, of the Spirit, of salvation, of God's care and love for people. This is the area Christ covered here. Today is the day of blessing.

> "Jesus answered and said unto them, Go and show John again those things which ye do hear and see: the blind receive their sight, and the lame walk, the lepers are cleansed, and the deaf hear, the dead are raised up, and the poor have the gospel preached to them" (Mt.11:4-5).
>
> "For God so loved the world, that he gave his only begotten Son, that whosoever believeth in him should not perish, but have everlasting life. For God sent not his Son into the world to condemn the world; but that the world through him might be saved" (Jn.3:16-17).
>
> "And if any man hear my words, and believe not, I judge him not: for I came not to judge the world, but to save the world" (Jn.12:47).
>
> "And the grace of our Lord was exceeding abundant with faith and love which is in Christ Jesus. This is a faithful saying, and worthy of all acceptation, that Christ Jesus came into the world to save sinners; of whom I am chief" (1 Tim.1:14-15).

    b.   The area of fire, of wrath, of judgment. The Messiah is to fulfill the judgment of God when He returns (see DEEPER STUDY # 2—Mt.1:18; DEEPER STUDY # 3—3:11; notes—11:1-6; 11:2-3; DEEPER STUDY # 2—11:6; DEEPER STUDY # 1—12:16; note—22:42 for discussion).

---

**DEEPER STUDY # 1**

(7:22) **Messiah, False Concepts**: Jesus was referring to Scripture in this verse. He was telling John that His actions were prophesied by the prophets (Is.35:5-6; 61:1-2; cp. Ps.72:2; 146:8; Zech.11:11). Note, however, that Jesus stressed the personal ministry and not the political. He omitted the phrases of Is.61:1 that could be interpreted that He was to be a political leader: "proclaiming liberty to the captives, and the opening of the prisons." He needed to get John's attention away from the wrong concept of the Messiah. He was reaching out in the power of the Spirit to individuals, saving and restoring them, not reaching out to mobilize people for the deliverance of Israel from the Roman enslavement.

---

**3** (7:24-27) **Messiah—John the Baptist**: the forerunner, John himself, proved Jesus was the Messiah (see outline and notes—Mt.11:7-15 for detailed discussion). As soon as John's disciples were gone, Jesus turned His attention to the crowd. This was necessary, for the people had heard all that had happened. Some thought John had wavered in his faith. If the people were allowed to think this, they would soon question if John were really the prophet who was to pave the way for the Messiah. Then following upon the heels of this question would be the questioning of Jesus' being the true Messiah. If this kind of talk and questioning got started, it would affect not only the crowd, but those who had already believed. It would be devastating to the Lord's mission. Note something in all this: how fickle people really are and how easily people forget a prophet's real calling and strength and pick up the news of his weak moment.

What Jesus did was reprimand the crowd. He vindicated John and his mission. He reminded the forgetful and fickle that John was the forerunner, and He claimed that He was the true Messiah.

1.    John was a man of conviction and staunchness. He was not like a reed shaken by the wind.

    ⇒  John's conviction that he was the forerunner proves Jesus is the Messiah.

    ⇒  John's conviction that the Messiah was coming proves Jesus is the Messiah.

⇒ John's conviction that He (Jesus) was the Lamb of God proves Jesus is the Messiah.
⇒ John's staunchness in standing up to the religionists proves Jesus is the Messiah.
⇒ John's staunchness in standing up to Herod proves Jesus is the Messiah.

"**Prove all things; hold fast that which is good**" (1 Th.5:21).
"**Therefore, my beloved brethren, be ye stedfast, unmovable, always abounding in the work of the Lord, forasmuch as ye know that your labour is not in vain in the Lord**" (1 Cor.15:58).
"**Let us hold fast the profession of our faith without wavering; (for he is faithful that promised)**" (Heb.10:23).

2.    John was a man of self-denial and sacrifice. He was not a man clothed in soft, extravagant, fashionable clothing. He denied himself and sacrificed the things of the world in order to carry out the work of God.

"**So likewise, whosoever he be of you that forsaketh not all that he hath, he cannot be my disciple**" (Lk.14:33).
"**Yea doubtless, and I count all things but loss for the excellency of the knowledge of Christ Jesus my Lord: for whom I have suffered the loss of all things, and do count them but dung, that I may win Christ**" (Ph.3:8).

3.    John was a prophet, a man sent on a prophetic mission. He proclaimed the Word of God, and his proclamation could not be denied. But John was more than a prophet.
    a.    He was the subject of prophecy as well as the messenger of it.
    b.    He was the herald who brought the message to the world that *the Lord had come*. In this John excelled over all other prophets. They only *foresaw* the Messiah's coming, but John *saw* Him come.
4.    John was the true forerunner. Note two critical points.
    a.    Jesus was saying that John was definitely the forerunner of the Messiah, the messenger predicted by the Scripture.
    b.    Jesus was *claiming* to be the Messiah before whom John ran and prepared the way.

"**The voice of him that crieth in the wilderness, Prepare ye the way of the LORD, make straight in the desert a highway for our God**" (Is.40:3).
"**Behold, I will send my messenger, and he shall prepare the way before me: and the Lord, whom ye seek, shall suddenly come to his temple, even the messenger of the covenant, whom ye delight in: behold, he shall come, saith the LORD of hosts**" (Mal.3:1).
"**In those days came John the Baptist, preaching in the wilderness of Judaea, and saying, Repent ye: for the kingdom of heaven is at hand. For this is he that was spoken of by the prophet Esaias, saying, The voice of one crying in the wilderness, Prepare ye the way of the Lord, make his paths straight**" (Mt.3:1-3).
"**And he shall go before him in the spirit and power of Elias, to turn the hearts of the fathers to the children, and the disobedient to the wisdom of the just; to make ready a people prepared for the Lord**" (Lk.1:17).
"**And thou, child, shalt be called the prophet of the Highest: for thou shalt go before the face of the Lord to prepare his ways**" (Lk.1:76).

**4**    (7:28) **Kingdom of God**: the Kingdom of God proved Jesus was the Messiah. Jesus' invasion into human history divided time and the ages. The period of history before Jesus came into the world is known as the age of promise. But since Jesus' coming, men are living in the time and age of God's kingdom. John lived in the age of promise, whereas the followers of Jesus live in the Kingdom of God. Therefore, the least in the Kingdom is greater than the greatest of prophets who lived in the age of promise. *Jesus Christ is the reason*: knowing Him personally makes all the difference in the privileges of a person. The citizen of God's kingdom knows the presence of Christ within his body in the Person of the Holy Spirit, and he knows the *active* rule and reign of God in life (1 Cor.6:19-20; cp. Jn.14:16-18, 20, 23). However, those who lived in the age of promise only had the hope of the promise (Ro.8:16-17; Gal.4:4-6). (See note—Mt.11:11 for more discussion.)

"**Whom [the prophets] having not seen, ye love; in whom, though now ye see him not, yet believing, ye rejoice with joy unspeakable and full of glory: receiving the end of your faith, even the salvation of your souls. Of which salvation the prophets have enquired and searched diligently, who prophesied of the grace that should come unto you: searching what, or what manner of time the Spirit of Christ which was in them did signify, when it testified beforehand the sufferings of Christ, and the glory that should follow. Unto whom it was revealed, that not unto themselves, but unto us they did minister the things, which are now reported unto you by them that have preached the gospel unto you with the Holy Ghost sent down from heaven; which things the angels desire to look into**" (1 Pt.1:8-12; cp. v.13-16).
"**Blessed be the God and Father of our Lord Jesus Christ, which according to his abundant mercy hath begotten us again unto a lively hope by the resurrection of Jesus Christ from the dead, to an inheritance incorruptible, and undefiled, and that fadeth not away, reserved in heaven for you**" (1 Pt.1:3-4).
"**Grace and peace be multiplied unto you through the knowledge of God, and of Jesus our Lord, according as his divine power hath given unto us all things that pertain unto life and godliness, through the knowledge of him that hath called us to glory and virtue: whereby are given unto us exceeding great and precious promises: that by these ye might be partakers of the divine nature, having escaped the corruption that is in the world through lust**" (2 Pt.1:2-4).

| | P. Jesus Reveals God's Verdict Upon this Generation & Age, 7:29-35 (Mt.11:16-27) | 32 They are like unto children sitting in the marketplace, and calling one to another, and saying, We have piped unto you, and ye have not danced; we have mourned to you, and ye have not wept. | 2 An age of childishness |
|---|---|---|---|
| 1 Reactions to John<br>a. The people & tax collectors who were baptized: Vindicated John<br>b. The religionists who were not baptized: Rejected God's purpose<br>c. Jesus warned His generation & age | 29 And all the people that heard him, and the publicans, justified God, being baptized with the baptism of John.<br>30 But the Pharisees and lawyers rejected the counsel of God against themselves, being not baptized of him.<br>31 And the Lord said, Whereunto then shall I liken the men of this generation? and to what are they like? | 33 For John the Baptist came neither eating bread nor drinking wine; and ye say, He hath a devil.<br>34 The Son of man is come eating and drinking; and ye say, Behold a gluttonous man, and a winebibber, a friend of publicans and sinners!<br>35 But wisdom is justified of all her children. | 3 An age of escapism: Seeking to escape responsibility<br>a. Accused John of conservatism: Too denying<br>b. Accused Jesus of license: Too loose<br><br>4 An age with only a few wise toward God |

# DIVISION III

## THE SON OF MAN'S ANNOUNCED MISSION AND PUBLIC MINISTRY, 4:16-9:17

## P. Jesus Reveals God's Verdict Upon This Generation and Age, 7:29-35

(7:29-35) **Introduction**: Jesus gave the verdict upon His generation. In so doing He gave a glimpse of God's verdict upon every generation of men. (See outline and notes—Mt.11:16-27 for more discussion.)

1. Reactions to John (v.29-31).
2. A generation and age of childishness (v.32).
3. A generation and age of escapism (v.33-34).
4. A generation and age with only a few wise toward God (v.35).

**1** (7:29-31) **John the Baptist—Religionists**: the reaction of the people to John was twofold. The common people and tax collectors accepted John and his ministry, but the religionists rejected him. Note several things.

1. The tax collectors were set apart from the people themselves. This was because they were so despised and ostracized. They were actually treated in a class all by themselves, a class of betrayers (usually wealthy) who had forsaken the common people. The tax collectors, of course, felt the sting of rejection; and in some cases sensed their sin and the need for repentance. These responded to John.

2. It was "the people that *heard him [Jesus]*" who repented:
   ⇒ the people who wanted forgiveness of sin, sensing the need for repentance.
   ⇒ the people who believed his message that the Messiah was coming.

3. The people who repented "justified God." By repenting and being baptized, they vindicated John's ministry. They proclaimed that God is just and righteous and that they owed their lives to Him. They accepted God, repenting and changing their lives. Their repentance proved that both God and John were just and true.

4. The religionists (Pharisees and lawyers) rejected the counsel of God. The evidence was clearly seen in what they failed to do: they did not repent and were not baptized by John. Being the religious leaders, they were the very ones who should have responded, but they did not. And what a surprise! The Pharisees were the practitioners of religion, a whole sect of men who had given their lives to live out the law—even to the most minute detail (see DEEPER STUDY # 3—Acts 23:8). The lawyers (Scribes) were those who gave their lives to study and learn the law to the fullest extent possible (see DEEPER STUDY # 1—Lk.6:2; DEEPER STUDY # 1—Mt.22:35).

5. Jesus warned His generation. It was a religious generation...
   • that should have known and been prepared for the prophet of God and his message.
   • that had God's Word, yet ignored it.
   • that had the worship of God and the ordinances of God, yet neglected them.
   • to whom God sent His prophet, yet they rejected him.
   • to whom God sent His Son, yet they rejected Him.
   • that was smug in its own adequacy and sufficiency.

**2** (7:32) **World—Generation—Perverse**: a generation of childishness. Note three things.

1. When looking at His own generation, Jesus asked: "Whereunto [to what] shall I liken this generation?" The most adequate illustration which came to His mind was that of children (see note—Mt.11:16-19). He was saying that His own generation was a *childish generation*. By childish He meant *perverse*. His generation was perverse. They turned away from that which was right and good to that which was corruptible; they acted contrary to the evidence; they were opposed to that which was right, reasonable, and acceptable; and they were obstinate in their opposition. They were mindless and contrary. They did not want the truth, so they made excuses for not receiving the truth.

2. The illustration Jesus used is clearly understood. Children are playing in the market place. A few begin to play wedding music on their pipes and cry out to others, "Let's play wedding." The others shout back, "No. We don't want to

129

dance around today." So the first group, still wanting to play, begins to play funeral music and shout back, "Well, let's play funeral." "No. We don't want to play funeral either. We don't feel like acting sad."

3.     Every generation is alike in that it has its privileges. The privileges are used by some and ignored and abused by others. Since the coming of Christ, God's very own Son, the greatest privilege in all the world has been the privilege of knowing Him personally and of being brought into a right relationship with God. As with all privileges, some have come to know Him personally, but the vast majority have ignored and abused Him.

> "For my people is foolish, they have not known me; they are sottish children, and they have none understanding: they are wise to do evil, but to do good they have no knowledge" (Jer.4:22).
>
> "That we henceforth be no more children, tossed to and fro, and carried about with every wind of doctrine, by the sleight of men, and cunning craftiness, whereby they lie in wait to deceive" (Eph.4:14).
>
> "And I, brethren, could not speak unto you as unto spiritual, but as unto carnal, even as unto babes in Christ. I have fed you with milk, and not with meat: for hitherto ye were not able to bear it, neither yet now are ye able" (1 Cor.3:1-2).
>
> "When I was a child, I spake as a child, I understood as a child, I thought as a child: but when I became a man, I put away childish things" (1 Cor.13:11).
>
> "For when for the time ye ought to be teachers, ye have need that one teach you again which be the first principles of the oracles of God; and are become such as have need of milk, and not of strong meat" (Heb.5:12).

**3** (7:33-34) **Escapism—License vs. Liberty:** a generation of escapism, of always seeking an excuse to escape *personal* responsibility. The generation was contrary, mindless, playful; they were faultfinders who could not be pleased. The people found fault with whatever was suggested. They just could not accept anything that put restrictions upon their loose play. They found fault with a separatist approach to the gospel, and they also find fault with a sociable approach to the gospel.

1.     They accused John of being too conservative and too self-denying. John came neither eating nor drinking; he was a separatist. He was from the desert; and he lived a strict, austere, highly disciplined life. He did not associate with people; he did not make friends. He just isolated himself, cut himself off from everyone and withdrew from society. His message was a gospel of repentance and of separation from the things of the world. Therefore, he was accused of having a "devil," of being mad and insane for choosing to live that way.

2.     They accused Jesus of license, of being too loose. Jesus was the very opposite of John. He lived and preached a gospel of liberty, eating and drinking with people. He was with them in their social moments; and He moved among all sorts of people—mixing, being friendly and open and accessible to all, no matter how terrible they were thought to be. Therefore, He was accused of being a sinner Himself: a glutton, a winebibber, and an immoral friend of sinners.

God clearly used both approaches to righteousness (cp. 1 Cor.12:6-7). Jesus did not condemn John's approach, and John did not condemn Jesus' approach. They supported each other, but the majority of people rejected any attempt to restrict their *own play*. They wished to continue doing their own thing: seeking pleasure, intellectual pursuit, secular interest, religious commitment. Most were willing to go only so far in restricting their own desires, wills, and way. Few were willing to deny self completely (see note and DEEPER STUDY # 1—Lk.9:23).

> "So I spake unto you; and ye would not hear, but rebelled against the commandment of the LORD" (Dt.1:43).
>
> "He, that being often reproved hardeneth his neck, shall suddenly be destroyed, and that without remedy" (Pr.29:1).
>
> "For thus saith the Lord GOD, the Holy One of Israel; In returning and rest shall ye be saved; in quietness and in confidence shall be your strength: and ye would not" (Is.30:15).
>
> "But these [unbelievers], as natural brute beasts, made to be taken and destroyed, speak evil of the things that they understand not; and shall utterly perish in their own corruption; and shall receive the reward of unrighteousness, as they that count it pleasure to riot in the day time. Spots they are and blemishes, sporting themselves with their own deceivings while they feast with you; having eyes full of adultery, and that cannot cease from sin; beguiling unstable souls: an heart they have exercised with covetous practices; cursed children: which have forsaken the right way" (2 Pt.2:12-15).
>
> "But exhort one another daily, while it is called To day; lest any of you be hardened through the deceitfulness of sin" (Heb.3:13).

**4** (7:35) **Wise, The—Liberty vs. Ascetic:** a generation with only a few wise toward God. Note what Jesus said: "Wisdom is justified of all her children."

1.     Wisdom does have children, wise children.
2.     Wise children will justify (declare wisdom) what is wise and right.
3.     Therefore, the wise will declare that both John and Jesus were right. The way they lived and preached, the ascetic vs. the social, are both right. They were both of God, one the forerunner and the other the Messiah, the Son of God. (See note, pt.2—Mt.11:16-19 and DEEPER STUDY # 1—Mt.11:19 for a different understanding of this verse.)
4.     The wise (children of wisdom) are the non-critical, the saved who know that God sent both John the ascetic and Jesus the Messiah. Very simply, the wise are the few who accept the ministry of both John and Jesus, both of whom fulfilled the *prophetic Word of God*.

> "But of him [God] are ye in Christ Jesus, who of God is made unto us wisdom, and righteousness, and sanctification, and redemption" (1 Cor.1:30; cp.1 Cor.1:24).
>
> "In whom [Christ] are hid all the treasures of wisdom and knowledge" (Col.2:3; cp. Is.11:2).
>
> "And unto man he said, Behold, the fear of the LORD, that is wisdom; and to depart from evil is understanding" (Job 28:28; cp. Hos.14:9).

| | Q. Jesus Contrasts the Attitudes of the Repentant & Self-Righteous, 7:36-50 | nothing to pay, he frankly forgave them both. Tell me therefore, which of them will love him most? | both debtors<br>c. A piercing question: Who appreciated & loved the most?<br>d. A begrudging answer |
|---|---|---|---|
| 1  Simon, a Pharisee, invited Jesus to dinner & Jesus accepted | 36 And one of the Pharisees desired him that he would eat with him. And he went into the Pharisee's house, and sat down to meat. | 43 Simon answered and said, I suppose that he, to whom he forgave most. And he said unto him, Thou hast rightly judged. | |
| 2  The attitude of the repentant: A woman prostitute<br>a. She sensed a desperate need | 37 And, behold, a woman in the city, which was a sinner, when she knew that Jesus sat at meat in the Pharisee's house, brought an alabaster box of ointment, | 44 And he turned to the woman, and said unto Simon, Seest thou this woman? I entered into thine house, thou gavest me no water for my feet: but she hath washed my feet with tears, and wiped them with the hairs of her head. | 5  The need of the self-righteous: To really see Jesus, who the repentant say He is<br>a. He is the One who deserves more than common courtesies<br>1) Common vs. worshipful respect |
| b. She approached the Lord despite all<br>c. She surrendered to the Lord in utter humility<br>d. She loved much, giving her most precious possession | 38 And stood at his feet behind him weeping, and began to wash his feet with tears, and did wipe them with the hairs of her head, and kissed his feet, and anointed them with the ointment. | 45 Thou gavest me no kiss: but this woman since the time I came in hath not ceased to kiss my feet. | 2) Common vs. humble greeting |
| 3  The attitude of the self-righteous<br>a. He was a considerate man, but self-righteous<br>b. He considered himself better than others<br>c. He sensed no need for forgiveness | 39 Now when the Pharisee which had bidden him saw it, he spake within himself, saying, This man, if he were a prophet, would have known who and what manner of woman this is that toucheth him: for she is a sinner. | 46 My head with oil thou didst not anoint: but this woman hath anointed my feet with ointment. | 3) Common vs. sacrificial gift |
| 4  The two attitudes illustrated: The parable of two debtors<br>a. One debtor owed much; the other little | 40 And Jesus answering said unto him, Simon, I have somewhat to say unto thee. And he saith, Master, say on. 41 There was a certain creditor which had two debtors: the one owed five hundred pence, and the other fifty. | 47 Wherefore I say unto thee, Her sins, which are many, are forgiven; for she loved much: but to whom little is forgiven, the same loveth little. 48 And he said unto her, Thy sins are forgiven. 49 And they that sat at meat with him began to say within themselves, Who is this that forgiveth sins also? | b. He is the One who has the power to forgive sins<br><br>c. He is the One whom people need to ask about |
| b. A free forgiveness of | 42 And when they had | 50 And he said to the woman, Thy faith hath saved thee; go in peace. | d. He is the One who saves the repentant |

# DIVISION III

## THE SON OF MAN'S ANNOUNCED MISSION AND PUBLIC MINISTRY, 4:16-9:17

## Q.  Jesus Contrasts the Attitudes of the Repentant and Self-Righteous, 7:36-50

(7:36-50) **Introduction**: the present passage contrasts the attitudes of the sinful (repentant) and the self-righteous. It needs to be studied carefully, for self-righteousness is a serious sin. It is both common and damning.

1. Simon, a Pharisee, invited Jesus to dinner and Jesus accepted (v.36).
2. The attitude of the repentant: a woman prostitute (v.37-38).
3. The attitude of the self-righteous (v.39).
4. The two attitudes illustrated: the parable of two debtors (v.40-43).
5. The need of the self-righteous: to really see Jesus, who the repentant say He is (v.44-50).

**1** (7:36) **Jesus Christ, Seeking Man**: Simon, a Pharisee, invited Jesus to dinner. Note several things.

1. Simon invited Jesus to his house, but he did not extend to Jesus the common courtesies (v.44-46). He was rude to the Lord. He was not even sure Jesus was a prophet, much less the Messiah (v.39). Why then did he invite Jesus to his house? We do not know; nothing is said as to why. The best speculation is that Simon enjoyed the company of celebrities, and he had heard so much about Jesus that he wanted to meet and talk with Him on an informal and friendly basis.

2. Jesus ate with both sinners and religionists (Pharisees) (Lk.5:29-30). No one was excluded from His attention or love, even when they lacked the common everyday courtesies and respect (v.44-46). He sought every man.

3. The house of Simon was a house of the rich. The rich always had an open courtyard, usually in the center of the house. Sometimes the host would allow the public to stand around in the courtyard and listen to the discussions, in particular when a rabbi or some celebrity was the chief guest.

**2** (7:37-38) **Repentance—Salvation—Humility—Jesus Christ, Seeking**: the attitude of the repentant. The woman was a sinner, a prostitute. She demonstrated what a sinner has to do in coming to Jesus.

1. She sensed a desperate need. She was either convicted of her sin while hearing Jesus or else she had heard Him before and came under heavy conviction. His plea for men and women to repent and prepare for the Kingdom of God pierced her heart. She knew she was a sinner: unclean, lost, condemned. The guilt and weight of her sin was more than she could bear. She ached for forgiveness and cleansing, for freedom and liberty.

2. She approached the Lord despite all. She knew that the public scorned and gossiped about her, and the so-called decent people wanted nothing to do with her. What would Jesus do—He who said, "Come unto me all ye that labor and are heavy laden and I will give you rest...." (Mt.11:28-30)? She knew that if she were recognized, the Pharisee might throw her out of the house. He knew about her (v.39). She thought about the situation, and her thinking turned into hope, and her hope into belief. Surely He who offered such an invitation would receive her. Before anyone could stop her, she rushed to Jesus and stood behind Him at His feet. (Remember, in the East people reclined to eat. They rested on their left arm facing each other around the table with their body and feet extending out away from the table.)

3. She surrendered to the Lord in utter humility. Standing there, she was overcome with conviction and emotion. She fell at Jesus' feet weeping—so broken that tears just flowed from her eyes. She unwound her hair and wiped and kissed Jesus' feet. Seldom has such love and devotion been shown Jesus.

Now note: there was only one thing that could make a prostitute enter a Pharisee's home—desperation. She was gripped with a sense of lostness, of helplessness, of urgency. The loosening of her hair to wipe Jesus' feet was forbidden of women in public. She must have been so desperate she was totally oblivious to the onlookers. The point is this: she was surrendering her heart and life to the Lord, begging Him to forgive her. She was so broken she was unable to speak, but Jesus knew her heart. Words were not necessary (v.47-48).

4. She loved much, giving her most precious possession. Perfume was highly valued by women of that day (see note—Mt.26:8-9). Apparently, by describing the perfume as he does, Luke is stressing the expense of the perfume and the great sacrifice she was making. It was probably the most costly possession she had, so she was giving it to her Lord. However, there is something more important here. Note what she did with the perfume. She anointed her Lord; anointed His feet in a supreme act of humility and love and surrender (see note—Lk.7:44-50).

> **Thought 1.** The person who comes to Christ must come with a broken and contrite heart.
>
> > "Come unto me, all ye that labour and are heavy laden, and I will give you rest" (Mt.11:28).
> >
> > "For we have not an high priest which cannot be touched with the feeling of our infirmities; but was in all points tempted like as we are, yet without sin. Let us therefore come boldly unto the throne of grace, that we may obtain mercy, and find grace to help in time of need" (Heb.4:15-16).
> >
> > "The LORD is nigh unto them that are of a broken heart; and saveth such as be of a contrite spirit" (Ps.34:18).
> >
> > "For thus saith the high and lofty One that inhabiteth eternity, whose name is Holy; I dwell in the high and holy place, with him also that is of a contrite and humble spirit, to revive the spirit of the humble, and to revive the heart of the contrite ones" (Is.57:15).
> >
> > "For all those things hath mine hand made, and all those things have been, saith the LORD: but to this man will I look, even to him that is poor and of a contrite spirit, and trembleth at my word" (Is.66:2).

**3** (7:39) **Self-righteousness**: the attitude of the self-righteous. The behavior of the self-righteous man revealed several things.

1. The man was considerate, but self-righteous. Note, he only thought these things; he would not say them publicly lest he embarrass his guests. (How like the self-righteous!)

2. The man considered himself better. He felt he was better than the sinful woman, so he would never allow her to touch him. He would keep his distance, ignore, and have nothing to do with her. But note something else. He considered his judgment and knowledge, opinions and behavior to be better than others. He expected others (Jesus) to judge and act as he did. He thought that if Jesus only knew who the lady was, then He would reject her.

> **Thought 1.** Many do live self-righteously. They feel that they live and act better than others. They feel and act superior because they have a...

|   |   |   |   |
|---|---|---|---|
| • a better house | • a better child | • a better position | • a better job |
| • a better profession | • a better heritage | • more ability | • better skills |
| • a better education | • a better income | • more success | • a better life |
| • a better religion | • a better discipline | • more recognition |   |

3. The man sensed no need for forgiveness and repentance. He thought of himself as *good enough* in two areas.
   a. He was *good enough in religion*. Note he was a Pharisee, a man who had given his life to practice religion. If anyone were ever *good enough*, he should have been (see DEEPER STUDY # 3—Acts 23:8).
   b. He was *good enough* in behavior. He was well behaved, decent and moral, just and equitable, respected and highly esteemed. He was not immoral; in fact, he would have nothing to do with immorality. He had not and never would commit a sin that would be publicly condemned. Therefore, he felt as though he had done nothing for which he needed forgiveness.

"Not every one that saith unto me, Lord, Lord, shall enter into the kingdom of heaven; but he that doeth the will of my Father which is in heaven" (Mt.7:21).

"He answered and said unto them, Well hath Esaias prophesied of you hypocrites, as it is written, This people honoureth me with their lips, but their heart is far from me" (Mk.7:6).

"For we dare not make ourselves of the number, or compare ourselves with some that commend themselves: but they measuring themselves by themselves, and comparing themselves among themselves, are not wise" (2 Cor.10:12).

"They profess that they know God; but in works they deny him, being abominable, and disobedient, and unto every good work reprobate" (Tit.1:16).

"My little children, let us not love in word, neither in tongue; but in deed and in truth" (1 Jn.3:18).

"Most men will proclaim every one his own goodness: but a faithful man who can find?" (Pr.20:6).

"There is a generation that are pure in their own eyes, and yet is not washed from their filthiness" (Pr.30:12).

**4** (7:40-43) **Jesus Christ, Deity; Knowledge**: the two attitudes illustrated. Jesus told a parable about two debtors. Note several things that say much to the self-righteous.

1. Jesus *announced* that He had something to say, something critically important. Undivided attention was needed. Every self-righteous person needs to listen and listen closely.

2. Jesus was a prophet and more—He was the Son of God; therefore, He not only knew the people who were sitting around Him, He knew their every thought. Note that from this point on, Jesus was answering the *thoughts* of Simon. Simon had never said a word about Jesus' not knowing who the woman was nor about his own question about Jesus' being a prophet. Simon had only been thinking these thoughts "within himself" (v.39).

**Thought 1.** Jesus is the Son of God; therefore, what a man thinks pales into insignificance when facing the One who knows all thoughts, including what one really thinks and feels *within*. Jesus knows the truth of every thought and feeling within a man. If a person is self-righteous, Jesus knows it. If a person is repentant, truly repentant, Jesus knows it. No one hides anything, no feeling, no thought from Him.

3. The meaning of the parable is strikingly clear. A glance at the verses and points in the outline show this. Note how clearly the parable illustrates the grace of God in freely forgiving sin (salvation) (cp. Eph.1:7; 2:8-9; 1 Jn.1:9; 2:1-2).

**5** (7:44-50) **Self-Righteousness**: the need of the self-righteous—to really see Jesus, who the repentant say He is. Note what Jesus asked Simon, "Seest thou this woman, this repentant?" The repentant had much to teach the self-righteous about Jesus. The repentant *really sees* Jesus, who He really is.

1. Jesus was the One who deserved more than common courtesies. The host usually showed respect by providing water for the guests to wash their dusty, sandaled feet. The kiss was the accepted greeting among friends, and oil was usually given for honored guests to refresh themselves after travelling under the hot sun. It was expensive, so it was usually reserved for honored guests.

   a. Jesus deserved *more than common respect* (water); He deserved a worshipful respect. He was seen as Lord and was respected as Lord by the repentant. He was the One who alone could meet the needs of the human heart; therefore, He was the One who was to be worshipped. The self-righteous needed to learn this.

   b. Jesus deserved *more than a common greeting*; He deserved a humble, brokenhearted greeting. He was approached with a sense of unworthiness and humility. The repentant saw the worthiness of Jesus and grasped something of His awesome person as the Son of God and as the sovereign Lord of the universe; therefore, He was the One to whom all men owed their allegiance, the One who alone had the power to forgive and accept men. The repentant saw Jesus as the One who alone could help her, the One who alone had the power to help, so the repentant approached Jesus and greeted Him with a deep sense of humility and unworthiness. The self-righteous needed to learn this.

   c. Jesus deserved *more than a common gift*; He deserved a sacrificial gift. He was seen as the hope and Savior of one's life, so the repentant gave Jesus her life, all she was and had. The repentant surrendered her life and gave the most precious gift she had to anoint her Lord. The self-righteous needed to learn this.

2. Jesus was the One who had the power to forgive sins. Three simple facts are imorant here.

   a. The woman's sins were many. Jesus did not overlook her sins, nor the seriousness of them. After all it was her sins and the sins of others that brought about *His humiliation*, His having to come to this sinful world and to die for the sins of men. However, He forgave her sins despite their awfulness. Every sinner should note this carefully.

   b. Self-righteousness sensed the need for *little* forgiveness; therefore, the self-righteous loved little. The self-righteous had only a formal, distant relationship with God. His relationship was cold, having only a small sense of sin and sensing only a little need for forgiveness. It was enough to have Jesus present at his table (the table was about the only place many acknowledged His presence).

   **Thought 1.** The self-righteous approach to God...
   • has only a little sense of sin; therefore senses only a little need for forgiveness.
   • is blinded to man's *state of sin*, to man's true being, that of being short of God's glory (Ro.3:23).
   • has little sense of the need for special mercy and grace, is blinded to God's Sovereign Majesty and Person.

- has only a formal, distant relationship with God, has little personal relationship with God.
- gives little honor to God, makes little sacrifice for God.

c. Jesus forgave sin. He had the power to forgive the sins of this repentant.

**Thought 1.** The fact of forgiveness, the very knowledge that millions have been truly forgiven, is proof that Christ is the Son of God, the One to whom men are to go for forgiveness.

3. Jesus was the One whom people needed to ask about.

**Thought 1.** The very fact that Jesus claimed the right and power to forgive sins should cause every man to sit up, take notice and ask, "Who is this?"

> "Him hath God exalted with his right hand to be a Prince and a Saviour, for to give repentance to Israel, and forgiveness of sins" (Acts 5:31).
> "Be it known unto you therefore, men and brethren, that through this man is preached unto you the forgiveness of sins" (Acts 13:38).
> "In whom we have redemption through his blood, the forgiveness of sins, according to the riches of his grace" (Eph.1:7).
> "Who forgiveth all thine iniquities; who healeth all thy diseases" (Ps.103:3).
> "But there is forgiveness with thee, that thou mayest be feared" (Ps.130:4).
> "I, even I, am he that blotteth out thy transgressions for mine own sake, and will not remember thy sins" (Is.43:25).
> "I have blotted out, as a thick cloud, thy transgressions, and, as a cloud, thy sins: return unto me; for I have redeemed thee" (Is.44:22).
> "Let the wicked forsake his way, and the unrighteous man his thoughts: and let him return unto the LORD, and he will have mercy upon him; and to our God, for he will abundantly pardon" (Is.55:7).
> "And I will cleanse them from all their iniquity, whereby they have sinned against me; and I will pardon all their iniquities, whereby they have sinned, and whereby they have transgressed against me" (Jer.33:8).

4. Jesus was the One who did save the repentant. The woman believed Christ to be the Savior, the One who could forgive her sins. Therefore, Christ saved her.

> "For God so loved the world, that he gave his only begotten Son, that whosoever believeth in him should not perish, but have everlasting life" (Jn.3:16).
> "Jesus saith unto him, I am the way, the truth, and the life: no man cometh unto the Father, but by me" (Jn.14:6).
> "That if thou shalt confess with thy mouth the Lord Jesus, and shalt believe in thine heart that God hath raised him from the dead, thou shalt be saved. For with the heart man believeth unto righteousness; and with the mouth confession is made unto salvation" (Ro.10:9-10).
> "This is a faithful saying, and worthy of all acceptation, that Christ Jesus came into the world to save sinners; of whom I am chief" (1 Tim.1:15).

| | | with him, | try of discipleship |
|---|---|---|---|
| | **CHAPTER 8** | 2 And certain women, which | 3 **They supported a minis-** |
| | | had been healed of evil spirits | **try of salvation** |
| | **R. Jesus and the Women** | and infirmities, Mary called | a. Mary Magdalene: A |
| | **Who Supported Him, 8:1-3** | Magdalene, out of whom | dark past [DS3] |
| | | went seven devils. | |
| **1 They supported a minis-** | And it came to pass after- | 3 And Joanna the wife of | b. Joanna: A lady of the |
| **try of preaching**[DS1,2] | ward, that he went through- | Chuza Herod's steward, and | King's court[DS4] |
| a. It reached out | out every city and village, | Susanna, and many others, | c. Susanna:[DS5] An unno- |
| b. It was true to the gos- | preaching and showing the | which ministered unto him of | ticed follower |
| pel: The K. of God | glad tidings of the kingdom | their substance. | d. Many others: Unknown[DS6] |
| **2 They supported a minis-** | of God: and the twelve were | | |

# DIVISION III

## THE SON OF MAN'S ANNOUNCED MISSION AND PUBLIC MINISTRY, 4:16-9:17

## R.    Jesus and the Women Who Supported Him, 8:1-3

(8:1-3) **Introduction**: this is an interesting passage. It shows that Jesus received financial support for His ministry. There were some women, apparently well-off financially, who supported Him.
1.    They supported a ministry of preaching (v.1).
2.    They supported a ministry of discipleship (v.1).
3.    They supported a ministry of salvation (v.2-3).

**1**  (8:1) **Preaching**: the women supported a preaching ministry. Preaching was Jesus' business; it was what He came to do, His primary call and mission. Note the word "afterward" (en toi kathexes). The word means one after the other, an orderly, successive step. The suggestion is that right after the banquet at Simon's home, Jesus got up and went about His primary task, that of preaching and proclaiming the gospel. He did not linger in fellowship or in any other pursuits, no matter their legitimacy or enjoyment. He was faithful and consistent in preaching and proclaiming the gospel. The point is this: the women supported a solid preaching ministry. They supported the Lord because He *preached* and was faithful to His call to preach. Note two facts in particular.
1.    They supported a ministry that reached out. Jesus "went throughout every city and village preaching." He had an ache, a compassion for all, not willing that any should perish. He sought everyone *within His reach*. Note that He did not seek the limelight of the cities. He went out into the villages of the countryside as well. He had been sent to preach, and He preached anywhere and everywhere He could reach. The whole thrust of His being was to reach people for God, to reach everyone He could. This was the kind of ministry the women supported.

> "Even as the Son of man came not to be ministered unto, but to minister, and to give his life a ransom for many" (Mt.20:28).
> "The Spirit of the Lord is upon me, because he hath anointed me to preach the gospel to the poor; he hath sent me to heal the brokenhearted, to preach deliverance to the captives, and recovering of sight to the blind, to set at liberty them that are bruised, to preach the acceptable year of the Lord" (Lk.4:18-19).
> "And he said unto them, I must preach the kingdom of God to other cities also: for therefore am I sent" (Lk.4:43).
> "For the Son of man is come to seek and to save that which was lost" (Lk.19:10).
> "The thief cometh not, but for to steal, and to kill, and to destroy: I am come that they might have life, and that they might have it more abundantly" (Jn.10:10).
> "And if any man hear my words, and believe not, I judge him not: for I came not to judge the world, but to save the world" (Jn.12:47).
> "To this end was I born, and for this cause came I into the world, that I should bear witness unto the truth. Every one that is of the truth heareth my voice" (Jn.18:37).
> "This is a faithful saying, and worthy of all acceptation, that Christ Jesus came into the world to save sinners; of whom I am chief" (1 Tim.1:15).
> "Behold, I stand at the door, and knock: if any man hear my voice, and open the door, I will come in to him, and will sup with him, and he with me" (Rev.3:20).

2.    They supported a ministry that was *true* to the gospel, a ministry that proclaimed the glad tidings of the Kingdom of God (see DEEPER STUDY # 3—Mt.19:23-24). Note that Jesus did not preach religion and ritual, ceremony and ordinance, laws and rules, works and deeds, mind and spirit, soul and body, thinking and reasoning. He touched on all these, but they were not His prime message. His message was the *good news*.

> "For God so loved the world, that he gave his only begotten Son, that whosoever believeth in him should not perish, but have everlasting life. For God sent not his Son into the world to condemn the world; but that the world through him might be saved. He that believeth on him is not condemned: but he that believeth not is condemned already, because he hath not believed in the name of the only begotten Son of God" (Jn.3:16-18).

"Verily, verily, I say unto you, He that heareth my word, and believeth on him that sent me, hath everlasting life, and shall not come into condemnation; but is passed from death unto life" (Jn.5:24).

"Little children, yet a little while I am with you. Ye shall seek me: and as I said unto the Jews, Whither I go, ye cannot come; so now I say to you. A new commandment I give unto you, that ye love one another; as I have loved you, that ye also love one another" (Jn.13:33-34).

"And this is his commandment, That we should believe on the name of his Son Jesus Christ, and love one another, as he gave us commandment" (1 Jn.3:23).

---

**DEEPER STUDY # 1**
(8:1) **Preach—Preaching** (kerusso): to proclaim, to publish, to be a herald, to preach the gospel as a herald.

---

**DEEPER STUDY # 2**
(8:1) **Showing the Glad Tidings—Preaching** (euaggelizomenos): to preach glad tidings, to announce glad tidings, to declare good news, to proclaim the gospel of Jesus Christ. Note the Greek word, how it resembles the word *evangelism*. The English word *evangelism* comes from it. By the very nature of his work, the preacher is an evangelist. He is a herald who comes in the name of the King, representing the King (cp. 2 Cor.5:20). He proclaims *only* the message of the King; he has no message of his own. If and when he begins to proclaim his own message, he is no longer the representative or the spokesman of the King.

---

[2] (8:1) **Discipleship—Stewardship**: they supported a ministry of discipleship. This was a critically important ministry, one which Christ stressed in His own life and practice. Making disciples of others was what He was doing with the twelve, and it was soon to be the *Great Commission* to all His followers. The support of the women in this ministry was critical, for it is doubtful that the disciples could have given their *full time* to Jesus without financial support. (See note—Mt.28:19-20 for detailed discussion.)

"Go ye therefore, and teach all nations, baptizing [making disciples of] them in the name of the Father, and of the Son, and of the Holy Ghost: teaching them to observe all things whatsoever I have commanded you: and, lo, I am with you alway, even unto the end of the world" (Mt.28:19-20).

"Then said Jesus to them again, Peace be unto you: as my Father hath sent me, even so send I you" (Jn.20:21).

"And the things that thou hast heard of me among many witnesses, the same commit thou to faithful men, who shall be able to teach others also" (2 Tim.2:2).

[3] (8:2-3) **Devotion—Stewardship**: they supported Jesus out of devotion. They were grateful for what He had done for them. Note that each one of them had been *reached and healed* by Jesus. They had received a very special touch from Him, and as a result they "ministered unto Him of their substance" (means, finances, property). Note the women who did minister (see DEEPER STUDY # 3-6—Lk.8:2-3).

---

**DEEPER STUDY # 3**
(8:2) **Mary Magdalene**: she was delivered from seven demons (Lk.8:2); was one of Jesus' primary financial supporters (Lk.8:3); was among the women who courageously stood at the cross (Mt.27:55-56); and was one to whom Jesus appeared after His resurrection (Mt.28:1; Mk.16:1; Lk.24:10; cp. Jn.20:11).

---

**DEEPER STUDY # 4**
(8:3) **Joanna**: her husband, Herod's steward, was the court official who looked after the king's estate and financial interests. Such was the task of the *steward*. The very nature of his job shows that he had to be a most-trusted official (cp. Lk.24:10).

---

**DEEPER STUDY # 5**
(8:3) **Susanna**: there is no other reference to Susanna. She represents the prominent disciple who is known by everyone but serves in a capacity that few ever notice. But note: she was such a devoted servant in giving, her name is known.

---

**DEEPER STUDY # 6**
(8:3) **Many others**: these represent the unknown and quiet, but all-important, followers of the Lord. They serve completely in the background, never up front; therefore, they are totally unknown. But note: they are faithful and do serve, consistently and faithfully.

| | S. Jesus Teaches The Sure Fate of the Word: How People Receive the Word, 8:4-15 (Mt.13:1-23; Mk.4:1-20) | 10 And he said, Unto you it is given to know the mysteries of the kingdom of God: but to others in parables; that seeing they might not see, and hearing they might not understand. | a. To reveal the truth to open hearts b. To conceal the truth from closed minds |
|---|---|---|---|
| 1 Crowds thronged Jesus—came from every city | 4 And when much people were gathered together, and were come to him out of every city, he spake by a parable: | 11 Now the parable is this: The seed is the word of God. | 4 The interpretation a. The seed is the Word of God |
| 2 The parable: A sower sowed seed a. Some fell by the wayside 1) Were trampled 2) Were devoured | 5 A sower went out to sow his seed: and as he sowed, some fell by the way side; and it was trodden down, and the fowls of the air devoured it. | 12 Those by the way side are they that hear; then cometh the devil, and taketh away the word out of their hearts, lest they should believe and be saved. | b. Some are by the wayside 1) They do hear 2) The devil snatches the Word away |
| b. Some fell upon rock 1) Were withered & scorched 2) Had no moisture or depth | 6 And some fell upon a rock; and as soon as it was sprung up, it withered away, because it lacked moisture. | 13 They on the rock are they, which, when they hear, receive the word with joy; and these have no root, which for a while believe, and in time of temptation fall away. | c. Some are on rock 1) They do hear 2) They have no root: When tempted, they fall away |
| c. Some fell among thorns: Were choked | 7 And some fell among thorns; and the thorns sprang up with it, and choked it. | 14 And that which fell among thorns are they, which, when they have heard, go forth, and are choked with cares and riches and pleasures of this life, and bring no fruit to perfection. | d. Some are among thorns 1) They do hear 2) They are choked with materialism & pleasure |
| d. Some fell on good ground: Were fruitful | 8 And other fell on good ground, and sprang up, and bare fruit an hundredfold. And when he had said these things, he cried, He that hath ears to hear, let him hear. | 15 But that on the good ground are they, which in an honest and good heart, having heard the word, keep it, and bring forth fruit with patience. | e. Some are on rich soil 1) They keep the Word 2) They have honest & good hearts 3) They bear fruit |
| 3 The reason why Jesus spoke in parables | 9 And his disciples asked him, saying, What might this parable be? | | |

# DIVISION III

## THE SON OF MAN'S ANNOUNCED MISSION AND PUBLIC MINISTRY, 4:16-9:17

**S.    Jesus Teaches the Sure Fate of the Word: How People Receive the Word, 8:4-15**

(8:4-15) **Introduction—Revival—Crowds—Worship—Church Attendance—Decision—Word of God**: the whole country was in a state of revival. It began with John the Baptist and continued with Jesus the Messiah. Multitudes of people were flocking to Jesus and being challenged to repent and follow God. The whole nation was charged with expectation, for the carpenter from Nazareth was not only claiming to be the Messiah, He was backing up His claims with a phenomenal demonstration of power—the power of God. But as Scripture says, "the Lord knew what was in man" (Jn.2:25). He knew that many were not really sincere. They did not have what it takes. They lacked…

- a real spirit of repentance
- a changed life
- an honest commitment
- a genuine faith
- a willingness to sacrifice
- a consistent obedience

Jesus knew that many were following Him not because they wanted to know God, not because they were genuine and sincere, but because of…

- family and friends
- the fellowship
- the social identification
- good feelings
- needs' being met

The insincerity of so many, of course, cut the heart of Jesus; but He still wanted to warn and reach as many as possible. This is what the parable of the seed is all about. Jesus wanted people to know that *hearing* the Word of God was not enough. There are many ways to hear the Word of God, but only one way bears fruit. Only one reception makes us acceptable to God. If we receive the Word of God any other way, then it becomes fruitless and does no good. It is snatched away or scorched or choked out. Only one reception will bear fruit.

Note how the parable speaks to every person. It is a *warning* to all hearers of the Word, especially to those who are not genuine followers of Christ. It gives great *assurance* to those who do hear: they shall definitely bear fruit. It is great encouragement to the preacher and teacher and to the lay witness. The seed they sow shall bear *some* fruit. (See outline and notes—Mt.13:1-9; Mk.4:1-20 for more discussion.)

1.    Crowds thronged Jesus, coming from every city (v.4).
2.    The parable: a sower sowed seed (v.5-8).
3.    The reason Jesus spoke in parables (v.9-10).
4.    The interpretation (v.11-15).

**1**  (8:4) **Multitudes—Jesus Christ, Multitudes Follow—Revival**: the crowds thronged Jesus, coming from every city. Note the words "much people" and "every city." Thousands were now flocking to Jesus from everywhere. One can estimate the numbers on the basis of His having fed five thousand men on one occasion. This does not count the women and children, each of which would outnumber the men by far. We are probably safe to say, as we can in every generation, that more women followed Jesus than men; and families were larger than the average of four persons per family today. Apparently the crowd was well over twenty thousand.

**2**  (8:5-8) **Sower, Parable of—Word of God**: the parable was taken from an everyday happening. It concerned a sower, a farmer, who went out to sow seed. Note: he did go out and he did sow.

> **Thought 1.** How many *do not* go out? Of those who do, how many really sow the seed of the Word? It is so easy for the minister and believer...
> - to sit in the comfort of the home or office and rest and work administratively instead of going out and sowing.
> - to visit and care for the flock in their needs instead of going out into the fields to sow.

In sharing the parable, Jesus said four things happened to the seed when it was sown.
1.  Some seed fell by the wayside, off to the side, out of the field upon the walking paths and roads. The paths and roads, of course, were trodden down and the soil was hard; therefore, the seed just lay on top and the birds came and devoured it.
2.  Some seed fell upon a rock, that is, a large layer of rock lying right under the surface. This seed, of course, grew quickly because of the water's lying upon the rock right after a rain. But it soon withered away because the water was soon evaporated, leaving nothing but dry soil. The sun scorched the young plant.
3.  Some seed fell among thorns. The seed sprouted, but the plants were soon choked to death by thorns.
4.  Other seed fell on good ground. The seed sprang up and was very fruitful, bearing an hundredfold.
Now note what Jesus did. Immediately upon finishing the parable, He cried (ephonei) with a loud shout: "He that hath ears to hear, let him hear." He warned: "Hear!"

**3**  (8:9-10) **Parables**: the reason why Jesus spoke in parables. Later, when Jesus and the disciples were all alone, the disciples asked Him to explain the parable. But Jesus used the occasion, first, to explain why He was now beginning to teach by parables. Up until now He had been teaching by direct statement and clear illustration, using few parables. But from now on, there was to be a difference. His primary method would be the parable. Why? Jesus gave two reasons.
1.  Jesus wanted the *open hearts*, the persons who were really seeking God, to learn all they could about the *mysteries* of the Kingdom of God. Parables required much thought in order to grasp their meaning. A person who really sought after God would seek, strive, think, and ask until he could find the meaning to the parable. And then he would chew upon the meaning, drawing all the meaning he could out of the parable so that he could learn everything possible about God.

> **Thought 1.** What Christ said about seeking the truth is especially true of those who already know God personally. However, it is also true of the crowd, of any who are genuine in their search for God but have not yet found Him. Christ longs to reach any who are truly seeking Him. The parable is an excellent method to arouse interest and curiosity among men. Of course, if a man is genuinely sincere in knowing *the Truth*, he will search out the meaning (Truth), no matter how much time and effort are required.

2.  Jesus wanted the truth concealed from closed minds. Closed minds are hardened and unwilling to consider the *mysteries* of the Kingdom of God. Sitting there in the audience, they heard and understood the words and the pictures which the words painted. But there was only a little interest in searching into the hidden meaning (mysteries) of the parable. The time and effort required were not worth it. The closed minded and carnal were just not that interested. Jesus and His message were interesting, for He was a very capable preacher, full of charisma and practical help for living. However, as far as committing one's life totally to His cause and commandments, as far as denying self completely and sacrificing all one is and has, it was not worth it, not to the carnal. Therefore, the carnal were not willing to take the time or effort required to search out the meaning of the parable. Jesus actually said that He wanted the meaning hidden from the closed minded.
Note something else as well. The closed-minded, hardhearted, and carnal often *react* to the truth when the truth points a finger at them and their wrong. (See outline and notes—Mt.13:10-17 for a full outline on why Jesus spoke in parables.)

**4**  (8:11-15) **Word of God—Witnessing—Profession—Worldliness—Conversion, Dramatic**: the interpretation of the parable was given by Jesus. The sower is the Lord Jesus Christ or a servant of His. The servants of the Lord, ministers or laymen, are "laborers together with God" (1 Cor.3:9). The seed is the Word of God or the Word of the kingdom. It is called (1) the "incorruptible seed" (1 Pt.1:23), and (2) "the gospel which...bringeth forth fruit" (Col.1:5-6).
The ground upon which the seed is sown is the heart of the hearer. Jesus said two significant things about the ground. (1) There are different ways to hear and receive the Word (seed). And (2) He warns all hearers (all types of ground): the fate of the Word, how well it grows, depends upon the hearer.

> **Thought 1.** The success of the seed depends upon one thing alone; the condition of the soil (heart) to receive the seed (Word). If the ground (heart) is soft and rich, being full of the right minerals (spiritual qualities) and cleared of all junk and brush, ploughed and turned over, then it is ready to receive the seed.

1.    The seed by the wayside. The person by the wayside does hear the Word of God. He is present, but he is off to the side, out of the way, not involved. He lets his mind wander and thinks little and involves himself even less. He respects Christ and the preacher and would not miss a service, but he is on the outer circle, paying little attention to the warnings and promises of the Word.

Note what happens. Before the person believes, the devil comes and snatches the Word away. It is taken from the person; the person never applies the Word to his life, never really lives sacrificially for Christ. (Cp. Judas Iscariot and cp. Herod who enjoyed listening to John the Baptist, Mk.6:20.)

> "For the heart of this people is waxed gross, and their ears are dull of hearing, and their eyes have they closed; lest they should see with their eyes, and hear with their ears, and understand with their ears, and understand with their heart, and should be converted, and I should heal them" (Acts 28:27).
>
> "Who [the hardhearted] being past feeling have given themselves over unto lasciviousness, to work all uncleanness with greediness" (Eph.4:19).
>
> "But exhort one another daily, while it is called To day; lest any of you be hardened through the deceitfulness of sin" (Heb.3:13).
>
> "Happy is the man that feareth always: but he that hardeneth his heart shall fall into mischief" (Pr.28:14).
>
> "He, that being often reproved hardeneth his neck, shall suddenly be destroyed, and that without remedy" (Pr.29:1).
>
> "But after thy hardness and impenitent heart treasurest up unto thyself wrath against the day of wrath and revelation of the righteous judgment of God" (Ro.2:5).

2.    The seed on the rock. This person hears the Word, and becomes excited over it. He receives the Word, professes belief in Christ, and makes a profession of faith before the world. But he fails to count the cost, to consider the commitment, the self-denial, the sacrifice, the study, the learning, the hours and effort required. He does not apply himself to *learn Christ*; therefore, he does not become rooted and grounded in the Word. He is only a superficial believer.

Note what happens. When trials and temptations come, he falls away. His profession is scorched and consumed, burned up by the heat of the trial and temptation. (Cp. John Mark who at first failed to endure, Acts 13:13; Demas, Phile.1:24; and the men who discovered that following Christ just cost too much, Lk.9:57-62.)

> "And because iniquity shall abound, the love of many shall wax cold" (Mt.24:12).
>
> "But he that heareth, and doeth not, is like a man that without a foundation built an house upon the earth; against which the stream did beat vehemently, and immediately it fell; and the ruin of that house was great" (Lk.6:49).
>
> "And Jesus said unto him, No man, having put his hand to the plough, and looking back, is fit for the kingdom of God" (Lk.9:62).
>
> "But now, after that ye have known God, or rather are known of God, how turn ye again to the weak and beggarly elements [the world], whereunto ye desire again to be in bondage?" (Gal.4:9).
>
> "Now the just shall live by faith: but if any man draw back, my soul shall have no pleasure in him" (Heb.10:38).
>
> "For if after they have escaped the pollutions of the world through the knowledge of the Lord and Saviour Jesus Christ, they are again entangled therein, and overcome, the latter end is worse with them than the beginning. For it had been better for them not to have known the way of righteousness, than, after they have known it, to turn from the holy commandment delivered unto them. But it is happened unto them according to the true proverb, The dog is turned to his own vomit again; and the sow that was washed to her wallowing in the mire" (2 Pt.2:20-22).
>
> "Nevertheless I have somewhat against thee, because thou hath left thy first love. Remember therefore from whence thou art fallen, and repent, and do the first works; or else I will come unto thee quickly, and will remove thy candlestick out of his place, except thou repent" (Rev.2:4-5)

3.    The seed among thorns. This is a person who receives the Word and *honestly tries* (professes) to live for Christ. Christ and His followers and the church and its activities appeal to him. So he joins right in, even professing Christ as he walks about his daily affairs. But there is one problem: the thorns or worldliness. He is unwilling to cut completely loose from the world: "[to] come out from among them and [to] be separate" (2 Cor.6:17-18). He lives a double life, trying to live for Christ and yet still live out in the world. He keeps right on growing in the midst of the thorns, giving his mind and attention to the *cares* and *riches* and *pleasures* of this world.

Note what happens. He bears fruit. Fruit does appear, but it never ripens; it is never able to be plucked. The thorns choke the life out of it. It never lives to be used. (Cp. the Rich Young Ruler, Lk.18:18f; Ananias and Sapphira, Acts 5:1f.)

**Thought 1.** Note the three areas that choke the life out of men.
1)    The cares of this life.

> "Therefore I say unto you, Take no thought for your life, what ye shall eat, or what ye shall drink; nor yet for your body, what ye shall put on. Is not the life more than meat, and the body than raiment?" (Mt.6:25).

"Therefore take no thought, saying, What shall we eat? or, What shall we drink? or, Wherewithal shall we be clothed?" (Mt.6:31).

"And seek not ye what ye shall eat, or what ye shall drink, neither be ye of doubtful mind" (Lk.12:29).

"And take heed to yourselves, lest at any time your hearts be overcharged with surfeiting, and drunkenness, and cares of this life, and so that day come upon you unawares" (Lk.21:34).

"Be careful for nothing; but in every thing by prayer and supplication with thanksgiving let your requests be made known unto God" (Ph.4:6).

"Casting all your care upon him; for he careth for you" (1 Pt.5:7).

"Surely every man walketh in a vain show: surely they are disquieted in vain: he heapeth up riches, and knoweth not who shall gather them" (Ps.39:6).

"It is vain for you to rise up early, to sit up late, to eat the bread of sorrows: for so he giveth his beloved sleep" (Ps.127:2).

2) The riches of this life.

"And the cares of this world, and the deceitfulness of riches, and the lusts of other things entering in, choke the word, and it becometh unfruitful" (Mk.4:19).

"But they that will be rich fall into temptation and a snare, and into many foolish and hurtful lusts, which drown men in destruction and perdition" (1 Tim.6:9).

"Your gold and silver is cankered; and the rust of them shall be a witness against you, and shall eat your flesh as it were fire. Ye have heaped treasure together for the last days" (Jas.5:3).

"Then said Jesus unto his disciples, Verily I say unto you, That a rich man shall hardly enter into the kingdom of heaven" (Mt.19:23).

"For we brought nothing into this world, and it is certain we can carry nothing out" (1 Tim.6:7).

"And when thy herds and thy flocks multiply, and thy silver and thy gold is multiplied, and all that thou hast is multiplied; then thine heart be lifted up, and thou forget the LORD thy God, which brought thee forth out of the land of Egypt, from the house of bondage" (Dt.8:13-14).

"The increase of his house shall depart, and his goods shall flow away in the day of his [God's] wrath" (Job 20:28).

"For he seeth that wise men die, likewise the fool and the brutish person perish, and leave their wealth to others" (Ps.49:10).

"Wilt thou set thine eyes upon that which is not? For riches certainly make themselves wings; they fly away as an eagle toward heaven" (Pr.23:5).

"Yea, I hated all my labor which I had taken under the sun: because I should leave it unto the man that shall be after me" (Eccl.2:18).

"As the partridge sitteth on eggs, and hatcheth them not; so he that getteth riches, and not by right, shall leave them in the midst of his days, and at his end shall be a fool" (Jer.17:11).

3) The pleasures of this life.

"And I will say to my soul, Soul, thou hast much goods laid up for many years; take thine ease, eat, drink, and be merry" (Lk.12:19).

"But she that liveth in pleasure is dead while she liveth" (1 Tim.5:6).

"This know also, that in the last days perilous times shall come. For men shall be lovers of their own selves....lovers of pleasures more than lovers of God" (2 Tim.3:1-2, 4).

"For we ourselves [believers] also were sometimes foolish, disobedient, deceived, serving divers lusts and pleasures, living in malice and envy, hateful, and hating one another" (Tit.3:3).

"Ye have lived in pleasure on the earth, and been wanton; ye have nourished your hearts, as in a day of slaughter" (Jas.5:5).

"And shall receive the reward of unrighteousness, as they that count it pleasure to riot [party, revel, carouse] in the day time. Spots they are and blemishes, sporting themselves with their own deceivings while they feast with you" (2 Pt.2:13).

"Therefore hear now this, thou that art given to pleasures, that dwellest carelessly, that sayest in thine heart, I am, and none else beside me; I shall not sit as a widow, neither shall I know the loss of children: but these two things shall come to thee in a moment in one day, the loss of children, and widowhood: they shall come upon thee in their perfection for the multitude of thy sorceries, and for the great abundance of thine enchantments" (Is.47:8-9).

4.   The seed on good ground. These are they who have an honest and good heart. Therefore, when they hear the Word, they keep it. Note several things.

a.  Their hearts are "honest" (kalei). The word means fair, noble, and just. It has the idea of holding fast. These people are honest and fair; they are noble people in listening and considering the Word. They honestly seek to learn and know the truth, spiritually as well as physically.

> "These were more noble than those in Thessalonica, in that they received the word with all readiness of mind, and searched the scriptures daily, whether those things were so" (Acts 17:11).
> "Then they that gladly received his word were baptized: and the same day there were added unto them about three thousand souls" (Acts 2:41).
> "For this cause also thank we God without ceasing, because, when ye received the word of God which ye heard of us, ye received it not as the word of men, but as it is in truth, the word of God, which effectually worketh also in you that believe" (1 Th.2:13).

b.  Their hearts are "good" (agathei), meaning devoted, committed, given over to the truth. Once the truth is known, they hold fast to it.

> "But God be thanked, that ye were the servants of sin, but ye have obeyed from the heart that form of doctrine which was delivered you" (Ro.6:17).
> "O that there were such a heart in them, that they would fear me, and keep all my commandments always, that it might be well with them, and with their children for ever!" (Dt.5:29).
> "This day the LORD thy God hath commanded thee to do these statutes and judgments: thou shalt therefore keep and do them with all thine heart, and with all thy soul" (Dt.26:16).
> "This book of the law shall not depart out of thy mouth; but thou shalt meditate therein day and night, that thou mayest observe to do according to all that is written therein: for then thou shalt make thy way prosperous, and then thou shalt have good success" (Josh.1:8).
> "My heart is fixed, O God, my heart is fixed: I will sing and give praise" (Ps.57:7).
> "And I will give them a heart to know me, that I am the LORD: and they shall be my people, and I will be their God: for they shall return unto me with their whole heart" (Jer.24:7).
> "A new heart also will I give you, and a new spirit will I put within you: and I will take away the stony heart out of your flesh, and I will give you a heart of flesh" (Ezk.36:26; cp. Ezk.11:19).

c.  They keep the Word. They do not let the devil snatch it, nor the trials and temptations of life scorch it, nor the cares and riches and pleasures of this life choke it.

> "Verily, verily, I say unto you, If a man keep my saying, he shall never see death" (Jn.8:51).
> "Jesus answered and said unto him, If a man love me, he will keep my words: and my Father will love him, and we will come unto him, and make our abode with him" (Jn.14:23).
> "I have manifested thy name unto the men which thou gavest me out of the world: thine they were, and thou gavest them me; and they have kept thy word" (Jn.17:6).
> "And hereby we do know that we know him, if we keep his commandments" (1 Jn.2:3).
> "I know thy works: behold, I have set before thee an open door, and no man can shut it: for thou hast a little strength, and hast kept my word, and hast not denied my name" (Rev.3:8).

d.  They bear fruit with *patience*. They endure and study, grow and serve more and more. They constantly water and pluck the weeds and thorns, and they continue to do so until the fruit is fully grown and plucked and *taken home* to the Master of the house.

> "Therefore if any man be in Christ, he is a new creature: old things are passed away; behold, all things are become new" (2 Cor.5:17).
> "Verily, verily, I say unto you, Except a corn of wheat fall into the ground and die, it abideth alone: but if it die, it bringeth forth much fruit" (Jn.12:24).
> "I am the vine, ye are the branches: He that abideth in me, and I in him, the same bringeth forth much fruit: for without me ye can do nothing" (Jn.15:5).
> "For the fruit of the Spirit is in all goodness and righteousness and truth" (Eph.5:9).
> "Being filled with the fruits of righteousness, which are by Jesus Christ, unto the glory and praise of God" (Ph.1:11).
> "That ye might walk worthy of the Lord unto all pleasing, being fruitful in every good work, and increasing in the knowledge of God" (Col.1:10).
> "Those that be planted in the house of the LORD shall flourish in the courts of our God. They shall still bring forth fruit in old age; they shall be fat and flourishing" (Ps.92:13-14).

| | T. Jesus Teaches Three Fundamental Principles of Life, 8:16-18 (Mt.5:15-16; 10:26-27; 13:12; Mk.4:21-23; cp. Lk.11:33-36) | enter in may see the light. 17 For nothing is secret, that shall not be made manifest; neither any thing hid, that shall not be known and come abroad. 18 Take heed therefore how ye hear: for whosoever hath, | 2 Secrecy is impossible: All things shall be found out |
|---|---|---|---|
| 1 A candle (life) is for the purpose of giving light*DS1* a. It is not covered, not hid b. It is made conspicuous | 16 No man, when he hath lighted a candle, covereth it with a vessel, or putteth it under a bed; but setteth it on a candlestick, that they which | to him shall be given; and whosoever hath not, from him shall be taken even that which he seemeth to have. | 3 Truth is very narrow a. A person must watch how he hears b. The reason: Truth shall be rewarded; but the "seemingly" true shall be stripped away |

# DIVISION III

## THE SON OF MAN'S ANNOUNCED MISSION AND PUBLIC MINISTRY, 4:16-9:17

### T.    Jesus Teaches Three Fundamental Principles of Life, 8:16-18

(8:16-18) **Introduction**: Christ gives three fundamental principles of life, principles that speak clearly to all believers, both layman and preacher.
1.    A candle or life is for the purpose of giving light (v.16).
2.    Secrecy is impossible: all things shall be found out (v.17).
3.    Truth is very narrow (v.18).

**1**    (8:16) **Light—Purpose—Life**: a candle, a life, is for the purpose of giving light. Note five simple facts about its purpose.
1.    The candle is a given candle. It is not purchased or earned. God gives the candle to every man. This is the key. The candle is a gift from God. A man has it, but a man has to use it for it to be of any benefit. The candle is a man's life, the life which he is given when he is born into the world.
2.    The candle is to be lit. The candle just exists until it is lit; it is not fulfilling its primary function. Its function is to give light, but it may be used for other things, useful things such as...
   • decorations to beautify (a life that beautifies).
   • wax to plug holes and fill gaps (a life that plugs and fills the gaps of society).
   • a stick-like object to push or pull (a life that pushes and pulls as it is needed).
   • an ornament to attract attention (a life that entices, centers on self).

Note a significant fact: in most of these cases the candle or life of a person is helpful and useful; but the candle has yet to fulfill its *primary* function, the very purpose for which it was made and formed. The candle has to be lit before it can give light. The man himself is the one who has to take the initiative to have his candle lit. He has to come to Christ, the Light of the World, and receive the quickening spark of His Light. A man has to reach out for the light that is Jesus Christ. Christ is the Light, but man has to put the candle of his life up to the light of Christ in order to be lit, ignited, and quickened (Jn.1:9; Jn.8:12; 11:9-10; 12:36, 46; Eph.5:8).
3.    The candle is not to be hid. Once the candle has been lit *no man* covers it with a vessel or puts it under a bed. Such is ludicrous, foolish, unreasonable. All the energy and effort as well as the purpose for lighting the candle are wasted if it is slid under a bed or covered. The candle and light are useless, of no purpose.

> **"Whosoever therefore shall be ashamed of me and of my words in this adulterous and sinful generation; of him also shall the Son of man be ashamed, when he cometh in the glory of his Father with the holy angels" (Mk.8:38).**
> **"For God hath not given us the spirit of fear; but of power, and of love, and of a sound mind. Be not thou therefore ashamed of the testimony of our Lord, nor of me his prisoner: but be thou partaker of the afflictions of the gospel according to the power of God" (2 Tim.1:7-8).**

4.    The candle is to be conspicuous, placed high upon a candlestick. Every genuine believer has had his candle ignited; he has touched Christ, the Light of the World, and Christ has given him light. Therefore, the believer burns and shows forth light. The only question is, how brightly does he shine? His light may be bright or dim, strong or weak, flickering or flaming, blinking or flooding, smoking or clear. Christ says it is foolish to have light and it not be turned on, conspicuously giving off light.

> **"According to my earnest expectation and my hope, that in nothing I shall be ashamed, but that with all boldness, as always, so now also Christ shall be magnified in my body, whether it be by life, or by death" (Ph.1:20).**
> **"Yet if any man suffer as a Christian, let him not be ashamed; but let him glorify God on this behalf" (1 Pt.4:16).**
> **"And now, little children, abide in him; that, when he shall appear, we may have confidence, and not be ashamed before him at his coming" (1 Jn.2:28).**

"Then shall I not be ashamed, when I have respect unto all thy commandments" (Ps.119:6).

"For the Lord GOD will help me; therefore shall I not be confounded: therefore have I set my face like a flint, and I know that I shall not be ashamed" (Is.50:7).

"And ye shall eat in plenty, and be satisfied, and praise the name of the LORD your God, that hath dealt wondrously with you: and my people shall never be ashamed" (Joel 2:26).

5.   The candle is to be seen by all who enter. Note a critical point. This is the very purpose of *the lighted candle, to provide light.* And light does numerous things (see DEEPER STUDY # 1, *Light, Purpose*—Lk.8:16).

"Ye are the light of the world. A city that is set on an hill cannot be hid. Neither do men light a candle, and put it under a bushel, but on a candlestick; and it giveth light unto all that are in the house. Let your light so shine before men, that they may see your good works, and glorify your Father which is in heaven" (Mt.5:14-16).

"For we cannot but speak the things which we have seen and heard" (Acts 4:20).

"Be filled with the Spirit; speaking to yourselves in psalms and hymns and spiritual songs, singing and making melody in your heart to the Lord" (Eph.5:18-19).

"But sanctify the Lord God in your hearts: and be ready always to give an answer to every man that asketh you a reason of the hope that is in you with meekness and fear" (1 Pt.3:15).

"I have set watchmen upon thy walls, O Jerusalem, which shall never hold their peace day nor night: ye that make mention of the LORD, keep not silence" (Is.62:6).

"The LORD hath brought forth our righteousness: come, and let us declare in Zion the work of the LORD our God" (Jer.51:10).

"Come and hear, all ye that fear God, and I will declare what he hath done for my soul" (Ps.66:16).

---

**DEEPER STUDY # 1**

(8:16) **Light—Purpose**: Christ said, "I am the Light of the world" (Jn.8:12; 9:5). Here He says the disciple is to be like Himself—"the light of the world." Therefore, the disciple is to undergo a radical transformation. He is to *become like Christ* more and more and *to reflect the light* of Christ (2 Cor.3:18; 4:6-7). Light is and does several things.

1.   Light is clear and pure. It is clean, that is, good, right, and true (Eph.5:8f).
2.   Light penetrates. It cuts through and eliminates darkness.
3.   Light enlightens. It enlarges one's vision and knowledge of an area.
4.   Light reveals. It opens up the truth of an area, a whole new world, and it clears the way so that a person can see the truth and the life (Jn.14:6).
5.   Light guides (Jn.12:36, 46). It directs the way to go and leads along the right path.
6.   Light strips away (Jn.3:19-20). It unclothes the darkness that blackens life.
7.   Light routes the chaos (cp. Gen.1:2-3). It brings peace to the disturbance caused by walking in pitch darkness.
8.   Light discriminates between the right way and the wrong way (see note—Eph.5:10; cp. 5:8-10).
9.   Light warns. It warns of dangers that lie ahead in one's path.

---

[2]   (8:17) **Sin, Secret—Judgment**: secrecy is impossible. All things shall be found out. Three things are said in this verse.

1.   Men try to hide things. They try to keep some things secret.
   a.   Men try to hide sin and shame. They sin in the dark and behind closed doors, when out and away from home and friends, and by keeping secret books or bank accounts.
   b.   Men try to hide possessions lest they have to give or spend more.
   c.   Men try to hide abilities and talents, lest they have to serve and use them. They prefer the ease and comfort of complacency and plenty instead of the rigors and sacrifice required to meet the needs of a suffering world.
   d.   Men try to hide the Light and the Truth they have come to know. They are lazy, complacent, embarrassed, apprehensive and fearful; or else they lack the vision, willingness, commitment, initiative, and endurance to set the Light and Truth out before men. They just keep quiet within their own world, unwilling to sacrifice and deny themselves in order *to go* and share with those in darkness and ignorance.
2.   Men think they will never be found out. They think their secrets will be hid forever and never discovered...
   - not by mom or dad
   - not by friend or acquaintance
   - not by preacher or God
   - not by wife or children
   - not by society or organization

Men feel they are safe with the secret. They feel bad consequences will never happen to them: suffering and punishment, bad and evil will never fall upon them. They will be able to keep the secret hid forever and escape punishment.

3.   Christ said nothing—not a single thing—will be hid forever. Every secret thing will be revealed and opened up. The thing hidden is seen, if not by men then by God, and it will be revealed. God will reveal the truth in the day of judgment if not before. The deceptions, the cloaks, the disguises, the secrets, the hidden things of all men shall be stripped away and unveiled; then all shall see, for it shall be manifested for all to see (Ro.2:2, 6, 11, 16).

"Therefore judge nothing before the time, until the Lord come, who both will bring to light the hidden things of darkness, and will make manifest the counsels of the hearts: and then shall every man have praise of God" (1 Cor.4:5).

"In the day when God shall judge the secrets of men by Jesus Christ according to my gospel" (Ro.2:16).

"Behold, ye have sinned against the LORD: and be sure your sin will find you out" (Num.32:23).

"If I sin, then thou markest me, and thou wilt not acquit me from mine iniquity" (Job 10:14).

"For now thou numberest my steps: dost thou not watch over my sin?" (Job 14:16).

"The heaven shall reveal his iniquity; and the earth shall rise up against him" (Job 20:27).

"For God shall bring every work into judgment, with every secret thing, whether it be good, or whether it be evil" (Eccl.12:14).

"For though thou wash thee with nitre, and take thee much soap, yet thine iniquity is marked before me, saith the Lord GOD" (Jer.2:22).

"For mine eyes are upon all their ways: they are not hid from my face, neither is their iniquity hid from mine eyes" (Jer.16:17).

"I the LORD search the heart, I try the reins, even to give every man according to his ways, and according to the fruit of his doings" (Jer.17:10).

"Can any hide himself in secret places that I shall not see him? saith the LORD. Do not I fill heaven and earth? saith the LORD" (Jer.23:24).

"And the spirit of the LORD fell upon me, and said unto me, Speak; Thus saith the LORD; Thus have ye said, O house of Israel: for I know the things that come into your mind, every one of them" (Ezk.11:5).

"And they consider not in their hearts that I remember all their wickedness: now their own doings have beset them about; they are before my face" (Hos.7:2).

"For I know your manifold transgressions and your mighty sins: they afflict the just, they take a bribe, and they turn aside the poor in the gate from their right" (Amos 5:12).

**3** (8:18) **Truth—Seeking**: truth is narrow, very narrow. This verse is a severe warning. It is referring back to the seed or the Word of God and the hearers. Very simply, Christ warns that we must hear and use what we hear if we want to be given things from God. If we hear and do not use what we hear, then what we have shall be taken away.

Note two points.

1. We must take heed *how* we hear. We can hear but hear wrongly. We can think and guess and suppose we know what we hear, but it is false and counterfeit and shall be stripped away. Note that we must "take heed," discern what we hear. We must make sure we have the truth. (See DEEPER STUDY # 1—Jn.1:9; DEEPER STUDY # 1—8:32; DEEPER STUDY # 2—14:6.)

2. The *reason* we need to watch how we hear is strikingly clear: the truth shall be rewarded, but the *seemingly true* shall be stripped away. If we use what we hear, we shall be given more; if we do not use what we have, even what we do possess will be taken away.

Seekers and achievers do receive and get more. The non-dreamer and complacent receive little and get less. This is a law of every realm.

1. It is the law of nature. The early get and survive. The early bird gets the worm; the late get little and suffer.

2. It is the law of man. Men reward energy and effort, production and results. They threaten and often take away from the lazy and inactive. Those who labor and practice and are diligent and persistent will always see and hear and get. They are in a position to get more and more and to be given more and more. But the lazy and non-worker, the neglectful and unfaithful will always lose.

All through life a man either gains or loses. He seldom, if ever, stands still. It all depends on the dreams, the effort, and the energy he is willing to exert.

3. It is the law of God.

"Blessed are they which do hunger and thirst after righteousness: for they shall be filled" (Mt.5:6).

"But seek ye first the kingdom of God and his righteousness; and all these things shall be added unto you" (Mt.6:33).

"Ask, and it shall be given you; seek, and ye shall find; knock, and it shall be opened unto you: for every one that asketh receiveth; and he that seeketh findeth; and to him that knocketh it shall be opened" (Mt.7:7-8).

"He that is faithful in that which is least is faithful also in much: and he that is unjust in the least is unjust also in much" (Lk.16:10).

"And the LORD thy God will make thee plenteous in every work of thine hand, in the fruit of thy body, and in the fruit of thy cattle, and in the fruit of thy land, for good: for the LORD will again rejoice over thee for good, as he rejoiced over thy fathers" (Dt.30:9).

**Thought 1.** This verse is both a great encouragement and a realistic threat.

1) It is a great encouragement to the...

- faithful
- diligent
- stedfast
- toiling
- persevering
- consistent
- enduring
- hardworking
- hardpracticing
- beginner and finisher
- initiator and finalizer
- hardstudying

2) It is a realistic and understandable threat to the...

| | | | |
|---|---|---|---|
| • lazy | • close-minded | • sluggish | • late sleeper |
| • idle | • close-eyed | • slothful | • late starter |
| • complacent | • close-eared | • shiftless | • time waster |
| • inconsistent | • self-satisfied | • purposeless | • misguided |

"And we desire that every one of you do show the same diligence to the full assurance of hope unto the end: that ye be not slothful, but followers of them who through faith and patience inherit the promises" (Heb.6:11-12).

"Not slothful in business; fervent in spirit; serving the Lord" (Ro.12:11; cp. Mt.25:24-27).

"For even when we were with you, this we commanded you, that if any would not work, neither should he eat. For we hear that there are some which walk among you disorderly, working not at all, but are busybodies. Now them that are such we command and exhort by our Lord Jesus Christ, that with quietness they work, and eat their own bread" (2 Th.3:10-12).

"Because thou servedst not the LORD thy God with joyfulness, and with gladness of heart, for the abundance of all things; therefore shalt thou serve thine enemies which the LORD shall send against thee, in hunger, and in thirst, and in nakedness, and in want of all things: and he shall put a yoke of iron upon thy neck, until he have destroyed thee" (Dt.28:47-48).

"He [the wicked man] wandereth abroad for bread, saying, Where is it? He knoweth that the day of darkness is ready at his hand" (Job 15:23).

"Give not sleep to thine eyes, nor slumber to thine eyelids" (Pr.6:4).

"Go to the ant, thou sluggard; consider her ways, and be wise: which having no guide, overseer, or ruler, provideth her meat in the summer, and gathereth her food in the harvest. How long wilt thou sleep, O sluggard? When wilt thou arise out of thy sleep? Yet a little sleep, a little slumber, a little folding of the hands to sleep: so shall thy poverty come as one that travelleth, and thy want as an armed man" (Pr.6:6-11).

"He that gathereth in summer is a wise son: but he that sleepeth in harvest is a son that causeth shame" (Pr.10:5).

"The soul of the sluggard desireth, and hath nothing: but the soul of the diligent shall be made fat" (Pr.13:4).

"The way of the slothful man is as a hedge of thorns: but the way of the righteous is made plain" (Pr.15:19).

"He also that is slothful in his work is brother to him that is a great waster" (Pr.18:9).

"Slothfulness casteth into a deep sleep; and an idle soul shall suffer hunger" (Pr.19:15).

"A slothful man hideth his hand in his bosom, and will not so much as bring it to his mouth again" (Pr.19:24).

"The sluggard will not plow by reason of the cold; therefore shall he beg in harvest, and have nothing" (Pr.20:4).

"Love not sleep, lest thou come to poverty: Open thine eyes, and thou shalt be satisfied with bread" (Pr.20:13).

"The desire of the slothful killeth him; for his hands refuse to labor. He coveteth greedily all the day long: but the righteous giveth and spareth not" (Pr.21:25-26).

"The slothful man saith, There is a lion without, I shall be slain in the streets" (Pr.22:13).

"For the drunkard and the glutton shall come to poverty: and drowsiness shall clothe a man with rags" (Pr.23:21).

"I went by the field of the slothful, and by the vineyard of the man void of understanding; and, lo, it was all grown over with thorns, and nettles had covered the face thereof, and the stone wall thereof was broken down. Then I saw, and considered it well: I looked upon it, and received instruction. Yet a little sleep, a little slumber, a little folding of the hands to sleep: so shall thy poverty come as one that travelleth; and thy want as an armed man" (Pr.24:30-34).

"The slothful man saith, There is a lion in the way; a lion is in the streets. As the door turneth upon his hinges, so doth the slothful upon his bed. The slothful hideth his hand in his bosom; it grieveth him to bring it again to his mouth. The sluggard is wiser in his own conceit than seven men that can render a reason" (Pr.26:13-16).

"By much slothfulness the building decayeth; and through idleness of the hands the house droppeth through" (Eccl.10:18).

| | U. Jesus Teaches the Basis of True Kinship, 8:19-21 (Mt.12:46-50; Mk.3:31-35) | 20 And it was told him by certain which said, Thy mother and thy brethren stand without, desiring to see thee. | 2 True kinship is not based upon human relationships |
|---|---|---|---|
| 1 Jesus' family sought Him | 19 Then came to him his mother and his brethren, and could not come at him for the press. | 21 And he answered and said unto them, My mother and my brethren are these which hear the word of God, and do it. | 3 True kinship is based upon the Word of God: Hearing & doing it |

# DIVISION III

## THE SON OF MAN'S ANNOUNCED MISSION AND PUBLIC MINISTRY, 4:16-9:17

## U.  Jesus Teaches the Basis of True Kinship, 8:19-21

(8:19-21) **Introduction**: the immediate family is generally looked upon as the closest bond on earth. Sometimes it is; sometimes it is not. It should always be very, very close. However, Christ teaches there is a closer tie than the family, the tie that binds Him and His followers together. This is the lesson of this passage, a lesson that teaches a phenomenal truth. (See outline and notes—Mt.12:46-50; Mk.3:31-35 for more discussion.)

1. Jesus' family sought Him (v.19).
2. True kinship is not based upon human relationships (v.20).
3. True kinship is based upon the Word of God: hearing and doing it (v.21).

**1** (8:19) **Jesus Christ, Family—Accusations, Insane**: Jesus' family sought Him. It is interesting to observe what they were *not* doing.

1. They were not making a social call. It was not a friendly visit, not family members visiting family members. Jesus was preaching and holding a service, yet His family interrupted Him right in the middle of the service. However, Jesus did not stop preaching; He continued right on. In fact, He used the occasion to teach a great spiritual truth.
2. They were not visiting Jesus to hear Him preach nor to learn from Him. This is known from the fact that His brothers did not believe in Him and the fact that the family did not enter the service. Note also that the family was late for the service; they arrived while He was already preaching and conducting the service.
3. They did not make their way through the crowd to Him. Instead they sent word by someone else for Him to come outside to them (Mt.12:47; Mk.3:31). Apparently, they were too embarrassed for one of them to try to reach Him.

Why was Jesus' family seeking Him? Several facts need to be considered in answering the question.

1. At first, some of the family supported Jesus and followed His leadership. They went with Him and His disciples on one of His very first evangelistic tours to Capernaum and remained with Him for a long time, apparently helping out in both practical and ministerial duties (Jn.2:12).
2. Second, the family witnessed two *unbelievable events* at the beginning of Jesus' ministry when He visited their hometown, Nazareth. They heard Jesus, one of their very own, claim to be the Messiah, the very One who was the fulfillment of the Holy Scripture. Imagine the shock of hearing one's own brother claiming to be Messiah, the Savior of the world. Then they witnessed their own hometown neighbors reject and attempt to kill Jesus. They actually saw their closest neighbors and dearest friends become insanely violent against their brother. Again, imagine the shock and the fear for Jesus' welfare, and the embarrassment as they walked among their friends throughout the coming days and weeks. It would be very difficult to live and face one's neighbors and townfolk after such an incident (Lk.4:16-31).
3. Third, the family was under constant pressure from friends to bring Jesus home—friends who counted themselves dear enough to advise the family. The friends thought Jesus was *mad* and *insane* by going about making the claims He was making, claims which included being the Son of God. Apparently, the family at some point gave permission for some friends to go bring Jesus home (Mk.3:21).
4. Fourth, Jesus' brothers did not support nor believe in Him. In fact, their disbelief eventually declined into ridicule. This is seen happening about six months before the crucifixion (Jn.7:5). As a point of interest, the brothers never did believe in Him until after the resurrection.

What seems to have been happening was that Mary and the family were coming to take Jesus home. The brothers had become convinced that Jesus was either insane or else caught up in the frenzy and honor of the people, and Mary feared for His life and welfare. Acting out of a mother's love and concern, she wanted to be a responsible mother and bring Him home to help Him all she could. (See notes—Mt.12:46-50; Mk.3:31-35.)

**2** (8:20) **Brotherhood—Family**: true kinship is not based upon human relationships. Picture the scene. Jesus was standing before the crowd preaching, and all of a sudden He was interrupted, being told that His mother and brothers were outside *desiring to see Him*. Of course, Jesus knew why they had come, and in this event He saw a unique opportunity to teach a profound truth, the truth that *true kinship* is not based upon human relationships.

> **Thought 1.** A true family, a true kinship does not exist just because some people have common blood, genes, and traits. This is clearly seen in the pages of family histories every day. Too many families are in turmoil, divided and being torn apart. Too many families are in constant conflict ranging from mild verbal attacks to murderous assaults. There is...
> - parent against child
> - child against parent
> - brother against brother
> - sister against sister
> - relative against relative
> - husband against wife

146

"But as many as received him, to them gave he power to become the sons of God, even to them that believe on his name: which were born, not of blood, nor of the will of the flesh, nor of the will of man, but of God" (Jn.1:12-13).

"Being born again, not of corruptible seed, but of incorruptible, by the word of God, which liveth and abideth for ever" (1 Pt.1:23).

**3** (8:21) **Brotherhood—Word of God—Believers**: true kinship is based upon the Word of God—hearing it and doing it.

The emphasis, of course, is upon doing the Word of God. The person who is closest to God is the person who obeys God, who takes His Word seriously. Any honest person knows that the child who obeys is the child closest to his parent's heart.

The deepest relationships in life are not determined by blood, but by hearts and minds being meshed together. The deepest relationships are founded upon common purposes and cares and behavior. However, the Christian believer has something even beyond this: he has the very *Word of God Himself*. When the believer hears and does the Word, that is, the will of God, five things happen.

1. God takes the believer's heart and life and welds it together with the hearts and lives of other believers—spiritually and supernaturally. They become the adopted children of God; therefore, the persons who hear the Word of God and do it are spiritually bound together in the family of God.

    a. Adoption by redemption.

> "But when the fulness of the time was come, God sent forth his Son, made of a woman, made under the law, to redeem them that were under the law, that we might receive the adoption of sons. And because ye are sons, God hath sent forth the Spirit of his Son into your hearts, crying, Abba, Father" (Gal.4:4-6).
>
> "But as many as received him, to them gave he power to become the sons of God, even to them that believe on his name" (Jn.1:12).
>
> "For ye have not received the spirit of bondage again to fear; but ye have received the Spirit of adoption, whereby we cry, Abba, Father. The Spirit itself beareth witness with our spirit, that we are the children of God: and if children, then heirs; heirs of God, and joint-heirs with Christ; if so be that we suffer with him, that we may be also glorified together" (Ro.8:15-17).
>
> "For through him we both have access by one Spirit unto the Father. Now therefore ye are no more strangers and foreigners, but fellowcitizens with the saints, and of the household of God" (Eph.2:18-19).
>
> "Fear not: for I have redeemed thee, I have called thee by thy name; thou art mine" (Is.43:1).

    b. Adoption by separation.

> "Wherefore come out from among them, and be ye separate, saith the Lord, and touch not the unclean thing; and I will receive you, and will be a Father unto you, and ye shall be my sons and daughters, saith the Lord Almighty" (2 Cor.6:17-18).
>
> "For both he that sanctifieth and they who are sanctified are all of one: for which cause he is not ashamed to call them brethren" (Heb.2:11).
>
> "For thou art a holy people unto the LORD thy God, and the LORD hath chosen thee to be a peculiar people unto himself, above all the nations that are upon the earth" (Dt.14:2).

2. Believers become a people who search God's Word out, absorb it into their lives and do it. His Word becomes their life and behavior. Believers obey the three basic commandments.

    a. The commandment of God.

> "And this is his commandment, That we should believe on the name of his Son Jesus Christ, and love one another, as he gave us commandment" (1 Jn.3:23).

    b. The commandment of Christ.

> "Verily, verily, I say unto you, He that heareth my word, and believeth on him that sent me, hath everlasting life, and shall not come into condemnation; but is passed from death unto life" (Jn.5:24).

    c. The greatest commandment.

> "Master, which is the great commandment in the law? Jesus said unto him, Thou shalt love the Lord thy God with all thy heart, and with all thy soul, and with all thy mind. This is the first and great commandment. And the second is like unto it, Thou shalt love thy neighbour as thyself" (Mt.22:36-40).

3. Believers live obediently in a very special relationship to God and Christ.

"He that hath my commandments, and keepeth them, he it is that loveth me: and he that loveth me shall be loved of my Father, and I will love him, and will manifest myself to him" (Jn.14:21).

"As newborn babes, desire the sincere milk of the word, that ye may grow thereby: is so be ye have tasted that the Lord is gracious" (1 Pt.2:2-3).

"Study to show thyself approved unto God, a workman that needeth not to be ashamed, rightly dividing the word of truth" (2 Tim.2:15).

4.    Believers act together and live together in *fellowship* within the church and society. They are knitted together by God's Word and God's true family. (See Deeper Study # 3, *Fellowship*—Acts 2:42 for more discussion.)

"And they continued stedfastly in the apostles' doctrine and fellowship, and in breaking of bread, and in prayers" (Acts 2:42).

"So we, being many, are one body in Christ, and every one members one of another" (Ro.12:5).

"For we being many are one bread, and one body: for we are all partakers of that one bread" (1 Cor.10:17).

"For as the body is one, and hath many members, and all the members of that one body, being many, are one body: so also is Christ. For by one Spirit are we all baptized into one body, whether we be Jews or Gentiles, whether we be bond or free; and have been all made to drink into one Spirit" (1 Cor.12:12-13).

"Now ye are the body of Christ, and members in particular" (1 Cor.12:27).

"Till we all come in the unity of the faith, and of the knowledge of the Son of God, unto a perfect man, unto the measure of the stature of the fulness of Christ" (Eph.4:13).

5.    Believers become God's new community, new society, new race, new nation of people. They become His church, His new creation—spiritually and supernaturally born again—who comprise the true family of God. (See Deeper Study # 8—Mt.21:43; note—Mk.3:34-35; Deeper Study # 1—Jn.4:22; notes—Eph.2:11-18; pt.4—Eph.2:14-15; 2:15; 4:17-19; cp. 1 Pt.2:9-10; Rev.21:1f for discussion.)

"For through him we both [Jew and Gentile] have access by one Spirit unto the Father. Now therefore ye are no more strangers and foreigners, but fellowcitizens with the saints, and of the household of God; and are built upon the foundation of the apostles and prophets, Jesus Christ himself being the chief corner stone; in whom all the building fitly framed together groweth unto an holy temple in the Lord: in whom ye also are builded together for an habitation of God through the Spirit" (Eph.2:18-22).

| | | | |
|---|---|---|---|
| **1 Jesus crossed the Sea of Galilee**<br>**2 Jesus' humanity: He was definitely a man**<br>a. He needed & requested the help of men<br><br>b. He became tired & slept | **V. Jesus Calms a Storm: Jesus' Deity & Sovereignty, 8:22-25**<br>(Mt.8:23-27; Mk.4:35-41)<br><br>22 Now it came to pass on a certain day, that he went into a ship with his disciples: and he said unto them, Let us go over unto the other side of the lake. And they launched forth.<br>23 But as they sailed he fell asleep: and there came down a storm of wind on the lake; | and they were filled with water, and were in jeopardy.<br>24 And they came to him, and awoke him, saying, Master, master, we perish. Then he arose, and rebuked the wind and the raging of the water: and they ceased, and there was a calm.<br>25 And he said unto them, Where is your faith? And they being afraid wondered, saying one to another, What manner of man is this! for he commandeth even the winds and water, and they obey him. | **3 Jesus' confidence in His men**<br>**4 Jesus' power & sovereignty: He was definitely God**<br>a. The disciples despaired<br>b. Jesus calmed the storm<br><br>**5 Jesus' faith in God**<br>a. He questioned the disciples' faith<br>b. He stirred the disciples to question who He was |

# DIVISION III

## THE SON OF MAN'S ANNOUNCED MISSION AND PUBLIC MINISTRY, 4:16-9:17

## V. Jesus Calms a Storm: Jesus' Deity and Sovereignty, 8:22-25

(8:22-25) **Introduction**: this event is a clear demonstration of the deity and sovereignty of the Lord Jesus Christ. It shows clearly the sovereign power of Christ to calm the storms that arise in man's life.

1. Jesus crossed the Sea of Galilee (v.22).
2. Jesus' humanity: He was definitely a man (v.22-23).
3. Jesus' confidence in His men (v.23).
4. Jesus' power and sovereignty: He was definitely God (v.24).
5. Jesus' faith in God (v.25).

[1] (8:22) **The Sea of Galilee**: Jesus crossed the Sea of Galilee (see note—Mk.1:16).

[2] (8:22-23) **Jesus Christ, Humanity—God, Power of—Jesus Christ, Incarnation**: two pictures of Jesus' humanity are clearly seen in these verses.

First, Jesus needed and requested the help of the disciples. He wanted to cross the lake. He could have walked around the lake; it was only a mile's journey, but He wanted to go by boat in order to get away from the crowd. They had been pressing in upon Him most of the day now, demanding and needing help. The *pressure and physical strain* had gotten to Jesus, wearing Him down. He needed time away from the crowds. If He walked, they would follow Him, so He requested the seamanship skills of the disciples to cross the lake. He could get alone off to the side someplace on the boat, away even from the disciples.

Second, Jesus was tired and needed sleep. He was fully man, flesh and blood; therefore, He sometimes suffered exhaustion just as any hardworking man does.

Now note: when studying the deity of Jesus, it helps to see His humanity, the fact that He was fully man. Seeing Jesus as Man helps tremendously in understanding God, for Jesus' humanity (being fully Man) highlights God more. It highlights and sets off His deity in at least two ways.

1. Christ's humanity, His having to suffer through life as a man, shows us the great love of God. In Christ, God identifies with man, and He identifies fully in every way and in everything. He knows how we feel and suffer because He was fully man. He knows all the trials and experiences and day-to-day routines of life; therefore, He is able to save us from the depths to the uttermost.

> "For verily he took not on him that nature of angels; but he took on him the seed of Abraham. Wherefore in all things it behoved him to be made like unto his brethren, that he might be a merciful and faithful high priest in things pertaining to God, to make reconciliation for the sins of the people. For in that he himself hath suffered being tempted, he is able to succour them that are tempted." (Heb.2:16-18).
>
> "For we have not an high priest which cannot be touched with the feeling of our infirmities; but was in all points tempted like as we are, yet without sin. Let us therefore come boldly unto the throne of grace, that we may obtain mercy, and find grace to help in time of need" (Heb.4:15-16).

2. Christ's humanity shows us the great power of God.
   a. It shows God's power to actually become a man, to bring about the Incarnation. Standing before us as flesh and blood, Jesus Christ is a powerful demonstration of God's great sovereignty. God is sovereign; He can do anything, even become a Man. By partaking of flesh and blood, Jesus Christ shows the enormous power (Sovereignty) of God.

"Therefore the Lord himself shall give you a sign; Behold, a virgin shall conceive, and bear a son, and shall call his name Emmanuel" (Is.7:14).

"For unto us a child is born, unto us a son is given: and the government shall be upon his shoulder: and his name shall be called Wonderful, Counselor, The mighty God, The everlasting Father, The Prince of Peace" (Is.9:6).

"Now the birth of Jesus Christ was on this wise: When as his mother Mary was espoused to Joseph, before they came together, she was found with child of the Holy Ghost. Then Joseph her husband, being a just man, and not willing to make her a public example, was minded to put her away privily. But while he thought on these things, behold, the angel of the Lord appeared unto him in a dream, saying, Joseph, thou son of David, fear not to take unto thee Mary thy wife: for that which is conceived in her is of the Holy Ghost. And she shall bring forth a son, and thou shalt call his name JESUS: for he shall save his people from their sins. Now all this was done, that it might be fulfilled which was spoken of the Lord by the prophet, saying, Behold, a virgin shall be with child, and shall bring forth a son, and they shall call his name Emmanuel, which being interpreted is, God with us" (Mt.1:18-23).

"And the Word was made flesh, and dwelt among us, (and we beheld his glory, the glory as of the only begotten of the Father,) full of grace and truth" (Jn.1:14).

"Men and brethren, let me freely speak unto you of the patriarch David, that he is both dead and buried, and his sepulchre is with us unto this day. Therefore being a prophet, and knowing that God had sworn with an oath to him, that of the fruit of his loins, according to the flesh, he would raise up Christ to sit on his throne; he seeing this before spake of the resurrection of Christ, that his soul was not left in hell, neither his flesh did see corruption. This Jesus hath God raised up, whereof we all are witnesses" (Acts 2:29-32).

"Paul, a servant of Jesus Christ, called to be an apostle, separated unto the gospel of God, (which he had promised afore by his prophets in the holy scriptures,) concerning his Son Jesus Christ our Lord, which was made of the seed of David according to the flesh; and declared to be the Son of God with power, according to the spirit of holiness, by the resurrection from the dead" (Ro.1:1-4).

"For what the law could not do, in that it was weak through the flesh, God sending his own Son in the likeness of sinful flesh, and for sin, condemned sin the flesh" (Ro.8:3).

"But [Christ] made himself of no reputation, and took upon him the form of a servant, and was made in the likeness of men" (Ph.2:7).

"And without controversy great is the mystery of godliness: God was manifest in the flesh, justified in the Spirit, seen of angels, preached unto the Gentiles, believed on in the world, received up into glory" (1 Tim.3:16).

"Forasmuch then as the children are partakers of flesh and blood, he also himself likewise took part of the same; that through death he might destroy him that had the power of death, that is, the devil" (Heb.2:14).

"Hereby know ye the Spirit of God: Every spirit that confesseth that Jesus Christ is come in the flesh is of God" (1 Jn.4:2).

"For many deceivers are entered into the world, who confess not that Jesus Christ is come in the flesh. This is a deceiver and an antichrist" (2 Jn.7).

b.   Christ's humanity shows God's power to control physical events. When Jesus the carpenter calms a storm and multiplies food, the power and sovereignty of God are stressed—stressed much more than when some mystical force or freak accident happens to intervene in physical events. When Jesus Christ stands and works a miracle before men's very eyes, *God's power is clearly seen*. It is visible and there is no question about it. The presence and power, the very Being and Sovereignty of God, are acting for all to see; and *only a hard and foolish heart would deny it*.

**3**   (8:23) **Ministers, Call—Believers—Trust:** Jesus demonstrated a very striking point. He had confidence in His men. He entrusted His life to them, which means He laid the completion of His mission into their hands. Note the enormous confidence He had in His men. He slept soundly, remaining off to the side even through the most fierce storm. The boat was filling with water. Note two things.
1.   He was definitely trusting His men and their ability. He was entrusting His life and mission into their hands.
2.   He was present, but not actively engaged in this particular task. The disciples had the natural skill to handle this work, so they were expected to do it themselves. And note: the task was difficult, demanding all the seamen's skills they had.

"And I thank Christ Jesus our Lord, who hath enabled me, for that he counted me faithful, putting me into the ministry" (1 Tim.1:12).
"Therefore seeing we have this ministry, as we have received mercy, we faint not" (2 Cor.4:1).

**4**   (8:24) **Jesus Christ, Power; Deity; Sovereignty:** Jesus' power and sovereignty are clearly seen in this event. He was definitely God, just as He was definitely man (cp. v.22).
1.   The disciples came to Him crying out, "Master, Master, we perish."
   a.   They had no problem realizing and acknowledging their need.

b. They believed and were sure that He could save them.

c. It was their cry—a desperate, fervent cry—that awakened Him and brought about the calm. He awakened to their need, and the danger and fear were relieved. The calm and stillness came because they cried in all earnestness.

2. Jesus rebuked the wind and raging water by simply speaking. It was His Word that removed the threat and that brought calm both within nature and within their fearful hearts (cp. Ps.89:9; Ph.4:6-7).

3. Jesus' mastery over the sea was absolute, clearly showing (revealing) that He was the Sovereign Lord of the universe. Moreover, Jesus' mastery over the fear of the human heart was absolute, clearly showing that He was the loving God so desperately needed by man.

**Thought 1.** Christ can calm the storms that so often confront man, the storms of...

- suffering
- loss
- lust
- anger
- bankruptcy
- hatred
- trouble
- grief
- temptation
- passion
- trial
- persecution

**Thought 2.** Bringing calm to the storms of life involves doing as the disciples did: coming to Christ.
1) Acknowledging that one is perishing.
2) Believing that Jesus can save.
3) Crying out for Jesus to save.

**Thought 3.** God's Word is the Source and Power that brings calmness to the storms of life.

"And Jesus came and spake unto them, saying, All power is given unto me in heaven and in earth" (Mt.28:18).

"Peace I leave with you, my peace I give unto you: not as the world giveth, give I unto you. Let not your heart be troubled, neither let it be afraid" (Jn.14:27).

"These things I have spoken unto you, that in me ye might have peace. In the world ye shall have tribulation: but be of good cheer; I have overcome the world" (Jn.16:33).

"And the Lord shall deliver me from every evil work, and will preserve me unto his heavenly kingdom: to whom be glory for ever and ever" (2 Tim.4:18).

"Fear thou not; For I am with thee: be not dismayed; for I am thy God: I will strengthen thee; yea, I will help thee; yea, I will uphold thee with the right hand of my righteousness" (Is.41:10).

"Call unto me, and I will answer thee, and show thee great and mighty things, which thou knowest not" (Jer.33:3).

**5** (8:25) **Faith—Jesus Christ, Deity**: Jesus' faith in God is demonstrated in this verse. Look carefully at Jesus' question, "Where is *your* faith?" He was contrasting His confidence with their confidence. He was trusting God (as Man); why were they not trusting God? Note three points.

1. Jesus was stressing the absolute necessity for His people to have faith in God. He demonstrated faith perfectly by sleeping in the midst of a storm. His life was in the hands of God; He had put it there. Therefore, His destiny was under God's control and at God's disposal. This was the lesson Christ wanted to teach His disciples.

2. Jesus was rebuking the disciples, their fear and lack of faith. They should not have been terrified and distrusting. They should have labored on against the storm knowing that He was nearby and would never have let them perish. They should have known that their lives and destiny were in His hands and under His love and care and power.

Note a crucial lesson. The faith of the disciples was to be used. Their faith was not to be dormant, lying within their hearts doing nothing. Faith existed for the purpose of struggling against the storm. They were to exercise their faith when the storm came.

**Thought 1.** The lesson is clear. The very time for us to use our faith is when the storms of life come. It is against the storms that our faith is to be aroused and exercised.

"Verily I say unto you, If ye have faith as a grain of mustard seed, ye shall say unto this mountain [trial], Remove hence to yonder place; and it shall remove; and nothing shall be impossible unto you" (Mt.17:20).

"Jesus said unto him, If thou canst believe, all things are possible to him that believeth" (Mk.9:23).

"Above all, taking the shield of faith, wherewith ye shall be able to quench all the fiery darts of the wicked" (Eph.6:16).

"But without faith it is impossible to please him: for he that cometh to God must believe that he is, and that he is a rewarder of them that diligently seek him" (Heb.11:6).

"If any of you lack wisdom, let him ask of God, that giveth to all men liberally, and upbraideth not; and it shall be given him. But let him ask in faith, nothing wavering. For he that wavereth is like a wave of the sea driven with the wind and tossed" (Jas.1:5-6).

"Believe in the LORD your God, so shall ye be established; believe his prophets, so shall ye prosper" (2 Chron.20:20).

3.   The disciples feared as those who stand in the presence of God Himself. They did not, of course, fully understand the Person of Christ. But they knew they stood in the presence of One who aroused the same fearful reverence due God. This is seen in three responses.
   a.   They were "afraid," stricken with awe and reverence.
   b.   They "wondered," that is, marvelled, at His enormous power and sovereignty.
   c.   They asked, "Who is this?" This was just the question Jesus wanted them to ask. They needed to be thinking about who He was.

"And fear not them which kill the body, but are not able to kill the soul: but rather fear him which is able to destroy both soul and body in hell" (Mt.10:28).

"And his mercy is on them that fear him from generation to generation" (Lk.1:50).

"But in every nation he that feareth him, and worketh righteousness, is accepted with him" (Acts 10:35).

"And if ye call on the Father, who without respect of persons judgeth according to every man's work, pass the time of your sojourning here in fear" (1 Pt.1:17).

"And now, Israel, what doth the LORD God require of thee, but to fear the LORD thy God, to walk in all his ways, and to love him, and to serve the LORD thy God with all thy heart and with all thy soul" (Dt.10:12).

"Now therefore fear the LORD, and serve him in sincerity and in truth (Josh.24:14).

"What man is he that feareth the LORD? Him shall he teach in the way that he shall choose" (Ps.25:12).

"Oh how great is thy goodness, which thou hast laid up for them that fear thee; which thou hast wrought for them that trust in thee before the sons of men!" (Ps.31:19).

"Let all the earth fear the LORD: let all the inhabitants of the world stand in awe of him" (Ps.33:8).

"God is greatly to be feared in the assembly of the saints, and to be had in reverence of all them that are about him" (Ps.89:7).

"Be not wise in thine own eyes: fear the LORD, and depart from evil" (Pr.3:7).

"Let us hear the conclusion of the whole matter: Fear God, and keep his commandments: for this is the whole duty of man" (Eccl.12:13).

"Sanctify the LORD of hosts himself; and let him be your fear, and let him be your dread" (Is.8:13).

"Who is among you that feareth the LORD, that obeyeth the voice of his servant, that walketh in darkness, and hath no light? let him trust in the name of the LORD, and stay upon his God" (Is.50:10).

| 1 The character of evil spirits | W. Jesus Casts out Demons in Gadara: Power to Free Men from Evil Spirits, 8:26-39 (Mt.8:28-34; Mk.5:1-20) | them. And he suffered them. 33 Then went the devils out of the man, and entered into the swine: and the herd ran violently down a steep place into the lake, and were choked. | j. Were subject to the Lord's command & power[DS1] |
| --- | --- | --- | --- |
| a. Possessed a man | 26 And they arrived at the country of the Gadarenes, which is over against Galilee. | 34 When they that fed them saw what was done, they | 2 The reaction of a covetous people |
| b. Caused a man to lose his sense of shame & conscience | 27 And when he went forth to land, there met him out of the city a certain man, which | fled, and went and told it in the city and in the country. | a. Saw a great deliverance & good done: Feared the strange, what they |
| c. Caused alienation | had devils long time, and | 35 Then they went out to | could not understand |
| d. Stripped a man of his necessities | ware no clothes, neither abode in any house, but in the tombs. | see what was done; and came to Jesus and found the man, out of whom the devils were | |
| e. Became enraged against the Lord 1) Knew Him 2) Opposed Him 3) Feared Him | 28 When he saw Jesus, he cried out, and fell down before him, and with a loud voice said, What have I to do with thee, Jesus, thou Son of God most high? I beseech thee, torment me not. | departed, sitting at the feet of Jesus, clothed, and in his right mind: and they were afraid. 36 They also which saw it told them by what means he that was possessed of the | b. Feared the great loss of property |
| f. Seized a man | 29 (For he had commanded | devils was healed. | 1) Rejected Jesus |
| g. Hated restraint, cp. v.31 | the unclean spirit to come out of the man. For oftentimes it had caught him: and he was | 37 Then the whole multitude of the country of the Gadarenes round about be- | |
| | kept bound with chains and in fetters; and he brake the bands, and was driven of the devil into the wilderness. | sought him to depart from them; for they were taken with great fear: and he went up into the ship, and returned | 2) Feared Him & feared more loss |
| h. Were numerous, formidable | 30 And Jesus asked him, saying, What is thy name? And he said, Legion: because | back again. 38 Now the man out of whom the devils were de- | 3 The spirit of a delivered man a. He desired discipleship |
| | many devils were entered into him. | parted besought him that he might be with him: but Jesus sent him away, saying, | |
| i. Desired a body to inhabit for the purpose of working evil | 31 And they besought him that he would not command them to go out into the deep. 32 And there was there an herd of many swine feeding on the mountain: and they besought him that he would suffer them to enter into | 39 Return to thine own house, and show how great things God hath done unto thee. And he went his way, and published throughout the whole city how great things Jesus had done unto him. | b. He was commissioned as a disciple—to his own hometown |

# DIVISION III

## THE SON OF MAN'S ANNOUNCED MISSION AND PUBLIC MINISTRY, 4:16-9:17

## W. Jesus Casts Out Demons in Gadara: Power to Free Men from Evil Spirits, 8:26-39

(8:26-39) **Evil Spirits—Unclean Spirits—Devils** (daimonia): evil spirits are demons. There is only one devil (see DEEPER STUDY # 1, *Satan, Diabolos*—Rev.12:9). However, there are many evil or unclean spirits or demons, and the New Testament has much to say about them.

The characteristics of demons other than the ones given in the outline above are said to be as follows:

1. They are spirits (Mt.12:43-45).
2. They are Satan's emissaries (Mt.12:26-27).
3. They know their fate is to be eternal doom (Mt.8:29; Lk.8:31).
4. They affect man's health (Mt.12:22; 17:15-18; Lk.13:16). Apparently, demon-possession is to be distinguished from mental illness.
5. They seduce men to a false religion of asceticism (1 Tim.4:1-3).
6. They seduce men to depart from the faith (1 Tim.4:1).
7. They are cast out of people (exorcism) in the name of Jesus Christ (Acts 16:18).
8. They shall participate in the apocalyptic judgment which is coming upon the earth (Rev.9:1-11, 20).

Evil spirits are enemies of Christ and of man. As such, they oppress, possess, and obsess people. (1) They delude the world and blind people to Christ (Eph.2:2). (2) They attack theology (1 Tim.4:1-3). (3) They attack society (Rev.9:3, 20-21). (4) They attack individuals (Lk.8:29). (5) They influence people to commit the sins of demon-worship, idolatry, sorcery, fornication, theft, murder, and much more (Rev.9:20-21).

The believer's defense is the Lord. The believer must pray and fast and take on the armor of God in order to stand against their power (Mt.17:21; Eph.6:12f).

This passage is excellent for studying the character of evil spirits and the Lord's power to deliver men from evil spirits.
1. The character of evil spirits (v.26-33).
2. The reaction of a covetous people (v.34-37).
3. The spirit of a delivered man (v.38-39).

**1** (8:26-33) **Evil Spirits—Demons—Devils**: the character of evil spirits. At least ten traits of evil spirits are seen in this passage. (See notes—Mt.8:28-31; Mk.5:2-5 for more discussion and thoughts for application.)
1. Evil spirits are enemies of man, possessing a man for long periods of time. They take hold of a man, controlling his faculties and causing him to act abnormally, hurting both himself and others.
2. Evil spirits cause men to lose their sense of shame and conscience. This man was driven to run around naked. The point is, evil spirits destroy man's sense of modesty, privacy, intimacy, and respect. Evil spirits cause men to enjoy the attention of public exposure and the embarrassment of others.
3. Evil spirits cause alienation, the loss of all friends and social life. They lead a man to be *cut off*, ostracized from others. They often force a man to withdraw into himself and away from others, including immediate family; or they cause society to push the man away, forcing him to live alone or with others like himself. Evil spirits often destroy a man by making him live as it were among the dead, among those who have no contact with the world of living men. This is seen in this man's being forced to live among the tombs of the dead.
4. Evil spirits are enraged against the Lord. Note three things in this verse. They knew that Jesus was the Son of the Most High God (cp. the Holy One of God, Mk.4:34). They also opposed Him and feared Him (see note—Mk.1:23-24; 5:6-7. Cp. Mt.8:31-32; Jas.2:19.)
5. Evil spirits seize men. Their influence and unrestrained nature seem to come and go, to lie calm and then to break forth in violence.
6. Evil spirits hate restraint and cause men to mistreat and oppose others. They drive men to struggle against morality and justice and against being governed, restricted, controlled, and disciplined. They drive men to live wild and loose lives, to do as they please. They cause men to become unclean, sullen, violent, and malicious (cp. Mt.8:28; 9:33; 10:1; 12:43; Mk.1:23; 5:3-5; 9:17-20; Lk.6:18; 9:39).
7. Evil spirits take away a man's name, his identity, and his recognition. They deprive a person of purpose, meaning, significance. They destroy his self-image and his public image.
Note that Christ asked the man what his name was. The Lord was stirring within the man fond memories of his name before he had become demon-possessed.
8. Evil spirits are numerous and formidable. The evil spirit cried out within the man that his name was *Legion*. The legion refers to the Roman military legion which included over six thousand men. This definitely indicates that the man's case was desperate; the evil spirits in him were formidable, just as a military legion was formidable. (Cp. Mary Magdalene who had been possessed by seven devils, Mk.16:9. Note how a specific number was known. Cp. also Mk.5:9 "many.")
9. Evil spirits desire a body to inhabit for the purpose of working evil. They desire to be malicious, violent, and destructive. The evil spirits are said to be the ones who are speaking here. They recognized Jesus' sovereignty. Note how the "evil spirits" thought and worked.
   a. They were indwelling and hurting this man physically, mentally, and spiritually.
   b. They wished (if exorcised from the human body) to hurt other men by damaging and destroying their property.
   c. They wished (if exorcised) to keep other men from Christ by destroying property and having them blame God for the devastation and loss.
10. Evil spirits are subject to the Lord's power. Christ had the power of His Word. The devil's power may be great, but the Word of Christ is omnipotent (all powerful), for all power belongs to Him.

> **"Greater is He that is in you, than he that is in the world"** (1 Jn.4:4).
> **"If God be for us, who can be against us?"** (Ro.8:31f. Read this whole passage for a beautiful and powerful description of the Lord's love and might.)

There was the result of Jesus' Word: the man was saved; the evil spirits were cast out of the man. Christ had the power to deliver and save. All He had to do was say, "Go," and whatever evil indwelt the man was gone. The man was delivered from all evil: its presence, guilt, and consequences. The man was "saved to the uttermost" (Heb.7:25). (See note—Mk.5:8-13 for more discussion and thoughts for application.)

> **"But that ye may know that the Son of man hath power on earth to forgive sins, (then saith he to the sick of the palsy,) Arise, take up thy bed, and go unto thine house"** (Mt.9:6).
> **"But Jesus beheld them, and said unto them, With men this is impossible; but with God all things are possible"** (Mt.19:26).
> **"And Jesus came and spake unto them, saying, All power is given unto me in heaven and in earth"** (Mt.28:18).
> **"For with God nothing shall be impossible"** (Lk.1:37).
> **"As thou hast given him power over all flesh, that he should give eternal life to as many as thou hast given him"** (Jn.17:2).
> **"How God anointed Jesus of Nazareth with the Holy Ghost and with power: who went about doing good, and healing all that were oppressed of the devil; for God was with him"** (Acts 10:38).

"Wherefore he is able also to save them to the uttermost that come unto God by him, seeing he ever liveth to make intercession for them" (Heb.7:25).

"I know that thou canst do every thing, and that no thought can be withholden from thee" (Job 42:2).

---

**DEEPER STUDY # 1**

(8:33) **Swine:** a question is often asked about the swine which were killed. This is discussed in Matthew (see DEEPER STUDY # 2—Mt.8:32).

---

**2** (8:34-37) **Covetousness:** the reaction of a covetous people (see DEEPER STUDY # 2—Mt.8:32; Mk.5:14-17 for more discussion and application). Note three things.

1. The people saw the great deed done, the marvelous deliverance of the demon-possessed man. However, their response was not one of rejoicing; it was fear—fear of Christ's power. They had known the demon-possessed man, how desperately hopeless his condition had been; and here he sat, delivered and made whole. What enormous power this man Jesus had!

2. The people rejected Jesus, being overwhelmed "with great fear." They were bound to be gripped with a sense of judgment because of their swine's being killed. They were also bound to be wondering if the proclaimed Messiah had come to judge them ahead of time or to destroy more of their property. They definitely knew they were breaking the law of God by *keeping swine* (cp. Lev.11:7; Is.65:3-4; 66:17). Because of this sin and other sins and their callousness toward the healed demonic, they were bound to be fearful standing there face to face with God's Son. They were unwilling to repent of their sins and to begin living for God. Thus, they could feel nothing else but fear.

3. Jesus did exactly what they asked. He left them. They chose the tasty, satisfying nourishment of the *swine of the world* over the joy and salvation of Christ. And so far as we know, He left forever, never to return to those who coveted this world more than Him.

> "Love not the world, neither the things that are in the world. If any man love the world, the love of the Father is not in him. For all that is in the world, the lust of the flesh, and the lust of the eyes, and the pride of life, is not of the Father, but is of the world" (1 Jn.2:15-16).
>
> "For what is a man profited, if he shall gain the whole world, and lose his own soul? or what shall a man give in exchange for his soul?" (Mt.16:26).
>
> "But whosoever shall deny me before men, him will I also deny before my Father which is in heaven" (Mt.10:33).
>
> "Whosoever therefore shall be ashamed of me and of my words in this adulterous and sinful generation; of him also shall the Son of man be ashamed, when he cometh in the glory of his Father with the holy angels" (Mk.8:38).
>
> "He that loveth silver shall not be satisfied with silver; nor he that loveth abundance with increase: this is also vanity" (Eccl.5:10).
>
> "Wherefore do ye spend money for that which is not bread? and your labor for that which satisfieth not? hearken diligently unto me, and eat ye that which is good, and let your soul delight itself in fatness" (Is.55:2).

**3** (8:38-39) **Witnessing—Call:** the spirit of a delivered man. The man was a dynamic example. As soon as he was delivered, he begged to be "with Christ," to travel all around, sharing the good news of Christ. He was *on fire* for the Lord and wanted to commit himself to the ministry. But note what Christ did. He redirected the man; He commissioned the man to go to his own hometown.

**Thought 1.** Christ often redirects our fervor and willingness. He knows where we can best serve Him and the cause of His kingdom.

**Thought 2.** Every man, when saved, should become a dynamic witness for the Lord and be willing to go anyplace.

**Thought 3.** We should never let a redirection or a call to go elsewhere kill our fervor.

> "Let your light so shine before men, that they may see your good works, and glorify your Father which is in heaven" (Mt.5:16).
>
> "Go ye therefore, and teach all nations, baptizing them in the name of the Father, and of the Son, and of the Holy Ghost: teaching them to observe all things whatsoever I have commanded you: and, lo, I am with you alway, even unto the end of the world" (Mt.28:19-20).
>
> "And he said unto them, Go ye into all the world, and preach the gospel to every creature" (Mk.16:15).
>
> "But ye shall receive power, after that the Holy Ghost is come upon you: and ye shall be witnesses unto me both in Jerusalem, and in all Judaea, and in Samaria, and unto the uttermost part of the earth" (Acts 1:8).
>
> "And brought them out, and said, Sirs, what must I do to be saved? And they said, Believe on the Lord Jesus Christ, and thou shalt be saved, and thy house" (Acts 16:30-31).
>
> "Therefore they that were scattered abroad went every where preaching the word" (Acts 8:4).
>
> "But sanctify the Lord God in your hearts: and be ready always to give an answer to every man that asketh you a reason of the hope that is in you with meekness and fear" (1 Pt.3:15).

**X. Jesus Raises Jairus' Daughter & Heals a Woman: The Reward of True Faith, 8:40-56** (Mt.9:18-26; Mk.5:21-43)

**1 The Gadarenes rejected Jesus, but the Galileans welcomed Him**

**2 The faith of a desperate ruler**
- a. His rank: A religious ruler
- b. His approach: He forgot pride & position—denied himself
- c. His faith: He believed Jesus could save His daughter
- d. The reward: Jesus went to help him

**3 The faith of an embarrassed, hopeless woman**
- a. Her hopelessness
- b. Her shame: Ceremonially unclean & socially outcast
- c. Her unusual "touch of faith": Many touched Jesus but only she was healed

- d. Her fearful awe & honest trust

40 And it came to pass, that, when Jesus was returned, the people gladly received him: for they were all waiting for him.
41 And, behold, there came a man named Jairus, and he was a ruler of the synagogue: and he fell down at Jesus' feet, and besought him that he would come into his house:
42 For he had one only daughter, about twelve years of age, and she lay a dying. But as he went the people thronged him.
43 And a woman having an issue of blood twelve years, which had spent all her living upon physicians, neither could be healed of any,
44 Came behind him, and touched the border of his garment: and immediately her issue of blood stanched.
45 And Jesus said, Who touched me? When all denied, Peter and they that were with him said, Master, the multitude throng thee and press thee, and sayest thou, Who touched me?
46 And Jesus said, Somebody hath touched me: for I perceive that virtue is gone out of me.
47 And when the woman saw that she was not hid, she

came trembling, and falling down before him, she declared unto him before all the people for what cause she had touched him, and how she was healed immediately.
48 And he said unto her, Daughter, be of good comfort: thy faith hath made thee whole; go in peace.
49 While he yet spake, there cometh one from the ruler of the synagogue's house, saying to him, Thy daughter is dead; trouble not the Master.
50 But when Jesus heard it, he answered him, saying, Fear not: believe only, and she shall be made whole.
51 And when he came into the house, he suffered no man to go in, save Peter, and James, and John, and the father and the mother of the maiden.
52 And all wept, and bewailed her: but he said, Weep not; she is not dead, but sleepeth.
53 And they laughed him to scorn, knowing that she was dead.
54 And he put them all out, and took her by the hand, and called, saying, Maid, arise.
55 And her spirit came again, and she arose straightway: and he commanded to give her meat.
56 And her parents were astonished: but he charged them that they should tell no man what was done.

- e. Her reward: Jesus' undivided attention & healing

**4 The faith of stubborn, helpless parents**
- a. The parents' helplessness: The daughter died
- b. The parents' need: A strong faith[DS1]
- c. The parents' strong faith: They followed Jesus despite the mockery

- d. The reward: Jesus' undivided attention & resurrection power

- e. The unusual command

# DIVISION III

## THE SON OF MAN'S ANNOUNCED MISSION AND PUBLIC MINISTRY, 4:16-9:17

## X. Jesus Raises Jairus' Daughter and Heals a Woman: The Reward of True Faith, 8:40-56

(8:40-56) **Introduction**: true faith will be rewarded. This passage gives a glimpse into just how enormously faith will be rewarded.
1. The Gadarenes rejected Jesus, but the Galileans welcomed Him (v.40).
2. The faith of a desperate ruler (v.41-42).
3. The faith of an embarrassed, hopeless woman (v.43-48).
4. The faith of stubborn, helpless parents (v.49-56).

**1** (8:40) **Minister—Jesus Christ, Rejection**: the Gadarenes rejected Jesus, but the Galileans welcomed Him. Note two points.
1. One people drove Him away; the other hoped in Him. One country was closed to Him; the other was opened to Him.
2. Jesus sought work to do. Note a crucial point. When He was rejected by a people...
- He did not retaliate, strike back.
- He did not begin to moan, grumble, or gripe.
- He did not slip into discouragement or depression.

- He did not quit.

What did He do? He immediately left the people, the country of those who rejected Him, but He sought to minister elsewhere.

**2** (8:41-42) **Faith—Self-Denial—Care—Humility**: the faith of a desperate ruler. One of the persons waiting for Jesus was a man named Jairus.

1. Jairus was a religious ruler, probably the highest-ranking official in the area. He was the head of the synagogue, the very center of Jewish life in the city. He was evidently well-to-do and highly esteemed among the people.

2. Jairus approached Jesus willing to pay the ultimate price.
   a. He laid his position on the line in order to secure Jesus' help. The religionists were now opposing Jesus with a fierceness seldom seen, and they were attacking Him publicly. By coming to Jesus, Jairus was running the risk of arousing the hostility of his peers and of being censored and losing his position.
   b. He denied and forgot self completely, laying all pride aside. He ran up to Jesus and fell down at Jesus' feet begging for help (see note and DEEPER STUDY # 1—Lk.9:23).

> "For whosoever will save his life shall lose it: but whosoever will lose his life for my sake, the same shall save it. For what is a man advantaged, if he gain the whole world, and lose himself, or be cast away? For whosoever shall be ashamed of me and of my words, of him shall the Son of man be ashamed, when he shall come in his own glory, and in his Father's, and of the holy angels" (Lk.9:24-26).
> "But he giveth more grace. Wherefore he saith, God resisteth the proud, but giveth grace unto the humble" (Jas.4:6).
> "Humble yourselves in the sight of the Lord, and he shall lift you up" (Jas.4:10).

3. Jairus' concern was over someone else. He was running the risk of losing everything for the sake of someone else: his twelve-year-old daughter. She was his only child and she was dying. Note Jairus' faith. He besought (begged) Jesus to help. He believed with all his heart that Jesus could save his daughter—if He would only come to his house.

> "He shall call upon me, and I will answer him: I will be with him in trouble; I will deliver him, and honour him" (Ps.91:15).
> "Then shalt thou call, and the LORD shall answer; thou shalt cry, and he shall say, Here I am. If thou take away from the midst of thee the yoke, the putting forth of the finger, and speaking vanity" (Is.58:9).
> "Call unto me, and I will answer thee, and show thee great and mighty things, which thou knowest not" (Jer.33:3).

4. Jairus' faith was immediately rewarded. "Jesus went"; He answered Jairus' plea. Jesus turned and began to move toward Jairus' house. The humble, self-denying approach of Jairus caused Jesus to turn and begin meeting his desperate need.
   > "And all things, whatsoever ye shall ask in prayer, believing, ye shall receive" (Mt.21:22).
   > "If ye shall ask any thing in my name, I will do it" (Jn.14:14).

**3** (8:43-48) **Hopelessness—Faith—Jesus Christ, Work of**: the faith of an embarrassed, hopeless woman. Five simple points are brought out about this woman.

1. She was hopeless.

2. She was ashamed, extremely embarrassed over her problem. The reason was twofold. First, she was considered ceremonially unclean; that is, she was cut off from society and religious worship (Lev.15:19-33). She had even been divorced, for the law required it (Lev.15:25-27). Imagine a woman's having to live with the shame of being divorced because of a medical problem. Second, she was hesitant about letting anyone know about her condition. Her hemorrhaging was a personal, intimate matter for her, something she did not want to be known and discussed publicly.

3. Her unusual *touch of faith*. Note that many were thronging Jesus and touching Him, but only one touched Him in faith. The woman had an *expectant, believing attitude*. She believed that if she could only touch Him she would be made whole (v.47; cp. Mt.9:21), and she was: "Her issue of blood stopped at once" (este).

> "Jesus said unto him, If thou canst believe, all things are possible to him that believeth" (Mk.9:23).
> "Oh how great is thy goodness, which thou hast laid up for them that fear thee; which thou hast wrought for them that trust in thee before the sons of men!" (Ps.31:19).
> "Commit thy way unto the LORD; trust also in him; and he shall bring it to pass" (Ps.37:5).

4. Her fearful awe and honest trust. Note what now happened.
   a. Jesus knew what had happened. He had allowed the woman to be healed in order to help her in her embarrassment. However, secret discipleship was impossible. She had to confess her deliverance.

> "Also I say unto you, Whosoever shall confess me before men, him shall the Son of man also confess before the angels of God" (Lk.12:8).
> "Whosoever therefore shall confess me before men, him will I confess also before my Father which is in heaven" (Mt.10:32).

**"That if thou shalt confess with thy mouth the Lord Jesus, and shalt believe in thine heart that God hath raised him from the dead, thou shalt be saved. For with the heart man believeth unto righteousness; and with the mouth confession is made unto salvation" (Ro.10:9-10).**

b. Serving and helping others cost Jesus, and cost Him dearly. Virtue (*dunamin*), spiritual power, flowed out from His being into the woman. It was that which healed her. Note that the disciples were unaware of what it cost Jesus to minister. They were insensitive to the spiritual energy He was exerting, ignorant of what Jesus was doing:
⇒ He was taking our infirmities upon Himself and bearing our sicknesses.

**"That it might be fulfilled which was spoken by Esaias the prophet, saying, Himself took our infirmities, and bare our sicknesses" (Mt.8:17; cp. Is.53:4).**

⇒ He was teaching that public confession of Him was essential.

Note what the woman did when she "saw that she was not hid." She knew that He who had such power knew who had touched Him, so she came as all should come in approaching the Lord: "trembling and falling down before Him," confessing all.

**Thought 1.** It is spiritual virtue that flows into and delivers any of us, the spiritual virtue (power) of Christ.

5. The woman's faith was rewarded, wonderfully so. Her faith caused Jesus to meet her face to face; her faith did some wonderful things for her.
a. She was called, "Daughter." This was the only time Jesus ever called a woman, "Daughter." What a distinct privilege! It meant she had become a child of God's.

**"For ye have not received the spirit of bondage again to fear; but ye have received the Spirit of adoption, whereby we cry, Abba, Father. The Spirit itself beareth witness with our spirit, that we are the children of God: and if children, then heirs; heirs of God, and joint-heirs with Christ; if so be that we suffer with him, that we may be also glorified together" (Ro.8:16-17).**
**"But when the fulness of the time was come, God sent forth his Son, made of a woman, made under the law, to redeem them that were under the law, that we might receive the adoption of sons. And because ye are sons, God hath sent forth the Spirit of his Son into your hearts, crying, Abba, Father" (Gal.4:4-6).**

b. She was given comfort (*tharsei*), or more accurately, cheer, courage, confidence, and boldness in her faith and healing.
c. She was assured that she was whole permanently. Her deliverance would last.
d. She was given peace (see note—Jn.14:27).

**"Be careful for nothing; but in every thing by prayer and supplication with thanksgiving let your requests be made known unto God. And the peace of God, which passeth all understanding, shall keep your hearts and minds through Christ Jesus" (Ph.4:6-7).**
**"Peace I leave with you, my peace I give unto you: not as the world giveth, give I unto you. Let not your heart be troubled, neither let it be afraid" (Jn.14:27).**
**"These things I have spoken unto you, that in me ye might have peace. In the world ye shall have tribulation: but be of good cheer; I have overcome the world" (Jn.16:33).**

**4** (8:49-56) **Faith—Helplessness:** the faith of stubborn, helpless parents. Five points are seen in the suspense of this scene.
1. The helplessness of Jairus: his daughter died. It was while Jesus was still speaking to the hemorrhaging woman that the news came to Jairus: his daughter was dead. Note three things.
a. Jairus' faith had been sorely tried. His daughter was critically ill, and he was forced to wait while Jesus ministered to another patient. What he feared had happened. Jesus was too late; his daughter had died.
b. Jairus was pulled off to the side and told not to bother the Lord any more now; the Master was too busy to bother with his situation since his daughter was now dead.
c. Jesus' power was thought to be limited and ineffective in the face of death. So the messenger suggested that Jairus could now go home. The point is that Jairus was totally helpless, and the power of Jesus was thought to be limited to the living. The thought that Jesus' power would be effective in dealing with the dead never crossed this gloomy messenger's mind.
2. The parents' need: a strong, stubborn faith. Jesus did not even give Jairus a chance to speak. Jesus forcibly said:
⇒ "Fear not" (*me phobou*): do not be gripped with terror, dread, fear, anxiety.
⇒ "Believe only" (see notes—Mk.11:22-23; DEEPER STUDY # 2—Jn.2:24; note—Ro.10:16-17; DEEPER STUDY # 1—Heb.10:38).
⇒ "And she shall be made whole" (*swthesetai*): restored, made alive, saved.
Imagine the strong faith required to believe simply because of Jesus' Word, because of what He said.
3. The parents' strong faith: they followed Jesus despite the mockery.

a.  Jesus took only the parents and His inner circle into the house. The parents and daughter would need quiet and time to be reunited and to regain their joyful composure before seeing people. The inner circle would give enough witness to verify and record the incident for all generations.

b.  The mourners who scorned Jesus would probably include relatives, friends, neighbors, and the professional mourners. The professional mourners were a custom in the East. Note how Jesus was scorned and ridiculed.

c.  The girl was dead. Some readers stress Jesus' words, "she is not dead, but sleepeth," saying that she was actually still alive (see DEEPER STUDY # 1, *Death*—Lk.8:50).

d.  The parents' stubborn faith was rewarded, greatly so. Their faith caused Jesus to save their daughter, to actually raise her up from the dead. Her spirit returned to her body and she arose.

Note Jesus commanded that food be given to her. This activity would help her mother handle the emotion of the moment and help to strengthen the daughter.

**Thought 1.** *Stubborn faith* is desperately needed by many parents in behalf of their children. However, note what must precede stubborn faith: a desperate faith that forgets and denies oneself, seeking Jesus no matter the cost. Difficult cases require both a desperate faith and a stubborn faith. It is such faith that receives the *great* reward.

"**Verily I say unto you, If ye have faith as a grain of mustard seed, ye shall say unto this mountain, Remove hence to yonder place; and it shall remove; and nothing shall be impossible unto you" (Mt.17:20; cp. Mt.21:21).**

"**And Jesus answering saith unto them, Have faith in God. For verily I say unto you, That whosoever shall say unto this mountain, Be thou removed, and be thou cast into the sea; and shall not doubt in his heart, but shall believe that those things which he saith shall come to pass; he shall have whatsoever he saith. Therefore I say unto you, What things soever ye desire, when ye pray, believe that ye receive them, and ye shall have them" (Mk.11:22-24).**

"**But when Jesus heard it, he answered him, saying, Fear not: believe only, and she shall be made whole" (Lk.8:50).**

"**And they rose early in the morning, and went forth into the wilderness of Tekoa: and as they went forth, Jehoshaphat stood and said, Hear me, O Judah, and ye inhabitants of Jerusalem; Believe in the LORD your God, so shall ye be established; believe his prophets, so shall ye prosper" (2 Chron.20:20).**

e.  Jesus gave an unusual command. He was probably commanding the parents to keep silent about the matter because the crowds surrounding Him were already too large.

---

**DEEPER STUDY # 1**

(8:50) **Death—Sleep**: some argue that this girl was actually alive and that Jesus knew it. But note several facts. (See DEEPER STUDY # 1—Jn.11:13 for more discussion.)

1.  Jesus and the Bible speak of death as nothing more than sleep. By sleep is meant *rest and comfort in God* (Mt.27:52; Acts 7:60; 1 Th.4:13-18). Many within the world think of death as annihilation or ceasing to exist. Jesus drew the contrast in order to say that death is not annihilation. Believers continue to exist, resting in the life and comfort of God.

2.  Note that Jesus knew the girl was dead (v.53). He clearly said so.

3.  Note the words "her spirit came again." The point is this: her spirit had left her body, and upon the command of Jesus, her spirit returned. Her life returned to the body immediately.

---

| | **CHAPTER 9** | 5 And whosoever will not receive you, when ye go out of that city, shake off the very dust from your feet for a testimony against them. | c. To warn rejecters |
|---|---|---|---|
| 1 **Their call: To come together for ministry**<br>2 **Their equipment: Power & authority**<br>3 **Their mission: To preach & minister**<br>4 **Their method**<br>  a. Not to seek success through personal appearance & materialism<br><br>  b. To minister in the homes, to the interested & the hospitable*DS1* | **Y. Jesus Commissions His Disciples, 9:1-9**<br>(Mt.9:35-10:42; Mk.6:7-13)<br><br>Then he called his twelve disciples together, and gave them power and authority over all devils, and to cure diseases.<br>2 And he sent them to preach the kingdom of God, and to heal the sick.<br>3 And he said unto them, Take nothing for your journey, neither staves, nor scrip, neither bread, neither money; neither have two coats apiece.<br>4 And whatsoever house ye enter into, there abide, and thence depart. | 6 And they departed, and went through the towns, preaching the gospel, and healing every where.<br>7 Now Herod the tetrarch heard of all that was done by him: and he was perplexed, because that it was said of some, that John was risen from the dead;<br>8 And of some, that Elias had appeared; and of others, that one of the old prophets was risen again.<br>9 And Herod said, John have I beheaded: but who is this, of whom I hear such things? And he desired to see him. | 5 **Their obedience: They went forth preaching & ministering**<br><br>6 **Their effect**<br>  a. Herod was disturbed by their message<br><br><br>  b. The people speculated about Jesus' identity<br><br>  c. Herod desired to know Jesus' identity |

# DIVISION III

## THE SON OF MAN'S ANNOUNCED MISSION AND PUBLIC MINISTRY, 4:16-9:17

**Y.    Jesus Commissions His Disciples, 9:1-9**

(9:1-9) **Introduction**: this was the first time Jesus sent His disciples out alone; therefore, it a significant event. The instructions given by Jesus to the early disciples are needed by every generation of believers. It is the only sure way the world can ever be reached and grounded in the Lord.

1.    Their call: to come together for ministry (v.1).
2.    Their equipment: power and authority (v.1).
3.    Their mission: to preach and minister (v.2).
4.    Their method (v.3-5).
5.    Their obedience: they went forth preaching and ministering (v.6).
6.    Their effect (v.7-9).

**1**    (9:1) **Ministers, Call—Unity—Jesus Christ, Ministry—Power**: the disciples' call was to come together for ministry. Jesus had to call His disciples back *together*. Note the word "together" (sunkalesamenos). The word reveals several things to us.

1.    The disciples had families and responsibilities. We tend to glamorize the disciples and Jesus, forgetting the disciples were ordinary men with day-to-day duties. They were not with the Lord at this time. They had to spend some time at home taking care of their families and whatever other duties they had. No doubt they did spend most of their time with Jesus as travelling evangelists, but at certain times, they returned home in order to tend to family affairs.

2.    The basic ingredient for ministry is *togetherness*. Note the words, "called...together." The very thrust of the words points to the importance of *coming together*.

> **"Little children, yet a little while I am with you. Ye shall seek me: and as I said unto the Jews, Whither I go, ye cannot come; so now I say to you. A new commandment I give unto you, That ye love one another; as I have loved you, that ye also love one another" (Jn.13:33-34).**
> **"Stand fast in one spirit, with one mind striving together for the faith of the gospel" (Ph.1:27).**

3.    The purpose for coming together is to minister. Jesus was completing His Galilean ministry. He was now ready to set His face toward Jerusalem (Lk.9:51). His ministry had been successful. Multitudes knew of His coming to earth, many had been helped and some did believe and trust. Now, before He left the area, He wanted to reach out one more time to those who were close to believing and to more deeply root and ground those who already believed.

4.    The call of Jesus was for the disciples to have power over "all devils, and to cure diseases."
  a.    "Power...over *all* devils." The word "all" means that the disciple was to have power over all kinds of evil, no matter how evil and enslaving, strong and fierce, subtle and undetected. It also points to the glorious purpose of Jesus. He had come to defeat and conquer the evil forces of this world, to rout and triumph over "all" of them.

"For we wrestle not against flesh and blood, but against principalities, against powers, against the rulers of the darkness of this world, against spiritual wickedness in high places" (Eph.6:12).

"Now is the judgment of this world: now shall the prince of this world be cast out" (Jn.12:31).

"Who hath delivered us from the power of darkness, and hath translated us into the kingdom of his dear Son: in whom we have redemption through his blood, even the forgiveness of sins" (Col.1:13-14).

"And having spoiled principalities and powers, he [Christ] made a show of them openly, triumphing over them in it" (Col.2:15).

"Forasmuch then as the children are partakers of flesh and blood, he also himself likewise took part of the same; that through death he might destroy him that had the power of death, that is, the devil; and deliver them who through fear of death were all their lifetime subject to bondage" (Heb.2:14-15).

"He that committeth sin is of the devil; for the devil sinneth from the beginning. For this purpose the Son of God was manifested, that he might destroy the works of the devil" (1 Jn.3:8).

    b.   "Power...to cure diseases." This would demonstrate the great compassion of the Lord and draw people to Him (Jn.12:32). It would also help tremendously in confirming the faith of some.

**2**  (9:1) **Power—Authority**: the disciples' equipment was to be power and authority. Jesus equipped His disciples with power and with the authority to use that power. Power is the *gift*, the necessary resource to minister; authority is the *right* to minister. The disciple has to decide when and where to exercise his power (resource). The awesome responsibility for such power should help to keep the disciple on his face before God, acknowledging his total dependence upon God. It should also help the disciple to seek a closeness with God, a true sensitivity to the Spirit of God.

    **Thought 1.** Think how little power is really seen in the lives and ministry of believers, lay and minister alike! How *displaced* or *misplaced* so many believers are. The *authority* to minister (where and when) has not been used as it should. The face of the Lord has not been sought, not to the point that a true closeness to His Spirit has directed our authority. We have taken the authority, the right to minister where we wish into our own hands. The evidence: after 2000 years so much of the world still has not heard the gospel.

       "Go ye therefore, and teach all nations, baptizing them in the name of the Father, and of the Son, and of the Holy Ghost: teaching them to observe all things whatsoever I have commanded you: and, lo, I am with you alway, even unto the end of the world" (Mt.28:19-20).

       "But ye shall receive power, after that the Holy Ghost is come upon you: and ye shall be witnesses unto me both in Jerusalem, and in all Judaea, and in Samaria, and unto the uttermost part of the earth" (Acts 1:8).

       "And with great power gave the apostles witness of the resurrection of the Lord Jesus: and great grace was upon them all" (Acts 4:33).

       "And my speech and my preaching was not with enticing words of man's wisdom, but in demonstration of the Spirit and of power" (1 Cor.2:4).

       "And I thank Christ Jesus our Lord, who hath enabled me, for that he counted me faithful, putting me into the ministry" (1 Tim.1:12).

       "Who also hath made us able ministers of the new testament; not of the letter, but of the spirit: for the letter killeth, but the spirit giveth life" (2 Cor.3:6).

       "And God is able to make all grace abound toward you; that ye, always having all sufficiency in all things, may abound to every good work" (2 Cor.9:8).

       "I can do all things through Christ which strengtheneth me" (Ph.4:13).

       "Now unto him that is able to do exceeding abundantly above all that we ask or think, according to the power that worketh in us" (Eph.3:20).

       "For our gospel came not unto you in word only, but also in power, and in the Holy Ghost, and in much assurance; as ye know what manner of men we were among you for your sake" (1 Th.1:5).

       "For God hath not given us the spirit of fear; but of power, and of love, and of a sound mind" (2 Tim.1:7).

**3**  (9:2) **Ministers, Duty—Mission**: the disciples' mission was to preach and minister. Note three points.

    1.    They were sent on the very same mission as Christ.

       "Then said Jesus to them again, Peace be unto you: as my Father hath sent me, even so send I you" (Jn.20:21).

       "And the people, when they knew it, followed him: and he received them, and spake unto them of the kingdom of God, and healed them that had need of healing" (Lk.9:11).

2.	They were to preach the Kingdom of God (see Deeper Study # 3—Mt.19:23-24). Preaching met the spiritual needs of the human soul.

> "For the Son of man is come to seek and to save that which was lost" (Lk.19:10; cp. Jn.20:31).

3.	They were to heal the sick. Healing met the physical needs of the human body.

> "Even as the Son of man came not to be ministered unto, but to minister, and to give his life a ransom for many" (Mt.20:28).
> "Finally, be ye all of one mind, having compassion one of another, love as brethren, be pitiful, be courteous" (1 Pt.3:8).
> "And of some have compassion, making a difference: and others save with fear, pulling them out of the fire; hating even the garment spotted by the flesh" (Jude 22-23).
> "Thus speaketh the LORD of hosts, saying, Execute true judgment, and show mercy and compassions every man to his brother" (Zech.7:9).
> "Who [ministers, believers] can have compassion on the ignorant, and on them that are out of the way; for that he himself also is compassed with infirmity" (Heb.5:2).

**4** (9:3-5) **Mission—Ministry—Method**: the disciples' method was threefold.

1.	They were not to seek success through personal appearance and materialism. They were to live in utter simplicity and humility. This was the point of the things Christ listed (v.3. See note—Mk.6:8-13 for more discussion.) Christ was saying three things to the disciples.
   a.	The need and the hour were urgent. Concentrate on preaching and ministering. Do not get sidetracked.

> "Set your affection on things above, not on things on the earth" (Col.3:2).

   b.	Learn to believe and trust God day by day. Become a living example of what is being preached: faith in God. Do not begin to trust in the things of the world. Learn to trust God daily, and then others can learn what is meant by "believing" and "trusting" God through your example.

> "But seek ye first the kingdom of God, and his righteousness; and all these things shall be added unto you" (Mt.6:33).

   c.	Avoid the very appearance of evil. Having your mind upon the things of this world will distract from God and from the needs of men and from the ministry. Become attached to God and to His kingdom alone; not to money, houses, lands, cars, clothes, hairstyles, appearance, food, buying, selling, and accumulating. Be heavenly-minded and ministry-centered, so that men may know there is a far better land than what this earth offers.

> "For they that are after the flesh do mind the things of the flesh; but they that are after the Spirit the things of the Spirit. For to be carnally minded is death; but to be spiritually minded is life and peace" (Ro.8:5-6).
> "These all died in faith, not having received the promises, but having seen them afar off, and were persuaded of them, and embraced them, and confessed that they were strangers and pilgrims on the earth. For they that say such things declare plainly that they seek a country. And truly, if they had been mindful of that country from whence they came out, they might have had opportunity to have returned. But now they desire a better country, that is, an heavenly: wherefore God is not ashamed to be called their God: for he hath prepared for them a city" (Heb.11:13-16).
> "By faith Moses, when he was come to years, refused to be called the son of Pharaoh's daughter; choosing rather to suffer affliction with the people of God, than to enjoy the pleasures of sin for a season; esteeming the reproach of Christ greater riches than the treasures in Egypt: for he had respect unto the recompence of the reward" (Heb.11:24-26).

2.	They were to minister in the homes to the interested and the hospitable families (see Deeper Study # 1—Lk.9:4).
3.	They were to warn rejecters. If a community or city did not receive their witness and if a home could not be found that would receive them, then the disciple was to leave.
   a.	He was not to force the issue or create a bad situation either for the rejecters or for himself. There was to be no tongue-lashing, accusation, or divisiveness created.
   b.	He was simply to leave; and as he left, he was to give a *silent* testimony against them. He was to shake the very dust from his feet. This was a symbol of serious judgment. It meant that not even the dust of that place was worthy of the gospel of God, much less the people. The place and its people were *left* to themselves just as they had wished. They were left *without God* and His glorious news of salvation, so they were to be left alone to govern their own lives just as they had willed. God would *abandon* them to their own way and choice of life.

**DEEPER STUDY # 1**

**(9:4) Church, In Homes:** the method Christ chose for evangelizing was the method of home evangelism (cp. 10:5f). Note this, for it should speak loudly and clearly to us. The disciple was to carefully investigate and search out a receptive family and home. He was to make that home the center for ministry. Note several things about this method.

a. It emphasizes the family, making it the very hub of ministry.

b. It stresses stability, security, and settledness. Nothing on earth is to be any more secure and stable than the family. By placing the center of ministry in the home, the Kingdom of God becomes secure and stable.

c. It centers preaching and ministering in the community, right where people live and walk. It makes the presence of Christ visible to all in day-to-day living.

d. It serves as the center from which the message can move out in an ever-widening circle, spreading from family to family.

**Thought 1.** The most ideal form of evangelism is probably this method given by Christ: a selected home and family serving as the center of witness within a community or town. The early church was definitely centered in the homes of committed believers (Acts 5:42; 12:12; 16:40; 20:20; 1 Cor.16:19; Col.4:15; Phile.2).

**5** (9:6) **Obedience:** they went forth and preached and ministered. The disciples did exactly what Christ had commissioned them to do. They did not fail in the least.

a. They departed. There was no hesitation, no question, no condition, no hanging back, no slowness to move.

b. They went through the towns. They reached a home and ministered to its surrounding community, ever moving farther and farther out into the whole town. And then they moved on to another town to bear witness to its people as well.

c. They preached and ministered "everywhere." They had an extensive ministry, very successful in its outreach, ministering to both soul (preaching) and body (healing).

"Therefore they that were scattered abroad went every where preaching the word" (Acts 8:4).

"Preach the word; be instant in season, out of season; reprove, rebuke, exhort with all longsuffering and doctrine" (2 Tim.4:2).

"Jesus said unto him, Let the dead bury their dead: but go thou and preach the kingdom of God" (Lk.9:60).

"Go, stand and speak in the temple to the people all the words of this life" (Acts 5:20).

**6** (9:7-9) **Jesus Christ, Response to:** their effect was phenomenal. The message and ministry of Jesus and His apostles reached even into the halls of government. The impact of the message and ministry reached far and wide during these days. (See outline and notes—Mt.14:1-14; Mk.6:14-29 for detailed discussion.)

1. Herod became disturbed. He had murdered John the Baptist, and some were saying that Jesus was John the Baptist risen from the dead. Of course, Herod's conscience was bothering him, just as all men are nagged by questions (at least questions about reality and the hereafter). He thought he had gotten rid of John's convicting preaching. Was it possible that John had arisen or that another like John had come on the scene? Herod wished to know.

2. The people were speculating about Jesus' identity (see outline and notes—Jn.7:37-53).

| | **Z. Jesus Teaches How to Minister, 9:10-17** (Mt.14:15-21; Mk.6:30-44; Jn.6:1-14) | for we are here in a desert place. | |
|---|---|---|---|
| **1 He demonstrated & taught the need for privacy & rest** | 10 And the apostles, when they were returned, told him all that they had done. And he took them, and went aside privately into a desert place belonging to the city called Bethsaida. | 13 But he said unto them, Give ye them to eat. And they said, We have no more but five loaves and two fishes; except we should go and buy meat for all this people. | b. The right attitude: Let the disciples meet the peoples'needs |
| a. The twelve returned & reported to Jesus | | | c. The problem: Inadequate resources |
| b. Jesus sought privacy with the disciples | | 14 For they were about five thousand men. And he said to his disciples, Make them sit down by fifties in a company. | **5 He approached needs in an orderly fashion** |
| **2 He allowed the needy to interrupt the much needed privacy & rest** | 11 And the people, when they knew it, followed him: and he received them, and spake unto them of the kingdom of God, and healed them that had need of healing. | 15 And they did so, and made them all sit down. | |
| **3 He met both spiritual & physical needs** | | 16 Then he took the five loaves and the two fishes, and looking up to heaven, he blessed them, and brake, and gave to the disciples to set before the multitude. | **6 He looked to God in meeting needs** |
| **4 He challenged the disciples to meet the people's needs** | 12 And when the day began to wear away, then came the twelve, and said unto him, Send the multitude away, that they may go into the towns and country round about, and lodge, and get victuals: | 17 And they did eat, and were all filled: and there was taken up of fragments that remained to them twelve baskets. | a. He thanked God for what He had |
| a. The wrong attitude: Let the people take care of themselves | | | b. He broke & gave what He had |
| | | | c. He utilized all for future ministering & feeding |

# DIVISION III

## THE SON OF MAN'S ANNOUNCED MISSION AND PUBLIC MINISTRY, 4:16-9:17

## Z.    Jesus Teaches How to Minister, 9:10-17

(9:10-17) **Introduction**: Jesus once said, "The Son of Man came not to be ministered unto, but to minister." So it is with the Lord's disciple. But how the disciple ministers is of vital concern, for how he ministers determines the eternal fate of men and the success or failure of the Lord's mission. In this passage Jesus teaches His followers *how to minister*. (See outlines and notes—Mt.14:15-21; Mk.6:30-44 for more discussion and applications.)

1.    He demonstrated and taught the need for privacy and rest (v.10).
2.    He allowed the needy to interrupt the much needed privacy and rest (v.11).
3.    He met both spiritual and physical needs (v.11).
4.    He challenged the disciples to meet the people's needs (v.12-13).
5.    He approached needs in an orderly fashion (v.14-15).
6.    He looked to God in meeting needs (v.16-17).

1 (9:10) **Devotion—Rest—Evaluation**: Jesus demonstrated and taught the need for privacy. The twelve returned from their mission and reported what had happened. Jesus had never needed time with them as much as He did now, for He was closing out His Galilean ministry. In fact, there was to be little public ministry hereafter. From this point onward He was to concentrate primarily on His disciples, giving them intensive training (see notes—Mt.16:13-20; 16:21-28; 17:1-13; 17:22; 17:24-27; 20:17; 20:20-28 to see the emphasis upon this intensive training).

1.    Jesus needed to discuss their witnessing tour with them. As they reported, He needed to point out both the strengths and weaknesses of how they went about it. They must learn to minister in the most effective way possible. An evaluation session was needed.

2.    The disciples needed to evaluate themselves; but they needed to do it in the presence of God alone so that they could restore both their spirits and bodies. They were physically exhausted and their spirits were drained.

What did Jesus do? "He took them, and went aside privately into a desert place belonging [somewhere near] to the city of Bethsaida." Note: He took them to a "desert place." Its quietness and privacy are mentioned twice, which indicates that they did not actually enter the city (v.10, 12).

The point was clearly demonstrated for the disciples. There is a time for ministry and for evaluating oneself and one's ministry; there is also a time for renewing one's spirit and body.

"**Come unto me, all ye that labour and are heavy laden, and I will give you rest**" (Mt.11:28).

"**And he said unto them, Come ye yourselves apart into a desert place, and rest a while: for there were many coming and going, and they had no leisure so much as to eat**" (Mk.6:31).

"**Six days thou shalt work, but on the seventh day thou shalt rest: in earing time and in harvest thou shalt rest**" (Ex.34:21; cp. Ex.23:12; 31:15; 35:2).

"**Six days shall work be done: but the seventh day is the sabbath of rest, a holy convocation; ye shall do no work therein: it is the sabbath of the LORD in all your dwellings**" (Lev.23:3).

"And I said, Oh that I had wings like a dove! For then would I fly away, and be at rest. Lo, then would I wander far off, and remain in the wilderness" (Ps.55:6-7).
"And he said, My presence shall go with thee, and I will give thee rest" (Ex.33:14).
"Return unto thy rest, O my soul; for the LORD hath dealt bountifully with thee" (Ps.116:7).
"To whom he said, This is the rest wherewith ye may cause the weary to rest; and this is the refreshing: yet they would not hear" (Is.28:12).
"For thus saith the Lord GOD, the Holy One of Israel; In returning and rest shall ye be saved; in quietness and in confidence shall be your strength: and ye would not" (Is.30:15).
"Meditate upon these things; give thyself wholly to them; that thy profiting may appear to all" (1 Tim.4:15).
"Take my yoke upon you, and learn of me; for I am meek and lowly in heart: and ye shall find rest unto your souls" (Mt.11:29).
"I will meditate also of all thy work, and talk of thy doings" (Ps.77:12).
"My meditation of him shall be sweet: I will be glad in the LORD" (Ps.104:34).
"I will meditate in thy precepts, and have respect unto thy ways" (Ps.119:15).
"I remember the days of old; I meditate on all thy works; I muse on the work of thy hands" (Ps.143:5).

**2** (9:11) **Ministry—Vision**: Jesus allowed the needy to interrupt the much needed privacy. The emphasis is on the words "the people followed Him and He received them." (See note—Mk.6:33 for the drama of the scene.) The people were disturbing and interrupting the disciples' need for privacy, for rest and spiritual renewal. The disciples had been ministering, doing all they could, yet here the people were demanding more. Note the contrast between Jesus and the disciples. The disciples became irritated (v.12; cp. the rude statement, "except we should go and buy meat for all this people" of v.13). Jesus, on the other hand, was filled with compassion for the people (cp. Mk.6:34). The disciples had a much needed lesson to learn, and they needed to learn the lesson more than they needed rest. The lesson was simple but dramatic: while one is resting the multitudes are still lost. They are as sheep without a shepherd (Mk.6:34). A disciple must not rest unless it is *absolutely necessary*. Too many are lost and hurting.

"Say not ye, There are yet four months, and then cometh harvest? behold, I say unto you, Lift up your eyes, and look on the fields; for they are white already to harvest" (Jn.4:35).
"I must work the works of him that sent me, while it is day: the night cometh, when no man can work" (Jn.9:4).
"For we cannot but speak the things which we have seen and heard" (Acts 4:20).
"For though I preach the gospel, I have nothing to glory of: for necessity is laid upon me; yea, woe is unto me, if I preach not the gospel!" (1 Cor.9:16).
"Preach the word; be instant in season, out of season; reprove, rebuke, exhort with all longsuffering and doctrine" (2 Tim.4:2).
"Wherefore I put thee in remembrance that thou stir up the gift of God, which is in thee by the putting on of my hands" (2 Tim.1:6).
"Whatsoever thy hand findeth to do, do it with thy might; for there is no work, nor device, nor knowledge, nor wisdom, in the grave, whither thou goest" (Eccl.9:10).
"For Zion's sake will I not hold my peace, and for Jerusalem's sake I will not rest, until the righteousness thereof go forth as brightness, and the salvation thereof as a lamp that burneth" (Is.62:1).
"Then I said, I will not make mention of him, nor speak any more in his name. But his word was in mine heart as a burning fire shut up in my bones, and I was weary with forbearing, and I could not stay" (Jer.20:9).

**3** (9:11) **Heals—Healing**: Jesus met both spiritual and physical needs. The people did not need preaching alone; they also needed help physically. Both body and soul needed to be saved and restored. So Jesus...
 • spoke (preached) unto them the Kingdom of God.
 • healed them that had need of healing.
Note two points.
1. Jesus preached the Kingdom of God—of which God is the ruler and man is the subject, of which the Word of God is Law and the obedience of man is demanded.
2. Jesus healed the people that "had need of healing." This is always true. A believer who really *needs healing* is blessed by God and healed. But note: *the need of healing is not always the greatest need of a person*. God sometimes uses the physical need to meet that which is far more important: the spiritual need and the glory of God. Therefore, not all believers are always healed. Sometimes the believer needs to learn love, joy, peace, endurance, prayer, trust, faith, and hope through his suffering. (See DEEPER STUDY # 3—Mt.8:1-4 for detailed discussion.)
However, there is and has been a problem with the truth of this down through the centuries. So many use the spiritual need as an excuse for not having the faith and godly power to be healed and to heal. As Jesus Himself said, it is much easier to tell a man his sins are forgiven than it is to tell him to take up his bed and walk. Jesus met both needs of a man, his spiritual needs and his physical needs: "healing them that *had need* of healing." (See DEEPER STUDY # 3—Mt.8:1-4 for detailed discussion.)
The disciples needed to learn that both the spiritual and physical needs of men were to be met.

"How God anointed Jesus of Nazareth with the Holy Ghost and with power: who went about doing good, and healing all that were oppressed of the devil; for God was with him" (Acts 10:38).

**4** (9:12-13) **Resources—Ministering—Needs, Attitudes Toward**: Jesus challenged the disciples to meet the people's needs. The people had been listening to Jesus for hours. Sundown was soon to come. There was danger the people would be caught out in the desert in the dark, unable to get food before the next day. Some had already gone most of the day without food. It was time for Jesus to stop and let the people go; however, He gave no sign of stopping. So the disciples suggested He dismiss the crowd. Note the two attitudes toward meeting the needs of people.

1. The wrong attitude was illustrated by the disciples. They suggested that Jesus let the people go and take care of their own needs. Keep in mind that the crowd was not welcomed by the disciples, not this day. It was to have been a day of rest and spiritual renewal for them. The point is, the disciples had not sensed any personal responsibility for the *hunger* (physical or spiritual) of the crowd. They were willing, even wanting the crowd to go away, no matter the difficulty they would have in fending for themselves.

2. The right attitude was illustrated by Jesus. He emphatically said, "Give ye them to eat." The "you" is emphatic in the Greek. Jesus was stressing that it was the disciples' responsibility. They were to take care of the people's needs. They were to "feed" the people (physically and spiritually). The people were not to be left to themselves. They could not fend nor provide for themselves.

Note something else: it was more important for the people to be hearing the gospel and receiving ministry than to be out seeking bread. "Man shall not live by bread alone, but by every word of God" (Lk.4:4). It is, of course, necessary to seek bread sometime in order to survive, but seeking spiritual food is absolutely essential. Seeking spiritual food must be interrupted only when necessary.

> "And Jesus answered and said unto her, Martha, Martha, thou are careful and troubled about many things: but one thing is needful [sitting at Jesus' feet learning]: and Mary hath chosen that good part, which shall not be taken away from her" (Lk.10:41-42).
>
> "And Jesus said unto them, I am the bread of life: he that cometh to me shall never hunger; and he that believeth on me shall never thirst" (Jn.6:35).
>
> "I am the living bread which came down from heaven: if any man eat of this bread, he shall live for ever: and the bread that I will give is my flesh, which I will give for the life of the world" (Jn.6:51).

3. The problem was inadequate resources. The disciples readily confessed that they had too little to meet the need of the people. Just think about the enormity of the situation for a moment. The crowd was huge; the task was *impossible*. There was no possibility the disciples could meet the need of the people. But note: they did exactly what needed to be done:

⇒ They told Jesus exactly what they did have.
⇒ They did the best thinking they could, giving the best solution they could.

What the disciples had was inadequate, but they did lay what they had before Jesus and discussed the only solution they knew (to go and buy food).

> "And I charged your judges at that time, saying, Hear the causes between your brethren, and judge righteously between every man and his brother, and the stranger that is with him. Ye shall not respect persons in judgment; but ye shall hear the small as well as the great; ye shall not be afraid of the face of man; for the judgment is God's: and the cause that is too hard for you, bring it unto me, and I will hear it" (Dt.1:16-17).
>
> "Upon the first day of the week let every one of you lay by him in store, as God hath prospered him, that there be no gatherings when I come" (1 Cor.16:2).
>
> "Give, and it shall be given unto you; good measure, pressed down, and shaken together, and running over, shall men give into your bosom. For with the same measure that ye mete withal it shall be measured to you again" (Lk.6:38).
>
> "Give to him that asketh thee, and from him that would borrow of thee turn not thou away" (Mt.5:42).
>
> "I have showed you all things, how that so labouring ye ought to support the weak, and to remember the words of the Lord Jesus, how he said, It is more blessed to give than to receive" (Acts 20:35).

**5** (9:14-15) **Organization**: Jesus approached needs in an orderly fashion. There were over five thousand men alone, not counting women and children. The need was so great, organization was necessary for the need to be met. The need was divided and spread about among the disciples by setting the people up in groups. Each group or company had fifty persons, or double rows of fifty each (Mk.6:40).

**Thought 1.** The task is enormous. It can be met only by an orderly, organized approach.

**6** (9:16-17) **Ministering**: Jesus looked to God in meeting needs. Note exactly what Jesus did.

1. Jesus looked up to heaven, giving thanks to God for what He did have. This is what is meant by the *blessing*.
2. Jesus broke and gave what He had. Note a crucial point. Jesus was doing what He could: looking up to God, giving thanks and then giving what He had. He could do no more.

**Thought 1.** The lesson is clear for every believer. Once we do our part, God will multiply our resources.

3.    Jesus utilized all. There was plenty to feed all, in fact more than enough.

**Thought 1.** There will always be enough to feed all—if we will only confess our inadequate resources, give thanks for what we have, and then give what we have.

> "But seek ye first the kingdom of God, and his righteousness; and all these things shall be added unto you" (Mt.6:33).
> "Bring ye all the tithes into the storehouse, that there may be meat in mine house, and prove me now herewith, saith the LORD of hosts, if I will not open you the windows of heaven, and pour you out a blessing, that there shall not be room enough to receive it" (Mal.3:10).
> "The earth is the LORD'S, and the fulness thereof; the world, and they that dwell therein" (Ps.24:1).
> "Blessed is he that considereth the poor: the LORD will preserve him, and keep him alive; and he shall be blessed upon the earth: and thou wilt not deliver him unto the will of his enemies" (Ps.41:1).
> "For every beast of the forest is mine, and the cattle upon a thousand hills" (Ps.50:10).
> "The liberal soul shall be made fat: and he that watereth shall be watered also himself" (Pr.11:25).
> "He that hath a bountiful eye shall be blessed; for he giveth of his bread to the poor" (Pr.22:9).
> "He that giveth unto the poor shall not lack: but he that hideth his eyes shall have many a curse" (Pr.28:27).
> "Cast thy bread upon the waters: for thou shalt find it after many days" (Eccl.11:1).
> "But the liberal deviseth liberal things; and by liberal things shall he stand" (Is.32:8).
> "And if thou draw out thy soul to the hungry, and satisfy the afflicted soul; then shall thy light rise in obscurity, and thy darkness be as the noonday" (Is.58:10).
> "The silver is mine, and the gold is mine, saith the LORD of hosts" (Hag.2:8).

| | | | |
|---|---|---|---|
| | IV. **THE SON OF MAN'S INTENSIVE PREPARA-TION OF HIS DISCI-PLES FOR JERUSA-LEM AND DEATH, 9:18-50** | 19 They answering said, John the Baptist; but some say, Elias; and others say, that one of the old prophets is risen again. | |
| | | 20 He said unto them, But whom say ye that I am? Peter answering said, The Christ of God. | 3 **The disciples' conviction: Jesus was Messiah** |
| | A. **The First Prediction of Death: Who Jesus Really Is, 9:18-22** (Mt.16:13-23; Mk.8: 27-33) | 21 And he straitly charged them, and commanded them to tell no man that thing; | 4 **The full meaning of the conviction** a. The full meaning: Was not yet grasped |
| 1 **Jesus was alone praying** | 18 And it came to pass, as he was alone praying, his disciples were with him: and he asked them, saying, Whom say the people that I am? | 22 Saying, The Son of man must suffer many things, and be rejected of the elders and chief priests and scribes, and be slain, and be raised the third day. | b. The full meaning: Jesus was the suffering & conquering Savior[DS1] |
| 2 **The people's belief: Jesus was only a great man** | | | |

# DIVISION IV

## THE SON OF MAN'S INTENSIVE PREPARATION OF HIS DISCIPLES FOR JERUSALEM AND DEATH, 9:18-50

### A.    The First Prediction of Death: Who Jesus Really Is, 9:18-22

(9:18-22) **Introduction**: Who is Jesus? The most critical time in a man's life is when he answers this question.
1.    Jesus was alone praying (v.18).
2.    The people's belief: Jesus was only a great man (v.18-19).
3.    The disciples' conviction: Jesus was the Messiah (v.20).
4.    The full meaning of the conviction (v.21-22).

1   (9:18) **Prayer**: Jesus was alone praying. He sensed a deep need for prayer.

1.    He needed personal strength. He was "setting His face toward Jerusalem," which means that He was setting His face toward the cross where He was to die for the sins of men (Lk.9:51). The days ahead held excruciating suffering for Him.
2.    The disciples needed a very special *quickening* from God. They, too, had to face the issue of the cross, that the Messiah had to die for the sins of the world in order to save men. This was a radically different concept of the Messiah than the popular concept. The popular concept said that the Messiah was to be the Son of David, the promised King who was to come and free Israel from her enemies and set up the Kingdom of God over all nations of the earth (see note—Mt.16:21-28).

The disciples also had an immediate need, the need for a very special *revelation* into His person. It was time for them to grasp and confess without any hesitation that He was the Messiah, the very Son of God. Jesus was now ready to examine their hearts and convictions about Him, so He went before God to beg a very *special insight*, a very special revelation of the Spirit for the disciples.

**Thought 1.** Three important lessons on prayer can be gleaned from what Christ was doing.
1)    We must pray before momentous events.

> **"Ask, and it shall be given you; seek, and ye shall find; knock, and it shall be opened unto you" (Mt.7:7).**
> **"Is any among you afflicted? let him pray. Is any merry? let him sing psalms" (Jas.5:13).**
> **"Call unto me, and I will answer thee, and show thee great and mighty things, which thou knowest not" (Jer.33:3)**

2)    We must pray for others, that they might have special insight and the quickening power of the Spirit upon their lives.

> **"Praying always with all prayer and supplication in the Spirit, and watching thereunto with all perseverance and supplication for all saints" (Eph.6:18).**

3)    We must pray for strength to withstand severe trials, that we might be enabled to bear whatever cross lies ahead.

> **"Watch and pray, that ye enter not into temptation: the spirit indeed is willing, but the flesh is weak" (Mt.26:41).**

"Likewise the Spirit also helpeth our infirmities: for we know not what we should pray for as we ought: but the Spirit itself maketh intercession for us with groanings which cannot be uttered" (Ro.8:26).

"He shall call upon me, and I will answer him: I will be with him in trouble; I will deliver him, and honour him" (Ps.91:15).

"When the poor and needy seek water, and there is none, and their tongue faileth for thirst, I the LORD will hear them, I the God of Israel will not forsake them" (Is.41:17).

"Then shalt thou call, and the LORD shall answer; thou shalt cry, and he shall say, Here I am. If thou take away from the midst of thee the yoke, the putting forth of the finger, and speaking vanity" (Is.58:9).

"And it shall come to pass, that before they call, I will answer; and while they are yet speaking, I will hear" (Is.65:24).

"And I will bring the third part through the fire, and will refine them as silver is refined, and will try them as gold is tried: they shall call on my name, and I will hear them: I will say, It is my people: and they shall say, The LORD is my God" (Zech.13:9).

**2** (9:18-19) **Jesus Christ, Concept of—Man, Concept of Christ:** the people's belief was that Jesus was only a great man. The scene was that of Jesus' being off to the side, away from the disciples and all alone. He was seeking the face of God and agonizing in prayer. Then all of a sudden He quit praying and arose, and walked over to the disciples. Immediately He asked them, "Whom say the people that I am?" Why did Christ ask this question? What was He doing?

1. The disciples' concept of the Messiah needed to be corrected. Their concept was the popular concept that saw the Messiah only as the greatest of men. They desperately needed to grasp and understand to the fullest measure who Jesus was. The very destiny of the world rested in their hands. Men were doomed and lost forever unless the disciples fully understood. Therefore, Jesus had to examine them to make sure they were thinking for themselves and rejecting the false ideas of Messiahship held by men.

2. The popular opinion of the Messiah was wrong. Most of the people honored Jesus highly, very highly. They saw Him as a great man; in fact, they saw Him as one of the greatest of men. However, such a concept would spell doom for the world if it were not corrected. Jesus had to make sure the people's idea had not influenced and corrupted the thinking of the disciples.

   a. Some thought Jesus was John the Baptist, that is, the forerunner of the Messiah (Mal.4:5). Both John and Jesus were doing a unique and great work for God. Both were divinely chosen and gifted by God, and both proclaimed the Kingdom of God and prepared men for it. Therefore, when some looked at Jesus and His ministry, they thought Jesus was not the Messiah Himself, but the promised forerunner of the Messiah (Mal.4:5).

   b. Some thought Jesus was Elijah. These were professing Jesus to be the greatest prophet and teacher of all time. Elijah was so considered, and Elijah was also predicted to be the forerunner of the coming Messiah (Mal.4:5). Even today the Jews expect Elijah to return before the Messiah. In celebrating the Passover, they always leave a chair vacant for him to occupy. Elijah had also been used by God to miraculously feed a widow woman and her son (1 Ki.17:14). The people connected Elijah's miracle and Jesus' feeding of the multitude.

   c. Some thought Jesus was one of the old prophets. These were professing Jesus to be a great prophet sent for their day and time. He was thought to be one of the great prophets brought back to life or one in whom the spirit of a great prophet dwelt (cp. Dt.18:15, 18).

**Thought 1.** Note that the same false confessions about Christ exist in every generation.

1) He was only a great man of righteousness, martyred for His faith. As such He leaves us a great example of how to live and stand up for what we believe.

2) He was one of the greatest teachers and prophets of all time.

3) He was a great man who revealed some very important things to us about God and religion. As such He can make a significant contribution to every man in His search for God.

4) He was a great man and prophet sent to the people (Jews) of His day; however, we can learn a great deal that will help us by studying His life.

"Is not this the carpenter, the son of Mary, the brother of James, and Joses, and of Juda, and Simon? and are not his sisters here with us? And they were offended at him" (Mk.6:3).

"He was in the world, and the world was made by him, and the world knew him not. He came unto his own, and his own received him not" (Jn.1:10-11).

"Who is a liar but he that denieth that Jesus is the Christ? He is antichrist, that denieth the Father and the Son. Whosoever denieth the Son, the same hath not the Father: [but] he that acknowledgeth the Son hath the Father also" (1 Jn.2:22-23).

"And every spirit that confesseth not that Jesus Christ is come in the flesh is not of God: and this is that spirit of antichrist, whereof ye have heard that it should come; and even now already is it in the world" (1 Jn.4:3).

**3** (9:20) **Jesus Christ, Concept—Man, Concept of Christ:** the disciples' conviction was that Jesus was the Messiah. Jesus sat and listened closely to what the disciples had to say about the people's ideas regarding the Messiah. Now He was ready for *the question...*

- the question whose answer determines a man's eternal salvation.
- the question which is the most significant question ever asked.

"But whom say ye that I am?" The "you" is emphatic. Jesus stressed the *personal*, the importance of a personal response: "But *you*, whom do *you* say that I am?" Note several things.

1. The answer was immediate and forceful: *the Christ of God*. Peter was the spokesman for all, and he emphatically declared that Jesus was *the Christ of God*. It was a powerful statement—a statement profound in meaning.

2. The answer was profound in its meaning, for Jesus was "the Christ," that is, "the Messiah," *the anointed One of God* (see DEEPER STUDY # 2—Mt.1:18). This means three things.
   a. Jesus was sent on a deliberate mission, the mission of saving man (Lk.19:10).
   b. Jesus was *sent and qualified* by God to carry out that mission (Jn.3:16; 4:34; 5:23-24, 30, 36-38; 6:29, 38-40, 44, 57; 7:16, 18, 28-29; 8:16, 18, 26, 29, 42; 9:4; 10:36; 11:42; 12:45, 49; 14:24; 15:21; 16:5; 17:3, 18, 21, 23, 25; 20:21; 1 Jn.4:9-10, 14).
   c. Jesus was the fulfillment of all the prophecies which promised the coming of the Messiah for man.

3. The question was very personal. It might even offend some. But Jesus meant the question to be personal. It had to be, for a man's eternal destiny and fate is determined by his answer. Jesus was not just a man as the popular idea of Him declared. He was more, much more. He was *the Christ of God*. Man's life, death, and eternal fate hinged on how he saw and confessed Christ.

"Whosoever therefore shall confess me before men, him will I also confess before my Father which is in heaven. But whosoever shall deny me before men, him will I also deny before my Father which is in heaven" (Mt.10:32-33).

"Whosoever therefore shall be ashamed of me and of my words in this adulterous and sinful generation; of him also shall the Son of man be ashamed, when he cometh in the glory of his Father with the holy angels" (Mk.8:38).

"Also I say unto you, Whosoever shall confess me before men, him shall the Son of man also confess before the angels of God" (Lk.12:8).

"That if thou shalt confess with thy mouth the Lord Jesus, and shalt believe in thine heart that God hath raised him from the dead, thou shalt be saved. For with the heart man believeth unto righteousness; and with the mouth confession is made unto salvation" (Ro.10:9-10).

"Whosoever denieth the Son, the same hath not the Father: [but] he that acknowledgeth the Son hath the Father also" (1 Jn.2:23).

"Whosoever shall confess that Jesus is the Son of God, God dwelleth in him, and he in God" (1 Jn.4:15).

"He that covereth his sins shall not prosper: but whoso confesseth and forsaketh them shall have mercy" (Pr.28:13).

"He first findeth his own brother Simon, and saith unto him, We have found the Messias, which is, being interpreted, the Christ" (Jn.1:41).

"Philip findeth Nathanael, and saith unto him, We have found him [the Messiah], of whom Moses in the law, and the prophets, did write, Jesus of Nazareth, the son of Joseph" (Jn.1:45).

"Nathanael answered and saith unto him, Rabbi, thou art the Son of God; thou art the King of Israel" (Jn.1:49).

"Come, see a man, which told me all things that ever I did: is not this the Christ?" (Jn.4:29).

"And we believe and are sure that thou art that Christ, the Son of the living God" (Jn.6:69).

"She saith unto him, Yea, Lord: I believe that thou art the Christ, the Son of God, which should come into the world" (Jn.11:27).

"And Thomas answered and said unto him, My Lord and my God" (Jn.20:28).

"And as they went on their way, they came unto a certain water: and the eunuch said, See, here is water; what doth hinder me to be baptized? And Philip said, If thou believest with all thine heart, thou mayest. And he answered and said, I believe that Jesus Christ is the Son of God" (Acts 8:36-37).

**4** (9:21-22) **Messiah—Messiahship—Jesus Christ, Death; Resurrection**: the full meaning of the conviction. There are two significant points here.

1. The full meaning of the Messiah was not yet fully grasped. The disciples were yet to experience the death and resurrection of Jesus Christ. The prophecies of the Messiah which stuck out in their minds were those dealing with His exaltation, sovereignty, power, and glory. They saw His ruling and reigning over the earth and subjecting men to God by force. Their idea of the Messiah was that of an earthly rule within the bounds of the physical and material world. They had little if any idea of the spiritual world; therefore, they were not ready to share the truth of the Messiah (see note—Eph.1:3). They would be sharing an incomplete message, a false message; so Jesus had to charge them to tell no man, not yet, not until they understood the real meaning of the spiritual salvation which He was bringing to man. Note the importance of understanding the full meaning of the Messiah. Jesus charged them and then commanded them to say nothing until they did understand.

2. Jesus began to clearly reveal that the Messiah had to be both a suffering and a conquering Savior. For some time Jesus had been telling His disciples about His death and resurrection, but they had not understood. Why? There are two reasons:

   ⇒ The idea of a suffering Messiah differed radically from their own idea of the Messiah (see notes—Mt.1:1; DEEPER STUDY # 2—1:18; DEEPER STUDY # 3—3:11; notes—11:1-6; 11:2-3; DEEPER STUDY # 1—11:5; DEEPER STUDY # 2—11:6; DEEPER STUDY # 1—12:16; note—Lk.7:21-23).
   ⇒ The revelation had been hid in pictures and symbols.

**"Destroy this temple, and in three days I will raise it up" (Jn.2:19).**

"As Moses lifted up the serpent in the wilderness, even so must the Son of Man be lifted up" (Jn.3:14).

"I am the living bread which came down from heaven: if any man eat of this bread, he shall live for ever: and the bread that I will give is my flesh, which I will give for the life of the world" (Jn.6:51).

The difference now was that Jesus no longer spoke in pictures and symbols, but He told them in simple and direct words (Mt.20:18-20; Lk.18:31-33). A new stage in the revelation of God's plan for the world was now taking place: God's Son was to die and be raised again for the sins of the world. God's plan for saving the world was to take place through a suffering Messiah, not a conquering Messiah who was going to deliver a *materialistic* world into the hands of His followers. His death was to usher in the Kingdom of God, making it possible for His followers to live eternally in the very presence of God Himself (see DEEPER STUDY # 3—Mt.19:23-24; cp. Jn.3:16; 5:24f).

Note the word "must" (dei). It is strong; it means a constraint, an imperative, a necessity was laid upon Him. He had no choice. His death and resurrection had been planned and willed by God through all eternity. The prophets had so predicted. He must fulfill the will of God, for God had ordained His death. (See DEEPER STUDY # 3—Acts 2:23 for more discussion. Cp. Mt.26:54.)

"Ought not Christ to have suffered these things, and to enter into his glory?" (Lk.24:26).

"And said unto them, Thus it is written, and thus it behoved Christ to suffer, and to rise from the dead the third day: and that repentance and remission of sins should be preached in his name among all nations, beginning at Jerusalem" (Lk.24:46-47).

**DEEPER STUDY # 1**

(9:22) **Jesus Christ, Opposition**: note the three Jewish groups who were to take the lead in killing Jesus. These were the three groups who made up the Sanhedrin, the supreme court of Jewish justice. It was comprised of seventy members (cp. the historical basis for this structure, 2 Chron.19:5-11).

1. The elders: these were the older, respected men of a community. The elders were judges of the civil courts, of temporal affairs (Ex.3:29; 12:21; 24:9; Num.11:25; 1 Sam.16:4; Ezra 10:14; Mt.27:12).

2. The chief priests: these were primarily leaders from among the Sadducees who held most of the high offices of Jewish government under Roman rule (see note—Acts 23:8). The chief priests were judges of religious affairs.

3. The Scribes: these were Pharisees who held the teaching positions of the nation (see DEEPER STUDY # 1—Lk.6:2).

| 1 The terms of discipleship<br>a. Must deny self<br>b. Must take up the cross—daily[DS1]<br>c. Must follow Jesus<br>2 The warning to the materialist<br>a. Do not save life for self<br>b. Spend life for Christ<br>3 The question for the | B. The Terms of Discipleship, 9:23-27<br>(Mt.16:24-28; Mk.8:34-9:1)<br><br>23 And he said to them all, If any man will come after me, let him deny himself, and take up his cross daily, and follow me.<br>24 For whosoever will save his life shall lose it: but whosoever will lose his life for my sake, the same shall save it.<br>25 For what is a man ad- | vantaged, if he gain the whole world, and lose himself, or be cast away?<br>26 For whosoever shall be ashamed of me and of my words, of him shall the Son of man be ashamed, when he shall come in his own glory, and in his Father's, and of the holy angels.<br>27 But I tell you of a truth, there be some standing here, which shall not taste of death, till they see the kingdom of God. | materialist<br>a. If he gains the world<br>b. And loses himself<br>c. What does he gain?[DS2]<br>4 The judgment of the materialist<br>a. The reason: He is ashamed of Jesus & His Words<br>b. The judgment: Counted unsuitable for glory<br>5 The disciple's reward: God's kingdom |

# DIVISION IV

## THE SON OF MAN'S INTENSIVE PREPARATION OF HIS DISCIPLES FOR JERUSALEM AND DEATH, 9:18-50

## B. The Terms of Discipleship, 9:23-27

(9:23-27) **Introduction**: Jesus was to bear the cross for man. He had just discussed this fact with His disciples (Lk.9:22). Now He said there was another cross—a cross which man was to bear for Him. If a man wished to follow Christ, he had to bear this cross. There was no option. Discipleship demanded it.

1. The terms of discipleship (v.23).
2. The warning to the materialist (v.24).
3. The question for the materialist (v.25).
4. The judgment of the materialist (v.26).
5. The disciple's reward: God's kingdom (v.27).

**1** (9:23) **Cross—Self-Denial—Death, to Self—Discipleship**: there are three terms of discipleship if a person wills to follow Christ.

1. A person must deny himself. Man's tendency is to indulge himself and do exactly what he desires; but the believer is not to indulge himself, his comfort and ease, appetites and urges, thoughts and feelings, deceptions and enticements, plots and intrigues, pride and boastings, reactions and disturbances. The believer is to deny himself by discipline and control and by loving and caring, sacrificing and giving, helping and ministering.

2. A person must take up his cross and do it daily (see DEEPER STUDY # 1, *Cross*—Lk.9:23).

3. A person must follow Jesus. However, man's tendency is to follow someone else and to give one's first allegiance to something else. Within the world, there are many things available for a man to serve and to put first. There are...

- service organizations
- humanitarian needs
- religion (institutional)
- family
- recreation
- hobby
- education

- profession
- houses
- business
- clubs
- self (fame, honor)
- comfort
- clothing

- social acceptance
- pleasure
- health
- looks
- sports
- fleshy stimulation

"Then spake Jesus again unto them, saying, I am the light of the world: he that followeth me shall not walk in darkness, but shall have the light of life" (Jn.8:12).

"My sheep hear my voice, and I know them, and they follow me: and I give unto them eternal life; and they shall never perish, neither shall any man pluck them out of my hand. My Father, which gave them me, is greater than all; and no man is able to pluck them out of my Father's hand" (Jn.10:27-29).

"If any man serve me, let him follow me; and where I am, there shall also my servant be: if any man serve me, him will my Father honour" (Jn.12:26).

"This I say then, Walk in the Spirit, and ye shall not fulfil the lust of the flesh" (Gal.5:16).

"Be ye therefore followers of God, as dear children; and walk in love, as Christ also hath loved us, and hath given himself for us an offering and a sacrifice to God for a sweetsmelling savour" (Eph.5:1-2).

"For this ye know, that no whoremonger, nor unclean person, nor covetous man, who is an idolater, hath any inheritance in the kingdom of Christ and of God" (Eph.5:5).

"As ye have therefore received Christ Jesus the Lord, so walk ye in him" (Col.2:6).

"For even hereunto were ye called: because Christ also suffered for us, leaving us an example, that ye should follow his steps" (1 Pt.2:21).

"He that saith he abideth in him ought himself also so to walk, even as he walked" (1 Jn.2:6).

## DEEPER STUDY # 1

(9:23) **Cross—Discipleship**: people in Jesus' day knew what it meant to "take up" a cross. They saw scores of criminals bear the cross to the place where they were to be executed, and they witnessed scores of crucifixions, some even by the side of the roads that led in and out of the cities.

The cross does not mean merely bearing one's particular hardship in life, such as poor health, abuse, unemployment, invalid parents, an unsaved spouse, a wayward child. The cross is always an instrument of death, not just an object to carry or bear. The Christian is to die mentally and actively. He is to deny himself daily. He is to let the mind of Christ, the mind of humbling himself to the point of death, be in him and fill his thoughts every day (Ph.2:5-8; 2 Cor.10:3-5). He is to put his will, his desires, his wants, his ambitions to death. In their stead, he is to follow Jesus and to do His will all day long. Note this is not negative, passive behavior. It takes positive, active behavior to *will*, to *deny self*, to *take up* one's *cross*, to *follow* Christ. A person has to act, work, get to it, be diligent, consistent, and enduring in order to die to self.

There are several ways the believer dies to self. Romans 6:11-13 spells out the ways as clearly as they can be.

> **"Likewise reckon ye also yourselves to be dead indeed unto sin, but alive unto God through Jesus Christ our Lord. Let not sin therefore reign in your mortal body, that ye should obey it in the lusts thereof. Neither yield ye your members as instruments of unrighteousness unto sin: but yield yourselves unto God, as those that are alive from the dead, and your members as instruments of righteousness unto God" (Ro.6:11-13; cp. Ro.6:2-10).**

1. The believer reckons or counts himself crucified with Christ.

   > **"Likewise reckon ye also yourselves to be dead indeed unto sin" (Ro.6:11$^a$).**
   > **"Knowing this, that our old man is [was] crucified with him, that the body of sin might be destroyed, that henceforth we should not serve sin" (Ro.6:6).**
   > **"I am crucified with Christ: nevertheless I live; yet not I, but Christ liveth in me: and the life which I now live in the flesh I live by the faith of the Son of God, who loved me, and gave himself for me" (Gal.2:20).**
   > **"And they that are Christ's have crucified the flesh with the affections and lusts" (Gal.5:24).**

2. The believer reckons or counts himself dead to sin, but alive to God.

   > **"Likewise reckon ye also yourselves to be dead indeed unto sin, but alive unto God through Jesus Christ our Lord (Ro.6:11).**
   > **"That he no longer should live the rest of his time in the flesh to the lusts of men, but to the will of God" (1 Pt.4:2).**

3. The believer does not let sin reign in his body.

   > **"Let not sin therefore reign in your mortal body, that ye should obey it in the lusts thereof" (Ro.6:12).**
   > **"Mortify therefore your members which are upon the earth; fornication, uncleanness, inordinate affection, evil concupiscence, and covetousness, which is idolatry" (Col.3:5).**

4. The believer does not yield his bodily members as instruments of sin.

   > **"Neither yield ye your members as instruments of unrighteousness unto sin" (Ro.6:13$^a$).**
   > **"For if ye live after the flesh, ye shall die: but if ye through the Spirit do mortify the deeds of the body, ye shall live" (Ro.8:13).**

5. The believer yields himself to God—as much as those who are alive from the dead are yielded to God.

   > **"But yield yourselves unto God, as those that are alive from the dead" (Ro.6:13$^b$).**
   > **"I beseech you therefore, brethren, by the mercies of God, that ye present your bodies a living sacrifice, holy, acceptable unto God, which is your reasonable service" (Ro.12:1).**
   > **"But put ye on the Lord Jesus Christ, and make not provision for the flesh, to fulfil the lusts thereof" (Ro.13:14).**

6. The believer yields his bodily members as instruments of righteousness.

   > **"But yield...your members as instruments of righteousness unto God" (Ro.6:13$^c$).**
   > **"This I say then, Walk in the Spirit, and ye shall not fulfil the lust of the flesh" (Gal.5:16).**

It should be noted that one's hardship or burden can bring a person to the place where the Lord can deal with him. It is then that the hardship becomes the cross and denial of self that Jesus is talking about. With an act of self-denial, the Christian can then reckon himself alive to God (Ro.6:13). He can then follow Jesus. This is an act which can be described as committing all that one is and has to Christ. It is an act that needs to be repeated every day (cp. Mt.10:38). (See outlines and notes—Mt.19:21-22; 19:23-26; 19:27-30.)

**2** (9:24) **Life:** the warning to the materialist is clear. Note the word "life" (psuche). In this context it means the natural, animal life; the earthly life that quickly passess away; the fading, aging, decaying, corruptible life of the earth. The warning is twofold. (See note—Mt.16:25-28 for more discussion.)

1. Do not save your life for yourself. If a person saves his life, that is, works to please himself on this earth, he will lose his life eternally. A man does not have life...

- to indulge himself: getting all he can of the comforts and pleasures and interests of life.
- to hoard life: keeping all the good things of life and seldom becoming involved in giving and sacrificing to help those who do not have.

"And that which fell among thorns are they, which, when they have heard, go forth, and are choked with cares and riches and pleasures of this life, and bring no fruit to perfection" (Lk.8:14).

"And I will say to my soul, Soul, thou hast much goods laid up for many years; take thine ease, eat, drink, and be merry. But God said unto him, Thou fool, this night thy soul shall be required of thee: then whose shall those things be, which thou hast provided? So is he that layeth up treasure for himself, and is not rich toward God" (Lk.12:19-21).

"But she that liveth in pleasure is dead while she liveth" (1 Tim.5:6).

"But these, as natural brute beasts, made to be taken and destroyed, speak evil of the things that they understand not; and shall utterly perish in their own corruption; and shall receive the reward of unrighteousness, as they that count it pleasure to riot [indulge, party, carouse] in the day time. Spots they are and blemishes, sporting themselves with their own deceivings while they feast with you; having eyes full of adultery, and that cannot cease from sin; beguiling unstable souls: an heart they have exercised with covetous practices; cursed children" (2 Pt.2:12-14).

"He that laboreth, laboreth for himself; for his mouth craveth it of him" (Pr.16:26).

"All the labor of man is for his mouth, and yet the appetite is not filled" (Eccl.6:7).

"It shall even be as when a hungry man dreameth, and, behold, he eateth; but he awaketh, and his soul is empty: or as when a thirsty man dreameth, and behold, he drinketh; but he awaketh, and, behold, he is faint, and his soul hath appetite: so shall the multitude of all the nations be, that fight against mount Zion" (Is.29:8).

"Blessed is the man that doeth this, and the son of man that layeth hold on it; that keepeth the sabbath from polluting it, and keepeth his hand from doing any evil" (Is.56:2).

2. Spend your life for Christ. Note the words "for my sake." The person who loses his life, that is, works to please Christ on this earth, shall save his life eternally.

a. A man has life to know God and fellowship with God.

"That which we have seen and heard declare we unto you, that ye also may have fellowship with us: and truly our fellowship is with the Father, and with his Son Jesus Christ" (1 Jn.1:3).

"Ye are my witnesses, saith the LORD, and my servant whom I have chosen: that ye may know and believe me, and understand that I am he: before me there was no God formed, neither shall there be after me" (Is.43:10).

b. A man has life to know men and fellowship with men.

"And the LORD God said, It is not good that the man should be alone; I will make him a help meet [fit] for him" (Gen.2:18).

"But if we walk in the light, as he is in the light, we have fellowship one with another, and the blood of Jesus Christ his Son cleanseth us from all sin" (1 Jn.1:7).

"And they continued stedfastly in the apostles' doctrine and fellowship, and in breaking of bread, and in prayers" (Acts 2:42).

"I am a companion of all them that fear thee, and of them that keep thy precepts" (Ps.119:63).

"Two are better than one; because they have a good reward for their labor. For if they fall, the one will lift up his fellow: but woe to him that is alone when he falleth; for he hath not another to help him up" (Eccl.4:9-10).

"Then they that feared the LORD spake often one to another: and the LORD hearkened, and heard it, and a book of remembrance was written before him for them that feared the LORD, and that thought upon his name" (Mal.3:16).

c. A man has life to help save a world lost in sin and shame and suffering.

"Even as the Son of man came not to be ministered unto, but to minister, and to give his life a ransom for many" (Mt.20:28).

"For the Son of man is come to seek and to save that which was lost" (Lk.19:10).

"Then said Jesus to them again, Peace be unto you: as my Father hath sent me, even so send I you" (Jn.20:21).

**"We then that are strong ought to bear the infirmities of the weak, and not to please ourselves"** (Ro.15:1).

**3** (9:25) **Materialism—Worldliness—Wealth—Soul—Life**: the materialist is questioned. The man who seeks to save his life, who works to please himself, is challenged to think honestly. Christ asks one question of the materialist, but it has two parts or pictures. (See note—Mt.16:25-28 for more discussion.)

1. The picture of gaining the *whole* world. Note that Christ did not say this: what if a man could gain and own all the land of Texas, or all of the wealth of Africa. He said what if a man could gain the *whole world*, all the world's...

- land
- honor
- gold
- wealth
- pleasure
- satisfaction

Imagine for a moment: What if a man could gain the whole world? No man can or will gain it all; but many pursue and some do gain a great deal of land, wealth, honor, pleasure, and carnal satisfaction.

2. The picture of losing self, of being cast away. Note that this is a stated fact, an inevitable and sure result. The man who seeks to please himself is doomed to "lose himself" and to "be cast away." He *tried to find himself* here on earth, but he never did. He *lost himself*. He lost the greatest things in all the world: certainty, assurance, confidence, and satisfaction of knowing that he is eternally secure and destined to live and serve God forever.

> **"What is a man advantaged, if he gain the whole world, and lose himself, or be cast away?"** (Lk.9:25).
>
> **"And I say unto you, That many shall come from the east and west, and shall sit down with Abraham, and Isaac, and Jacob, in the kingdom of heaven. But the children of the kingdom [false professions] shall be cast out into outer darkness: there shall be weeping and gnashing of teeth"** (Mt.8:11-12).
>
> **"And he saith unto him, Friend, how camest thou in hither not having a wedding garment [righteousness]? and he was speechless. Then said the king to the servants, Bind him hand and foot, and take him away, and cast him into outer darkness; there shall be weeping and gnashing of teeth"** (Mt.22:12-13).
>
> **"And cast ye the unprofitable servant into outer darkness: there shall be weeping and gnashing of teeth"** (Mt.25:30).
>
> **"Ye have not chosen me, but I have chosen you, and ordained you, that ye should go and bring forth fruit, and that your fruit should remain: that whatsoever ye shall ask of the Father in my name, he may give it you"** (Jn.15:16).
>
> **"But I keep under my body, and bring it into subjection: lest that by any means, when I have preached to others, I myself should be a castaway"** (1 Cor.9:27).
>
> **"And take heed to yourselves, lest at any time your hearts be overcharged with surfeiting, and drunkenness, and cares of this life, and so that day come upon you unawares"** (Lk.21:34).

---

**DEEPER STUDY # 2**
(9:25) **Castaway** (zemiotheis): to suffer the loss of, to forfeit, to lose what is of greatest value, to be punished by forfeiting and losing.

---

**4** (9:26) **Judgment—Jesus Christ, Coming Again—Ashamed, of Christ—Rejection, of Christ**: the judgment of the materialist is tragic. He did not have to suffer the judgment of God, but the materialist chose the world and its things and pleasures over Christ. Why is the materialist to be judged?

1. There is basically one reason: the materialist is ashamed of *Jesus and His words*. He is embarrassed and ashamed by such things as...

- being known as a true believer.
- following and obeying Christ completely.
- witnessing and standing up for Christ and morality.
- living less extravagantly than others.
- having less because of giving so much.
- associating with the needy to help them.
- driving a cheaper car.
- living in a less expensive home.
- not socializing with the worldly.
- not compromising and going along.
- not having the things others have.
- not joining in off-colored talk and jokes.

Simply stated, the man *loved* the acceptance and recognition of society, the comfort and pleasure of the world too much—he loved it all too much to give up his life and bear the reproach of Christ. He misjudged, counting the few years (ten to thirty years) of plenty on this earth as worth the unending years of the new earth and heavens.

2. Judgment is the most tragic event imaginable in the life of the materialist. He is counted unsuitable for glory.
   a. The Lord is coming. It is stated without equivocation. It is definite, even fixed. Jesus said He shall come.
   b. The Lord is coming in a threefold glory.
      ⇒ There is His own glory, exalted as the Messiah, the Christ of God (Ph.2:9-11).

⇒ There is the glory of God in all the brilliance and splendor of His person (1 Tim.6:16; 1 Jn.1:5; Rev.22:15).
⇒ There is the glory of the angels in their magnificence of being and brightness. They shall accompany Jesus when He returns to judge the earth.

The point is clear: when Jesus comes in His glory, the materialist will not join Him. He will not be welcomed into the glory of the Lord. Why? Christ will be *ashamed* of him. He will be embarrassed by the man, too embarrassed to acknowledge that He knows the man. The man is...
- not properly dressed (with the righteousness of God).
- not employed (in the things of God).
- too dirty (morally and righteously).
- too poor (in the spirit).
- too immoral (not repenting).
- too unjust (not changing).
- too disliked (by being obstinate in unbelief).
- too different (from the children of God).
- too uneducated (in the things of God).

"And then will I profess unto them, I never knew you: depart from me, ye that work iniquity" (Mt.7:23).
"But he answered and said, Verily I say unto you, I know you not" (Mt.25:12).
"But he that denieth me before men shall be denied before the angels of God" (Lk.12:9).
"But he shall say, I tell you, I know you not whence ye are; depart from me, all ye workers of iniquity" (Lk.13:27).

**5** (9:27) **Reward—Kingdom of God**: the reward of the disciple is God's kingdom. The believer enters the Kingdom of God immediately upon believing (see DEEPER STUDY # 3—Mt.19:23-24). Standing there in the crowd before Christ, some were to be eye-witnesses of the death and resurrection of Christ and the coming of the Holy Spirit. They were to taste and experience the Kingdom of God. Since that day, many have been saved and have seen the Kingdom of God before experiencing *physical death* (cp. Jn.3:16; 5:24; 8:52; Heb.2:9, 14-15).

| | C. The Events of the Transfiguration: A Glimpse into Glory, 9:28-36 (Mt.17:1-13; Mk.9:2-13) | were awake, they saw his glory, and the two men that stood with him. | a. Peter, James, & John |
|---|---|---|---|
| **1 Jesus took three disciples up into a mountain** | 28 And it came to pass about an eight days after these sayings, he took Peter and John and James, and went up into a mountain to pray. | 33 And it came to pass, as they departed from him, Peter said unto Jesus, Master, it is good for us to be here: and let us make three tabernacles; one for thee, and one for Moses, and one for Elias: not knowing what he said. | b. They desired to retain the experience |
| **2 Event 1: Jesus was praying** | | | |
| **3 Event 2: The countenance & clothing of Jesus were changed—a glittering white** | 29 And as he prayed, the fashion of his countenance was altered, and his raiment was white and glistering. | 34 While he thus spake, there came a cloud, and overshadowed them: and they feared as they entered into the cloud. | **6 Event 5: A cloud overshadowed them** |
| **4 Event 3: Two men appeared & talked with Jesus** | 30 And, behold, there talked with him two men, which were Moses and Elias: | | |
| a. Moses, the lawgiver; Elijah, the great prophet | 31 Who appeared in glory, and spake of his decease which he should accomplish at Jerusalem. | 35 And there came a voice out of the cloud, saying, This is my beloved Son: hear him. | **7 Event 6: A voice spoke to them** |
| b. They discussed His death | | 36 And when the voice was past, Jesus was found alone. And they kept it close, and | **8 Event 7: A stunned silence fell upon them** |
| **5 Event 4: Three disciples witnessed the event** | 32 But Peter and they that were with him were heavy with sleep: and when they | told no man in those days any of those things which they had seen. | |

# DIVISION IV

## THE SON OF MAN'S INTENSIVE PREPARATION OF HIS DISCIPLES FOR JERUSALEM AND DEATH, 9:18-50

## C. The Events of the Transfiguration: A Glimpse into Glory, 9:28-36

(9:28-36) **Introduction—Transfiguration**: there were at least seven reasons for the transfiguration.

1. Jesus needed a very special strength to face the pressure of the cross. In the transfiguration and in the Garden of Gethsemane, God is shown strengthening His Son in a marvelous way. Jesus was enabled to become the sin-bearer for the world (2 Cor.5:21).

2. The disciples needed their faith strengthened to face what lay ahead. Therefore, God gave them a glimpse of the glory of Jesus, that He is "the brightness of His glory, the express image of His Person" (Heb.1:3).

3. The disciples needed the quickening power and insight of God's Spirit, for Jesus was to be killed (Mt.16:21; cp. Mt.17:1-2). After the resurrection, the disciples' memory would need to be *quickened* to understand the spiritual significance of the cross. They would thereby become dynamic witnesses for Him. Remembering the transfiguration would stir their conviction.

4. The disciples needed to know that Jesus was more than a great lawgiver and a great prophet. In fact, He was the very Son of God who fulfilled all the Law and the Prophets (the Old Testament). He was the One who was to usher in the New Testament or covenant between God and man (see outline and notes—Mt.5:17-18; 2 Cor.3:6-18; cp. Mt.9:16-17).

5. The disciples needed to see into the glory of the spiritual world and into the reality of life after death. The disciples needed to understand God's purpose in Christ: to save man eternally and to make it possible for man to be transferred from this world into the next upon death. The Messiah of the cross was God's way, not a messiah of power and dominion.

6. The disciples would need to be reminded of the glory of Christ in the future, for the cross was an ugly sight because of the blood and suffering and sin and death. But it was also a glorious event planned by God, through which He revealed His love and grace and through which He saves the world. (See outline and notes—Mt.16:21-28.)

7. The disciples needed some glimpse into the glory that will be experienced when all believers are raised and transformed into the Lord's image. By seeing Moses and Elijah, the disciples saw two Old Testament believers who were *still living*, and they were living in a glorious state (v.30-31). They also knew that Christ had power over life and death. He could raise whom He wished from the dead to be in glory with Him.

The transfiguration was a striking event, an event that both interests and intrigues men. But, as has already been seen, intrigue was not its purpose. We should learn from the transfiguration, learn more about who Jesus really is and more about the life we are to live.

1. Jesus took three disciples up into a mountain (v.28).
2. Event 1: Jesus was praying (v.28).
3. Event 2: Jesus' countenance and clothing were changed—a glittering white (v.29).
4. Event 3: two men appeared and talked with Jesus (v.30-31).
5. Event 4: three disciples witnessed the event (v.32-33).
6. Event 5: a cloud overshadowed them (v.34).
7. Event 6: a voice spoke to them (v.35).
8. Event 7: a stunned silence fell upon them (v.36).

**1** (9:28) **Inner Circle**: Jesus took three disciples up into a mountain. The disciples were Peter, James, and John—His inner circle (see Deeper Study # 1, *Inner Circle*—Mk.9:2). Why did He take just these three disciples? The answer is not given. Perhaps it was for the same reason that leaders sometimes need to be alone with only a few of their closest friends.

⇒ There is the need for supportive companionship and prayer because of severe pressure.
⇒ There is the need to guard what is happening from spreading out into the public before it should.

The leader knows that the fewer witnesses to an event the less likely something will spread. In Jesus' case, He was under severe pressure, and the transfiguration and the glory of His person could not be understood until after the cross and the resurrection. He had to keep the matter quiet for now (cp. v.36).

**2** (9:28) **Jesus Christ, Prayer of—Prayer**: the first event was Jesus' praying. The transfiguration was a spectacular event—one that met the special needs of Jesus Christ. Note that Jesus went up into the mountain for the express purpose of praying (v.28). At least two things drove Him to pray at this time.

1. The cross lay right before Him. The *weight* and *load* of bearing the sin of the world was closing in on Him, and the pressure was almost more than He could bear. The terrifying strain and pressure are seen in three significant events that lay just ahead: the need for Moses and Elijah to talk with Him about His death; the excruciating pressure of Gethsemane; and the terrifying cry on the cross (Mt.26:36-46; see note—Mt.27:46-49).
2. The disciples had so much to learn and time was short. Jesus faced a tremendous problem: how to make them understand that God's way was not the way of earthly power and might (see notes—Mt.1:1; Deeper Study # 2—1:18; Deeper Study # 3—3:11; notes—11:1-6; 11:2-3; Deeper Study # 1—11:5; Deeper Study # 2—11:6; Deeper Study # 1—12:16; note—Lk.7:21-23), but the way of spiritual and eternal salvation (Jn.3:16; 2 Cor.5:21; 1 Pt.2:24; 3:18).

Jesus had no choice with such pressure and responsibility bearing in upon Him. He had to seek God and trust God to meet His need, and God did—in a most remarkable and encouraging way. While He met Jesus' need, God also met the needs of the three disciples who accompanied Him.

**Thought 1.** God will always meet the needs of the person who prays and seeks His help.

"He shall call upon me, and I will answer him: I will be with him in trouble; I will deliver him, and honour him" (Ps.91:15).
"When the poor and needy seek water, and there is none, and their tongue faileth for thirst, I the LORD will hear them, I the God of Israel will not forsake them" (Is.41:17).
"Then shalt thou call, and the LORD shall answer; thou shalt cry, and he shall say, Here I am. If thou take away from the midst of thee the yoke, the putting forth of the finger, and speaking vanity" (Is.58:9).
"And it shall come to pass, that before they call, I will answer; and while they are yet speaking, I will hear" (Is.65:24).
"Call unto me, and I will answer thee, and show thee great and mighty things, which thou knowest not" (Jer.33:3).
"And I say unto you, Ask, and it shall be given you; seek, and ye shall find; knock, and it shall be opened unto you. For every one that asketh receiveth; and he that seeketh findeth; and to him that knocketh it shall be opened" (Lk.11:9-10).
"If ye shall ask any thing in my name, I will do it" (Jn.14:14).
"If ye abide in me, and my words abide in you, ye shall ask what ye will, and it shall be done unto you" (Jn.15:7).
"And whatsoever we ask, we receive of him, because we keep his commandments, and do those things that are pleasing in his sight" (1 Jn.3:22).

**3** (9:29) **Jesus Christ, Deity—Glory**: the second event was the change of Jesus' countenance and clothing. Note three points.
1. His countenance or face was altered and became different. "His face did shine as the sun" (Mt.17:2). Imagine being as bright "as the sun!"
2. His clothing was altered and became different, a glittering or dazzling white. The word "glistering" or "dazzling" (exastrapton) means to flash like lightning, to gleam, brighten, be radiant.

"White as light" (Mt.17:2).
"White as snow" (Mk.9:3).
"White and glistering" (Lk.9:29).

3. Jesus was praying when these changes took place. Apparently, He was concentrating so intensely and was so wrapped up in God that God transformed Him, that is, allowed His Godly nature to shine right through Him.

**Thought 1.** Note several lessons.
1) The divine nature of Christ is seen in this event. God is showing man that Christ is definitely His Son. There is no excuse for unbelief.
2) The need of Christ was desperate, so God was meeting His need in a very special way. When our need is desperate, God will meet our need in a very special way if we will come to Him in intense prayer.

**Thought 2.** When a genuine believer prays with intensity and heavy concentration, his countenance is sometimes changed. He experiences a precious glow, a brightness, a light about his whole countenance.

> "But we all, with open face beholding as in a glass the glory of the Lord, are changed into the same image from glory to glory, even as by the Spirit of the Lord" (2 Cor.3:18).
> "That ye may be blameless and harmless, the sons of God, without rebuke, in the midst of a crooked and perverse nation, among whom ye shine as lights in the world" (Ph.2:15).
> "If thou prepare thine heart, and stretch out thine hands toward him [God]; if iniquity be in thine hand, put it far away, and let not wickedness dwell in thy tabernacles. For then shalt thou lift up thy face without spot; yea, thou shalt be steadfast, and shalt not fear: because thou shalt forget thy misery, and remember it as waters that pass away: and thine age shall be clearer than the noonday; thou shalt shine forth, thou shalt be as the morning" (Job 11:13-17).
> "They looked unto him [God], and were lightened: and their faces were ashamed" (Ps.34:5).
> "Who is as the wise man? and who knoweth the interpretation of a thing? a man's wisdom maketh his face to shine, and the boldness of his face shall be changed" (Eccl.8:1).
> "And they that be wise shall shine as the brightness of the firmament; and they that turn many to righteousness as the stars for ever and ever" (Dan.12:3).

**4** (9:30-31) **Jesus Christ, Death—Moses—Elijah—Exodus—Salvation:** the third event was the two men who appeared and talked with Jesus. Note two things.

1. Moses and Elijah appeared and talked with Jesus. Moses was the great lawgiver and Elijah was the greatest of the prophets. These two men were honoring and ministering to Jesus. By such they were *symbolizing* that the law and the prophets found their fulfillment in Jesus. Jesus was the One of whom the law and the prophets spoke; He was the One to whom they pointed (cp. Lk.24:26-27; 1 Pt.1:11).

2. The conversation concerned the death of Jesus. Jesus was sensing extreme pressure in thinking about His death, and the thought probably never left His mind. Death for Him meant so much more than the death of men. He was going to die for the sins of all men of all generations, and God was going to separate Himself from Jesus. The pressure and suffering were to be unbearable (see note—Mt.20:19; Mk.10:33). He desperately needed to be strengthened—inwardly and spiritually—to bear the suffering of the cross.

Apparently, Jesus needed a very special kind of encouragement, an encouragement from two Old Testament believers—believers who had lived in the faith and expectation of His coming to save them. Sharing their love for Him and their trust and hope in His dying for them, they would stir Him to continue on for the sake of mankind. It must have been a precious moment for all three. Luke gives some hint of this. His word for "decease" (exodos) means exodus. There stood Moses sharing how God had so miraculously saved and delivered the children of Israel out of bondage and how the exodus (deliverance) was only a picture of the marvelous deliverance that He, God's Son, was to accomplish for man. Jesus was to accomplish a new exodus, a new *saving deliverance*, except this time it was to be for all men. All men were to be delivered from the bondage of sin and death, from the devil and hell—delivered into the glorious liberty of God and life, both abundant and eternal life. Jesus' dying was to be well worth it, Moses and Elijah stressed. Note: the very encouragement that our Lord needed as Man was given by two who had believed and hoped in His coming. Being reminded of the marvelous deliverance (exodus) that had happened so long ago was bound to strengthen and lift the heart of Christ. Just seeing Moses and Elijah stand there, two who had trusted and believed and hoped, was bound to cause the Lord's spirit to rise. He was greatly encouraged and knew that He could not fail these men who had trusted and hoped in Him so much.

Elijah's stress, of course, would have been the many prophecies concerning the sufferings of Jesus and the glory that should follow. Again, Luke hints at this in the word "accomplish" (pleroo).

> "Then he took unto him the twelve, and said unto them, Behold, we go up to Jerusalem, and all things that are written by the prophets concerning the son of man shall be accomplished" (Lk.18:31. Cp. Lk.12:50; 22:37.)
> "Of which salvation the prophets have enquired and searched diligently, who prophesied of the grace that should come unto you: searching what, or what manner of time the Spirit of Christ which was in them did signify, when it testified beforehand the sufferings of Christ, and the glory that should follow" (1 Pt.1:10-11).

**Thought 1.** Our faith and hope are realized and fulfilled in Christ. He is our Deliverer or Exodus out of the grip of sin and death, the devil and hell. We can be free in Christ, free to live abundantly and eternally.

> "Verily, verily, I say unto you, The hour is coming, and now is, when the dead shall hear the voice of the Son of God: and they that hear shall live" (Jn.5:24).
> "Who gave himself for our sins, that he might deliver us from this present evil world, according to the will of God and our Father" (Gal.1:4).
> "Who gave himself for us, that he might redeem us from all iniquity, and purify unto himself a peculiar people, zealous of good works" (Tit.2:14).
> "Forasmuch then as the children are partakers of flesh and blood, he also himself likewise took part of the same; that through death he might destroy him that had the power of death, that is, the devil; and deliver them who through fear of death were all their lifetime subject to bondage" (Heb.2:14-15).

179

"And from Jesus Christ, who is the faithful witness, and the first begotten of the dead, and the prince of the kings of the earth. Unto him that loved us, and washed us from our sins in his own blood" (Rev.1:5).

"There is therefore now no condemnation to them which are in Christ Jesus, who walk not after the flesh, but after the Spirit. For the law of the Spirit of life in Christ Jesus hath made me free from the law of sin and death. For what the law could not do, in that it was weak through the flesh, God sending his own Son in the likeness of sinful flesh, and for sin, condemned sin in the flesh: that the righteousness of the law might be fulfilled in us, who walk not after the flesh, but after the Spirit" (Ro.8:1-4).

**Thought 2.** Discussing death should not be feared, not if we are genuine believers. Sharing with other believers will encourage us in our faith and hope.

**5** (9:32-33) **Spiritual Experiences—Glory**: the fourth event was the presence of three disciples to witness the event. Apparently it was night (v.37). The three had fallen asleep. Suddenly something woke them—more than likely the brilliance of the light, the Shekinah glory upon Christ. The three were *tasting glory*. They were in the very presence of God Himself and were tasting some of heaven's perfection: joy, peace, security, fulfillment. They did not want to leave this hallowed ground.

Note what Peter did.

1.     Peter offered to build three *shelters* (skenas) for Jesus and the two prophets. By this act he hoped to extend the stay of the heavenly guests and the glorious experience. The shelters offered were the booths made of branches and grass which could be quickly built, the kind often built by travellers on their stops along the road night by night.

2.     Peter said, "Let us." Even in a moment as glorious as this, Peter would not act against His Lord's will. Imagine the devotion and loyalty.

**Thought 1.** There is always a pull to live in the glory and forget the human need, to experience the high and neglect the low. We must always remember: it is the discipline of serving where there is need and ministering to the low that results in glory and the experiences of highs.

"Is it not [your purpose] to deal thy bread to the hungry, and that thou bring the poor that are cast out to thy house? when thou seest the naked, that thou cover him; and that thou hide not thyself from thine own flesh?" (Is.58:7).

"I have showed you all things, how that so labouring ye ought to support the weak, and to remember the words of the Lord Jesus, how he said, It is more blessed to give than to receive" (Acts 20:35).

"We then that are strong ought to bear the infirmities of the weak, and not to please ourselves" (Ro.15:1).

"Bear ye one another's burdens, and so fulfil the law of Christ" (Gal.6:2).

"Remember them that are in bonds, as bound with them; and them which suffer adversity, as being yourselves also in the body" (Heb.13:3).

"Pure religion and undefiled before God and the Father is this, To visit the fatherless and widows in their affliction, and to keep himself unspotted from the world" (Jas.1:27).

"Finally, be ye all of one mind, having compassion one of another, love as brethren, be pitiful, be courteous" (1 Pt.3:8).

**6** (9:34) **Jesus Christ, Deity—Covenants—Law vs. Grace**: the fifth event was the cloud that overshadowed them. The cloud and the voice of God terrified the disciples and caused them to fall immediately upon their faces, prostrate and unable to look up. As mortal men they were crouched in fear, and paralyzed in terror. Note three facts.

1.     The cloud was "a bright cloud." This was the Shekinah glory, the cloud that symbolized God's presence. It was the cloud that guided Israel out of Egypt and that rested upon the tabernacle and above the Mercy Seat in the Most Holy Place (Ex.40:34-38). God "only hath immortality, dwelling in the light which *no man can approach* unto" (1 Tim.1:16). God dwells in unapproachable light upon which no man can look. Peter later called it "the excellent glory" (2 Pt.1:17).

2.     The "bright cloud" overshadowing Christ was a sharp contrast to the dark and threatening cloud that overshadowed the giving of the old covenant to Moses, that is, the law (Ex.19:18; 20:21). There is a point to be made here. The law (old covenant) was dark and threatening (see notes—Gal.3:10). The new covenant (the love of Christ) is bright: it is given to save and bless, not to threaten and condemn (Heb.12:18-24. Cp. Heb.8:6-13.)

3.     The voice which spoke actually said, "This is My Son, the Beloved One" (Greek). Note the two facts stressed: Christ is God's Son, and He is the Beloved One. The idea is that Christ is the *only begotten Son* who was to be given for the world.

"For God so loved the world, that he gave his only begotten Son, that whosoever believeth in him should not perish, but have everlasting life" (Jn.3:16).

"He that spared not his own Son, but delivered him up for us all, how shall he not with him also freely give us all things?" (Ro.8:32).

**7** (9:35) **Jesus Christ, Deity**: the sixth event was the voice that spoke out of the cloud. The message was clear: "This is my Son, my chosen One [ho huios mou, ho eklelegmenos], hear ye him!" "Listen to Him, for He is my Son, my chosen One." God was both telling and warning the disciples to listen to Christ…

- He was God's Son, the beloved and chosen One.
- What Jesus spoke was the truth, even when He predicted His death and resurrection.

**Thought 1.** God warns every living man to listen to Christ for the same two reasons.

> "If we receive the witness of men, the witness of God is greater: for this is the witness of God which he hath testified of his Son. He that believeth on the Son of God hath the witness in himself: he that believeth not God hath made him a liar; because he believeth not the record that God gave of his Son. And this is the record, that God hath given to us eternal life, and this life is in his Son. He that hath the Son hath life; and he that hath not the Son of God hath not life" (1 Jn.5:9-12).
>
> "I have many things to say and to judge of you: but he that sent me is true; and I speak to the world those things which I have heard of him" (Jn.8:26).
>
> "For I have not spoken of myself; but the Father which sent me, he gave me a commandment, what I should say, and what I should speak" (Jn.12:49).
>
> "Believest thou not that I am in the Father, and the Father in me? the words that I speak unto you I speak not of myself: but the Father that dwelleth in me, he doeth the works" (Jn.14:10).
>
> "He that loveth me not keepeth not my sayings: and the word which ye hear is not mine, but the Father's which sent me" (Jn.14:24).
>
> "For I have given unto them the words which thou gavest me; and they have received them, and have known surely that I came out from thee, and they have believed that thou didst send me" (Jn.17:8).
>
> "For Moses truly said unto the fathers, A prophet [Christ] shall the Lord your God raise up unto you of your brethren, like unto me; him shall ye hear in all things whatsoever he shall say unto you" (Acts 3:22).

**8** (9:36) **Quietness:** the seventh event was the stunned silence. Jesus was standing there all alone. There was stone silence. No one said anything, not even Jesus. We can picture the silence throughout the night. They were apparently on the mountain all night (v.37). Note the disciples said nothing about the experience during those days (see note, *Inner Circle*—Lk.9:28).

**Thought 1.** There is a time for silence, for being still and meditating upon the Lord.

> "Stand in awe, and sin not: commune with your own heart upon your bed, and be still" (Ps.4:4).
>
> "Be still, and know that I am God: I will be exalted among the heathen, I will be exalted in the earth" (Ps.46:10).
>
> "Now therefore stand still, that I may reason with you before the LORD of all the righteous acts of the LORD, which he did to you and to your fathers" (1 Sam.12:7).
>
> "Oh that ye would altogether hold your peace! And it should be your wisdom" (Job 13:5).
>
> "Hearken unto this, O Job: stand still, and consider the wondrous works of God" (Job 37:14).
>
> "In the multitude of words there wanteth not sin: but he that refraineth his lips is wise" (Pr.10:19).
>
> "Even a fool, when he holdeth his peace, is counted wise: and he that shutteth his lips is esteemed a man of understanding" (Pr.17:28).
>
> "A time to rend, and a time to sew; a time to keep silence, and a time to speak" (Eccl.3:7).
>
> "But the LORD is in his holy temple: let all the earth keep silence before him" (Hab.2:20).
>
> "Holy thy peace at the presence of the Lord GOD: for the day of the LORD is at hand: for the LORD hath prepared a sacrifice, he hath bid his guests" (Zeph.1:7).
>
> "Be silent, O all flesh, before the LORD: for he is raised up out of his holy habitation" (Zech.2:13).
>
> "Seeing then that these things cannot be spoken against, ye ought to be quiet, and to do nothing rashly" (Acts 19:36).
>
> "And that ye study to be quiet, and to do your own business, and to work with your own hands, as we commanded you" (1 Th.4:11).
>
> "But let it [one's dress or clothing] be the hidden man of the heart, in that which is not corruptible, even the ornament of a meek and quiet spirit, which is in the sight of God of great price" (1 Pt.3:4).

| | D. The Second Prediction of Death: A Rebuke of the Present Generation, 9:37-45<br>(Mt.17:14-23; Mk.9:14-32) | O faithless and perverse generation, how long shall I be with you, and suffer you? Bring thy son hither. | & a wayward heart*DS2,3* |
|---|---|---|---|
| **1 The next day after the transfiguration**<br>a. Jesus was met by a crowd<br>b. A man cried out in desperation<br><br>1) For his only son<br><br>2) The problem: An evil spirit possessed him*DS1* | 37 And it came to pass, that on the next day, when they were come down from the hill, much people met him.<br>38 And, behold, a man of the company cried out, saying, Master, I beseech thee, look upon my son: for he is mine only child.<br>39 And, lo, a spirit taketh him, and he suddenly crieth out; and it teareth him that he foameth again, and bruising him hardly departeth from him. | 42 And as he was yet a coming, the devil threw him down, and tare him. And Jesus rebuked the unclean spirit, and healed the child, and delivered him again to his father.<br>43 And they were all amazed at the mighty power of God. But while they wondered every one at all things which Jesus did, he said unto his disciples, | **3 Rebuke 2: A lack of God's power**<br>a. Jesus rebuked the disciples' lack of power by His own act of healing<br><br><br>b. The people were amazed |
| c. The disciples were powerless<br><br>**2 Rebuke 1: A lack of faith** | 40 And I besought thy disciples to cast him out; and they could not.<br>41 And Jesus answering said, | 44 Let these sayings sink down into your ears: for the Son of man shall be delivered into the hands of men.<br>45 But they understood not this saying, and it was hid from them, that they perceived it not: and they feared to ask him of that saying. | **4 Rebuke 3: A slowness to grasp the Messiah's death** |

# DIVISION IV

## THE SON OF MAN'S INTENSIVE PREPARATION OF HIS DISCIPLES FOR JERUSALEM AND DEATH, 9:18-50

### D. The Second Prediction of Death: A Rebuke of the Present Generation, 9:37-45

(9:37-45) **Introduction**: Jesus was rebuking His generation (v.41). They deserved to be rebuked—so does any generation which stands guilty of such faithless living.
1. The next day after the transfiguration (v.37-40).
2. Rebuke 1: a lack of faith and a wayward heart (v.41).
3. Rebuke 2: a lack of God's power (v.42-43).
4. Rebuke 3: a slowness to grasp the Messiah's death (v.44-45).

[1] (9:37-40) **Powerlessness—Seeking Christ**: it was the next day after the transfiguration. Jesus and the three disciples were coming down from having spent the night on the mountain. A huge crowd ran to meet Jesus, and from their midst a man broke forth, elbowing his way up to Jesus (Mt.17:14; Mk.9:15).
1. The man cried out in desperation: "Master, I beseech thee." The words "cried" and "beseeched" are strong; he shouted and begged for Jesus to meet his need.

"Look upon my son: for he is mine only child." The word for "look upon" (epiblepsai) is a medical term. It means to carefully examine the patient, to look upon with pity. The son had an evil spirit that abused him physically (see DEEPER STUDY # 1—Lk.9:39).
2. The disciples were powerless in helping the man, despite his desperate need. This was tragic, for it meant that the power of God had left them. They had just demonstrated the power to cast out demons on their preaching tour (Lk.9:1-6, 10), but now they had no power. There was something wrong in their lives, some sin, some lack which was blocking the power of God. Jesus later told them they had not been praying and fasting as they should (Mt.17:21).

**DEEPER STUDY # 1**
(9:39) **Evil Spirits**: the son's illness seemed to have been both physical and spiritual. The description of the illness in Mark points toward what is known today as epilepsy and demon-possession (Mt.17:15; Mk.9:17-18). The demon-possession in particular seems to have heightened and aggravated the condition, perhaps causing some suicidal tendencies (Mt.17:15; Mk.9:22). Throughout the gospels this seems to be one of the major works of evil spirits: to *heighten and aggravate* existing conditions.

[2] (9:41) **Unbelief—Heart, Wayward**: the first rebuke was for a lack of faith and a wayward heart. Note three things.

1. Jesus spoke to His whole generation. He enlarged His comments beyond the disciples. They had no power; neither did anyone else in His generation. What the disciples lacked was lacked by all. Their sins were the sins of all, the sins of *being faithless and perverse* (see DEEPER STUDY # 2,3—Lk.9:41).

2.  Jesus actually said that His presence would not always be available; He would not be patient with man's unbelief forever. Note: there is a point of coming judgment in this statement.
3.  Jesus was looked upon only as a great prophet and minister...
    * not as the very presence of God in their midst.
    * not as the true Messiah before whom a person must repent.
    * not as the Christ to whom a person owed his life and service.
Thus, the generation of people were walking around faithless and perverse before God, as powerless and helpless as ever.

> "And he said unto them, Why are ye so fearful? how is it that ye have no faith?" (Mk.4:40).
> "But without faith it is impossible to please him: for he that cometh to God must believe that he is, and that he is a rewarder of them that diligently seek him" (Heb.11:6).
> "Art thou the Christ? tell us. And he said unto them, If I tell you, ye will not believe" (Lk.22:67).
> "Verily, verily, I say unto thee, We speak that we do know, and testify that we have seen; and ye receive not our witness" (Jn.3:11).
> "Then came the Jews round about him, and said unto him, How long dost thou make us to doubt? If thou be the Christ, tell us plainly. Jesus answered them, I told you, and ye believed not: the works that I do in my Father's name, they bear witness of me" (Jn.10:24-25).
> "But though he had done so many miracles before them, yet they believed not on him" (Jn.12:37).
> "Who hath believed our report? and to whom is the arm of the LORD revealed?" (Is.53:1).

---

**DEEPER STUDY # 2**
(9:41) **Faithless** (apistos): disbelieving; being without faith; being out of faith; not keeping faith, unbelieving (cp. Tit.1:15).

---

**DEEPER STUDY # 3**
(9:41) **Perverse** (diastrepho): to distort, to twist, to turn aside or away, to be torn in two, to be corrupted (cp. Acts 20:30; Ph.2:15).

> "That ye may be blameless and harmless, the sons of God, without rebuke, in the midst of a crooked and perverse nation, among whom ye shine as lights in the world" (Ph.2:15).
> "Also of your own selves shall men arise, speaking perverse things, to draw away disciples after them" (Acts 20:30).
> "Perverse disputings of men of corrupt minds, and destitute of the truth, supposing that gain is godliness: from such withdraw thyself" (1 Tim.6:5).
> "The integrity of the upright shall guide them: but the perverseness of transgressors shall destroy them" (Pr.11:3).
> "A man shall be commended according to his wisdom: but he that is of a perverse heart shall be despised" (Pr.12:8).
> "A wholesome tongue is a tree of life: but perverseness therein is a breach in the spirit" (Pr.15:4).
> "Better is the poor that walketh in his uprightness, than he that is perverse in his ways, though he be rich" (Pr.28:6).

---

**3** (9:42-43) **Minister, Duty**: the second rebuke was for a lack of God's power. Note two significant points.

1.  Jesus rebuked the disciples' lack of power by His own act of healing.
    a.  Jesus healed the boy while the evil spirit was actually attacking the boy, while he was at his very worst. The Lord's power was clearly demonstrated.

> "But that ye may know that the Son of man hath power on earth to forgive sins, (then saith he to the sick of the palsy,) Arise, take up thy bed, and go unto thine house" (Mt.9:6).
> "And Jesus came and spake unto them, saying, all power is given unto me in heaven and in earth" (Mt.28:18).
> "For with God nothing shall be impossible" (Lk.1:37).
> "How God anointed Jesus of Nazareth with the Holy Ghost and with power: who went about doing good, and healing all that were oppressed of the devil; for God was with him" (Acts 10:38).
> "I know that thou canst do every thing, and that no thought can be withholden from thee" (Job 42:2).

b. Jesus rebuked the spirit, broke the devil's power by *His Word*. Satan could not stand before God's Word. Jesus had purposed to spoil principalities and powers.

> "Now is the judgment of this world: now shall the prince of this world be cast out" (Jn.12:31).
> "Who hath delivered us from the power of darkness, and hath translated us into the kingdom of his dear Son: in whom we have redemption through his blood, even the forgiveness of sins" (Col.1:13-14).
> "And having spoiled principalities and powers, he made a show of them openly, triumphing over them in it" (Col.2:15).
> "Forasmuch then as the children are partakers of flesh and blood, he also himself likewise took part of the same; that through death he might destroy him that had the power of death, that is, the devil; and deliver them who through fear of death were all their lifetime subject to bondage" (Heb.2:14-15).
> "He that committeth sin is of the devil; for the devil sinneth from the beginning. For this purpose the Son of God was manifested, that he might destroy the works of the devil" (1 Jn.3:8).

c. Jesus showed tenderness for men. He delivered the little boy to his father.

2. The people were all amazed (exeplessonto depantes). They marvelled, were astonished at "the mighty power of God." The Greek word is "megaleioteti," which means majesty. They marvelled at "the majesty of God." Note that Jesus brought honor to God, not to Himself.

**Thought 1.** Powerlessness is inexcusable. Why? Because Christ has revealed how the believer can possess the power and strength of God.

> "And Jesus said unto them, Because of your unbelief: for verily I say unto you, If ye have faith as a grain of mustard seed, ye shall say unto this mountain, Remove hence to yonder place; and it shall remove; and nothing shall be impossible unto you. Howbeit this kind goeth not out but by prayer and fasting" (Mt.17:20-21).
> "John answered and said, A man can receive nothing, except it be given him from heaven" (Jn.3:27).
> "I am the vine, ye are the branches: He that abideth in me, and I in him, the same bringeth forth much fruit: for without me ye can do nothing" (Jn.15:5).
> "Not that we are sufficient of ourselves to think any thing as of ourselves; but our sufficiency is of God" (2 Cor.3:5).
> "But ye shall receive power, after that the Holy Ghost is come upon you: and ye shall be witnesses unto me both in Jerusalem, and in Judaea, and in Samaria, and unto the uttermost part of the earth" (Acts 1:8. See outline—Ro.8:1-17.)

**4** (9:44-45) **Dullness—Understanding, Lack of**: the third rebuke was for a slowness to grasp the Messiah's death. Apparently, the disciples began to think about the earthly reign of Jesus. The power of God demonstrated that Jesus had the power to conquer the earth and subject all men to Himself. Their hopes were stirred.

But note what Jesus did. He rebuked their thoughts of a physical and material Messiah. He again had to show them that God's Messiah had to die in order to save the world.

1. Jesus strongly exhorted: "Let these sayings sink down into your ears." The Greek is, "Put these sayings into your ears." Give special attention to them.

2. The word "delivered" (paradidosthai) means to be ordained, predetermined in the counsel and plan of God. (See note—Mt.17:22.)

> "Him, being delivered by the determinate counsel and foreknowledge of God, ye have taken, and by wicked hands have crucified and slain" (Acts 2:23).
> "He that spared not his own Son, but delivered him up for us all, how shall he not with him also freely give us all things?" ( Ro.8:32).

3. The disciples did not grasp the Messiah's death. They just did not understand. Note why: it was hidden from them, so that they could not perceive it.

Why was it hid from them? Certainly not because of God. The reason had to be because of their unbelief and perverseness. They just refused to see it. They were spiritually dull, lacking a sensitivity to spiritual truth.

> "Then he said unto them, O fools, and slow of heart to believe all that the prophets have spoken" (Lk.24:25).
> "Ye hypocrites, ye can discern the face of the sky and of the earth; but how is it that ye do not discern this time [the day and age of Christ]?" (Lk.12:56).
> "Why do ye not understand my speech? even because ye cannot hear my word" (Jn.8:43).
> "For the heart of this people is waxed gross, and their ears are dull of hearing, and their eyes have they closed; lest they should see with their eyes, and hear with their ears, and understand with their heart, and should be converted, and I should heal them" (Acts 28:27).

"There is none that understandeth, there is none that seeketh after God" (Ro.3:11).

"But the natural man receiveth not the things of the Spirit of God: for they are foolishness unto him: neither can he know them, because they are spiritually discerned" (1 Cor.2:14).

"Ever learning, and never able to come to the knowledge of the truth" (2 Tim.3:7).

"Of whom we have many things to say, and hard to be uttered, seeing ye are dull of hearing" (Heb.5:11).

"I will instruct thee and teach thee in the way which thou shalt go: I will guide thee with mine eye. Be ye not as the horse, or as the mule, which have no understanding: whose mouth must be held in with bit and bridle" (Ps.32:8-9).

"Man that is in honour, and understandeth not, is like the beasts that perish" (Ps.49:20).

"When the boughs thereof are withered, they shall be broken off: the women come, and set them on fire: for it is a people of no understanding: therefore he that made them will not have mercy on them, and he that formed them will show them no favor" (Is.27:11).

"For my people is foolish, they have not known me; they are sottish children, and they have none understanding: they are wise to do evil, but to do good they have no knowledge" (Jer.4:22).

"Hear now this, O foolish people, and without understanding; which have eyes, and see not; which have ears, and hear not: fear ye not me? saith the LORD: will ye not tremble at my presence, which have placed the sand for the bound of the sea by a perpetual decree, that it cannot pass it: and though the waves thereof toss themselves, yet can they not prevail; though they roar, yet can they not pass over it? But this people hath a revolting and a rebellious heart; they are revolted and gone. Neither say they in their heart, Let us now fear the LORD our God, that giveth rain, both the former and the latter, in his season: he reserveth unto us the appointed weeks of the harvest" (Jer.5:21-24).

"But they know not the thoughts of the LORD, neither understand they his counsel" (Mic.4:12).

| | E. The Way of Greatness: Humility, 9:46-50 (Mt.18:1-4; Mk.9:33-41) | and whosoever shall receive me receiveth him that sent me: for he that is least among you all, the same shall be great. | Jesus' name b. Reward 1) Will receive Jesus 2) Will receive God 3) Will be great |
|---|---|---|---|
| 1 The desire for greatness: Wanting place, recognition & power | 46 Then there arose a reasoning among them, which of them should be greatest. | | |
| 2 The picture of greatness a. Jesus took a child b. Jesus held the child | 47 And Jesus, perceiving the thought of their heart, took a child, and set him by him, | 49 And John answered and said, Master, we saw one casting out devils in thy name; and we forbad him, because he followeth not with us. | 4 The right to greatness: Not an exclusive right |
| 3 The right concept of greatness a. Receiving a child in | 48 And said unto them, Whosoever shall receive this child in my name receiveth me: | 50 And Jesus said unto him, Forbid him not: for he that is not against us is for us. | |

# DIVISION IV

## THE SON OF MAN'S INTENSIVE PREPARATION OF HIS DISCIPLES FOR JERUSALEM AND DEATH, 9:18-50

## E.  The Way of Greatness: Humility, 9:46-50

(9:46-50) **Introduction**: people are interested in greatness to varying degrees. It is enough for some people to simply be accepted and approved by friends and neighbors; that is enough *greatness* for them. Others want more: to be elevated to a particular position, to live in a particular neighborhood, to own a certain kind of car, to hold a particular club membership—they want something that gives them greater recognition and greater prestige. They crave for more greatness than others. Some crave the greatness of authority and rule, of power and fame, of position and wealth. They want the prestige and honor and recognition far above the ordinary.

Note another fact: the nature of a person determines whether he secures his greatness by hook or crook or by respect and honesty, by meanness and depravity or by right and goodness. A man's heart determines whether people are blessed or hurt by his greatness. A good neighbor or ruler blesses others. A bad neighbor or ruler hurts others.

Jesus teaches the way to greatness.

1. The desire for greatness: wanting place, recognition, and power (v.46).
2. The picture of greatness (v.47).
3. The right concept of greatness (v.48).
4. The right to greatness is not an exclusive right (v.49-50).

[1] (9:46) **Greatness—Worldliness—Material vs. Spiritual—Selfishness**: the disciples desired greatness in the Kingdom of Christ. They desired places of honor, recognition, and power.

1. The disciples were actually arguing over the highest positions in the Lord's kingdom. The word "reasoning" (dialogismos) means a dispute, debate, or argument. They were maneuvering for positions of leadership. Later, James and John were even to manipulate their mother into asking Jesus for the highest positions.

2. The disciples were thinking of an earthly kingdom, a physical and material rule right here on earth. Their desire was for worldly position, name, recognition, honor, authority, challenge, duties, pleasure, and wealth. They were not thinking in terms of goodness or character. They did not mean the greatest in love and care, in ministry and help, but in position and rule, name and recognition.

3. The disciples were full of self, just as all men are. They were thinking of self, not of others, not how they could be great in helping others. They were not even thinking of Jesus. And remember, He had just been revealing that He was to *give* His life for the salvation of the world (v.44. Cp. Mk.9:33-34.) Their thoughts should have been on Jesus and the meaning of what He had said. They should have been seeking to encourage Him and to learn all they could from Him. Instead they were so full of self, they could think of nothing but themselves.

**Thought 1.** It is difficult to admit that we are full of self, that is, self-centered and selfish. The fact hurts; we revolt against it. But the truth has to be faced before we can become what we should be.

"And whosoever shall exalt himself shall be abased; and he that shall humble himself shall be exalted" (Mt.23:12).

"How can ye believe, which receive honour one of another, and seek not the honour that cometh from God only?" (Jn.5:44).

"For I say, through the grace given unto me, to every man that is among you, not to think of himself more highly than he ought to think; but to think soberly, according as God hath dealt to every man the measure of faith" (Ro.12:3).

"Be of the same mind one toward another. Mind not high things, but condescend to men of low estate. Be not wise in your own conceits" (Ro.12:16).

"For if a man think himself to be something, when he is nothing, he deceiveth himself" (Gal.6:3).

"Let nothing be done through strife or vainglory; but in lowliness of mind let each esteem other better than themselves. Look not every man on his own things, but every man also on the things of others" (Ph.2:3-4).

186

"So then because thou art lukewarm, and neither cold nor hot, I will spue thee out of my mouth. Because thou sayest, I am rich, and increased with goods, and have need of nothing; and knowest not that thou art wretched, and miserable, and poor, and blind, and naked" (Rev.3:16-17).

"For the wicked boasteth of his heart's desire, and blesseth the covetous, whom the LORD abhorreth" (Ps.10:3).

"They that trust in their wealth, and boast themselves in the multitude of their riches; none of them can by any means redeem his brother, nor give to God a ransom for him" (Ps.49:6-7).

"Whoso boasteth himself of a false gift is like clouds and wind without rain" (Pr.25:14).

"For thou hast trusted in thy wickedness: thou hast said, None seeth me. Thy wisdom and thy knowledge, it hath perverted thee; and thou hast said in thine heart, I am, and none else beside me" (Is.47:10).

"Though thou exalt thyself as the eagle, and though thou set thy nest among the stars, thence will I bring thee down, saith the LORD" (Obad.4).

4.     The disciples did not understand what the Kingdom of Heaven was. They still saw an earthly and temporal kingdom and not a spiritual and eternal kingdom. They still thought in terms of getting all they could for a few short years while on this earth. They had not grasped the hope and reality of the spiritual world, of eternal life and blessings. (See DEEPER STUDY # 3—Mt.19:23-24; Eph.1:3 for more discussion.)

**2** (9:47) **Greatness—Salvation—Deliverance—Freedom—Bondage**: the picture of greatness was acted out by Jesus. Note that He pictured what greatness was before He explained the right concept. The picture involved two acts. First, He reached out and took a child; and second, He set the child by His side. What was Jesus doing?

Very simply, Jesus was *showing* the disciples what greatness was. A person is great when he takes a child and brings that child to Jesus. Greatness surrounds Christ and children, children who are *willing* to be brought to Christ. Greatness is setting children, the people of the world, by the side of Christ, beside the One who can meet all their needs.

1.     Greatness is bringing people to the One who can give them freedom from the bondages of this world. Imagine how great the person is who shows men how to be liberated from...

- sin
- guilt
- drunkenness
- immorality
- oppression

- loneliness
- suffering
- lying
- stealing
- emptiness

- death
- laziness
- cursing
- selfishness
- hatred

2.     Greatness is bringing people to the One who can give them the right to live, to live abundantly on this earth and eternally when entering the next world.

"But as many as received him, to them gave he power to become the sons of God, even to them that believe on his name" (Jn.1:12).

"For God so loved the world, that he gave his only begotten Son, that whosoever believeth in him should not perish, but have everlasting life" (Jn.3:16).

"Verily, verily, I say unto you, He that heareth my word, and believeth on him that sent me, hath everlasting life, and shall not come into condemnation; but is passed from death unto life" (Jn.5:24).

"And this is the record, that God hath given to us eternal life, and this life is in his Son. He that hath the Son hath life; and he that hath not the Son of God hath not life. These things have I written unto you that believe on the name of the Son of God; that ye may know that ye have eternal life, and that ye may believe on the name of the Son of God" (1 Jn.5:11-13).

"That being justified by his grace, we should be made heirs according to the hope of eternal life" (Tit.3:7).

"The Spirit itself beareth witness with our spirit, that we are the children of God: and if children, then heirs; heirs of God, and joint-heirs with Christ; if so be that we suffer with him, that we may be also glorified together" (Ro.8:16-17).

"The fruit of the righteous is a tree of life; and he that winneth souls is wise" (Pr.11:30).

"And they that be wise shall shine as the brightness of the firmament; and they that turn many to righteousness as the stars for ever and ever" (Dan.12:3).

**3** (9:48) **Greatness**: the right concept of greatness is explained. Greatness is *receiving* a child, that is, a person, in the name of Jesus. To receive a child means at least three things.

1.     It means doing just what Jesus did: we *reach out and welcome and accept* a person into our arms. This sounds easy—taking a child into our arms—but it is not always so. Sometimes a person...

- is unkempt, dirty, even filthy.
- is acting ugly, mean, misbehaving.
- is disliked, rejected, unacceptable to others.

And there is always the threat that receiving a person will cause our own friends to withdraw their friendship because the person is unacceptable to them.

2.     It means sharing the best news that we have: the *good news of God's kingdom*. Note: Jesus did not say that greatness is *just* receiving a child. He adds that the child must be received *in His name*. The name of Jesus has to be shared

with the person. The person is to be told and shown that we act in the name and cause of Jesus. The kingdom of God is to be shared with the child (the person received).

3. It means that we help the person in every way possible, no matter the cost. We do our best to meet his...
- physical and mental needs.
- material and social needs.
- spiritual and godly needs.

"Even as the Son of man came not to be ministered unto, but to minister, and to give his life a ransom for many" (Mt.20:28).

"Then said Jesus to them again, Peace be unto you: as my Father hath sent me, even so send I you" (Jn.20:21).

"I have showed you all things, how that so labouring ye ought to support the weak, and to remember the words of the Lord Jesus, how he said, It is more blessed to give than to receive" (Acts 20:35).

"We then that are strong ought to bear the infirmities of the weak, and not to please ourselves" (Ro.15:1).

"Bear ye one another's burdens, and so fulfil the law of Christ" (Gal.6:2).

Now, note what Jesus covered in this point. He revealed what the reward will be for receiving people in His name. This stresses the importance of receiving people. It is close to His heart, the very purpose for which He came to earth (Mt.20:28). It is the thing His followers are to be doing, the very thing to which we are to commit our lives. Therefore, He wants to challenge His followers to get to it. There is no better challenge than to lay the reward out in front of them. The reward is threefold for the man who receives persons *in the name of Jesus Christ*.

1. The disciple receives Christ. Note, it is in the very act of receiving others that we receive Christ. This means that the disciple receives a very special presence of Christ, an abiding presence, a presence that cares for and looks after and guides and directs his life.

Another way to see what Christ is saying is this...
- Receiving our neighbor *equals* receiving Christ.
- Loving our neighbor *equals* loving Christ.

"If a man say, I love God [Christ], and hateth his brother, he is a liar: for he that loveth not his brother whom he hath seen, how can he love God whom he hath not seen?" (1 Jn.4:20. Cp. Mt.22:36-39.)

2. The disciple receives God. Again, this is active, that is, it is *in the very act* of receiving Christ that we receive God. God enters the disciple's life *at the very moment* the disciple receives Christ.

"But love ye your enemies, and do good, and lend, hoping for nothing again; and your reward shall be great, and ye shall be the children of the Highest: for he is kind unto the unthankful and to the evil. Be ye therefore merciful, as your Father also is merciful" (Lk.6:35-36).

3. The disciple shall be great. Note: Jesus did not say *greatest*; He said "great." Every one who serves by bringing men to Christ by receiving others *in the name of Christ* shall be great.

Note a crucial point. It is the person who receives others and who is actually reaching out to others in the name of Jesus who *receives Christ*. Reaching and receiving others is the evidence that one has received Christ. A person's heart has to be opened both to Christ and to others before Christ can ever enter his life. To open one's heart to Christ is to open one's heart to others. There is no such thing as an open heart to God and a closed hand to man. It is out of the heart that man acts. If his heart belongs to God, then his hand (life) belongs to man. He will do all he can to love and help man, receiving and welcoming every child who will be brought to Christ. That person "shall be great."

"And whosoever shall give to drink unto one of these little ones a cup of cold water only in the name of a disciple, verily I say unto you, he shall in no wise lose his reward" (Mt.10:42).

"Then shall the righteous shine forth as the sun in the kingdom of their Father. Who hath ears to hear, let him hear" (Mt.13:43).

"And every one that hath forsaken houses, or brethren, or sisters, or father, or mother, or wife, or children, or land, for my name's sake, shall receive an hundredfold, and shall inherit everlasting life" (Mt.19:29).

"His lord said unto him, Well done, good and faithful servant; thou hast been faithful over a few things, I will make thee ruler over many things: enter thou into the joy of thy lord" (Mt.25:23).

"If any man serve me, let him follow me; and where I am, there shall also my servant be: if any man serve me, him will my Father honour" (Jn.12:26).

"But glory, honour, and peace, to every man that worketh good, to the Jew first, and also to the Gentile" (Ro.2:10).

"The Spirit itself beareth witness with our spirit, that we are the children of God: and if children, then heirs; heirs of God, and joint-heirs with Christ; if so be that we suffer with him, that we may be also glorified together" (Ro.8:16-17).

"For our conversation [citizenship] is in heaven; from whence also we look for the Saviour, the Lord Jesus Christ: who shall change our vile body, that it may be fashioned like unto his glorious body, according to the working whereby he is able even to subdue all things unto himself" (Ph.3:20-21).

"When Christ, who is our life, shall appear, then shall ye also appear with him in glory" (Col.3:4).

"If we suffer, we shall also reign with him: if we deny him, he also will deny us" (2 Tim.2:12).

"For ye had compassion of me in my bonds, and took joyfully the spoiling of your goods, knowing in yourselves that ye have in heaven a better and an enduring substance" (Heb.10:34).

"Esteeming the reproach of Christ greater riches than the treasures in Egypt: for he had respect unto the recompence of the reward" (Heb.11:26).

"And when the chief Shepherd shall appear, ye shall receive a crown of glory that fadeth not away" (1 Pt.5:4).

"Behold, I come quickly; hold that fast which thou hast, that no man take thy crown" (Rev.3:11).

**4** (9:49-50) **Tolerance**: the right to greatness is not an exclusive right. John knew that the apostles had done just what Christ had demonstrated they should not do. They had just failed to receive a man; in fact, they had rejected the man. And to top it off, the man was ministering in the name of Christ. John wanted to find out if they were right in forbidding others to preach in Jesus' name. John felt there were bound to be limits to what Jesus was saying—certainly not everyone was to be received and welcomed and brought to Jesus—some people "followeth not with us." They were...

- different
- untrained
- uneducated
- immoral
- doctrinally unsound
- unruly
- unauthorized
- too far right
- too far left

What Jesus said is pointed and clear, yet it is difficult for some to accept.

⇒ "Forbid him not."
⇒ "He that is *not against* us is for us."

Note: Jesus said, "*against us.*" Jesus and His followers are one. The man who stands against us stands against Jesus, and he who stands against Jesus stands against us. A person's attitude and behavior are to be watched. The way he acts toward Christ and His followers determines whether we receive him or not. A person who is against Jesus and His followers is not to be received. The person who receives Jesus and His followers is to be received (cp. Lk.9:5; 10:10-11). (See outline and notes—Mk.9:38-41 for more discussion.)

"And into whatsoever city or town ye shall enter, enquire who in it is worthy; and there abide till ye go thence. And when ye come into an house, salute it. And if the house be worthy, let your peace come upon it: but if it be not worthy, let your peace return to you. And whosoever shall not receive you, nor hear your words, when ye depart out of that house or city, shake off the dust of your feet. Verily I say unto you, It shall be more tolerable for the land of Sodom and Gomorrha in the day of judgment, than for that city" (Mt.10:11-15).

"And other sheep I have, which are *not of this fold*: them also I must bring, and they shall hear my voice; and there shall be one fold, and one shepherd" (Jn.10:16).

"Some indeed preach Christ even of envy and strife; and some also of good will: the one preach Christ of contention, not sincerely, supposing to add affliction to my bonds: but the other of love, knowing that I am set for the defence of the gospel. What then? notwithstanding, every way, whether in pretence, or in truth, Christ is preached; and I therein do rejoice, yea, and will rejoice" (Ph.1:15-18).

"He that heareth you heareth me; and he that despiseth you despiseth me; and he that despiseth me despiseth him that sent me" (Lk.10:16).

"He that is not with me is against me: and he that gathereth not with me scattereth" (Lk.11:23).

"No servant can serve two masters: for either he will hate the one, and love the other; or else he will hold to the one, and despise the other. Ye cannot serve God and mammon" (Lk.16:13).

"But when ye sin so against the brethren, and wound their weak conscience, ye sin against Christ" (1 Cor.8:12).

| 1 His mission: To secure salvation<br>  a. By the ascension[DS1]<br>  b. By death: He set His face toward Jerusalem<br>2 His mission misunderstood<br>  a. He sent forerunners to prepare the way | V. THE SON OF MAN'S GREAT JOURNEY TO JERUSALEM (STAGE I): HIS MISSION AND PUBLIC CHALLENGE, 9:51-13:21<br><br>A. The Son of Man's Mission: Jesus' Mission Misunderstood, 9:51-56<br><br>51 And it came to pass, when the time was come that he should be received up, he stedfastly set his face to go to Jerusalem,<br>52 And sent messengers before his face: and they went, and entered into a village of the Samaritans, to make ready | for him.<br>53 And they did not receive him, because his face was as though he would go to Jerusalem.<br>54 And when his disciples James and John saw this, they said, Lord, wilt thou that we command fire to come down from heaven, and consume them, even as Elias did?<br>55 But he turned, and rebuked them, and said, Ye know not what manner of spirit ye are of.<br>56 For the Son of man is not come to destroy men's lives, but to save them. And they went to another village. | b. He was rejected by the Samaritans[DS2]<br><br>c. The disciples reacted against the Samaritans<br><br><br>3 His mission explained<br><br><br>a. He did not come to use His power to destroy men's lives<br>b. He came to use His power to save men |

# DIVISION V

## THE SON OF MAN'S GREAT JOURNEY TO JERUSALEM (STAGE I): HIS MISSION AND PUBLIC CHALLENGE, 9:51-13:21

### A.    The Son of Man's Mission: Jesus' Mission Misunderstood, 9:51-56

(9:51-19:28) **DIVISION OVERVIEW: Jesus' Purpose**: this passage marks a significant turning point in Jesus' ministry. Chapters 9:51-19:28 have no parallel in the other Gospels. Most of the events are recorded by Luke alone. The thrust of the passage is that Jesus' face is set—it is fixed toward Jerusalem.

Luke divides this journey of Jesus into three stages. Each stage begins by strongly emphasizing Jesus' journey toward Jerusalem (Lk.9:51, 53; 13:22; 17:11). There are also several passages that hint or mention the journey (Lk.9:53, 57; 10:1, 38; 13:33; 14:25; 18:31; 19:11, 28).

(9:51-56) **Introduction**: Jesus turned and set His face toward Jerusalem and death. This was one of the turning points of His life. As He launched forth in this new direction, the first subject covered is His mission. The mission of the Son of Man is seen in clear terms—terms so clear that the follower of the Lord cannot miss the meaning.
1.    His mission: to secure salvation (v.51).
2.    His mission misunderstood (v.52-54).
3.    His mission explained (v.55-56).

**1** (9:51) **Jesus Christ, Mission**: Jesus' mission upon earth was to secure salvation. Jesus knew His mission; He knew why He had come to earth. He also knew that the time for Him to die for the salvation of men was at hand. Note the words, "when the time was come." He was fully aware that the time had come (Lk.9:22, 27, 31). Therefore, He turned around and "set His face to go to Jerusalem."

What is so significant about Jerusalem? Very simply, it was in Jerusalem that Jesus was to die for the salvation of men and be received up, that is, ascend into heaven. When Jesus "set His face to go to Jerusalem," Jerusalem symbolized the death, resurrection, and ascension of our Lord. It was in Jerusalem that He secured salvation for man through His death, resurrection, and ascension.
1.    Jesus Christ secured salvation by His ascension (see DEEPER STUDY # 1, *Ascension*—Lk.9:51 for discussion).
2.    Jesus Christ secured salvation by His death.

       **"But God commendeth his love toward us, in that, while we were yet sinners, Christ died for us" (Ro.5:8).**
       **"Christ hath redeemed us from the curse of the law, being made a curse for us: for it is written, Cursed is every one that hangeth on a tree" (Gal.3:13).**
       **"[God] who hath delivered us from the power of darkness, and hath translated us into the kingdom of his dear Son: in whom we have redemption through his blood, even the forgiveness of sins" (Col.1:13-14).**
       **"For this is good and acceptable in the sight of God our Saviour; who will have all men to be saved, and to come unto the knowledge of the truth. For there is one God, and one mediator between God and men, the man Christ Jesus; who gave himself a ransom for all, to be testified in due time" (1 Tim.2:3-6).**
       **"But we see Jesus, who was made a little lower than the angels for the suffering of death, crowned with glory and honour; that he by the grace of God should taste death for every man" (Heb.2:9).**

"So Christ was once offered to bear the sins of many; and unto them that look for him shall he appear the second time without sin unto salvation" (Heb.9:28).

"Who his own self bare our sins in his own body on the tree, that we, being dead to sins, should live unto righteousness: by whose stripes ye were healed" (1 Pt.2:24; cp. 1 Pt.3:18).

"But he was wounded for our transgressions, he was bruised for our iniquities: the chastisement of our peace was upon him; and with his stripes we are healed" (Is.53:5).

---

**DEEPER STUDY # 1**

(9:51) **Jesus Christ, Ascension**: the words "received up" (analempseos) mean taken up. They refer to the ascension of Christ (cp. analambano, Acts 1:2, 11, 22; 1 Tim.3:16). Salvation was to be secured by the ascension of Christ. How? The Ascended Lord means at least four things.

1. It means *the Risen Lord*. The ascension means that Christ arose from the dead. If He had remained in the grave, He would still be there in the form of dust. He could not have ascended. If He were to be "received up," He had to be *raised up—quickened—made alive—taken up*. No one can be *taken up* without first being raised up. Therefore, to speak of the ascension is to mean that Christ is risen. Death is conquered; man can now be saved from death.

"Now if Christ be preached that he rose from the dead, how say some among you that there is no resurrection of the dead? But if there be no resurrection of the dead, then is Christ not risen: and if Christ be not risen, then is our preaching vain, and your faith is also vain. Yea, and we are found false witnesses of God; because we have testified of God that he raised up Christ: whom he raised not up, if so be that the dead rise not. For if the dead rise not, then is not Christ raised: and if Christ be not raised, your faith is vain; ye are yet in your sins. Then they also which are fallen asleep in Christ are perished. If in this life only we have hope in Christ, we are of all men most miserable. But now is Christ risen from the dead, and become the firstfruits of them that slept. For since by man came death, by man came also the resurrection of the dead. For as in Adam all die, even so in Christ shall all be made alive. But every man in his own order: Christ the firstfruits; afterward they that are Christ's at his coming. Then cometh the end, when he shall have delivered up the kingdom to God, even the Father; when he shall have put down all rule and all authority and power" (1 Cor.15:12-24).

"[Christ] made himself of no reputation, and took upon him the form of a servant, and was made in the likeness of men: and being found in fashion as a man, he humbled himself, and became obedient unto death, even the death of the cross. Wherefore God also hath highly exalted him, and given him a name which is above every name" (Ph.2:7-9).

"How it was not written for his sake alone, that it [righteousness] was imputed to him; but for us also, to whom it [righteousness] shall be imputed, if we believe on him that raised up Jesus our Lord from the dead; who was delivered for our offences, and was raised again for our justification" (Ro.4:23-25).

2. It means *the Advocate or Representative Lord*. On earth Christ lived a perfect life; He was without sin (2 Cor.5:21; Heb.4:15; 1 Pt.1:19; 2:22; Jn.8:46). He was "obedient unto death, even the death of the cross. Wherefore God also hath highly exalted Him" (Ph.2:8-9). He is "sitting on the right hand of God (Col.3:1). He is "Jesus Christ the righteous"; therefore, He is our "advocate with the Father" (1 Jn.2:1). He is able to represent us before God because He has lived upon earth and secured a perfect righteousness. He is the Ideal Man (see note—Mt.5:17-18), our advocate, the One who is qualified to plead our case before God and see to it that we are saved.

"Wherefore he is able also to save them to the uttermost that come unto God by him, seeing he ever liveth to make intercession for them" (Heb.7:25).

3. It means *the Priestly or Intercessory Lord*. Every man suffers while on earth: suffers pain, trial, need, want, temptation, loss, illness, and eventually death. We are incapable of even knowing how to pray as we ought in order to secure the help we need. But Christ knows and understands. He has been to earth and suffered just as we suffer. Therefore, He knows how to intercede for us and how to deliver us.

"Seeing then that we have a great high priest, that is passed into the heavens, Jesus the Son of God, let us hold fast our profession. For we have not an high priest which cannot be touched with the feeling of our infirmities; but was in all points tempted like as we are, yet without sin. Let us therefore come boldly unto the throne of grace, that we may obtain mercy, and find grace to help in time of need" (Heb.4:14-16).

"For verily he took not on him the nature of angels; but he took on him the seed of Abraham. Wherefore in all things it behoved him to be made like unto his brethren, that he might be a merciful and faithful high priest in things pertaining to God, to make reconciliation for the sins of the people. For in that he himself hath suffered being tempted, he is able to succour them that are tempted" (Heb.2:16-18).

"Who shall lay any thing to the charge of God's elect? It is God that justifieth. Who is he that condemneth? It is Christ that died, yea rather, that is risen again, who is even at the right hand of God, who also maketh intercession for us" (Ro.8:33-34).

4.    It means *the exalted Lord*. Christ has ascended to be exalted, to rule and reign over the universe for God. There is a great day of judgment coming upon the world, a day when all men shall bow the knee and acknowledge that Jesus is Lord, the Son of the living God.

> "Wherefore God also hath highly exalted him, and given him a name which is above every name: that at the name of Jesus every knee should bow, of things in heaven, and things in earth, and things under the earth: and that every tongue should confess that Jesus Christ is Lord, to the glory of God the Father" (Ph.2:9-11).
> "And what is the exceeding greatness of his power to us-ward who believe, according to the working of his mighty power, which he wrought in Christ, when he raised him from the dead, and set him at his own right hand in the heavenly places, far above all principality, and power, and might, and dominion, and every name that is named, not only in this world, but also in that which is to come: and hath put all things under his feet, and gave him to be the head over all things to the church, which is his body, the fulness of him that filleth all in all" (Eph.1:19-23).
> "Then cometh the end, when he shall have delivered up the kingdom to God, even the Father; when he shall have put down all rule and all authority and power. For he must reign, till he hath put all enemies under his feet. The last enemy that shall be destroyed is death" (1 Cor.15:24-26).

**2**    (9:52-54) **Jesus Christ, Mission**: Jesus' mission upon earth was misunderstood. Note three things of vital importance.

1.    Jesus sent some disciples to run ahead of Him, to prepare the way for His coming. Apparently, this was the *method* Christ used to let the people of an area know He was soon to enter their city. Those who had interest could thereby be prepared for His coming.
2.    Jesus was rejected by the Samaritans. Why? Because He was heading for Jerusalem, going to a place they despised. The Jews were unacceptable to them; therefore, they would have nothing to do with Jesus if He were going to minister in Jerusalem. Jerusalem had its own worship and priests, and the Samaritans had theirs. If Jesus would be theirs alone, they would gladly receive Him; if not, then He was not welcomed in their circles. (See Deeper Study # 2, *Samaritans*—Lk.10:33 for more detailed discussion.)
3.    James and John were upset, fiery and angry over such rejection. They asked Jesus if they should destroy the village by calling fire from heaven to consume the people. Note two crucial points.
   a.    The faith of James and John in Jesus was strong. They believed without question that Jesus had the authority to control the power of heaven, either through Himself or through them.
   b.    The wrong understanding of Jesus' mission that James and John had was also strong. They thought in terms of a Messianic Ruler on earth, subjecting men and forcing them to worship and serve God. They saw the Messiah's judging those who rejected Him.
      Note that James and John were guilty of the very some error that the Samaritans had just committed. They were full of bitterness, wrath, and vengeance, reacting against the Samaritans just as the Samaritans had reacted against the Jews and Jesus. They wanted to destroy the Samaritans because the Samaritans were not willing to worship (Jesus) and live as James and John wished.

> "For God sent not his son into the world to condemn the world; but that the world through him might be saved" (Jn.3:17).
> "And if any man hear my words, and believe not, I judge him not: for I came not to judge the world, but to save the world" (Jn.12:47).

**DEEPER STUDY # 2**
(9:53) **Samaritans**: see Deeper Study # 2—Lk.10:33.

**3**    (9:55-56) **Jesus Christ, Mission**: Jesus' mission explained. Jesus' mission was not to destroy life, but to save it. This is repeated time and time again.

> "For the Son of man is come to seek and to save that which was lost" (Lk.19:10).
> "Verily, verily, I say unto you, He that heareth my word, and believeth on him that sent me, hath everlasting life, and shall not come into condemnation; but is passed from death unto life" (Jn.5:24).
> "The thief cometh not, but for to steal, and to kill, and to destroy: I am come that they might have life, and that they might have it more abundantly" (Jn.10:10).
> "There is therefore now no condemnation to them which are in Christ Jesus, who walk not after the flesh, but after the Spirit" (Ro.8:1).
> "Who is he that condemneth? It is Christ that died, yea rather, that is risen again, who is even at the right hand of God, who also maketh intercession for us" (Ro.8:34).
> "This is a faithful saying, and worthy of all acceptation, that Christ Jesus came into the world to save sinners; of whom I am chief" (1 Tim.1:15).

**Thought 1.** Note several facts.
1) Christ proclaimed that today is the day of salvation, and He proclaimed it loudly and clearly.

> "For he saith, I have heard thee in a time accepted, and in the day of salvation have I succoured thee: behold, now is the accepted time; behold, now is the day of salvation" (2 Cor.6:2).
> "Behold, I stand at the door, and knock: if any man hear my voice, and open the door, I will come into him, and will sup with him, and he with me" (Rev.3:20).
> "For the Son of man is come to seek and to save that which was lost" (Lk.19:10).

2) Scripture pronounces that judgment is *to come*. There is a day "appointed unto men once to die, after this the judgment."

> "And as it is appointed unto men once to die, but after this the judgment" (Heb.9:27)

| 1 A person must count the cost<br>a. The man offered himself<br><br>b. Jesus offered no luxury, no materialism—only self-denial & sacrifice[DS1]<br><br>2 A person must follow immediately | B. The Great Cost of Discipleship, 9:57-62<br>(Mt.8:18-22)<br><br>57 And it came to pass, that, as they went in the way, a certain man said unto him, Lord, I will follow thee whithersoever thou goest.<br>58 And Jesus said unto him, Foxes have holes, and birds of the air have nests; but the Son of man hath not where to lay his head.<br>59 And he said unto another, Follow me. But he | said, Lord, suffer me first to go and bury my father.<br>60 Jesus said unto him, Let the dead bury their dead: but go thou and preach the kingdom of God.<br>61 And another also said, Lord, I will follow thee; but let me first go bid them farewell, which are at home at my house.<br>62 And Jesus said unto him, No man, having put his hand to the plough, and looking back, is fit for the kingdom of God. | a. Jesus invited the man<br>b. The man had divided attention<br>c. Jesus' demand<br>　1) A sense of urgency<br>　2) Go now & preach<br><br>3 A person must not look back<br>a. Another man offered himself<br>b. The man's double allegiance<br>c. Jesus' judgment: Looking back disqualifies a person |

# DIVISION V

## THE SON OF MAN'S GREAT JOURNEY TO JERUSALEM (STAGE I): HIS MISSION AND PUBLIC CHALLENGE, 9:51-13:21

### B.　The Great Cost of Discipleship, 9:57-62

(9:57-62) **Introduction**: some people desire to follow Christ; therefore, they attach themselves to Him and join the church. Yet they come ever so short and miss eternal life. Why? Because they never knew the price of discipleship. They were to pay a great price, but they knew nothing about it or else were unwilling to pay the price. True discipleship costs everything a person is and has.

1. One must count the cost (v.57-58).
2. One must follow immediately (v.59-60).
3. One must not look back (v.61-62).

1 (9:57-58) **Discipleship**: one must count the cost. A man offered to become a follower of Jesus, and he made an unusual promise: he would follow Jesus wherever He led. Why? For the same reasons so many are attracted to the Lord.

⇒ He enjoyed the presence of the Lord and His followers.
⇒ He was motivated by the Lord's wisdom and teaching.
⇒ He appreciated the good the Lord did.

Jesus' reply was to the point. The man had to count the cost, for Jesus offered no luxury and no material comfort—only self-denial. The man had to deny himself and sacrifice all he was and had. Note several facts. (See note—Mt.8:19-20 for more discussion.)

1. Jesus Himself was the prime example. He denied Himself completely. He sacrificed and gave all, both Himself and all He had. He did not even have a place to lay His head. The animals of the world did; the birds had their nests and the foxes had their holes, but Jesus had no place. He gave all to meet the needs of a dying and desperate world.

2. Jesus told the man to count the cost. A profession was not enough. Being *willing to follow* was not enough. The man must deny himself completely, sacrificing and giving all he was and had to meet the needs of a lost and desperate world (see note and DEEPER STUDY # 1—Lk.9:23 for discussion).

3. Jesus called Himself the Son of Man (see DEEPER STUDY # 1—Lk.9:58 for discussion). This pictures exactly who He was. The man was to follow Jesus, accepting Him as the Son of Man. He was to accept Jesus as the Ideal Servant of man, the Ideal Man who loved and cared and ministered and felt for all, and who did it perfectly.

**Thought 1.** Some persons are willing and determined to go to the ends of the earth. However Jesus said that *He—the Son of Man, His pattern of life—*must be accepted.

Many are committed, but their commitments are *self-commitments*, not Christ-centered commitments. We must realize that self-commitments can arise from (1) strong wills, (2) strong determinations, and (3) strong discipline. And the person can follow through in a great way. But self-commitment is not enough for Christ. There has to be a total commitment to the Son of Man, abandoning all of self and all of the world.

"And he said to them all, If any man will come after me, let him deny himself, and take up his cross daily, and follow me" (Lk.9:23).

"For even hereunto were ye called: because Christ also suffered for us, leaving us an example, that ye should follow his steps" (1 Pt.2:21).

"Let this mind be in you, which was also in Christ Jesus: who, being in the form of God, thought it not robbery to be equal with God: but made himself of no reputation, and took upon him the form of a servant, and was made in the likeness of men: and being found in fashion as a man, he humbled himself, and became obedient unto death, even the death of the cross" (Ph.2:5-8).

"For we which live are alway delivered unto death for Jesus' sake, that the life also of Jesus might be made manifest in our mortal flesh" (2 Cor.4:11).

"For ye know the grace of our Lord Jesus Christ, that, though he was rich, yet for your sakes he became poor, that ye through his poverty might be rich" (2 Cor.8:9).

---

**DEEPER STUDY # 1**

(9:58) **Son of Man**: Jesus was not only what an ordinary man is, a son of man; but Jesus was what every man ought to be, the Son of Man Himself. As such, He has become the *Ideal Man*, the *Representative Man*, the *Perfect Man*, the *Pattern*, the *Embodiment* of everything a man ought to be (see DEEPER STUDY # 3—Mt.1:16). Jesus Christ is the *perfect picture* of a man. Everything God wants a man to be is seen perfectly in Jesus Christ (cp. Jn.1:14; Col.2:9-10; Heb.1:3). The title also means the *Ideal Servant* of man. It stresses His sympathy for the poor, the brokenhearted, the captives, the blind, the bruised, the outcasts, the bereaved (cp. Lk.4:18). Jesus is the pattern, the model, the perfect example of concern and caring. He served just like every man ought to serve others.

Jesus called Himself "the Son of Man" about eighty times. It was His favorite term. The title *Son of Man* is probably based upon the Son of Man of Daniel 7:13-14. There is a picture of Jesus as the heavenly Son of Man contrasted with Adam as the earthly Man in 1 Cor.15:45-47. Each served as a Representative Man in God's plan for world history.

---

**2** (9:59-60) **Discipleship—Decision—Call**: one must follow Jesus immediately. Note three things.

1. It was Jesus who invited the man to follow Him. There was something very special within the man that caught Jesus' eye, and Jesus was moved to call him. In fact, the *specialness* within the man was of such quality that Jesus stayed after the man even after the man hesitated. The man was of too much value to let go, so Jesus pleaded and argued and even commanded, "Go thou and preach."

> **Thought 1.** Note two important points.
> 1) Every person is of extreme value to Jesus. Therefore, the Spirit stays after a man as long as the man allows Him, despite man's selfishness.
> 2) Every person who is called by Christ to "preach" must take heed and respond immediately. The Lord's call is to be the primary thrust of a person's life.

2. The man had divided attention. The call of God came to this man, yet he hesitated (see note—Mt.8:21). Note two facts.
   a. The man's hesitation was legitimate. Caring for parents is essential. His father was either already dead or on the verge of death. He was legitimately needed at home.
   b. The man's problem was *divided attention*. When he felt God's call, he looked at his situation and did not yield immediately. What happened so often happens. His circumstances and problems overwhelmed him, so he wanted to wait and handle them. As soon as the problems were handled, he would leave and follow Jesus.

> "If any man come to me, and hate not his father, and mother, and wife, and children, and brethren, and sisters, yea, and his own life also, he cannot be my disciple. And whosoever doth not bear his cross, and come after me, cannot be my disciple" (Lk.14:26-27).
>
> "Then Peter began to say unto him, Lo, we have left all, and have followed thee. And Jesus answered and said, Verily I say unto you, There is no man that hath left house, or brethren, or sisters, or father, or mother, or wife, or children, or lands, for my sake, and the gospel's, but he shall receive an hundredfold now in this time, houses, and brethren, and sisters, and mothers, and children, and lands, with persecutions; and in the world to come eternal life" (Mk.10:28-30).
>
> "And the things that thou hast heard of me among many witnesses, the same commit thou to faithful men, who shall be able to teach others also. Thou therefore endure hardness, as a good soldier of Jesus Christ. No man that warreth entangleth himself with the affairs of this life; that he may please him who hath chosen him to be a soldier" (2 Tim.2:2-4).
>
> "And the servant of the Lord must not strive; but be gentle unto all men, apt to teach, patient, in meekness instructing those that oppose themselves; if God peradventure will give them repentance to the acknowledging of the truth; and that they may recover themselves out of the snare of the devil, who are taken captive by him at his will" (2 Tim.2:24-26).
>
> "But watch thou in all things, endure afflictions, do the work of an evangelist, make full proof of thy ministry" (2 Tim.4:5).

3. Jesus demanded that the man act now and not wait. Jesus saw through the man's partial commitment. He saw through the man's lack of trust in God. Jesus expects us to take care of our parents (1 Tim.5:3-8), but He demands first loyalty and immediate response. He demands two things in particular.
   a. A sense of urgency. Imagine! Jesus refused to give the man time to bury the dead. Why? Because the need is so great, and men are dying every hour without Christ. Nothing can be done for the dead (his father), but the living can be reached and snatched out of the grip of death and saved unto eternal life. If we hesitate, for whatever reason, some whom we might have reached will die and be doomed. The point is forceful: the hour is urgent.

"And Jesus said unto them, Come ye after me, and I will make you to become fishers of men. And straightway [immediately] they forsook their nets, and followed him" (Mk.1:17-18).

"Jesus saith unto them, My meat is to do the will of him that sent me, and to finish his work" (Jn.4:34).

"I must work the works of him that sent me, while it is day: the night cometh, when no man can work" (Jn.9:4)

"And that, knowing the time, that now it is high time to awake out of sleep: for now is our salvation nearer than when we believed. The night is far spent, the day is at hand" (Ro.13:11-12).

"But this I say, brethren, the time is short" (1 Cor.7:29).

"Redeeming the time, because the days are evil" (Eph.5:16).

"Walk in wisdom toward them that are without, redeeming the time" (Col.4:5).

"Stir up the gift of God which is in thee" (2 Tim.1:6).

"Yea, I think it meet, as long as I am in this tabernacle, to stir you up by putting you in remembrance" (2 Pt.1:13).

"As many as I love, I rebuke and chasten: be zealous therefore, and repent" (Rev.3:19).

"So teach us to number our days, that we may apply our hearts unto wisdom" (Ps.90:12).

"Remember now thy Creator in the days of thy youth, while the evil days come not, nor the years draw nigh, when thou shalt say, I have no pleasure in them" (Eccl.12:1).

b.  Go and preach the Kingdom of God. Note that Christ tells His messengers what to preach, yet how little the real message of God's kingdom is preached (see note—Mt.19:23-24).

"For we cannot but speak the things which we have seen and heard" (Acts 4:20).

"And when Silas and Timotheus were come from Macedonia, Paul was pressed in the spirit, and testified to the Jews that Jesus was Christ" (Acts 18:5).

"For though I preach the gospel, I have nothing to glory of: for necessity is laid upon me; yea, woe is unto me, if I preach not the gospel!" (1 Cor.9:16).

"Preach the word; be instant in season, out of season; reprove, rebuke, exhort with all longsuffering and doctrine" (2 Tim.4:2).

"Then I said, I will not make mention of him, nor speak any more in his name. But his word was in mine heart as a burning fire shut up in my bones, and I was weary with forbearing, and I could not stay" (Jer.20:9).

"The lion hath roared, who will not fear? the Lord GOD hath spoken, who can but prophesy?" (Amos 3:8).

**3**  (9:61-62) **Decision—Discipleship**: one must not look back. Note three things.

1.  This man offered himself to Jesus. He was *willing* to follow Jesus. Something about the Lord touched his heart or else the Lord's teaching and ministry appealed to him. He saw the enormous benefit to men and to society as Christ ministered to the needs of men. In either case, he made a decision to follow Jesus. He was *willing*.

2.  The man had a *double allegiance*. Note the words "but" and "first." The man had thought through his decision and concluded that he was willing to follow Christ, *but* something else needed to be handled *first*: a family affair, a business affair, an employment affair, a financial affair—some other concern was put first (as is the case with so many).

Something else could have been concerning the man. He may have wanted his family's counsel and advice, to see how they felt about his decision. Perhaps he felt their approval was needed. Then again, he could have been putting his love for family before his love for Christ. Perhaps he was attached to his family more than he was attached to Christ. Family should be our *first* attachment *after* our attachment to Christ. Christ is to be first in our lives.

"But seek ye first the kingdom of God, and his righteousness; and all these things shall be added unto you" (Mt.6:33).

"He that is not with me is against me; and he that gathereth not with me scattereth abroad" (Mt.12:30).

"Then shall the King say unto them on his right hand, Come, ye blessed of my Father, inherit the kingdom prepared for you from the foundation of the world: for I was an hungred, and ye gave me meat: I was thirsty, and ye gave me drink: I was a stranger, and ye took me in: naked, and ye clothed me: I was sick, and ye visited me: I was in prison, and ye came unto me" (Mt.25:34-36).

"Which now of these three, thinkest thou, was neighbour unto him that fell among the thieves? And he said, He that showed mercy on him. Then said Jesus unto him, Go, and do thou likewise" (Lk.10:36-37).

"So likewise, whosoever he be of you that forsaketh not all that he hath, he cannot be my disciple" (Lk.14:33).

"No servant can serve two masters: for either he will hate the one, and love the other; or else he will hold to the one, and despise the other. Ye cannot serve God and mammon" (Lk.16:13).

> "So when they had dined, Jesus saith to Simon Peter, Simon, son of Jonas, lovest thou me more than these? He saith unto him, Yea, Lord; thou knowest that I love thee. He saith unto him, Feed my lambs. He saith to him again the second time, Simon, son of Jonas, lovest thou me? He saith unto him, Yea, Lord; thou knowest that I love thee. He saith unto him, Feed my sheep. He saith unto him the third time, Simon, son of Jonas, lovest thou me? Peter was grieved because he said unto him the third time, Lovest thou me? And he said unto him, Lord, thou knowest all things; thou knowest that I love thee. Jesus saith unto him, Feed my sheep" (Jn.21:15-17).

> "Yea doubtless, and I count all things but loss for the excellency of the knowledge of Christ Jesus my Lord: for whom I have suffered the loss of all things, and do count them but dung, that I may win Christ" (Ph.3:8).

> "Feed the flock of God which is among you, taking the oversight thereof, not by constraint, but willingly; not for filthy lucre, but of a ready mind" (1 Pt.5:2).

> "And now, Israel, what doth the LORD thy God require of thee, but to fear the LORD thy God, to walk in all his ways, and to love him, and to serve the LORD thy God with all thy heart and with all thy soul" (Dt.10:12).

> "Now therefore fear the LORD, and serve him in sincerity and in truth" (Josh.24:14).

> "And Samuel said, Hath the LORD as great delight in burnt offerings and sacrifices, as in obeying the voice of the LORD? and to hearken than the fat of rams" (1 Sam.15:22).

> "And Elijah came unto all the people, and said, How long halt ye between two opinions? if the LORD be God, follow him: but if Baal, then follow him" (1 Ki.18:21).

> "And thou, Solomon my son, know thou the God of thy father, and serve him with a perfect heart and with a willing mind: for the LORD searcheth all hearts, and understandeth all the imaginations of the thoughts: if thou seek him, he will be found of thee; but if thou forsake him, he will cast thee off for ever" (1 Chron.28:9).

> "Serve the LORD with fear, and rejoice with trembling" (Ps.2:11).

> "Stand in the gate of the LORD'S house, and proclaim there this word, and say, Hear the word of the LORD, all ye of Judah, that enter in at these gates to worship the LORD" (Jer.7:2).

> "Son of man, I have made thee a watchman unto the house of Israel: therefore hear the word at my mouth, and give them warning from me" (Ezk.3:17).

3.   Jesus' judgment was descriptively stated—stated in such a way that once heard or read, it would be difficult to forget: "No man, having put his hand to the plough, and looking back, is fit for the kingdom of God." The man got the point, and he probably never forgot it. It more than likely pricked his conscience and disturbed him often as the saying flashed across his mind. He had willed to follow Christ, but he "had looked back"; therefore, he was not fit for the Kingdom of God.

The idea is this. A man who begins to plough and then looks back...

* ploughs a crooked row. No row (person) is ever straight, not like it should be. (Each row or person receives only partial teaching.)
* ploughs an inconsistent field. The field under his care is never matured; it never receives consistent work.
* ploughs in a spirit lacking total commitment. He may turn away at any time, leaving a job unfinished.
* ploughs but allows distractions and disruptions which affect the crops (the plants are not cared for).

> "Not every one that saith unto me, Lord, Lord, shall enter into the kingdom of heaven; but he that doeth the will of my Father which is in heaven" (Mt.7:21).

> "And every one that heareth these sayings of mine, and doeth them not, shall be likened unto a foolish man, which built his house upon the sand: and the rain descended, and the floods came, and the winds blew, and beat upon that house; and it fell: and great was the fall of it" (Mt.7:26-27).

> "Jesus said unto him, If thou wilt be perfect, go and sell that thou hast, and give to the poor, and thou shalt have treasure in heaven: and come and follow me. But when the young man heard that saying, he went away sorrowful: for he had great possessions. Then said Jesus unto his disciples, Verily I say unto you, That a rich man shall hardly enter into the kingdom of heaven" (Mt.19:21-23).

> "And that servant, which knew his lord's will, and prepared not himself, neither did according to his will, shall be beaten with many stripes" (Lk.12:47).

> "It is the spirit that quickeneth; the flesh profiteth nothing: the words that I speak unto you, they are spirit, and they are life. But there are some of you that believe not. For Jesus knew from the beginning who they were that believed not, and who should betray him. And he said, Therefore said I unto you, that no man can come unto me, except it were given unto him of my Father. From that time many of his disciples went back, and walked no more with him. Then said Jesus unto the twelve, Will ye also go away? Then Simon Peter answered him, Lord, to whom shall we go? thou hast the words of eternal life. And we believe and are sure that thou art that Christ, the Son of the living God. Jesus answered them, have not I chosen you twelve, and one of you is a devil?" (Jn.6:63-70).

> "So then every one of us shall give account of himself to God" (Ro.14:12).

> "I marvel that ye are so soon removed from him that called you into the grace of Christ unto another gospel: which is not another; but there be some that trouble you, and would pervert the gospel of Christ" (Gal.1:6-7).

"But now, after that ye have known God, or rather are known of God, how return ye again to the weak and beggarly elements, whereunto ye desire again to be in bondage?" (Gal.4:9).

"Now the just shall live by faith: but if any man draw back, my soul shall have no pleasure in him" (Heb.10:38).

"For consider him that endured such contradiction of sinners against himself, lest ye be wearied and faint in your minds" (Heb.12:3).

"A double minded man is unstable in all his ways" (Jas.1:8).

"Draw nigh to God, and he will draw nigh to you. Cleanse your hands, ye sinners; and purify your hearts, ye double minded" (Jas.4:8).

"Therefore to him that knoweth to do good, and doeth it not, to him it is sin" (Jas.4:17).

"For if after they have escaped the pollutions of the world through the knowledge of the Lord and Saviour Jesus Christ, they are again entangled therein, and overcome, the latter end is worse with them than the beginning" (2 Pt.2:20).

"Ye therefore, beloved, seeing ye know these things before, beware lest ye also, being led away with the error of the wicked, fall from your own stedfastness" (2 Pt.3:17).

"They went out from us, but they were not of us; for if they had been of us, they would no doubt have continued with us: but they went out, that they might be made manifest that they were not all of us" (1 Jn.2:19).

"Nevertheless I have somewhat against thee, because thou hast left thy first love. Remember therefore from whence thou art fallen, and repent, and do the first works; or else I will come unto thee quickly, and will remove thy candlestick out of his place, except thou repent" (Rev.2:4-5).

"Cursed be he that doeth the work of the LORD deceitfully, and cursed be he that keepeth back his sword from blood" (Jer.48:10).

**CHAPTER 10**

**C. The Seventy Sent Forth: Great Purpose, 10:1-16**
(cp. Mt.10)

1 **Jesus appointed seventy disciples to prepare the way for Him**
  a. Had many disciples
  b. Sent two by two
  c. Saw tremendous need
  d. Sent as forerunners

2 **First, pray for more laborers**

3 **Second, go into an antagonistic world**

4 **Third, trust God & sense the hour's urgency**

5 **Fourth, guard the message—do not force it upon people**

6 **Fifth, accept compensation, but do not seek luxury**

7 **Sixth, be accommodating & adaptable**
  a. Identify with people

After these things the Lord appointed other seventy also, and sent them two and two before his face into every city and place, whither he himself would come. 2 Therefore said he unto them, The harvest truly is great, but the labourers are few: pray ye therefore the Lord of the harvest, that he would send forth labourers into his harvest. 3 Go your ways: behold, I send you forth as lambs among wolves. 4 Carry neither purse, nor scrip, nor shoes: and salute no man by the way. 5 And into whatsoever house ye enter, first say, Peace be to this house. 6 And if the son of peace be there, your peace shall rest upon it: if not, it shall turn to you again. 7 And in the same house remain, eating and drinking such things as they give: for the labourer is worthy of his hire. Go not from house to house. 8 And into whatsoever city ye enter, and they receive you, eat such things as are set before you:

9 And heal the sick that are therein, and say unto them, The kingdom of God is come nigh unto you. 10 But into whatsoever city ye enter, and they receive you not, go your ways out into the streets of the same, and say, 11 Even the very dust of your city, which cleaveth on us, we do wipe off against you: notwithstanding be ye sure of this, that the kingdom of God is come nigh unto you. 12 But I say unto you, that it shall be more tolerable in that day for Sodom, than for that city. 13 Woe unto thee, Chorazin! woe unto thee, Bethsaida! for if the mighty works had been done in Tyre and Sidon, which have been done in you, they had a great while ago repented, sitting in sackcloth and ashes. 14 But it shall be more tolerable for Tyre and Sidon at the judgment, than for you. 15 And thou, Capernaum, which art exalted to heaven, shalt be thrust down to hell. 16 He that heareth you heareth me; and he that despiseth you despiseth me; and he that despiseth me despiseth him that sent me.

  b. Minister to people
  c. Proclaim the Kingdom of God

8 **Seventh, walk away from rejecters**
  a. Any city & people who reject
    1) Symbolize God's rejection by wiping off the very dust of the city
    2) Reason: Kingdom of Heaven came near, but they rejected it
    3) Judgment: Shall be greater than Sodom's
  b. Any who *only profess* to be God's people[DS1]
    1) Illust. by two Jewish cities
    2) The reason: The works of Christ were seen, yet He was rejected
    3) The judgment: To be more terrible
  c. Any who have a constant witness but reject: To receive the greatest judgment—hell

9 **Eighth, know that the Christian laborer represents the Lord**

# DIVISION V

## THE SON OF MAN'S GREAT JOURNEY TO JERUSALEM (STAGE I): HIS MISSION AND PUBLIC CHALLENGE, 9:51-13:21

**C.    The Seventy Sent Forth: Great Purpose, 10:1-16**

(10:1-16) **Introduction**: this passage tells the Christian laborer how he is to labor and tells the hearer how he is to treat the laborer of God.

1. Jesus appointed seventy disciples to prepare the way for Him (v.1).
2. First, pray for more laborers (v.2).
3. Second, go into an antagonistic world (v.3).
4. Third, trust God and sense the hour's urgency (v.4).
5. Fourth, guard the message—do not force it upon people (v.5-6).
6. Fifth, accept compensation, but do not seek luxury (v.7).
7. Sixth, be accommodating and adaptable (v.8-9).
8. Seventh, walk away from rejecters (v.10-15).
9. Eighth, know that the Christian laborer represents the Lord (v.16).

**1** (10:1) **Apostles—Disciples—Jesus Christ, Followers—Witnessing**: Jesus appointed seventy disciples to prepare the way for Him. The number seventy is disputed, for some very good manuscripts say seventy-two were appointed. No matter which number is adopted, the number is held to be symbolic just as the appointment of twelve apostles is said to be symbolic. The twelve apostles are said to symbolize…

- the twelve patriarchs.
- the twelve tribes of Israel.
- the twelve leaders of the tribes.

The seventy are said to symbolize...

- the nations of the world (cp. Gen.10 where seventy names are listed; seventy-two in the Septuagint Greek Version of the Old Testament). The point being made in the symbolism is that the gospel is to go into all the world.
- the seventy elders who saw the glory of God (Ex.24:1, 9).
- the seventy elders of Israel (Num.11:16f).
- the seventy palm trees at Elim (Ex.15:27). (Note there were also twelve wells of water at Elim said to represent the twelve apostles.)
- the great Sanhedrin, the ruling body of the Jews, which had seventy members.

Whatever the case may be, the verse does point out four significant things.

1. Jesus had many disciples, many more than just the twelve often pictured. There were at least seventy disciples who followed Jesus so closely that He could send them out as witnesses for Him. Peter spoke of the witnesses as "these men which have companied with us all the time that the Lord Jesus went in and out among us" (Acts 1:21; cp.1:15).
2. Jesus sent them out two by two for mutual encouragement and help.
3. Jesus saw a tremendous need, a need so great that a great corps of witnesses was needed.
4. Jesus sent the seventy forth as forerunners. They were to prepare the people for His coming (cp. Tit.2:12-13).

**Thought 1.** All four points are applicable to us. Think them through. How many of us follow Christ so closely that He can send us out as witnesses for Him?

**2** (10:2) **Prayer—World—Ministers—Vision—Laborers**: first, pray for more laborers (see outline and notes—Mt.9:37-38 for more discussion). This was the very first duty. There were not enough laborers because the need was so overwhelming. (We must always be praying diligently for laborers.) Jesus gave four reasons.

1. There was a great harvest of precious souls to be reached with the gospel. The number was staggering, and the vast majority were without Jesus, reeling to and fro under the weight of the problems of a sinful and dying world.

> "Say not ye, There are yet four months, and then cometh harvest? behold, I say unto you, Lift up your eyes, and look on the fields; for they are white already to harvest. And he that reapeth receiveth wages, and gathereth fruit unto life eternal: that both he that soweth and he that reapeth may rejoice together" (Jn.4:35-36).
> "And let us not be weary in well doing: for in due season we shall reap, if we faint not" (Gal.6:9).

2. The laborers were few, very few.
3. The need was urgent: the crop was ripe, ready for *harvest*. Some wanted the *gospel*, the answer to life. They were actually ready to be reaped, wanting purpose, meaning, and significance in their lives. They might not know what was causing the longing and aching within their hearts; they might not know how to identify it, but they were ready to listen and grab hold of the answer. And Jesus was the answer.
4. God was the One who had to send forth laborers. He was the Source of laborers, and prayer was the method He used to send them forth.

**Thought 1.** Note a crucial point. A generation's concern determines how well that generation gets along under God's care. A generation that longs for God—that seeks after God to send forth laborers—will have laborers and see a good deal of righteousness prevail during its life. A generation that ignores God finds immorality and ungodliness, injustice and evil getting worse and worse. The answer to a solid generation, to a moral and just generation is prayer—prayer for laborers to be sent forth to reap the precious harvest of souls. If voices are not proclaiming love and morality and justice, then sin and death will reign.

> "But when the fruit is brought forth, immediately he putteth in the sickle, because the harvest is come" (Mk.4:29).
> "They that sow in tears shall reap in joy. He that goeth forth and weepeth, bearing precious seed, shall doubtless come again with rejoicing, bringing his sheaves with him" (Ps.126:5-6).
> "Sow to yourselves in righteousness, reap in mercy; break up your fallow ground: for it is time to seek the LORD, till he come and rain righteousness upon you" (Hos.10:12).

**3** (10:3) **Persecution—Sheep—Wolves**: second, go into an antagonistic world (see note, pt.2—Mt.10:16 for more discussion). Note two points.

1. The threat or danger of persecution. Jesus said that some men would be as wolves...
   - protecting their territory, snarling and putting down the messenger of God, trying to scare him away from trying to tame the world.
   - growling and threatening the believer who opposes the way of the world.
   - hungry and ready to hunt down, attack and consume.
2. The spirit of the Christian laborer. He was to be as a sheep: meek, harmless, and non-combative.

> "Take heed therefore unto yourselves, and to all the flock, over the which the Holy Ghost hath made you overseers, to feed the church of God, which he hath purchased with his own blood. For I know this, that after my departing shall grievous wolves enter in among you, not sparing the flock. Also of your own selves shall men arise, speaking perverse things, to draw away disciples after them. Therefore watch, and remember" (Acts 20:28-31).
> "Remember the word that I said unto you, The servant is not greater than his lord. If they have persecuted me, they will also persecute you; if they have kept my saying, they will keep yours also" (Jn.15:20).

200

"These things have I spoken unto you, that ye should not be offended. They shall put you out of the synagogues: yea, the time cometh, that whosoever killeth you will think that he doeth God service. And these things will they do unto you, because they have not known the Father, nor me. But these things have I told you, that when the time shall come, ye may remember that I told you of them. And these things I said not unto you at the beginning, because I was with you" (Jn.16:1-4).

"For unto you it is given in the behalf of Christ, not only to believe on him, but also to suffer for his sake" (Ph.1:29).

"That no man should be moved by these afflictions: for yourselves know that we are appointed thereunto" (1 Th.3:3).

"Yea, and all that will live godly in Christ Jesus shall suffer persecution" (2 Tim.3:12).

"Beloved, think it not strange concerning the fiery trial which is to try you, as though some strange thing happened unto you: but rejoice, inasmuch as ye are partakers of Christ's sufferings; that, when his glory shall be revealed, ye may be glad also with exceeding joy. If ye be reproached for the name of Christ, happy are ye; for the spirit of glory and of God resteth upon you: on their part he is evil spoken of, but on your part he is glorified. But let none of you suffer as a murderer, or as a thief, or as an evildoer, or as a busybody in other men's matters. Yet if any man suffer as a Christian, let him not be ashamed; but let him glorify God on this behalf" (1 Pt.4:12-16).

"Not as Cain, who was of that wicked one, and slew his brother. And wherefore slew he him? Because his own works were evil, and his brother's righteous" (1 Jn.3:12).

"Fear none of those things which thou shalt suffer: behold, the devil shall cast some of you into prison, that ye may be tried; and ye shall have tribulation ten days: be thou faithful unto death, and I will give thee a crown of life" (Rev.2:10).

"But beware of men: for they will deliver you up to the councils, and they will scourge you in their synagogues" (Mt.10:17).

**4** (10:4) **Conversation—Trust—Necessities—Minister**: third, trust God and sense the hour's urgency. The charge was twofold.

1.    Trust God. They were not to carry a money-bag (purse, ballantion) or a traveller's bag (pera) or two pair of sandals. They were to trust God for provisions, not worrying about money for food, housing, or clothing (Mt.6:24-34). Worrying about such things would be cumbersome, taking away precious time that should be spent in ministering. Also, they were preaching a message of faith and trust in God. They needed to live what they were preaching and become a living picture of the dependency that God wants from every man.

"But seek ye first the kingdom of God, and his righteousness; and all these things shall be added unto you" (Mt.6:33).

"Not that I speak in respect of want: for I have learned, in whatsoever state I am, therewith to be content. I know both how to be abased, and I know how to abound: every where and in all things I am instructed both to be full and to be hungry, both to abound and to suffer need. I can do all things through Christ which strengtheneth me" (Ph.4:11-13).

"Trust in the LORD, and do good; so shalt thou dwell in the land, and verily thou shalt be fed" (Ps.37:3).

"Commit thy way unto the LORD; trust also in him; and he shall bring it to pass" (Ps.37:5).

"Ye that fear the LORD, trust in the LORD: he is their help and their shield" (Ps.115:11).

"It is better to trust in the LORD than to put confidence in man" (Ps.118:8).

"Trust in the LORD with all thine heart; and lean not unto thine own understanding" (Pr.3:5).

"Thou wilt keep him in perfect peace, whose mind is stayed on thee: because he trusteth in thee. Trust ye in the LORD for ever: for in the LORD JEHOVAH is everlasting strength" (Is.26:3-4).

"Who is among you that feareth the LORD, that obeyeth the voice of his servant, that walketh in darkness, and hath no light? let him trust in the name of the LORD, and stay upon his God" (Is.50:10).

2.    Act now, the hour is urgent. They were not to waste time by stopping along the way and carrying on needless conversation. Such time was to be spent in ministry or prayer. Their mission was focused upon another world that lasted forever, a world into which every man was to eventually enter. Man desperately needed to sense the urgency and commitment necessary to enter the Kingdom of God. This world and its needless affairs were not to be engaged in by the Christian laborer. (Note: all affairs are not needless, but so many often are.)

"I must work the works of him that sent me, while it is day: the night cometh, when no man can work" (Jn.9:4).

"But this I say, brethren, the time is short" (1 Cor.7:29).

"Redeeming the time, because the days are evil" (Eph.5:16).

"Walk in wisdom toward them that are without, redeeming the time" (Col.4:5).

"So teach us to number our days, that we may apply our hearts unto wisdom" (Ps.90:12).

**5** (10:5-6) **Peace**: fourth, guard the message, do not force it upon people. Three points were stressed by Jesus.

1.    The message of the laborer was peace (see note, *Peace*—Jn.14:27 for discussion)...
- the peace with God.
- the peace of God dwelling within a person's heart.
- the peace between men.

"Therefore being justified by faith, we have peace with God through our Lord Jesus Christ" (Ro.5:1).

"And how shall they preach, except they be sent? as it is written, How beautiful are the feet of them that preach the gospel of peace, and bring glad tidings of good things!" (Ro.10:15).

"But now in Christ Jesus ye who sometimes were far off are made nigh by the blood of Christ. For he is our peace, who hath made both one, and hath broken down the middle wall of partition between us; having abolished in his flesh the enmity, even the law of commandments contained in ordinances; for to make in himself of twain one new man, so making peace; and that he might reconcile both unto God in one body by the cross, having slain the enmity thereby: and came and preached peace" (Eph.2:13-17).

"[Have] your feet shod with the preparation of the gospel of peace" (Eph.6:15).

2. The laborer was to proclaim peace to whatever house he entered. If the "son of peace," that is, the head of the household, was a man of peace, then the message of peace was to be continued. But if the message of peace was not accepted, then it was to be taken away. The disciple was not to proclaim the message of peace to anyone who was not willing to receive it. Neither the messenger nor the message was to be forced upon anyone.

"And when ye come into an house, salute it. And if the house be worthy, let your peace come upon it: but if it be not worthy, let your peace return to you. And whosoever shall not receive you, nor hear your words, when ye depart out of that house or city, shake off the dust of your feet. Verily I say unto you, It shall be more tolerable for the land of Sodom and Gomorrha in the day of judgment, than for that city" (Mt.10:12-15).

3. The method Christ used was *house evangelism* (see DEEPER STUDY # 1—Lk.9:4 for discussion).

**6** (10:7) **Stewardship—Minister, Compensation**: fifth, accept compensation, but do not seek luxury. There were three things being stressed.

1. "The laborer is worthy of his hire"; therefore, he should be given compensation and taken care of (1 Tim.5:18). Scripture says the laborer is really worth double compensation and such appreciation should be expressed to him (1 Tim.5:17). He is never to be taken advantage of. He is to be looked after by seeing that he has a house, food, and drink—all the necessities of life.

"Even so hath the Lord ordained that they which preach the gospel should live of the gospel" (1 Cor.9:14).

"Let him that is taught in the word communicate [give, support] unto him that teacheth in all good things" (Gal.6:6).

"Notwithstanding ye have well done, that ye did communicate [give, share] with my affliction" (Ph.4:14).

"For the scripture saith, Thou shalt not muzzle the ox that treadeth out the corn. And, The labourer is worthy of his reward" (1 Tim.5:18).

"Charge them that are rich in this world, that they be not highminded, nor trust in uncertain riches, but in the living God, who giveth us richly all things to enjoy; that they do good, that they be rich in good works, ready to distribute, willing to communicate" (1 Tim.6:17-18).

2. The laborer was to accept compensation. He was not to be self-conscious or embarrassed in receiving payment for his labor.

3. *However*, he was not to seek luxury, going from house to house and person to person seeking more and more of the better things of life. *The laborer was to live in simplicity, giving all that he had beyond his own needs—giving all to meet the needs of others.* He was to seek to meet the needs of men, not to secure the things of this world. What a contrast of value: things vs. people. How mixed up men allow their values to become.

"If ye then be risen with Christ, seek those things which are above, where Christ sitteth on the right hand of God. Set your affection on things above, not on things on the earth" (Col.3:1-2).

"For they that are after the flesh do mind the things of the flesh; but they that are after the Spirit the things of the Spirit. For to be carnally minded is death; but to be spiritually minded is life and peace" (Ro.8:5-6).

"These all died in faith, not having received the promises, but having seen them afar off, they were persuaded of them, and embraced them, and confessed that they were strangers and pilgrims on the earth. For they that say such things declare plainly that they seek a country. And truly, if they had been mindful of that country from whence they came out, they might have had opportunity to have returned. But now they desire a better country, that is, an heavenly: wherefore God is not ashamed to be called their God: for he hath prepared for them a city" (Heb.11:13-16).

"By faith Moses, when he was come to years, refused to be called the son of Pharaoh's daughter; choosing rather to suffer affliction with the people of God, than to enjoy the pleasures of sin for a season; esteeming the reproach of Christ greater riches than the treasures in Egypt: for he had respect unto the recompence of the reward" (Heb.11:24-26).

**7** (10:8-9) **Missions—Missionaries**: sixth, be hospitable, accommodating, and adaptable. Jesus gave three charges that will help His messenger reach those to whom he goes.

1. Identify with the people. This is the point Jesus was making. He simply used the most sensitive and basic thing to

stress its importance, that of food. If necessary, God's messenger was to change his customs and habits to reach the people. He was to accommodate and adapt himself to the people he was trying to reach, even down to the food eaten. The people were to see that he accepted and received them into his life and heart.

> "But a lover of hospitality, a lover of good men, sober, just, holy, temperate" (Tit.1:8).
> "Let brotherly love continue. Be not forgetful to entertain strangers: for thereby some have entertained angels unawares" (Heb.13:1-2).
> "Use hospitality one to another without grudging" (1 Pt.4:9).
> "Thou shalt love thy neighbour as thyself. There is none other commandment greater than these" (Mk.12:31; cp. Gal.5:14; Jas.2:8).
> "Love worketh no ill to his neighbour: therefore love is the fulfilling of the law" (Ro.13:10).
> "Let every one of us please his neighbour for his good to edification" (Ro.15:2).

2. Minister to the people. The messenger was to minister to the people's physical needs, even to the point of healing the sick.

> "Even as the Son of man came not to be ministered unto, but to minister, and to give his life a ransom for many" (Mt.20:28).
> "Then said Jesus to them again, Peace be unto you: as my Father hath sent me, even so send I you" (Jn.20:21).
> "How God anointed Jesus of Nazareth with the Holy Ghost and with power: who went about doing good, and healing all that were oppressed of the devil; for God was with him" (Acts 10:38).
> "I have showed you all things, how that so labouring ye ought to support the weak, and to remember the words of the Lord Jesus, how he said, It is more blessed to give than to receive" (Acts 20:35).
> "We then that are strong ought to bear the infirmities of the weak, and not to please ourselves" (Ro.15:1).
> "Bear ye one another's burdens, and so fulfil the law of Christ" (Gal.6:2).

3. Proclaim the Kingdom of God. Note: the message was given by Christ; it was not created in the mind of the messenger. Note also that the kingdom was near people, right before them. The opportunity to receive the kingdom was present, right then and there (see DEEPER STUDY # 3, *Kingdom of God*—Mt.19:23-24 for discussion).

> "From that time Jesus began to preach, and to say, Repent: for the kingdom of heaven is at hand" (Mt.4:17).
> "And as ye go, preach, saying, The kingdom of heaven is at hand" (Mt.10:7).
> "And he said unto them, I must preach the kingdom of God to other cities also: for therefore am I sent" (Lk.4:43).
> "And it came to pass afterward, that he went throughout every city and village, preaching and showing the glad tidings of the kingdom of God: and the twelve were with him" (Lk.8:1).
> "And he sent them to preach the kingdom of God, and to heal the sick" (Lk.9:2).
> "The law and the prophets were until John: since that time the kingdom of God is preached, and every man presseth into it" (Lk.16:16).
> "So likewise ye, when ye see these things come to pass, know ye that the kingdom of God is nigh at hand" (Lk.21:31).
> "To whom also he showed himself alive after his passion by many infallible proofs, being seen of them forty days, and speaking of the things pertaining to the kingdom of God" (Acts 1:3).
> "But when they believed Philip preaching the things concerning the kingdom of God, and the name of Jesus Christ, they were baptized, both men and women" (Acts 8:12).
> "And now, behold, I know that ye all, among whom I have gone preaching the kingdom of God, shall see my face no more" (Acts 20:25).
> "And when they had appointed him a day, there came many to him into his lodging; to whom he expounded and testified the kingdom of God, persuading them concerning Jesus, both out of the law of Moses, and out of the prophets, from morning till evening" (Acts 28:23).

**8** (10:10-15) **Rejection—Judgment, Degrees of—Profession Only**: seventh, walk away from rejecters. This, of course, protected the messenger from harm, at least to some degree. It also served as an immediate warning to any who rejected, perhaps causing them to think about the matter more deeply and changing their minds and hearts toward Jesus. Jesus discussed three classes of rejecters.

1. There would be cities that would reject Him (v.10-12). The messenger was to symbolize God's rejection of them by shaking the dust off his feet. This was a silent testimony that God was doing just what they wanted, leaving them alone to walk through life as they desired (see note, pt.3—Lk.9:3-5 for more discussion).

The reason for God's judgment was that they rejected the Kingdom of God. The kingdom came near them; the opportunity was there, but they rejected it. They shut their doors to God. Their judgment was, therefore, to be greater than Sodom's (see DEEPER STUDY # 4—Mt.10:15; DEEPER STUDY # 4—11:23 for more discussion).

2. There would be those who *only professed* to be God's people. These were illustrated by two towns that were heavily populated by Jewish people who professed to be the people of God. Yet they *only professed*. They rejected God's Son, despite the mighty works done among them. Therefore, they were to be judged. Their profession was profession only. Therefore, their judgment was to be greater than the judgment which was to come upon the heathen. Why? Because they had the opportunity to accept Christ, an opportunity that the heathen never had (Tyre and Sidon). Note the degrees of judgment taught. (See outline and notes—Mt.11:20-24; Ro.2:11-15 for more discussion.)

3.    There would be those who had a constant witness. These were to receive the greatest judgment of all, hell itself. Capernaum was the *chosen* city and headquarters of Christ (Mt.9:1), yet they rejected Christ. (See outline and notes—Mt.11:20-24 for more discussion.)

**Thought 1.** Judgment is definitely coming, and everyone who rejects the Lord Jesus Christ will be condemned.

"Whosoever therefore shall be ashamed of me and of my words in this adulterous and sinful generation; of him also shall the Son of man be ashamed, when he cometh in the glory of his Father with the holy angels" (Mk.8:38).

"But he that knew not, and did commit things worthy of stripes, shall be beaten with few stripes. For unto whomsoever much is given, of him shall be much required: and to whom men have committed much, of him they will ask the more" (Lk.12:48).

"And this is the condemnation, that light is come into the world, and men loved darkness rather than light, because their deeds were evil" (Jn.3:19).

"But after thy hardness and impenitent heart treasurest up unto thyself wrath against the day of wrath and revelation of the righteous judgment of God" (Ro.2:5).

"So then every one of us shall give account of himself to God" (Ro.14:12).

"And to you who are troubled rest with us, when the Lord Jesus shall be revealed from heaven with his mighty angels, in flaming fire taking vengeance on them that know not God, and that obey not the gospel of our Lord Jesus Christ" (2 Th.1:7-8).

"But exhort one another daily, while it is called To day; lest any of you be hardened through the deceitfulness of sin" (Heb.3:13).

"Wherein they [unbelievers] think it strange that ye run not with them to the same excess of riot [partying], speaking evil of you: who shall give account to him that is ready to judge the quick and the dead" (1 Pt.4:4-5).

"And Enoch also, the seventh from Adam, prophesied of these, saying, Behold, the Lord cometh with ten thousands of his saints, to execute judgment upon all, and to convince all that are ungodly among them of all their ungodly deeds which they have ungodly committed, and of all their hard speeches which ungodly sinners have spoken against him" (Jude 14-15).

"...every man shall be put to death for his own sin" (Dt.24:16).

"He, that being often reproved hardeneth his neck, shall suddenly be destroyed, and that without remedy" (Pr.29:1).

"And now, because ye have done all these works, saith the LORD, and I spake unto you, rising up early and speaking, but ye heard not; and I called you, but ye answered not; therefore will I do unto this house, which is called by my name, wherein ye trust, and unto the place which I gave to you and to your fathers, as I have done to Shiloh. And I will cast you out of my sight, as I have cast out all your brethren, even the whole seed of Ephraim" (Jer.7:13-15).

"But every one shall die for his own iniquity" (Jer.31:30).

"The soul that sinneth, it shall die" (Ezk.18:20).

---

**DEEPER STUDY # 1**

(10:13) **Woe:** not a call for vengeance, but an expression of deep regret, of warning (cp. 6:24).

---

**9** (10:16) **Ministers, Rejection; Acceptance; Treatment of:** eighth, know that the messenger represents the Lord. This stresses two critical points.

1.    The messenger's position and message were of the highest value. The messenger represented Christ and was to be given the most serious hearing possible. He was counted as though Christ Himself were speaking.

2.    The rejection of the messenger was the most serious offense. It was counted as the rejection of God Himself.

"He that receiveth you receiveth me, and he that receiveth me receiveth him that sent me" (Mt.10:40).

"And whoso shall receive one such little child [believer] in my name receiveth me" (Mt.18:5).

"And the King shall answer and say unto them, Verily I say unto you, Inasmuch as ye have done it unto one of the least of these my brethren, ye have done it unto me" (Mt.25:40).

"Then shall he answer them, saying, Verily I say unto you, Inasmuch as ye did it not to one of the least of these, ye did it *not* to me. And these shall go away into everlasting punishment: but the righteous into life eternal" (Mt.25:45-46).

"And Saul, yet breathing out threatenings and slaughter against the disciples of the Lord, went unto the high priest, and desired of him letters to Damascus to the synagogues, that if he found any of this way, whether they were men or women, he might bring them bound unto Jerusalem. And as he journeyed, he came near Damascus: and suddenly there shined round about him a light from heaven: and he fell to the earth, and heard a voice saying unto him, Saul, Saul, why persecutest thou me?" (Acts 9:1-4).

"But when ye sin so against the brethren, and wound their weak conscience, ye sin against Christ" (1 Cor.8:12).

| | D. The Seventy Return (Part I): Great Power, 10:17-20 | from heaven.<br>19 Behold, I give unto you power to tread on serpents and scorpions, and over all the power of the enemy: and nothing shall by any means hurt you. | 3 The Christian laborer has power over all enemies: perfect security |
|---|---|---|---|
| 1 The seventy returned<br>　a. With joy<br>　b. With great results & a<br>　　testimony of power<br><br>2 The Christian laborer<br>　has power over Satan | 17 And the seventy returned again with joy, saying, Lord, even the devils are subject unto us through thy name.<br>18 And he said unto them, I beheld Satan as lightning fall | 20 Notwithstanding in this rejoice not, that the spirits are subject unto you; but rather rejoice, because your names are written in heaven. | 4 The Christian laborer is to rejoice in his salvation, not in his power |

# DIVISION V

## THE SON OF MAN'S GREAT JOURNEY TO JERUSALEM (STAGE I): HIS MISSION AND PUBLIC CHALLENGE, 9:51-13:21

## D. The Seventy Return (Part I): Great Power, 10:17-20

(10:17-20) **Introduction**: Christ gives great power to the person who truly labors for Him. The presence of God's power in the laborer's life is a wonderful thing; however, it is something that can be misunderstood and abused. When the seventy returned, Jesus used the occasion to teach a much needed lesson on the power of God in a person's life.

1. The seventy returned (v.17).
2. The Christian laborer has power over Satan (v.18).
3. The Christian laborer has power over all enemies—perfect security (v.19).
4. The Christian laborer is to rejoice in his salvation, not in his power (v.20).

1 (10:17) **Power—Ministry, Results; Praise for**: the seventy returned. The testimony of their return has several significant lessons for every generation of Christian laborers.

1. They returned with joy (chara). The word means joy and rejoicing, a heart full of gladness. Frankly, their spirit was different from what so many express after an arduous ministry. They were not sharing and reveling in...

- how much they had done for Christ.
- how taxing the work had been.
- how strong the opposition and enemy had fought.

The very opposite was true. They were filled with joy and were rejoicing in Christ over the phenomenal power of Christ's name.

2. They returned with astounding results—results that were wrought through the name of Christ. The seventy expressed surprise: "Lord, even the devils are subject unto us." But note two facts.

　a. The power had come *through Christ's name*.

> "Neither is there salvation in any other: for there is none other name under heaven given among men, whereby we must be saved" (Acts 4:12).

　b. Their shock at such power or results led to a confession of their own weakness and nothingness before Christ. They knew and readily confessed that the power to do the work had not come from them. Only the name of Christ could give genuine power and results.

3. They returned giving glory to Christ. They praised Him for the glorious experience He had granted them "through His name." They were not in any sense of the term drawing attention to themselves. They were lifting up Christ and praising Him. The devils were subject unto them through *Christ's name*.

4. They returned having ministered to both body and soul. Men's bodies were healed (v.9), and they were freed spiritually when the demons and forces of evil were cast out of their lives. (See outline and notes—Mt.8:28-34 for more discussion and thoughts.)

2 (10:18) **Power—Satan, Defeat of**: there was power over Satan (see DEEPER STUDY # 1, *Satan*—Rev.12:9). Satan "falling from heaven" means falling from the height and the summit of power. The word "beheld" (etheoroun) means that Jesus thought upon, gave full attention to, contemplated, envisioned Satan's falling from his summit of power as the *god and prince* of this world (see DEEPER STUDY # 1, *Satan*—Rev.12:9). The idea is that Jesus saw the seventy's victorious mission as a sign of the total defeat of Satan that was now beginning.

1. Jesus saw Satan defeated in the souls of men.

> "And you hath he quickened, who were dead in trespasses and sins; wherein in time past ye walked according to the course of this world, according to the prince of the power of the air, the spirit that now worketh in the children of disobedience" (Eph.2:1-2; cp. v.3-10).
> "Who [God] hath delivered us from the power of darkness [Satan], and hath translated us into the kingdom of his dear Son: in whom we have redemption through his blood, even the forgiveness of sins" (Col.1:13-14).

2.　Jesus saw Satan defeated through the spread of the gospel.

> "Now is the judgment of this world: now shall the prince of this world be cast out. And I, if I be lifted up from the earth, will draw all men unto me" (Jn.12:31-32).
>
> "Nevertheless I tell you the truth; It is expedient for you that I go away: for if I do go not away, the Comforter will not come unto you; but if I depart, I will send him unto you. And when he is come, he will reprove the world of sin, and of righteousness, and of judgment: of sin, because they believe not on me; of righteousness, because I go to my Father, and ye see me no more; of judgment, because the prince of this world is judged" (Jn.16:7-11).
>
> "In whom the god of this world hath blinded the minds of them which believe not, lest the light of the glorious gospel of Christ, who is the image of God, should shine unto them" (2 Cor.4:4).

3.　Jesus saw Satan defeated in the daily strategies and struggles which he wages against the individual believer (See note—Ro.8:2-4.)

> "He that committeth sin is of the devil; for the devil sinneth from the beginning. For this purpose the Son of God was manifested, that he might destroy the works of the devil" (1 Jn.3:8).
>
> "Finally, my brethren, be strong in the Lord, and in the power of his might. Put on the whole armour of God, that ye may be able to stand against the wiles of the devil. For we wrestle not against flesh and blood, but against principalities, against powers, against the rulers of the darkness of this world, against spiritual wickedness in high places" (Eph.6:10-12; cp. v.13-18).

4.　Jesus saw Satan defeated in His power over death.

5.　Jesus saw Satan defeated through His death on the cross.

> "And having spoiled principalities and powers, he made a show of them openly, triumphing over them in it [the cross]" (Col.2:15).
>
> "Who his own self bare our sins in his own body on the tree, that we, being dead to sins, should live unto righteousness: by whose stripes ye were healed" (1 Pt.2:24. Cp. Jn.12:32.)

6.　Jesus saw Satan defeated in the end of the world, in the consummation of the ages and time. (See outlines and notes—Rev.20:1-3; 20:7-10.)

> "And the devil that deceived them was cast into the lake of fire and brimstone, where the beast and the false prophet are, and shall be tormented day and night for ever and ever" (Rev.20:10).

> **Thought 1.** We are to "behold" the power of God in the same way that Christ "beheld" it. God's power is for the purpose of defeating Satan, of delivering men from the power of Satan.

**3**　(10:19) **Power—Deliverance—Satan, Power Over**: the Christian believer has power over all enemies; he has perfect security. Are the words "power over serpents and scorpions" to be taken literally or figuratively? (Cp. Mk.16:15-18.)

1.　There is a literal meaning in this sense. If it is God's purpose to continue using His servant, then God will protect His servant no matter the threat or injury, whether by shipwreck (Acts 28:14f) or snake bite (Acts 28:3-5). The life of a genuine believer is in the hands of God every moment of his life, and God looks after the believer. Whatever befalls him is under the will and care of God (Ro.8:28f; cp. 2 Cor.11:23-30 for a descriptive picture of what does befall God's servant and a picture of how God delivers until He is ready to take His servant home.)

But note a crucial point. A man does not test God; he does not presume upon the power of God. The true servant of God does not put himself in *harm's way* where he will be threatened. Such a person is busy at the wrong thing. The servant is to be busy reaching people for Christ, not proving his ability with animals or his immunity to their bites.

2.　There is a spiritual meaning. Power is given over the enemy (Satan). Note five points.

　　a.　The enemy does have power; the idea is that he has enormous power.

> "For we wrestle not against flesh and blood, but against principalities, against powers, against the rulers of the darkness of this world, against spiritual wickedness in high places" (Eph.6:12).

　　b.　The Lord's power is greater, much greater.

> "What shall we then say to these things? If God be for us, who can be against us?" (Ro.8:31).
>
> "Greater is he that is in you, than he that is in the world" (1 Jn.4:4; Heb.2:14-15; 1 Jn.3:8).

　　c.　The Lord gives His power to His laborer.

> "Then he called his twelve disciples together and gave them power and authority over all devils, and to cure diseases" (Lk.9:1).

"For God hath not given us the spirit of fear; but of power, and of love, and of a sound mind" (2 Tim.1:7).

d.  The laborer's power is over *all* the power of the enemy.

"And what is the exceeding greatness of his power to us-ward who believe, according to the working of his mighty power" (Eph.1:19).
"Now unto him that is able to do exceeding abundantly above all that we ask or think, according to the power that worketh in us" (Eph.3:20).

e.  The laborer is *perfectly secure* against all enemies. No spiritual power shall by any means be able to touch him. He is secure in the hands of God.

"My Father, which gave them me, is greater than all; and no man is able to pluck them out of my Father's hand" (Jn.10:29; cp. Eph.6:10-18).
"And now I am no more in the world, but these are in the world, and I come to thee. Holy Father, keep through thine own name those whom thou hast given me, that they may be one, as we are" (Jn.17:11).
"Being confident of this very thing, that he which hath begun a good work in you will perform it until the day of Jesus Christ" (Ph.1:6).
"But the Lord is faithful, who shall stablish you, and keep you from evil" (2 Th.3:3).
"For the which cause I also suffer these things: Nevertheless I am not ashamed: for I know whom I have believed, and am persuaded that he is able to keep that which I have committed unto him against that day" (2 Tim.1:12).
"And the Lord shall deliver me from every evil work, and will preserve me unto his heavenly kingdom: to whom be glory for ever and ever" (2 Tim.4:18).
"Who [believers] are kept by the power of God through faith unto salvation ready to be revealed in the last time" (1 Pt.1:5).
"Now unto him that is able to keep you from falling, and to present you faultless before the presence of his glory with exceeding joy, to the only wise God our Saviour, be glory and majesty, dominion and power, both now and ever" (Jude 24-25).
"And, behold, I am with thee, and will keep thee in all places whither thou goest, and will bring thee again into this land [promised land, heaven]; for I will not leave thee, until I have done that which I have spoken to thee of" (Gen.28:15).

**4** (10:20) **Joy—Book of Life—Salvation**: the Christian laborer is to rejoice in his salvation, not in his power. Note two points.
1.  The real basis for joy is not power, but salvation. The great privilege of a believer is not his work and ministry, but the fact that he is a child of God's and has been given eternal life.
⇒  He has been adopted as a son or daughter of God.

"But when the fulness of the time was come, God sent forth his Son, made of a woman, made under the law, to redeem them that were under the law, that we might receive the adoption of sons. And because ye are sons, God hath sent forth the Spirit of his Son into your hearts, crying, Abba, Father" (Gal.4:4-6).
"Wherefore come out from among them, and be ye separate, saith the Lord, and touch not the unclean thing; and I will receive you, and will be a Father unto you, and ye shall be my sons and daughters, saith the Lord Almighty" (2 Cor.6:17-18).

⇒  He has received the Spirit of adoption which gives him open access into the very presence of God.

"For ye have not received the spirit of bondage again to fear; but ye have received the Spirit of adoption, whereby we cry, Abba, Father" (Ro.8:15).
"Likewise the Spirit also helpeth our infirmities: for we know not what we should pray for as we ought: but the Spirit itself maketh intercession for us with groanings which cannot be uttered" (Ro.8:26).
"Hitherto [before Jesus' death, salvation] have ye asked nothing in my name: ask, and ye shall receive, that your joy may be full" (Jn.16:24).

⇒  He has been made an heir of God and, unbelievably, an equal heir with Christ.

"The Spirit itself beareth witness with our spirit, that we are the children of God: and if children, then heirs; heirs of God, and joint-heirs with Christ; if so be that we suffer with him, that we may be also glorified together" (Ro.8:16-17).
"That being justified by his grace, we should be made heirs according to the hope of eternal life" (Tit.3:7).
"Blessed be the God and Father of our Lord Jesus Christ, which according to his abundant mercy hath begotten us again unto a lively hope by the resurrection of Jesus

Christ from the dead, to an inheritance incorruptible, and undefiled, and that fadeth not away, reserved in heaven for you" (1 Pt.1:3-4).

2.  The believer's name is written down in heaven (cp. Rev.13:8; 17:8; 20:12; 22:19).

"He that overcometh, the same shall be clothed in white raiment; and I will not blot out his name out of the book of life, but I will confess his name before my Father, and before his angels" (Rev.3:5).

"And I intreat thee also, true yokefellow, help those women which laboured with me in the gospel, with Clement also, and with other my fellowlabourers, whose names are in the book of life" (Ph.4:3).

"But ye are come unto mount Sion, and unto the city of the living God, the heavenly Jerusalem, and to an innumerable company of angels, to the general assembly and church of the firstborn, which are written in heaven, and to God the Judge of all, and to the spirits of just men made perfect" (Heb.12:22-23).

"And there shall in no wise enter into it [heaven] any thing that defileth, neither whatsoever worketh abomination, or maketh a lie: but they which are written in the Lamb's book of life" (Rev.21:27).

"Yet now, if thou wilt forgive their sin—and if not, blot me, I pray thee, out of thy book which thou hast written. And the LORD said unto Moses, Whosoever hath sinned against me, him will I blot out of my book" (Ex.32:32-33).

"Let them be blotted out of the book of the living, and not be written with the righteous" (Ps.69:28; cp. Jer.17:13).

"And at that time shall Michael stand up, the great prince which standeth for the children of thy people: and there shall be a time of trouble, such as never was since there was a nation even to that same time: and at that time thy people shall be delivered, every one that shall be found written in the book" (Dan.12:1).

| | E. The Seventy Return (Part II): Great Privileges, 10:21-24 (Mt.11:25-27) | man knoweth who the Son is, but the Father; and who the Father is, but the Son, and he to whom the Son will reveal him. | only Son a. God & the Son alone know one another b. The Son reveals God to some |
|---|---|---|---|
| 1 Jesus rejoiced 2 Privilege 1: The spiritual insight into truth a. Into "these things" b. God hides truth from the wise & prudent c. God reveals truth to babes d. Such action is well pleasing to God 3 Privilege 2: The knowledge of God & of His | 21 In that hour Jesus rejoiced in spirit, and said, I thank thee, O Father, Lord of heaven and earth, that thou hast hid these things from the wise and prudent, and hast revealed them unto babes: even so, Father; for so it seemed good in thy sight. 22 All things are delivered to me of my Father: and no | 23 And he turned him unto his disciples, and said privately, Blessed are the eyes which see the things that ye see: 24 For I tell you, that many prophets and kings have desired to see those things which ye see, and have not seen them; and to hear those things which ye hear, and have not heard them. | 4 Privilege 3: The insight & privilege of learning God's full revelation |

# DIVISION V

## THE SON OF MAN'S GREAT JOURNEY TO JERUSALEM (STAGE I): HIS MISSION AND PUBLIC CHALLENGE, 9:51-13:21

## E. The Seventy Return (Part II): Great Privileges, 10:21-24

(10:21-24) **Introduction**: the Christian laborer has three great privileges. Jesus was filled with such a joy over these privileges that He broke forth in praise to God. How the Lord's heart longs to share these privileges with every person.

1. Jesus rejoiced (v.21).
2. Privilege 1: the spiritual insight into truth (v.21).
3. Privilege 2: the knowledge of God and of His only Son (v.22).
4. Privilege 3: the insight and privilege of learning God's full revelation (v.23-24).

**1** (10:21) **Joy—Rejoicing**: Jesus rejoiced (egalliasato). The word is much stronger than the English *rejoice*. The Greek means great joy and exultation. It means to be filled with joy or thrilled with joy. There is the idea of *victorious joy* because of the glorious triumph over the arch-enemy Satan (v.18-20). Note: this joy comes only from the Spirit; it cannot be worked up. It is a joy of confidence and assurance that arises from down deep within—a confidence and assurance that all is well with God and the victory is won over evil. This was the joy experienced by Christ when the seventy returned. Souls had been snatched from the grip of sin and death, for the power of God over evil had been exercised by men. Satan's fall was assured. God would be victorious within the world as the gospel was carried forth by His servants; the Spirit of God stirred Jesus to rejoice greatly over the victory won.

> **"Looking unto Jesus the author and finisher of our faith; who for the joy that was set before him endured the cross, despising the shame, and is set down at the right hand of the throne of God" (Heb.12:2).**

**2** (10:21) **Truth—Self-Sufficient—Predestination—Humanism—Unbelief—"Babes"—"Wise and Prudent of World"**: first, there is the privilege of spiritual insight into truth. The Christian laborer is able to grasp the spiritual truth of things. Note four points.

1. The term "these things" refers to the gospel of the Lord Jesus Christ. More specifically, however, it refers to the truth which the seventy had learned (v.19-20); that is, that God is active in the world. God saves men and cares for men, giving them power over the forces of evil and writing their names in heaven. Note an important fact: knowing "these things" is the greatest knowledge in all the world. No other knowledge could ever surpass knowing God in such a personal way, knowing...

- that He has saved us.
- that He cares and looks after us.
- that He delivers us from the power of evil.
- that He infuses us with assurance and confidence and perfect security.

2. God hides "these things" from the wise and prudent. Such people are those who think themselves wise and intelligent. They are the self-sufficient, the proud, the wise of this world (1 Cor.1:21, 25-29; 2:14). These are blind to the Lord of heaven and earth and to the truth. The proud and self-sufficient by their very nature sense no need for help and refuse to receive help. They rest in their own ability and achievements.

   a. Spiritual truth is *hid*. Where? In God. God has done the logical thing. He has taken spiritual truth and locked it up in Himself. The only access to truth is through God. The only key to spiritual truth is faith and trust in God.

   The man who considers himself wise and intelligent and sufficient enough without God never comes to God. Therefore, a personal relationship with God is never known. The self-sufficient person never comes to know God nor the spiritual truth *hid* in God (Ro.1:18-22). God and His presence and His plan for the ages are foreign to the self-sufficient person. He does not believe God—not enough to come to Him. Therefore, the things of the Spirit and of the gospel are hid from him. However, God's heart and truths are open to the one who comes in dependency and trust.

Note a crucial point. What Christ condemns is not intelligence and wisdom, but intellectual pride and self-sufficiency. God made man to think and reason and seek and search in order to discover and build, but God expects man "not to think of himself too highly" (Ro.12:3; cp. Ph.2:3-4). A man is to walk humbly during his short stay on earth, knowing from whom he has come and to whom he is going. He is to trust God, putting his time and destiny in God's hands.

b. God is helpless to reveal truth to the "wise and prudent" of this world. Why? Because they *rest* in their own ability and achievements and *sense no need* beyond themselves. They sense no need for God. They...

⇒ keep God out of their lives.  ⇒ question the value of God.
⇒ push God away.  ⇒ believe they have no need for God, not now.
⇒ deny God's existence.  ⇒ believe God is irrelevant in a scientific, technological world.

c. God is not the Author of man's self-sufficiency and pride. Man is the one who makes himself his own *god* and creates the religion of humanism (that man is sufficient unto himself). God has no choice. He has to do two things.

First, God has to leave such persons to themselves. God cannot force man to worship Him, for forced behavior would be making robots out of man. And God wants to be loved and worshipped by men because men *choose* to worship Him. Therefore, man's sin becomes his punishment; his rejection becomes harder and harder, and he is removed farther and farther away from God—exactly what the man had desired (Jn.12:39-40; Ro.1:18-32. Cp. Acts 28:26-27; Ro.11:7-8.)

Second, God has to hide the truth from such persons because their *evil hearts* would only corrupt the truth. They would mix the truth with their own *rationalized and humanistic ideas*. Note another fact: if the self-sufficient knew the truth, they would be honored as the creators of the truth. They would lift man up as the source of truth. Unfortunately, this is exactly the claim made by so many. However, God will not share the honor due His Son with anyone. His Son, the only Son He has, is to receive all the honor and praise of this earth. Why? Because He is the One who has loved perfectly, loved so much that He laid down His life to save the world.

d. If a man honors God with what he has (his intelligence, abilities, and achievements), God will give "these things" to that man. But if the man takes what he has and claims to be self-sufficient, then God has no choice but to hide "these things" from his understanding.

"And he spake this parable unto certain which trusted in themselves that they were righteous" (Lk.18:9).

"Jesus said unto them, If God were your Father, ye would love me: for I proceeded forth and came from God; neither came I of myself, but he sent me. Why do ye not understand my speech? even because ye cannot hear my word" (Jn.8:42-43).

"Which of you convinceth me of sin? And if I say the truth, why do ye not believe me? He that is of God heareth God's words: ye therefore hear them not, because ye are not of God" (Jn.8:46-47).

"Therefore they could not believe, because that Esaias said again, He hath blinded their eyes, and hardened their heart; that they should not see with their eyes, nor understand with their heart, and be converted, and I should heal them" (Jn.12:39-40).

"And if any man hear my words, and believe not, I judge him not: for I came not to judge the world, but to save the world. He that rejecteth me, and receiveth not my words, hath one that judgeth him: the word that I have spoken, the same shall judge him in the last day. For I have not spoken of myself; but the Father which sent me, he gave me a commandment, what I should say, and what I should speak. And I know that his commandment is life everlasting: whatsoever I speak therefore, even as the Father said unto me, so I speak" (Jn.12:47-50).

"He that loveth me not keepeth not my sayings: and the word which ye hear is not mine, but the Father's which sent me" (Jn.14:24).

"For the invisible things of him from the creation of the world are clearly seen, being understood by the things that are made, even his eternal power and Godhead; so that they are without excuse: because that, when they knew God, they glorified him not as God, neither were thankful; but became vain in their imaginations, and their foolish heart was darkened. Professing themselves to be wise, they became fools" (Ro.1:20-22; cp. v.18-32).

"Be of the same mind one toward another. Mind not high things, but condescend to men of low estate. Be not wise in your own conceits" (Ro.12:16).

"For the preaching of the cross is to them that perish foolishness; but unto us which are saved it is the power of God. For it is written, I will destroy the wisdom of the wise, and will bring to nothing the understanding of the prudent. Where is the wise? where is the scribe? where is the disputer of this world? hath not God made foolish the wisdom of this world? For after that in the wisdom of God the world by wisdom knew not God, it pleased God by the foolishness of preaching to save them that believe" (1 Cor.1:18-21; cp. 1 Cor.3:19-21).

"And if any man think that he knoweth any thing, he knoweth nothing yet as he ought to know" (1 Cor.8:2).

"Wherefore let him that thinketh he standeth take heed lest he fall" (1 Cor.10:12).

"For if a man think himself to be something, when he is nothing, he deceiveth himself" (Gal.6:3).

"And the afflicted people thou wilt save: but thine eyes are upon the haughty, that thou mayest bring them down" (2 Sam.22:28).

"Be not wise in thine own eyes: fear the LORD, and depart from evil" (Pr.3:7).

"Most men will proclaim every one his own goodness: but a faithful man who can find?" (Pr.20:6).

"Seest thou a man wise in his own conceit? There is more hope of a fool than of him" (Pr.26:12).

"He that trusteth in his own heart is a fool: but whoso walketh wisely, he shall be delivered" (Pr.28:26).

"Woe unto them that are wise in their own eyes, and prudent in their own sight!" (Is.5:21).

"The earth mourneth and fadeth away, the world languisheth and fadeth away, the haughty people of the earth do languish" (Is.24:4).

"Therefore hear now this, thou that art given to pleasures, that dwellest carelessly, that sayest in thine heart, I am, and none else beside me; I shall not sit as a widow, neither shall I know the loss of children: but these two things shall come to thee in a moment in one day, the loss of children, and widowhood: they shall come upon thee in their perfection for the multitude of thy sorceries and for the great abundance of thine enchantments. For thou hast trusted in thy wickedness: thou hast said, None seeth me. Thy wisdom and thy knowledge, it hath perverted thee; and thou hast said in thine heart, I am, and none else beside me" (Is.47:8-10).

"Ye have plowed wickedness, ye have reaped iniquity; ye have eaten the fruit of lies: because thou didst trust in thy way, in the multitude of thy mighty men" (Hos.10:13).

"The pride of thine heart hath deceived thee, thou that dwellest in the clefts of the rock, whose habitation is high; that saith in his heart, Who shall bring me down to the ground? though thou exalt thyself as the eagle, and though thou set thy nest among the stars, thence will I bring thee down, saith the LORD" (Obad.3-4).

"This is the rejoicing city that dwelt carelessly, that said in her heart, I am, and there in none beside me: how is she become a desolation, a place for beasts to lie down in! every one that passeth by her shall hiss, and wag his hand" (Zeph.2:15).

3.     God reveals "these things" to *babes* (see DEEPER STUDY # 4—Mk.10:14). The babes are the humble before God, those who acknowledge...
*   that this world is not all there is.
*   that a few short years of life are not all there is.
*   that they have an inadequacy in solving the *seed of corruption*, that is, the seed of sin and death in the world.
*   that God is, and that He is their Father.
*   that God is, and that He is a rewarder of those who diligently seek Him (Heb.11:6).

The *babes* are those who look up to God as their Father because they are...
*   open and receptive within their spirits.
*   dependent and trusting spiritually.
*   responsive and submissive to spiritual truth.
*   teachable and obedient to God.
*   loving and forgiving toward others (Mt.22:36-40; 1 Jn.4:20-21; Mt.6:14-15).
(See Pt.1 of this note to see what it is that God reveals to babes.)

4.     It pleases God enormously that He is able to reveal "these things" to the "babes" of the earth.

"Then said Jesus to those Jews which believed on him, If ye continue in my word, then are ye my disciples indeed; and ye shall know the truth, and the truth shall make you free" (Jn.8:31-32).

"Ye are my friends, if ye do whatsoever I command you. Henceforth I call you not servants; for the servant knoweth not what his lord doeth: but I have called you friends; for all things that I have heard of my Father I have made known unto you" (Jn.15:14-15).

"But as it is written, Eye hath not seen, nor ear heard, neither have entered into the heart of man, the things which God hath prepared for them that love him. But God hath revealed them unto us by his Spirit: for the Spirit searcheth all things, yea, the deep things of God" (1 Cor.2:9-10).

"As newborn babes, desire the sincere milk of the word, that ye may grow thereby: if so be ye have tasted that the Lord is gracious" (1 Pt.2:2-3).

**3** (10:22) **Revelation—Spiritual World—Jesus Christ, Deity; Knows God; Sovereignty:** second, there is the privilege of knowing God and Christ in a very personal way. Four things are being said by Christ.

1.     Christ holds the supreme place in the universe. All things have been delivered into the hands of God's Son, for all things have been made for God's Son (Col.1:16-17). Jesus Christ is the supreme Authority over the universe; therefore, He is to oversee and rule the universe. However, His sovereignty is not seen, not right now, not by the vast majority of men. He was not understood nor accepted by the people of His day, nor is He understood and accepted by the people of today (Jn.1:10-11). But the truth will be obvious some day, for the day is coming when the Son of God will be revealed to the world.

"Because he hath appointed a day, in the which he will judge the world in righteousness by that man whom he hath ordained; whereof he hath given assurance unto all men, in that he hath raised him from the dead" (Acts 17:31).

"Then cometh the end, when he shall have delivered up the kingdom to God, even the Father; when he shall have put down all rule and all authority and power. For he must reign, till he hath put all enemies under his feet" (1 Cor.15:24-25).

"And to you who are troubled rest with us, when the Lord Jesus shall be revealed from heaven with his mighty angels, in flaming fire taking vengeance on them that know not God, and that obey not the gospel of our Lord Jesus Christ: who shall be punished with everlasting destruction from the presence of the Lord, and from the glory of his power; when he shall come to the glorified in his saints, and to be admired in all them that believe (because our testimony among you was believed) in that day" (2 Th.1:7-10).

"And being found in fashion as a man, he humbled himself, and became obedient unto death, even the death of the cross. Wherefore God also hath highly exalted him, and given him a name which is above every name: that at the name of Jesus every knee should bow, of things in heaven, and things in earth, and things under the earth; and that every tongue should confess that Jesus Christ is Lord, to the glory of God the Father" (Ph.2:8-11).

2. God and Christ alone have perfect knowledge. Therefore, a complete knowledge of God can be grasped only by the Son, and a complete knowledge of the Son can be grasped only by God the Father.

"Then cried Jesus in the temple as he taught, saying, Ye both know me, and ye know whence I am: and I am not come of myself, but he that sent me is true, whom ye know not. But I know him: for I am from him, and he hath sent me" (Jn.7:28-29).

"Jesus answered, If I honour myself, my honour is nothing: it is my Father that honoureth me; of whom ye say, that he is your God: yet ye have not known him; but I know him: and if I should say, I know him not, I shall be a liar like unto you: but I know him, and keep his saying" (Jn.8:54-55).

"As the Father knoweth me, even so know I the Father: and I lay down my life for the sheep" (Jn.10:15).

"O righteous Father, the world hath not known thee: but I have known thee, and these have known that thou hast sent me" (Jn.17:25).

3. God is Spirit (Jn.4:24). He is of another dimension of being entirely. If man is to know the spiritual world, then God must reveal that spiritual world and the things of that world to man. This is what Jesus is profoundly claiming. He and God alone know each other; but He has chosen to reveal the Father, who is Spirit, to some. Passages such as v.21 show that the persons chosen to receive this revelation are the humble who truly seek God and trust the Son's testimony. (See outline and notes—1 Cor.2:6-13; 2:14—3:4; Jn.4:23-24.)

"Howbeit we speak wisdom among them that are perfect: yet not the wisdom of this world, nor of the princes of this world, that come to nought: but we speak the wisdom of God in a mystery, even the hidden wisdom, which God ordained before the world unto our glory: which none of the princes of this world knew: for had they known it, they would not have crucified the Lord of glory" (1 Cor.2:6-8).

"But the natural man receiveth not the things of the Spirit of God: for they are foolishness unto him: neither can he know them, because they are spiritually discerned. But he that is spiritual judgeth all things, yet he himself is judged of no man. For who hath known the mind of the Lord, that he may instruct him? But we have the mind of Christ" (1 Cor.2:14-16).

4. The persons chosen to receive this revelation are the babes who truly seek God and trust the *Son's* testimony (see note, *Truth*, pt.3—Lk.10:21).

**4** (10:23-24) **Revelation—Knowledge, Hidden—Prophets, Salvation Predicted**: third, there is the privilege of seeing and learning God's full revelation. Note several things.

1. Jesus shared this point with His disciples alone. What He said is understood only by His disciples.

2. Jesus said that He himself was the great salvation which the godly prophets and kings of old desired to see and hear. Jesus was claiming to be the Messiah, the Son of the Living God. He was the One promised by God down through the ages. (Cp. Is.53:1f.)

"I have waited for thy salvation, O LORD" (Gen.49:18).

"And now I [Paul] stand and am judged for the hope of the promise made of God unto our fathers: unto which promise our twelve tribes, instantly serving God day and night, hope to come. For which hope's sake, king Agrippa, I am accused of the Jews. Why should it be thought a thing incredible with you, that God should raise the dead?" (Acts 26:6-8).

"Which in other ages was not made known unto the sons of men, as it is now revealed unto his holy apostles and prophets by the Spirit" (Eph.3:5).

"Of which salvation the prophets have enquired and searched diligently, who prophesied of the grace that should come unto you: searching what, or what manner of time the Spirit of Christ which was in them did signify, when it testified beforehand the sufferings of Christ, and the glory that should follow. Unto whom it was revealed, that not unto themselves, but unto us they did minister the things, which are now reported unto you by them that have preached the gospel unto you with the Holy Ghost sent down from heaven; which things the angels desire to look into" (1 Pt.1:10-12).

3. Jesus was saying that His disciples were highly privileged to know Him, to see and hear Him and the truth which He revealed.

"Verily, verily, I say unto you, He that heareth my word, and believeth on him that sent me, hath everlasting life, and shall not come into condemnation; but is passed from death and life" (Jn.5:24; cp. 1 Pt.1:10-13).

| | F. The Parable of the Good Samaritan: The Two Supreme Questions of Life, 10:25-37 (cp. Mt.22:34-40; Mk.12:28-34) | 31 And by chance there came down a certain priest that way: and when he saw him, he passed by on the other side. | b. The priest: Placed work above people 1) Saw the injured traveller 2) Rushed by him |
|---|---|---|---|
| 1 A lawyer tempted Jesus | 25 And, behold, a certain lawyer stood up, and tempted him, saying, Master, what shall I do to inherit eternal life? | 32 And likewise a Levite, when he was at the place, came and looked on him, and passed by on the other side. | c. The Levite: Placed safety before compassion 1) Saw him 2) Stopped & looked |
| 2 Question 1: How do we inherit eternal life?[DS1] a. First, the law has the answer | 26 He said unto him, What is written in the law? how readest thou? | 33 But a certain Samaritan, as he journeyed, came where he was: and when he saw him, he had compassion on him, | d. The Samaritan:[DS2] Placed compassion before prejudice & opinion 1) Gave his heart: Compassion |
| b. Second, love God supremely | 27 And he answering said, Thou shalt love the Lord thy God with all thy heart, and with all thy soul, and with all thy strength, and with all thy mind; and thy neighbour as | 34 And went to him, and bound up his wounds, pouring in oil and wine, and set him on his own beast, and brought him to an inn, and took care of him. | 2) Sacrificed his work, time, energy, goods, and money |
| c. Third, love your neighbor as yourself d. Fourth, obey & you shall live | thyself. 28 And he said unto him, Thou hast answered right: this do, and thou shalt live. | 35 And on the morrow when he departed, he took out two pence, and gave them to the host, and said unto him, Take care of him; and whatsoever thou spendest more, when I come again, I will repay thee. | 3) Saw to it that continued care was given |
| 3 Question 2: Who is my neighbor? a. The traveller: Was foolish & irresponsible 1) Travelled alone | 29 But he, willing to justify himself, said unto Jesus, And who is my neighbour? 30 And Jesus answering said, A certain man went down from Jerusalem to Jericho, and fell among | 36 Which now of these three, thinkest thou, was neighbour unto him that fell among the thieves? | e. The Lord's commission: Go & do likewise |
| 2) Was robbed 3) Was assaulted & left half-dead | thieves, which stripped him of his raiment, and wounded him, and departed, leaving him half dead. | 37 And he said, He that showed mercy on him. Then said Jesus unto him, Go, and do thou likewise. | |

# DIVISION V

## THE SON OF MAN'S GREAT JOURNEY TO JERUSALEM (STAGE I): HIS MISSION AND PUBLIC CHALLENGE, 9:51-13:21

### F. The Parable of the Good Samaritan: The Two Supreme Questions of Life, 10:25-37

(10:25-37) **Introduction**: there are two supreme questions of life, questions that could revolutionize the world if men would ask them and then heed their answers.
1. A lawyer tempted Jesus (v.25).
2. Question 1: how do we inherit eternal life (v.25-28)?
3. Question 2: who is my neighbor (v.29-37)?

**1** (10:25) **Jesus Christ, Questioned**: a lawyer tempted Jesus (see DEEPER STUDY # 1, *Lawyer*—Mt.22:35). The lawyer was not seeking the truth. He was not really trying to discover the way to God. His purpose was to trip Jesus, to lead Jesus to discredit Himself by giving some unusual answer that would arouse the people against Him.

**2** (10:25-28) **Eternal Life—Love**: the first supreme question of life is: How do we inherit eternal life? Note that the lawyer's question stressed works. He asked, "What shall I do?" To him, salvation was by works. God was going to accept him because he was or could become *good enough*. He had no concept of the part that God's love and grace played in salvation (cp. Eph.2:8-8; Tit.3:5-7 for a description of what he failed to see).
Note how clearly Jesus led the conversation to spell out the steps to eternal life.
1. First, the law has the answer to eternal life. If a man wishes eternal life, he must look into the law of God. Note Jesus' instructions to the lawyer, "How readest them?" The lawyer had a little leather box called a phylactery. Several passages of Scripture were in the box, two of which were Dt.6:3 and Dt.6:11. These were the two verses which he quoted.

**Thought 1.** God has given us the answer to eternal life in clear terms—so clear we are left without excuse.
1) He has given us the answer in written words. It is in black and white, certain and unmistakable.
2) He has given us the answer in the life of Christ Himself. God has caused the words to be lived out in a human life, giving us the example of the Ideal Life (see DEEPER STUDY # 1, *Jesus Christ, The Word*—Jn.1:1-5).

2.     Second, love God supremely.
    a.     "Love the Lord thy God." Love God as *your* very own God. This is a personal relationship, not a distant relationship. God is not impersonal, not far out in space someplace, distant and removed. God is personal, ever so close, and we are to be personally involved with God as though face to face. The command is to *"love the Lord thy God."* Loving God is alive and active, not dead and inactive. We are, therefore, to maintain a personal relationship with God that is alive and active.
    b.     Love God with all that you are, with all of your being, all of your nature. Jesus breaks our being into three parts: the heart, the soul, and the mind (see notes—Mk.12:29-31 for more discussion).

> **"And the Lord direct your hearts into the love of God, and into the patient waiting for Christ" (2 Th.3:5).**
>
> **"Keep yourselves in the love of God, looking for the mercy of our Lord Jesus Christ unto eternal life" (Jude 21).**
>
> **"And thou shalt love the LORD thy God with all thine heart, and with all thy soul, and with all thy might" (Dt.6:5).**
>
> **"And now, Israel, what doth the LORD thy God require of thee, but to fear the LORD thy God, to walk in all his ways, and to love him, and to serve the LORD thy God with all thy heart and with all thy soul" (Dt.10:12).**
>
> **"Therefore thou shalt love the LORD thy God, and keep his charge, and his statutes, and his judgments, and his commandments, always" (Dt.11:1).**
>
> **"But take diligent heed to do the commandment and the law, which Moses the servant of the LORD charged you, to love the LORD your God, and to walk in all his ways, and to keep his commandments, and to cleave unto him, and to serve him with all your heart and with all your soul" (Josh.22:5).**
>
> **"O love the LORD, all ye his saints: for the LORD preserveth the faithful, and plentifully rewardeth the proud doer" (Ps.31:23).**

3.     Third, love your neighbor as yourself. If a man wishes eternal life, he has to love his *neighbor*. The first commandment, "Love God," is abstract; it cannot be seen or understood standing by itself. There has to be a *demonstration, an act, something done* for love to be seen and understood. A profession of love without demonstration is empty. It is profession only. Love is not known without showing it. Several important things need to be said about love at this point.
    a.     Love is an active experience, not inactive and dormant. This was the point Jesus was making. Love for God *acts*. Love acts by showing and demonstrating itself. It is inaccurate and foolish for a man to say, "I love God," and then be inactive and dormant, doing nothing for God. If he truly loves God, he will *do things* for God. Any person who loves does things for the one loved.
    b.     The *primary thing* God wants from us is to love our neighbor, not to do religious things. Doing religious things is good, but it is not the first thing God wants. God wants us to make loving our neighbor the first order of our lives. To do religious things is only dealing with things such as rituals, observances, ordinances, laws. Such things are lifeless, unfeeling and unresponsive. They are material objects; therefore, they are not helped by our doing them. Only we are helped. They make us feel good and religious, which is beneficial to our growth, but religious things are not what demonstrate our love for God. Loving our neighbor is what proves our love for God. A man may say he loves God, but if he hates and acts unkindly toward his neighbor, everyone knows his religion is profession only. (See note—Mt.22:39 for more discussion.)

4.     Fourth, obey and you shall live eternally.

> **"We know that we have passed from death unto life, because we love the brethren. He that loveth not his brother abideth in death" (1 Jn.3:14).**
>
> **"If a man say, I love God, and hateth his brother, he is a liar: for he that loveth not his brother whom he hath seen, how can he love God whom he hath not seen? and this commandment have we from him, That he who loveth God love his brother also" (1 Jn.4:20-21).**
>
> **"But I say unto you, Love your enemies, bless them that curse you, do good to them that hate you, and pray for them which despitefully use you, and persecute you" (Mt.5:44).**
>
> **"And the second is like, namely this, Thou shalt love thy neighbour as thyself. There is none other commandment greater than these" (Mk.12:31).**
>
> **"A new commandment I give unto you, That ye love one another; as I have loved you, that ye also love one another. By this shall all men know that ye are my disciples, if ye have love one to another" (Jn.13:34-35).**
>
> **"This is my commandment, That ye love one another, as I have loved you" (Jn.15:12).**
>
> **"Let love be without dissimulation [hypocrisy]. Abhor that which is evil; cleave to that which is good" (Ro.12:9).**
>
> **"Owe no man anything, but to love one another: for he that loveth another hath fulfilled the law. For this, Thou shalt not commit adultery, Thou shalt not kill, Thou shalt not steal, Thou shalt not bear false witness, Thou shalt not covet; and if there be any other commandment, it is briefly comprehended in this saying, namely, Thou shalt love thy neighbour as thyself. Love worketh no ill to his neighbour: therefore love is the fulfilling of the law" (Ro.13:8-10).**
>
> **"For all the law is fulfilled in one word, even in this; Thou shalt love thy neighbour as thyself" (Gal.5:14).**
>
> **"And the Lord make you to increase and abound in love one toward another, and toward all men, even as we do toward you" (1 Th.3:12).**

"Let brotherly love continue" (Heb.13:1).

"If ye fulfil the royal law according to the scripture, Thou shalt love thy neighbour as thyself, ye do well" (Jas.2:8).

"Seeing ye have purified your souls in obeying the truth through the Spirit unto unfeigned love of the brethren, see that ye love one another with a pure heart fervently" (1 Pt.1:22).

"Beloved, let us love one other: for love is of God; and every one that loveth is born of God, and knoweth God. He that loveth not knoweth not God; for God is love. In this was manifested the love of God toward us, because that God sent his only begotten Son into the world, that we might live through him. Herein is love, not that we loved God, but that he loved us, and sent his Son to be the propitiation for our sins. Beloved, if God so loved us, we ought also to love one another" (1 Jn.4:7-11).

"But the stranger that dwelleth with you shall be unto you as one born among you, and thou shalt love him as thyself" (Lev.19:34).

---

**DEEPER STUDY # 1**
(10:25) **Eternal Life:** see Deeper Study # 2—Jn.1:4; Deeper Study # 1—Jn.10:10; Deeper Study # 1—Jn.17:2-3.

---

**3** (10:29-37) **Love—Brotherhood—Compassion—Ministering—Care:** the second supreme question of life is: Who is my neighbor? Note the lawyer sought to "justify himself." He sensed that Jesus was saying that he had not done the law; he had failed to love his neighbor. So he asked the logical question, "Who is my neighbor?" Jesus answered and drove the point home to the human heart by doing what He had so often done—He gave an illustration.

1. There was a traveller who was foolish and irresponsible. He was foolish because he travelled the road between Jerusalem and Jericho that was known for its danger. It was about twenty one miles in distance, in a wild country, a rugged, rocky pass much of the way. It was a favorite habitat for marauding thieves, so much so it was called *the Way of Blood.* Travellers never journeyed there alone. They always travelled with caravans. Therefore, this traveller was irresponsible, foolish, and reckless. Some would even argue that such foolishness was undeserving of help.

**Thought 1.** How many are foolish and reckless in life, exposing and destroying their bodies by walking where they should not and by doing what they should not?

"A prudent man foreseeth the evil, and hideth himself: but the simple pass on, and are punished" (Pr.22:3).
"Who is wise, and he shall understand these things? prudent, and he shall know them? for the ways of the LORD are right, and the just shall walk in them: but the transgressors shall fall therein" (Hos.14:9).

2. There was the priest who placed his religious work and ceremony before the welfare of the man. Note this was a religionist, and he did not even make a move toward helping the man. He "passed by on the other side" which means he rushed away. The priest was probably hurrying to meet his evening religious duties. The trip was a day's journey, and he would have to rush to make it. There was also a religious rule that made a person unclean for seven days after touching a dead body. This ceremonial ritual caused a priest to lose his turn of duty at the temple. The priest was not about to sacrifice his primary work and privilege for the man.

**Thought 1.** How many put work, even religious works, and *busyness* before helping others?

**Thought 2.** How many put their church and its ceremony and ritual before the needs of desperate men? How much less would be invested in buildings and facilities if men were seen as half dead travellers who needed our compassion and help?

"Then shall he say also unto them on the left hand, Depart from me, ye cursed, into everlasting fire, prepared for the devil and his angels: for I was an hungred, and ye gave me no meat: I was thirsty, and ye gave me no drink: I was a stranger, and ye took me not in: naked, and ye clothed me not: sick, and in prison, and ye visited me not" (Mt.25:41-43).
"And that servant, which knew his lord's will, and prepared not himself, neither did according to his will, shall be beaten with many stripes" (Lk.12:47).
"Therefore to him that knoweth to do good, and doeth it not, to him it is sin" (Jas.4:17).
"For I desired mercy, and not sacrifice; and the knowledge of God more than burnt offerings" (Hos.6:6).
"He hath showed thee, O man, what is good; and what doth the LORD require of thee, but to do justly, and to love mercy, and to walk humbly with thy God?" (Mic.6:8).

3. There was the Levite who placed safety before compassion. The Levite was touched with enough feeling to walk over and look upon the man. But he shrank from helping. Perhaps He...
- feared being identified with the robbers.
- feared that the robbers might still be lurking behind the shadows of the surrounding cliffs.
- felt that meddling with the poor soul was just too much bother to undergo.

"There was a certain rich man, which was clothed in purple and fine linen, and fared sumptuously every day: and there was a certain beggar named Lazarus, which was laid at his gate, full of sores, and desiring to be fed with the crumbs which fell from the rich man's table: moreover the dogs came and licked his sores. And it came to pass, that the beggar died, and was carried by the angels into Abraham's bosom: the rich man also died, and was buried; and in hell he lift up his eyes, being in torments" (Lk.16:19-23).

"What doth it profit, my brethren, though a man say he hath faith, and have not works? can faith save him? If a brother or sister be naked, and destitute of daily food, and one of you say into them, Depart in peace, be ye warmed and filled; notwithstanding ye have given them not those things which are needful to the body; what doth it profit? Even so faith, if it hath not works, is dead, being alone" (Jas.2:14-16).

"But whoso hath this world's good, and seeth his brother have need, and shutteth up his bowels of compassion from him, how dwelleth the love of God in him? My little children, let us not love in word, neither in tongue; but in deed and in truth" (1 Jn.3:17-18).

"Because that he remembered not to show mercy, but persecuted the poor and needy man, that he might even slay the broken in heart. As he loved cursing, so let it come unto him: as he delighted not in blessing, so let it be far from him" (Ps.109:16-17).

"Whoso stoppeth his ears at the cry of the poor, he also shall cry himself, but shall not be heard" (Pr.21:13).

"If thou forbear to deliver them that are drawn unto death, and those that are ready to be slain; if thou sayest, Behold, we knew it not; doth not he that pondereth the heart consider it? And he that keepeth thy soul, doth not he know it? And shall not he render to every man according to his works?" (Pr.24:11-12).

"The diseased have ye not strengthened, neither have ye healed that which was sick, neither have ye bound up that which was broken, neither have ye brought again that which was driven away, neither have ye sought that which was lost; but with force and with cruelty have ye ruled them" (Ezk.34:4; cp. v.5-10).

4.   The good Samaritan placed compassion before everything: prejudice, opinion, work, time, energy, and money. The *good Samaritan* teaches beyond question who our neighbor is. The good Samaritan gave his heart, his compassion, his all in order to help the desperate man.

   a.   The injured man was a Jew. The good Samaritan and the Jew were of different races—races who hated and despised each other. No prejudice has ever run any deeper than the prejudice between these two (see note—Lk.10:33). Yet the good Samaritan had a sense of *common humanity*. He was a man who saw another man—not as a Jew and not as an enemy. This was most strange, for the Jews cursed the Samaritans, and there was the likelihood that the injured Jew would curse the Samaritan when he had recovered. However, despite all, the good Samaritan saw a fellow human being in desperate need, and he was moved with compassion for him.

   b.   The good Samaritan gave up his work, time, and energy to help the man. Note what he did. Each step is significant in showing how we are to love our neighbors.
   ⇒   He went to him: went forth, reached out personally to help.
   ⇒   He bound up his wounds: eased his pain.
   ⇒   He poured oil and wine into his wounds: gave of his own goods.
   ⇒   He set him on his own beast: sacrificed his own comfort.
   ⇒   He provided rooming for him: provided the basic necessities.
   ⇒   He took care of him: nursed, looked after him personally.
   Note the time, energy, and money involved in this. Showing love to one's neighbor is putting love into action; and putting love into action requires time, energy, and money. Love is not just an idea or a feeling toward God. It is *practical acts and commitment* to help any who need help.

   c.   The good Samaritan saw to it that continued compassion and care were given. *Two denarii* amounted to somewhere between twenty-four to forty-eight days of room and board, a considerable sum. And note: the good Samaritan said that if it cost more, he would pay it when he returned. The good Samaritan saw a desperate need and did *all he could* to help.

5.   The Lord's commission was forceful: go and do likewise. Note a striking point: Christ still did not answer the lawyer. There was no need. The answer was strikingly clear. If the lawyer wished eternal life, he had to "go and do likewise." He now knew who his neighbor was: it was any man who needed mercy, whether a friend or just an acquaintance or even an enemy. The lawyer was forced to admit this. However, more than just confession was needed. Love was needed. The lawyer and all of us need to demonstrate love as we go about our daily affairs. We must help our neighbors—all those around us who hurt and are suffering.

"For I was an hungred, and ye gave me meat: I was thirsty, and ye gave me drink: I was a stranger, and ye took me in: naked, and ye clothed me: I was sick, and ye visited me: I was in prison, and ye came unto me. Then shall the righteous answer him, saying, Lord, when saw we thee an hungred, and fed thee? or thirsty, and gave thee drink? When saw we thee a stranger, and took thee in? or naked, and clothed thee? Or when saw we thee sick, or in prison, and came unto thee? And the King shall answer and say unto them, Verily I say unto you, Inasmuch as ye have done it unto one of the least of these my brethren, ye have done it unto me" (Mt.25:35-40).

"I have showed you all things, how that so labouring ye ought to support the weak, and to remember the words of the Lord Jesus, how he said, It is more blessed to give than to receive" (Acts 20:35).

"Therefore if thine enemy hunger, feed him; if he thirst, give him drink: for in so doing thou shalt heap coals of fire on his head" (Ro.12:20).

"Bear ye one another's burdens, and so fulfil the law of Christ" (Gal.6:2).

"Remember them that are in bonds, as bound with them; and them which suffer adversity, as being yourselves also in the body" (Heb.13:3).

"If thou meet thine enemy's ox or his ass going astray, thou shalt surely bring it back to him again" (Ex.23:4).

"And if thy brother be waxen poor, and fallen in decay with thee; then thou shalt relieve him: yea, though he be a stranger, or a sojourner; that he may live with thee" (Lev.25:35).

"For the LORD your God is God of gods, and Lord of lords, a great God, a mighty, and a terrible, which regardeth not persons, nor taketh reward: He doth execute the judgment of the fatherless and widow, and loveth the stranger, in giving him food and raiment. Love ye therefore the stranger: for ye were strangers" (Dt.10:17-19).

"Rejoice not when thine enemy falleth, and let not thine heart be glad when he stumbleth" (Pr.24:17).

"If thine enemy be hungry, give him bread to eat; and if he be thirsty, give him water to drink: for thou shalt heap coals of fire upon his head, and the LORD shall reward thee" (Pr.25:21-22).

"Is not this the fast [religion] that I have chosen? to loose the bands of wickedness, to undo the heavy burdens, and to let the oppressed go free, and that ye break every yoke? Is it not to deal thy bread to the hungry, and that thou bring the poor that are cast out to thy house? when thou seest the naked, that thou cover him; and that thou hide not thyself from thine own flesh?" (Is.58:6-7).

---

**DEEPER STUDY # 2**

(10:33) **Samaritans**: Samaria was the central part of Palestine. Palestine was a small country, reaching only one hundred twenty miles north to south. The country was divided into three sections:
- ⇒ Judea, the southern section
- ⇒ Galilee, the northern section
- ⇒ Samaria, the central section, lying right between the two

There was bitter hatred between the Jews and the Samaritans. Two things in particular caused this hatred.

1. The Samaritans were mongrel or half-Jews, a mixed breed by birth. What had happened was this. Centuries before (about 720 B.C.), the King of Assyria had captured the ten tribes of Israel and deported a large number of the people, scattering them throughout Media (cp. 2 Ki.17:6-41). He then took people from all over the Assyrian empire and transplanted them into Samaria to repopulate the land. The result was only natural. Intermarriage took place and the people became a mixed breed, a breed including...
- • the transplanted people
- • the weak of the land who had been left behind
- • the outcast and irreligious who had intermarried with the original Samaritans

The fact of a mixed breed, of course, infuriated the strict Jews who held to a pure race.

2. The Samaritans were mongrel or half-Jews, a mixed breed by religion as well as by birth. The transplanted heathen, of course, brought their gods with them. The God of Israel eventually won out, but the religion of the Samaritans never became pure Judaism. Three things happened to cause this.
- a. When Ezra led the Jews back from exile in Babylon, the first thing the Jews did was to start rebuilding their temple. The Samaritans offered to help them but the Jews rejected their help, declaring that the Samaritans, through intermarriage and worship of false gods, had lost their purity and forfeited their right to worship the only true God. This severe denunciation, of course, embittered the Samaritans against the Jews in Jerusalem.
- b. The Samaritans built a rival temple on Mount Gerizim to stand in competition with the Jewish temple at Jerusalem (cp. Jn.4:20-21).
- c. The Samaritans twisted both the Scripture and history to favor their own people and nation.
  - ⇒ They twisted Scripture by accepting only the first five books of the Bible, the Pentateuch. Just imagine! They missed all the richness and depth of the Psalms and prophets.
  - ⇒ They twisted history by claiming that three great events took place on Mt. Gerizim, events that set it apart as a place of worship. It was the place where Abraham offered Isaac, where Melchizedek met Abraham, and where Moses built his first altar after leading Israel out of Egyptian bondage.

| | G. The One Thing Needed: To Sit at Jesus' Feet, 10:38-42 | 40 But Martha was cumbered about much serving, and came to him, and said, Lord, dost thou not care that my sister hath left me to serve alone? bid her therefore that she help me. | 3 Martha's problem: She was distracted<br>a. Distracted by serving<br>b. Distracted by material things: Food, necessities & the cares of the world |
|---|---|---|---|
| 1 Jesus entered a village<br>2 Two strong characters<br>  a. Martha's character<br>    1) Giving<br>    2) Courageous<br>    3) Caring & loving<br>  b. Mary's character<br>    1) Loving & humble<br>    2) Gripped with a<br>      spiritual hunger | 38 Now it came to pass, as they went, that he entered into a certain village: and a certain woman named Martha received him into her house.<br>39 And she had a sister called Mary, which also sat at Jesus' feet, and heard his word. | 41 And Jesus answered and said unto her, Martha, Martha, thou art careful and troubled about many things:<br>42 But one thing is needful: and Mary hath chosen that good part, which shall not be taken away from her. | 4 Martha's one need: To sit quietly & listen to Jesus' words |

# DIVISION V

## THE SON OF MAN'S GREAT JOURNEY TO JERUSALEM
### (STAGE I): HIS MISSION AND PUBLIC CHALLENGE, 9:51-13:21

## G.   The One Thing Needed: To Sit at Jesus' Feet, 10:38-42

(10:38-42) **Introduction—Devotion**: this event is historically misplaced, for Mary and Martha lived in Bethany, a suburb two to three miles outside of Jerusalem. Why then does Luke place it here on Jesus' journey to Jerusalem? Perhaps he feared the Parable of the Good Samaritan might be construed to teach salvation by works. Mary and Martha's experience teaches that waiting and sitting at Jesus' feet is much more important than running to and fro trying to work one's way into God's favor. There is one basic essential in life, and that is sitting at Jesus' feet and hearing His Word.

1.   Jesus entered a village (v.38).
2.   Two strong characters (v.38-39).
3.   Martha's problem: she was distracted (v.40).
4.   Martha's one need: to sit quietly and listen to Jesus' words (v.41-42).

**1** (10:38) **Bethany**: Jesus entered a certain village. The village was Bethany which was a suburb of Jerusalem only about two miles away (see note, *Bethany*—Mt.21:17; cp. Jn.11:1).

**2** (10:38-39) **Spiritual Hunger—Character—Mary—Martha**: the scene pictures two strong characters.

1.   Martha is the first person seen, and she has a highly commendable character. It is said that "Jesus loved Martha" (Jn.11:5). Therefore, it is important to see the strong points of her character and to see what it was that caused a person who was so strong to fail.
    a.   Martha was a *giving* person. Note that she owned a house so large she could give lodging to Jesus and His apostles. Taking care of so many was expensive, yet she willingly entertained them. The next two traits also show how giving she was.
    b.   Martha was a *courageous* person. It was now dangerous to associate too closely with Jesus, especially around Jerusalem. The authorities were seeking some way to kill Jesus (see Jn.7:25, 30, 32). Many of His own disciples had forsaken Him (Jn.5:66) and others were now speaking against Him (Jn.7:20, 43-44). Even His own family had rejected Him (Jn.7:3-5). Nevertheless, Martha welcomed Him; she was willing to let the world know of her devotion to Him.
    c.   Martha was a caring and loving person. She loved and cared for her sister Mary. Note that Mary was living with Martha and that her brother Lazarus was also living there (Jn.11:1f). For some unknown reason, Martha was taking care of them both. She felt a deep devotion for her family, loving and caring for them very much. This was apparent even in the midst of the disturbance she felt toward Mary (v.40).
2.   Mary also had a commendable character. (Her name was *Miriam* in the Hebrew.)
    a.   She was loving and humble. Note how she loved Jesus; she attached herself to Him. Her love and devotion ran deep, so deep that nothing else mattered except being right next to Him. Note also her humility. She *sat* at His feet, not by His side and not in front of Him. The room or courtyard was large enough to entertain a large crowd, so she could have chosen to sit elsewhere. Mary definitely had a devoted love and a sense of humility toward her Lord.
    b.   She had a spiritual hunger for the Word of the Lord: she "heard His Word." She sat there, fixing her eyes and attention upon Him. She centered her mind upon what He said, listening and concentrating and hearing every word. She did not take His message lightly. She hungered for the Word of Christ, so she absorbed His words and took them to heart. This means that she had...
        • a spiritual hunger
        • a readiness to hear
        • a desire to surrender
        • a willingness to do

**3** (10:40) **Service—Ministry, Burdened Down—Stress—Pressure—Busyness—Murmuring—Complaining**: Martha's problem was that she became distracted. The word "cumbered" (periespato) means to draw around, to twist, to be drawn here and there, to be distracted. The idea is that Martha was drawn around and twisted with anxiety and worry. She was distracted, running here and there, being drawn by the cares of this person and that person. There are two ways Martha's distraction can be viewed and applied to our lives.

1. She was distracted by "much serving." She loved others; so she ministered to them, helping whomever and wherever she could, even using her own home as a center for caring. But Martha had a problem. She was "cumbered," loaded down with the cares and needs of others. She became so weighed and burdened down, so tired and fatigued, so pressured and tense...

- that she lost sight of her priority
- that she became aggravated and critical of those who were not helping

2. Martha could also be distracted by material things, by the food and necessities and cares of this world. Martha had wealth, which is indicated by her entertaining Jesus and His large group. Apparently, she was a very active lady, possessing initiative and some management ability. She had much to look after, including a brother and sister who lived with her. It was the things of this world—food, necessities, cares, and social entertaining—that had distracted her.

As any lady of the house would do, she felt a keen responsibility for taking care of the guests and meeting their needs. When Jesus and His large group arrived, she naturally expected her sister to help with the preparation of the meals and lodging. The problem in her mind was that even Jesus did not suggest that Mary help. Martha was disturbed with Jesus as well as with Mary.

Martha had a legitimate complaint, and that legitimacy points out the importance of sitting at Jesus' feet and hearing His Word (v.39). No matter *how* important anything else is, sitting at Jesus' feet is the one thing that is to be given priority.

The fact that Martha owned a house, entertained Jesus and His large group, and took care of her sister shows that Martha was loving and concerned about people. But evidently she had become too busy. Perhaps her wealth, initiative, hospitality, social status, and management ability were the things that had priority in her mind and life. As good as they were, they were not enough, for they did not meet the one basic essential in life: having her spiritual hunger fed with the Word of Christ Himself.

**Thought 1.** Man needs food and necessities and some social entertainment. But he is not to be distracted by these. He is not to be choked by the cares of this world.

> "And that which fell among thorns are they, which, when they have heard, go forth, and are choked with cares and riches and pleasures of this life, and bring no fruit to perfection" (Lk.8:14).
> "And seek not ye what ye shall eat, or what ye shall drink, neither be ye of doubtful mind" (Lk.12:29).
> "And take heed to yourselves, lest at any time your hearts be overcharged with surfeiting, and drunkenness, and cares of this life, and so that day come upon you unawares" (Lk.21:34).
> "No man that warreth entangleth himself with the affairs of this life; that he may please him who hath chosen him to be a soldier" (2 Tim.2:4).

**Thought 2.** We should seek out opportunities to serve, working to meet the needs of a desperate world. But we must not become cumbered and burdened down to the point...

- that the pressure gets to us
- that we become critical of others

> "Jesus therefore answered and said unto them, Murmur not among yourselves" (Jn.6:43).
> "Neither murmur ye, as some of them also murmured, and were destroyed of the destroyer" (1 Cor.10:10).
> "Do all things without murmurings and disputings: that ye may be blameless and harmless, the sons of God, without rebuke, in the midst of a crooked and perverse nation, among whom ye shine as lights in the world" (Ph.2:14-15).
> "Surely every man walketh in a vain show: surely they are disquieted in vain: he heapeth up riches, and knoweth not who shall gather them" (Ps.39:6).
> "The foolishness of man perverteth his way: and his heart fretteth against the LORD" (Pr.19:3).
> "Then I looked on all the works that my hands had wrought, and on the labor that I had labored to do: and, behold, all was vanity and vexation of spirit, and there was no profit under the sun" (Eccl.2:11).
> "Yea, I hated all my labor which I had taken under the sun: because I should leave it unto the man that shall be after me" (Eccl.2:18).
> "Wherefore doth a living man complain, a man for the punishment of his sins?" (Lam.3:39).

**4** (10:41-42) **Devotions—Worship—Quiet Time—Anxiety—Busyness**: Martha's one need was to sit quietly and listen to Jesus' words. Note four things.

1. Jesus loved and was tender toward Martha despite her failure. This is seen in His double address, "Martha, Martha." Jesus was deeply concerned for her. She was under stress and pressure and she had become disturbed. So many men

had moved in upon her, and she was trying her best to meet the needs of all. Jesus' heart went out to her, wanting to ease the pressuring and stressful situation and her sense of anger with Mary (cp. Lk.22:31; Acts 9:4 for double addresses tenderly spoken).

2.      Jesus reproved her because she was anxious and troubled about "many things." The word "anxious" (merimnais) means to worry. It has the idea of being inwardly torn and divided in two, of being distracted from what one's mind and heart and life should be focused upon. The word "troubled" (thorubazei) means to be disturbed, agitated, in turmoil, stirred up, ruffled. Martha sought to please Jesus with her service and ministering, but two things were wrong.

⇒ She was looking after "many things," too many. She was trying to do *too much* for so many.
⇒ She had become anxious and troubled.

3.      Jesus said, "One thing is needful." What was the one thing? He clearly said that it was the *good part* which Mary chose. And in the words of Scripture, *"Mary...sat at Jesus' feet, and heard His Word."* Martha's mistake was failing to do what Mary did. She let "many things" distract her from her *devotion* to the Lord, from sitting at His feet and hearing His Word. Note what Jesus meant by the "many things," what it actually was that distracted Martha from her devotions:

⇒ giving lodging and food to those who needed such
⇒ preparing the food for those who needed it
⇒ serving the hungry
⇒ making the needy comfortable

(Remember that Jesus was poor in worldly goods, having no place to lay His head, and apparently He sometimes had no money for food. Yet, He still stressed the spiritual over the physical.)

4.      Jesus said that the "good part" chosen by Mary would not be taken away. The hunger and thirst after righteousness (God's Word) would be filled and never taken away (Mt.5:6).

**Thought 1.** Our devotion to Christ is a daily affair (Lk.9:23). Therefore, seeking to hear His Word is to be a daily experience. Every believer should have what is commonly called *daily devotions*, a time set aside every day when he gets alone with God and sits at God's feet to seek His Word.

> "And in the morning, rising up a great while before day, he went out, and departed into a solitary place, and there prayed" (Mk.1:35).
> "And she was a widow of about fourscore and four years, which departed not from the temple, but served God with fastings and prayers night and day" (Lk.2:37).
> "These were more noble than those in Thessalonica, in that they received the word with all readiness of mind, and searched the scriptures daily, whether those things were so" (Acts 17:11).
> "For whatsoever things were written aforetime were written for our learning, that we through patience and comfort of the scriptures might have hope" (Ro.15:4).
> "Meditate upon these things; give thyself wholly to them; that thy profiting may appear to all" (1 Tim.4:15).
> "And it shall be with him, and he shall read therein all the days of his life: that he may learn to fear the LORD his God, to keep all the words of this law and these statutes, to do them" (Dt.17:19).
> "This book of the law shall not depart out of thy mouth; but thou shalt meditate therein day and night, that thou mayest observe to do according to all that is written therein: for then thou shalt make thy way prosperous, and then thou shalt have good success" (Josh.1:8).
> "But his delight is in the law of the LORD; and in his law doth he meditate day and night. And he shall be like a tree planted by the rivers of water, that bringeth forth his fruit in his season; his leaf also shall not wither; and whatsoever he doeth shall prosper" (Ps.1:2-3).
> "Stand in awe, and sin not: commune with your own heart upon your bed, and be still" (Ps.4:4; cp. Ps.63:6).
> "My voice shalt thou hear in the morning, O LORD; in the morning will I direct my prayer unto thee, and will look up" (Ps.5:3).
> "Let the words of my mouth, and the meditation of my heart, be acceptable in thy sight, O LORD, my strength, and my redeemer" (Ps.19:14).
> "Evening, and morning, and at noon, will I pray, and cry aloud: and he shall hear my voice" (Ps.55:17).
> "I will remember the works of the LORD: surely I will remember thy wonders of old. I will meditate also of all thy work, and talk of thy doings" (Ps.77:11-12; cp. Ps.104:34; 119:15-16; 119:47; 119:96-100; 119:148; 127:1-2; 143:5).
> "Thou wilt keep him in perfect peace, whose mind is stayed on thee: because he trusteth in thee. Trust ye in the LORD for ever: for in the LORD JEHOVAH is everlasting strength" (Is.26:3-4).
> "Now when Daniel knew that the writing was signed, he went into his house; and his windows being open in his chamber toward Jerusalem, he kneeled upon his knees three times a day, and prayed, and gave thanks before his God, as he did aforetime" (Dan.6:10).

**CHAPTER 11**

**H. The Great Subject of Prayer, 11:1-13**
(cp. Mt.6:5-15; cp. Mk.11:20-26)

**1 Jesus prayed**
a. The disciples asked Jesus to teach them how to pray
b. John had taught his disciples to pray
**2 Jesus' model prayer**
a. Thank God
1) For being our Father
2) For heaven
b. Praise His name
c. Pray
1) For His kingdom
2) For daily bread

3) For forgiveness

4) For deliverance
**3 Man's part in prayer**[DS1]
a. The illust.: Man is to persevere & endure in prayer

And it came to pass, that, as he was praying in a certain place, when he ceased, one of his disciples said unto him, Lord, teach us to pray, as John also taught his disciples.
2 And he said unto them, When ye pray, say, Our Father which art in heaven, Hallowed be thy name. Thy kingdom come. Thy will be done, as in heaven, so in earth.
3 Give us day by day our daily bread.
4 And forgive us our sins; for we also forgive every one that is indebted to us. And lead us not into temptation; but deliver us from evil.
5 And he said unto them, Which of you shall have a friend, and shall go unto him at midnight, and say unto him, Friend, lend me three loaves;
6 For a friend of mine in his journey is come to me, and I have nothing to set before

Him?
7 And he from within shall answer and say, Trouble me not: the door is now shut, and my children are with me in bed; I cannot rise and give thee.
8 I say unto you, Though he will not rise and give him, because he is his friend, yet because of his importunity he will rise and give him as many as he needeth.
9 And I say unto you, Ask, and it shall be given you; seek, and ye shall find; knock, and it shall be opened unto you.
10 For every one that asketh receiveth; and he that seeketh findeth; and to him that knocketh it shall be opened.
11 If a son shall ask bread of any of you that is a father, will he give him a stone? or if he ask a fish, will he for fish give him a serpent?
12 Or if he shall ask an egg, will he offer him a scorpion?
13 If ye then, being evil, know how to give good gifts unto your children: how much more shall your heavenly Father give the Holy Spirit to them that ask him?

b. The point: Perseverance & endurance receive what is requested

c. The exhortation
1) Ask—shall be given
2) Seek—shall find
3) Knock—shall be opened
d. The answer assured

**4 God's part in prayer**
a. The illust.: God is not evil, but He is good— He is just like a father

b. The point: God is *most* willing to give—especially the Holy Spirit to dwell within man's heart & life

# DIVISION V

## THE SON OF MAN'S GREAT JOURNEY TO JERUSALEM
## STAGE I): HIS MISSION AND PUBLIC CHALLENGE, 9:51-13:21

## H.    The Great Subject of Prayer, 11:1-13

(11:1-13) **Introduction**: this is one of the most thorough passages in all of Scripture dealing with the great subject of prayer. It is a passage that should be studied time and again.
1.    Jesus prayed (v.1).
2.    Jesus' model prayer (v.2-4).
3.    Man's part in prayer (v.5-10).
4.    God's part in prayer (v.11-13).

**1** (11:1) **Jesus Christ, Prayer Life**: Jesus prayed. It had been predicted that He would give Himself to prayer (Ps.109:4), and He was always praying. (See Introduction, Special Features, pt.7 for a complete list of Jesus' recorded prayer times.)
⇒  He prayed at His baptism (Lk.3:21).
⇒  He prayed during His temptation (Lk.5:16).
⇒  He continued all night in prayer (Lk.6:12).
⇒  He was alone praying (Lk.9:18).
⇒  He went up into a mountain to pray (Lk.9:28).
⇒  He was now praying in a certain place (Lk.11:1).
While Jesus prayed, something caught the eye and ear of the disciples. Apparently, they were off to the side someplace but within sight and hearing. Three things stirred them to ask Jesus to teach them to pray.
1.    Jesus often prayed, and He emphasized prayer as one of the greatest needs of human life. He always insisted that it was the source of His strength in living and serving God. Therefore, the disciples were aroused to hunger after the same strength for life and service.
2.    Jesus prayed as a Son to His Father, and such intimacy stirred the disciples to want the same kind of relationship with God.
3.    John had taught His disciples to pray. It was a common practice for a teacher to instruct his disciples in prayer. Jesus' disciples used this as the basis to ask Him: "Lord, teach us to pray."

**2** (11:2-4) **Prayer**: Jesus' model prayer. Naturally, Jesus will teach anyone to pray—anyone who is really sincere and wants to begin praying. Note what Jesus did. He said, "*When ye pray, say....*" or "*After this manner...pray ye*" or "*Pray then like this.*" He was giving a *model prayer* upon which we are to base our praying. It is a guide, the points of which are to be *prayed through*. The believer is to develop the points as He prays. (See note—Mt.6:9-13 for more discussion.)

1. Thank God for two things.
   a. Thank God for being "our Father." This is a personal relationship, a family relationship, the relationship of a child to a parent. It is a family relationship wrought by a person's being born anew (Jn.1:12-13; 2 Cor.6:17-18. Cp. Gal.4:4-7.) A person needs to thank God for being his Father, for creating the family of God and allowing him to be a part of so glorious a family.
   b. Thank God for heaven. Heaven is the spiritual dimension of being; it is the real world, incorruptible and undefiled, and it does not fade away. More importantly, it is where God is, and it is where we shall be. We need to thank God for heaven, that He is there and that we shall be in heaven with Him.
2. Praise God. His name is hallowed, set apart, different. God is holy, righteous, pure, loving, kind, merciful, gracious. Therefore, God is to be praised for who He is.
3. Request four things in particular. But note: these should be prayed for only after we have thanked and praised God.
   a. Pray for God's kingdom to come. Christ needs to be enthroned, His rule and reign established on earth. His will needs to be done in all of our lives just as it is done in heaven. We need to pray for such to come. (See DEEPER STUDY # 3—Mt.19:23-24 for a discussion of the kingdom which shows that for which we should pray.)
   b. Pray for daily bread, that is, for the necessities of life. People are hungry, starving both physically and spiritually. We all need to be fed both without and within. We need to pray both for our bodies and spirits—*daily* (cp. Mt.6:24-32).
   c. Pray for forgiveness. We should pray for the Father to forgive our sins, and we need to take some time in discussing the matter with our Father. But note the word "our." We are to ask God to forgive "our sins," the sins of our family, neighbors, city, state, nation, and world. Sin is a shame, an affront to God. Sin is the most serious matter and most tragic event to ever occur in the universe. It is to be discussed with the Father every day—not just our own sins, but the world's sins. Intercessory prayer for the sinners of the world is to be a daily event in the life of every believer. But note a crucial fact: old sins that have been confessed and covered by the blood of Christ are not to be brought back up to God. They are already forgiven, hid and cast away by God. He does not want them remembered anymore. They are too painful and hurtful. However, there are new sins—new things committed every day—so many within our hearts and throughout the world that it would stagger the human mind. We are ever so short of God's glory—*unconformed* to the image of Christ, undeveloped and immature—so far short of what we should be. It is these and the unconfessed sins of the world and the new sins of the human heart that need to be forgiven. The believer needs to come every day begging for a fresh experience of forgiveness both for himself and for the world.

      Note there is a condition for forgiveness. We must forgive those who sin against us. We sin and sin often against God. If we expect Him to forgive us, we have to forgive those who offend us.

   > **"For if ye forgive men their trespasses, your heavenly Father will also forgive you: but if ye forgive not men their trespasses, neither will your Father forgive your trespasses" (Mt.6:14-15).**
   > **"And when ye stand praying, forgive, if ye have ought against any: that your Father also which is in heaven may forgive you your trespasses" (Mk.11:25).**

   d. Pray for deliverance. The idea of God's leading men into temptation bothers some people. God tempts no one to do evil (Jas.1:13). What this request means is, "Pray for God to deliver us from temptation and from the evil one, Satan" (cp. Lk.22:40; 1 Cor.10:13).

**3** (11:5-10) **Prayer**: man's part in prayer. No clearer explanation of man's part in prayer could be given than what is taught here.
1. Jesus *illustrated* very simply what man's part is. The story explains itself.
2. Jesus drove *the point* home: perseverance and endurance receives what it asks. The believer shall get what he asks if he...
   - will not leave the throne of God.
   - will not go away.
   - will not let God alone.

The whole point is that the person who prays must be sincere, fervent, constant, persistent, persevering, and enduring in seeking the face of God for whatever he wants.
3. Jesus gave an exhortation, a mini-sermon, to persevere and endure in prayer, and he stated it perfectly in two ways.
   a. The person who prays is to continue asking for what he needs.
      ⇒ Ask, and it shall be given you. But if asking does not receive it, then...
      ⇒ seek, and ye shall find. But if seeking does not receive it, then...
      ⇒ knock, and it shall be opened unto you.
      The point is this: we must mean what we pray, and the way we show God our sincerity is by continuing to ask for what we need.

b. The verbs ask, seek, and knock are all *continuous action*. We are to keep on asking and seeking and knocking, ever beseeching God to hear us.

4. The answer is assured. God will hear and answer the person who perseveres and endures in prayer. The believer always receives the need desired. In the parable shared by Jesus, the friend was occupied with a very needed and worthy matter—he was rejuvenating his body with sleep. The point is this: most have experienced being disturbed while sleeping (whether by a crying child or some other noise) and being slow to arise. Few arise unless the beckoning call persists. But one always arises if the child coughs or cries enough or the noise repeats itself enough. Persistence proves one's sincerity. There are certain requests that need a "continual coming" (Lk.18:5). (See note and DEEPER STUDY # 1—Mt.7:7.)

God is most willing to give. The child of God can rest assured that when the circumstances of life become hard, God will give the presence and power of the Holy Spirit to see His child through.

Now note another fact: God is not only willing to answer, He is *most willing* to answer. He loves and cares for man in all his needs. This must always be remembered. (See DEEPER STUDY # 1—Lk.11:5-10.) Note something else: God always answers our prayers, but sometimes the answer has to be "no." Why? Because what we asked is not always for our good, and God is always going to do what is best for us.

"Watch and pray, that ye enter not into temptation: the spirit indeed is willing, but the flesh is weak" (Mt.26:41).

"And he spake a parable unto them to this end, that men ought always to pray, and not to faint" (Lk.18:1).

"Watch ye therefore, and pray always, that ye may be accounted worthy to escape all these things that shall come to pass, and to stand before the Son of man" (Lk.21:36).

"Praying always with all prayer and supplication in the Spirit, and watching thereunto with all perseverance and supplication for all saints" (Eph.6:18).

"Be careful for nothing; but in every thing by prayer and supplication with thanksgiving let your requests be made known unto God" (Ph.4:6).

"Continue in prayer, and watch in the same with thanksgiving" (Col.4:2).

"Pray without ceasing" (1 Th.5:17).

"But if from thence thou shalt seek the LORD thy God, thou shalt find him, if thou seek him with all thy heart and with all thy soul" (Dt.4:29).

"Seek the LORD and his strength, seek his face continually" (1 Chron.16:11).

"Seek ye the LORD while he may be found, call ye upon him while he is near" (Is.55:6).

"And ye shall seek me, and find me, when ye shall search for me with all your heart" (Jer.29:13).

"Seek the LORD, and his strength: seek his face evermore" (Ps.105:4).

"I love them that love me; and those that seek me early shall find me" (Pr.8:17).

---

**DEEPER STUDY # 1**

(11:5-10) **Prayer—Fellowship**: Why does God not always answer our prayers immediately? Why is it necessary to ask and seek and knock and to keep on asking and seeking and knocking? Why do we need to ask at all when God knows our needs even before we ask?

There are at least four reasons.

1. Prayer teaches us to communicate and fellowship with God and to trust and seek after God more and more. When God holds back the giving, we keep coming to talk and share with Him more and more. Just as a human father longs for such fellowship and trust, our heavenly Father longs for such fellowship and trust.

2. Prayer teaches us both patience and hope in God and His promises. When God does not give immediately, we patiently (enduringly) keep coming into His presence, waiting for and hoping in what He has promised us (Mt.21:22; Jn.14:26; 1 Jn.5:14-15).

3. Prayer teaches us to love God as our Father more and more. Knowing that what we ask is coming and having to wait on it causes us to draw closer and closer to God and His gifts. And then when the gift is given, our hearts are endeared ever so much more to Him.

4. Prayer demonstrates how deeply we trust God and how much we love and depend upon Him. A person who really trusts God—who really knows that what he asks is going to be received—will bring more and more to God. He will come to God in prayer more and more. But the person who is not quite sure about receiving will only occasionally come, usually only in emergencies. God easily sees how much we really love and trust Him by our prayer life.

---

**4** (11:11-13) **Prayer**: God's part in prayer. No clearer explanation of God's part in prayer could be given than what is taught here.

1. Jesus illustrated what God's part is. God is not evil; He is good just as an earthly father is good. Jesus stressed the point with three simple illustrations. Note all three illustrations had to do with a father and his son.

2. Jesus drove the point home: God is most willing to give. Note two points.

a. Man is evil, full of selfishness and sin, yet he gives to his child when asked. (Note the enormous contrast being made between evil man and God, who is perfectly good. If evil man gives, it is impossible that God, who is good, would not give.)

b. Our heavenly Father gives us the very Source of all good things, the Holy Spirit Himself. Just imagine the very presence of God dwelling within our hearts and bodies! If He dwells within us, then every good thing is assured. Once we have the Holy Spirit, we do not have to pray to God who is *way off* in outer space somewhere. We do not have to wait upon His gifts to arrive. We have His presence within...

- to accompany and be with us.

    "Nevertheless I tell you the truth; It is expedient for you that I go away: for if I go not away, the Comforter will not come unto you; but if I depart, I will send him unto you" (Jn.16:7).

- to look after and care for us.

    "But the fruit of the Spirit is love, joy, peace, longsuffering, gentleness, goodness, faith, meekness, temperance: against such there is no law" (Gal.5:22-23).

- to direct and guide us.

    "For as many as are led by the Spirit of God, they are the sons of God" (Ro.8:14).
    "Howbeit when he, the Spirit of truth, is come, he will guide you into all truth: for he shall not speak of himself; but whatsoever he shall hear, that shall he speak: and he will show you things to come" (Jn.16:13).

- to assure and comfort us.

    "But the Comforter, which is the Holy Ghost, whom the Father will send in my name, he shall teach you all things, and bring all things to your remembrance, whatsoever I have said unto you" (Jn.14:26).
    "For ye have not received the spirit of bondage again to fear; but ye have received the Spirit of adoption, whereby we cry, Abba, Father. The Spirit itself beareth witness with our spirit, that we are the children of God: and if children, then heirs; heirs of God, and joint-heirs with Christ; if so be that we suffer with him, that we may be also glorified together" (Ro.8:15-17).

- to pray and intercede for us.

    "Likewise the Spirit also helpeth our infirmities: for we know not what we should pray for as we ought: but the Spirit itself maketh intercession for us with groanings which cannot be uttered" (Ro.8:26).

**Thought 1.** God does answer prayer.

    "And all things, whatsoever ye shall ask in prayer, believing, ye shall receive" (Mt.21:22).
    "Therefore I say unto you, What things soever ye desire, when ye pray, believe that ye receive them, and ye shall have them" (Mk.11:24).
    And whatsoever ye shall ask in my name, that will I do, that the Father may be glorified in the Son. If ye shall ask any thing in my name, I will do it" (Jn.14:13-14).
    "If ye abide in me, and my words abide in you, ye shall ask what ye will, and it shall be done unto you" (Jn.15:7).
    "Hitherto have ye asked nothing in my name: ask, and ye shall receive, that your joy may be full" (Jn.16:24).
    "If any of you lack wisdom, let him ask of God, that giveth to all men liberally, and upbraideth not; and it shall be given him. But let him ask in faith, nothing wavering. For he that wavereth is like a wave of the sea driven with the wind and tossed" (Jas.1:5-6).
    "And whatsoever we ask, we receive of him, because we keep his commandments, and do those things that are pleasing in his sight" (1 Jn.3:22).
    "And this is the confidence that we have in him, that, if we ask any thing according to his will, he heareth us: and if we know that he hear us, whatsoever we ask, we know that we have the petitions that we desired of him" (1 Jn.5:14-15).
    "If my people, which are called by my name, shall humble themselves, and pray, and seek my face, and turn from their wicked ways; then will I hear from heaven, and will forgive their sin, and will heal their land" (2 Chron.7:14).
    "He shall call upon me, and I will answer him: I will be with him in trouble; I will deliver him, and honor him" (Ps.91:15).
    "When the poor and needy seek water, and there is none, and their tongue faileth for thirst, I the LORD will hear them, I the God of Israel will not forsake them" (Is.41:17).
    "Then shalt thou call, and the LORD shall answer; thou shalt cry, and he shall say, Here I am" (Is.58:9).
    "And it shall come to pass, that before they call, I will answer; and while they are yet speaking, I will hear" (Is.65:24).
    "Call unto me, and I will answer thee, and show thee great and mighty things, which thou knowest not" (Jer.33:3).
    "They shall call on my name, and I will hear them: I will say, It is my people: and they shall say, The LORD is my God" (Zech.13:9).

224

| | I. The Proof that Jesus is the Messiah, 11:14-28 (Mt.12:22-30; Mk.3:22-30) | keepeth his palace, his goods are in peace: | He claimed to be stronger than Satan |
|---|---|---|---|
| 1 Jesus proved He was the Messiah—He cast a devil out of a man<br>a. The people wondered: Who was Jesus?<br><br>b. Some accused Him: He was a deceiver, of Beelzebub<br><br>c. Some tested Him: Sought a sign<br><br>2 Illust.1: A kingdom & a house—He claimed to be of another kingdom & house than Satan's kingdom & house<br><br><br><br><br><br><br><br><br><br>3 Illust.2: Religious exorcist—He claimed the right to be respected, at least as much as other ministers<br><br>4 Illust.3: The finger of God—He claimed to possess the power to usher in the Kingdom of God<br>5 Illust.4: A stronger man— | 14 And he was casting out a devil, and it was dumb. And it came to pass, when the devil was gone out, the dumb spake; and the people wondered.<br>15 But some of them said, He casteth out devils through Beelzebub the chief of the devils.<br>16 And others, tempting him, sought of him a sign from heaven.<br>17 But he, knowing their thoughts, said unto them, Every kingdom divided against itself is brought to desolation; and a house divided against a house falleth.<br>18 If Satan also be divided against himself, how shall his kingdom stand? because ye say that I cast out devils through Beelzebub.<br>19 And if I by Beelzebub cast out devils, by whom do your sons cast them out? therefore shall they be your judges.<br>20 But if I with the finger of God cast out devils, no doubt the kingdom of God is come upon you.<br>21 When a strong man armed | 22 But when a stronger than he shall come upon him, and overcome him, he taketh from him all his armour wherein he trusted, and divideth his spoils.<br>23 He that is not with me is against me: and he that gathereth not with me scattereth.<br>24 When the unclean spirit is gone out of a man, he walketh through dry places, seeking rest; and finding none, he saith, I will return unto my house whence I came out.<br>25 And when he cometh, he findeth it swept and garnished.<br>26 Then goeth he, and taketh to him seven other spirits more wicked than himself; and they enter in, and dwell there; and the last state of that man is worse than the first.<br>27 And it came to pass, as he spake these things, a certain woman of the company lifted up her voice, and said unto him, Blessed is the womb that bare thee, and the paps which thou hast sucked.<br>28 But he said, Yea rather, blessed are they that hear the word of God, and keep it. | <br><br><br>6 Illust.5: A shepherd & a flock—He claimed to be the pivotal figure of history<br>7 Illust.6: An empty house—He claimed that a man must turn from self-reformation to Him & be infilled with His very presence<br><br><br><br><br><br><br><br><br><br>8 Conclusion: The necessary thing—to hear the Word of God & keep it |

# DIVISION V

## THE SON OF MAN'S GREAT JOURNEY TO JERUSALEM (STAGE I): HIS MISSION AND PUBLIC CHALLENGE, 9:51-13:21

### I.    The Proof that Jesus is the Messiah, 11:14-28

(11:14-28) **Introduction**: Jesus has been rejected, denied, and cursed by most men. Yet there is enormous evidence that He is just who He claimed to be. Jesus Himself gave some of the indisputable evidence in this passage.

1. Jesus proved that He was the Messiah—He cast a devil out of a man (v.14-16).
2. Illustration.1: a kingdom and a house—He claimed to be of another kingdom and house than Satan's kingdom and house (v.17-18).
3. Illustration 2: religious exorcist—He claimed the right to be respected, at least as much as other ministers (v.19).
4. Illustration 3: the finger of God—He claimed to possess the power to usher in the Kingdom of God (v.20).
5. Illustration 4: a stronger man—He claimed to be stronger than Satan (v.21-22).
6. Illustration 5: a shepherd and a flock—He claimed to be the pivotal or decisive figure of history (v.23).
7. Illustration 6: an empty house—He claimed that a man must turn from self-reformation to Him and be infilled with His very presence (v.24-26).
8. Conclusion: the necessary thing—to hear the Word of God and keep it (v.27-28).

[1] (11:14-16) **Signs, Seeking—Jesus Christ, Charges Against**: Jesus proved that He was the Messiah by casting a devil out of a man. He demonstrated that He...
- was waging war against the evil forces of this world (Eph.6:12).
- had come to destroy the works of the devil (Jn.3:8).

Jesus saw a man gripped by evil, by some spirit that made him dumb and blind (cp. Mt.12:22). Jesus' heart went out to the man, and He was moved with compassion for him. Jesus cast out the evil spirit and healed the man. By doing so, He demonstrated to all that He was the true Messiah, the One who possessed the power of God perfectly. The response of the people was threefold.

1. Some were amazed and astonished, wondering just who Jesus might be.

2.     Others immediately rejected Jesus. But note they did not question His power. They had to admit He possessed the power to do marvelous things. The tragedy of their rejection was this: they said the power was of Beelzebub, the chief of the devils. (See Deeper Study # 1—Mk.3:22 for more discussion.)

3.     Others sought fleshly, carnal signs that would satisfy their worldly desires. To confess Christ would cost them everything they had, both wealth and friends (see note and Deeper Study # 1—Lk.9:23; note—Mt.19:16-22). There was already plenty of evidence that Jesus was the true Messiah; they were just unwilling to give all they had to meet the needs of a desperate world and to be ridiculed and abused by the world (see note—Mt.16:2-4). Therefore, they demanded a sign—a sign so great that it would convert everyone and everything all at once. If everything could be miraculously converted all at once, then heaven would be on earth and all man's carnal desires would be met. (See outline and notes—Jn.6:22-29, esp. 6:26-27, 30.) Therefore, they asked for a sign from heaven, a sign that would convert all men. (Note: if God did this, it would be treating us as robots, eliminating our freedom of choice and will.)

> **Thought 1.** Men think that if they had a spectacular sign, then all men would believe and two things would happen. (1) There would be no abuse, ridicule, or persecution by friends or neighbors or anyone else. (2) The whole world would be converted. The Kingdom of God would come to earth and there would be plenty for everyone. There would be no need to protect what one has nor to fear the selfishness and evil of others. This, of course, is untrue, for man is *selfish and self-centered*, seeking to control his own life. Man would still disbelieve and distrust God and would still choose to do what he desired instead of God's will.

> **"The heart is deceitful above all things, and desperately wicked: who can know it?" (Jer.17:9).**

> Jesus knew the thoughts of the unbelievers standing there, so He delivered a crushing blow to their thoughts and unbelief. He did so by giving six illustrations.

**2**  (11:17-18) **Jesus Christ, Deity—Messiah, Proof of—Satan, Purpose of**: Illustration 1—a kingdom. Jesus claimed to be of another kingdom and house than Satan's. Note several facts.

1.     Jesus used a very simple illustration to make His claim, that of a divided kingdom and a house. It is an illustration that is clearly understood by all because everyone knows of kingdoms and houses that are divided and that crumble every day.

2.     Jesus assumed the existence of Satan and his kingdom, both of which struggle against righteousness and good. He did not deny Satan's existence nor try to correct man's *mistaken notion* about the devil and his kingdom. Why? Because the devil and his kingdom are not *mistaken notions*. They are very, very real (see Deeper Study # 1—Rev.12:9).

3.     Jesus said Satan is not divided against himself. He is not going to do good nor is he going to build up God's kingdom. The very opposite is true. Satan is going to build his own kingdom, his own rule and reign. He desires to oppose and exalt himself against God. He wants men to follow him and his way of evil and by such to cut the heart of God. He wants God to hurt, and he knows that God hurts when man goes astray and turns from God's kingdom (see Deeper Study # 3—Mt.19:23-24). Therefore, Satan seeks to lead men into evil by enticing them through the fleshly and carnal desires of human nature. Satan knows that sin leads to disease and to the destruction of the human body and family. He knows that such destruction causes great pain and hurt and suffering for God, which apparently is his ultimate motive.

The point is clear: Satan is not going to be casting out evil. Therefore, the power of Christ has to be of God. His power is good; it casts out evil. Therefore He, the Messiah, is of God's kingdom and house, not of Satan's kingdom and house.

> **"He that believeth on him is not condemned: but he that believeth not is condemned already, because he hath not believed in the name of the only begotten Son of God" (Jn.3:18).**
> **"Say ye of him, whom the Father hath sanctified, and sent into the world, Thou blasphemest; because I said, I am the Son of God? If I do not the works of my Father, believe me not. But if I do, though ye believe not me, believe the works: that ye may know, and believe, that the Father is in me, and I in him" (Jn.10:36-38).**
> **"Of how much sorer punishment, suppose ye, shall he be thought worthy, who hath trodden under foot the Son of God, and hath counted the blood of the covenant, wherewith he was sanctified, an unholy thing, and hath done despite unto the Spirit of grace?" (Heb.10:29).**

**3**  (11:19) **Jesus Christ, Response to**: Illustration 2—religious exorcists. Jesus claimed the right to be respected, at least as much as other ministers. This is a simple argument. There were Jewish exorcists, sons of the Jewish nation, who tried to cast out devils in the name of God. Jesus argued that they were not accused of hellish power. Why was He being accused? The question is pointed and instructive, for Jesus always healed and was always successful in casting out evil. Certainly He should be respected as much if not more than other ministers.

> **Thought 1.** The mistake of the Jews was that they exalted priests (ministers) and religion above God. Many do the same today. They read, quote, and use other ministers as their source much more than they use Jesus and the Holy Scripture.

> **Thought 2.** Jesus Christ should be exalted as the Messiah, the Son of God who alone can cast out evil. Therefore, He must be read, quoted, and preached day in and day out. Jesus Christ must be honored by every man.

> **"That all men should honour the Son, even as they honour the Father. He that honoureth not the Son honoureth not the Father which hath sent him. Verily, verily, I say unto**

you, He that heareth my word, and believeth on him that sent me, hath everlasting life, and shall not come into condemnation; but is passed from death unto life" (Jn.5:23-24).

"Search the scriptures; for in them ye think ye have eternal life: and they are they which testify of me" (Jn.5:39; cp. v.40-47).

"Then Simon Peter answered him, Lord, to whom shall we go? thou hast the words of eternal life" (Jn.6:68).

"The officers answered, Never man spake like this man" (Jn.7:46).

"Jesus answered and said unto him, If a man love me, he will keep my words: and my Father will love him, and we will come unto him, and make our abode with him. He that loveth me not keepeth not my sayings: and the word which ye hear is not mine, but the Father's which sent me" (Jn.14:23-24).

"And hereby we do know that we know him, if we keep his commandments" (1 Jn.2:3).

"I know thy works: behold, I have set before thee an open door, and no man can shut it: for thou hast a little strength, and hast kept my word, and hast not denied my name" (Rev.3:8).

"Give unto the LORD the glory due unto his name; worship the LORD in the beauty of holiness" (Ps.29:2).

"O magnify the LORD with me, and let us exalt his name together" (Ps.34:3).

"Let the redeemed of the LORD say so, whom he hath redeemed from the hand of the enemy" (Ps.107:2).

"O LORD, thou art my God; I will exalt thee, I will praise thy name; for thou hast done wonderful things; thy counsels of old are faithfulness and truth" (Is.25:1).

**4** (11:20) **Kingdom of God—Messiah**: Illustration 3—the finger of God. Jesus claimed to possess the power to usher in the Kingdom of God. The finger of God is the same as the Spirit of God (cp. Mt.12:28). The power that cast out devils is the power of God. It comes from God and from no one else (see note, pt.3—Lk.11:17-18).

Now note something of crucial importance. Jesus said, "If I possess the power of God, then I am bringing the kingdom of God to you. Wherever the power of God is, there is the Kingdom of God, for the power of God is used to bring about the rule and reign of God. Therefore, the Kingdom of God is come upon you and is beginning in this day and age. The power of evil is now being cast out." Jesus is, of course, urging that no one miss the Kingdom of God. He is ushering the kingdom in, but it has to be accepted (see DEEPER STUDY # 3—Mt.19:23-24).

"The law and the prophets were until John: since that time the kingdom of God is preached, and every man presseth into it" (Lk.16:16).

"And when he was demanded of the Pharisees, when the kingdom of God should come, he answered them and said, The kingdom of God cometh not with observation; neither shall they say, Lo here! or, lo there! for, behold, the kingdom of God is within you" (Lk.17:20-21).

"Now after that John was put in prison, Jesus came into Galilee, preaching the gospel of the kingdom of God, and saying, The time is fulfilled, and the kingdom of God is at hand: repent ye, and believe the gospel" (Mk.1:14-15).

"Verily I say unto you, Whosoever shall not receive the kingdom of God as a little child, he shall not enter therein" (Mk.10:15).

"And he lifted up his eyes on his disciples, and said, Blessed be ye poor [in spirit]: for yours is the kingdom of God" (Lk.6:20).

"Jesus answered and said unto him, Verily, verily, I say unto thee, except a man be born again, he cannot see the kingdom of God....Jesus answered, Verily, verily, I say unto thee, Except a man be born of water and of the Spirit, he cannot enter into the kingdom of God" (Jn.3:3, 5).

"And when Jesus saw that he answered discreetly, he said unto him, Thou art not far from the kingdom of God. And no man after that durst ask him any question" (Mk.12:34).

"And he said unto them, Verily I say unto you, There is no man that hath left house, or parents, or brethren, or wife, or children, for the kingdom of God's sake, who shall not receive manifold more in this present time, and in the world to come life everlasting" (Lk.18:29-30).

"For the kingdom of God is not meat and drink; but righteousness, and peace, and joy in the Holy Ghost" (Ro.14:17).

**5** (11:21-22) **Satan—Jesus Christ, Destroys Satan**: Illustration 4—a stronger man. Jesus claimed to be stronger than Satan.

1. Satan is the strong man. Note he is armed.
2. Satan's "goods" are men who are subjected to him: men who follow the way of the world, that is, selfishness, the rejection of God, and rebellion against righteousness.
3. Satan works to keep his palace (kingdom) and "goods" in peace, that is, under his rule and reign. There is some *peace and comfort* in Satan's realm. Satan will give pleasures to secure a person in his kingdom. But note, it is only for a season (Heb.11:25; 9:27).
4. The stronger Man is Jesus Christ.
   ⇒ Jesus Christ came upon Satan.

"He that committeth sin is of the devil; for the devil sinneth from the beginning. For this purpose the Son of God was manifested, that he might destroy the works of the devil" (1 Jn.3:8).

"**Forasmuch then as the children are partakers of flesh and blood, he also himself likewise took part of the same; that through death he might destroy him that had the power of death, that is, the devil; and deliver them who through fear of death were all their lifetime subject to bondage**" (Heb.2:14-15).

⇒ Jesus Christ overcame Satan.

"**And having spoiled principalities and powers, he made a show of them openly, triumphing over them in it**" (Col.2:15).
"**Who [God] hath delivered us from the power of darkness, and hath translated us into the kingdom of his dear Son: in whom we have redemption through his blood, even the forgiveness of sins**" (Col.1:13-14).

⇒ Jesus Christ delivered men from Satan's strategies.

"**Finally, my brethren, be strong in the Lord, and in the power of his might. Put on the whole armour of God, that ye may be able to stand against the wiles of the devil**" (Eph.6:10-11; cp. v.12-18).

⇒ Jesus Christ divided Satan's spoils: the spoils of a clear mind, clean body, pure heart, and the gifts of the Spirit.

"**Wherefore he saith, When he ascended up on high, he led captivity captive, and gave gifts unto men. (Now that he ascended, what is it but that he also descended first into the lower parts of the earth? He that descended is the same also that ascended up far above all heavens, that he might fill all things)**" (Eph.4:8-11; cp. Gal.5:22-23).

**6** (11:23) **Shepherd—Decision—History, Pivotal Point of**: Illustration 5—a shepherd and a flock. Jesus claimed to be the pivotal or decisive figure of history. Gathering and scattering is a picture of the shepherd and his flock. The person who does not stand with Christ does not gather, but scatters the flock. Where a person stands in relation to Jesus Christ determines the success and impact of his life. Jesus Christ is the decisive figure of history that determines a person's destiny (see note—Lk.7:28).

There is *no neutrality* with Christ: a person is either with Him or against Him. A person either fights against evil or against righteousness, either fights for the Kingdom of God or for the kingdom of evil. Standing still is impossible, for standing still is doing nothing for God. Standing still, being neutral, is working for evil by allowing evil to continue and to grow without opposition. A voice of silence is a voice for evil.

"**Ye cannot drink the cup of the Lord, and the cup of devils: ye cannot be partakers of the Lord's table, and of the table of devils**" (1 Cor.10:21).
"**A double minded man is unstable in all his ways**" (Jas.1:8).
"**Draw nigh to God, and he will draw nigh to you. Cleanse your hands, ye sinners; and purify your hearts, ye double minded**" (Jas.4:8).
"**And Jesus said unto him, No man, having put his hand to the plough, and looking back, is fit for the kingdom of God**" (Lk.9:62).
"**No servant can serve two masters: for either he will hate the one, and love the other; or else he will hold to the one, and despise the other. Ye cannot serve God and mammon**" (Lk.16:13).
"**See, I have set before thee this day life and good, and death and evil**" (Dt.30:15).
"**I call heaven and earth to record this day against you, that I have set before you life and death, blessing and cursing: therefore choose life, that both thou and thy seed may live**" (Dt.30:19).
"**And Elijah came unto all the people, and said, How long halt ye between two opinions? if the LORD be God, follow him: but if Baal, then follow him. And the people answered him not a word**" (1 Ki.18:21).
"**They feared the LORD, and served their own gods, after the manner of the nations whom they carried away from thence**" (2 Ki.17:33).
"**Their heart is divided; now shall they be found faulty: he shall break down their altars, he shall spoil their images**" (Hos.10:2).

**7** (11:24-26) **Reformation—Regeneration—New Birth**: Illustration 6—an empty house. Jesus claimed that a man must turn from self-reformation to Him and be infilled with His very presence. Note three things.
1. What happens when a man casts the evil (spirit) out of his life?
   a. A man experiences many "dry places." No matter where he goes or what he does, there is an emptiness, a void. Nothing seems to fill the evil (spirit) put out of his life.
   b. The evil (spirit) that was in man and has been put aside seeks rest, but finds none. Man's evil spirit, when it is subdued or cast aside, becomes restless. It goes about in *restless wanderings*, yet it finds no rest.
   c. A man always experiences the craving of the evil to return. The evil (spirit) says, "I will return." Note the words, "into my house," the place that was so comfortable, that made him feel so good and at ease. He says in essence, "I will return to that which always looked good, tasted good, and felt good."
2. All the above has to do with a man's reforming and cleaning up his life. However, note what happened when the evil (spirit) returned to the man and knocked on the door of his thoughts and pried at the windows of his desires.

    a.  He found the house empty and *unoccupied*.

    b.  He found the house swept; it was clean and put in order—ready for occupancy. The man had removed all the rubbish and swept out all the dirt. He had cleaned the house (his life), but he had not invited the *tenant* (the Lord Jesus Christ) to move in and occupy the premises.

3.    What happened when the evil (spirit) found the house empty and unoccupied?

    a.  The evil swarmed and flooded in with more force than ever. The man indulged much more than before.

    b.  The evil brought more evil with him—launched out and did more evil than ever.

    c.  The evil *dwelt* there. It is unlikely the man would ever clean his house again.

> "And because iniquity shall abound, the love of many shall wax cold" (Mt.24:12).
>
> "Howbeit then, when ye knew not God, ye did service unto them which by nature are no gods. But now, after that ye have known God, or rather are known of God, how turn ye again to the weak and beggarly elements, whereunto ye desire again to be in bondage? Ye observe days, and months, and times, and years [religious ritual]" (Gal.4:8-10).
>
> "But evil men and seducers shall wax worse and worse, deceiving, and being deceived" (2 Tim.3:13).
>
> "After they have escaped the pollutions of the world through the knowledge of the Lord and Saviour Jesus Christ, [if] they are again entangled therein, and overcome, the latter end is worse with them than the beginning. For it had been better for them not to have known the way of righteousness, than, after they have known it, to turn from the holy commandment delivered unto them" (2 Pt.2:20-21).
>
> "Nevertheless I have somewhat against thee, because thou hast left thy first love" (Rev.2:4).

**Thought 1.** The answer to being infilled with the presence of Christ is not reformation—not the changing of the outside or the external—but the transformation or regeneration of man's heart. It is the filling of the human heart and of society with Christ Himself and with acts of Christian love and care. The message and acts of love and care are to be carried to a world suffering and reeling in pain and war, doomed to die and to be without God's presence forever.

**8**   (11:27-28) **Word of God**: the necessary thing is to hear the Word of God and keep it. Luke is the only Gospel writer to mention this incident. Apparently what happened was that some woman in the crowd was caught up in Jesus' teaching and presence. She just exclaimed that a woman who could bear One like Jesus was to be blessed. But note what Jesus said. There is a greater blessing than what even Mary had. Imagine! A greater blessing than being able to testify that one had given birth to Jesus! What is it? "Blessed are they that hear the Word of God and keep it" (v.28).

> "He that hath my commandments, and keepeth them, he it is that loveth me: and he that loveth me shall be loved of my Father, and I will love him, and will manifest myself to him" (Jn.14:21).
>
> "But whoso looketh into the perfect law of liberty, and continueth therein, he being not a forgetful hearer, but a doer of the work, this man shall be blessed in his deed" (Jas.1:25).
>
> "And whatsoever we ask, we receive of him, because we keep his commandments, and do those things that are pleasing in his sight" (1 Jn.3:22).
>
> "Blessed are they that do his commandments, that they may have right to the tree of life, and may enter in through the gates into the city" (Rev.22:14).
>
> "Now therefore, if ye will obey my voice indeed, and keep my covenant, then ye shall be a peculiar treasure unto me above all people: for all the earth is mine" (Ex.19:5).
>
> "When thou art in tribulation, and all these things are come upon thee, even in the latter days, if thou turn to the LORD thy God, and shalt be obedient unto his voice; (for the LORD thy God is a merciful God;) he will not forsake thee, neither destroy thee, nor forget the covenant of thy fathers which he sware unto them" (Dt.4:30-31).
>
> "O that there were such a heart in them, that they would fear me, and keep all my commandments always, that it might be well with them, and with their children for ever!" (Dt.5:29).
>
> "And if thou wilt walk in my ways, to keep my statutes and my commandments, as thy father David did walk, then I will lengthen thy days" (1 Ki.3:14).
>
> "If they obey and serve him, they shall spend their days in prosperity, and their years in pleasures" (Job 36:11).
>
> "Whoso keepeth the law is a wise son: but he that is a companion of riotous men shameth his father" (Pr.28:7).

| | J. The Great Proof that Jesus is the Messiah: The Resurrection, 11:29-36 (Mt.5:14-16; 12:38-42; Mk.4:21-22; cp.Lk.8:16) | 32 The men of Nineve shall rise up in the judgment with this generation, and shall condemn it: for they repented at the preaching of Jonas; and, behold, a greater than Jonas is here. | b. Bc. they did not repent with Christ's preaching (as Nineveh) |
|---|---|---|---|
| 1 The crowds thronged Jesus<br>a. Jesus charged: This is an evil generation<br>b. The reason: They sought a sign<br>2 The one & only sign: The sign of Jonah, that is, the resurrection | 29 And when the people were gathered thick together, he began to say, This is an evil generation: they seek a sign; and there shall no sign be given it, but the sign of Jonas the prophet.<br>30 For as Jonas was a sign unto the Ninevites, so shall also the Son of man be to this generation. | 33 No man, when he hath lighted a candle, putteth it in a secret place, neither under a bushel, but on a candlestick, that they which come in may see the light.<br>34 The light of the body is the eye: therefore when thine eye is single, thy whole body also is full of light; but when thine eye is evil, thy body also is full of darkness. | 4 The sign's (resurrection) visibility: It is as clearly seen as a shining candle<br>a. A fact: A shining candle is not hid but is placed where it gives light<br>b. A choice: To see the sign (resurrection) with a healthy eye or a diseased eye |
| 3 The sign's (resurrection) effect: It will condemn this evil generation<br>a. Bc. they did not seek Christ (as the queen sought wisdom) | 31 The queen of the south shall rise up in the judgment with the men of this generation, and condemn them: for she came from the utmost parts of the earth to hear the wisdom of Solomon; and, behold, a greater than Solomon is here. | 35 Take heed therefore that the light which is in thee be not darkness.<br>36 If thy whole body therefore be full of light, having no part dark, the whole shall be full of light, as when the bright shining of a candle doth give thee light. | c. A warning: Beware of a diseased eye, of a body full of darkness<br>d. A promise: A healthy eye will give great light |

# DIVISION V

## THE SON OF MAN'S GREAT JOURNEY TO JERUSALEM
## (STAGE I): HIS MISSION AND PUBLIC CHALLENGE, 9:51-13:21

## J. The Great Proof that Jesus is the Messiah: The Resurrection, 11:29-36

(11:29-36) **Introduction**: the great proof that Jesus Christ is the Messiah, the Son of the living God, is the resurrection. Men may seek for other proofs and other signs, but God has given this one supreme sign. No other sign will ever be given to man. The resurrection leaves man without excuse.
1. The crowds thronged Jesus (v.29).
2. The one and only sign: the sign of Jonah, that is, the resurrection (v.29-30).
3. The sign's (resurrection) effect: it will condemn this evil generation (v.31-32).
4. The sign's (resurrection) visibility: it is as clearly seen as a shining candle (v.33-36).

**1** (11:29) **Man, Unbelief—Jesus Christ, Deity—Signs**: crowds thronged Jesus. As soon as the crowd settled down, Jesus began to preach, and what He had to say was strong. He made a serious charge against His generation: "This is an evil generation." Why? They sought a sign.

1. What is wrong with seeking a sign, with seeking some proof that Jesus is who He claims to be? Nothing. There is nothing wrong with seeking evidence that Jesus is the Son of God. The problem is not in seeking evidence; the problem is in seeking *more and more* evidence. Think for a moment. What greater sign could God have given than to *reveal Himself* to man? The greatest sign in all the world was to have God's very own Son stand in the presence of men so that they could see and touch Him.

> "And the Word [Jesus Christ] was made flesh, and dwelt among us, (and we beheld his glory, the glory as of the only begotten of the Father,) full of grace and truth. John bare witness of him, and cried, saying, this was he of whom I spake, He that cometh after me is preferred before me: for he was before me. And of his fulness have all we received, and grace for grace" (Jn.1:14-16).
> "That which was from the beginning, which we have heard, which we have looked upon, and our hands have handled, of the Word of life; (For the life was manifested, and we have seen it, and bear witness, and show unto you that eternal life, which was with the Father, and was manifested unto us;) that which we have seen and heard declare we unto you, that ye also may have fellowship with us: and truly our fellowship is with the Father, and with his Son Jesus Christ" (1 Jn.1:1-3).

2. What greater evidence could God give that Jesus is His Son? God met *all the needs of men* while Jesus was among them. The greatest evidence in all the world is seeing Jesus demonstrate the *love and power* of God...
- by feeding the hungry.
- by calming both nature and the fear of men.
- by preaching and teaching as no other man has ever done.
- by healing all manner of sicknesses and infirmities.

- by casting out evil spirits.
- by raising the dead.

> "Blessed are they which do hunger and thirst after righteousness: for they shall be filled" (Mt.5:6).
> "But whosoever drinketh of the water that I shall give him shall never thirst; but the water that I shall give him shall be in him a well of water springing up into everlasting life" (Jn.4:14).
> "In the last day, that great day of the feast, Jesus stood and cried, saying, If any man thirst, let him come unto me, and drink" (Jn.7:37).
> "But my God shall supply all your need according to his riches in glory by Christ Jesus" (Ph.4:19).
> "They shall be abundantly satisfied with the fatness of thy house; and thou shalt make them drink of the river of thy pleasures" (Ps.36:8; cp. Ps.23:1f).
> "And the LORD shall guide thee continually, and satisfy thy soul in drought, and make fat thy bones: and thou shalt be like a watered garden, and like a spring of water, whose waters fail not" (Is.58:11).

3. What greater proof (sign) could God give that He was bringing salvation to man? God sent His Son into the world to personally save man. What greater evidence could God give than...
- to have His Son live as a Man, living a perfect and sinless life, and by His perfection to secure righteousness for man.
- to have His Son die *for men*.
- to raise His Son from the dead.

The Jews and all men are totally unjustified in seeking additional signs. God has given the greatest signs that could ever be given. If a man rejects the signs already given, he will reject any sign no matter what the sign might be. Signs and evidence are not man's problem. Man's problem is twofold.

1. Man just does not believe because he does not want to believe. He wants to live like he wants, to do his own thing. Man wants no Lord over him, not One who demands all he is and has. Man's heart is hard, and he is obstinate in his unbelief (see notes—Lk.10:21; Deeper Study # 4—Mt.12:24; note—12:31-32).

2. Man does not understand the love and the faith of God, that is, the true religion of God. He fails to see what God is after and has always been after: faith and love, not signs and works. God wants a man to simply believe and love Him because of who He is and because of what He does for man. The true religion of God is not a religion of works and signs, but of faith and love in Christ Jesus, His own Son (see Deeper Study # 2—Jn.2:24; Deeper Study # 1—4:22; note—4:48-49; Deeper Study # 1—Ro.4:1-25; note—4:4-5. Cp. Acts 2:22.)

2 (11:29-30) **Jesus Christ, Deity—Resurrection**: the one and only sign—the sign of Jonah, that is, of the resurrection (cp. v.32). The sign of Jonah pointed to the resurrection of Jesus from the dead (see note—Mt.12:38-40). The resurrection is the *great proof* that Jesus is the Messiah, the Savior of the world. He is "declared to be the son of God with power...by the resurrection from the dead" (Ro.1:4).

Jesus claimed to be greater than Jonah. He claimed to be the greatest messenger who had ever come, the Messiah Himself. Since His coming, all men are definitely without excuse. The worst sinners in history repented at the preaching of a mere man, the prophet Jonah. Now the Messiah Himself, God's own Son, has come. And He has preached and announced that the Kingdom of God itself is at hand. Every person is now, beyond question, without excuse.

3 (11:31-32) **Jesus Christ, Deity; Resurrection—Queen of Sheba—Seeking Jesus—Wisdom**: the sign's (resurrection) effect—it will condemn this evil generation. There are two reasons for this:

1. This evil generation did not seek Jesus, the One who knew the truth. Jesus gave a prime example in the Queen of Sheba of what He meant (cp. 1 Ki.10:1f; 2 Chron.9:1f). The Queen of Sheba demonstrated how a person is to seek the truth and how important it is to seek Christ. She had to seek as diligently and go through as much as anyone ever has in seeking the truth.
   a. She had a long and perilous search. She had to travel from "the utmost parts of the earth" to seek the truth.
   b. She had extreme responsibility. She was a queen with demanding duties and a busy schedule as the Head of State. As with all Heads of State, she had much demanding her time and presence and depending upon her care, yet she let nothing stop her search for the truth.
   c. She had uncertain seeking. Her search was a gamble, uncertain in at least two senses.
      ⇒ She could not be absolutely certain that Solomon was as wise in the truth as he was said to be. Reputations become exaggerated when spread by word of mouth, and she knew this.
      ⇒ She had no personal invitation to visit Solomon. Fame flatters men and causes them to become inaccessible in order to enhance their fame of being busy and laden with heavy responsibility and of being surrounded with greatness. She could not be sure he would see her nor grant much time to her.
   d. She had to bear terrible prejudice. She was a woman in a man's world. In her day women were nothing more than chattel property, possessed and used by men for their own pleasure as they so desired.

The Queen of Sheba will be used as a testimony in the day of judgment. Her diligent seeking will stand as a testimony against all who fail to seek after Christ. Her seeking will leave all without excuse. There is no distance too far, no road too perilous, no responsibility so important, no question so weighty, no prejudice or opposition so strong that it should keep a person from seeking after Christ. The Queen of Sheba faced all this, yet despite all, she sought the truth. It was the primary drive of her life; therefore, her example leaves everyone without excuse.

> "But seek ye first the kingdom of God, and his righteousness; and all these things [provisions] shall be added unto you" (Mt.6:33).
> "And I say unto you, Ask, and it shall be given you; seek, and ye shall find; knock, and it shall be opened unto you. For every one that asketh receiveth; and he that seeketh findeth; and to him that knocketh it shall be opened" (Lk.11:9-10; cp. v.5-8).
> "And [God] hath made of one blood all nations of men for to dwell on all the face of the earth, and hath determined the times before appointed, and the bounds of their habitation; that they should seek the Lord, if haply they might feel after him, and find him, though he be not far from every one of us" (Acts 17:26-27).
> "But if from thence [idolatry] thou shalt seek the LORD thy God, thou shalt find him, if thou seek him with all thy heart and with all thy soul" (Dt.4:29).
> "But where shall wisdom be found? And where is the place of understanding?...And unto man he said, Behold, the fear of the LORD, that is wisdom; and to depart from evil is understanding" (Job 28:12, 28; cp. v.13-27).
> "Seek the LORD, and his strength: seek his face evermore" (Ps.105:4).
> "Yea, if thou criest after knowledge, and liftest up thy voice for understanding; if thou seekest her as silver, and searchest for her as for hid treasures; then shalt thou understand the fear of the LORD, and find the knowledge of God" (Pr.2:3-5).
> "Seek ye the LORD while he may be found, call ye upon him while he is near" (Is.55:6).
> "For I know the thoughts that I think toward you, saith the LORD, thoughts of peace, and not of evil, to give you an expected end. Then shall ye call upon me, and ye shall go and pray unto me, and I will hearken unto you. And ye shall seek me, and find me, when ye shall search for me with all your heart" (Jer.29:11-13).
> "For thus saith the LORD unto the house of Israel, Seek ye me, and ye shall live" (Amos 5:4).
> "Sow to yourselves in righteousness, reap in mercy; break up your fallow ground: for it is time to seek the LORD, till he come and rain righteousness upon you" (Hos.10:12).
> "Seek ye the LORD, all ye meek of the earth, which have wrought his judgment; seek righteousness, seek meekness: it may be ye shall be hid in the day of the LORD'S anger" (Zeph.2:3).

Note that Jesus claimed to be greater than Solomon. He claimed to be the way, the truth, and the life. Imagine! He claimed to be *life* itself (Jn.14:6). He claimed to be the One whom all men must seek and find or else face condemnation.

Since His coming, all men are definitely without excuse. The most improbable person (the Queen of Sheba) went to the farthest extremes possible to seek after the truth from a mere man, Solomon. Now the Messiah, who is *the truth* Himself, has come and revealed the truth of God. Beyond question, every person is now without excuse.

> "And the Word was made flesh, and dwelt among us, (and we beheld his glory, the glory as of the only begotten of the Father,) full of grace and truth" (Jn.1:14).
> "Jesus saith unto him, I am the way, the truth, and the life: no man cometh unto the Father, but by me" (Jn.14:6).
> "Jesus saith unto him, Have I been so long time with you, and yet hast thou not known me, Philip? he that hath seen me hath seen the Father; and how sayest thou then, Show us the Father? Believest thou not that I am in the Father, and the Father in me? the words that I speak unto you I speak not of myself: but the Father that dwelleth in me, he doeth the works. Believe me that I am in the Father, and the Father in me: or else believe me for the very works' sake" (Jn.14:9-11).
> "For there is one God, and one mediator between God and men, the man Christ Jesus" (1 Tim.2:5).
> "But now hath he obtained a more excellent ministry, by how much also he is the mediator of a better covenant, which was established upon better promises" (Heb.8:6).
> "And for this cause he is the mediator of the new testament, that by means of death, for the redemption of the transgressions that were under the first testament, they which are called might receive the promise of eternal inheritance" (Heb.9:15).
> "For Christ is not entered into the holy places made with hands, which are the figures of the true; but into heaven itself, now to appear in the presence of God for us" (Heb.9:24).
> "And to Jesus the mediator of the new covenant, and to the blood of sprinkling, that speaketh better things than that of Abel. See that ye refuse not him that speaketh. For if they escaped not who refused him that spake on earth, much more shall not we escape, if we turn away from him that speaketh from heaven" (Heb.12:24-25).
> "My little children, these things write I unto you, that ye sin not. And if any man sin, we have an advocate with the Father, Jesus Christ the righteous" (1 Jn.2:1).

2.  This evil generation did not repent with Jesus' preaching. Note several things.
    a.  A whole generation can be evil and adulterous—so evil and adulterous that its lifestyle and dominant character can be called "evil and adulterous" (Mt.12:39).
    b.  The Ninevites gave a prime example of *repentance* and just how essential repentance is. A person must repent or else he shall be condemned.

c. There is a day of judgment out in the future. Note the words, "in judgment" and "in the judgment." Both phrases point to a definite day of judgment.

d. The Ninevites' repentance will be used as a testimony in the day of judgment. The people of Nineveh are the prime example of people's turning to God from the depth of sin. They had fallen into the pit of sin, as deeply as a people can fall. Yet, they repented at the preaching of Jonah.

e. The Ninevites' repentance leaves all *without excuse*. Why? There is no one who has fallen any deeper into sin than they did, yet they repented. They show that anyone can turn to God from sin no matter how terrible his sin is. No man has an excuse for not turning to God.

> **"Blessed are they that mourn: for they shall be comforted" (Mt.5:4)**
>
> **"I tell you, Nay: but, except ye repent, ye shall all likewise perish" (Lk.13:3).**
>
> **"Then Peter said unto them, Repent, and be baptized every one of you in the name of Jesus Christ for the remission of sins, and ye shall receive the gift of the Holy Ghost" (Acts 2:38).**
>
> **"Repent ye therefore, and be converted, that your sins may be blotted out, when the times of refreshing shall come from the presence of the Lord" (Acts 3:19).**
>
> **"Repent therefore of this thy wickedness, and pray God, if perhaps the thought of thine heart may be forgiven thee" (Acts 8:22).**
>
> **"And the times of this ignorance God winked at; but now commandeth all men every where to repent" (Acts 17:30).**
>
> **"If my people, which are called by my name, shall humble themselves, and pray, and seek my face, and turn from their wicked ways; then will I hear from heaven, and will forgive their sin, and will heal their land" (2 Chron.7:14).**
>
> **"Let the wicked forsake his way, and the unrighteous man his thoughts: and let him return unto the LORD, and he will have mercy upon him; and to our God, for he will abundantly pardon" (Is.55:7).**
>
> **"Go and proclaim these words toward the north, and say, Return, thou backsliding Israel, saith the LORD; and I will not cause mine anger to fall upon you: for I am merciful, saith the LORD, and I will not keep anger for ever" (Jer.3:12).**
>
> **"But if the wicked will turn from all his sins that he hath committed, and keep all my statutes, and do that which is lawful and right, he shall surely live, he shall not die" (Ezk.18:21).**
>
> **"Therefore say thou unto them, Thus saith the LORD of hosts; Turn ye unto me, saith the LORD of hosts, and I will turn unto you, saith the LORD of hosts" (Zech.1:3).**

f. Jesus claimed to be greater, to be superior to Jonah (see note—Lk.11:30).

**4** (11:33-36) **Jesus Christ, Resurrection**: the sign's (resurrection) visibility. It is as clearly seen as a shining candle. Note four points.

1. A fact: a lit candle is not hid but placed where it can give light and be seen. Jesus said that the lit candle, the *resurrection*, would not be done in secret nor would it be a secret. Jesus was resurrected openly and publicly so that all who were to "come in [might] see the light" and be convinced that He is the true Messiah.

2. A choice: to see the sign (resurrection) with a healthy eye or a diseased eye. The healthy eye is the single eye, the eye that concentrates on seeing the light, the way of God and righteousness. The diseased eye is the evil eye, the eye which centers upon the world and material things, the flesh and passion, pleasure and stimulation, self and wealth. Note: the one sign that God has given is dramatically clear: it is the resurrection. God has not kept the sign a secret nor has He hidden it. The sign can be seen just as clearly as a candle lit in the dark of midnight. The only conceivable thing that can prevent a person from seeing it is an unhealthy or evil eye; and if a person's eye is evil, his whole body is full of darkness, that is, full of evil and death.

3. A warning: beware of a diseased eye, of a body full of darkness. Every man thinks he sees light and has light, sees truth and has truth. Simply said, every man thinks that what he sees (believes) and embraces is the truth. The warning is clear. Take heed...

- make sure that what you see is seen with a healthy eye.
- make sure that what is in you is light and not darkness.

The *resurrection is the light of God. Seeing any other light or truth is darkness*. It is looking for light and truth with a diseased eye.

4. A promise: a healthy eye will give great light. Very simply, if a man is "full of light"...

- from having seen the resurrection,
- and allows no part of darkness (doubt, unbelief, false belief) to enter...

...then his whole being shall be full of light. He will be as full of light as the brightest light of a candle.

**Thought 1.** Jesus Christ is the Light of the world; He is the Light to which men must open the door of their dark hearts. He is the light which men must take into their sinful lives and world of darkness.

> **"In him was life; and the life was the light of men" (Jn.1:4).**
>
> **"That was the true Light, which lighteth every man that cometh into the world" (Jn.1:9).**
>
> **"Then spake Jesus again unto them, saying, I am the light of the world: he that followeth me shall not walk in darkness, but shall have the light of life" (Jn.8:12).**

"Then Jesus said unto them, Yet a little while is the light with you. Walk while ye have the light, lest darkness come upon you: for he that walketh in darkness knoweth not whither he goeth" (Jn.12:35).

"I am come a light into the world, that whosoever believeth on me should not abide in darkness" (Jn.12:46).

"For God, who commanded the light to shine out of darkness, hath shined in our hearts, to give the light of the knowledge of the glory of God in the face of Jesus Christ" (2 Cor.4:6).

"For ye were sometimes darkness, but now are ye light in the Lord: walk as children of light" (Eph.5:8).

"Wherefore he saith, Awake thou that sleepest, and arise from the dead, and Christ shall give thee light" (Eph.5:14).

"That ye may be blameless and harmless, the sons of God, without rebuke, in the midst of a crooked and perverse nation, among whom ye shine as lights in the world" (Ph.2:15).

"Again, a new commandment I write unto you, which thing is true in him and in you: because the darkness is past, and the true light now shineth" (1 Jn.2:8).

"And the city had no need of the sun, neither of the moon, to shine in it: for the glory of God did lighten it, and the Lamb is the light thereof" (Rev.21:23).

"The people that walked in darkness have seen a great light: they that dwell in the land of the shadow of death, upon them hath the light shined" (Is.9:2).

"I the LORD have called thee [Jesus Christ, His Son] in righteousness, and will hold thine hand, and will keep thee, and give thee for a covenant of the people, for a light of the Gentiles; to open the blind eyes, to bring out the prisoners from the prison, and them that sit in darkness out of the prison house" (Is.42:6-7; cp. Mt.4:14-16; Lk.1:79).

| | | | |
|---|---|---|---|
| **1 A Pharisee invited Jesus to dine**<br>a. Jesus accepted the invitation<br>b. Jesus was questioned about ceremonial cleanliness<br><br>**2 Charge 1: Religionists are ceremonially clean, but inwardly unclean**<br>a. They clean the outside & not the inside<br><br>b. God made both the outside & the inside (heart) of man<br><br>c. The giving of one's heart cleanses everything<br><br>**3 Charge 2: Religionists obey God in tithing but ignore justice & love**<br><br><br>**4 Charge 3: Religionists crave prominence & honor**<br><br>**5 Charge 4: Religionists mislead others, causing them to become unclean & corrupt**<br><br><br>**6 Charge 5: Religionists burden men with rules & regulations** | **K. The Severe Charges Against Religionists, 11:37-54**<br>(cp. Mt.23:13-36; Mk.12:38-40)<br><br>37 And as he spake, a certain Pharisee besought him to dine with him: and he went in, and sat down to meat.<br>38 And when the Pharisee saw it, he marvelled that he had not first washed before dinner.<br>39 And the Lord said unto him, Now do ye Pharisees make clean the outside of the cup and the platter; but your inward part is full of ravening and wickedness.<br>40 Ye fools, did not he that made that which is without make that which is within also?<br>41 But rather give alms of such things as ye have; and, behold, all things are clean unto you.<br>42 But woe unto you, Pharisees! for ye tithe mint and rue and all manner of herbs, and pass over judgment and the love of God: these ought ye to have done, and not to leave the other undone.<br>43 Woe unto you, Pharisees! for ye love the uppermost seats in the synagogues, and greetings in the markets.<br>44 Woe unto you, scribes and Pharisees, hypocrites! for ye are as graves which appear not, and the men that walk over them are not aware of them.<br>45 Then answered one of the lawyers, and said unto him, Master, thus saying thou | reproachest us also.<br>46 And he said, Woe unto you also, ye lawyers! for ye lade men with burdens grievous to be borne, and ye yourselves touch not the burdens with one of your fingers.<br>47 Woe unto you! for ye build the sepulchres of the prophets, and your fathers killed them.<br>48 Truly ye bear witness that ye allow the deeds of your fathers: for they indeed killed them, and ye build their sepulchres.<br>49 Therefore also said the wisdom of God, I will send them prophets and apostles, and some of them they shall slay and persecute:<br>50 That the blood of all the prophets, which was shed from the foundation of the world, may be required of this generation;<br>51 From the blood of Abel unto the blood of Zacharias, which perished between the altar and the temple: verily I say unto you, It shall be required of this generation.<br>52 Woe unto you, lawyers! for ye have taken away the key of knowledge: ye entered not in yourselves, and them that were entering in ye hindered.<br>53 And as he said these things unto them, the scribes and the Pharisees began to urge him vehemently, and to provoke him to speak of many things:<br>54 Laying wait for him, and seeking to catch something out of his mouth, that they might accuse him. | a. A lawyer's spiritual blindness<br><br>b. Jesus' charge<br><br>**7 Charge 6: Religionists honor the true prophets of God—so long as they are dead**<br>a. The honor of the past servants of God<br><br>b. The rejection of the present servants of God<br><br><br>c. The judgment to be required[DS1,2]<br><br><br>**8 Charge 7: Religionists have taken away the key to the truth about God**<br><br>**9 Conclusion: A reaction of hostility toward Jesus** |

# DIVISION V

## THE SON OF MAN'S GREAT JOURNEY TO JERUSALEM (STAGE I):HIS MISSION AND PUBLIC CHALLENGE, 9:51-13:21

### K. The Severe Charges Against Religionists, 11:37-54

(11:37-54) **Introduction:** most people feel they are *religious*. For that reason, the religious person needs to pay close attention to what Jesus says in this passage. The religious person needs to examine his heart and life to make sure his religion is genuine. Jesus was severe in His charges against false religionists. (See outline and notes—Mt.23:1-12; 23:13-36; Lk.15:25-32; 18:9-12; Ro.2:17-29 for more discussion and application.)

1. A Pharisee invited Jesus to dine (v.37-38).
2. Charge 1: religionists are ceremonially clean, but inwardly unclean (v.39-41).
3. Charge 2: religionists obey God in tithing, but ignore justice and love (v.42).
4. Charge 3: religionists crave prominence and honor (v.43).
5. Charge 4: religionists mislead others to become unclean and corrupted (v.44).
6. Charge 5: religionists burden men with rules and regulations (v.45-46).
7. Charge 6: religionists honor the true prophets of God—so long as they are dead (v.47-51).
8. Charge 7: religionists have taken away the key to the truth about God (v.52).
9. Conclusion: a reaction of hostility (v.53-54).

**1** (11:37-38) **Scribal Law—Washing the Hands**: a Pharisee invited Jesus to dine with him. The Pharisee had probably been in the audience of Jesus and had become interested in Jesus' teaching. He wanted to talk personally with Jesus, so he invited Him to a meal. What happened was this. When Jesus entered the man's home, He went straight to the food and sat down to eat; He did not wash His hands. This astonished the Pharisee, for it was a serious violation of religious law. It had nothing to do with cleanliness, but with ceremonial purity. It was taught that a person's hands had been in contact with a sinful world; therefore, the person was to wash his hands before eating to prevent impurity from entering into his body. The Pharisee (religionist) was thinking to himself that Jesus had seriously violated the law of purity. Jesus, of course, knew His thoughts and began to reply. His reply was in the form of seven severe charges.

**2** (11:39-41) **Religionists—Heart, Good vs. Evil—Depravity—Ritual—Self-righteousness**: the first charge was that religionists were clean ceremonially but unclean within. They kept their religious ceremonies, but they did nothing about the human heart.

1. Religionists cleaned the outside and not the inside. They treated religion like a person who would be washing dishes. The person washed the outside of the cup and platter but left the inside dirty. The heart of the religionist was full of...
   - ravening (harpazo), which means plunder, seizing, extortion, robbery, taking by force
   - wickedness (ponerias)

Most religionists deny, just as they did in the day of Jesus, that they plunder and do wickedness. But note: Jesus said that a religionist not only does these things but he is full of plunder and wickedness. What did Jesus mean? A religionist is *plundering* the way of God, trying to *seize* God's kingdom his own way instead of following the way of God. He is committing extortion against God by robbing God of the salvation He has set up. The religionist is "full of... wickedness," that is, disobeying God and refusing to follow Jesus, who is the way of righteousness established by God (Ro.10:3-4; Ph.3:9). Instead of coming to God by the Messiah, a religionist comes to God by his own righteousness. He tries to make himself clean by keeping the religious ceremonies and worship. (See note—Mt.23:25-26 for more discussion and a different explanation.)

> **Thought 1.** Note two critical lessons that must be heeded by the religionists.
> 1) Jesus Christ is God's righteousness.
>
>> "For they being ignorant of God's righteousness, and going about to establish their own righteousness, have not submitted themselves unto the righteousness of God. For Christ is the end of the law for righteousness to every one that believeth. For Moses describeth the righteousness which is of the law, That the man which doeth those things shall live by them" (Ro.10:3-5).
>> "But now the righteousness of God without the law [and works] is manifested, being witnessed by the law and the prophets; even the righteousness of God which is by faith of Jesus Christ unto all and upon all them that believe: for there is no difference: for all have sinned, and come short of the glory of God; being justified freely by his grace through the redemption that is in Christ Jesus: whom God hath set forth to be a propitiation through faith in his blood, to declare his righteousness for the remission of sins that are past" (Ro.3:21-25).
>> "[That I may] be found in him, not having mine own righteousness, which is of the law, but that which is through the faith of Christ, the righteousness which is of God by faith" (Ph.3:9).
>
> 2) A man, religious or non-religious, cannot establish his own righteousness. He cannot make himself clean enough to approach God: not by works, nor by religious ceremony and worship, nor by cleaning up the outside of his platter or life.
>
>> "For I say unto you, That except your righteousness shall exceed the righteousness of the scribes and Pharisees, ye shall in no case enter into the kingdom of heaven" (Mt.5:20).
>> "Many will say to me in that day, Lord, Lord, have we not prophesied in thy name? and in thy name have cast out devils? and in thy name done many wonderful works? And then will I profess unto them, I never knew you: depart from me, ye that work iniquity" (Mt.7:22-23).
>> "Therefore by the deeds of the law there shall no flesh be justified in his sight: for by the law is the knowledge of sin" (Ro.3:20).
>> "Knowing that a man is not justified by the works of the law, but by the faith of Jesus Christ, even we have believed in Jesus Christ, that we might be justified by the faith of Christ, and not by the works of the law: for by the works of the law shall no flesh be justified" (Gal.2:16).
>> "For by grace are ye saved through faith; and that not of yourselves: it is the gift of God: not of works, lest any man should boast" (Eph.2:8-9).
>> "Who hath saved us, and called us with an holy calling, not according to our works, but according to his own purpose and grace, which was given us in Christ Jesus before the world began" (2 Tim.1:9).

"But after that the kindness and love of God our Saviour toward man appeared, not by works of righteousness which we have done, but according to his mercy he saved us, by the washing of regeneration, and renewing of the Holy Ghost; which he shed on us abundantly through Jesus Christ our Saviour; that being justified by his grace, we should be made heirs according to the hope of eternal life" (Tit.3:4-7).

2. God made both the outside and the inside (the heart) of man. Jesus said the outside is not all that is unclean. The inside is also unclean and must be cleansed to become acceptable to God. Note that He calls religionists "fools." God made the whole man, the heart as well as the body. A man has to give God a clean heart and a clean body, a spiritual heart as well as a religious body.

**Thought 1.** The heart is the source of evil; therefore, it has to be cleansed by Christ—even the heart of the religionist.

"For from within, out of the heart of men, proceed evil thoughts, adulteries, fornications, murders" (Mk.7:21).
"Take heed, brethren, lest there be in any of you an evil heart of unbelief, in departing from the living God" (Heb.3:12).
"But there were false prophets also among the people, even as there shall be false teachers among you, who privily shall bring in damnable heresies, even denying the Lord that bought them, and bring upon themselves swift destruction. And many shall follow their pernicious ways; by reason of whom the way of truth shall be evil spoken of. And through covetousness shall they with feigned words make merchandise of you: whose judgment now of a long time lingereth not, and their damnation slumbereth not....[these false teachers] having eyes full of adultery, and that cannot cease from sin; beguiling unstable souls: an heart they have exercised with covetous practices; cursed children" (2 Pt.2:1-3, 15; cp. v.1-22).
"There is an evil among all things that are done under the sun, that there is one event unto all: yea, also the heart of the sons of men is full of evil, and madness is in their heart while they live, and after that they go to the dead" (Eccl.9:3).
"The heart is deceitful above all things, and desperately wicked: who can know it?" (Jer.17:9).

3. The giving of one's heart cleanses everything. Note what Jesus said: "Give alms [gifts] of such things as ye have [within, in your heart]." The one thing that a man has which he can give is his heart. If he gives his heart to God, then he will become clean in all things. He will be giving instead of taking, giving to God and giving to men. Simply stated, Jesus said that a man is...
- to give *all he is* to God, by which he *will become* clean within.
- to give *all he has* to God, by which he *will demonstrate* that he is clean within.

"That if thou shalt confess with thy mouth the Lord Jesus, and shalt believe in thine heart that God hath raised him from the dead, thou shalt be saved. For with the heart man believeth unto righteousness; and with the mouth confession is made unto salvation" (Ro.10:9-10).
"But God be thanked, that ye were the servants of sin, but ye have obeyed from the heart that form of doctrine which was delivered you. Being then made free from sin, ye became the servants of righteousness....For when ye were the servants of sin, ye were free from righteousness. What fruit had ye then in those things whereof ye are now ashamed? for the end of those things is death. But now being made free from sin, and become servants to God, ye have your fruit unto holiness, and the end everlasting life. For the wages of sin is death; but the gift of God is eternal life through Jesus Christ our Lord" (Ro.6:17-18, 20-23).
"But that [seed] on the good ground are they, which in an honest and good heart, having heard the word, keep it, and bring forth fruit with patience" (Lk.8:15).
"Let us draw near with a true heart in full assurance of faith, having our hearts sprinkled from an evil conscience, and our bodies washed with pure water. Let us hold fast the profession of our faith without wavering; (for he is faithful that promised)" (Heb.10:22-23).
"And he [a lawyer] answering said, Thou shalt love the Lord thy God with all thy heart, and with all thy soul, and with all thy strength, and with all thy mind; and thy neighbour as thyself. And he [Jesus] said unto him, Thou hast answered right: this, do, and thou shalt live" (Lk.10:27-28).

**3** (11:42) **Tithe—Justice—God, Love of—Poor—Oppressed:** the second charge was that religionists obeyed God in tithing but ignored justice and love. Note several things.

1. The religionists took tithing very seriously. Tithing is the command of God and was meant to be a joyful experience (Dt.14:22-23; Lev.27:30). The religionists wanted to make sure they did exactly what God wanted, so they went beyond what God required. They tithed every little thing, even the plants of their gardens and the little potted plants they might have in their homes. (See DEEPER STUDY # 6, *Tithe*—Mt.23:23 for more discussion.)

2.     Jesus did not say that going beyond the tithe is wrong. In fact, God demands everything (see outline and notes—Mt.19:16-22. Cp. Lk.9:23.) Jesus was not discussing the tithe; He was simply using the tithe to illustrate His point.

3.     The point was that religionists stressed outward duties such as tithing and ceremony, ritual and ordinances, works and form; but they neglected the inward duties such as *justice and love of God.*

⇒     *Justice* is the way we treat others. Religionists and their church organizations are the recipients of the tithe and offerings of God's people. The monies and gifts are too often coveted for oneself and the building of one's organization more than for ministering to the poor, the oppressed, and the lost. Too often monies are kept for extravagant buildings and livelihoods and personal comfort—monies that God wants used to feed the hungry, clothe the naked, house the orphan, care for the widows and reach the lost. Such extravagance and misuse of the tithe reveals an unjust heart. It is cheating the needy of the world. It is as Jesus said, passing over justice. It is overlooking what is right and just in a world that just reels under the weight of millions who are in desperate need.

⇒     *The love of God* is both the love He has given us in Christ and the love we are to have for Him and others.

> "Jesus said unto him, If thou wilt be perfect, go and sell that thou hast, and give to the poor, and thou shalt have treasure in heaven: and come and follow me" (Mt.19:21).
>
> "And the second is like unto it, Thou shalt love thy neighbour as thyself" (Mt.22:39).
>
> "Let love be without dissimulation [hypocrisy]. Abhor that which is evil; cleave to that which is good" (Ro.12:9).
>
> "Owe no man any thing, but to love one another: for he that loveth another hath fulfilled the law" (Ro.13:8).
>
> "Masters, give unto your servants that which is just and equal; knowing that ye also have a Master in heaven" (Col.4:1).
>
> "If a brother or sister be naked, and destitute of daily food, and one of you say unto them, Depart in peace, be ye warmed and filled; notwithstanding ye give them not those things which are needful to the body; what doth it profit?" (Jas.2:15-16).
>
> "Thou shalt not oppress a hired servant [employee] that is poor and needy, whether he be of thy brethren, or of thy strangers that are in thy land within thy gates" (Dt.24:14).
>
> "If there be among you a poor man of one of thy brethren within any of thy gates in thy land which the LORD thy God giveth thee, thou shalt not harden thine heart, nor shut thine hand from thy poor brother" (Dt.15:7).
>
> "That which is altogether just shalt thou follow, that thou mayest live, and inherit the land which the LORD thy God giveth thee" (Dt.16:20).
>
> "Blessed is he that considereth the poor: the LORD will deliver him in time of trouble" (Ps.41:1).
>
> "Trust not in oppression, and become not vain in robbery: if riches increase, set not your heart upon them" (Ps.62:10).
>
> "Defend the poor and fatherless: do justice to the afflicted and needy" (Ps.82:3).
>
> "He that despiseth his neighbor sinneth: but he that hath mercy on the poor, happy is he" (Pr.14:21).
>
> "He that oppresseth the poor reproacheth his Maker: but he that honoreth him hath mercy on the poor" (Pr.14:31).
>
> "He that hath pity upon the poor lendeth unto the LORD; and that which he hath given will he pay him again" (Pr.19:17).
>
> "To do justice and judgment is more acceptable to the LORD than sacrifice" (Pr.21:3).
>
> "Whoso stoppeth his ears at the cry of the poor, he also shall cry himself, but shall not be heard" (Pr.21:13).
>
> "He that oppresseth the poor to increase his riches, and he that giveth to the rich, shall surely come to want" (Pr.22:16).
>
> "To have respect of persons is not good: for, for a piece of bread that man will transgress" (Pr.28:21).
>
> "If thou seest the oppression of the poor, and violent perverting of judgment and justice in a province, marvel not at the matter: for he that is higher than the highest regardeth; and there be higher than they" (Eccl.5:8).
>
> "Thus saith the LORD, Keep ye judgment, and do justice: for my salvation is near to come, and my righteousness to be revealed" (Is.56:1).
>
> "He judged the cause of the poor and needy; then it was well with him: was not this to know me? saith the LORD" (Jer.22:16).
>
> "Thus speaketh the LORD of hosts, saying, Execute true judgment, and show mercy and compassions every man to his brother: and oppress not the widow, nor the fatherless, the stranger, nor the poor; and let none of you imagine evil against his brother in your heart" (Zech.7:9-10).

**4**  (11:43) **Self-seeking—Tithes—Honor—Position**: the third charge was that religionists crave prominence and honor. Jesus mentioned two things.

1.     Religionists loved the most prominent positions and seats. In the synagogues they sat at the front, facing the congregation. Every church has its individuals who seek prominent positions and seats.

2.    They loved the titles that honored and recognized them. In Jesus' day it was "Rabbi." In our day it is the various titles we give to honor a man above others. However, Jesus did not say that position or title is wrong. It is the *love* of these that is condemned. But we must be open with ourselves and search our hearts honestly.

> "How can ye believe, which receive honour one of another, and seek not the honour that cometh from God only?" (Jn.5:44).
> "For all flesh is as grass, and all the glory of man as the flower of grass. The grass withereth, and the flower thereof falleth away" (1 Pt.1:24).
> "I wrote unto the church: but Diotrephes, who loveth to have the preeminence among them, receiveth us not" (3 Jn.9).
> "Nevertheless man being in honour abideth not: he is like the beasts that perish. This their way is their folly: yet their posterity approve their sayings" (Ps.49:12-13).
> "For when he dieth he shall carry nothing away: his glory shall not descend after him" (Ps.49:17).
> "For that which befalleth the sons of men befalleth beasts; even one thing befalleth them: as the one dieth, so dieth the other; yea, they have all one breath; so that a man hath no preeminence above a beast: for all is vanity" (Eccl.3:19).
> "Therefore hell hath enlarged herself, and opened her mouth without measure: and their glory, and their multitude, and their pomp, and he that rejoiceth, shall descend into it" (Is.5:14).

5    (11:44) **Sin, Misleading Others—Hypocrisy**: the fourth charge was that religionists misled others and made them unclean and corrupt. Again, Jesus was talking about ceremonial and religious uncleanness. A man was considered to be unclean and corrupt if he walked over a grave. Therefore, men were walking over them and not aware of the defilement and corruption they were picking up. Note exactly what Jesus said. Religionists were as graves, as men declared dead and buried, but their graves were unmarked. People could not look at the religionists and tell that they were misleading people and corrupting them. (See note—Mt.23:27-28 for more discussion.)

> "Even so ye also outwardly appear righteous unto men, but within ye are full of hypocrisy and iniquity" (Mt.23:28).
> "Beware ye of the leaven of the Pharisees, which is hypocrisy. For there is nothing covered, that shall not be revealed; neither hid, that shall not be known" (Lk.12:1-2).
> "For it is a shame even to speak of those things which are done of them in secret" (Eph.5:12).
> "Now the Spirit speaketh expressly, that in the latter times some shall depart from the faith, giving heed to seducing spirits, and doctrines of devils; speaking lies in hypocrisy; having their conscience seared with a hot iron" (1 Tim.4:1-2).
> "They profess that they know God; but in works they deny him, being abominable, and disobedient, and unto every good work reprobate" (Tit.1:16).

6    (11:45-46) **Burdens—Rules and Regulations—Word of God, Adding to**: the fifth charge was that religionists burdened men with rules and regulations. Note three things.

1.    A lawyer, up to this point, had excluded himself and his profession. He was applying all that Jesus was saying to someone else. It never dawned upon him that Jesus could be talking to him! All of a sudden something struck the lawyer's mind, and he felt Jesus was including his profession. Jesus proceeded to leave no doubt in anyone's mind. He was speaking to all who put religion, ritual, ceremony, heritage, and anything else before God. Man's duty, even the duty of religionists, is to turn his  heart and being over to God.

2.    Jesus now charged the religionist with creating man-made rules and regulations. Jesus was speaking of the Scribal law (see DEEPER STUDY # 1—Lk.6:2). The Scribal law was considered even more important than the Word of God itself. In the minds of the religionists, the law of God was sometimes hard to understand, but not the rules and regulations of the religionists. Therefore, any breaking of the Scribal law was considered deliberate and much more serious. Jesus also charged the religionists with failing to lift one finger to help a man in keeping the law. Instead of helping the man, the religionist condemned the man.

> "And every one that heareth these sayings of mine [the Word of God], and doeth them not, shall be likened unto a foolish man, which built his house upon the sand: and the rain descended, and the floods came, and the winds blew, and beat upon that house; and it fell: and great was the fall of it" (Mt.7:26-27).
> "And that servant, which knew his lord's will, and prepared not himself, neither did according to his will, shall be beaten with many stripes" (Lk.12:47).
> "Therefore to him that knoweth to do good, and doeth it not, to him it is sin" (Jas.4:17).
> "Thou therefore which teachest another, teachest thou not thyself? thou that preachest a man should not steal, dost thou steal?" (Ro.2:21).

3.    Jesus said that the Law, the Word of God, was adequate by itself. Man did not have to add rules and regulation to it. (See note—Mt.23:4 for more discussion.)

7    (11:47-51) **Heritage—Roots**: the sixth charge was that religionists honored the true prophets of God as long as they were dead.

1.    The religionists honored the past. They showed great respect for the prophets of old—renovating, adorning, and looking after their sepulchres and relics. They took great pride in their roots.

"Bring forth therefore fruits worthy of repentance, and begin not to say within yourselves, We have Abraham to our father: for I say unto you, That God is able of these stones to raise up children unto Abraham" (Lk.3:8).

"They answered him, We be Abraham's seed, and were never in bondage to any man: how sayest thou, Ye shall be made free?" (Jn.8:33).

"They answered and said unto him, Abraham is our father. Jesus saith unto them, If ye were Abraham's children, ye would do the works of Abraham" (Jn.8:39).

"Then they reviled him, and said, Thou art his disciple; but we are Moses' disciples" (Jn.9:28).

2.　The religionists, however, rejected the present. They *rejected the teaching and godly lives* of the prophets and apostles whom God sent. They reverenced the past—Abraham and Moses, Jeremiah and Zachariah—but they rejected God's very own Son. In rejecting Him, they bore witness that they were just as their father's were: murderers (v.48).

"And the Pharisees went forth, and straightway took counsel with the Herodians against him, how they might destroy him" (Mk.3:6).

"And the scribes and chief priests heard it, and sought how they might destroy him: for they feared him, because all the people was astonished at his doctrine" (Mk.11:18).

"After two days was the feast of the passover, and of unleavened bread: and the chief priests and the scribes sought how they might take him by craft, and put him to death. But they said, Not on the feast day, lest there be an uproar of the people" (Mk.14:1-2).

3.　The judgment upon religionists will be more severe than upon others. The blood of all the prophets, ranging from Abel to Zacharias, will fall upon their head. Why the blood of all? Because Jesus' generation had the greatest privilege and opportunity known to man. God's Son Himself, the summit of the prophets, now stood before the world, in particular before the religionists. To reject Him was to reject all the prophets. He was *the One Prophet* who embraced all prophets, the One to whom all prophets had looked. (See notes—-Mt.23:29-33; 23:34-36; Deeper Study # 10,11—23:35; *Deeper Study # 12*—23:36.)

"For the Son of man shall come in the glory of his Father with his angels; and then he shall reward every man according to his works" (Mt.16:27).

"But after thy hardness and impenitent heart treasurest up unto thyself wrath against the day of wrath and revelation of the righteous judgment of God; who will render to every man according to his deeds" (Ro.2:5-6).

"For we must all appear before the judgment seat of Christ; that every one may receive the things done in his body, according to that he hath done, whether it be good or bad" (2 Cor.5:10).

"And if ye call on the Father, who without respect of persons judgeth according to every man's work, pass the time of your sojourning here in fear" (1 Pt.1:17).

"All the churches shall know that I am he which searcheth the reins and hearts: and I will give unto every one of you according to your works" (Rev.2:23).

"And I saw the dead, small and great, stand before God; and the books were opened: and another book was opened, which is the book of life: and the dead were judged out of those things which were written in the books, according to their works" (Rev.20:12; cp. Rev.22:12).

"Also unto thee, O Lord, belongeth mercy: for thou renderest to every man according to his work" (Ps.62:12).

"If thou sayest, Behold, we knew it not; doth not he that pondereth the heart consider it? And he that keepeth thy soul, doth not he know it? And shall not he render to every man according to his works?" (Pr.24:12).

"I the LORD search the heart, I try the reins, even to give every man according to his ways, and according to the fruit of his doings" (Jer.17:10).

"Great in counsel, and mighty in work: for thine eyes are open upon all the ways of the sons of men: to give every one according to his ways, and according to the fruit of his doings" (Jer.32:19).

"Therefore I will judge you, O house of Israel, every one according to his ways, saith the Lord GOD. Repent, and turn yourselves from all your transgressions; so iniquity shall not be your ruin" (Ezk.18:30).

---

**DEEPER STUDY # 1**
(11:51) **Zacharias**: see Deeper Study # 11—Mt.23:35.

---

**DEEPER STUDY # 2**
(11:51) **Abel**: cp. Gen.4:8.

---

**8** (11:52) **Religionists—Stumbling Block—Teachers, False**: the seventh charge was that religionists had taken away the key to the truth about God. They had taken away the key that unlocked the Scriptures and the way to God.
　⇒　They stressed the external, the ceremony, the religious form over the heart and repentance, the Scripture and obedience.
　⇒　They turned men away from the Scripture to their own ideas and thoughts, rules and regulations.

"Jesus answered and said unto them, Ye do err, not knowing the scriptures, nor the power of God" (Mt.22:29).

"For we are not as many, which corrupt the word of God: but as of sincerity, but as of God, in the sight of God speak we in Christ" (2 Cor.2:17).

"As also in all his [Paul's] epistles, speaking in them of these things; in which are some things hard to be understood, which they that are unlearned and unstable wrest, as they do also the other scriptures, unto their own destruction" (2 Pt.3:16).

Note that some persons were entering into the truth until the religionists got hold of them. The religionist stopped them from entering.

"But woe unto you, scribes and Pharisees, hypocrites! for ye shut up the kingdom of heaven against men: for ye neither go in yourselves, neither suffer ye them that are entering to go in" (Mt.23:13).

"For the priest's lips should keep knowledge, and they should seek the law at his mouth: for he is the messenger of the LORD of hosts. But ye are departed out of the way; ye have caused many to stumble at the law; ye have corrupted the covenant of Levi, saith the LORD of hosts" (Mal.2:7-8).

⑨ (11:53-54) **Jesus Christ, Response to**: the conclusion was hostility. The religionists could not accept the truth. They were incensed and set aflame against Jesus. They tried to trap Him so they could arrest and stop Him.

| | | | |
|---|---|---|---|
| | **CHAPTER 12**<br><br>**L. The Things Men Should Fear, 12:1-12** | into hell; yea, I say unto you, Fear him.<br>  6 Are not five sparrows sold for two farthings, and not one of them is forgotten before God? | b. Do not fear the lack of necessities: God cares |
| **1 An innumerable multitude of people gathered around Jesus** | In the mean time, when there were gathered together an innumerable multitude of people, insomuch that they trode one upon another, he began to say unto his disciples first of all, Beware ye of the leaven of the Pharisees, which is hypocrisy. | 7 But even the very hairs of your head are all numbered. Fear not therefore: ye are of more value than many sparrows. | |
| **2 Message 1: To the disciples—fear hypocrisy**[DS1]<br><br>  a. Deeds are to be exposed | 2 For there is nothing covered, that shall not be revealed; neither hid, that shall not be known. | 8 Also I say unto you, Whosoever shall confess me before men, him shall the Son of man also confess before the angels of God: | c. Fear the spirit of disloyalty, of denying Christ |
|   b. Words are to be exposed | 3 Therefore whatsoever ye have spoken in darkness shall be heard in the light; and that which ye have spoken in the ear in closets shall be proclaimed upon the housetops. | 9 But he that denieth me before men shall be denied before the angels of God.<br>  10 And whosoever shall speak a word against the Son of man, it shall be forgiven him: but unto him that blasphemeth against the Holy Ghost it shall not be forgiven. | d. Fear the unpardonable sin |
| **3 Message 2: To the friends of Christ—what to fear**[DS2]<br>  a. Do not fear men, but God and God alone | 4 And I say unto you my friends, Be not afraid of them that kill the body, and after that have no more that they can do.<br>  5 But I will forewarn you whom ye shall fear: Fear him, which after he hath killed hath power to cast | 11 And when they bring you unto the synagogues, and unto magistrates, and powers, take ye no thought how or what thing ye shall answer, or what ye shall say:<br>  12 For the Holy Ghost shall teach you in the same hour what ye ought to say. | e. Do not fear persecution & trials: The Holy Spirit empowers |

# DIVISION V

## THE SON OF MAN'S GREAT JOURNEY TO JERUSALEM (STAGE I): HIS MISSION AND PUBLIC CHALLENGE, 9:51-13:21

## L.　The Things Men Should Fear, 12:1-12

(12:1-12) **Introduction**: there are things to fear in life, some very serious things. However, there is a vast difference between what men usually fear and what God says to fear. The things men fear are usually of their own making, and men would not have to fear them if they trusted God (war, deception, evil, stealing, bankruptcy, and other fears of men).

Jesus covered what men *should* fear. Note: He spoke first to the disciples (v.1-3), then to His *friends* (v.4-12). There was one thing in particular that His disciples needed to fear, and that one thing needs to be feared by everyone. That one thing is hypocrisy.

1.　An innumerable multitude of people gathered around Jesus (v.1).
2.　Message 1: to the disciples—fear hypocrisy (v.1-3).
3.　Message 2: to the friends of Christ—what to fear (v.4-12).

**1**　(12:1) **Jesus Christ, Crowds Followed**: a vast crowd now gathered around Jesus, a crowd so large it could not be numbered. Many thousands (muriadon) is the Greek word. Note: so many had gathered that they were pushing and stepping upon each other. They were so eager to hear the Word of God that they were trying to get as close as possible.

> **Thought 1.** What a lesson for modern man—to be so hungry for the Word of God that we flock to His preaching and struggle to get up front!

**2**　(12:1-3) **Hypocrisy—Sin, Exposed**: the first message was to the disciples of Christ. He said, "Fear hypocrisy." Hypocrisy was the leaven of the religionists. (See DEEPER STUDY # 3—Mt.16:12; note and DEEPER STUDY # 1,2—Mk.8:15 for more discussion and application.)

1.　The religionists, surprisingly, were the ones who were guilty of hypocrisy, that is, saying one thing and doing another. (See DEEPER STUDY # 2, *Hypocrisy*—Mt.23:13.) They claimed to be followers of God, to lead men to God...

* in their ceremony and ritual.
* in their form of worship and teaching.
* in their doctrine and preaching.

However, Jesus said that what the religionists were doing was hypocrisy, for religious form is not God's way of salvation.

        "**Ye hypocrites, well did Esaias prophesy of you, saying, This people draweth nigh unto me with their mouth, and honoureth me with their lips; but their heart is far from me. But in vain they do worship me, teaching for doctrines the commandments of men**" (Mt.15:7-9).

        "**But woe unto you, scribes and Pharisees, hypocrites! for ye shut up the kingdom of heaven against men: for ye neither go in yourselves, neither suffer ye them that are entering to go in**" (Mt.23:13).

        "**Even so ye also outwardly appear righteous unto men, but within ye are full of hypocrisy and iniquity**" (Mt.23:28).

        "**And why beholdest thou the mote that is in thy brother's eye, but perceivest not the beam that is in thine own eye? Either how canst thou say to thy brother, Brother, let me pull out the mote that is in thine eye, when thou thyself beholdest not the beam that is in thine own eye? Thou hypocrite, cast out first the beam out of thine own eye, and then shalt thou see clearly to pull out the mote that is in thy brother's eye. For a good tree bringeth not forth corrupt fruit: neither doth a corrupt tree bring forth good fruit**" (Lk.6:41-43).

        "**Ye hypocrites, ye can discern the face of the sky and of the earth; but how is it that ye do not discern this time? Yea, and why even of yourselves judge ye not what is right?**" (Lk.12:56-57).

        "**Now I beseech you, brethren, mark them which cause divisions and offences contrary to the doctrine which ye have learned; and avoid them. For they that are such serve not our Lord Jesus Christ, but their own belly; and by good words and fair speeches deceive the hearts of the simple**" (Ro.16:17-18).

        "**Now the Spirit speaketh expressly, that in the latter times some shall depart from the faith, giving heed to seducing spirits, and doctrines of devils; speaking lies in hypocrisy; having their conscience seared with a hot iron**" (1 Tim.4:1-2).

        "**They profess that they know God; but in works they deny him, being abominable, and disobedient, and unto every good work reprobate**" (Tit.1:16).

        "**For as he thinketh in his heart, so is he: Eat and drink, saith he to thee; but his heart is not with thee**" (Pr.23:7).

2.     The religionists' hypocrisy was like leaven (see DEEPER STUDY # 1, *Leaven*—Lk.12:1).

        "**Then understood they how that he bade them not beware of the leaven of bread, but of the doctrine of the Pharisees and of the Sadducees**" (Mt.16:12).

        "**Beware lest any man spoil you through philisophy and vain deceit, after the tradition of men, after the rudiments of the world, and not after Christ**" (Col.2:8).

        "**Be not carried about with divers and strange doctrines. For it is a good thing that the heart be established with grace**" (Heb.13:9).

The disciples of Jesus were the ones in particular who were to fear hypocrisy. Why? Because they were the teachers, the preachers of righteousness. They were both to proclaim the truth and live the truth.

1.     The disciples' deeds were to be exposed. There is nothing covered or hid that will remain so. Every act—whether done behind closed doors, in the dark, placed in a file or deposit box, or written in a book, pamphlet or letter—will be revealed and known.

2.     The disciples' words were to be exposed. There is no word that will not be heard and proclaimed for all to hear. Every word—whether spoken in the dark or whispered in the ear of someone or just conceived in the mind—will come to light.

        "**For nothing is secret, that shall not be made manifest; neither any thing hid, that shall not be known and come abroad**" (Lk.8:17).

        "**But they shall proceed no further: for their folly shall be manifest unto all men, as theirs also was**" (2 Tim.3:9).

        "**Therefore judge nothing before the time, until the Lord come, who both will bring to light the hidden things of darkness, and will make manifest the counsels of the hearts: and then shall every man have praise of God**" (1 Cor.4:5).

        "**Behold, ye have sinned against the LORD: and be sure your sin will find you out**" (Num.32:23).

        "**If I sin, then thou markest me, and thou wilt not acquit me from mine iniquity**" (Job 10:14).

        "**For now thou numberest my steps: dost thou not watch over my sin?**" (Job 14:16).

        "**The heaven shall reveal his iniquity; and the earth shall rise up against him**" (Job 20:27).

        "**For his eyes are upon the ways of man, and he seeth all his goings**" (Job 34:21).

        "**For the ways of man are before the eyes of the LORD, and he pondereth all his goings**" (Pr.5:21).

        "**For God shall bring every work into judgment, with every secret thing, whether it be good, or whether it be evil**" (Eccl.12:14).

        "**For though thou wash thee with nitre, and take thee much soap, yet thine iniquity is marked before me, saith the Lord GOD**" (Jer.2:22).

        "**For mine eyes are upon all their ways: they are not hid from my face, neither is their iniquity hid from mine eyes**" (Jer.16:17).

"Great in counsel, and mighty in work: for thine eyes are open upon all the ways of the sons of men: to give every one according to his ways, and according to the fruit of his doings" (Jer.32:19).

"I know the things that come into your mind, every one of them" (Ezk.11:5).

"For I know your manifold transgressions and your mighty sins: they afflict the just, they take a bribe, and they turn aside the poor in the gate from their right" (Amos 5:12).

---

**DEEPER STUDY # 1**

(12:1) **Leaven**: leaven is inserted in dough, and once it is, it does at least four things.

1. Leaven penetrates, seeps, and works its way through the dough. It cannot be seen, but it still works.
2. Leaven spreads. It spreads slowly, but once it is inserted, it cannot be stopped. It continues to spread until the whole dough is leavened.
3. Leaven swells the dough. It puffs dough up, making dough look much larger than it really is. Note: it does not add to the dough. It only changes its appearance.
4. Leaven ferments and sours the dough. It changes the dough's very nature.

---

**3** (12:4-12) **Fear—God, Care of—Unpardonable Sin—Jesus Christ, Son of Man**: the second message was to the friends of Jesus. He told them what to fear.

1. Do not fear men, but God alone. The reason is logical: men can only kill the body. God can cast both body and soul "into hell." (See DEEPER STUDY # 2, *Fear*—Lk.12:4; note and DEEPER STUDY # 1—Mt.10:28; DEEPER STUDY # 2—5:22.)

2. Do not fear the lack of necessities. Note the word "forgotten." The friend of the Lord is not forgotten, no matter the circumstance. There is something very precious here, yet there is a revelation of power as well.

⇒ There is a preciousness in the thought that every sparrow, no matter how common or forgotten or ignored, is very dear to God.

⇒ There is power in that God knows every single sparrow on the earth, and not a single one falls but what He knows about its injury. The idea is that injury to the sparrow causes pain and hurt which God feels. Suffering is due to the corruption and evil in the world, and corruption and evil always cause pain for God.

    a. There is God's providence. God sees, knows, cares, and oversees all the events and happenings on earth—even for the little sparrow that is so common and forgotten.

> "Therefore I say unto you, Take no thought for your life, what ye shall eat, or what ye shall drink; nor yet for your body, what ye shall put on. Is not the life more than meat, and the body than raiment? Behold the fowls of the air: for they sow not, neither do they reap, nor gather into barns; yet your heavenly Father feedeth them. Are ye not much better than they?" (Mt.6:25-26).
>
> "Casting all your care upon him; for he careth for you" (1 Pt.5:7).

    b. There is God's knowledge (omniscience). God knows every little happening and all that is, even to the most minute detail. He knows when a single sparrow falls to the ground. He knows every hair of a person's head, even the number of hairs.

> "Be not ye therefore like unto them [heathen]: for your Father knoweth what things ye have need of, before ye ask him" (Mt.6:8).
>
> "Now are we sure that thou knowest all things, and needest not that any man should ask thee: by this we believe that thou camest forth from God" (Jn.16:30).
>
> "And again, The Lord knoweth the thoughts of the wise, that they are vain. Therefore let no man glory in men. For all things are yours" (1 Cor.3:20-21).
>
> "Talk no more so exceeding proudly; let not arrogancy come out of your mouth: for the LORD is a God of knowledge, and by him actions are weighed" (1 Sam.2:3).
>
> "Hast thou not known? hast thou not heard, that the everlasting God, the LORD the Creator of the ends of the earth, fainteth not, neither is weary? there is no searching of his understanding" (Is.40:28).

    c. There is God's power (omnipotence). God is able to control the events that happen to the believer, no matter how detailed and minute. He can control and work them out for good to such an extent that there is no need for the believer to fear.

> "And we know that all things work together for good to them that love God, to them who are the called according to his purpose" (Ro.8:28).
>
> "For our light affliction, which is but for a moment, worketh for us a far more exceeding and eternal weight of glory" (2 Cor.4:17).
>
> "And he said unto me, My grace is sufficient for thee: for my strength is made perfect in weakness. Most gladly therefore will I rather glory in my infirmities, that the power of Christ may rest upon me" (2 Cor.12:9).

    d. There is God's love. Nothing can separate us from the love of Christ and of God.

> "Who shall separate us from the love of Christ? Shall tribulation, or distress, or persecution, or famine, or nakedness, or peril, or sword?....For I am persuaded, that neither death, nor life, nor angels, nor principalities, nor powers, nor things present, nor things to come, Nor height, nor depth, nor any other creature, shall be able to separate us from the love of God, which is in Christ Jesus our Lord" (Ro.8:35, 38-39).

3. Fear the spirit of disloyalty, of denying Christ. Note three points.
   a. Men shall be judged before the angels of God. Angels will witness either our acceptance or rejection by God.
   b. The judgment will be executed by the Son of Man Himself. He alone is the One Man who lived and experienced all the temptations and trials of life, yet He never sinned. He alone has been through it all and conquered all. He alone is worthy to judge. He alone knows...
      • what a man is.
      • what a man believes and does not believe.
      • what a man can and can not do.
      • what a man does and fails to do.

> "And before him [Christ] shall be gathered all nations: and he shall separate them one from another, as a shepherd divideth his sheep from the goats" (Mt.25:32).
> "For the Father judgeth no man, but hath committed all judgment unto the Son" (Jn.5:22).
> "And he commanded us to preach unto the people, and to testify that it is he which was ordained of God to be the Judge of quick [living] and dead" (Acts 10:42).
> "Because he hath appointed a day, in the which he will judge the world in righteousness by that man [Christ] whom he hath ordained; whereof he hath given assurance unto all men, in that he hath raised him from the dead" (Acts 17:31).
> "In the day when God shall judge the secrets of men by Jesus Christ according to my gospel" (Ro.2:16).
> "We shall all stand before the judgment seat of Christ" (Ro.14:10).
> "I charge thee therefore before God, and the Lord Jesus Christ, who shall judge the quick [living] and the dead at his appearing and his kingdom" (2 Tim.4:1).

   c. The basis of judgment is a man's attitude toward the Son of Man (see note—Mt.8:20).
      ⇒ The man who truly confesses (lives for) Christ before men, shall be confessed (given life) before the angels of God.

> "Whosoever therefore shall confess me before men, him will I confess also before my Father which is in heaven" (Mt.10:32).
> "That if thou shalt confess with thy mouth the Lord Jesus, and shalt believe in thine heart that God hath raised him from the dead, thou shalt be saved. For with the heart man believeth unto righteousness; and with the mouth confession is made unto salvation" (Ro.10:9-10).
> "Whosoever denieth the Son, the same hath not the Father: [but] he that acknowledgeth the Son hath the Father also" (1 Jn.2:23).
> "Whosoever shall confess that Jesus is the Son of God, God dwelleth in him, and he in God" (1 Jn.4:15).

      ⇒ The man who denies (fails to live for) Christ before men shall be denied (not given life) before the angels of God.

> "But whosoever shall deny me before men, him will I also deny before my Father which is in heaven" (Mt.10:33).
> "Whosoever therefore shall be ashamed of me and of my words in this adulterous and sinful generation; of him also shall the Son of man be ashamed, when he cometh in the glory of his Father with the holy angels" (Mk.8:38).
> "If we suffer, we shall also reign with him: if we deny him, he also will deny us" (2 Tim.2:12).
> "They profess that they know God; but in works they deny him, being abominable, and disobedient, and unto every good work reprobate" (Tit.1:16).
> "But there were false prophets also among the people, even as there shall be false teachers among you, who privily shall bring in damnable heresies, even denying the Lord that bought them, and bring upon themselves swift destruction" (2 Pt.2:1).
> "Who is a liar but he that denies that Jesus is the Christ? He is antichrist, that denieth the Father and the Son" (1 Jn.2:22).

4. Fear the unpardonable sin. Note two crucial points.
   a. Blasphemy against Christ, the Son of Man, can be forgiven. If a person is guilty of cursing Christ and he really wants forgiveness, he can ask for forgiveness and God will forgive him if he repents.

b. Blasphemy against the Holy Spirit is not forgiven. This sin is not referring to just *speaking* words against the Spirit. It means setting one's mind and heart and life against the Spirit. It means that the words spoken against the Spirit come from a heart set against the Spirit and the work of the Spirit (see note—Mt.12:31-32 for more discussion).

5. Do not fear persecution and trials. Why? Because the Holy Spirit empowers the believer. This point has to do with persecution, whether mild ridicule or physical abuse and martyrdom. The Holy Spirit will give power to the Lord's friend (follower), the strength to bear and the words to speak.

Very simply, God is to be trusted in the hour of trial, trusted for the strength to bear whatever men may do to us. This does not mean we should not be praying and thinking, but it means that God is to be trusted for the defense. There is a reason for this. Only God knows the heart of the persecutors and any others who are present. Thus, He alone knows what needs to be said to touch their hearts or else to serve as a witness against them in the future.

> "But when they deliver you up, take no thought how or what ye shall speak: for it shall be given you in that same hour what ye shall speak" (Mt.10:19).
> "For I will give you a mouth and wisdom, which all your adversaries shall not be able to gainsay [refute] nor resist" (Lk.21:15).
> "Which [spiritual] things also we speak, not in the words which man's wisdom teacheth, but which the Holy Ghost teacheth; comparing spiritual things with spiritual" (1 Cor.2:13).
> "Now therefore go, and I will be with thy mouth, and teach thee what thou shalt say" (Ex.4:12).
> "The Lord GOD hath given me the tongue of the learned, that I should know how to speak a word in season to him that is weary: he wakeneth morning by morning, he wakeneth mine ear to hear as the learned" (Is.50:4).
> "And I have put my words in thy mouth, and I have covered thee in the shadow of mine hand, that I may plant the heavens, and lay the foundations of the earth, and say unto Zion, Thou art my people" (Is.51:16).
> "Wherefore thus saith the LORD God of hosts, Because ye speak this word, behold, I will make my words in thy mouth fire, and this people wood, and it shall devour them" (Jer.5:14).

---

**DEEPER STUDY # 2**

(12:4) **Fear—Persecution**: fear of man is a terrible thing. It is a subject that needs to be looked at closely. Jesus said that fear can cost a person his eternal destiny, even if the person is a friend, a follower, of His. (Note that Jesus is addressing His "friends," His followers, v.4.)

1. The fear of men causes several things.
   ⇒ It causes a person to become disturbed within heart and mind: the loss of peace.
   ⇒ It causes a person to lose fervor: the loss of commitment.
   ⇒ It causes a person to be either sidetracked from or to give up what he knows to be God's will: the loss of mission and meaning and purpose.

> "For God hath not given us the spirit of fear; but of power, and of love, and of a sound mind" (2 Tim.1:7).
> "There is no fear in love; but perfect love casteth out fear: because fear hath torment. He that feareth is not made perfect in love" (1 Jn.4:18).
> "Fear thou not; For I am with thee: be not dismayed; for I am thy God: I will strengthen thee; yea, I will help thee; yea, I will uphold thee with the right hand of my righteousness" (Is.41:10).
> "Fear not: for I have redeemed thee, I have called thee by thy name; thou art mine. When thou passest through the waters, I will be with thee; and through the rivers, they shall not overflow thee: when thou walkest through the fire, thou shalt not be burned; neither shall the flame kindle upon thee. For I am the LORD thy God" (Is.43:1-3).

2. There are several reasons why men are not to be feared.
   a. Men can only kill the body, not the soul. Their power is limited; they can go no further. They cannot touch a person's soul or life.
   b. Men can only send us out of this world, not out of heaven. "To be with Christ...is far better" anyway (Ph.1:23; 3:20-21).
   c. Men can only separate us from this world, not from life. We have eternal life. Death is not a part of the experience of the believer, for the believer will not "taste" death. Christ "tasted," that is, experienced, death for the believer (Heb.2:9). The believer has already passed from death to life and lives forever (Jn.5:24). When he faces death, he is merely transferred from this world, from the physical dimension of being, into the next world, the heavenly or spiritual dimension of being (see DEEPER STUDY # 1—2 Tim.4:18).

> "Verily, verily, I say unto you, He that heareth my word, and believeth on him that sent me, hath everlasting life, and shall not come into condemnation; but is passed from death unto life" (Jn.5:24).
> "But we see Jesus, who was made a little lower than the angels for the suffering of death, crowned with glory and honour; that he by the grace of God should taste death for every man. For it became him, for whom are all things, and by whom are all things, in

bringing many sons unto glory, to make the captain of their salvation perfect through sufferings. For both he that sanctifieth and they who are sanctified are all of one: for which cause he is not ashamed to call them brethren" (Heb.2:9-11; cp. v.12-18).

"And the Lord shall deliver me from every evil work, and will preserve me unto his heavenly kingdom: to whom be glory for ever and ever" (2 Tim.4:18).

d. Men can only cut us off from the unbelievers and believers of this earth, not from the love of God and the saints in glory.

"Who shall separate us from the love of Christ? shall tribulation, or distress, or persecution, or famine, or nakedness, or peril, or sword? As it is written, For thy sake we are killed all the day long; we are accounted as sheep for the slaughter. Nay, in all these things we are more than conquerors through him that loved us. For I am persuaded, that neither death, nor life, nor angels, nor principalities, nor powers, nor things present, nor things to come, nor height, nor depth, nor any other creature, shall be able to separate us from the love of God, which is in Christ Jesus our Lord" (Ro.8:35-39).

3. There are two *primary* reasons why we should not fear men and persecution.

a. God has given us a great and glorious cause: to reach men for Christ. Very practically some men do not want to be reached; therefore, they rail and react and become our persecutors. But some do want to be saved, and the fact that they can receive eternal life is so glorious that it is worth whatever price we have to pay in order to see them saved.

"Let him know, that he which converteth the sinner from the error of his way shall save a soul from death, and shall hide a multitude of sins" (Jas.5:20).

"For God so loved the world, that he gave his only begotten Son, that whosoever believeth in him should not perish, but have everlasting life. For God sent not his Son into the world to condemn the world; but that the world through him might be saved" (Jn.3:16-17).

"For the wages of sin is death; but the gift of God is eternal life through Jesus Christ our Lord" (Ro.6:23).

"For to be carnally minded is death; but to be spiritually minded is life and peace" (Ro.8:6).

"Wherefore he is able also to save them to the uttermost that come unto God by him, seeing he ever liveth to make intercession for them" (Heb.7:25).

"There is no fear in love; but perfect love casteth out fear: because fear hath torment. He that feareth is not made perfect in love" (1 Jn.4:18).

b. God has given us a great hope (see thought—Mt.10:26-27).

"Verily, verily, I say unto you, If a man keep my saying, he shall never see death" (Jn.8:51).

"And whosoever liveth and believeth in me shall never die. Believest thou this?" (Jn.11:26).

"And [I] have hope toward God, which they themselves also allow, that there shall be a resurrection of the dead, both of the just and unjust. And herein do I exercise myself, to have always a conscience void of offence toward God, and toward men" (Acts 24:15-16).

"To them who by patient continuance in well doing seek for glory and honour and immortality, eternal life" (Ro.2:7).

"For we know that if our earthly house of this tabernacle were dissolved, we have a building of God, an house not made with hands, eternal in the heavens" (2 Cor.5:1).

"For the hope which is laid up for you in heaven, whereof ye heard before in the word of the truth of the gospel" (Col.1:5).

"For our conversation [citizenship] is in heaven; from whence also we look for the Saviour, the Lord Jesus Christ: who shall change our vile body, that it may be fashioned like unto his glorious body, according to the working whereby he is able even to subdue all things unto himself" (Ph.3:20-21).

"Looking for that blessed hope, and the glorious appearing of the great God and our Saviour Jesus Christ" (Tit.2:13).

"Wherein God, willing more abundantly to show unto the heirs of promise the immutability of his counsel, confirmed it by an oath: that by two immutable things, in which it was impossible for God to lie, we might have a strong consolation, who have fled for refuge to lay hold upon the hope set before us: which hope we have as an anchor of the soul, both sure and stedfast, and which entereth into that within the veil [heaven]; whither the forerunner is for us entered, even Jesus, made an high priest for ever" (Heb.6:17-20).

"Blessed by the God and Father of our Lord Jesus Christ, which according to his abundant mercy hath begotten us again unto a lively hope by the resurrection of Jesus Christ from the dead, to an inheritance incorruptible, and undefiled, and that fadeth not away, reserved in heaven for you" (1 Pt.1:3-4).

4. There is a remedy to keep us from fearing men: God. God is to be feared (see note—Mt.10:28). Note several things.

   a. God can destroy us, both body and soul, and put both "in hell" (see DEEPER STUDY # 2—Mt.5:22). By "destroy" Jesus did not mean our body and soul would cease to exist, but they would live a worthless existence, be ruined and suffer in ruin forever (see DEEPER STUDY # 1—Mt.10:28).

   b. Jesus was speaking to believers in this passage. God is to be feared much more and much sooner than men. The terror of men pales into absolute insignificance in comparison to God's terror. Imagine this one fact alone. Man's terror is but for a short while at most, but God's terror is *forever*. The Bible says it never ends. The point is clear: before caving in to man's persecution, we need to remember the *fear of God*.

   c. The destruction of the soul comes from God, not from man. The power to destroy the soul is God's power alone. How fearful we must be of God—even we who are believers (see note—Mt.10:28)!

   > "And fear not them which kill the body, but are not able to kill the soul: but rather fear him which is able to destroy both soul and body in hell" (Mt.10:28).

   > "And if ye call on the Father, who without respect of persons judgeth according to every man's work, pass the time of your sojourning here in fear" (1 Pt.1:17).

   > "Honour all men. Love the brotherhood. Fear God. Honour the king" (1 Pt.2:17).

   > "And if the righteous scarcely be saved, where shall the ungodly and the sinner appear?" (1 Pt.4:18).

   > "Saying with a loud voice, Fear God, and give glory to him; for the hour of his judgment is come: and worship him that made heaven, and earth, and the sea, and the fountains of waters" (Rev.14:7).

   > "Wherefore now let the fear of the LORD be upon you; take heed and do it: for there is no iniquity with the LORD our God, nor respect of persons, nor taking of gifts" (2 Chron.19:7).

| | M. The Parable of the Rich Fool: The Man of Wealth & What He Should Fear, 12:13-21 | 17 And he thought within himself, saying, What shall I do, because I have no room where to bestow my fruits? | |
|---|---|---|---|
| **1 A request for Jesus to give a judicial decision** a. Brother's desire for an inheritance & wealth b. Jesus' stern refusal | 13 And one of the company said unto him, Master, speak to my brother, that he divide the inheritance with me. 14 And he said unto him, Man, who made me a judge or a divider over you? | 18 And he said, This will I do: I will pull down my barns, and build greater; and there will I bestow all my fruits and my goods. 19 And I will say to my soul, Soul, thou hast much goods laid up for many years; take thine ease, eat, drink, and be merry. | **d. The big mistake: Self-indulgence & extravagant living** |
| **2 Fear this: Life does not consist in things** a. The serious charge: Take heed—beware b. The big sin: Covetousness[DS1] c. The big "I" (6 times, 16-19a): Aggressively self-centered | 15 And he said unto them, Take heed, and beware of covetousness: for a man's life consisteth not in the abundance of the things which he possesseth. 16 And he spake a parable unto them, saying, The ground of a certain rich man brought forth plentifully: | 20 But God said unto him, Thou fool, this night thy soul shall be required of thee: then whose shall those things be, which thou hast provided? 21 So is he that layeth up treasure for himself, and is not rich toward God. | **3 Fear this: The soul may be required & demanded tonight** **4 Fear this: Wealth is not a permanent possession—someone else gets it** |

# DIVISION V

## THE SON OF MAN'S GREAT JOURNEY TO JERUSALEM STAGE I): HIS MISSION AND PUBLIC CHALLENGE, 9:51-13:21

## M. The Parable of the Rich Fool: The Man of Wealth and What He Should Fear, 12:13-21

(12:13-21) **Introduction**: the man of wealth is often self-sufficient, but there are some things he needs to fear.
1. A request for Jesus to give a judicial decision (v.13-14).
2. Fear: life does not consist in things (v.15-19).
3. Fear: the soul may be required and demanded tonight (v.20).
4. Fear: wealth is not a permanent possession—someone else gets it (v.20-21).

**1** (12:13-14) **Worldliness—Materialism**: there was a request for Jesus to give a judicial decision. A man was having a dispute with his brother over the inheritance of his father's estate. The law gave two-thirds to the older son and one third to the younger son. The man felt he was not getting his legal share, so he appealed to Jesus for help in getting his share. It was a common practice for Rabbis to settle legal disputes. Note five things.
1. The man was in the congregation listening to Jesus preach. There is a strong possibility that the man was even a follower of Jesus. This is seen in that Jesus had apparently paused for a brief rest between sermons, and the man knew Jesus well enough to approach Him about the matter in the midst of a huge crowd.
2. What the man wanted was significant. He wanted material wealth, money, and property. Note: he appealed to Jesus for help in getting what had probably been *stolen from him*. More than likely the property was rightfully his anyway. It would have been an act of justice to straighten out the inheritance.
3. Jesus refused rather sternly. He forcefully addressed the man as a stranger: "Man." He treats the man as one who is alien to the Lord and His purpose on earth. Jesus refused to become involved in worldly affairs, in settling property and money disputes.
4. The man exposed a serious flaw in his spiritual life. Jesus had just preached a message on trusting God for the necessities of life, for God cares and will provide. Apparently, the man *had not heard the message*. He was bodily present, but he was too preoccupied with the thoughts of property and money to really hear the Word and receive the message.

> **Thought 1.** Listening to the Word's being preached does not mean that we "hear the Word," nor that we learn from it. The Word, salvation, and spiritual maturity do not *rub off on a wandering mind or on a worldly life*.

5. The contrast between the mind and attitude of the man and of Jesus is significant. The man's mind was set on the things of the earth and the world, on property and money, wealth and selfishness. The Lord's mind was set on the higher and more noble, on salvation and life, on heaven and eternity. The mission of Jesus was not to give man property, but to give man life, both abundant and eternal. Property is nothing without life.

**2** (12:15-19) **Fear—Worldliness—Selfishness—Indulgence**: fear—life does not consist in things. Note four points.
1. The charge of Jesus was strong. There was a double warning: *"take heed, beware."* The warning was to be given close attention. The word "beware" (phulassesthe) means to guard oneself from some enemy.
2. The big sin of man is *covetousness* (see Deeper Study # 1—Lk.12:15; Deeper Study # 1—Jas.4:1-3 for more discussion). This is the big sin of the world—desiring more and more. However, a man's happiness and comfort, soul and body do not depend upon what he has; *many poor people* are happy and comfortable with healthy souls and bodies. Life does not consist in possessions—a beautiful home, the latest clothes, a new car, property, money, wealth.

249

3. The *big "I"* shows that the covetous man is *aggressively self-centered*. Note how Jesus gets the fact of man's covetousness across. He shares a parable about a man who was also *aggressively self-centered*. In just three short verses describing his thoughts, the rich man in the parable said, "I" six times and "my" five times. The man's attention was solely upon himself. Now note the parable.

    a. The man was blessed materially, tremendously blessed, but he did not *thank God* for his blessing.

    b. The man called the fruits of the ground and the possessions he had, "*my fruit*" and "*my goods*" (v.17-18).

    c. The man called his soul, "*my soul*." There is no indication he had given his soul to God.

    d. He became *puffed up*, prideful with what he had done. He began to think of *bigger and bigger*, of *I and I*, of *my and my*.

4. The big mistake of man is *selfishness*, self-indulgence, and extravagant living (see Deeper Study # 1—Lk.16:19-21). Note the sole purpose of man is to be at ease, to have plenty to eat and drink, and to enjoy life as he wishes. Note several facts about the man in the parable.

    a. He thought only of self, of living at ease and in comfort, of indulging self and being as extravagant as he wished. He gave no thought to helping others. He forgot that he lived in a needy world that was lost and dying.

    b. He put off living and enjoying life until he got his barns built. The idea is that he was a *workaholic*, who was consumed with the passion to get what he wanted. (How many are just like him when they want something!)

    c. Now note the most shocking point: he only *thought* these things. He never did them; they were only thoughts of his heart.

> "Beware that thou forget not the LORD thy God, in not keeping his commandments, and his judgments, and his statutes, which I command thee this day: lest when thou hast eaten and art full, and hast built goodly houses, and dwelt therein; and when thy herds and thy flocks multiply, and thy silver and thy gold is multiplied, and all that thou hast is multiplied; then thine heart be lifted up, and thou forget the LORD thy God" (Dt.8:11-14).
>
> "There is that scattereth, and yet increaseth; and there is that withholdeth more than is meet, but it tendeth to poverty" (Pr.11:24).
>
> "Whoso stoppeth his ears at the cry of the poor, he also shall cry himself, but shall not be heard" (Pr.21:13).
>
> "If thou forbear to deliver them that are drawn unto death, and those that are ready to be slain; if thou sayest, Behold, we knew it not; doth not he that pondereth the heart consider it? And he that keepeth thy soul, doth not he know it? And shall not he render to every man according to his works?" (Pr.24:11-12).
>
> "He that giveth unto the poor shall not lack: but he that hideth his eyes shall have many a curse" (Pr.28:27).
>
> "Woe unto them that join house to house, that lay field to field, till there be no place, that they may be placed alone in the midst of the earth!" (Is.5:8).
>
> "There is a sore evil which I have seen under the sun, namely, riches kept for the owners thereof to their hurt" (Eccl.5:13).
>
> "And when ye did eat, and when ye did drink, did not ye eat for yourselves, and drink for yourselves?" (Zech.7:6).
>
> "Then said Jesus unto his disciples, Verily I say unto you, That a rich man shall hardly enter into the kingdom of heaven" (Mt.19:23).
>
> "For I was an hungred, and ye gave me no meat: I was thirsty, and ye gave me no drink: I was a stranger, and ye took me not in: naked, and ye clothed me not: sick, and in prison, and ye visited me not" (Mt.25:42-43).
>
> "And the cares of this world, and the deceitfulness of riches, and the lusts of other things entering in, choke the word, and it becometh unfruitful" (Mk.4:19).
>
> "But they that will be rich fall into temptation and a snare, and into many foolish and hurtful lusts, which drown men in destruction and perdition" (1 Tim.6:9).
>
> "But whoso hath this world's good, and seeth his brother have need, and shutteth up his bowels of compassion from him, how dwelleth the love of God in him?" (1 Jn.3:17).

---

**DEEPER STUDY # 1**

(12:15) **Covetousness** (pleonexia): a craving, a desire for more. It is greediness, a dissatisfaction with what is enough. It includes the cravings for both material things and fleshly indulgence. It is desiring what belongs to others; snatching at something that belongs to others; a love of having, a cry of *give me, give me* (cp. 2 Pt.2:14).

    ⇒ It is a lust so deep within a man that he finds his happiness in things instead of in God.

    ⇒ It is a covetousness so deep that it desires the power that things bring more than the things themselves.

    ⇒ It is an intense appetite for gain; a passion for the pleasure that things can bring. It goes beyond the pleasure of possessing things for their own sakes.

> "Lay not up for yourselves treasures upon earth, where moth and rust doth corrupt, and where thieves break through and steal: but lay up for yourselves treasures in heaven, where neither moth nor rust doth corrupt, and where thieves do not break through nor steal: for where your treasure is, there will your heart be also" (Mt.6:19-21).

"No man can serve two masters: for either he will hate the one, and love the other; or else he will hold to the one, and despise the other. Ye cannot serve God and mammon" (Mt.6:24).

"For what is a man profited, if he shall gain the whole world, and lose his own soul? or what shall a man give in exchange for his soul?" (Mt.16:26).

"But fornication, and all uncleanness, or covetousness, let it not be once named among you, as becometh saints....For this ye know, that no whoremonger, nor unclean person, nor covetous man, who is an idolater, hath any inheritance in the kingdom of Christ and of God" (Eph.5:3, 5).

"Mortify therefore your members which are upon the earth; fornication, uncleanness, inordinate affection, evil concupiscence, and covetousness, which is idolatry: for which things' sake the wrath of God cometh on the children of disobedience" (Col.3:5-6).

"For many walk, of whom I have told you often, and now tell you even weeping, that they are the enemies of the cross of Christ: whose end is destruction, whose God is their belly, and whose glory is in their shame, who mind earthly things" (Ph.3:18-19).

"A bishop [minister] then must be blameless....not covetous" (1 Tim.3:2-3; cp. Tit.1:7).

"For we brought nothing into this world, and it is certain we can carry nothing out. And having food and raiment let us be therewith content. But they that will be rich fall into temptation and a snare, and into many foolish and hurtful lusts, which drown men in destruction and perdition. For the love of money is the root of all evil: which while some coveted after, they have erred from the faith, and pierced themselves through with many sorrows" (1 Tim.6:7-10).

"Charge them that are rich in this world, that they be not highminded, nor trust in uncertain riches, but in the living God, who giveth us richly all things to enjoy" (1 Tim.6:17).

"For men shall be lovers of their own selves, covetous, boasters, proud, blasphemers, disobedient to parents, unthankful, unholy" (2 Tim.3:2).

"Let your conversation [behavior] be without covetousness; and be content with such things as ye have: for he hath said, I will never leave thee, nor forsake thee" (Heb.13:5).

"Ye lust, and have not: ye kill, and desire to have, and cannot obtain: ye fight and war, yet ye have not, because ye ask not. Ye ask, and receive not, because ye ask amiss, that ye may consume it upon your lusts" (Jas.4:2-3).

"Go to now, ye rich men, weep and howl for your miseries that shall come upon you. Your riches are corrupted, and your garments are motheaten. Your gold and silver is cankered; and the rust of them shall be a witness against you, and shall eat your flesh as it were fire. Ye have heaped treasure together for the last days" (Jas.5:1-3; cp. v.4-6).

"Feed the flock of God which is among you, taking the oversight thereof, not by constraint, but willingly; not for filthy lucre, but of a ready mind" (1 Pt.5:2).

"And through covetousness shall they [false teachers] with feigned words make merchandise of you: whose judgment now of a long time lingereth not, and their damnation slumbereth not" (2 Pt.2:3).

"[False teachers] having eyes full of adultery, and that cannot cease from sin; beguiling unstable souls: an heart they have exercised with covetous practices; cursed children" (2 Pt.2:14).

"Thou shalt not covet thy neighbor's house, thou shalt not covet thy neighbor's wife, nor his manservant, nor his maidservant, nor his ox, nor his ass, nor any thing that is thy neighbor's" (Ex.20:17).

"If I have made gold my hope, or have said to the fine gold, Thou art my confidence; if I rejoiced because mine hand had gotten much....this also were an iniquity to be punished by the judge: for I should have denied the God that is above" (Job 31:24-25, 28).

"For the wicked boasteth of his heart's desire, and blesseth the covetous, whom the LORD abhorreth" (Ps.10:3).

"Trust not in oppression, and become not vain in robbery: if riches increase, set not your heart upon them" (Ps.62:10).

"Incline my heart unto thy testimonies, and not to covetousness" (Ps.119:36).

"He that is greedy of gain troubleth his own house; but he that hateth gifts shall live" (Pr.15:27).

"The desire of the slothful killeth him; for his hands refuse to labor. He coveteth greedily all the day long: but the righteous giveth and spareth not" (Pr.21:25-26).

"He that oppresseth the poor to increase his riches, and he that giveth to the rich, shall surely come to want" (Pr.22:16).

"Labor not to be rich: cease from thine own wisdom. Wilt thou set thine eyes upon that which is not? For riches certainly make themselves wings; they fly away as an eagle toward heaven" (Pr.23:4-5).

"For riches are not for ever: and doth the crown endure to every generation?" (Pr.27:24).

"Whoso causeth the righteous to go astray in an evil way, he shall fall himself into his own pit: but the upright shall have good things in possession" (Pr.28:10).

"A faithful man shall abound with blessings: but he that maketh haste to be rich shall not be innocent" (Pr.28:20).

"Remove far from me vanity and lies; give me neither poverty nor riches; feed me with food convenient for me" (Pr.30:8).

"He that loveth silver shall not be satisfied with silver; nor he that loveth abundance with increase: this is also vanity" (Eccl.5:10).

"Thy princes are rebellious, and companions of thieves: every one loveth gifts, and followeth after rewards: they judge not the fatherless, neither doth the cause of the widow come unto them" (Is.1:23).

"Yea, they [watchmen, false ministers] are greedy dogs which can never have enough, and they are shepherds that cannot understand: they all look to their own way, every one for his gain, from his quarter" (Is.56:11).

"For the iniquity of his covetousness was I wroth, and smote him: I hid me, and was wroth, and he went on frowardly in the way of his heart" (Is.57:17).

"For from the least of them even unto the greatest of them every one is given to covetousness; and from the prophet even unto the priest every one dealeth falsely" (Jer.6:13; cp. Jer.8:10).

"But thine eyes and thine heart are not but for thy covetousness, and for to shed innocent blood, and for oppression, and for violence, to do it" (Jer.22:17).

"O thou that dwellest upon many waters, abundant in treasures, thine end is come, and the measure of thy covetousness" (Jer.51:13).

"In thee have they taken gifts to shed blood; thou hast taken usury and increase, and thou hast greedily gained of thy neighbors by extortion, and hast forgotten me, saith the Lord GOD" (Ezk.22:12).

"And they come unto thee as the people cometh, and they sit before thee as my people, and they hear thy words, but they will not do them: for with their mouth they show much love, but their heart goeth after their covetousness" (Ezk.33:31).

"And they covet fields, and take them by violence; and houses, and take them away: so they oppress a man and his house, even a man and his heritage" (Mic.2:2).

"The heads thereof judge for reward, and the priests thereof teach for hire and the prophets thereof divine for money: yet will they lean upon the LORD, and say, Is not the LORD among us? none evil can come upon us" (Mic.3:11).

"That they may do evil with both hands earnestly, the prince asketh, and the judge asketh for a reward; and the great man, he uttereth his mischievous desire: so they wrap it up" (Mic.7:3).

"Woe to him that coveteth an evil covetousness to his house, that he may be delivered from the power of evil! Thou hath consulted shame to thy house by cutting off many people, and hast sinned against thy soul" (Hab.2:9-10).

"Ye have sown much, and bring in little; ye eat, but there is none warm; and he that earneth wages earneth wages to put it into a bag with holes" (Hag.1:6).

**3** (12:20) **Death—Fear—Judgment**: fear—the soul may be required and demanded tonight. Note several things.

1. It was God who now spoke. It was God who knew the thoughts of the man. It was God who knew the man was to die that very night. The man did not know it, nor did anyone else.

2. The man was to die that night. Everyone has his night (day) to die, and this was his night.

3. The man's "soul" was required. God required and demanded it. His soul was not going to cease existing. It was to exist in another world. Existence was not over for the man. The man's soul was simply to be in another world, in the spiritual dimension of existence.

4. The man was called a "fool" by God. He had lived as a fool, lived entirely for himself. He had refused to think about the truth, about the uncertainty of life. There was a good possibility that he might not live as long as he wished to live.

"And this know, that if the goodman of the house had known what hour the thief would come, he would have watched, and not have suffered his house to be broken through. Be ye therefore ready also: for the Son of man cometh at an hour when ye think not" (Lk.12:39-40).

"What fruit had ye then in those things whereof ye are now ashamed? for the end of those things is death" (Ro.6:21).

"But that which beareth thorns and briers is rejected, and is nigh unto cursing: whose end is to be burned" (Heb.6:8).

"But the end of all things is at hand: be ye therefore sober, and watch unto prayer" (1 Pt.4:7).

"For the time is come that judgment must begin at the house of God: and if it first begin at us, what shall the end be of them that obey not the gospel of God? And if the righteous scarcely be saved, where shall the ungodly and the sinner appear?" (1 Pt.4:17-18).

"These [the wicked] are wells without water, clouds that are carried with a tempest; to whom the mist of darkness is reserved for ever" (2 Pt.2:17).

"Raging waves of the sea, foaming out their own shame; wandering stars, to whom [the wicked] is reserved the blackness of darkness for ever" (Jude 13).

"But the fearful, and unbelieving, and the abominable, and murderers, and whoremongers, and sorcerers, and idolaters, and all liars, shall have their part in the lake which burneth with fire and brimstone: which is the second death" (Rev.21:8).

"The wicked shall be turned into hell, and all the nations that forget God" (Ps.9:17).

"For they shall soon be cut down like the grass, and wither as the green herb" (Ps.37:2).

"For yet a little while, and the wicked shall not be: yea, thou shalt diligently consider his place, and it shall not be" (Ps.37:10).

"I have seen the wicked in great power, and spreading himself like a green bay tree. Yet he passed away, and, lo, he was not: yea, I sought him, but he could not be found" (Ps.37:35-36).

"But thou, O God, shalt bring them down into the pit of destruction: bloody and deceitful men shall not live out half their days; but I will trust in thee" (Ps.55:23).

"When the wicked spring as the grass, and when all the workers of iniquity do flourish; it is that they shall be destroyed for ever" (Ps.92:7).

"The wicked shall see it, and be grieved; he shall gnash with his teeth, and melt away: the desire of the wicked shall perish" (Ps.112:10).

"For the ways of man are before the eyes of the LORD, and he pondereth all his goings. His own iniquities shall take the wicked himself, and he shall be holden with the cords of his sins. He shall die without instruction; and in the greatness of his folly he shall go astray" (Pr.5:21-23).

"And behold at eveningtide trouble; and before the morning he is not. This is the portion of them that spoil us, and the lot of them that rob us" (Is.17:14).

"Have I any pleasure at all that the wicked should die? saith the Lord GOD: and not that he should return from his ways, and live?" (Ezk.18:23).

**4** (12:20-21) **Spiritual Dimension—Death—Judgment—Wealth**: fear—wealth is not a permanent possession; someone else gets it. The man left every penny behind. He took nothing with him. Now note why. This is a point seldom thought about. *He could take nothing with him because the strength, the energy, the power, the life of his body had left.* The Bible reveals...

- that the life of a man's body is his spirit.
- that the spirit lives forever.

Note: when the spirit left, the man's strength and energy and power were gone. His body had to lie down. Note something else: *his spirit was spiritual,* of another dimension of being. It belonged to another world, another life. Therefore, all *material* possessions had to be left behind.

"For we brought nothing into this world, and it is certain we can carry nothing out" (1 Tim.6:7).

"By faith Moses, when he was come to years, refused to be called the son of Pharaoh's daughter; choosing rather to suffer affliction with the people of God, than to enjoy the pleasures of sin for a season" (Heb.11:24-25).

"Your gold and silver is cankered; and the rust of them shall be a witness against you, and shall eat your flesh as it were fire. Ye have heaped treasure together for the last days" (Jas.5:3).

"So then because thou art lukewarm, and neither cold nor hot, I will spue thee out of my mouth. Because thou sayest, I am rich, and increased with goods, and have need of nothing; and knowest not that thou art wretched, and miserable, and poor, and blind, and naked" (Rev.3:16-17).

"The increase of his house shall depart, and his goods shall flow away in the day of his wrath" (Job 20:28).

"Surely every man walketh in a vain show: surely they are disquieted in vain: he heapeth up riches, and knoweth not who shall gather them" (Ps.39:6).

"For he seeth that wise men die, likewise the fool and the brutish person perish, and leave their wealth to others" (Ps.49:10).

"Yea, I hated all my labor which I had taken under the sun: because I should leave it unto the man that shall be after me" (Eccl.2:18).

"For God giveth to a man that is good in his sight wisdom, and knowledge, and joy: but to the sinner he giveth travail, to gather and to heap up, that he may give to him that is good before God. This also is vanity and vexation of spirt" (Eccl.2:26).

"As the partridge sitteth on eggs, and hatcheth them not; so he that getteth riches, and not by right, shall leave them in the midst of his days, and at his end shall be a fool" (Jer.17:11).

"Now therefore thus saith the LORD of hosts; Consider your ways. Ye have sown much, and bring in little; ye eat, but ye have not enough; ye drink, but ye are not filled with drink; ye clothe you, but there is none warm; and he that earneth wages earneth wages to put it into a bag with holes" (Hag.1:5-6).

| 1 Do not be anxious about food & clothing | N. The Genuine Believer: Worry Not About Necessities, 12:22-34 (Mt.6:25-34) | one of these. |  |
|---|---|---|---|
|  |  | 28 If then God so clothe the grass, which is to day in the field, and to morrow is cast into the oven; how much more will he clothe you, O ye of little faith? |  |
|  | 22 And he said unto his disciples, Therefore I say unto you, Take no thought for your life, what ye shall eat; neither for the body, what ye shall put on. | | e. A tragic truth: Little faith[DS1] |
| a. Illust.1: Life & body—mean more than things | 23 The life is more than meat, and the body is more than raiment. | 29 And seek not ye what ye shall eat, or what ye shall drink, neither be ye of doubtful mind. | 2 Do not be wrapped up in seeking food & drink, nor in doubting God's care |
| b. Illust.2: The ravens—are fed by God | 24 Consider the ravens: for they neither sow nor reap; which neither have storehouse nor barn; and God feedeth them: how much more are ye better than the fowls? | 30 For all these things do the nations of the world seek after: and your Father knoweth that ye have need of these things. | a. Such is worldliness<br><br>b. God knows your needs |
| c. Illust.3: A man's height—is not altered an inch by worry | 25 And which of you with taking thought can add to his stature one cubit? | 31 But rather seek ye the kingdom of God; and all these things shall be added unto you. | 3 Seek the Kingdom of God<br>a. God provides necessities |
|  | 26 If ye then be not able to do that thing which is least, why take ye thought for the rest? | 32 Fear not, little flock; for it is your Father's good pleasure to give you the kingdom. | b. God gives you the kingdom |
| d. Illust.4: The lilies & grass—are clothed by God | 27 Consider the lilies how they grow: they toil not, they spin not; and yet I say unto you, that Solomon in all his glory was not arrayed like | 33 Sell that ye have, and give alms; provide yourselves bags which wax not old, a treasure in the heavens that faileth not, where no thief approacheth, neither moth corrupteth. | c. God gives treasures that do not age, fail, corrupt—nor can they be stolen |
|  |  | 34 For where your treasure is, there will your heart be also. | d. God warns: Your heart shall be where your treasure is |

# DIVISION V

## THE SON OF MAN'S GREAT JOURNEY TO JERUSALEM (STAGE I): HIS MISSION AND PUBLIC CHALLENGE, 9:51-13:21

## N. The Genuine Believer: Worry Not About Necessities, 12:22-34

(12:22-34) **Introduction**: this message is not for the world; it is for disciples, the followers of Jesus. Jesus spoke "to His disciples" (v.22). "Taking thought" (merimnan), that is, worrying, being anxious and overly concerned, is a constant problem among men. It is not to be so among God's people. (See outline and notes—Mt.6:25-34 for more discussion and application.)

1. Do not be anxious about food and clothing (v.22-28).
2. Do not be wrapped up in seeking food and drink, nor in doubting God's care (v.29-30).
3. Seek the Kingdom of God (v.31-34).

**1** (12:22-28) **Necessities—Food—Clothing—Body—Life—Birds**: do not be anxious about food and clothing. One of the great sins of men is their desire for better and better things, such as food and clothing, houses and furnishings, position and recognition, property and wealth. The sin is covetousness (v.15). It is so common that Jesus warned His disciples not to be taken in by it. They were not to be anxious and worrying over such things. Jesus drove the point home with four illustrations.

1. The first illustration was that of the life and the body. The life and the body mean much more than the food we eat and the clothes we wear. Think for a moment. What means the most? A steak or one's life? A dress or one's body? The answer is clear. Therefore, a person's concern needs to be his life and his body, not delicious foods and the latest styles in clothes. He needs to give his time, energy, and effort to taking care of his life and body, not the delicious and stylish things of the world. Note two points.
   a. A *healthy body* will extend a person's time on earth, and a *well-kept life* will assure a person of living forever in the presence of God. The life and body are to be the concern of man, not food and clothing. (See note—Mt.6:25 for more discussion.)
   b. Jesus did not say we are not to think and plan for the necessities of life. He said we are not to worry and be anxious over the necessities of life. Everything in life takes some thought and some planning, but nothing should be so coveted that it causes anxiety and worry for us.
2. The second illustration was that of the ravens (crows). They were fed by God. Jesus said, "Consider"—think about the birds. Learn from what happens to them.
   ⇒ They do not sow or reap their food.
   ⇒ They do not store up their food.

⇒ Yet, God provides food for them.
⇒ They are able to pluck up the food that they need.

Learn that the believer is of much more value than the birds.

  a. He is a higher being, on a much higher level of creation. He is more noble and excellent, a spiritual being capable of a personal relationship with God (Job 35:11; Jn.3:16).
  b. The believer is a child of God. God is the Creator of birds, but He is the Father of believers (Ro.8:15-16; Gal.4:4-6).
  c. The believer is an heir of God. He is to receive all that God possesses in that glorious day of redemption (Ro.8:16-17; Tit.3:7; 1 Pt.1:3-4).

Again, however, Jesus was not pampering His followers. He was talking about worrying and being anxious over food and clothing and shelter. God does not put up with laziness and slothfulness, nor with lack of planning and initiative and effort. Jesus planned ahead (Jn.12:6) and preached industriousness (Lk.16:8; cp. 1-10). The Bible is clear about man's faithfully working at his employment, even working for extra in order to have enough to give and to help meet the needs of a desperate world (Eph.4:28). (See note—Mt.6:25-34.)

"For what is a man advantaged, if he gain the whole world, and lose himself, or be cast away?" (Lk.9:25).

"Be careful [anxious] for nothing; but in every thing by prayer and supplication with thanksgiving let your requests be made known unto God. And the peace of God, which passeth all understanding, shall keep your hearts and minds through Christ Jesus" (Ph.4:6-7).

"But I would have you without carefulness [anxiety, to be free from care]" (1 Cor.7:32).

"Thou wilt keep him in perfect peace, whose mind is stayed on thee: because he trusteth in thee" (Is.26:3).

"Trust ye in the LORD for ever: for in the LORD JEHOVAH is everlasting strength" (Is.26:4).

"Oh how great is thy goodness, which thou hast laid up for them that fear thee; which thou hast wrought for them that trust in thee before the sons of men!" (Ps.31:19).

"Now therefore thus saith the LORD of hosts; Consider your ways" (Hag.1:5).

**Thought 1.** The believer who truly trusts Jesus Christ shall never be forsaken by God. This does not mean the believer will never suffer nor that the believer will never have to face martyrdom. Suffering is sometimes necessary for the growth of the believer's faith and as a testimony to the world (see notes—Mt.5:10-12; 10:24-25). However, God never forsakes the believer. He takes care of the believer no matter what circumstances confront him. God cares for the believer and feeds him far more quickly than He feeds the ravens of the air.

"And he commanded the multitude to sit down on the grass, and took the five loaves, and the two fishes, and looking up to heaven, he blessed, and brake, and gave the loaves to his disciples, and the disciples to the multitude. And they did all eat, and were filled: and they took up of the fragments that remained twelve baskets full" (Mt.14:19-20).

"Not that I speak in respect of want: for I have learned, in whatsoever state I am, therewith to be content. I know both how to be abased, and I know how to abound: every where and in all things I am instructed both to be full and to be hungry, both to abound and to suffer need. I can do all things through Christ which strengtheneth me" (Ph.4:11-13).

"But my God shall supply all your need according to his riches in glory by Christ Jesus" (Ph.4:19).

"Trust in the LORD, and do good; so shalt thou dwell in the land, and verily thou shalt be fed" (Ps.37:3).

"Thou visitest the earth, and waterest it: thou greatly enrichest it with the river of God, which is full of water: thou preparest them corn, when thou hast so provided for it" (Ps.65:9).

"Blessed be the Lord, who daily loadeth us with benefits, even the God of our salvation" (Ps.68:19; cp. Ps.107:31-38; 114:11-15 for the basis of God's blessings).

"And even to your old age I am he; and even to hoar hairs will I carry you: I have made, and I will bear; even I will carry, and will deliver you" (Is.46:4).

"Blessed is the man that trusteth in the LORD, and whose hope the LORD is. For he shall be as a tree planted by the waters, and that spreadeth out her roots by the river, and shall not see when heat cometh, but her leaf shall be green; and shall not be careful in the year of drought, neither shall cease from yielding fruit" (Jer.17:7-8).

3. The third illustration was that of a man's height. The word "stature" (helikia) means height, quality, or status gained by growth; but sometimes it also means age. The word "cubit" (pechus) literally means measure of space, or distance (approximately 18 inches); but it can also mean a measure of time or age (Jn.9:21). So the verse can read either "who can add one cubit to his stature" or "one minute to his life span."

The point is striking: worry is senseless—just as senseless as trying to add to one's height or lengthen a minute to one's life span (when it is time for one to pass on). All statures and all bodies are not normal and perfectly formed. The world is corruptible and imperfect (see note—Mt.6:19-20). But there is a glorious hope in God—a hope that acknowledges that God does love and does care and has promised a new heavens and earth that shall be perfect. In that perfect heavens and earth, all bodies shall be normal and perfectly formed. God shall "wipe away all tears" (Rev.21:4; cp. 1-7).

"For our conversation [citizenship] is in heaven; from whence also we look for the Saviour, the Lord Jesus Christ: who shall change our vile body, that it may be fashioned like unto his glorious body, according to the working whereby he is able even to subdue all things unto himself" (Ph.3:20-21).

"So also is the resurrection of the dead. It is sown in corruption; it is raised in incorruption: it is sown in dishonour; it is raised in glory: it is sown in weakness; it is raised in power: it is sown a natural body: it is raised a spiritual body. There is a natural body, and there is a spiritual body" (1 Cor.15:42-44).

"And as we have borne the image of the earthy, we shall also bear the image of the heavenly" (1 Cor.15:49).

"For in this we groan, earnestly desiring to be clothed upon with our house [body] which is from heaven" (2 Cor.5:2).

"But they which shall be accounted worthy to obtain that world, and the resurrection from the dead, neither marry, nor are given in marriage: neither can they die any more: for they are equal unto the angels; and are the children of God, being the children of the resurrection" (Lk.20:35-36).

"For the Lamb which is in the midst of the throne shall feed them, and shall lead them unto living fountains of waters: and God shall wipe away all tears from their eyes" (Rev.7:17).

"And God shall wipe away all tears from their eyes; and there shall be no more death, neither sorrow, nor crying, neither shall there be any more pain: for the former things are passed away" (Rev.21:4).

**Thought 1.** Note the rich fool could not add one minute to his life. There was a night (day) appointed for his death, and he could not change that night (cp. Lk.12:16-21).

Very practically, some do have imperfect or abnormal bodies. How do they keep from being anxious and worrying?
1) There is a glorious hope for all (see note—Mt.6:27 for discussion).
2) There is the assuring promise of God to work all things out for good to those who truly love God.

> "And we know that all things work together for good to them that love God, to them who are the called according to his purpose" (Ro.8:28).

3) There is the strong challenge to be content with one's state or lot in life.

> "But as God hath distributed to every man, as the Lord hath called every one, so let him walk. And so ordain I in all churches....Let every man abide in the same calling wherein he was called....Brethren, let every man, wherein he is called, therein abide with God" (1 Cor.7:17, 20, 24; cp. v.7-24).
>
> "Not that I speak in respect of want: for I have learned, in whatsoever state I am, therewith to be content. I know both how to be abased, and I know how to abound: every where and in all things I am instructed both to be full and to be hungry, both to abound and to suffer need. I can do all things through Christ which strengtheneth me" (Ph.4:11-13).
>
> "Let the brother of low degree rejoice in that he is exalted: but the rich, in that he is made low: because as the flower of the grass he shall pass away. For the sun is no sooner risen with a burning heat, but it withereth the grass, and the flower thereof falleth, and the grace of the fashion of it perisheth: so also shall the rich man fade away in his ways" (Jas.1:9-11).

4) There is the challenge to trust God's care.

> "Casting all your care upon him; for he careth for you" (1 Pt.5:7).
>
> "It is vain for you to rise up early, to sit up late, to eat the bread of sorrows: for so he giveth his beloved sleep" (Ps.127:2).

4. The fourth illustration was that of the lilies and the grass. They are clothed by God. Again Jesus said, "Consider"—look at and think about the lilies of the field. Learn from what happens to them.
⇒ Lilies do not toil for money to buy their clothing.
⇒ Lilies do not spin to make their clothing.
⇒ Yet, lilies are more arrayed than Solomon in all his glory.
⇒ Lilies pass away almost overnight, yet God cares enough for them to clothe them.
Learn that you are of much more value than lilies. God will clothe you.

There are three concerns surrounding clothing. (Sometimes the concern becomes so strong it turns into a literal fear.)
1. The concern of popularity. A person fears not having the right clothing necessary to make him popular. Sometimes the concern is so great that he refuses to go to a particular function without the proper clothing.
2. The concern of style and fashion. A person is concerned with the very latest in style and fashion. He cannot accept his clothing's being the least bit outdated.

3.    The concern of acceptability. Most adults would fall into this category. Clothing is a matter that actually involves inward feelings. The concern is really there. Time and thought and effort are expended to stay in style, at least enough to be acceptable.

The point Jesus was making is this: fret not, worry not, be not anxious over clothing. But seek ye first—center your life and thoughts and efforts upon God and His righteousness and not upon popularity, fashion and acceptability—and then all these things (clothing) will be added unto you (Mt.6:33).

> "He also that received seed among the thorns is he that heareth the word; and the care of this world, and the deceitfulness of riches, choke the word, and he becometh unfruitful" (Mt.13:22).
>
> "In like manner also, that women adorn themselves in modest apparel, with shamefacedness and sobriety; not with broided hair, of gold, or pearls, or costly array; but (which becometh women professing godliness) with good works" (1 Tim.2:9-10).
>
> "While they [husbands] behold your chaste conversation [behavior] coupled with fear. Whose adorning let it not be that outward adorning of plaiting the hair, and of wearing of gold, or of putting on of apparel; but let it be the hidden man of the heart, in that which is not corruptible, even the ornament of a meek and quiet spirit, which is in the sight of God of great price. For after this manner in the old time the holy women also, who trusted in God, adorned themselves" (1 Pt.3:2-5).
>
> "Let thy garments be always white [cleaned, washed]; and let thy head lack no ointment [well-groomed, cared for]" (Eccl.9:8).
>
> "The women shall not wear that which pertaineth unto a man, neither shall a man put on a woman's garment: for all that do so are abomination unto the LORD thy God" (Dt.22:5).
>
> "Moreover the LORD saith, Because the daughters of Zion are haughty, and walk with stretched forth necks and wanton eyes, walking and mincing as they go, and making a tinkling with their feet: therefore the Lord will smite with a scab the crown of the head of the daughters of Zion, and the LORD will discover their secret parts. In that day the Lord will take away the bravery of their tinkling ornaments about their feet, and their cauls, and their round tires like the moon, the chains, and the bracelets, and the mufflers, the bonnets, and the ornaments of the legs, and the headbands, and the tablets, and the earrings, the rings, and nose jewels, the changeable suits of apparel, and the mantles, and the wimples, and the crisping pins, the glasses, and the fine linen, the hoods, and the veils. And it shall come to pass, that instead of sweet smell there shall be stink; and instead of a girdle a rent; and instead of well set hair baldness; and instead of a stomacher a girding of sackcloth; and burning instead of beauty" (Is.3:16-24).

---

**DEEPER STUDY # 1**
(12:28) "O Ye of Little Faith": see DEEPER STUDY # 1—Mt.6:30 for discussion.

---

[2]    (12:29-30) **Worldliness—Materialism**: do not be wrapped up in seeking food and drink, nor in doubting God's care.
Note a significant fact: this is not a challenge; *it is a command*. The believer is to center his mind and life upon the Lord and the work God has given him to do, not upon *making a living and eating and drinking*. There are two reasons Jesus commands this.

1.    Being wrapped up in seeking food and drink is worldliness. It is what the nations of the world, the Gentiles, the heathen, the lost, do. They center their whole life around getting more and more of the things of this world. They talk and talk, think and think about food and drink and clothing. It consumes their whole beings. All they know is getting more of what the world has to offer. Life to them is food and drink and possessions (houses, furnishings, position, promotion, recognition, money, the latest styles, keeping up with everyone else). The believer is not to be seeking after these things. He is different. He is to be seeking the Kingdom of God and not doubting God's care and provision.

> "For after all these things do the Gentiles seek: for your heavenly Father knoweth that ye have need of all these things" (Mt.6:32).
>
> "For what is a man profited, if he shall gain the whole world, and lose his own soul? or what shall a man give in exchange for his soul [life]?" (Mt.16:26).
>
> "And take heed to yourselves, lest at any time your hearts be overcharged with surfeiting [self-indulgence, extravagance], and drunkenness, and cares of this life, and so that day come upon you unawares" (Lk.21:34).
>
> "Set your affection on things above, not on things on the earth" (Col.3:2).
>
> "Teaching us that, denying ungodliness and worldly lusts, we should live soberly, righteously, and godly, in this present world; looking for that blessed hope, and the glorious appearing of the great God and our Saviour Jesus Christ" (Tit.2:12-13).
>
> "Ye adulterers and adulteresses, know ye not that the friendship of the world is enmity with God? whosoever therefore will be a friend of the world is the enemy of God" (Jas.4:4).

2.    God knows that the believer has needs. The believer is...
- to know that God knows about his needs.
- not to have a *doubtful* and *anxious mind*.
- to trust God and His ability to meet the need for food and clothing (the necessities of life).

257

"Jesus said unto him, If thou canst believe, all things are possible to him that believeth" (Mk.9:23).

"For whatsoever is born of God overcometh the world: and this is the victory that overcometh the world, even our faith" (1 Jn.5:4).

"The LORD redeemeth the soul of his servants: and none of them that trust in him shall be desolate" (Ps.34:22).

"Commit thy way unto the LORD; trust also in him; and he shall bring it to pass" (Ps.37:5).

"The LORD hath been mindful of us: he will bless us; he will bless the house of Israel; he will bless the house of Aaron" (Ps.115:12).

"It is better to trust in the LORD than to put confidence in man" (Ps.118:8).

"Trust in the LORD with all thine heart; and lean not unto thine own understanding" (Pr.3:5).

"Trust ye in the LORD for ever: for in the LORD JEHOVAH is everlasting strength" (Is.26:4).

"Who is among you that feareth the LORD, that obeyeth the voice of his servant, that walketh in darkness, and hath no light? let him trust in the name of the LORD, and stay upon his God" (Is.50:10).

**3** (12:31-34) **Service—Giving—Wealth, True**: seek the Kingdom of God (see DEEPER STUDY # 3—Mt.19:23-24). The believer is not to seek after the things of the world. He is to focus his life upon the Kingdom of God and the work God has given him to do. He is to leave his welfare in the hands of God. Jesus made three great promises and one significant warning.

1. God will provide the necessities of life for the person who seeks God first.

"And I say unto you, Ask, and it shall be given you; seek, and ye shall find; knock, and it shall be opened unto you. For every one that asketh receiveth; and he that seeketh findeth; and to him that knocketh it shall be opened. If a son shall ask bread of any of you that is a father, will he give him a stone? or if he ask a fish, will he for a fish give him a serpent? Or if he shall ask an egg, will he offer him a scorpion? If ye then, being evil, know how to give good gifts unto your children: how much more shall your heavenly Father give the Holy Spirit to them that ask him?" (Lk.11:9-13).

"And shall not God avenge his own elect, which cry day and night unto him, though he bear long with them?" (Lk.18:7).

"If ye shall ask [keep on asking, persevering] any thing in my name, I will do it" (Jn.14:14)

2. God will give the kingdom to His "little flock," those who truly seek God's kingdom first and trust Him to care for them. Note the term "little flock." It tells us two things.
   a. The number is small. Only a few really seek God's kingdom first.

"Because strait is the gate, and narrow is the way, which leadeth unto life, and few there be that find it" (Mt.7:14).

"For many are called, but few are chosen" (Mt.22:14).

"Blessed are the poor in spirit: for theirs is the kingdom of heaven" (Mt.5:3).

"Then shall the King say unto them on his right hand, Come, ye blessed of my Father, inherit the kingdom prepared for you from the foundation of the world: for I was an hungred, and ye gave me meat: I was thirsty, and ye gave me drink: I was a stranger, and ye took me in" (Mt.25:34-35).

"For the kingdom of God is not meat and drink; but righteousness, and peace, and joy in the Holy Ghost" (Ro.14:17).

"Now this I say, brethren, that flesh and blood cannot inherit the kingdom of God; neither doth corruption inherit incorruption" (1 Cor.15:50).

"Hearken, my beloved brethren, Hath not God chosen the poor of this world rich in faith, and heirs of the kingdom which he hath promised to them that love him?" (Jas.2:5).

   b. The care of God is sure. He is the Shepherd and His true followers are the sheep of *His pasture*.

"To him the porter openeth; and the sheep hear his voice: and he calleth his own sheep by name, and leadeth them out. And when he putteth forth his own sheep, he goeth before them, and the sheep follow him: for they know his voice" (Jn.10:3-4).

"I am the good shepherd, and know my sheep, and am known of mine....And other sheep I have, which are not of this fold: them also I must bring, and they shall hear my voice; and there shall be one fold, and one shepherd" (Jn.10:14, 16).

"The LORD is my shepherd; I shall not want" (Ps.23:1; cp. v.2-6).

3. God gives treasures that do not age, fail, nor corrupt; neither can they be stolen. What Jesus said is revolutionary: "Sell what ye have, and give alms." Very simply, once our needs have been met, we do not need more. We can do nothing more with it...
   • unless we waste it.
   • unless we store it up.

This is exactly what Jesus preached against so strongly. When we live in a world so full of needs, a world lost and dying, once we have met our own needs, we are to give what is left to meet the needs of others. It does not matter what position or profession or kind of income we have, once we meet our needs, we are to begin meeting the needs of the world. In fact, the believer is commanded to seek the *good professions and jobs* so that he can have *more* to give to the needy (Eph.4:28). Note the purpose: it is not to hold a reputable position nor to gain wealth. It is for the purpose of seeking God's kingdom, of spreading the love of God by meeting the needs of others.

    a.    The believer is to fill his bag (billfold, pocket, bank account) with the *gifts or giving* of money and *deeds* of helps. Such will never age.

> **"Give to him that asketh thee, and from him that would borrow of thee turn not thou away: (Mt.5:42).**
> **"He answereth and saith unto them, He that hath two coats, let him impart to him that hath none; and he that hath meat, let him do likewise" (Lk.3:11).**
> **"I have showed you all things, how that so labouring ye ought to support the weak [needy], and to remember the words of the Lord Jesus, how he said, It is more blessed to give than to receive" (Acts 20:35).**
> **"Distributing to the necessity of saints; given to hospitality" (Ro.12:13).**
> **"As we have therefore opportunity [to give], let us do good unto all men, especially unto them who are of the household of faith" (Gal.6:10).**
> **"...let him labour, working with his hands the thing which is good, that he may have to give to him that needeth" (Eph.4:28).**
> **"That they do good, that they be rich in good works, ready to distribute, willing to communicate [give]" (1 Tim.6:18).**
> **"But to do good and to communicate [give] forget not: for with such sacrifices God is well pleased" (Heb.13:16).**

    b.    The believer is to secure the treasures of God's approval and of souls won in heaven. These treasures will never fail nor corrupt nor be stolen.

> **"For what is our hope, or joy, or crown of rejoicing? Are not even ye [saved souls] in the presence of our Lord Jesus Christ at his coming?" (1 Th.2:19).**

Everything on this earth ages, fails, corrupts, and can be stolen. But the man who uses only what he needs and then gives the rest fills his bag with *real money and real treasure*, money and treasure that shall...

- never age.
- never fail.
- never corrupt.
- never be stolen.

> **"Yea doubtless, and I count all things but loss for the excellency of the knowledge of Christ Jesus my Lord: for whom I have suffered the loss of all things, and do count them but dung, that I may win Christ" (Ph.3:8).**
> **"Laying up in store for themselves a good foundation against the time to come, that they may lay hold on eternal life" (1 Tim.6:19).**
> **"Blessed be the God and Father of our Lord Jesus Christ, which according to his abundant mercy hath begotten us again unto a lively hope by the resurrection of Jesus Christ from the dead, to an inheritance incorruptible, and undefiled, and that fadeth not away, reserved in heaven for you" (1 Pt.1:3-4).**
> **"I counsel thee to buy of me gold tried in the fire, that thou mayest be rich; and white raiment, that thou mayest be clothed, and that the shame of thy nakedness do not appear; and anoint thine eyes with eyesalve, that thou mayest see" (Rev.3:18).**

4.    Jesus warned His followers: their hearts would be where their treasure is. If their treasure is in the world, if they live indulgent and extravagant lives, their hearts will be in the world.

> **"But lay up for yourselves treasures in heaven, where neither moth nor rust doth corrupt, and where thieves do not break through nor steal" (Mt.6:20).**
> **"Again, the kingdom of heaven is like unto treasure hid in a field; the which when a man hath found, he hideth, and for joy thereof goeth and selleth all that he hath, and buyeth that field" (Mt.13:44).**
> **"Jesus said unto him, If thou wilt be perfect, go and sell that thou hast, and give to the poor, and thou shalt have treasure in heaven: and come and follow me" (Mt.19:21).**
> **"Love not the world, neither the things that are in the world. If any man love the world, the love of the Father is not in him. For all that is in the world, the lust of the flesh, and the lust of the eyes, and the pride of life, is not of the Father, but is of the world. And the world passeth away, and the lust thereof: but he that doeth the will of God abideth forever" (1 Jn.2:15-17).**

| | O. The Parable of the Faithful & Unfaithful Steward: A Strong Warning—Be Prepared, 12:35-48 (Mt.24:37-25:30) | him, Lord, speakest thou this parable unto us, or even to all? 42 And the Lord said, Who then is that faithful and wise steward, whom his lord shall make ruler over his household, to give them their portion of meat in due season? | steward (manager) a. There was Peter's question b. There is a faithful & wise steward 1) He is a steward |
|---|---|---|---|
| 1 The charge: Be watching—be ready for the Lord's return a. Bc. the Lord is returning | 35 Let your loins be girded about, and your lights burning; 36 And ye yourselves like unto men that wait for their lord, when he will return from the wedding; that when he cometh and knocketh, they may open unto him immediately. | 43 Blessed is that servant, whom his lord when he cometh shall find so doing. 44 Of a truth I say unto you, that he will make him ruler over all that he hath. | 2) He is a servant 3) He is found "doing": Serving faithfully 4) He is to be rewarded: Made a ruler |
| b. Bc. you shall be served by Christ Himself | 37 Blessed are those servants, whom the lord when he cometh shall find watching: verily I say unto you, that he shall gird himself, and make them to sit down to meat, and will come forth and serve them. | 45 But and if that servant say in his heart, My lord delayeth his coming; and shall begin to beat the menservants and maidens, and to eat and drink, and to be drunken; | c. There is an unfaithful & unwise steward (manager) 1) He says there is "plenty of time" 2) He does his own will, his own thing |
| c. Bc. you shall be blessed | 38 And if he shall come in the second watch, or come in the third watch, and find them so, blessed are those servants. | 46 The lord of that servant will come in a day when he looketh not for him, and at an hour when he is not aware, and will cut him in sunder, and will appoint him his portion with the unbelievers. | 3) He is to be judged with the unbelievers |
| d. Bc. Christ shall come suddenly, unexpectedly | 39 And this know, that if the goodman of the house had known what hour the thief would come, he would have watched, and not have suffered his house to be broken through. | 47 And that servant, which knew his lord's will, and prepared not himself, neither did according to his will, shall be beaten with many stripes. | d. There is the unfaithful steward identified 1) The 1st class of unfaithful stewards: Sinned deliberately—knew the Lord's will |
| e. Bc. Christ shall come when least expected | 40 Be ye therefore ready also: for the Son of man cometh at an hour when ye think not. | 48 But he that knew not, and did commit things worthy of stripes, shall be beaten with few stripes. For unto whomsoever much is given, of him shall be much required: and to whom men have committed much, of him they will ask the more. | 2) The 2nd class of unfaithful stewards: Sinned in ignorance—did not know the Lord's will 3) The principle of judgment: Having much requires giving much |
| 2 The parable of the | 41 Then Peter said unto | | |

# DIVISION V

## THE SON OF MAN'S GREAT JOURNEY TO JERUSALEM (STAGE I): HIS MISSION AND PUBLIC CHALLENGE, 9:51-13:21

**O.** The Parable of the Faithful and Unfaithful Steward: A Strong Warning—Be Prepared, 12:35-48

(12:35-48) **Introduction**: Jesus was still dealing with the subject of men who want things—wealth and riches and plenty. He was still dealing with covetousness (Lk.12:13-21; 12:22-34). The believer's mind is to be upon purity of life and service, not upon possessions and cares of this world. Jesus strongly warned: be prepared.
1. The charge: be watching—be ready for the Lord's return (v.35-40).
2. The parable of the steward (manager) (v.41-48).

**1** (12:35-40) **Jesus Christ, Return**: the charge—be watching, be ready for the Lord's return. Jesus shared a striking illustration. The picture was that of a Lord who had gone off to attend a great marriage celebration. His servants had been left behind to look after the household and to wait for his return. The servants should be full of joy and rejoicing for their master's privilege in celebrating the marriage. They may not be, but they should be, and they should be looking after everything with all diligence until he returns. Jesus took the picture and applied it to Himself and His disciples.

The believer is to be in a state of readiness. He is always to be prepared, always watching and waiting for his Lord's return.

⇒ He is to be fully dressed, even to having his belt tight around his waist. This refers to personal preparation: purity of heart and life and keeping one's body ready to move and meet the Lord. In the East men wore robes that had to be tied with a belt at the waist or else the loose robes hampered movement and work. It was impossible to move quickly and freely without the belt being tight.

⇒ The Lord's servant is to have the lights burning, never allowing them to go out. Keeping the lights burning refers to serving and laboring for the Lord. He is to keep the lights of labor burning by faithfully serving and working for the Lord.

The idea with both the belt and the light is, of course, *readiness*: being prepared in body and labor, being pure and faithful. The believer must never lie down or slumber, never be caught off guard or unprepared. Jesus gave six reasons for living in a state of readiness, of purity and faithfulness.

1. The believer is to stay ready because the Lord is returning. He is the Head of the house; He owns the property. He did not desert the house and the property. He left to attend a great marriage feast. He will be returning to *His home and His property* (world). Note: the words "your" (v.35) and "you yourselves" are emphatic. No matter what others may do, "your loins...your lights" must be prepared. You must be like men who wait and stay awake and look and are prepared for their Lord. You must be *ready* to open the door *immediately* when He knocks, for He is going to return and knock. His return is an absolute certainty (cp. Jn.14:2-3; Tit.2:12-13).

"But he held his peace, and answered nothing. Again the high priest asked him, and said unto him, Art thou the Christ, the Son of the Blessed? And Jesus said, I am: and ye shall see the Son of man sitting on the right hand of power, and coming in the clouds of heaven" (Mk.14:61-62).

"And then shall they see the Son of man coming in a cloud with power and great glory" (Lk.21:27).

"Which also said, Ye men of Galilee, why stand ye gazing up into heaven? this same Jesus, which is taken up from you into heaven, shall so come in like manner as ye have seen him go into heaven" (Acts 1:11).

"But I would not have you to be ignorant, brethren, concerning them which are asleep, that ye sorrow not, even as others which have no hope. For if we believe that Jesus died and rose again, even so them also which sleep in Jesus will God bring with him, For this we say unto you by the word of the Lord, that we which are alive and remain unto the coming of the Lord shall not prevent [precede] them which are asleep. For the Lord himself shall descend from heaven with a shout, with the voice of the archangel, and with the trump of God: and the dead in Christ shall rise first: then we which are alive and remain shall be caught up together with them in the clouds, to meet the Lord in the air: and so shall we ever be with the Lord. Wherefore comfort one another with these words" (1 Th.4:13-18).

"So Christ was once offered to bear the sins of many; and unto them that look for him shall he appear the second time without sin unto salvation" (Heb.9:28).

**Thought 1.** There is a message on salvation here as well. A person must be ready to open the door of his heart immediately when Jesus knocks.

"Behold, I stand at the door, and knock: if any man hear my voice, and open the door, I will come in to him, and will sup with him, and he with me" (Rev.3:20).

2. The believer is to stay ready because he will be served by Christ Himself. This is a most precious and wonderful promise, a most unusual promise. Imagine the Lord of the universe *serving* us at a banquet, yet it is the promise made by Jesus! Why would such a promise be made to the believer?

God has only one Son, and God loves His only Son *so much* that He promises to elevate to the highest position any man who honors His Son. Any man who honors God's Son will be highly honored by God.

"If any man serve me, let him follow me: and where I am, there shall also my servant be: if any man serve me, him will my Father honour" (Jn.12:26).

The person who honors God's Son is adopted as a child of God's, and that person becomes a brother to Christ and an heir of God.

"But when the fulness of the time was come, God sent forth his Son, made of a woman, made under the law, to redeem them that were under the law, that we might receive the adoption of sons. And because ye are sons, God hath sent forth the Spirit of his Son into your hearts, crying, Abba, Father. Wherefore thou art no more a servant, but a son; and if a son, then an heir of God through Christ" (Gal.4:4-7).

"For ye have not received the spirit of bondage again to fear; but ye have received the Spirit of adoption, whereby we cry, Abba, Father. The Spirit itself beareth witness with our spirit, that we are the children of God: and if children, then heirs; heirs of God, and joint-heirs with Christ; if so be that we suffer with him, that we may be also glorified together. For I reckon that the sufferings of this present time are not worthy to be compared with the glory which shall be revealed in us" (Ro.8:15-18).

"In my Father's house are many mansions: if it were not so, I would have told you. I go to prepare a place for you. And if I go and prepare a place for you, I will come again, and receive you unto myself; that where I am, there ye may be also" (Jn.14:2-3).

"Therefore judge nothing before the time, until the Lord come, who both will bring to light the hidden things of darkness, and will make manifest the counsels of the hearts: and then shall every man have praise of God" (1 Cor.4:5).

3. The believer is to stay ready because the very thing for which he has been working is Christ's return. When Christ gathers us all together, His heart will be so overflowing with love and joy (as will ours) that He will begin serving us immediately: conforming us to His image, explaining and discussing everything with us, assigning us our eternal duties.

> "For our conversation [citizenship] is in heaven; from whence also we look for the Saviour, the Lord Jesus Christ: who shall change our vile body, that it may be fashioned like unto his glorious body, according to the working whereby he is able even to subdue all things unto himself" (Ph.3:20-21).
>
> "When Christ, who is our life, shall appear, then shall ye also appear with him in glory" (Col.3:4).
>
> "To the end he may stablish your hearts unblameable in holiness before God, even our Father, at the coming of our Lord Jesus Christ with all his saints" (1 Th.3:13).
>
> "Beloved, now are we the sons of God, and it doth not yet appear what we shall be: but we know that, when he shall appear, we shall be like him; for we shall see him as he is" (1 Jn.3:2).

3. The believer is to stay ready because he will be blessed. The word "blessed" (makarioi) means to pronounce a person happy or blessed. The idea is that Christ is going to make the believer happy and blessed. Happiness and blessedness will become a state of being, the constant experience of the believer. But note two points.

    a. It is conditional. The believer must be watching and ready for the Lord's coming (pure and faithful) if he is to be blessed.

    b. The Lord is not returning in the first watch. His return is going to be in the second or third watch. The night was divided into four watches by the Romans and into three watches by the Jews. The point is the importance of being ready: the hour of His return is unknown, but He is returning. It may be immediately; it may be later. The idea is that no one knows the time, but be ready—be prepared—if you wish to be blessed.

> "Let your moderation be known unto all men. The Lord is at hand" (Ph.4:5).
>
> "Be ye also patient; stablish your hearts: for the coming of the Lord draweth nigh" (Jas.5:8).
>
> "Behold, I come quickly; hold that fast which thou hast, that no man take thy crown" (Rev.3:11).

4. The believer is to stay ready because Christ will come unexpectedly. The parable is clear: the hour of the Lord's return is not known; His return is going to be unexpected. The believer...

- must not be careless: get tired of waiting up, get sleepy, be caught off guard, begin to disbelieve. (All of this can happen to a houseowner waiting on a burglar.)
- must watch: secure, sit up, stay awake, listen, look, take notice of all noises and sights (signs). (The burglar always comes in an unexpected hour.)

The believer must watch and be prepared as much as a houseowner would watch and prepare if he knew a burglar were coming.

> "For as the lightning cometh out of the east, and shineth even unto the west; so shall also the coming of the Son of man be" (Mt.24:27).
>
> "But of that day and hour knoweth no man, no, not the angels of heaven, but my Father only" (Mt.24:36).
>
> "Watch ye therefore: for ye know not when the master of the house cometh, at even, or at midnight, or at the cockcrowing, or in the morning" (Mk.13:35).

5. The believer is to stay ready because Christ will come when *least* expected. Jesus could not have stated it any clearer; He could not have spoken any plainer. "When ye think not," He will come. He will be coming when we least expect Him to come. "Be ye therefore ready."

> "Therefore be ye also ready: for in such an hour as ye think not the Son of man cometh" (Mt.24:44).
>
> "And while they went to buy, the bridegroom came; and they that were ready went in with him to the marriage: and the door was shut. Afterward came also the other virgins, saying, Lord, Lord, open to us. But he answered and said, Verily I say unto you, I know you not. Watch therefore, for ye know neither the day nor the hour wherein the Son of man cometh" (Mt.25:10-13, cp. v.6-9).
>
> "For yourselves know perfectly that the day of the Lord so cometh as a thief in the night" (1 Th.5:2).
>
> "Remember therefore how thou hast received and heard, and hold fast, and repent. If therefore thou shalt not watch, I will come on thee as a thief, and thou shalt not know what hour I will come upon thee" (Rev.3:3).
>
> "Behold, I come as a thief. Blessed is he that watcheth, and keepeth his garments, lest he walk naked, and they see his shame" (Rev.16:15).

**2** (12:41-48) **Steward—Dedication—Faithfulness vs. Unfaithfulness—Rewards—Punishment, Degrees:** the parable of the steward.

1. Peter wanted to know if the message on *watching and readiness* was for the disciples only or did it apply to the world as well. Jesus answered by giving a parable known as the parable of the steward.

2. There was a faithful and wise steward. Jesus said four things about this steward.

    a. He was a steward. A steward was just what Jesus said he was: a man who was made ruler over his Lord's household. He was the manager of the Lord's estate, responsible for all of it.

> "For the kingdom of heaven is as a man [Christ] travelling into a far country, who called his own servants, and delivered unto them his goods. And unto one he gave five talents, to another two, and to another one; to every man according to his several ability; and straightway took his journey" (Mt.25:14-15).

"And he called his ten servants, and delivered them ten pounds, and said unto them, Occupy till I come" (Lk.19:13).

b.  He was a slave (doulos), a bond-slave, a man under the Lord's will entirely. He was possessed by the Lord and his very life depended upon doing everything the Lord said (see note, *Slave*—Ro.1:1).

c.  He was found "doing," that is, serving faithfully when the Lord returned. The Lord found him *doing exactly* what he should have been doing (1 Cor.4:2).

⇒ He was overseeing the Master's household.

"For ye are bought with a price: therefore glorify God in your body, and in your spirit, which are God's" (1 Cor.6:20).

"Therefore, my beloved brethren, be ye stedfast, unmoveable, always abounding in the work of the Lord, forasmuch as ye know that your labour is not in vain in the Lord" (1 Cor.15:58).

"With good will doing service, as to the Lord, and not to men" (Eph.6:7).

"Obey them that have the rule over you, and submit yourselves: for they watch for your souls, as they that must give account, that they may do it with joy, and not with grief: for that is unprofitable for you" (Heb.13:17).

"O Timothy, keep that which is committed to thy trust, avoiding profane and vain babblings, and oppositions of science falsely so called" (1 Tim.6:20).

"That good thing which was committed unto thee keep by the Holy Ghost which dwelleth in us" (2 Tim.1:14).

"Feed the flock of God which is among you, taking the oversight thereof, not by constraint, but willingly; not for filthy lucre, but of a ready mind; neither as being lords over God's heritage, but being ensamples to the flock" (1 Pt.5:2-3)

⇒ He was feeding the Master's family faithfully.

"So when they had dined, Jesus saith to Simon Peter, Simon, son of Jonas, lovest thou me more than these? He saith unto him, Yea, Lord; thou knowest that I love thee. He saith unto him, Feed my lambs" (Jn.21:15; cp. v.16-17).

"Moreover it is required in stewards, that a man be found faithful" (1 Cor.4:2).

"Take heed unto thyself, and unto the doctrine; continue in them: for in doing this thou shalt both save thyself, and them that hear thee" (1 Tim.4:16).

"As every man hath received the gift, even so minister the same one to another, as good stewards of the manifold grace of God" (1 Pt.4:10).

d.  He was to be rewarded, made *ruler* and *promoted over all* that the Lord had. The idea is that the faithful and wise believer will be placed as highly as he can be placed. He will be given all that the Master and Lord has, that is, a complete estate to manage (see notes—Lk.16:10-12; 19:15-23; 22:28-30).

"His lord said unto him, Well done, good and faithful servant; thou hast been faithful over a few things, I will make thee ruler over many things: enter thou into the joy of thy lord" (Mt.25:23).

"Then shall the King say unto them on his right hand, Come, ye blessed of my Father, inherit the kingdom prepared for you from the foundation of the world" (Mt.25:34).

"But love ye your enemies, and do good, and lend, hoping for nothing again; and your reward shall be great, and ye shall be the children of the Highest: for he is kind unto the unthankful and to the evil" (Lk.6:35).

"And he said unto him, Well, thou good servant: because thou hast been faithful in a very little, have thou authority over ten cities" (Lk.19:17).

"Ye are they which have continued with me in my temptations. And I appoint unto you a kingdom, as my Father hath appointed unto me" (Lk.22:28-29).

"For if by one man's offence death reigned by one; much more they which receive abundance of grace and of the gift of righteousness shall reign in life by one, Jesus Christ" (Ro.5:17).

"Do ye not know that the saints shall judge [rule, have authority over] the world?" (1 Cor.6:2).

"If we suffer, we shall also reign with him: if we deny him, he also will deny us" (2 Tim.2:12).

"And from Jesus Christ, who is the faithful witness, and the first begotten of the dead, and the prince of the kings of the earth. Unto him that loved us, and washed us from our sins in his own blood, and hath made us kings and priests unto God and his Father; to him be glory and dominion for ever and ever" (Rev.1:5-6).

"To him that overcometh will I grant to sit with me in my throne, even as I also overcame, and am set down with my Father in his throne" (Rev.3:21).

"And I saw thrones, and they sat upon them, and judgment was given unto them: and I saw the souls of them that were beheaded for the witness of Jesus, and for the word of God, and which had not worshipped the beast, neither his image, neither had received his mark upon their foreheads, or in their hands; and they lived and reigned with Christ a thousand years" (Rev.20:4).

"And there shall be no night there; and they need no candle, neither light of the sun; for the Lord God giveth them light: and they shall reign for ever and ever" (Rev.22:5).

3. There was an unfaithful, an unwise steward (manager). Jesus said three things about this steward.

a. The unfaithful steward said there is *plenty of time.* Why? Because the Lord had delayed His coming; therefore, the steward thought the Lord's return was a long way off. Note: he did not doubt the Lord's return. He knew the Lord was returning, but he did not think it would be soon.

"And I will say to my soul, Soul, thou hast much goods laid up for many years; take thine ease, eat, drink, and be merry" (Lk.12:19).

"And as he reasoned of righteousness, temperance, and judgment to come, Felix trembled, and answered, Go thy way for this time; when I have a convenient season, I will call for thee" (Acts 24:25).

"Go to now, ye that say, To day or to morrow we will go into such a city, and continue there a year, and buy and sell, and get gain: whereas ye know not what shall be on the morrow. For what is your life? It is even a vapour, that appeareth for a little time, and then vanisheth away" (Jas.4:13-14).

"Boast not thyself of tomorrow; for thou knowest not what a day may bring forth" (Pr.27:1).

"Come ye, say they, I will fetch wine, and we will fill ourselves with strong drink; and tomorrow shall be as this day, and much more abundant" (Is.56:12).

b. He did his own will, his own thing. He mistreated and abused others, both male and female, using and misusing, deceiving and taking advantage as he willed. And he lived a worldly life, indulging in the fleshly pleasures of partying and carousing, eating and drinking.

"And that which fell among thorns are they, which, when they have heard, go forth, and are choked with cares and riches and pleasures of this life, and bring no fruit to perfection" (Lk.8:14).

"He that is faithful in that which is least is faithful also in much: and he that is unjust in the least is unjust also in much" (Lk.16:10).

"But she that liveth in pleasure is dead while she liveth" (1 Tim.5:6).

"This know also, that in the last days perilous times shall come. For men shall be lovers of their own selves, covetous, boasters, proud, blasphemers, disobedient to parents, unthankful, unholy, without natural affection, trucebreakers, false accusers, incontinent, fierce, despisers of those that are good, traitors, heady, highminded, lovers of pleasures more than lovers of God" (2 Tim.3:1-4).

"For we ourselves also were sometimes foolish, disobedient, deceived, serving divers lusts and pleasures, living in malice and envy, hateful, and hating one another" (Tit.3:3).

"Ye have lived in pleasure on the earth, and been wanton; ye have nourished your hearts, as in a day of slaughter" (Jas.5:5).

"And shall receive the reward of unrighteousness, as they that count it pleasure to riot [carouse, party, indulge] in the day time. Spots they are and blemishes, sporting themselves with their own deceivings while they feast with you" (2 Pt.2:13).

"Thou shalt not oppress a hired servant that is poor and needy, whether he be of thy brethren, or of thy strangers that are in thy land" (Dt.24:14).

"Trust not in oppression, and become not vain in robbery: if riches increase, set not your heart upon them" (Ps.62:10).

"How long will ye judge unjustly, and accept the persons of the wicked?" (Ps.82:2).

"Envy thou not the oppressor, and choose none of his ways" (Pr.3:31).

"He that oppresseth the poor reproacheth his Maker: but he that honoreth him hath mercy on the poor" (Pr.14:31).

"He that oppresseth the poor to increase his riches, and he that giveth to the rich, shall surely come to want" (Pr.22:16).

"If thou seest the oppression of the poor, and violent perverting of judgment and justice in a province, marvel not at the matter: for he that is higher than the highest regardeth; and there be higher than they" (Eccl.5:8).

c. He was to be judged with the unbelievers. The Lord was very clear about this.

⇒ The unfaithful steward shall be caught by the Lord, caught *unaware,* "in a day when he looks not for the Lord."

"And take heed to yourselves, lest at any time your hearts be overcharged with surfeiting, and drunkenness, and cares of this life, and so that day come upon you unawares. For as a snare shall it come on all them that dwell on the face of the whole earth" (Lk.21:34-35).

"For man also knoweth not his time: as the fishes that are taken in an evil net, and as the birds that are caught in the snare; so are the sons of men snared in an evil time, when it falleth suddenly upon them" (Eccl.9:12).

"For as in the days that were before the flood they were eating and drinking, marrying and giving in marriage, until the day that Noe entered into the ark, and knew not until the flood came, and took them all away; so shall also the coming of the Son of man be" (Mt.24:38-39).

⇒ The Lord will "cut the unfaithful steward in sunder." This means he will be condemned to death, cut off from among the living, exiled from eternal life. Most tragic, he shall be *cut asunder, cut off* from God's presence.

⇒ The Lord will appoint the unfaithful steward his portion with the unbelievers. Why? Because he was not genuine. He was a hypocrite.

> "And shall cut him asunder, and appoint him his portion with the hypocrites: there shall be weeping and gnashing of teeth" (Mt.24:51).
>
> "When he is about to fill his belly, God shall cast the fury of his wrath upon him, and shall rain it upon him while he is eating....The heaven shall reveal his iniquity; and the earth shall rise up against him. The increase of his house shall depart, and his goods shall flow away in the day of his wrath. This is the portion of a wicked man from God, and the heritage appointed unto him by God" (Job 20:23, 27-29).
>
> "Upon the wicked he shall rain snares, fire and brimstone, and a horrible tempest: this shall be the portion of their cup" (Ps.11:6).
>
> "This is thy lot, the portion of thy measures from me, saith the LORD; because thou hast forgotten me, and trusted in falsehood. Therefore will I discover thy skirts upon thy face, that thy shame may appear. I have seen thine adulteries, and thy neighings, the lewdness of thy whoredom, and thine abominations on the hills in the fields. Woe unto thee" (Jer.13:25-27).

4. There was the unfaithful steward identified. Note that Jesus answered Peter's question in these two verses. He was speaking to both believers and unbelievers. Who is to be watching and living in a state of readiness? Who is to be served by Christ and greatly blessed? The answer is clear: the faithful steward, not the unfaithful steward. Who then is the unfaithful steward? There are two classes named:

a. Class 1: the *servant* who knew the Lord's will and did not prepare himself (v.35), nor did he do the Lord's will (cp. 1 Jn.3:23). This servant's judgment is tragic, for he knew God's will, but deliberately rejected it. Therefore, he will be beaten with many stripes, that is, due much more judgment and punishment.

> "And these shall go away into everlasting punishment: but the righteous into life eternal" (Mt.25:46; cp. v.25-45).
>
> "But he that shall blaspheme against the Holy Ghost hath never forgiveness, but is in danger of eternal damnation" (Mk.3:29).
>
> "...he [Christ] will thoroughly purge his floor, and will gather the wheat into his garner; but the chaff he will burn with fire unquenchable" (Lk.3:17).
>
> "But unto them that are contentious, and do not obey the truth, but obey unrighteousness, indignation and wrath, tribulation and anguish, upon every soul of man that doeth evil, of the Jew first, and also of the Gentile" (Ro.2:8-9).
>
> "And to you who are troubled rest with us, when the Lord Jesus shall be revealed from heaven with his mighty angels, in flaming fire taking vengeance on them that know not God, and that obey not the gospel of our Lord Jesus Christ: who shall be punished with everlasting destruction from the presence of the Lord, and from the glory of his power" (2 Th.1:7-9).
>
> "Of how much sorer punishment, suppose ye, shall he be thought worthy, who hath trodden under foot the Son of God, and hath counted the blood of the covenant, wherewith he was sanctified, an unholy thing, and hath done despite unto the Spirit of grace? For we know him that hath said, Vengeance belongeth unto me, I will recompense, saith the Lord. And again, The Lord shall judge his people" (Heb.10:29-30).
>
> "The Lord knoweth how to deliver the godly out of temptations, and to reserve the unjust unto the day of judgment to be punished" (2 Pt.2:9).
>
> "And whosoever was not found written in the book of life was cast into the lake of fire" (Rev.20:15).
>
> "But the fearful, and unbelieving, and the abominable, and murderers, and whoremongers, and sorcerers, and idolaters, and all liars, shall have their part in the lake which burneth with fire and brimstone: which is the second death" (Rev.21:8).

b. Class 2: the men who did not know the Lord's will; therefore, they were not able to prepare themselves as they should have, nor were they able to faithfully serve the Lord.

However, note a critical point. Even the stewards committed things worthy of punishment. Therefore, they will be judged and condemned as well, but not as severely (cp. Ro.1:20f; 2:11-16).

The principle of judgment is perfect justice: having many gifts and possessing much wealth means a person is to serve and give much. A person is to use and give all he is and has—holding nothing back. Note that degrees of rewards and punishment are being taught. (See Master Subject Index, *Rewards*.)

| | P. The Three Gross Misconceptions of Man, 12:49-59 | people, When ye see a cloud rise out of the west, straightway ye say, There cometh a shower; and so it is. | Messiah has not yet come |
|---|---|---|---|
| 1 **Misconception 1: The Messiah was to bring peace on earth**<br>a. Truth 1: He came to bring judgment, v.49<br>b. Truth 2: He came to suffer & die<br>c. Truth 3: He came to bring division | 49 I am come to send fire on the earth; and what will I, if it be already kindled?<br>50 But I have a baptism to be baptized with; and how am I straitened till it be accomplished!<br>51 Suppose ye that I am come to give peace on earth? I tell you, Nay; but rather division:<br>52 For from henceforth there shall be five in one house divided, three against two, and two against three.<br>53 The father shall be divided against the son, and the son against the father; the mother against the daughter, and the daughter against the mother; the mother in law against her daughter in law, and the daughter in law against her mother in law.<br>54 And he said also to the | 55 And when ye see the south wind blow, ye say, There will be heat; and it cometh to pass.<br>56 Ye hypocrites, ye can discern the face of the sky and of the earth; but how is it that ye do not discern this time?<br>57 Yea, and why even of yourselves judge ye not what is right?<br>58 When thou goest with thine adversary to the magistrate, as thou art in the way, give diligence that thou mayest be delivered from him; lest he hale thee to the judge, and the judge deliver thee to the officer, and the officer cast thee into prison.<br>59 I tell thee, thou shalt not depart thence, till thou hast paid the very last mite. | a. Truth 1: People discern the weather, i.e. earthly events<br><br><br>b. Truth 2: People do not discern the signs of the times, the Messianic age<br><br>c. Truth 3: People do not discern spiritual matters<br><br>3 **Misconception 3: Men have no need to make peace with God**<br>a. Truth 1: People have a bad case before God, the Judge.<br>b. Truth 2: The time is urgent—"give diligence"<br><br>c. Truth 3: The surety of payment, that is, judgment |
| 2 **Misconception 2: The** | | | |

# DIVISION V

## THE SON OF MAN'S GREAT JOURNEY TO JERUSALEM
## (STAGE I): HIS MISSION AND PUBLIC CHALLENGE, 9:51-13:21

**P.    The Three Gross Misconceptions of Man, 12:49-59**

(12:49-59) **Introduction**: forcibly, Jesus covered three gross misconceptions of man.
1.    Misconception 1: the Messiah was to bring peace on earth (v.49-53).
2.    Misconception 2: the Messiah has not yet come (v.54-57).
3.    Misconception 3: men have no need to make "peace with God" (v.58-59).

1    (12:49-53) **Peace—Judgment—Jesus Christ, Work—Sin**: the first misconception is that the Messiah came to bring peace on earth. Men usually think of Christ as having brought the message of peace to earth, and He did. He brought *peace with God* to a man's heart and the *peace of God* to a man's life (see note, *Peace*—Jn.14:27). But note three significant truths about what Christ says in this point.
1.    Christ brought not only peace but fire on the earth, that is, judgment. Fire is usually the symbol of judgment (cp. the term *hell fire*). This is the clearest meaning here, for Christ was talking about His death (v.50).
   a.    The word "what" (ti) can be and probably should be translated *how*,: "how I wish the fire were already kindled." Christ was wishing that the cross was already over with. The judgment as the *sin-bearer* of the world was almost too much for Him to bear (cp. Lk.22:39-46, Gethsemane).
   b.    It was Christ's death that brought the fire of judgment to the world.
   ⇒    His death judged (condemned) sin in the flesh.

> **"For what the law could not do, in that it was weak through the flesh, God sending his own Son in the likeness of sinful flesh, and for sin, condemned sin in the flesh" (Ro.8:3).**
> **"For Christ also hath once suffered for sins, the just for the unjust, that he might bring us to God, being put to death in the flesh, but quickened by the Spirit" (1 Pt.3:18).**

   ⇒    His death judged (condemned) the prince of this world.

> **"Now is the judgment of this world: now shall the prince of this world be cast out. And I, if I be lifted up from the earth, will draw all men unto me" (Jn.12:31-32).**
> **"Of judgment, because the prince of this world is judged" (Jn.16:11).**

   ⇒    His death caused men to judge themselves to be sinners, sinners who were spiritually dead to God.

> **"For the love of Christ constraineth us; because we thus judge, that if one died for all, then were all dead: and that he died for all, that they which live should not hence-**

forth live unto themselves, but unto him which died for them, and rose again"
(2 Cor.5:14-15).
"Who his own self bare our sins in his own body on the tree, that we, being dead
to sins, should live unto righteousness: by whose stripes ye were healed" (1 Pt.2:24).

⇒ His death caused men to judge themselves in the flesh, that is, to judge their flesh as being weak and subject to sin. The flesh of men needs to be controlled and denied and brought into subjection to Christ.

"For I know that in me (that is, in my flesh,) dwelleth no good thing: for to will is
present with me; but how to perform that which is good I find not. For the good that I
would I do not: but the evil which I would not, that I do. Now if I do that I would not,
it is no more I that do it, but sin that dwelleth in me" (Ro.7:18-20).
"For if we would judge ourselves, we should not be judged" (1 Cor.11:31).
"Knowing this, that our old man is [was, Greek] crucified with him, that the body
of sin might be destroyed, that henceforth we should not serve sin....For in that he
died, he died unto sin once: but in that he liveth, he liveth unto God. Likewise reckon
ye also yourselves to be dead indeed unto sin, but alive unto God through Jesus Christ
our Lord. Let not sin therefore reign in your mortal body, that ye should obey it in the
lusts thereof. Neither yield ye your members [body parts] as instruments of unrighteousness unto sin: but yield yourselves unto God, as those that are alive from the dead,
and your members as instruments of righteousness unto God" (Ro.6:6, 10-13).
"And he said to them all, If any man will come after me, let him deny himself, and
take up his cross daily, and follow me" (Lk.9:23).

2. Christ came to suffer and die, that is, to be baptized with the judgment of death and to be separated from God. The term "a baptism to be baptized with" refers to Christ's death. He was to be immersed, placed into a state of death, of separation from God *for man*. His suffering in bearing the judgment of God was to be beyond imagination. Note that He used the metaphor of both *fire and baptism* to describe His death. Note also that He was *straightened*, pressured to get the ordeal of the judgment over, to have the judgment accomplished and man's salvation completed.

"And they were in the way going up to Jerusalem; and Jesus went before them: and they were
amazed; and as they followed, they were afraid. And he took again the twelve, and began to tell
them what things should happen unto him, saying, Behold we go up to Jerusalem; and the Son of
man shall be delivered unto the chief priests, and unto the scribes; and they shall condemn him to
death, and shall deliver him to the Gentiles: and they shall mock him, and shall scourge him, and
shall spit upon him, and shall kill him: and the third day he shall rise again....But Jesus said unto
them, Ye know not what ye ask: can ye drink of the cup that I drink of? and be baptized with the
baptism that I am baptized with?" (Mk.10:32-34, 38).

3. Christ came to bring division to the earth. (See outline and notes—Mt.10:34-37 for more discussion and application.) Note three things.
   a. It is Christ who *sets* a family member against his family. It is important to see this. Christ calls a person out of the world: to be separate from the world and to go about correcting the sin and evil of the world. If a family continues to live in sin and to walk ever onward toward the grave without turning to God and a life of righteousness, two things usually happen.
      1) The believer struggles to witness to his loved ones, no matter the cost and opposition he may face.
      2) The family members often rebel against the righteousness and efforts of the believer.
   b. The believer is called to a life of righteousness and to a warfare against sin and evil. If a member of his family is engaged on the side of evil, there is *a natural conflict* between the believer and the family member.
      1) The family member is still of the earth and living primarily to satisfy his earthly desires. The thought of God is repressed and subdued so that he can pursue his physcal and material desires.
      2) The believer is of the earth, but he is also of heaven. He is physical and spiritual, and more importantly, he is living primarily for God and His righteousness, to reach men with the glorious gospel of Christ.
         The two natures differ drastically. They are diametrically opposed to one another. The person of the world primarily talks about the world and lives for the pursuit of the world. The person of the spirit makes God the primary force of his life: he talks about God and the things of righteousness, and he pursues God and His righteousness.
   c. A believer is to love his family, but he is to love God first and foremost. Our first loyalty is to God. Two terrible things happen when we put our family before God.
      1) Our families cannot be what they should be without God. No family can reach its full potential without God. There will be a lack of spiritual growth and strength, of conviction and commitment, of confidence and assurance, of purpose and meaning, of life and God—a lack of all—it will be for eternity. There will be no sense, no assurance of anything beyond this life.
      2) Our families cannot be looked after by God unless God is given His rightful place in the family. If the family takes control over its own life, ignoring God and His control, then what happens to the family is in its hands. God is put off to the side, excluded and shut out. He has no say so over the welfare of the family. The family is left all to itself, and all kinds of trouble usually follows. There is certainly a lack of spiritual strength to face the trials and crises that confront every family during life.

What these two facts teach is this: we must love God supremely, putting Him before all—even before our families. When we do, our families are assured of being everything they should be and of being looked after and cared for by God (Mt.6:33). Therefore, a man's decision to follow Christ, no matter the sacrifice to his family, is a wise decision; in fact, it is the only reasonable decision.

> "Think not that I am come to send peace on earth: I came not to send peace, but a sword. For I am come to set a man at variance against his father, and the daughter against her mother, and the daughter in law against her mother in law. And a man's foes shall be they of his own household. He that loveth father or mother more than me is not worthy of me: and he that loveth son or daughter more than me is not worthy of me" (Mt.10:34-37).
>
> "I beseech you therefore, brethren, by the mercies of God, that ye present your bodies a living sacrifice, holy, acceptable unto God, which is your reasonable service. And be not conformed to this world: but be ye transformed by the renewing of your mind, that ye may prove what is that good, and acceptable, and perfect, will of God" (Ro.12:1-2).
>
> "Jesus said unto him, Thou shalt love the Lord thy God with all thy heart, and with all thy soul, and with all thy mind. This is the first and great commandment" (Mt.22:37-38).
>
> "Keep yourselves in the love of God, looking for the mercy of our Lord Jesus Christ unto eternal life" (Jude 21).
>
> "And thou shalt love the LORD thy God with all thine heart, and with all thy soul, and with all thy might" (Dt.6:5).
>
> "What doth the LORD thy God require of thee, but to fear the LORD thy God, to walk in all his ways, and to love him, and to serve the LORD thy God with all thy heart and with all thy soul" (Dt.10:12).

**[2]** (12:54-57) **Messiah—Unbelief—Incarnation:** the second misconception is that the Messiah has not yet come. People in Jesus' day did not believe that He was the Messiah, and people today do not believe that He is the Messiah. Jesus stated two truths to all unbelievers.

1. People discern the weather, that is, physical matters of the world. Man's natural senses can be very discerning and sharp. He is skillful in studying and experimenting and in drawing conclusions from the natural world. Weather is the example Christ used; but the subject could be finances, medicine, society, or any other earthly subject. Jesus said people are very capable in discerning the material and physical matters of their world.

2. People do not discern spiritual matters. When it comes to the spiritual senses, man is dead and undiscerning. He does not take time to observe nor to experience the spiritual world, not really.

   a. People had *failed to discern the time*, that is, the coming of the Messiah. The signs that pointed to Jesus being the Messiah were visible. A thoughtful and genuinely spiritual person could see the signs, and some had seen them such as Simeon and Anna (Lk.3:25f). Some of the signs were as follows:
      ⇒ The sceptre, that is, the lawgiver had actually come from Judah in the person of Jesus Christ (Mt.1:2).
      ⇒ The weeks and ages predicted by Daniel were closing out (see note and DEEPER STUDY # 1—Mt.24:15).
      ⇒ The prophet Elijah, the forerunner of the Messiah, had come and proclaimed the Messiah to be Jesus (Mt.3:1-12).
      ⇒ The baby Jesus had been born in Bethlehem (Mt.2:1).
      ⇒ Many throughout the world were expecting the coming of some great person, some Messiah (Mt.1:18).
      ⇒ Many godly Jews were looking for the coming of the Messiah, God's great Deliverer of Israel (Lk.2:25f).
      ⇒ The message and works of Jesus were great evidence, phenomenal miracles given by God to substantiate His claims (see note and DEEPER STUDY # 1—Jn.14:11).

      In addition to these what greater signs could God give than the signs which change lives, radically change them? Unbelief is without excuse. The problem is that men want signs of their own choosing, not the signs which God has chosen to give. Men are always wanting God to deal with them through some...

      - spectacular sign
      - brilliant sight
      - astounding truth
      - irrefutable argument
      - miraculous experience
      - unbelievable deliverance

      God's great concern is not *signs from heaven*, not signs outside man. God's great concern is meeting people in their lives, within their hearts, where they really need help. People must discern the times if they are to live abundantly while on this earth and live eternally in the next world. God wants to meet people in their sickness and sorrow and lostness. Meeting man in the areas of his need are irrefutable signs given to every generation.

   b. They *failed to discern and judge what was right*. This was one of the most honest, thought-provoking, and revealing questions ever asked of man. It takes a man who is honestly open—a man who is willing to have his heart exposed for what it really is—to answer the question. "Why...judge ye not what is right?"

**Thought 1.** Why do men not discern, not judge what is right?

1) Why do men not discern that God *is*, that He exists?

"In the beginning God" (Gen.1:1).

"Thou, even thou, art LORD alone; thou hast made heaven, the heaven of heavens, with all their host, the earth, and all things that are therein, the seas, and all that is therein, and thou preservest them all; and the host of heaven worshipeth thee" (Neh.9:6).

"The LORD he is God; there in none else beside him" (Dt.4:35).

"The LORD our God is one LORD: and thou shalt love the LORD thy God with all thine heart, and with all thy soul, and with all thy might" (Dt.6:4-5).

"That men may know that thou, whose name alone is JEHOVAH, art the Most High over all the earth" (Ps.83:18).

"For thou art great, and doest wondrous things: thou art God alone" (Ps.86:10).

"I am the LORD; and beside me there is no savior. I have declared, and have saved, and I have showed, when there was no strange god among you: therefore ye are my witnesses, saith the LORD, that I am God" (Is.43:11-12).

"Thus saith the LORD the King of Israel, and his Redeemer the LORD of hosts; I am the first, and I am the last; and beside me there is no God" (Is.44:6).

"For thus saith the LORD that created the heavens; God himself that formed the earth and made it; he hath established it, he created it not in vain, he formed it to be inhabited: I am the LORD; and there is none else" (Is.45:18).

"And Jesus answered him, The first of all the commandments is, Hear, O Israel; The Lord our God is one Lord: and thou shalt love the Lord thy God with all thy heart, and with all thy soul, and with all thy mind, and with all thy strength: this is the first commandment" (Mk.12:29-30).

"We know that an idol is nothing in the world, and that there is none other God but one" (1 Cor.8:4).

"There is one body, and one Spirit, even as ye are called in one hope of your calling; one Lord, one faith, one baptism, one God and Father of all, who is above all, and through all, and in you all" (Eph.4:4-6).

"For there is one God, and one mediator between God and men, the man Christ Jesus; who gave himself a ransom for all, to be testified in due time" (1 Tim.2:5-6).

"For there are three that bear record in heaven, the Father, the Word, and the Holy Ghost: and these three are one" (1 Jn.5:7).

2) Why do men not discern that Jesus Christ is truly the Son of God.

"Then they that were in the ship came and worshipped him, saying, Of a truth thou art the Son of God" (Mt.14:33).

"The beginning of the gospel of Jesus Christ, the Son of God" (Mk.1:1).

"And I [John the Baptist] saw, and bare record that this is the Son of God" (Jn.1:34).

"For God so loved the world, that he gave his only begotten Son, that whosoever believeth in him should not perish, but have everlasting life. For God sent not his Son into the world to condemn the world; but that the world through him might be saved. He that believeth on him is not condemned: but he that believeth not is condemned already, because he hath not believed in the name of the only begotten Son of God" (Jn.3:16-18).

"Jesus heard that they had cast him out; and when he had found him, he said unto him, Dost thou believe on the Son of God? He answered and said, Who is he, Lord, that I might believe on him? And Jesus said unto him, Thou hast both seen him, and it is he that talketh with thee" (Jn.9:35-37).

"Say ye of him, whom the Father hath sanctified, and sent into the world, Thou blasphemest; because I said, I am the Son of God?" (Jn.10:36).

"Jesus said unto her, I am the resurrection, and the life: he that believeth in me, though he were dead, yet shall he live: and whosoever liveth and believeth in me shall never die. Believest thou this? She saith unto him, Yea, Lord: I believe that thou art the Christ, the Son of God, which should come into the world" (Jn.11:25-27).

"Of how much sorer punishment, suppose ye, shall he be thought worthy, who hath trodden under foot the Son of God, and hath counted the blood of the covenant, wherewith he was sanctified, an unholy thing, and hath done despite unto the Spirit of grace?" (Heb.10:29).

"Whosoever shall confess that Jesus is the Son of God, God dwelleth in him, and he in God" (1 Jn.4:15).

3) Why do men not discern that righteousness is the way for men to live and the way for communities and the world to conduct their affairs.

"For I say unto you, That except your righteousness shall exceed the righteousness of the scribes and Pharisees, ye shall in no case enter into the kingdom of heaven" (Mt.5:20).

"For the kingdom of God is not meat and drink; but righteousness, and peace, and joy in the Holy Ghost" (Ro.14:17).

"Awake to righteousness, and sin not; for some have not the knowledge of God: I speak this to your shame" (1 Cor.15:34).

"For the love of money is the root of all evil: which while some coveted after, they have erred from the faith, and pierced themselves through with many sorrows. But thou, O man of God, flee these things; and follow after righteousness, godliness, faith, love, patience, meekness. Fight the good fight of faith, lay hold on eternal life, whereunto thou art also called, and hast professed a good profession before many witnesses" (1 Tim.6:10-12).

"Teaching us that, denying ungodliness and worldly lusts, we should live soberly, righteously, and godly, in this present world; looking for that blessed hope, and the glorious appearing of the great God and our Saviour Jesus Christ" (Tit.2:12-13).

"The Lord is not slack concerning his promise, as some men count slackness; but is long-suffering to us-ward, not willing that any should perish, but that all should come to repentance. But the day of the Lord will come as a thief in the night; in the which the heavens shall pass away with a great noise, and the elements shall melt with fervent heat, the earth also and the works that are therein shall be burned up. Seeing then that all these things shall be dissolved, what manner of persons ought ye to be in all holy conversation and godliness, looking for and hasting unto the coming of the day of God, wherein the heavens being on fire shall be dissolved, and the elements shall melt with fervent heat? Nevertheless we, according to his promise, look for new heavens and a new earth, wherein dwelleth righteousness. Wherefore, beloved, seeing that ye look for such things, be diligent that ye may be found of him in peace, without spot, and blameless" (2 Pt.3:9-14).

Jesus was saying that the signs of the times—the signs of every generation—the signs of nature itself—are enough to point toward God in all His love and righteousness. "Why...judge ye not what is right?"

**3** (12:58-59) **Messiah, Misconception—Man, Need**: the third misconception is that men have no need to make *peace with God*. Jesus used an earthly illustration to stress three truths.
1. Men have a bad case before God, the Judge.
2. When a man has a hopeless case with an adversary, the best thing for him to do is to hasten for *settlement out of court*.
3. Otherwise, he is going to be judged in court and have to *pay every penny*.

So it is with God. The hour is urgent. Man needs to make peace with God; he needs to give all diligence to the effort immediately. If he fails to make peace, then he will have to pay the most severe penalty, to the very last mite.

"Ye serpents, ye generation of vipers, how can ye escape the damnation of hell?" (Mt.23:33).

"And thinkest thou this, O man, that judgest them which do such things, and doest the same, that thou shalt escape the judgment of God?" (Ro.2:3).

"For when they shall say, Peace and safety; then sudden destruction cometh upon them, as travail upon a woman with child; and they shall not escape" (1 Th.5:3).

"How shall we escape, if we neglect so great salvation; which at the first began to be spoken by the Lord, and was confirmed unto us by them that heard him" (Heb.2:3).

"See that ye refuse not him that speaketh. For if they escaped not who refused him that spake on earth, much more shall not we escape, if we turn away from him that speaketh from heaven" (Heb.12:25).

"Though hand join in hand, the wicked shall not be unpunished: but the seed of the righteous shall be delivered" (Pr.11:21).

"Every one that is proud in heart is an abomination to the LORD: though hand join in hand, he shall not be unpunished" (Pr.16:5).

"Therefore thus saith the LORD, Behold, I will bring evil upon them, which they shall not be able to escape; and though they shall cry unto me, I will not hearken unto them" (Jer.11:11).

"Woe unto you [false professors] that desire the day of the LORD! to what end is it for you? the day of the LORD is darkness, and not light. As if a man did flee from a lion, and a bear met him; or went into the house, and leaned his hand on the wall, and a serpent bit him. Shall not the day of the LORD be darkness, and not light? even very dark, and no brightness in it?" (Amos 5:18-20).

"Though they dig into hell, thence shall mine hand take them; though they climb up to heaven, thence will I bring them down" (Amos 9:2).

**CHAPTER 13**

**Q. The Truth About Suffering and Sin: The Great Need for All to Repent, 13:1-9**

(cp. Mt.21:18-21; Mk.11:12-14, 20-26; Is.5:1-7)

There were present at that season some that told him of the Galilaeans, whose blood Pilate had mingled with their sacrifices.

2 And Jesus answering said unto them, Suppose ye that these Galilaeans were sinners above all the Galilaeans, because they suffered such things?

3 I tell, you, Nay: but, except ye repent, ye shall all likewise perish.

4 Or those eighteen, upon whom the tower in Siloam fell, and slew them, think ye that they were sinners above all men that dwelt in Jerusalem?

5 I tell you, Nay: but, except ye repent, ye shall all likewise perish.

6 He spake also this parable; A certain man had a fig tree planted in his vineyard; and he came and sought fruit thereon, and found none.

7 Then said he unto the dresser of his vineyard, Behold, these three years I come seeking fruit on this fig tree, and find none: cut it down; why cumbereth it the ground?

8 And he answering said unto him, Lord, let it alone this year also, till I shall dig about it, and dung it:

9 And if it bear fruit, well: and if not, then after that thou shalt cut it down.

**1 Men do not suffer because they are greater sinners than others**[DS1]
  a. Event 1: The latest news of a horrible murderous event
    1) Did not suffer because they were greater sinners
    2) *All* must repent or perish
  b. Event 2: The latest news of a terrible tragedy
    1) Did not suffer because they were greater sinners
    2) *All* must repent or perish

**2 Men must bear fruit or else they will perish**
  a. The fig tree's privilege: In the vineyard
  b. The fig tree's purpose: To bear fruit
  c. The day for reaping came
    1) Found no fruit
    2) Found that the tree was using up space on the ground & producing nothing
  d. The mercy of God
    1) Gave another chance
    2) Fertilized & fed
  e. The judgment was based on fruit

# DIVISION V

## THE SON OF MAN'S GREAT JOURNEY TO JERUSALEM (STAGE I): HIS MISSION AND PUBLIC CHALLENGE, 9:51-13:21

### Q. The Truth About Suffering and Sin: The Great Need for All to Repent, 13:1-9

(13:1-9) **Introduction**: one of the world's most perplexing problems is, why do men suffer? Some say that men suffer because they are greater sinners. The result, too often, is that many who suffer feel this is true; consequently, they end up with all sorts of guilt and emotional problems. They think their suffering is due to some great sin they have committed and that God is punishing them because they have been such great sinners. It is this subject that is dealt with in this passage.
  1.    Men do not suffer because they are *greater sinners* (v.1-5).
  2.    Men must bear fruit or else they will perish (v.6-9).

**1**  (13:1-5) **Suffering—Sin—Repentance**: men do not suffer because they are *greater sinners* than others. Jesus used two of the latest news events of His day to teach this lesson.
  1.    Some shared with Jesus the latest news of a horrible massacre. Some Galileans were in the temple in the midst of worship, offering their sacrifices to God, when Herod had them attacked and slaughtered by his soldiers (see DEEPER STUDY # 1—Lk.13:1-5). The crowd was being harsh and making a very harsh judgment. They were saying the Galileans were murdered because they were *great sinners*. The crowd was responding to what Jesus had taught, that men must make peace with God before it is too late (Lk.12:58-59). They were saying the Galileans were swept down upon, just like Jesus had described; therefore, they must have been great sinners.
    Jesus was pointed and clear in refuting their thoughts. Note: the people had not spoken their thoughts; they had *only related* the story. However, the thought in their minds was that the Galileans had suffered such a horrible death because they were great sinners, or to express it as it is so often stated: suffering is due to sin.
    Jesus said, "No! But except you repent, you shall all likewise perish!" Such an argument has its basis in self-righteousness. The point is unmistakable: all men must repent of sin, for all men are sinners, just as sinful as the Galileans.
  2.    Now note: the subject is so important and men need to grasp its lesson so much that Jesus referred to another late-news event—the terrible tragedy of a tower's falling on eighteen construction workers. It is significant that Jesus used a tragedy as a second illustration instead of an event similar to the murderous act just discussed. His point is unquestionable; suffering is not necessarily due to sin or to degrees of sin. If suffering were due to sin, then there would be no life whatsoever. Why? Because *all men are so sinful* that they are worthy of only the most horrible suffering—death itself. Thus, Jesus made His point: all men must repent or else perish. (See DEEPER STUDY # 2—Lk.5:23; note—Jn.9:1-3.)

Note what Jesus had said.
  1.    Suffering is not always due to *greater sins*.

    **"Or how wilt thou say to thy brother, Let me pull out the mote out of thine eye; and, behold, a beam is in thine own eye?" (Mt.7:4).**
    **"And when the barbarians saw the venomous beast hang on his hand, they said among themselves, No doubt this man is a murderer, whom, though he hath escaped the sea, yet vengeance suffereth not to live" (Acts 28:4; see outline and notes—1 Cor.1:3-11; 1:3-4 for more discussion and verses).**

2.   All men are guilty of great sin, sin great enough to perish.

"As it is written, There is none righteous, no, not one: there is none that understandeth, there is none that seeketh after God. They are all gone out of the way, they are together become unprofitable; there is none that doeth good, no, not one. Their throat is an open sepulchre; with their tongues they have used deceit; the poison of asps is under their lips: whose mouth is full of cursing and bitterness: their feet are swift to shed blood: destruction and misery are in their ways: and the way of peace have they not known: there is no fear of God before their eyes" (Ro.3:10-18).
"For all have sinned, and come short of the glory of God" (Ro.3:23).
"Now the works of the flesh are manifest, which are these; adultery, fornication, uncleanness, lasciviousness, idolatry, witchcraft, hatred, variance, emulations, wrath, strife, seditions, heresies, envyings, murders, drunkenness, revellings, and such like: of the which I tell you before, as I have also told you in time past, that they which do such things shall not inherit the kingdom of God" (Gal.5:19-21).

3.   All men are doomed to perish.

"For the wages of sin is death; but the gift of God is eternal life through Jesus Christ our Lord" (Ro.6:23).
"For to be carnally minded is death; but to be spiritually minded is life and peace" (Ro.8:6).
"But the fearful, and unbelieving, and the abominable, and murderers, and whoremongers, and sorcerers, and idolaters, and all liars, shall have their part in the lake which burneth with fire and brimstone: which is the second death" (Rev.21:8).
"The soul that sinneth, it shall die" (Ezk.18:20).

4.   There is only one way to keep from perishing: repent.

"Repent, and be baptized every one of you in the name of Jesus Christ for the remission of sins, and ye shall receive the gift of the Holy Ghost" (Acts 2:38).
"Repent ye therefore, and be converted, that your sins may be blotted out, when the times of refreshing shall come from the presence of the Lord" (Acts 3:19).
"Repent therefore of this thy wickedness, and pray God, if perhaps the thought of thine heart may be forgiven thee" (Acts 8:22).
"And the times of this ignorance God winked at; but now commandeth all men every where to repent" (Acts 17:30).

---

**DEEPER STUDY # 1**
(13:1-5) **Suffering—Galileans—Construction Workers:** Who were the Galileans slaughtered by Herod and the construction workers upon whom the tower fell? There is no sure record of either group other than what is given here. The best *guesses* are these.
   Two suggestions are made about the Galileans. First, they were followers of Judas of Galilee who opposed taxation imposed by the Romans (Acts 5:37). Herod either knew that some of Judas' followers were in the temple worshipping or mistook some group of Galileans as his followers and had them slaughtered. This much is known. Pilate set out to build a new water system for Jerusalem. It was a huge construction project, and to finance the work, Pilate had to insist that the money be taken from the temple finances. This of course enraged the Jews, for the temple monies were gifts to God and belonged to God. The Galileans were an inflammable people; therefore, they were usually in the forefront of trouble. Second, some commentators think that the slaughtered Galileans were revolutionaries who had moved into the city to carry out terrorist acts against the government. Herod knew about it and caught them off guard while they were worshipping. Note they were caught so much by surprise that their blood actually flowed and mingled with the blood of the animal sacrifices they were offering to God.
   The construction workers are thought by most to have been repairing one of the towers which served as part of the fortifications on the walls of Jerusalem. It is thought to have been near the pool of Siloam.

---

[2]   (13:6-9) **Fruit-Bearing:** men must bear fruit or else they shall perish. Jesus wanted to drive home the need for repentance by sharing the parable of a man's seeking fruit. The man represents God; the vineyard dresser represents Christ; the vineyard represents either the world or Israel. Note these facts about the fig tree.
   1.   The fig tree was greatly privileged. It was *in the vineyard*, which meant several things.
        a.   It was planted (born) by the vineyard keeper (God or Christ) himself. God causes every man to be born into the world. He stands behind every person as that person's Creator and Lord.

"For in him we live, and move, and have our being; as certain also of your own poets have said, for we are also his offspring" (Acts 17:28).
"The Spirit of God hath made me, and the breath of the Almighty hath given me life" (Job 33:4).
"Know ye that the LORD he is God: it is he that hath made us, and not we ourselves; we are his people, and the sheep of his pasture" (Ps.100:3).

"And forgettest the LORD thy maker, that hath stretched forth the heavens, and laid the foundations of the earth" (Is.51:13).

"Have we not all one father? hath not one God created us? why do we deal treacherously every man against his brother, by profaning the covenant of our fathers?" (Mal.2:10).

b. It was planted in the vineyard itself, right where there were other trees bearing fruit. It had the same soil, nourishment, rain, and sun from heaven. This is true of all persons who are born in nations where the gospel is freely preached.

"Hear another parable: There was a certain householder, which planted a vineyard, and hedged it round about, and digged a winepress in it, and built a tower, and let it out to husbandmen, and went into a far country" (Mt.21:33).

2. The fig tree's purpose was to bear fruit. It had been *planted* to bear fruit and it *existed* to bear fruit. It was by nature a *fruit* tree; therefore, it was supposed to bear fruit. It had no other purpose for existing. So it is with man (Lk.10:27; Gal.5:22-23. See DEEPER STUDY # 1—Jn.15:1-8.)

"Bring forth therefore fruits meet for repentance" (Mt.3:8).

"For the kingdom of heaven is like unto a man that is an householder, which went out early in the morning to hire labourers into his vineyard" (Mt.20:1).

"Herein is my Father glorified, that ye bear much fruit; so shall ye be my disciples" (Jn.15:8).

"Ye have not chosen me, but I have chosen you, and ordained you, that ye should go and bring forth fruit, and that your fruit should remain: that whatsoever ye shall ask of the Father in my name, he may give it you" (Jn.15:16).

3. The day for reaping came. Jesus said five things about the day of reaping.
a. The vineyard owner, God Himself, was the One who came looking for fruit. The reaper was not someone else; it was God Himself.
⇒ He planted the tree to get fruit (God put man on earth to bear fruit).
⇒ He expected fruit, for He was the One who had planted the tree.

"Even so every good tree bringeth forth good fruit; but a corrupt tree bringeth forth evil fruit" (Mt.7:17).

"I am the vine, ye are the branches: He that abideth in me, and I in him, the same bringeth forth much fruit: for without me ye can do nothing" (Jn.15:5).

"But the fruit of the Spirit is love, joy, peace, longsuffering, gentleness, goodness, faith, meekness, temperance: against such there is no law" (Gal.5:22-23).

b. The vineyard owner found no fruit. The tree was bare.
⇒ It failed in its purpose. (So many have all the privileges, yet so few ever honor God or bear fruit as they should.)
⇒ The investment in the life of the tree was wasted.

"He also that received seed among the thorns is he that heareth the word; and the care of this world, and the deceitfulness of riches, choke the word, and he becometh unfruitful" (Mt.13:22).

"And he fenced it, and gathered out the stones thereof, and planted it with the choicest vine, and built a tower in the midst of it, and also made a winepress therein: and he looked that it should bring forth grapes, and it brought forth wild grapes" (Is.5:2).

"Ye have plowed wickedness, ye have reaped iniquity; ye have eaten the fruit of lies: because thou didst trust in thy way, in the multitude of thy mighty men" (Hos.10:13).

c. The vineyard owner had waited a long time. He had come time after time looking for fruit.
⇒ The tree had plenty of time to bear fruit if it were ever going to bear fruit.
⇒ The Owner's patience was extremely long-suffering.

"The Lord is not slack concerning his promise, as some men count slackness; but is long-suffering to us-ward, not willing that any should perish, but that all should come to repentance" (2 Pt.3:9).

d. The tree was wasting and misusing space. The purpose of the vineyard, the very reason for its existence, was to produce fruit for the Owner.
⇒ All space was needed for fruit.
⇒ No space could be allowed to be wasted, not forever.
⇒ The tree was hurting the production of the vineyard. The example of false believers affects the whole vineyard. They cheapen the vineyard (world, church), causing others not to want its fruit.

"Because he hath appointed a day, in the which he will judge the world in righteousness by that man whom he hath ordained; whereof he hath given assurance unto all men, in that he hath raised him from the dead" (Acts 17:31).

"Thou that makest thy boast of the law, through breaking the law *dishonourest thou God*? For the name of God is blasphemed among the Gentiles through you, as it is written" (Ro.2:23-24).

"And many shall follow their pernicious ways; by reason of whom the way of truth shall be evil spoken of" (2 Pt.2:2).

e. The tree was to be cut down. The Owner pronounced judgment.

"Be not deceived; God is not mocked: for whatsoever a man soweth, that shall he also reap. For he that soweth to his flesh shall of the flesh reap corruption; but he that soweth to the Spirit shall of the Spirit reap life everlasting" (Gal.6:7-8).

"For the wages of sin is death; but the gift of God is eternal life through Jesus Christ our Lord" (Ro.6:23).

"And before him shall be gathered all nations: and he shall separate them one from another, as a shepherd divideth his sheep from the goats" (Mt.25:32).

4. The mercy of God. The vineyard dresser interceded for the unfruitful tree. He asked for another year, one last chance for the tree.
⇒ God granted one last chance, one last opportunity.
⇒ Next year, however, was to be the last chance, the last opportunity for the tree.

"Who is he that condemneth? It is Christ that died, yea rather, that is risen again, who is even at the right hand of God, who also *maketh intercession for us*" (Ro.8:34).

"Wherefore he is able also to save them to the uttermost that come unto God by him, seeing he *ever liveth to make intercession* for them" (Heb.7:25).

"Then said Jesus, Father, forgive them; for they know not what they do. And they parted his raiment, and cast lots" (Lk.23:34).

"For their vine is of the vine of Sodom, and of the fields of Gomorrah: their grapes are grapes of gall, their clusters are bitter: their wine is the poison of dragons, and the cruel venom of asps. Is not this laid up in store with me, and sealed up among my treasures? To me belongeth vengeance, and recompense; their foot shall slide in due time: for the day of their calamity is at hand, and the things that shall come upon them make haste" (Dt.32:32-35)

5. The judgment was based upon fruit (see outline and notes—Jn.15:1-8; Gal.5:22-23).

"And now also the axe is laid unto the root of the trees: therefore every tree which bringeth not forth good fruit is hewn down, and cast into the fire" (Mt.3:10).

"If a man abide not in me, he is cast forth as a branch, and is withered; and men gather them, and cast them into the fire, and they are burned" (Jn.15:6).

"But that which beareth thorns and briers is rejected, and is nigh unto cursing: whose end is to be burned" (Heb.6:8).

| | | R. People vs. Religion: Which is More Important? 13:10-17 | and said unto the people, There are six days in which men ought to work: in them therefore come and be healed, and not on the sabbath day. | a. He became angry with the people<br>b. He corrupted God's Word[DS2]<br>c. He rejected Christ |
|---|---|---|---|---|
| 1 Jesus taught in the synagogue on the Sabbath | | 10 And he was teaching in one of the synagogues on the sabbath. | | d. He was hypocritical<br>1) He placed animals above people[DS3] |
| 2 The woman was a worshipper of God<br>a. She was worshipping<br>b. She had a curvature of the spine | | 11 And, behold, there was a woman which had a spirit of infirmity eighteen years, and was bowed together, and could in no wise lift up herself. | 15 The Lord then answered him, and said, thou hypocrite, doth not each one of you on the sabbath loose his ox or his ass from the stall, and lead him away to watering? | |
| c. She was seen & called by Jesus | | 12 And when Jesus saw her, he called her to him, and said unto her, Woman, thou art loosed from thine infirmity. | 16 And ought not this woman, being a daughter of Abraham, whom Satan hath bound, lo, these eighteen years, be loosed from this bond on the sabbath day? | 2) He placed religion above people |
| d. She received Jesus' word & touch<br>e. She glorified God first | | 13 And he laid his hands on her: and immediately she was made straight, and glorified God. | | 4 The effect of Jesus' works & words |
| 3 The ruler (religionist) was a worshipper of God[DS1] | | 14 And the ruler of the synagogue answered with indignation, because that Jesus had healed on the sabbath day, | 17 And when he had said these things, all his adversaries were ashamed: and all the people rejoiced for all the glorious things that were done by him. | a. The opponents: Were humiliated<br>b. The crowds: Rejoiced |

# DIVISION V

## THE SON OF MAN'S GREAT JOURNEY TO JERUSALEM (STAGE I): HIS MISSION AND PUBLIC CHALLENGE, 9:51-13:21

### R. People vs. Religion: Which is More Important? 13:10-17

(13:10-17) **Introduction**: one of the great tragedies of religion is that religion is so often placed before man and his needs. Jesus met this problem head-on.
1. Jesus taught in the synagogue on the Sabbath (v.10).
2. The woman was a worshipper of God (v.11-13).
3. The ruler (religionist) was a worshipper of God (v.14-16).
4. The effect of Jesus' works and words (v.17).

**1** (13:10) **Jesus Christ, Worship of**: Jesus taught in the synagogue on the Sabbath. Three significant facts need to be seen in this point.
1. This was the last time Jesus was ever in a synagogue as far as we know. From this point on He was such a controversial figure that no synagogue would allow Him in the pulpit.
2. This healing miracle took place on the Sabbath, and healing was not allowed on the Sabbath. It was considered work unless it was a matter of life and death. The fact that Jesus broke the Sabbath law was what caused the present dispute.
3. Note that both the woman and the religionist were worshippers of God (v.11-16).

**Thought 1.** Jesus was worshipping on the Sabbath, doing exactly what He should have been doing.

**Thought 2.** There is a difference between worshippers. This is seen in the woman and the man (v.11-16). She sought to draw near the Lord for deliverance, whereas the man only practiced his ceremony and ritual.

**2** (13:11-13) **Salvation—Worship—Jesus Christ, Heals—Compassion**: the woman was a worshipper of God. Note five things about her.
1. She was worshipping. It was her habit to worship, to seek the face of God in looking after her life. Therefore, she was where she was supposed to be on this particular Sabbath: in worship. And because she was there, she was to receive a very special touch from God. She did not know it yet, but she was. Why her? Because she was sincere, ever so sincere in seeking God and His care.

> "Then saith Jesus unto him, Get thee hence, Satan: for it is written, Thou shalt worship the Lord thy God, and him only shalt thou serve" (Mt.4:10).
> "God is a Spirit: and they that worship him must worship him in spirit and in truth" (Jn.4:24).
> "Give unto the LORD the glory due unto his name: bring an offering, and come before him: worship the LORD in the beauty of holiness" (1 Chron.16:29).

"Surely goodness and mercy shall follow me all the days of my life: and I will dwell in the house of the LORD for ever" (Ps.23:6).

"LORD, I have loved the habitation of thy house, and the place where thine honour dwelleth" (Ps.26:8).

"One thing have I desired of the LORD, that will I seek after; that I may dwell in the house of the LORD all the days of my life, to behold the beauty of the LORD, and to enquire in his temple" (Ps.27:4).

"Blessed is the man whom thou choosest, and causest to approach unto thee, that he may dwell in thy courts: we shall be satisfied with the goodness of thy house, even of thy holy temple" (Ps.65:4).

"My soul longeth, yea, even fainteth for the courts of the LORD: my heart and my flesh crieth out for the living God" (Ps.84:2).

"For a day in thy courts is better than a thousand. I had rather be a doorkeeper in the house of my God, than to dwell in the tents of wickedness" (Ps.84:10).

"I was glad when they said unto me, Let us go into the house of the LORD" (Ps.122:1).

2.   She had a curvature of the spine. This sounds like some form of arthritis where the joints of the spine fuse together. Luke, the physician, gives the medical description of his day for the disease. She had been deformed for eighteen yars. Two facts need to be noted.
   a.   She had been afflicted with "a spirit of infirmity." Jesus said the spirit was an *evil spirit of infirmity*: "[She was] a daughter...whom Satan hath bound" (v.16). Thus, the woman needed spiritual healing as well as physical healing.
   b.   She was in worship *despite* her deformity, and note her deformity was severe. She was all bent over and unable to rise up. The pain was sometimes severe. Yet, her habit was to attend worship and to seek the favor and help of God upon her life.

   "But seek ye first the kingdom of God, and his righteousness; and all these things shall be added unto you" (Mt.6:33).

   "And I say unto you, Ask, and it shall be given you; seek, and ye shall find; knock, and it shall be opened unto you. For every one that asketh receiveth; and he that seeketh findeth; and to him that knocketh it shall be opened" (Lk.11:9-10).

   "That they should seek the Lord, if haply they might feel after him, and find him, though he be not afar from every one of us" (Acts 17:27).

   "Seek the LORD, and his strength: seek his face evermore" (Ps.105:4).

   "Seek ye me, and ye shall live" (Amos 5:4).

3.   She was seen and called by Jesus. The woman's faithfulness in the worship of God, despite deformity and pain, attracted Jesus. He knew both her condition with all its pain and inconvenience and the great sacrifice she made to worship God. He was moved with compassion. Note: she did not have to call to Him for help; Jesus called her *to Him*.

   "But the mercy of the LORD is from everlasting to everlasting upon them that fear him, and his righteousness unto children's children" (Ps.103:17).

   "In all their affliction he was afflicted, and the angel of his presence saved them: in his love and in his pity he redeemed them; and he bare them, and carried them all the days of old" (Is.63:9).

   "For we have not an high priest which cannot be touched with the feeling of our infirmities; but was in all points tempted like as we are, yet without sin" (Heb.4:15).

   "Who shall separate us from the love of Christ? shall tribulation, or distress, or persecution, or famine, or nakedness, or peril, or sword?" (Ro.8:35).

   "Casting all your care upon him; for he careth for you" (1 Pt.5:7).

   "It is of the LORD'S mercies that we are not consumed, because his compassions fail not" (Lam.3:22).

4.   She received Jesus' Word and touch. This was crucial. Jesus had called her to come "to Him." She had to respond to His call; He could not come for her. She had to take the step of coming herself. When she obeyed, Jesus spoke the Word, the *good news* to her: "Thou art loosed from thine infirmity." (Keep in mind that her problem had been both spiritual and physical.) Jesus reached out and touched her, and she was "made straight." She stood upright. *She experienced both the power of Jesus' Word and touch.* But note: it was because she came when Jesus called, and she was able to hear Jesus' call because she was worshipping God, seeking His grace and care.

**Thought 1.** The Lord alone can heal those who are bowed down.

   **"The LORD openeth the eyes of the blind: the LORD raiseth them that are bowed down: the LORD loveth the righteous" (Ps.146:8).**

**Thought 2.** Souls that are bent or bowed down can be lifted up by Jesus, no matter what it is that has caused the bowing:

| | |
|---|---|
| ⇒ humiliation and shame | ⇒ accident |
| ⇒ sin | ⇒ disease |
| ⇒ lack of education | ⇒ appearance and looks |
| ⇒ loss of everything | ⇒ personality |

"I am troubled; I am bowed down greatly; I go mourning all the day long. For my loins are filled with a loathsome disease: and there is no soundness in my flesh. I am feeble and sore broken: I have roared by reason of the disquietness of my heart. Lord, all my desire is before thee; and my groaning is not hid from thee. My heart panteth, my strength faileth me: as for the light of mine eyes, it also is gone from me" (Ps.38:6-10).

"Even as the Son of man came not to be ministered unto, but to minister, and to give his life a ransom for many" (Mt.20:28).

"When the even was come, they brought unto him many that were possessed with devils: and he cast out the spirits with his word, and healed all that were sick: that it might be fulfilled which was spoken by Esaias the prophet, saying, Himself took our infirmities, and bare our sicknesses" (Mt.8:16-17).

"And Jesus answering said unto them, They that are whole need not a physician; but they that are sick. I came not to call the righteous, but sinners to repentance" (Lk.5:31-32).

"How God anointed Jesus of Nazareth with the Holy Ghost and with power: who went about doing good, and healing all that were oppressed of the devil; for God was with him" (Acts 10:38).

"For thou hast been a strength to the poor, a strength to the needy in his distress, a refuge from the storm, a shadow from the heat, when the blast of the terrible ones is as a storm against the wall" (Is.25:4).

"Surely he hath borne our griefs, and carried our sorrows: yet we did esteem him stricken, smitten of God, and afflicted" (Is.53:4).

5.  She glorified God first. Note the word "immediately."

"But thanks be to God, which giveth us the victory through our Lord Jesus Christ" (1 Cor.15:57).

"For ye are bought with a price: therefore glorify God in your body, and in your spirit, which are God's" (1 Cor.6:20).

"Thanks be unto God for his unspeakable gift" (2 Cor.9:15).

"Giving thanks always for all things unto God and the Father in the name of our Lord Jesus Christ" (Eph.5:20).

"In every thing give thanks: for this is the will of God in Christ Jesus concerning you" (1 Th.5:18).

"By him therefore let us offer the sacrifice of praise to God continually, that is, the fruit of our lips giving thanks to his name" (Heb.13:15).

"But ye are a chosen generation, a royal priesthood, an holy nation, a peculiar people; that ye should show forth the praises of him who hath called you out of darkness into his marvellous light" (1 Pt.2:9).

"Give thanks unto the LORD, call upon his name, make known his deeds among the people" (1 Chron.16:8).

"Sing praises to the LORD, which dwelleth in Zion: declare among the people his doings" (Ps.9:11).

"Offer unto God thanksgiving; and pay thy vows unto the most High" (Ps.50:14).

"Let the people praise thee, O God; let all the people praise thee" (Ps.67:3).

"Blessed be the Lord, who daily loadeth us with benefits, even the God of our salvation" (Ps.68:19).

"It is a good thing to give thanks unto the LORD, and to sing praises unto thy name, O most High" (Ps.92:1).

**3** (13:14-16) **Religionists—Tradition—Hypocrisy:** the ruler (religionist) was a worshipper of God. He was the head of the synagogue (see DEEPER STUDY # 2—Mt.4:23; 9:18-19). He was a different kind of worshipper than the deformed woman. Whereas the woman sought God *through her need and dependency* to favor and help her personally, the ruler sought God *through form and ritual*, ceremony and rules. There is a vast difference between the two approaches. The one thing God teaches is that a man has to approach Him as a child, dependent and needy. Note four faults or sins of the religionist. (See outline and notes—Mt.12:1-8; 12:9-13 for more discussion and application.)

1.  The ruler got angry with people. In fact, the very people with whom he became angry were his neighbors, the very persons who sat in worship with him every week. He allowed his temper to get out of control. The people were merely seeking help, for they were in desperate need, especially the woman; and he knew it. However, because he differed with them, he flared up against them.

**Thought 1.** How many have hot tempers! How many strike out when they differ! How few control themselves!

**Thought 2.** Note two things.
1)  The man lost his temper in the presence of Jesus. Every flare-up is seen by God, and He knows the sin being committed.

2) The man was really upset with Jesus as well as the people. However, he *feared* to take Jesus on, for he felt Jesus was stronger and more able than himself. So he struck out against the weaker persons. How like the *angry* person!

2. The ruler misunderstood and corrupted God's law (Sabbath). In his mind, Jesus had committed a serious crime. He had healed on the Sabbath day (see Deeper Study # 1,2—Lk.13:14 for discussion).

3. He refused to acknowledge the Messiah, God's Son, who actually stood right before him (see outline and notes—Ro.11:28-29; 1 Th.2:15-16 for discussion).

**"Not every one that saith unto me, Lord, Lord, shall enter into the kingdom of heaven; but he that doeth the will of my Father which is in heaven" (Mt.7:21).**

**"Whosoever therefore shall confess me before men, him will I confess also before my Father which is in heaven. But whosoever shall deny me before men, him will I also deny before my Father which is in heaven" (Mt.10:32-33).**

**"Jesus saith unto him, I am the way, the truth, and the life: no man cometh unto the Father, but by me" (Jn.14:6).**

**"For there is one God, and one mediator between God and men, the man Christ Jesus; who gave himself a ransom for all, to be testified in due time" (1 Tim.2:5-6).**

**"And this is his commandment, That we should believe on the name of his Son Jesus Christ, and love one another, as he gave us commandment" (1 Jn.3:23).**

4. He was hypocritical. He placed both animals and *man-made* religious rules above people. He allowed tradition and ritual, ceremony and rules to become more important than meeting the basic needs of human life: the need for God and the need for spiritual, physical, and mental help—all were to take a back seat to religious form. The religionist's offense was serious. Note the woman was...
*   a "daughter of Abraham," a professed believer in God.
*   a woman who had a spiritual need. She had been bound by Satan.
*   a woman who had suffered for eighteen years.

**"But if ye had known what this meaneth, I will have mercy, and not sacrifice, ye would not have condemned the guiltless. For the Son of man is Lord even of the sabbath day" (Mt.12:7-8).**

**"Master, which is the great commandment in the law? Jesus said unto him, Thou shalt love the Lord thy God with all thy heart, and with all thy soul, and with all thy mind. This is the first and great commandment. And the second is like unto it, Thou shalt love thy neighbour as thyself" (Mt.22:36-39).**

**"Woe unto you, scribes and Pharisees, hypocrites! for ye make clean the outside of the cup and of the platter, but within they are full of extortion and excess. Thou blind Pharisee, cleanse first that which is within the cup and platter, that the outside of them may be clean also. Woe unto you, scribes and Pharisees, hypocrites! for ye are like unto whited sepulchres, which indeed appear beautiful outward, but are within full of dead men's bones, and of all uncleanness. Even so ye also outwardly appear righteous unto men, but within ye are full of hypocrisy and iniquity" (Mt.23:25-28).**

**"He answered and said unto them, Well hath Esaias prophesied of you hypocrites, as it is written, This people honoureth me with their lips, but their heart is far from me. Howbeit in vain do they worship me, teaching for doctrines the commandments of men. For laying aside the commandment of God, ye hold the tradition of men, as the washing of pots and cups: and many other such like things ye do. And he said unto them, Full well ye reject the commandment of God, that ye may keep your own tradition" (Mk.7:6-9).**

**"And why call ye me, Lord, Lord, and do not the things which I say?" (Lk.6:46).**

**"Love worketh no ill to his neighbour: therefore love is the fulfilling of the law" (Ro.13:10).**

**"Beware lest any man spoil you through philosophy and vain deceit, after the tradition of men, after the rudiments of the world, and not after Christ" (Col.2:8).**

**"Having a form of godliness, but denying the power thereof: from such turn away" (2 Tim.3:5).**

**"They profess that they know God; but in works they deny him, being abominable, and disobedient, and unto every good work reprobate" (Tit.1:16).**

**"Rebuke them sharply, that they may be sound in the faith; not giving heed to Jewish fables, and commandments of men, that turn from the truth" (Tit.1:13-14).**

**"Pure religion and undefiled before God and the Father is this, To visit the fatherless and widows in their affliction, and to keep himself unspotted from the world" (Jas.1:27).**

**"Hereby perceive we the love of God, because he laid down his life for us: and we ought to lay down our lives for the brethren. But whoso hath this world's good, and seeth his brother have need, and shutteth up his bowels of compassion from him, how dwelleth the love of God in him? My little children, let us not love in word, neither in tongue; but in deed and in truth. And hereby we know that we are of the truth, and shall assure our hearts before him" (1 Jn.3:16-19).**

"For I desired mercy, and not sacrifice; and the knowledge of God more than burnt offerings" (Hos.6:6).
"He hath showed thee, O man, what is good; and what doth the LORD require of thee, but to do justly, and to love mercy, and to walk humbly with thy God?" (Mic.6:8).

---

**DEEPER STUDY # 1**

(13:14) **Sabbath Law—Religionists**: the crime committed by Jesus was "breaking the sabbath law," that is, *working* on the Sabbath day. This was a serious matter to the orthodox Jew. Just how serious can be seen in the strict demands governing the Sabbath. Law after law was written to govern all activity on the Sabbath. A person could not travel, fast, cook, buy, sell, draw water, walk beyond a certain distance, lift anything, fight in a war, or heal on the sabbath unless life was at stake. A person was not even to contemplate any kind of work or activity. A good example of the legal restriction and the people's loyalty to it is seen in the women who witnessed Jesus' crucifixion. Despite their enormous love for Him, they would not even walk to His tomb to prepare the body for burial until the Sabbath was over (Mk.16:1f, Mt.28:1f).

It was a serious matter to break the Sabbath law. A person who broke the law was condemned, and if the offence were serious enough, the person was to die.

This may seem harsh to some. But when dealing with the Jewish nation, one must remember that it was their religion that held them together as a nation through centuries and centuries of exile. Their religion—in particular their beliefs about God's call to their nation, the temple, and the Sabbath—became the *binding force* that kept Jews together and maintained their distinctiveness as a people. It protected them from alien beliefs and from being swallowed up by other people through intermarriage. No matter where they were, they met together and associated together and held on to their beliefs. A picture of this can be seen in the insistence of Nehemiah when he led some Jews back to Jerusalem (Neh.13:15-22; cp. Jer.17:19-27; Ezk.46:1-7).

All the above explains to some degree why the religionists opposed Jesus with such hostility. Their problem was that they had allowed religion and ritual, ceremony and liturgy, and probably position, security, and recognition to become more important than the basic essentials of human life: personal need and compassion, and the true worship and mercy of God. (See note and DEEPER STUDY # 1—Mt.12:10. This is an important note for more discussion on this point.)

---

**DEEPER STUDY # 2**

(13:14) **Religionists—Word of God**: the religionists (Jewish teachers) corrupted God's Word. There are two ways this is done (Rev.22:18-19; Pr.30:6).

1. By taking away from the words of God's Scripture. A person takes away from God's Word by denying sections that he does not like or understand, by neglecting to live the whole counsel of God, and by interpreting some commandments too loosely.

2. By adding to the words of God's Scripture. A person adds to God's Word by interpreting and living too strictly. Such exalts the flesh and is nothing more than extreme discipline and self-control. Of course, both discipline and self-control are commendable and are qualities demanded by God's Word, but they are not an end in themselves.

God's Word is practical and leads to an abundant life, to real living. It is not cold, harsh, restrictive, monastic, unrealistic, or impractical. God did not give His Word for a select group (clergy); He gave it for the common man. "His commandments are not grievous" (1 Jn.5:3).

The Sadducees were especially guilty of taking away from God's Word, whereas the Pharisees and Scribes were especially guilty of adding to God's Word (see DEEPER STUDY # 2—Acts 23:8; DEEPER STUDY # 1—Lk.6:2).

"For verily I say unto you, Till heaven and earth pass, one jot or one tittle shall in no wise pass from the law, till all be fulfilled" (Mt.5:18).
"And if any man shall take away from the words of the book of this prophecy, God shall take away his part out of the book of life, and out of the holy city, and from the things which are written in this book" (Rev.22:19).
"Ye shall not add unto the word which I command you, neither shall ye diminish aught from it, that ye may keep the commandments of the LORD your God which I command you" (Dt.4:2).
"What thing soever I command you, observe to do it: thou shalt not add thereto, nor diminish from it" (Dt.12:32).
"Every word of God is pure: he is a shield unto them that put their trust in him. Add thou not unto his words, lest he reprove thee, and thou be found a liar" (Pr.30:5-6).

---

**DEEPER STUDY # 3**

(13:15-16) **Man, Deceived**: the ruler became angry with Jesus, but he camouflaged it by attacking the people over a religious tradition. His life had become so routine that it was warped: he showed more concern for animals than he did for human beings. Jesus' frontal rebuke indicates that the man had probably never even thought of his plight. If he had, Jesus would probably have tried to stir him to a proper decision.

---

**4** (13:17) **Jesus Christ, Impact**: the effect of Jesus' work and words was the humiliation of those who opposed Him and the rejoicing of those who were open to Him.

| | | | |
|---|---|---|---|
| | **S. The Parables of the Mus-**<br>**tard Seed and Leaven:**<br>**The Kingdom of God,**<br>**13:18-21**<br>(Mt.13:31-33; Mk.4:<br>30-32) | tard seed, which a man took,<br>and cast into his garden; and<br>it grew, and waxed a great<br>tree; and the fowls of the air<br>lodged in the branches of<br>it.<br> 20 And again he said,<br>Whereunto shall I liken the | a. It is planted by God<br>  1) As a seed<br>  2) In His garden<br>b. It grows to be great[DS2]<br>c. It is lodging for all<br><br>**3 It is like leaven's working**<br>**in bread[DS3,4]** |
| **1 The Kingdom of God illus-**<br>**trated** | 18 Then said he, Unto what<br>is the kingdom of God like?<br>and whereunto shall I re-<br>semble it? | kingdom of God?<br>21 It is like leaven, which a<br>woman took and hid in three<br>measures of meal, till the | a. It is taken & placed in<br>  meal<br>b. It works until the whole<br>  is changed |
| **2 It is like a mustard seed[DS1]** | 19 It is like a grain of mus- | whole was leavened. | |

# DIVISION V

## THE SON OF MAN'S GREAT JOURNEY TO JERUSALEM
## (STAGE I): HIS MISSION AND PUBLIC CHALLENGE, 9:51-13:21

**S.    The Parables of the Mustard Seed and Leaven: The Kingdom of God, 13:18-21**

(13:18-21) **Introduction**: Jesus was still in the synagogue teaching. Some had rejected Him; others had accepted Him (v.17). This stirred His mind to think about the Kingdom of God, a subject that people needed to understand fully.
1.    The Kingdom of God illustrated (v.18).
2.    It is like a mustard seed (v.19).
3.    It is like leaven's working in bread (v.20-21).

**1**  (13:18) **Kingdom of God**: the Kingdom of God illustrated. Jesus stirred thought about the kingdom by asking two questions.
1.    What is the Kingdom of God like?
2.    To what shall the Kingdom of God be compared?

**2**  (13:19) **Kingdom of God—Christianity, Growth of—Mustard Seed**: the Kingdom of God is like a mustard seed. Jesus said three things about this particular mustard seed.
1.    The mustard seed was planted by God. The man in the parable is God or Christ. Note the word "took" (labon, having taken). It means to deliberately take, to take with purpose and thought. The seed was not planted by chance; it did not just happen. With purpose and thought, God planted and nourished the seed (kingdom).
  a.   He planted it as a small seed (see Deeper Study # 1, *Mustard Seed*—Lk.13:19 for discussion).
  b.   He planted it in His garden. God's garden is the world, the creation of His own hand.

> "In the beginning God created the heaven and the earth" (Gen.1:1).
> "Thou, even thou, art LORD alone; thou hast made heaven, the heaven of heavens, with all their host, the earth, and all things that are therein, the seas, and all that is therein, and thou preservest them all; and the host of heaven worshippeth thee" (Neh.9:6).
> "Of old hast thou laid the foundation of the earth: and the heavens are the work of thy hands" (Ps.102:25).

2.    The mustard seed grew to be great. This is really the major point of Luke, to show how the kingdom was to grow from a few persons into a great movement. Imagine the scene. There stood Jesus in the synagogue with only a few persons who truly believed that He was bringing the Kingdom of God to earth. In fact, most of the ones sitting before Him did not believe in Him at all; they opposed Him. But He knew something. God was planting the kingdom on earth through Him; therefore the kingdom was destined to grow and succeed. (See Deeper Study # 2, *Christianity*—Lk.13:19.)

> "And when the Gentiles heard this, they were glad, and glorified the word of the Lord: and as many as were ordained to eternal life believed" (Acts 13:48).
> "Be it known therefore unto you, that the salvation of God is sent unto the Gentiles, and that they will hear it" (Acts 28:28).
> "And that the Gentiles might glorify God for his mercy; as it is written, For this cause I will confess to thee among the Gentiles, and sing unto thy name" (Ro.15:9).
> "That the blessing of Abraham might come on the Gentiles through Jesus Christ; that we might receive the promise of the Spirit through faith" (Gal.3:14).
> "That the Gentiles should be fellowheirs [with Jewish believers], and of the same body, and partakers of his promise in Christ by the gospel" (Eph.3:6).
> "There shall be a handful of corn in the earth upon the top of the mountains; the fruit thereof shall shake like Lebanon: and they of the city shall flourish like grass of the earth" (Ps.72:16).
> "Of the increase of his government and peace there shall be no end, upon the throne of David, and upon his kingdom, to order it, and to establish it with judgment and with justice from henceforth even for ever. The zeal of the LORD of hosts will perform this" (Is.9:7).

"For thou shalt break forth on the right hand and on the left; and thy seed shall inherit the Gentiles, and make the desolate cities to be inhabited" (Is.54:3).

"Behold, thou shalt call a nation that thou knowest not, and nations that knew not thee shall run unto thee because of the LORD thy God, and for the Holy One of Israel; for he hath glorified thee" (Is.55:5).

"Then thou shalt see, and flow together, and thine heart shall fear, and be enlarged; because the abundance of the sea shall be converted unto thee, the forces of the Gentiles shall come unto thee" (Is.60:5).

"A little one shall become a thousand, and a small one a strong nation: I the LORD will hasten it in his time" (Is.60:22).

3. The mustard bush provided lodging for the birds of the air. The birds' flocking to the tree is a picture of the people and nations of the earth seeking refuge in the covering of Christianity.
   a. Some say the birds are those in the world who find their lodging in the kingdom—the kingdom (the church, Christianity) that had so small a beginning but is now growing into a stately movement. Many in the world, believers and non-believers alike, have found help and safety under its branches. To a large extent laws and institutions of mercy, justice, and honor have evolved from this magnificent movement. This interpretation relies heavily upon the picture painted by the Old Testament. A great empire is said to be like a tree, and conquered nations are said to be like birds who lodge under its shadow (Ezk.17:22-24; 31:6; Dan.4:14).
   b. Others say the birds are the children of the evil one who see the lodging facilities and protective covering of the kingdom and seek lodging therein.

"The law and the prophets were until John: since that time the kingdom of God is preached, and every man presseth into it" (Lk.16:16).

---

**DEEPER STUDY # 1**
(13:19) **Mustard Seed**: the mustard seed was not actually the smallest seed known in Jesus' day, but the seed was small and the mustard bush grew as large as some trees. It has been reported that a rider on horseback could find shade under its branches. The fact that such a small seed could produce such huge results caused people to use the mustard seed as a proverbial saying to describe smallness.

---

**DEEPER STUDY # 2**
(13:19) **Christianity—Kingdom of God**: there are several facts that show just how small the beginning of the kingdom or of Christianity really was.
   1. It began in the soul of a single person. Jesus launched the movement all by Himself. The idea, the dream, was in no one else's soul but His. He moved out alone—in God's strength.
   2. It was born in the soul of a carpenter from an obscure village, Nazareth, and from an obscure and despised nation, Israel (see note—Mt.8:5-13; Lk.7:4-5).
   3. It was carried forth by men with no position and no prestige. There were no mighty, no noble, no famous persons among its early followers. They were but common folk, some from honorable professions such as the fishing industry (Mt.4:18-21), and some from despised professions such as tax collecting (Mt.9:9). (Cp. 1 Cor.1:26.)
   4. It grew from just a few persons who had very *little faith* (cp. Mt.14:31; Lk.12:32).
   5. It was formed as a church and numbered only one hundred and twenty in the very beginning (Acts 1:15).

---

**3** (13:20-21) **Kingdom of God—Christianity—Leaven**: the Kingdom of God is like leaven's working in bread. Quickly note what Jesus said: the Kingdom of God is like leaven which is placed in meal (the world) until the whole (world) is changed. Note two major points.
   1. The leaven (kingdom) is taken and placed into the meal (world).
      a. The kingdom or gospel is deliberately taken and placed into the world. The kingdom and the gospel of God are not by chance (see DEEPER STUDY # 2, pt.1, *Kingdom of God*—Lk.13:19).

"For God so loved the world, that he gave his only begotten Son, that whosoever believeth in him should not perish, but have everlasting life" (Jn.3:16).

"But God commendeth his love toward us, in that, while we were yet sinners, Christ died for us" (Ro.5:8).

"For there is no difference between the Jew and the Greek: for the same Lord over all is rich unto all that call upon him" (Ro.10:12).

"Who will have all men to be saved, and to come unto the knowledge of the truth" (1 Tim.2:4).

"He [Jesus Christ] is the propitiation for our sins: and not for ours only, but also for the sins of the whole world" (1 Jn.2:2).

"Look unto me, and be ye saved, all the ends of the earth: for I am God, and there is none else" (Is.45:22).

b. The purpose of the kingdom is to leaven, that is, to change the whole of an individual and of society itself.
⇒ It seeks to leaven individuals: to penetrate them with the gospel until the *whole* being is transformed.
⇒ It seeks to leaven society as a whole: to penetrate society with the gospel until the whole of society is transformed.

> "Therefore if any man be in Christ, he is a new creature: old things are passed away; behold, all things are become new" (2 Cor.5:17).
> "For in Christ Jesus neither circumcision availeth any thing, nor uncircumcision, but a new creature" (Gal.6:15).
> "And be renewed in the spirit of your mind; and that ye put on the new man, which after God is created in righteousness and true holiness" (Eph.4:23-24).
> "And have put on the new man, which is renewed in knowledge after the image of him that created him" (Col.3:10).

c. Leaven has a changing, transforming, fulfilling, and satisfying power (see DEEPER STUDY # 3—Lk.1:21 for discussion).

2. The leaven (kingdom) works until the whole (world) is changed. (See DEEPER STUDY # 4, *Leaven*—Lk.13:21 for discussion.)

> "Then Jesus said unto them, Verily, verily, I say unto you, Moses gave you not that bread from heaven; but my Father giveth you the true bread from heaven. For the bread of God is he which cometh down from heaven, and giveth life unto the world" (Jn.6:32-33).
> "And Jesus said unto them, I am the bread of life: he that cometh to me shall never hunger; and he that believeth on me shall never thirst" (Jn.6:35).
> "I am that bread of life. Your fathers did eat manna in the wilderness, and are dead. This is the bread which cometh down from heaven, that a man may eat thereof, and not die. I am the living bread which came down from heaven: if any man eat of this bread, he shall live for ever: and the bread that I will give is my flesh, which I will give for the life of the world" (Jn.6:48-51).
> "This is that bread which came down from heaven: not as your fathers did eat manna, and are dead: he that eateth of this bread shall live for ever" (Jn.6:58).
> "The thief cometh not, but for to steal, and to kill, and to destroy: I am come that they might have life, and that they might have it more abundantly" (Jn.10:10).
> "And to know the love of Christ, which passeth knowledge, that ye might be filled with all the fulness of God" (Eph.3:19).
> "Who [the Lord] satisfieth thy mouth with good things; so that thy youth is renewed like the eagle's" (Ps.103:5).
> "For he satisfieth the longing soul, and filleth the hungry soul with goodness" (Ps.107:9).

---

**DEEPER STUDY # 3**

(13:21) **Leaven—Transformation—Gospel—Kingdom of God**: leaven changes and transforms bread. Bread made from water is hard, dry, and not too nourishing; but leaven, mixed in with dough, changes and transforms bread tremendously. It does at least four things for bread.

1. Leaven makes bread soft, no longer hard. The leaven of the gospel does the same: it penetrates the heart of man and softens the hardness of his life. Thereby the man becomes much softer toward the Lord and toward the needs of others. He becomes a more caring and giving person. Softness is definitely one of the trademarks of a transformed person.

2. Leaven makes bread porous and moist, no longer dry. The leaven of the gospel does the same: it penetrates the dryness of a man's heart and life. Thereby the gospel penetrates, creates pores in his life, and moistens his heart so that he can grow into a moist or fruitful person.

3. Leaven makes bread satisfying, no longer dissatisfying. Again, the gospel does the same for the man who lives a dissatisfied life with no purpose, meaning, or significance. The gospel leavens, that is, transforms a person's heart and life, giving purpose and joy and hope—all the satisfaction a person could ever desire.

4. Leaven makes bread nourishing, no longer of little benefit. The leaven of the gospel does the same thing for the man who seems to accomplish so little in life. The gospel not only gives *purpose* but it *inspires, commissions,* and causes a man to *feed others.* A person transformed by the gospel is able to feed the truth to the world. The gospel is able to explain the reasons for the emptiness and loneliness of the human heart and God's provision for such.

---

**DEEPER STUDY # 4**

(13:21) **Leaven**: note several important facts about how leaven works.

1. Leaven works quietly and silently. It works without fanfare and the spectacular. There is a thoughtful lesson here on how the gospel should be presented (see outline and notes—Mt.4:5-7; 12:38-40).

> "And the servant of the Lord must not strive; but be gentle unto all men, apt to teach, patient, in meekness instructing those that oppose themselves; if God peradventure will give them repentance to the acknowledging of the truth" (2 Tim.2:24-25).
> "To speak evil of no man, to be no brawlers, but gentle, showing all meekness unto all men" (Tit.3:2).

"Who is a wise man and endued with knowledge among you? let him show out of a good conversation his works with meekness of wisdom" (Jas.3:13).

"But sanctify the Lord God in your hearts: and be ready always to give an answer to every man that asketh you a reason of the hope that is in you with meekness and fear" (1 Pt.3:15).

2. Leaven finishes its work. Once it is inserted into the dough, nothing can stop it or ever pluck it out. It will transform the dough. This is a great lesson on the security of the person who genuinely allows the gospel to penetrate his heart and life.

"And I give unto them eternal life; and they shall never perish, neither shall any man pluck them out of my hand" (Jn.10:28).

"Being confident of this very thing, that he which hath begun a good work in you will perform it until the day of Jesus Christ" (Ph.1:6).

"For the which cause I also suffer these things: nevertheless I am not ashamed: for I know whom I have believed, and am persuaded that he is able to keep that which I have committed unto him against that day" (2 Tim.1:12).

"But the Lord is faithful, who shall stablish you, and keep you from evil" (2 Th.3:3).

"Who are kept by the power of God through faith unto salvation ready to be revealed in the last time" (1 Pt.1:5).

"Now unto him that is able to keep you from falling, and to present you faultless before the presence of his glory with exceeding joy, to the only wise God our Saviour, be glory and majesty, dominion and power, both now and ever" (Jude 24-25).

"Because thou hast kept the word of my patience, I also will keep thee from the hour of temptation, which shall come upon all the world, to try them that dwell upon the earth" (Rev.3:10).

"And now I am no more in the world, but these are in the world, and I come to thee. Holy Father, keep through thine own name those whom thou hast given me, that they may be one, as we are" (Jn.17:11).

"And, behold, I am with thee, and will keep thee in all places whither thou goest, and will bring thee again into this land; for I will not leave thee, until I have done that which I have spoken to thee of" (Gen.28:15).

"The LORD is thy keeper: the LORD is thy shade upon thy right hand. The sun shall not smite thee by day, nor the moon by night. The LORD shall preserve thee from all evil: he shall preserve thy soul. The LORD shall preserve thy going out and thy coming in from this time forth, and even for evermore" (Ps.121:5-8).

3. Leaven works slowly and gradually, yet consistently. It takes time for it to leaven the whole lump. The believer can learn at least two lessons from this fact.
   a. It will take time for him to personally grow in the gospel. Just as a child grows physically through proper nourishment, so the believer will grow spiritually if he receives proper nourishment. His spiritual growth will take time; but it will be consistent and sure.

"And now, brethren, I commend you to God, and to the word of his grace, which is able to build you up, and to give you an inheritance among all them which are sanctified" (Acts 20:32).

"As newborn babes, desire the sincere milk of the word, that ye may grow thereby: if so be ye have tasted that the Lord is gracious" (1 Pt.2:2-3).

"Study to show thyself approved unto God, a workman that needeth not to be ashamed, rightly dividing the word of truth" (2 Tim.2:15).

"All scripture is given by inspiration of God, and is profitable for doctrine, for reproof, for correction, for instruction in righteousness" (2 Tim.3:16).

   b. It will take time for his own witnessing and work to produce bread. Yet his leavening (service and ministry) will leaven the lump of meal (people) he handles and works.
4. Leaven changes the quality, not the substance, of the dough. It is still dough, yet it is changed. A man who receives the gospel remains a man; but he is a changed man, a man of quality, a man of God.
5. Leaven changes the whole lump. It permeates every pore of the dough's being. So it is with a man. Once the gospel honestly penetrates, it permeates and affects all of his life (cp. 2 Cor.5:17; Gal.6:15; Eph.4:23-24; Col.3:10).

| | VI. THE SON OF MAN'S GREAT JOURNEY TO JERUSALEM (STAGE II): HIS TEACHING AND PUBLIC CONFLICT, 13:22-17:10 | and he shall answer and say unto you, I know you not whence ye are: | |
|---|---|---|---|
| | **A. The Saved Discussed, 13:22-30** | 26 Then shall ye begin to say, We have eaten and drunk in thy presence, and thou hast taught in our streets. | 4 The saved are not the citizens of so-called Christian nations nor members of certain fellowships |
| 1 Jesus journeyed toward Jerusalem<br>  a. Taught in the cities & villages<br>  b. Along the way someone questioned Jesus about salvation | 22 And he went through the cities and villages, teaching, and journeying toward Jerusalem.<br>23 Then said one unto him, Lord, are there few that be saved? And he said unto them, | 27 But he shall say, I tell you, I know you not whence ye are; depart from me, all ye workers of iniquity. | 5 The saved shall be separated from the lost & the lost shall see them enter God's Kingdom[DS1,2] |
| 2 The saved strive to enter the narrow gate | 24 Strive to enter in at the strait gate: for many, I say unto you, will seek to enter in, and shall not be able. | 28 There shall be weeping and gnashing of teeth, when ye shall see Abraham, and Isaac, and Jacob, and all the prophets, in the kingdom of God, and you yourselves thrust out. | |
| 3 The saved act soon enough: A man can move too late | 25 When once the master of the house is risen up, and hath shut to the door, and ye begin to stand without, and to knock at the door, saying, Lord, Lord, open unto us; | 29 And they shall come from the east, and from the west, and from the north, and from the south, and shall sit down in the kingdom of God.<br>30 And, behold, there are last which shall be first, and there are first which shall be last. | 6 The saved will come from all nations & classes of society |

# DIVISION VI

## THE SON OF MAN'S GREAT JOURNEY TO JERUSALEM (STAGE II): HIS TEACHING AND PUBLIC CONFLICT, 13:22-17:10

## A.    The Saved Discussed, 13:22-30

(13:22-30) **Introduction**: Who are the saved? Will many be saved? Christ answers these questions in this passage. However, He does not answer the questions to satisfy curiosity. He answers them to challenge us so that we will make sure we are saved.

1.    Jesus journeyed toward Jerusalem (v.22-23).
2.    The saved strive to enter the narrow gate (v.24).
3.    The saved act soon enough: a man can move too late (v.25).
4.    The saved are not the citizens of so-called Christian nations nor members of certain fellowships (v.26).
5.    The saved shall be separated from the lost and the lost shall see them enter God's Kingdom (v.27-28).
6.    The saved will come from all nations and classes of society (v.29-30).

[1] (13:22-23) **Jesus Christ, Cross—Salvation**: Jesus journeyed toward Jerusalem. This is the second stage of Jesus' great journey to the cross. (See DEEPER STUDY # 1—Lk.9:51; cp. Lk.17:11.) Note: as He travelled along, He taught wherever He was. He kept on doing what God sent Him to do, not slacking off nor forgetting His call and mission. Whether he was in a large city or a small village, it did not matter; He reached out to as many as He could reach.

Somewhere along the way, someone asked Him point blank: "Lord, are there few that be saved?" The man was not asking how he might be saved but if the saved would be many or few. His question was probably one of two things. It was a question of curiosity, a question often discussed among people: Are most people saved or lost? However, it could have been a legitimate question asking for clarification. The Jews taught that all would be saved just because they were Jews by birth and circumcision. But Jesus taught that nationality and ritual had nothing to do with salvation, and He was always stressing that many are called, but few are chosen. Perhaps the man was asking how to reconcile the two teachings. Note: Jesus used the occasion to speak "unto them" all, the whole multitude.

**Thought 1.** Many are curious, but not curious enough to really seek after the Lord for personal salvation. They are ready and willing to discuss *religious subjects* but unwilling to deny themselves and to diligently seek after God.

**Thought 2.** Birth and ritual are not enough to save a person, not even if the ritual is circumcision (for the Jew) or baptism (for the Christian). Baptism no more saves a person *born within Christian circles* than circumcision saved a Jew *born within Jewish circles*.

[2] (13:24) **Salvation—Narrow Gate—Jesus Christ, Mediator—Seeking**: the saved strive to enter the narrow gate. Note three significant facts.
1.    The entrance to salvation is a *narrow gate*. This means at least three things.
  a.    The way to salvation is specific, very specific.

284

b.  The way to salvation is the only way. There are not many ways to be saved; there is only one way.

> "Jesus saith unto him, I am the way, the truth, and the life: no man cometh unto the Father, but by me" (Jn.14:6).
> "Neither is there salvation in any other: for there is none other name under heaven given among men, whereby we must be saved" (Acts 4:12).
> "For there is one God, and one mediator between God and men, the man Christ Jesus; who gave himself a ransom for all, to be testified in due time" (1 Tim.2:5-6).
> "But now hath he obtained a more excellent ministry, by how much also he is the mediator of a better covenant, which was established upon better promises" (Heb.8:6).
> "And for this cause he is the mediator of the new testament, that by means of death, for the redemption of the transgressions that were under the first testament, they which are called might receive the promise of eternal inheritance" (Heb.9:15).
> "And to Jesus the mediator of the new covenant, and to the blood of sprinkling, that speaketh better things than that of Abel" (Heb.12:24).
> "My little children, these things write I unto you, that ye sin not. And if any man sin, we have an advocate with the Father, Jesus Christ the righteous" (1 Jn.2:1).

c.  The way to salvation is straight. It is not crooked in direction or purpose or morals. It is the straight way.

2.  A person has to "*strive*" (agonizesthe) to be saved. The word means to agonize, struggle, contend, exert to the fullest, labor fervently. *Whole-hearted dedication and effort* are required. But note a critical point: the idea is not that a person works for his salvation, but that he *diligently seeks* God. He casts himself totally upon the *belief that God is*, that God actually exists (cp. Heb.11:6). It is the spirit, the attitude, the heart that sets itself upon God, refusing to be diverted or to be committed to anything else. It is the total commitment of one's life to God for salvation.

> "And I say unto you, Ask, and it shall be given you; seek, and ye shall find; knock, and it shall be opened unto you. For every one that asketh receiveth; and he that seeketh findeth; and to him that knocketh it shall be opened" (Lk.11:9-10).
> "That they should seek the Lord, if haply they might feel after him, and find him, though he be not far from every one of us" (Acts 17:27; cp. v.24-28).
> "But without faith it is impossible to please him: for he that cometh to God must believe that he is, and that he is a rewarder of them that diligently seek him" (Heb.11:6).
> "But if from thence thou shalt seek the LORD thy God, thou shalt find him, if thou seek him with all thy heart and with all thy soul" (Dt.4:29).
> "Seek ye the LORD while he may be found, call ye upon him while he is near" (Is.55:6).
> "And ye shall seek me, and find me, when ye shall search for me with all your heart" (Jer.29:13).
> "Sow to yourselves in righteousness, reap in mercy; break up your fallow ground: for it is time to seek the LORD, till he come and rain righteousness upon you" (Hos.10:12).
> "For thus saith the LORD unto the house of Israel, Seek ye me, and ye shall live" (Amos 5:4).
> "Seek ye the LORD, all ye meek of the earth, which have wrought his judgment; seek righteousness, seek meekness: it may be ye shall be hid in the day of the LORD'S anger" (Zeph.2:3).

3.  Many will seek to enter the door of salvation but "shall not be able." The reason is what Jesus said. One must "*strive*" to enter and few are willing to pay the price of self-denial. It costs too much for them to give up the world (see note and DEEPER STUDY # 1—Lk.9:23).

> "And he said to them all, If any man will come after me, let him deny himself, and take up his cross daily, and follow me. For whosoever will save his life shall lose it: but whosoever will lose his life for my sake, the same shall save it" (Lk.9:23-24).

[3]  (13:25) Salvation—Decision—Accepted Time: the saved act soon enough; a man can move too late. The parable is simple and clearly understood. Note three things.

1.  The person who strives *now* can enter salvation. This is seen in the words "will seek" (v.24). The words are in the future tense; that is, it is in the future that many "will seek to enter in, and shall not be able." Right now, all who "strive" to enter salvation can be saved.

> "For he saith, I have heard thee in a time accepted, and in the day of salvation have I succoured thee: behold, now is the accepted time; behold, now is the day of salvation" (2 Cor.6:2).
> "I acknowledged my sin unto thee, and mine iniquity have I not hid. I said, I will confess my transgressions unto the LORD; and thou forgavest the iniquity of my sin. Selah. For this shall every one that is godly pray unto thee in a time when thou mayest be found: surely in the floods of great waters they shall not come nigh unto him. Thou art my hiding place; thou shalt preserve me from trouble; thou shalt compass me about with songs of deliverance. Selah" (Ps.32:5-7).
> "But as for me, my prayer is unto thee, O LORD, in an acceptable time: O God, in the multitude of thy mercy hear me, in the truth of thy salvation" (Ps.69:13).
> "For he is our God; and we are the people of his pasture, and the sheep of his hand. To day if ye will hear his voice" (Ps.95:7).

> "Thus saith the LORD, In an acceptable time have I heard thee, and in a day of salvation have I helped thee: and I will preserve thee, and give thee for a covenant of the people, to establish the earth" (Is.49:8).

2. The Master shall rise up and shut the door to salvation. There is a time limit to salvation. The door will not always be opened.
    a. It is shut at a person's death. No man who is presently living has yet had the door shut; but for some, the door will be shut within the very next minute, the next hour, the next day (Heb.9:27).
    b. It is shut when the Lord returns and the great day of judgment takes place. The age of grace and the day of salvation will be closed for the whole world, for every man and woman and child who is of responsible age.
3. Many shall rise up and knock at the closed door and beg to enter. This is the scene painted by Christ: men's rising up and crying for mercy and salvation after it is too late. Once a man dies, it is too late. Once Christ returns, it will be too late.

> "For unto every one that hath shall be given, and he shall have abundance: but from him that hath not shall be taken away even that which he hath. And cast ye the unprofitable servant into outer darkness: there shall be weeping and gnashing of teeth" (Mt.25:29-30; cp. v.24-30).
> "Then shall he say also unto them on the left hand, Depart from me, ye cursed, into everlasting fire, prepared for the devil and his angels: for I was an hungred, and ye gave me no meat: I was thirsty, and ye gave me no drink: I was a stranger, and ye took me not in: naked, and ye clothed me not: sick, and in prison, and ye visited me not. Then shall they also answer him, saying, Lord, when saw we thee an hungred, or athirst, or a stranger, or naked, or sick, or in prison, and did not minister unto thee? Then shall he answer them, saying, Verily I say unto you, Inasmuch as ye did it not to one of the least of these, ye did it not to me. And these shall go away into everlasting punishment: but the righteous into life eternal" (Mt.25:41-46).
> "And as it is appointed unto men once to die, but after this the judgment" (Heb.9:27).
> "For ye know how that afterward, when he would have inherited the blessing, he was rejected: for he found no place of repentance, though he sought it carefully with tears" (Heb.12:17).
> "The harvest is past, the summer is ended, and we are not saved" (Jer.8:20).

**4** (13:26) **False Profession—Heritage—Christian Nation**: the saved are not the citizens of so-called Christian nations nor members of certain fellowships or churches. Note the exact words of men when they stand before Christ in that day:
1. "We have *eaten* and *drunk* in thy presence." They were...
    • where He was, in His very presence (in church, in the presence of believers).
    • where His Word was taught.
    • where His works were performed.
2. "Thou hast taught in our streets."
    • They were citizens of nations which allowed His teaching.
    • They allowed His teaching in their own streets, neighborhoods, cities, and homes.
However, they are *only professing believers*; they are not genuine believers. They are people who had all the privileges of the gospel; some are even baptized church members and moral persons, but they never dedicated their whole beings to *strive* after salvation (see outline and notes—Jn.1:12-13; Ph.3:7-11). They continued to live worldly and unrighteous lives, seeking the comforts and possessions of this world.

> "Not every one that saith unto me, Lord, Lord, shall enter into the kingdom of heaven; but he that doeth the will of my Father which is in heaven" (Mt.7:21).
> "He answered and said unto them, Well hath Esaias prophesied of your hypocrites, as it is written, This people honoureth me with their lips, but their heart is far from me" (Mk.7:6).
> "And why call ye me, Lord, Lord, and do not the things which I say?" (Lk.6:46).
> "They profess that they know God; but in works they deny him, being abominable, and disobedient, and unto every good work reprobate" (Tit.1:16).
> "My little children, let us not love in word, neither in tongue; but in deed and in truth" (1 Jn.3:18).
> "And they remembered that God was their rock, and the high God their redeemer" (Ps.78:35).
> "And they come unto thee [the prophet, preacher] as the people cometh, and they sit before thee as my people, and they hear thy words, but they will not do them: for with their mouth they show much love, but their heart goeth after their covetousness. And, lo, thou art unto them as a very lovely song of one that hath a pleasant voice, and can play well on an instrument: for they hear thy words, but they do them not" (Ezk.33:31-32).

**5** (13:27-28) **Judgment—Lost, Rejected by God**: the saved shall be separated from the lost, and the lost shall see them enter God's kingdom. (See DEEPER STUDY # 3, *Kingdom of God*—Mt.19:23-24.) Note several tragic facts.
1. The Master will not know the lost nor from where they came. They had lived in a different life and realm, a different world of thought and behavior than He had. They will have come from a different background entirely than the Master. Therefore, He will not know them nor from where they came.

> "For I say unto you, That except your righteousness shall exceed the righteousness of the scribes and Pharisees, ye shall in no case enter into the kingdom of heaven" (Mt.5:20).

"And said, Verily I say unto you, Except ye be converted, and become as little children, ye shall not enter into the kingdom of heaven" (Mt.18:3; cp. Mk.10:15).

"Know ye not that the unrighteous shall not inherit the kingdom of God? Be not deceived: neither fornicators, nor idolaters, nor adulterers, nor effeminate, nor abusers of themselves with mankind" (1 Cor.6:9; cp. Gal.5:19-21; cp. v.22-23).

"Now this I say, brethren, that flesh and blood cannot inherit the kingdom of God; neither doth corruption inherit incorruption" (1 Cor.15:50).

"And there shall in no wise enter into it any thing that defileth, neither whatsoever worketh abomination, or maketh a lie: but they which are written in the Lamb's book of life" (Rev.21:27).

2. The Master will have to reject the lost, because they have been "workers of iniquity" (cp. Ps.6:8).

"Many will say to me in that day, Lord, Lord, have we not prophesied in thy name? and in thy name have cast out devils? and in thy name done many wonderful works? And then will I profess unto them, I never knew you: depart from me, ye that work iniquity" (Mt.7:22-23).

"Let both grow together until the harvest: and in the time of harvest I will say to the reapers, Gather ye together first the tares, and bind them in bundles to burn them: but gather the wheat into my barn" (Mt.13:30).

"So shall it be at the end of the world: the angels shall come forth, and sever the wicked from among the just" (Mt.13:49).

"Then shall two be in the field; the one shall be taken, and the other left. Two women shall be grinding at the mill; the one shall be taken, and the other left" (Mt.24:40-41; cp. Lk.17:34-36).

"Afterward came also the other virgins, saying, Lord, Lord, open to us. But he answered and said, Verily I say unto you, I know you not" (Mt.25:11-12).

"And these shall go away into everlasting punishment: but the righteous into life eternal" (Mt.25:46).

"And beside all this, between us and you there is a great gulf fixed: so that they which would pass from hence to you cannot; neither can they pass to us, that would come from thence" (Lk.16:26).

3. The lost will weep and gnash their teeth (see DEEPER STUDY # 1,2—Lk.13:28). Note the reason: they will actually see their fathers, godly men from whose roots they came, enter God's kingdom; but they themselves shall be thrust out. Note: the lost are able to see believers in heaven, in God's kingdom (see note, pt.2—Lk.16:23-31).

**Thought 1.** How many will see godly parents, children, friends, neighbors, and acquaintences enter God's kingdom and find themselves shut out? There will be weeping and gnashing of teeth in that tragic day. Why? Simply because they (the lost) would not "strive" to enter salvation. They would not deny themselves (see note and DEEPER STUDY # 1—Lk.9:23).

---

**DEEPER STUDY # 1**
(13:28) **Weeping**: loud grief, mourning, groaning, wailing, floods and floods of tears.

---

**DEEPER STUDY # 2**
(13:28) **Gnashing** (brugmos): grinding; biting in hostility and bitterness and indignation; spitefully snapping the teeth; rage, fury, and despair because nothing can be done. A person's state is permanently determined (cp. Is.51:20).

---

[6] (13:29-30) **Gentile, Conversion—Salvation, Universal—Reward**: the saved will come from all nations and classes of society. This is a prediction of the great Gentile revival and conversion to take place. We are, of course, in the midst of this great revival today. Note three facts.

1. The saved will come from the four corners of the world. Salvation is not from one corner nor from one nation of the earth. It is of God, who rules over all the earth, and it is by faith, by *striving* to enter God's kingdom (see notes—Ro.4:11-12. See outline and DEEPER STUDY # 1—Ro.4:1-25.)

"Go ye therefore into the highways, and as many as ye shall find, bid to the marriage" (Mt.22:9).

"Go ye therefore, and teach all nations, baptizing them in the name of the Father, and of the Son, and of the Holy Ghost: teaching them to observe all things whatsoever I have commanded you: and, lo, I am with you alway, even unto the end of the world" (Mt.28:19-20).

"In the last day, that great day of the feast, Jesus stood and cried, saying, If any man thirst, let him come unto me, and drink" (Jn.7:37).

"For there is no difference between the Jew and the Greek: for the same Lord over all is rich unto all that call upon him" (Ro.10:12).

"And the Spirit and the bride say, Come. And let him that heareth say, Come. And let him that is athirst come. And whosoever will, let him take the water of life freely" (Rev.22:17).

"Look unto me, and be ye saved, all the ends of the earth: for I am God, and there is none else" (Is.45:22).

"Ho, every one that thirsteth, come ye to the waters, and he that hath no money; come ye, buy, and eat; yea, come, buy wine and milk without money and without price" (Is.55:1).

2. The saved will sit down in the Kingdom of God. The picture is that of the great marriage supper of the Messiah. (See outline and notes—Lk.14:15-24; Mt.22:1-14 for discussion.)

"To him that overcometh will I grant to sit with me in my throne, even as I also overcame, and am set down with my Father in his throne" (Rev.3:21).

3. The saved come from all classes, even from those who are classified as "last" by men. *Classes* do not matter to God. He is no respecter of persons. He saves any man who *strives* to enter salvation. Thus, many who are first (safe and secure) in the minds of themselves and others shall be last (lost), and many considered as last shall be first.

"Then Peter opened his mouth, and said, Of a truth I perceive that God is no respecter of persons: but in every nation he that feareth him, and worketh righteousness, is accepted with him" (Acts 10:34-35).

"But glory, honour, and peace, to every man that worketh good, to the Jew first, and also to the Gentile: for there is no respect of persons with God" (Ro.2:10-11).

"For there is no difference between the Jew and the Greek: for the same Lord over all is rich unto all that call upon him" (Ro.10:12).

"God accepteth no man's person" (Gal.2:6).

"He hath put down the mighty from their seats, and exalted them of low degree" (Lk.1:52).

"Woe unto you that are full! for ye shall hunger. Woe unto you that laugh now! for ye shall mourn and weep" (Lk.6:25).

| | B. The Tragic Rejection of Jesus, 13:31-35 (Mt.23:37-39; cp. Lk.19:41-44) | the day following: for it cannot be that a prophet perish out of Jerusalem. | c. His death must be diligently pursued in Jerusalem |
|---|---|---|---|
| **1 Some Pharisees warned Jesus about a plot to kill Him** | 31 The same day there came certain of the Pharisees, saying unto him, Get thee out, and depart hence: for Herod will kill thee. | 34 O Jerusalem, Jerusalem, which killest the prophets, and stonest them that are sent unto thee; how often would I have gathered thy children together, as a hen doth gather | **3 The rejection by the religionists & the people** a. They killed God's prophets & messengers |
| **2 The rejection by political leaders** a. His ministry will be perfected, that is, completed | 32 And he said unto them, Go ye, and tell that fox, Behold, I cast out devils, and I do cures to day and to morrow, and the third day I shall be perfected. | her brood under her wings, and ye would not! | b. They rejected the Messiah's salvation |
| b. His walk today, tomorrow, & the day after "must be" | 33 Nevertheless I must walk to day and to morrow, and | 35 Behold, your house is left unto you desolate: and verily I say unto you, Ye shall not see me, until the time come when ye shall say, Blessed is he that cometh in the name of the Lord. | **4 The warning to all those who reject Jesus** a. They will be forsaken by God b. There will be a day when Jesus will return & rule supremely |

# DIVISION VI

## THE SON OF MAN'S GREAT JOURNEY TO JERUSALEM (STAGE II): HIS TEACHING AND PUBLIC CONFLICT, 13:22-17:10

## B. The Tragic Rejection of Jesus, 13:31-35

(13:31-35) **Introduction**: Jesus Christ has always been rejected and opposed by men. He has been and still is opposed by the ordinary man, the religionist, and the ruler. There is not a single class of men who flocks to Christ, not in *true* belief. The opposition to Jesus ranges from ignoring Him to trying to stamp out His witness through His followers. Some people ridicule and abuse the followers of the Lord, while others persecute and kill them. This passage deals with persons who rejected Jesus Christ.

1. Some Pharisees warned Jesus about Herod's plot to kill Him (v.31).
2. The rejection by political leaders (v.31-33).
3. The rejection by the religionists and the people (v.34).
4. The warning to all those who reject Jesus (v.35).

(13:31-35) **Another Outline**. Some Unusual Things About Jesus.

1. Some Pharisees cared for Jesus (v.31).
2. Herod plotted against Jesus (v.31).
3. Jesus used sharp language: "That fox" (v.32).
4. Jesus knew the duration of His life (v.33).
5. Jesus knew the place of His death (v.33).
6. Jesus deliberately walked into the murderous trap set for Him (v.33).
7. Jesus lamented over those who rejected Him (v.34).
8. Jesus foretold a future day of Godly supremacy (v.35).

**1** (13:31) **Pharisees**: some Pharisees warned Jesus about Herod's plot. This verse shows that some Pharisees respected Jesus and were not hostile toward Him. Apparently, the vast majority did reject and stand against Him, but there were a few who *truly* loved and believed God. Therefore, they would never think of plotting to kill a man, much less to kill Jesus. When they looked at Jesus, they felt He was a good man—perhaps a prophet, maybe even the Messiah. We do know that some Pharisees did accept Jesus as the Messiah (Acts 6:7; 15:5; 18:8, 17). It was probably some of these who warned Jesus against Herod.

**2** (13:31-33) **Jesus Christ, Rejection**: the rejection by political leaders. Herod plotted to kill Jesus. This is a fact seldom considered, but the plot was real and dangerous. The Lord's words to Herod show this (v.32). Remember the scene. Jesus was in Herod's territory, Galilee, and thousands were following Him throughout the whole area. The whole country was aroused with the rumor of the Messiah. And when the subject of a Jewish Messiah arose, the authorities paid close attention. Usually when a man claimed to be a Messiah, an uprising of some sort took place. Herod was bound to be paying close attention and keeping watch over Jesus and His movements.

**Thought 1.** The Pharisees who warned Jesus bucked the tide. What they did was not popular among their peers, but they did what they knew to be the right thing. They *stood up for Christ*.

Another factor is known about Herod. He had reacted against the righteousness of John the Baptist and had him killed. Herod fell sway to what so many political leaders experience:

⇒ The fear of the people's *first* loyalty going to God instead of the state. (Government leaders often fail to see that Christ's kingdom is not of this earth and that God demands loyalty to the state. See notes—Lk.20:19-26; Mt.22:15-22; 17:24-27.)
⇒ The fear of the teaching of Christ: the responsibility of men to God.
⇒ The fear of *true* righteousness and justice and love. (Such virtues often run contrary to what government leaders really want.)

It is for these reasons that men try to stamp out the witness of Christ. Note that Jesus called Herod "that fox." The *fox* was a symbol of...

- a sly man
- a subtle man
- a base man
- a crafty man
- a treacherous man
- a destructive man
- a worthless man

Men will attack the witness of Christ by being...

- sly
- subtle
- base
- crafty
- treacherous
- destructive
- worthless

Jesus said three revealing things about the attack against His witness.

1. His ministry and witness will be *"perfected"* (teleioumai). The word means completed and finished. His ministry of delivering men spiritually and physically (casting out evil spirits and healing) will not be stopped by any man, even rulers such as Herod.

The words "the third day I shall be perfected" mean that His witness and delivering power will be completed and finished. There is a *definite time* for it, then His witness will stop. It will be no more. But until that day, nothing can stop His ministry and witness. This is, of course, a reference to Jesus' death and His resurrection on the third day. Note that His resurrection is the perfection of His ministry. It is by arising from the dead that death is conquered and man's salvation is completed.

> "But ye denied the Holy One and the Just, and desired a murderer to be granted unto you; and killed the Prince of life, whom God hath raised from the dead; whereof we are witnesses" (Acts 3:14-15).
>
> "And we are witnesses of all things which he did both in the land of the Jews, and in Jerusalem; whom they slew and hanged on a tree: him God raised up the third day, and showed him openly; not to all the people, but unto witnesses chosen before of God, even to us, who did eat and drink with him after he rose from the dead" (Acts 10:39-41).
>
> "And declared to be the Son of God with power, according to the spirit of holiness, by the resurrection from the dead" (Ro.1:4).
>
> "But now is Christ risen from the dead, and become the firstfruits of them that slept. For since by man came death, by man came also the resurrection of the dead. For as in Adam all die, even so in Christ shall all be made alive. But every man in his own order: Christ the firstfruits; afterward they that are Christ's at his coming" (1 Cor.15:20-23).
>
> "Knowing that he which raised up the Lord Jesus shall raise up us also by Jesus, and shall present us with you" (2 Cor.4:14).
>
> "But for us also, to whom it [righteousness] shall be imputed, if we believe on him that raised up Jesus our Lord from the dead; who was delivered for our offences, and was raised again for our justification" (Ro.4:24-25).
>
> "That if thou shalt confess with thy mouth the Lord Jesus, and shalt believe in thine heart that God hath raised him from the dead, thou shalt be saved" (Ro.10:9).
>
> "For if we believe that Jesus died and rose again, even so them also which sleep in Jesus will God bring with him" (1 Th.4:14).
>
> "Blessed be the God and Father of our Lord Jesus Christ, which according to his abundant mercy hath begotten us again unto a lively [living] hope by the resurrection of Jesus Christ from the dead, to an inheritance incorruptible, and undefiled, and that fadeth not away, reserved in heaven for you" (1 Pt.1:3-4).

2. His walk today and tomorrow and the day after *"must be."* The word "must" (dei) means necessary, being necessary by the very nature of the case. The witness of Jesus was a divine necessity overseen and ordained by God, and it could not be stopped. Jesus' walk and witness were directed by God.

> "Him, being delivered by the determinate counsel and foreknowledge of God, ye have taken, and by wicked hands have crucified and slain: whom God hath raised up, having loosed the pains of death: because it was not possible that he should be holden of it" (Acts 2:23-24. See DEEPER STUDY # 3, Determinate Counsel—Acts 2:23.)
>
> "And Paul, as his manner was, went in unto them, and three sabbath days reasoned with them out of the scriptures, opening and alleging, that Christ must needs have suffered, and risen again from the dead; and this Jesus, whom I preach unto you, is Christ" (Acts 17:2-3).

**Thought 1.** Note two critical questions.
1. How many of us know the *divine necessity* of God to witness?
2) How many of us walk *today and tomorrow* under the direction (divine necessity) of God?

3. His death *must be in Jerusalem.* Jerusalem was the capital of the nation, the symbolic center of the people's government, religion, and hopes. It was there that their temple stood and that their ruling body (the Sanhedrin) governed and judged the nation. If a prophet were to die, the decision for death was made in Jerusalem. Therefore, Jesus was saying this about His death:

⇒ When the people kill Him (God's Son), He must be killed in the place that symbolized all the hopes and activities of man (government and religion). Why? Because He was to die for all men everywhere: for all their corruptions in government and religion and for all their injustices in both. They did not understand the reason yet, but they soon would.

> **"Who his own self bare our sins in his own body on the tree, that we, being dead to sins, should live unto righteousness: by whose stripes ye were healed" (1 Pt.2:24).**
> **"For Christ also hath once suffered for sins, the just for the unjust, that he might bring us to God, being put to death in the flesh, but quickened by the Spirit" (1 Pt.3:18).**

**3** (13:34) **Jesus Christ, Rejection:** the rejection by the religionists and the people. When Jesus looked upon Jerusalem, He wept. He wept because he saw the city as the symbol of all formal religion and of all men who rejected His witness. (See note, pt.3—Lk.13:31-33.) It is because of this that this passage is known as Jesus' lament over Jerusalem (see outline and notes—Mt.23:37-39 for more discussion).

1. The religionists and people rejected, ridiculed, abused, persecuted, and killed God's prophets and messengers. Something needs to be remembered by people who abuse God's messengers. God holds His messengers very dear to His heart; and He is extremely protective of them. To ridicule and abuse one of His true followers is a very serious offense. Jerusalem and the people of Israel were guilty of many sins, but it was this sin that Jesus pointed out as the *most condemning*. In conjunction with this thought is the fact that it was primarily the *grumbling* of Israel in the wilderness against Moses and God that caused God to judge that generation so severely.

Scripture says:

> **"Who are thou that judgest another man's servant? To his own master [the Lord] he standeth or falleth. Yea, he shall be holden up: for God is able to make him stand" (Ro.14:4). (See note, Jews, Sins of—Mt.23:37 for a list of the prophets abused by the people.)**

2. The people rejected the Messiah's salvation.
   a. Note the enormous patience of God. Despite continued rejection and even murder of the godly, God kept after the people.
   b. Note the continued patience and love of Christ. "How often would I have gathered [you]." He would have saved the people time and again, for He desired to save them, not to condemn them.

> **"For the Son of man is come to seek and to save that which was lost" (Lk.19:10).**
> **"For God sent not his Son into the world to condemn the world; but that the world through him might be saved" (Jn.3:17).**
> **"The thief cometh not, but for to steal, and to kill, and to destroy: I am come that they might have life, and that they might have it more abundantly" (Jn.10:10).**
> **"And if any man hear my words, and believe not, I judge him not: for I came not to judge the world, but to save the world" (Jn.12:47).**
> **"Pilate therefore said unto him, Art thou a king then? Jesus answered, Thou sayest that I am a king. To this end was I born, and for this cause came I into the world, that I should bear witness unto the truth. Every one that is of the truth heareth my voice" (Jn.18:37).**
> **"This is a faithful saying, and worthy of all acceptation, that Christ Jesus came into the world to save sinners" (1 Tim.1:15).**

   c. Note the tragic words, "Ye would not." He would save them, but they would not be saved. The people had every privilege and opportunity imaginable. They heard Christ and learned of Him, yet they rejected Him. Their rejection was a *deliberate decision*.

> **"He came unto his own, and his own received him not" (Jn.1:11).**
> **"I am come in my Father's name, and ye receive me not: if another shall come in his own name, him ye will receive" (Jn.5:43).**
> **"He that rejecteth me, and receiveth not my words, hath one that judgeth him: the word that I have spoken, the same shall judge him in the last day" (Jn.12:48).**

**4** (13:35) **Jesus Christ, Exaltation—Judgment—Rejection:** the warning to all those who reject Christ is twofold.

1. They and their house are to be forsaken by God. The house may be a literal house, a nation, a religious body, a city, a local group—it does not matter—if they reject Christ time after time, reject the privileges they have, God will leave them all alone. They will be deserted, left without the presence of God. And a place without the presence of God is like a wilderness or a desert—deserted and left all alone to waste away. (See outlines and notes—Mt.23:38-39; Ro.1:24-32.)

> **"But the children of the kingdom shall be cast out into outer darkness: there shall be weeping and gnashing of teeth" (Mt.8:12).**
> **"Then said the king to the servants, Bind him hand and foot, and take him away, and cast him into outer darkness; there shall be weeping and gnashing of teeth" (Mt.22:13).**
> **"And cast ye the unprofitable servant into outer darkness: there shall be weeping and gnashing of teeth" (Mt.25:30).**

"If a man abide not in me, he is cast forth as a branch, and is withered; and men gather them, and cast them into the fire, and they are burned" (Jn.15:6).

"Then God turned, and gave them up to worship the host of heaven [cp. astrology]" (Acts 7:42).

"Wherefore God also gave them up to uncleanness through the lusts of their own hearts, to dishonour their own bodies between themselves: who changed the truth of God into a lie, and worshipped and served the creature more than the Creator, who is blessed for ever. Amen. For this cause God gave them up unto vile affections: for even their women did change the natural use into that which is against nature: and likewise also the men, leaving the natural use of the woman, burned in their lust one toward another; men with men working that which is unseemly, and receiving in themselves that recompence of their error which was meet. And even as they did not like to retain God in their knowledge, God gave them over to a reprobate mind, to do those things which are not convenient; being filled with all unrighteousness, fornication, wickedness, covetousness, maliciousness; full of envy, murder, debate, deceit, malignity; whisperers, backbiters, haters of God, despiteful, proud, boasters, inventors of evil things, disobedient to parents, without understanding, covenentbreakers, without natural affection, implacable, unmerciful: who knowing the judgment of God, that they which commit such things are worthy of death, not only do the same, but have pleasure in them that do them" (Ro.1:24-32).

"For I have told him that I will judge his house for ever for the iniquity which he knoweth; because his sons made themselves vile, and he restrained them not" (1 Sam.3:13).

"And be not ye like your fathers, and like your brethren, which trespassed against the LORD God of their fathers, who therefore gave them up to desolation, as ye see" (2 Chron.:7).

"But my people would not hearken to my voice; and Israel would none of me. So I gave them up unto their own hearts' lust: and they walked in their own counsels" (Ps.81:11-12).

"Then shall they call upon me, but I will not answer; they shall seek me early, but they shall not find me: for that they hated knowledge, and did not choose the fear of the LORD: they would none of my counsel: they despised all my reproof. Therefore shall they eat of the fruit of their own way, and be filled with their own devices. For the turning away of the simple shall slay them, and the prosperity of fools shall destroy them. But whoso hearkeneth unto me shall dwell safely, and shall be quiet from fear of evil" (Pr.1:28-33).

"Ephraim is joined to idols: let him alone" (Hos.4:17).

2.　There is to be a day when He will return and rule supremely. This is a definite reference to Jesus' return to earth (cp. Ps.118:26). Note: every one who rejected Jesus Christ will see Him return, but then it will be too late. He will be returning in judgment, to bow the knee of all those who rejected His supremacy.

"Wherefore God also hath highly exalted him, and given him a name which is above every name: that at the name of Jesus every knee should bow, of things in heaven, and things in earth, and things under the earth; and that every tongue should confess that Jesus Christ is Lord, to the glory of God the Father" (Ph.2:9-11).

"Teaching us that, denying ungodliness and worldly lusts, we should live soberly, righteously, and godly, in this present world; looking for that blessed hope, and the glorious appearing of the great God and our Saviour Jesus Christ" (Tit.2:12-13).

"So then after the Lord had spoken unto them, he was received up into heaven, and sat on the right hand of God" (Mk.16:19).

"Hereafter shall the Son of man sit on the right hand of the power of God" (Lk.22:69).

"He that cometh from above is above all: he that is of the earth is earthly, and speaketh of the earth: he that cometh from heaven is above all" (Jn.3:31).

"Ye call me Master and Lord: and ye say well; for so I am" (Jn.13:13).

"Therefore let all the house of Israel know assuredly, that God hath made that same Jesus, whom ye have crucified, both Lord and Christ" (Acts 2:36).

"Let us therefore follow after the things which make for peace, and things wherewith one may edify another" (Ro.14:19).

"For he must reign, till he hath put all enemies under his feet" (1 Cor.15:25).

"Which he wrought in Christ, when he raised him from the dead, and set him at his own right hand in the heavenly places" (Eph.1:20).

"Who is gone into heaven, and is on the right hand of God; angels and authorities and powers being made subject unto him" (1 Pt.3:22).

"And I beheld, and I heard the voice of many angels round about the throne and the beasts and the elders: and the number of them was ten thousand times ten thousand, and thousands of thousands; saying with a loud voice. Worthy is the Lamb that was slain to receive power, and riches, and wisdom, and strength, and honour, and glory, and blessing. And every creature which is in heaven, and on the earth, and under the earth, and such as are in the sea, and all that are in them, heard I saying, Blessing, and honour, and glory, and power, be unto him that sitteth upon the throne, and unto the Lamb for ever and ever. And the four beasts said, Amen. And the four and twenty elders fell down and worshipped him that liveth for ever and ever" (Rev.5:11-14).

| | CHAPTER 14 | 3 And Jesus answering spake unto the lawyers and Pharisees, saying Is it lawful to heal on the sabbath day? | 3 The religionists made religious form more important than healing men |
|---|---|---|---|
| | C. The Religionists & Their Error, 14:1-6 (cp. Mt.12:9-13) | 4 And they held their peace. And he took him, and healed him, and let him go; | 4 The religionists refused to confess the truth taught by Jesus |
| 1 The religionists watched Jesus critically | And it came to pass, as he went into the house of one of the chief Pharisees to eat bread on the sabbath day, that they watched him. | 5 And answered them, saying, Which of you shall have an ass or an ox fallen into a pit, and will not straightway pull him out on the sabbath day? | 5 The religionists failed to see the inconsistency of their belief & behavior |
| 2 The religionists overlooked what was really needful | 2 And, behold, there was a certain man before him which had the dropsy. | 6 And they could not answer him again to these things. | 6 Conclusion: The religionists were silenced |

# DIVISION VI

## THE SON OF MAN'S GREAT JOURNEY TO JERUSALEM (STAGE II): HIS TEACHING AND PUBLIC CONFLICT, 13:22-17:10

### C.    The Religionists and Their Error, 14:1-6

(14:1-6) **Introduction**: a chief Pharisee invited Jesus to a meal on the Sabbath. Some commentators think the invitation was deceptive, a plot to entrap Jesus into breaking the Sabbath law and to disqualify Him in the eyes of the people as a lawbreaker. However, we are not told this; and usually when the religionists were trying to entrap Jesus, the gospel writer said so. This much is known: Jesus was sitting at the meal surrounded by religionists, and He saw a unique opportunity to point out the errors of the religionists. The same errors are common to every generation of religionists.

1.    The religionists watched Jesus critically (v.1).
2.    The religionists overlooked what was really needful (v.2).
3.    The religionists made religious form more important than healing men (v.3).
4.    The religionists refused to confess the truth taught by Jesus (v.4).
5.    The religionists failed to see the inconsistency of their belief and behavior (v.5).
6.    The conclusion: the religionists were silenced (v.6).

**1** (14:1) **Religionists, Error—Denial**: the religionists "watched" Jesus with critical eyes. The word "watched" (parateroumenoi) means to observe with a sinister purpose: to look for something wrong, to search for the incorrect, to watch for error. It means to look with critical and cynical eyes. The religionists sat there watching Jesus, looking for some mistake, some wrong He might do.

> **Thought 1.** Men should be trying to learn of Christ, but too often they search for ways to deny Him. They seek for error in His Word and for wrong in His behavior in order to deny His claim upon their lives. They feel that if they can disprove His Word and Person, they are then free to live as they wish.

> "And they watched him, whether he would heal him on the sabbath day; that they might accuse him" (Mk.3:2).
> "And they watched him, and sent forth spies, which should feign themselves just men, that they might take hold of his words, that so they might deliver him unto the power and authority of the governor" (Lk.20:20).
> "The wicked watcheth the righteous, and seeketh to slay him" (Ps.37:32).
> "All that watch for iniquity are cut off" (Is.29:20).
> "For I heard the defaming of many, fear on every side. Report, say they, and we will report it. All my familiars watched for my halting, saying, Peradventure he will be enticed, and we shall prevail against him, and we shall take our revenge on him. But the LORD is with me as a mighty terrible one: therefore my persecutors shall stumble, and they shall not prevail: they shall be greatly ashamed; for they shall not prosper: their everlasting confusion shall never be forgotten. But, O LORD of hosts, that triest the righteous, and seest the reins of the heart, let me see thy vengeance on them: for unto thee have I opened my cause. Sing unto the LORD, praise ye the LORD: for he hath delivered the soul of the poor from the hand of the evildoers" (Jer.20:10-13).

**2** (14:2) **Religionists, Errors of—Need**: the religionists overlooked what was really needful. The man with dropsy was not an invited guest; he just appeared. He either came on his own, hoping for help from Jesus, or he had been planted there by the religionists to see if Jesus would break the Sabbath law. In either case, a real failure of the religionists is seen. They did not see the *need* of the man. He was a reject, an abnormal person who was *down and out* in society, a man who was in desperate need. However, the religionists failed to see his need and to reach out to help him. If they had planted him, then their failure was even more severe, for they were using him for their own purposes instead of reaching out to help him.

> **Thought 1.** There are two serious failures seen in this event.
> 1) The failure of going about one's business and not reaching out to help the needy. In this case, it was the religionists who were going about their religious business.

2)  The using of the needy for one's own purpose. The purpose may be to show that one is benevolent, or to ease one's conscience, or to add to one's statistics by bringing them into church. Whatever the case, the motive is impure and regretful.

**Thought 2.** This point forces several critical questions that should touch the heart of every person who has had a roof over his head and a hot meal in the last twelve hours.
1)  How many within the church ever *see* the needful? How many *overlook* the needful? How many of the needful, of those who are *down and out*, walk into the church and have others *sit away* from them? How many have come to church for help and been sent away empty?
2)  How many churches sit empty for days upon days and are not in use while so many walk the streets cold and freezing? Are they being overlooked deliberately? Or are the churches just ignoring and neglecting them?
3)  How many believers and churches have nice houses and buildings and plenty of food, yet their own communities or cities are full of needy people who are hungry and unclothed and unsheltered?
4)  How many ever think about a world full of teeming millions who are desperately needful? Who are suffering and lost, never having heard the gospel?

> "Is it not [your purpose] to deal thy bread to the hungry, and that thou bring the poor that are cast out to thy house? when thou seest the naked, that thou cover him; and that thou hide not thyself from thine own flesh?" (Is.58:7).
> "[Religionists] which say, Stand by thyself, come not near to me; for I am holier than thou. These are a smoke in my nose, a fire that burneth all the day" (Is.65:5).

**3** (14:3) **Religionists, Errors of—Ritual—Ceremony—Need**: the religionists made their religious form more important than *healing* men. Note: the man stood "before" Jesus, and Jesus was touched by the man's needs. Jesus knew it was the Sabbath, the day when the Jews allowed no work whatsoever (see DEEPER STUDY # 1, *Sabbath*—Lk.13:14). He saw a unique opportunity to teach a much needed truth: the truth that healing and helping a needy man is much more important than religious form and ceremony, than religious ritual and rules.

Note the question of Jesus: "Is it lawful to heal on the sabbath day?" The law said absolutely not. No work whatsoever, not even the healing of a man could be done on the Sabbath. (See DEEPER STUDY # 1—Lk.13:14; note and DEEPER STUDY # 1—Mt.12:10 for a clear understanding of this discussion.)

What Jesus did was show that the very purpose of God is the *healing of man*. God is seeking to save man, to reconcile man unto Himself. Therefore, the very object of true religion becomes the *healing of man*, not form and ceremony, not ritual and rules.

**Thought 1.** Religionists are always putting their *form and practices* of religion before meeting the healing needs of men. People can be desperately in need within a few miles of a church, yet the religionists...
*  will shelter their religious services for only a few hours each week (no matter the cost) while so many never have shelter.
*  will feed their own flocks three meals a day while so many eat less than one meal a day, and multitudes starve to death every day of the week.
*  will clothe their own flocks in the latest fashion while so many go cold, some even freezing to death.
*  will fill their own religious buildings with the finest facilities and warmth while so many are so desperately needful.
*  will preach and teach the man, exalting messages of self-help and social improvement, while so many are dying without ever hearing of God's personal salvation for the human soul.
*  will observe their worship and ritual, their rules and ceremonies without ever reaching out to help those who surround them and are in such desperate need.

> "But if ye had known what this meaneth, I will have mercy, and not sacrifice, ye would not have condemned the guiltless. For the Son of man is Lord even of the sabbath day" (Mt.12:7-8).
> "Thou shalt love thy neighbour as thyself" (Mt.22:39).
> "And he said unto them, Full well ye reject the commandment of God, that ye may keep your own tradition" (Mk.7:9).
> "Love worketh no ill to his neighbour: therefore love is the fulfilling of the law" (Ro.13:10).
> "They profess that they know God; but in works they deny him, being abominable, and disobedient, and unto every good work reprobate" (Tit.1:16).
> "Hereby perceive we the love of God, because he laid down his life for us: and we ought to lay down our lives for the brethren. But whoso hath this world's good, and seeth his brother have need, and shutteth up his bowels of compassion from him, how dwelleth the love of God in him?" (1 Jn.3:16-17).

**Thought 2.** A religionist will observe his religious worship and form without ever repenting of his sin and turning to God in complete surrender and self-denial. Too often he places his trust in his baptism, religious ceremony, church membership, worship attendance, rules, and regulations instead of in Christ Himself.

**4** (14:4) **Religionists, Errors of—Church, Problems**: the religionists refused to confess the truth taught by Jesus. Jesus had asked if it were lawful to heal a man on the Sabbath day. "They held their peace." They said nothing in reply to

Jesus' question. No matter how they answered the question, they would offend a large number of people and run the risk of losing their loyalty. Therefore, they said nothing.

⇒ They could have agreed with Christ and said "Yes, it is lawful to help a man before keeping one's religious rule." But if they had answered "Yes," other religionists would have charged them with disloyalty and with being loose with the law.

⇒ They could have said, "No, it is not lawful to help a man on the Sabbath, unless he is dying, no matter how serious his case." This answer would have caused honest and thoughtful people to charge them with being *hard and indifferent* to human suffering.

Therefore, the religionists said nothing. They sat there ignoring Jesus. It seemed ridiculous, for Jesus was there, and He had just asked a question of them. Yet they refused to answer lest they entrap themselves. After a long silence and some pause in activity, Jesus apparently took the man into His arms and healed him.

**Thought 1.** There are reasons why the religionist refuses to confess the truth taught by Jesus, reasons why religious form and the present order of things are put before man and the meeting of his real needs.
1) Too many of us slip into a routine, a way of doing things, and just continue in it because it is comfortable.
2) Too many of us fear change lest we lose some people and their support.
3) Too many of us fear the loss of position and security.
4) Too many of us fear failure, the weakening of what we already have, of losing the loyalty of our followers to our own religious position and practices.

**Thought 2.** Nothing should keep us from meeting man's needs, from putting him and his needs first, before all religious ritual and form.
1) It is the only way the heart of man can be reached and satisfied (Col.2:9-10; Jn.10:10).
2) It is the only way we can stop the loss of people who are being lost by the droves. As the saying goes: they come in the front door and leave just as quickly by the back door. Why? Their needs are not being met.

Something else needs to be asked of our hearts. Are that many really coming? Are people really accepting Christ by the droves? Why not? Did not the Lord say the fields are white unto *harvest*? Could it be we are so steeped in *religion* that we are putting religion before meeting the real needs of men?

**Thought 3.** Man's basic need is to know and worship God in a personal way. Yet we put worship and form and order and ritual before trying to reach out to man and actually meeting his need. Too often, we act as though...
⇒ man exists for religion, instead of religion's existing for man.
⇒ man exists for worship services, instead of worship services' existing for man.
⇒ man exists for maintaining the organization, instead of the organization's existing for man.
⇒ man exists for the rules and rituals instead of the rules and rituals' existing for man.

"Even as the Son of man came not to be ministered unto, but to minister, and to give his life a ransom for many" (Mt.20:28).

"I have showed you all things, how that so labouring ye ought to support the weak, and to remember the words of the Lord Jesus, how he said, It is more blessed to give than to receive" (Acts 20:35).

"We then that are strong ought to bear the infirmities of the weak, and not to please ourselves" (Ro.15:1).

"Bear ye one another's burdens, and so fulfil the law of Christ" (Gal.6:2).

**5** (14:5) **Religionists, Errors of—Needs:** the religionists failed to see the inconsistency in their belief and behavior. The illustration by Christ was powerful. A man would set aside his religious rule to help his oxen out of a ditch. His oxen or personal property was quickly put before his religious rule. Why then should a man who was in need not be put before religious rules?

**Thought 1.** The world reels with teeming millions' dying from starvation and disease, from the elements of nature and war, from spiritual ignorance and eternal death while religionists who profess belief in God...
• build newer buildings to be used for only a few hours a week.
• stress attendance to church services instead of stressing Christ.
• preach and teach physical well-being instead of spiritual salvation and peace of heart and mind.
• covet the latest styles in cars and clothing, hairdo's and furnishings.
• desire better houses and positions, more pay and security.

"Not every one that saith unto me, Lord, Lord, shall enter into the kingdom of heaven; but he that doeth the will of my Father which is in heaven" (Mt.7:21).

"He answered and said unto them, Well hath Esaias prophesied of you hypocrites, as it is written, This people honoureth me with their lips, but their heart is far from me" (Mk.7:6).

"And they come unto thee as the people cometh, and they sit before thee as my people, and they hear thy words, but they will not do them: for with their mouth they show much love, but their heart goeth after their covetousness" (Ezk.33:31).

**6** (14:6) **Religionists, Errors of—Guilt:** the conclusion is that the religionists were silenced. What can any of us say against what Christ has just taught if we are truly honest and thoughtful?

| | D. The Importance of Humility, 14:7-14 | go up higher: then shalt thou have worship in the presence of them that sit at meat with thee. | 2) Is rewarded with a higher position<br>3) Is honored by all |
|---|---|---|---|
| **1 Jesus attended a banquet**<br>a. He noticed some choosing the chief seats<br>b. He shared a parable | 7 And he put forth a parable to those which were bidden, when he marked how they chose out the chief rooms; saying unto them, | 11 For whosoever exalteth himself shall be abased; and he that humbleth himself shall be exalted. | **3 The parable's point**<br>a. Self-exaltation abases<br>b. Humility exalts[DS1] |
| **2 The parable: The ambitious guest**<br>a. The first man: Seeks the place of honor<br>1) Is displaced<br>2) Finds all other seats already taken<br>3) Has to take the lowest seat<br>4) Is embarrassed<br>b. The second man: Takes the lowest place of honor<br>1) Is acknowledged | 8 When thou art bidden of any man to a wedding, sit not down in the highest room; lest a more honourable man than thou be bidden of him;<br>9 And he that bade thee and him come and say to thee, Give this man place; and thou begin with shame to take the lowest room.<br>10 But when thou art bidden, go and sit down in the lowest room; that when he that bade thee cometh, he may say unto thee, Friend, | 12 Then said he also to him that bade him, When thou makest a dinner or a supper, call not thy friends, nor thy brethren, neither thy kinsmen, nor thy rich neighbours; lest they also bid thee again, and a recompence be made thee.<br>13 But when thou makest a feast, call the poor, the maimed, the lame, the blind:<br>14 And thou shalt be blessed; for they cannot recompense thee: for thou shalt be recompensed at the resurrection of the just. | **4 The demonstration of humility**<br>a. Humility is not serving those who can repay<br><br><br><br>b. Humility is serving those who are needy & cannot repay<br>c. Humility shall be rewarded |

# DIVISION VI

## THE SON OF MAN'S GREAT JOURNEY TO JERUSALEM (STAGE II): HIS TEACHING AND PUBLIC CONFLICT, 13:22-17:10

### D.    The Importance of Humility, 14:7-14

(14:7-14) **Introduction**: the importance of humility is the thrust of this passage.
1.    Jesus attended a banquet (v.7).
2.    The parable: the ambitious guest (v.8-10).
3.    The parable's point (v.11).
4.    The demonstration of humility (v.12-14).

**1** (14:7) **Jesus Christ, Social Life**: Jesus was still at the banquet of the chief Pharisee (v.1). It was time for everyone to be seated for the meal, and Jesus noticed how some guests scrambled for the chief seats. Today we usually place the names of the most honored guests at the plates. However, in Jesus' day the highest seat of honor was on the right of the host and the next highest on his left, and so the ranking continued alternating back and forth until the lowest ranked person sat the farthest away from the host. Very simply, the closer one sat to the host, the higher the honor. When Jesus saw how some quickly moved up close to the host, He saw an opportunity to teach the great importance of humility. The phrase "the chief rooms" (tas protoklisias) means the chief seats.

**2** (14:8-10) **Ambition—Self-Seeking—Parable**: the parable is that of the ambitious guest. Jesus spoke directly to the man of ambition, the man who wants more recognition, honor, and position. Jesus said something that is very practical and should be clearly seen even by the ambitious man: the ambitious man should not sit in a seat that is higher than his position or capability lest a man more honorable enters and replaces him. If the ambitious man takes a higher seat, four things are likely to happen.
1.    He will be displaced.
2.    He will then find all the other seats taken.
3.    He will have to take a lower seat.
4.    He will be embarrassed.

What the ambitious man should take is the lowest seat and place of honor. Three things happen when he does.
1.    His presence is acknowledged by the host.
2.    He is rewarded, moved up to a higher seat and position.
3.    He is recognized and honored by all, no matter how high or how far from the top the position is.
The point of the parable is twofold: self-exaltation abases and humility exalts.

**3** (14:11) **Self-Exaltation—Pride—Arrogance—Self-Seeking—Ambition**: the parable's point is clearly contrary to the ambitions and behavior of most men. The man who exalts himself shall be abased. It is not just a possibility; he *will* be abased. Jesus said so.
1.    The man who exalts himself does at least four things.

296

a. He debases others. He has to treat others as less and lower than himself in order to exalt himself.
⇒ He degrades others: downplaying their ability or person, position or performance, appearance or acceptance.
⇒ He demeans others: trying to wound and injure, shame and humiliate.
⇒ He debases others: trying to tear down, hurt, lower, and damage.

b. He acts self-sufficient. He may not be self-sufficient, but if he is going to exalt himself, he is forced to act...
- in control
- in charge
- very capable
- independent
- above others

Note: the great problem with being self-sufficient is that a person feels he does not even need God in his life. He may be religious, but he does not live a changed life that demonstrates a true trust and dependency upon God for salvation and life.

c. He corrupts morality and justice. The man who exalts himself governs all things by whatever moves him ahead and gives him the greatest position and recognition. True morality and justice may be thought about, but they are set aside if needed. The ambitious man who exalts himself often has to...
- lie
- steal
- cheat
- abuse
- ridicule
- shame
- not give due recognition
- hold others back or down
- hurt, damage or kill

d. He lives a life of struggle. He always feels torn within to maneuver and outdo others in order to get the highest seat or recognition possible. He seldom knows peace within, no matter the appearance given.

2. The man who exalts himself is to be abased. As mentioned above, it is not just a possibility; it is a sure thing. He shall be abased. The likelihood is that he will be abased in this life, but if not, then he will be abased by God in eternity (cp. v.14). Four things will happen to him.

a. He will be displaced. He will be removed from his seat of position and recognition. It probably will happen in this world, for people can be fooled and misused for only so long. Eventually they catch on and react. More tragically, the self-exalting (prideful) man will be displaced by God. He will lose his place in heaven and be put out of heaven.

b. He will find all other seats and positions already taken. There will be no room for him. This often happens in business when a man is demoted or released. A suitable position cannot be found to match his ability and true worth. The same will happen in heaven. If a man has exalted himself, he will find all available seats taken. His name will not be written by any seat in heaven. He will move farther and farther down the line, finding no empty seat.

c. He will have to take the lowest seat. Note: this man was invited to the feast and he responded. He walked in the midst of all the guests. But he had a problem. He exalted himself, so he had to be moved down to the lowest seat. The lowest seat was the place of the least recognition and honor, doomed to be the seat for all hypocrites (cp. Mt.25:41. See note, pt.3—Lk.12:41-48.)

d. He will be embarrassed and shamed by being debased.

"Be of the same mind one toward another. Mind not high things, but condescend to men of low estate. Be not wise in your own conceits" (Ro.12:16).

"And if any man think that he knoweth any thing, he knoweth nothing yet as he ought to know" (1 Cor.8:2).

"For if a man think himself to be something, when he is nothing, he deceiveth himself" (Gal.6:3).

"For all that is in the world, the lust of the flesh, and the lust of the eyes, and the pride of life, is not of the Father, but is of the world" (1 Jn.2:16).

"Thine eyes are upon the haughty, that thou mayest bring them down" (2 Sam.22:28).

"The wicked in his pride doth persecute the poor: let them be taken in the devices that they have imagined" (Ps.10:2).

"When pride cometh, then cometh shame: but with the lowly is wisdom" (Pr.11:2).

"Only by pride cometh contention: but with the well advised is wisdom" (Pr.13:10).

"Pride goeth before destruction, and a haughty spirit before a fall" (Pr.16:18).

"A high look, and a proud heart, and the plowing of the wicked, is sin" (Pr.21:4).

"Seest thou a man wise in his own conceit? There is more hope of a fool than of him" (Pr.26:12).

"He that is of a proud heart stirreth up strife: but he that putteth his trust in the LORD shall be made fat" (Pr.28:25).

"Woe unto them that are wise in their own eyes, and prudent in their own sight!" (Is.5:21).

"The earth mourneth and fadeth away, the world languisheth and fadeth away, the haughty people of the earth do languish" (Is.24:4).

"Though thou exalt thyself as the eagle, and though thou set thy nest among the stars, thence will I bring thee down, saith the LORD" (Obad.4).

"Behold, his soul which is lifted up is not upright in him" (Hab.2:4).

"In that day shalt thou not be ashamed for all thy doings, wherein thou hast transgressed against me: for then I will take away out of the midst of thee them that rejoice in thy pride, and thou shalt no more be haughty because of my holy mountain" (Zeph.3:11).

**DEEPER STUDY # 1**

(14:11) **Humility—Exaltation:** the man who humbles himself shall be exalted. Exaltation is a certainty, and a man can ask for nothing more than to be assured that he will be exalted.

Humility (tareinophrosune) means lowliness of mind. It is a word that was coined by Christianity. Before Christ, a humble man was looked upon as a coward: a cringing, unappealing, effeminate type of person. However after Christ, humility was elevated to the most praise-worthy level. When men looked at Christ, they saw the strength of humility through the influence of One Who was perfect in meekness and lowliness of heart. Humility means five things.

1. To *walk* as a servant to others, always ready and willing to help (cp. Ph.2:8).

2. To *behave* in an unassuming manner, not being showy or pretentious, prideful or haughty, arrogant or assertive.

> "Whosoever therefore shall humble himself as this little child, the same is greatest in the kingdom of heaven" (Mt.18:4).
> "For I say, through the grace given unto me, to every man that is among you, not to think of himself more highly than he ought to think; but to think soberly, according as God hath dealt to every man the measure of faith" (Ro.12:3).

3. To *assume* a spirit of lowliness and submission, of oneness and identification with others, not showing conceit or superiority or being boastful.

> "But Jesus called them unto him, and said, Ye know that the princes of the Gentiles exercise dominion over them, and they that are great exercise authority upon them. But it shall not be so among you: but whosoever will be great among you, let him be your minister; and whosoever will be chief among you, let him be your servant: even as the Son of man came not to be ministered unto, but to minister, and to give his life a ransom for many" (Mt.20:25-28).
> "And he said unto them, The kings of the Gentiles exercise lordship over them; and they that exercise authority upon them are called benefactors. But ye shall not be so: but he that is greatest among you, let him be as the younger; and he that is chief, as he that doth serve" (Lk.22:25-26).
> "Serving the Lord with all humility of mind, and with many tears, and temptations, which befell me by the lying in wait of the Jews" (Acts 20:19).
> "Likewise, ye younger, submit yourselves unto the elder. Yea, all of you be subject one to another, and be clothed with humility: for God resisteth the proud, and giveth grace to the humble. Humble yourselves therefore under the mighty hand of God, that he may exalt you in due time" (1 Pt.5:5-6).

4. To *possess* a sense of lowliness and unworthiness, to have a modest opinion of oneself, knowing that others are just as significant and valuable.

> "Let nothing be done through strife or vainglory; but in lowliness of mind let each esteem others better than themselves. Look not every man on his own things, but every man also on the things of others" (Ph.2:3-4).
> "I therefore, the prisoner of the Lord, beseech you that ye walk worthy of the vocation wherewith ye are called, with all lowliness and meekness, with longsuffering, forbearing one another in love" (Eph.4:1-2).
> "Put on therefore, as the elect of God, holy and beloved, bowels of mercies, kindness, humbleness of mind, meekness, longsuffering" (Col.3:12).

5. To *come* to God on a regular basis and confess one's spiritual need and unworthiness.

> "Humble yourselves in the sight of the Lord, and he shall lift you up" (Jas.4:10).

Humility is a problem to most men. Why? Because the world looks upon humility as a sign of weakness and cowardice. They see a humble person as a person who cowers and cringes before others, as a person who the world takes and...
- uses and misuses.
- overlooks and bypasses.
- ignores and neglects.
- enslaves and abuses.
- shuns and despises.

Men fear humility. They fear humility will make them the object of contempt and abuse, causing them to be passed over. However, the very opposite is true. Humility leads a person...
- to Christ and to conversion.
- to realize his full potential.
- to evaluate himself and to work at improving himself.
- to become all that he can and should be.
- to develop more healthy relationships with people.
- to a stronger and more productive community and world.

When men consider others (humble themselves), they win friends and influence people. They build and strengthen everyone and everything involved.

The results of humility are threefold.

1. The humble man will be acknowledged. Both men and God will notice his spirit and energy in serving others, no matter how lowly his position. His putting others first, whether person, project, work or company, will not go unnoticed for long. His dedication to serving and working and helping others will be seen and acknowledged.

2. The humble man will be rewarded. He will be approached; and his presence, energy, and effort will be desired and promoted and placed where he can serve to the maximum.

3. The humble man will be honored by all. He will have lived to serve and help others; therefore, when he is exalted, all will rejoice with him.

> "By humility and the fear of the LORD are riches, and honor, and life" (Pr.22:4).
> "A man's pride shall bring him low: but honor shall uphold the humble in spirit" (Pr.29:23).
> "For thus saith the high and lofty One that inhabiteth eternity, whose name is Holy; I dwell in the high and holy place, with him also that is of a contrite and humble spirit, to revive the spirit of the humble, and to revive the heart of the contrite ones" (Is.57:15).
> "Whosoever therefore shall humble himself as this little child, the same is greatest in the kingdom of heaven" (Mt.18:4).
> "I tell you, this man went down to his house justified rather than the other: for every one that exalteth himself shall be abased; and he that humbleth himself shall be exalted" (Lk.18:14).

Humility comes from three things. (These ideas come from William Barclay in his *Letters to the Galatians and Ephesians,* Eph.4:1-3.)

a. Humility comes from measuring ourselves against the Lord Jesus. When a man measures himself against Christ, he measures himself against Perfection, for Christ was without sin (Jn.8:46; 2 Cor.5:21; Heb.4:15; 7:26; 1 Pt.1:19; 2:22). When measured against other men, a man may be morally good, but God demands that every man measure himself against the perfection of Christ. Against such a One and such a demand, there is no room for pride. (See DEEPER STUDY # 3—Mt.8:20.)

b. Humility comes from a continued consciousness of God's presence. No man has anything, not in reality: not air, not food, not clothing—nothing. All we have and all we know deteriorates and decays, even our own bodies. And all that crosses our path is held but for a short time, for the end of all things comes ever so quickly. We are completely dependent upon God who has given all and controls all and, in the end, shall take all. Before Him we can only walk humbly.

c. Humility comes from knowing ourselves, just who we really are. It comes from an honest appraisal of ourselves. It takes courage to look at ourselves and it takes honesty to see ourselves as we really are: basically self-centered, a bundle of self-admiration and self-love. We tend to dramatize ourselves. We tend to see ourselves through rose-colored glasses. We see ourselves...

- at the center of action.
- as the hero of some spectacular rescue.
- as the great politician marching to victory.
- as the reknown sportsman saving the game in the last second or bagging a record catch.
- as the beauty queen dazzling the crowds.
- as the laborer of brilliance.
- as Prince Charming or Cinderella sweeping others off their feet.

We are always at the center of the picture. Humility begins to come when we honestly face ourselves and admit our self-centeredness. Self-centeredness weakens and limits and destroys relationships and achievements. Humility reaches its height when we lose our lives in the cause of Christ and welfare of others.

**4** (14:12-14) **Humility—Ministry—Service—Needy, The**: the demonstration of humility was clearly stated by Jesus. He addressed His words to the chief Pharisee, the most proud and ambitious man present. What He said was forceful; it served as a strong warning, for no man can enter the Kingdom of Heaven without true humility.

1. Humility is not serving or centering one's life around those who can repay. Jesus used the banquet as an illustration. If the host courts the presence of those who can repay him for his favor, then the host has received his reward. He will receive their favors, but that is all he will receive. He will not have God's favor; he will be left with only human favor.

Note: Jesus was not downgrading normal social life and Christian fellowship. He was saying that the host had not shown humility and lowliness of mind, the giving of himself and his goods to those who really needed his gifts and services. The host served only those who could repay by adding to his welfare. He had not humbled himself to help anyone who really needed help.

2. Humility is serving those who are needy and cannot repay. Now, if a man serves the poor, the maimed, the lame, the blind—that man demonstrates humility. His motive is pure; he has a lowly spirit, a spirit willing to get down with a needy person and help him. By "*host*" Jesus means any man who is able to help others because he has the health, position, or finances. When he gives himself and his goods to help those who need help, he is demonstrating humility. Man lives in a world full of desperate needs; therefore, a man should live being kind and giving generously. But note the crucial point: he should not be giving to receive back, but rather to help and to encourage and to build others up.

> "Jesus said unto him, If thou wilt be perfect, go and sell that thou hast, and give to the poor, and thou shalt have treasure in heaven: and come and follow me" (Mt.19:21).

"Give, and it shall be given unto you; good measure, pressed down, and shaken together, and running over, shall men give into your bosom. For with the same measure that ye mete withal it shall be measured to you again" (Lk.6:38).

"He that hath pity upon the poor lendeth unto the LORD; and that which he hath given will he pay him again" (Pr.19:17).

"Blessed is he that considereth the poor: the LORD will deliver him in time of trouble" (Ps.41:1).

"He that despiseth his neighbor sinneth: but he that hath mercy on the poor, happy is he" (Pr.14:21).

"He that giveth unto the poor shall not lack: but he that hideth his eyes shall have many a curse" (Pr.28:27).

"And if thou draw out thy soul to the hungry, and satisfy the afflicted soul; then shall thy light rise in obscurity, and thy darkness be as the noonday" (Is.58:10).

3.  Humility shall be rewarded. Note when: at the resurrection of the just.
    a.  A humble person is a *just* and righteous person, a person who does what is right.
    b.  A humble person shall be raised from the dead to live eternally with all the other just persons and, of course, with God Himself who is the very embodiment of righteousness. (See note, pts.2, 3—Lk.14:11.)

> "Verily, verily, I say unto you, He that heareth my word, and believeth on him that sent me, hath everlasting life, and shall not come into condemnation; but is passed from death unto life. Verily, verily, I say unto you, The hour is coming, and now is, when the dead shall hear the voice of the son of God: and they that hear shall live" (Mt.5:24-25).
>
> "And this is the will of him that sent me, that every one which seeth the Son, and believeth on him, may have everlasting life: and I will raise him up at the last day" (Jn.6:40).
>
> "Jesus said unto her, I am the resurrection, and the life: he that believeth in me, though he were dead, yet shall he live" (Jn.11:25).
>
> "And [I, Paul] have hope toward God, which they themselves also allow, that there shall be a resurrection of the dead, both of the just and unjust" (Acts 24:15).
>
> "Knowing that he which raised up the Lord Jesus shall raise up us also by Jesus, and shall present us with you" (2 Cor.4:14).
>
> "If by any means I [Paul] might attain unto the resurrection of the dead" (Ph.3:11).
>
> "For the Lord himself shall descend from heaven with a shout, with the voice of the archangel, and with the trump of God: and the dead in Christ shall rise first: then we which are alive and remain shall be caught up together with them in the clouds, to meet the Lord in the air: and so shall we ever be with the Lord. Wherefore comfort one another with these words" (1 Th.4:16-18).
>
> "Teaching us that, denying ungodliness and worldly lusts, we should live soberly, righteously, and godly, in this present world; looking for that blessed hope, and the glorious appearing of the great God and our Saviour Jesus Christ" (Tit.2:12-13).

| | E. The Parable of the Great Supper: The Invitation and Man's Excuses, 14:15-24 (cp. Mt.22:1-14) | bought five yoke of oxen, and I go to prove them: I pray thee have me excused.<br>20 And another said, I have married a wife, and therefore I cannot come. | b. Excuse 2: Too wrapped up in new purchases<br><br>c. Excuse 3: Too wrapped up with family |
|---|---|---|---|
| 1 Jesus was still at the feast of the chief Pharisee (v.1)<br>a. A Pharisee's joy<br>b. Jesus' parable: A great supper<br><br>2 The invitation to "God's Great Supper" goes out to many guests | 15 And when one of them that sat at meat with him heard these things, he said unto him, Blessed is he that shall eat bread in the kingdom of God.<br>16 Then said he unto him, A certain man made a great supper, and bade many:<br>17 And sent his servant at supper time to say to them that were bidden, Come; for all things are now ready. | 21 So that servant came, and showed his lord these things. Then the master of the house being angry said to his servant, Go out quickly into the streets and lanes of the city, and bring in hither the poor, and the maimed, and the halt, and the blind.<br>22 And the servant said, Lord, it is done as thou hast commanded, and yet there is room. | 4 The Lord becomes angry at the busy guests who reject<br>5 The Lord sends invitations to outsiders—quickly<br><br>a. He has a difficult time filling the kingdom even then |
| 3 The invited guests make excuses<br>a. Excuse 1: Too involved in business | 18 And they all with one consent began to make excuse. The first said unto him, I have bought a piece of ground, and I must needs go and see it: I pray thee have me excused.<br>19 And another said, I have | 23 And the Lord said unto the servant, Go out into the highways and hedges, and compel them to come in, that my house may be filled.<br>24 For I say unto you, That none of those men which were bidden shall taste of my supper. | b. He demands a double, strenuous effort<br><br>6 The guests who rejected are excluded |

# DIVISION VI

## THE SON OF MAN'S GREAT JOURNEY TO JERUSALEM (STAGE II): HIS TEACHING AND PUBLIC CONFLICT, 13:22-17:10

### E. The Parable of the Great Supper: The Invitation and Man's Excuses, 14:15-24

(14:15-24) **Introduction**: this passage gives a clear picture of the Lord's great invitation to mankind and the flimsy excuses men give for not accepting His invitation. The scene is known as *The Great Supper of God*. The Great Marriage Feast of Matthew should be compared with this passage. There are some similarities, but the differences are many (see outline and note—Mt.22:1-14).

1. Jesus was still at the feast of the chief Pharisee (v.15).
2. The invitation to God's Great Supper went out to many guests (v.16-17).
3. The invited guests make excuses (v.18-20).
4. The Lord becomes angry at the guests who reject (v.21).
5. The Lord sends invitations to outsiders—"quickly" (v.21-23).
6. The guests who rejected are excluded (v.24).

**1** (14:15) **Great Supper of God**: Jesus was still at the feast of the chief Pharisee (v.1). When Jesus mentioned the resurrection (v.14), all of a sudden one of the Pharisees broke forth in joyful praise: "Blessed is he that shall eat bread in the kingdom of God" (v.15). What the Pharisee meant was the Jewish picture of the great Messianic Feast. The Feast was to be given by God for His people when He set up His kingdom on earth.

The Pharisee saw himself and the Jewish nation only as being invited to God's Great Supper. No outsider, no Gentile or serious sinner, would ever be an invited guest. Jesus knew what was in the mind of the Pharisee, so He sets out to correct his misconception of the Great Supper of God. Note three things.

1. *The Great Supper of God* will be held. The Pharisee was right in his picture of a great gathering and feast in "the resurrection" (v.14).
2. *The Great Supper of God* will include guests from the highways and hedges of the world, not just Jews. The Pharisee was wrong about this. It was this that Jesus set out to correct.
3. The parable can apply to Israel in verses 16-22 and to the Gentiles in verses 23-24. However, the parable has a strong personal message to all men everywhere: men are saved by responding to God's invitation, and they are lost by making excuses. Note something else of significance: God is planning a *Great Supper* where all who accept His invitation will be gathered together. Once the guest list is filled, time will be no more; all things will end. The doors to His banquet hall will be closed forever.

**2** (14:16-17) **Invitation—Decision**: the invitation to *God's Great Supper* goes out to many. Note four things.

1. "All things are now ready" (v.17). Christ has purchased salvation for every man through His death and resurrection. The provisions for God's Great Supper have now been secured and are waiting for the guests to accept.

2.    The invitation is to "many." The many are those who hear the gospel...
- in church
- over television or radio
- from a preacher
- by reading
- from a witnessing believer
- through conscience

The many are all those who hear, see, or read the gospel and who sense a personal invitation to join God at His great feast.

3.    The invitation is given more than once; it comes in the future as well as in the past. This is seen in v.16-17. The invitation was sent out to inform people of the upcoming Supper. Then it was followed up as soon as "all things were ready." (See note—Mt.22:3-7 for application to Israel.)

4.    The invitation is accepted by all. Note this, for this is a most critical point. The servant was sent "to them that were bidden [invited before]." They had already accepted; now they were being told to come, for the day of the Supper had arrived. The point is this: these claim to have accepted God's invitation, but they have only professed. They are not preparing to attend, not cleaning up or getting dressed (Tit.3:5; 2 Cor.5:21).

> **"For many are called, but few are chosen" (Mt.22:14).**
>
> **"He answered and said unto them, Well hath Esaias prophesied of you hypocrites, as it is written, This people honoureth me with their lips, but their heart is far from me" (Mk.7:6).**
>
> **"They profess that they know God; but in works they deny him, being abominable, and disobedient, and unto every good work reprobate" (Tit.1:16).**
>
> **"He that believeth on him is not condemned: but he that believeth not is condemned already, because he hath not believed in the name of the only begotten Son of God" (Jn.3:18).**

**3**    (14:18-20) **Excuses—Decision**: the invited guests make excuses.

1.    Excuse 1: one man said he was too involved in business. The man had bought a piece of ground and needed to look after it. A man can become too involved in any business, not just the business of developing property and farming. A person's business, profession, and affairs must not be allowed to consume his life. God is to be the center of a person's life, and God is to be the one around whom all else revolves.

> **"For what is man profited, if he shall gain the whole world, and lose his own soul? or what shall a man give in exchange for his soul? (Mt.16:26).**
>
> **"And that which fell among thorns are they, which, when they have heard, go forth, and are choked with cares and riches and pleasures of this life, and bring forth fruit with patience" (Lk.8:14).**
>
> **"And seek not ye what ye shall eat, or what ye shall drink, neither be ye of doubtful mind" (Lk.12:29).**
>
> **"No man that warreth entangleth himself with the affairs of this life; that he may please him who hath chosen him to be a soldier" (2 Tim.2:4).**
>
> **"Surely every man walketh in a vain show: surely they are disquieted in vain: he heapeth up riches, and knoweth not who shall gather them" (Ps.39:6).**
>
> **"Therefore I went about to cause my heart to despair of all the labor which I took under the sun" (Eccl.2:20).**

2.    Excuse 2: another man said that he was too wrapped up in new purchases. The oxen had just been purchased. They were a new possession, and the owner wanted to *try them out*. So it is with new purchases such as houses, lands, cars, bikes, records, books, radios, televisions, and a host of other material things. However, this is the point: things should never keep us from God.

> **"And take heed to yourselves, lest at any time your hearts be overcharged with surfeiting, and drunkenness, and cares of this life, and so that day come upon you unawares" (Lk.21:34).**
>
> **"And be not conformed to this world: but be ye transformed by the renewing of your mind, that ye may prove what is that good, and acceptable, and perfect, will of God" (Ro.12:2).**
>
> **"Teaching us that, denying ungodliness and worldly lusts, we should live soberly, righteously, and godly, in this present world" (Tit.2:12).**
>
> **"Ye adulterers and adulteresses, know ye not that the friendship of the world is enmity with God? whosoever therefore will be a friend of the world is the enemy of God" (Jas.4:4).**
>
> **"Love not the world, neither the things that are in the world. If any man love the world, the love of the Father is not in him. For all that is in the world, the lust of the flesh, and the lust of the eyes, and the pride of life, is not of the Father, but is of the world" (1 Jn.2:15-16).**
>
> **"Thou sayest, I am rich, and increased with goods, and have need of nothing; and knowest not that thou art wretched, and miserable, and poor, and blind, and naked" (Rev.3:17).**
>
> **"...thou art waxen fat, thou art grown thick, thou art covered with fatness; then he forsook God which made him, and lightly esteemed the Rock of his salvation" (Dt.32:15).**
>
> **"They are enclosed in their own fat: with their mouth they speak proudly" (Ps.17:10).**
>
> **"Therefore hear now this, thou that art given to pleasures, that dwellest carelessly, that sayest in thine heart, I am, and none else beside me" (Is.47:8).**
>
> **"They are waxen fat, they shine: yea, they overpass the deeds of the wicked: they judge not the cause, the cause of the fatherless, yet they prosper; and the right of the needy do they not judge" (Jer.5:28).**

3. Excuse 3: still another man said that he was too wrapped up with his family. This man had just been married, and it is true that marriage is ordained by God. However, it is not to be put before God. The man should have prepared for *The Great Feast* before marrying. Nothing—family, friends, or important social functions—should be put before attending *The Great Supper of God*.

> "So likewise, whosoever he be of you that forsaketh not all that he hath [friends, family], he cannot be my disciple" (Lk.14:33).
> "So when they had dined, Jesus saith to Simon Peter, Simon, son of Jonas, lovest thou me more than these? He saith unto him, Yea Lord; thou knowest that I love thee. He saith unto him, Feed my lambs. He saith to him again the second time, Simon, son of Jonas, lovest thou me? He saith unto him, Yea Lord; thou knowest that I love thee. He saith unto him, Feed my sheep. He saith to him again the third time, Simon, son of Jonas, lovest thou me? Peter was grieved because he said unto him the third time, Lovest thou me? And he said unto him, Lord, thou knowest all things; thou knowest that I love thee. He saith unto him, Feed my sheep" (Jn.21:15-17).
> "And now, Israel, what doth the LORD thy God require of thee, but to fear the LORD thy God, to walk in all his ways, and to love him, and to serve the LORD thy God with all thy heart and with all thy soul" (Dt.10:12).
> "Now therefore fear the LORD, and serve him in sincerity and in truth" (Josh.24:14).

**4** (14:21) **Jesus Christ, Rejected—Response**: the Lord becomes angry at the *busy* guests who make excuses. Note three things.
1. The guests who rejected showed both unconcern and contempt for the invitation.
   a. They showed unconcern over the *great cost* to God in preparing and providing "all things" (Christ's death, v.17). The great cost and price He paid was of little, if any, concern to them.
   b. They showed contempt in that they deceived the Lord. They accepted the first invitation, but they never began to clean themselves nor to dress properly for the feast.
2. The Lord had reason to be angry. The guests who had rejected His invitation had deceived and shown the utmost contempt, giving no thought to the great price He had paid for them.
3. Note a critical fact. Not a single one of the guests who rejected His invitation were allowed to *taste of His supper* (v.24).

> "For this ye know, that no whoremonger, nor unclean person, nor covetous man, who is an idolater, hath any inheritance in the kingdom of Christ and of God. Let no man deceive you with vain words: for because of these things cometh the wrath of God upon the children of disobedience" (Eph.5:5-6).
> "For the wrath of God is revealed from heaven against all ungodliness and unrighteousness of men, who hold the truth in unrighteousness" (Ro.1:18).
> "But unto them that are contentious, and do not obey the truth, but obey unrighteousness, indignation and wrath" (Ro.2:8).

**5** (14:21-23) **Evangelism—Witnessing—Decision—Invitation**: the Lord sends invitations to outsiders *quickly*. Note several facts.
1. The Lord will not allow His plan to be halted. He has planned a feast and no one will be allowed to stop it.
2. The Lord is going to fill His banquet hall quickly. Note: He sends His servant forth saying, "Go quickly." (What a challenge to all believers! God wants the job done quickly. What excitement to think of being with Him at *The Great Supper* soon!)
3. The Lord's servant is to "go out" into the streets and lanes of the city. He is to leave the homes of the rich and luxurious, the self-sufficient and worldly-minded, the religionists and self-righteous. He is to "go out" from among the acceptable and established to reach out to the people of the streets and the highways.
4. The Lord's servant is to go to those who will need assistance in order to come; he is to go to those who know and readily admit that they need help. Note the servant is to "bring in" these to whom he is now sent.
   a. He is to bring in the poor, those who will need new and appropriate clothing. Some of the poor will accept the clothing.

> "For he hath made him to be sin for us, who knew no sin; that we might be made the righteousness of God in him" (2 Cor.5:21).
> "Blessed are the poor in spirit: for theirs is the kingdom of heaven" (Mt.5:3).

   b. He is to bring in the maimed and the halt, those who will need to be supported and perhaps carried to the banquet hall.
   c. He is to bring in the blind, those who will need to be guided and directed.

Note: some of these know their need. Their need is evident, and they readily *confess their need and accept the help*.

Now note two critical points.
1. The Lord's servant still has a difficult time in getting enough people to accept the invitation. Some of the poor, maimed, halt, and blind care nothing about coming. They are too prideful or bitter, too embarrassed or ashamed, too self-centered or self-pitying to receive help or to accept an invitation that is being rejected by so many.

2.   The Lord demands a double, strenuous effort. He sends His servant into the highways and hedges to invite whomever he can find. Note three facts.

    a.   This refers either to the Gentiles or to the greatest of sinners, depending on how a person is approaching the passage.

    b.   The Lord says, "compel them." This does not mean to compel by physical force but by the force of preaching and persuasion, by the power of the Holy Spirit.

> "Knowing therefore the terror of the Lord, we persuade men" (2 Cor.5:11).
>
> "For I know the forwardness of your mind, for which I boast of you to them of Macedonia, that Achaia was ready a year ago; and your zeal hath provoked very many" (2 Cor.9:2).
>
> "Preach the word; be instant in season, out of season; reprove, rebuke, exhort with all longsuffering and doctrine" (2 Tim.4:2).
>
> "As ye go, preach, saying, The kingdom of heaven is at hand" (Mt.10:7).
>
> "What I tell you in darkness, that speak ye in light: and what ye hear in the ear, that preach ye upon the housetops" (Mt.10:27).
>
> "And he said unto them, Go ye into all the world, and preach the gospel to every creature" (Mk.16:15).
>
> "Jesus said unto him, Let the dead bury their dead: but go thou and preach the kingdom of God" (Lk.9:60).
>
> "Go, stand and speak in the temple to the people all the words of this life" (Acts 5:20).

    c.   The Lord says, "My house shall be filled." Remember the command "go quickly." Connect the command to this promise, and the time frame seems to be soon. However, we must keep in mind that a thousand years is as one day to the Lord (2 Pt.3:8).

> "In the last day, that great day of the feast, Jesus stood and cried, saying, If any man thirst, let him come unto me, and drink" (Jn.7:37).
>
> "For whosoever shall call upon the name of the Lord shall be saved" (Ro.10:13).
>
> "Who will have all men to be saved and to come unto the knowledge of the truth" (1 Tim.2:4).
>
> "And the Spirit and the bride say, Come. And let him that heareth say, Come. And let him that is athirst come. And whosoever will, let him take the water of life freely" (Rev.22:17).
>
> "Ho, every one that thirsteth, come ye to the waters, and he that hath no money; come ye, buy, and eat; yea, come, buy wine and milk without money and without price" (Is.55:1).

**6**  (14:24) **Judgment—Salvation, Rejected**: the rejecters are excluded. This is a tragic pronouncement, but a very deserving verdict. The Lord says that not a single rejecter "shall taste of my supper." There is no second chance.

> "And while they went to buy, the bridegroom came; and they that were ready went in with him to the marriage: and the door was shut" (Mt.25:10).
>
> "Verily I say unto you, Whosoever shall not receive the kingdom of God as a little child, he shall not enter therein" (Mk.10:15).
>
> "Know ye not that the unrighteous shall not inherit the kingdom of God? Be not deceived: neither fornicators, nor idolaters, nor adulterers, nor effeminate, nor abusers of themselves with mankind, nor thieves, nor covetous, nor drunkards, nor revilers, nor extortioners, shall inherit the kingdom of God" (1 Cor.6:9-10).
>
> "Now this I say, brethren, that flesh and blood cannot inherit the kingdom of God; neither doth corruption inherit incorruption" (1 Cor.15:50).
>
> "And there shall in no wise enter into it any thing that defileth, neither whatsoever worketh abomination, or maketh a lie: but they which are written in the Lamb's book of life" (Rev.21:27).
>
> "Your iniquities have turned away these things, and your sins have withholden good things from you" (Jer.5:25).
>
> "My God will cast them away, because they did not hearken unto him: and they shall be wanderers among the nations" (Hos.9:17).

| | F. The Cost of Discipleship, 14:25-35 (cp. Mt.5:13; cp. Mt.10:37-39; Mk.9:50) | 30 Saying, This man began to build, and was not able to finish. | |
|---|---|---|---|
| 1 Huge crowds followed Jesus & He challenged them<br>2 A man must put Christ first: Before family & even before himself | 25 And there went great multitudes with him: and he turned, and said unto them,<br>26 If any man come to me, and hate not his father, and mother, and wife, and children, and brethren, and sisters, yea, and his own life also, he cannot be my disciple. | 31 Or what king, going to make war against another king, sitteth not down first, and consulteth whether he be able with ten thousand to meet him that cometh against him with twenty thousand?<br>32 Or else, while the other is yet a great way off, he sendeth an ambassage, and desireth conditions of peace. | b. Illust.2: A king at war—must count the consequences |
| 3 A man must bear the cross of death: Death to self<br>4 A man must give thought to discipleship: Count the cost & the consequences<br><br>  a. Illust.1: A builder—must count his resources | 27 And whosoever doth not bear his cross, and come after me, cannot be my disciple.<br>28 For which of you, intending to build a tower, sitteth not down first, and counteth the cost, whether he have sufficient to finish it?<br>29 Lest haply, after he hath laid the foundation, and is not able to finish it, all that behold it begin to mock him, | 33 So likewise, whosoever he be of you that forsaketh not all that he hath, he cannot be my disciple.<br>34 Salt is good: but if the salt have lost his savour, wherewith shall it be seasoned?<br>35 It is neither fit for the land, nor yet for the dunghill; but men cast it out. He that hath ears to hear, let him hear. | c. The point: A man must pay the ultimate price—forsake all<br>5 A man must have the salt of discipleship: The salt of self-denial<br>  a. A half-hearted choice<br>    1) Is worthless<br>    2) Is to be cast out<br><br>  b. An invitation: Hearing is a choice |

# DIVISION VI

## THE SON OF MAN'S GREAT JOURNEY TO JERUSALEM (STAGE II): HIS TEACHING AND PUBLIC CONFLICT, 13:22-17:10

## F.     The Cost of Discipleship, 14:25-35

(14:25-35) **Introduction**: Christ is not interested in cheap invitations and discipleship. Too often the call to discipleship is to receive the great benefits and advantages offered by God. There are eternal benefits and advantages, but salvation and discipleship involve much more. They involve an unbelievable cost, the supreme sacrifice. A person must pay the ultimate price, all that one *is and has* to follow Christ. Just what does it cost to follow Christ? This is the all important subject of this passage.

1. Huge crowds followed Jesus and He challenged them (v.25).
2. A man must put Christ first: before family, even before self (v.26).
3. A man must bear the cross of death: death to self (v.27).
4. A man must give thought to discipleship: count the cost and the consequences (v.28-33).
5. A man must have the salt of discipleship: the salt of self-denial (v.34-35).

(14:25-35) **Another Outline**: *The cost or conditions of discipleship* might be outlined as follows.
1. Renunciation (v.26).
2. Self-denial (v.27).
3. Thoughtfulness—counting the cost (v.28-32).
4. Forsaking all (v.33-35).

There are three other *conditions for discipleship* given by Christ elsewhere.
1. Love to others: "By this shall all men know that ye are my disciples, if ye have love one to another" (Jn.13:35; cp. 34).
2. Stedfastness: "If ye continue in my word then are ye my disciples indeed" (Jn.8:31).
3. Fruitfulness: "Herein is my Father glorified, that ye bear much fruit; so shall ye be my disciples" (Jn.15:8).

**1** (14:25) **Discipleship**: huge crowds were following Jesus. The cross and the desperate needs of the world were upon His mind (v.27). The enormous sacrifice and cost it was going to take to reach the world consumed His thoughts. He must have followers who would sacrifice themselves totally if the message of salvation were to be carried to the world. He could not have second best. God would not accept any place other than first place in a man's life. He must make clear what it meant and what it cost to be His disciple.

**2** (14:26) **Family—Self-Denial—Dedication—Discipleship**: a man must put Christ first, even before his family and himself. (See outline and note—Mt.10:35-37.) The words "hate not" (ou misei) are strong. They mean not showing preference, indifference, aversion, disregard (cp. Gen.29:31, 33; Dt.21:15). Christ was not saying that one's family and one's self were to be literally hated. The true believer is to love *even* his enemies (Lk.6:27). What then did Christ mean? Very simply...

⇒ Christ is to be *first* in a person's life: before family, even before self.
⇒ Christ is to be put before family: even if one's family opposes his decision to follow Christ.
⇒ Christ is to be put *first*: before the companionship and comfort and pleasure of family and home.
⇒ All—even family and self—are to be put behind Christ and His mission. All must be denied and put behind a person's love and devotion to Christ and His cause.

"Then Peter began to say unto him, Lo, We have left all, and have followed thee" (Mk.10:28).
"And when they had brought their ships to land, they forsook all, and followed him" (Lk.5:11).
"And after these things he went forth, and saw a publican, named Levi, sitting at the receipt of custom: and he said unto him, follow me" (Lk.5:27).
"And he said unto them, Verily I say unto you, There is no man that hath left house, or parents, or brethren, or wife, or children, for the kingdom of God's sake, who shall not receive manifold more in this present time, and in the world to come life everlasting" (Lk.18:29-30).
"Yea doubtless, and I count all things but loss for the excellency of the knowledge of Christ Jesus my Lord: for whom I have suffered the loss of all things, and do count them but dung, that I may win Christ" (Ph.3:8).

3 (14:27) **Self-denial**: a man must bear the cross of death—to self. (See notes and DEEPER STUDY # 1—Lk.9:23; Mt.16:24 for discussion and application.)

4 (14:28-33) **Decision—Discipleship—Thought—Mind**: a man must think and give thought to discipleship; he must count the cost and the consequences. Christ used two parables to get His point across.

1. A man who wants to build a tower, first sits down to *think* about the project and to count the cost. Does he have *sufficient resources*, enough of what it takes to finish the task? He has to make sure, or else he will not be able to finish the task and will end up being mocked. The point is clear: before a person begins to follow Christ, Christ wants that person to think about it. He wants the person to be sure, absolutely sure. Can he afford to follow through; does he have what it takes to build the tower (life)? Why? Because a false profession damages the Kingdom of God.

A false profession causes...
• the world to mock and charge true believers with being hypocritical.
• prospective believers to turn sour.
• believers to be hampered and hindered in their ministry.
• some believers to become discouraged.

2. The second parable concerned two kings at war. The king being attacked had only ten thousand soldiers, whereas the king marching against him had twenty thousand soldiers. The defending king sat down and thought long and hard about his resources and the consequences. He was forced to think about the loss of life and property even if he did win. Note: this king had to make a decision. He was being invaded. He had to decide to fight against the invading king or to surrender. He had to *think through the consequences both ways*, the consequences of fighting or surrendering. (Cp. the invading king to Christ and the defending king to the individual.)

The point of the two parables is clear: a man must pay the ultimate price. He must forsake all, renounce and give up all that he *is and has*; or else "he cannot be my disciple." When a man counts the cost of following Christ, he needs to think about two things.

1. It will cost him *all he is*. The man must be willing to center his life around Christ and His mission to reach a world lost and full of desperate needs. It will cost the man...
• his heart: total devotion and commitment.
• his mind: being permeated and controlled by Christ.
• his eyes: watching what he looks at.
• his ears: watching what he listens to.
• his hands: watching what he touches and picks up.
• his feet: watching where he goes.
• his mouth: watching what he eats and drinks and says.
• his desires: watching, controlling, and changing his urges and desires.
• his energy: committing his strength, initiative, and will to Christ.
• his effort and work: dedicating and centering all in Christ, using his efforts and work in the cause of Christ.

"Knowing this, that our old man is crucified with him, that the body of sin might be destroyed, that henceforth we should not serve sin" (Ro.6:6).
"I beseech you therefore, brethren, by the mercies of God, that ye present your bodies a living sacrifice, holy, acceptable unto God, which is your reasonable service" (Ro.12:1).
"It is good neither to eat flesh, nor to drink wine, nor any thing whereby thy brother stumbleth, or is offended, or is made weak" (Ro.14:21).
"What? know ye not that your body is the temple of the Holy Ghost which is in you, which ye have of God, and ye are not your own? For ye are bought with a price: therefore glorify God in your body, and in your spirit, which are God's" (1 Cor.6:19-20).

"Let no man seek his own, but every man another's wealth" (1 Cor.10:24).

"Wherefore come out from among them, and be ye separate, saith the Lord, and touch not the unclean thing; and I will receive you, and will be a Father unto you, and ye shall be my sons and daughters, saith the Lord Almighty" (2 Cor.6:17-18).

"I am crucified with Christ: nevertheless I live; yet not I, but Christ liveth in me: and the life which I now live in the flesh I live by the faith of the Son of God, who loved me, and gave himself for me" (Gal.2:20).

"And they that are Christ's have crucified the flesh with the affections and lusts" (Gal.5:24).

"For ye are dead, and your life is hid with Christ in God" (Col.3:3).

2.    It will cost him *all he has*. The man must be willing to give everything he has to Christ, without watering down the cost. It is this point that will cause so many to be lost and doomed (see outline and notes—Lk.18:18-30; Mt.10:16-22). To really follow Christ will cost...

- family: being put after Christ.
- friends: being put after Christ and centered around Christ.
- home: all the comforts and extravagances.
- job: being centered around Christ and being used to earn enough to give to those who do not have (Eph.4:28).
- cars: not being extravagant, so as to have more to give to a needful world.
- investments: using for God's cause.
- money: taking care of personal necessities and then using the rest for God's cause.

Whatever a person has, it will cost him. He must surrender it to Christ, which is to say, he must be willing to use it in the Lord's mission, the mission of helping a world lost and reeling under the weight of enormous needs.

When a man counts the cost of following Christ, he must think about the consequences of both fighting against Christ and surrendering to Christ. If the man chooses to reject Christ, to struggle against Him, the man will...

- never experience abundant life, deep satisfaction (Jn.10:10).
- never know God, His love and care, on a daily basis.
- never have an *eternal sense* of purpose, meaning, and significance.
- never know nor have the assurance of eternal life.
- never be free from the uncertainty of life.
- never be free from the dread and fear of death.
- never be free of some sense of judgment and of what lies ahead.
- never be freed from a sense of false security.

The consequences of surrendering to Christ are, of course, the very opposite of the above.

"Jesus said unto him, If thou wilt be perfect, go and sell that thou hast, and give to the poor, and thou shalt have treasure in heaven: and come and follow me" (Mt.19:21; cp. Lk.18:22).

"And the cares of this world, and the deceitfulness of riches, and the lusts of other things entering, choke the word, and it becometh unfruitful" (Mk.4:19).

"Sell that ye have, and give alms; provide yourselves bags which wax not old, a treasure in the heavens that faileth not, where no thief approacheth, neither moth corrupteth. For where your treasure is, there will your heart be also" (Lk.12:33-34).

"And Zacchaeus stood, and said unto the Lord; Behold, Lord, the half of my goods I give to the poor; and if I have taken any thing from any man by false accusation, I restore him fourfold" (Lk.19:8).

"Even as I please all men in all things, not seeking mine own profit, but the profit of many, that they may be saved" (1 Cor.10:33).

"For ye know the grace of our Lord Jesus Christ, that, though he was rich, yet for your sakes he became poor, that ye through his poverty might be rich" (2 Cor.8:9).

"But they that will be rich fall into temptation and a snare, and into many foolish and hurtful lusts, which drown men in destruction and perdition" (1 Tim.6:9).

"But whoso hath this world's good, and seeth his brother have need, and shutteth up his bowels of compassion from him, how dwelleth the love of God in him?" (1 Jn.3:17).

5  (14:34-35) **Decision, Half-hearted—Dedication**: a man must have the salt of discipleship which is self-denial, renunciation, the sacrifice and giving, of all one is and has. (See notes—Mt.5:13; Mk.9:50 for more discussion.) Christ said three very pointed things.

1.    A half-hearted choice is worthless. It *cannot season or penetrate*; it cannot help anything or anyone.

"And Jesus said unto him, No man, having put his hand to the plough, and looking back, is fit for the kingdom of God" (Lk.9:62).

2.    A half-hearted choice is to be cast out. Salt that is worthless and useless is always cast out, for it is good for nothing.

"But the children of the kingdom shall be cast out into outer darkness: there shall be weeping and gnashing of teeth" (Mt.8:12).

"Then said the King to the servants, Bind him hand and foot, and take him away, and cast him into outer darkness; there shall be weeping and gnashing of teeth" (Mt.22:13).

"And cast ye the unprofitable servant into outer darkness: there shall be weeping and gnashing of teeth" (Mt.25:30).

"But he shall say, I tell you, I know you not whence ye are; depart from me, all ye workers of iniquity" (Lk.13:27).

"If a man abide not in me, he is cast forth as a branch, and is withered; and men gather them, and cast them into the fire, and they are burned" (Jn.15:6).

"Let him that is taught in the word communicate unto him that teacheth in all good things. Be not deceived; God is not mocked: for whatsoever a man soweth, that shall he also reap. For he that soweth to his flesh shall of the flesh reap corruption; but he that soweth to the Spirit shall of the Spirit reap life everlasting" (Gal.6:6-8).

"Now the just shall live by faith: but if any man draw back, my soul shall have no pleasure in him. But we are not of them who draw back unto perdition; but of them that believe to the saving of the soul" (Heb.10:38-39).

"For if after they have escaped the pollutions of the world through the knowledge of the Lord and Saviour Jesus Christ, they are again entangled therein, and overcome, the latter end is worse with them than the beginning" (2 Pt.2:20).

3.    A man with ears needs to hear the invitation. Hearing spiritual truth is a choice which a man must make. He chooses whether to hear or not to hear the truth.

"Therefore whosoever heareth these sayings of mine, and doeth them, I will liken him unto a wise man, which built his house upon a rock: and the rain descended, and the floods came, and the winds blew, and beat upon that house; and it fell not: for it was founded upon a rock. And every one that heareth these sayings of mine, and doeth them not, shall be likened unto a foolish man, which built his house upon the sand: and the rain descended, and the floods came, and the winds blew, and beat upon that house; and it fell: and great was the fall of it" (Mt.7:24-27).

"The good ground are they, which in an honest and good heart, having heard the word, keep it, and bring forth fruit with patience" (Lk.8:15).

"And he said unto him, If they hear not Moses and the prophets, neither will they be persuaded, though one rose from the dead" (Lk.16:31).

"For this cause also thank we God without ceasing, because, when ye received the word of God which ye heard of us, ye received it not as the word of men, but as it is in truth, the word of God, which effectually worketh also in you that believe" (1 Th.2:13).

"For if any be a hearer of the word, and not a doer, he is like unto a man beholding his natural face in a glass: for he beholdeth himself, and goeth his way, and straightway forgetteth what manner of man he was" (Jas.1:23-24).

"The ear that heareth the reproof of life abideth among the wise" (Pr.15:31).

| | | one of them, doth not leave the ninety and nine in the wilderness, and go after that which is lost, until he find it? | **because of self** |
|---|---|---|---|
| | **CHAPTER 15** | | 4 **The sheep was lost "in the wilderness"** |
| | | | 5 **The sheep was sought until found** |
| | **G. The Parable of the Lost Sheep: The Lost Sinner Out in the World, 15:1-7** (cp. Mt.18:11-14) | 5 And when he hath found it, he layeth it on his shoulders, rejoicing. | 6 **The sheep, once found, brings great joy** |
| | | 6 And when he cometh home, he calleth together his friends and neighbours, saying unto them, Rejoice with me; for I have found my sheep which was lost. | |
| 1 **Tax collectors & sinners drew near Jesus** | Then drew near unto him all the publicans and sinners for to hear him. | | |
| a. The religionists: Grumbled against Jesus associating with "sinners" | 2 And the Pharisees and scribes murmured, saying, This man receiveth sinners, and eateth with them. | 7 I say unto you, that likewise joy shall be in heaven over one sinner that repenteth, more than over ninety and nine just persons, which need no repentance. | 7 **The sheep represented a repentant sinner** |
| b. Jesus: Shared a parable | 3 And he spake this parable unto them, saying, | | |
| 2 **The sheep was lost**[DS1] | 4 What man of you, having an hundred sheep, if he lose | | |
| 3 **The sheep was lost** | | | |

# DIVISION VI

## THE SON OF MAN'S GREAT JOURNEY TO JERUSALEM (STAGE II): HIS TEACHING AND PUBLIC CONFLICT, 13:22-17:10

### G. The Parable of the Lost Sheep: The Lost Sinner Out in the World, 15:1-7

(15:1-7) **Introduction**: Chapter 15 is one of the most important chapters in all the Bible. It includes three of the most famous parables ever told. The parables deal with the lost sinner and the great love of God in seeking and receiving the lost sinner when the sinner repents and returns home. The first parable is that of the Lost Sheep in the wilderness of the world.

1. Tax collectors and sinners drew near Jesus (v.1-3).
2. The sheep was lost (v.4).
3. The sheep was lost because of self (v.4).
4. The sheep was lost "in the wilderness" (v.4).
5. The sheep was sought until found (v.4).
6. The sheep, once found, brought great joy (v.5-6).
7. The sheep represented a repentant sinner (v.7).

**1** (15:1-3) **Separation—Spiritual Hunger**: tax-collectors and sinners drew near Jesus. Note they "all" drew near to Him. This shows two things.

1. They were hungry for His message. They were not coming out of curiosity, nor to observe, nor to seek physical blessings; they were coming out of a spiritual need, out of the need to receive His message of salvation.

2. They acknowledged their great need. Publicans, that is, tax-collectors, worked for the Roman government, the nation that had conquered Israel. Therefore, they were considered traitors to both Israel and God. Consequently, they were despised by the people and were cut off and shut out by the religionists. Sinners were the rank immoral and unjust who did not keep the law, such as harlots (cp. Mt.21:32), liars, thieves, murderers. All these were *sinners*, traitors to both God and man, and they knew it. So when Christ came along preaching deliverance from sin and hope of the Kingdom of God, they flocked to Him.

The attitude of the religionists was tragic. They grumbled against Jesus because He associated and ate with such terrible sinners. They felt it was beneath the dignity of any respectable person to associate with such vile sinners. Note an important point: Christ was not *of the world*, but He was *out in the world* trying to reach men for God. It is this that is often overlooked by both the liberals and the separatists.

⇒ The true believer is to "come out from among them [the worldly] and be ye separate, saith the Lord, and touch not the unclean thing; and I will receive you, and will be a Father unto you, and ye shall be my sons and daughters, saith the Lord Almighty" (2 Cor.6:17-18). He is not to be out in the world with sinners doing worldly things and carrying on worldly conversation (Eph.4:29; Col.4:6).

⇒ The true believer is to "go ye into all the world and preach the gospel to every creature [sinner]" (Mk.16:15). The believer *goes*; he does not sit back and wait on sinners to come to him and the church. He goes out where the sinners are.

**Thought 1.** If the *whole gospel* were preached today in power and authority, how many would be flocking to hear...
- the gospel of salvation from sin and death?
- the gospel of the hope for the Kingdom of God (see DEEPER STUDY # 3, *Kingdom of God*—Mt.19:23-24)?

Christ answered the religionists by sharing three great parables. The first parable is one of the most-loved stories ever told, the parable of the lost sheep.

**2** (15:4) **Sheep**: the sheep was lost. The sheep represents the unbeliever, the sinner who wanders out in the wilderness of the world, the person who has gone astray and is lost to God. Note the meaning of the word "lost" (see DEEPER STUDY # 1, *Lost*—Lk.15:4).

309

---

**DEEPER STUDY # 1**

(15:4) **Lost (apollumi)**: to perish, to destroy, to lose, to lose eternal life, to be spiritually destitute, to be cut off.

---

**3** (15:4) **Sheep, Lost—Man, Lost**: the sheep was lost because of self. A sheep loses itself in one of five ways.

1. The sheep is attracted by something out "in the wilderness," away from the flock of the shepherd. What the sheep sees is more attractive and appealing. It tempts and seduces him, and he lusts after it ("the lust of the flesh and the lust of the eyes," 1 Jn.2:16).

2. The sheep is aimless, not paying attention to what is going on. It aimlessly wanders off, and while it is *getting lost*, the sheep does not know it is losing its way. The sheep is already lost when it discovers it has lost its way.

3. The sheep refuses to heed the warnings of the shepherd and the example of the other sheep ("the pride of life," 1 Jn.2:16).

4. The sheep is not attached enough to the shepherd or to the other sheep. There is not the bond or union there should be. Therefore, he stays off by himself, eating and resting and working alone until eventually he wanders off without anyone's knowing it, including himself (Heb.10:25).

5. The sheep does not trust the shepherd. It does not think the shepherd will take care and see that there is satisfying food. It goes astray in search of *greener pasture and more satisfying food* (see note—Mt.18:14 for the help of others needed by the shepherd to care for the sheep).

> "All we like sheep have gone astray, we have turned every one to his own way; and the LORD hath laid on him the iniquity of us all" (Is.53:6).
>
> "The man that wandereth out of the way of understanding shall remain in the congregation of the dead" (Pr.21:16).
>
> "As a bird that wandereth from her nest, so is a man that wandereth from his place" (Pr.27:8).
>
> "They have wandered as blind men in the streets, they have polluted themselves with blood, so that men could not touch their garments (Lam.4:14).
>
> "For my people have committed two evils; they have forsaken me the fountain of living waters, and hewed them out cisterns, broken cisterns, that can hold no water" (Jer.2:13).
>
> "Thou hast forsaken me, saith the LORD, thou art gone backward: therefore will I stretch out my hand against thee, and destroy thee; I am weary with repenting" (Jer.15:6).
>
> "And because iniquity shall abound, the love of many shall wax cold" (Mt.24:12).
>
> "If any man draw back, my soul shall have no pleasure in him" (Heb.10:38).
>
> "Which have forsaken the right way, and are gone astray, following the way of Balaam the son of Bosor, who loved the wages of unrighteousness" (2 Pt.2:15).
>
> "Raging waves of the sea, foaming out their own shame: wandering stars, to whom is reserved the blackness of darkness for ever" (Jude 13).

**4** (15:4) **World—Worldliness—Wilderness—Lost**: the sheep was lost in the wilderness. The wilderness had an excitement about it. The unknown and the risk aroused the emotions; but once the sheep ventured out into the wilderness, he found its terrain rugged, full of narrow ridges and deep ravines and crevices. It was rough going, heavy with thick underbrush, pricking thorns, dangerous footing; and, if the way out were never found, it would sap the sheep's strength and age him ever so rapidly. Eventually the wilderness would take its life.

The wilderness and thrills of the world do attract a person. The world has much to offer.

1. The world gives a man...
   - occupation & purpose
   - lifestyle & acceptance
   - ego & self-esteem
   - recognition & privilege
   - more & more honor
   - position & image
   - plenty & wealth
   - opportunity & satisfaction
   - authority & power

2. The world stimulates and arouses a man, causing...
   - his blood to rush
   - his heart to beat faster
   - goose bumps
   - butterflies
   - desires
   - cravings
   - escape
   - relaxation

> "Love not the world, neither the things that are in the world. If any man love the world, the love of the Father is not in him, for all that is in the world, the lust of the flesh, and the lust of the eyes, and the pride of life, is not of the Father, but is of the world" (1 Jn.2:15-16).
>
> "Now the works of the flesh are manifest, which are these; adultery, fornication [pre-marital sex], uncleanness, lasciviousness [all forms of immorality], idolatry, witchcraft [sorcery], hatred, variance [strife], emulations [jealousy], wrath, strife, seditions [divisions], heresies, envyings, murders, drunkenness, revellings, and such like: of the which I tell you before, as I have also told you in time past, that they which do such things shall not inherit the kingdom of God" (Gal.5:19-21).

"My people hath been lost sheep: their shepherds have caused them to go astray, they have turned them away on the mountains: they have gone from mountain to hill, they have forgotten their resting place" (Jer.50:6).

"My sheep wandered through all the mountains, and upon every high hill: yea, my flock was scattered upon all the face of the earth, and none did search or seek after them" (Ezk.34:6).

"But when he saw the multitudes, he was moved with compassion on them, because they fainted, and were scattered abroad, as sheep having no shepherd" (Mt.9:36).

**5** (15:4) **Ministry—Seeking Lost**: the sheep was sought until found. Note four things.

1. The lost sheep was sought (v.4). The shepherd left the ninety-nine to seek the one lost sheep. The ninety-nine were safe; they were already in the shepherd's fold. But the one sheep was lost. It was the one that needed to be sought. It was this sheep that needed the attention of the shepherd and was to occupy the time, energy, and effort of the shepherd. As long as the sheep was lost, seeking it was the primary purpose and reason for the shepherd. (What a lesson for the church and ministers!)

2. The search was urgent. The shepherd *went after* that which was lost (v.4). He was gripped with concern. He went after the one lost sheep as though it were the only one. Note the shepherd's dedication and commitment to seeking the lost.

3. The shepherd sought until he found the sheep. He did not seek complacently or slowly, as though there were plenty of time. Nor did he give up, despite the difficulties that lay along the rough terrain and the weariness of the long hours and the tediousness of running into dead end after dead end. He sought and kept on seeking until he found the lost sheep. He never slackened, never backed off, never gave up.

4. When the shepherd found the sheep, he embraced the sheep and threw it over his shoulders. He received it...

- with arms wide open.
- embracing it.
- rejoicing in heart.
- supporting and carrying it to his home (v.6).

"Surely he hath borne our griefs, and carried our sorrows: yet we did esteem him stricken, smitten of God, and afflicted. But he was wounded for our transgressions, he was bruised for our iniquities: the chastisement of our peace was upon him; and with his stripes we are healed. All we like sheep have gone astray; we have turned every one to his own way; and the LORD hath laid on him the iniquity of us all" (Is.53:4-6).

"Ye were as sheep going astray; but are now returned unto the Shepherd and Bishop of your souls" (1 Pt.2:25).

"I have gone astray like a lost sheep; seek thy servant; for I do not forget thy commandments" (Ps.119:176).

**6** (15:5-6) **Salvation, Results**: once found, the sheep bought great joy. Note what the shepherd did.

1. He called all his neighbors together. He wanted everyone to know that the lost sheep had been found. Everyone had been so concerned—praying, hoping, waiting. They wanted to join in the rejoicing.

2. Everyone rejoiced because the shepherd's labor was not in vain.

3. The shepherd tenderly called the lost sheep "*my sheep*"—"my sheep which was lost." It was his, no matter how dirty, filthy, unclean, destitute, depraved, ugly or lost it had been. It was still the shepherd's sheep.

Note that God did not send an angel as a servant, but He sent His Son to seek the lost (cp. Is.53:4-6, 10-12).

"For God so loved the world, that he gave his only begotten Son, that whosoever believeth in him should not perish, but have everlasting life" (Jn.3:16).

"Who his own self bare our sins in his own body on the tree, that we, being dead to sins, should live unto righteousness: by whose stripes ye were healed. For ye were as sheep going astray; but are now returned unto the Shepherd and Bishop of your souls" (1 Pt.2:24-25).

"For the Son of man is come to seek and to save that which was lost" (Lk.19:10).

**7** (15:7) **Repentance**: the sheep represents a repentant sinner. A sinner must repent (see note and DEEPER STUDY # 1—Acts 17:29-30).

"Then Peter said unto them, Repent, and be baptized every one of you in the name of Jesus Christ for the remission of sins, and ye shall receive the gift of the Holy Ghost" (Acts 2:38).

"Repent ye therefore, and be converted, that your sins may be blotted out, when the times of refreshing shall come from the presence of the Lord" (Acts 3:19).

"Let the wicked forsake his way, and the unrighteous man his thoughts: and let him return unto the LORD, and he will have mercy upon him; and to our God, for he will abundantly pardon" (Is.55:7).

"But if the wicked will turn from all his sins that he hath committed, and keep all my statutes, and do that which is lawful and right, he shall surely live, he shall not die" (Ezk.18:21).

| | H. The Parable of the Lost Coin: The Lost Sinner Within the Home, 15:8-10 |
|---|---|
| 1 The coin was lost | 8 Either what woman having ten pieces of silver, if she lose one piece, doth not light a candle, and sweep the house, and seek diligently till she find it? |
| 2 The coin was lost because of others | |
| 3 The coin was lost in the house | |
| 4 The coin was sought until found | 9 And when she hath found it, she calleth her friends and her neighbours together, saying, Rejoice with me; for I have found the piece which I had lost. |
| 5 The coin, once found, brought great joy | |
| 6 The coin represented a repentant sinner | 10 Likewise, I say unto you, there is joy in the presence of the angels of God over one sinner that repenteth. |

# DIVISION VI

## THE SON OF MAN'S GREAT JOURNEY TO JERUSALEM (STAGE II): HIS TEACHING AND PUBLIC CONFLICT, 13:22-17:10

### H. The Parable of the Lost Coin: The Lost Sinner Within the Home, 15:8-10

(15:8-10) **Introduction**: this passage is often preached and taught right along with the Parable of the Lost Sheep (Lk.15:1-7). The lost sheep was lost out in the wilderness of the world, whereas the lost coin was lost in the house. Note the points are the same for each parable, but the application is different.

1. The coin was lost (v.8).
2. The coin was lost because of others (v.8).
3. The coin was lost in the house (v.8).
4. The coin was sought until found (v.9).
5. The coin, once found, brought great joy (v.9).
6. The coin represented a repentant sinner (v.10).

**1** (15:8) **Lost—Coin**: the lost coin represents the unbeliever, the sinner who is lost within the house, the family member who has gone astray and is lost both to God and to the mother. Note two facts.
1. The coin was silver, of extreme worth, and greatly desired.
2. The coin was lost and doomed to be lost forever if not found (see DEEPER STUDY # 1, *Lost*—Lk.15:4 for discussion).

**2** (15:8) **Lost—Family—Witnessing**: the coin was lost because of others. This is a striking picture of the responsibility family members have for one another. A coin (person) within the home is lost in one of four ways.
1. Ignoring the coin. It is set aside and forgotten. Once it has been brought into the house, little if any thought is given to it. Being too busy, not knowing its value, and confusing priorities can cause a coin to be ignored.
2. Neglecting the coin. A person can know the coin is there and know its value, yet neglect it. He can just fail to pay attention to the coin for such a long period of time that he forgets where it is.
3. Carelessly handling the coin. It is badly handled, dropped, and lost.
4. Unconsciously placing the coin someplace. Placing the coin can be unplanned; therefore, little attention is given to it. A person just goes about his daily affairs without ever planning any use for the coin. Eventually, it is forgotten.

> "That they may teach the young women to be sober, to love their husbands, to love their children, to be discreet, chaste, keepers at home, good, obedient to their own husbands, that the word of God be not blasphemed" (Tit.2:4-5).
>
> "So when they had dined, Jesus saith to Simon Peter, Simon, son of Jonas, lovest thou me more than these? He saith unto him, Yea, Lord; thou knowest that I love thee. He saith unto him, Feed my lambs" (Jn.21:15).
>
> "Behold, the third time I am ready to come to you; and I will not be burdensome to you: for I seek not yours, but you: for the children ought not to lay up for the parents, but the parents for the children" (2 Cor.12:14).
>
> "And thou shalt teach [God's Word] diligently unto thy children, and shalt talk of them when thou sittest in thine house, and when thou walkest by the way, and when thou liest down, and when thou risest up" (Dt.6:7).
>
> "And ye shall teach them [God's Word] your children, speaking of them when thou sittest in thine house, and when thou walkest by the way, when thou liest down, and when thou risest up" (Dt.11:19).
>
> "Train up a child in the way he should go: and when he is old, he will not depart from it" (Pr.22:6).
>
> "Whom shall he teach knowledge? and whom shall he make to understand doctrine? them that are weaned from the milk and drawn from the breasts" (Is.28:9).

"The living, the living, he shall praise thee, as I do this day: the father to the children shall make known thy truth" (Is.38:19).

"Arise, cry out in the night: in the beginning of the watches pour out thine heart like water before the face of the Lord: lift up thy hands toward him [God] for the life of thy young children" (Lam.2:19).

**3** (15:8) **Lost—Family—Witnessing**: the coin was lost in the house. Note three points.

1. The coin, although lost in the house, was lost in the dust and dirt of the floor. It was not clean like the other nine coins sitting on the dresser. The dust and dirt was slowly covering and tarnishing it in its filth.

2. The coin's experience, although in the house, was terrible. Being lost, it was...
   - useless: unable to contribute to family needs.
   - helpless: unable to fulfill its purpose.
   - gone: not present to participate in family functions.
   - bypassed: not seen, it could not be polished and cared for.
   - stepped upon and walked upon: down upon the floor covered with dust and dirt, it was not seen; therefore, it was misused and abused.

> "The rod and reproof give wisdom: but a child left to himself bringeth his mother to shame" (Pr.29:15).
> "And the younger of them said to his father, Father, give me the portion of goods that falleth to me. And he divided unto them his living. And not many days after the younger son gathered all together, and took his journey into a far country, and there wasted his substance with riotous living" (Lk.15:12-13).
> "And she, being before instructed of her mother, said, Give me here John Baptist's head in a charger" (Mt.14:8).
> "For I have told him [Eli] that I will judge his house for ever for the iniquity which he knoweth; because his sons made themselves vile, and he restrained them not" (1 Sam.3:13).
> "And his [Samuel's] sons walked not in his ways, but turned aside after lucre, and took bribes, and perverted judgment" (1 Sam.8:3).
> "And he did evil in the sight of the LORD, and walked in the way of his fahter, and in the way of his mother, and in the way of Jeroboam the son of Nebat, who made Israel to sin" (1 Ki.22:52).
> "He also walked in the ways of the house of Ahab: for his mother was his counselor to do wickedly" (2 Chron.22:3).
> "But have walked after the imagination of their own heart, and after Baalim, which their fathers taught them" (Jer.9:14).
> "But I said unto their children in the wilderness, Walk ye not in the statutes of your fathers, neither observe their judgments, nor defile yourselves with their idols: I am the LORD your God; walk in my statutes, and keep my judgments, and do them" (Ezk.20:18-19).

3. The coin was not aware it was lost. Note three things.
   a. A family member may have no consciousness or sensation of being lost. There may be no discomfort, distress, or anxiety; however, there is still personal responsibility. Everyone, no matter who he is, is responsible for his own life and salvation. He cannot blame his parents, mother, father, brother, sister, son or daughter. The family member who sins is responsible for his own behavior. He is the one who is lost in the dirt of the earth.
   b. There is no excuse for following peers and stronger personalities. There is no excuse for being passive, weak, or easily misled. A family member is eventually responsible for his own life.
   c. The other family members may not know the *truth* about the love of God and Christ, about the privilege of being saved and having one's sins forgiven and inheriting eternal life. Therefore, a family member is responsible to get out and seek the truth from those who do know the truth.

> "All therefore whatsoever they bid you observe, that observe and do; but do not ye after their works: for they say, and do not" (Mt.23:3).
> "Take heed to thyself that thou be not snared by following them, after that they be destroyed from before thee" (Dt.12:30).
> "And they rejected his statutes, and his covenant that he made with their fathers, and his testimonies which he testified against them; and they followed vanity, and became vain, and went after the heathen that were round about them, concerning whom the LORD had charged them, that they should not do like them" (2 Ki.17:15).
> "Thus saith the LORD; For three transgressions of Judah, and for four, I will not turn away the punishment thereof; because they have despised the law of the LORD, and have not kept his commandments, and their lies caused them to err, after the which their fathers have walked" (Amos 2:4).

**4** (15:9) **Witnessing—Lost, Seeking**: the coin was sought until found. There are several significant facts in this point.

1. The woman changed the whole atmosphere of the house. She lit a candle, for the houses of that day were very dark. Most had only one small window less than two feet across. The woman's only hope of finding the coin was to secure light.

The light represents Christ, the Light of the World (see Deeper Study # 1—Jn.8:12). The woman turned to Christ to bring light to her dark house. Note she used the light in her search, looking behind every door, under every table, in every drawer, and everywhere else. She went nowhere without the Light. (The light also represents the light of her life, that is, her trust in the righteousness of God. See notes—Mt.5:14; Deeper Study # 5—Jn.12:35:36.)

2. The woman swept throughout the house. She swept all the loose and clinging dirt and filth out of her house (cp. sin in the house). She knew two things.
   a. As long as there was loose dirt and filth in the house (sin), she might never find her precious coin.
   b. If she did not clean out all the loose dirt and filth (sin), she might lose another coin.
3. The woman searched for the coin immediately and urgently. The longer the coin stayed lost...
   * the dirtier it became.
   * the more scarred it became.
   * the more it settled in the dirt.
   * the harder it was to find.
4. The woman searched diligently for the coin until she found it. There was great loss felt, as though there were no other silver piece. There was no comfort in knowing the other pieces were safe. So much depended upon finding this one lost coin.

The coin's very purpose and usefulness in life depended upon being found and saved from the dirt of the earth, so one thing was set: she would not give up until she had found it.
   ⇒ She *willed* to find the coin: dedicated and committed her life to finding it, always praying for God's direction and trusting Him for His help.
   ⇒ She *labored* diligently: poured all the thought and energy and effort of her being into seeking her lost coin. Seeking the coin became the focus of her life until she found it.
   ⇒ She *endured*: the work was tedious and hard, for it involved sweeping away the dirt and filth under everything and in every little corner and unseen place.

She looked and prayed while walking upright, bowing, bending, and kneeling. Despite the inconvenience and difficulty, she shifted, removed, and rearranged all the furniture in order to clean and reach out to unnoticed areas—all in an attempt to reach and find the lost coin.

"For the Son of man is come to seek and to save that which was lost" (Lk.19:10).

"Afterward Jesus findeth him in the temple, and said unto him, Behold, thou art made whole: sin no more, lest a worse thing come unto thee" (Jn.5:14).

"They answered and said unto him, Thou wast altogether born in sins, and dost thou teach us? And they cast him out. Jesus heard that they had cast him out; and when he had found him, he said unto him, Dost thou believe on the Son of God?" (Jn.9:34-35).

"And if any man hear my words, and believe not, I judge him not: for I came not to judge the world, but to save the world" (Jn.12:47).

"As many as I love, I rebuke and chasten: be zealous therefore, and repent. Behold, I stand at the door, and knock: if any man hear my voice, and open the door, I will come in to him, and will sup with him, and he with me" (Rev.3:19-20).

"Nevertheless we, according to his promise, look for new heavens and a new earth, wherein dwelleth righteousness. Wherefore, beloved, seeing that ye look for such things, be diligent that ye may be found of him in peace, without spot, and blameless" (2 Pt.3:13-14).

"Return to thine own house, and show how great things God hath done unto thee. And he want his way, and published throughout the whole city how great things Jesus had done unto him" (Lk.8:39).

"For I could wish that myself were accursed from Christ for my brethren, my kinsmen according to the flesh" (Ro.9:3).

**5** (15:9) **Salvation—Joy—Witnessing**: the coin, once found, brought great joy. Note several things.

1. The woman's prayers and efforts payed off. She found her lost coin. Such prayer and diligence are rewarded by God.
2. The woman called her friends and neighbors together for a glorious celebration. Her lost coin had been found. It was a joyous moment, and she wanted those dearest to her to share in the joyful moment.
3. This is critical to remember. Note her words, "the piece which *I had* lost." She had been the one who had lost the coin. Why had she lost it? Note that the candle had not been lit. The house had only natural light shining through a small man-made window. The light of the candle (Christ) did not shine throughout the house.
4. The woman could now rejoice because...
   * she had secured light (Christ)
   * she had swept all the dirt and filth out of her house
   * she had prayed and sought diligently for her lost coin
   * her efforts and prayer led her to the coin

**6** (15:10) **Repentance**: the coin represented a repentant sinner. Note two simple but profound points.

1. The sinner who is found is a man who repents (see note and Deeper Study # 1—Acts 17:29-30).
2. God and all the angels rejoice greatly when one sinner repents.

"Then Peter said unto them, Repent, and be baptized every one of you in the name of Jesus Christ for the remission of sins, and ye shall receive the gift of the Holy Ghost" (Acts 2:38).

"Let the wicked forsake his way, and the unrighteous man his thoughts: and let him return unto the LORD, and he will have mercy upon him; and to our God, for he will abundantly pardon" (Is.55:7).

| | I. The Parable of the Prodigal Son: The Wayward Son, 15:11-24 | | |
|---|---|---|---|
| **1 He said, "Give me"** | | have bread enough and to spare, and I perish with hunger! | a. Thought of his father & his enormous provision |
| a. My inheritance*DS1* | 11 And he said, A certain man had two sons: | 18 I will arise and go to my father, and will say unto him, Father, I have sinned against heaven, and before thee, | b. Thought of his plight |
| | | | c. Thought of humbling himself: |
| | 12 And the younger of them said to his father, Father, give me the portion of goods that falleth to me. And he divided unto them his living. | | 1) Of repenting |
| | | 19 And am no more worthy to be called thy son: make me as one of thy hired servants. | 2) Of confessing his sin & unworthiness |
| b. My independence | | | **4 He arose & returned to his father** |
| | 13 And not many days after the younger son gathered all together, and took his journey into a far country, and there wasted his substance with riotous living. | 20 And he arose, and came to his father. But when he was yet a great way off, his father saw him, and had compassion, and ran, and fell on his neck, and kissed him. | a. He repented—turned from his sinful life |
| c. The result: He wasted his life in riotous living | | | b. He was accepted even before he confessed |
| **2 He met the day when he suffered & was in want** | 14 And when he had spent all, there arose a mighty famine in that land; and he began to be in want. | 21 And the son said unto him, Father, I have sinned against heaven, and in thy sight, and am no more worthy to be called thy son. | c. He confessed |
| a. He suffered being destitute | | | |
| b. He suffered natural disaster | 15 And he went and joined himself to a citizen of that country; and he sent him into his fields to feed swine. | 22 But the father said to his servants, Bring forth the best robe, and put it on him; and put a ring on his hand, and shoes on his feet: | **5 He was accepted when he returned to the father** |
| c. He suffered humiliation*DS2* | | | a. The father restored him |
| d. He suffered hunger | 16 And he would fain have filled his belly with the husks that the swine did eat: and no man gave unto him. | 23 And bring hither the fatted calf, and kill it; and let us eat, and be merry: | b. The father fed the son & celebrated his son's return |
| e. He suffered the loss of friends | | | |
| **3 He came to himself & snapped out of his insanity, back to reality** | 17 And when he came to himself, he said, How many hired servants of my father's | 24 For this my son was dead, and is alive again; he was lost, and is found. And they began to be merry. | c. The father proclaimed his son's new life |

# DIVISION VI

## THE SON OF MAN'S GREAT JOURNEY TO JERUSALEM (STAGE II): HIS TEACHING AND PUBLIC CONFLICT, 13:22-17:10

## I. The Parable of the Prodigal Son: The Wayward Son, 15:11-24

(15:11-24) **Introduction**: the parable of the Prodigal Son is the greatest and most-beloved story ever told in human language. God loves and reaches out to the most prodigal of men, and He runs to embrace any prodigal son who *repents and returns home*. God forgives His prodigal son and restores him, no matter how terrible the sin and failure of the prodigal.

1. He said, "Give me" (v.11-13).
2. He met the day when he suffered and was in want (v.14-16).
3. He came to himself and snapped out of his insanity, back to reality (v.17-19).
4. He arose and returned to his father (v.20-21).
5. He was accepted when he returned to the father (v.22-24).

**1** (15:11-13) **Selfishness—Hardness—Independence—Self—Stubborn—Worldliness**: the prodigal said, "Give me." Note the son was a child of the father's by birth. He belonged to the estate (world) of the father's by natural birth. But it is clear from what follows that the son did not belong to the father *in heart*, *mind*, or *spirit*. The prodigal wanted two things.

1. He said, "*Give me* my inheritance." He wanted money and the things and possessions of the estate (world) which he was to inherit. He wanted to get all the Father would give him so that he could enjoy it now.
   a. He had not earned it, not yet; therefore, he did not deserve it.
   b. He was selfish and self-centered, rude and unkind. He said, "Give me," not "Please" nor "May I have." The effect upon his father and the estate was of little, if any, concern to the prodigal. The father could be hurt and the estate could suffer from the loss of the money and goods; it mattered little to the prodigal.

> **"And the cares of this world, and the deceitfulness of riches, and the lusts of other things entering in, choke the word, and it becometh unfruitful" (Mk.4:19).**
> **"And he said unto them, Take heed, and beware of covetousness: for a man's life consisteth not in the abundance of the things which he possesseth" (Lk.12:15).**
> **"But they that will be rich fall into temptation and a snare, into many foolish and hurtful lusts, which drown men in destruction and perdition. For the love of money is the root of all evil: which while some coveted after, they have erred from the faith, and pierced themselves through with many sorrows" (1 Tim.6:9-10).**

"This know also, that in the last days perilous times shall come. For men shall be lovers of their own selves" (2 Tim.3:1-2).

"But whoso hath this world's good, and seeth his brother have need, and shutteth up his bowels of compassion from him, how dwelleth the love of God in him?" (1 Jn.3:17).

"Israel is an empty vine, he bringeth forth fruit unto himself" (Hos.10:1).

"From the least of them even unto the greatest of them every one is given to covetousness" (Jer.6:13).

"And when ye did eat, and when ye did drink, did not ye eat for yourselves, and drink for yourselves?" (Zech.7:6).

2.   He said, "Give me my independence." This is what the prodigal was really after, the right to his own life. He was tied down to the father's property and was held responsible for the care of the property. He wanted to *cut loose—to be away* from the father and to be relieved of the responsibility of the property. He wanted to live his own life, to do his own thing (Lk.15:12).

The prodigal rejected and turned from the father and his way of life because he felt the father would...
*   demand and require too much work.
*   curtail and limit his freedom.
*   disallow and restrict his fun and pleasure.
*   be unfair and not understand.
*   control and discipline too much.
*   keep an eye and hand upon him.

Note a crucial point: the father gave the son his freedom and possessions. The son was able to do what he wanted with his life and goods (abilities, talents, money, things). All was placed into the son's hands. He could use his life and what he had as he wished without any interference from the father. Since he was an adult son, he wanted to be free from the father and the father respected his adulthood. The father could do nothing about the choice of life chosen by the son. He had to let him go and live as he wished.

"Ye stiffnecked and uncircumcised in heart and ears, ye do always resist the Holy Ghost: as your fathers did, so do ye" (Acts 7:51).

"But chiefly them [the wicked] that walk after the flesh in the lust of uncleanness, and despise government [authority]. Presumptuous are they, selfwilled, they are not afraid to speak evil of dignities [authority]" (2 Pt.2:10).

"I have seen this people, and behold, it is a stiffnecked people" (Ex.32:9).

"He sent prophets to them, to bring them again unto the LORD; and they testified against them: but they would not give ear" (2 Chron.24:19).

"Now be ye not stiffnecked, as your fathers were, but yield yourselves unto the LORD, and enter into his sanctuary, which he hath sanctified for ever: and serve the LORD your God, that the fierceness of his wrath may turn away from you" (2 Chron.30:8).

"To whom he said, This is the rest wherewith ye may cause the weary to rest; and this is the refreshing: yet they would not hear" (Is.28:12).

"For thus saith the Lord GOD, the Holy One of Israel; In returning and rest shall ye be saved; in quietness and in confidence shall be your strength: and ye would not" (Is.30:15).

"Be ye not as the horse, or as the mule, which have no understanding: whose mouth must be held in with bit and bridle, lest they come near unto thee" (Ps.32:9).

"Happy is the man that feareth always: but he that hardeneth his heart shall fall into mischief" (Pr.28:14).

"He, that being often reproved hardeneth his neck, shall suddenly be destroyed, and that without remedy" (Pr.29:1).

"Hearken unto me, ye stouthearted, that are far from righteousness" (Is.46:12).

"I knew that thou art obstinate, and thy neck is an iron sinew, and thy brow brass" (Is.48:4).

"And they have turned unto me the back, and not the face: though I taught them, rising up early and teaching them, yet they have not hearkened to receive instruction" (Jer.32:33).

"As for the word that thou hast spoken unto us in the name of the LORD, we will not hearken unto thee" (Jer.44:16).

"But they refused to hearken, and pulled away the shoulder, and stopped their ears, that they should not hear" (Zech.7:11).

"If ye will not hear, and if ye will not lay it to heart, to give glory unto my name, saith the LORD of hosts, I will even send a curse upon you, and I will curse your blessings: yea, I have cursed them already, because ye do not lay it to heart" (Mal.2:2).

3.   The prodigal wasted his life in riotous living.
a.   He left his father—he rebelled and revolted and journeyed to a *far country*. He chose a country that was drastically different from his father's, a country that was full of carousing and drunkenness, partying and immorality, selfishness and greed, sin and shame, death and hell.
b.   He lived a worldly, fleshly life—living for the pleasure of this life only. "Riotous living" means loose, reckless, wild, extravagant living. It means...

| | | | |
|---|---|---|---|
| • careless spending | • being loose | • gluttonous eating | • dressing to attract |
| • carousing in the forbidden bed | • cursing | • drinking | • having a foul mouth |
| • drunkenness | • telling off-colored jokes | • partying | |

"And that which fell among thorns are they, which, when they have heard, go forth, and are choked with cares and riches and pleasures of this life, and bring no fruit to perfection" (Lk.8:14).

"And I will say to my soul, Soul, thou hast much goods laid up for many years; take thine ease, eat, drink, and be merry" (Lk.12:19).

"Now the works of the flesh are manifest, which are these; adultery, fornication, uncleanness, lasciviousness, idolatry, witchcraft, hatred, variance, emulations, wrath, strife, seditions, heresies" (Gal.5:19-21).

"But she that liveth in pleasure is dead while she liveth" (1 Tim.5:6).

"This know also, that in the last days perilous times shall come. For men shall be lovers of their own selves....lovers of pleasures more than lovers of God" (2 Tim.3:1-2, 4).

"For we ourselves also were sometimes foolish, disobedient, deceived, serving divers lusts and pleasures, living in malice and envy, hateful, and hating one another" (Tit.3:3).

"Ye have lived in pleasure on the earth, and been wanton; ye have nourished your hearts, as in a day of slaughter" (Jas.5:5).

"And shall receive the reward of unrighteousness, as they that count it pleasure to riot [party, revel, carouse] in the day time. Spots they are and blemishes, sporting themselves with their own deceivings while they feast with you" (2 Pt.2:13).

"One sinner destroyeth much good" (Eccl.9:18.)

"Therefore hear now this, thou that art given to pleasures, that dwellest carelessly, that sayest in thine heart, I am, and none else beside me; I shall not sit as a widow, neither shall I know the loss of children" (Is.47:8).

---

**DEEPER STUDY # 1**
(15:12) **Inheritance**: by law the younger son received one-third and the older son two-thirds of a father's estate when the father died. However, if the father wished, he could make gifts to his children throughout his life. The prodigal son was asking for a huge gift amounting to what his final inheritance would be.

---

**2** (15:14-16) **Worldliness—Sin—Enslavement—Bondage—Suffering—Friends—Dissatisfaction—Emptiness—Destitute—Spiritual Poverty**: the prodigal son met the day when he suffered and was in want. He suffered five things.
1. He suffered being *destitute*. He "spent all." He squandered and wasted and misused...

- his money
- his property
- his talents
- his purpose
- his opportunities

- his mind
- his thoughts
- his hands
- his body
- his soul

He misused all these in the lust of his flesh. Note: all these things, ranging from his money to his soul, came from God. They had been given to the son from the Father, either through nature at birth or through a direct gift. The son owed everything to the Father. He should have been working to hold up the name of the Father, serving and repaying the Father for all His marvelous gifts. But instead, the son became a rebel, a prodigal and "spent all" upon "riotous living."

The point is this: the prodigal had nothing on earth to help him. He had wrapped his life up in the pleasure and security of the world; but now, when they were all gone, there was nothing left to help him. He stood *bare*, *empty*, *alone*, and *destitute*. All that he had based his life upon was now gone. He now knew that the world was corruptible and that it passed away. Note: he had cut himself off from his Father (God), so he had no security from God. He was completely void of the confidence and spiritual strength that God would look after him and help him recover. He had not looked to God nor trusted and honored God with his life and goods. Therefore, he was destitute of all spiritual help, left out in the world all alone, having "spent all."

"What fruit had ye then in those things whereof ye are now ashamed? for the end of those things is death....For the wages of sin is death" (Ro.6:21, 23).

"...he that pursueth evil pursueth it to his own death" (Pr.11:19).

"At that time ye were without Christ, being aliens from the commonwealth of Israel, and strangers from the covenants of promise, having no hope, and without God in the world" (Eph.2:12).

"Because thou sayest, I am rich, and increased with goods, and have need of nothing; and knowest not that thou art wretched, and miserable, and poor, and blind, and naked" (Rev.3:17).

"But as for me, my feet were almost gone; my steps had well nigh slipped" (Ps.73:2).

"And the destruction of the transgressors and of the sinners shall be together, and they that forsake the LORD shall be consumed. For they shall be ashamed of the oaks which ye have desired, and ye shall be confounded for the gardens that ye have chosen. For ye shall be as an oak whose leaf fadeth, and as a garden that hath no water" (Is.1:28-30).

"O LORD, are not thine eyes upon the truth? thou hast stricken them, but they have not grieved; thou hast consumed them, but they have refused to receive correction: they have made their faces harder than a rock; they have refused to return. Therefore I said, Surely these are poor; they are foolish: for they know not the way of the LORD, nor the judgment of their God" (Jer.5:3-4).

"Ye have plowed wickedness, ye have reaped iniquity; ye have eaten the fruit of lies: because thou didst trust in thy way, in the multitude of thy mighty men" (Hos.10:13).

"Behold, the days come, saith the Lord GOD, that I will send a famine in the land, not a famine of bread, nor a thirst for water, but of hearing the words of the LORD: and they shall wander from sea to sea, and from the north even to the east, they shall run to and fro to seek the word of the LORD, and shall not find it" (Amos 8:11-12).

2. He suffered *natural disaster*. A famine struck. This refers to all the severe trials and disasters in life because of the very nature of the world. It may be storm, sickness, accident, death. Whatever it is, it is disastrous and causes great loss. Again, the prodigal son was all alone without God's presence; therefore, he had to face the disaster without God's care and help.

"And every one that heareth these sayings of mine, and doeth them not, shall be likened unto a foolish man, which built his house upon the sand: and the rain descended, and the floods came, and the winds blew, and beat upon that house; and it fell: and great was the fall of it" (Mt.7:26-27).

"Every man's work shall be made manifest: for the day shall declare it, because it shall be revealed by fire; and the fire shall try every man's work of what sort it is" (1 Cor.3:13).

3. He suffered *enslavement and humiliation* (see DEEPER STUDY # 2—Lk.15:15 for discussion).

4. He suffered *hunger*. The world's garbage (riotous living) will always leave a man empty and hungry. The world, its pleasures and wealth and styles, will please the body but leave the soul empty. The world cannot permanently...

- satisfy
- fill
- nourish

- provide
- supply
- please

The world will leave a man (deep within, within his soul)...

- dissatisfied
- unfulfilled
- unnourished

- empty
- unsupplied
- displeased

In contrast, only the man who hungers and thirsts after righteousness will be filled and bear the fruit of God's Spirit (see outlines, notes, and DEEPER STUDY # 5,6—Mt.5:6; Gal.5:22-23).

"Jesus answered and said unto her, Whosoever drinketh of this water shall thirst again: but whosoever drinketh of the water that I shall give him shall never thirst; but the water that I shall give him shall be in him a well of water [earthly water, pleasures] springing up into everlasting life" (Jn.4:13-14).

"And when the tempter came to him, he said, If thou be the Son of God, command that these stones be made bread" (Mt.4:3).

"And the fruits that thy soul lusted after are departed from thee, and all things which were dainty and goodly are departed from thee, and thou shalt find them no more at all" (Rev.18:14).

"Meats for the belly, and the belly for meats: but God shall destroy both it and them. Now the body is not for fornication, but for the Lord; and the Lord for the body" (1 Cor.6:13).

"He wandereth abroad for bread, saying, Where is it? He knoweth that the day of darkness is ready at his hand" (Job 15:23).

"All the labor of man is for his mouth, and yet the appetite is not filled" (Eccl.6:7).

"He feedeth on ashes: a deceived heart hath turned him aside, that he cannot deliver his soul" (Is.44:20).

"Wherefore do ye spend money for that which is not bread? and your labor for that which satisfieth not? hearken diligently unto me, and eat ye that which is good, and let your soul delight itself in fatness" (Is.55:2; cp. Is.29:8; 65:13).

5. He suffered *the loss of friends*. The *so-called friends* who surrounded him when he had plenty were now gone. Note two things.

a. When he had plenty and was able to maintain the same social class as his friends, they were all glad to call him friend. But when he was not able to *keep up* with their standard of living, he was not welcomed. They were *above* him, and he was *below* them. He was, in fact, an embarrassment to them. They did not want him around lest others associate them with a person who was unsuccessful and a failure.

b. The friends, at least some of them, were feeling the pinch of the famine as well. Note the selfishness of the world: "no man gave unto him." How like the vast majority of people today! And so many have so much that could be given!

"All my inward friends abhorred me: and they whom I loved are turned against me" (Job 19:19).

"My lovers and my friends stand aloof from my sore; and my kinsmen stand afar off" (Ps.38:11).

"I watch, and am as a sparrow alone upon the housetop" (Ps.102:7).

"I looked on my right hand, and beheld, but there was no man that would know me: refuge failed me; no man cared for my soul" (Ps.142:4).

"Trust ye not in a friend, put ye not confidence in a guide" (Mic.7:5).

**DEEPER STUDY # 2**

(15:15) **Sin**: a Jew was forbidden by law to be attached to a Gentile, a man of a "far country." But even disregarding this prohibition, the humiliation of cleaning hog pens was a horrible pain for a formerly fine rich young man to suffer. There are three pictures here.

   1.   The picture of being spiritually and emotionally and mentally drained. He ran out of spiritual strength, spent his inheritance.

   2.   The picture of attaching himself and becoming enslaved to a person of a "far country." Being spiritually drained, he sought refuge with a man of a "far country," a man away from God.

   3.   The picture of sin's leading and enslaving a man to the "hog pens" of the world.

> "Jesus answered them, Verily, verily, I say unto you, Whosoever committeth sin is the servant of sin" (Jn.8:34).
>
> "Know ye not, that to whom ye yield yourselves servants to obey, his servants ye are to whom ye obey; whether of sin unto death, or of obedience unto righteousness?" (Ro.6:16; cp. Ro.6:21).
>
> "But I see another law in my members, warring against the law of my mind [which tells me better], and bringing me into captivity to the law of sin which is in my members" (Ro.7:23).
>
> "While they [the wicked] promise them liberty, they themselves are the servants of corruption: for of whom a man is overcome, of the same is he brought in bondage" (2 Pt.2:19).
>
> "If a man therefore purge himself from these, he shall be a vessel unto honour, sanctified, and meet for the master's use, and prepared unto every good work" (2 Tim.2:21).
>
> "His own iniquities shall take the wicked himself, and he shall be holden with the cords of his sins" (Pr.5:22).
>
> "Therefore my people are gone into captivity, because they have no knowledge: and their honorable men are famished, and their multitude dried up with thirst" (Is.5:13).

---

**3** (15:17-19) **Sin—Repentance—Thinking**: the prodigal came to himself, snapped out of his insanity, back to reality. Note the words "came to himself." Jesus considers a person away from God to be *mad, insane, living in an unreal world*.

> "This is an evil among all things that are done under the sun, that there is one event unto all: yea, also the heart of the sons of men is full of evil, and madness is in their heart while they live, and after that they go to the dead" (Eccl.9:3).

Two things are indicated about repentance.

⇒   Repentance is the beginning of sanity and reality, the very basis for building a sound life.

⇒   The beginning of repentance is thought, thinking about one's need to repent and turn back to God.

Note the words, "When he came to himself, he said"; that is, he began to think to himself. He thought long and hard upon these things.

   1.   He thought upon his Father (God) and His enormous provision.

   a.   The Father's "many servants" would be the believers, the children of God.

   b.   The Father's "bread" was enough to feed all, and then there was even more to spare.

The prodigal remembered how his father had been able to provide for all. He remembered the sense of belonging, of being a family and of fellowshipping together among all the servants of God, the great provision of love and joy and peace, of purpose and meaning and significance. His father had it all and more to spare.

   2.   He thought upon his plight: "I perish" (v.17). The meaning is both now and future.

   a.   He was perishing now: empty, lonely, unhappy, humiliated, destitute, without purpose, meaning, or significance, without family or friend.

   b.   He was doomed to perish eternally (Jn.3:16; see DEEPER STUDY # 1—Heb.9:27).

   3.   He thought about humbling himself. Humbling himself would involve two significant steps.

   a.   Repenting. Note the prodigal would have to "arise," that is, turn from and leave the far country, and go to his father. These are the steps involved in repentance...

   •   arising, getting up.
   •   turning away from one's sinful life.
   •   turning toward and moving toward God.

Note that repentance is simply a changed life, a life that turns from sin to righteousness, from self to God, from this world to heaven, from the temporal to the eternal.

   b.   Confessing. The prodigal would have to confess...

   •   his sin.
   •   his unworthiness to be called God's son.

**Thought 1.** Note that the prodigal was only thinking of these things, not doing them—not yet. However, the desire and longing to return to his father was gnawing at his heart deeply.

> "Blessed are they which do hunger and thirst after righteousness: for they shall be filled" (Mt.5:6; cp. Lk.6:21).

"In the last day, that great day of the feast, Jesus stood and cried, saying, If any man thirst, let him come unto me, and drink" (Jn.7:37).

"I stretch forth my hands unto thee: my soul thirsteth after thee, as a thirsty land" (Ps.143:6; cp. Ps.42:2; 38:9; 63:1; 119:174).

"Ho, every one that thirsteth, come ye to the waters, and he that hath  no money; come ye, buy, and eat; yea, come, buy wine and milk without money and without price" (Is.55:1).

**4** (15:20-21) **Repentance—Confession—God, Seeking Men—Contrition:** the prodigal arose and returned to his father. This was the greatest of moments for the prodigal, the most momentous event in the life of any sinner. It is the summit of human experience. The prodigal returned to God: he sought reconciliation with his Father.

1. He repented: he did get up and turn from his sinful life and go to his Father. He was no longer just thinking about it; he was now repenting and going to the Father.

"Blessed are they that mourn: for they shall be comforted" (Mt.5:4).

"Repent ye therefore, and be converted, that your sins may be blotted out, when the times of refreshing shall come from the presence of the Lord" (Acts 3:19).

"Repent therefore of this thy wickedness, and pray God, if perhaps the thought of thine heart may be forgiven thee" (Acts 8:22).

"For godly sorrow worketh repentance to salvation not to be repented of: but the sorrow of the world worketh death" (2 Cor.7:10).

"Let the wicked forsake his way, and the unrighteous man his thoughts: and let him return unto the LORD, and he will have mercy upon him; and to our God, for he will abundantly pardon" (Is.55:7).

"But if the wicked will turn from all his sins that he hath committed, and keep all my statutes, and do that which is lawful and right, he shall surely live, he shall not die" (Ezk.18:21; cp. Ezk.18:31).

"Say unto them, As I live, saith the Lord GOD, I have no pleasure in the death of the wicked; but that the wicked turn from his way and live: turn ye, turn ye from your evil ways; for why will ye die?" (Ezk.33:11; cp. Joel 2:12).

"Therefore say thou unto them, Thus saith the LORD of hosts; Turn ye unto me, saith the LORD of hosts, and I will turn unto you, saith the LORD of hosts" (Zech.1:3; cp. Mal.3:7).

2. He was accepted even before he confessed. This is a significant point to note. Repentance is the sign that we are sincere when we confess, and God knows we are sincere when He sees us actually turn from our wicked ways. He forgives when we repent, when we truly want Him to forgive. This is the reason the Father runs to meet His son. The son had turned away from the far country and *had come* to the Father. Note:

⇒ the Father's eyes were merciful: no matter what He had seen, He wanted to have mercy.
⇒ the Father's heart was merciful: He wanted to reach out in compassion to the sinning son.
⇒ the Father's feet were merciful: He wanted to run and meet and *escort* the sinner home.
⇒ the Father's arms were merciful: He wanted to embrace the prodigal son and weep with him.
⇒ the Father's lips were merciful: He wanted to welcome the prodigal son home with all the tenderness of a true Father.

"The LORD is nigh unto them that are of a broken heart; and saveth such as be of a contrite spirit" (Ps.34:18).

"The sacrifices of God are a broken spirit: a broken and a contrite heart, O God, thou wilt not despise" (Ps.51:17).

"Sing forth the honour of his name: make his praise glorious" (Ps.66:2).

"And rend your heart, and not your garments, and turn unto the LORD your God: for he is gracious and merciful, slow to anger, and of great kindness, and repenteth him of the evil" (Joel 2:13).

3. He confessed. He needed to confess his terrible evil: that he had rebelled, rejected, and sinned against the Father. He had sinned against heaven, all that heaven stood for in all its righteousness and godliness; and sinned in the sight of God, going against all that the Father stood for and knew to be best.

"If we confess our sins, he is faithful and just to forgive us our sins, and to cleanse us from all unrighteousness" (1 Jn.1:9).

"Now therefore make confession unto the LORD God of your fathers, and do his pleasure: and separate yourselves from the people of the land, and from the strange wives" (Ezra 10:11).

"He that covereth his sins shall not prosper: but whoso confesseth and forsaketh them shall have mercy" (Pr.28:13).

"Only acknowledge thine iniquity, that thou hast transgressed against the LORD thy God, and hast scattered thy ways to the strangers under every green tree, and ye have not obeyed my voice, saith the LORD" (Jer.3:13).

"He [God] looketh upon men, and if any say, I have sinned, and perverted that which was right, and it profited me not; he will deliver his soul from going into the pit, and his life shall see the light" (Job 33:27-28).

**5** (15:22-24) **Forgiveness—Restoration**: the prodigal was accepted and restored. But note: he would not have been accepted and restored if he had not returned. The key to being accepted by God is *repentance*. We must always remember this fact, a fact which determines our eternal destiny.

1. The father restored him.
   a. The "*robe*" restored him to a position of sonship and honor. It symbolized being clothed with the righteousness of Christ.

> "For he hath made him to be sin for us, who knew no sin; that we might be made the righteousness of God in him" (2 Cor.5:21).
> "But put ye on the Lord Jesus Christ, and make not provision for the flesh, to fulfil the lusts thereof" (Ro.13:14).
> "And that ye put on the new man, which after God is created in righteousness and true holiness" (Eph.4:24).
> "And have put on the new man, which is renewed in knowledge after the image of him that created him" (Col.3:10).

   b. The "*ring*" restored him to a position of authority. The son was now to represent the father and his kingdom.

> "And because ye are sons, God hath sent forth the Spirit of his Son into your hearts, crying, Abba, Father. Wherefore thou art no more a servant, but a son; and if a son, then an heir of God through Christ" (Gal.4:6-7).
> "To him that overcometh will I grant to sit with me in my throne, even as I also overcame, and am set down with my Father in his throne" (Rev.3:21).
> "For ye have not received the spirit of bondage again to fear; but ye have received the Spirit of adoption, whereby we cry, Abba, Father. The Spirit itself beareth witness with our spirit, that we are the children of God: and if children, then heirs; heirs of God, and joint-heirs with Christ; if so be that we suffer with him, that we may be also glorified together" (Ro.8:15-17).
> "That being justified by his grace, we should be made heirs according to the hope of eternal life" (Tit.3:7).

   c. The "*shoes*" immediately restored and elevated him above servanthood, which means he became a *free man*. The son was now shod with shoes to carry the gospel of peace wherever he went.

> "And ye shall know the truth, and the truth shall make you free" (Jn.8:32).
> "Being then made free from sin, ye became the servants of righteousness" (Ro.6:18).
> "For the law of the Spirit of life in Christ Jesus hath made me free from the law of sin and death" (Ro.8:2).
> "Now the Lord is that Spirit: and where the Spirit of the Lord is, there is liberty" (2 Cor.3:17).
> "But take heed lest by any means this liberty of yours become a stumblingblock to them that are weak" (1 Cor.8:9).
> "For, brethren, ye have been called unto liberty; only use not liberty for an occasion to the flesh, but by love serve one another" (Gal.5:13).
> "And your feet shod with the preparation of the gospel of peace" (Eph.6:15).
> "As free, and not using your liberty for a cloke of maliciousness, but as the servants of God" (1 Pt.2:16).

   d. The "*celebration*" pictures reconciliation, full acceptance, and the great joy of the occasion.

> "But after that the kindness and love of God our Saviour toward man appeared, not by works of righteousness which we have done, but according to his mercy he saved us, by the washing of regeneration, and renewing of the Holy Ghost; which he shed on us abundantly through Jesus Christ our Saviour; that being justified by his grace, we should be made heirs according to the hope of eternal life" (Tit.3:4-7).

2. The father fed the son and celebrated his son's return. Both facts are important. All that the son needed was fed to him. He was fully accepted into the family; therefore, all the food of heaven was laid out before him. It was there to nourish him. But even more: there was celebration and great joy over the son's return. The whole household celebrated in joy.

> "That in the ages to come he might show the exceeding riches of his grace in his kindness toward us through Christ Jesus" (Eph.2:7).
> "But my God shall supply all your need according to his riches in glory by Christ Jesus" (Ph.4:19).
> "And the grace of our Lord was exceeding abundant with faith and love which is in Christ Jesus" (1 Tim.1:14).
> "Riches and honor are with me; yea, durable riches and righteousness" (Pr.8:18).
> "The blessing of the LORD, it maketh rich, and he addeth no sorrow with it" (Pr.10:22).

3.  The Father proclaimed His son's new life.
    a.  He "was dead and is alive again."

> "For God so loved the world, that he gave his only begotten Son, that whosoever believeth in him should not perish, but have everlasting life" (Jn.3:16).
> "Verily, verily, I say unto you, He that heareth my word, and believeth on him that sent me, hath everlasting life, and shall not come into condemnation; but is passed from death unto life" (Jn.5:24).
> "And you hath he quickened, who were dead in trespasses and sins" (Eph.2:1).
> "Being born again, not of corruptible seed, but of incorruptible, by the word of God, which liveth and abideth for ever" (1 Pt.1:23).

    b.  "He was lost and is found."

> "All we like sheep have gone astray, we have turned every one to his own way; and the LORD hath laid on him the iniquity of us all" (Is.53:6).
> "And when he cometh home, he calleth together his friends and neighbours, saying unto them, Rejoice with me; for I have found my sheep which was lost....And when she hath found it, she calleth her friends and her neighbours together, saying, Rejoice with me; for I have found the piece which I had lost" (Lk.15:6, 9).
> "For the Son of man is come to seek and to save that which was lost" (Lk.19:10).
> "Who his own self bare our sins in his own body on the tree, that we, being dead to sins, should live unto righteousness: by whose stripes ye were healed. For ye were as sheep going astray; but are now returned unto the Shepherd and Bishop of your souls" (1 Pt.2:24-25).

| | | | |
|---|---|---|---|
| **1 Fault 1: He was in the field away from home** | **J. The Parable of the Elder Son: The Self-Righteous Religionist, 15:25-32**<br><br>25 Now his elder son was in the field: and as he came and drew nigh to the house, he heard musick and dancing.<br>26 And he called one of the servants, and asked what these things meant.<br>27 And he said unto him, Thy brother is come; and thy father hath killed the fatted calf, because he hath received him safe and sound. | 29 And he answering said to his father, Lo, these many years do I serve thee, neither transgressed I at any time thy commandment: and yet thou never gavest me a kid, that I might make merry with my friends:<br>30 But as soon as this thy son was come, which hath devoured thy living with harlots, thou hast killed for him the fatted calf.<br>31 And he said unto him, Son, thou art ever with me, and all that I have is thine. | **3 Fault 3: He was self-righteous**<br>a. He claimed to be religious<br>b. He claimed to be moral & just<br>c. He felt he deserved more, that he was not recognized enough<br>**4 Fault 4: He lacked compassion & the understanding of sinners** |
| **2 Fault 2: He shut himself out** | 28 And he was angry, and would not go in: therefore came his father out, and in-treated him. | 32 It was meet that we should make merry, and be glad: for this thy brother was dead, and is alive again; and was lost, and is found. | **5 Fault 5: He failed to see two critical facts**<br>a. He had the same blessings available<br>b. His brother was truly saved |

# DIVISION VI

## THE SON OF MAN'S GREAT JOURNEY TO JERUSALEM (STAGE II): HIS TEACHING AND PUBLIC CONFLICT, 13:22-17:10

## J.    The Parable of the Elder Son: The Self-Righteous Religionist, 15:25-32

(15:25-32) **Introduction**: this passage is about the second son of the father (v.11, 25). The elder son represents the self-righteous religionist—the moral, the just, the good—the man who has never committed gross and visible sin. He is religious and does religious works; therefore, he feels and believes he is acceptable to God. In this parable Jesus pointed out five faults with the self-righteous religionist. (See outlines and notes—Lk.11:37-54; 18:9-12; Ro.2:17-29 for more discussion.)

1.    Fault 1: he was in the field away from home (v.25-27).
2.    Fault 2: he shut himself out (v.28).
3.    Fault 3: he was self-righteous (v.29).
4.    Fault 4: he lacked compassion and the understanding of sinners (v.30).
5.    Fault 5: he failed to see two critical facts (v.31-32).

**1** (15:25-27) **Religionists—Errors of**: the first fault of the religionist is his tragic position. He was "in the field" away from the house. He was in the field of religion, but not in the house of salvation. He was unaware of his father's affairs (v.26-27).

1.    The elder son was *in the field* of his father. He was working diligently, looking after the responsibilities of the field. So it is with the religionist. He is working diligently at the field of religious things: services, rituals, ceremonies, ordinances, prayers. He even uses religious talk and terms in his daily conversation. He attends services and prays and talks as much as he needs to satisfy his conscience.

The point is this: the religionist is "in the field" of religion. He professes to know God and to be a follower of religion. Just how much religion he practices depends upon how much religion he needs to salve his conscience and to feel acceptable to God. Most men want to feel acceptable to God, so they do whatever amount of religion makes them feel acceptable.

> **Thought 1.** How much religion does a man need to salve his conscience and make him feel acceptable to God?
> 1)    Some men sense the need for *very little religious activity*.
> 2)    Other men sense the need for *a great deal of religious activity*, even to becoming professional ministers.

2.    The elder son was in the field, not in the house of his father.
⇒    He did not know what was going on in the house (of salvation and repentance), only what was happening in the field (of religion).
⇒    When he looked at the *celebration* of repentant sinners, he questioned. He did not understand.
⇒    He had to ask what the celebration meant (what the celebration of repentance and salvation meant).

> **"Having a form of godliness, but denying the power thereof" (2 Tim.3:5).**
> **"Woe unto you scribes and Pharisees [religionists], hypocrites! for ye pay tithe...and have omitted the weightier matters of the law, judgment, mercy, and faith: these ought ye to have done, and not to leave the other undone" (Mt.23:23).**
> **"Ye observe [rituals] days, and months, and times and years. I am afraid of you, lest I have bestowed upon you labour in vain" (Gal.4:10-11).**
> **"For by grace are ye saved through faith; and that not of yourselves: it is the gift of God: not of works, lest any man should boast" (Eph.2:8-9).**

"[God] who hath saved us, and called us with an holy calling, not according to our works, but according to his own purpose and grace, which was given us in Christ Jesus before the world began" (2 Tim.1:9).

"But after that the kindness and love of God our Saviour toward man appeared, not by works of righteousness which we have done, but according to his mercy he saved us, by the washing of regeneration, and renewing of the Holy Ghost; which he shed on us abundantly through Jesus Christ our Saviour; that being justified by his grace, we should be made heirs according to the hope of eternal life" (Tit.3:4-7).

**2** (15:28) **Religionists—Jealousy—Unbelief**: the second fault of the religionist is his tragic rejection of God. He shuts himself out. Note the son in the field became angry at the repentant son who was now in the father's house. He did not understand repentance, how a man who had been so immoral, dirty, and unclean could change so much. The claims of being safe and secure and the sound of celebration and testimony disturbed the son from the field. So it is with the religionist. He does not understand such claims as...

- being saved.
- being saved *by God Himself.*
- being filled with power
- being filled with joy.
- being delivered *immediately* from enslaved habits (such as alcohol, smoking, immorality, cursing, covetousness, selfishness).
- being healed.
- being indwelt and given power by the Holy Spirit.

The religionist reacts against such claims. How? He wants nothing to do with such a *house of repentance and salvation.* He shuts himself out. Sometimes he even talks against and criticizes such a celebration and house.

"But woe unto you, scribes and Pharisees, hypocrites! for ye shut up the kingdom of heaven against men: for ye neither go in yourselves, neither suffer ye them that are entering to go in" (Mt.23:13).

"Wherefore the Lord said, Forasmuch as this people draw near me with their mouth, and with their lips do honour me, but have removed their heart far from me, and their fear toward me is taught by the precept of men....the wisdom of their wise men shall perish, and the understanding of their prudent men shall be hid" (Is.29:13-14; cp. Mk.7:6).

"For the priest's lips should keep knowledge, and they should seek the law at his mouth: for he is the messenger of the LORD of hosts. But ye are departed out of the way; ye have caused many to stumble at the law; ye have corrupted the covenant of Levi, saith the LORD of hosts" (Mal.2:7-8).

Note a significant fact: the religionist *shut himself out.* God does not shut him out. The *father* "came...out and intreated him" to come in. The father does even more for the religionist in that he comes seeking him, whereas the prodigal had to return home before the father could run out to meet him. The father came out and begged the religious son to understand repentance and salvation and to come in. (The religionist is already in the field of religion and close to the gospel, whereas the prodigal son is out in the field of the world far removed from the church and the gospel.)

Note the terrible jealousy and envy in the heart of the elder son. He was jealous of the treatment, of the fruit and blessing's being given to the prodigal son. (See DEEPER STUDY # 1, *Fruit-bearing*—Jn.15:1-8; cp. Gal.5:22-23 for more discussion.)

**3** (15:29) **Religionists—Self-righteousness**: the third fault of the religionist is his tragic self-righteousness. Note the elder son claimed three things.

1. He claimed to be religious: "I serve thee." A religionist does serve God through religious things: he worships, prays, tithes, witnesses, reads his Bible, and teaches.

2. He claimed to be moral and just: "Neither transgressed I at any time thy commandment." He never committed immorality, not any other dirty or unclean act that could be visibly or publicly seen. He never stole, cheated, lied, or cursed. He was obedient to his parents and responsible in his work and duties both to God and man.

3. He felt he deserved more, that he was not recognized enough: "Thou never gavest me a kid," that is, the spiritual food of power, love, joy, peace, confidence, joy, and the absolute assurance of heaven and eternal life. He felt he did not get enough, that he deserved more than those who were now filled with so much spiritual food and celebration.

Note what the religionist lacks: *faith* (Mt.23:23). He just does not *trust* the Father's love and judgment, His plan of salvation and repentance *for all.*

"Yet thou sayest, Because I am innocent, surely his anger shall turn from me. Behold, I will plead with thee, because thou sayest, I have not sinned" (Jer.2:35).

"Many will say to me in that day, Lord, Lord, have we not prophesied in thy name? and in thy name have cast out devils? and in thy name done many wonderful works? And then will I profess unto them, I never knew you: depart from me, ye that work iniquity" (Mt.7:22-23).

"Knowing that a man is not justified by the works of the law, but by the faith of Jesus Christ, even we have believed in Jesus Christ, that we might be justified by the faith of Christ, and not by the works of the law: for by the works of the law shall no flesh be justified" (Gal.2:16).

"Woe unto you, scribes and Pharisees, hypocrites! for ye make clean the outside of the cup and of the platter, but within they are full of extortion and excess" (Mt.23:25).

"Even so ye also outwardly appear righteous unto men, but within ye are full of hypocrisy and iniquity" (Mt.23:28).

**4** (15:30) **Self-righteousness—Compassion, Lack of—Hardness—Pride**: the fourth fault of the religionist is his tragic lack of compassion and the understanding of God's spiritual feast. Note three things about the elder son.

1. He did not call the prodigal son his brother. He said with arrogance, "*thy son.*" He felt *above* and *better* than the prodigal son, despite the change of heart and life that existed within the repentant son. He felt no compassion or joy whatsoever. But note something: his statement was true. The repentant son was *God's true son.*

2. He focused on the prodigal's faults, especially his immoral past. He ignored the prodigal son's repentance, his return home, and the glorious reunion. He ignored God's...

- great love
- great forgiveness
- great joy

3. He did not understand God's spiritual feast. The fatted calf would symbolize the spiritual food God gives to the repentant sinner.

    a. There was the food of absolute assurance of salvation and eternal life.

> "For ye have not received the spirit of bondage again to fear; but ye have received the Spirit of adoption, whereby we cry, Abba, Father. The Spirit itself beareth witness with our spirit, that we are the children of God: and if children, then heirs; heirs of God, and joint-heirs with Christ; if so be that we suffer with him, that we may be also glorified together" (Ro.8:15-17).
>
> "But when the fulness of the time was come, God sent forth his Son, made of a woman, made under the law, to redeem them that were under the law, that we might receive the adoption of sons. And because ye are sons, God hath sent forth the Spirit of his Son into your hearts, crying, Abba, Father" (Gal.4:4-6).

    b. There was the food of love, joy, and peace.

> "But the fruit of the Spirit is love, joy, peace, longsuffering, gentleness, goodness, faith, meekness, temperance: against such there is no law" (Gal.5:22-23).
>
> "Not every one that saith unto me, Lord, Lord, shall enter into the kingdom of heaven; but he that doeth the will of my Father which is in heaven" (Mt.7:21).
>
> "My little children, let us not love in word, neither in tongue; but in deed and in truth" (1 Jn.3:18).
>
> "And this is his commandment, That we should believe on the name of his Son Jesus Christ, and love one another, as he gave us commandment" (1 Jn.3:23).

**5** (15:31-32) **Religionists—Blindness—Unbelief—Rejection**: the fifth fault of the religionist is his tragic blindness. He fails to see two critical facts.

1. The religionist has the same privileges as the repentant prodigal. Note the words, "All that I have is thine." He has the worship, the Word, the promises, the preaching, and the teaching. He has constant exposure to all that is God's (see outline and notes—Ro.9:4-5 for more discussion). He can enter God's "house of salvation" anytime. All he has to do is repent, turn from trusting the field of religion, and enter God's house. He simply needs to believe in and trust the love of God. He is to stop opposing God's love to the prodigal sinner and come in himself.

2. The salvation of the repentant prodigal was real.

    ⇒ This thy brother was dead, and is alive.

> "Verily, verily, I say unto you, He that heareth my word, and believeth on him that sent me, hath everlasting life, and shall not come into condemnation; but is passed from death unto life" (Jn.5:24).
>
> "And you hath he quickened, who were dead in trespasses and sins" (Eph.2:1).
>
> "Being born again, not of corruptible seed, but of incorruptible, by the word of God, which liveth and abideth for ever" (1 Pt.1:23).
>
> "For God so loved the world, that he gave his only begotten Son, that whosoever believeth in him should not perish, but have everlasting life" (Jn.3:16).

    ⇒ This thy brother was lost, and is found.

> "All we like sheep have gone astray, we have turned every one to his own way; and the LORD hath laid on him the iniquity of us all" (Is.53:6).
>
> "And when he cometh home, he calleth together his friends and neighbours, saying unto them, Rejoice with me; for I have found my sheep which was lost....And when she hath found it, she calleth her friends and her neighbours together, saying, Rejoice with me; for I have found the piece which I had lost" (Lk.15:6, 9).
>
> "For the Son of man is come to seek and to save that which was lost" (Lk.19:10).
>
> "Who his own self bare our sins in his own body on the tree, that we, being dead to sins, should live unto righteousness: by whose stripes ye were healed. For ye were as sheep going astray; but are now returned unto the Shepherd and Bishop of your souls" (1 Pt.2:24-25).

**CHAPTER 16**

**K. The Parable of the Unjust Steward: Man and Money, 16:1-13**

**1 The unjust steward**

a. He was charged with embezzlement, with wasting the Lord's goods
b. He was required to prepare a final accounting

c. He knew he was guilty & was unwilling to change & cry for mercy

d. He decided what to do: He would forget the Lord & court the favor & rewards of men[DS1]

And he said also unto his disciples, There was a certain rich man, which had a steward; and the same was accused unto him that he had wasted his goods.

2 And he called him, and said unto him, How is it that I hear this of thee? give an account of thy stewardship; for thou mayest be no longer steward.

3 Then the steward said within himself, What shall I do? for my lord taketh away from me the stewardship: I cannot dig; to beg I am ashamed.

4 I am resolved what to do, that, when I am put out of the stewardship, they may receive me into their houses.

5 So he called every one of his lord's debtors unto him, and said unto the first, How much owest thou unto my lord?

6 And he said, An hundred measures of oil. And he said unto him, Take thy bill, and sit down quickly, and write fifty.

7 Then said he to another, And how much owest thou? And he said, An hundred measures of wheat. And he said unto him, Take thy bill, and write fourscore.

8 And the lord commended the unjust steward, because he had done wisely: for the children of this world are in their generation wiser than the children of light.

9 And I say unto you, Make to yourselves friends of the mammon of unrighteousness; that, when ye fail, they may receive you into everlasting habitations.

10 He that is faithful in that which is least is faithful also in much: and he that is unjust in the least is unjust also in much.

11 If therefore ye have not been faithful in the unrighteous mammon, who will commit to your trust the true riches?

12 And if ye have not been faithful in that which is another man's, who shall give you that which is your own?

13 No servant can serve two masters: for either he will hate the one, and love the other; or else he will hold to the one, and despise the other. Ye cannot serve God and mammon.

**2 The worldly are more wise in their material pursuits than God's people are in their spiritual pursuits**

**3 The Christian is to use material wealth for good**
a. Wealth will fail—at death
b. Giving will be reciprocated

**4 The Christian is to be faithful in handling possessions: Will determine what he will be trusted with eternally**
a. Money is the least trust
b. Unfaithfulness disqualifies one from true, heavenly riches
c. Unfaithfulness disqualifies one from all he would receive

**5 The Christian cannot serve two masters: Must choose God or riches**

# DIVISION VI

## THE SON OF MAN'S GREAT JOURNEY TO JERUSALEM (STAGE II): HIS TEACHING AND PUBLIC CONFLICT, 13:22-17:10

## K. The Parable of the Unjust Steward: Man and Money, 16:1-13

(16:1-13) **Introduction—Unjust Steward**: this passage is looked upon as one of the most difficult passages in all of Scripture to understand. Verse eight is the primary reason. In studying the passage, two overall approaches can be taken. A person can read the parable and the comments about the parable made by Christ and take it only for what it says, that is, without adding any comment or seeing any application in it. However, a person can also see application in the parable as well as in the points taught by Christ. To help those interested in the latter approach, some application is given to the points of the parable.

The steward was a trusted slave who was put in charge of the landowner's estate. He was highly regarded and esteemed, considered to be completely trustworthy. The term "*steward*" is applied to ministers (1 Cor.4:1) and to believers in general (1 Pt.4:10; Lk.16:1). (See note, pt.2—Lk.12:41-48.)

1. The unjust steward (v.1-7).
2. The worldly are more wise in their material pursuits than God's people are in their spiritual pursuits (v.8).
3. The Christian is to use material wealth for good (v.9).
4. The Christian is to be faithful in handling possessions: how he handles his possessions will determine what he will be trusted with eternally (v.10-12).
5. The Christian cannot serve two masters: he must choose God or riches (v.13).

**1** (16:1-7) **Parable, Unjust Steward**: in the parable itself Jesus said four things about the unjust steward.

1. The steward was charged with embezzlement, with *wasting the Lord's "goods."* The steward was in charge of the Lord's property, of all the Lord's goods. Therefore, it was easy for him to use the goods for his own purposes just as he desired. The point is, God has given every man some "goods": life, talents, house, property, money, duty, a sense of re-

sponsibility, conscience, family, and a host of other goods. Every man is charged with embezzlement, with misusing the goods to some degree

> "For the kingdom of heaven is as a man travelling into a far country, who called his own servants, and delivered unto them his goods. And unto one he gave five talents, to another two, and to another one; to every man according to his several ability; and straightway took his journey" (Mt.25:14-15; cp. Ro.12:6-8; 1 Cor.12:7f).
> "And he called his ten servants, and delivered them ten pounds, and said unto them, Occupy till I come" (Lk.19:13).
> "Moreover it is required in stewards, that a man be found faithful" (1 Cor.4:2).
> "As every man hath received the gift, even so minister the same one to another, as good stewards of the manifold grace of God" (1 Pt.4:10).

2.  The steward was required to prepare a final accounting. Two facts are important in this point.
    a.  The Lord hears that the steward has been misusing His "goods." Note: the Lord had only *heard* about the embezzlement. The full evidence against the steward was not yet fully known. The Lord gave the steward a chance to prove his trust and faithfulness. The accounting did not mean that the steward would be dismissed from the Lord's estate (heaven, Kingdom of God), only that he must prove his trust and faithfulness. Of course, if the steward had not been faithful in looking after the Lord's goods, then he would be dismissed: "Thou canst no longer [ougardunei] be steward."
    b.  The final accounting is at death (Heb.9:27). If the steward is found to have been untrustworthy, he will be *dismissed and discharged* from the Lord's estate (kingdom, heaven, eternal life. See DEEPER STUDY # 3—Mt.19:23-24.)

**Thought 1.** Death will take us away from all our earthly goods. If our accounting justifies us, then we shall be given a much greater responsibility, an eternal responsibility, for the Lord.

> "Therefore is the kingdom of heaven likened unto a certain king, which would take account of his servants" (Mt.18:23).
> "And when the time of the fruit drew near, he sent his servants to the husbandmen, that they might receive the fruits of it" (Mt.21:34).
> "After a long time the lord of those servants cometh, and reckoneth with them" (Mt.25:19).
> "And it came to pass, that when he was returned, having received the kingdom, then he commanded these servants to be called unto him, to whom he had given the money, that he might know how much every man had gained by trading" (Lk.19:15).
> "So then every one of us shall give account of himself to God" (Ro.14:12).
> "And as it is appointed unto men once to die, but after this the judgment" (Heb.9:27).
> "Wherein they think it strange that ye run not with them to the same excess of riot, speaking evil of you" (1 Pt.4:4).

3.  The steward knew he was guilty and was unwilling to change or ask for mercy. Note two things.
    a.  The words "What shall I do...?" The steward knew he was guilty and that the Lord was going to dismiss him.
    b.  The steward thought over what he should do. He reasoned out two courses of action.
        ⇒ He could dig. However, he was not willing to dig, not willing to be demoted to a field laborer and to serve in such a low capacity.
        ⇒ He could beg. However, he was *too proud* to leave the Lord and openly beg. He would be ashamed.
Now note something not mentioned. He was too proud to beg forgiveness of the Lord, too proud to be known as a repentant embezzler (sinner). This is the dominant point, although not mentioned. Begging for forgiveness was the steward's only hope. He considered every course of action but this one.

> "He that covereth his sins shall not prosper: but whoso confesseth and forsaketh them shall have mercy" (Pr.28:13).
> "Woe unto them that seek deep to hide their counsel from the LORD, and their works are in the dark, and they say, Who seeth us? and who knoweth us?" (Is.29:15).
> "Woe to the rebellious children, saith the LORD, that take counsel, but not of me; and that cover with a covering, but not of my spirit, that they may add sin to sin" (Is.30:1).

4.  The steward decided what to do: he would forget the Lord and court the favor and returns of men. He did what he could to secure the acceptance and favor of men.
    a.  He led them to be dishonest, to dismiss and lower their debts to the Lord. They were led to *embezzle and hold back* some of their goods. Note: the steward was in a responsible position (a religionist) and misled others.

    **Thought 1.** How many religionists mislead others through false teaching, causing so many not to use their lives and gifts for God.

    b.  This act *stole* from the Lord; it stole the goods (life and gifts) of others from the Lord.

c. The steward misled others to benefit himself, to secure his position and livelihood. And he did it in a most shrewd way, a way that was pleasing and profitable to the debtors. Anyone of them would gladly help the steward when he needed their support. (See DEEPER STUDY # 1—Lk.16:6-7.)

> "But ye are departed out of the way; ye have caused many to stumble at the law" (Mal.2:8).
> "...judge this rather, that no man put a stumblingblock or an occasion to fall in his brother's way" (Ro.14:13).

---

**DEEPER STUDY # 1**
(16:6-7) **Measure—Oil—Wealth**: a measure of oil (botos) was about 8 3/4 gallons. Therefore, the payment was a sizeable 800 gallons. The measure of wheat (koros) was about 10 bushels. This too was sizeable, about 1,000 bushels.

---

**2** (16:8) **Dedication—Worldly—Materialism**: the worldly are more wise in their material pursuits than God's people are in their spiritual pursuits. Note two points.
1. Jesus said the unjust steward did "wisely."
   ⇒ He looked out for himself, his personal welfare. In this he was very wise.
   ⇒ He was dedicated and sold out to taking care of his future.

Jesus was not commending the steward for his cunning deceit. He commended him for his concern about the future and his dedication and energy. The steward was *sold out* to pursuing a goal, and that part of his life was commendable. His mistake was being sold out to pursuing material wealth and comfort instead of Christ.
2. Jesus said the worldly are wiser "in their generation" than believers. Why? Because they dedicate so much energy and effort to caring for their earthly welfare.

The point is clear. Every disciple should be just as dedicated and sold out in spiritual pursuits as the worldly are in their material pursuits. The disciple is not to be outdone in the exertion of energy and dedication.

**Thought 1.** Note how much more initiative and energy this man of the world exerted in his pursuits than many Christians exert in theirs.

> "But he that received seed into the good ground is he that heareth the word, and understandeth it; which also beareth fruit, and bringeth forth, some an hundredfold, some sixty, some thirty" (Mt.13:23).
> "And he said to them all, If any man will come after me, let him deny himself, and take up his cross daily, and follow me. For whosoever will save his life shall lose it: but whosoever will lose his life for my sake, the same shall save it" (Lk.9:23-24).
> "I beseech you therefore, brethren, by the mercies of God, that ye present your bodies a living sacrifice, holy, acceptable unto God, which is your reasonable service" (Ro.12:1).
> "Trust in the LORD with all thine heart; and lean not unto thine own understanding" (Pr.3:5).
> "My son, give me thine heart, and let thine eyes observe my ways" (Pr.23:26).

**3** (16:9) **Stewardship—Wealth—Riches—Materialism**: the Christian is to use material wealth for good. The Christian is not being told to seek the friendship of the wealthy; he is being told to use his wealth to help others. By so helping, the disciple will gain friends and influence them for Christ. Then when the disciple finds himself without resources in this life, he will more likely be helped by those whom he helped.

> "But seek ye first the kingdom of God, and his righteousnnss; and all these things shall be added unto you" (Mt.6:33).
> "And he said unto them, Verily I say unto you, There is no man that hath left house, or parents, or brethren, or wife, or children, for the kingdom of God's sake, who shall not receive manifold more in this present time, and in the world to come life everlasting" (Lk.18:29-30).
> "And ye shall serve the LORD your God, and he shall bless thy bread, and thy water; and I will take sickness away from the midst of thee" (Ex.23:25).
> "Bring ye all the tithes into the storehouse, that there may be meat in mine house, and prove me now herewith, saith the LORD of hosts, if I will not open you the windows of heaven, and pour you out a blessing, that there shall not be room enough to receive it" (Mal.3:10).

Note another significant point: if the Christian is not helped in this life, then at death he will certainly be welcomed abundantly into heaven. His compassionate initiative in helping others will assure God's approval. (See note—Jas.1:10-11 for more discussion.)

> "But lay up for yourselves treasures in heaven, where neither moth nor rust doth corrupt, and where thieves do not break through nor steal" (Mt.6:20).
> "Jesus said unto him, If thou wilt be perfect, go and sell that thou hast, and give to the poor, and thou shalt have treasure in heaven: and come and follow me" (Mt.19:21).
> "Sell that ye have, and give alms; provide yourselves bags which wax not old, a treasure in the heavens that faileth not, where no thief approacheth, neither moth corrupteth" (Lk.12:33).

"So likewise, whosoever he be of you that forsaketh not all that he hath, he cannot be my disciple" (Lk.14:33).

"For we know that if our earthly house of this tabernacle were dissolved, we have a building of God, an house not made with hands, eternal in the heavens" (2 Cor.5:1).

"Yea doubtless, and I count all things but loss for the excellency of the knowledge of Christ Jesus my Lord: for whom I have suffered the loss of all things, and do count them but dung, that I may win Christ" (Ph.3:8).

"Laying up in store for themselves a good foundation against the time to come, that they may lay hold on eternal life" (1 Tim.6:19).

"Wherefore the rather, brethren, give diligence to make your calling and election sure: for if ye do these things, ye shall never fall: for so an entrance shall be ministered unto you abundantly into the everlasting kingdom of our Lord and Saviour Jesus Christ" (2 Pt.1:10-11).

"I counsel thee to buy of me gold tried in the fire, that thou mayest be rich; and white raiment, that thou mayest be clothed, and that the shame of thy nakedness do not appear; and anoint thine eyes with eyesalve, that thou mayest see" (Rev.3:18).

**4** (16:10-12) **Rewards**: the Christian is to be faithful in handling possessions, for his faithfulness determines what he will be trusted with eternally.

1. Money and possessions are the least trust given a person (v.10). They are nothing compared to eternal salvation and to love, joy, peace, and the absolute assurance and confidence of life eternal. They are nothing compared to the presence and companionship, the power and leadership of the Holy Spirit. They are nothing compared to possessing the Word of God and the promises of God. They are nothing compared to knowing God personally and to being made an heir of God and a joint heir with Christ.

2. Unfaithfulness in the use of money and possessions disqualifies a person from true, heavenly riches. A person may think his life and possessions are his own to do with as he wills, but they are not. His life and possessions are God's. God has trusted the person with life and possessions only as long as he is on this earth. The holder is only a steward of all he is and has. He cannot take his life or possessions with him out of this world when he dies. He has both life and possessions only temporarily—as a trust. If he handles his life and possessions badly, he shows he is not fit to be trusted with responsibility in the new heavens and earth.

Scripture says that the *true heavenly riches* and rewards are beyond comprehension:

*Rewards Dealing with our Nature or State of Being*
⇒ Being adopted as a son of God (Gal.4:4-7; 1 Jn.3:1).
⇒ Being made blameless and harmless (Ph.2:15).
⇒ Being given eternal life (Jn.3:16; 1 Tim.6:19).
⇒ Being given an enduring substance (Heb.10:34).
⇒ Being given a glorious body (Ph.3:11, 21; 1 Cor.15:42-44).
⇒ Being given eternal glory and honor and peace (Ro.2:10).
⇒ Being given eternal rest and peace (Heb.4:9; Rev.14:13).
⇒ Being given the blessings of the Lord (Pr.10:22).
⇒ Being given the knowledge of Christ Jesus (Ph.3:8).
⇒ Being given durable riches and righteousness (Pr.8:18).
⇒ Being made priests (Rev.20:6).
⇒ Being given a crown of incorruption (1 Cor.9:25).
⇒ Being given a crown of righteousness (2 Tim.4:8).
⇒ Being given a crown of life (Jas.1:12).
⇒ Being given a crown of glory (1 Pt.5:4).

*Rewards Dealing with Work or Position or Rule*
⇒ Being made exalted beings (Rev.7:9-12).
⇒ Being made ruler over many things (Mt.25:23).
⇒ Being given the Kingdom of God (Jas.2:5; Mt.25:34).
⇒ Being given a position or rule and authority (Lk.12:42-44; Lk.22:28-29; 1 Cor.6:2-3).
⇒ Being given eternal responsibility and joy (Mt.25:21, 23).
⇒ Being given rule and authority over cities (Lk.19:17, 19).
⇒ Being given thrones and the privilege of reigning forever (Rev.20:4; 22:5).
⇒ Being given the privilege of surrounding the throne of God (Rev.7:9-13; 20:4).
⇒ Being made priests (Rev.20:6).
⇒ Being made kings (Rev.1:5; 5:10).

*Rewards Dealing with our Inheritance or Wealth*
⇒ Being made an heir of God (Ro.8:16-17; Tit.3:7).
⇒ Being given an incorruptible inheritance (1 Pt.1:3-4).
⇒ Being given the blessings of the Lord (Pr.10:22).
⇒ Being given durable riches and righteousness (Pr.8:18).
⇒ Being given unsearchable riches (Eph.3:8).
⇒ Being given treasures in heaven (Mt.19:21; Lk.12:33).

3.     Unfaithfulness disqualifies a person from all he would receive. The other man in verse 12 refers to God. Our lives and possessions are His. If we are not faithful in using them, how can we expect to be compensated? Note a person never has all he would have if he fails to pursue God and to give others what is due them. (Cp. Mt.19:29; Mk.10:29-30; Lk.18:30.)

> "Thou oughtest therefore to have put my money to the exchangers, and then at my coming I should have received mine own with usury. Take therefore the talent from him, and give it unto him which hath ten talents. For unto every one that hath shall be given, and he shall have abundance: but from him that hath not shall be taken away even that which he hath" (Mt.25:27-29).
>
> "For what shall it profit a man, if he shall gain the whole world, and lose his own soul?" (Mk.8:36).
>
> "Every man's work shall be made manifest: for the day shall declare it, because it shall be revealed by fire; and the fire shall try every man's work of what sort it is. If any man's work abide which he hath built thereupon, he shall receive a reward. If any man's work shall be burned, he shall suffer loss: but he himself shall be saved; yet so as by fire" (1 Cor.3:13-15).
>
> "Your iniquities have turned away these things, and your sins have withholden good things from you" (Jer.5:25).

**5**   (16:13) **Decision—Spiritual Struggle**: the Christian cannot serve two masters; he must choose God or riches. Note three significant points.

1.     There are two masters in life, either God or the things and riches of this world.
2.     A person serves one of the two masters. He gives himself either to one or the other...
- He focuses himself upon the things and riches of the world or upon God.
- He turns himself over to the things and riches of the world or to God.
- He thinks primarily upon the things of the world or upon God.
- He gives his time, energy, and effort to the things of the world or to God.
- He allows his worldly pursuits to control Christ, or Christ to control his pursuits.
3.     A person struggles against God or else struggles against the things and riches of the world. No man can serve both God and mammon.
- ⇒ He hates the one and loves the other.
- ⇒ He holds to one and despises the other.

> "Then saith Jesus unto him, Get thee hence, Satan: for it is written, Thou shalt worship the Lord thy God, and him only shalt thou serve" (Mt.4:10).
>
> "Then Jesus beholding him loved him, and said unto him, One thing thou lackest: go thy way, sell whatsoever thou hast, and give to the poor, and thou shalt have treasure in heaven: and come, take up the cross, and follow me" (Mk.10:21).
>
> Ye cannot drink the cup of the Lord, and the cup of devils: ye cannot be partakers of the Lord's table, and of the table of devils" (1 Cor.10:21).
>
> "Of his own will begat he us with the word of truth, that we should be a kind of firstfruits of his creatures" (Jas.1:18).
>
> "Draw nigh to God, and he will draw nigh to you. Cleanse your hands, ye sinners; and purify your hearts, ye double minded" (Jas.4:8).
>
> "See, I have set before thee this day life and good, and death and evil" (Dt.30:15).
>
> "And if it seem evil unto you to serve the LORD choose you this day whom ye will serve" (Josh.24:15).
>
> "How long halt ye between two opinions? if the LORD be God, follow him: but if Baal, then follow him. And the people answered him not a word" (1 Ki.18:21).

| 1 The misunderstanding of money & possessions<br>a. Man tends to use his possessions to justify himself<br>b. God knows the heart<br>c. God detests men who center their esteem around money & possessions | L. The Misunderstanding About Wealth and God's Kingdom, 16:14-18<br><br>14 And the Pharisees also, who were covetous, heard all these things: and they derided him.<br>15 And he said unto them, Ye are they which justify yourselves before men; but God knoweth your hearts: for that which is highly esteemed among men is abomination in the sight of God. | 16 The law and the prophets were until John: since that time the kingdom of God is preached, and every man presseth into it.<br>17 And it is easier for heaven and earth to pass, than one tittle of the law to fail.<br>18 Whosoever putteth away his wife, and marrieth another, committeth adultery: and whosoever marrieth her that is put away from her husband committeth adultery. | 2 The misunderstanding of the new kindgom & world or social order<br>a. It is of God, not of earth<br>b. It is for "every man"<br>3 The misunderstanding of the law<br>a. It is not destroyed by the new kingdom<br>b. Marriage is an example of the unfailing law in both kingdoms |

# DIVISION VI

## THE SON OF MAN'S GREAT JOURNEY TO JERUSALEM (STAGE II): HIS TEACHING AND PUBLIC CONFLICT, 13:22-17:10

## L. The Misunderstanding About Wealth and God's Kingdom, 16:14-18

(16:14-18) **Introduction**: three of the greatest misunderstandings among men are covered in this passage. This is a critical message. It needs to be heeded by men so they can correct their misunderstanding.

1. The misunderstanding of money and possessions (v.14-15).
2. The misunderstanding of the new kingdom and world or social order (v.16).
3. The misunderstanding of the law (v.17-18).

1 (16:14-15) **Money—Wealth—Materialism—Heart**: the misunderstanding of money and possessions. Jesus had just said: "No servant can serve two masters: for either he will hate the one, and love the other; or else he will hold to the one, and despise the other. Ye cannot serve God and mammon" (Lk.16:13).

The religionists and others standing before Jesus could not believe what they were hearing.

⇒ Jesus was saying that a man's energy and effort in seeking and looking after money was wrong, that a man could not seek money and at the same time keep his mind and thoughts upon God. It was impossible to concentrate on both. Jesus was demanding total allegiance, all of one's mind and thoughts, energy and effort. Those who heard Jesus knew exactly what He was saying.

⇒ Jesus was saying that a man must not give himself to seek the comfort and ease and pleasures and possessions of the world.

⇒ Jesus was going against the philosophy of the world, a philosophy that had even permeated religious circles: that money and possessions are a sign of the blessings of God.

What Jesus was teaching bothered men, in particular the religionists. The reason has to do with the nature of man. By nature, men want money and possessions, comfort and ease, acceptance and recognition; and at the same time, they want to be known as *close to God*. A man wants to fit in and be acceptable to the world and, at the same time, to feel acceptable to God. Therefore, a man becomes disturbed, sometimes extremely disturbed, when he is told...

⇒ that he cannot give his mind and thought, energy and effort to both God and money (the possessions of the world).

⇒ that he cannot serve both God and money at the same time.

⇒ that God demands a person's total allegiance, all of a person's mind and thoughts, energy and effort.

Note four things.

1. Men can be both religious and covetous; in fact, the most covetous men are sometimes the most religious. These men who were ridiculing Jesus were Pharisees, probably the most religious sect who had ever lived, yet they were said to be covetous. They wanted things of the world and the things of God at the same time.

"No man can serve two masters: for either he will hate the one, and love the other; or else he will hold to the one, and despise the other. Ye cannot serve God and mammon" (Mt.6:24).

"For many walk, of whom I have told you often, and now tell you even weeping, that they are the enemies of the cross of Christ: whose end is destruction, whose God is their belly, and whose glory is in their shame, who mind earthly things" (Ph.3:18-19).

"For the love of money is the root of all evil: which while some coveted after, they have erred from the faith, and pierced themselves through with many sorrows" (1 Tim.6:10).

2. Jesus said that men tend to use their wealth to justify themselves before other men.
   a. They use their wealth to court the favor and honor of men and women. Even if they secured their wealth unjustly, they compensate for it by being generous, by entertaining, or by giving to some worthy need or project. And unfortunately, men and women alike give in to and go along with the wealthy.

b. Some rich persons are conscious of their need for a right relationship with God and of their obligation to help people. Therefore, they live strict religious lives and use some of their wealth to court the favor and honor of people through religious causes. The world, including the religious world, honors such benevolent giving by the wealthy.

> "He answered and said unto them, Well hath Esaias prophesied of you hypocrites, as it is written, This people honoureth me with their lips, but their heart is far from me" (Mk.7:6).
> "For we dare not make ourselves of the number, or compare ourselves with some that commend themselves: but they measuring themselves by themselves, and comparing themselves among themselves, are not wise" (2 Cor.10:12).
> "They profess that they know God; but in works they deny him, being abominable, and disobedient, and unto every good work reprobate" (Tit.1:16).
> "My little children, let us not love in word, neither in tongue; but in deed and in truth" (1 Jn.3:18).
> "Most men will proclaim every one his own goodness: but a faithful man who can find?" (Pr.20:6).
> "There is a generation that are pure in their own eyes, and yet is not washed from their filthiness" (Pr.30:12).

3. Jesus said, "But God knoweth your hearts." What did He mean?
   a. A man is acceptable to God because his heart is right before God, not because he has a lot of money. Money does not mean that a man is greatly blessed by God. God's blessings are not in material things.
   ⇒ Some people are wealthy, yet they are as ungodly and dirty as they can be.
   ⇒ Some people are poor, yet they are very godly, having little money and few things of the world.
   ⇒ Some people have some money and possessions, yet they are very godly.

   The point is this: the heart is that which *makes* a man acceptable to God, not money. Money does not mean that a man is blessed by God. It is the heart of a man that shows the blessings of God. God's blessings are not material things, they are spiritual things (see notes—Mt.19:25; Eph.1:3).

> "Then said Jesus unto his disciples, Verily I say unto you, That a rich man shall hardly enter into the kingdom of heaven. And again I say unto you, It is easier for a camel to go through the eye of a needle, than for a rich man to enter into the kingdom of God. When his disciples heard it, they were exceedingly amazed, saying, Who then can be saved?" (Mt.19:23-25).
> "Blessed be the God and Father of our Lord Jesus Christ, who hath blessed us with all spiritual blessings in heavenly places in Christ" (Eph.1:3).

   b. Note another important fact. When Jesus said that a man cannot serve God and money, He did not mean that a man's mind and thought could not be put upon his profession and work.

> "Finally, brethren, whatsoever things are true, whatsoever things are honest, whatsoever things are just, whatsoever things are pure, whatsoever things are lovely, whatsoever things are of good report; if there be any virtue, and if there be any praise, think on these things" (Ph.4:8).
> "Casting down imaginations, and every high thing that exalteth itself against the knowledge of God, and bringing into captivity every thought to the obedience of Christ" (2 Cor.10:5).

   The Scripture is very clear about this. A person's profession and the beneficial activities of life are included in the things of God. The legitimate things of life are true and honest. Therefore, a man is to live and work well. Living and working well are a great testimony to God's name; therefore, a genuine believer should be the very best at living and working, demonstrating that God's people are the most true and honest, pure and lovely people on earth.

   c. When dealing with the money and possessions of the world, we are to provide adequately for our families. But after adequate provision, the question arises, what are we to do? God is clear in His instructions: we are to work in order to have enough to help the needy. We are to help meet the needs of a desperate world.

> "Jesus said unto him, If thou wilt be perfect, go and sell that thou hast, and give to the poor, and thou shalt have treasure in heaven: and come and follow me" (Mt.19:21).
> "Let him that stole steal no more: but rather let him labour, working with his hands the thing which is good, that he may have to give to him that needeth" (Eph.4:28).

4. God detests the esteem of men being centered around money and things. God wants men to center their lives and esteem around the things of the heart, not around the things they possess. Material possessions pass away; spiritual possessions endure forever (see note—Eph.1:3. See outlines and notes—Mt.19:16-22; 19:23-26; 19:27-30 for more discussion on Christ's teaching concerning wealth.)

"But lay up for yourselves treasures in heaven, where neither moth nor rust doth corrupt, and where thieves do not break through nor steal" (Mt.6:20).

"Sell that ye have, and give alms; provide yourselves bags which wax not old, a treasure in the heavens that faileth not, where no thief approacheth, neither moth corrupteth" (Lk.12:33).

**2** (16:16) **Kingdom of God—Wealth—New Order—Old and New Testaments**: the misunderstanding of the new kingdom and order. Note three things.

1. Jesus sees the *period of Israel* (the law and the prophets) lasting up to and including the ministry of John the Baptist. As God's Messiah He ushered in a *new period and social order*, that is, the Kingdom of God. The Kingdom of God is presently a spiritual kingdom that occurs within a man and takes effect in the acts and behavior of men. Since Jesus has come, every man is to let God rule and reign in his heart and life (see DEEPER STUDY # 3—Mt.19:23-24 for more discussion).

2. The kingdom is now preached, a message which does not value what a man has, but what a man is—what he is within his heart. The message now centers upon the individual and his eternal potential in God, not upon material and temporal blessings. (See DEEPER STUDY # 3—Mt.19:23-24; note—Eph.1:3.)

"And when he was demanded of the Pharisees, when the kingdom of God should come, he answered them and said, The kingdom of God cometh not with observation: neither shall they say, Lo here! or, lo there! for, behold, the kingdom of God is within you" (Lk.17:20-21).

"The kingdom of God is at hand: repent ye, and believe the gospel" (Mk.1:15).

"And he lifted up his eyes on his disciples, and said, Blessed be ye poor: for yours is the kingdom of God" (Lk.6:20).

"For the kingdom of God is not meat and drink; but righteousness, and peace, and joy in the Holy Ghost" (Ro.14:17).

3. Every man presses into the kingdom. The Kingdom of God is not for any single race; the kingdom is for all people everywhere. When people hear the glorious message of the kingdom, they press and struggle to get into it. They no longer want a cheap, formal religion and an easy message. They cannot be content with such, not when they *really get a glimpse* of the Kingdom of God. Once they have seen the glory and value of God's kingdom, they press and struggle to enter, no matter the odds.

"Blessed are they which do hunger and thirst after righteousness: for they shall be filled" (Mt.5:6).

"And I, if I be lifted up from the earth, will draw all men unto me" (Jn.12:32).

"These were more noble than those in Thessalonica, in that they received the word with all readiness of mind, and searched the scriptures daily, whether those things were so" (Acts 17:11).

"Sow to yourselves in righteousness, reap in mercy; break up your fallow ground: for it is time to seek the LORD, till he come and rain righteousness upon you" (Hos.10:12).

"With my soul have I desired thee in the night; yea, with my spirit within me will I seek thee early: for when thy judgments are in the earth, the inhabitants of the world will learn righteousness" (Is.26:9).

**3** (16:17-18) **Old Testament—Law, The—Word of God Enslaves**: the misunderstanding of the law. In this point Jesus dealt with a very serious question—a question that bothers men. Is there a *higher law*, a law of God to which men are to subject their lives? Since Christ has come, since there is now a new order and a New Testament, what about the Old Testament, the law and the prophets? Is the Old Testament and its laws still to be used and followed by us? What is the place of the law? Is it erased? Does it have a place in God's new kingdom? Jesus said that there is a *higher law*, a law of God that is given in the Old Testament. It is not erased; it has a place in the new order. In fact, the Old Testament is fulfilled in the new kingdom, and it shall outlast heaven and earth. An example is the law governing marriage. It is the law for both social orders. It never changes. (See note—Mt.5:17-18; DEEPER STUDY # 2—Ro.8:3 for detailed discussion of Christ fulfilling the law; see DEEPER STUDY # 1—Mt.19:1-12 for detailed discussion of marriage.)

**Thought 1.** There is a *higher law*, a law of God given by God in the Old Testament, that is, in the old dispensation. It has been fulfilled in Christ; therefore, all men are to obey *the Law of God*. (Again, see note—Mt.5:17-18. This is an extremely important note to see how the Old Testament law was fulfilled in Christ.)

"Think not that I am come to destroy the law, or the prophets: I am not come to destroy, but to fulfil. For verily I say unto you, Till heaven and earth pass, one jot or one tittle shall in no wise pass from the law, till all be fulfilled" (Mt.5:17-18).

"Heaven and earth shall pass away, but my words shall not pass away" (Mt.24:35).

"But the word of the Lord endureth for ever. And this is the word which by the gospel is preached unto you" (1 Pt.1:25).

"For ever, O LORD, thy word is settled in heaven" (Ps.119:89).

"Concerning thy testimonies, I have known of old that thou hast founded them for ever" (Ps.119:152).

"The grass withereth, the flower fadeth: because the spirit of the LORD bloweth upon it: surely the people is grass" (Is.40:8).

| | M. The Rich Man and Lazarus: The Self-Indulgent vs. The Man of Faith, 16:19-31 | | |
|---|---|---|---|
| **1 A difference in life**[DS1]<br> a. Rich man nameless; Lazarus named<br> b. Rich man wealthy; Lazarus poor<br> c. Rich man healthy; Lazarus disabled<br><br> d. Rich man fared sumptuously; Lazarus begged, being helpless<br><br>**2 A difference in death: Lazarus died & was escorted to Paradise; rich man died & was buried**[DS2]<br><br>**3 A difference in eternity**<br> a. Rich man in hell;[DS3] Lazarus in Paradise<br> b. Rich man *saw* glory; Lazarus was *in* glory<br> c. Rich man was alone; Lazarus had fellowship<br> d. Rich man had burning sensation; Lazarus had water<br> e. Rich man tormented;[DS4] | 19 There was a certain rich man, which was clothed in purple and fine linen, and fared sumptuously every day:<br> 20 And there was a certain beggar named Lazarus, which was laid at his gate, full of sores,<br> 21 And desiring to be fed with the crumbs which fell from the rich man's table: moreover the dogs came and licked his sores.<br> 22 And it came to pass, that the beggar died, and was carried by the angels into Abraham's bosom: the rich man also died, and was buried;<br> 23 And in hell he lift up his eyes, being in torments, and seeth Abraham afar off, and Lazarus in his bosom.<br> 24 And he cried and said, Father Abraham, have mercy on me, and send Lazarus, that he may dip the tip of his finger in water, and cool my tongue; for I am tormented | in this flame.<br> 25 But Abraham said, Son, remember that thou in thy lifetime receivedst thy good things, and likewise Lazarus evil things: but now he is comforted, and thou art tormented.<br> 26 And beside all this, between us and you there is a great gulf fixed: so that they which would pass from hence to you cannot; neither can they pass to us, that would come from thence.<br> 27 Then he said, I pray thee therefore, father, that thou wouldest send him to my father's house:<br> 28 For I have five brethren; that he may testify unto them, lest they also come into this place of torment.<br> 29 Abraham saith unto him, They have Moses and the prophets; let them hear them.<br> 30 And he said, Nay, father Abraham: but if one went unto them from the dead, they will repent.<br> 31 And he said unto him, If they hear not Moses and the prophets, neither will they be persuaded though one rose from the dead. | Lazarus comforted<br> f. Rich man remembered his former life; Lazarus was silent<br><br><br> g. Rich man was fixed in hell; Lazarus was fixed in Paradise<br><br><br> h. Rich man agonized for loved ones; Lazarus was settled in eternity<br><br><br><br> i. Rich man begged for another chance; Lazarus was silently at peace<br><br> j. Rich man was unable to intercede for his family; Lazarus was at rest in God's promises |

## DIVISION VI

## THE SON OF MAN'S GREAT JOURNEY TO JERUSALEM (STAGE II): HIS TEACHING AND PUBLIC CONFLICT, 13:22-17:10

## M. The Rich Man and Lazarus: The Self-Indulgent vs. the Man of Faith, 16:19-31

(16:19-31) **Introduction**: note two things. Jesus identified Lazarus; Lazarus was named. When giving a parable, Jesus never named a character—not even once. Also note: Jesus did not say that this was a parable. These two facts, plus the language used to begin the account, point to it as an actual experience. Of course, it must always be remembered that spiritual and eternal truths have to be described with human and earthly language. This does not in any way lessen the blessing nor the terror of the truth; contrariwise, the eternal truth is *much more blessed* and *much more terrifying* than any mere human description.

1. A difference in life (v.19-21).
2. A difference in death: Lazarus died and was escorted to paradise; the rich man died and was buried (v.22).
3. A difference in eternity (v.23-31).

**1** (16:19-21) **Life—Christians**: there is a difference in life. The differences are fourfold.

1. There was one main difference between Lazarus and the rich man: the rich man was nameless, but Lazarus was named. The difference is ever so important. It is the difference between being known and honored by God and not being known or honored by God. The rich man did not know God; therefore, he was unknown to God and God was not able to honor him. He was nameless to God. Lazarus knew God and was known by God. His very name, Lazarus, means *God is my Help or Helper*. He trusted God to look after him, and his eyes were upon heaven and the blessings of heaven, not upon the earth. The Latin word for "rich" is Dives. This is the reason the rich man is often called *Dives*. However, we must always remember it was not his name; he was a nameless man to God.

> "I am the good shepherd, and know my sheep, and am known of mine" (Jn.10:14; cp. Jn.10:27).
> "But if any man love God, the same is known of him" (1 Cor.8:3).
> "For now we see through a glass, darkly; but then face to face: now I know in part; but then shall I know even as also I am known" (1 Cor.13:12).

**"Howbeit then, when ye knew not God, ye did service unto them which by nature are no gods. But now, after that ye have known God, or rather are known of God, how turn ye again to the weak and beggarly elements, whereunto ye desire again to be in bondage?" (Gal.4:8-9).**

2.     The rich man was wealthy; Lazarus was poor. (See DEEPER STUDY # 1, *Sin*—Lk.16:19-21 for discussion.)

3.     The rich man was healthy; Lazarus was disabled. Lazarus was full of ulcerated sores, unable to work and earn a living. He was either carried to the rich man's gate or else barely able to walk to the gate. He was what is called a *street person*—not by choice, but by being handicapped and without a family or friends who loved enough to care for him. How tragic! What an indictment against *men*. Note the charge is against the rich man and not *society*. Society is only an *idea*; men are a reality. The term or *idea of society* allows some men, including some social workers, to escape responsibility and to build up good salaries, healthy standards of living, and personal wealth while the needful continue to suffer. Each man is personally responsible for the poor and needy of the earth. That is Christ's point. In this case the rich man was responsible for Lazarus.

4.     The rich man fared sumptuously; Lazarus had to beg because he was helpless. The picture is that of Lazarus' lying at the rich man's gate (most people would not allow this). The rich man was too occupied with his own estate, interests and pleasures; he ignored Lazarus' lying at his gate. The rich man neither helped nor seemed to care. While Lazarus waited for the crumbs from the rich man's table, too weak to fight off the dogs from licking his sores, he found hope and peace in God. The wealthy used large pieces of bread to wipe their hands and then threw the hunks away. It was this bread that Lazarus waited for.

---

**DEEPER STUDY # 1**

(16:19-21) **Sin**: the sin of the rich man would not be a sin in the eyes of most societies. There is no record of a vicious, glaring sin; no record of a vulgar, public sin. He was not cruel—he never ordered Lazarus from his gate nor refused Lazarus the crumbs from his table. He was not a tyrant, not an oppressor of the poor, not a monstrous member of society. Rather, he was socially responsible, an upright citizen, respected and well-liked. No earthly court would ever think of arresting or condemning him. In society's eyes he was honored and highly esteemed. People liked him and spoke well of him. What then was his sin?

1.     The word "sumptuously" (lampros) means that he was flamboyant, displaying his wealth in materialistic ways.

2.     The "gate" was a large gate indicating that his home was a large house or a mansion.

3.     The purple and fine linen show that he had the latest styles and the ultimate in luxury.

4.     The words "every day" show that he feasted every day. His sin was *self-indulgence, comfort, ease, luxury, extravagant living*. He sought the things and pleasures of this world. He was complacent, hoarding and allowing money to lie around making more and more for himself and his estate while needs lay all around him—right at his gate. He neglected and ignored others, most significantly, Lazarus. The needs of a degenerate world concerned him little, if at all. He wanted what others in the world had, plenty for themselves and more. The world acknowledged and honored those who had plenty, and he wanted such recognition and honor for himself. He wanted what others had and he wanted to keep up with them.

> **"I was a stranger, and ye took me not in: naked, and ye clothed me not: sick, and in prison, and ye visited me not" (Mt.25:43).**
>
> **"But whoso hath this world's good, and seeth his brother have need, and shutteth up his bowels of compassion from him, how dwelleth the love of God in him?" (1 Jn.3:17).**
>
> **"And the cares of this world, and the deceitfulness of riches, and the lusts of other things entering in, choke the word, and it becometh unfruitful" (Mk.4:19).**
>
> **"But they that will be rich fall into temptation and a snare, and into many foolish and hurtful lusts, which drown men in destruction and perdition" (1 Tim.6:9).**
>
> **"And when ye did eat, and when ye did drink, did not ye eat for yourselves, and drink for yourselves?" (Zech.7:6).**
>
> **"If there be among you a poor man of one of thy brethren within any of thy gates in thy land which the LORD thy God giveth thee, thou shalt not harden thine heart, nor shut thine hand from thy poor brother" (Dt.15:7).**

---

**2** (16:22) **Death**: there was a difference in death. Lazarus died and was escorted to Paradise; the rich man died and was buried. Note the only words said about the rich man's death: "He died and was buried." What a terrible and disappointing legacy for a man to leave behind. The rich man was probably buried in state in the finest clothes and within the very best grave and cemetary. He had a most impressive funeral—a funeral well attended by the upper social class of his community. The words spoken over him were probably words of praise, words that recognized his respectability and contribution to society in providing so much for his community and religion. An expensive monument was probably set over his grave. However, the *tragedy of tragedies* was his experience. He knew *nothing* about it. He was not there to enjoy it. He just died and was buried.

However, note what is said about Lazarus. He "died and was carried by angels into Abraham's bosom" (see DEEPER STUDY # 2, *Abraham's Bosom*—Lk.16:22) or Paradise. Three facts are important here.

1.     Lazarus lived on despite his body's being dead. His being—his spirit and soul—did not die, nor cease to exist, nor fall into a state of sleep.

2.     Lazarus' soul was immediately met by angels. Instantaneously—as quick as the blinking of an eye—when Lazarus died, the angels stood by his body and carried his soul into Paradise.

3.    Lazarus was carried into the very place where the *Source* of all wealth is, where all who have trusted God are, the place where Abraham is: the Paradise of God Himself. (See Deeper Study # 3, *Paradise*—Lk.16:23 for discussion.)

"For God so loved the world, that he gave his only begotten Son, that whosoever believeth in him should not perish, but have everlasting life" (Jn.3:16).
"He that believeth on the Son hath everlasting life: and he that believeth not the Son shall not see life; but the wrath of God abideth on him" (Jn.3:36).
"Verily, verily, I say unto you, He that heareth my word, and believeth on him that sent me, hath everlasting life, and shall not come into condemnation; but is passed from death unto life" (Jn.5:24).
"For our light affliction, which is but for a moment, worketh for us a far more exceeding and eternal weight of glory" (2 Cor.4:17).
"For he that soweth to his flesh shall of the flesh reap corruption; but he that soweth to the Spirit shall of the Spirit reap life everlasting" (Gal.6:8).
"Wherefore the rather, brethren, give diligence to make your calling and election sure: for if ye do these things, ye shall never fall: for so an entrance shall be ministered unto you abundantly into the everlasting kingdom of our Lord and Saviour Jesus Christ" (2 Pt.1:10-11).

---

**DEEPER STUDY # 2**
(16:22) **Abraham's Bosom**: this refers to Paradise. It is a term that expressed the happiness that believers could expect upon death. It had the idea of sitting down and feasting with Abraham in Paradise. The bosom of Abraham was referred to because he was the father of the Jewish nation.

---

**3**    (16:23-31) **Eternal Life**: there was a difference in eternity. Ten facts are contrasted here.
1.    The rich man was in hell; Lazarus was in Paradise (see Deeper Study # 3, *Hell*—Lk.16:23).
   a.    Death snatched the rich man from his comfort and pleasures and from the material goods and wealth of this life. And he was immediately in hell, the place of misery and torment. (See Deeper Study # 3, *Hell*—Lk.16:23.)

"And these shall go away into everlasting punishment: but the righteous into life eternal" (Mt.25:46).
"And the smoke of their torment ascendeth up for ever and ever: and they have no rest day nor night" (Rev.14:11).

   b.    The rich man was unfit for Paradise. Why? Because he had lived in a *worldly paradise* while others were hungry and starving, diseased and helpless, cold and unclothed, unsaved and dying. He had possessed the "good things" of life while others had nothing; and he had kept back, banked, and hoarded beyond what he really needed—all for the sake of recognition from people. Justice had to be executed. He was unfit to live in a paradise of justice and love. He deserved to be tormented and left without the "good things," for he had added to and refused to ease the torments of others while on earth.

"Whoso stoppeth his ears at the cry of the poor, he also shall cry himself, but shall not be heard" (Pr.21:13).

2.    The rich man only saw glory: Lazarus was sharing in and experiencing glory. Note three things.
   a.    The rich man was able to see Paradise, but it was far, far off and way out of reach.
   b.    The rich man was able to see into Paradise, able to see both Abraham and Lazarus there. He saw all the glory and comfort, perfection and joy of Paradise. He saw the man Lazarus whom he had neglected and treated so lowly. He saw Lazarus in all the glory and perfection of heaven, and he envied and regretted what he saw.

"There shall be weeping and gnashing of teeth, when ye shall see Abraham, and Isaac, and Jacob, and all the prophets, in the kingdom of God, and you yourselves thrust out" (Lk.13:28).

   c.    Note that Lazarus seemed to be totally unaware of hell. He lived only in Paradise, only in the glory and perfection of God.

"For this corruptible must put on incorruption, and this mortal must put on immortality" (1 Cor.15:53).

3.    The rich man was painfully alone; Lazarus had companionship. Nothing is said about another soul around the rich man. He stood all alone, talking to no one else in hell. He only saw those in Paradise. What a drastic difference from what

336

is so often pictured and expressed by the lost of this world, thinking they will have plenty of company in hell. The true picture painted by Christ is that a person will be tormented with loneliness, that the person will...

- be all alone
- see no one
- sense no one
- be cut off from others
- be desolate
- be bleak

Lazarus had the company of Abraham and of the saints in glory. Christ had earlier taught the same point to the "workers of iniquity":

> **"There shall be weeping and gnashing of teeth, when ye shall see Abraham, and Isaac, and Jacob, and all the prophets, in the kingdom of God, and you yourselves [workers of iniquity] thrust out" (Lk.13:28).**

4. The rich man had a burning sensation; Lazarus had water. The contrast here is dramatic. The rich man was burning with such misery and pain from the "flame" (the wrath of God) that he begged for mercy: if he could not be freed from the flame and the misery, then he begged for just a drop of water to feel a momentary coolness. However, look at Lazarus. He had water; he had the coolness of whatever he needed to refresh his body.

> **"...the chaff he will burn with fire unquenchable" (Lk.3:17).**
> **"And he showed me a pure river of water of life, clear as crystal, proceeding out of the throne of God and of the Lamb" (Rev.22:1).**

5. The rich man was tormented; Lazarus was comforted (see DEEPER STUDY # 4, *Hell*—Lk.16:24).

> **"But the children of the kingdom shall be cast out into outer darkness: there shall be weeping and gnashing of teeth" (Mt.8:12).**
> **"And shall cast them into a furnace of fire: there shall be wailing and gnashing of teeth" (Mt.13:42).**
> **"And whosoever was not found written in the book of life was cast into the lake of fire" (Rev.20:15).**

6. The rich man remembered his former life; Lazarus was silent.
   a. Note the word "they" or "your." It is emphatic. The rich man had what *he* chose to have when on earth. He had received *his* "good things" (what he considered "good") in *his* lifetime, and he *saw* to it that Lazarus had "evil things." Now note: he did not beat, injure, or persecute Lazarus; *but he did not help Lazarus either*. He could have helped, for he had an estate and a bank full of money; but he did not help. Therefore, he *kept* Lazarus down and destitute in this world. He saw to it that Lazarus had "evil things" when he could have seen to it that Lazarus was helped.
   b. Lazarus was not responsible for the evil things that came upon him. Lazarus was *dished out* the evil things of this world by circumstances and by men like the rich man who neglected, ignored, and abused him.
   c. The rich man remembered...
      - his sins (comfort, ease, indulgence, pleasure, extravagance).
      - his missed opportunities (to help Lazarus).
      - his deaf ear to conscience, God, the Word, Lazarus, and all others who were so needy.
      - his failure to seek the truth (Heb.11:6).
      - his rejection of warning after warning.

7. The rich man was fixed in hell; Lazarus was fixed in Paradise. There was no passing from hell into Paradise or from Paradise into hell. There was a permanent gulf, and it was there for the *purpose* of keeping one from passing over. The sinner, who chooses to be cut off from God and Paradise, has his wish. He is cut off.

> **"Let both grow together until the harvest: and in the time of harvest I will say to the reapers, Gather ye together first the tares, and bind them in bundles to burn them: but gather the wheat into my barn" (Mt.13:30).**
> **"So shall it be at the end of the world: the angels shall come forth, and sever the wicked from among the just" (Mt.13:49).**
> **"And these shall go away into everlasting punishment: but the righteous into life eternal" (Mt.25:46).**

8. The rich man agonized for loved ones; Lazarus was settled in eternity. The rich man had five brothers. He had set such a bad example for them they were also heading for hell. Note that the rich man was saying two things.
   a. Hell is such a horrible place that it is not worth all the wealth and comfort and ease and pleasure of this world. Christ had said the same thing:

> **"For what shall it profit a man, if he shall gain the whole world, and lose his own soul?" (Mk.8:36).**

   b. Hell is such a horrible place that the world must be told to flee it. (Note that Christ is sharing how terrible hell is and how desperately we must seek to avoid it.)

The rich man was told that his brothers had the Scriptures, the Word of God, which explained and warned them of the future. They were to hear the Scripture, for the Scripture is a sufficient witness.

Lazarus was settled in eternity. He was a great contrast with the rich man's brothers. Why? Because he had believed the Scriptures, trusting God and His promises.

> **"Verily, verily, I say unto you, He that heareth my word, and believeth on him that sent me, hath everlasting life, and shall not come into condemnation; but is passed from death unto life"** (Jn.5:24).

9. The rich man begged for another chance as Lazarus was silently at peace as the Scriptures promised. This is seen by looking behind the words of the rich man. If Abraham were to allow one to arise to tell the living, the rich man could then plead less opportunity. He, too, would be entitled to another chance, to a sensational and miraculous sign, or so he felt.

Note that Lazarus was at peace just as the Scriptures had promised. Lazarus had believed and was thereby saved.

10. The rich man was unable to intercede for his family; Lazarus rested in God's presence. Note the words, "Neither will they be persuaded though one rose from the dead."

    a. A Man, the Lord Jesus Christ, has risen from the dead, yet men do not believe. Man's unbelief is not due to lack of signs; it is due to their love for the world with all its creature comforts and recognition, indulgence and selfishness, pleasures and honors.

> **"But after thy hardness and impenitent heart treasurest up unto thyself wrath against the day of wrath and revelation of the righteous judgment of God"** (Ro.2:5).

    b. The Scriptures and their testimony of the Lord's resurrection are much greater testimony than a dead man's standing before us in some *ghostly, mysterious form*.

> **"Search the scriptures; for in them ye think ye have eternal life: and they are they which testify of me"** (Jn.5:39).
>
> **"It [righteousness] shall be imputed, if we believe on him that raised up Jesus our Lord from the dead; who was delivered for our offences, and was raised again for our justification"** (Ro.4:24-25).

---

**DEEPER STUDY # 3**

(16:23) **Paradise—Hell (Hades)**: the Greek word *Hades* is the same as the Hebrew word *Sheol* (see DEEPER STUDY # 3—Gen.37:35). The picture of Hades revealed by Jesus is that of the other world: the unseen world, the spiritual world, the spiritual dimension of being. Jesus says that Hades is a place which is divided into two huge areas or sections or compartments. The two areas are separated by a great gulf that is impassible (v.26). One area is the place of sorrow (v.23-24, 28). The other area is the place of Paradise where believers go. To say that a person is dead is to say that one is in hades, in the other world.

Note a critical fact: the other world, the spiritual world and the spiritual dimension of being, does exist. And there are two areas or two places in the other world: Paradise, the place of glory, and hell, the place of torment. Jesus said they both actually exist. (Cp. 22-23, see outline and notes—Lk.16:19-31; see DEEPER STUDY # 4—Lk.16:24; notes—Mt.27:52-53; Eph.4:8-10; DEEPER STUDY # 1—1 Pt.3:19-20.)

---

**DEEPER STUDY # 4**

(16:24) **Hell—Torment**: to be anguished, tortured, and greatly distressed; to suffer pain and sorrow. The Bible unquestionably teaches there is to be a torment for unbelievers in fire. However, it must be remembered that the fire we know is material and temporal; it is not spiritual or eternal. Earthly fire does not last forever. Nothing on earth does. Earthly fire is of the physical dimension of being. The fire of hell, whatever its nature and qualities, is spiritual and eternal. It never ends. And men must face this; they must not shrink from the truth of hell. Why? Because hell, that is, separation from God, is much worse than any experience here on earth. It will be much worse than any physical experience imaginable. This is the teaching of Scripture. This is the point Jesus was making. Man absolutely must flee from hell. Man absolutely must flee to Christ for salvation (see DEEPER STUDY # 2—Mt.5:22). (Cp. Mt.5:22, 29; 10:28; 18:9; 23:15, 33; 25:41; Mk.9:43-48; Lk.12:5; 16:23; 2 Th.1:8-9; 2 Pt.2:4; Rev.14:10-11; 16:10; 18:10; 19:20; 20:10-15; 21:8.)

**CHAPTER 17**

**N. The Christian Disciple and Four Laws, 17:1-10**
(cp. Mt.18:6, 15; 17:20)

**1 Law 1: Leading another to sin brings judgment**
  a. Sin is inevitable
  b. Leading others to sin is terrible
  c. Leading others to sin is condemned[DS1]

**2 Law 2: Forgiving others is essential**
  a. If one sins, he is to be rebuked
  b. If one repents, he is to be forgiven
  c. How often: Time after time

**3 Law 3: Having faith is**

Then said he unto the disciples, It is impossible but that offences will come: but woe unto him, through whom they come!

2 It were better for him that a millstone were hanged about his neck, and he cast into the sea, than that he should offend one of these little ones.

3 Take heed to yourselves: If thy brother trespass against thee, rebuke him; and if he repent, forgive him.

4 And if he trespass against thee seven times in a day, and seven times in a day turn again to thee, saying, I repent; thou shalt forgive him.

5 And the apostles said unto the Lord, Increase our faith.

6 And the Lord said, If ye had faith as a grain of mustard seed, ye might say unto this sycamine tree, Be thou plucked up by the root, and be thou planted in the sea; and it should obey you.

7 But which of you, having a servant plowing or feeding cattle, will say unto him by and by, when he is come from the field, Go and sit down to meat?

8 And will not rather say unto him, Make ready wherewith I may sup, and gird thyself, and serve me, till I have eaten and drunken; and afterward thou shalt eat and drink?

9 Doth he thank that servant because he did the things that were commanded him? I trow not.

10 So likewise ye, when ye shall have done all those things which are commanded you, say, We are unprofitable servants: we have done that which was our duty to do.

essential—one of most powerful forces in the world[DS2]

**4 Law 4: Obeying God is a duty, not a service**
  a. The illust.: A servant is a slave who serves his master
    1) To serve all day
    2) To serve all evening
    3) To serve until all others have retired

    4) To serve whether or not one is thanked or appreciated

  b. The believer is to serve & obey until all of God's commandments are done
  c. The believer is to be humble in his service for the Lord

# DIVISION VI

## THE SON OF MAN'S GREAT JOURNEY TO JERUSALEM (STAGE II): HIS TEACHING AND PUBLIC CONFLICT, 13:22-17:10

### N. The Christian Disciple and Four Laws, 17:1-10

(17:1-10) **Introduction**: there are four laws in this passage that could revolutionize society. They are to revolutionize the believer's life. The believer is "to take heed" to the laws (v.3).
1. Law 1: leading another into sin brings judgment (v.1-2).
2. Law 2: forgiving others is essential (v.3-4).
3. Law 3: having faith is essential: one of the most powerful forces in the world (v.5-6).
4. Law 4: obeying God is a duty, not a service (v.7-10).

**1** (17:1-2) **Sin, Leading Others—Stumbling Blocks**: the first law is a severe warning: leading another person into sin brings heavy judgment. Note several facts.
1. The Lord was speaking to His disciples. The disciple had to guard against this grave sin. He was always subject to temptation, and if he yielded, he was going to mislead others. No sin will be condemned any more than the sin of misleading others into sin.
2. Sin is inevitable. Note the exact words of Jesus, "It is impossible but that offences will come."

**Thought 1.** Sin enters the world. Sin enters the business, the office, the marketplace, the play field, the club, even the home and the church. No place ever escapes sin, for no person is perfect. Wherever a person is, there is sin. No person is without sin.

3. Committing sin is a terrible thing, but leading others to sin is even more terrible. The word "offend" means to be a stumbling block; to bait, lure, and trip someone (see note, *Offend*—Mt.17:27 for more discussion). Who are these, the ones who cause others to stumble? In one simple statement, it is anyone who *practices sin*, who *continues in sin*.
  a. A stumbling block is anyone who *seduces others to sin*. Many persons seduce others into the sins...
    • of grumbling, complaining, and criticizing.
    • of taking sides against others.
    • of being worldly and materialistic.
    • of craving more and more.
    • of being conceited and prideful.
    • of living loose and immoral lives.
    • of cursing and talking filthy.

b. A stumbling block is anyone who *makes a false profession*, anyone who claims to be a follower of Christ, but who is not. The person who makes a false profession scandalizes the name of Christ. He is a hypocrite who causes others to stay away and to detest Christ and the church. False professors not only shut themselves out of the kingdom, but they lead their children into a false, hypocritical religion which shuts them out. The false professor causes others to say they want nothing to do with the church because it is full of hypocrites.

c. A stumbling block is anyone who *discourages a person* from following and serving Christ by...
- word or deed
- abuse or neglect
- persecution or injury
- gossip or slander
- anger or hostility

4. Leading others to sin is heavily condemned (see DEEPER STUDY # 1—Lk.17:2).

"And whosoever shall offend one of these little ones that believe in me, it is better for him that a millstone were hanged about his neck, and he were cast into the sea" (Mk.9:42).

"Let us not therefore judge one another any more: but judge this rather, that no man put a stumbling block or an occasion to fall in his brother's way" (Ro.14:13).

"But if thy brother be grieved with thy meat, now walkest thou not charitably. Destroy not him with thy meat, for whom Christ died" (Ro.14:15).

"It is good neither to eat flesh, nor to drink wine, nor any thing whereby thy brother stumbleth, or is offended, or is made weak" (Ro.14:21).

"Give none offence" (1 Cor.10:32).

"Giving no offence in any thing" (2 Cor.6:3).

"He that loveth his brother abideth in the light, and there is none occasion of stumbling in him" (1 Jn.2:10).

---

**DEEPER STUDY # 1**

(17:2) **Millstone** (monos onikos): the word *onos* is the word for a donkey. The word *mulos* is the word for the millstone that the donkey pulled around and around to grind the grain. Thus, the millstone Jesus spoke of is the huge millstone, not the small hand millstone used by the women to grind a little grain at a time. Note: the very fact that Jesus chose the huge millstone shows how great this sin is. The person would be held to the bottom of the sea by the most awful and terrible weight. The sin of leading others astray is the most awful sin that can be committed. Jesus is stressing that its condemnation will be awful and terrible.

---

[2] (17:3-4) **Forgiveness—Church, Discipline—Rebuke**: the second law is that forgiving others is essential. Note the words, "Take heed to yourselves." What Jesus said was of critical importance. If a person sins against us, we are to rebuke him; but if he repents, we are to forgive him. The point is strong. There is to be no sense of unforgiveness among God's people, no matter how grave the sin against us, no matter how big a stumbling block is put in our path (cp. v.1-2).

The word "rebuke" (epitimeson) is important. It means to charge, to be emphatic with. The believer is to confront the person who *offends* and puts a *stumbling block* in his way. We are to do what we can to correct an offending brother, but the correction is to be done in love and compassion, not in a censoring and judgmental spirit. The whole theme of this instruction is forgiveness, which means that a spirit of love and compassion exists. The instruction does not mean that the believer is weak or indifferent to sin, but rather that he responds to being mistreated by being loving and compassionate.

**Thought 1.** Believers are to correct those who sin against them and do them wrong. To allow sin to continue is to indulge and to give license to sin, and the last thing God wants is for sin to be indulged in and given the license to run wild.

"And have no fellowship with the unfruitful works of darkness, but rather reprove them" (Eph.5:11).

"Now we exhort you, brethren, warn them that are unruly, comfort the feebleminded, support the weak, be patient toward all men" (1 Th.5:14).

"Yet count him not as an enemy, but admonish him as a brother" (2 Th.3:15).

"Rebuke not an elder, but intreat him as a father; and the younger men as brethren; the elder women as mothers; the younger as sisters, with all purity" (1 Tim.5:1-2).

"Preach the word; be instant in season, out of season; reprove, rebuke, exhort with all longsuffering and doctrine" (2 Tim.4:2).

"These things speak, and exhort, and rebuke with all authority. Let no man despise thee" (Tit.2:15).

"A man that is an heretick after the first and second admonition reject" (Tit.3:10).

"And ye have forgotten the exhortation which speaketh unto you as unto children, My son, despise not thou the chastening of the Lord, nor faint when thou art rebuked of him" (Heb.12:5).

"The world cannot hate you; but me it hateth, because I testify of it, that the works thereof are evil" (Jn.7:7).

"I write not these things to shame you, but as my beloved sons I warn you" (1 Cor.4:14).

"Let the righteous smite me; it shall be a kindness: and let him reprove me; it shall be an excellent oil, which shall not break my head: for yet my prayer also shall be in their calamities" (Ps.141:5).

"But ye have set at nought all my counsel, and would none of my reproof" (Pr.1:25).

"He is in the way of life that keepeth instruction: but he that refuseth reproof erreth" (Pr.10:17).

"Whoso loveth instruction loveth knowledge: but he that hateth reproof is brutish" (Pr.12:1).

"A fool despiseth his father's instruction: but he that regardeth reproof is prudent" (Pr.15:5).

"Correction is grievous unto him that forsaketh the way: and he that hateth reproof shall die" (Pr.15:10).

"He, that being often reproved hardeneth his neck, shall suddenly be destroyed, and that without remedy" (Pr.29:1).

"It is better to hear the rebuke of the wise, than for a man to hear the song of fools" (Eccl.7:5).

"They hate him that rebuketh in the gate, and they abhor him that speaketh uprightly" (Amos 5:10).

The command to forgive is also strong. In fact, this is one of the most beautiful pictures of God's unlimited forgiveness. He continues to forgive and forgive. True, the believer does not have license to sin; the Bible is very clear about this (Ro.6:1-2; Gal.5:13; 1 Pt.2:16). The believer is not to take advantage of the forgiveness of God, for judgment awaits the person who so abuses the grace of God. However, the Bible is equally strong in proclaiming that God forgives and forgives the believer who truly repents—even if he sins time and again. It is God's unlimited forgiveness that requires the believer to forgive anyone who offends him and truly repents—even if the believer has to forgive the offender seven times a day for having wronged him. (See Deeper Study # 4—Mt.26:28.)

"Blessed are the merciful: for they shall obtain mercy" (Mt.5:7).

"And when ye stand praying, forgive, if ye have ought against any: that your Father also which is in heaven may forgive you your trespasses" (Mk.11:25).

"Be ye therefore merciful, as your Father also is merciful" (Lk.6:36).

"And be ye kind one to another, tenderhearted, forgiving one another, even as God for Christ's sake hath forgiven you" (Eph.4:32).

"Forbearing one another, and forgiving one another, if any man have a quarrel against any: even as Christ forgave you, so also do ye" (Col.3:13).

"Let not mercy and truth forsake thee: bind them about thy neck; write them upon the table of thine heart" (Pr.3:3).

"The merciful man doeth good to his own soul: but he that is cruel troubleth his own flesh" (Pr.11:17).

"Therefore turn thou to thy God: keep mercy and judgment, and wait on thy God continually" (Hos.12:6).

"He hath showed thee, O man, what is good; and what doth the LORD require of thee, but to do justly, and to love mercy, and to walk humbly with thy God?" (Mic.6:8).

**3** (17:5-6) **Faith—Boldness**: the third law is that faith is essential; faith is a powerful force. The disciples realized something: their faith was weak—too weak to ever live like Jesus was talking about. He was insisting on a faith so strong that they would...
- be free from ever causing another person to stumble.
- be so loving and compassionate they could forgive a person time and again, even seven times in a single day.

They knew that they desperately needed greater faith in the power and love of Christ, that the power and love of Christ would infill and permeate their whole beings. They knew that they had to believe and trust His presence more and more. Note what Jesus answered.

1. Genuine faith is what is needed, not great faith. The stress is not quantity, not on how much faith a person has. It is not a matter of *increasing faith*; it is a matter of *possessing* and *having* faith. It is a matter of *genuine* faith. The very smallest amount of genuine faith, a faith as small as a mustard seed, can do the impossible. Nothing is impossible to him who has a faith that is genuine, even if the faith is the smallest amount possible. (See Deeper Study # 2, *Mustard Seed*—Lk.17:6.)

2. Boldness is needed. It takes boldness to walk up to a tree and tell it to be removed. Imagine—to really believe that the request is done! We either believe it or not. It is not a matter of how much belief; it is a matter of genuine belief. If one's belief is genuine, then it is done.

"Jesus answered and said unto them, Verily I say unto you, If ye have faith, and doubt not, ye shall not only do this which is done to the fig tree, but also if ye shall say unto this mountain, Be thou removed, and be thou cast into the sea; it shall be done. And all things, whatsoever ye shall ask in prayer, believing, ye shall receive" (Mt.21:21-22).

"Jesus said unto him, If thou canst believe, all things are possible to him that believeth" (Mk.9:23).

"Now faith is the substance of things hoped for, the evidence of things not seen" (Heb.11:1).

"But without faith it is impossible to please him: for he that cometh to God must believe that he is, and that he is a rewarder of them that diligently seek him" (Heb.11:6).

"Oh how great is thy goodness, which thou hast laid up for them that fear thee; which thou hast wrought for them that trust in thee before the sons of men!" (Ps.31:19).

"Commit thy way unto the LORD; trust also in him; and he shall bring it to pass" (Ps.37:5).

---

**DEEPER STUDY # 2**

(17:6) **Mustard Seed—Faith**: What did Jesus mean by "faith as a grain of mustard seed"? The mustard seed was known for its small size, yet it grew to be a very large bush (see note—Mt.13:32). Picture a mustard seed lying in one's hand. It is *real and very small*, yet imagine the potential for *growth and use*. So is "faith as a grain of mustard seed." Faith is *real and small*, yet it has enormous power for growth and ministry.

---

**4** (17:7-10) **Service—Ministry—Faithfulness—Labor—Steadfastness**: the fourth law concerns obedience: to obey God is a duty not a service. There is danger that believers will become prideful and puffed up because of the gifts and power God gives, especially if they begin to live victoriously in faith as just described (v.5-6). Jesus used an illustration, making three points to combat this danger.

1. The believer is a servant, and a servant is a slave who serves his Master. (The parable is clear, but see note, *Servant*—Ro.1:1 for more discussion.)

2. The believer is to serve and obey the commandments of God until all the work is done. He is to feed the cattle and plough the fields, then in the evenings he is to serve the household by feeding and waiting on tables. Ploughing and feeding are tough work, requiring a sound and disciplined body and spirit. They require endurance. Note that the servant labors all day and all through the evening until all others have gone to bed. He goes to bed *after* all others have retired, and he arises *before* all others arise. *The servant serves his Master.* (What a lesson Christ lays out for the believer! How few serve the Lord so diligently! How many arise before others in order to spend time alone with the Lord, and then spend the last minutes of a day with the Lord after all others have retired?)

"But so shall it not be among you: but whosoever will be great among you, shall be your minister: and whosoever of you will be the chiefest, shall be servant of all" (Mk.10:43-44).

"Jesus saith unto them, My meat is to do the will of him that sent me, and to finish his work" (Jn.4:34).

"I must work the works of him that sent me, while it is day: the night cometh, when no man can work" (Jn.9:4).

"And when they had appointed him [Paul] a day, there came many to him into his lodging; to whom he expounded and testified the kingdom of God, persuading them concerning Jesus, both out of the law of Moses, and out of the prophets, from morning till evening" (Acts 28:23).

"Not slothful in business; fervent in spirit; serving the Lord" (Ro.12:11).

"Therefore, my beloved brethren, be ye stedfast, unmoveable, always abounding in the work of the Lord, forasmuch as ye know that your labour is not in vain in the Lord" (1 Cor.15:58).

"And let us not be weary in well doing: for in due season we shall reap, if we faint not. As we have therefore opportunity, let us do good unto all men, especially unto them who are of the household of faith" (Gal.6:9-10).

"Wherefore I put thee in remembrance that thou stir up the gift of God, which is in thee by the putting on of my hands" (2 Tim.1:6).

"But watch thou in all things, endure afflictions, do the work of an evangelist, make full proof of thy ministry" (2 Tim.4:5).

"And we desire that every one of you do show the same diligence to the full assurance of hope unto the end: that ye be not slothful, but followers of them who through faith and patience inherit the promises" (Heb.6:11-12).

"Wherefore seeing we also are compassed about with so great a cloud of witnesses, let us lay aside every weight, and the sin which doth so easily beset us, and let us run with patience the race that is set before us" (Heb.12:1).

"Ye therefore, beloved, seeing ye know these things before, beware lest ye also, being led away with the error of the wicked, fall from your own stedfastness" (2 Pt.3:17).

"Whatsoever thy hand findeth to do, do it with thy might; for there is no work, nor device, nor knowledge, nor wisdom, in the grave, whither thou goest" (Eccl.9:10).

3. The believer is to be humble in his service for the Lord. No matter what we do for Christ, it is our *duty* to do it. We are unworthy of the privilege to serve Him. We are to count ourselves "*unprofitable servants*." No man can claim he has done all he should; we know this. We all come short, no matter how much we do or how great the work. There is no room for pride or arrogance or boasting. God commands perfection; therefore, He expects humility.

"Be ye therefore perfect, even as your Father which is in heaven is perfect" (Mt.5:48).

"Whosoever therefore shall humble himself as this little child, the same is greatest in the kingdom of heaven" (Mt.18:4).

"Every one that exalteth himself shall be abased; and he that humbleth himself shall be exalted" (Lk.18:14).

"Be not highminded, but fear" (Ro.11:20).

"For I say, through the grace given unto me, to every man that is among you, not to think of himself more highly than he ought to think; but to think soberly, according as God hath dealt to every man the measure of faith" (Ro.12:3).

"Let nothing be done through strife or vainglory; but in lowliness of mind let each esteem other better than themselves. Look not every man on his own things, but every man also on the things of others" (Ph.2:3-4).

"Let this mind be in you, which was also in Christ Jesus: who, being in the form of God, thought it not robbery to be equal with God: but made himself of no reputation, and took upon him the form of a servant, and was made in the likeness of men: and being found in fashion as a man, he humbled himself, and became obedient unto death, even the death of the cross" (Ph.2:5-8).

"Humble yourselves in the sight of the Lord, and he shall lift you up" (Jas.4:10).

"Likewise, ye younger, submit yourselves unto the elder. Yea, all of you be subject one to another, and be clothed with humility: for God resisteth the proud, and gives grace to the humble" (1 Pt.5:5).

| | VII. THE SON OF MAN'S GREAT JOURNEY TO JERUSALEM (STAGE III): HIS LESSONS AND WARNINGS, 17:11-19:27 | 14 And when he saw them, he said unto them, Go show yourselves unto the priests. And it came to pass, that, as they went, they were cleansed. | d. There was perseverance<br><br>e. There was believing, being tested, obeying |
|---|---|---|---|
| | | 15 And one of them, when he saw that he was healed, turned back, and with a loud voice glorified God, | 3 The lesson on gratitude<br>a. All were blessed<br>b. One gave thanks |
| | A. The Lesson on Need and Gratitude, 17:11-19 | 16 And fell down on his face at his feet, giving him thanks: and he was a Samaritan. | 1) Glorified God<br>2) Worshipped Jesus<br>3) Was a Samaritan |
| 1 Jesus went toward Jerusalem | 11 And it came to pass, as he went to Jerusalem, that he passed through the midst of Samaria and Galilee. | 17 And Jesus answering said, Were there not ten cleansed? but where are the nine? | c. Most did not give thanks |
| 2 The lesson on need: Ten lepers were healed<sup>DS1</sup><br>a. There was desperation<br>b. There was humility<br>c. There was a cry for mercy | 12 And as he entered into a certain village, there met him ten men that were lepers, which stood afar off:<br>13 And they lifted up their voices, and said, Jesus, Master, have mercy on us. | 18 There are not found that returned to give glory to God, save this stranger.<br>19 And he said unto him, Arise, go thy way: thy faith hath made thee whole. | d. The one who was the most rejected was the most thankful<br>e. The thankful one shall be the one assured of salvation |

# DIVISION VII

## THE SON OF MAN'S GREAT JOURNEY TO JERUSALEM (STAGE III): HIS LESSONS AND WARNINGS, 17:11-19:27

## A.  The Lesson on Need and Gratitude, 17:11-19

(17:11-19) **Introduction**: this passage teaches two powerful lessons, one on how to have needs met and the other on gratitude.
1. Jesus went toward Jerusalem (v.11).
2. The lesson on need: ten lepers are healed (v.12-14).
3. The lesson on gratitude (v.15-19).

[1] (17:11) **Jesus Christ, Purpose**: Jesus went toward Jerusalem. His face was set to fulfill His purpose on earth: to die *for* man (see DEEPER STUDY # 1—Lk.9:51; note—13:22).

[2] (17:12-14) **Need—Cleansing—Faith—Perseverance—Prayer, Answer**: the lesson on need—ten lepers are healed. (See DEEPER STUDY # 1, *Leper*—Lk.17:12-14.) There were five things that led to their need's being met.
1. There was desperation. The men had leprosy, the most feared disease of that day (see DEEPER STUDY # 1, *Leprosy*—Lk.17:12-14). They met Jesus as He was entering the city, coming in from a long journey. The lepers had no idea where He was going: He could have been heading for an important meeting, or been tired and exhausted, or had no time for interruptions; but the lepers did not care. They were so desperate they would interrupt Him no matter what.

> **Thought 1.** One thing is basic to having a need met: a sense of desperation. When we sense a need so desperately that nothing can stop us from reaching Jesus, our needs will be met.
>
> > **"Seek the LORD, and his strength: seek his face evermore" (Ps.105:4).**
> > **"For thus saith the LORD unto the house of Israel, Seek ye me, and ye shall live" (Amos 5:4).**
> > **"Seek ye the LORD while he may be found, call ye upon him while he is near" (Is.55:6).**

2. There was humility. Note: they "stood afar off." They respected the law which demanded they stand at least six feet away from a person. These lepers were, of course, many yards away from Jesus because of the large crowd's following Him. They showed a great respect for the law by remaining on the outskirts of the crowd. On other occasions those seeking healing had ignored the law, bursting through crowds and running up to Jesus. Jesus was bound to note their humility and their acknowledgment of being unclean.

> **Thought 1.** Every man must recognize his uncleanness in approaching Jesus. He must come in humility...
> ⇒ *confessing unworthiness* to approach One so holy.
>
> > **"Humble yourselves in the sight of the Lord, and he shall lift you up" (Jas.4:10).**
> > **"The LORD is nigh unto them that are of a broken heart; and saveth such as be of a contrite spirit" (Ps.34:18).**
> > **"For thus saith the high and lofty One that inhabiteth eternity, whose name is Holy; I dwell in the high and holy place, with him also that is of a contrite and humble spirit, to revive the spirit of the humble, and to revive the heart of the contrite ones" (Is.57:15).**
>
> ⇒ *confessing need* for the cleansing touch of the Holy One of God, even the Lord Jesus Christ.

3. There was a cry for mercy. Note two things.
   a. They called Jesus "Master." The Greek word for "Master" is not *Rabbi*, the Teacher; but it is *epistata*, which means the Chief, the Commander, the Overseer, the One who has the power to meet needs. Note: the need is not for instruction (Rabbi) but for healing. By healing, they meant both the cleansing of their physical bodies and the spiritual sin which had caused their disease. The Jews always connected leprosy with sin, so this is definitely what they meant. They recognized Jesus to be the Master who could cleanse both the body and spirit, who could give them both healing and forgiveness of sins.
   b. They cried out for mercy. They did not ask only for physical healing; they asked for spiritual healing, for the forgiveness of sins as well. They cried out for mercy upon all of their being.

> "For we have not an high priest which cannot be touched with the feeling of our infirmities; but was in all points tempted like as we are, yet without sin. Let us therefore come boldly unto the throne of grace, that we may obtain mercy, and find grace to help in time of need" (Heb.4:15-16).
> "O LORD, rebuke me not in thine anger, neither chasten me in thy hot displeasure. Have mercy upon me, O LORD; for I am weak: O LORD, heal me; for my bones are vexed" (Ps.6:1-2).
> "Hear, O LORD, when I cry with my voice: have mercy also upon me, and answer me" (Ps.27:7).
> "This poor man cried, and the LORD heard him, and saved him out of all his troubles" (Ps.34:6).
> "Have mercy upon me, O God, according to thy lovingkindness: according unto the multitude of thy tender mercies blot out my transgressions" (Ps.51:1).
> "Show us thy mercy, O LORD, and grant us thy salvation" (Ps.85:7).
> "My mercy will I keep for him for evermore, and my covenant shall stand fast with him" (Ps.89:28).
> "The LORD is merciful and gracious, slow to anger, and plenteous in mercy" (Ps.103:8).
> "But the mercy of the LORD is from everlasting to everlasting upon them that fear him, and his righteousness unto children's children" (Ps.103:17).
> "Let thy tender mercies come unto me, that I may live: for thy law is my delight" (Ps.119:77).
> "Have mercy upon us, O LORD, have mercy upon us: for we are exceedingly filled with contempt. Our soul is exceeding filled with the scorning of those that are at ease, and with the contempt of the proud" (Ps.123:3-4).
> "Let the wicked forsake his way, and the unrighteous man his thoughts: and let him return unto the LORD, and he will have mercy upon him; and to our God, for he will abundantly pardon" (Is.55:7).

4. There was perseverance. Jesus did not notice them immediately. He ignored their cry in order to test them. They needed to cry and cry for mercy in order to show their sincerity and to build up their sense of need. These two things are important to note. God does not always answer our prayers immediately. Sometimes we need to learn to trust Him more or to build up a greater sense of need and desperation. Forcing us to seek and knock and persevere does both. Once God answers our prayer, we learn to trust Him more. There is another crucial matter as well. Forcing us to stay on our knees and to persevere in prayer day after day keeps us in His presence. Deep concentrated prayer provides some of the sweetest communion and fellowship ever experienced, and such communion and fellowship is what God is after.

> "And I say unto you, Ask, and it shall be given you; seek, and ye shall find; knock, and it shall be opened unto you" (Lk.11:9).
> "But if from thence thou shalt seek the LORD thy God, thou shalt find him, if thou seek him with all thy heart and with all thy soul" (Dt.4:29).
> "And ye shall seek me, and find me, when ye shall search for me with all your heart" (Jer.29:13).

5. There was *believing and obeying*. Jesus did not heal the lepers immediately. There were things they had to do, instructions that had to be obeyed, to have their needs met. They were to obey the law, go to the priest and report that they had been cleansed. If they obeyed the law and believed the Lord's Word (promise of cleansing), they would be cleansed. Now note: they were cleansed "as they went." This was a great legacy of faith to leave for succeeding generations (cp. Heb.11:7f). Think about the great belief they had in Jesus' word and power! They had to strike out for the temple to be inspected and pronounced cleansed—and they were not even healed yet! While they were obeying the Jewish law of cleansing, they were to be healed (Lev.14:1f).

> "Jesus saith unto him, Go thy way; thy son liveth. And the man believed the word that Jesus had spoken unto him, and he went his way" (Jn.4:50).
> "But without faith it is impossible to please him: for he that cometh to God must believe that he is, and that he is a rewarder of them that diligently seek him" (Heb.11:6).
> "And being made perfect, he became the author of eternal salvation unto all them that obey him" (Heb.5:9).

"Oh how great is thy goodness, which thou hast laid up for them that fear thee; which thou hast wrought for them that trust in thee before the sons of men!" (Ps.31:19).

"The Lord redeemeth the soul of his servants: and none of them that trust in him shall be desolate" (Ps.34:22).

"Commit thy way unto the LORD; trust also in him; and he shall bring it to pass" (Ps.37:5).

---

**DEEPER STUDY # 1**

(17:12-14) **Leprosy**: leprosy was the most terrible disease in the day of Jesus; it was greatly feared. It was disfiguring and sometimes fatal. In the Bible, leprosy is a type of sin.

1.    The leper himself was considered *utterly unclean*—physically and spiritually. He could not approach within six feet of any person including family members. "His clothes shall be rent, and his head bare, and he shall put a covering upon his upper lip, and shall cry, 'Unclean, unclean'" (Lev.13:45).

2.    He was judged to be *dead—the living dead*. He had to wear a black garment so he could be recognized as from among the dead.

3.    He was banished as an outcast, totally ostracized from society—earthly and heavenly. "All the days wherein the plague shall be in him he shall be *defiled*; he is *unclean*; he shall *dwell alone; without the camp* shall his habitation be" (Lev.13:46). He could not live within the walls of any city; his dwelling had to be outside the city gates.

4.    He was thought to be polluted, incurable by any human means whatsoever. Leprosy could be cured by God and His power alone. (Note how Jesus proved His Messiahship and deity by healing the leper.)

Imagine the anguish and heartbreak of the leper, being completely cut off from family and friends and society. Imagine the emotional and mental pain. There are other recorded instances of lepers' being healed (cp. Lk.7:22; Mt.8:1; 10:8; 11:5; Mk.1:40; and perhaps Mt.26:6; cp. Mk.14:3).

---

**[3]**  (17:15-19) **Gratitude**: there are five points to note on the lesson of gratitude.

1.    All the lepers were blessed and should have been thankful. This was true of the ten lepers, and it should be true of every man. Every one of the ten should have turned back and given thanks. They had all been blessed by Christ. Note they had all...

- recognized their need.
- shown humility.
- cried for mercy.
- persevered.
- believed and obeyed.

Their need had been met: they had all been healed. They now needed to turn back to give thanks and show appreciation.

"Let your light so shine before men, that they may see your good works, and glorify your Father which is in heaven" (Mt.5:16).

"That ye may with one mind and one mouth glorify God, even the Father of our Lord Jesus Christ" (Ro.15:6).

"For ye are bought with a price: therefore glorify God in your body, and in your spirit, which are God's" (1 Cor.6:20).

"By him therefore let us offer the sacrifice of praise to God continually, that is, the fruit of our lips giving thanks to his name" (Heb.13:15).

"Sing praises to the LORD, which dwelleth in Zion: declare among the people his doings" (Ps.9:11).

"And my tongue shall speak of thy righteousness and of thy praise all the day long" (Ps.35:28).

"Let the people praise thee, O God; let all the people praise thee" (Ps.67:3).

2.    One did give thanks. He was a Samaritan, the most despised and rejected of the men. (See DEEPER STUDY # 2, *Samaritan*—Lk.10:33.) Note what he did.

    a.  He glorified God immediately. He shouted at the top of his lungs with the loudest voice possible. He *witnessed* for God. God had cleansed him and he wanted all to know the great mercy and love of God.

    b.  He worshipped Jesus. Note that he fell down on his face at the feet of Jesus. This was both humility and recognition of the power of God in Christ, two essentials for true spiritual cleansing (salvation, v.19).

3.    Most did not give thanks. They kept going about their business at hand. They did not stop what they were doing nor return to the Lord to give thanks. But note something: they did return to their former world, the lives they used to live.

**Thought 1.** There is a lesson in the behavior of the lepers. Christ expects us to return to Him continually, to return, glorify, and worship Him as the Source of our power and strength for life.

"For men shall be lovers of their own selves, covetous, boasters, proud, blasphemers, disobedient to parents, unthankful, unholy" (2 Tim.3:2).

"Because that, when they knew God, they glorified him not as God, neither were thankful; but became vain in their imaginations, and their foolish heart was darkened" (Ro.1:21).

"Do ye thus requite [repay] the LORD, O foolish people and unwise? Is not he thy father that hath bought thee? Hath he not made thee, and established thee?" (Dt.32:6).

4.      The most rejected was the most thankful. Note the word "stranger" (allogenes, v.18). It means that he was a *"stranger* from the covenants of promise, having no hope, and without God in the world" (Eph.2:12). He had felt his need more keenly and deeply. He knew he needed to be saved, genuinely saved—spiritually as well as physically. Despite the fact that he had never known the real promises of God and that he had been without God in this world, he now knew God. His heart just broke forth to give glory to God. Jesus had saved him from so much.

> **"Giving thanks unto the Father, which hath made us meet to be partakers of the inheritance of the saints in light" (Col.1:12).**
> **"But ye are a chosen generation, a royal priesthood, an holy nation, a peculiar people; that ye should show forth the praises of him who hath called you out of darkness into his marvellous light" (1 Pt.2:9).**
> **"In every thing give thanks: for this is the will of God in Christ Jesus concerning you" (1 Th.5:18).**

5.      The thankful man shall be the one truly saved—spiritually. The verb "made whole" (sesoken) is literally "has saved you." The man was clearly whole in body. This could be easily seen, but one could not see the spiritual and inward cleansing. Jesus was telling the man that his sins were forgiven; He was giving the man the assurance of salvation.

Now note an important question. Had the nine been spiritually cleansed as well as physically cleansed? Or was it lack of being spiritually cleansed that kept them from returning to give thanks? Or was Jesus just giving this man a strong assurance of salvation?

We are not told, but one crucial factor is known. This man, the grateful and thankful leper, was the man who received *assurance of being cleansed and of having his sins forgiven*. The others did not. They failed to be grateful and thankful.

Another important fact to note is this: gratitude and praise bring assurance to the heart. They stir Christ to speak to the human heart, giving assurance of acceptance and cleansing.

> **"Therefore if any man be in Christ, he is a new creature: old things are passed away; behold, all things are become new" (2 Cor.5:17).**
> **"Not by works of righteousness which we have done, but according to his mercy he saved us, by the washing of regeneration, and renewing of the Holy Ghost" (Tit.3:5).**
> **"Being born again, not of corruptible seed, but of incorruptible, by the word of God, which liveth and abideth for ever" (1 Pt.1:23).**
> **"I said, LORD, be merciful unto me: heal my soul; for I have sinned against thee" (Ps.41:4).**
> **"But he was wounded for our transgressions, he was bruised for our iniquities: the chastisement of our peace was upon him; and with his stripes we are healed" (Is.53:5).**

| | | and destroyed them all. | judgment will fall |
|---|---|---|---|
| | **B. The Coming Day of God's Kingdom and Jesus' Return, 17:20-37** (cp. Mt.24; Mk.13) | 28 Likewise also as it was in the days of Lot; they did eat, they drank, they bought, they sold, they planted, they builded; | b. The days of Lot 1) Normal affairs will be going on |
| **1 The coming of God's Kingdom** | 20 And when he was demanded of the Pharisees, when the kingdom of God should come, he answered them and said, The kingdom of God cometh not with observation: | 29 But the same day that Lot went out of Sodom it rained fire and brimstone from heaven, and destroyed them all. | 2) Suddenly, unexpectedly, judgment will fall |
| a. It cannot be observed b. It is within | 21 Neither shall they say, Lo here! or, lo there! for, behold, the kingdom of God is within you. | 30 Even thus shall it be in the day when the Son of man is revealed. | c. The day of the Son of Man will be the same: Sudden, unexpected |
| **2 The day will be longed for** | 22 And he said unto the disciples, The days will come, when ye shall desire to see one of the days of the Son of man, and ye shall not see it. | 31 In that day, he which shall be upon the housetop, and his stuff in the house, let him not come down to take it away: and he that is in the field, let him likewise not return back. | **6 The day will be a day of urgency for all men** a. The urgency illust. |
| **3 The day is unknown; it is coming suddenly & visibly** | 23 And they shall say to you, See here; or, see there: go not after them, nor follow them. 24 For as the lightning, that lighteneth out of the one part under heaven, shineth unto the other part under heaven; so shall also the Son of man be in his day. | 32 Remember Lot's wife. 33 Whosoever shall seek to save his life shall lose it; and whosoever shall lose life shall preserve it. 34 I tell you, in that night there shall be two men in one bed; the one shall be taken, and the other shall be left. | b. The doom of turning back illustrated c. The one essential: Total abandonment **7 The day will be a day of separation** |
| **4 The day cannot come until some things happen first** | 25 But first must he suffer many things and be rejected of this generation. | 35 Two women shall be grinding together; the one shall be taken, and the other left. | |
| **5 The day will be as the days of Noah & Lot: Men will be occupied with normal, routine affairs** a. The days of Noah 1) Normal affairs will be going on 2) Suddenly, unexpectedly, | 26 And as it was in the days of Noe, so shall it be also in the days of the Son of man. 27 They did eat, they drank, they married wives, they were given in marriage, until the day that Noe entered into the ark, and the flood came, | 36 Two men shall be in the field; the one shall be taken, and the other left. 37 And they answered and said unto him, Where, Lord? And he said unto them, Wheresoever the body is, thither will the eagles be gathered together. | **8 The day will be universal, worldwide** |

# DIVISION VII

## THE SON OF MAN'S GREAT JOURNEY TO JERUSALEM (STAGE III): HIS LESSONS AND WARNINGS, 17:11-19:27

**B.  The Coming Day of God's Kingdom and Jesus' Return, 17:20-37**

(17:20-37) **Introduction**: the religionists (Pharisees) asked when the Kingdom of God was going to come. The Kingdom of God was the focus of Jesus' preaching and conversation. It was the topic of conversation being buzzed about by everyone. The Messiah had come and the Kingdom of God was to be ushered in. The religionists (Pharisees) in particular were interested.

⇒ They had heard Jesus preach, "Repent, for the kingdom of God is at hand." They wanted to know when it was coming, for it meant great blessings both for Israel and for them personally as religious leaders.
⇒ They had heard Jesus instruct His disciples to pray for the Kingdom of God to come. Their curiosity was aroused, and they wanted to know when to expect it.

Jesus answered their question in a very simple statement of two verses (v.20-21). Then, note what He did. He turned to His disciples (v.22) and gave them a dynamic message on *the coming day of God's Kingdom and on His own return*. It is important to see two things (see DEEPER STUDY # 3—Mt.19:23-24 for more discussion).

⇒ Two stages of God's kingdom are covered here: the spiritual kingdom that is within a person (v.20-21), and the coming kingdom to be set up on earth when Christ returns (v.24).
⇒ The Kingdom of God and of the Lord (Son of Man) refer to the same kingdom (v.20-21, 24, 26, 30).

1.  The coming of God's Kingdom (v.20-21).
2.  The day will be longed for (v.22).
3.  The day is unknown; it is coming suddenly and visibly (v.23-24).
4.  The day cannot come until some things happen first (v.25).

5.  The day will be as the days of Noah and Lot: men will be occupied with normal, routine affairs (v.26-30).
6.  The day will be a day of urgency for all men (v.31-33).
7.  The day will be a day of separation (v.34-36).
8.  The day will be universal, worldwide (v.37).

**1** (17:20-21) **Kingdom of God**: the coming of God's kingdom. When will it come?

1.  The Kingdom of God cannot be observed (paratereseos). The word means to watch closely, to give close observation to (as in astronomical observations). The kingdom cannot be seen with the naked eye. This means at least two things.
    a.  The Kingdom of God does not come with an outward, dramatic, thunderous show. It does not come in such a way that men say, "Lo here! or, lo there!" It comes with a silent, pervasive influence. It is coming, and its coming will permeate the whole world; but its coming is to be silent, not showy (cp. the leaven which silently permeates the whole lump, see note—Mt.13:33).
    b.  The Kingdom of God cannot be seen with the naked eye. The Lord's kingdom is not of this world, not of the physical and material dimension of being. It is not the kind of kingdom men see when they observe the nations of the world.
2.  The Kingdom of God is "within you" (entos humon). Some say this should be translated "among you." If so, then Christ is saying that He is the embodiment of the Kingdom of God. He is setting up the Kingdom of God among them, there and then. God is already beginning to rule and reign in the lives He is touching.
    Others say the words mean "within you." If so, then the kingdom is to be looked for within the hearts and lives of people. The Kingdom of God is spiritual; it is the changing of hearts, the rule and reign of God within men's lives. It is the power of God to change a sinful, immoral, and unjust man into a servant of God.

> "Now after that John was put in prison, Jesus came into Galilee, preaching the gospel of the kingdom of God, and saying, The time is fulfilled, and the kingdom of God is at hand: repent ye, and believe the gospel" (Mk.1:14-15).
> "And he lifted up his eyes on his disciples, and said, Blessed be ye poor: for yours is the kingdom of God" (Lk.6:20).
> "For the kingdom of God is not meat and drink; but righteousness, and peace, and joy in the Holy Ghost" (Ro.14:17).

**2** (17:22) **Jesus Christ, Return—Kingdom of God**: the day will be longed for. Note: from this point on Jesus began to speak to the disciples, but He was still dealing with the same subject: the coming of the Son of Man and of God's kingdom.
1.  The Kingdom of God is internal, but it is to be external also.
    ⇒ The term the "days of the Son of Man" refers to the Messianic kingdom.
    ⇒ The Son of Man is the title used by Daniel when describing the kingdom of the Messiah (cp. Dan.7:13-14).
2.  Men cannot control the Kingdom of God. This is a crucial point to note. They may wish to see the kingdom…
    •  as being prepared by the hands of men,
    •  as being close at hand, coming soon,
    •  as being now—existing on earth with God's ruling and reigning,
    …but man has nothing to do with its control. No matter how much men may "desire to see one of the days," they do not control even one day of it. They cannot create a single day of the kingdom so that they can see it.
3.  What is it that makes a believer ache to see the Son of Man and to be with Him in His kingdom (heaven)?
    ⇒ tough and terrible trials
    ⇒ persecution, personal abuse, and mistreatment
    ⇒ divisions, torn families and social groups
    ⇒ death, separation from family and dear friends
    ⇒ worship, a close sense and deep experience with God
Now note something ever so wonderful and precious. In every one of the above situations, God takes His dear child and meets his need. God draws his dear child near Him to give His child a sense of His presence and care and love. Even if the moment for the child's death and entrance into heaven has arrived, God draws near and carries His child in His arms of love, carries him through the "valley of the shadow of death" (Ps.23:4). However, the point made by Jesus is not the closeness of His presence in the death of the believer. It is the closeness of His presence through the great trials and troubles of life that causes the believer to ache for heaven. God does infuse a deep desire for heaven into the heart of the genuine believer, and He does it often. Such a consciousness of God's presence causes the genuine believer to long and ache for God's presence all the time.

> "Looking for and hasting unto the coming of the day of God, wherein the heavens being on fire shall be dissolved, and the elements shall melt with fervent heat? Nevertheless we, according to his promise, look for new heavens and a new earth, wherein dwelleth righteousness" (2 Pt.3:12-13).
> "My soul, wait thou only upon God; for my expectation is from him" (Ps.62:5).

**3** (17:23-24) **Jesus Christ, Return—Kingdom of God**: the day is unknown; it is coming suddenly. Some men will always be saying the kingdom has come and is present on earth. The kingdom…
    •  is here, "See here."
    •  is there, "See there."
Jesus said there is an *internal kingdom*, a kingdom "within you" which is the rule and reign of God within the human heart (v.21). But there is also an *external kingdom*, a heaven for which men shall long and not be *able* to see (v.22). The

external kingdom is coming "in His day" (v.24). When that day comes, it shall come suddenly and visibly, just as quickly and visibly as a flash of lightning.

Jesus was teaching an important lesson here. Since the day cannot be known, believers are to be busy about their labor for the Lord.

> "Therefore, my beloved brethren, be ye stedfast, unmoveable, always abounding in the work of the Lord, forasmuch as ye know that your labour is not in vain in the Lord" (1 Cor.15:58).
> "For as the lightning cometh out of the east, and shineth even unto the west; so shall also the coming of the Son of man be" (Mt.24:27).
> "Wherefore, beloved, seeing that ye look for such things [God's kingdom], be diligent that ye may be found of him in peace, without spot, and blameless" (2 Pt.3:14).

**4** (17:25) **Jesus Christ, Return**: the day cannot come until some things happen first. This was, of course, a reference to the Lord's death. Before the Kingdom of God could ever come to earth, He had to suffer and die. It was His death that would make it possible for His kingdom to come to earth.

> "And being found in fashion as a man, he humbled himself, and became obedient unto death, even the death of the cross. Wherefore God also hath highly exalted him, and given him a name which is above every name: that at the name of Jesus every knee should bow, of things in heaven, and things in earth, and things under the earth; and that every tongue should confess that Jesus Christ is Lord, to the glory of God the Father" (Ph.2:8-11; cp. 1 Cor.15:22-24).
> "Let not your heart be troubled: ye believe in God, believe also in me. In my Father's house are many mansions: if it were not so, I would have told you. I go to prepare a place for you. And if I go and prepare a place for you, I will come again, and receive you unto myself; that where I am, there ye may be also" (Jn.14:1-3).

**5** (17:26-30) **Noah—Lot—Jesus Christ, Return—Judgment**: the day will be as the days of Noah and Lot; men will be occupied with normal, routine affairs.

1. The affairs listed are the routine affairs of every day life. Men...

- ate
- drank
- married
- bought
- sold
- planted
- built

This is just the point. Men will be going about their daily lives without giving any attention to God or to the warnings of coming judgment (see note—Mt.24:37-39. Cp. 1 Pt.3:18-22; Gen.6:1f; 7:11f.)

2. Noah and Lot were not men who had reached spiritual maturity. They were not examples of spiritual men for others to follow. However, they did one thing which others failed to do: they believed God's Word when God said to prepare for the flood and for the coming judgment of fire. Despite all their shortcomings and failures, all their sensual and loose living, when the Word came to prepare, they *believed* and they *prepared*.

3. The people of Noah's and Lot's day did not believe and did not prepare. They went right on with their normal routine, living and focusing their minds upon...

- the world and its things.
- the flesh and its pleasures.

4. The people of Noah's and Lot's day were caught unaware. Unexpectedly—suddenly...

- "The flood came and destroyed them *all*" (v.27).
- "It rained fire and brimstone from heaven, and destroyed them *all*" (v.29).

5. God took care of Noah and Lot, the two who really believed His warning and prepared. He saved them from the coming judgment.

6. This is the crucial point. When the Son of Man returns, the world will be the same as it was in the days of Noah and Lot.

   a. Men will be going about their routine day-to-day affairs.
   b. Men will not believe God's warnings.
   c. Men will be caught unaware. Unexpectedly, suddenly Christ will appear and men will be judged.
   d. True believers who have really prepared themselves will be saved and delivered.

> "Teaching us that, denying ungodliness and worldly lusts, we should live soberly, righteously, and godly, in this present world; looking for that blessed hope, and the glorious appearing of the great God and our Saviour Jesus Christ" (Tit.2:12-13).
> "Seeing then that all these things shall be dissolved, what manner of persons ought ye to be in all holy conversation [behavior] and godliness" (2 Pt.3:11).
> "And the very God of peace sanctify you wholly; and I pray God your whole spirit and soul and body be preserved blameless unto the coming of our Lord Jesus Christ" (1 Th.5:23).
> "And this is his commandment, That we should believe on the name of his Son Jesus Christ, and love one another, as he gave us commandment" (1 Jn.3:23).
> "That thou keep this commandment without spot, unrebukeable, until the appearing of our Lord Jesus Christ" (1 Tim.6:14).

**6** (17:31-33) **Jesus Christ, Return—Judgment—Decision**: the day will be a day of urgency for all men. These verses are applied by some to the destruction of Jerusalem and by others to the return of Christ. They are applicable to both.

1. "In that day" when God gives the indication that His return is imminent, a man must act quickly, not wasting a moment's time. When is the Lord's return imminent? When are we to prepare and act?

Jesus said *now*: "Behold, I come quickly." Since He is coming soon, there is no "stuff in the house" (v.31)—no possessions—worth our attention and loyalty. Christ and Christ alone is worthy of our devotion and attention.

2. "Remember Lot's wife." She illustrates the doom of turning back. She came close to being saved; she had prepared. She was faithful to her husband, listening to his spiritual warnings, walking with him through the sinful city (world), and walking toward God's designated safety. But she walked behind her husband, not by his side; therefore, she was able to look back upon her sensual experiences in the world of Sodom. When she did, she perished with the worldly. "Remember Lot's wife" who came so close but who tried to hang on to the delights of the world (Gen.19:26).

> "And Jesus said unto him, No man, having put his hand to the plough, and looking back, is fit for the kingdom of God" (Lk.9:62).
>
> "Now the just shall live by faith: but if any man draw back, my soul shall have no pleasure in him" (Heb.10:38).
>
> "For if after they have escaped the pollutions of the world through the knowledge of the Lord and Saviour Jesus Christ, they are again entangled therein, and overcome, the latter end is worse with them than the beginning" (2 Pt.2:20).

3. The one essential is total abandonment to Christ and the warnings of judgment to come. We must not try to save (live) our lives for this world in its worldly ways. We must not do as Lot's wife and the people in the days of Noah and Lot. We must lose our lives for *Christ and His coming kingdom*. (See outline and notes—Lk.9:24 for more discussion.)

> "And every one that hath forsaken houses, or brethren, or sisters, or father, or mother, or wife, or children, or lands, for my name's sake, shall receive an hundredfold, and shall inherit everlasting life" (Mt.19:29).
>
> "And he said to them all, If any man will come after me, let him deny himself, and take up his cross daily, and follow me" (Lk.9:23).
>
> "Verily, verily, I say unto you, Except a corn of wheat fall into the ground and die, it abideth alone: but if it die, it bringeth forth much fruit" (Jn.12:24).
>
> "Yea doubtless, and I count all things but loss for the excellency of the knowledge of Christ Jesus my Lord: for whom I have suffered the loss of all things, and do count them but dung, that I may win Christ" (Ph.3:8).

**[7]** (17:34-36) **Jesus Christ, Return**: the day will be a day of separation. The point is clear: the day will come when all men will be going about their affairs, working or resting as usual. Then all of a sudden, unexpectedly, one here and there will be taken and the other left behind. The believer who has truly prepared himself will be taken home to the Lord. All who reject and oppose the Lord will be left behind. (See outline and notes—1 Th.4:13-5:3.)

> "Let both grow together until the harvest: and in the time of harvest I will say to the reapers, Gather ye together first the tares, and bind them in bundles to burn them: but gather the wheat into my barn" (Mt.13:30).
>
> "So shall it be at the end of the world: the angels shall come forth, and sever the wicked from among the just" (Mt.13:49).
>
> "And shall cast them into the furnace of fire: there shall be wailing and gnashing of teeth. Jesus saith unto them, Have ye understood all these things?" (Mt.13:50-51).
>
> "And before him shall be gathered all nations: and he shall separate them one from another, as a shepherd divideth his sheep from the goats" (Mt.25:32).
>
> "And to you who are troubled rest with us, when the Lord Jesus shall be revealed from heaven with his mighty angels, in flaming fire taking vengeance on them that know not God, and that obey not the gospel of our Lord Jesus Christ: who shall be punished with everlasting destruction from the presence of the Lord, and from the glory of his power; when he shall come to be glorified in his saints, and to be admired in all them that believe (because our testimony among you was believed) in that day" (2 Th.1:7-10).

**[8]** (17:37) **Jesus Christ, Return**: the day will be universal, that is, worldwide. Note the disciples asked where His return and kingdom was to take place. Jesus used an illustration to teach that His return would be universal. The "eagles" (hoi aetoi) can mean either eagle or vulture. It probably should be translated vulture here, for they are the ones who gather universally as scavengers over dead bodies. Vultures gather where the dead are and feast upon them. Since death is universal, vultures are found everywhere. Therefore, the coming of Jesus Christ and of God's kingdom will be the same as the coming of vultures. He shall come to the whole earth, to the place where men die. The moral corruption throughout the world necessitates the Lord's return in divine judgment (see note—Mt.24:25-28; cp. Job 39:27-30).

> "And then shall appear the sign of the Son of man in heaven: and then shall all the tribes of the earth mourn, and they shall see the Son of man coming in the clouds of heaven with power and great glory" (Mt.24:30).
>
> "Behold, he cometh with clouds; and every eye shall see him, and they also which pierced him: and all kindreds of the earth shall wail because of him. Even so, Amen" (Rev.1:7).

| | CHAPTER 18 | while: but afterward he said within himself, Though I fear not God, nor regard man; | He was hard & harsh |
|---|---|---|---|
| | C. The Parable of the Unjust Judge: The Secret of Prayer—Persistence, 18:1-8 | 5 Yet because this widow troubleth me, I will avenge her, lest by her continual coming she weary me. | d. The point: The judge honored her request because she continued to come |
| 1 The great duty to persevere in prayer | And he spake a parable unto them to this end, that men ought always to pray, and not to faint; | 6 And the Lord said, Hear what the unjust judge saith. | 3 The lesson on persevering prayer<br>a. Hear this point |
| | | 7 And shall not God avenge his own elect, which cry day and night unto him, though he bear long with them? | b. God avenges the elect who persevere in prayer<sup>DS1</sup> |
| 2 The parable of persevering prayer<br>a. The unjust judge | 2 Saying, There was in a city a judge, which feared not God, neither regarded man; | | c. He waits & bears long with unbelievers |
| b. The poor widow: Was all alone & persecuted | 3 And there was a widow in that city; and she came unto him, saying, Avenge me of mine adversary. | 8 I tell you that he will avenge them speedily. Nevertheless when the Son of man cometh, shall he find faith on the earth? | d. God will avenge His elect speedily |
| c. The silence of the judge: | 4 And he would not for a | | 4 The great tragedy: In the last days few will persevere in prayer & faith |

# DIVISION VII

## THE SON OF MAN'S GREAT JOURNEY TO JERUSALEM (STAGE III): HIS LESSONS AND WARNINGS, 17:11-19:27

**C.    The Parable of the Unjust Judge: The Secret of Prayer—Persistence, 18:1-8**

(18:1-8) **Introduction**: the secret to prayer is persistence. This is the great lesson Jesus taught in this passage.
1.    The great duty to persevere in prayer (v.1).
2.    The parable of persevering prayer (v.2-5).
3.    The lesson on persevering prayer (v.6-7).
4.    The great tragedy: in the last days few will persevere in prayer and faith (v.8).

1    (18:1) **Prayer—Perseverance—Jesus Christ, Return**: the great duty to persevere in prayer. Jesus was strong and forceful in stressing the believer's duty to persevere in prayer.
1.    This discussion follows the passage dealing with the return of Christ. There is need for perseverance in prayer, for praying over a long period of time and not giving in and becoming discouraged. God's people are to pray and keep on praying until Christ returns, no matter how long He may be delayed.
2.    The words "to this end" and "ought" (pros to dein) have the idea of necessity. It is absolutely necessary that men persevere in prayer.
3.    The word "always" means at all times. The believer is to develop a constant spirit of prayer, to maintain an unbroken consciousness of God's presence, to practice the very presence of God, to walk in a constant state of prayer.
4.    The words "not to faint" (me egkakein) mean not to lose heart, not to turn coward, or give up, or give in to evil.

"Seek the LORD and his strength, seek his face continually" (1 Chron.16:11).
"And ye shall seek me, and find me, when ye shall search for me with all your heart" (Jer.29:13).
"Ask, and it shall be given you; seek, and ye shall find; knock, and it shall be opened unto you: for every one that asketh receiveth; and he that seeketh findeth; and to him that knocketh it shall be opened" (Mt.7:7-8).
"Watch and pray, that ye enter not into temptation: the spirit indeed is willing, but the flesh is weak" (Mt.26:41).
"Praying always with all prayer and supplication in the Spirit, and watching thereunto with all perseverance and supplication for all saints" (Eph.6:18).
"Be careful for nothing; but in every thing by prayer and supplication with thanksgiving let your requests be made known unto God" (Ph.4:6).
"Continue in prayer, and watch in the same with thanksgiving" (Col.4:2).
"Pray without ceasing" (1 Th.5:17).

2    (18:2-5) **Prayer—Perseverance**: the parable of persevering prayer. The parable shows clearly the *power of persistence* even in the business and judicial affairs of men.
1.    There was the unjust judge. He had no fear of God and cared even less for what men said. The idea is that he took bribes and gave favors to persons who held position and authority. He did not care for conscience or law, for morality or justice. He was out to fill his pockets and to gain honor and esteem, recognition and position from those who were influential, those who held position, power, and wealth (cp. Eccl.3:16).
2.    There was the poor widow.
    ⇒  She was poor, without money to bribe the judge.

⇒ She was a widow, a woman all alone in a man's world, with no man and no money to secure legal counsel to plead her case.

⇒ She held no position or authority, no rights to commend her to the judge.

⇒ She was persecuted, being taken advantage of and abused by some adversary.

Note what she did: she let none of this stop her. She came to the judge and asked him to avenge her, to get rid of her adversary.

3. There was the silence of the judge. The judge did not move to help her. His heart was hard and harsh; he had no interest in helping anyone who would not benefit his career or fill his pockets.

4. The point is this: the judge gave in. He "would not for a while," but the poor widow kept on coming and coming, pleading and pleading. She would not let the judge rest. Now note the stress. The judge...

- did not fear God,
- did not regard man's opinions,

...yet he gave in to the widow, avenging her of her adversary.

Why? Because of her *"continual coming."* He could not get rid of her. She would not accept silence nor take *no* for an answer. She kept coming and coming. The judge said, "Lest she wear me out" (hina me hupopiazei me). The literal meaning is unless she "give me a black eye." The word can mean to *annoy* or to *damage a reputation.* She was persistent—refusing to let the judge go!

**3** (18:6-7) **Believers, Avenged—Judgment—Prayer, Persevering**: the lesson on persevering prayer. The lesson has four points.

1. Hear the lesson. The unjust judge holds a great lesson for believers. Hear, give attention and thought to what he teaches.

2. God avenges His elect who persevere in prayer.

   a. The elect are God's "own elect," the followers of His dear Son (see DEEPER STUDY # 1, *Elect*—Lk.18:7).

   b. God will avenge His elect. This indicates that they are in trouble; they need to be avenged and delivered from being...

   | | | |
   |---|---|---|
   | • ridiculed | • cursed | • passed over |
   | • ignored | • criticized | • persecuted |
   | • slandered | • abused | • injured |

   c. The reason God avenges His elect is because they persevere in prayer. They pray *day and night.*

   ⇒ They have great need.

   ⇒ They recognize that God alone can meet their need.

   Therefore, they go before God as the just Judge of the universe. They are one of His own elect, and they cry day and night to be avenged of their adversaries (spiritual as well as human adversaries). They plead and plead their case before God. They do not let God remain silent nor let Him refuse His delivering power.

   > **"Watch and pray, that ye enter not into temptation [trial]: the spirit indeed is willing, but the flesh is weak" (Mt.26:41).**

   > **"Watch ye therefore, and pray always, that ye may be accounted worthy to escape all these things that shall come to pass, and to stand before the Son of man" (Lk.21:36).**

   > **"If ye abide in me, and my words abide in you, ye shall ask what ye will, and it shall be done unto you" (Jn.15:7).**

   > **"He shall call upon me, and I will answer him: I will be with him in trouble; I will deliver him and honour him" (Ps.91:15).**

   > **"And it shall come to pass, that before they call, I will answer; and while they are yet speaking, I will hear" (Is.65:24).**

   > **"Call unto me, and I will answer thee, and show thee great and mighty things, which thou knowest not" (Jer.33:3).**

   > **"And I will bring the third part through the fire, and will refine them as silver is refined, and will try them as gold is tried: they shall call on my name, and I will hear them: I will say, It is my people: and they shall say, The LORD is my God" (Zech.13:9).**

3. God waits and bears a long time; He is *long-suffering* toward unbelievers. This is part of His purpose: to have mercy upon all who can be reached, not willing that any should perish (2 Pt.3:9). Note a significant point: the believer, bearing up under trial and persecution, is a dynamic witness of the strength of Christ. Some unbelievers are reached, and eventually they turn to Christ because of the strong witness of suffering believers. The point is this: God does not always answer the cry of a believer immediately. God allows the believer to suffer trial.

   a. A believer is allowed to suffer in order to be a dynamic witness to others. The presence and power of Christ is sufficient to help the believer stand faithfully.

   > **"The Lord is not slack concerning his promise, as some men count slackness; but is longsuffering to us-ward, not willing that any should perish, but that all should come to repentance" (2 Pt.3:9).**

   > **"That the trial of your faith, being much more precious than of gold that perisheth, though it be tried with fire, might be found unto praise and honour and glory at the appearing of Jesus Christ" (1 Pt.1:7).**

"[God] who comforteth us in all our tribulation, that we may be able to comfort them which are in any trouble, by the comfort wherewith we ourselves are comforted of God" (2 Cor.1:4).

"Likewise, ye wives, be in subjection to your own husbands; that, if any obey not the word, they also may without the word be won by the conversation [behavior] of the wives; while they behold your chaste conversation coupled with fear" (1 Pt.3:1-2).

b. A believer is allowed to suffer in order to become stronger and stronger in trusting and hoping in God (see note—Ro.5:3-5).

"We glory in tribulations also: knowing that tribulation worketh patience; and patience, experience; and experience, hope: and hope maketh not ashamed; because the love of God is shed abroad in our hearts by the Holy Ghost which is given unto us" (Ro.5:3-5).

"My brethren, count it all joy when ye fall into divers temptations; knowing this, that the trying of your faith worketh patience. But let patience have her perfect work, that ye may be perfect and entire, wanting nothing" (Jas.1:2-4).

4. God will avenge His elect speedily; that is, in God's time He will act quickly, suddenly, and without hesitation. He will avenge His elect. His wrath will come upon the world.

"Dearly beloved, avenge not yourselves, but rather give place unto wrath: for it is written, Vengeance is mine; I will repay, saith the Lord. Therefore if thine enemy hunger, feed him; if he thirst, give him drink: for in so doing thou shalt heap coals of fire on his head" (Ro.12:19-20).

"[God] who delivered us from so great a death, and doth deliver: in whom we trust that he will yet deliver us; ye also helping together by prayer for us" (2 Cor.1:10-11).

"And the Lord shall deliver me from every evil work, and will preserve me unto his heavenly kingdom: to whom be glory for ever and ever" (2 Tim.4:18).

"And to you who are troubled rest with us, when the Lord Jesus shall be revealed from heaven with his mighty angels, in flaming fire taking vengeance on them that know not God, and that obey not the gospel of our Lord Jesus Christ" (2 Th.1:7-8).

"And deliver them who through fear of death were all their lifetime subject to bondage" (Heb.2:15).

"They cried unto thee, and were delivered: they trusted in thee, and were not confounded" (Ps.22:5).

"In thee, O LORD, do I put my trust: let me never be put to confusion" (Ps.71:1).

"The hope of the righteous shall be gladness: but the expectation of the wicked shall perish" (Pr.10:28).

"And even to your old age I am he; and even to hoar hairs will I carry you: I have made, and I will bear; even I will carry, and will deliver you" (Is.46:4).

"Be not afraid of their faces: for I am with thee to deliver thee, saith the LORD" (Jer.1:8).

---

**DEEPER STUDY # 1**

(18:7) **Elect** (eklektos): the chosen, the person picked out. The elect are the believers, the disciples of Christ, the people who genuinely belong to God (Mt.24:22, 24, 31; Mk.13:20, 22, 27; Ro.8:33; Col.3:12; 2 Tim.2:10; Tit.1:1; 1 Pt.1:1; 2:9. Also cp. where the word is translated "chosen," Mt.20:16; 22:14; Ro.16:13; 2 Jn.1:1, 13; Rev.17:14.)

The focus of the word is upon God's choice. There is no doubt about this, for the word itself means that God does the choosing and the picking out. But note: the choosing is for service, not for salvation or position (Jn.15:16). The believer is chosen to bear fruit (see DEEPER STUDY # 1—Jn.15:1-8).

---

**4** (18:8) **Prayer, Persevering**: the great tragedy is this: in the last days few will persevere in prayer and faith. Most will fall away. This is the implication of Christ. Note three significant facts.

1. Faith is the one thing Christ is after. He wants trust and belief in Him, in His Word, in His promises and warnings.

2. The greatest evidence of faith is persevering prayer. Faith and persevering prayer are tied together. The person who truly believes will be talking and sharing, communing and fellowshipping, living and moving with God day and night. The person will be praying always.

3. There will be few men of faith and prayer when He returns to earth. There will be some, but the number will be few.

"Now the Spirit speaketh expressly, that in the latter times some shall depart from the faith, giving heed to seducing spirits, and doctrines of devils" (1 Tim.4:1).

"This know also, that in the last days perilous times shall come. For men shall be lovers of their own selves, covetous, boasters, proud, blasphemers, disobedient to parents, unthankful, unholy, without natural affection, trucebreakers, false accusers, incontinent, fierce, despisers of those that are good, traitors, heady, highminded, lovers of pleasures more than lovers of God; having a form of godliness, but denying the power thereof: from such turn away" (2 Tim.3:1-5).

"Knowing this first, that there shall come in the last days scoffers, walking after their own lusts, and saying, Where is the promise of his coming? for since the fathers fell asleep, all things continue as they were from the beginning of the creation" (2 Pt.3:3-4).

"Little children, it is the last time: and as ye have heard that antichrist shall come, even now are there many antichrists; whereby we know that it is the last time" (1 Jn.2:18).

"How that they told you there should be mockers in the last time, who should walk after their own ungodly lusts" (Jude 18).

"The LORD looked down from heaven upon the children of men, to see if there were any that did understand, and seek God. They are all gone aside, they are all together become filthy: there is none good, no, not one" (Ps.14:2-3).

"For I beheld, and there was no man; even among them, and there was no counselor, that, when I asked of them, could answer a word" (Is.41:28).

"And he saw that there was no man, and wondered that there was no intercessor" (Is.59:16).

"And I looked, and there was none to help; and I wondered that there was none to uphold" (Is.63:5).

"And I sought for a man among them, that should make up the hedge, and stand in the gap before me for the land, that I should not destroy it: but I found none" (Ezk.22:30).

| | D. The Parable of the Pharisee and the Publican: The Spirit Needed for Prayer, 18:9-14 | tioners, unjust, adulterers, or even as this publican.<br>12 I fast twice in the week, I give tithes of all that I possess.<br>13 And the publican, standing afar off, would not lift up so much as his eyes unto heaven, but smote upon his breast, saying, God be merciful to me a sinner.<br>14 I tell you, this man went down to his house justified rather than the other: for every one that exalteth himself shall be abased; and he that humbleth himself shall be exalted. | making him what he is<br><br>c. He rededicates himself—he reaffirms his commitment<br>4 The sinner prays<br>a. He stands "afar off"<br>b. He feels unworthy to face God<br>c. He cries for mercy<br><br>5 The major lesson: Justification<br>a. A humble approach is heard<br>b. A proud approach is not heard |
|---|---|---|---|
| 1 A parable of warning<br>a. To the self-righteous<br>b. To those who despise<br><br>2 The scene: Two men are praying in the temple<br>a. One is a Pharisee<br>b. One is a sinner<br>3 The religionist prays<br>a. He stands—prays only with himself<br>b. He thanks God for | 9 And he spake this parable unto certain which trusted in themselves that they were righteous, and despised others:<br>10 Two men went up into the temple to pray; the one a Pharisee, and the other a publican.<br>11 The Pharisee stood and prayed thus with himself, God, I thank thee, that I am not as other men are, extor- | | |

# DIVISION VII

## THE SON OF MAN'S GREAT JOURNEY TO JERUSALEM (STAGE III): HIS LESSONS AND WARNINGS, 17:11-19:27

### D. The Parable of the Pharisee and the Publican: The Spirit Needed for Prayer, 18:9-14

(18:9-14) **Introduction**: two striking things are seen in this passage—both the spirit needed for prayer and the spirit needed for one to be saved.
1. A parable of warning (v.9).
2. The scene: two men are praying in the temple (v.10).
3. The religionist prays (v.11-12).
4. The sinner prays (v.13).
5. The major lesson: justification (v.14).

**1** (18:9) **Self-righteousness—Religionists—Self-sufficient**: this parable is directed to three self-centered persons.

1. Those who trust (peitho) in themselves; that is, those who feel they are completely self-sufficient and have no need for anyone else. They feel all they need dwells within their own bodies and minds. There is a feeling that neither God nor anyone else is really needed—not too often, if ever—as one ploughs through life. Note the pride and conceit in the self-sufficient.

> **"And if any man think that he knoweth any thing, he knoweth nothing yet as he ought to know" (1 Cor.8:2).**
> **"Wherefore let him that thinketh he standeth take heed lest he fall" (1 Cor.10:12).**
> **"For if a man think himself to be something, when he is nothing, he deceiveth himself" (Gal.6:3).**
> **"Seest thou a man wise in his own conceit? There is more hope of a fool than of him" (Pr.26:12).**
> **"Woe unto them that are wise in their own eyes, and prudent in their own sight!" (Is.5:21).**
> **"Ye have plowed wickedness, ye have reaped iniquity; ye have eaten the fruit of lies: because thou didst trust in thy way, in the multitude of thy mighty men" (Hos.10:13).**

2. Those who are self-righteous. (See notes—Lk.11:37-54; 15:25-32; note and DEEPER STUDY # 1—Ro.2:17-29 for more discussion.) The self-righteous differ from the self-sufficient in that they are interested in righteousness and in God. The self-righteous can be divided into two classes.
   a. There are those who feel they are *good enough* for God as they are. They have done and are doing enough good for God to accept them. They think that when they stand face to face with God, He will never reject them. True, they do wrong; but not that much wrong, not enough for God to reject and condemn them, not for eternity. They go about life living as they wish, worshipping God only enough to satisfy their consciences.

**Thought 1.** The vast majority of people are in this class of self-righteousness. Few men believe they will be rejected by God and refused entrance into heaven. They feel they have enough *goodness* to make them acceptable to God.

> **"For we dare not make ourselves of the number, or compare ourselves with some that commend themselves: but they measuring themselves by themselves, and comparing themselves among themselves, are not wise" (2 Cor.10:12).**

356

"If I justify myself, mine own mouth shall condemn me: if I say, I am perfect, it shall also prove me perverse" (Job.9:20).

"I am clean without transgression, I am innocent; neither is there iniquity in me" (Job 33:9).

"Thinkest thou this to be right, that thou saidst, My righteousness is more than God's?" (Job 35:2).

"All the ways of a man are clean in his own eyes; but the LORD weigheth the spirits" (Pr.16:2).

"Most men will proclaim every one his own goodness: but a faithful man who can find?" (Pr.20:6).

"Every way of a man is right in his own eyes: but the Lord pondereth the hearts" (Pr.21:2).

"He that trusteth in his own heart is a fool: but whoso walketh wisely, he shall be delivered" (Pr.28:26).

"There is a generation that are pure in their own eyes, and yet is not washed from their filthiness" (Pr.30:12).

"Yet thou sayest, Because I am innocent, surely his anger shall turn from me. Behold, I will plead with thee, because thou sayest, I have not sinned" (Jer.2:35).

b. There are those who have a sensitive conscience and feel the need to give themselves to *good works* as much as is humanly possible. They work and do good in order to secure the favor of God. They believe their good works are what make them *good and righteous* and build them up in the eyes of God. Thus, they labor all their lives trying to build up virtue and merit before God. They try their best to make themselves acceptable to God.

"For I say unto you, That except your righteousness shall exceed the righteousness of the scribes and Pharisees, ye shall in no case enter into the kingdom of heaven" (Mt.5:20).

"Many will say to me in that day, Lord, Lord, have we not prophesied in thy name? and in thy name have cast out devils? and in thy name done many wonderful works? And then will I profess unto them, I never knew you: depart from me, ye that work iniquity" (Mt.7:22-23).

"Therefore by the deeds of the law there shall no flesh be justified in his sight: for by the law is the knowledge of sin" (Ro.3:20).

"Knowing that a man is not justified by the works of the law, but by the faith of Jesus Christ, even we have believed in Jesus Christ, that we might be justified by the faith of Christ, and not by the works of the law: for by the works of the law shall no flesh be justified" (Gal.2:16).

"For by grace are ye saved through faith; and that not of yourselves: it is the gift of God: not of works, lest any man should boast" (Eph.2:8-9).

"Who hath saved us, and called us with an holy calling, not according to our works, but according to his own purpose and grace, which was given us in Christ Jesus before the world began" (2 Tim.1:9).

"But after that the kindness and love of God our Saviour toward man appeared, not by works of righteousness which we have done, but according to his mercy he saved us, by the washing of regeneration, and renewing of the Holy Ghost; which he shed on us abundantly through Jesus Christ our Saviour; that being justified by his grace, we should be made heirs according to the hope of eternal life" (Tit.3:4-7).

3. Those who despise others. The word "despise" (exouthenountas) means to set at naught; to count as nothing, as unimportant and insignificant. Such persons feel and act as though they are above and better, more important and significant than others. They shy away from, ignore and neglect, pass by and downgrade, criticize and talk about...

- the poor
- the unfortunate
- the poorly dressed
- the homeless
- the downcast
- the derelict
- the undernourished
- the sinner

"Behold, ye despisers, and wonder, and perish: for I work a work in your days, a work which ye shall in no wise believe, though a man declare it unto you" (Acts 13:41).

"Or despisest thou the riches of his goodness and forbearance and longsuffering; not knowing that the goodness of God leadeth thee to repentance?" (Ro.2:4).

"He that despised Moses' law died without mercy under two or three witnesses: of how much sorer punishment, suppose ye, shall he be thought worthy, who hath trodden under foot the Son of God, and hath counted the blood of the covenant, wherewith he was sanctified, an unholy thing, and hath done despite unto the Spirit of grace?" (Heb.10:28-29).

Now note: it is these people to whom Jesus directed this parable. He both appealed to and warned the self-sufficient, the self-righteous, and the man who despises others.

**2** (18:10) **Seeking God—Prayer**: two men are praying in the temple. One was a Pharisee, a religionist; the other was a publican, a tax collector who was a great sinner. Note two points.

1. Both men went to the most prominent place to pray, to the temple, the house of prayer itself. There is no better place to pray, no better place to seek God's face. Both men were seeking God's face right where they should have been.

2. Both men went to pray in order to please God. They were both seeking God, wanting God to accept them and to be present with them throughout all their life.

> **"But if from thence thou shalt seek the LORD thy God, thou shalt find him, if thou seek him with all thy heart and with all thy soul" (Dt.4:29).**

**3** (18:11-12) **Self-Righteousness—Religionists**: there is the prayer of the religionist.

1. The religionist stood and prayed only "with himself." Standing was the posture used for public prayer in that day. But note the significant fact: he prayed only "*with himself,*" that is, only to himself. He called "God" by name and addressed his words to God, but his words were not going up to God. They were not a true prayer. He was speaking only with himself and perhaps to others who could hear him. His time and words were wasted except for their personal value, that is, to build his self-confidence and social acceptance. As far as God was concerned, no prayer was being offered to Him. The man's so-called prayer was only a *formal prayer.* There was no true worship or personal communion in it.

> **"Now we know that God heareth not sinners: but if any man be a worshipper of God, and doeth his will, him he heareth" (Jn.9:31).**
> **"Ye ask, and receive not, because ye ask amiss, that ye may consume it upon your lusts" (Jas.4:3).**
> **"If I regard iniquity in my heart, the Lord will not hear me" (Ps.66:18).**
> **"Then shall they call upon me, but I will not answer; they seek me early, but they shall not find me" (Pr.1:28).**
> **"Whoso stoppeth his ears at the cry of the poor, he also shall cry himself, but shall not be heard" (Pr.21:13).**
> **"He that turneth away his ear from hearing the law, even his prayer shall be abomination" (Pr.28:9).**
> **"And when ye spread forth your hands, I will hide mine eyes from you: yea, when ye make many prayers, I will not hear: your hands are full of blood" (Is.1:15).**
> **"But your iniquities have separated between you and your God, and your sins have hid his face from you, that he will not hear" (Is.59:2).**
> **"Then shall they cry unto the LORD, but he will not hear them: he will even hide his face from them at that time, as they have behaved themselves ill in their doings" (Mic.3:4).**

2. The religionist thanked God for making him what he was. Note several things that should be eye-openers to us. (See note—Lk.18:9 for Scripture on the self-righteous attitude.)
   a. He *thanked God that he had been kept* from the sins which people counted as *public sins* or *scandalous sins.* God had kept him from falling into the *great public sins.* He acknowledged that "but for the grace [strength] of God, there go I," and he thanked God that he had been kept from such terrible sins.
   b. He said that other men had fallen and committed such sins. He said that…
      • God had His hand upon his life and had kept him from sin, so he thanked God for keeping him.
      • God did not have His hand upon the lives of sinners, so he thanked God that he was not like such men.
      • God looked upon him as the favored one and upon the sinner as the unfavored one.
   c. He listed some of the *more serious* public or scandalous sins that he had not fallen into. He thanked God that he was not…
      • an extortioner: in dealing with others he had always been fair and just, kind and giving, rather than coming across as not being fair or as taking advantage of others.
      • unjust: he treated all men justly by recognizing, commending, and promoting them and their welfare. He moved to the side himself and pushed others ahead rather than running the risk of appearing unjust and demonstrating a bad testimony.
      • an adulterer: he was faithful and moral, never going astray in his behavior.
      • a betrayer or non-religious person: he was not as the tax collectors who sold their loyalty and religious privileges to serve the Roman empire, by which they betrayed their own nation (see DEEPER STUDY # 1, *Tax Collector*—Lk.5:27).
   d. He listed two very positive and worshipful acts which he did.
      ⇒ He fasted twice a week. Imagine going without food two days every week just to seek to worship and please God. The religionist was as sincere as he could be about God and righteousness.
      ⇒ He tithed not only ten percent of his income but also ten percent of all that he possessed. Imagine!
   (Again, see note—Lk.18:9 for Scripture on the self-righteous attitude.)

**4** (18:13) **Lost, The—Confession—Mercy**: there is the prayer of the sinner. Note three significant points.

1. The sinner stood "afar off." He was ashamed and embarrassed by his sin. He felt cut off both by God and man. He felt isolated and alone, estranged and separated, dirty and unclean. He also knew that others were embarrassed and shamed

by his sin, and he did not want them to be, so he kept his distance: he stood "afar off." But note: he is genuinely worshipping God, even if he is standing "afar off."

2. The sinner felt he was unworthy to face God. This is seen in two acts.

    a. He would not so much as lift his eyes up to heaven. He did lift his heart, but not his eyes. His sins weighed him down ever so heavily, for he had fallen into gross sin. He was a terrible sinner and he knew it. He was unworthy of the least of God's favors and he knew it. He did not deserve God's forgiveness and acceptance, and he knew it. He could not lift up his eyes, for he had hurt God too much.

    b. He beat upon his breast and did it often. Why? Because he could not help it. Sometimes he was disappointed in himself and angry at himself; at other times his heart burst with tears of pleading, begging God to forgive him. He was so unworthy that the tension, emotions, and strain burst forth.

> **"All things are delivered unto me of my Father: and no man knoweth the Son, but the Father; neither knoweth any man the Father, save the Son, and he to whomsoever the Son will reveal him" (Mt.11:27).**
>
> **"When Jesus heard it, he saith unto them, They that are whole have no need of the physician, but they that are sick: I came not to call the righteous, but sinners to repentance" (Mk.2:17).**
>
> **"For we have not an high priest which cannot be touched with the feeling of our infirmities; but was in all points tempted like as we are, yet without sin. Let us therefore come boldly unto the throne of grace, that we may obtain mercy, and find grace to help in time of need" (Heb.4:15-16).**
>
> **"Humble yourselves in the sight of the Lord, and he shall lift you up" (Jas.4:10).**
>
> **"The LORD is nigh unto them that are of a broken heart; and saveth such as be of a contrite spirit" (Ps.34:18).**
>
> **"But I am poor and needy; yet the Lord thinketh upon me: thou art my help and my deliverer; make no tarrying, O my God" (Ps.40:17).**
>
> **"Wash me thoroughly from mine iniquity, and cleanse me from my sin" (Ps.51:2).**
>
> **"The sacrifices of God are a broken spirit: a broken and a contrite heart, O God, thou wilt not despise" (Ps.51:17).**
>
> **"Help us, O God of our salvation, for the glory of thy name: and deliver us, and purge away our sins, for thy name's sake" (Ps.79:9).**
>
> **"For thus saith the high and lofty One that inhabiteth eternity, whose name is Holy; I dwell in the high and holy place, with him also that is of a contrite and humble spirit, to revive the spirit of the humble, and to revive the heart of the contrite ones" (Is.57:15).**
>
> **"For all those things hath mine hand made, and all those things have been, saith the LORD: but to this man will I look, even to him that is poor and of a contrite spirit, and trembleth at my word" (Is.66:2).**
>
> **"And rend your heart, and not your garments, and turn unto the LORD your God: for he is gracious and merciful, slow to anger, and of great kindness, and repenteth him of the evil" (Joel 2:13).**

3. The sinner cried for mercy. There are two things to note.

    a. He called himself *"the sinner"* (to hamartolo). This is critical: he did not feel he was just "a sinner" like everyone else, which would mean he was also as good as everyone else. But he felt he was *the sinner*, the one who had hurt and shamed God more than anyone else, the one who was more undeserving than anyone else. There was nothing *good* within him, nothing to commend him to God, nothing to make him acceptable to God.

    b. He cried for mercy. The word "mercy" (hilastheti) is really the word for *"propitiated."* He prayed for God to remove His anger and judgment from him. He deserved God's anger and judgment, but he begged God to turn His anger and judgment away. He felt he would die from the pressure within his chest unless God forgave him and gave him peace and assurance of forgiveness. He wanted to be reconciled to God; he wanted God to remove His judgment from him and to accept him.

    Now note: he knew the only way he could ever be accepted by God was for God to have mercy upon him and to forgive his sins. He had *no good* thing about him, no righteousness to offer God. If he were going to be saved by God, God had to accept him simply because he came to God in all the desperation and sincerity of his heart and begged God for mercy. God alone was his hope, and mercy alone was all he could plead.

> **"And his mercy is on them that fear him from generation to generation" (Lk.1:50).**
>
> **"Not by works of righteousness which we have done, but according to his mercy he saved us, by the washing of regeneration, and renewing of the Holy Ghost" (Tit.3:5; cp. v.4-7).**
>
> **"But God, who is rich in mercy, for his great love wherewith he loved us, even when we were dead in sins, hath quickened us together with Christ, (by grace ye are saved)" (Eph.2:4-5).**
>
> **"Who is a God like unto thee, that pardoneth iniquity, and passeth by the transgression of the remnant of his heritage? he retaineth not his anger for ever, because he delighteth in mercy" (Mic.7:18).**

**5** (18:14) **Justification—Salvation**: the major lesson of these verses is justification. The words of Jesus are shocking, contrary to what the world teaches, contrary to the opinions of men, and even contrary to the way many believers act. The *scandalous sinner is the one "justified"* in the sight of God. Why? There are two reasons given by Jesus.

1. Because of what justification means. It means that a person...
   - acknowledges his sinfulness and unworthiness.
   - cries for God to have mercy.

The justified person is *not righteous*, but he is *counted righteous* by God. The justified person has genuinely cried for mercy and turned from his sin to God. Because of his cry and repentance, God has taken his cry and counted it as righteousness. He has accepted the person because his heart was really set upon God. (See DEEPER STUDY # 2, *Justification*—Ro.4:22; 5:1. Cp. Ro.4:5; 4:1-3; 4:1-25 for more discussion.)

> **"They that are whole have no need of the physician, but they that are sick: I came not to call the righteous, but sinners to repentance"** (Mk.2:17).
> **"And therefore it [faith] was imputed to him for righteousness"** (Ro.4:22).
> **"But for us also, to whom it [righteousness] shall be imputed, if we believe on him that raised up Jesus our Lord from the dead; who was delivered for our offences, and was raised again for our justification"** (Ro.4:24-25).
> **"Therefore being justified by faith, we have peace with God through our Lord Jesus Christ"** (Ro.5:1).

2. Because a proud approach is not heard (see note and DEEPER STUDY # 1—Lk.14:11 for complete discussion).

> **"For whosoever exalteth himself shall be abased; and he that humbleth himself shall be exalted"** (Lk.14:11).
> **"A man's pride shall bring him low: but honor shall uphold the humble in spirit"** (Pr.29:23).

| | E. The Little Children and Jesus, 18:15-17 (Mt.19:13-15; Mk.10:13-16) | 16 But Jesus called them unto him, and said, Suffer little children to come unto me, and forbid them not: for of such is the kingdom of God. | 2 | Jesus wanted to receive little children & He called them to Him |
|---|---|---|---|---|
| | | | 3 | Little children are in the Kingdom of Heaven |
| 1 Little children were brought to Jesus a. By parents b. For Jesus to touch c. Against the disciples' judgment | 15 And they brought unto him also infants, that he would touch them: but when his disciples saw it, they rebuked them. | 17 Verily I say unto you, Whosoever shall not receive the kingdom of God as a little child shall in no wise enter therein. | 4 | Only children are in the Kingdom of Heaven |

# DIVISION VII

## THE SON OF MAN'S GREAT JOURNEY TO JERUSALEM (STAGE III): HIS LESSONS AND WARNINGS, 17:11-19:27

## E.     The Little Children and Jesus, 18:15-17

(18:15-17) **Introduction**: What is it that makes a man acceptable to God? The answer had just been given by Jesus in the story of the Pharisee and the publican (Lk.18:9-14). Now Jesus gave a living demonstration. He took a few small children into His arms and sat them upon His lap, and He told everyone exactly what they must do to be acceptable to God.

1.     Little children were brought to Jesus (v.15).
2.     Jesus wanted to receive little children and He called them to Him (v.16).
3.     Little children are in the Kingdom of Heaven (v.16).
4.     Only children are in the Kingdom of Heaven. (v.17).

1  (18:15) **Children—Parents**: little children were brought to Jesus. Note three things.

1.     The children were brought by their parents. It is not actually said that the parents brought the children, but it was certainly their parents. They were brought by parents who had already been blessed by Jesus, parents who had already heard Him and been touched by Him. They had been so deeply touched that they wanted their children to be touched.

> **Thought 1.** The point is clear. Parents need to expose themselves to the gospel; they need to be touched by Christ. Parents need to experience true repentance and salvation, and then they need to bring their children to Christ.

2.     The children were brought to Jesus for Him to touch. The parents cared for their children and cared deeply. They believed that the thing needed by their children was the *touch* of Jesus. They believed that His touch would bring blessings to their children's lives. But the children were unable to come by themselves. The children would not receive the touch of Jesus unless the parents brought them. To these parents, the touch of Jesus was powerful.

> "So when they had dined, Jesus saith to Simon Peter, Simon, son of Jonas, lovest thou me more than these? He saith unto him, Yea, Lord; thou knowest that I love thee. He saith unto him, Feed my lambs" (Jn.21:15).
> "Behold, the third time I am ready to come to you; and I will not be burdensome to you: for I seek not yours, but you: for the children ought not to lay up for the parents, but the parents for the children" (2 Cor.12:14).
> "And, ye fathers, provoke not your children to wrath: but bring them up in the nurture and admonition of the Lord" (Eph.6:4).
> "Only take heed to thyself, and keep thy soul diligently, lest thou forget the things which thine eyes have seen, and lest they depart from thy heart all the days of thy life: but teach them thy sons, and thy sons' sons" (Dt.4:9).
> "And thou shalt teach them diligently unto thy children, and shalt talk of them when thou sittest in thine house, and when thou walkest by the way, and when thou liest down, and when thou risest up" (Dt.6:7).

3.     The disciples rebuked the parents, refusing to let them reach Jesus. They probably felt the parents were only trying to show off their children, and Jesus was just too busy for such frivolous pride. They made two serious errors in stopping children from coming to Jesus.
a.     They were determining who could and who could not be touched by Jesus. Of course, no man has the right to dictate who can and cannot be touched by Jesus.
b.     They were not grasping the importance of Jesus' touch, even for little children. Their understanding of the blessing and power of God was immature. No one should ever be stopped or discouraged from coming or from being brought to Jesus.

2  (18:16) **Children—Man, Growth Process—Creation**: Jesus wanted to receive little children and He called them to Him. There are at least two reasons for this.

1.    Little children were formed in the mind of God. God is the One who planned for a person to grow from a little child. God cares about every stage of the process of human growth. Therefore, He cares for every single child. As the song says, "He holds the tiny little baby in His hands."

2.    Jesus is love, and as love He cares for all, no matter the size or age, looks or appearance, abilities or capabilities. Jesus loves the person even if the person is only a *baby* who has to be carried in the arms of a parent.

> "For in him we live, and move, and have our being; as certain also of your own poets have said, For we are also his offspring" (Acts 17:28).
>
> "The Spirit of God hath made me, and the breath of the Almighty hath given me life" (Job 33:4).
>
> "Know ye that the Lord he is God: it is he that hath made us, and not we ourselves; we are his people, and the sheep of his pasture" (Ps.100:3).
>
> "Lo, children are an heritage of the LORD: and the fruit of the womb is his reward" (Ps.127:3).
>
> "Behold, I and the children whom the LORD hath given me are for signs and for wonders in Israel from the LORD of hosts, which dwelleth in mount Zion" (Is.8:18).
>
> "Even every one that is called by my name: for I have created him for my glory, I have formed him; yea, I have made him" (Is.43:7).
>
> "This people have I formed for myself; they shall show forth my praise" (Is.43:21).
>
> "Thus saith the LORD that made thee, and formed thee from the womb, which will help thee; Fear not" (Is.44:2).
>
> "Before I formed thee in the belly I knew thee; and before thou camest forth out of the womb I sanctified thee" (Jer.1:5).
>
> "The burden of the word of the LORD for Israel, saith the LORD, which stretcheth forth the heavens, and layeth the foundation of the earth, and formeth the spirit of man within him" (Zech.12:1).

**3** (18:16) **Children—Kingdom of Heaven**: little children are in the Kingdom of Heaven. Jesus was saying at least two significant things.

1.    Little children are in the *keeping* hands and care of God. "Of such [as these little children] is the kingdom of God." God is looking after little children, loving and caring for them, at least until they reach the point of deliberately rejecting Him and His righteousness.

2.    Little children possess the traits that exist in heaven. (See notes—Mt.18:3; DEEPER STUDY # 5—Mk.10:15 for more discussion.)

    a.    A child is usually dependent and trusting. He knows little and can do little in taking care of himself. To him *big people*, especially mommy and daddy, know everything and can do everything. The child trusts everyone; anyone can take the child into his arms, for the child has not learned to suspect the world. Everyone is a friend; no one is an enemy, and few are strangers.

> "Be ye therefore followers of God, as dear children" (Eph.5:1).
>
> "Come, ye children, hearken unto me: I will teach you the fear of the LORD" (Ps.34:11).
>
> "Surely I have behaved and quieted myself, as a child that is weaned of his mother: my soul is even as a weaned child" (Ps.131:2).
>
> "Both young men, and maidens; old men, and children: let them praise the name of the LORD: for his name alone is excellent; his glory is above the earth and heaven" (Ps.148:12-13).
>
> "Remember now thy Creator in the days of thy youth, while the evil days come not, nor the years draw nigh, when thou shalt say, I have no pleasure in them" (Eccl.12:1).
>
> "But I said unto their children in the wilderness, Walk ye not in the statutes of your fathers, neither observe their judgments, nor defile yourselves with their idols: I am the LORD your God; walk in my statutes, and keep my judgments, and do them" (Ezk.20:18-19).

    b.    A child is usually responsive and submissive. A child responds to an adult. He will come, go, pick up, do whatever is suggested to him. He will drop whatever he is doing, surrender whatever is occupying his thoughts and behavior and respond.

> "If ye keep my commandments, ye shall abide in my love; even as I have kept my Father's commandments, and abide in his love....Ye are my friends, if ye do whatsoever I command you" (Jn.15:10, 14).
>
> "But ye shall not be so: but he that is greatest among you, let him be as the younger; and he that is chief, as he that doth serve" (Lk.22:26).
>
> "Likewise, ye younger, submit yourselves unto the elder, Yea, all of you be subject one to another, and be clothed with humility: for God resisteth the proud, and giveth grace to the humble. Humble yourselves therefore under the mighty hand of God, that he may exalt you in due time" (1 Pt.5:5-6).
>
> "Even a child is known by his doings, whether his work be pure, and whether it be right" (Pr.20:11).

c.   A child is usually obedient and learning. He will do exactly what he is asked to do and learn by it. He has not yet learned too much pride nor to act too independently—not while small and innocent. The terrible tragedy is, he is soon taught to be self-centered and pridefully independent just by the example of adults.

> "That we henceforth be no more children, tossed to and fro, and carried about with every wind of doctrine, by the sleight of men, and cunning craftiness, whereby they lie in wait to deceive" (Eph.4:14).
> "Children, obey your parents in the Lord: for this is right. Honour thy father and mother; (which is the first commandment with promise;) that it may be well with thee, and thou mayest live long on the earth" (Eph.6:1-3).
> "Children, obey your parents in all things: for this is well pleasing unto the Lord" (Col.3:20).
> "As newborn babes, desire the sincere milk of the word, that ye may grow thereby" (1 Pt.2:2).
> "Come, ye children, hearken unto me: I will teach you the fear of the LORD" (Ps.34:11).
> "Hearken unto thy father that begat thee, and despise not thy mother when she is old" (Pr.23:22).
> "He hath showed thee, O man, what is good; and what doth the LORD require of thee, but to do justly, and to love mercy, and to walk humbly with thy God?" (Mic.6:8).

d.   A child is usually humble and forgiving. He is not interested in prominence, fame, power, wealth, or position. He does not push himself forward. He does not want to *sit around* in the midst of a group of adults. He has not been taught to think in terms of *self-importance*, not yet. The child also forgives ever so easily. He can be disciplined, neglected, even abused; and before the adult turns around the child forgives and forgets (unless, of course, it is extreme abuse. We must remember that Christ is talking about the child in a normal, healthy environment.)

> "Blessed are the peacemakers: for they shall be called the children of God" (Mt.5:9).
> "Brethren, be not children in understanding: howbeit in malice be ye children, but in understanding be men" (1 Cor.14:20).
> "And ye have forgotten the exhortation which speaketh unto you as unto children, My son, despise not thou the chastening of the Lord, nor faint when thou are rebuked of him: for whom the Lord loveth he chasteneth, and scourgeth every son whom he receiveth" (Heb.12:5-6).

**4**   (18:17) **Children—Kingdom of Heaven**: only children are in the Kingdom of Heaven. This point is critical to see, for Christ used strong words about some persons not being able to enter the Kingdom of Heaven: "[Some persons] shall in no wise enter therein." There is nothing, absolutely nothing that can get a man into the Kingdom of Heaven except receiving the kingdom like a little child. There is no one in heaven except little children, people who have become children of God. (See note, *Child*—Mt.18:3 for more explanation of this fact.)

> "And if so be that he find it, verily I say unto you, he rejoiceth more of that sheep, than of the ninety and nine which went not astray" (Mt.18:13).
> "But as many as received him, to them gave he power to become the sons of God, even to them that believe on his name: which were born, not of blood, nor of the will of the flesh, nor of the will of man, but of God" (Jn.1:12-13).
> "Jesus answered and said unto him, Verily verily, I say unto thee, Except a man be born again, he cannot see the kingdom of God" (Jn.3:3).
> "For as many as are led by the Spirit of God, they are the sons of God. For ye have not received the spirit of bondage again to fear; but ye have received the Spirit of adoption, whereby we cry, Abba, Father. The Spirit itself beareth witness with our spirit, that we are the children of God" (Ro.8:14-16).
> "Wherefore come out from among them, and be ye separate, saith the Lord, and touch not the unclean thing; and I will receive you, and will be a Father unto you, and ye shall be my sons and daughters, saith the Lord Almighty" (2 Cor.6:17-18).
> (Cp. also Gal.4:4-7; Ph.2:15; 1 Jn.3:1.)

| 1 **Example 1: The ruler** | **F. The Rich Young Ruler: The Cost of Eternal Life, 18:18-30** (Mt.19:16-30; Mk.10: 17-31) | 23 And when he heard this, he was very sorrowful: for he was very rich. | d. He rejects sorrowfully |
|---|---|---|---|
| a. He must acknowledge Jesus as God | | 24 And when Jesus saw that he was very sorrowful, he said, How hardly shall they that have riches enter into the kingdom of God! | 2 **Example 2: The wealthy** a. It is difficult for a wealthy person to enter God's Kingdom |
| 1) Ruler called Him "Good Master" | 18 And a certain ruler asked him, saying, Good Master, what shall I do to inherit eternal life? | | b. The misconception about wealthy persons |
| 2) God is the only good one | 19 And Jesus said unto him, Why callest thou me good? none is good, save one, that | 25 For it is easier for a camel to go through a needle's eye, than for a rich man to enter into the kingdom of | |
| 3) Jesus asked: Are you calling me God? | is, God. | God. | |
| b. He must keep the commandments | 20 Thou knowest the commandments, Do not commit adultery, Do no kill, Do not steal, Do not bear false witness, Honour thy father and thy mother. | 26 And they that heard it said, Who then can be saved? 27 And he said, The things which are impossible with men are possible with God. | c. The only possible way for wealthy persons to be saved: God |
| | 21 And he said, All these have I kept from my youth up. | 28 Then Peter said, Lo, we have left all, and followed thee. | 3 **Example 3: The disciples** a. They left all to follow Christ |
| c. He must *give up* all that he has | 22 Now when Jesus heard these things, he said unto him, Yet lackest thou one thing: sell all that thou hast, and distribute unto the poor, and thou shalt have treasure in heaven: and come, follow me. | 29 And he said unto them, Verily I say unto you, There is no man that hath left house, or parents, or brethren, or wife, or children, for the kingdom of God's sake, 30 Who shall not receive manifold more in this present time, and in the world to come life everlasting. | b. They & all other followers shall be greatly rewarded<br><br>1) In this world: "Much more" 2) In the world to come: "Life everlasting" |

# DIVISION VII

## THE SON OF MAN'S GREAT JOURNEY TO JERUSALEM (STAGE III): HIS LESSONS AND WARNINGS, 17:11-19:27

## F.     The Rich Young Ruler: The Cost of Eternal Life, 18:18-30

(18:18-30) **Introduction**: many people think that eternal life is free, that it costs nothing. This is a false concept. Eternal life does cost. It costs a man everything he is and has. The message of this passage is probably the most demanding message ever preached.

1.     Example 1: the ruler (v.18-23).
2.     Example 2: the wealthy (v.24-27).
3.     Example 3: the disciples (v.28-30).

1 (18:18-23) **Eternal Life—Jesus Christ, Deity—Needs—Self-Denial**: the first example is that of the rich young ruler. When the other gospel accounts of this event are compared, the ruler is seen to be young and rich. But it does not matter, not for the purpose Luke is stressing. The cost of eternal life is the *same* for all persons, rich or poor, young or old.

1.     The person who seeks eternal life must acknowledge Jesus as God. The ruler called Jesus "Good Master." The word "good" was a word that was ascribed only to God. It was never used in reference to a man. This is critical to see, for it meant that the ruler was calling Jesus "good" in the sense that God would be called "good." He saw something in Jesus *like God*. It was not just flattery; he esteemed Jesus highly, probably believing or else coming close to believing Jesus' claim to be the Son of God.

Now note what Jesus did. The man had called Him "good," a word used only in addressing God. Jesus asked the man, "Why callest me good? God alone is good. Are you saying I am God?" Jesus is unquestionably claiming to be God. He was saying, "*If I am a mere man*, a good teacher, then I am not good and do not have the words of eternal life. *But if I am God*, then you can truly call me good, and I do have the words of eternal life." The point is this: Jesus told the man how to receive eternal life. He was claiming to be God, the One who could give eternal life to a person.

"**For God so loved the world, that he gave his only begotten Son, that whosoever believeth in him should not perish, but have everlasting life**" (Jn.3:16).

"**Then Simon Peter answered him, Lord, to whom shall we go? Thou hast the words of eternal life**" (Jn.6:68).

"**I said therefore unto you, that ye shall die in your sins: for if ye believe not that I am he, ye shall die in your sins**" (Jn.8:24).

"Jesus saith unto him, I am the way, the truth, and the life: no man cometh unto the Father, but by me. If ye had known me, ye should have known my Father also: and from henceforth ye know him, and have seen him" (Jn.14:6-7).

"Neither is there salvation in any other: for there is none other name under heaven given among men, whereby we must be saved" (Acts 4:12).

"For there is one God, and one mediator between God and men, the man Christ Jesus; who gave himself a ransom for all, to be testified in due time" (1 Tim.2:5-6).

2. The man must keep the commandments. He had asked, "What shall I do to inherit eternal life?" In his mind he had to do something, some great work—and he did. He had to trust and love God so much that he would keep God's commandments. He had to keep the commandments *after* he had accepted Jesus as God.

Jesus said to the man, "I am good, just as God is good; therefore, I am God. Now, once accepting this fact, you must obey the commandments and learn to love your neighbor. First, trust and love God, then trust and love your neighbor." Note two facts.

    a. The man had to see that Jesus was God, and as God He was to be trusted and loved. Then he had to see that he was to love his neighbor *as* himself. Jesus was simply covering the two great commandments with the man, and He was going to show the man how desperately short he was. (See outlines and notes— Mt.22:34-40.)

> "Not every one that saith unto me, Lord, Lord, shall enter into the kingdom of heaven; but he that doeth the will of my Father which is in heaven" (Mt.7:21).
>
> "He that hath my commandments, and keepeth them, he it is that loveth me: and he that loveth me shall be loved of my Father, and I will love him, and will manifest myself to him" (Jn.14:21).
>
> "Jesus answered and said unto him, If a man love me, he will keep my words: and my Father will love him, and we will come unto him, and make our abode with him" (Jn.14:23).
>
> "If ye keep my commandments, ye shall abide in my love; even as I have kept my Father's commandments, and abide in his love....Ye are my friends, if ye do whatsoever I command you" (Jn.15:10, 14).
>
> "Blessed are they that do his commandments, that they may have right to the tree of life, and may enter in through the gates into the city" (Rev.22:14).

    b. The man made a phenomenal claim: he had kept all these commandments from his youth up. He, of course, had not kept them, not like he should. He was sincere, but this picture of God was a surface picture. He was not perfect in all his dealings with men and women, not in the eyes of God. In fact, it was just this, the way he looked at men and the desperate needs of the world, that was his problem. He was not *giving* to help the needs of the world like he should. It was this that was keeping him out of heaven.

3. The man must *give up* all he had. This is exactly what Jesus said, "Sell, give all that thou hast and distribute to the poor." Was this unreasonable? Did Jesus really mean it? Could such radical action be demanded even by God?

Why not? Why would God *not* demand just this? Especially when the world is full of little children (and men and women) who are starving and diseased, without shelter or clothing, and dying being doomed to hell? And why are they in such a condition when there is enough of everything to go around, and the gospel that can save them is known? Let no one ever say that God does not demand the giving of all after a man has taken care of his own necessities. And let no one ever think that the doom of God will not fall upon the man...

- who shuts his eyes to the massive needs of the world.
- who hoards and banks his money.
- who lets money just sit and sit, doing nothing except causing men to say "My, what a rich man."

How empty words really are. There is but one question for the man who builds up and keeps: "Who do you think you are, God? Beware of God if you think He does not demand the giving of all you are and have to help the desperate millions of this earth." Jesus hit the very nerve of the man's problem: coveting—lusting after money, material goods, possessions, and wealth—instead of longing to help the needy of the world.

Note the glorious promise: give all you have and you shall have treasure in heaven and be allowed to follow Christ. It is *only after* we give all we have (beyond our own true needs) that we are allowed to enter heaven. That is the Word of Christ, His answer to the question, "How do I inherit eternal life?"

The man rejected Jesus—Jesus had asked too much. The man was unwilling to give all he was and had; he was sorrowful about his decision, but he did reject.

> "And he said to them all, If any man will come after me, let him deny himself, and take up his cross daily, and follow me" (Lk.9:23).
>
> "But lay up for yourselves treasures in heaven, where neither moth nor rust doth corrupt, and where thieves do not break through nor steal" (Mt.6:20).
>
> "Sell that ye have, and give alms; provide yourselves bags which wax not old, a treasure in the heavens that faileth not, where no thief approacheth, neither moth corrupteth" (Lk.12:33).
>
> "So likewise, whosoever he be of you that forsaketh not all that he hath, he cannot be my disciple" (Lk.14:33).
>
> "Yea doubtless, and I count all things but loss for the excellency of the knowledge of Christ Jesus my Lord: for whom I have suffered the loss of all things, and do count them but dung, that I may win Christ" (Ph.3:8).

"Charge them that are rich in this world, that they be not highminded, nor trust in uncertain riches, but in the living God, who giveth us richly all things to enjoy; that they do good, that they be rich in good works, ready to distribute, willing to communicate [give]; laying up in store for themselves a good foundation against the time to come, that they may lay hold on eternal life" (1 Tim.6:17-19).

"I counsel thee to buy of me gold tried in the fire, that thou mayest be rich; and white raiment, that thou mayest be clothed, and that the shame of thy nakedness do not appear; and anoint thine eyes with eyesalve, that thou mayest see" (Rev.3:18).

**2** (18:24-27) **Wealth—Rich—Salvation—Needy**: the second example is that of wealthy persons. Jesus made three striking points.

1. It is extremely difficult, almost impossible, for a rich person to enter heaven. It is as difficult as a camel's going through the eye of a needle. Why? Because the rich man has kept his wealth, hoarded and stored it up. He has not served God by *loving his neighbor as himself.* The rich man has used his talents to make money so that he could buy the *latest styles and be called rich* by other men. He failed to use his talents to make money to meet the desperate needs of children (and men and women). The world desperately needs food, shelter, clothes, medicine, and above all, the gospel. It is no wonder a rich man will not enter heaven when most of the world is in such desperate need. Why would God accept a man who has wealth when that man would not take the time to seek and reach out to the child who was starving and dying both physically and spiritually?

Attempts are sometimes made to lessen the cost of the Lord's demands.

⇒ Some say that what Christ means is this: a man *must be willing* to give his wealth, not actually give it. This is tragic, for there is *no meaning in willingness*—no act, no true decision, no work, no evidence, no proof, no demonstration. Willingness is nothing more than a word. It is empty without action to back it up. A man who is truly willing does something. Conversely, a man is *not really willing* if he does not do something.

⇒ Others try to explain away the impossibility of a camel's going through the eye of a needle. They say that a sewing needle is not what is meant (see note, *Camel*—Mt.19:24). Again, this view misses the whole point. Jesus is saying this: a man who does not give all his wealth (beyond his *true* necessities) to meet the needs of the world shall find it no easier entering heaven than a camel does going through the eye of a needle.

**Thought 1.** Let none of us miss heaven or cause another to miss heaven by trying to lessen the demand of Christ. Any honest man—if he were responsible for overseeing the children of the world—would condemn another person who had the money but who let a child die of starvation or exposure.

**Thought 2.** It is time for us to be honest and let the Savior of the world speak with the force with which He spoke. The world is desperate. Children and their mothers and fathers are dying from the agonizing pain of hunger and disease, and the terrorizing elements of nature. They are dying without ever having heard of the eternal salvation that is in Christ. The rich, who have the talents to earn more than they need, must use their talents to earn more to save the children and adults of the world who are in such a desperate plight. Jesus said no rich man shall enter heaven who does not give all he has.

"For where your treasure is, there will your heart be also" (Mt.6:21).

"Go and sell that thou hast, and give to the poor, and thou shalt have treasure in heaven: and come and follow me" (Mt.19:21).

"And the second is like unto it, Thou shalt love thy neighbor as thyself" (Mt.22:39).

"For ye know the grace of our Lord Jesus Christ, that, though he was rich, yet for your sakes he became poor, that ye through his poverty might be rich" (2 Cor.8:9).

"Let him that stole steal no more: but rather let him labour, working with his hands the thing which is good, that he may have to give to him that needeth" (Eph.4:28).

"Lo, this is the man that made not God his strength; but trusted in the abundance of his riches, and strengthened himself in his wickedness" (Ps.52:7).

"He that trusteth in his riches shall fall: but the righteous shall flourish as a branch" (Pr.11:28).

2. The misconception about wealth. The disciples were shocked, thoroughly dismayed. Jesus was saying something diametrically opposed to what they and everyone else had always thought. They had always been taught (as have succeeding generations, even the church):

⇒ that prosperity (wealth, comfort, and things) is God's blessing.

⇒ that a person receives because God is blessing him.

⇒ that prosperity is the reward of righteousness and obedience.

⇒ that God blesses a person with the things of this earth if he is righteous and obedient.

However, Jesus was saying the very opposite: that a prosperous person will most likely never enter heaven; that prosperity poses such a dangerous threat to a person that his eternal doom is almost assured. The disciples knew that God would never put a person in such a precarious, dangerous position. They knew that Jesus was attacking the world's most cherished and ardent belief: be good (righteous) and you will be blessed by God (and the thought of blessing is always of material blessing. See note—Eph.1:3.)

They were shocked, thoroughly dismayed: Who then can be saved? The vast majority of people were threatening their own eternal destiny. They were dooming themselves. Since prosperity is not the reward (sign) for righteousness and the rich are barred from heaven, that means that the poor, too, are barred; for they are spending most of their time in dreaming about and seeking prosperity.

"And the cares of this world, and the deceitfulness of riches, and the lusts of other things entering in, choke the word, and it becometh unfruitful" (Mk.4:19).

"And I will say to my soul, Soul, thou hast much goods laid up for many years; take thine ease, eat, drink, and be merry. But God said unto him, Thou fool, this night thy soul shall be required of thee: then whose shall those things be, which thou hast provided?" (Lk.12:19-20).

"But they that will be rich fall into temptation and a snare, and into many foolish and hurtful lusts, which drown men in destruction and perdition" (1 Tim.6:9).

"Charge them that are rich in this world, that they be not highminded, nor trust in uncertain riches, but in the living God, who giveth us richly all things to enjoy" (1 Tim.6:17).

"And when thy herds and thy flocks multiply, and thy silver and thy gold is multiplied, and all that thou hast is multiplied; then thine heart be lifted up, and thou forget the LORD thy God" (Dt.8:13-14).

"The rich man's wealth is his strong city, and as a high wall in his own conceit" (Pr.18:11).

3. The only possibility for wealthy persons to be saved is God. Very simply...
   - it is impossible for a rich man to save himself.
   - the rich man must turn to God and love God and do God's will by loving his neighbor as himself. God alone can save a rich man.
   - the decision is up to the rich man. He can turn to be *with God* in eternity, or he can continue to live for himself now and can suffer eternal condemnation.

"For with God nothing shall be impossible" (Lk.1:37).

"I know that thou canst do every thing, and that no thought can be withholden from thee" (Job 42:2).

"Charge them that are rich in this world, that they be not highminded, nor trust in uncertain riches, but in the living God, who giveth us richly all things to enjoy; that they do good, that they be rich in good works, ready to distribute, willing to communicate; laying up in store for themselves a good foundation against the time to come, that they may lay hold on eternal life" (1 Tim.6:17-19).

"For other foundation can no man lay than that is laid, which is Jesus Christ" (1 Cor.3:11).

**3** (18:28-30) **Reward:** the third example is that of the disciples. Note two points.

1. The disciples were examples of what Christ meant. They had left all to follow Christ. (See note and DEEPER STUDY # 1—Lk.9:23 for discussion.)
2. The disciples and all other followers of Christ will be richly rewarded. Note three points.
   a. The reason for the reward is clearly stated. They left all, gave up all for Christ, in order to meet the desperate needs of the world, and they gave up the most cherished things on earth: their property and family.
   b. Their reward in this world was to be *much more*. The Gospel of Mark makes it clear that Christ was speaking of present reward on earth (Mk.10:21). No true follower of Christ has ever forsaken persons or things and then been left alone and destitute by Christ. Christ rewards His true follower manyfold. Note: the reward is both human and material.
      1) The human reward is most fulfilling: a real and true fellowship among genuine believers. Christ knows when a follower of His has been turned against by those whom He loves ever so deeply. He knows when to send someone into the life of His followers, when to meet the aching need of His follower for true friendship. He more than abundantly meets the need.

"That which we have seen and heard declare we unto you, that ye also may have fellowship with us: and truly our fellowship is with the Father, and with his Son Jesus Christ" (1 Jn.1:3).

"But if we walk in the light, as he is in the light, we have fellowship one with another, and the blood of Jesus Christ his Son cleanseth us from all sin" (1 Jn.1:7).

"And they continued stedfastly in the apostles' doctrine and fellowship, and in breaking of bread, and in prayers" (Acts 2:42).

"I am a companion of all them that fear thee, and of them that keep thy precepts" (Ps.119:63).

"Then they that feared the LORD spake often one to another: and the LORD hearkened, and heard it, and a book of remembrance was written before him for them that feared the LORD, and that thought upon his name" (Mal.3:16).

   2) The material reward is most assuring: the meeting of necessities and whatever else God wants us to have so that we can help meet the needs of others.

The idea that Christ was conveying is that of perfect care and security. Fear and insecurity cause us to crave and to be greedy for more, and fear and insecurity are most unhealthy and destabilizing. When we forsake all to genuinely follow Christ, He gives us the greatest peace and security possible: Himself and His power to provide our necessities. We never have to worry or be anxious again (see notes—

Lk.16:10-12; Mt.6:25-34. Cp. Lk.18:30; Mk.10:30; Eph.4:28.) There is much more in Christ than in any amount of possessions or worldly companionship and friendship. In Christ the believer has…

- happiness
- peace
- assurance
- satisfaction
- fulfillment

- joy
- security
- confidence
- completeness

"But seek ye first the kingdom of God, and his righteousness; and all these things shall be added unto you" (Mt.6:33; cp. Mt.6:25-34).

"The thief cometh not, but for to steal, and to kill, and to destroy: I am come that they might have life, and that they might have it more abundantly" (Jn.10:10).

"But my God shall supply all your need according to his riches in glory by Christ Jesus" (Ph.4:19).

"And ye shall serve the LORD your God, and he shall bless thy bread, and thy water; and I take sickness away from the midst of thee" (Ex.23:25).

"Blessed be the Lord, who daily loadeth us with benefits, even the God of our salvation" (Ps.68:19).

"Then shall he give the rain of thy seed, that thou shalt sow the ground withal; and bread of the increase of the earth, and it shall be fat and plenteous: in that day shall thy cattle feed in large pastures" (Is.30:23).

"And ye shall eat in plenty, and be satisfied, and praise the name of the Lord your God, that hath dealt wondrously with you: and my people shall never be ashamed" (Joel 2:26).

"Bring ye all the tithes into the storehouse, that there may be meat in mine house, and prove me now herewith, saith the LORD of hosts, if I will not open you the windows of heaven, and pour you out a blessing, that there shall not be room enough to receive it" (Mal.3:10).

c. Their reward in the world to come is to be "life everlasting." (see DEEPER STUDY # 1—Jn.17:2-3; cp. Jn.1:4 and Mt.19:28. Cp. Ro.8:16-18.)

"Then Jesus beholding him loved him, and said unto him, One thing thou lackest: go thy way, sell whatsoever thou hast, and give to the poor, and thou shalt have treasure in heaven: and come, take up the cross, and follow me" (Mk.10:21).

"Verily, verily, I say unto you, He that heareth my word, and believeth on him that sent me, hath everlasting life, and shall not come into condemnation; but is passed from death unto life" (Jn.5:24).

| 1 The purpose of Jesus: To fullfill the Scripture | G. The Prediction of the Cross, 18:31-34 (Mt.20:17-19; Mk.10: 32-34)<br><br>31 Then he took unto him the twelve, and said unto them, Behold, we go up to Jerusalem, and all things that are written by the prophets concerning the Son of man shall be accomplished. | 32 For he shall be delivered unto the Gentiles, and shall be mocked, and spitefully entreated, and spitted on:<br>33 And they shall scourge him, and put him to death: and the third day he shall rise again.<br>34 And they understood none of these things: and this saying was hid from them, neither knew they the things which were spoken. | 2 The prophecies to be fulfilled<br>a. He was to be tortured & disgraced<br>b. He was to be put to death<br>c. He was to rise again*DSI*<br><br>3 The disciples' response: Confusion |

# DIVISION VII

## THE SON OF MAN'S GREAT JOURNEY TO JERUSALEM (STAGE III): HIS LESSONS AND WARNINGS, 17:11-19:27

## G.  The Prediction of the Cross, 18:31-34

(18:31-34) **Jesus' Death—Bible**: note that Jesus pulled the twelve disciples off to the side. He wanted to continue drilling into them the fact of His death and resurrection. It was through these two phenomenal events that He was to save the world; therefore, they had to be indoctrinated with the glorious truth of the two events.
1. The purpose of Jesus: to fulfill Scripture (v.31).
2. The prophecies to be fulfilled (v.32-33).
3. The disciples' response: confusion (v.34).

**1** (18:31) **Jesus Christ, Mission—Purpose—Scripture—Prophecy**: the purpose of Jesus was to fulfill Scripture. Note three points.
1. Jesus said, "We go up to Jerusalem." This was His purpose, to set His face toward Jerusalem. By this He meant His death and His sufferings. The focus of His purpose on earth was to suffer for the salvation of men (see notes—Lk.9:51-13:21; 9:51-56).
2. Jesus claimed to be the Son of Man. He said that all things written concerning the Son of Man would be fulfilled in Him. He was the One who was sent to fulfill God's purposes on earth (see DEEPER STUDY # 3—Mt.8:20).
3. Jesus said that His sufferings were the prophetic fulfillment of Scripture. In Him all the prophecies of Scripture are to be fulfilled. Note how this supports both the truth of the Scripture and of Christ. The Scriptures have to be fulfilled, and they have to be fulfilled in Christ. Not one jot or tittle can fail. Jesus was the Son of Man, the very One of whom Scripture spoke and the very One in whom all Scripture was to be fulfilled.

> **"For verily I say unto you, Till heaven and earth pass, one jot or one tittle shall in no wise pass from the law, till all be fulfilled" (Mt.5:18).**
> **"Heaven and earth shall pass away: but my words shall not pass away" (Lk.21:33).**
> **"The works of his hands are verity and judgment; all his commandments are sure" (Ps.111:7).**
> **"For I am the LORD: I will speak, and the word that I shall speak shall come to pass" (Ezk.12:25).**

**2** (18:32-33) **Prophecy—Scripture**: the prophecies to be fulfilled. Note the reference to the Gentiles. Jesus was to be delivered to the Gentiles. The Jews were going to be the ones to deliver Him into Gentile hands. This fact was to symbolize both the religionists and the world—both were going to reject and put God's Son to death. Neither could accept Him and His message of total self-denial. There were three prophecies in particular to be fulfilled. (Cp. Ps.22:1f; Is.53:1f.)
1. Jesus was to be tortured and disgraced, injured and insulted. There were four forms of disgrace and torture mentioned.
   a. To mock: to ridicule, scorn, insult, humiliate, defy, jeer.
   b. To spitefully treat (hubristhsetai): to reproach; to treat with insolence and contempt; to be outraged; to treat shamefully and despitefully.
   c. To spit upon: a sign of monstrous disrespect and gross insult.
   d. To scourge: to beat with a rod or a whip weighted with either jagged metal or bone chips. Thirty-nine or forty lashes were inflicted. The whole purpose of scourging was to inflict severe pain.
2. Jesus was to be put to death. In this passage He was predicting His death. We, of course, look back upon it. Jesus bore the sins of men, suffering the ultimate degree of pain. He suffered pain in an absolute sense.
   a. Mentally, while He was being tortured, His mind was bound to be upon why He was suffering. He was thinking about the sin of man and the problem sin had caused God. Imagine all the world's sin, the enormity and awfulness of it, consuming His mind. He was suffering mentally to the ultimate degree.
   b. Spiritually, His heart was being broken. Those whom He loved so much were committing a sin so horrendous it defied imagination. They were rebelling against God so much that they were killing God's own Son.
       Even more terrible, His own Father, God Himself, was to turn His back upon Him. Because of sin, God was forced to separate Himself from His Son (see notes—Mt.27:46-49; Mk.15:34). Jesus was going to

369

bear spiritual pain in an absolute sense (1 Pt.2:24; 2 Cor.5:21. Cp. Is.53:4-7 for a descriptive account of His bearing our sin.)

    c. Physically, the pain of the crucifixion was to be more severe because of the mental and spiritual pressure He was having to bear. There is also truth to the fact that the more ridicule within a persecutor's heart, the more he tortures his victim (cp. the crown of thorns, royal robe, and excessive mockery of the soldiers). The fact that Jesus claimed to be the Son of God aroused the heart of the persecutors to inflict more scorn and torture.

> "I am the good shepherd: the good shepherd giveth his life for the sheep" (Jn.10:11).
>
> "As the Father knoweth me, even so know I the Father: and I lay down my life for the sheep" (Jn.10:15).
>
> "Therefore doth my Father love me, because I lay down my life, that I might take it again. No man taketh it from me, but I lay it down of myself. I have power to lay it down, and I have power to take it again. This commandment have I received of my Father" (Jn.10:17-18).
>
> "Who gave himself for our sins, that he might deliver us from this present evil world, according to the will of God and our Father" (Gal.1:4).
>
> "And walk in love, as Christ also hath loved us, and hath given himself for us an offering and a sacrifice to God for a sweetsmelling savour....Husbands, love your wives, even as Christ also loved the church, and gave himself for it" (Eph.5:2, 25).
>
> "Who gave himself for us, that he might redeem us from all iniquity, and purify unto himself a peculiar people, zealous of good works" (Tit.2:14).
>
> "Who his own self bare our sins in his own body on the tree, that we, being dead to sins, should live unto righteousness: by whose stripes ye were healed" (1 Pt.2:24).
>
> "For Christ also hath once suffered for sins, the just for the unjust, that he might bring us to God, being put to death in the flesh, but quickened by the Spirit" (1 Pt.3:18).
>
> "Hereby perceive we the love of God, because he laid down his life for us: and we ought to lay down our lives for the brethren" (1 Jn.3:16).
>
> "Unto him that loved us, and washed us from our sins in his own blood" (Rev.1:5).

3.    Jesus was to rise from the dead (see DEEPER STUDY # 1—Lk.18:33).

> "Him, being delivered by the determinate counsel and foreknowledge of God, ye have taken, and by wicked hands have crucified and slain: whom God hath raised up, having loosed the pains of death: because it was not possible that he should be holden of it" (Acts 2:23-24).
>
> "But ye denied the Holy One and the Just, and desired a murderer to be granted unto you; and killed the Prince of life, whom God hath raised from the dead; whereof we are witnesses" (Acts 3:14-15).
>
> "And with great power gave the apostles witness of the resurrection of the Lord Jesus: and great grace was upon them all" (Acts 4:33).
>
> "And we are witnesses of all things which he did both in the land of the Jews, and in Jerusalem; whom they slew and hanged on a tree: him God raised up the third day, and showed him openly; not to all the people, but unto witnesses chosen before of God, even to us, who did eat and drink with him after he rose from the dead" (Acts 10:39-41).
>
> "Who was delivered for our offences, and was raised again for our justification" (Ro.4:25).
>
> "That if thou shalt confess with thy mouth the Lord Jesus, and shalt believe in thine heart that God hath raised him from the dead, thou shalt be saved" (Ro.10:9).
>
> "For I delivered unto you first of all that which I also received, how that Christ died for our sins according to the scriptures; and that he was buried, and that he rose again the third day according to the scriptures" (1 Cor.15:3-4).
>
> "After that, he was seen of James; then of all the apostles" (1 Cor.15:7).
>
> "[Christ] died for all, that they which live should not henceforth live unto themselves, but unto him which died for them, and rose again" (2 Cor.5:15).
>
> "Which he wrought in Christ, when he raised him from the dead, and set him at his own right hand in the heavenly places" (Eph.1:20).
>
> "For if we believe that Jesus died and rose again, even so them also which sleep in Jesus will God bring with him" (1 Th.4:14).
>
> "Blessed be the God and Father of our Lord Jesus Christ, which according to his abundant mercy hath begotten us again unto a lively hope by the resurrection of Jesus Christ from the dead" (1 Pt.1:3).
>
> "For Christ also hath once suffered for sins, the just for the unjust, that he might bring us to God, being put to death in the flesh, but quickened by the Spirit" (1 Pt.3:18).

---

**DEEPER STUDY # 1**

(18:33) **Jesus Christ, Resurrection**: Jesus was to be raised from the dead. Covering the resurrection in the same discussion with His death did three major things.

1.    It drove the point of the resurrection into the minds of the disciples. They must forever remember the resurrection. The death of Jesus was not the final word.

"Remember that Jesus Christ of the seed of David was raised from the dead according to my gospel" (2 Tim.2:8)

2. It foreshadowed the power of God. After His resurrection the disciples would remember, and the glorious truth of God's power would be reinforced in their minds and hearts forever.
   a. The power of God was victorious.

   "O death, where is thy sting? O grave, where is thy victory?...But thanks be to God, which giveth us the victory through our Lord Jesus Christ" (1 Cor.15:55, 57).

   b. The power of God did triumph.

   "And having spoiled principalities and powers, he made a show of them openly, triumphing over them in it" (Col.2:15).

   c. The power of God did conquer.

   "Nay, in all these things we are more than conquerors through him that loved us" (Ro.8:37).
   "Forasmuch then as the children are partakers of flesh and blood, he also himself likewise took part of the same; that through death he might destroy him that had the power of death, that is, the devil; and deliver them who through fear of death were all their lifetime subject to bondage" (Heb.2:14-15).

3. It foreshadowed the stirring that God's power was going to work in their lives.
   a. The power to encourage and motivate.

   "And what is the exceeding greatness of his power to us-ward who believe, according to the working of his mighty power, which he wrought in Christ, when he raised him from the dead, and set him at his own right hand in the heavenly places" (Eph.1:19-20).
   "For God hath not given us the spirit of fear; but of power, and of love, and of a sound mind" (2 Tim.1:7).

   b. The power to assure and build confidence.

   "Then saith he to Thomas, Reach hither thy finger, and behold my hands; and reach hither thy hand, and thrust it into my side: and be not faithless, but believing. And Thomas answered and said unto him, My Lord and my God. Jesus saith unto him, Thomas, because thou hast seen me, thou hast believed: blessed are they that have not seen, and yet have believed" (Jn.20:27-29).

   c. The power to give courage and boldness.

   "And now, Lord, behold their threatenings: and grant unto thy servants, that with all boldness they may speak thy word, by stretching forth thine hand to heal; and that signs and wonders may be done by the name of thy holy child Jesus" (Acts 4:29-30).
   "Be not thou therefore ashamed of the testimony of our Lord, nor of me his prisoner: but be thou partaker of the afflictions of the gospel according to the power of God; who hath saved us, and called us with an holy calling, not according to our works, but according to his own purpose and grace, which was given us in Christ Jesus before the world began" (2 Tim.1:8-9).

**3** (18:34) **Jesus Christ, Death, Misunderstood**: the disciples' response was that of confusion. (See notes—Mt.17:22; Lk.9:44-45 for more discussion.) Note an interesting fact. This verse says the same thing over and over in three different ways. The disciples were totally confused.
   ⇒ They understood none of these things. They *would not* accept nor understand the death of Christ literally. They refused to take His words at face value; therefore, they *did not* understand these things.
   ⇒ His saying was hid from them. Since they *would not* literally accept His words, they *could not* understand. What He said was a puzzle, a mystery, a riddle. The meaning was completely hidden from them. The word "hid" (kekrummenon) has the sense of completion in it.
   ⇒ They did not know the things which were spoken. They did not perceive, and they *kept on* not perceiving.

The disciples were familiar with the Old Testament, but they had never seen *within* the passages that predicted the Messiah's death. They were so intent on the predicted blessings that the Messiah was to bring that they were blind to the predicted sufferings. They could see nothing that could be accomplished by the disgrace of death; therefore, they had only a partial grasp of prophetic truth. (See note—Mk.10:32.)

**Thought 1.** When the Scriptures are not taken at face value—when they are not accepted for exactly what they say—the result for anyone is always…

- not understanding *these things*.
- having the *saying* hid from them.
- not knowing *the things* which are spoken.

> "Then he said unto them, O fools, and slow of heart to believe all that the prophets have spoken" (Lk.24:25).
>
> "But the natural man receiveth not the things of the Spirit of God: for they are foolishness unto him: neither can he know them, because they are spiritually discerned" (1 Cor.2:14).
>
> "Man that is in honour, and understandeth not, is like the beasts that perish" (Ps.49:20).
>
> "But they know not the thoughts of the LORD, neither understand they his counsel" (Mic.4:12).

| | H. The Healing of Blind Bartimaeus: Steps to Getting Help from God, 18:35-43 (cp. Mt.20:29-34; Mk.10:46-52) | before rebuked him, that he should hold his peace: but he cried so much the more, Thou Son of David, have mercy on me. | in seeking Jesus that would not quit |
|---|---|---|---|
| 1 Jesus approached Jericho<br>2 A man had great need<br>  a. He was blind<br>  b. He was poor<br>3 A man had great hope in Jesus<br><br>  a. He believed the reports he had heard about Jesus<br>  b. He acknowledged Jesus as the Messiah[DS1]<br>  c. He cried for mercy<br>4 A man had a persistence | 35 And it came to pass, that as he was come nigh unto Jericho, a certain blind man sat by the way side begging:<br>36 And hearing the multitude pass by, he asked what it meant.<br>37 And they told him, that Jesus of Nazareth passeth by.<br>38 And he cried, saying, Jesus, thou Son of David, have mercy on me.<br>39 And they which went | 40 And Jesus stood, and commanded him to be brought unto him: and when he was come near, he asked him,<br>41 Saying, What wilt thou that I shall do unto thee? And he said, Lord, that I may receive my sight.<br>42 And Jesus said unto him, Receive thy sight: thy faith hath saved thee.<br>43 And immediately he received his sight, and followed him, glorifying God: and all the people, when they saw it, gave praise unto God. | 5 A man had the boldness to ask great things of God<br>  a. Jesus stood still & called for him<br>  b. The man expressed his longing<br><br>  c. The man was saved by faith<br><br>6 A man had the appreciation to glorify God |

# DIVISION VII

## THE SON OF MAN'S GREAT JOURNEY TO JERUSALEM (STAGE III): HIS LESSONS AND WARNINGS, 17:11-19:27

## H. The Healing of Blind Bartimaeus: Steps to Getting Help from God, 18:35-43

(18:35-43) **Introduction**: blind Bartimaeus demonstrated ever so clearly how men can get help from God.
1. Jesus approached Jericho (v.35).
2. A man had great need (v.35).
3. A man had great hope in Jesus (v.36-38).
3. A man had a persistence in seeking Jesus that would not quit (v.39).
4. A man had the boldness to ask great things of God (v.40-42).
5. A man had the appreciation to glorify God (v.43).

**1** (18:35) **Scripture, Discrepancies**: Jesus was near Jericho, about to enter the city. He was on His way to Jerusalem where He was to die. His face was set to accomplish the purpose for which God had sent Him into the world. (See DEEPER STUDY # 1—Lk.9:51.) Jericho was only about seventeen miles from Jerusalem, so the journey was about over. The cross was ever so near, hanging immediately before His face.
There are two apparent conflicts among the three gospel accounts of this event that need to be mentioned.
1. The actual location where the healing of Bartimaeus took place. Luke said it took place as Jesus "came near" to Jericho; Matthew and Mark said the event took place as He "departed from Jericho." What happened was apparently what often happens in a big city. There was an old Jericho (the one so often mentioned in the Old Testament), and a new Jericho built by Herod the Great; or as we might say today, an old section of town and a new section. Matthew and Mark were apparently referring to the old or new city Jesus was leaving and Luke to the other city He was entering. There is also the possibility that the two blind men began to cry as Jesus entered the city. However, since they needed their faith strengthened by persisting, Jesus waited until they were close to leaving the city before hearing their cry.
2. The number of blind men involved. Matthew said there were two; Mark and Luke said one, and Mark gave his name as Bartimaeus. The simplest explanation of what happened is what often happens in an ordinary conversation when an event is being explained: the spokesman or prominent person is the only one mentioned. In this particular case, the prominent person was Bartimaeus. Therefore, Bartimaeus is the only blind man referred to by Mark and Luke.
Note: we do not know what actually happened. However when we get to heaven, God will reveal that what *appeared* to be discrepancies were only that, apparent discrepancies that gave us another opportunity to trust Him and His Word.

**2** (18:35) **Needy, The**: a man had great need. The blind man was as needful as he could be, desperately needful. He had been blind for years, perhaps for life, with no hope of ever seeing. All he knew about things and people was what he could imagine from touching and hearing and tasting. The only places he could go were the places where people led him or else where he could safely feel his way along. Even then he would sometimes stumble and fall. He was doomed to live in total darkness, never to see anything but pitch black as long as he lived. The worst fact of all was that he knew it. He had to live with the knowledge that he was doomed to a world of darkness. It preyed and preyed upon his mind. He knew that he could never be normal, never fit in, and never be fully accepted by normal people.
He was also poor. He had to beg to survive, and he suffered the humiliation of being a beggar every day. There was no one to care for him—not family or neighbor or social group. He was left on his own, entirely alone in fending for himself and struggling for survival. How many days he must have gone to bed hungry, his stomach suffering sharp pains or nausea from lack of food. He was desperately needful, and he knew it.

**3** (18:36-38) **Seeking Jesus—Hope**: a man had great hope in Jesus. As the blind man sat by the wayside, he heard all kinds of commotion throughout the day. The road was a major highway, one of the major commercial routes of the day. During this particular time, pilgrims from all over the known world were flooding the road; therefore the commotion was noisier and more hectic than usual. All of a sudden, the blind man heard a huge throng of people passing by. When he asked about the crowd, someone told him Jesus of Nazareth was coming.

1.    The blind man had heard about Jesus of Nazareth, and he had *believed the reports* about Him. Apparently the blind man hoped for "the consolation of Israel." As soon as he heard that Jesus of Nazareth was passing by, he knew who Jesus was and he began to cry out immediately. This tells us that he had already been thinking about the possibility of Jesus' coming his way. Hope had already risen in his heart, and now, despite the fact that he could not see, the opportunity of his life stared him in the face. The point to note is this: he had already *believed the report* that the Messiah had come. Belief had already been stirred in his heart—at least to some degree.

> "Who hath believed our report? and to whom is the arm of the LORD revealed?" (Is.53:1; cp. Jn.12:38; Ro.10:16).
> "For he saith, I have heard thee in a time accepted, and in the day of salvation have I succoured thee: behold, now is the accepted time; behold, now is the day of salvation" (2 Cor.6:2).

2.    The blind man acknowledged Jesus as Messiah. He called Jesus "thou Son of David." This term is used only two times in Luke (cp. Lk.20:41). It was a title of the Messiah. (See *notes*—Lk.3:24-31; DEEPER STUDY # 1—18:38; note—7:21-23.) It was an inadequate concept of Jesus, although it was a true fact. He was the Son of David predicted from the beginning, but He was more, much more. He was the very Son of God Himself. But note: the blind man approached Jesus with what knowledge he had. He used what he understood and cried out to Jesus in his desperate need.

> **Thought 1.** All a man needs to do is *use what knowledge* he has and call out to God. God will help a man grow in knowledge as the man continues to seek God's help, no matter the need.

> "That they should seek the Lord, if haply they might feel after him, and find him, though he be not far from every one of us" (Acts 17:27).
> "Seek the LORD, and his strength: seek his face evermore" (Ps.105:4).
> "Seek ye the LORD, all ye meek of the earth, which have wrought his judgment; seek righteousness, seek meekness: it may be ye shall be hid in the day of the LORD'S anger" (Zeph.2:3).
> "Seek ye the LORD while he may be found, call ye upon him while he is near" (Is.55:6).

3.    The blind man cried for mercy. This is significant. He was blind and poor and he had to beg for daily survival. But note: he did not cry for food, clothing, or shelter. The basic necessities of life were not his primary concern. The mercy of God upon his life was his concern.

> "And his mercy is on them that fear him from generation to generation" (Lk.1:50).
> "And the publican, standing afar off, would not lift up so much as his eyes unto heaven, but smote upon his breast, saying, God be merciful to me a sinner. I tell you, this man went down to his house justified" (Lk.18:13-14).
> "But God, who is rich in mercy, for his great love wherewith he loved us, even when we were dead in sins, hath quickened us together with Christ, (by grace ye are saved)" (Eph.2:4-5).
> "Have mercy upon me, O LORD; for I am weak: O LORD, heal me; for my bones are vexed: my soul is also sore vexed: but thou, O LORD, how long?" (Ps.6:2-3).
> "Hear, O LORD, when I cry with my voice: have mercy also upon me, and answer me" (Ps.27:7).
> "Have mercy upon me, O God, according to thy lovingkindness: according unto the multitude of thy tender mercies blot out my transgressions" (Ps.51:1).
> "Show us thy mercy, O LORD, and grant us thy salvation" (Ps.85:7).
> "Let thy tender mercies come unto me, that I may live: for thy law is my delight" (Ps.119:77).
> "And rend your heart, and not your garments, and turn unto the LORD your God: for he is gracious and merciful, slow to anger, and of great kindness, and repenteth him of the evil" (Joel 2:13).
> "Rejoice not against me, O mine enemy: when I fall, I shall arise; when I sit in darkness, the LORD shall be a light unto me" (Mic.7:8).

---

**DEEPER STUDY # 1**

(18:38) **Jesus Christ, Titles, Son of David**: the title the Son of David is a common title throughout the Bible. (Cp. Mt.12:23; 15:22; 20:30-31; 21:9, 15; Acts 2:29-36; Ro.1:3; 2 Tim.2:8; Rev.22:16.) It was the common title and popular concept of the Messiah. Generation after generation of Jews longed and looked for the promised deliverer of Israel. The people expected Him to be a great general who would deliver and restore the nation to its greatness. In fact, they expected Him to make the nation the center of universal rule. Under God He would conquer the world and center the glory and majesty of God Himself in Jerusalem. From His throne, the throne of David, He (the Son of David, the Messiah) would execute "the Messianic fire of judgment" upon the nations and people of the world (see DEEPER STUDY # 2—Mt.1:18; DEEPER STUDY #

3—3:11; notes—11:1-6; 11:2-3; DEEPER STUDY # 1—11:5; DEEPER STUDY # 2—11:6; DEEPER STUDY # 1—12:16; 22:42; Lk.7:21-23.
Referring to these notes will show what the Jewish concept of the Messiah was.)

**4** (18:39) **Persistence**: a man had a persistence that would not quit. This is an excellent example of the kind of persistence that gets help from God.

1.    Some of the people with Jesus rebuked the blind man. They tried to silence and stop him from crying out to the Lord. Why we are not told, but they did oppose him. He had every reason to be discouraged, for he was blind and could not see to make his way through the crowd. All he could do was shout out, and some were even trying to stop him from doing that. He could have easily quit and given up, for it seemed so useless.

2.    Note what he did: he "cried so much the more." He would not quit and would not be silenced. Jesus was his hope, the only chance he had for mercy. No other man could have mercy upon him or meet his need. They might feed, clothe, and house him; but they could not meet the crying need of his heart, the blindness of his eyes and spirit. His faith in Jesus was strong; therefore, he was not to be stopped. His faith fought against all odds: the opposition of the crowd and the noise above which he had to be heard. His faith cried out louder and louder, desperately hoping that God would help Jesus hear.

> "**Ask, and it shall be given you; seek, and ye shall find; knock, and it shall be opened unto you**" (Mt.7:7).
> "**But if from thence thou shalt seek the LORD thy God, thou shalt find him, if thou seek him with all thy heart and with all thy soul**" (Dt.4:29).
> "**Seek ye me, and ye shall live**" (Amos 5:4).

**Thought 1.** Perseverance—resisting and standing against all odds—is the answer to being helped by God. God cannot turn a deaf ear to the persevering cry of a desperate need, not if the person cries and cries for help, never quitting. God has promised to hear and answer *undying perseverance* (cp. Lk.11:8-13; 18:1-8).

**5** (18:40-42) **Prayer—Seeking**: a man had the boldness to ask great things of God. Note three significant facts.

1.    The man's persistence caused Jesus to stop and to stand still. Imagine the scene. Jesus heard the cry and its sound of desperation. He stopped and looked about, standing perfectly still with a hush sweeping over the crowd until there was nothing but stone silence. Then piercing through the silence, the desperate cry came: "Thou Son of David, have mercy on me."

**Thought 1.** There is symbolism in the scene: the great need for quietness and silence for Jesus to hear us. There are times when the crowd must be silenced, hushed so that Christ can hear our cries for mercy. Nothing should ever be allowed to interfere with our daily *quiet time* with the Lord. How many of our needs would be met so much quicker if we persevered daily in a *quiet time*, crying out to the Lord for mercy.

> "**Be still, and know that I am God: I will be exalted among the heathen, I will be exalted in the earth**" (Ps.46:10).
> "**But the LORD is in his holy temple: let all the earth keep silence before him**" (Hab.2:20).
> "**Be silent, O all flesh, before the LORD: for he is raised up out of his holy habitation**" (Zech.2:13).

2.    The blind man asked for a great thing to be done. Imagine—being truly blind and asking a man standing there to heal your eyes. An unbelievable thing, yet the blind man believed. He believed in the One who stood before Him, *believing what he had heard*: that this Jesus was the Messiah who possessed the very power of God. He was able to do anything, so the blind man asked for the greatest need in his life to be met. There was no need to ask for anything less, for Jesus was the One possessing the power of God. And Jesus had called him to come forward and to ask for whatever he needed. It was a time for courage, the kind of courage that asks great things of God, even if they seem impossible.

> "**And all things, whatsoever ye shall ask in prayer, believing, ye shall receive**" (Mt.21:22).
> "**And whatsoever ye shall ask in my name, that will I do, that the Father may be glorified in the Son**" (Jn.14:13).
> "**If ye abide in me, and my words abide in you, ye shall ask what ye will, and it shall be done unto you**" (Jn.15:7).
> "**Hitherto have ye asked nothing in my name: ask, and ye shall receive, that your joy may be full**" (Jn.16:24).
> "**And this is the confidence that we have in him, that, if we ask any thing according to his will, he heareth us: and if we know that he hear us, whatsoever we ask, we know that we have the petitions that we desired of him**" (1 Jn.5:14-15).
> "**And it shall come to pass, that before they call, I will answer; and while they are yet speaking, I will hear**" (Is.65:24).
> "**Call unto me, and I will answer thee, and show thee great and mighty things, which thou knowest not**" (Jer.33:3).

3.    Jesus granted his request. He gave him sight and saved him. The blind man had taken three critical steps. He had...
*    believed the reports that Jesus was the promised Messiah (Ro.10:13-17, esp. 16).
*    cried out for mercy.
*    persevered and persisted and refused to give up despite all kinds of odds.

Therefore, Jesus saved him by giving him sight and saving his soul. This was a complete healing that included both the inner and outer person: the spirit as well as the body (see note—Mt.14:36).

"Wherefore he is able also to save them to the uttermost that come unto God by him, seeing he ever liveth to make intercession for them" (Heb.7:25).

"But without faith it is impossible to please him: for he that cometh to God must believe that he is, and that he is a rewarder of them that diligently seek him" (Heb.11:6).

"Commit thy way unto the LORD; trust also in him; and he shall bring it to pass" (Ps.37:5).

"Trust in the LORD with all thine heart; and lean not unto thine own understanding" (Pr.3:5).

"Trust ye in the LORD for ever: for in the LORD JEHOVAH is everlasting strength" (Is.26:4).

6    (18:43) **Witnessing—Courage**: a man had the appreciation to glorify God, the courage to become a witness for Christ.

1.    Note that he followed Christ immediately.

"And he said to them all, If any man will come after me, let him deny himself, and take up his cross daily, and follow me" (Lk.9:23).

"My sheep hear my voice, and I know them, and they follow me" (Jn.10:27).

"If any man serve me, let him follow me; and where I am, there shall also my servant be: if any man serve me, him will my Father honour" (Jn.12:26).

"Be ye therefore followers of God, as dear children" (Eph.5:1).

"As ye have therefore received Christ Jesus the Lord, so walk ye in him" (Col.2:6).

"For even hereunto were ye called: because Christ also suffered for us, leaving us an example, that ye should follow his steps" (1 Pt.2:21).

"He that saith he abideth in him ought himself also so to walk, even as he walked" (1 Jn.2:6).

2.    Note that he glorified God and caused others to praise God.

"Let your light so shine before men, that they may see your good works, and glorify your Father which is in heaven" (Mt.5:16).

"That ye may with one mind and one mouth glorify God, even the Father of our Lord Jesus Christ" (Ro.15:6).

"For ye are bought with a price: therefore glorify God in your body, and in your spirit, which are God's" (1 Cor.6:20).

"That the name of our Lord Jesus Christ may be glorified in you, and ye in him, according to the grace of our God and the Lord Jesus Christ" (2 Th.1:12).

"By him therefore let us offer the sacrifice of praise to God continually, that is, the fruit of our lips giving thanks to his name" (Heb.13:15).

"But ye are a chosen generation, a royal priesthood, an holy nation, a peculiar people; that ye should show forth the praises of him who hath called you out of darkness into his marvellous light" (1 Pt.2:9).

"Sing praises to the LORD, which dwelleth in Zion: declare among the people his doings" (Ps.9:11).

"Let the people praise thee, O God; let all the people praise thee" (Ps.67:3).

| | | | |
|---|---|---|---|
| | **CHAPTER 19**<br><br>**I. The Conversion of Zac-<br>chaeus: The Meaning of<br>Conversion, 19:1-10** | Zacchaeus, make haste, and<br>come down; for to day I must<br>abide at thy house.<br>6 And he made haste, and<br>came down, and received<br>him joyfully.<br>7 And when they saw it, | b. Jesus called him by name<br>c. Jesus asked to be<br>received<br>d. Zacchaeus obeyed |
| **1 Zacchaeus, the chief tax-<br>collector—a man who was<br>very rich** | And Jesus entered and<br>passed through Jericho.<br>2 And, behold, there was a<br>man named Zacchaeus, which<br>was the chief among the<br>publicans, and he was rich. | they all murmured, saying,<br>That he was gone to be guest<br>with a man that is a sinner.<br>8 And Zacchaeus stood, and<br>said unto the Lord; Behold,<br>Lord, the half of my goods I<br>give to the poor; and if I have | **4 Third, repenting, that is,<br>changing one's whole way<br>of life**<br>a. He was a sinner<br>b. He repented, changed<br>his life |
| **2 First, being desperate to<br>see Jesus: Who He is**<br>a. He was thrust back<br>b. He persisted | 3 And he sought to see<br>Jesus who he was; and could<br>not for the press, because he<br>was little of stature.<br>4 And he ran before, and<br>climbed up into a sycamore<br>tree to see him: for he was to<br>pass that way. | taken any thing from any<br>man by false accusation, I<br>restore him fourfold.<br>9 And Jesus said unto him,<br>This day is salvation come to<br>this house, forsomuch as he<br>also is a son of Abraham. | **5 Fourth, looking to Jesus<br>as the Savior**<br>a. The One who pro-<br>claims salvation |
| **3 Second, receiving the<br>invitation of Jesus**<br>a. Jesus saw him | 5 And when Jesus came to<br>the place, he looked up, and<br>saw him, and said unto him, | 10 For the Son of man is<br>come to seek and to save that<br>which was lost. | b. The One who seeks &<br>saves the lost |

# DIVISION VII

## THE SON OF MAN'S GREAT JOURNEY TO JERUSALEM<br>(STAGE III): HIS LESSONS AND WARNINGS, 17:11-19:27

## I. The Conversion of Zacchaeus: The Meaning of Conversion, 19:1-10

(19:1-10) **Introduction**: the meaning of conversion is clearly illustrated in the experience of Zacchaeus. The fact that man can be converted should stir hope within every heart that truly senses need and wants to meet God as though face to face.

1. Zacchaeus, the chief tax-collector—a man who was very rich (v.1-2).
2. First, being desperate to see Jesus: who He is (v.3-4).
3. Second, receiving the invitation of Jesus (v.5-6).
4. Third, repenting, that is, changing one's whole way of life (v.7-8).
5. Fourth, looking to Jesus as the Savior (v.9-10).

**1** (19:1-2) **Tax Collector**: Zacchaeus, the chief tax-collector, was a very rich man. This is the only time the title "chief" is used with a tax collector. Its meaning is not known. It probably refers to the head of the local taxation office; therefore, Zacchaeus would be responsible to the Roman government for the employment and management of the local tax-collectors and their monies. (See DEEPER STUDY # 1—Lk.5:27.) Note two things about Zacchaeus.

1. He had all the pleasures and comforts of life which money could buy.
2. He was a man who would find it very difficult to enter the Kingdom of Heaven. His money was a serious threat to his salvation, as it is with all rich men. It was going to be difficult to give up all he had to follow Christ. A man tends to *love* his money and the things it does for him (see outline and notes—Lk.18:24-27).

**2** (19:3-4) **Seeking Jesus—Conversion**: first, conversion is being desperate to see Jesus, just who He is. Note three facts.

1. Zacchaeus showed a desperation in trying to see Jesus. Despite his wealth and the pleasures and comfort enjoyed by wealth, he was apparently empty and lonely within his heart. This can be imagined because tax-collectors were bitterly hated by the people. (See DEEPER STUDY # 1—Lk.5:27.) Zacchaeus was also small of stature, which means that he was probably self-conscious and felt inferior and had a low self-image. Being so little in stature, it was dangerous for him to be out in the midst of a crowd that despised him. From all indications he was denied passage through the crowd, probably being shoved back and abused. Therefore, his desperate determination and persistence is even more evident.

> **"But if from thence thou shalt seek the LORD thy God, thou shalt find him, if thou seek him with all thy heart and with all thy soul" (Dt.4:29).**
> **"Seek ye the LORD while he may be found, call ye upon him while he is near" (Is.55:6).**
> **"And ye shall seek me, and find me, when ye shall search for me with all your heart" (Jer.29:13).**
> **"Sow to yourselves in righteousness, reap in mercy; break up your fallow ground: for it is time to seek the LORD, till he come and rain righteousness upon you" (Hos.10:12).**

2. Zacchaeus persevered in his attempt to see Jesus, and he had to humble himself to do it. Imagine Zacchaeus, a man of position and wealth, climbing a tree just to see an important person pass by. He wanted to see Jesus so badly he

forgot everyone around and humbled himself to climb a tree. He was determined to see the Lord, and nothing was going to stop him.

3.     Zacchaeus had most likely experienced the stirring of faith within his heart for some time. He had heard reports about Jesus being the Messiah, and perhaps had heard about Jesus saving and calling Matthew, another tax-collector, to be one of His apostles. Zacchaeus had begun to *believe the reports* or at least to wonder and hope that the reports were true. His efforts to see Jesus and what follows are evidence of some stirring, of some hope that drove him to seek Jesus.

> "Ho, every one that thirsteth, come ye to the waters, and he that hath no money; come ye, buy, and eat; yea, come, buy wine and milk without money and without price" (Is.55:1).
>
> "Come unto me, all ye that labour and are heavy laden, and I will give you rest" (Mt.11:28).
>
> "For we have not an high priest which cannot be touched with the feeling of our infirmities; but was in all points tempted like as we are, yet without sin. Let us therefore come boldly unto the throne of grace, that we may obtain mercy, and find grace to help in time of need" (Heb.4:15-16).

**3**   (19:5-6) **Conversion**: second, conversion is receiving the invitation of Jesus. Note several points.

1.     Jesus "looked up, and saw him." Jesus sees every man, no matter where he is: in the dark places of his sin and shame, in his home and work and play, in his seeking to know the truth. Jesus sees everything about a man, but there is one person in particular whom he sees. He sees the man who is seeking Him. Jesus sees him in the sense of knowing about his need and reaching out to meet that need.

Zacchaeus is an example. He was desperate to see Jesus, so he had struggled against the odds and found a place where he could see Jesus. Even though the place he chose meant humiliating himself and exposing himself to people who were bitterly opposed to him, he was willing to suffer whatever it took to get a look at the Savior. And, because Zacchaeus sought so diligently to see Jesus, Jesus saw him.

2.     Jesus knew and called him by name. This was bound to strike Zacchaeus and be very meaningful to him. When anyone, especially a stranger, calls us by name, our ears perk up and our senses become more alert. Jesus knows every man's name (cp. Jn.1:48; Is.43:1). He wants to address every one of us by name, but we must let Him. We have to do as Zacchaeus did: seek to find the place and vantage point where we can see Jesus, then Jesus will see us and call us by name.

> "And he brought him to Jesus. And when Jesus beheld him, he said, Thou art Simon the son of Jona: thou shalt be called Cephas, which is by interpretation, A stone" (Jn.1:42).
>
> "To him the porter openeth; and the sheep hear his voice: and he calleth his own sheep by name, and leadeth them out" (Jn.10:3).
>
> "I am the good shepherd, and know my sheep, and am known of mine" (Jn.10:14).
>
> "But if any man love God, the same is known of him" (1 Cor.8:3).
>
> "But now, after that ye have known God, or rather are known of God, how turn ye again to the weak and beggarly elements, whereunto ye desire again to be in bondage?" (Gal.4:9).
>
> "Nevertheless the foundation of God standeth sure, having this seal, The Lord knoweth them that are his. And, Let every one that nameth the name of Christ depart from iniquity" (2 Tim.2:19).
>
> "Fear not: for I have redeemed thee, I have called thee by thy name; thou art mine" (Is.43:1).

3.     Jesus asked to be received and to be received with haste. He was set for Jerusalem and must not delay too long. There was no time to waste. Jesus wanted to be welcomed, received, and entertained by Zacchaeus; but Zacchaeus had to act then and there. Jesus had only a couple of hours before He had to move on to fulfill His purpose. The moment of opportunity was then and there, that day. The next day it would be gone. There would be no pull, no struggle, no spirit of seeking within Zacchaeus' heart.

> "Come unto me, all ye that labour and are heavy laden, and I will give you rest" (Mt.11:28).
>
> "Behold, I stand at the door, and knock: if any man hear my voice, and open the door, I will come in to him, and will sup with him, and he with me" (Rev.3:20).
>
> "That which we have seen and heard declare we unto you, that ye also may have fellowship with us: and truly our fellowship is with the Father, and with his Son Jesus Christ" (1 Jn.1:3).
>
> "God is faithful, by whom ye were called unto the fellowship of his Son Jesus Christ our Lord" (1 Cor.1:9).
>
> "And the Spirit and the bride say, Come. And let him that heareth say, Come. And let him that is athirst come. And whosoever will, let him take the water of life freely" (Rev.22:17).
>
> "Come now, and let us reason together, saith the LORD: though your sins be as scarlet, they shall be as white as snow; though they be red like crimson, they shall be as wool" (Is.1:18).
>
> "Ho, every one that thirsteth, come ye to the waters, and he that hath no money; come ye, buy, and eat; yea, come, buy wine and milk without money and without price" (Is.55:1).

4.     Zacchaeus *obeyed*; he made haste and received Christ joyfully.

> "But as many as received him, to them gave he power to become the sons of God, even to them that believe on his name" (Jn.1:12).
>
> "For he saith, I have heard thee in a time accepted, and in the day of salvation have I succoured thee: behold, now is the accepted time; behold, now is the day of salvation" (2 Cor.6:2).

**4** (19:7-8) **Conversion—Repentance—Restitution**: third, conversion is repenting, that is, changing one's whole way of life.

1. Zacchaeus was a sinner. Note "all murmured." Everyone knew that Zacchaeus was a betrayer of his country, serving the alien power of Rome. And Zacchaeus himself knew that he was a sinner, both a betrayer and a thief, having stolen much from many. The point is twofold.
   a. Zacchaeus knew he was a sinner and readily confessed his need for the Savior.

> "Whosoever therefore shall confess me before men, him will I confess also before my Father which is in heaven" (Mt.10:32).
> "That if thou shalt confess with thy mouth the Lord Jesus, and shalt believe in thine heart that God hath raised him from the dead, thou shalt be saved" (Ro.10:9).
> "Whosoever denieth the Son, the same hath not the Father: [but] he that acknowledgeth the Son hath the Father also" (1 Jn.2:23).
> "Whosoever shall confess that Jesus is the Son of God, God dwelleth in him, and he in God" (1 Jn.4:15).

   b. The crowd, that is, the general populace, demonstrated self-righteousness. They did not like Jesus' eating and associating with a known and confessed sinner. Note: their sin was murmuring and grumbling and complaining—the great sins of Israel in the wilderness. They just misunderstood Jesus' purpose for coming to earth, that of saving sinners.

> "And Jesus answering said unto them, They that are whole need not a physician; but they that are sick. I came not to call the righteous, but sinners to repentance" (Lk.5:31-32).
> "But God commendeth his love toward us, in that, while we were yet sinners, Christ died for us" (Ro.5:8).
> "This is a faithful saying, and worthy of all acceptation, that Christ Jesus came into the world to save sinners; of whom I am chief" (1 Tim.1:15).

2. Zacchaeus repented and changed his whole life; he completely turned around from his sinful life to God and His way of righteousness.
   a. He gave half his goods to the poor. He did exactly what Jesus had said time after time, and he did exactly what the rich young ruler had refused to do (Lk.18:18-24).

> "And he said to them all, If any man will come after me, let him deny himself, and take up his cross daily, and follow me. For whosoever will save his life shall lose it: but whosoever will lose his life for my sake, the same shall save it. For what is a man advantaged, if he gain the whole world, and lose himself, or be cast away?" (Lk.9:23-25).
> "But rather give alms of such things as ye have; and, behold, all things are clean unto you" (Lk.11:41).
> "Sell that ye have, and give alms; provide yourselves bags which wax not old, a treasure in the heavens that faileth not, where no thief approacheth, neither moth corrupteth" (Lk.12:33).
> "Now when Jesus heard these things, he said unto him, Yet lackest thou one thing: sell all that thou hast, and distribute unto the poor, and thou shalt have treasure in heaven: and come, follow me" (Lk.18:22).
> "Let him that stole steal no more: but rather let him labour, working with his hands the thing which is good, that he may have to give to him that needeth" (Eph.4:28).
> "Charge them that are rich in this world, that they be not highminded, nor trust in uncertain riches, but in the living God, who giveth us richly all things to enjoy; that they do good, that they be rich in good works, ready to distribute, willing to communicate" (1 Tim.6:17-18).

   b. He gave back to those whom he had cheated; he gave *four times* what he had taken. *Restitution* became the thrust of his life for the next while. Think of the people he had cheated, stealing everything he could from them. Imagine the list of people and how long it would take to track them down.

> "Then it shall be, because he hath sinned, and is guilty, that he shall restore that which he took violently away, or the thing which he hath deceitfully gotten, or that which was delivered him to keep, or the lost thing which he found" (Lev.6:4).
> "But if he be found, he shall restore sevenfold; he shall give all the substance of his house" (Pr.6:31).
> "I will seek that which was lost, and bring again that which was driven away, and will bind up that which was broken, and will strengthen that which was sick: but I will destroy the fat and the strong; I will feed with judgment" (Ezk.34:16; cp. 1 Ki.20:34; 2 Ki.8:6; Neh.5:12).

The point is that this sinner, Zacchaeus, truly repented. He was serious about following Christ and living righteously. (See notes and DEEPER STUDY # 1, *Repentance*—Acts 17:29-30.)

"I tell you, Nay: but, except ye repent, ye shall all likewise perish" (Lk.13:3).

"Repent ye therefore, and be converted, that your sins may be blotted out, when the times of refreshing shall come from the presence of the Lord" (Acts 3:19).

"Repent therefore of this thy wickedness, and pray God, if perhaps the thought of thine heart may be forgiven thee" (Acts 8:22).

"Let the wicked forsake his way, and the unrighteous man his thoughts: and let him return unto the LORD, and he will have mercy upon him; and to our God, for he will abundantly pardon" (Is.55:7).

"But if the wicked will turn from all his sins that he hath committed, and keep all my statutes, and do that which is lawful and right, he shall surely live, he shall not die" (Ezk.18:21).

**5** (19:9-10) **Jesus Christ, Mission:** fourth, conversion is looking to Jesus as the Savior.

1. Jesus is the One who proclaims salvation. He proclaimed two things:
   a. That repentance saved Zacchaeus, and that Zacchaeus would bring the message of salvation to his whole household.

   "He that believeth and is baptized shall be saved; but he that believeth not shall be damned" (Mk.16:16).

   "And brought them out, and said, Sirs, what must I do to be saved? And they said, Believe on the Lord Jesus Christ, and thou shalt be saved, and thy house" (Acts 16:30-31).

   b. That Zacchaeus was a true son of Abraham, a spiritual son.

   "That he [Abraham] might be the father of all them that believe, though they be not circumcised [have undergone a ritual]; that righteousness might be imputed unto them also" (Ro.4:11).

   "Therefore we conclude that a man is justified by faith without the deeds of the law" (Ro.3:28).

2. Jesus is the One who seeks and saves the lost.
   a. The lost are the ones who are perishing, being destroyed, losing eternal life, and being cut off from God. The lost are spiritually destitute.
   b. Jesus, the One who seeks and saves the lost, is the One who sought Zacchaeus. Zacchaeus put himself in a position to see Jesus, but Jesus did the speaking to Zacchaeus' heart, asking Zacchaeus to receive him. Note: only after Zacchaeus received Jesus did Jesus save him. (See notes—Ro.10:16-17; note and DEEPER STUDY # 1—1 Cor.1:18 for more discussion.)

   "What man of you, having an hundred sheep, if he lose one of them, doth not leave the ninety and nine in the wilderness, and go after that which is lost, until he find it?" (Lk.15:4).

   "Jesus heard that they had cast him out; and when he had found him, he said unto him, Dost thou believe on the Son of God? He answered and said, Who is he, Lord, that I might believe on him? And Jesus said unto him, Thou hast both seen him, and it is he that talketh with thee" (Jn.9:35-37).

   "But they have not all obeyed the gospel. For Esaias saith, Lord, who hath believed our report? So then faith cometh by hearing, and hearing by the word of God" (Ro.10:16-17).

| | | | |
|---|---|---|---|
| | **J. The Parable of the Pounds: Every Man is Being Tested, 19:11-27** | saying, Lord, thy pound hath gained five pounds. | 500% receives 500% |
| **1 Jesus tried to correct a wrong idea about the Kingdom of God** | 11 And as they heard these things, he added and spake a parable, because he was nigh to Jerusalem, and because they thought that the kingdom of God should immediately appear. | 19 And he said likewise to him, Be thou also over five cities. 20 And another came, saying, Lord, behold, here is thy pound, which I have kept laid up in a napkin: | **c. The believer who does not work receives nothing** |
| **2 He went to a far country to receive a kingdom, but He will return** | 12 He said therefore, A certain nobleman went into a far country to receive for himself a kingdom, and to return. | 21 For I feared thee, because thou art an austere man: thou takest up that thou layedst not down, and reapest that thou didst not sow. | |
| **3 He insisted: Occupy till I come**[DS1,2] | 13 And he called his ten servants, and delivered them ten pounds, and said unto them, Occupy till I come. | 22 And he saith unto him, Out of thine own mouth will I judge thee, thou wicked servant. Thou knewest that I was an austere man, taking up that I laid not down, and reaping that I did not sow: | |
| **4 The citizens of the world hate Him & reject His rule** | 14 But his citizens hated him, and sent a message after him, saying, We will not have this man to reign over us. | 23 Wherefore then gavest not thou my money into the bank, that at my coming I might have required mine own with usury? | |
| **5 His servants are to be rewarded according to the percent of their labor**[DS3] | 15 And it came to pass, that when he was returned, having received the kingdom, then he commanded these servants to be called unto him, to whom he had given the money, that he might know how much every man had gained by trading. | 24 And he said unto them that stood by, Take from him the pound, and give it to him that hath ten pounds. 25 (And they said unto him, Lord, he hath ten pounds.) | **6 The servant who labors 1000% will be given the reward of the unfaithful plus his own reward** a. Other servants wonder why b. Because the servant was so faithful—ever increasing, 1 Cor.15:58 |
| a. The believer who works 1000% receives 1000% | 16 Then came the first, saying, Lord, thy pound hath gained ten pounds. 17 And he said unto him, Well, thou good servant: because thou hast been faithful in a very little, have thou authority over ten cities. | 26 For I say unto you, That unto every one which hath shall be given; and from him that hath not, even that he hath shall be taken away from him. | |
| b. The believer who works | 18 And the second came, | 27 But those mine enemies, which would not that I should reign over them, bring hither, and slay them before me. | **7 The citizens who are enemies of His rule are to be slain** |

# DIVISION VII

## THE SON OF MAN'S GREAT JOURNEY TO JERUSALEM (STAGE III): HIS LESSONS AND WARNINGS, 17:11-19:27

**J.    The Parable of the Pounds: Every Man is Being Tested, 19:11-27**

(19:11-27) **Introduction**: the Lord trusts us; He believes in us. He gives us gifts and responsibilities to look after until He returns. He longs for us to be faithful and diligent in doing our duty, and He is going to greatly reward those who are faithful. But He is going to severely judge those who do nothing to help a lost and needful world. (See outline and notes—Mt.25:14-30 for more discussion.)

1.    Jesus tried to correct a wrong idea about the Kingdom of God (v.11).
2.    He went to a far country to receive a kingdom, but He will return (v.12).
3.    He insisted: occupy till I come (v.13).
4.    The citizens of the world hate Him and reject His rule (v.14).
5.    His servants are to be rewarded according to the percent of their labor (v.15-23).
6.    The servant who labors 1000 percent shall be given the reward of the unfaithful plus his own reward (v.24-26).
7.    The citizens who are enemies of His rule are to be slain (v.27).

**1**    (19:11) **Kingdom of God—Messiah, Misconception of**: Jesus tried to correct a wrong idea about the Kingdom of God. Jesus was near Jerusalem. The disciples and people with Him believed that the capital of God's kingdom was to be set up in Jerusalem. They were very aware of how He had been talking about Jerusalem and setting His face like a flint for the city. They also thought that the kingdom "should *immediately* appear." They believed that as soon as they reached Jerusalem, Jesus was going to usher in the Kingdom of God, freeing Israel from Roman domination and establishing the rule of God over all the earth. In their minds the climax of human history and the beginning of God's reign upon earth was at hand. They knew that with His power, He could do whatever was necessary to subdue the nations of the earth and bring God's righteousness to earth.

Now note, all their thoughts were upon this earth: upon the temporal and the worldly, the physical and the material. They saw themselves in positions of leadership and honor, as the princes and counsellors of state (cp. Lk.22:24-30; Mt.20:20-28; Mk.9:33-37). There is a problem with this concept: at most a person would enjoy an earthly kingdom for only a few short years of a life time. The disciples were just not thinking in terms of the spiritual world:

⇒ an eternal life which lives on forever.
⇒ an eternal world which actually exists.
⇒ an eternal world in another dimension of being.
⇒ an eternal world which is the real world.
⇒ an eternal world which is much more real than this physical world which fades away in its corruption.

Jesus had to correct their misconcept and teach them the truth about the Kingdom of God. In the parable, Jesus is the nobleman; the citizens are the unbelievers of the world; the servants are the professing believers of the Lord.

**2** (19:12) **Jesus Christ, Return**: the Lord went to a "far country" to receive a kingdom, but He will return. The following facts are important.

1. The "far country" indicates He will be gone for a while. It takes time to travel a long distance and handle the affairs and return.

2. He has gone to receive a kingdom from the King of the *whole realm of the universe*, God Himself. The picture is that of Jesus' sitting at the right hand of God in glory while He and God discuss the kingdom and its affairs.

3. He is to return. He will be gone a long time, for the "far country" is a long way off. The discussions surrounding His kingdom, His rule, and His reign will take time; but He will return. The day of His arrival will come. (See DEEPER STUDY # 3, *Kingdom of Heaven*—Mt.19:23-24.)

"In my Father's house are many mansions: if it were not so, I would have told you. I go to prepare a place for you. And if I go and prepare a place for you, I will come again, and receive you unto myself; that where I am, there ye may be also" (Jn.14:2-3).

"But Jesus held his peace. And the high priest answered and said unto him, I adjure thee by the living God, that thou tell us whether thou be the Christ, the Son of God. Jesus saith unto him, Thou hast said: nevertheless I say unto you, Hereafter shall ye see the Son of man sitting on the right hand of power, and coming in the clouds of heaven" (Mt.26:63-64).

"And then shall they see the Son of man coming in a cloud with power and great glory" (Lk.21:27).

"So Christ was once offered to bear the sins of many; and unto them that look for him shall he appear the second time without sin unto salvation" (Heb.9:28).

**3** (19:13) **Dedication—Ministering—Service**: the Lord insisted, "Occupy till I come." Note what He did.

1. He called His servants. They were already His servants and already belonged to His household; therefore, He believed in them, feeling that He could trust them. They were supposed to be responsible persons, completely trustworthy, for they belonged to the household of the Lord Himself.

2. He put His business affairs into their hands while He was gone. Jesus illustrated this with money (see DEEPER STUDY # 1, *Pound*—Lk.19:13). The Lord said, "Occupy till I come." That was all He said: four exact, straightforward, and powerful words. Yet, they were so full of meaning. The servant of God is to take what Jesus has given him and use it until Jesus returns. The word "occupy" (pragmateuomai) is a word of diligent action. It is from the root word meaning to walk, to set in motion, and to continue in motion. The servant is to labor diligently, never letting up and using all the Lord has given him to look after (see DEEPER STUDY # 2, *Occupy*—Lk.19:13).

**Thought 1.** Every believer is called and gifted by Christ to serve (cp. Ro.12:3f; 1 Cor.12:7f; Eph.4:11f; 1 Pt.4:10).

"Say not ye, There are yet four months, and then cometh harvest? behold, I say unto you, Lift up your eyes, and look on the fields; for they are white already to harvest" (Jn.4:35).

"I must work the works of him that sent me, while it is day: the night cometh, when no man can work" (Jn.9:4).

"Moreover it is required in stewards, that a man be found faithful" (1 Cor.4:2).

"For ye are bought with a price: therefore glorify God in your body, and in your spirit, which are God's" (1 Cor.6:20).

"As every man hath received the gift, even so minister the same one to another, as good stewards of the manifold grace of God" (1 Pt.4:10).

"Wherefore I put thee in remembrance that thou stir up the gift of God, which is in thee by the putting on of my hands" (2 Tim.1:6).

"Greatly desiring to see thee, being mindful of thy tears, that I may be filled with joy" (2 Tim.1:4).

"Whatsoever thy hand findeth to do, do it with thy might; for there is no work, nor device, nor knowledge, nor wisdom, in the grave, whither thou goest" (Eccl.9:10).

---

**DEEPER STUDY # 1**
(19:13) **Pound**: the word in the Greek testament is *mna* which was a Greek coin worth about one hundred drachmai. One drachmai was about one days' wage for a laborer.

**DEEPER STUDY # 2**
(19:13) **Occupy** (pragmateuomai): to do business; to get busy; to work for gain; to trade. This is the only time the word is used in the New Testament (cp. Is.35:3; Heb.12:28; 12:12).

**4** (19:14) **Jesus Christ, Response to—Unbelief**: the citizens of the world hate Him and reject His rule. This, of course, describes the unbeliever who refuses to acknowledge Christ and surrender his life to the rule of Christ. It can also apply to Israel's rejection of Christ. Men are rejecting Christ every day. Why? Very simply because they will not let Him rule over them. They want to control their own lives, do their own thing just as they wish.

> "He came unto his own, and his own received him not" (Jn.1:11).
> "I am come in my Father's name, and ye receive me not: if another shall come in his own name, him ye will receive. How can ye believe, which receive honour one of another, and seek not the honour that cometh from God only?" (Jn.5:43-44).
> "He that rejecteth me, and receiveth not my words, hath one that judgeth him: the word that I have spoken, the same shall judge him in the last day" (Jn.12:48).
> "To whom he said, This is the rest wherewith ye may cause the weary to rest; and this is the refreshing: yet they would not hear" (Is.28:12).
> "For thus saith the Lord GOD, the Holy One of Israel; In returning and rest shall ye be saved; in quietness and in confidence shall be your strength: and ye would not" (Is.30:15).

**5** (19:15-23) **Faithfulness—Dedication—Gifts—Unfaithfulness—Service**: the Lord's servants are to be rewarded according to the percent of their labor. The story is clear, but note these points.
1.    Scripture is clear about judgment: there is to be a day of judgment.

> "For the Son of man shall come in the glory of his Father with his angels; and then he shall reward every man according to his works" (Mt.16:27).
> "When the Son of man shall come in his glory, and all the holy angels with him, then shall he sit upon the throne of his glory: and before him shall be gathered all nations: and he shall separate them one from another, as a shepherd divideth his sheep from the goats" (Mt.25:31-32).
> "So then every one of us shall give account of himself to God" (Ro.14:12).
> "For we must all appear before the judgment seat of Christ; that every one may receive the things done in his body, according to that he hath done, whether it be good or bad" (2 Cor.5:10).
> "I charge thee therefore before God, and the Lord Jesus Christ, who shall judge the quick and the dead at his appearing and his kingdom" (2 Tim.4:1).

2.    In the parable the Lord did return. The day of accounting did arrive. Every servant was called to report on what he had done with the gifts Christ had given him.
3.    Only the servants of the Lord are pictured as appearing before the Lord. The three results illustrate the three courses of action taken by God's servants: being very faithful, faithful, and unfaithful.
4.    The first two servants were both faithful. Both labored diligently, but there was a difference. One labored ever so diligently: daily, hourly, every day and every hour. He was always walking with the Lord, never slacking up or allowing the trials of life to hinder his labor. He worked to increase the Lord's property regardless of circumstances. He was 1000 percent faithful. The other servant was not quite as sold out; he did not strain and sacrifice as much. He was 500 percent faithful.

> "And he said to them all, If any man will come after me, let him deny himself, and take up his cross daily, and follow me" (Lk.9:23).
> "He that is faithful in that which is least is faithful also in much: and he that is unjust in the least is unjust also in much" (Lk.16:10).
> "I beseech you therefore, brethren, by the mercies of God, that ye present your bodies a living sacrifice, holy, acceptable unto God, which is your reasonable service" (Ro.12:1).
> "Not slothful in business; fervent in spirit; serving the Lord" (Ro.12:11).
> "Therefore, my beloved brethren, be ye stedfast, unmoveable, always abounding in the work of the Lord, forasmuch as ye know that your labour is not in vain in the Lord" (1 Cor.15:58).
> "With good will doing service, as to the Lord, and not to men" (Eph.6:7).
> "And we desire that every one of you do show the same diligence to the full assurance of hope unto the end: that ye be not slothful, but followers of them who through faith and patience inherit the promises" (Heb.6:11-12).
> "Feed the flock of God which is among you, taking the oversight thereof, not by constraint, but willingly; not for filthy lucre, but of a ready mind; neither as being lords over God's heritage, but being ensamples to the flock" (1 Pt.5:2-3).
> "Wherefore the rather, brethren, give diligence to make your calling and election sure: for if ye do these things, ye shall never fall" (2 Pt.1:10).
> "Wherefore, beloved, seeing that ye look for such things, be diligent that ye may be found of him in peace, without spot, and blameless" (2 Pt.3:14).

5.    The two faithful servants were rewarded. But note three facts.
  a.    The servant who labored 1000 percent was commended by the Lord, "Well, thou good servant." The servant who served 500 percent was not personally commended.

b.   The servants were rewarded *exactly* as they labored. A city for each pound. *Perfect justice* was executed. Each servant determined exactly what his own reward would be. The amount or the percent of energy and labor put into increasing the Lord's property determined his reward.

c.   The reward involved responsibility, the assigning of duties to perform for the Lord. The two faithful believers reigned with the Lord: they were put in charge of certain territories that included several cities or kingdoms. The point to see is this: they were definitely assigned certain areas of responsibility to oversee *for the Lord*, and the areas of responsibility were based upon how trustworthy they had been while He had been gone. This is the picture of rewards always painted by the Lord and Scripture (see Rev.2:26).

> "His lord said unto him, Well done, good and faithful servant; thou hast been faithful over a few things, I will make thee ruler over many things: enter thou into the joy of thy lord" (Mt.25:23).
>
> "Then shall the King say unto them on his right hand, Come, ye blessed of my Father, inherit the kingdom prepared for you from the foundation of the world" (Mt.25:34).
>
> "But love ye your enemies, and do good, and lend, hoping for nothing again; and your reward shall be great, and ye shall be the children of the Highest: for he is kind unto the unthankful and to the evil" (Lk.6:35).
>
> "Ye are they which have continued with me in my temptations. And I appoint unto you a kingdom, as my Father hath appointed unto me" (Lk.22:28-29).
>
> "For if by one man's offence death reigned by one; much more they which receive abundance of grace and of the gift of righteousness shall reign in life by one, Jesus Christ" (Ro.5:17).
>
> "Do ye not know that the saints shall judge [reign over, hold authority over] the world? and if the world shall be judged by you, are ye unworthy to judge the smallest matters? Know ye not that we shall judge angels? how much more things that pertain to this life?" (1 Cor.6:2-3).
>
> "If we suffer, we shall also reign with him: if we deny him, he also will deny us" (2 Tim.2:12).
>
> "And from Jesus Christ, who is the faithful witness, and the first begotten of the dead, and the prince of the kings of the earth. Unto him that loved us, and washed us from our sins in his own blood, and hath made us kings and priests unto God and his Father; to him be glory and dominion for ever and ever" (Rev.1:5-6).
>
> "And he that overcometh, and keepeth my works unto the end, to him will I give power over the nations" (Rev.2:26).
>
> "To him that overcometh will I grant to sit with me in my throne, even as I also overcame, and am set down with my Father in his throne" (Rev.3:21).
>
> "And there shall be no night there; and they need no candle, neither light of the sun; for the Lord God giveth them light: and they shall reign for ever and ever" (Rev.22:5).

6.   The servant who did not work received nothing. Note two facts.

a.   The unfaithful servant did nothing, absolutely nothing with what Christ had given him.

     ⇒  He had no vision of what could be done.
     ⇒  He had no sense of responsibility to the Lord.
     ⇒  He had no concern for the growth of the Lord's kingdom and property.
     ⇒  He felt the gift given him did not matter that much and was not needed that much.
     ⇒  He did not look for the blessed moment of his Lord's return.
     ⇒  He had a *false security*, believing the Lord would accept him and understand even if he did fail to use the gifts.

b.   He tried to justify his behavior. He accused the Lord of being "austere" (austeros), which means sharp, stringent. He felt the Lord was too demanding and strict, that if he committed himself to the Lord's affairs, he would lose out on too much of the pleasures and comforts of life. But note: this was merely an excuse for his failure. He had chosen to live a life of selfishness and comfort and worldliness in the kingdom of the Lord without paying the price of helping to build it. He had been complacent and idle, doing very little. He had to cover up his failure or else face judgment, but his excuse was unacceptable. Perfect justice was executed again. "Out of thy mouth will I judge thee." The very excuse as well as the life of the unfaithful servant determined his judgment.

Note the unfaithful servant is called "thou *wicked* servant." He was not being condemned for what he did, but for what he *had not* done. He was moral and decent, a good and ethical person, but he failed to use his gifts for the Lord in building up the Lord's kingdom. His sin was the sin of omission, not the sin of commission. He was not actively working with the faithful servants of the Lord. He felt the Lord required too much, that the Lord was too strict.

> "And every one that heareth these sayings of mine, and doeth them not, shall be likened unto a foolish man, which built his house upon the sand: and the rain descended, and the floods came, and the winds blew, and beat upon that house; and it fell: and great was the fall of it" (Mt.7:26-27).
>
> "And that which fell among thorns are they, which, when they have heard, go forth, and are choked with cares and riches and pleasures of this life, and bring no fruit to perfection" (Lk.8:14).

"He spake also this parable; A certain man had a fig tree planted in his vineyard; and he came and sought fruit thereon, and found none" (Lk.13:6).

"And take heed to yourselves, lest at any time your hearts be overcharged with surfeiting, and drunkenness, and cares of this life, and so that day come upon you unawares. For as a snare shall it come on all them that dwell on the face of the whole earth" (Lk.21:34-35).

"Therefore to him that knoweth to do good, and doeth it not, to him it is sin" (Jas.4:17).

"Ye have lived in pleasure on the earth, and been wanton; ye have nourished your hearts, as in a day of slaughter" (Jas.5:5).

"And shall receive the reward of unrighteousness, as they that count it pleasure to riot in the day time. Spots they are and blemishes, sporting themselves with their own deceivings while they feast with you" (2 Pt.2:13).

"Ye have plowed wickedness, ye have reaped iniquity; ye have eaten the fruit of lies: because thou didst trust in thy way, in the multitude of thy mighty men" (Hos.10:13).

---

**DEEPER STUDY # 3**

(19:15-19) **Rewards—Responsibility**: moneymaking was not the purpose of the servants (see note 3—Lk.19:13). The purpose was to test them, to show how capable and responsible they were. Could they be trusted with responsibility, with the authority of God? The leaders who are needed to rule God's universe in the coming kingdom and world order must be strong and responsible. The dominant idea is that of testing, a time of trial. The Nobleman's purpose is to develop distinguished rulers: leaders that are decisive, firm, and strong.

It is interesting that the Lord spoke in the hundreds of percent—interesting that the one who really pleased the Lord exerted not 100 percent energy but 1000 percent, and the one who showed some fruitfulness labored not just 50 percent but 500 percent. Is there some significance in these percentages? Some message for God's people? Is there a servant who dares to waste a moment of time after studying what the Lord said?

---

**6** (19:24-26) **Reward**: the Lord's servant who labors 1000 percent shall be given the reward of the unfaithful. Why? Very simply, because he has proven he can handle any amount of responsibility. He had taken a little (one pound) and used it to the maximum. He was as responsible as he could be. He could and would handle and oversee whatever the Lord gave him to oversee.

Note: there were some who objected. Who it was that objected is not known. Jesus simply answered that he who had labored ever so diligently to increase would receive more and more. But the person who did not work to increase would lose even what he had (cp. 1 Cor.15:58). If a man does not use his gift, he will lose it just as a man would lose his arm if he did not use it.

"And they that be wise shall shine as the brightness of the firmament; and they that turn many to righteousness as the stars for ever and ever" (Dan.12:3).

"And whosoever shall give to drink unto one of these little ones a cup of cold water only in the name of a disciple, verily I say unto you, he shall in no wise lose his reward" (Mt.10:42).

"His lord said unto him, Well done, good and faithful servant; thou hast been faithful over a few things, I will make thee ruler over many things: enter thou into the joy of thy lord" (Mt.25:23).

"But love ye your enemies, and do good, and lend, hoping for nothing again; and your reward shall be great, and ye shall be the children of the Highest: for he is kind unto the unthankful and to the evil" (Lk.6:35).

"Knowing that whatsoever good thing any man doeth, the same shall he receive of the Lord, whether he be bond or free" (Eph.6:8).

**7** (19:27) **Judgment**: the citizens who are enemies of the Lord's rule are to be slain. There are two points to note here.

1. The man who rejects Christ and His reign over his life is an enemy of Christ. He opposes and stands against Christ.

2. The enemy of Christ shall be condemned *before Christ*. He shall suffer doom, be slain, be put to death, and be separated from God eternally and spiritually (see DEEPER STUDY # 1, *Death*—Heb.9:27).

"But the children of the kingdom shall be cast out into outer darkness: there shall be weeping and gnashing of teeth" (Mt.8:12).

"And cast ye the unprofitable servant into outer darkness: there shall be weeping and gnashing of teeth" (Mt.25:30).

"Then shall he say also unto them on the left hand, Depart from me, ye cursed, into everlasting fire, prepared for the devil and his angels" (Mt.25:41).

"And these shall go away into everlasting punishment: but the righteous into life eternal" (Mt.25:46).

"But after thy hardness and impenitent heart treasurest up unto thyself wrath against the day of wrath and revelation of the righteous judgment of God" (Ro.2:5).

"And to you who are troubled rest with us, when the Lord Jesus shall be revealed from heaven with his mighty angels, in flaming fire taking vengeance on them that know not God, and that obey not the gospel of our Lord Jesus Christ" (2 Th.1:7-8).

| | | | |
|---|---|---|---|
| | **VIII. THE SON OF MAN'S DRAMATIC ENTRANCE INTO JERUSALEM: HIS CLAIM AND CONFLICT, 19:28-21:4**<br><br>**A. The Triumphal Entry: Jesus' Claim to be King, 19:28-40**<br>(Mt.21:1-11; Mk.11:1-11; Jn.12:12-19) | even as he had said unto them.<br> 33 And as they were loosing the colt, the owners thereof said unto them, Why loose ye the colt?<br> 34 And they said, The Lord hath need of him.<br> 35 And they brought him to Jesus: and they cast their garments upon the colt, and they set Jesus thereon.<br> 36 And as he went, they spread their clothes in the way. | d. He accepted the recognition of the disciples<br><br>**3 There was the people's proclaiming Him to be King** |
| **1 There was the constraint to go to Jerusalem: To suffer & die**<br>**2 There was the deliberate claim to be King**DS1,2 | 28 And when he had thus spoken, he went before, ascending up to Jerusalem.<br> 29 And it came to pass, when he was come nigh to Bethphage and Bethany, at the mount called the mount of Olives, he sent two of his disciples, | 37 And when he was come nigh, even now at the descent of the mount of Olives, the whole multitude of the disciples began to rejoice and praise God with a loud voice for all the mighty works that they had seen; | |
| a. He planned a dramatic demonstration in detailDS3 | 30 Saying, Go ye into the village over against you; in the which at your entering ye shall find a colt tied, whereon yet never man sat: loose him, and bring him hither. | 38 Saying, Blessed be the King that cometh in the name of the Lord: peace in heaven, and glory in the highest.<br> 39 And some of the Pharisees from among the multitude said unto him, Master, rebuke thy disciples. | **4 There was the insistent claim of Jesus; He was to be proclaimed King by the people**<br>a. The religionists rebuked Him |
| b. He used the title "the Lord" in laying claim to men's property | 31 And if any man ask you, Why do ye loose him? thus shall ye say unto him, Because the Lord hath need of him. | 40 And he answered and said unto them, I tell you that, if these should hold their peace, the stones would immediately cry out. | b. Jesus insisted that proclaiming Him King was inevitable |
| c. His instructions were carefully followed | 32 And they that were sent went their way, and found | | |

# DIVISION VIII

## THE SON OF MAN'S DRAMATIC ENTRANCE INTO JERUSALEM: HIS CLAIM AND CONFLICT, 19:28-21:4

### A.    The Triumphal Entry: Jesus' Claim to be King, 19:28-40

(19:28-40) **Introduction**: this was a dramatic picture. Jesus' arrival into Jerusalem began the last week of His life. It is what we call *Holy Week* or *Palm Sunday*. Jesus was unquestionably claiming to be King, but He was claiming to be a different kind of King, a King who was different from what men usually conceived. He was claiming to be the King of Peace, the King whose kingdom is not of this earth (Jn.19:36).

1.    There was the constraint to go to Jerusalem: to suffer and die (v.28).
2.    There was the deliberate claim to be King (v.29-35).
3.    There was the people's proclaiming Him to be King (v.36-38).
4.    There was the insistent claim of Jesus: He was to be proclaimed King by the people (v.39-40).

[1]  (19:28) **Jesus Christ, Death**: there was the constraint, the drive to suffer and die. Right after Jesus had finished sharing the parable of the pounds, He felt the driving constraint to move on toward Jerusalem. There the climax of His purpose was to take place. He was to suffer and die for man. Jesus was constrained, compelled with an iron determination, to complete His purpose. Jesus was driven to die for man. His whole spirit is pictured in the words, "Therefore have I set my face like a flint" (Is.50:7. See DEEPER STUDY # 1—Lk.9:51; Mk.10:32.) Remember, Jerusalem was only about seventeen miles away. The final events were now to begin.

[2]  (19:29-35) **Jesus Christ, Claim—Messiah**: there was the deliberate claim to be King. Note four things. (See notes—Mt.21:2-5 for more discussion.)

1.    Jesus planned a dramatic demonstration in detail. The whole scene was to center around His riding into the city on a colt (see DEEPER STUDY # 3—Lk.19:30 for discussion).

2.    Jesus used the title "the Lord" in laying claim upon men and their property. "The Lord" (o kurios) is a strong expression; it is the same as saying Jehovah. Jesus was claiming the right to use the colt because He was "the Lord." The owner was bound to have been a disciple who would allow "the Lord" to borrow his animals. A man of the world might not allow the claim of the Lord to affect him.

3.    Jesus' instructions were followed carefully.

**Thought 1.** Note a crucial point. The task given to the two disciples to go and secure the colt may have seemed small, but no task is small in the proclamation of Jesus as King. Fetching the colt was extremely important if Christ were to be proclaimed as King before the people. The task was essential.

4.    Jesus accepted the recognition of the disciples. The disciples knew exactly what Jesus was doing. They acknowledged His claim by three acts.
    ⇒    They obeyed His instructions explicitly.
    ⇒    They used their own garments as a saddle.
    ⇒    They sat Jesus upon the colt.
The point is this: Jesus accepted their homage and thereby claimed to be the Messiah.

---

**DEEPER STUDY # 1**
(19:29) **Bethphage**: means *House of Figs*. It was a suburb of Jerusalem, lying toward the Mount of Olives. Note that Jesus arrived in Bethphage by foot. This pictures the great humiliation to which the Son of God subjected Himself in order to come to earth and save man. While on earth, He had no means of travelling except by walking.

---

**DEEPER STUDY # 2**
(19:29) **Bethany**: it was a suburb of Jerusalem, about two miles east. The city was the home of Lazarus, Mary, and Martha. Jesus stayed with the family when ministering in and around Jerusalem. One must remember that Jesus apparently had no home of His own. His immediate family did not believe in His claims (Jn.7:1-5, esp.5). He Himself said, "The foxes have holes, and the birds of the air have nests, but the Son of man hath not where to lay his head" (Mt.8:20). The only housing He had was the home of others such as Martha and Mary (Jn.11:1f; cp. Lk.11:1f; Lk.10:38-42; Jn.12:1f).

---

**DEEPER STUDY # 3**
(19:30) **Colt—Ass**: in ancient days the colt or donkey was a noble animal. It was used as a beast of service to carry the burdens of men. More significantly, it was used by Kings and their emissaries when they entered a city in peace. They rode a colt to symbolize their peaceful intentions (cp. the judges of Israel and the chieftains throughout the land, Judges 5:10; 10:4). This differed dramatically from a conquering King. When a King entered a city as a conqueror, he rode a stallion.
    Jesus was dramatically demonstrating two things: first, He was unquestionably the promised King, the Savior of the people; and second, He was not coming as the people expected. He was not coming as a conquering king or as a worldly potentate in pomp and ceremony, nor as the leader of an army to kill, injure, and maim. Therefore, the people must change their concept of the Messiah, for He was coming as the Savior of Peace. He was coming to save men not to destroy them. He was coming to show men that God is the God of love and reconciliation.
    1.    The colt was a symbol of peace. Jesus came to bring peace, as pointed out in the above discussion.
    2.    The colt symbolized service. It was a noble animal, an animal used in the service of men to carry their burdens. Jesus came upon the colt symbolizing that He came to serve men, to bear their burdens for them.
    3.    The colt symbolized sacredness, for it had never been ridden before (v.2). Animals and things used for sacred or religious purposes had to be animals and things that had never been used before (Num.10:2; Dt.21:3; 1 Sam.6:7). This detail points to the sacredness of the event. It pictured that Jesus was deliberately taking every precaution to proclaim that *He is the sacred hope*, the promised Messiah of the people.

---

**3**    (19:36-38) **Messiah, Misconceptions**: there was the people's proclaiming Him to be King. Three facts need to be noted in this point.
    1.    The people praised God for all the mighty works they had seen. There were teeming thousands lining the roadway, throwing their cloaks down ahead of Him. (See note—Mt.21:8-9 for more discussion.) The people had just recently seen miracle after miracle including the raising of Lazarus from the dead. The whole atmosphere was electric with excitement and expectation. The people knew Jesus had the power to do anything: He could bring the Kingdom of God to earth.

> **"How God anointed Jesus of Nazareth with the Holy Ghost and with power: who went about doing good, and healing all that were oppressed of the devil; for God was with him" (Acts 10:38).**
> **"I know that thou canst do every thing, and that no thought can be withholden from thee" (Job 42:2).**
> **"But our God is in the heavens: he hath done whatsoever he hath pleased" (Ps.115:3).**

    2.    They proclaimed Jesus to be "the King that cometh in the name of the Lord." They thought the hour had arrived. Jesus was going to usher in the Kingdom of God *now*. (See note—Lk.19:11.) God was going...
    •    to free all the nations of the earth from Roman domination.
    •    to set up the throne of Jesus in Jerusalem from which the rule and reign of righteousness would be executed.
    •    to establish Israel as the leading nation of the earth.

> **"And as they heard these things, he added and spake a parable, because he was nigh to Jerusalem, and because they thought that the kingdom of God should immediately appear" (Lk.19:11).**

3. The people failed to see several things.
   a. They failed to see that Jesus was riding a colt, coming as the King of Peace.

   > "Through the tender mercy of our God; whereby the dayspring [Christ] from on high hath visited us, to give light to them that sit in darkness and in the shadow of death, to guide our feet into the way of peace" (Lk.1:78-79).
   > "Glory to God in the highest, and on earth peace, good will toward men" (Lk.2:14).
   > "Peace I leave with you, my peace I give unto you: not as the world giveth, give I unto you. Let not your heart be troubled, neither let it be afraid" (Jn.14:27; cp. Jn.16:33).
   > "For the kingdom of God is not meat and drink; but righteousness, and peace, and joy in the Holy Ghost" (Ro.14:17).
   > "The LORD will give strength unto his people; the LORD will bless his people with peace" (Ps.29:11).

   b. They failed to see that Jesus was riding the animal of burdens, coming as the King who wished to bear the burdens of men.

   > "Wherefore in all things it behoved him to be made like unto his brethren, that he might be a merciful and faithful high priest in things pertaining to God, to make reconciliation for the sins of the people. For in that he himself hath suffered being tempted, he is able to succour them that are tempted" (Heb.2:17-18).
   > "For we have not an high priest which cannot be touched with the feeling of our infirmities; but was in all points tempted like as we are, yet without sin" (Heb.4:15-16).

   c. They failed to see that Jesus was riding the animal that symbolized sacredness, coming for the purpose of saving the people spiritually. (See note—Eph.1:1-3.)
   d. They failed to see that Jesus was riding the animal that symbolized meekness, coming as the King of meekness.

   > "Come unto me, all ye that labour and are heavy laden, and I will give you rest. Take my yoke upon you, and learn of me; for I am meek and lowly in heart: and ye shall find rest unto your souls" (Mt.11:28-29).
   > "Who, when he was reviled, reviled not again; when he suffered, he threatened not; but committed himself to him that judgeth righteously: who his own self bare our sins in his own body on the tree, that we, being dead to sins, should live unto righteousness: by whose stripes ye were healed" (1 Pt.2:23-24).

**4** (19:39-40) **Jesus Christ, Claim—Praise**: there was the insistent claim of Jesus. He was to be proclaimed King by the people. The religious authorities were hostile. They had already given the word to hunt Jesus down and arrest Him (Jn.11:57). Despite this threat, Jesus publicly and triumphantly entered Jerusalem. The great weight and importance of His mission, "to seek and save that which was lost," is clearly seen in such courageous behavior. (See notes—Mk.11:1-11.)

> "Nathanael answered and saith unto him, Rabbi, thou art the Son of God; thou art the King of Israel" (Jn.1:49).
> "Pilate therefore said unto him, Art thou a king then? Jesus answered, Thou sayest that I am a king. To this end was I born, and for this cause came I into the world, that I should bear witness unto the truth. Every one that is of the truth heareth my voice" (Jn.18:37).

Note the clear declaration to deity that Jesus made: "I tell you that, if these [the praising crowds] should hold their peace, the stones would immediately cry out." Nature did cry out when He hung upon the cross. The world and the disciples had forsaken Him, but the sun hid its face and the earth split asunder in a demonstration of the cry of nature (cp. Mt.27:45, 51-52).

> "Let the heaven and earth praise him, the seas, and every thing that moveth therein" (Ps.69:34).
> "Sing, O ye heavens; for the LORD hath done it: shout, ye lower parts of the earth: break forth into singing, ye mountains, O forest, and every tree therein: for the LORD hath redeemed Jacob, and glorified himself in Israel" (Is.44:23).
> "Sing, O heavens; and be joyful, O earth; and break forth into singing, O mountains: for the LORD hath comforted his people, and will have mercy upon his afflicted" (Is.49:13).

| | B. The Dramatic Prediction: Judgment Upon Jerusalem, 19:41-44 (cp. Mt.23:37-39; Lk.13:34-35) | eyes. 43 For the days shall come upon thee, that thine enemies shall cast a trench about thee, and compass thee round, and keep thee in on every side, | 2 The terrible fate of the city foretold a. Was to be encircled |
|---|---|---|---|
| 1 The great love of Jesus for the city a. He wept over the city b. The city had rejected the way of peace; that is, it rejected the Messiah*DS1* | 41 And when he was come near, he beheld the city, and wept over it, 42 Saying, If thou hadst known, even thou, at least in this thy day, the things which belong unto thy peace! but now they are hid from thine | 44 And shall lay thee even with the ground, and thy children within thee; and they shall not leave in thee one stone upon another; because thou knewest not the time of thy visitation. | b. Was to be utterly destroyed c. Was to be personally judged 3 The cause of the city's doom |

# DIVISION VIII

## THE SON OF MAN'S DRAMATIC ENTRANCE INTO JERUSALEM: HIS CLAIM AND CONFLICT, 19:28-21:4

## B. The Dramatic Prediction: Judgment Upon Jerusalem, 19:41-44

**(19:41-44) Introduction**: this passage is covered only by Luke. It is full of prophecy and compassion, the prediction of Jerusalem's terrible fate and the compassion of our Lord for a people doomed to utter destruction. The truth of Scripture is also demonstrated in this passage, the truth that Scripture is God's Word. There is also the truth that sin dooms a nation, but righteousness exalts a nation and its people.

1. The great love of Jesus for the city (v.41-42).
2. The terrible fate of the city foretold (v.43-44).
3. The cause for the city's doom (v.44).

**(19:41-48) Another Outline**. A Look at Jesus.
1. The compassion of Jesus (v.41-44).
2. The anger of Jesus (v.45-46).
3. The courage of Jesus (v.47-48).

**1** (19:41-42) **Jerusalem—Jesus Christ, Compassion**: the city was greatly loved by Jesus (see outline and notes—Mt.23:37-39; Lk.13:34-35).
1. Jesus wept over the city. Note three facts.
   a. The word "wept" (eklausen) means to burst into tears, to weep out loud, to sob, to wail, to mourn. Jesus was literally heartbroken over Jerusalem.
   b. The words "beheld the city" mean He was looking and gazing upon the city with **deep** intensity. He was looking upon, considering, regarding the city in all its tragic state.
   c. Jesus was weeping while the city was engaged in the excitement of feasting and **fellowshipping** in a jovial, party-like spirit. The whole atmosphere was like that of a present-day **convention**. The scene can be imagined. But while the people were in such a partying mood, Jesus was off on the **hillside** weeping over the city and its people.
2. The reason for Jesus' weeping was stated by Jesus Himself: the city and its people had rejected the way of peace, that is, the Messiah Himself. Another way to say it is, they had rejected the things which make for peace.
   a. Jesus was not weeping because He was to suffer and die in the city. He was not weeping over Himself, not yet. He was weeping over the city and its people, weeping because they did not know the way of peace.
   b. There are things which make for peace, things which bring peace both to the hearts of men and to the society and world of men (see DEEPER STUDY # 1—Lk.19:42 for discussion).
   c. The things that bring peace are "hid from [the people's] eyes." This statement has two possible meanings. First, the people closed their eyes to Jesus and His message of peace. They refused to see; therefore, they did not see. Second, God counted Jerusalem as having lost its opportunity. He had shown patience for generation after generation (see outline and notes—Mt.23:37); now the time for judgment had come. God hid "the things of peace" from their eyes. He turned Jerusalem over to their blindness (see notes, *Judicial Judgment*—Mt.13:13-15; DEEPER STUDY # 1—Jn.12:39-41; note—Ro.1:24-25; DEEPER STUDY # 2—11:7-10).

> "For this people's heart is waxed gross, and their ears are dull of hearing, and their ears are dull of hearing, and their eyes they have closed; lest at any time they should see with their eyes, and hear with their ears, and should understand with their heart, and should be converted, and I should heal them" (Mt.13:15).

---

**DEEPER STUDY # 1**
(19:42) **Peace** (eriene): to bind together, to join and weave together. It means that one is bound, woven, joined together with himself and with God and with others.

The Hebrew word is *shalom*. It means freedom from trouble and much, much more. It means experiencing the highest good, enjoying the very best, possessing all the inner good possible.

There are two kinds of peace mentioned in the Scripture.
1.    There is the *peace of the world*. This is a peace of escapism, of avoiding trouble, of refusing to face things, of unreality.
2.    There is the *peace of Christ and of God*. This is a *bosom peace*, a peace deep within. It is a tranquility of mind, a composure, a peace that settles and strengthens the believer even through the most terrible circumstances and situations. It is more than feelings, even more than attitude and thought.
    a.    God's bosom peace is the *peace of conquest*. It is the peace independent of conditions and environment; the peace which no sorrow, danger, suffering, or experience can take away.

> **"Peace I leave with you, my peace I give unto you: not as the world giveth, give I unto you. Let not your heart be troubled, neither let it be afraid" (Jn.14:27).**
> **"These things I have spoken unto you, that in me ye might have peace. In the world ye shall have tribulation: but be of good cheer; I have overcome the world" (Jn.16:33)**

    b.    God's bosom peace is the *peace of perfect assurance*. It is the peace of unquestionable confidence; the peace with a sure knowledge that a person's life is in the hands of God and that all things will work out for good to those who love God and are called according to His purpose.

> **"And we know that all things work together for good to them that love God, to them who are the called according to his purpose" (Ro.8:28).**
> **"Being confident of this very thing, that he which hath begun a good work in you will perform it until the day of Jesus Christ" (Ph.1:6).**
> **"I know whom I have believed, and am persuaded that he is able to keep that which I have committed unto him against that day" (2 Tim.1:12).**

    c.    God's bosom peace is the *peace of intimacy with God*. It is the peace of the highest good. It is the peace that settles the mind, strengthens the will, and establishes the heart.

> **"Therefore being justified by faith, we have peace with God through our Lord Jesus Christ" (Ro.5:1; cp. v.2-5).**
> **"Be careful for nothing; but in every thing by prayer and supplication with thanksgiving let your requests be made known unto God" (Ph.4:6-7).**

There is *the source of peace*. Peace is always born out of reconciliation. Its source is found only in the reconciliation wrought by Jesus Christ. Peace always has to do with personal relationships: a man's relationship to himself, to God, and to his fellow man. A man must be bound, woven, and joined together with himself, with God, and with his fellow man (cp. Eph.2:13-14).

*Man secures peace* in the following manner.
1.    By justification (Ro.5:1)
2.    By loving God's Word (Ps.119:165; Jn.16:33)
3.    By praying about everything (Ph.4:7)
4.    By being spiritually minded (Ro.8:6)
5.    By keeping his mind upon God (Is.26:3; Ph.4:8)
6.    By keeping God's commandments (Is.48:18; Ph.4:9)

The *subject of peace* is often divided as (1) Peace with God (Ro.5:1; Eph.2:14-17), (2) the Peace of God (Lk.7:50; Ph.4:6-7), and (3) Peace from God (Ro.1:7; 1 Cor.1:3).

**2**    (19:43-44) **Jerusalem—Judgment, Upon Nations**: the city's terrible fate. Three major things were to be involved in Jerusalem's destruction.
1.    The city was to have a trench dug around it, completely encircling the city. The ditch and dirt mound shoveled from it served as a protective wall for the Roman army. Sharp-pointed wooden stakes were driven into the mound of dirt, sticking up facing the encircled city in the event that the city's army launched a counterattack. The city was to have an army launched against it in a full-fledged military attack.
2.    The city was to be utterly destroyed. It was to be completely demolished and razed to the ground; not one stone was to be left upon another.
3.    The people were to be *personally* judged. Note the words, "Thy children within thee" shall be laid to the ground. Also note that the word "you" is used ten times in two verses (v.42-44). The prediction is very personal. Cities and nations may fall under the judgment of God, but it is the people who are at fault and who shall be personally judged.

What Christ said was literally fulfilled by the attack of Titus in 70 A.D. In 66 A.D. the Jews revolted and the Roman army was swift to attack, but the city was difficult to take, primarily for two reasons. It sat upon a hill, well protected by the terrain, and the leaders of the revolt were religious fanatics. Well over a million people had fled into the city behind its protective walls.

As the siege wore on, the predictions of Christ were literally fulfilled. Outside the walls sat the Roman army with all the maiming and killing of war. Inside the walls neighbor after neighbor faced famine, pestilence, false deliverers (messiahs), betrayal, murder, revolt, rebellion, and hatred—and all took their toll. Josephus says over 1,000,000 people died and 97,000 were taken captive. He describes well the horrors of the siege (see notes—Mt.24:7; 24:10; 24:11. See Flavius Josephus. *Josephus Complete Works*, translated by William Whiston. Grand Rapids, MI: Kregel, 1960. <u>Wars</u>. 5. 12:3; 6. 3:4; 6. 8:5.)

> **"It appears to me that the misfortunes of all men, from the beginning of the world, if they be compared to these of the Jews, are not so considerable as they were" (Josephus, <u>Wars</u>. Preface 4). (See outline and notes—Mt.24:1-14 for a descriptive picture of the utter destruction of Jerusalem.)**

**Thought 1.** Jerusalem is a prime example of the fate of a nation that rejects God. It is doomed to fall.

> **"He that believeth on the Son hath everlasting life: and he that believeth not the Son shall not see life; but the wrath of God abideth on him" (Jn.3:36).**
> **"I said therefore unto you, that ye shall die in your sins: for if ye believe not that I am he, ye shall die in your sins" (Jn.8:24).**
> **"All day long I have stretched forth my hands unto a disobedient and gainsaying people" (Ro.10:21).**
> **"By the blessing of the upright the city is exalted: but it is overthrown by the mouth of the wicked" (Pr.11:11).**
> **"Righteousness exalteth a nation: but sin is a reproach to any people" (Pr.14:34).**
> **"It is an abomination to kings to commit wickedness: for the throne is established by righteousness" (Pr.16:12).**
> **"Take away the wicked from before the king, and his throne shall be established in righteousness" (Pr.25:5).**

**3** (19:44) **Jerusalem—Judgment Upon Nations**: the cause of the city's doom. The people rejected the day of the Messiah or the day of their salvation.

1. Their day of visitation came. God had always visited Israel; they had the revelation...
   - of God Himself down through the centuries.
   - of God's Word, the Scriptures of the Old Testament.
   - of God's messengers and prophets.
   - of God's active presence in the lives of believers.

Now they had the very presence of God's Messiah, the Son of God Himself (cp. Ro.9:4-5).

2. They did not know Him, and there was no excuse, for they could clearly see that God was at work once again among His people. It had been three to four hundred years since the Old Testament had closed and the last prophet had appeared. The evidence was clear and strong that the day of prophecy had been opened once again. The promised Messiah, the day of Israel's salvation had come, but the people rejected the evidence. They were doomed by their rejection, and Jesus wept because they refused to see the day of their salvation.

> **"O Jerusalem, Jerusalem, which killest the prophets, and stonest them that are sent unto thee; how often would I have gathered thy children together, as a hen doth gather her brood under her wings, and ye would not! Behold, your house is left unto you desolate: and verily I say unto you, Ye shall not see me, until the time come when ye shall say, Blessed is he that cometh in the name of the Lord" (Lk.13:34-35).**

| | | written, My house is he house of prayer: but ye have made it a den of thieves. | a. The place of His presence & dwelling |
|---|---|---|---|
| **C. The Cleansing of the Temple: The Righteous Anger of Jesus, 19:45-48** (Mt.21:12-16; Mk.11:15-19; cp. Jn.2:13-16) | | 47 And he taught daily in the temple. But the chief priests and the scribes and the chief of the people sought to destroy him, | b. The place of prayer c. The place for teaching the Word of God **3 The results of His cleansing the temple** a. The leaders: Sought to destroy Him |
| **1 How He cleansed the temple: Cast people out** a. Those who profaned b. Those who exploited **2 Why He cleansed the temple** | 45 And he went into the temple, and began to cast out them that sold therein, and them that bought; 46 Saying unto them, It is | 48 And could not find what they might do: for all the people were very attentive to hear him. | b. The people: Listened to Him attentively |

# DIVISION VIII

## THE SON OF MAN'S DRAMATIC ENTRANCE INTO JERUSALEM: HIS CLAIM AND CONFLICT, 19:28-21:4

## C. The Cleansing of the Temple: The Righteous Anger of Jesus, 19:45-48

(19:45-48) **Introduction**: the anger of Jesus is seen in this passage. It is important to note what angered Him: the abuse of God's temple.

⇒ The believer's body is the temple of God, and it angered Him to see the body abused (1 Cor.6:19-20).
⇒ The church is the temple of God, and it angered Him to see the church abused (see note—1 Cor.3:16; 3:17).

The church is the temple of God. This fact is often de-emphasized by believers and overlooked by the world. But no matter how man treats the church, Jesus proclaims the church to be God's, to be His holy temple. The church is the place that is set apart for prayer, worship, and communion with God.
1. How He cleansed the temple: cast people out (v.45).
2. Why He cleansed the temple (v.46).
3. The results of His cleansing the temple (v.47-48).

**1** (19:45) **Temple—Church**: How did Jesus cleanse the temple? He "cast out" those who profaned and exploited the temple. This took place in the outer court of the temple, the court of the Gentiles, which was where Gentiles worshipped. It was tragically abused. It had become nothing more than a commercial marketplace owned and, in many cases, operated by the priests. It was used for the selling and buying of sacrificial animals which included oxen and sheep as well as smaller doves and pigeons. It was also used for the inspection of the animals' purity and for the exchanging of foreign currencies. Every Passover season found thousands of pilgrims coming to the temple from all over the world travelling great distances. It was usually impossible for a pilgrim to bring his own animal for sacrifice; but if he did, he had to get it by the inspector, which often cost a fee. The bickering back and forth created an atmosphere of utter chaos that apparently gave off the sound of a human volcanic uproar. Picture a modern-day trade show—large, crowded, extremely noisy—and add to that the presence of animals and the exchanging of thousands of coins (see note, pt.2—Eph.2:14-15).

Hundreds of thousands of animals were sold at the great feasts, and unfortunately, the High Priest and other priests were often in the middle of the commercialism. It is this commercialism and secularism of religion that Jesus lashed out against. (See note—Mt.21:12-16 for detailed discussion and thoughts.)

> "And said unto them that sold doves, Take these things hence; make not my Father's house an house of merchandise" (Jn.2:16).
> "What? have ye not houses to eat and to drink in [businesses to buy and sell in]? or despise ye the church of God, and shame them that have not? What shall I say to you? shall I praise you in this? I praise you not" (1 Cor.11:22).
> "Ye shall keep my sabbaths, and reverence my sanctuary: I am the LORD" (Lev.19:30).
> "Keep thy foot when thou goest to the house of God, and be more ready to hear, than to give the sacrifice of fools: for they consider not that they do evil" (Eccl.5:1).
> "For the children of Judah have done evil in my sight, saith the LORD: they have set their abominations in the house which is called by my name, to pollute it" (Jer.7:30).
> "Her [the temple, the churches] prophets are light and treacherous persons: her priests have polluted the sanctuary, they have done violence to the law" (Zeph.3:4).

**2** (19:46-47) **Temple**: Why did Jesus cleanse the temple? Jesus' attitude toward the temple is clearly seen in this verse. The same attitude, of course, would be true of the church. He held the temple in the highest regard.
1. Jesus called the temple (church) "My house." This says at least two things to people of every generation.
   a. The temple or church is the place where He dwells and lives: it is the place where His presence is. However, considering that God is omnipresent (everywhere) what could Jesus have meant? Very simply, the church is a place that has been *set apart* (sanctified) especially for Him. The church is the very special place designated for Him; it is the place that is different from all other places, different in that it is the place set aside for God's very own presence to be known.

Note: Jesus said in another place that the temple is related so closely to God that it actually *reveals and reflects God's nature*. This is seen in His demand that men not swear by the temple. Why? Because the temple or church is God's, of His plan and purpose; therefore, the church is of Him, of His very nature (Mt.23:16f).

> **"God is a Spirit: and they that worship him must worship him in spirit and in truth" (Jn.4:24).**
> **"But unto the place which the LORD your God shall choose out of all your tribes to put his name there, even unto his habitation shall ye seek, and thither thou shalt come" (Dt.12:5).**
> **"LORD, I have loved the habitation of thy house, and the place where thine honour dwelleth" (Ps.26:8).**
> **"One thing have I desired of the LORD, that will I seek after; that I may dwell in the house of the LORD all the days of my life, to behold the beauty of the LORD, and to enquire in his temple" (Ps.27:4).**
> **"Blessed is the man whom thou choosest, and causest to approach unto thee, that he may dwell in thy courts: we shall be satisfied with the goodness of thy house, even of thy holy temple" (Ps.65:4).**

b. The word "My" is possessive: the temple is the Lord's; it belongs to Him. He possesses and owns it. The people in the temple are only ministers, not owners; therefore, whatever is done in the temple is to be what He wants done. His house is to be operated as He wills, and His servants are to do His bidding, not violating, profaning, or exploiting His house. (See note—1 Cor.3:16; 3:17.)

> **"Surely goodness and mercy shall follow me all the days of my life: and I will dwell in the house of the LORD for ever" (Ps.23:6).**
> **"For a day in thy courts is better than a thousand. I had rather be a doorkeeper in the house of my God, than to dwell in the tents of wickedness" (Ps.84:10).**
> **"I was glad when they said unto me, Let us go into the house of the LORD" (Ps.122:1).**

2. Jesus called the temple "the house of prayer." Jesus' words are actually a quotation from two Scriptures.

> **"Mine house shall be called an house of prayer for all people" (Is.56:7).**
> **"Is this house, which is called by my name, become a den of robbers in your eyes?" (Jer.7:11).**

Note three points.

a. The temple or church is called a house of prayer, not a house of sacrifice, nor a house of offerings, teaching, prophecy, or preaching. Everything done within the House of God is to lead to prayer, the *worship of and communion with* the Father.

b. The temple or church is to be the house of prayer. Men are to pray everywhere, but they are to go to the church to pray also. The church is the very special place *set aside* for God. It is the place where all of God's people come together; therefore, it is a very special place for prayer.

> **"And he came to Nazareth, where he had been brought up: and, as his custom was, he went into the synagogue on the sabbath day, and stood up for to read" (Lk.4:16).**
> **"And they worshipped him, and returned to Jerusalem with great joy: and were continually in the temple, praising and blessing God" (Lk.24:52-53).**
> **"Give unto the LORD the glory due unto his name: bring an offering, and come before him: worship the LORD in the beauty of holiness" (1 Chron.16:29).**
> **"Give unto the LORD the glory due unto his name; worship the LORD in the beauty of holiness" (Ps.29:2).**
> **"O come, let us worship and bow down: let us kneel before the LORD our maker" (Ps.95:6).**
> **"O worship the LORD in the beauty of holiness: fear before him, all the earth" (Ps.96:9).**
> **"Exalt ye the LORD our God, and worship at his footstool; for he is holy" (Ps.99:5).**
> **"And the inhabitants of one city shall go to another, saying, Let us go speedily to pray before the LORD, and to seek the LORD of hosts: I will go also" (Zech.8:21).**

c. The temple or church is not to be used as a commercial place. It is not to be a place of buying and selling, marketing and retailing, stealing and cheating. It is not to be profaned. The church is the House of God, God's House of Prayer. It is to be a place of sanctity, refined and purified by God Himself. It is to be a place of quietness and meditation, a place set aside for worship, not for buying and selling and securing gain.

> **"Ye shall keep my sabbaths, and reverence my sanctuary: I am the LORD" (Lev.19:30).**

"And he said, Draw not nigh hither: put off thy shoes from off thy feet, for the place whereon thou standest is holy ground" (Ex.3:5).

"God is greatly to be feared in the assembly of the saints, and to be had in reverence of all them that are about him" (Ps.89:7).

"But the LORD is in his holy temple: let all the earth keep silence before him" (Hab.2:20).

3. Christ used the temple as a place for teaching. Note three things.

   a. He taught daily in the temple. It was the place where the people had gathered for the purpose of hearing the Word of God, so He met their need and fulfilled that purpose.

   b. It was not enough to cleanse the temple. He was compelled to be about God's business, that of proclaiming God's Word in God's house.

   c. He was about God's business while others were still misusing the temple and plotting against His life. He was busy carrying out the purpose of the temple while others were profaning and misusing it. He used the temple as the house of teaching, teaching which led men into prayer and worship and communion with God.

   "And he said unto them, How is it that ye sought me [in the temple]? wist ye not that I must be about my Father's business?" (Lk.2:49).

   "And many people shall go and say, Come ye, and let us go up to the mountain of the LORD, to the house of the God of Jacob; and he will teach us of his ways, and we will walk in his paths: for out of Zion shall go forth the law, and the word of the LORD from Jerusalem" (Is.2:3).

   "And many nations shall come, and say, Come, and let us go up to the mountain of the LORD, and to the house of the God of Jacob; and he will teach us of his ways, and we will walk in his paths: for the law shall go forth of Zion, and the word of the LORD from Jerusalem" (Mic.4:2).

[3] (19:47-48) **Temple—Church**: the results of Christ's cleansing the temple were twofold.

1. The leaders sought to destroy Christ. The leaders were the chief priests and Scribes, that is, those who were *professional religionists*. There were also "the chief of the people," that is, lay leaders and people from among the ruling class.

Note two things.

   a. The leaders were actively seeking to "destroy" (apolesai) Christ. The word means to *utterly destroy*. (Imagine *religious leaders'* being so disturbed that they seek to destroy and ruin the ministry of a person.)

   b. The reason why the leaders were so disturbed was twofold: first, they were losing control of the temple; and second, they were losing control of the people. Jesus had invaded their temple by cleansing it, and He was teaching the true gospel of the Kingdom of God and righteousness. They were losing money because Jesus had cast out the vendors, and their own personal ideas and control were being undermined. They were unwilling to accept the truth personally and to surrender their lives to Jesus. (See notes—Mt.12:1-8; note and DEEPER STUDY # 1—12:10 for more discussion.)

**Thought 1.** The leaders were making the same two mistakes made by men of every generation.

1) They were letting their *greed* keep them from Christ.

   "For the love of money is the root of all evil: which while some coveted after, they have erred from the faith, and pierced themselves through with many sorrows" (1 Tim.6:10).

   "Your gold and silver is cankered; and the rust of them shall be a witness against you, and shall eat your flesh as it were fire. Ye have heaped treasure together for the last days" (Jas.5:3).

   "Better is a little with righteousness, than great revenues without right" (Pr.16:8).

   "As the partridge sitteth on eggs, and hatcheth them not; so he that getteth riches, and not by right, shall leave them in the midst of his days, and at his end shall be a fool" (Jer.17:11).

2) They were letting their self-confidence and self-righteousness keep them from Christ. Just think about it! Not a single leader, civil or religious, thought God would ever reject him or keep him out of heaven. Every one of them thought he was good enough to be acceptable to God, yet not a single one is in heaven today.

   "Not every one that saith unto me, Lord, Lord, shall enter into the kingdom of heaven; but he that doeth the will of my Father which is in heaven" (Mt.7:21).

   "He answered and said unto them, Well hath Esaias prophesied of you hypocrites, as it is written, This people honoureth me with their lips, but their heart is far from me" (Mk.7:6).

   "They profess that they know God; but in works they deny him, being abominable, and disobedient, and unto every good work reprobate" (Tit.1:16).

"Most men will proclaim every one his own goodness: but a faithful man who can find?" (Pr.20:6).

"There is a generation that curseth their father, and doth not bless their mother" (Pr.30:12).

"Ye have plowed wickedness, ye have reaped iniquity; ye have eaten the fruit of lies: because thou didst trust in thy way, in the multitude of thy mighty men" (Hos.10:13).

"The pride of thine heart hath deceived thee, thou that dwellest in the clefts of the rock, whose habitation is high; that saith in his heart, Who shall bring me down to the ground? Though thou exalt thyself as the eagle, and though thou set thy nest among the stars, thence will I bring thee down, saith the LORD" (Obad.3-4).

2.   The people listened to Jesus. The word "attentive" (exekremeto) means they hung upon Jesus, gave Him rapt attention, were struck by Him. The picture is this: since the Triumphal Entry the day before, *teeming thousands* were clinging to Him, anxious to hear His word as much as they could. Note: it was His popularity among the people that kept the leaders from arresting Him. They just could not find a time or place to carry out their terrible scheme without causing an uprising among the people.

**Thought 1.** How many give rapt attention to Jesus today? If we were truly concentrating our attention upon Him like we should, would there be so much opposition to the gospel? Would society be different? Would evil be held back and controlled more?

"With my soul have I desired thee in the night; yea, with my spirit within me will I seek thee early: for when thy judgments are in the earth, the inhabitants of the world will learn righteousness" (Is.26:9).

"Blessed are they which do hunger and thirst after righteousness: for they shall be filled" (Mt.5:6).

"Lord, all my desire is before thee; and my groaning is not hid from thee" (Ps.38:9; cp. Ps.63:1).

| | | CHAPTER 20 | 3 And he answered and said unto them, I will also ask you one thing; and answer me: | d. Jesus appealed to the logic of men: Was John the Baptist of God of or men? |
|---|---|---|---|---|
| | | **D. The Question of Authority: Who is Jesus? 20:1-8** (Mt.21:23-27; Mk.11:27-33) | 4 The baptism of John, was it from heaven, or of men? | |
| **1 The unbelief of men vs. Jesus** | | And it came to pass, that on one of those days, as he taught the people in the temple, and preached the gospel, the chief priests and the scribes came upon him with the elders, | 5 And they reasoned with themselves, saying, If we shall say, From heaven; he will say, Why then believed ye him not? | **2 Possibility 1: His authority was of God** |
| a. Jesus taught & preached the gospel | | | | |
| b. Unbelief caused men to close their ears to the gospel | | | 6 But and if we say, Of men; all the people will stone us: for they be persuaded that John was a prophet. | **3 Possibility 2: His authority was of men** |
| c. Unbelief caused men to question the authority of Jesus | | 2 And spake unto him, saying, Tell us, by what authority doest thou these things? or who is he that gave thee this authority? | 7 And they answered, that they could not tell whence it was. | **4 Possibility 3: Indecision & silence** |
| | | | 8 And Jesus said unto them, Neither tell I you by what authority I do these things. | |

# DIVISION VIII

## THE SON OF MAN'S DRAMATIC ENTRANCE INTO JERUSALEM: HIS CLAIM AND CONFLICT, 19:28-21:4

## D. The Question of Authority: Who is Jesus? 20:1-8

(20:1-8) **Introduction**: this passage begins a series of attacks upon Jesus. Question after question was asked Him in an attempt to discredit His claim to be the true Messiah, the Son of God. But the questions were to no avail. The present passage is basic, it is the question of authority: Who is Jesus?

1. The unbelief of men vs. Jesus (v.1-4).
2. Possibility 1: His authority was of God (v.5).
3. Possibility 2: His authority was of men (v.6).
4. Possibility 3: indecision and silence (v.7-8).

1 (20:1-4) **Unbelief**: there was unbelief vs. Jesus. This is a striking picture.

1. Jesus was teaching and preaching the gospel. He shared the good news about the Kingdom of God and the great hope for man through repentance. A large crowd listened "very attentively" (Lk.19:48), soaking up every word He said and having the hope of God stirred within their hearts. The words of the Lord were being driven home to the need of the human heart.

2. But note what happened. Unbelief caused men to close their ears to the gospel. The religionists were standing there listening to Jesus just as so many others were, yet their motives differed from the crowd. They were not seeking God beyond their own ideas of religion. They had...

- critical and unbelieving hearts.
- a fear of worldly ridicule, disapproval, and unacceptance.
- a concern for livelihood, security, profession, and position.

They were not interested in discovering the truth about Jesus. They were only interested in tricking Him and discrediting Him before the people. They wanted the people's loyalty to their own *religious position*. The truth mattered little. Their ears were closed and their eyes were blinded to the truth because of their obstinate unbelief.

3. Note another fact about unbelief. Unbelief caused men to question the authority of Jesus, just who He really was. This was the basic question to ask, a question that probed into the very nature of Jesus. What was His authority, who sent Him, who empowered Him, who gave Him the right to do as He was doing? Where had He come from? Just who was He?

The leaders wanted to know what right He had to interfere with their lives and area of responsibility. They were the authorized guardians and rulers of the temple and of the people. He was interfering with their management and had no right to do so. They asked Him two questions.

a. What was the authority for His works? "By what authority doest thou *these things*?" He had marched triumphantly into the city of Jerusalem as a King, receiving the homage of the Messianic King from the people; He had cast the market traders out of the temple; He had healed the blind and lame (Mt.21:14); and He had accepted the homage of small children proclaiming Him to be the Messiah. What authority did He have to do such things?

**Thought 1.** The leaders were asking the basic question that needed to be asked. It is the question that every man needs to ask: What is the authority, the explanation for the works of Christ? The works of...

| | |
|---|---|
| • ministry | • preaching |
| • healing | • calming the storms of nature |
| • teaching | • foretelling the future |
| • raising the dead | • dying and fulfilling Scripture |
| • rising again | • ascending into heaven |

b. What was the authority of His person: *"Who gave thee* this authority?" He *was claiming...*
- to be the promised Messianic King by entering the city as He did.
- to be the Head, the God of the Temple: "My house."
- to be the Light of the world to the blind and the Messianic Healer to the lame (Mt.21:14).
- to be the Messianic fulfillment of Scripture by receiving the praise of the children.

The authorities knew who Jesus was claiming to be. They just rejected His claim and refused to believe. They chose the course of obstinate unbelief, still refusing to believe despite having proof upon proof.

There were two possible answers to the question of who Jesus was.
⇒ Jesus could have claimed to be acting by His own authority, saying that His power was His own. This, of course, would have made Him an ego-maniac or a great imposter (the greatest in history). Of course, if He had claimed to act by His own authority, they would have discredited Him immediately and arrested Him for causing so much havoc.
⇒ Jesus could have claimed to be acting by the authority of God, to be of and from God. Now note: this was the claim that Jesus made time and again. But if He had made it then and there in the face of the authorities, they would have arrested Him immediately for blasphemy. They would claim that God would never give orders to cause such turmoil in the temple.

Again the leaders were asking the basic question that needs to be asked by every man. *Who gave Jesus* His authority? Who is He: a mere man or truly the Son of God? Is He *of man* or *of God*? Is His authority of men or inherent, that is, from within, of His very own nature as God?
4. Very simply, Jesus appealed to the truth and logic of John the Baptist: "Was [John] from heaven, or of men?"

**2** (20:5) **Jesus Christ, Deity—Unbelief**: the first possibility was that Jesus' authority was *of God. John pointed* toward Christ and proclaimed...
- "Behold the Lamb of God" (Jn.1:29).
- "I saw and *bare record* that this is the Son of God" (Jn.1:34).

If John were from God, a true messenger of God, then Jesus was the true Messiah, the Son of God. This would mean that Jesus' message of the Kingdom of God, of hope for man through repentance, was true. Man could be saved from sin, death, and hell.

Note the words, "they reasoned with themselves." They discussed the matter among themselves. However, they were not searching their hearts and seeking for the truth. Their minds were already made up. Their preconceived ideas were not going to be set aside, not even by the truth. They were deliberately rejecting Jesus, being obstinate in their unbelief.

**Thought 1.** Christ and His message were from God; therefore, there is great hope for man. Man can be saved eternally, saved for the Kingdom of God. However, man has a twofold problem.
1) There is the problem of obstinate unbelief.

**"He that believeth on him is not condemned: but he that believeth not is condemned already, because he hath not believed in the name of the only begotten Son of God" (Jn.3:18).**
**"He that believeth on the Son hath everlasting life: and he that believeth not the Son shall not see life; but the wrath of God abideth on him" (Jn.3:36).**
**"I said therefore unto you, that ye shall die in your sins: for if ye believe not that I am he, ye shall die in your sins" (Jn.8:24).**
**"Take heed, brethren, lest there be in any of you an evil heart of unbelief, in departing from the living God" (Heb.3:12).**
**"He, that being often reproved hardeneth his neck, shall suddenly be destroyed, and that without remedy" (Pr.29:1).**

2) There is the problem of being unwilling to give up this world, of being unwilling to deny oneself, one's own desires and preconceived ideas. Man loves the money, acceptance, positions, and possessions of the world too much.

**"No man can serve two masters: for either he will hate the one, and love the other; or else he will hold to the one, and despise the other. Ye cannot serve God and mammon" (Mt.6:24).**
**"And the cares of this world, and the deceitfulness of riches, and the lusts of other things entering in, choke the word, and it becometh unfruitful" (Mk.4:19).**
**"For many walk, of whom I have told you often, and now tell you even weeping, that they are the enemies of the cross of Christ: whose end is destruction, whose God is their belly, and whose glory is in their shame, who mind earthly things" (Ph.3:18-19).**
**"But they that will be rich fall into temptation and a snare, and into many foolish and hurtful lusts, which drown men in destruction and perdition" (1 Tim.6:9).**

**3** (20:6) **Jesus Christ, Deity—Unbelief**: the second possibility was that Jesus' authority was *of men*. Again, whatever was true of John was true of Jesus. However, if John's ministry was of men, how could so many *changed lives* be accounted for? Thousands had repented and been transformed, turning their lives completely around and following God with a new vigor. To say that John was *not of God*, that he had received his power and his authority from men, was foolish and absurd (cp. Lk.7:29; Jn.10:41-42).

The authorities knew that if they publicly held this position, the people would rise up against them. They would lose whatever grip they had over the people, for the people believed that John was a great prophet of God.

> **Thought 1.** Down through the centuries thousands of lives have been changed by Christ. Thousands would lay down their lives in testimony of His transforming power. No greater evidence exists for the deity of Christ. The changed lives of many proclaim the glorious truth of the gospel. Christ is the true Messiah, the Son of God.

> > **"And all the people that heard him, and the publicans, justified God, being baptized with the baptism of John" (Lk.7:29).**

> > **"Jesus answered them, I told you, and ye believed not: the works that I do in my Father's name, they bear witness of me" (Jn.10:25).**

> > **"Say ye of him, whom the Father hath sanctified, and sent into the world, Thou blasphemest; because I said, I am the Son of God? If I do not the works of my Father, believe me not. But if I do, though ye believe not me, believe the works: that ye may know, and believe, that the Father is in me, and I in him" (Jn.10:36-38).**

> > **"And many resorted unto him, and said, John did no miracle: but all things that John spake of this man were true. And many believed on him there" (Jn.10:41-42).**

> > **"Believest thou not that I am in the Father, and the Father in me? the words that I speak unto you I speak not of myself: but the Father that dwelleth in me, he doeth the works" (Jn.14:10).**

**4** (20:7-8) **Jesus Christ, Deity—Unbelief:** the third possibility was indecision and silence. This was tragic. It is always tragic when a person's concern is to save face not to discover the truth. It is always tragic when a person is so concerned with his position, esteem, and security that he ignores or denies the truth. This was the very response of these men, and it is often the response of men to Christ.

1. They chose expediency, to be deliberately ignorant. They feared being shamed, embarrassed, and ridiculed. To confess Jesus would have meant confessing they had been wrong all along. It would have meant denying self completely and doing so publicly.

2. They denied Jesus. To confess that John was of God would have forced them to acknowledge Jesus, and they were not willing to confess Him. They feared the loss of all they possessed: position, power, wealth, esteem, image, security, and livelihood.

> **"And he said to them all, If any man will come after me, let him deny himself, and take up his cross daily, and follow me. For whosoever will save his life shall lose it: but whosoever will lose his life for my sake, the same shall save it" (Lk.9:23-24).**

> **"For what shall it profit a man, if he shall gain the whole world, and lose his own soul?" (Mk.8:36).**

**Thought 1.** The tragedy of tragedies is that most men...
- choose expediency rather than principle.
- choose to play it safe rather than to stand for the truth.
- choose to say "I don't know" rather than to speak the truth.

> > **"Whosoever therefore shall be ashamed of me and of my words in this adulterous and sinful generation; of him also shall the Son of man be ashamed, when he cometh in the glory of his Father with the holy angels" (Mk.8:38).**

> > **"If we suffer, we shall also reign with him: if we deny him, he also will deny us" (2 Tim.2:12).**

> > **"But there were false prophets also among the people, even as there shall be false teachers among you, who privily shall bring in damnable heresies, even denying the Lord that bought them, and bring upon themselves swift destruction" (2 Pt.2:1).**

> > **"Who is a liar but he that denieth that Jesus is the Christ? He is antichrist, that denieth the Father and the Son" (1 Jn.2:22).**

| | E. The Parable of the Wicked Husbandmen: The Overview of World History, 20:9-18 (Mt.21:33-46; Mk.12: 1-12; cp. Is.5:1-7) | will send my beloved son: it may be they will reverence him when they see him. | a. He sent His own Son to collect the fruit |
|---|---|---|---|
| **1 A man founded a vineyard** a. Leased it to tenants b. Went to a far country | 9 Then began he to speak to the people this parable; A certain man planted a vineyard, and let it forth to husbandmen, and went into a far country for a long time. | 14 But when the husbandmen saw him, they reasoned among themselves, saying, This is the heir: come, let us kill him, that the inheritance may be ours. | b. The tenants saw the Son c. The tenants plotted the Son's death d. The tenants planned to seize the inheritance e. The tenants rejected & killed the Son |
| **2 A day of accounting came** a. He sent servants to collect b. The husbandmen mistreated His servants & refused to pay them | 10 And at the season he sent a servant to the husbandmen, that they should give him of the fruit of the vineyard: but the husbandmen beat him, and sent him away empty. | 15 So they cast him out of the vineyard, and killed him. What therefore shall the lord of the vineyard do unto them? | **4 A just judgment was pronounced** a. He shall come to destroy them b. He shall give the world to others |
| c. He showed patience | 11 And again he sent another servant: and they beat him also, and entreated him shamefully, and sent him away empty. 12 And again he sent a third: and they wounded him also, and cast him out. | 16 He shall come and destroy these husbandmen, and shall give the vineyard to others. And when they heard it, they said, God forbid. 17 And he beheld them, and said, What is this then that is written, The stone which the builders rejected, the same is become the head of the corner? | **5 A sure proof of coming judgment was given: Scripture** a. Jesus' solemn look b. The rejected Stone's exaltation c. The rejected Stone's destructive power |
| **3 A special appeal was made to the tenants** | 13 Then said the lord of the vineyard, What shall I do? I | 18 Whosoever shall fall upon that stone shall be broken; but on whomsoever it shall fall, it will grind him to powder. | |

# DIVISION VIII

## THE SON OF MAN'S DRAMATIC ENTRANCE INTO JERUSALEM: HIS CLAIM AND CONFLICT, 19:28-21:4

## E. The Parable of the Wicked Husbandmen: The Overview of World History, 20:9-18

(20:9-18) **Introduction—World**: the parable was directed to Israel, but it is a panoramic view of world history as well. (See note—Mt.21:33-46 for the interpretation of Israel.) In the view of world history, God is the man who founded the world; the husbandmen or tenants are men and nations responsible for certain areas of production; the servants are God's messengers sent to secure His fruit; the Son is Jesus Christ Himself. Every man or nation who rejects God's Son finds God turning elsewhere and giving the vineyard and the responsibility to others.

1. A man founded a vineyard (v.9).
2. A day of accounting came (v.10-12).
3. A special appeal was made to the tenants (v.13-15).
4. A just judgment was pronounced (v.15-16).
5. A sure proof of coming judgment was given: Scripture (v.17-18).

**1** (20:9) **Labor—Man, Duty—World**: a man (God) founded a vineyard. He planted the world; He also planted Israel. He leased the world to men, and Israel to the Jews. Now note two critical facts.

1. It was God, not man, who created the world and created Israel. Neither the world nor Israel happened by chance. God made both, each one for a very specific purpose.

> "For in him we live, and move, and have our being; as certain also of your own poets have said, for we are also his offspring" (Acts 17:28).
> "The Spirit of God hath made me, and the breath of the Almighty hath given me life" (Job 33:4).
> "Know ye that the LORD he is God: it is he that hath made us, and not we ourselves; we are his people, and the sheep of his pasture" (Ps.100:3).
> "And forgettest the LORD thy maker, that hath stretched forth the heavens, and laid the foundations of the earth" (Is.51:13).
> "Have we not all one father? hath not one God created us? why do we deal treacherously every man against his brother, by profaning the covenant of our fathers?" (Mal.2:10).

2. God has given man the highest of privileges: the privilege of life and the privilege of caring for His world. (See DEEPER STUDY # 1—Jn.4:22 for Israel's privilege and purpose.) God has given man life and the potential of the earth in which to live, and He has placed both life and the earth into man's hands. The world is in no one else's hands; therefore, man is responsible for the world, to manage it for God and to give God the fruit of his hands. The point is simply this: man is to labor ever so vigorously, making every contribution He can both for God and for his fellow man (society). Why? Because

he is privileged ever so highly, privileged with life and privileged with the beauty and potential of the earth. He is to labor out of love and appreciation for all God has given him.

> "So God created man in his own image, in the image of God created he him; male and female created he them. And God blessed them, and God said unto them, Be fruitful, and multiply, and replenish the earth, and subdue it: and have dominion over the fish of the sea, and over the fowl of the air, and over every living thing that moveth upon the earth" (Gen.1:27-28).
>
> "Thou madest him to have dominion over the works of thy hands; thou hast put all things under his feet" (Ps.8:6).
>
> "For the kingdom of heaven is as a man travelling into a far country, who called his servants, and delivered unto them his goods" (Mt.25:14).
>
> "Moreover it is required in stewards, that a man be found faithful" (1 Cor.4:2).
>
> "Keep that which is committed to thy trust, avoiding profane and vain babblings, and oppositions of science falsely so called" (1 Tim.6:20).
>
> "And he called his ten servants, and delivered them ten pounds, and said unto them, Occupy till I come" (Lk.19:13).

**2** (20:10-12) **Judgment**: a day of accounting came; the day for payment came. Note the words "and the season." The season came when fruit was to be offered up to God.

1. God sent servants to collect. Fruit was expected, and it was time for payment. God *sent* servants to ask for the fruit. Every man was *expected* to pay his dues, to contribute for the wonderful privilege of living in the beautiful vineyard of the world.

> "Bring forth therefore fruits meet for repentance" (Mt.3:8).
>
> "He spake also this parable; A certain man had a fig tree planted in his vineyard; and he came and sought fruit thereon, and found none" (Lk.13:6).
>
> "Every branch in me that beareth not fruit he taketh away: and every branch that beareth fruit, he purgeth it, that it may bring forth more fruit" (Jn.15:2).
>
> "Herein is my Father glorified, that ye bear much fruit; so shall ye be my disciples" (Jn.15:8).
>
> "Ye have not chosen me, but I have chosen you, and ordained you, that ye should go and bring forth fruit, and that your fruit should remain: that whatsoever ye shall ask of the Father in my name, he may give it you" (Jn.15:16).
>
> "Wherefore, my brethren, ye also are become dead to the law by the body of Christ; that ye should be married to another, even to him who is raised from the dead, that we should bring forth fruit unto God" (Ro.7:4).
>
> "That ye might walk worthy of the Lord unto all pleasing, being fruitful in every good work, and increasing in the knowledge of God" (Col.1:10).

2. God's servants were mistreated and were refused payment. Note three things.
   a. Man deliberately rebels against God. Man wants to rule the vineyard himself. He wants to be the king of the kingdom, the ruler of the earth, and even the head of the church. He wants things to go his way, to rule and reign as he desires and wills. He wants no authority above him. He wants to live as he wishes and do things as he wishes. He wants to claim the fruits for himself.
   b. Man wants his own way so much that he criticizes, ridicules, slanders, persecutes and even murders the true servants of God.

> "Which of the prophets have not your fathers persecuted? and they have slain them which showed before of the coming of the Just One; of whom ye have been now the betrayers and murderers" (Acts 7:52. Cp. Mt.23:34-37; Heb.11:36-38.)

   c. The servant of God must understand that he is called to suffer (see DEEPER STUDY # 2—Mt.20:22-23).

> "For unto you it is given in the behalf of Christ, not only to believe on him, but also to suffer for his sake" (Ph.1:29).
>
> "Yea, and all that will live godly in Christ Jesus shall suffer persecution" (2 Tim.3:12).
>
> "Beloved, think it not strange concerning the fiery trial which is to try you, as though some strange thing happened unto you: but rejoice, inasmuch as ye are partakers of Christ's sufferings; that, when his glory shall be revealed, ye may be glad also with exceeding joy" (1 Pt.4:12-13; cp. 1 Pt.2:21; 4:5-6; Mt.19:29; Ro.8:16-17).

3. God showed patience. He did not strike out in anger at the first sign of rebellion, even when men brutally attacked His servants. He continued to send messengers to Israel (the world), giving man chance after chance.

> "Which of the prophets have not your fathers persecuted? and they have slain them which showed before of the coming of the Just One; of whom ye have been now the betrayers and murderers" (Acts 7:52. Cp. Mt.23:34-37; Heb.11:36-38.)
>
> "Then said he unto the dresser of the vineyard, Behold, these three years I come seeking fruit on this fig tree, and find none: cut it down; why cumbereth it the ground? And he answering said

unto him, Lord, let it alone this year also, till I shall dig about it, and dung it: and if it bear fruit, well: and if not, then after that thou shalt cut it down" (Lk.13:7-9).

"The Lord is not slack concerning his promise, as some men count slackness; but is longsuffering to usward, not willing that any should perish, but that all should come to repentance" (2 Pt.3:9).

"For my name's sake will I defer mine anger, and for my praise will I refrain for thee, that I cut thee not off" (Is.48:9).

**3** (20:13-15) **Jesus Christ, Rejection of**: a special appeal was made to the tenants. This was a very special appeal. It was God's sending His own "beloved Son" into the world to collect the fruit. Five significant facts are spelled out.

1. Jesus claimed to be God's Son. He was different from all the servants sent before. He was more than another man-servant; He was God's very own Son. There was no question that Jesus was clearly making this unique claim for Himself.

2. The cultivators saw God's Son. There were all kinds of evidence: Old Testament prophecies, the testimony of John the Baptist, the claims of Jesus Himself, the miraculous works, the signs of the times (Gal.4:4). There was a feeling that He was the promised Messiah even among those who now opposed Him (see note—Jn.3:2; cp. Jn.11:47-52). This was the tragic indictment against the Jews. Down deep within, they had a sense that Jesus really was the Messiah; but sin or greed for position, esteem, power, and security kept them from acknowledging Him. Their unbelief was deliberate—obstinate (see outline and notes—Mt.21:23-27).

3. The cultivators plotted His death (cp. Mt.12:14; Jn.11:53).

4. The cultivators planned to seize His inheritance. Man wants to possess the kingdom, the nation, the property, the power, the rule, the reign, the position, the esteem, the fame, the recognition, the wealth. Whatever the possession is, man always wants the possession himself. He will deny, deceive, lie, cheat, steal, and even kill to get it. (See note—Mt.12:1-8; note and DEEPER STUDY # 1—12:10; note—15:1-20; DEEPER STUDY # 2—15:6-9.)

5. The cultivators murdered the Son. They committed the worst crime of human history: they killed the Son of God Himself. Note two things: (1) Jesus was predicting His death, and (2) His death was to be a voluntary act on His part. He knew death lay ahead and could have escaped, but He chose to die. It was in "the determinate counsel of God" (Acts 2:23).

"For God so loved the world, that he gave his only begotten Son, that whosoever believeth in him should not perish, but have everlasting life" (Jn.3:16).

"But God commendeth his love toward us, in that, while we were yet sinners, Christ died for us" (Ro.5:8).

"But God, who is rich in mercy, for his great love wherewith he loved us, even when we were dead in sins, hath quickened us together with Christ, (by grace ye are saved)" (Eph.2:4-5).

"[God] who hath delivered us from the power of darkness, and hath translated us into the kingdom of his dear Son" (Col.1:13).

**4** (20:15-16) **Judgment**: a just judgment was pronounced. The crime was the most terrible and tragic crime in all the universe: the rejection and killing of God's *only* Son. Therefore, the judgment was to be the most tragic and extreme judgment in all the universe.

1. The rebellious tenants will be destroyed (see note—Lk.20:17-18).

2. The vineyard (world) will be given to others. The vineyard will not be left uncultivated; it will not be left untended to bear no fruit. God will raise up a new people to care for it (the church, the new creation of God. See notes—Eph.2:11-18; pt.4, 2:14-15; 4:17-19.)

When the Jews heard this statement, they knew what Jesus meant. They could not believe their ears. There was no chance whatsoever that they could be rejected by God, not in their minds. They burst forth in outrage, interrupting His warning, "God forbid."

"And now also the axe is laid unto the root of the trees: therefore every tree which bringeth not forth good fruit is hewn down, and cast into the fire" (Mt.3:10).

"If a man abide not in me, he is cast forth as a branch, and is withered; and men gather them, and cast them into the fire, and they are burned" (Jn.15:6).

"But that which beareth thorns and briers is rejected, and is nigh unto cursing: whose end is to be burned" (Heb.6:8).

**5** (20:17-18) **Judgment**: a sure proof of coming judgment was given—the proof of Scripture. Note His solemn look, "He beheld them and said...The stone which the builders rejected." The stone is a symbol of Jesus Christ. Note two facts.

1. The rejected Stone's exaltation. Christ is the Head or Chief Cornerstone, the Foundation Stone. He is the Foundation, the Stone upon which every man must build his life. There is no other Foundation upon which man can build and be secure. Similarly, He is the Foundation and Cornerstone of the church (see DEEPER STUDY # 6—Mt.21:42).

"For other foundation can no man lay than that is laid, which is Jesus Christ" (1 Cor.3:11).

"And are built upon the foundation of the apostles and prophets, Jesus Christ himself being the chief corner stone; in whom all the building fitly framed together groweth unto an holy temple in the Lord: in whom ye also are builded together for an habitation of God through the Spirit" (Eph.2:20-22).

"To whom [Christ] coming, as unto a living stone, disallowed indeed of men, but chosen of God, and precious, ye also, as lively stones, are built up a spiritual house, an holy priesthood, to offer up spiritual sacrifices, acceptable to God by Jesus Christ" (1 Pt.2:4-5.)

2.     The rejected Stone's destructive power. The destructive power of a stone against flesh and blood is well-known. A man who stumbles or falls over the stone, Jesus Christ, is hurt. A man upon whom the huge stone, Jesus Christ, falls is ground to powder, utterly destroyed—permanently. (See DEEPER STUDY # 6—Mt.21:42; DEEPER STUDY # 8,9—21:44 for more discussion.)

"The wicked shall fall by his own wickedness" (Pr.11:5).
"Were they ashamed when they had committed abomination? nay, they were not at all ashamed, neither could they blush: therefore they shall fall among them that fall: at the time that I visit them they shall be cast down, saith the LORD" (Jer.6:15).
"Moreover thou shalt say unto them, Thus saith the LORD; Shall they fall, and not arise? shall he turn away, and not return?" (Jer.8:4).
"The people that doth not understand shall fall" (Hos.4:14).

| 1 The cause of the question: The religionists sought to destroy Jesus | F. The Question of Government and Religion: Which is Supreme? 20:19-26 (Mt.22:15-22; Mk.12: 13-17) | thou sayest and teachest rightly, neither acceptest thou the person of any, but teachest the way of God truly: | |
|---|---|---|---|
| | | 22 Is it lawful for us to give tribute unto Caesar, or no? | 2 The two false concepts of citizenship |
| a. Their reason: They feared losing control of the people | 19 And the chief priests and the scribes the same hour sought to lay hands on him; and they feared the people: for they perceived that he had spoken this parable against them. | 23 But he perceived their craftiness, and said unto them, Why tempt ye me? | |
| | | 24 Show me a penny. Whose image and superscription hath it? They answered and said, Caesar's. | 3 The image stamped on coins is the government's image a. The government owns some things |
| b. Their method: They sought to discredit Him | 20 And they watched him, and sent forth spies, which should feign themselves just men, that they might take hold of his words, that so they might deliver him unto the power and authority of the governor. | 25 And he said unto them, Render therefore unto Caesar the things which be Caesar's, and unto God the things which be God's. | b. The government is due some things 4 The image stamped upon man is God's image |
| 1) Before the people 2) Before Rome: Committing treason | | | |
| 3) Through deception & flattery | 21 And they asked him, saying, Master, we know that | 26 And they could not take hold of his words before the people: and they marvelled at his answer, and held their peace. | 5 Conclusion: The religionists were silenced |

# DIVISION VIII

## THE SON OF MAN'S DRAMATIC ENTRANCE INTO JERUSALEM: HIS CLAIM AND CONFLICT, 19:28-21:4

## F. The Question of Government and Religion: Which is Supreme? 20:19-26

(20:19-26) **Introduction**: one of the major questions throughout history has dealt with government and religion—Which is supreme? Jesus deals with the subject in this passage.
1. The cause of the question: the religionists sought to destroy Jesus (v.19-21).
2. The two false concepts of citizenship (v.22-23).
3. The image stamped on coins is the government's image (v.24-25).
4. The image stamped upon man is God's image (v.25).
5. Conclusion: the religionists were silenced (v.26).

**1** (20:19-21) **Religionists, Opposed Jesus**: the cause of the question. The religionists sought to destroy Jesus. Note how institutionalized and political Jewish religion had become. The priesthood had begun with Aaron right after Moses had led the Israelites out of Egyptian bondage. Now, after just a few centuries, the priests were seen maneuvering to discredit and destroy Jesus just like secular rulers seek to destroy political opponents. There is no testimony of godliness in their lives. The very persons who were to be God's testimony in righteousness had become engrossed in selfish ambition and political intrigue.

The religionists feared they were losing their control over the people. The people were flocking to Jesus by the droves (Lk.19:37), and Jesus had...
- proclaimed Himself to be the Messiah (Lk.19:30, 37, 46; 20:2-6, 13, 17-18).
- cleansed the temple, accusing them of misusing it (Lk.19:25).
- confounded their attempt to discredit Him (Lk.20:7-8).
- accused them of being wicked husbandmen who had failed to care for God's vineyard (Lk.20:9-18).

If the people rose up against the leaders and proclaimed Jesus to be the Messiah, the Romans would step in to put down the revolt. The leaders would lose their position, authority, livelihood—everything. They felt they must stop Jesus at any cost.

The method they chose to stop Jesus was to pose trick questions to Him. If they could get Jesus to take some position against the people, the people would forsake Him. He could then be arrested and destroyed. On the other hand, if they could get Him to take some position against Rome, He would be arrested for preaching treason.

Note the deception and drooling flattery used on Jesus (v.21). It turns the reader's stomach, yet how characteristic of men who seek their own ends. (Cp. Job 15:5; Ps.5:9; Pr.12:3; 29:5.)

**Thought 1.** Too often religion becomes institutionalized and political. God's people must always guard against seeking...
- recognition
- honor
- position
- power
- worldly security
- selfish loyalty

> **"How can ye believe, which receive honour one of another, and seek not the honour that cometh from God only?" (Jn.5:44).**

"But Jesus called them unto him, and said, Ye know that the princes of the Gentiles exercise dominion over them, and they that are great exercise authority upon them. But it shall not be so among you: but whosoever will be great among you, let him be your minister; and whosoever will be chief among you, let him be your servant" (Mt.20:25-27).

"But he that is greatest among you shall be your servant. And whosoever shall exalt himself shall be abased; and he that shall humble himself shall be exalted" (Mt.23:11-12).

**2** (20:22-23) **Citizenship—State—Caesar**: the two false concepts of citizenship are seen in this question.

1. There was the concept of the religionists who were asking the question. They believed religion was supreme. They believed strongly in the heavenly, spiritual world. They believed all obedience and loyalty were due God and God alone. In fact, all things on earth were due God. The state and all other power and authority were to be subject to religious rule. Therefore, they were strongly against paying taxes to a foreign king. Paying taxes was an infringement upon God's right.

2. There was the concept of the secularist or humanist. These believed the state was supreme. They did not hold to the supernatural, not in the sense that a Supreme Being was the creator and sovereign power who was to be actively involved in the affairs of men. Religion, if it were to be practiced at all, was to be subject to the state. Religion existed to serve and benefit the state. God was either ignored or denied, viewed only as a tool to benefit the state.

**Thought 1.** Both concepts are always present among men. There will always be those who hold religion to be supreme and those who hold humanism and secularism to be supreme.

"For all flesh is as grass, and all the glory of man as the flower of grass. The grass withereth, and the flower thereof falleth away" (1 Pt.1:24).

"For when he dieth he shall carry nothing away: his glory shall not descend after him" (Ps.49:17).

"Therefore hell hath enlarged herself, and opened her mouth without measure: and their glory, and their multitude, and their pomp, and he that rejoiceth, shall descend into it" (Is.5:14).

"Hear the word of the LORD, ye that tremble at his word; Your brethren that hated you, that cast you out for my name's sake, said, Let the LORD be glorified: but he shall appear to your joy, and they shall be ashamed" (Is.66:5).

"Also, thou son of man, shall it not be in the day when I take from them their strength, the joy of their glory, the desire of their eyes, and that whereupon they set their minds, their sons and their daughters" (Ezk.24:25).

"As they were increased, so they sinned against me: therefore will I change their glory into shame" (Hos.4:7).

Note that Christ saw through the deception and flattery. He was the Son of God, so He knew *their craftiness* and knew...
- every self-seeking ambition.
- every deception and flattering word.
- every pretension to honor Him.
- every man who ignored and denied Him.
- every secular and humanistic claim.

**3** (20:24-25) **Citizenship—State**: the image stamped on coins is the government's image. As Jesus pointed to the image on the coin, this could not be denied. The government had made the coin and stamped its inscription on it. God did not make the coin; therefore, the government owned the coin and the government could demand the coin. The point was clear.

1. The coin and some other things produced by the state belonged to the state, things such as roads, buildings, sewage, and public transportation.

2. The government was due some things. In particular, the state was due a man's allegiance and support. A man was a citizen of this world as long as he was in the world. The world provided him with everything necessary to sustain physical life; and the government under which he lived provided protection, roads, water, and laws. Therefore, man owed his *due share* to the state. (See note—Ro.13:1-7 for more discussion.)

"Let every soul be subject unto the higher powers. For there is no power but of God: the powers that be are ordained of God" (Ro.13:1).

"Notwithstanding, lest we should offend them, go thou to the sea, and cast an hook, and take up the fish that first cometh up; and when thou hast opened his mouth, thou shalt find a piece of money: that take, and give unto them for me and thee" (Mt.17:27).

"Put them in mind to be subject to principalities and powers, to obey magistrates, to be ready to every good work" (Tit.3:1).

"Submit yourselves to every ordinance of man for the Lord's sake: whether it be to the king, as supreme; or unto governors, as unto them that are sent by him for the punishment of evildoers, and for the praise of them that do well. For so is the will of God, that with well doing ye may put to silence the ignorance of foolish men" (1 Pt.2:13-15).

"Honour all men. Love the brotherhood. Fear God. Honour the king" (1 Pt.2:17).

"And whosoever will not do the law of thy God, and the law of the king, let judgment be executed speedily upon him, whether it be unto death, or to banishment, or to confiscation of goods, or to imprisonment" (Ezra 7:26).

"I counsel thee to keep the king's commandment, and that in regard of the oath of God" (Eccl.8:2).

**4** (20:25) **Citizenship—State—Man, Image of God**: the image stamped upon man is God's image. The Jews frantically held that God created man and that He stamped His very image upon man. Therefore, man owed his total obedience to God and to no one other than God. What they failed to grasp was what Jesus was pointing out. Man is presently a citizen of two worlds: this world (cosmos) and the world of God or of the Spirit. Therefore, man owes to Caesar whatever carries Caesar's stamp, and he owes to God whatever carries God's stamp.

1. The stamp of God is upon *man's life*; therefore man owes God his life—life that was made to exist with God forever.

> "For God so loved the world, that he gave his only begotten Son, that whosoever believeth in him should not perish, but have everlasting life" (Jn.3:16).
> "And this is life eternal, that they might know thee the only true God, and Jesus Christ, whom thou hast sent" (Jn.17:3).
> "For he that soweth to his flesh shall of the flesh reap corruption; but he that soweth to the Spirit shall of the Spirit reap life everlasting" (Gal.6:8).

2. The stamp of God is upon *man's life*; therefore man owes God his world—a world that is ever so beautiful and needs to be looked after and cared for by man.

> "So God created man in his own image, in the image of God created he him; male and female created he them. And God blessed them, and God said unto them, Be fruitful, and multiply, and replenish the earth, and subdue it: and have dominion over the fowl of the air, and over every living thing that moveth upon the earth" (Gen.1:27-28).
> "Herein is my Father glorified, that ye bear much fruit; so shall ye be my disciples" (Jn.15:8).
> "Ye have not chosen me, but I have chosen you, and ordained you, that ye should go and bring forth fruit, and that your fruit should remain: that whatsoever ye shall ask of the Father in my name, he may give it you" (Jn.15:16).

3. The stamp of God is upon *man's life*; therefore man owes God his spirit—a spirit that can be *born again* and live a self-denying life of love and peace for the sake of all men everywhere.

> "Seeing ye have purified your souls in obeying the truth through the Spirit unto unfeigned love of the brethren, see that ye love one another with a pure heart fervently: being born again, not of corruptible seed, but of incorruptible, by the word of God, which liveth and abideth for ever" (1 Pt.1:22-23).
> "And he said to them all, If any man will come after me, let him deny himself, and take up his cross daily, and follow me. For whosoever will save his life shall lose it: but whosoever will lose his life for my sake, the same shall save it" (Lk.9:23-24).
> "[Christ] whom we preach, warning every man, and teaching every man in all wisdom; that we may present every man perfect in Christ Jesus" (Col.1:28).
> "The thief cometh not, but for to steal, and to kill, and to destroy: I am come that they might have life, and that they might have it more abundantly" (Jn.10:10).

4. The stamp of God is upon man's mind and body; therefore man owes God his mind and body—a mind and body that have the power to produce for the betterment of all mankind.

> "I beseech you therefore, brethren, by the mercies of God, that ye present your bodies a living sacrifice, holy, acceptable unto God, which is your reasonable service. And be not conformed to this world: but be ye transformed by the renewing of your mind, that ye may prove what is that good and acceptable, and perfect, will of God" (Ro.12:1-2).
> "What? know ye not that your body is the temple of the Holy Ghost which is in you, which ye have of God, and ye are not your own? For ye are bought with a price: therefore glorify God in your body, and in your spirit, which are God's" (1 Cor.6:19-20).
> "But the fruit of the Spirit is love, joy, peace, longsuffering, gentleness, goodness, faith, meekness, temperance: against such there is no law" (Gal.5:22-23).
> "Whoso sheddeth man's blood, by man shall his blood be shed: for in the image of God made he man" (Gen.9:6).
> "For a man indeed ought not to cover his head, forasmuch as he is the image and glory of God" (1 Cor.11:7).
> "And have put on the new man, which is renewed in knowledge after the image of him that created him" (Col.3:10).

**5** (20:26) **Citizenship**: the conclusion was that the religionists were silenced. Two things happened: first, they were unable to discredit Jesus; and second, they were struck with amazement. They marvelled at His answer.

**Thought 1.** Men have to stand in amazement at the Lord's concept of dual citizenship. A man is to be a citizen both of this world and of heaven: rendering to Caesar what is due him, and rendering to God what is due Him.

> "Fear God. Honor the King" (1 Pt.2:17).

| | **G. The Question of the Resurrection: The Two Worlds—Earth & Heaven—Differ, 20:27-38** (Mt.22:23-33; Mk.12:18-27) | died also.<br>33 Therefore in the resurrection whose wife of them is she? for seven had her to wife. | c. They asked an egotistical & blind question |
|---|---|---|---|
| **1 The Sadducees, the liberal-minded, tried to discredit Jesus**[DS1] | 27 Then came to him certain of the Sadducees, which deny that there is any resurrection; and they asked him, | 34 And Jesus answering said unto them, The children of this world marry, and are given in marriage: | **2 Marriage is different**<br>a. This world: There is marriage |
| a. They referred to Levrite marriage[DS2] | 28 Saying, Master, Moses wrote unto us, If any man's brother die, having a wife, and he die without children, that his brother should take his wife, and raise up seed unto his brother. | 35 But they which shall be accounted worthy to obtain that world, and the resurrection from the dead, neither marry, nor are given in marriage: | b. Next world: There is no marriage<br>**3 Entrance is different: Must be counted worthy** |
| b. They presented a logical situation | 29 There were therefore seven brethren: and the first took a wife, and died without children.<br>30 And the second took her to wife, and he died childless.<br>31 And the third took her; and in like manner the seven also: and they left no children, and died.<br>32 Last of all the woman | 36 Neither can they die any more: for they are equal unto the angels; and are the children of God, being the children of the resurrection.<br>37 Now that the dead are raised, even Moses showed at the bush, when he calleth the Lord the God of Abraham, and the God of Isaac, and the God of Jacob.<br>38 For he is not a God of the dead, but of the living: for all live unto him. | **4 Death is different: No longer can die**<br>**5 Personal being (nature) is different**<br>a. Are like angels<br>b. Are children of God<br>**6 Life is different: It is a resurrected life**<br>a. It is life after death<br>b. Illustrated by Moses<br><br>c. Purpose: To live for God |

# DIVISION VIII

## THE SON OF MAN'S DRAMATIC ENTRANCE INTO JERUSALEM: HIS CLAIM AND CONFLICT, 19:28-21:4

### G. The Question of the Resurrection: The Two Worlds (Earth and Heaven) Differ, 20:27-38

(20:27-38) **Introduction**: this world and the other world—earth and heaven—differ. They differ drastically. Jesus used the attack of the Sadducees to discuss the differences.

1. Sadducees, the liberal-minded, tried to discredit Jesus(v.27-33).
2. Marriage is different (v.34-35).
3. Entrance is different: must be counted worthy (v.35).
4. Death is different: no longer can die (v.36).
5. Personal being (nature) is different (v.36).
6. Life is different: it is a resurrected life (v.37-38).

**1** (20:27-33) **Religionists, Oppose Christ—Question**: The Sadducees, the liberal-minded, tried to discredit Jesus. Note three points.

1. They referred to Levrite marriage (see DEEPER STUDY # 2—Lk.20:28).
2. They presented a logical situation: there were seven brothers. The first brother married but died without having children. Each of the other brothers obeyed the law, but each brother *died before having children*. Finally the woman died also. The point was logical, but most unlikely. (See DEEPER STUDY # 2—Lk.20:28 for discussion of the Levrite law.)
3. They asked an egotistical and blind question. The question was logical, but note two things:
   a. The spirit that lay behind the questioning. The situation was absurd; the spirit was cold and coarse, egotistical and unbelieving, regrettable and revolting. The unbeliever's spirit is often self-incriminating and self-condemning.
   b. The blindness and human frailty of the question. The human mind *cannot know* the spiritual world apart from *revelation*. The Sadducees were thinking that the spiritual world would be just like the physical world, that it would be nothing more than a continuation of this world both in *its nature and in its relationships*.

> **"But the natural man receiveth not the things of the Spirit of God: for they are foolishness unto him: neither can he know them, because they are spiritually discerned"** (1 Cor.2:14).

---

**DEEPER STUDY # 1**

(20:27) **Sadducees**: these were the religious and political liberals of Jesus' day. They were the wealthy, the aristocratic, the governing class of leaders in Israel. Many Sadducees served on the nation's governing body, the Sanhedrin. The Chief Priest himself was usually a Sadducee who presided over the Sanhedrin. The Sanhedrin ruled the people in behalf of the

Roman empire (Acts 4:1-2; 5:27). The Romans readily saw to it that the Sadducees held the positions of leadership in the nation, for the Sadducees favored Greek customs over Jewish customs. They willingly aided the Romans in doing away with religious practices and instituting Greek and Roman customs (Hellenism).

The Sadducees are thought to have arisen out of the same struggle as the Pharisees around 175 B.C. However, they were always the fewest in number among the various sects of Jewish belief.

Several things should be noted.

1.   The Sadducees were secular and materialistic. They were the independent thinkers, the rationalists of their day.

2.   They were heavily entrenched in the priesthood of Jesus' day (cp. Acts 4:1-2; 5:17). They readily collaborated with the Roman government in order to protect their position, power, and wealth.

3.   They denied the supernatural to a great degree: the resurrection and miracles, life after death, and the existence of beings in other dimensions such as angels and spirits (Mt.22:23; Acts 23:8). To them there was no heaven or hell, no existence whatsoever except on this earth. A man died and was annihilated; he ceased to exist. There was no such thing as rewards or punishment in an afterlife; there was no such thing as life that continued eternally. (See notes—Mt.22:23-33.)

4.   The only Scripture they accepted was the Pentateuch, the first five books of the Old Testament. They felt these books were the only Scripture that was binding. They rejected the Oral and Scribal Law. They did not accept the prophets nor the poetic books of the Scripture.

5.   By practice, they bordered on being humanists, believing that man was in control of his own life and destiny. God had little if anything to do with life, for there was no afterlife. Whatever was achieved was to be done by man's own will and energy and effort.

6.   They were diametrically opposed to the Pharisees.

The liberal position of the Sadducees caused two things.

1.   It caused them to stumble at the spiritual and supernatural. They ridiculed and scorned both. Therefore, in their minds, the teachings of Jesus were the teachings of an unthinking and illogical man, lacking philosophical analysis and natural proof.

2.   Their liberal position caused them to feel threatened and to oppose Jesus. The people were flocking to Jesus and soaking up His teachings. This meant the Sadducees were losing their grip on the people. Their position and wealth were being jeopardized; therefore, they were compelled to attack and discredit Him before the people.

---

**DEEPER STUDY # 2**

(20:28) **Levrite Marriage**: when a husband died without a son, the Levrite law said that his brother was to marry his wife and bear a son. By law, the son was considered the firstborn son of the deceased brother. This assured two things: (a) that the family name continued, and (2) that the property holdings were kept in the family. This was a law that had been given to help preserve and enlarge the nation of Israel (cp. Ruth 4:5).

---

[2]   (20:34-35) **Heaven—Marriage—Resurrection**: marriage differs in the two worlds. In this world there is marriage, but in the other world there will be no marriage. There is a very special and wonderful reason why there is no marriage in the other world: *love is perfected*. Future life and relationships will exceed earthly relationships, even the bond of marital relationships. The strong union and bond of earthly marriage will not be less, it will be greater and stronger in heaven, but so will all other relationships.

In heaven our relationships will cease to be as they are on earth. They will be changed in an absolute sense: selfishness and sin will not affect our love and lives. Our love will be perfected; therefore, we will love everyone perfectly. A wife on this earth will not be loved as she was on this earth—imperfectly. She will be loved more, *loved perfectly*. Everyone will love everyone else perfectly. God will change all relationships into perfection, even as the relationships between angels and God are perfected.

[3]   (20:35) **Worthy—Justification—Heaven—World**: entrance into the two worlds differs. A man has nothing to do with his entrance into this world. He is conceived and born by the act of a man and a woman. But note three facts about the next world.

1.   Only those who are *accounted worthy* shall obtain that world. This is significant. A man does not work or earn his way into the next world. He is not worthy; he is only *counted* worthy. Worthiness is accounted to him, merely laid to his account. Scripture says that it is his *faith* that is counted as making him worthy. God takes a man's faith and counts it as "righteousness" (see DEEPER STUDY # 2, *Justification*—Ro.4:22; 5:1. Cp. Ro.4:5; 4:1-3; 4:1-25.)

> **"Therefore being justified by faith, we have peace with God through our Lord Jesus Christ" (Ro.5:1).**
> **"Now it was not written for his sake alone, that it [righteousness] was imputed to him; but for us also, to whom it shall be imputed, if we believe on him that raised up Jesus our Lord from the dead; who was delivered for our offences, and was raised again for our justification" (Ro.4:23-25).**
> **"Even as Abraham believed God, and it was accounted to him for righteousness" (Gal.3:6).**

2.   Jesus was speaking of the resurrection of believers only. He did not say "the resurrection *of the dead*" which would mean all the dead, but He said "the resurrection from the dead" which means the resurrection of believers *from among* the dead.

> **"Verily, verily, I say unto you, The hour is coming, and now is, when the dead shall hear the voice of the Son of God: and they that hear shall live" (Jn.5:25).**

"And this is the will of him that sent me, that every one which seeth the Son, and believeth on him, may have everlasting life: and I will raise him up at the last day" (Jn.6:40).

"And have hope toward God, which they themselves also allow, that there shall be a resurrection of the dead, both of the just and unjust" (Acts 24:15).

"Blessed and holy is he that hath part in the first resurrection: on such the second death hath no power, but they shall be priests of God and of Christ, and shall reign with him a thousand years" (Rev.20:6).

3. Every man continues to exist after this world, but all will not enter "that world," that is, heaven. Those who have not lived a life of faith in Christ, who are not counted worthy, will not enter "that world," but will enter hell (see DEEPER STUDY # 4—Lk.16:24; DEEPER STUDY # 2—Mt.5:22).

"And he cried and said, Father Abraham, have mercy on me, and send Lazarus, that he may dip the tip of his finger in water, and cool my tongue; for I am tormented in this flame" (Lk.16:24).

"Marvel not at this: for the hour is coming, in the which all that are in the graves shall hear his voice, and shall come forth; they that have done good, unto the resurrection of life; and they that have done evil, unto the resurrection of damnation" (Jn.5:28-29).

"And have hope toward God, which they themselves also allow, that there shall be a resurrection of the dead, both of the just and unjust" (Acts 24:15).

"And many of them that sleep in the dust of the earth shall awake, some to everlasting life, and some to shame and everlasting contempt" (Dan.12:2).

**4** (20:36) **Death—Eternal Life**: death differs in the two worlds. In the next world there is no death (see DEEPER STUDY #1, *Death*—Heb.9:27 for more discussion). Note: Jesus said a man "cannot die any more." A man is locked in, given an incorruptible body and existence, living forever with God. (See DEEPER STUDY #1—Jn.17:2-3. Cp. Jn.1:4.)

"Then we which are alive and remain shall be caught up together with them in the clouds, to meet the Lord in the air: and so shall we ever be with the Lord" (1 Th.4:17).

"For this corruptible must put on incorruption, and this mortal must put on immortality. So when this corruptible shall have put on incorruption, and this mortal shall have put on immortality, then shall be brought to pass the saying that is written, Death is swallowed up in victory" (1 Cor.15:53-54).

"And the Lord shall deliver me from every evil work, and will preserve me unto his heavenly kingdom: to whom be glory for ever and ever" (2 Tim.4:18).

**5** (20:36) **Believers, Nature—Reward—Eternal Life—Heaven**: personal being, that is, man's nature, differs in the two worlds. Two things are said about believers.

1. Believers shall be "equal unto the angels." The Greek word *isangelloi* means that believers shall have a nature like the angels: be glorified, be their peers, living in the joy of working and serving God just as the angels do. It means believers will have all the glorious being and privileges and responsibilities that angels have.

"So also is the resurrection of the dead. It is sown in corruption; it is raised in incorruption: it is sown in dishonour; it is raised in glory: it is sown in weakness; it is raised in power: it is sown a natural body: it is raised a spiritual body. There is a natural body, and there is a spiritual body" (1 Cor.15:42-44).

"And as we have borne the image of the earthy, we shall also bear the image of the heavenly. Now this I say, brethren, that flesh and blood cannot inherit the kingdom of God; neither doth corruption inherit incorruption. Behold, I show you a mystery; We shall not all sleep, but we shall all be changed, in a moment, in the twinkling of an eye, at the last trump: for the trumpet shall sound, and the dead shall be raised incorruptible, and we shall be changed. For this corruptible must put on incorruption, and this mortal must put on immortality" (1 Cor.15:49-53).

2. But there is even more than what angels have. Believers are the children of God, the adopted children of God. (See note—Gal.4:5-6.)

"For ye have not received the spirit of bondage again to fear; but ye have received the Spirit of adoption, whereby we cry, Abba, Father. The Spirit itself beareth witness with our spirit, that we are the children of God: and if children, then heirs, heirs of God, and joint-heirs with Christ; if so be that we suffer with him, that we may be also glorified together" (Ro.8:15-17).

"But when the fulness of the time was come, God sent forth his Son, made of a woman, made under the law, to redeem them that were under the law, that we might receive the adoption of sons. And because ye are sons, God hath sent forth the Spirit of his Son into your hearts, crying, Abba, Father. Wherefore thou art no more a servant, but a son; and if a son, then an heir of God through Christ" (Gal.4:4-7).

"That being justified by his grace, we should be made heirs according to the hope of eternal life" (Tit.3:7).

**6** (20:37-38) **Life—Eternal Life—Heaven**: life differs in the two worlds. In the other world, it is a *resurrected life*, a real life, a life that is more real than the life of this world. It is a perfect life that lives for God perfectly. Note three facts.

1.  God is the God of Abraham, Isaac, and Jacob. Jesus meant at least two things in this point.
    a.  God's relationships are active relationships, not inactive. God says, "I am the God of...." not, "I was the God of...." His relationships with His subjects are maintained even after departing this world. God is eternal; therefore, He creates and maintains eternal, active relationships. God's subjects enter into the spiritual realm of His presence and actively relate to Him. The resurrection is a fact.
    b.  God's relationships are good and rewarding. The patriarchs of old were promised very personal rewards (cp. Heb.11:13-16). There has to be a resurrection if our relationship with God is good and rewarding. To die and to be left dead as a decayed corpse is not good nor rewarding. Abraham, Isaac, and Jacob have a good and rewarding relationship with God. They are more alive today than they were while on earth, for they are perfected and eternal. They are with God Himself, and so shall we be. The resurrection is a fact.
2.  *God is—God exists.* Note the two simple words in v.38. The fact that *God is*, that God exists, proves the resurrection. The Greek (ego eimi) means the self-existent, eternal One (see DEEPER STUDY # 1—Jn.6:20; note—18:4-6).

> **"I am the God...." (Mt.22:32).**
> **"He that cometh to God must believe that He is" (Heb.11:6).**

Since God exists, He is God with omnipotent power—power that is perfect and eternal. God can do anything and all things, perfectly and eternally. He can call the elements of a decayed body back together again and raise it up to live in the spiritual dimension, both perfectly and eternally.

Note carefully: *God exists* (lives)—the argument is irrefutable. Note carefully the great passage in Ephesians dealing with the spiritual blessings that are ours in Christ.

> **"We have obtained an inheritance....That we should be [exist]" (Eph.1:11-12).**

The resurrection is a fact. It will be experienced by all men of all ages because *God is.* God has willed to give us an inheritance—an inheritance *to be*, that is, *to live eternally* with Him. We will undergo a transformation of nature, a transformation of perfection and permanency. For this reason, we need to pay close attention to what Scripture says.

> **"But without faith it is impossible to please him: for he that cometh to God must believe that he [God] is, and that he is a rewarder of them that diligently seek him" (Heb.11:6).**

We must believe that *God is* and that *He is a rewarder* of all those who diligently seek Him; that is, He rewards all of us who seek to live eternally with Him.

> **"If by any means I might attain unto the resurrection of the dead" (Ph.3:11).**
> **"Teaching us that, denying ungodliness and worldly lusts, we should live soberly, righteously, and godly, in this present world; looking for that blessed hope, and the glorious appearing of the great God and our Saviour Jesus Christ" (Tit.2:12-13).**
> **"Beloved, now are we the sons of God, and it doth not yet appear what we shall be: but we know that, when he shall appear, we shall be like him; for we shall see him as he is" (1 Jn.3:2).**
> **"And I saw a new heaven and a new earth: for the first heaven and the first earth were passed away....Behold, I make all things new. And he said unto me, Write: for these words are true and faithful" (Rev.21:1, 5).**

3.  God is not the God of the dead but of the living. God is the God of Abraham, Isaac, and Jacob, not the God of dead and decayed corpses. When Moses wrote these words, the three patriarchs had been dead for centuries. If they were dead, God was not their God. Since He was their God, they were alive; they were living in God's presence and in a relationship to Him that was perfect and eternal. There is to be a resurrection.

> **"For none of us liveth to himself, and no man dieth to himself. For whether we live, we live unto the Lord; and whether we die, we die unto the Lord: whether we live therefore, or die, we are the Lord's. For to this end Christ both died, and rose, and revived, that he might be Lord both of the dead and living" (Ro.14:7-9).**

One simple fact comes to the forefront ever so clearly in these points made by Jesus: *since God is*, God is not the God of the dead but of the living.

> **"Why should it be thought a thing incredible with you, that God should raise the dead?" (Acts 26:8).**
> **"There shall be a resurrection of the dead, both of the just and unjust" (Acts 24:15).**

Note also that all believers live. They live unto God, for God is the God of the living. Death cannot break the believer's relationship to God. The believer goes to live with the Lord forever. (See notes, *Reward*—Lk.12:41-48; 16:10-12; DEEPER STUDY # 3—19:15-19 for more discussion.)

| | H. The Question of David's Son: Two Misunderstandings Corrected, 20:39-47 (Mt.22:41-46; 23:6-7, 14; Mk.12:35-40) | Sit thou on my right hand, 43 Till I make thine enemies thy footstool. 44 David therefore calleth him Lord, how is he then his son? 45 Then in the audience of all the people he said unto his disciples, | b. David himself called the Messiah "Lord" 3 Misunderstanding 2: Religionists are genuine a. Their desire & love: Self-esteem & praise |
|---|---|---|---|
| 1 The response of the religionists to Jesus a. Some were impressed b. All were silenced | 39 Then certain of the scribes answering said, Master, thou hast well said. 40 And after that they durst not ask him any question at all. | 46 Beware of the scribes, which desire to walk in long robes, and love greetings in the markets, and the highest seats in the synagogues, and the chief rooms at feasts; | |
| 2 Misunderstanding 1: The Messiah is David's Son[DS1] a. David said that God called the Messiah "Lord" | 41 And he said unto them, How say they that Christ is David's son? 42 And David himself saith in the book of Psalms, The LORD said unto my Lord, | 47 Which devour widows' houses, and for a show make long prayers: the same shall receive greater damnation. | b. Their terrible sin: Devour widows c. Their condemnation: Is to be greater |

# DIVISION VIII

## THE SON OF MAN'S DRAMATIC ENTRANCE INTO JERUSALEM: HIS CLAIM AND CONFLICT, 19:28-21:4

## H. The Question of David's Son: Two Misunderstandings Corrected, 20:39-47

(20:39-47) **Introduction**: there are two ideas among men that desperately need correcting. It is absolutely essential that they be corrected, for they both lead to gross error and damnation (v.47). What are the erroneous ideas?
1. The response of the religionists to Jesus (v.39-40).
2. Misunderstanding 1: the Messiah is David's Son (v.41-44).
3. Misunderstanding 2: religionists are genuine (v.45-47).

**1** (20:39-40) **Religionists, Response to Jesus**: the response of the religionists to Jesus was twofold.

1. Some were impressed with the Lord's answers to their questions (cp. Lk.19:47-20:38). They shared very honestly with Him, "Master, thou hast well said." This was an amazing statement, for remember, the religionists were out to kill Jesus. They had engaged Him in argument time and again, trying to entrap Him in His words. They tried their best to turn the people against Him. They had to break His hold on the people before they dared arrest Him. But He had answered their questions so wisely and with so much authority, some of the very ones engaged in the plot were impressed.
2. All the religionists were silenced. They had been so routed and embarrassed before the people that they dared not ask any more questions.

**2** (20:41-44) **Messiah—Jesus Christ, Claims**: the first misunderstanding was that the Messiah was David's Son. Many believed that Jesus was a mere man, of human origin. The idea that the Messiah might be of divine origin, of God Himself, was unacceptable, and still is unacceptable, to some people. However, Jesus makes Himself perfectly clear. He is not the son of David, not born of man. He is the Lord from heaven. His argument is *forceful*.
1. David said in Scripture that God called the Messiah, "Lord." Note four facts.
   a. Fact 1: David called the Messiah "Lord" in the Psalms. That is, David's words are recorded in Scripture under the *inspiration of the Spirit*. God was directing him (cp. Mt.22:43; 2 Pt.1:21; 1 Cor.12:3).
   b. Fact 2: David said that "the Lord [Jehovah God] said to *my* Lord [the Messiah]." David unquestionably called the Messiah "*My Lord*."
   c. Fact 3: David said that *my* Lord "sits on God's right hand." The Messiah is *Lord*, for He is *exalted* by God.

   > "[God's mighty power] which he wrought in Christ, when he raised him from the dead, and set him at his own right hand in the heavenly places" (Eph.1:20).
   > "Wherefore God also hath highly exalted him, and given him a name which is above every name" (Ph.2:9).
   > "Now of the things which we have spoken this is the sum: We have such an high priest, who is set on the right hand of the throne of the Majesty in the heavens" (Heb.8:1).

   d. Fact 4: David said that my Lord's "enemies are to be made His footstool." The Messiah is Lord, for all His enemies are to be subjected under Him (Ph.2:10-11).
2. David himself called Messiah "Lord." Jesus asked a pointed question. How could the Messiah be both David's Lord and his Son? Jesus was doing at least two things by asking this question.
   a. Jesus was saying this: to think of the Messiah only in human terms is totally inadequate. It is not enough to think in terms of earthly power, of national, political, military, and institutional leadership. There is no way a mere man can bring perfect deliverance, leadership, and utopia to this earth. The Messiah is not only man; He is the Lord from heaven.

410

b. Jesus was claiming to be the Son of God Himself. Man's concept has to go beyond the mere human and physical. Man's idea has to stretch upward into God's very own heart. God loves this earth; therefore, God sent His Son to earth, sacrificing Him in order to save it and all those within it.

> "For God so loved the world, that he gave his only begotten Son, that whosoever believeth in him should not perish, but have everlasting life" (Jn.3:16).
> "But God commendeth his love toward us, in that, while we were yet sinners, Christ died for us" (Ro.5:8).
> "And Simon Peter answered and said, Thou art the Christ, the Son of the living God" (Mt.16:16).
> "The woman saith unto him, I know that Messias cometh, which is called Christ: when he is come, he will tell us all things. Jesus saith unto her, I that speak unto thee am he" (Jn.4:25-26).
> "Then said Jesus unto the twelve, Will ye also go away? Then Simon Peter answered him, Lord, to whom shall we go? thou hast the words of eternal life. And we believe and are sure that thou art that Christ, the Son of the living God" (Jn.6:67-69).
> "I said therefore unto you, that ye shall die in your sins: for if ye believe not that I am he, ye shall die in your sins" (Jn.8:24).
> "Then said Jesus unto them, When ye have lifted up the Son of man, then shall ye know that I am he, and that I do nothing of myself; but as my Father hath taught me, I speak these things" (Jn.8:28).

---

**DEEPER STUDY # 1**

(20:41) **Messiah—Son of David**: The common title for the Messiah was *the Son of David*. The Old Testament definitely said the Messiah was to come from the line of David. It was from such passages as these that the Messiah was known as *the Son of David*. (See notes—Lk.3:24-31; Deeper Study # 3—Jn.1:45 for most verses and their fulfillment dealing with the Messiah's being the Son of David.)

> "Once have I sworn by my holiness that I will not lie unto David. His seed shall endure for ever, and his throne as the sun before me" (Ps.89:35-36).
> "For unto us a child is born, unto us a son is given: and the government shall be upon his shoulder: and his name shall be called Wonderful, Counselor, the mighty God, the everlasting Father, the Prince of Peace. Of the increase of his government and peace there shall be no end, upon the throne of David, and upon his kingdom, to order it, and to establish it with judgment and with justice from henceforth even for ever. The zeal of the Lord of hosts will perform this" (Is.9:6-7).
> "And there shall come forth a rod out of the stem of Jesse, and a Branch shall grow out of his roots: and the spirit of the Lord shall rest upon him, the spirit of wisdom and understanding, the spirit of counsel and might, the spirit of knowledge and of the fear of the Lord; and shall make him of quick understanding in the fear of the Lord: and he shall not judge after the sight of his eyes, neither reprove after the hearing of his ears: but with righteousness shall he judge the poor, and reprove with equity for the meek of the earth: and he shall smite the earth with the rod of his mouth, and with the breath of his lips shall he slay the wicked. And righteousness shall be the girdle of his loins, and faithfulness the girdle of his reins" (Is.11:1-5).

The Messiah was to do four specific things. (See notes—Mt.1:1; Deeper Study # 2—1:18; Deeper Study # 3—3:11; notes—11:1-6; 11:2-3; Deeper Study # 1—11:5; Deeper Study # 2—11:6; Deeper Study # 1—12:16; notes—22:42; Lk.7:21-23. These notes will help in understanding concept of the Messiah.)

1.   He was to free Israel from all enslavement. Enslavement was to be abolished and all men set free under God's domain.
2.   He was to give victory over all enemies. Israel was to be established as the seat of His rule. This, of course, meant Israel was to be the leading nation of the world.
3.   He was to bring peace to earth. All were to serve God under the government established by the Messiah.
4.   He was to provide plenty for all. The Messiah was to bring all the benefits of both God's rule and care in providing the necessities of life and in bringing utopia (the Kingdom of God) to earth.

---

**3** (20:45-47) **Religionists—Widows—Dress**: the second misunderstanding was that religionists were genuine. Jesus was forceful in this fact. He said to all men: "Beware of the scribes" (religionists).
1.   Their "desire...and love" was self-esteem and praise.
   a.   They dressed to draw attention to themselves. There were two ways this was done.
       First, a person could desire to wear the clothing of the extravagant and wasteful. The long robe was the dress of the nobility, the rich, the well-known, the person of style. It was a long robe reaching to the ground. A man was unable to work in it; therefore, it was the sign of *higher society* and of a man of leisure. Note: Jesus was not speaking against fine clothing. What He said was, "Beware of [those] who *love* to go in long robes" (fine clothing). He condemned the person who was extravagant and wasteful, whose mind was on attracting attention, on self, on appearance.

**Thought 1.** A person's mind is not to be on clothing, but...

> **"Whatsoever things are true, whatsoever things are honest, whatsoever things are just, whatsoever things are pure, whatsoever things are lovely, whatsoever things are of good report; if there be any virtue, and if there be any praise, think on these things" (Ph.4:8).**

**Thought 2.** A man's life consists not in the things he has, but in the service he renders to others. The world is desperate, swamped with enormous needs. God wills for all persons to be wrapped up in meeting the needs of others and not wrapped up in clothing—especially the believer. The believer's concern is to be righteousness. He is to work for Christ and His kingdom, not for expensive, flamboyant, ostentatious clothing (cp. 1 Pt.3:3-4).

> **"Let him that stole steal no more: but rather let him labour, working with his hands the thing which is good, that he may have to give to him that needeth" (Eph.4:28).**

Second, a person can change his clothing and his appearance *in order to attract attention*. He desires and loves the attention, so he seeks to attract by being different and by making himself stand out. This was a prominent sin of the religionists in Jesus' day.
- ⇒ They wore phylacteries. These were little leather-type boxes which contained a piece of parchment with four passages of Scripture written on it. The scriptures were Ex.13:1-10; 13:11-16; Dt.6:4-9; and 11:13-21. The use of the phylacteries seems to have arisen from a literal translation of Ex.13:9 and Pr.7:3. However, the true meaning of these two passages seems to be that we are to have the Word of God in our minds just as clearly as if we had them before our eyes. The great fault of these religionists was that they not only interpreted the passages literally and wore the little leather boxes, but they enlarged the boxes to draw attention to themselves as being religious.
- ⇒ They also enlarged the borders of their garments; that is, they wore tassels on their outside robes. God had instructed the Jews to make fringes or tassles on the borders of their outer robes. When a person noticed them, he was to be reminded to keep God's commandments. Again, the error was that the religionist changed his appearance from others; he enlarged his tassels, drawing attention to his being more religious than others.

**Thought 1.** A person can wear clothes to attract attention by either overdressing or underdressing. A person can overdress to attract and focus attention upon himself, and a person can wear clothes that expose the body, that actually attract attention to certain parts of the body. A person can wear clothes that are too tight, too low cut, too high cut, too thin. A person can wear too little clothing and clothing that fails to cover enough of the body.

Jesus very simply says to beware of dressing to attract attention. The religionists did it to appear *righteous*. Others do it to appear *worldly* (appealing).

> **"Neither yield ye your members [bodily parts] as instruments of unrighteousness unto sin: but yield yourselves unto God, as those that are alive from the dead, and your members as instruments of righteousness unto God" (Ro.6:13).**
> **"In like manner also, that women adorn themselves in modest apparel, with shamefacedness and sobriety; not with broided hair, or gold, pearls, or costly array; but (which becometh women professing godliness) with good works" (1 Tim.2:9-10).**
> **"Whose [wives] adorning let it not be that outward adorning of plaiting the hair, and of wearing of gold, or of putting on of apparel; but let it be the hidden man of the heart, in that which is not corruptible, even the ornament of a meek and quiet spirit, which is in the sight of God of great price" (1 Pt.3:3-5).**

b. The religionists loved the greetings and titles that exalted men with honor. Note: the title was "Rabbi" which meant teacher or master. It was only a simple title, yet some loved and revelled in the recognition above other men. It took a man that was supposed to be God's messenger and said, "Here he is; this is he." It honored the man and not the Lord.

> **"And whosoever shall exalt himself shall be abased; and he that shall humble himself shall be exalted" (Mt.23:12).**
> **"Though thou exalt thyself as the eagle, and though thou set thy nest among the stars, thence will I bring thee down, saith the LORD" (Obad.4).**
> **"For all flesh is as grass, and all the glory of man as the flower of grass. The grass withereth, and the flower thereof falleth away" (1 Pt.1:24).**
> **"Nevertheless man being in honour abideth not: he is like the beasts that perish" (Ps.49:12).**

c. The religionists loved the front seats and high places in the synagogues and feasts that were seen, admired, and showed their prominence. In the synagogue the leaders and distinguished persons sat on a bench in front of the ark (where the Scripture was kept), and they sat facing the congregation. No leader could be missed. On social occasions the most honored sat at the right hand of the host, then the next honored at his left hand, and so on, alternating from the right to the left down the table. Position and recognition were set.

**Thought 1.** Some love the titles and esteem, the special seats and places of recognition. There are those who love the restricted neighborhoods and clubs, the preferred lists. They love the preeminence. Note what is condemned: not being in these positions and places, but the *love* of them. Someone has to hold the upper positions and fill the major places. It is the *love* and feeling of pride because of the title and the place and position that is wrong.

> "How can ye believe, which receive honour one of another, and seek not the honour that cometh from God only?" (Jn.5:44).
>
> "Nevertheless man being in honour abideth not: he is like the beasts that perish" (Ps.49:12).
>
> "I wrote unto the church: but Diotrephes, who loveth to have the preeminence among them, receiveth us not" (3 Jn.9).

2.    The terrible sin of the religionists was that they devoured widows' houses; that is, they used widows for gain. This was and is a gross sin, and it is common. There are some preachers and leaders, professing hypocrites, who court the attention and favor of people (especially widows) for the purpose of securing money. They seek large donations, endowments, trusts, investments, and gifts *to promote themselves and their institution*. The great tragedy is that such false and hypocritical hearts use the guise of religion to promote themselves and their false ideas. Their call to people is to institutional religion, not to the honor of God and the spirit of self-denial. Vain men, of course, are succeptible to such appeals; but widows in particular are exposed to those who seem to be so devoted to God.

3.    The condemnation of religionists and any one else who is guilty of such sins is to be greater. There are some sins more horrible than others. Using religion for selfish ends is one of them. Such will receive a greater damnation. A fact should be noted here: widows hold a special place in God's heart. He has always instructed His people to care for them in a very special way.

> "He doth execute the judgment of the fatherless and widow, and loveth the stranger, in giving him food and raiment" (Dt.10:18).
>
> "Cursed be he that perverteth the judgment of the stranger, fatherless, and widow" (Dt.27:19).
>
> "A father of the fatherless, and a judge of the widows, is God in his holy habitation" (Ps.68:5).
>
> "Learn to do well; seek judgment, relieve the oppressed, judge the fatherless, plead for the widow" (Is.1:17).
>
> "And there was a widow in that city; and she came unto him, saying, Avenge me of mine adversary. And he would not for a while: but afterward he said within himself, Though I fear not God, nor regard man; yet because this widow troubleth me, I will avenge her, lest by her continual coming she weary me. And the Lord said, hear what the unjust judge saith. And shall not God avenge his own elect, which cry day and night unto him, though he bear long with them?" (Lk.18:3-7).

## CHAPTER 21

### I. The Widow's Mite: The Question of Giving, 21:1-4 (Mk.12:41-44)

| | |
|---|---|
| 1 Jesus sat & rested<sup>DS1</sup><br>  a. Saw the rich give<br>  b. Saw a poor widow give<br>2 Giving must be in the right spirit | And he looked up, and saw the rich men casting their gifts into the treasury.<br>2 And he saw also a certain poor widow casting in thither two mites. |
| 3 Giving must not be based on the amount given, but on the amount kept back | 3 And he said, of a truth I say unto you, that this poor widow hath cast in more than they all: |
| 4 Giving must be sacrificial, given because a person has need | 4 For all these have of their abundance cast in unto the offerings of God: but she of her penury hath cast in all the living that she had. |

# DIVISION VIII

## THE SON OF MAN'S DRAMATIC ENTRANCE INTO JERUSALEM: HIS CLAIM AND CONFLICT, 19:28-21:4

## I. The Widow's Mite: The Question of Giving, 21:1-4

(21:1-4) **Introduction—Stewardship**: giving to the church and charity is a thorn in the side of many. Most persons give a little money or a few worn out or unwanted items, but few give much of value. However, if the needs of a world that reels in desperation are to be met, many must begin to give and to give sacrificially. Something needs to be seen: giving may be debated among men, but it is not debatable with Jesus. Jesus answered the questions about giving, and He did so strongly—without hesitation and debate. Every person must give *everything he is and has* to meet the needs of a world that has thousands *dying every day*, dying because they lack the very necessities of life and have never heard the gospel of His glorious love and deliverance.

1. Jesus sat and rested (v.1-2).
2. Giving must be in the right spirit (v.2).
3. Giving must not be based on the amount given, but on the amount kept back (v.3).
4. Giving must be sacrificial, given because a person has need (v.4).

**1** (21:1-2) **Jesus Christ, Tired—Vision**: Jesus sat and rested. He had suffered a great deal of pressure and tension over the past few hours. The authorities had baited Him time and again with trick questions, trying to trap and discredit Him before the people (Lk.20:1-47). He was tired and mentally exhausted. Note the words, "He looked up." He had walked out of the court of the Gentiles into the court of the women and sat down to rest over by the treasury (see DEEPER STUDY # 1—Lk.21:1). His elbows were upon His knees and His face and head were resting in the palms of His hands. Sitting there with His eyes closed and resting, He heard the clanging of the money being dropped into the collection boxes. At some point "He looked up and saw" what must have been an impressive sight. It was Passover week and teeming thousands would be streaming by the boxes making their contributions. In fact, Mark says *"many that were rich cast in much"* (Mk.12:41). Jesus saw the rich making their contributions. In some cases the gifts were very large. Then all of a sudden out of nowhere something caught Jesus' eye. A poor widow cast in "two mites," which were the smallest coins—coins that had the least value in that day.

The point is this: Jesus saw in the widow's mite a timely illustration, an illustration that would answer man's question about giving to the work of God and meeting the desperate needs of the world.

---

**DEEPER STUDY # 1**

(21:1) **Temple—Treasury**: the treasury (gazophulakion) was in the court of the women. A section of the court had thirteen trumpet shaped collection boxes. Each box had written on it the purpose for which the offerings were to be used. People simply dropped their offerings into the box of the ministry they wished to support.

---

**2** (21:2) **Stewardship—Tithing**: giving must be in the right spirit. The widow was very poor. Jesus used two different words for "poor" to describe just how poor the woman really was. In verse two the word is *penichran* which means a person who earns only a meager, pitiful wage. In verse three the word is *ptoche* which means abject poverty, utter destitution, poverty that is visible and unquestionable. It is the poverty that forces one to beg and seek alms in order to survive. In that day there was little work for a widow. Poor widows had to struggle for their very survival. Such was the case of this poor widow; she was desperately poor. Note: she had cast in two mites, and the two coins were all she had (v.4).

1.    She was giving to God's work because she wanted to give. She wanted God to have what she had to use in His service. She did not give grudgingly or reluctantly, but willingly.

> "Every man according as he purposeth in his heart, so let him give; not grudgingly, or of necessity: for God loveth a cheerful giver" (2 Cor.9:7).
> "For if there be first a willing mind, it is accepted according to that a man hath, and not according to that he hath not" (2 Cor.8:12).

2.    Her trust was not in money. Her trust was in God. She literally gave all she had to God. Her spirit was right; it was reaching out to God, saying that all she had belonged to God. Both she and her possessions were the Lord's.

> "But rather give alms of such things as ye have; and, behold, all things are clean unto you" (Lk.11:41).
> "Charge them that are rich in this world, that they be not highminded, nor trust in uncertain riches, but in the living God, who giveth us richly all things to enjoy" (1 Tim.6:17).
> "The LORD redeemeth the soul of his servants: and none of them that trust in him shall be desolate" (Ps.34:22).
> "Trust in the LORD, and do good; so shalt thou dwell in the land, and verily thou shalt be fed....Commit thy way unto the LORD; trust also in him; and he shall bring it to pass" (Ps.37:3, 5).
> "Thou wilt keep him in perfect peace, whose mind is stayed on thee: because he trusteth in thee" (Is.26:3).
> "Blessed is the man that trusteth in the LORD, and whose hope the LORD is" (Jer.17:7).

**3**  (21:3) **Stewardship—Tithing**: giving must not be based on the amount given, but on the amount kept back. This is difficult for men to accept, in particular rich men, but it is definitely one of the points Jesus was making. Wealth and money are not for the purpose of hoarding and storing and banking, not in a world reeling with poverty and need, sin and death. The needs of all men must be met and the message of salvation and eternal life must to be proclaimed. The imperative of the need and command of God is unequivocal and irrevocable.

Note what Jesus said. She "hath cast in more than they all." Jesus was not saying that she cast in more than any *one* of them, but she cast in more than *all of them put together*. This was shocking! How could He make such a statement, for some had cast in much more money than she? And all the rich combined had cast in an enormous sum. Very simply, God measured what was kept back, not how much was given.

⇒ The widow had less remaining; the others still had much.
⇒ The widow had given more of what she had; the others had given less of what they had.
⇒ The widow had sacrificed more; the others had sacrificed less.

In proportion to what she had, the widow gave a larger percent. The others gave a much smaller percent. After they had given, they still had 85 percent or 95 percent to spend on themselves.

> "For where your treasure is, there will your heart be also" (Mt.6:21).
> "Sell that ye have, and give alms; provide yourselves bags which wax not old, a treasure in the heavens that faileth not, where no thief approacheth, neither moth corrupteth" (Lk.12:33).
> "Now when Jesus heard these things, he said unto him, Yet lackest thou one thing: sell all that thou hast, and distribute unto the poor, and thou shalt have treasure in heaven: and come, follow me" (Lk.18:22).
> "And Zacchaeus stood, and said unto the Lord; Behold, Lord, the half of my goods I give to the poor; and if I have taken any thing from any man by false accusation, I restore him fourfold" (Lk.19:8).
> "And though I bestow all my goods to feed the poor, and though I give my body to be burned, and have not charity, it profiteth me nothing" (1 Cor.13:3).
> "And God is able to make all grace abound toward you; that ye, always having all sufficiency in all things, may abound to every good work" (2 Cor.9:8).

**4**  (21:4) **Stewardship—Tithing**: giving must be sacrificial—given because a person has need. This is a critical point, a truth that must be heeded by all givers of every generation.

1.    The rich gave *out of their abundance*. They believed in God and trusted Him, and they were appreciative and thankful for the blessings of God. They were even concerned about the needs and welfare of God's work, concerned enough to give *sizable offerings*. It is important to see this fact in order to clearly see what Jesus was saying. The rich were giving and giving much because they cared deeply about the work of God.

2.    The widow gave sacrificially; she gave "out of her need." She "gave all the *living* she had." Why? Because she had a need, a great need. She desperately needed food, clothing, and shelter. She was so desperate she seldom knew where her next meal was coming from. The pressure and pain of being destitute and hungry and exposed to the elements was a daily experience for her, and no one cared or helped. But she knew something: God cared. She could trust God, so she took her need and gave it to God. Her need was financial, so she took what money she had and gave it all to God. She simply said, "God, I have need, the need for money. I do not even have enough money to buy food. If I am to eat, you have to provide—somehow, some way. I have worked as hard as I can at the jobs I have been able to find. Here is all I have. Take it; use it in your kingdom. I cast myself upon You. You take care of me."

She knew the great principle that God would take care of those who give all they *are and have* to Him. She knew that if she were to be *assured* of God's care, she had to give *all* to God. If she gave *all*, God would not deny anything to her. He would provide all the necessities of life (Mt.6:33). She took her need and all that was involved in it and gave it to God. She sought God to meet her need by giving to God *all that she had*.

Note another fact. Two needs are present and being met.
1.   God's temple (church) had need. The widow, though poor, gave to help the temple carry on the ministry of God.
2.   The poor widow had need. She gave believing God would see to it that she had food, clothing, and shelter. And note: God saw her, and although we are not told about how He did it, He took her under His wing and took care of her.

> "But seek ye first the kingdom of God, and his righteousness; and all these things shall be added unto you" (Mt.6:33).
> "Bring ye all the tithes into the storehouse, that there may be meat in mine house, and prove me now herewith, saith the LORD of hosts, if I will not open you the windows of heaven, and pour you out a blessing, that there shall not be room enough to receive it" (Mal.3:10).
> "The earth is the LORD'S, and the fulness thereof; the world, and they that dwell therein" (Ps.24:1).
> "Blessed is he that considereth the poor: the LORD will preserve him, and keep him alive; and he shall be blessed upon the earth: and thou wilt not deliver him unto the will of his enemies" (Ps.41:1).
> "The liberal soul shall be made fat: and he that watereth shall be watered also himself" (Pr.11:25).
> "He that hath a bountiful eye shall be blessed; for he giveth of his bread to the poor" (Pr.22:9).
> "But the liberal deviseth liberal things; and by liberal things shall he stand" (Is.32:8).
> "And if thou draw out thy soul to the hungry, and satisfy the afflicted soul; then shall thy light rise in obscurity, and thy darkness be as the noonday" (Is.58:10).

| | IX. THE SON OF MAN'S PROPHETIC SIGNS: HIS PREDICTION CONCERNING THE FATE OF JERUSALEM AND THE WORLD,*DS1* 21:5-38 (Mt.24-25; Mk.13) | ing, Master, but when shall these things be? and what sign will there be when these things shall come to pass? 8 And he said, Take heed that ye be not deceived: for many shall come in my name, saying, I am Christ; and the time draweth near: go ye not therefore after them. | questions 1) When was it to be destroyed 2) What were the signs c. The warning: Be not deceived |
|---|---|---|---|
| | A. The Predicted Signs of the Present Age, 21:5-11 (Mt.24:1-14; Mk.13:1-13) | 9 But when ye shall hear of wars and commotions, be not terrified: for these things must first come to pass; but the end is not by and by. | **2 Sign 1: False Christs** |
| **1 The disciples admired the temple's beauty** a. Jesus predicted the temple's utter destruction | 5 And as some spake of the temple, how it was adorned with goodly stones and gifts, he said, 6 As for these things which ye behold, the days will come, in the which there shall not be left one stone upon another, that shall not be thrown down. | 10 Then said he unto them, Nation shall rise against nation, and kingdom against kingdom: 11 And great earthquakes shall be in divers places, and famines, and pestilences; and fearful sights and great signs shall there be from heaven. | **3 Sign 2: Conflict of nations** **4 Sign 3: Natural disasters** |
| b. The disciples asked two | 7 And they asked him, say- | | |

# DIVISION IX

## THE SON OF MAN'S PROPHETIC SIGNS: HIS PREDICTION CONCERNING THE FATE OF JERUSALEM AND THE WORLD, 21:5-38

### A.     The Predicted Signs of the Present Age, 21:5-11

(21:5-38) **DIVISION OVERVIEW:** this chapter is known as the *Olivet Discourse* (see outlines and notes—Mt.24:1-25:46; DEEPER STUDY # 1,2,*3*—Mk.13:1-37 for more discussion). It deals with *three great subjects* that lay out in the future when they were predicted by Christ.

1.     The destruction of Jerusalem (v.6-7; cp. Mt.24:2-3).
2.     The Lord's return (v.7; cp. Mt.24:3).
3.     The end of the world (v.7; cp. Mt.24:3).

Matthew and Mark's account of what happens in this passage should be read along with Luke for a clearer understanding.

---

**DEEPER STUDY # 1**

(21:5-38) **End Time:** four things will help in understanding what Jesus was doing in the discussion of the end times.

1.     It will help to remember that Jesus was preparing His disciples for His death and departure from this world and preparing them to carry on after He was gone. His immediate disciples were to face some terrible times, ranging all the way from personal trials brought on by their witness for Jesus to national trials involving the utter destruction of their nation. In addition, it would be generations stretching into centuries before He returned to earth. No one knew this at that time, but He did. Therefore, He needed to prepare His future disciples as well, for they too were going to face all kinds of trials. There was the danger that His disciples might tire waiting for His return; moreover, they were to see and experience so much trouble in the world, their faith might falter. They, along with many in the world, might begin to ask:

**"Where is the promise of his coming? for since the fathers fell asleep, all things continue as they were from the beginning of the creation" (2 Pt.3:4).**

What Jesus did was use this occasion to reveal some of the events that were to take place upon the earth during these *"last days,"* the days of the church (Acts 2:16-17; 1 Jn.2:18). By knowing some of the events, His disciples would be better prepared to endure and to keep their hope for His return alive.

⇒     They would know that God is never caught off guard. God is still on the throne and still in control of all world events.

⇒     They would not be caught off guard themselves. They would know what to expect in this corruptible and sinful world. Therefore, when the events happened, they would not be as likely to become discouraged.

⇒     They would be challenged to *keep themselves* ever so close to God in order to be as strong as possible to face the trials coming upon earth.

⇒     They would be encouraged to place their hope in God and in the new heavens and earth and not in this corruptible world. They would be "looking for that blessed hope, and the glorious appearing of the great God and our Savior Jesus Christ" (Tit.2:13).

2.     Remembering that Jesus was dealing with two questions will also help in understanding what was being said. He was answering the questions: When will the temple be destroyed, and what shall be the sign of His return and of the end of the world?

Note something: Jesus was dealing with *the end of the temple and with the end of the world, the destruction of the temple and the destruction of the world*. He was covering the signs, the events that cause and occur during the judgment of *both the temple and the world*. What is the point? Simply this. Scripture teaches that the same sins and events cause the judgment of anything. That is, the events (sins) that cause judgment upon one thing are the same events that will bring judgment upon everything else. Therefore, the signs that surrounded the destruction of Jerusalem are much the same as the signs that will surround the end of the world. What Jesus was saying has a double meaning and application (see notes— Mt.24:1-14; 24:15-28. Both notes will help to see the double application.)

The Lord's words applied both to the disciples of His day and to all disciples who were to follow in succeeding generations. As long as the earth stands, the disciples of "the last days" (or ages) will face many of the same signs faced by those who experienced the destruction of Jerusalem. However, there is to be one difference. At the end of the world, the signs will *increase and intensify*. The day is coming; it will be so terrible that it can be called *the beginning of sorrows* (Mt.24:8), and the *great tribulation* (Mt.24:21). (See notes—Mt.24:1-28; 24:15-28 for a discussion of these two lessons.)

3.     The present age is considered by God to be "the age of the last days" or "the last time." According to God's timetable, the history of the church, its presence on earth takes place in "the last days" or during "the last times."

> **"But this is that which was spoken by the prophet Joel: And it shall come to pass in the last days, saith God, I will pour out of my Spirit upon all flesh: and your sons and your daughters shall prophesy, and your young men shall see visions, and your old men shall dream dreams" (Acts 2:16-17).**
>
> **"[God] hath in these last days spoken unto us by his Son, whom he hath appointed heir of all things, by whom also he made the worlds" (Heb.1:2).**
>
> **"Little children, it is the last time" (1 Jn.2:18).**

4.     A quick overview of the passages in this chapter also helps in understanding what Jesus was doing.
    a.    The signs of the present age (Lk.21:5-11).
    b.    The tragic sign prior to the end: persecution (Lk.21:12-19).
    c.    The destruction of Jerusalem (Lk.21:20-24).
    d.    The Coming of the Son of Man (Lk.21:25-28).
    e.    The Parable of the Fig Tree: the signs are clearly seen (Lk.21:29-33).

(21:5-11) **Introduction—End Time**: there is a matter of critical importance when looking at the end time. In understanding what Jesus was saying, we have to be very careful not to add to or take away from what He said. Both mistakes were made by religionists concerning Jesus' first coming (Mt.2:4-6).

A major fact to keep in mind is this. The disciples *did think* that all three events (Jerusalem's destruction, the Lord's return, and the world's end) would happen at about the same time. They did think in terms of the Messianic Kingdom of God. Comparing Acts 1:6 with the Jewish concept of the Messiah shows this. (See notes—Mt.1:1; DEEPER STUDY # 2—1:18; DEEPER STUDY # 3—3:11; notes—11:1-6; 11:2-3; DEEPER STUDY # 1—11:5; DEEPER STUDY # 2—11:6; DEEPER STUDY # 1—12:16; notes— 22:42; Lk.7:23-23.) When Jesus said that the temple would be destroyed, the disciples assumed it would happen at the same time that He returned to end the world, thereby restoring the kingdom to Israel.

Jesus, however, gave no timetable. He did not say when the three events would occur. What He did was give signs that would occur before the events, signs that would point toward His return and toward the end of Jerusalem and toward the end of the world.

It is also important to keep in mind that most of the signs happen *all through history*. However, there is this difference: the signs increase and intensify right before the end of Jerusalem and the end of the world. There will be a period known as *the beginning of sorrows* (Mt.24:8) and a period launched by *the abomination of desolation* known as the "great tribulation, such as was not since the beginning of the world" (Mt.24:21).

The signs of the present age are three.
1.     The disciples admired the temple's beauty (v.5-8).
2.     Sign 1: false Christs (v.8).
3.     Sign 2: conflict of nations (v.9-10).
4.     Sign 3: natural disasters (v.11).

**1** (21:5-8) **End Time**: the disciples admired the temple's beauty. The temple was magnificent. It sat upon the towering summit of Mount Zion. It was built of white marble plated with gold. The temple was a massive structure that could hold thousands of people. (Cp. Acts 4:4 which perhaps took place in the temple. Five thousand men were saved among a crowd which probably numbered many thousands more.) The temple had several porches such as Solomon's Porch and the Royal Porch that were supported with huge, towering pillars. The pillars were so large that it took three to four men's reaching arm to arm to encircle each one. The temple was a striking sight, one of the building wonders of the world. The disciples apparently stood some place where the temple in all its magnificent beauty struck them with awe, and they wanted Jesus to see the beautiful sight. When they drew His attention to it, three things happened.

1.     Jesus used the occasion to arouse the disciples' interest in coming events. He predicted the temple's utter destruction.

2.     The disciples were shocked and aroused to ask two questions of the Lord. To understand the questions, the beliefs of the disciples must be remembered. Their thoughts were filled with the idea of Israel's glory as the greatest nation upon earth. They had finally accepted the fact that Jesus was the Messiah, God's appointed instrument to free Israel and to raise the nation to its destined glory. Therefore, when Jesus began to talk about the temple's being razed to the ground, they

were utterly shocked. "Master, when shall these things be?" They could hardly believe their ears. The thought that flashed across their minds was *the end time*. "These things will occur in *the end time*, will they not, Master? Just when will they take place? What signs will there be to show they are about to take place?" (Cp. Mt.24:1-3, 15-31.) In their minds the temple could not possibly be destroyed until the end of all things came about. They were thinking that the glory of Israel was to be set up when all of a sudden, Jesus began to talk about the utter destruction of the temple, the very center of their nation. They wanted to know two things.

⇒ When was the temple to be destroyed?

⇒ What would be the signs "when these things shall come to pass," that is, the destruction of Jerusalem, the end of the world, and the Lord's return (see DEEPER STUDY # 1—Lk.21:5-38)?

3.    Jesus warned His disciples not to be deceived. This can mean one or two things.

    a.    A person can be easily deceived when dealing with end time prophecies.

    b.    A person can be easily deceived when facing the end time events. He can be deceived into thinking that certain cataclysmic events are infallible signs that the end is at hand. Too often cataclysmic events result in wild guesses about the end time. They result in...

        • universal predictions.

        • the deceiving of others.

        • discouragement of one's faith when the end does not come.

**2**    (21:8) **Messiah, False**: the first sign will be *false messiahs*. Jesus said three things about this sign.

1.    There will be *many*, not just a few but *many,* false messiahs.

2.    They will make two claims.

    a.    The claim of deity. Note the words, "I Am" (eimi). This is the name which was used by God to reveal Himself to Moses. It is the most basic name of Deity. "I Am" equals *Being*, the most basic Being of the Universe. It is the claim used by God to tell man that He is the Supreme Being of the universe, the Messiah, the Deliverer of all mankind (see note—Jn.6:20).

    b.    The claim that the end time—the Messianic Age, the age when Israel and the world are to be delivered—*is at hand*. (How often this claim is made, even by some well-meaning men! But note what Jesus said in the next point.)

3.    "Go...not...after them." They are false messiahs. The real Messiah has already come, Jesus Christ, the Son of God Himself. It is He and He alone who has "the words of eternal life." As Peter exclaimed:

**"Lord, to whom shall we go? thou hast the words of eternal life" (Jn.6:68).**

**Thought 1.** Note to whom Christ was speaking: His disciples. Disciples can be misled by false teachers and prophets.

        **"Beware of false prophets, which come to you in sheep's clothing, but inwardly they are ravening wolves" (Mt.7:15).**

        **"For many shall come in my name, saying, I am Christ; and shall deceive many" (Mt.24:5).**

        **"And many false prophets shall rise, and shall deceive many" (Mt.24:11).**

        **"For there shall arise false Christs, and false prophets, and shall show great signs and wonders; insomuch that, if it were possible, they shall deceive the very elect" (Mt.24:24; cp. Mk.13:22).**

        **"Also of your own selves shall men arise, speaking perverse things, to draw away disciples after them" (Acts 20:30).**

        **"For they that are such serve not our Lord Jesus Christ, but their own belly; and by good words and fair speeches deceive the hearts of the simple" (Ro.16:18).**

        **"For such are false apostles, deceitful workers, transforming themselves into the apostles of Christ" (2 Cor.11:13).**

        **"That we henceforth be no more children, tossed to and fro, and carried about with every wind of doctrine, by the sleight of men, and cunning craftiness, whereby they lie in wait to deceive" (Eph.4:14).**

        **"Now the Spirit speaketh expressly, that in the latter times some shall depart from the faith, giving heed to seducing spirits, and doctrines of devils; speaking lies in hypocrisy; having their conscience seared with a hot iron" (1 Tim.4:1-2).**

        **"But evil men and seducers shall wax worse and worse, deceiving, and being deceived" (2 Tim.3:13).**

        **"For the time will come when they will not endure sound doctrine; but after their own lusts shall they heap to themselves teachers, having itching ears; and they shall turn away their ears from the truth, and shall be turned unto fables" (2 Tim.4:3-4).**

        **"For there are many unruly and vain talkers and deceivers, specially they of the circumcision [the doctrine of the law, of works]: whose mouths must be stopped, who subvert whole houses, teaching things which they ought not, for filthy lucre's sake" (Tit.1:10-11).**

        **"But there were false prophets also among the people, even as there shall be false teachers among you, who privily shall bring in damnable heresies, even denying the Lord that bought them, and bring upon themselves swift destruction" (2 Pt.2:1).**

"Little children, it is the last time: and as ye have heard that antichrist shall come, even now are there many antichrists; whereby we know that it is the last time. They went out from us, but they were not of us; for if they had been of us, they would no doubt have continued with us: but they went out, that they might be made manifest that they were not all of us" (1 Jn.2:18-19).

"Who is a liar but he that denieth that Jesus is the Christ? He is antichrist, that denieth the Father and the Son" (1 Jn.2:22).

"For many deceivers are entered into the world, who confess not that Jesus Christ is come in the flesh. This is a deceiver and an antichrist" (2 Jn.7).

**3** (21:9-10) **World Violence—War**: the second sign will be *conflict of nations*. Four things were said here.

1. Believers will hear of wars and commotions (akatastasias), which means tumults, uproars, riots, terrorism, insurrections, treasons, confusions of governments. There will be uprisings within governments, and governments will be overthrown. Believers can become extremely disturbed over the news.

2. Believers are not to be "terrified" (ptoethete). They are not to let their hearts "be troubled" (Jn.14:1). World violence can trouble people; but the believer's heart and life are to be centered upon God, trusting His presence, care, and security—eternally.

"Let not your heart be troubled: ye believe in God, believe also in me. In my Father's house are many mansions: if it were not so, I would have told you. I go to prepare a place for you" (Jn.14:1-2).

"These things I have spoken unto you, that in me ye might have peace. In the world ye shall have tribulation: but be of good cheer; I have overcome the world" (Jn.16:33).

"And I say unto you my friends, Be not afraid of them that kill the body, and after that have no more that they can do. But I will forewarn you whom ye shall fear: Fear him, which after he hath killed hath power to cast into hell; yea, I say unto you, Fear him" (Lk.12:4-5).

3. World violence "must first come to pass." It does not come to pass because God destines it, but because men's hearts are gripped by passion, lust, greed, and evil.

"Woe unto the world because of offences! for it must needs be that offences come; but woe to that man by whom the offence cometh!" (Mt.18:7).

"From whence come wars and fightings among you? come they not hence, even of your lusts that war in your members? Ye lust, and have not: ye kill, and desire to have, and cannot obtain: ye fight and war, yet ye have not, because ye ask not" (Jas.4:1-3).

4. World violence can so dominate the news that men are led to believe that the end is at hand. However, Jesus warned, "The end is not by and by," not yet. Remember the words just spoken, "Take heed that ye be not deceived."

"And nation was destroyed of nation, and city of city: for God did vex them with all adversity. Be ye strong therefore, and let not your hands be weak: for your work shall be rewarded" (2 Chron.15:6-7).

"My people, go ye out of the midst of her, and deliver ye every man his soul from the fierce anger of the LORD. And lest your heart faint, and ye fear for the rumor that shall be heard in the land; a rumor shall both come one year, and after that in another year shall come a rumor, and violence in the land, ruler against ruler" (Jer.51:45-46).

"And take heed to yourselves, lest at any time your hearts be overcharged with surfeiting, and drunkenness, and cares of this life, and so that day come upon you unawares" (Lk.21:34).

"Be careful for nothing; but in every thing by prayer and supplication with thanksgiving let your requests be made known unto God" (Ph.4:6).

"Casting all your care upon him; for he careth for you" (1 Pt.5:7).

**4** (21:11) **Nature—Earthquakes—Famines—Pestilence**: the fourth sign will be *natural disasters*. Five disasters in nature were mentioned in particular.

1. Earthquakes. Great earthquakes cause enormous damage to buildings, disrupting and destroying the lives of people, cities, and communitites. Earthquakes are one of the most alarming and frightening disasters among men. Josephus records the fulfillment of Jesus' prophecy. He even hints that the natural disasters which happened were a sign of coming destruction.

"...there broke out a prodigious storm in the night, with the utmost violence, and very strong winds, with the largest showers of rain, and continual lightnings, terrible thunderings, and amazing concussions and bellowings of the earth, that was in an earthquake. These things were a manifest indication that some destruction was coming upon men, when the system of the world was put into this disorder; and any one would guess that these wonders forshowed some grand calamities that were coming" (Josephus, Wars. 4. 4:5).

Earthquakes will occur in many places during the last days of the earth (Rev.6:12; 11:12-13, 19; 16:17-19).

2. Famines. Food is one of the most basic necessities of men. Without food men die. Jesus said that in the last days, right before Jerusalem's fall and right before the end of the world, there shall be terrible famine. Scripture speaks of a "great famine throughout all the world which came to pass in the days of Claudius Caesar" (Acts 11:28-30). Josephus describes the famine as being so terrible that when flour "was brought into the temple...not one of the priests was so hardy as

to eat one crumb of it... while so great a distress was upon the land" (Josephus, *Ant.* 3. 15:3). He says in another place, "A famine did oppress them [Jerusalem]...and many people died for want of what was necessary to procure food" (Josephus, *Ant.* 20:25).

In the very last days before Jerusalem's fall, Josephus speaks of another terrible famine:

> "It was now a miserable case, and a sight that would justly bring tears into our eyes, how men stood to their food, while the more powerful had more than enough, and the weaker were lamenting (for want of it)" (Josephus, Wars. 5. 10:3).
> "Then did the famine widen its progress, and devoured the people by whole houses and families; the upper rooms were full of women and children that were dying by famine; and the lanes of the city were full of the dead bodies of the aged; the children also and the young men wandered about the marketplaces like shadows, all swelled with famine, and fell down dead wheresoever their misery seized them" (Josephus, Wars. 5. 12:3).

There is evidently to be terrible famine in the last days. The black horse of the four horsemen of the Apocalypse indicates terrible famine (see note—Rev.6:5-6). The unbearable pain and terrible evil that hunger can cause is graphically described by Scripture.

> **"They that be slain with the sword are better than they that be slain with hunger: for these pine away, stricken through for want of the fruits of the field. The hands of the pitiful women have sodden [boiled] their own children: they were their meat [food] in the destruction of the daughter of my people" (Lam.4:9-10).**

Luke adds a third disaster of nature: pestilence. Earthquakes and famines, of course, cause disease and pestilence (see note—Mt.24:7).

3. Pestilence. Disease is often the result of war and widespread disasters such as earthquakes. Pestilence shows no partiality. The rich may be able to buy food during a famine, but they cannot buy their way out of an epidemic of disease. Death by disease and other natural causes shows no partiality.

Josephus' record of a great pestilence that struck during the days of Herod is evidence of the fact.

> "When he [Herod] was in the way, there arose a pestilential disease, and carried off the greatest part of the multitude, and of his best and most esteemed friends [the wealthy]" (Josephus, Ant. 15. 7:7).

Pestilence will also be one of the terrible sufferings at the end time. Part of the suffering caused by the pale horse of the four horsemen of the Apocalypse includes pestilences.

> **"Power was given unto (Death and Hell) over the fourth part of the earth, to kill with sword [war], and with hunger [famine], and with death [pestilence resulting from war and famine]" (Rev.6:8; see note—Rev.6:8).**

4. Astronomical happenings. There will be "fearful sights and great signs" happening in the sky at the end of the world. Very practically, such astronomical happenings occur now. The earth is sometimes darkened by dust from earthly catastrophes such as volcanic eruptions, wind storms, and smoke from huge fires. Of course, whatever darkens the sun, hides the light of the moon from earth. The stars, that is, meteorites of varying sizes, fall through space often. The point is, the events of the end time are going to trigger astronomical happenings worldwide, universally. (See notes—Mk.13:24; Mk.13:24-25 for more discussion.)

> **"But in those days, after that tribulation, the sun shall be darkened, and the moon shall not give her light, and the stars of heaven shall fall, and the powers that are in heaven shall be shaken" (Mk.13:24-25).**
> **"But the same day that Lot went out of Sodom it rained fire and brimstone from heaven, and destroyed them all. Even thus shall it be in the day when the Son of man is revealed" (Lk.17:29-30).**
> **"And there shall be signs in the sun, and in the moon, and in the stars; and upon the earth distress of nations, with perplexity; the sea and the waves roaring; men's hearts failing them for fear, and for looking after those things which are coming on the earth: for the powers of heaven shall be shaken" (Lk.21:25-26).**
> **"And I will show wonders in heaven above, and signs in the earth beneath; blood, and fire, and vapor of smoke: the sun shall be turned into darkness, and the moon into blood, before that great and notable day of the Lord come" (Acts 2:19-20).**
> **"And I beheld when he had opened the sixth seal, and, lo, there was a great earthquake; and the sun became black as sackcloth of hair, and the moon became as blood; and the stars of heaven fell unto the earth, even as a fig tree casteth her untimely figs, when she is shaken of a mighty wind. And the heaven departed as a scroll when it is rolled together; and every mountain and island were moved out of their places. And the kings of the earth, and the great men, and the rich men, and the chief captains, and the mighty men, and every bondman, and every free man, hid themselves in the dens and in the rocks of the mountains; and said to the mountains and rocks, Fall on us, and hide us from the face of him that sitteth on the throne, and from the wrath of the Lamb: for the great day of his wrath is come; and who shall be able to stand?" (Rev.6:12-17).**

| | **B. The Tragic Sign Prior to the End: Persecution, 21:12-19** (Mt.24:9-10, 13; Mk.13:9, 11-12) | ye shall answer: 15 For I will give you a mouth and wisdom, which all your adversaries shall not be able to gainsay nor resist. | defense 2) A supernatural answer will be given |
|---|---|---|---|
| **1 The persecution of believers** a. The persecutors: Religious & civil authorities b. The reason: Believers are followers of Christ | 12 But before all these, they shall lay their hands on you, and persecute you, delivering you up to the synagogues, and into prisons, being brought before kings and rulers for my name's sake. | 16 And ye shall be betrayed both by parents, and brethren, and kinsfolks, and friends; and some of you shall they cause to be put to death. 17 And ye shall be hated of all men for my name's sake. | **2 The betrayers of believers** a. Relatives b. All men |
| c. The result: A glorious testimony d. The preparation 1) Do not prepare a | 13 And it shall turn to you for a testimony. 14 Settle it therefore in your hearts, not to meditate before | 18 But there shall not an hair of your head perish. 19 In your patience possess ye your souls. | **3 The promise to believers** a. God is in control b. Eternal security: *If* endure |

# DIVISION IX

## THE SON OF MAN'S PROPHETIC SIGNS: HIS PREDICTION CONCERNING THE FATE OF JERUSALEM AND THE WORLD, 21:5-38

## B. The Tragic Sign Prior to the End: Persecution, 21:12-19

(21:12-19) **Introduction**: the discussion of the present passage focuses upon the signs of the end time (see *Deeper Study # 1*—Lk.21:5-38). There is one sign of the end time that must be proclaimed to all believers. It is the sign of *persecution*. It is true that believers are persecuted in every generation, but right before the end time there will be a great intensification of persecution throughout the whole world. Believers will be persecuted as never before. Note the words, "But before all these, they shall lay their hands on you, and persecute you." Believers must be prepared. This is the purpose of the present passage. The passage can be applied to believers in every generation to prepare them for facing persecution.

1. The persecution of believers (v.12-15).
2. The betrayers and traitors of believers (v.16-17).
3. The promise to believers (v.18-19).

**1** (21:12-15) **Persecution, Reasons; Results**: the persecution of believers. Note three facts.

1. The persecution will be carried out by both civil and religious authorities. Both the government and religion will persecute true believers right before the end time. The idea is, of course, an intensification of persecution in the end time (see note—Lk.21:5-8). This is the very reason Jesus made a distinction between the end time and the church age persecutors. Right before the end of the world, believers will be opposed, abused, arrested, tried, and martyred as never before in human history. Both the courts of the world and the councils of religion will take believers and rake them over the hot coals of persecution. Believers will be...

- afflicted (cp. Acts 4:3; 8:1; 12:4; 13:50; 14:19; 2 Cor.11:23-25).
- killed (Acts 7:59; 12:2).
- hated by all nations (Acts 28:22. See outline and notes—Mt.10:16-23. Cp. Jn.15:20; 16:2.)

2. The reason believers will be persecuted is clearly stated by Jesus: *"For my name's sake."* The world will try to stamp out and silence believers because they are true followers of Christ. Their intense hatred of the believer will be due to at least three reasons.

   a. The standard of true godliness. The believer sets before the world a different standard—the standard of true godliness. The world is not godly nor is its standard godly. Therefore by his *very nature*, any man who lives for the world and does not wish to change opposes godliness.

   > **"Wherefore come out from among them, and be ye separate, saith the Lord, and touch not the unclean thing; and I will receive you, and will be a Father unto you, and ye shall be my sons and daughters, saith the Lord Almighty" (2 Cor.6:17-18).**
   > **"Love not the world, neither the things that are in the world. If any man love the world, the love of the Father is not in him. For all that is in the world, the lust of the flesh, and the lust of the eyes, and the pride of life, is not of the Father, but is of the world" (1 Jn.2:15-16).**

   b. The life of purity. The genuine believer lives a life of purity, clean and just. True morality and godliness controls the mind, dresses modestly, converses respectfully, and behaves justly. The worldly live to fulfill the lust of their flesh and to have possessions as they wish. Therefore, the believer is opposed by any person who does not wish to live a pure and just life.

   > **"Now the works of the flesh are manifest, which are these; Adultery, fornication, uncleanness, lasciviousness, idolatry, witchcraft, hatred, variance, emulations, wrath, strife, seditions, heresies, envyings, murders, drunkenness, revellings, and such like: of the which**

I tell you before, as I have also told you in time past, that they which do such things shall not inherit the kingdom of God. But the fruit of the Spirit is love, joy, peace, longsuffering, gentleness, goodness, faith, meekness, temperance: against such there is no law. And they that are Christ's have crucified the flesh with the affections and lusts" (Gal.5:19-24).

c. The message of repentance and of self-denial. The genuine believer proclaims the message of Christ: repentance and self-denial. Very practically, few men are willing to change (repent) to the degree that self is totally denied (person and possessions) in order to meet the needs of desperate people. Therefore most, even the religious, oppose the idea that men are to live sacrificially in order to save a starving and dying world (both a physically and spiritually starving and dying world). (See outline and notes—Mt.19:21-22; 19:23-26.)

"And he said to them all, If any man will come after me, let him deny himself, and take up his cross daily, and follow me. For whosoever will save his life shall lose it: but whosoever will lose his life for my sake, the same shall save it" (Lk.9:23-24).
"For if ye live after the flesh, ye shall die: but if ye through the Spirit do mortify the deeds of the body, ye shall live" (Ro.8:13).
"Jesus said unto him, If thou wilt be perfect, go and sell that thou hast, and give to the poor, and thou shalt have treasure in heaven: and come and follow me" (Mt.19:21).
"It is good neither to eat flesh, nor to drink wine, nor any thing whereby thy brother stumbleth, or is offended, or is made weak" (Ro.14:21).
"Let no man seek his own, but every man another's wealth [welfare]" (1 Cor.10:24).

3. The result of the persecution will be a glorious witness for the Lord. The persecutors will try to silence the believer, but the very persecution itself will turn out to be a glorious witness for the Lord. How? The believer, standing there suffering, will show such loyalty and supernatural strength that some, even some of the persecutors, will be attracted to Christ. The believer will show that Christ and eternity are real, and he will be a testimony even as he receives the beatings and the swords of the persecutors.

"For I will show him how great things he must suffer for my name's sake" (Acts 9:16).
"Blessed be God, even the Father of our Lord Jesus Christ, the Father of mercies, and the God of all comfort; who comforteth us in all our tribulation, that we may be able to comfort them which are in any trouble, by the comfort wherewith we ourselves are comforted of God" (2 Cor.1:3-4).
"For we which live are alway delivered unto death for Jesus' sake, that the life also of Jesus might be made manifest in our mortal flesh" (2 Cor.4:11).

4. The preparation of a defense will not be necessary. When the genuine believer has to give an answer or a defense to his persecutors, God will fill his heart and mouth with a reply. The believer will be so filled with wisdom that his persecutors will not be able to resist his defense.
Note: Jesus was not promising the believer that he would be freed. He was promising a strong, unanswerable testimony. It will be time for many believers to go on home with the Lord. The end time will be filled with the blood of many martyrs for the Lord.

"At my first answer no man stood with me, but all men forsook me: I pray God that it may not be laid to their charge. Notwithstanding the Lord stood with me, and strengthened me; that by me the preaching might be fully known, and that all the Gentiles might hear: and I was delivered out of the mouth of the lion. And the Lord shall deliver me from every evil work, and will preserve me unto his heavenly kingdom: to whom be glory for ever and ever" (2 Tim.4:16-18).
"So that we may boldly say, The Lord is my helper, and I will not fear what man shall do unto me" (Heb.13:6).
"Fear thou not; For I am with thee: be not dismayed; for I am thy God: I will strengthen thee; yea, I will help thee; yea, I will uphold thee with the right hand of my righteousness" (Is.41:10).
"Behold, the Lord GOD will help me; who is he that shall condemn me? lo, they all shall wax old as a garment; the moth shall eat them up" (Is.50:9).

**2** (21:16-17) **Persecution**: the betrayal of believers will be heartrending. Believers will be betrayed by their *own families and relatives*, friends and neighbors. Some believers will even be put to death because of their betrayal. Note three points.
1. Jesus was speaking of the end time. Betrayal by loved ones will intensify in the end time.
2. The reason for the betrayal will cut the human heart. Families and friends will hate the believer because of Christ (v.17). The believer will stand for the name and righteousness of Christ; therefore, loved ones will betray him...
- to save their own lives
- to secure some favor
- to escape embarrassment
- to secure vengeance
- to escape persecution themselves
- to gain the favor of authorities
- to escape fear
- to preserve selfish honor or position

"And the brother shall deliver up the brother to death, and the father the child: and the children shall rise up against their parents, and cause them to be put to death" (Mt.10:21).

423

3.    *All* shall hate the believer. Few will be kind, tender, and loving; dissension and division will prevail in the last days. Most will begrudge what another has or is doing or is not doing. Unfortunately, such behavior has been the case down through the centuries, and too often the church has experienced one person's disliking and opposing another person. Envy, greed, and concern for security and recognition—all the sins of selfishness—have caused too many to stand against another person's position, beliefs, abilities, and leadership. Criticism and judging, dissension and division among believers have been and are some of the most visible traits of the church, both locally and universally. Jesus said that such hatred will increase and intensify in the end time.

> **"But beware of men: for they will deliver you up to the councils, and they will scourge you in their synagogues" (Mt.10:17).**
> **"Then shall they deliver you up to be afflicted, and shall kill you: and ye shall be hated of all nations for my name's sake" (Mt.24:9; cp. Lk.21:12-13).**
> **"Remember the word that I said unto you, The servant is not greater than his lord. If they have persecuted me, they will also persecute you; if they have kept my saying, they will keep yours also" (Jn.15:20).**
> **"These things have I spoken unto you, that ye should not be offended. They shall put you out of the synagogues: yea, the time cometh, that whosoever killeth you will think that he doeth God service. And these things will they do unto you, because they have not known the Father, nor me" (Jn.16:1-3).**
> **"Yea, and all that will live godly in Christ Jesus shall suffer persecution" (2 Tim.3:12).**
> **"O LORD my God, in thee do I put my trust: save me from all them that persecute me, and deliver me" (Ps.7:1).**
> **"My times are in thy hand: deliver me from the hand of mine enemies, and from them that persecute me" (Ps.31:15).**
> **"All thy commandments are faithful: they persecute me wrongfully; help thou me" (Ps.119:86).**
> **"For the enemy hath persecuted my soul; he hath smitten my life down to the ground; he hath made me to dwell in darkness, as those that have been long dead" (Ps.143:3).**

**3**    (21:18-19) **Persecution**: the promise is glorious and assuring to the believer. It is twofold.

1.    First, the promise is that God is in control of the believer's life, total control. "Not an hair of your head shall perish." Jesus meant, of course, spiritual security. He had just said some would "be put to death" (v.16). God knows every hair on the believer's head (Lk.12:7); God is in total control of every single thing concerning the believer. Therefore, if the believer is persecuted, he is under God's care; and if he is being killed, he is under God's care. No matter the persecution and suffering...

- God sees and is in control. He holds the believer in His hands.
- God turns the suffering into a "far more exceeding and eternal weight of glory" and reward (2 Cor.4:17).

2.    Second, the promise is the eternal security of the believer's soul. If the believer endures the persecution, he shall possess his soul eternally. The idea is that endurance to the end is *required*. The genuine believer *will* stand fast and endure. He will *not deny* his Lord; he could never give in to such, for he knows the presence and salvation (deliverance) of the Lord. (See note—Mk.13:13.)

Very simply, persecution is not to be feared by the Christian believer. Persecution, even martyrdom, is nothing in light of eternity (cp. Rev.6:9-11). Despite death (v.16) and hatred (v.17), Jesus promised "there shall not a hair of your head perish" (v.18). The believer is secure in the arms of Jesus eternally.

> **"Fear none of those things which thou shalt suffer: behold, the devil shall cast some of you into prison, that ye may be tried; and ye shall have tribulation ten days: be thou faithful unto death, and I will give thee a crown of life" (Rev.2:10).**
> **"To them who by patient continuance in well doing seek for glory and honour and immortality, *eternal life*: but unto them that are contentious, and do not obey the truth, but obey unrighteousness, indignation and wrath, tribulation and anguish, upon every soul of man that doeth evil, of the Jew first, and also of the Gentile (Ro.2:7-9).**
> **"Blessed is the man that endureth temptation [trial]: for when he is tried, he shall receive the crown of life, which the Lord hath promised to them that love him" (Jas.1:12).**
> **"Behold, we count them happy which endure. Ye have heard of the patience of Job, and have seen the end of the Lord; that the Lord is very pitiful, and of tender mercy" (Jas.5:11).**
> **"But ye are a chosen generation, a royal priesthood, an holy nation, a peculiar people; that ye should show forth the praises of him who hath called you out of darkness into this marvellous light (1 Pt.2:9).**

| | C. The Destruction of Jerusalem, 21:20-24 (Mt.24:15-28; Mk.13:14-23) | vengeance, that all things which are written may be fulfilled. | |
|---|---|---|---|
| 1 A sign for which to look: Jerusalem surrounded by armies | 20 And when ye shall see Jerusalem compassed with armies, then know that the desolation thereof is nigh. | 23 But woe unto them that are with child, and to them that give suck, in those days! for there shall be great distress in the land, and wrath upon this people. | 4 A time of woe: Distress & wrath, death & captivity |
| 2 A time to flee | 21 Then let them which are in Judaea flee to the mountains; and let them which are in the midst of it depart out; and let not them that are in the countries enter thereinto. | 24 And they shall fall by the edge of the sword, and shall be led away captive into all nations: and Jerusalem shall be trodden down of the Gentiles, until the times of the Gentiles be fulfilled. | 5 A time numbered by the Gentiles |
| 3 A time of vengeance[DS1] | 22 For these be the days of | | |

# DIVISION IX

## THE SON OF MAN'S PROPHETIC SIGNS: HIS PREDICTION CONCERNING THE FATE OF JERUSALEM AND THE WORLD, 21:5-38

## C. The Destruction of Jerusalem, 21:20-24

(21:20-24) **Introduction—End Time**: this passage is definitely dealing with the destruction of Jerusalem in A.D. 70 and with the Jewish nation throughout history (v.24).

⇒ The desolation mentioned is the desolation of Jerusalem, not the *abomination of desolation* (that is, the antichrist spoken of by Matthew and Mark, Mt.24:15; Mk.13:14).

⇒ Verse 24 makes it clear that the period covered by Jesus stretches from the time "ye shall see Jerusalem compassed with armies" (v.20) "until the times of the Gentiles be fulfilled" (v.24).

However, the points of this Scripture can also be applied to the end time as well. Matthew and Mark definitely give a double meaning to the words of Jesus. The disciples had asked two questions. First, when was Jerusalem to be destroyed? They thought it could be destroyed only in the end time. Second, what were the signs of the end time, or the destruction and remaking of all things which would usher in the Kingdom of God? (See note—Lk.21:5-8. Cp. notes—Lk.21:5-38 for more discussion.) What Jesus says in Matthew and Mark can be applied here in Luke. The fall of Jerusalem is judgment upon sin, and the fall of the world will be judgment upon sin. The questions asked by the disciples (v.7) refer to similar conditions that bring about judgment. Therefore, the signs of both the fall of Jerusalem and the end of the world are similar. The only difference is that there will be an intensification of the signs in the end time (see notes—Mt.24:15-28; Mk.13:14-23).

1. A sign for which to look: Jerusalem surrounded by armies (v.20).
2. A time to flee (v.21).
3. A time of vengeance (v.22).
4. A time of woe, distress and wrath, death and captivity (v.23).
5. A time numbered by the Gentiles (v.24).

**1** (21:20) **Jerusalem**: a sign to look for is that of Jerusalem's being surrounded by armies. In A.D. 66-70 Jerusalem experienced one of the most terrible sieges in history. In A.D. 66 the Jews revolted and the Roman army was swift to attack. However, the city was difficult to take primarily for two reasons. It sat upon a hill, well protected by the terrain, and the leaders of the revolt were religious fanatics. Well over a million people had fled into the city behind its protective walls.

Jesus made two points.
1. Some standing there with Him were to *see* and be witnesses of the sign. They were to actually see judgment fall upon Jerusalem.
2. All of His followers were to be *looking* for and alert to the sign. They were to be prepared at all times for the coming judgment.

> **Thought 1.** The point is clear. We are to be prepared for the coming judgment of the end time. Some of us will be the actual witnesses of the sign. (See outline, note, and DEEPER STUDY # 1—Mt.24:15 for more discussion and application.)

**2** (21:21) **End Time—Judgment**: the sign of Jerusalem's being surrounded will be a time to flee. Jesus warned His disciples to flee and to flee immediately. The danger would be imminent and urgency would be needed. Believers...

• in the *surrounding areas* around Jerusalem are to flee to the mountains.
• in the *midst* of Jerusalem are to get out and leave the city immediately.
• in other countries are to stay away and give no thought to entering Jerusalem (Israel).

Note two things.
1. The believers did heed the warning of Jesus. They fled Jerusalem before the attack, sometime around A.D. 66. They fled to a small town called *Pella* in the district of Decapolis.

2.	Matthew points out that Jesus said to forget all comfort of home and personal possessions, that the danger was so close and terrible that believers should think only about escaping. Nothing else mattered, nothing except fleeing the coming judgment.

> **Thought 1.** Too many minds are centered upon comfort and possessions, the world and money. The coming judgment is so close and terrible, it alone should consume our thoughts. We must flee to Christ for safety when the signs are seen, and they are definitely seen today. We who live in these "last days" must heed the warning of Christ even as believers of the first century heeded.

> **Thought 2.** The judgment that fell upon Jerusalem is a picture of the coming judgment upon the world. We must be prepared to flee to Christ for safety.

>> "Therefore whosoever heareth these sayings of mine, and doeth them, I will liken him unto a wise man, which built his house upon a rock: and the rain descended, and the floods came, and the winds blew, and beat upon that house; and it fell not: for it was founded upon a rock" (Mt.7:24-25).
>> "Laying up in store for themselves a good foundation against the time to come, that they may lay hold on eternal life" (1 Tim.6:19).
>> "Nevertheless the foundation of God standeth sure, having this seal, The Lord knoweth them that are his. And, Let every one that nameth the name of Christ depart from iniquity" (2 Tim.2:19).
>> "Let your conversation be without covetousness; and be content with such things as ye have: for he hath said, I will never leave thee, nor forsake thee" (Heb.13:5).

**3** (21:22) **Judgment—End Time**: the sign of Jerusalem's being surrounded will be a time of vengeance. Note two points.

1.	"The days of vengeance" will be the fulfillment of Scripture, the days of God's wrath (see DEEPER STUDY # 1, *Vengeance*—Lk.21:22). God had been patient and long-suffering with Israel for generations, in fact, from the very beginning of their history. But Israel had always rejected God's pleadings. Therefore, the predicted judgment had to fall. What Israel had sown was to be reaped. (See DEEPER STUDY # 1—Jn.4:22.)

2.	The terrible desolation that took place upon Jerusalem and that is to take place at the end of the world—all the desolation—is due to sin. Jerusalem committed the most heinous sin in human history: the people rejected God for centuries and eventually killed God's very own Son. Therefore, Jerusalem was utterly destroyed.

> **Thought 1.** There is a severe warning here for believers and nations. Sin results in desolation. Rejection of God's Son will bring judgment upon any person and any nation of people.

---

**DEEPER STUDY # 1**

(21:22) **Vengeance** (ekdikeseos): executing perfect justice, retribution, satisfaction. It is judgment that flows out of righteousness and justice. It is not the retaliation that flows from human anger and hurt feelings. There is no self-gratification or selfish reaction in the word at all. It is judgment that executes perfect justice. It is judgment that makes things right, exactly as they should be.

> "Dearly beloved, avenge not yourselves, but rather give place unto wrath: for it is written, Vengeance is mine; I will repay, saith the Lord" (Ro.12:19).
> "And to you who are troubled rest with us, when the Lord Jesus shall be revealed from heaven with his mighty angels, in flaming fire taking vengeance on them that know not God, and that obey not the gospel of our Lord Jesus Christ" (2 Th.1:7-8).
> "For we know him that hath said, Vengeance belongeth unto me, I will recompense, saith the Lord. And again, The Lord shall judge his people. It is a fearful thing to fall into the hands of the living God" (Heb.10:30-31).
> "To me belongeth vengeance, and recompense; their foot shall slide in due time: for the day of their calamity is at hand, and the things that shall come upon them make haste" (Dt.32:35).
> "O LORD God, to whom vengeance belongeth; O God, to whom vengeance belongeth, show thyself. Lift up thyself, thou judge of the earth: render a reward to the proud" (Ps.94:1-2).
> "And I will execute great vengeance upon them with furious rebukes; and they shall know that I am the LORD, when I shall lay my vengeance upon them" (Ezk.25:17).
> "And I will execute vengeance in anger and fury upon the heathen, such as they have not heard" (Mic.5:15).
> "God is jealous, and the LORD revengeth; the LORD revengeth, and is furious; the LORD will take vengeance on his adversaries, and he reserveth wrath for his enemies" (Nah.1:2).

---

**4** (21:23) **End Time—Judgment**: the sign of Jerusalem's being surrounded will be a time of woe, distress and wrath, death and captivity. Four pictures are painted to describe the awfulness of the hour.

1.	Women who were pregnant and carrying small children would find it difficult to flee. They would be too slow to escape the onrushing judgment.

2. There would be great "distress" in the land. As the siege wore on, the predictions of Jesus were literally fulfilled. There was the killing and maiming of loved ones in war, the famine and pestilence and false deliverers (messiahs). There was the betrayal and murder of neighbors in stealing food and seeking the favor of authorities in order to survive. Everyone was fending for himself. There was the utter chaos and collapse of order. There was the pressure and tension, the suffering and pain that one's nation and people were about to be wiped off the face of the earth. Distress swept over the whole land.

3. The wrath of man (Rome) and the wrath of God fell upon the people.

4. An unbelievable number fell by the sword; over one million people died and about ninety-seven thousand were taken captive (see notes—Mt.24:7; 24:10; 24:11. See Josephus, *Wars* 5. 12:3; 6. 3:4; 6. 8:5.)

> *"It appears to me that the misfortunes of all men, from the beginning of the world, if they be compared to these of the Jews, are not so considerable as they were"* (Josephus, *Wars*. Preface 4).

In the end time, the world will experience great tribulations—unparalleled in history. Note that Jesus did not describe the great trials beyond what He had already said in these verses. A quick glance at the great tribulation period covered in Revelation will give some idea of the trials (see outlines and notes—all of the following. Cp. Dan.12:1-2.)

⇒ Thunderings, lightnings, and an earthquake (Rev.8:5; cp. 8:1-5).
⇒ Natural catastrophes (Rev.8:6-12).
⇒ Demonic-like locust or plagues (Rev.8:13-9:11).
⇒ Demonic-like army (Rev.9:12-21).
⇒ Nations angry, destroying the earth (Rev.11:18; cp. 11:14-19).
⇒ An evil political ruler (Rev.13:1-10).
⇒ A false religious ruler (Rev.13:11-18).
⇒ Terrible destruction and suffering both upon nature and men (Rev.16:1-21).
⇒ An evil, deceptive world power (Rev.17:1-18:24).

**5** (21:24) **Gentiles, Times of**: the sign of Jerusalem's being surrounded will be a time numbered by the Gentiles. The Jewish nation was to be scattered and Jerusalem trodden down until "the times of the Gentiles be fulfilled." Note two things.

1. The word "fulfilled" (plerothosin) means that God is in control of the times. There is a purpose to "the times of the Gentiles" and to what has happened and is yet to happen to Israel. God is in control of history.

> **"And saying, The time is fulfilled, and the kingdom of God is at hand: repent ye, and believe the gospel" (Mk.1:15).**
>
> **"But when the fulness of the time was come, God sent forth his Son, made of a woman, made under the law, to redeem them that were under the law, that we might receive the adoption of sons. And because ye are sons, God hath sent forth the Spirit of his Son into your hearts, crying, Abba, Father" (Gal.4:4-6).**
>
> **"That in the dispensation of the fulness of times he might gather together in one all things in Christ, both which are in heaven, and which are on earth; even in him" (Eph.1:10).**
>
> **"For there is one God, and one mediator between God and men, the man Christ Jesus; who gave himself a ransom for all, to be testified in due time" (1 Tim.2:5-6).**
>
> **"In hope of eternal life, which God, that cannot lie, promised before the world began; but hath in due times manifested his word through preaching, which is committed unto me according to the commandment of God our Saviour" (Tit.1:2-3).**

2. There is to be an end to the Jews' captivity and to Jerusalem's being trodden down. The nation will be restored to its land. When? When "the times of the Gentiles be fulfilled." (See outline and notes, *Israel's Restoration*—Ro.11:25-36; note and DEEPER STUDY # 1—11:25-26 for more discussion.)

> **"For I would not, brethren, that ye should be ignorant of this mystery, lest ye should be wise in your own conceits; that blindness in part is happened to Israel, until the fulness of the Gentiles be come in. And so all Israel shall be saved: as it is written, There shall come out of Sion the Deliverer, and shall turn away ungodliness from Jacob: for this is my covenant unto them, when I shall take away their sins" (Ro.11:25-27).**

| | D. The Coming of Jesus: The Son of Man, 21:25-28 (Mt.24:29-31; Mk.13:24-27) | for fear, and for looking after those things which are coming on the earth: for the powers of heaven shall be shaken. | & fearing d. Reason reemphasized: Heavenly bodies shaken |
|---|---|---|---|
| 1  The signs of astronomical happenings & their results a. Distress of nations b. Oceans affected | 25 And there shall be signs in the sun, and in the moon, and in the stars; and upon the earth distress of nations, with perplexity; the sea and the waves roaring; | 27 And then shall they see the Son of man coming in a cloud with power and great glory. 28 And when these things begin to come to pass, then look up, and lift up your heads; for your redemption | 2  The actual coming of Jesus, the Son of Man 3  The great encouragement to the believer: Look up— your redemption is near |
| c. Men's hearts failing | 26 Men's hearts failing them | draweth nigh. | |

# DIVISION IX

## THE SON OF MAN'S PROPHETIC SIGNS: HIS PREDICTION CONCERNING THE FATE OF JERUSALEM AND THE WORLD, 21:5-38

### D.  The Coming of Jesus: The Son of Man, 21:25-28

(21:25-28) **Introduction**: the Lord now begins to cover the most significant event yet to occur in human history: His own personal return. The language points toward the Lord's personal return to earth (Lk.21:27, 35). The point is this: there are signs that precede His coming, signs that will enable His followers to be prepared and strengthened to the utmost in endurance.

1.  The signs of astronomical happenings and their results (v.25-26).
2.  The actual coming of Jesus, the Son of Man (v.27).
3.  The great encouragement to the believer: look up—your redemption is near (v.28).

[1]  (21:25-26) **End Time—Jesus Christ, Return—Heavenly Bodies—Outer Space**: the signs of astronomical happenings and their results. There shall be signs in the sun, moon, and stars. What will happen is described in both Matthew and Mark (Mt.24:29; Mk.13:24). Mark says...

- "The sun shall be darkened."
- "The moon shall not give her light."
- "The stars of heaven shall fall."
- "The powers that are in heaven shall be shaken."

Very practically, such astronomical happenings occur now. The earth is sometimes darkened by dust from earthly catastrophes such as volcanic eruptions, wind storms, and smoke from huge fires. Of course, whatever darkens the sun, hides the light of the moon from earth. The stars, that is, meteorites of varying sizes, fall throughout space often. "The powers of the heavens" being shaken could mean the heavenly bodies outside our solar system that are called by the Bible "the host of heaven" (Dt.4:19).

Something should be mentioned about the power of the atom. The atom exploded on earth is powerful enough to darken the sun and moon from earth's view. Worldwide atomic warfare would cause so much dust and pollution it would be difficult for any man to see anything in outer space. But as the atom is known today, it could not affect the axis or rotation (the falling or shaking) of the sun and moon and stars unless there were to be an inter-galactical war of some sort way out in the future, and unless there was a power much greater than what we know today. This is not to say that atomic warfare will never happen. There will be wars and rumors of war as long as the earth stands. But what the Bible teaches is that God is going to end all things, not man. When the world ends, it will be God's ending it by His own will and act.

An extreme literalism needs to be avoided when interpreting these verses, for there is so much we do not know about the laws (powers) of nature and the forces God has put in motion throughout the universe. However, there is absolutely no reason for not understanding the Lord's words as actual or literal events.

What the present passage seems to mean is that the whole universe is going to be affected by Christ's coming to earth. The sun and moon, the stars and powers (laws) of heaven will be affected in the sense that they will *open up and receive Him* and serve notice that He is the Creator, the Son of Man, God's very own Son, who is now coming to earth in great power and glory. Imagine a spectacular universal fireworks display, and perhaps what Christ is saying is being pictured. A simple question is: Why would not everything, including the heavenly bodies, put on a display (that would be terrifying to man) when its Creator, the Son of God, returns?

The astronomical bodies are affected because of the *evil of men and the wrath of God*. The scene of falling stars (meteorites) will not be for man to witness a spectacular event; it will be to point to the Son of God, to His judgment falling upon the earth. Every man is going to know beyond any doubt that Jesus Christ is coming in all the power and the glory of God Himself. As Jesus said, "with power and great glory" He is coming. He is coming that "every knee should bow, of things in heaven, and things in earth, and things under the earth; and that every tongue should confess that Jesus Christ is Lord, to the glory of God the Father" (Ph.2:10-11). (See notes—Mt.24:29 for more discussion.)

The astronomical happenings will, of course, have devastating results upon earth. These results are the very point of Luke.

⇒  There will be distress and perplexity of nations. The picture is that of leaders' and governments' meeting and trying to figure out what is happening to the heavenly bodies in the sky above. However, they will not know nor be able to cope. They are perplexed and distressed, sensing the doom of the universe.

⇒ There will be the roaring effect upon the oceans and the upheaval of their waves and tides. This, of course, is to be expected since the oceans are controlled by the heavenly bodies.

⇒ There will be men's hearts' failing them; men will be gripped by fear, a desperate fear, sensing the end of the world is at hand. And note: the end *will* be at hand.

> "But in those days, after that tribulation, the sun shall be darkened, and the moon shall not give her light, and the stars of heaven shall fall, and the powers that are in heaven shall be shaken" (Mk.13:24-25).

> "But the same day that Lot went out of Sodom it rained fire and brimstone from heaven, and destroyed them all. Even thus shall it be in the day when the Son of man is revealed" (Lk.17:29-30).

> "And there shall be signs in the sun, and in the moon, and in the stars; and upon the earth distress of nations, with perplexity; the sea and the waves roaring; men's hearts failing them for fear, and for looking after those things which are coming on the earth: for the powers of heaven shall be shaken" (Lk.21:25-26).

> "And I will show wonders in heaven above, and signs in the earth beneath; blood, and fire, and vapor of smoke: the sun shall be turned into darkness, and the moon into blood, before that great and notable day of the Lord come" (Acts 2:19-20).

> "And I beheld when he had opened the sixth seal, and, lo, there was a great earthquake; and the sun became black as sackcloth of hair, and the moon became as blood; and the stars of heaven fell unto the earth, even as a fig tree casteth her untimely figs, when she is shaken of a mighty wind. And the heaven departed as a scroll when it is rolled together; and every mountain and island were moved out of their places. And the kings of the earth, and the great men, and the rich men, and the chief captains, and the mighty men, and every bondman, and every free man, hid themselves in the dens and in the rocks of the mountains; and said to the mountains and rocks, Fall on us, and hide us from the face of him that sitteth on the throne, and from the wrath of the Lamb: for the great day of his wrath is come; and who shall be able to stand?" (Rev.6:12-17).

> "For the stars of heaven and the constellations thereof shall not give their light: the sun shall be darkened in his going forth, and the moon shall not cause her light to shine. And I will punish the world for their evil, and the wicked for their iniquity; and I will cause the arrogancy of the proud to cease, and will lay low the haughtiness of the terrible. I will make a man more precious than fine gold; even a man than the golden wedge of Ophir. Therefore I will shake the heavens, and the earth shall remove out of her place, in the wrath of the Lord of hosts, and in the day of his fierce anger" (Is.13:10-13).

> "Fear, and the pit, and the snare, are upon thee, O inhabitant of the earth. And it shall come to pass, that he who fleeth from the noise of the fear shall fall into the pit; and he that cometh up out of the midst of the pit shall be taken in the snare: for the windows from on high are open, and the foundations of the earth do shake. The earth is utterly broken down, the earth is clean dissolved, the earth is moved exceedingly. The earth shall reel to and fro like a drunkard, and shall be removed like a cottage; and the transgression thereof shall be heavy upon it; and it shall fall, and not rise again. And it shall come to pass in that day, that the Lord shall punish the host of the high ones that are on high, and the kings of the earth upon the earth. And they shall be gathered together, as prisoners are gathered in the pit, and shall be shut up in the prison...." (Is.24:17-22).

> "And I will show wonders in the heavens and in the earth, blood, and fire, and pillars of smoke. The sun shall be turned into darkness, and the moon into blood, before the great and the terrible day of the Lord come" (Joel 2:30-31).

> "The sun and the moon shall be darkened, and the stars shall withdraw their shining. The Lord also shall roar out of Zion, and utter his voice from Jerusalem; and the heavens and the earth shall shake: but the Lord will be the hope of his people, and the strength of the children of Israel" (Joel 3:15-16).

**2** (21:27) **Jesus Christ, Return**: the actual coming of Jesus, the Son of Man. There are three significant points in this verse.

1. It will be the Son of Man who comes. Jesus claimed to be the Son of Man, God's very own Son incarnate in human flesh as Perfect Man (see DEEPER STUDY # 3—Mt.8:20). In that day, there will be no doubt about who He is (cp. Mk.14·61-62). Right now He is recognized only by believers, but then His identity will be unmistakable: He is the Son of Man.

2. Every eye, all men, shall see Him return. This is what is meant by "they." Matthew actually says, "All the tribes of the earth mourn, and they shall see the Son of Man coming" (Mt.24:30). His return will be visible to every man on earth, and every man shall then acknowledge Him to be Lord, God's very own Son (Ph.2:9-11; cp. Rev.1:7).

3. He is coming "in the clouds with great power and glory." Picture the scene. The backdrop of heaven is pitch dark, without any major light from the sun and moon. And then, suddenly, as quickly as the flash of lightning, the most brilliant focus of light ever known to man appears. The Shekinah glory of God will shine in the person of Jesus Christ as He appears to the world. The Son of Man is there, in the clouds, having returned in great power and glory just as He said He would.

"Which also said, Ye men of Galilee, why stand ye gazing up into heaven? this same Jesus, which is taken up from you into heaven, shall so come in like manner as ye have seen him go into heaven" (Acts 1:11).

"And to you who are troubled rest with us, when the Lord Jesus shall be revealed from heaven with his mighty angels, in flaming fire taking vengeance on them that know not God, and that obey not the gospel of our Lord Jesus Christ: Who shall be punished with everlasting destruction from the presence of the Lord, and from the glory of his power; when he shall come to be glorified in his saints, and to be admired in all them that believe (because our testimony among you was believed) in that day" (2 Th.1:7-10).

"And then shall that Wicked be revealed, whom the Lord shall consume with the spirit of his mouth, and shall destroy with the brightness of his coming" (2 Th.2:8).

"Behold, he cometh with clouds; and every eye shall see him, and they also which pierced him: and all kindreds of the earth shall wail because of him. Even so, Amen" (Rev.1:7).

"And I saw heaven opened, and behold a white horse; and he that sat upon him was called Faithful and True, and in righteousness he doth judge and make war. His eyes were as a flame of fire, and on his head were many crowns; and he had a name written, that no man knew, but he himself. And he was clothed with a vesture dipped in blood: and his name is called The Word of God. And the armies which were in heaven followed him upon white horses, clothed in fine linen, white and clean. And out of his mouth goeth a sharp sword, that with it he should smite the nations: and he shall rule them with a rod of iron: and he treadeth the winepress of the fierceness and wrath of Almighty God. And he hath on his vesture and on his thigh a name written, KING OF KINGS, AND LORD OF LORDS" (Rev.19:11-16).

**3** (21:28) **Jesus Christ, Return**: the great encouragement to the believer. What a glorious hope the believer has! When the terrible events come in the heavens and upon the earth, he is...
- not to be distressed and perplexed, as the nations will be.
- not to fear and have a failing heart, as men will have.

Believers are not to be discouraged, but encouraged. They are to look up and lift up their heads, for their redemption draweth near. The consummation of their salvation and hope is about to take place.

"Teaching us that, denying ungodliness and worldly lusts, we should live soberly, righteously, and godly, in this present world; looking for that blessed hope, and the glorious appearing of the great God and our Saviour Jesus Christ; who gave himself for us, that he might redeem us from all iniquity, and purify unto himself a peculiar people, zealous of good works" (Tit.2:12-14).

"In whom we have redemption through his blood, even the forgiveness of sins" (Col.1:14).

"And you, that were sometime alienated and enemies in your mind by wicked works, yet now hath he reconciled [redeemed] in the body of his flesh through death, to [eternally] present you holy and umblameable and unreproveable in his sight" (Col.1:21-22).

"Looking for that blessed hope, and the glorious appearing of the great God and our Saviour Jesus Christ; who gave himself for us, that he might redeem us [eternally] from all iniquity, and purify unto himself a peculiar people, zealous of good works" (Tit.2:13-14).

"And for this cause he is the mediator of the new testament, that by means of death, for the redemption of the transgressions that were under the first testament, they which are called might receive the promise of eternal inheritance" (Heb.9:15).

"And they sung a new song, saying, Thou art worthy to take the book, and to open the seals thereof: for thou wast slain, and hast redeemed us to God by thy blood out of every kindred, and tongue, and people, and nation; and hast made us unto our God kings and priests: and we shall reign on the earth" (Rev.5:9-10).

"I will lift up mine eyes unto the hills, from whence cometh my help" (Ps.121:1).

"Praise ye the LORD. Praise, O ye servants of the LORD, praise the name of the LORD" (Ps.113:1).

"To whom then will ye liken me, or shall I be equal? saith the Holy One. Lift up your eyes on high, and behold who hath created these things, that bringeth out their host by number: he calleth them all by names by the greatness of his might, for that he is strong in power; not one faileth" (Is.40:25-26).

| | E. The Parable of the Fig Tree: The Signs are Clearly Seen, 21:29-33 (Mt.24:32-35; Mk.13:28-34) | your own selves that summer is now nigh at hand. 31 So likewise ye, when ye see these things come to pass, know ye that the kingdom of God is nigh at hand. | b. Will show the Kingdom of God is at hand |
|---|---|---|---|
| 1 The signs can be seen—are discernable | | 32 Verily I say unto you, This generation shall not pass away, till all be fulfilled. | 2 The signs will occur within one generation |
| a. Will be seen just as the leaves of a fig tree are seen when they first appear | 29 And he spake to them a parable; Behold the fig tree, and all the trees; 30 When they now shoot forth, ye see and know of | 33 Heaven and earth shall pass away: but my words shall not pass away. | 3 The signs are sure—eternally set |

# DIVISION IX

## THE SON OF MAN'S PROPHETIC SIGNS: HIS PREDICTION CONCERNING THE FATE OF JERUSALEM AND THE WORLD, 21:5-38

### E. The Parable of the Fig Tree: The Signs are Clearly Seen, 21:29-33

(21:29-33) **Introduction**: when will Christ return to earth? The signs covered in v.5-28 will be clearly seen. The day and hour are known only by God, but believers are to be ready. There will be no excuse for being caught off guard.
1. The signs can be seen—are discernable (v.29-31).
2. The signs will occur within one generation (v.32).
3. The signs are sure—eternally set (v.33).

1 (21:29-31) **End Time—Jesus Christ, Return**: the signs can be seen; they are discernable. Jesus said two things.
1. The signs are to be just as clear as the leaves appearing on a fig tree. Note exactly what Jesus said.
    a. Behold the fig tree and all the other trees. Observe and study this truth. If a person is not looking and thinking about the fact, he will miss the truth. Looking, observing, studying, thinking about the fact is essential in order to see the truth.
    b. When the leaves shoot forth, if a person sees and notices them, he *knows* something. Summer is *now* near.
2. The signs will show that the Kingdom of God is at hand, that Jesus Christ is ready to return to earth and set up the Kingdom of God (see DEEPER STUDY # 3, *Kingdom of God*—Mt.19:23-24). Note that Jesus used the word "know." When the signs are seen, believers are to *know* that the end is at hand and not question, wonder, doubt, disbelieve, or fall away.
    ⇒ When believers see false messiahs and prophets arise, they can *know* that a large number of the lost and carnal will be tragically deceived.
    ⇒ When believers see conflict of nations, they can *know* terrible times lie ahead.
    ⇒ When believers see natural disasters, they can *know* that the worst periods of human suffering ever experienced are about to occur.
    ⇒ When believers see intensified persecution, they can *know* God is about to straighten out the injustices and crimes of men.
    ⇒ When believers see armies amassing against Jerusalem, they can *know* the time of the Gentiles is about to end and Israel restored once-for-all.
    ⇒ When believers see astronomical happenings, they can *know* the Lord's return is at hand.

The point is strikingly clear: signs are just that, signs. And signs do at least four things.
1. They point toward an object, helping us to see the object (Christ) and to anticipate knowing the object (Christ).
2. They focus attention upon an object (Christ). Signs keep our thoughts upon Christ and His glorious return.
3. They give direction, keeping us on the right track, helping to guard and protect us from going astray.
4. They give assurance and confidence, assurance that we will not be caught off guard and taken by surprise.

2 (21:32) **End Time—Jesus Christ, Return**: the signs will occur in one generation. Jesus warned: the events will occur rapidly. They will happen in one generation. Just what is meant by "generation" is often disputed, but it must *always* be kept in mind that the disciples had asked two questions: one about Jerusalem's destruction and one about the end of the world. In answering their questions, Jesus nowhere drew a definite line between the two questions. The signs and events that precede one shall precede the other. Therefore, just as the signs and destruction of Jerusalem took place within a generation, the signs and destruction of the world will also occur within a generation. (See DEEPER STUDY # 2, pt.2—Mt.24:1-31 for more discussion.)

3 (21:33) **End Time—Jesus Christ, Return**: the signs are sure, eternally set. The events are sure and irrevocable. Jesus was definite about what He had said. "Heaven and earth *shall* pass away, but my words shall not pass away." Note two things.
1. Heaven and earth shall pass away. Jesus was saying they were actually going to be done away with (2 Pt.3:10-11).
2. All that He had said—all about the great tribulation and His return—would happen. The great tribulation and His return were more sure than heaven and earth.

In the eyes of men, it has been a long, long time since Jesus spoke these words; and an innumerable list of events have happened. Therefore, they assume the whole idea of the second coming is a fable, the figment of hopeful imagination. God knew this would happen.

> "Knowing this first, that there shall come in the last days scoffers, walking after their own lusts, and saying, Where is the promise of his coming? for since the fathers fell asleep, all things continue as they were from the beginning of the creation....But, beloved, be not ignorant of this one thing, that one day is with the Lord as a thousand years, and a thousand years as one day. The Lord is not slack concerning his promise, as some men count slackness; but is longsuffering to usward, not willing that any should perish, but that all should come to repentance. But the day of the Lord will come as a thief in the night; in the which the heavens shall pass away with a great noise, and the elements shall melt with fervent heat, the earth also and the works that are therein shall be burned up. Seeing then that all these things shall be dissolved, what manner of persons ought ye to be in all holy conversation and godliness, looking for and hasting unto the coming of the day of God, wherein the heavens being on fire shall be dissolved, and the elements shall melt with fervent heat? Nevertheless we, according to this promise, look for new heavens and a new earth, wherein dwelleth righteousness" (2 Pt.3:3-4, 8-13).

Three things are certain to happen in human history:
⇒ "the beginning of sorrows" (Mt.24:8).
⇒ "the great tribulation, such as was not since the beginning of the world" ((Mt.24:21).
⇒ "the Son of Man coming in the clouds of heaven with power and great glory" (Lk.21:27).

Heaven and earth shall pass away but not the words Jesus spoke, not what He said would happen. What He said would happen will happen. The three events are certain.

> "But the day of the Lord will come as a thief in the night; in the which the heavens shall pass away with a great noise, and the elements shall melt with fervent heat, the earth also and the works that are therein shall be burned up" (2 Pt.3:10).
>
> "And I saw a new heaven and a new earth: for the first heaven and the first earth were passed away" (Rev.21:1).
>
> "And the world passeth away, and the lust thereof: but he that doeth the will of God abideth for ever"(1 Jn.2:17).
>
> "And they that use this world, as not abusing it: for the fashion of this world passeth away" (1 Cor.7:31).
>
> "While we look not at the things which are seen, but at the things which are not seen: for the things which are seen are temporal; but the things which are not seen are eternal" (2 Cor.4:18).
>
> "Of old hast thou laid the foundation of the earth: and the heavens are the work of thy hands. They shall perish, but thou shalt endure: yea, all of them shall wax old like a garment; as a vesture shalt thou change them, and they shall be changed" (Ps.102:25-26).
>
> "The earth mourneth and fadeth away, the world languisheth and fadeth away, the haughty people of the earth do languish" (Is.24:4).
>
> "And all the host of heaven shall be dissolved, and the heavens shall be rolled together as a scroll: and all their host shall fall down, as the leaf falleth off from the vine, and as a falling fig from the fig tree" (Is.34:4).
>
> "Lift up your eyes to the heavens, and look upon the earth beneath: for the heavens shall vanish away like smoke, and the earth shall wax old like a garment, and they that dwell therein shall die in like manner: but my salvation shall be for ever, and my righteousness shall not be abolished" (Is.51:6).
>
> "And I will say to my soul, Soul, thou hast much goods laid up for many years; take thine ease, eat, drink, and be merry. But God said unto him, Thou fool, this night thy soul shall be required of thee: then whose shall those things be, which thou hast provided?" (Lk.12:19-20).

| | F. The Warning: Watch & Pray for The Day of Jesus' Return, 21:34-36 (Mt.24:42-44; Mk.13:35-37) |
|---|---|
| **1 It demands taking heed**<br>  a. By not engaging in worldliness<br>    1) Partying & drunkenness<br>    2) Cares of life<br><br>  b. Reason: Lest the believer be caught unaware— snared—trapped[DS1] | 34 And take heed to yourselves, lest at any time your hearts be overcharged with surfeiting, and drunkenness, and cares of this life, and so that day come upon you unawares.<br>35 For as a snare shall it come on all them that dwell on the face of the whole earth. |
| **2 It demands watching & praying always**<br>  a. To be counted worthy<br>  b. To escape the things coming to earth<br>  c. To stand justified | 36 Watch ye therefore, and pray always, that ye may be accounted worthy to escape all these things that shall come to pass, and to stand before the Son of man. |

# DIVISION IX

## THE SON OF MAN'S PROPHETIC SIGNS: HIS PREDICTION CONCERNING THE FATE OF JERUSALEM AND THE WORLD, 21:5-38

## F. The Warning: Watch and Pray for the Day of Jesus' Return, 21:34-36

(21:34-36) **Introduction**: the universe is to suffer much in coming days. Sometime out in the future, the world will experience disasters and calamities as never before. There will be an increase...

- in wars and conflicts of nations (v.9-10).
- in natural disasters such as earthquakes, famines, disease (v.11).
- in persecution of believers (v.12-19).
- in attacks upon Israel (v.20-24).
- in astronomical happenings (v.25-26).
- in distress of nations (v.25).
- in ocean disturbances (v.25).
- in men's hearts' failing and fearing (v.26).

Jesus warned the believer. The believer must watch and pray for that day.
1. It demands taking heed (v.34-35).
2. It demands watching and praying always (v.36).

**1** (21:34-35) **End Time—Jesus Christ, Return—Indulgence—Drunkenness—Worldliness**: that day (the end time and the day of the Lord's return) demands taking heed. The word "take heed" (prosexete) means to give attention, to focus one's mind, to guard, to beware, to take care. Note the believer is to take heed to *himself*, that is, to guard his life. *How*? By not engaging in worldliness. His heart is not to be overcharged (barethosin): heavy, weighed down, burdened, overloaded, filled up, indulged. Three worldly acts in particular are mentioned.

1. Surfeiting (kraipale). The word means to be lighthearted, silly, frivolous, giddy. Medically, it referred to drunken nausea or headaches. It is the kind of lightheartedness, silliness, frivolity, and giddiness that comes from partying and drinking. It is the loose, giddy, suggestive movements and talk that take place...

- at parties
- at social gatherings
- on dates
- behind closed doors
- at luncheons & dinner engagements
- at dances
- at clubs
- on business trips
- in the dark (cp. 1 Th.5:5-10)

2. Drunkenness (methei). The word comes from the word meaning *wine* (methu). It means to be drunk with wine (or any other strong drink or drug), to be intoxicated. Drinking wine (or any other strong drink or drug) has several bad effects:

⇒ It indulges the lust, the appetite of the flesh.
⇒ It *loosens up* a person's moral restraints and allows the indulging of sexual and immoral cravings.
⇒ It dulls the mind to responsibility.
⇒ It burdens the heart and conscience and causes guilt, at least until a person becomes hardened in his sin.
⇒ It deadens feelings for spouses and loved ones, causing distance and withdrawal (such is seldom, if ever, regained).
⇒ It harms the body.

"Let us walk honestly, as in the day; not in rioting [revelling, carousing, partying] and drunkenness, not in chambering [immorality] and wantonness [debauchery, sensuality, licentiousness], not in strife and envying" (Ro.13:13).

"Now the works of the flesh are manifest, which are these...drunkenness, revellings, and such like: of the which I tell you before, as I have also told you in time past, that they which do such things shall not inherit the kingdom of God" (Gal.5:19, 21).

"And be not drunk with wine, wherein is excess; but be filled with the Spirit" (Eph.5:18).

3. Cares of this life. This means to indulge one's cravings for more and more of the things of this world. Man too often gives his attention and focuses his mind upon more and more of this world. *He desires far more than what he needs*, more...

- food and delicacies
- clothes and the latest styles
- houses and furnishings
- property and holdings
- cars and other vehicles
- free time and recreation
- money and wealth
- recognition and esteem

"For the time past of our life may suffice us to have wrought the will of the Gentiles, when we walked in lasciviousness, lusts, excess of wine, revellings, banquetings, and abominable idolatries: wherein they think it strange that ye run not with them to the same excess of riot, speaking evil of you" (1 Pt.4:3-4).

"But these, as natural brute beasts, made to be taken and destroyed, speak evil of the things that they understand not; and shall utterly perish in their own corruption; and shall receive the reward of unrighteousness, as they that count it pleasure to riot [party, indulge] in the day time. Spots they are and blemishes, sporting themselves with their own deceivings while they feast with you" (2 Pt.2:12-13).

Why is the believer to take heed, to guard himself against these things? The point is crucial. The believer can be focusing upon the things and possessions of the world so much that he is caught unaware, snared and entrapped in the end time. That day, the day of the Lord's return, can catch him unexpectedly and unprepared.

"For as in the days that were before the flood they were eating and drinking, marrying and giving in marriage, until the day that Noe entered into the ark, and knew not until the flood came, and took them all away; so shall also the coming of the Son of man be" (Mt.24:38-39).

"For man also knoweth not his time: as the fishes that are taken in an evil net, and as the birds that are caught in the snare; so are the sons of men snared in an evil time, when it falleth suddenly upon them" (Eccl.9:12).

---

**DEEPER STUDY # 1**

(21:35) **Snare—End Time—Jesus Christ, Return—World, Judgment Upon**: the word "snare" (pagis) means to trap as in a net. That day, the end time, is going to catch the whole world unprepared. The terrible events and calamities of the end times are going to fall upon the earth and entrap all. All who dwell upon the earth shall be caught in the disastrous events, the destruction and devastation, distress and misery, misfortune and loss, suffering and affliction. (See outline and notes—Lk.21:5-33.)

Jesus warned the believer. He must "take heed," for in the end time the world will experience great tribulations unparalleled in history. A quick glance at the great tribulation period covered in Revelation will give some idea of the trials (see outlines and notes—all of the following. Cp. Dan.12:1-2.)

⇒ Thunderings, lightnings, and an earthquake (Rev.8:5; cp. 8:1-5).
⇒ Natural catastrophes (Rev. 8:6-12).
⇒ Demonic-like locust or plagues (Rev.8:13-9:11).
⇒ Demonic-like army (Rev.9:12-21).
⇒ Nations angry and destroying the earth (Rev.11:18; cp. 11:14-19).
⇒ An evil political ruler (Rev.13:1-10).
⇒ A false and evil religious ruler (Rev.13:11-18).
⇒ Terrible destruction and suffering both upon nature and men (Rev.16:1-21).
⇒ An evil, deceptive world power (Rev.17:1-18:24).

---

**2** (21:36) **End Times—Watching—Praying—Believers, Duties**: that day (the end time and the day of the Lord's return) demands watching and praying *always*. The word "watch" (agrupneite) means to be sleepless, awake, on guard. It means a spirit of being wakeful, of being restless, of guarding.

Praying always means the believer is to live in a spirit of prayer...

- praying all day, as he walks throughout the day.
- praying on all occasions and about everything.
- praying at appointed times, times set aside for nothing but prayer and devotions or quiet times.

There are three reasons why the believer is to watch and pray.

1.    Watching and praying cause God to count the believer "worthy." The man who watches and prays for the Lord's return truly believes in the Lord, and God takes that man's belief and counts it worthy. Note: God does not *make* the man worthy; He counts the man worthy. The man's faith, his watching and praying, are counted as righteousness. (See note, *Justification*—Lk.20:35; DEEPER STUDY # 2—Ro.4:22; 5:1. Cp. Ro.4:5 and 4:1-3; 4:1-25.)

2.    Watching and praying cause the believer to escape the things coming to earth (see DEEPER STUDY # 1, *Snare*—Lk.21:35). This can mean...

- to escape the presence of the coming judgments altogether (by being raptured away).
- to escape the sufferings of the judgments (by being supernaturally protected; for example, Israel was protected during the Egyptian plagues, Exodus 5:1f).

3.    Watching and praying cause the believer to stand justified before the Son of Man (see DEEPER STUDY # 3, *Son of Man*—Mt.8:20). The picture is that the faithful believer will have no fear or dread, no apprehension or hesitation in facing the Son of Man. He will stand before his Lord...

- justified.
- ready to be "fashioned like unto His glorious body" (Ph.3:21).
- ready "to be conformed to His image" (Ro.8:29).
- ready to "behold the face of the Father" (Mt.18:10).
- ready to "serve God day and night in His temple" or world (Rev.7:15).

> "Watch therefore; for ye know neither the day nor the hour wherein the Son of man cometh" (Mt.25:13).
>
> "Blessed are those servants, whom the lord when he cometh shall find watching: verily I say unto you, that he shall gird himself, and make them to sit down to meat, and will come forth and serve them" (Lk.12:37).
>
> "Ye are all the children of light, and the children of the day: we are not of the night, nor of darkness. Therefore let us not sleep, as do others; but let us watch and be sober" (1 Th.5:5-6).
>
> "Behold, I come quickly: hold that fast which thou hast, that no man take thy crown" (Rev.3:11).
>
> "Behold, I come as a thief. Blessed is he that watcheth, and keepeth his garments, lest he walk naked, and they see his shame" (Rev.16:15).
>
> "Watch and pray, that ye enter not into temptation: the spirit indeed is willing, but the flesh is weak" (Mt.26:41).
>
> "Wherefore let him that thinketh he standeth take heed lest he fall" (1 Cor.10:12).
>
> "Continue in prayer, and watch in the same with thanksgiving" (Col.4:2).
>
> "Be sober, be vigilant; because your adversary the devil, as a roaring lion, walketh about, seeking whom he may devour" (1 Pt.5:8).

| | G. The Daily Ministry of Jesus, 21:37-38 |
|---|---|
| 1 The daytime: Jesus taught in the temple<br>2 The night: Jesus was alone with God<sup>DS1</sup> | 37 And in the day time he was teaching in the temple; and at night he went out, and abode in the mount that is called the mount of Olives. |
| 3 The morning: Jesus began early in the morning | 38 And all the people came early in the morning to him in the temple, for to hear him. |

# DIVISION IX

## THE SON OF MAN'S PROPHETIC SIGNS: HIS PREDICTION CONCERNING THE FATE OF JERUSALEM AND THE WORLD, 21:5-38

### G. The Daily Ministry of Jesus, 21:37-38

(21:37-38) **Introduction**: this passage very simply tells how Jesus spent His days and nights during the last days of His life. The picture is both interesting and informative.
1. The daytime: Jesus taught in the temple (v.37).
2. The night: Jesus was alone with God (v.37).
3. The morning: Jesus began early in the morning (v.38).

**1** (21:37) **Jesus Christ, Teaching**: during the daytime Jesus taught in the temple. Several facts are seen in this point.

1. Jesus was a tireless teacher. He taught not only on Sunday, but every day of the week. He taught at every opportunity, and He made as many opportunities as He could. He taught all through the day. He sought the chance to teach, using day-to-day events and experiences to teach. He never tired of teaching even in the face of exhaustion. (Cp. all that happened during this last week of His life, beginning with the Triumphal Entry. Despite the pressure, tension, and fatigue, He continued to teach.)

> "And he said unto them, How is it that ye sought me? wist ye not that I must be about my Father's business?" (Lk.2:49).
> "And he taught daily in the temple. But the chief priests and the scribes and the chief of the people sought to destroy him" (Lk.19:47).
> "Jesus saith unto them, My meat is to do the will of him that sent me, and to finish his work" (Jn.4:34).
> "I must work the works of him that sent me, while it is day: the night cometh, when no man can work" (Jn.9:4).

2. Jesus was a fearless teacher. The authorities were seeking to arrest and kill Him. The opposition was constant: questioning, arguing, plotting, and threatening. However, He did not flee, nor did He retaliate. He simply went about fulfilling God's will, teaching those who so desperately needed God's message.

> "And he taught daily in the temple, But the chief priests and the scribes and the chief of the people sought to destroy him, and could not find what they might do: for all the people were very attentive to hear him" (Lk.19:47-48).

3. Jesus was a faithful teacher, ever meeting the needs of people. Men needed the gospel of God, needed to hear the glorious message of the Kingdom of God. The only way they could ever know how to live day by day was to be taught. Christ wanted to grasp every opportunity He could before He departed this world. (See DEEPER STUDY # 3, Kingdom of God—Mt.19:23-24.)

> "But this I say, brethren, the time is short: it remaineth, that both they that have wives be as though they had none" (1 Cor.7:29).
> "Redeeming the time, because the days are evil" (Eph.5:16).

4. Jesus was a teacher of conviction. Note where He taught: in the temple. The temple was corrupt, being misused and abused and made into a center of commercialism. Yet, the temple was supposed to be God's house of prayer. Jesus refused to desert it; He used the temple as it should be used, making it the center for teaching the gospel of God.

> "And his disciples remembered that it was written, The zeal of thine house hath eaten me up" (Jn.2:17).

**2** (21:37) **Devotion—Mount of Olives—Preparation**: during the night, Jesus got all alone with God. This is a striking point, for it is information about our Lord that deeply moves and touches the heart. "At night, He went out, and abode in the mount that is called the mount of Olives." He was facing so much, the final preparation of His disciples and His

436

own final hours on earth, and He was facing it all in just *one week's time*. He needed time alone with God, a very special time, for He needed great strength, and the source of His strength was God. Every muscle in His body and every thought of His mind must have been craving for God's presence and wisdom and strength. He needed...

- to make maximum use of time in teaching the disciples, teaching exactly what they needed in these final hours.
- to have His own heart prepared to the maximum, ready to bear all the punishment of sin that was to be laid upon Him.

"And in the morning, rising up a great while before day, he went out, and departed into a solitary place, and there prayed" (Mk.1:35).

"And when he had sent them away, he departed into a mountain to pray" (Mk.6:46).

"And he withdrew himself into the wilderness, and prayed" (Lk.5:16).

"And it came to pass, as he was alone praying, his disciples were with him: and he asked them, saying, Whom say the people that I am?" (Lk.9:18).

"And he was withdrawn from them about a stone's cast, and kneeled down, and prayed" (Lk.22:41).

"He shall call upon me, and I will answer him: I will be with him in trouble; I will deliver him, and honour him" (Ps.91:15).

"Call unto me, and I will answer thee, and show thee great and mighty things, which thou knowest not" (Jer.33:3).

"Likewise the Spirit also helpeth our infirmities: for we know not what we should pray for as we ought: but the Spirit itself maketh intercession of us with groanings which cannot be uttered" (Ro.8:26).

---

**DEEPER STUDY # 1**

(21:37) **Mount of Olives or Olivet**: the mountain range was a little more than one-half mile from the city limits of Jerusalem. The range of mountains lie on the east of Jerusalem and stretch only about one or two miles across. The mountain range was loved by Jesus. It was...

- where Jesus often resorted (Lk.22:39).
- where Jesus often spent the night when in Jerusalem (Jn.7:53-8:1).
- where Jesus spent the nights of His last week on earth—praying and seeking God (Lk.29:37).
- where Jesus first went when He approached Jerusalem to face His last week on earth (Mt.21:1f; Mk.11:1f).
- where the great sermon on the end time was preached (Mt.24:3f; Mk.13:3f).
- where (at the descent) the Triumphal Entry began (Lk.19:37f).
- where Jesus' terrible agony in the Garden of Gethsemane took place. The Garden of Gethsemane was on the side of the mountain (Mt.26:30f; Mk.14:26).
- where the ascension took place (Acts 1:12).

---

**3** (21:38) **Teaching—Prayer**: Jesus began early in the morning. Note four significant facts.

1. The first thing Jesus did after prayer and spending time alone with God was teach.
2. Jesus spent time alone with God before teaching. The *presence and power* of God was necessary before teaching.

"My voice shalt thou hear in the morning, O Lord; in the morning will I direct my prayer unto thee, and will look up" (Ps.5:3).

"Evening, and morning, and at noon, will I pray, and cry aloud: and he shall hear my voice" (Ps.55:17).

"Awake up, my glory; awake, psaltery and harp: I myself will awake early" (Ps.57:8).

"I prevented the dawning of the morning, and cried: I hoped in thy word" (Ps.119:147).

"Night and day praying exceedingly that we might see your face, and might perfect that which is lacking in your faith?" (1 Th.3:10; cp. Dan.6:10).

3. The first duty of Jesus after prayer was teaching the gospel. He did not seek relaxation, recreation, fellowship or some social function. After praying, He sought to teach the message of the glorious gospel.

"And he said unto them, Let us go into the next towns, that I may preach there also: for therefore came I forth" (Mk.1:38).

"And he said unto them, I must preach the kingdom of God to other cities also: for therefore am I sent" (Lk.4:43).

4. The people hungered and thirsted after righteousness. Note the word "all." All the people came early in the morning to hear Him.

**Thought 1.** What a difference between the people of that day and other generations! Why? Is it because people's hearts no longer cry out for righteousness? Or, is it because ministers do not seek the face of God *all night* in prayer like Jesus was doing?

"Blessed are ye that hunger now: for ye shall be filled. Blessed are ye that weep now: for ye shall laugh" (Lk.6:21).

"But whosoever drinketh of the water that I shall give him shall never thirst: but the water that I shall give him shall be in him a well of water springing up into everlasting life" (Jn.4:14).

"In the last day, that great day of the feast, Jesus stood and cried, saying, If any man thirst, let him come unto me, and drink" (Jn.7:37).

"Lord, all my desire is before thee; and my groaning is not hid from me" (Ps.38:9).

"For he satisfieth the longing soul, and filleth the hungry soul with goodness" (Ps.107:9).

"Ho, every one that thirsteth, come ye to the waters, and he that hath no money; come ye, buy, and eat; yea, come, buy wine and milk without money and without price" (Is.55:1).

| | CHAPTER 22 | might kill him; for they feared the people. | a. Used deception |
|---|---|---|---|
| | | | b. Feared the people |
| | X. THE SON OF MAN'S LAST SUPPER: HIS TRAITOR, INSTRUCTIONS AND WARNINGS, 22:1-38 | 3 Then entered Satan into Judas surnamed Iscariot, being of the number of the twelve. | **3 Satan: Used an available disciple** |
| | A. The Plot Against Jesus, 22:1-6 (Mt.26:14-16; Mk.14: 1-2, 10-11) | 4 And he went his way, and communed with the chief priests and captains, how he might betray him unto them. | **4 A covetous man: Went his own way** |
| | | | a. Was a professing disciple |
| | | 5 And they were glad, and covenanted to give him money. | b. Communed with world |
| | | | c. Made the enemies of Jesus glad |
| **1 The Passover is tied to the death of Christ**DS1 | Now the feast of unleavened bread drew nigh, which is called the Passover. | 6 And he promised, and sought opportunity to betray him unto them in the absence of the multitude. | d. Coveted money |
| **2 The unbelieving religionists**DS2 | 2 And the chief priests and scribes sought how they | | e. Made a covenant with the world |

# DIVISION X

## THE SON OF MAN'S LAST SUPPER: HIS TRAITOR, INSTRUCTIONS AND WARNINGS, 22:1-38

### A. The Plot Against Jesus, 22:1-6

(22:1-6) **Introduction—Jesus Christ, Opposition**: Jesus Christ was seriously opposed by formidable foes. The religionists rejected Him lest they lose the favor, security, and position of the world. Satan opposed His work of salvation lest men give their lives and worship to God. Men rebelled against His demand for self-denial, for the commitment of all one is and has to the cause of God.
1. The Passover is tied to the death of Christ (v.1).
2. The unbelieving religionists (v.2).
3. Satan: used an available man (v.3).
4. A covetous man: went his own way (v.4-6).

**1** (22:1) **Passover**: the Passover is tied to the death of Christ. This passage begins the final stage of Jesus' life before He was killed. In dramatic fashion Luke sets the stage for what was coming. He mentions the Passover and then points out those who are plotting Jesus' death, two scenes as opposite from one another as can be imagined. The Passover was a feast, a joyous and festive occasion. It was a feast when all of God's people were to be celebrating God's glorious deliverance of Israel out of the bondage of Egypt. However, during the very days of this joyous celebration, Jesus' murder was being plotted. Tragically, it was being plotted by religionists, the very people who should have been taking the lead in the Passover. On the one hand is the celebration of deliverance, the saving of life; on the other hand is the plotting of death, the taking of life. This passage deliberately sets the stage for what was to come. (See DEEPER STUDY # 1, Passover—Mt.26:2.)

**DEEPER STUDY # 1**
(22:1) **Feast of Unleavened Bread**: this feast is another name for the Passover Feast (see Lev.23:5-8; Lk.22:1). However on the first day of the Passover week, the Feast of Unleavened Bread had special significance. It was the day that all preparations were made to celebrate the Passover. (See DEEPER STUDY # 1—Mt.26:2; cp. Ex.12:1-51, esp. v.11-28 for the background of the Passover.) Preparations included securing the lamb and taking it to the temple to be sacrificed. Preparations also included securing the items of food and drink necessary for the Passover and arranging the room for the Feast. However, there were two preparations from which the Feast of Unleavened Bread received its name.
1. There was the baking of unleavened bread. On the night of the Passover, God had told Israel to make final preparations for being delivered from Egyptian bondage. However, the Israelites did not have time to bake leavened bread. They had to bake bread without leaven because of the time it takes for leavened bread to rise. The Feast of Unleavened Bread is simply one of the Passover ceremonies by which Israel remembered God's glorious deliverance of their forefathers from Egyptian bondage. (See DEEPER STUDY # 1—Mt.26:2.)
2. There was a ceremony by which all leaven within the house had to be removed. It must be remembered that leaven was a symbol of evil to the Jews. In removing all leaven, they were picturing the need for putting evil out of their lives and household. There was an actual search made throughout the rooms of the house. The people looked for any crumb of leaven that might have fallen upon the floor and under or between some furniture. Whatever leaven was found, no matter how small a crumb, it was removed from the house. By removing all leaven from their households, the Jews were saying they wanted to be included among the faithful of their forefathers. They wanted to be counted as the faithful who purified and cleansed their lives and households for the journey of deliverance from bondage and slavery.

**2** (22:2) **Religionists**: the first opponents to Jesus were unbelieving religionists. Luke paints a dramatic picture. While the people were in the streets openly preparing to praise God for His delivering power and the saving of life, the religionists were behind closed doors plotting to murder the very One who had come to be their great Deliverer (Savior). Note two facts.

1.     The religionists plotted to use deception and lies (Mt.26:4; Mk.14:1).

"**Their throat is an open sepulchre; with their tongues they have used deceit; the poison of asps is under their lips**" (Ro.3:13).

"**Know ye not that the unrighteous shall not inherit the kingdom of God? Be not deceived**" (1 Cor.6:9).

"**Be not deceived; God is not mocked: for whatsoever a man soweth, that shall he also reap**" (Gal.6:7).

"**Let no man deceive you with vain words: for because of these things cometh the wrath of God upon the children of disobedience**" (Eph.5:6).

"**Little children, let no man deceive you: he that doeth righteousness is righteous, even as he is righteous. He that committeth sin is of the devil; for the devil sinneth from the beginning. For this purpose the Son of God was manifested, that he might destroy the works of the devil**" (1 Jn.3:7-8).

"**But be ye doers of the word, and not hearers only, deceiving your own selves**" (Jas.1:22).

"**For he flattereth himself in his own eyes, until his iniquity be found to be hateful**" (Ps.36:2).

"**All the ways of a man is right in his own eyes: but the Lord weigheth the spirits**" (Pr.16:2).

"**Every way of a man is right in his own eyes: but the Lord pondereth the hearts**" (Pr.21:2).

"**There is a generation that are pure in their own eyes, and yet is not washed from their filthiness**" (Pr.30:12).

"**Most men will proclaim every one his own goodness: but a faithful man who can find?**" (Pr.20:6).

"**And they will deceive every one his neighbor, and will not speak the truth: they have taught their tongue to speak lies, and weary themselves to commit iniquity**" (Jer.9:5).

"**The heart is deceitful above all things, and desperately wicked: who can know it?**" (Jer.17:9).

2.     The reason they sought to get rid of Jesus was because they feared the people. This means that they feared both losing the support of the people and the reaction of the people against them if the people knew they were killing Jesus. (See DEEPER STUDY # 2, *Religionists*—Lk.22:2 for more discussion and application as to why the religionists opposed Jesus.)

---

**DEEPER STUDY # 2**

(22:2) **Religionists**: the religionists' conflict with Jesus is often misunderstood. This is because so much of the conflict had to do with rules and regulations that seem petty and meaningless to modern minds (cp. Mk.2:23-28; 3:1-6; 3:22-30. See notes—Mt.12:1-8; note and DEEPER STUDY # 1—12:10; note—15:1-20; DEEPER STUDY # 2—15:6-9.) Four facts will help in understanding why the conflicts happened and were life threatening, ending in the murder of Jesus Christ.

1.     The Jewish nation had been held together by their religious beliefs. Through the centuries the Jewish people had been conquered by army after army, and by the millions they had been deported and scattered over the world. Even in the day of Jesus, they were enslaved by Rome. Their religion was the binding force that kept Jews together, in particular...

⇒   their belief that God had called them to be a distinctive people (who worshipped the only true and living God).

⇒   their rules governing the Sabbath and the temple.

This belief and these rules protected them from alien beliefs and from being swallowed up by other peoples through intermarriage. Their religion was what maintained their distinctiveness as a people and as a nation.

Jewish leaders knew this. They knew that their religion was the binding force that held their nation together. Therefore, they opposed anyone or anything that threatened or attempted to break the laws of their religion.

2.     The religionists were men of deep conviction. They were strong in their beliefs. Therefore, they became steeped in religious belief and practice, law and custom, tradition and ritual, ceremony and liturgy, rules and regulations. To break any law or rule governing any belief or practice was a serious offense, for it taught loose behavior. And loose behavior, once it had spread enough, would weaken their religion which was the binding force that held their people together. Therefore, Jesus was committing a great offense by breaking their law. He was weakening their religion and threatening their nation.

3.     The religionists were men who had profession, position, recognition, esteem, livelihood and security. Anyone who went contrary to what they believed and taught was a threat to all they had. Some religionists felt that Jesus was a threat to them. Every time Jesus broke their law, He was undermining their very position and security.

4.     The religionists were exposed by Jesus. In order for the religionists and the people to know the truth, Jesus had to point out where they were wrong and what they needed to do to get right with God. Both the sin of men and the truth of God had to be proclaimed. The religionists could not take it. They refused to accept the fact that they were unacceptable to God. They were, after all, the religious of the day, the very ones who professed God. They felt they had no sin, at least not enough sin to bar them from God. Anyone who accused them of being so wrong and so depraved could not conceivably be of God. He must be of Beelzebub (see outline and note—Mk.3:22-30).

There were at least four responses to Jesus by the religionists.

1.     Some were sincere men of deep conviction. They actually thought Jesus was an imposter, a deceiver, a false messiah. Paul, Saul of Tarsus, would be an example of this position.

2.    Some were open-minded enough to seek the truth about Jesus. They observed and reasoned, being honest enough to consider what He was saying, and they sought Him out to find the truth. Nicodemus is an example of this.

3.    Some did believe and trust Christ (see note—Lk.13:31; pt.4—Mt.23:13-36).

4.    Some were just professional priests and ministers who looked upon Jesus as a threat. They held the position because of the prestige, comfort, livelihood, and security they received from it. Therefore, they opposed Christ rather vehemently. Caiaphas and Annas are examples of this response.

The error of the religionists was fourfold.

1.    They misinterpreted and corrupted God's Word (see notes—Mt.12:1-3; DEEPER STUDY # 1—Jn.4:22; cp. Ro.9:4).

2.    They committed serious sin after serious sin in God's eyes (see notes—1 Th.2:15-16; cp. Ro.2:17-29).

3.    They rejected God's way of righteousness, God's Messiah, which is Jesus Christ (see notes—Ro.11:18; 1 Th.2:15-16; cp. Ro.10:1-21, esp. 1-4, 19-21).

4.    They allowed religion in its tradition and ritual, ceremony and rules, to become more important than meeting the basic needs of human life: the need for God and the need for spiritual, mental, and physical health. Jesus, being the true Messiah, was bound to expose such error. Therefore, the battle lines were drawn.

The Messiah had to liberate people from such enslaving behavior. He had to liberate them so they could be saved and worship God in freedom of spirit. The religionists had to oppose anyone who broke their law. They had to oppose Jesus because He was a threat to their nation and to their own personal position and security.

**3**    (22:3) **Satan, Work of**: the second opponent to Jesus was Satan. Satan is the spiritual being who is out to destroy the relationship between God and men. In wrath and bitter hostility he opposes God. (See DEEPER STUDY # 1, *Satan*—Rev.12:9 for more discussion on just who Satan is and on his terrible work.) Satan is seen entering Judas, stirring him to strike up a bargain to betray Jesus. Later Satan will enter Judas again and urge him to go ahead and finish his work of betrayal (Jn.13:27. See note, pt.4—Mk.14:10-11.) The point is, if Satan could destroy Jesus, keep Him from fulfilling His work on earth, then man could never be saved. Satan, of course, had no idea that God was going to save the world through the death of Jesus. Satan is not omniscient; he could not know the future any more than anyone else. Therefore, he had attempted to have Jesus killed time and again, even as a child (Mt.2:13, 16, 22; Lk.4:8, 29). Satan's opposition to God and man is clearly seen in Scripture.

1.    He tempts to disobey God (Gen.3:4-5; Mt.4:4; 1 Th.3:5).

2.    He snatches the Word out of man's heart (Mt.13:19).

3.    He plants unbelievers in the midst of believers, the church (Mt.13:38-39).

4.    He afflicts people with sickness and disease (Job 2:7; Lk.13:16).

5.    He tries to sift, shake men in their faith (Lk.22:31).

6.    He causes murder and killing (Jn.8:44; 1 Jn.3:12).

7.    He lies and is the father of lies (Jn.8:44).

8.    He enters men's lives (Lk.22:3; Jn.13:27).

9.    He plants evil into the hearts of men (Jn.13:2).

10.   He leads men to steal from God (Acts 5:3).

11.   He tempts married couples sexually (1 Cor.7:5).

12.   He tries to keep people from forgiving others (2 Cor.2:10-11).

13.   He blinds the minds of unbelievers lest they believe (2 Cor.4:4).

14.   He deceives the minds of men (2 Cor.11:3).

15.   He transforms himself into a messenger of light to deceive man (2 Cor.11:14).

16.   He transforms some ministers into ministers of righteousness to deceive men (2 Cor.11:15).

17.   He works in the disobedient (Eph.2:2).

18.   He launches powerful strategies against believers (Eph.6:11).

19.   He rules the principalities and powers, the darkness and spiritual wickedness, of this world (Eph.6:12; Col.2:15).

20.   He hinders the work of believers (1 Th.2:18).

21.   He works with power and signs and lying wonders (2 Th.2:9).

22.   He leads men to blaspheme (1 Tim.1:20).

23.   He condemns men and causes men to condemn themselves (1 Tim.3:6).

24.   He snares and entraps people (1 Tim.3:7; 2 Tim.2:26).

25.   He turns people aside to go after him (1 Tim.5:15).

26.   He did hold the power of death (Heb.2:14).

27.   He seeks to prey upon men and devour them (1 Pt.5:8).

28.   He sins and works against men and God (1 Jn.3:8).

29.   He opposes the angels of God (Jude 6).

30.   He possesses, rules, and controls some churches and worship centers (Rev.2:9; 3:9).

31.   He causes believers to be cast into prison (Rev.2:10).

32.   He deceives the whole world (Rev.12:9; 20:7-8, 10).

33.   He accuses believers before God (Rev.12:10).

34.   He causes great havoc upon the earth (Rev.12:12).

(See notes, *Satan*—Col.2:15; DEEPER STUDY # 1—Jas.4:7; DEEPER STUDY # 1—Rev.12:9 for more discussion.)

**4**    (22:4-6) **Judas—Unbeliever—Devil—Apostasy**: the third opponent to Jesus was a covetous man, a man who went his own way in life. Judas was such a man. Several facts show this.

1.    Judas was a professing disciple. In fact, he was one of the twelve apostles. Just think about the fact: Judas had been personally chosen by Jesus. Judas had some great potential, some unique qualities that attracted the Lord, and the

Lord gaveJudas the most honored opportunity in all the world to develop his abilities, the privilege of walking with Him personally.

⇒ Judas knew Jesus face to face.

⇒ Judas walked with Jesus day after day.

⇒ Judas heard most, if not all, that Jesus taught.

⇒ Judas saw most, if not all, that Jesus did—miracles and wondrous works.

⇒ Judas was trained to be an apostle by Jesus Himself.

⇒ Judas served as an apostle even on witnessing tours under Jesus' personal command (Mk.6:7f).

⇒ Judas was warned of sin's consequences by Jesus Himself.

Despite all this, Judas' life was a terrible tragedy. He was so gifted and had so much opportunity, yet he lost it all. Why? Simply because he turned his back on the Lord Jesus Christ. He went to the chief priests of this earth and put his fate into their hands instead of placing his life into the hands of Jesus. He had allowed his craving for more and more to blind him to the truth about Jesus—that He was truly the Son of God who demanded loyalty—even when man cannot understand the events and happenings that surround Him (see note—Mt.26:14. This note will explain what is behind this statement.) Judas simply did not believe that Jesus was truly God's Son. Therefore, he did not give his heart and life to Jesus—not really. He was a follower of Jesus; he was even one of the first twelve apostles, but he was not a genuine believer who entrusted his life to Jesus.

**"And he said to them all, If any man will come after me, let him deny himself, and take up his cross daily, and follow me. For whosoever will save his life shall lose it: but whosoever will lose his life for my sake, the same shall save it" (Lk.9:23-24).**

2. Judas communed with the world. He was definitely worldly; his mind and heart were upon worldly acceptance, position, recognition, prestige, influence, power, and wealth. Note: he approached and communed with the world, the chief priests of the world. He thought they who were of the world were the winning side and could offer much more than Jesus.

**"But it shall not be so among you: but whosoever will be great among you, let him be your minister; and whosoever will be chief among you, let him be your servant: even as the Son of man came not to be ministered unto, but to minister, and to give his life a ransom for many" (Mt.20:26-28).**

**"And whosoever shall exalt himself shall be abased; and he that shall humble himself shall be exalted" (Mt.23:12).**

**"How can ye believe, which receive honour one of another, and seek not the honour that cometh from God only?" (Jn.5:44).**

3. Judas coveted the world and its money. Judas' gnawing sin was greed and the love of money. Various commentators pose different reasons why Judas may have betrayed Jesus, but the Scripture pointedly says that the reason was greed: "What will ye give me, and I will give [betray] Him to you."

Judas' gnawing greed was a growing sin. This is seen by looking at what is said about him in the Scripture.

a. Judas was chosen by Jesus to be an apostle (Mt.10:4). Therefore, we know he was sincere in the beginning. There was something within Judas—qualities that attracted Jesus, qualities that Jesus knew could mean a lot to the Kingdom of God.

b. Judas was a gifted man in financial affairs. Apparently he was even more gifted in financial affairs than Matthew, the wealthy tax collector, and the businessmen who were among the apostles such as Peter, James, and John (see Subject Index under each name for references to notes on their business background). Among all these, Judas was placed in charge of the Lord's funds and the purchasing of whatever was needed (Jn.12:6; 13:29; cp. Lk.8:2-3 for some who supported Jesus' ministry). His appointment from among so many was bound to be due to unusual spiritual qualities as well as financial management.

c. Judas, at some unknown point, began to embezzle from the Lord's funds. John says unmistakably that Judas was a thief (Jn.12:6). John relates this fact when he says that Judas was greatly disturbed with Mary, the sister of Martha. Mary used some very expensive perfume to annoint Jesus instead of selling it to secure money for the Lord's treasury. John says the reason for Judas' disturbance was because Judas was a thief and could have embezzled some of the money (Jn.12:5-6).

d. Judas refused to repent, and he hardened his heart more and more in his sin. Jesus knew of Judas' embezzlement and hinted at it, giving Judas opportunity time and again to repent.

**"But there are some of you that believe not. For Jesus knew from the beginning who they were that believed not, and who should betray him....Jesus answered them, have not I chosen you twelve, and one of you is a devil? He spake of Judas Iscariot the son of Simon: for he it was that should betray him, being one of the twelve" (Jn.6:64, 70-71).**

Judas was bound to feel the pangs of guilt at such times, yet he continued to deceive himself, believing that Jesus did not really know and had no real proof. Judas kept right on taking what he felt he could safely embezzle, hardening his heart more and more.

e. Judas apparently followed Jesus out of a heart of greed and worldly ambition, not out of a heart of love and faith in Him as the Son of God. This seems to be indicated by two facts.

1) He felt that wealth, power, and position would be his when Jesus set up his kingdom. The other apostles thought the same, but there was a vast difference. They mistook the Messiah's method of saving the world, not His person. Judas mistook both the Lord's method and person. He did not believe and trust the Lord to be the Son of God, whereas the others did.

2) He apparently was disillusioned in Jesus after the triumphal entry. Jesus did not immediately set up His kingdom, and as the days passed, the fact that He was not going to set up His kingdom became more and more apparent. The authorities were mobilizing against Jesus to kill Him, and it seemed as though they were going to be successful. Jesus had even been teaching that they were to be successful. He was to be killed by their hands (Mt.16:21).

Judas became convinced he had been mistaken about Jesus. Jesus was not the real Messiah; He was just another mistaken self-proclaimed messiah; He was doomed and there was no way out. Judas experienced his dreams of wealth and power and position with Jesus being shattered. Therefore, what he was trying to do was to get what he could out of the situation. He wanted to be in good standing with the winning side and to secure a sizeable amount of money for betraying Jesus. Note: Judas apparently expected to get much more from the religionists than he got. Once he had approached the religionists, he had to follow through with the betrayal and accept whatever they offered.

f. Judas filled his heart with the lust for more and more instead of filling it with Jesus. He went too long without repenting and letting Jesus into his life, and the devil was able to fill his being. The devil blinded and took control of his rationale, hence Judas was able to justify his betrayal in his own mind. He was, after all, helping the religious body and himself. Therefore, he betrayed Jesus of Nazareth who apparently in Judas' mind was just another mistaken self-proclaimed messiah.

> **"And he said unto them, Take heed, and beware of covetousness: for a man's life consisteth not in the abundance of the things which he possesseth" (Lk.12:15).**
>
> **"For the love of money is the root of all evil: which while some coveted after, they have erred from the faith, and pierced themselves through with many sorrows" (1 Tim.6:10).**
>
> **"Your gold and silver is cankered; and the rust of them shall be a witness against you, and shall eat your flesh as it were fire. Ye have heaped treasure together for the last days" (Jas.5:3).**
>
> **"He that loveth silver shall not be satisfied with silver; nor he that loveth abundance with increase" (Eccl.5:10).**

4. Judas makes a covenant with the world. Note the words, "He promised, and sought opportunity to betray Him." Judas made a covenant with the world, a pact to betray Jesus. The picture is that of being on the prowl, searching and seeking, looking here and there for the right moment. Judas' heart was set, full of intrigue, plotting evil and planning its strategy. He did not believe, but unbelief was not enough. He willed to do evil against Jesus, to hurt Him, to destroy Him. And he sought opportunity to do so. Just how deceitful Judas was can be seen by noticing that immediately after bargaining with the authorities, he sat down to eat with Jesus. He sat at the very table where the Lord's Supper was being instituted.

**Thought 1.** Judas not only rejected but sought to destroy Jesus. Many reject Christ, but not all seek to harm and destroy Him. Some do, but not all.
⇒ Some curse and curse Him, consciously and unconsciously dishonoring His name.
⇒ Some talk and teach against His divine nature, saying that He is not the Son of God.
⇒ Some talk and teach against the written revelation of Himself and the truth, that is, the Word.
⇒ Some talk and teach against His active presence in the life of the genuine believer.

> **"Beware of false prophets, which come to you in sheep's clothing, but inwardly they are ravening wolves" (Mt.7:15).**
>
> **"Now the Spirit speaketh expressly, that in the latter times some shall depart from the faith, giving heed to seducing spirits, and doctrines of devils; speaking lies in hypocrisy; having their conscience seared with a hot iron" (1 Tim.4:1-2).**
>
> **"This know also, that in the last days perilous times shall come. For men shall be lovers of their own selves, covetous, boasters, proud, blasphemers, disobedient to parents, unthankful, unholy, without natural affection, trucebreakers, false accusers, incontinent, fierce, despisers of those that are good, traitors, heady, highminded, lovers of pleasures more than lovers of God; having a form of godliness, but denying the power thereof: from such turn away" (2 Tim.3:1-5).**

| | B. The Lord's Supper, 22:7-23 (Mt.26:17-30; Mk.14: 12-25; Jn.13) | twelve apostles with him. | |
|---|---|---|---|
| **1 The great purpose of the Lord's Supper**[DS1] a. To show how Christ fulfilled the Passover Feast: Delivers man from judgment b. To stress the need to remember & celebrate the Lord's death 1) Despite obstacles 2) The prearranged sign c. To stress the need for cautious preparations in approaching Christ & His death | 7 Then came the day of unleavened bread, when the passover must be killed. 8 And he sent Peter and John, saying, Go and prepare us the passover, that we may eat. 9 And they said unto him, Where wilt thou that we prepare? 10 And he said unto them, Behold, when ye are entered into the city, there shall a man meet you, bearing a pitcher of water; follow him into the house where he entereth in. 11 And ye shall say unto the goodman of the house, The Master saith unto thee, Where is the guestchamber, where I shall eat the passover with my disciples? 12 And he shall show you a large upper room furnished: there make ready. 13 And they went, and found as he had said unto them: and they made ready the passover. 14 And when the hour was come, he sat down, and the | 15 And he said unto them, With desire I have desired to eat this passover with you before I suffer: 16 For I say unto you, I will not any more eat thereof, until it be fulfilled in the kingdom of God. 17 And he took the cup, and gave thanks, and said, Take this, and divide it among yourselves: 18 For I say unto you, I will not drink of the fruit of the vine, until the kingdom of God shall come. 19 And he took bread, and gave thanks, and brake it, and gave unto them, saying, This is my body which is given for you: this do in remembrance of me. 20 Likewise also the cup after supper, saying, This cup is the new testament in my blood, which is shed for you. 21 But, behold, the hand of him that betrayeth me is with me on the table. 22 And truly the Son of man goeth, as it was determined: but woe unto that man by whom he is betrayed! 23 And they began to enquire among themselves, which of them it was that should do this thing. | **2 The great significance of the Lord's Supper** a. It is tied to the Lord's death & the Passover b. It pictures a greater supper, a glorious promise **3 The great meaning of the Lord's Supper**[DS2] a. The Bread: Symbolizes Christ's body, broken for us b. The Cup: Symbolizes Christ's blood, shed for us **4 The great appeal of the Lord's Supper** a. It is used to appeal to a sinner b. It is used to warn a sinner c. It is used to stir the searching of hearts |

# DIVISION X

## THE SON OF MAN'S LAST SUPPER: HIS TRAITOR, INSTRUCTIONS, AND WARNINGS, 22:1-38

### B.    The Lord's Supper, 22:7-23

(22:7-23) **Introduction**: this is a great passage on the subject of the Lord's Supper.
1.    The great purpose of the Lord's Supper (v.7-14).
2.    The great significance of the Lord's Supper (v.15-18).
3.    The great meaning of the Lord's Supper (v.19-20).
4.    The great appeal of the Lord's Supper (v.21-23).

[1]    (22:7-14) **Lord's Supper**: the great purpose of the Lord's Supper is threefold.

1.    It shows how Jesus fulfilled the great Passover Feast (see DEEPER STUDY # 1—Lk.22:7).
2.    It stresses the great need and helps a person to remember the Lord's death. Scripture is pointedly clear about this. The Lord's Supper helps us to keep our minds upon Christ, and at the same time it demonstrates that our minds are upon Him.

> **"This do in remembrance of me" (Lk.22:19; 1 Cor.11:24-25).**
> **"For as often as ye eat this bread, and drink this cup, ye do show the Lord's death till he comes" (1 Cor.11:26).**

The Lord's Supper is to be kept even in the *face of difficulty*. Note the difficulty Jesus faced. There were those who were seeking to find out where He was so they might arrest and kill Him. Even one of His own disciples had betrayed Him and was only waiting for an opportunity to inform the authorities where He was and where He could be quietly arrested. However, despite this terrible difficulty, Jesus was determined to observe the celebration. (What an indictment against *loose attitudes and approaches* to the Lord's Supper! Believers are to be obedient to the religious ordinances despite difficulty.)

444

3.    It stresses the need for cautious preparation in approaching Christ and His death. Note the words "made ready" in all three gospels.

> **"And they went, and found as he had said unto them: and they *made ready* the passover"** (Lk.22:13).
> **"And the disciples did as Jesus had appointed them; and they *made ready* the passover"** (Mt.26:19).
> **"And his disciples went forth, and came into the city, and found as he had said unto them: and they *made ready* the passover"** (Mk.14:16).

The point is this: detailed preparations were required for observing the Passover (see DEEPER STUDY # 1—Lk.22:7). The stringent preparations taught that God was to be *approached carefully*, exactly as prescribed. Why? Because God is holy, and there is only one way to approach Him—through the blood of the Passover Lamb. Three acts in this passage stress the need for approaching Christ carefully.

⇒  He went to great pains to keep the Passover despite extreme danger.
⇒  He had personally made preparations for the observance (v.9-12).
⇒  The disciples found the arrangements made just as He had said and did their part in preparing the observance.

**Thought 1.** Christ kept the Passover even in the face of death. How few value the Lord's Supper enough! How many observe it too little! How many could care less if it is observed or not! How many place the comfort of home, recreation, and the doing of one's own thing before observing the Lord's Supper!

---

**DEEPER STUDY # 1**

(22:7) **Passover—Lord's Supper**: historically, the Passover refers back to the time when God delivered Israel from Egyptian bondage (Ex.11:1f). He had pronounced judgment, the taking of the firstborn, upon the people of Egypt for their injustices. As He prepared to execute the final judgment, those who believed God were instructed to slay a pure lamb and sprinkle its blood over the door posts of their homes. The blood of the innocent lamb would then serve as a sign that the coming judgment had already been carried out upon the sacrificial lamb. When seeing the blood, God would *pass over* that house. Those who believed God applied the blood to their homes and were saved, but those who did not believe did not apply the blood to their homes, and they were destroyed.

Symbolically, the Passover pictured the coming of Jesus Christ as the Savior. The *lamb without blemish* pictured His sinless life (cp. Jn.1:29), and the *blood sprinkled on the door posts* pictured His blood shed for the believer. It was a sign that the life and blood of the innocent lamb had been substituted for the firstborn. The "eating of the lamb" pictured the need for spiritual nourishment gained by feeding on Christ, the Bread of Life. The unleavened bread (bread without yeast) pictured the need for putting evil out of one's life and household. (See DEEPER STUDY # 1, *Feast of Unleavened Bread*—Mt.26:17.)

In addition to the lamb and unleavened bread, the Jewish Passover Feast was celebrated by using four food and drink items. (1) A bowl of salt water was conspicuously placed on the table to remind the family of the tears shed by their forefathers in their 430 years of Egyptian bondage. (2) A bitter salad-like plate was to remind them of their forefather's bitter experiences of slavery. (3) A paste-like mixture of fruit (charosheth) with cinnamon sticks was to remind them of their forefather's toil in making bricks from clay and straw for the Egyptian cities and buildings. (4) Four cups of wine were used to remind them of God's four promises in Ex.6:6-8 to deliver their forefathers from Egyptian slavery.

The one thing to be noted about the Passover celebration is that it is all historical. It is celebrating an act of the past, whereas the Lord's Supper is much more than mere history. It is a celebration of the living Christ in the heart and life of the believer until He returns. It is a remembrance of the potential power of the living Christ within the life of the believer right now—an explosive power that is made possible through the cross (cp. 1 Cor.11:26).

---

**2**   (22:15-18) **Lord's Supper**: the great significance of the Lord's Supper is shown by two things.

1.    The Lord's Supper is tied to the Lord's death. Note the Lord's words:
⇒  "Before I suffer" (v.15).
⇒  "I will not any more eat thereof, *until*...." (v.16).
⇒  "I will not drink of the fruit of the vine, *until*...." (v.18).

Jesus was definitely tying both the Passover and the Lord's Supper to His death. And, of course, His death is what the Lord's Supper is all about (see DEEPER STUDY # 2—Lk.22:19-20).

2.    The Lord's Supper pictures a great supper, a glorious promise (v.16-18). Note carefully the promise of Jesus. He said He was going to eat and drink again when all things were "fulfilled in the kingdom of God." Jesus was *promising* to celebrate the Supper with His followers in the future. Believers shall sit down with Christ at the great *Marriage Feast of the Lamb* (see outline and notes—Mt.20:1-16; 20:2). It is the promise of sitting with Christ in His glorious kingdom, of being a part of the new heavens and earth, of being perfected and living forever (see DEEPER STUDY # 3, *Kingdom of God*—Mt.19:23-24; *Rewards*—Lk.16:10-12).

> **"The Spirit itself beareth witness with our spirit, that we are the children of God: and if children, then heirs; heirs of God, and joint-heirs with Christ; if so be that we suffer with him, that we may be also glorified together"** (Ro.8:16-17).

"When Christ, who is our life, shall appear, then shall ye also appear with him in glory" (Col.3:4).

"For our light affliction, which is but for a moment, worketh for us a far more exceeding and eternal weight of glory" (2 Cor.4:17).

"The elders which are among you I exhort, who am also an elder, and a witness of the sufferings of Christ, and also a partaker of the glory that shall be revealed" (1 Pt.5:1).

"For so an entrance shall be ministered unto you abundantly into the everlasting kingdom of our Lord and Saviour Jesus Christ" (2 Pt.1:11).

**3** (22:19-20) **Lord's Supper**: the great meaning of the Lord's Supper.

1. There is the meaning of the bread. Jesus took the bread and broke it. This symbolized His broken body. His body was broken, that is, sacrificed, as a victim for man's deliverance (Is.53:5). This act was so significant that the early church sometimes called the Lord's Supper simply *the breaking of bread* (Acts 2:42, 46; 1 Cor.10:16). Under the Old Testament the broken bread pictured the sufferings of the Israelites. Now, under the New Testament, the bread was to picture the broken body of Christ (1 Cor.11:24).

Note: Jesus said His body was broken and given for us. He suffered and died *for us*: in our behalf, in our stead, in our place. He bore the judgment of God against sin by dying *for us*.

"This is the bread which cometh down from heaven, that a man may eat thereof, and not die. I am the living bread which came down from heaven: if any man eat of this bread, he shall live for ever: and the bread that I will give is my flesh, which I will give for the life of the world" (Jn.6:50-51).

"And when he had given thanks, he brake it, and said, Take, eat: this is my body, which is broken for you: this do in remembrance of me" (1 Cor.11:24).

"But he was wounded for our transgressions, he was bruised for our iniquities: the chastisement of our peace was upon him; and with his stripes we are healed" (Is.53:5).

2. There is the meaning of the cup. Jesus identified the cup as His blood of the New Testament. He simply meant that His blood establishes a new covenant with God; His blood allows a new relationship between God and man. Note the Lord's exact words.

a. "This is my blood": His blood, which was shed from His body, was to become the sign or symbol of the new covenant. His blood was to take the place of the sacrifice of animals.

b. "The new testament": His blood, the sacrifice of His life established a New Testament, a new covenant between God and man (cp. Heb.9:11-15). Faith in His blood and sacrifice is the way man is now to approach God. Under the Old Testament, a man who wanted a right relationship with God approached God through the sacrifice of the animal's blood. The Old Testament believer believed that God accepted him because of the sacrifice of the animal. Now, under the New Testament, the believer believes that God accepts him because of the sacrifice of Christ. This is what Jesus said: "This is my blood of the New Testament, which is shed for many" (Mk.14:24. See note Mt.26:28; cp. Eph.1:7; 1 Jn.2:1-2; Heb.9:22.) A man's sins are forgiven and he becomes acceptable to God by believing that Christ's blood was shed for him (1 Jn.1:7).

"In whom we have redemption through his blood, the forgiveness of sins, according to the riches of his grace" (Eph.1:7).

"But if we walk in the light, as he is in the light, we have fellowship one with another, and the blood of Jesus Christ his Son cleanseth us from all sin" (1 Jn.1:7).

"My little children, these things write I unto you, that ye sin not. And if any man sin, we have an advocate with the Father, Jesus Christ the righteous: and he is the propitiation for our sins: and not for ours only, but also for the sins of the whole world" (1 Jn.2:1-2).

"Whoso eateth my flesh, and drinketh my blood, hath eternal life; and I will raise him up at the last day. For my flesh is meat indeed, and my blood is drink indeed. He that eateth my flesh, and drinketh my blood, dwelleth in me, and I in him. As the living Father hath sent me, and I live by the Father: so he that eateth me, even he shall live by me. This is the bread which came down from heaven: not as your fathers did eat manna, and are dead: he that eateth of this bread shall live for ever" (Jn.6:54-58).

---

**DEEPER STUDY # 2**

(22:19-20) **Lord's Supper—Passover**: note the words "in remembrance of me." By fulfilling the Passover with the shedding of His own blood, Jesus was tying the Lord's Supper to the Passover Feast. In instituting the Lord's Supper, Jesus was showing His disciples that He was, first of all, the great Liberator. A *liberator* differs from a *deliverer*. A deliverer might deliver a person into something as bad or even worse than that which enslaves him, but not a liberator. A liberator sets a person free from whatever bondage grips him. As the disciples partook of the Supper, they were to:

1. Remember how God liberated Israel from Egyptian slavery.

2. Remember how the Lord's blood liberated them from earthly and sinful slavery. The Lord's Supper is to remind the disciples how the blood of the Lamb keeps them safe from the terrible hand of God's judgment.

3. Remember how the blood of Christ makes it possible for Him to return and to liberate them into the eternal presence of God's glory.

**4** (22:21-23) **Judas Iscariot**: the great appeals of the Supper. Jesus used the Supper to make three appeals.

1.    Jesus used the Supper to appeal to a sinner. Judas had forsaken Jesus. He thought his sin was hid and unknown, but Jesus knew. He had seen all, everything that Judas had done.

2.    Jesus used the Supper to warn the sinner. "*Woe* unto that man," Jesus said. The word "woe" means wrath and sorrow, anger and pity. It was a grieving denunciation, a heartrending pronouncement of judgment. Terrible judgment was a sure thing for the sinner Judas, and it broke the heart of God.

> **Thought 1.** Jesus knows the destiny of the sinner, the terrible fate that awaits him. It would be better never to be born than to deny and betray Christ. Note the grace of God in warning the sinner of judgment.
>
> 1)    The sinner is told in *advance*, before judgment ever comes or is ever pronounced. Judas was told. The sinner can still repent when he *first* hears about judgment. He can still be saved as long as he is living. It is God's grace that warns us of the consequences of our sin, of coming judgment.
> 2)    The sinner is never compelled to repent of his denial or betrayal of Christ. Judas was not forced to turn from his evil; neither is any other sinner. It is God's grace that respects our will and desires. God loves and cares, warns and speaks frankly, but He never forces obedience.
>
>> "I tell you, Nay: but, except ye repent, ye shall all likewise perish" (Lk.13:3, 5).
>> "Repent ye therefore, and be converted, that your sins may be blotted out, when the times of refreshing shall come from the presence of the Lord" (Acts 3:19).
>> "Repent therefore of this thy wickedness, and pray God, if perhaps the thought of thine heart may be forgiven thee" (Acts 8:22).

3.    Jesus used the Supper to stir the searching of hearts. The disciples were stirred to ask, "Is it I?" (Mt.26:22; Mk.14:19). They looked at themselves. They were not accusing one another; rather each one feared lest he be so weak he might fall.

> "Watch and pray, that ye enter not into temptation: the spirit indeed is willing, but the flesh is weak" (Mt.26:41).
> "Wherefore let him that thinketh he standeth take heed lest he fall" (1 Cor.10:12).
> "Watch ye, stand fast in the faith, quit you like men, be strong" (1 Cor.16:13).
> "Be sober, be vigilant; because your adversary the devil, as a roaring lion, walketh about, seeking whom he may devour" (1 Pt.5:8).

| | C. The Dispute Over Greatness, 22:24-30 (Mt.20:20-28; Mk.10:35-45) | er; and he that is chief, as he that doth serve. | b. To act as a servant |
|---|---|---|---|
| **1 The disciples argued over position and power** | 24 And there was also a strife among them, which of them should be accounted the greatest. | 27 For whether is greater, he that sitteth at meat, or he that serveth? is not he that sitteth at meat? but I am among you as he that serveth. | c. To follow the example of the Lord—to be as He that serveth |
| **2 The world's attitude about greatness** <br> a. To hold authority over people <br> b. To be recognized & honored as a benefactor | 25 And he said unto them, The kings of the Gentiles exercise lordship over them; and they that exercise authority upon them are called benefactors. | 28 Ye are they which have continued with me in my temptations. <br> 29 And I appoint unto you a kingdom, as my Father hath appointed unto me; | **4 The Lord's encouragement to serve faithfully** <br> a. He gives assurance: They have proven themselves <br> b. He makes a covenant <br> 1) They are to inherit a kingdom[DS1] |
| **3 The Lord's attitude toward greatness** <br> a. To act as the youngest | 26 But ye shall not be so: but he that is greatest among you, let him be as the young- | 30 That ye may eat and drink at my table in my kingdom, and sit on thrones judging the twelve tribes of Israel. | 2) They are to rule |

# DIVISION X

## THE SON OF MAN'S LAST SUPPER: HIS TRAITOR, INSTRUCTIONS, AND WARNINGS, 22:1-38

### C. The Dispute Over Greatness, 22:24-30

(22:24-30) **Introduction**: men desire recognition, prestige, position, honor, power, authority. The disciples had such desires. Jesus used their power struggle to teach the world a much needed lesson, a lesson that speaks directly and forcibly to every person.

1. The disciples argued over position and power (v.24).
2. The world's attitude about greatness (v.25).
3. The Lord's attitude about greatness (v.26-27).
4. The Lord's encouragement to serve faithfully (v.28-30).

**1** (22:24) **Division—Strife—Position**: the disciples argued. Note three facts.

1. The word "strife" (philoneikia) means being eager and ready to argue and contend; being alert to strive for one's position. It conveys the idea of giving no ground, of standing up no matter what, of being stubborn, of resisting regardless of circumstances.

2. The disciples were still thinking about an earthly kingdom. They thought Jesus was about to lead an uprising against the Romans and free Palestine, establishing the Messiah's kingdom in Israel. From Israel the Messiah was to rule and reign over the whole earth in behalf of God. (See note, pt.2—Lk.7:21-23. Also see notes—Mt.1:1; DEEPER STUDY # 2—1:18; DEEPER STUDY # 3—3:11; notes—11:1-6; 11:2-3; DEEPER STUDY # 1—11:5; DEEPER STUDY # 2—11:6; DEEPER STUDY # 1—12:16; note—22:42.)

3. The disciples were in the upper room *jockeying* for position. As in most societies, the highest in position sat on the right of the host and the next highest on the left. The highest in position continued to alternate between the right and left until everyone was seated.

Since Jesus was about to set up His kingdom, now was the time to seize the positions of rule and power in His kingdom. Now was the time to assume the seats of honor and authority in His presence. The disciples were trying to assure themselves of key seats and positions in His government. (See outline and notes—-Mt.18:1-4.)

**2** (22:25) **Greatness**: the world's attitude about greatness involves two key concepts.

1. There is the concept that greatness is holding authority over people or *lording it over* people: holding position and authority, influence and power, rank and dominion, money and property. Men seek position and wealth for the sake of power. They want to rule or manage people, exercise authority over them, and control their lives.

2. There is the concept of being known and called a benefactor (euergetai), a man who gives and helps others. Note the word "called." The worldly benefactor wants to be known and called a benefactor, recognized and honored for his help and contribution. He desires to be known as a great man, a man who is generous, thoughtful, concerned, honorable.

> "And whosoever shall exalt himself shall be abased; and he that shall humble himself shall be exalted" (Mt.23:12).
>
> "How can ye believe, which receive honour one of another, and seek not the honour that cometh from God only?" (Jn.5:44).
>
> "For the wicked boasteth of his heart's desire, and blesseth the covetous, whom the LORD abhorreth" (Ps.10:3).
>
> "Whoso boasteth himself of a false gift is like clouds and wind without rain" (Pr.25:14).

"For thou hast trusted in thy wickedness: thou hast said, None seeth me. Thy wisdom and thy knowledge, it hath perverted thee; and thou hast said in thine heart, I am, and none else beside me" (Is.47:10).

"Though thou exalt thyself as the eagle, and though thou set thy nest among the stars, thence will I bring thee down, saith the LORD" (Obad.4).

**3** (22:26-27) **Greatness**: the Lord's attitude about greatness. The Lord rejected the world's attitude of greatness. True greatness does not seek to hold authority nor to lord it over people; it does not seek position for the sake of authority and power, nor to give and help for the sake of being known and called a benefactor. True greatness is not self-centered and selfish, not worldly-minded.

Note a crucial point: Jesus did not forbid a man from holding a position of greatness or authority. What He was doing was giving instructions to the person who is "greatest among you" (v.26). The Lord's attitude of greatness involves two key concepts.

1. There is the concept of acting as the *youngest*, that is, of taking the last seat, of assuming the lowliest position. In the ancient world, the younger always honored and gave way to the older. Age was looked up to and honored. Jesus was saying that the person who was truly great was the person who took the lowest seat and last place, the person who did not seek the recognition and honor, the credit and esteem, because he held some position or had done some special work or made some unusual gift or given extraordinary help.

"But when thou art bidden, go and sit down in the lowest room; that when he that bade thee cometh, he may say unto thee, Friend, go up higher: then shalt thou have worship in the presence of them that sit at meat with thee" (Lk.14:10).

"For I say, through the grace given unto me, to every man that is among you, not too think of himself more highly than he ought to think; but to think soberly, according as God hath dealt to every man the measure of faith" (Ro.12:3).

"Humble yourselves in the sight of the Lord, and he shall lift you up" (Jas.4:10).

"Likewise, ye younger, submit yourselves unto the elder. Yea, all of you be subject one to another, and be clothed with humility: for God resisteth the proud, and giveth grace to the humble. Humble yourselves therefore under the mighty hand of God, that he may exalt you in due time" (1 Pt.5:5-6).

2. There is the concept of acting as a servant. The chief person is to serve. The picture Jesus painted is descriptive. The truly great man will serve others just as a table waiter serves the guests at a banquet. The table waiter in Jesus' day was a bond-slave (doulos). The bond-slave was bound every moment of his life, always serving, no matter the hour or call or difficulty (see note, *Slave*—Ro.1:1).

The truly great person looks for people to help and for ways to help them, whether at work, home, play, or church. He is always seeking those who need a visit, care, attention, company, food, clothing, shelter, money. He seeks for the sake of ministering (cp. Mt.25:34-40).

"And whosoever shall give to drink unto one of these little ones a cup of cold water only in the name of a disciple, verily I say unto you, he shall in no wise lose his reward" (Mt.10:42).

"Let nothing be done through strife or vainglory; but in lowliness of mind let each esteem other better than themselves. Look not every man on his own things, but every man also on the things of others" (Ph.2:3-4).

3. There is the concept of following the example of the Lord. The follower is to be like his Lord, yet he is to humble himself and serve and minister to men. Of course, the man who sits at the table is greater than the man who serves. He holds a higher position, but he is not to *act* like it, lording it over the servant. He is to behave like the Lord, serving and ministering to men, even to the servants who are waiting upon him. (See notes—Mk.10:45 for three supreme ways Christ served.)

"After that he poureth water into a bason, and began to wash the disciples' feet, and to wipe them with the towel wherewith he was girded" (Jn.13:5).

"With good will doing service, as to the Lord, and not to men" (Eph.6:7).

"Let this mind be in you, which was also in Christ Jesus: who, being in the form of God, thought it not robbery to be equal with God: but made himself of no reputation, and took upon him the form of a servant, and was made in the likeness of men" (Ph.2:5-8).

**4** (22:28-30) **Faithfulness**: the Lord's encouragement to serve faithfully.

Jesus gave assurance to the disciples who proved themselves. The disciples who *continued* with Jesus, who were faithful, standing by Him and clinging to Him, were given a great promise. The promise was a covenant. Note the word "appoint." The promise was set and fixed in eternity. It could not be revoked nor changed in any form or fashion. The covenant was twofold.

1. The faithful disciple is to be a citizen of the Lord's kingdom (see Deeper Study # 3—Mt.19:23-24). The picture is that of the Marriage Feast of the Lamb. (See note, pt.2—Lk.22:15-18. Also see note—Mt.20:2.)

2. The faithful disciple is to rule (see Deeper Study # 1—Lk.22:30).

**DEEPER STUDY # 1**

**(22:30) Reward**: Jesus said that the disciples would be rewarded with twelve thrones, each one governing one of the twelve tribes of Israel. When are they to govern? "In the regeneration" when the new order of things shall be set up under the rule and reign of Christ. But when is the new order of things to be? There are two possible answers: either the millenial reign of Christ (see DEEPER STUDY # 3—Mt.19:23-24; note—Rev.20:4-6) or the new heavens and earth (Rev.21:1f; cp. 1 Cor.15:23-28).

There are three passages where Christ dealt with the regeneration as predicted here.

> "Ye which have followed me, in the regeneration when the Son of man shall sit in the throne of his glory, ye also shall sit upon twelve thrones, judging the twelve tribes of Israel" (Mt.19:28).
> The request of James' and John's mother: "Grant that these my two sons may sit, the one on thy right hand, and the other on the left, in thy kingdom....And he saith unto them, Ye shall drink indeed of my cup, and be baptized with the baptism that I am baptized with: but to sit on my right hand, and on my left, is not mine to give, but it shall be given to them for whom it is prepared of my Father" (Mt.20:21, 23).
> "Ye are they which have continued with me in my temptations. And I appoint unto you a kingdom, as my Father hath appointed unto me; that ye may eat and drink at my table in my kingdom, and sit on thrones judging the twelve tribes of Israel" (Lk.22:28-30).

The fulfillment of this promise seems to be the Messianic kingdom or millenial reign of Christ on earth. This seems to be the way Christ's promise to Israel will be fulfilled.

> "And I will restore thy judges as at the first, and thy counselors as at the beginning: afterward thou shalt be called, The city of righteousness, the faithful city" (Is.1:26).

Note three things.

1. Some commentators find great difficulty in saying there is ever again to be a distinction between Jew and Gentile, for Christ came to bring peace between all men, breaking down the wall of partition between all. They say that the great weight of Scripture is opposed to there being a distinction between Jew and Gentile again. This interpretation simply says that when Christ returns, that is it: He sets up His *eternal reign and rule forever*. Therefore, the apostles are to rule and reign over the church, spiritual Israel, the true Israel of God (Gal.6:15-16; cp. Ro.2:28-29).

2. Jesus said He will reward the disciples with *a particular honor*. Why? The disciples believed and followed Christ in the embryo stage of Christianity. They adhered to their belief and endured in the face of unbelievable odds.

⇒ Imagine standing before a man who looked like all other men, merely a man, and believing that man to really be the *Son of God*.

⇒ Imagine clinging to and continuing to follow Christ when everyone else turned away from Him (cp. Jn.6:67).

⇒ Imagine following immediately upon the heels of the risen Lord and being instantly responsible for reaching the world. (No wonder God had to plan for His Spirit to infill the disciples and to live within our bodies as He does. See notes—1 Cor.3:16; 6:19-20.)

⇒ Imagine continuing on and on, trying to be obedient and to reach the world for Christ, despite unbelievable odds.

⇒ Imagine confronting and enduring through unbelievable persecution launched from both an immoral government and a fierce religion.

The disciples were not only responsible for more and faced more than most of us will ever know; they were responsible for and faced more than we can ever imagine (cp. 1 Cor.4:9-13; 2 Cor.11:24-28).

3. The disciples were not the only ones to be rewarded. Every true follower of Christ will be greatly rewarded (see notes—Mt.19:29; Lk.16:1-13 for discussion).

| | | | |
|---|---|---|---|
| | **D. The Denial of Peter Foretold: The Great Warning of Satan's Attack, 22:31-38** (Mt.26:31-35; Mk.14:27-31; Jn.13:36-38) | thou shalt thrice deny that thou knowest me. 35 And he said unto them, When I sent you without purse, and scrip, and shoes, lacked ye anything? And they said, Nothing. | b. Not forgetting Jesus' resources |
| **1 The warning: Satan's desire is to sift—separate from God** | 31 And the Lord said, Simon, Simon, behold, Satan hath desired to have you, that he may sift you as wheat: | 36 Then said he unto them, But now, he that hath a purse, let him take it, and likewise his scrip: and he that hath no sword, let him sell his garment, and buy one. | c. Knowing difficult days lie ahead 1) Friends will forsake 2) Enemies will be fierce |
| **2 The answer to Satan's attack** a. Jesus' interceding b. Turning back c. Helping others | 32 But I have prayed for thee, that thy faith fail not: and when thou art converted, strengthen thy brethren. | 37 For I say unto you, that this that is written must yet be accomplished in me, And he was reckoned among the transgressors: for the things concerning me have an end. | d. Knowing Jesus is the Suffering Servant 1) Prophecy refers to Him (Is.53) 2) He is counted as a sinner 3) Salvation will be fulfilled |
| **3 The preventions against Satan's attack** a. Knowing the difference between carnal & spiritual commitment | 33 And he said unto him, Lord, I am ready to go with thee, both into prison, and to death. 34 And he said, I tell thee, Peter, the cock shall not crow this day before that | 38 And they said, Lord, behold, here are two swords. And he said unto them, It is enough. | **4 Conclusion: The disciples still do not understand— still think in terms of earthly Messiah** |

# DIVISION X

## THE SON OF MAN'S LAST SUPPER: HIS TRAITOR, INSTRUCTIONS, AND WARNINGS, 22:1-38

## D. The Denial of Peter Foretold: The Great Warning of Satan's Attack, 22:31-38

(22:31-38) **Introduction**: Satan attacks God's people. Knowing and understanding this fact helps the believer tremendously. It helps him...

- to recognize and stand against the attacks.
- to recover himself when caving in to the attacks.
- to strengthen others in their stand against the attacks.

Jesus knew the attack which was about to be launched against the disciples. This passage shows how He prepared His disciples. It is a strong warning that Satan does attack the believer.

1. The warning: Satan's desire is to sift the believer, to separate him from God (v.31).
2. The answer to Satan's attack (v.32).
3. The preventions against Satan's attack (v.33-37).
4. Conclusion: the disciples still do not understand—still think in terms of an earthly Messiah (v.38).

[1] (22:31) **Temptation—Satan—Spiritual Struggle**: there is the warning. Satan's desire is to sift the believer, that is, to separate him from God. This verse reveals a great deal about temptation. Note three things.

1. The word "you" is plural in the Greek. Satan desires to tempt all the disciples. Jesus addressed the warning to Peter because he was the leader of the group and because he was to go beyond desertion and actually deny Jesus. Peter needed some very special attention.

2. The word "desired" (exeitesato) means to beg for something, to obtain by asking. Jesus pictured Satan as begging permission of God to trip the disciples. It is the same picture that is found in Job (Job 1:6f). The Bible is clear in its teaching: God is supreme; anything that goes on in the universe goes on because God allows it, even temptation. Just why He allows temptation is covered in the next point. The truth to see right now is that...

- Jesus did give a glimpse into the spiritual world.
- Satan begged God to let him test and try the disciples.
- Satan is subject to God and has no right or power to *tempt believers* unless God allows it.
- The Lord's prayer does include the words, "Deliver us from the evil one" (a po tou poneron) (see DEEPER STUDY #9—Mt.6:13).

3. The word "sift" (siniasai) means to shake, to sift in a sieve in order to separate the good grain from the chaff. The picture is that Satan wished...

- to sift and shake the disciples.
- to test and try them.
- to prove they were not genuine.
- to cut the heart of God by showing they were not genuine.
- to disgrace God by proving their disloyalty.

Satan's primary purpose in temptation is to disgrace and cut the heart of God. He does this by challenging God to remove the *sense* of His presence and His blessings from the believer. Satan feels that the believer will fall and turn from God. He suggests to God that the believer will not stand by faith through trial after trial, not without the evidence of some *physical* or *material* blessing. His suggestion seems to be that the believer loves God not for Himself, not because of what Christ has done for him, but because of what he gets out of God. (Cp. Job 1:6-12.)

The presence of Jesus *was* about to be removed from the disciples. He was to die. And the disciples were thinking in terms of a physical kingdom and material rewards (cp. Lk.22:24-30). They did, of course, fail in the trial. However, we must always remember they did not yet know the full meaning of the cross and resurrection. They were living through the events while we are looking back upon them; we have complete understanding of what took place. Their love and devotion for Jesus ran deep. They did repent, returning and committing their lives fully to Him.

**Thought 1.** Satan's purpose in temptation is to disgrace and cut the heart of God. This should drive us to stand firm through all temptation, no matter the cost—by faith in the power of the Lord. (See note, *Satan*—Lk.22:3 for a list of the works of Satan.)

"There hath no temptation taken you but such as is common to man: but God is faithful, who will not suffer you to be tempted above that ye are able; but will with the temptation also make a way to escape, that ye may be able to bear it" (1 Cor.10:13).

"Lest Satan should get an advantage of us: for we are not ignorant of his devices" (2 Cor.2:11).

"But I fear, lest by any means, as the serpent beguiled Eve through his subtilty, so your minds should be corrupted from the simplicity that is in Christ" (2 Cor.11:3).

"For we wrestle not against flesh and blood, but against principalities, against powers, against the rulers of the darkness of this world, against spiritual wickedness in high places. Wherefore take unto you the whole armour of God, that ye may be able to withstand in the evil day, and having done all, to stand" (Eph.6:12-13).

"But they that will be rich fall into temptation and a snare, and into many foolish and hurtful lusts, which drown men in destruction and perdition" (1 Tim.6:9).

"But every man is tempted, when he is drawn away of his own lust, and enticed" (Jas.1:14).

"Be sober, be vigilant; because your adversary the devil, as a roaring lion, walketh about, seeking whom he may devour" (1 Pt.5:8).

**2** (22:32) **Repentance—Discipleship**: there is the answer when failing and falling under Satan's attack. Jesus wanted Peter to know three things.

1. Jesus is the believer's Intercessor. He was Peter's advocate before God. He had prayed that Peter's faith would not fail. This means Jesus prayed that Peter would not *permanently fall*, that his faith would not *totally fail and be absolutely ruined*, that he would not make a *final and lasting denial* of Jesus. Peter and the others would stumble and fall, but Jesus prayed that they would...
- not remain down.
- not stay in sin.
- not make a final and lasting rejection.
- not desert forever.

Jesus prayed that they would be kept by the power of God and not be plucked out of God's hand (Jn.10:29; 1 Pt.1:5).

"My little children, these things write I unto you, that ye sin not. And if any man sin, we have an advocate with the Father, Jesus Christ the righteous: and he is the propitiation for our sins: and not for ours only, but also for the sins of the whole world" (1 Jn.2:1-2).

"Who is he that condemneth? It is Christ that died, yea rather, that is risen again, who is even at the right hand of God, who also maketh intercession for us" (Ro.8:34).

"Wherefore he is able also to save them to the uttermost that come unto God by him, seeing he ever liveth to make intercession for them" (Heb.7:25).

2. The believer is to turn back to God after falling. The word "converted" (epistrepho) means to turn around, to turn back to, to turn again. The believer is to repent, turn back to God (see note and DEEPER STUDY # 1, *Repentance*—Acts 17:29-30).

"And said, Verily I say unto you, Except ye be converted, and become as little children, ye shall not enter into the kingdom of heaven" (Mt.18:3).

"Repent ye therefore, and be converted, that your sins may be blotted out, when the times of refreshing shall come from the presence of the Lord" (Acts 3:19).

"The place of the scripture which he read was this, He was led as a sheep to the slaughter; and like a lamb dumb before his shearer, so opened he not his mouth" (Acts 8:32).

3. The believer is to strengthen his brothers once he has returned to God. The believer is to take what he has learned from falling and...
- teach others how to find the mercy of God.
- help others who have fallen to return.
- strengthen the faith of others to keep them from falling.

"Brethren, if any of you do err from the truth, and one convert him; let him know, that he which converteth the sinner from the error of his way shall save a soul from death, and shall hide a multitude of sins" (Jas.5:19-20).

"Brethren, if a man be overtaken in a fault, ye which are spiritual, restore such an one in the spirit of meekness; considering thyself, lest thou also be tempted. Bear ye one another's burdens, and so fulfil the law of Christ" (Gal.6:1-2).

"Him that is weak in the faith receive ye, but not to doubtful disputations" (Ro.14:1).

"We then that are strong ought to bear the infirmities of the weak, and not to please ourselves" (Ro.15:1).

"Now we exhort you, brethren, warn them that are unruly, comfort the feebleminded, support the weak, be patient toward all men" (1 Th.5:14).

"Restore unto me the joy of thy salvation; and uphold me with thy free spirit. Then will I teach transgressors thy ways; and sinners shall be converted unto thee" (Ps.51:12-13).

**3** (22:33-37) **Commitment—Cross—Flesh—Carnal—Desires—Persecution**: the prevention against Satan's attack is fourfold.

1.   Prevention 1: knowing the difference between a carnal and a spiritual commitment. Peter immediately declared his loyalty to Jesus. He did not know the difference between a carnal and spiritual commitment to God. There are three differences.

a.   There is the difference between purposes and desires.
⇒ A carnal commitment purposes and desires to have *earthly and material things*.
⇒ A spiritual commitment purposes and desires to have *spiritual and heavenly things*.

Peter was committed to Jesus in the establishment of an earthly kingdom. That was what he wanted, and he was willing to follow Jesus to achieve the end—even to the point of dying in combat against the Romans (cp. Jn.13:33, 36-14:3). However, when he saw Jesus arrested and tried and apparently powerless, Peter's personal ambition was being crushed. Therefore, his succumbing to temptation was inevitable—not because of his lack of commitment, but because his *purpose and motive for committing himself was wrong*.

"And whosoever shall exalt himself shall be abased; and he that shall humble himself shall be exalted" (Mt.23:12).

"For I say, through the grace given unto me, to every man that is among you, not to think of himself more highly than he ought to think; but to think soberly, according as God hath dealt to every man the measure of faith" (Ro.12:3).

"For if a man think himself to be something, when he is nothing, he deceiveth himself" (Gal.6:3).

"Wherefore let him that thinketh he standeth take heed lest he fall" (1 Cor.10:12).

"Many seek the ruler's favor; but every man's judgment cometh from the LORD" (Pr.29:26).

b.   There is the difference between seeing and being blind to the cross.
⇒ A carnal commitment ignores or rejects or spiritualizes the real meaning of the cross.
⇒ A spiritual commitment sees the cross and leads a person to crucify his flesh by the cross. (See note and DEEPER STUDY # 1—Lk.9:23. Cp. Ro.6:6; 8:13; Gal.2:20; 5:24; Col.3:5.)

Peter's overconfidence was caused by being blind to the cross. It was Jesus hanging upon the cross that was going to cause Peter to deny Jesus. Jesus had told him all about the cross; but Peter had refused to believe it (see notes—Mt.17:22; 18:1-2). The fact that human flesh was so sinful and so depraved that God would have to crucify it was just too much to grasp (see outline and notes—Mt.26:33-34; Ro.6:6-13; pt.2—Gal.2:19-21; 5:24; 6:14-17. Cp. Ro.6:2; Col.3:3.)

"And he said to them all, If any man will come after me, let him deny himself, and take up his cross daily, and follow me" (Lk.9:23).

"Knowing this, that our old man is crucified with him, that the body of sin might be destroyed, that henceforth we should not serve sin" (Ro.6:6).

"For if ye live after the flesh, ye shall die: but if ye through the Spirit do mortify the deeds of the body, ye shall live" (Ro.8:13).

"I am crucified with Christ: nevertheless I live; yet not I, but Christ liveth in me: and the life which I now live in the flesh I live by the faith of the Son of God, who loved me, and gave himself for me" (Gal.2:20).

"And they that are Christ's have crucified the flesh with the affections and lusts" (Gal.5:24).

"Mortify [put to death] therefore your members which are upon the earth; fornication, uncleanness, inordinate affection, evil concupiscence, and covetousness, which is idolatry" (Col.3:5).

c.   There is the difference between knowing and not knowing the weakness of the human flesh. Peter boasted confidence in himself, in his own natural strength. *As with all men*, his natural strength failed. The need for the Lord's strength, the presence of the Holy Spirit to conquer self and evil, was the great lesson Peter had to learn. Very simply, he and the others had to learn to trust the strength of Jesus, not their own flesh, not if they wished to please God and to be acceptable to Him.

"For they that are after the flesh do mind the things of the flesh; but they that are after the Spirit the things of the Spirit. For to be carnally minded is death; but to be spiritually minded is life and peace. Because the carnal mind is enmity against God: for it is not subject to the law of God, neither indeed can be. So then they that are in the flesh cannot please God" (Ro.8:5-8).

"And if any man think that he knoweth any thing, he knoweth nothing yet as he ought to know" (1 Cor.8:2).

"For if a man think himself to be something, when he is nothing, he deceiveth himself" (Gal.6:3).

"Be not wise in thine own eyes: fear the LORD, and depart from evil" (Pr.3:7).

Note: the cock's crowing was probably mentioned to trigger the warning about the weakness of the flesh in the mind of Peter and the others. For the person who has the privilege of hearing the rooster crow, it is a good trigger to remind him of the weakness of his own flesh and the great need to walk with the Spirit of God. (See note, pt.2—Mt.26:33-35.)

2. Prevention 2: not forgetting Jesus' resources. Jesus reminded His disciples how God had taken care of them when He sent them out to preach (see outline and notes—Lk.9:3-5; 10:4 for the background of this event). God provided everything they needed. One of the preventatives against Satan's attacks is to remember God's glorious provisions.

"There hath no temptation taken you but such as is common to man: but God is faithful, who will not suffer you to be tempted above that ye are able; but will with the temptation also make a way to escape, that ye may be able to bear it" (1 Cor.10:13).

"Not that I speak in respect of want: for I have learned, in whatsoever state I am, therewith to be content. I know both how to be abased, and I know how to abound: every where and in all things I am instructed both to be full and to be hungry, both to abound and to suffer need. I can do all things through Christ which strengtheneth me" (Ph.4:11-13).

"But my God shall supply all your need according to his riches in glory by Christ Jesus" (Ph.4:19).

"But seek ye first the kingdom of God, and his righteousness; and all these things shall be added unto you" (Mt.6:33).

3. Prevention 3: knowing that very difficult days lie ahead. Jesus was warning of the perilous days that lay ahead and the need for the disciples to prepare for those days. He was speaking symbolically—of spiritual warfare and spiritual preparation. Two things were to happen to the followers of the Lord.
   a. Their friends were to forsake them. They would have to earn their own livelihood while preaching and ministering. They would need their purses and money. No man would help them nor provide housing or upkeep; no man would free them to preach the gospel or minister. They should, but they would not.

"Let the elders that rule well be counted worthy of double honour, especially they who labour in the word and doctrine. For the scripture saith, Thou shalt not muzzle the ox that treadeth out the corn. And, The labourer is worthy of his reward" (1 Tim.5:17-18).

   b. Their enemies would be fierce. Jesus was not telling His disciples to arm themselves. He was simply using symbolic language to stress a spiritual truth. The persecution they were to face would be so fierce that they must clothe themselves with courage, the kind of courage...
      • that is determined to stand and conquer.
      • that considers a weapon more important than clothing.
      • that gives up its last possession before surrendering.
4. Prevention 4: knowing that Jesus is the Suffering Servant of God. Jesus said three things.
   a. The Scripture included prophecies of Him and they "must yet be accomplished *in me*." He was claiming deity, to be the Messiah, the Son of the living God. He was claiming that the prophecy of the Suffering Servant in Isaiah 53 concerned Him. He was the Suffering Servant of God.

"Surely he hath borne our griefs, and carried our sorrows: yet we did esteem him stricken, smitten of God, and afflicted. But he was wounded for our transgressions, he was bruised for our iniquities: the chastisement of our peace was upon him; and with his stripes we are healed" (Is.53:4-5).

   b. He was to be reckoned and counted among the transgressors. This means that God was to look at Him and count Him as a sinner just like all other men. He was to become one with man even in sin, yet He was to be without sin. Why? So that He could take the place of sinful men, bearing their sins for them. He was to become the substitute for men in bearing both their sins and the guilt and judgment of their sins (see note—Lk.22:43-44).

"Christ hath redeemed us from the curse of the law, being made a curse for us: for it is written, Cursed is every one that hangeth on a tree" (Gal.3:13).

"But we see Jesus, who was made a little lower than the angels for the suffering of death, crowned with glory and honour; that he by the grace of God should taste death for every man" (Heb.2:9).

"So Christ was once offered to bear the sins of many; and unto them that look for him shall he appear the second time without sin unto salvation" (Heb.9:28).

"Who his own self bare our sins in his own body on the tree, that we, being dead to sins, should live unto righteousness: by whose stripes ye were healed" (1 Pt.2:24).

"For Christ also hath once suffered for sins, the just for the unjust, that he might bring us to God, being put to death in the flesh, but quickened by the Spirit" (1 Pt.3:18).

"And ye know that he was manifested to take away our sins; and in him is no sin" (1 Jn.3:5).

c. The things concerning Him "have an end" (telos echei): an accomplishment, fulfillment, completion. The Suffering Servant of God would fulfill Isaiah 53, and man's salvation would be finally settled, finished. He was to proclaim upon the cross "It is finished" and then bow His head and give up the ghost.

"Jesus saith unto them, My meat is to do the will of him that sent me, and to finish his work" (Jn.4:34).

"I have glorified thee on the earth: I have finished the work which thou gavest me to do" (Jn.17:4).

"When Jesus therefore had received the vinegar, he said, It is finished: and he bowed his head, and gave up the ghost" (Jn.19:30).

**4** (22:38) **Conclusion**: the disciples still did not understand. The warning was not grasped. They still thought in terms of an earthly Messiah, of a Messiah who needed their help in the fight against the evil forces of the world. They still refused to accept the spiritual kingdom of the Messiah. Jesus' words "it is enough" did not mean that two swords were enough, but "enough of this kind of talk."

| | XI. THE SON OF MAN'S SUFFERINGS: HIS AGONY, TRIALS, AND CRUCIFIXION, 22:39-23:56 | from them about a stone's cast, and kneeled down, and prayed, 42 Saying, Father, if thou be willing, remove this cup from me: nevertheless not my will, but thine be done. | cup of suffering[DS1] |
|---|---|---|---|
| | A. Jesus' Great Agony: Bearing Unbelievable Weight, 22:39-46 (Mt.26:36-46; Mk.14:32-42; Jn.18:1; cp. Heb.5:7-8; 12:3-4) | 43 And there appeared an angel unto him from heaven, strengthening him. 44 And being in an agony he prayed more earnestly: and his sweat was as it were great drops of blood falling down to the ground. | 4 The awful weight of His intense agony[DS2] a. Seen in the angel's visit b. Seen in His intense praying c. Seen in His sweat |
| 1 Jesus in the Mount of Olives a. His custom to withdraw there for prayer b. His disciples follow 2 The weight of His disciples' great trial 3 The weight of His own | 39 And he came out, and went, as he was wont, to the mount of Olives and his disciples also followed him. 40 And when he was at the place, he said unto them, Pray that ye enter not into temptation. 41 And he was withdrawn | 45 And when he rose up from prayer, and was come to his disciples, he found them sleeping for sorrow, 46 And said unto them, Why sleep ye? rise and pray, lest ye enter into temptation. | 5 The weight of the disciples' continued weakness |

# DIVISION XI

## THE SON OF MAN'S SUFFERINGS: HIS AGONY, TRIALS, AND CRUCIFIXION, 22:39-23:56

## A.    Jesus' Great Agony: Bearing Unbelievable Weight, 22:39-46

(22:39-46) **Introduction**: this passage shows the great weight of suffering Jesus underwent in facing the cross.
1.    Jesus in the Mount of Olives (v.39).
2.    The weight of His disciples' great trial (v.40).
3.    The weight of His own cup of suffering (v.41-42).
4.    The awful weight of the intense agony (v.43-44).
5.    The weight of the disciples' continued weakness (v.45-46).

[1]  (22:39) **Prayer—Jesus Christ, Prayer Life of**: Jesus entered the Mount of Olives. His disciples were with Him. The significant thing to note is this: it was His custom to seek time alone with God on the mount when in Jerusalem. During the last week of His life, He was spending every night in prayer (see note 2 and DEEPER STUDY # 1—Lk.21:37).

[2]  (22:40) **Jesus Christ, Sufferings—Discipleship**: Jesus bore the weight of His disciples' great trial. The greatest trial the disciples were to ever know was at hand, and they did not know it. In just a few hours they were going to fall away. They desperately needed to pray that they "enter not into temptation" (v.40), that they not be so gripped by temptation and sin that they would be too weak to repent when Jesus arose and confronted them. Jesus knew the enormous temptation that was coming upon these men, and He loved and cared for them, so He was bound to feel the pressure of their trial.

> "For we have not an high priest which cannot be touched with the feeling of our infirmities; but was in all points tempted like as we are, yet without sin. Let us therefore come boldly unto the throne of grace, that we may obtain mercy, and find grace to help in time of need" (Heb.4:15-16).
> "For we wrestle not against flesh and blood, but against principalities, against powers, against the rulers of the darkness of this world, against spiritual wickedness in high places. Wherefore take unto you the whole armour of God, that ye may be able to withstand in the evil day, and having done all, to stand" (Eph.6:12-13).
> "Ye therefore, beloved, seeing ye know these things before, beware lest ye also, being led away with the error of the wicked, fall from your own stedfastness" (2 Pt.3:17).

[3]  (22:41-42) **Jesus Christ, Sufferings**: Jesus bore the weight of His own cup of suffering. In confronting death Jesus turned to God, crying with *strong cries and tears* (cp. Heb.5:7). Four things are seen in this verse.
1.    Jesus got all alone and prostrated Himself before God. Luke says He withdrew "about a stone's cast" from the three disciples. Note two significant points. (1) He needed to be alone with God—He was desperate. (b) He fell on His face—the pressure and weight were unbearable.
2.    Jesus prayed, "Father (pater)." It is the address of a child's love and dependency and trust. The child knows that His father will hear and turn to him when he calls "Father." But note also the words, "O my Father." Jesus was broken and weighted down; He had fallen prostrate upon the ground with His face buried in His hands. In desperation He cried out "O my Father" (cp. Mt.26:39). Just like a child, He cried out to His Father in brokenness and dependency, knowing that His Father would hear Him and turn to help Him.

3.     Jesus asked God to remove the cup from Him. (See DEEPER STUDY # 4, *Cup*—Mt.26:39. Also see DEEPER STUDY # 1—Mt.27:26-44; cp. Mt.20:19.) The human nature and will of Jesus is clearly seen in this experience. He was as much flesh as any man is; therefore, He begged God to choose another way other than the cup, if possible. The experience of being *separated from God* upon the cross was too much to bear.

4.     The divine nature and will of Jesus is also clearly seen in this experience. Note the Lord's words: "Let this cup pass from me: nevertheless...." The first act, the first impulse and struggle of His will, had come from His flesh: to escape the cup of separation from God. But immediately, the second act, the second impulse and struggle of His will, came from His Godly nature: not to do as He willed, but as God willed.

Jesus' surrender to do God's perfect will in the Garden of Gethsemane was critical.

⇒     It was in His surrender that He was made perfect and was able to stand before God as the Ideal, Perfect Man.

⇒     It was in His surrender to be the Ideal, Perfect Man that His righteousness was able to stand for every man.

⇒     It was in His surrender to be the Ideal, Perfect Man that He was able to bear the cup of God's wrath against sin *for every man.*

⇒     It was in His surrender to be the Ideal, Perfect Man that His sacrifice and sufferings were able to stand for every man.

> **"But we see Jesus, who was made a little lower than the angels for the suffering of death, crowned with glory and honor; that he by the grace of God should taste death for every man. For it became him, for whom are all things, and by whom are all things, in bringing many sons unto glory, to make the captain of their salvation perfect through sufferings" (Heb.2:9-10).**
>
> **"Though he were a Son, yet learned he obedience by the things which he suffered; and being made perfect, he became the author of eternal salvation unto all them that obey him" (Heb.5:8-9).**
>
> **"For he hath made him to be sin for us, who knew no sin; that we might be made the righteousness of God in him" (2 Cor.5:21).**

---

**DEEPER STUDY # 1**

(22:42) **Cup**: Jesus Christ was not fearing nor shrinking from death itself. This is clearly seen in Jn.10:17-18. Death for a cause is not such a great price to pay. Many men have died for causes fearlessly and willingly, some perhaps even more cruelly than Jesus Himself. Shrinking from betrayal, beatings, humiliation, and death—increased by foreknowledge—is not what was happening to Jesus. As stated, some men have faced such trials courageously, even inviting martyrdom for a cause. The Lord knew He was to die from the very beginning, and He had been preparing His disciples for His death (see DEEPER STUDY # 1—Lk.9:22). It was not human and physical suffering from which Jesus was shrinking. Such an explanation is totally inadequate in explaining Gethsemane. The great cup or trial Jesus was facing was separation from God (see note, pt.1—Mt.26:37-38). He was to be the sacrificial *Lamb of God* who was to take away the sins of the world (Jn.1:29). He was to bear the judgment of God for the sins of the world (see note—Mt.27:46-49; cp. Is.53:10). Jesus Himself had already spoken of the "cup" when referring to His sacrificial death (see DEEPER STUDY # 2—Mt.20:22-23; note—Mk.14:41-42; DEEPER STUDY # 2—Jn.18:11).

Scripture speaks of the cup in several ways.

1.     The cup is called "the cup of the Lord's fury" (Is.51:17).

2.     The cup is associated with suffering and God's wrath (cp. Ps.11:6; Is.51:17; Lk.22:42).

3.     The cup is also associated with salvation. Because Jesus drank the cup of suffering and wrath for us, we can "take the cup of salvation and call upon the name of the Lord" (Ps.116:13). He bears the judgment of God for the sins of the world (Is.53:10).

---

**4** (22:43-44) **Jesus Christ, Suffering**: Jesus bore the awful weight of intense agony. This is seen in three facts.

1.     God had to send an angel to strengthen Jesus. What did the angel do? We are not told, but certainly the angel would have shared how His death...

•     was an act that glorified and honored God because it was doing exactly what His Father wanted. It was an act of obedience, of love and adoration for God. It was an offering, the perfect offering to God (see note—Eph.5:2).

•     was to result in His own glory and honor and exaltation (Heb.12:2; Ph.2:6-11).

•     was the only way man could be saved eternally.

Also, the angel probably did some very practical things. We can imagine the angel's embracing His Lord, just holding Him ever so tightly, perhaps infusing strength into His being. The scene of our Lord's being so weak that He had to be embraced and engulfed in the arms of an angel should break the believer's heart. Perhaps the angel wiped the perspiration and blood and tears off His brow. Whatever the scene, we need to see the awful weight and intensity of our Lord's agony.

2.     He prayed "more earnestly," more intensely. The reason is seen in the Greek words for "being in an agony" (genomenos en agonia). The Greek (aorist participle) means Jesus experienced a growing agony. The weight upon Him was not only intense, it grew more and more intense. The pressure and sense of suffering became heavier and heavier. The picture is that of His becoming engrossed and embodied in agony. Thus, He prayed more and more earnestly. His prayer grew and increased in intensity even as His agony intensified.

3.    He sweat great drops of blood. The words "great drops" (thromboi) mean thick clots of blood. Apparently Jesus was under so much pressure the capillary veins right under the skin burst and the blood mingled with sweat and poured through the enlarged pores. What Jesus was experiencing can never be known (see DEEPER STUDY # 2, *Jesus Christ, Suffering*—Lk.22:43-44).

---

**DEEPER STUDY # 2**
(22:43-44) **Jesus Christ, Suffering**: words could never express what Jesus experienced. Words to describe the suffering of Jesus are totally inadequate. Using all the descriptive words in the world would be as inadequate as using a syringe to drain an ocean.

1.    There was the *mental and emotional agony*: the weight, pressure, anguish, sorrow, and excessive strain such as no man has ever experienced. He was the Son of God, the Maker of heaven and earth; but *now* pressing in ever so heavily upon His mind and spirit were the images, the thoughts of...

- the *hardness and unbelief* of all men everywhere.
- the *rejection* of His own people, the Jews.
- the *malice* of the world's leaders, both Jew and Gentile, religious and civil.
- the *betrayal* of one of His own, Judas.
- the *desertion* of all His men.
- the *denial* by the leader of His own men, Peter.
- the *injustice and condemnation* of His trial.
- the *ridicule and pain* of being scourged, spit upon, slugged, cursed, mocked, crowned with thorns, nailed to the cross and killed.
- the *wrath of God* that was soon to be cast upon Him as the Sin-Bearer of the world.
- the *departure of God's Spirit* from Him as He bore the sins of the world.

2.    There was the *physical experience of death while being the Son of God*. What was it like for the Son of God to die just as all men die? If just the physical aspect of Jesus' death is considered, His death was still different from all other men.

a.    Jesus as the Son of God possessed the very seed of life within His being (see DEEPER STUDY # 1—Jn.17:2-3).
b.    Jesus as the Son of God possessed no seed of death (Jn.14:6; 1 Tim.6:16; 1 Jn.1:1-2. Cp. Jn.1:4.) But man does. Man possesses the seed of corruption and death; man's sinful nature knows nothing and expects nothing but death. However, the sinless nature of Jesus knew nothing of sin and death. Therefore, the agony and pain of death was bound to be as different from man's death as white is different from black.
        There is another fact to note as well. Man suffers the depth of humiliation in death. No matter how much man struggles to live, he irrevocably wastes and wastes away until he is carried into the grave and dust of the ground. But not Jesus. Again He was sinless, perfect even in His human nature. Imagine the humiliation: the Son of God—Perfect Man, Perfect God—having to die upon this earth! No wonder He "began to be sorrowful and *very heavy*!" No wonder He could say, "My soul is exceeding sorrowful, *even unto death.*" In some mysterious way, God made Jesus to become sin for us (2 Cor.5:21).

3.    There was *the spiritual experience of death* while being the Son of Man (see note—Mt.5:17-18; DEEPER STUDY # 3—8:20; DEEPER STUDY # 2—Ro.8:3). There is so much in this fact, yet so little can ever be known.

a.    First, what is it like to be without sin? Although being fully man, Jesus was sinless. He lived as all men live facing all the trials and temptations that men face, yet He never sinned. He became the Perfect Man, the Ideal Man—all that God wants man to be. Therefore, He became the Pattern for all men.

> "For we have not an high priest which cannot be touched with the feeling of our infirmities; but was in all points tempted like as we are, yet without sin" (Heb.4:15; cp. 2 Cor.5:21; 1 Pt.2:22; 1 Jn.3:5).
> "Though he were a Son, yet learned he obedience by the things which he suffered; and being made perfect, he became the author of eternal salvation unto all them that obey him" (Heb.5:8-9).

b.    Second, what is it like to bear all the sins of the world? What is it like to be perfect and sinless, and then *all of a sudden* to have all the sins of the world laid upon Oneself? In some mysterious way, God took all the sins of the world and laid the whole *body of sin* upon Jesus. In some mysterious way, God made Jesus to become sin for us (2 Cor.5:21). Jesus, as the Ideal Man, became the Ideal Sin-Bearer. He bore all the sins and all that sin causes, all the...

| | | | |
|---|---|---|---|
| darkness | weight | worry | strife |
| pollution | pressure | guilt | warring |
| filth | anxiety | savagery | torture |
| dirt | turmoil | conflict | enmity |
| poison | corrosion | consumption | disturbance |

> "All we like sheep have gone astray; we have turned every one to his own way; and the Lord hath laid on him the iniquity of us all" (Is.53:6).
> "In due time Christ died for the ungodly" (Ro.5:6).
> "For he hath made him to be sin for us, who knew no sin; that we might be made the righteousness of God in him" (2 Cor.5:21).

"So Christ was once offered to bear the sins of many; and unto them that look for him shall he appear the second time without sin unto salvation" (Heb.9:28).

"Who his own self bare our sins in his own body on the tree, that we, being dead to sins, should live unto righteousness: by whose stripes ye were healed" (1 Pt.2:24).

c. Third, what is it like to bear all the judgment and condemnation of sin for all men? What is it like to be judged and condemned for *all the sins ever committed*? Jesus suffered for the sins of *the whole world*, suffered *separation* from God. The terrifying mystery of this hellish experience is seen in His cry upon the cross, "My God, My God, why hast thou forsaken me?" (See notes—Mt.27:26-44; 27:46-49; 1 Pt.2:21-25.)

"But he was wounded for our transgressions, he was bruised for our iniquities: the chastisement of our peace was upon him; and with his stripes we are healed" (Is.53:5).

"Christ hath redeemed us from the curse of the law, being made a curse for us: for it is written, Cursed is every one that hangeth on a tree" (Gal.3:13).

"But we see Jesus, who was made a little lower than the angels for the suffering of death, crowned with glory and honor; that he by the grace of God should taste death for every man" (Heb.2:9).

"For Christ also hath once suffered for sins, the just for the unjust, that he might bring us to God, being put to death in the flesh, but quickened by the Spirit" (1 Pt.3:18).

---

**5** (22:45-46) **Jesus Christ, Suffering**: Jesus bore the weight of the disciples' continued weakness. The disciples were weak, so weak in fact that they were of no help to Jesus as He faced the most severe crises of His life. Jesus had to face the cross knowing the terrible weakness of His own men. Note what happened.

1. Jesus arose from prayer and went to the three who were supposed to be praying with Him. They were asleep. The companionship and spirit of prayer and comfort He had sought were not there. All were asleep. He had been left alone to wrestle with God by Himself.

2. Jesus warned them of temptation. They had failed to pray for Him, but they must not fail to pray for themselves. Jesus said, "Watch and pray." Both were important. *Watchfulness* sees and *praying* prepares. They must watch in order to see temptation's coming, and they must pray in order to be prepared when temptation struck.

3. Jesus warned of the flesh and its weakness. They were sleeping because of the emotional strain and distress of the evening. As Luke says, they slept because of "sorrow," that is, sadness (Lk.22:45). The evening had been shocking and taxing. They were weary, fatigued, and preoccupied. Concentration in prayer was difficult. They probably fought to stay awake and to pray for their Lord, but the importance of prayer and of spiritual dependancy upon God in facing trials had not yet been learned. They were making two mistakes common among believers.

a. They were depending upon their own wisdom and strength instead of God's Spirit to fight whatever battles lay ahead.

b. They were taking God's deliverance for granted instead of assuring themselves of His deliverance through the testimony of prayer. They believed Christ to be the Messiah; therefore, they believed that God was going to deliver them from the Romans no matter what. As carnal, fleshy men are apt to do, the disciples no doubt thought prayer mattered little. They were just presuming upon God, taking His deliverance for granted. What Jesus said was, "Watch and pray, for only as you watch and pray can you keep from falling when the trial comes."

A point needs to be noted here: watchfulness and prayer bear *testimony* to God. When men watch and pray, they demonstrate that dependency and trust in God are well founded. When God answers the prayers of men, He demonstrates that He loves and delivers those who truly look up to Him. Without watching and praying, God allows the disciples to fall in order to teach that dependency and trust in Him are absolutely essential.

4. They were failing to stay awake to pray, to watch and be watchful in prayer. Their spirits were not alive and alert enough to overcome the flesh. The drowsiness and slumber of the flesh were stronger than the spirit (see note, pt.2—Mt.26:42-44; cp. Eph.6:18).

"Watch and pray, that ye enter not into temptation: the spirit indeed is willing, but the flesh is weak" (Mt.26:41).

"Wherefore let him that thinketh he standeth take heed lest he fall" (1 Cor.10:12).

"Continue in prayer, and watch in the same with thanksgiving" (Col.4:2).

"Be sober, be vigilant; because your adversary the devil, as a roaring lion, walketh about, seeking whom he may devour" (1 Pt.5:8).

| | B. Jesus' Arrest: Terrible Sins Against Jesus, 22:47-53 (Mt.26:47-56; Mk.14:43-52; Jn.18:3-11) | sword? 50 And one of them smote the servant of the high priest, and cut off his right ear. | |
|---|---|---|---|
| **1 Deserting Jesus: The betrayer** a. A professing disciple b. A leader of sinners | 47 And while he yet spake, behold a multitude, and he that was called Judas, one of the twelve, went before them, and drew near unto Jesus to kiss him. | 51 And Jesus answered and said, Suffer ye thus far. And he touched his ear, and healed him. 52 Then Jesus said unto the | **b. Jesus rebuked the disciples** **3 Being blind to the Son of God: The religionists** |
| c. A deceptive commitment **2 Misunderstanding the Lord's will: The disciples** a. The disciples misunderstood & ignored Jesus' will | 48 But Jesus said unto him, Judas, betrayest thou the Son of man with a kiss? 49 When they which were about him saw what would follow, they said unto him, Lord, shall we smite with the | chief priests, and captains of the temple, and the elders, which were come to him, Be ye come out, as against a thief, with swords and staves? 53 When I was daily with you in the temple, ye stretched forth no hands against me: but this is your hour, and the power of darkness. | **4 Joining forces with the power of darkness** |

# DIVISION XI

## THE SON OF MAN'S SUFFERINGS: HIS AGONY, TRIALS, AND CRUCIFIXION, 22:39-23:56

## B.    Jesus' Arrest: Terrible Sins Against Jesus, 22:47-53

(22:47-53) **Introduction**: it took only a few minutes to arrest Jesus. However, in those few minutes was painted a dramatic picture of four terrible sins against the Lord, sins that are repeated by too many in every generation.
1.    Deserting Jesus: the betrayer (v.47-48).
2.    Misunderstanding and ignoring the Lord's will: the disciples (v.49-51).
3.    Being blind to the Son of God: the religionists (v.52).
4.    Joining forces with the power of darkness (v.53).

[1]    (22:47-48) **Unbelief—Desertion—Apostasy—Judas**: deserting the Lord, the sin committed by Judas the betrayer. Three things are seen in Judas' desertion.
1.    He was a *professing* disciple, a man who claimed to be a follower of the Lord. In fact, he had actually been with the Lord and His followers for over two years. On this very evening, just a few hours before, he had been eating and fellowshipping with the Lord and the other disciples; but ever so quickly, he had turned away.
2.    He was a *leader* of sinners, leading the world in its opposition to Jesus. Note the words "went before them." As pointed out earlier, he chose the world before Jesus—the world's money, position, and recognition (fame). (See note—Mk.14:10.)
The crowd which Judas led is identified by Matthew and Mark as being arresting officers or temple police from the Sanhedrin. John says they included Roman soldiers. Matthew and Mark say they were armed. The soldiers, of course, had their swords; the elders and other officials of the High Priest had armed themselves with boards and sticks (cp. Mt.26:47).
3.    He had a *deceptive* commitment to the Lord. Note what happened. It was dark. How would the temple guards be able to recognize Jesus in the dark and keep Him from slipping away? Judas thought and came up with a plan. He would identify Jesus for them by walking up and greeting Jesus with a kiss. A kiss was a sign of friendship and commitment among people in the East, in particular among friends. Judas felt he could deceive the disciples; they would never suspect his sin.
What Judas planned, he did. The sin was bad, but the deception was worse. Jesus' question was searching: "Betrayest thou the Son of man with a kiss?" Note: the question was not a rebuke or reproach. Jesus was forcing Judas to think, to search his deceptive heart. He still wanted to reach Judas, if possible (see note—Mt.26:48-50).

> **Thought 1.** How many profess Christ but do not really know Christ nor live for Christ? How many are deceivers just as Judas was: trying to make others think they are followers of Christ when they are really living *for themselves*? How many began to follow Christ but are now falling back into sin just as Judas did?
>
> > "And they will deceive every one his neighbour, and will not speak the truth: they have taught their tongue to speak lies, and weary themselves to commit iniquity" (Jer.9:5).
> > "The heart is deceitful above all things, and desperately wicked: who can know it?" (Jer.17:9).
> > "That we henceforth be no more children, tossed to and fro, and carried about with every wind of doctrine, by the sleight of men, and cunning craftiness, whereby they lie in wait to deceive" (Eph.4:14).
> > "But evil men and seducers shall wax worse and worse, deceiving, and being deceived" (2 Tim.3:13).
> > "For there are many unruly and vain talkers and deceivers" (Tit.1:10).

"Take heed, brethren, lest there be in any of you an evil heart of unbelief, in departing from the living God" (Heb.3:12).

"[These] shall receive the reward of unrighteousness, as they that count it pleasure to riot [party] in the day time. Spots they are and blemishes, sporting themselves with their own deceivings while they feast with you [the church]; having eyes full of adultery, and that cannot cease from sin; beguiling unstable souls: an heart they have exercised with covetous practices; cursed children" (2 Pt.2:13-14).

"For many deceivers are entered into the world, who confess not that Jesus Christ is come in the flesh. This is a deceiver and an antichrist" (2 Jn.7).

**2** (22:49-51) **Flesh—Commitment—Carnal**: misunderstanding and ignoring the Lord's will, the sin committed by the disciples. Note two things.

1. The disciples misunderstood the Lord's will and the spiritual nature of His kingdom. They were ready to *war in the flesh*. The disciple referred to in v.50 was Peter, and the servant whose ear was cut off was Malchus (Jn.18:10). Jesus restored the ear, miraculously healed it (Lk.22:51).

Peter thought the Messiah's hour had come, that Jesus was now ready to free Israel and establish the throne of David as the dominant nation in the world (see notes—Mt.1:1; DEEPER STUDY # 2—1:18; DEEPER STUDY # 3—3:11; notes—11:1-6; 11:2-3; DEEPER STUDY # 1—11:5; DEEPER STUDY # 2—11:6; DEEPER STUDY # 1—12:16; notes—22:42; Lk.7:21-23). Peter drew his sword (note he had one) and struck, slashing off the ear of Malchus.

2. Jesus rebuked the disciples: their carnal commitment, their warring in the flesh.
   ⇒ He told Peter to put his sword back into its sheath where it belonged (Mt.26:52).
   ⇒ He healed Malchus' ear (Lk.22:51).

The picture painted by the disciples' behavior is carnal commitment, that is, acting and struggling in the flesh. The disciples took their stand for Jesus *in the flesh*. Therefore they failed, and eventually they deserted Jesus. Acting in the flesh will always result in failing and deserting Christ. The disciples' carnal commitment is seen in four mistakes. Each mistake is too often seen in the life of believers.

1. The disciples misunderstood the Lord's Word. First, they thought Jesus was to establish an earthly kingdom. They thought in terms of the earthly, the physical, the material. Therefore, they *failed to grasp the spiritual and eternal kingdom* proclaimed by Jesus. Second, they never accepted the Lord's Word. Jesus had predicted His death and forewarned the disciples, giving them extensive training for months (see notes—Mt.16:13-20; 16:21-28; 17:1-13; 17:22; 17:24-27). Yet they refused to give up their preconceived ideas to accept what Jesus was saying. Therefore, they did not see the eternal world of the Spirit nor the eternal salvation which Jesus was securing.

2. The disciples did not wait for instructions from Jesus. They acted on their own, took matters into their own hands. The disciples had asked, "Lord, shall we smite with the sword?" But Jesus had not yet answered. However, this did not stop them; they went ahead and acted on their own.

**Thought 1.** How like so many of us! Too often, we act without waiting on the Lord.

3. The disciples did not ask Jesus what to do, not again and again. They did not *persist* until Jesus answered.

"Watch and pray, that ye enter not into temptation: the spirit indeed is willing, but the flesh is weak" (Mt.26:41).

"Watch ye therefore, and pray always, that ye may be accounted worthy to escape all these things that shall come to pass, and to stand before the Son of man" (Lk.21:36).

"Seek the LORD and his strength, seek his face continually" (1 Chron.16:11).

4. The disciples did not think clearly nor act wisely. Their actions could have led to the failure of God's will. It could have led to the death of many. That is what Jesus was saying: "Violence leads to violence. If you draw the sword, the soldiers will cut you down." Among God's people, the place of the sword is in the sheath, not drawn and slashing at people. God's people are to proclaim love and peace, not war and violence, not carnal and fleshly behavior.

"Not by might, nor by power, but by my spirit, saith the LORD of hosts" (Zech.4:6).

"As many as I love, I rebuke and chasten: be zealous therefore, and repent" (Rev.3:19).

"But sanctify the Lord God in your hearts: and be ready always to give an answer to every man that asketh you a reason of the hope that is in you with meekness and fear" (1 Pt.3:15).

**3** (22:52) **Sin—Unbelief—Blindness**: being blind to the Son of God, the sin committed by the religionists. The religionists refused to accept Jesus as the Messiah (see note and DEEPER STUDY # 1—Mk.14:1-2). The question of Jesus was piercing. Why did the world treat Him as a thief? They acted as though He stole from them. He did not preach a message that allowed them to live as they wished; it was as though He took the right to live as they wished away from them. He did not praise them, boost their egos, honor their service and gifts. Rather, He told them they were lacking in discernment and sinful, dying and doomed if they did not repent and begin to live as God said (see note—Mt.26:55-56).

**Thought 1.** Note a crucial point so often not seen. Jesus had to tell the truth in order for men to be saved. God is love, but His love is not like a grandfather's indulgence that accepts wrongdoing. His love is the father's ache and acceptance of repentance and obedience. *Only through repentance and obedience can a man ever know the love of God* (cp. Jn.14:21, 23-24; 15:10, 14). God does not accept a man who does wrong and lives unrighteously. Jesus had to tell men the truth, for He could not deceive men. If men wanted to be acceptable to God and live in His love, then they had to turn away from sin and come to God, believing that He exists and diligently seeking Him.

> "But without faith it is impossible to please him: for he that cometh to God must believe that he is, and that he is a rewarder of them that diligently seek him" (Heb.11:6).
>
> "He that hath my commandments, and keepeth them, he it is that loveth me: and he that loveth me shall be loved of my Father, and I will love him, and will manifest myself to him" (Jn.14:21).
>
> "Jesus answered and said unto him, If a man love me, he will keep my words: and my Father will love him, and we will come unto him, and make our abode with him. He that loveth me not keepeth not my sayings: and the word which ye hear is not mine, but the Father's which sent me" (Jn.14:23-24).
>
> "If ye keep my commandments, ye shall abide in my love; even as I have kept my Father's commandments, and abide in his love....Henceforth I call you not servants; for the servant knoweth not what his lord doeth: but I have called you friends; for all things that I have heard of my Father I have made known unto you" (Jn.15:10, 14).

**4** (22:53) **Satan**: joining forces with the power of darkness. What Jesus said was alarming: "This is your hour, *and* the power of darkness." Those who opposed Jesus had joined forces with the power of darkness against Jesus. The power of darkness refers to the forces of evil, the evil one himself, Satan (Eph.6:12; Col.1:13). Note these points about the word "hour."

1. An hour is only a short time. It soon passes. Therefore, the power of darkness and those who oppose the Lord will last but a short time. Their hour will soon pass.

2. The power of darkness is always broken and conquered by light. When light appears, the presence and power of darkness are destroyed. So it is with God's Son, the Light of the world. The power of darkness and those who oppose Christ may have their hour now, but their hour is to end. He, the Light of the world, will arise and dispel the darkness and completely do away with it.

3. An hour soon passes, but then what is left? All the hours of life and of eternity. The power of darkness and those who oppose Christ may have an hour, but that will be all. However He, the Light of the world, will give Light to the world forever.

> "For we wrestle not against flesh and blood, but against principalities, against powers, against the rulers of the darkness of this world, against spiritual wickedness in high places" (Eph.6:12).
>
> "Who hath delivered us from the power of darkness, and hath translated us into the kingdom of his dear Son: in whom we have redemption through his blood, even the forgiveness of sins" (Col.1:13-14).

| | C. Peter's Denial: The Great Tragedy of Denial, 22:54-62 (Mt.26:57, 69-75; Mk.14:53-54, 66-72; Jn.18:15-18, 25-27) | not. 58 And after a little while another saw him, and said, Thou art also of them. And Peter said, Man, I am not. | 3 The denial of discipleship: Denying that one is a follower of Jesus |
|---|---|---|---|
| 1 The cause of denial | 54 Then took they him, and led him, and brought him into the high priest's house. And Peter followed afar off. | 59 And about the space of one hour after another confidently affirmed, saying, Of a truth this fellow also was with him: for he is a Galilaean. | 4 The denial of ignorance: Claiming to know nothing about what is being said |
| a. "Followed afar off" b. "Sat down" in the midst of the crowd | 55 And when they had kindled a fire in the midst of the hall, and were set down together, Peter sat down among them. | 60 And Peter said, Man, I know not what thou sayest. And immediately, while he yet spake, the cock crew. | a. The charge: Emphatic—was with Jesus b. The denial: Emphatic—know nothing about Him |
| 2 The denial of pretension: Pretending not to know Jesus | 56 But a certain maid beheld him as he sat by the fire, and earnestly looked upon him, and said, This man was also with him. | 61 And the Lord turned, and looked upon Peter. And Peter remembered the word of the Lord, how he had said unto him, Before the cock crow, thou shalt deny me thrice. | 5 The answer to denial a. Remembering the Lord's word |
| a. The charge: Was with Jesus b. The denial: Pretends not to know Jesus | 57 And he denied him, saying, Woman, I know him | 62 And Peter went out, and wept bitterly. | b. Getting alone c. Expressing godly sorrow[DS1] |

# DIVISION XI

## THE SON OF MAN'S SUFFERINGS: HIS AGONY, TRIALS, AND CRUCIFIXION, 22:39-23:56

## C. Peter's Denial: The Great Tragedy of Denial, 22:54-62

(22:54-62) **Introduction**: denying Jesus is one of the greatest tragedies in all of life. Yet Jesus is denied often, not only by unbelievers but by believers as well. This passage is a study of denial, the awful tragedy of denying Jesus.

1. The cause of denial (v.54-55).
2. The denial of pretension: pretending not to know Jesus (v.56-57).
3. The denial of discipleship: denying that one is a follower of Jesus (v.58).
4. The denial of ignorance: claiming that one knows nothing about what is being said (v.59-60).
5. The answer to denial (v.61-62).

**1** (22:54-55) **Apostasy—Jesus Christ, Denied**: the cause of denial given in these verses is twofold. Peter failed Jesus and failed Him miserably.

1. "Peter followed afar off." *Following Jesus afar off* means not walking close to Him, not standing and being identified with Him. A man who follows *afar off* is not focusing on Christ. His mind and life are not fixed upon the Lord. His commitment is weak; therefore, he is easily…

* distracted by the world and drawn into its ways.
* stricken with fear—the fear of ridicule, embarrassment, abuse, persecution, being cut off, shunned, ignored, ostracized.

> **"For God hath not given us the spirit of fear; but of power, and of love, and of a sound mind. Be not thou therefore ashamed of the testimony of our Lord" (2 Tim.1:7-8).**

2. Peter "sat down among" the crowd, the crowd which represented the world of rejecters. Very frankly, Peter was failing Jesus miserably. Sitting down among the crowd was the last place he should have been. He, of course, should have never forsaken Jesus. But having fled, he should have been off alone with God in prayer, seeking answers and understanding from God (see notes—Mt.26:51-52; 26:55-56). Or he should have been with the other apostles, leading them to seek the face of God for understanding and direction.

> **"Wherefore come out from among them, and be ye separate, saith the Lord, and touch not the unclean thing; and I will receive you, and will be a Father unto you, and ye shall be my sons and daughters, saith the Lord Almighty" (2 Cor.6:17-18).**

**2** (22:56-57) **Apostasy—Jesus Christ, Denied**: the denial of pretension—pretending not to know Jesus. When confronted, this denial says, "I have nothing to do with Christ."

Note what happened. A maid "earnestly looked" at Peter. She stared at him, observed him closely, thinking she had seen him with Jesus. She concluded that Peter was one of the Lord's followers: "This man was also with Him." There seems to be no threat or danger in this statement to Peter. At worst it seems that it would have led only to some bantering fsand ridicule. The rejecters standing around were naturally bantering back and forth about Jesus and His claims, considering Him to have been a fool. Peter had an opportunity, perhaps, to be a witness for Jesus, humbly sharing about the love and enormous care of Jesus for people. Perhaps he could have helped to turn some who were standing there to Jesus, or at least stopped some of the mob's ridiculing. We must always remember that John was somewhere in the palace as well, and as far as we know, he was maintaining his composure and testimony for Jesus.

Peter cracked under his fear. He denied Jesus, pretending he did not know Him or have anything to do with Him.

> **Thought 1.** Weak believers fear the crowd. When in church they readily profess Christ, but out in the world, at work or at school, they fear being known as believers. They pretend not to know Christ.
>
> > "But whosoever shall deny me before men, him will I also deny before my Father which is in heaven" (Mt.10:33).
> > "A false witness shall not be unpunished; and he that speaketh lies shall not escape" (Pr.19:5).
> > "But sanctify the Lord God in your hearts: and be ready always to give an answer to every man that asketh you a reason of the hope that is in you with meekness and fear" (1 Pt.3:15).

**3** (22:58) **Apostasy—Jesus Christ, Denied**: the denial of discipleship—denying that one is a follower of Jesus. When confronted, this denial is more emphatic and vocal, "I am not a disciple, not a follower of Christ."

Note the charge: "Thou art also *of them*." The charge was true.

⇒ Peter had been with Jesus. He was an apostle; in fact, he was the leader of the apostles.
⇒ Peter was the disciple who had professed that Jesus was the Christ, the Son of God (Mt.16:16).
⇒ Peter was the disciple who had sworn loyalty to Jesus even if it meant death (Mt.26:33-35).

Peter emphatically denied that he was a disciple, a follower of Jesus: "I am not!" Peter was falling (progressing) more and more into sin. He was denying Jesus because he was not by His side, but *standing among* the Lord's rejecters.

⇒ He was standing among the Lord's rejecters because he had fled the Lord.
⇒ He had fled the Lord because he had acted in the flesh (see note—Lk.22:49-51).
⇒ He had acted in the flesh because he had not accepted the Lord's words for what they said.

> "Whosoever therefore shall be ashamed of me and of my words in this adulterous and sinful generation; of him also shall the Son of man be ashamed, when he cometh in the glory of his Father with the holy angels" (Mk.8:38).
> "Be not thou therefore ashamed of the testimony of our Lord, nor of me his prisoner: but be thou partaker of the afflictions of the gospel according to the power of God" (2 Tim.1:8).
> "Be strong and of a good courage, fear not, nor be afraid of them: for the LORD thy God, he it is that doth go with thee; he will not fail thee, nor forsake thee" (Dt.31:6).

**4** (22:59-60) **Apostasy—Jesus Christ, Denied**: the denial of ignorance—claiming that one knows nothing about what is being said. This is the denial that claims ignorance, "I do not know what you are talking about; I know absolutely nothing about the matter." Matthew and Mark say Peter began to curse and swear, *denying any knowledge whatsoever about Jesus.*

Note: this accuser is sure Peter was a follower of Jesus. The man "confidently affirmed," insisted upon the fact. He even identified Peter's nationality, a Galilaean Jew. It was common knowledge that Jesus' disciples were Galilaeans.

Peter's chest was bound to be pounding with emotion and fear. His thoughts were flying, trying to figure how to escape. His emotions just burst forth in cursing and swearing, a forceful denial: "I know not what thou sayest." Note that this denial occurred about one hour after the last one. Peter's failure was a deteriorating failure.

⇒ At first, he pretended not to know Jesus.
⇒ Then he fell even farther. He emphatically denied being a disciple.
⇒ Now, he claimed total ignorance of all. He cursed and swore that he knew absolutely nothing about Jesus.

This is the point: Peter stayed in the crowd, still stood around the rejecters of Jesus—even after they had led him to deny Jesus twice. He was trying to be *of the world*, one of the crowd, when he should have been off praying and seeking to understand the ways of God.

> "Enter not into the path of the wicked, and go not in the way of evil men" (Pr.4:14).
> "Ye therefore, beloved, seeing ye know these things before, beware lest ye also, being led away with the error of the wicked, fall from your own stedfastness" (2 Pt.3:17).
> "They profess that they know God; but in works they deny him, being abominable, and disobedient, and unto every good work reprobate" (Tit.1:16).
> "If we suffer, we shall also reign with him: if we deny him, he also will deny us" (2 Tim.2:12).
> "And in nothing terrified by your adversaries: which is to them an evident token of perdition, but to you of salvation, and that of God" (Ph.1:28).
> "And with many other words did he testify and exhort, saying, Save yourselves from this untoward generation" (Acts 2:40).

**5** (22:60-62) **Repentance—Confession**: three steps were involved in Peter's repentance.

1. Remembering the Lord's words. Apparently while the rooster was crowing, the Lord, standing in the chamber of the palace, turned around and caught the eye of Peter (Lk.22:61). And Peter, eye to eye with the Lord, remembered the words the Lord had spoken to him:

> "And the Lord said, Simon, Simon, behold, Satan hath desired to have you, that he may sift you as wheat: but I have prayed for thee, that thy faith fail not: and when thou art converted, strengthen thy brethren" (Lk.22:31-32).

In the midst of all His own pain and suffering, the Lord's look told Peter that His Lord had not forgotten him. The Lord still loved and cared for Him and wanted his loyalty and service. Jesus had prayed for Peter, and the power of that prayer was now moving in Peter's heart and life. Peter now remembered His Lord's word and that word began to take effect.

2.    Getting alone. Peter left as fast as he safely could from the porch or courtyard through the gate out into the night to get alone at last with God. He was broken, full of anguish and pain for having failed his Lord: he "wept bitterly."

3.    Expressing godly sorrow: repentance (see DEEPER STUDY # 1—2 Cor.7:10).

> "If we confess our sins, he is faithful and just to forgive us our sins, and to cleanse us from all unrighteousness" (1 Jn.1:9).
> "Repent therefore of this thy wickedness, and pray God, if perhaps the thought of thine heart may be forgiven thee" (Acts 8:22).
> "And said, O my God, I am ashamed and blush to lift up my face to thee, my God: for our iniquities are increased over our head, and our trespass is grown up unto the heavens" (Ezra 9:6).
> "Now therefore make confession unto the LORD God of your fathers, and do his pleasure: and separate yourselves from the people of the land" (Ezra 10:11).
> "For mine iniquities are gone over mine head: as an heavy burden they are too heavy for me" (Ps.38:4).
> "For I acknowledge my transgressions: and my sin is ever before me" (Ps.51:3).
> "Thus my heart was grieved, and I was pricked in my reins" (Ps.73:21; cp. Jn.16:8).
> "He that covereth his sins shall not prosper: but whoso confesseth and forsaketh them shall have mercy" (Pr.28:13).
> "Only acknowledge thine iniquity, that thou hast transgressed against the LORD thy God, and hast scattered thy ways to the strangers under every green tree, and ye have not obeyed my voice, saith the LORD" (Jer.3:13).

---

**DEEPER STUDY # 1**

(22:62) **Repentance**: see note and DEEPER STUDY # 1—Acts 17:29-30.

| | | |
|---|---|---|
| | **D. Jesus Tried Before the Sanhedrin Court: The Phenomenal Claims of Jesus, 22:63-71** (Mt.26:57-68; 27:1; Mk.14:53-65; 15:1; Jn.18:12-14, 19-24) | and the chief priests and the scribes came together, and led him into their council, saying, |
| **1 The attitude of religion & the world toward Jesus' claims** <br> a. There is physical & verbal abuse | 63 And the men that held Jesus mocked him, and smote him, <br> 64 And when they had blindfolded him, they struck him on the face, and asked him, saying, Prophesy, who is it that smote thee? <br> 65 And many other things blasphemously spake they against him. | 67 Art thou the Christ? tell us. And he said unto them, If I tell you, ye will not believe: <br> 68 And if I also ask you, ye will not answer me, nor let me go. <br> 69 Hereafter shall the Son of man sit on the right hand of the power of God. <br> 70 Then said they all, Art thou then the Son of God? And he said unto them, Ye say that I am. |
| b. There is formal & legal abuse—a formal trial[DS1] | 66 And as soon as it was day, the elders of the people | 71 And they said, What need we any further witness? for we ourselves have heard of his own mouth. |

Additional right-column headings:

**2 Claim 1: He is the Messiah**

**3 Claim 2: He is the Son of Man, exalted**

**4 Claim 3: He is the Son of God**

**5 Conclusion: The claims understood, but rejected**

# DIVISION XI

## THE SON OF MAN'S SUFFERINGS: HIS AGONY, TRIALS, AND CRUCIFIXION, 22:39-23:56

## D. Jesus Tried Before the Sanhedrin Court: The Phenomenal Claims of Jesus, 22:63-71

(22:63-71) **Introduction**: this is the first trial of Jesus covered by Luke. The thrust of the trial was the phenomenal claims of Jesus, claims which demand a decision from every man.

1. The attitude of religion and the world toward Jesus' claims (v.63-66).
2. Claim 1: the Messiah (v.67-68).
3. Claim 2: the Son of Man, exalted (v.69).
4. Claim 3: the Son of God (v.70).
5. Conclusion: the claims understood, but rejected (v.71).

**1** (22:63-66) **World, Response to Jesus—Persecution, of Jesus Christ—Jesus Christ, Trials of**: the attitude of religion and the world to Jesus' claims. The world and formal religion opposed Jesus. This is clearly seen in the treatment of Jesus during the night while He was being held for trial the next morning.

1. There was (and is today) physical and verbal abuse. They ridiculed and mocked and shamed and beat Him. Why? Because of His claims.

> **"Remember the word that I said unto you, The servant is not greater than his lord. If they have persecuted me, they will also persecute you; if they have kept my saying, they will keep yours also" (Jn.15:20. Also refer to Jn.15:20-25.)**

2. There was ridicule of His spiritual power. If He were the Son of God, He should know all things, so they mocked and challenged His power: "Prophesy, who is it that smote thee?" But God gives no signs, not to the mocking and obstinate and devilish unbeliever. (See note—Mk.8:12.)
3. There were all kinds of blasphemy and cursing spoken against Him. (How tragic! Yet, how much like men today!)

Note the setting for the formal trial of Jesus. This was a trial by the Sanhedrin, the ruling body of the Jews which included both religious and lay leaders (see DEEPER STUDY # 1, *Sanhedrin*—Mt.26:59). Jesus stood before them all on trial for His life. Note the words "came together": they gathered, resorted, *flocked together* just as a body of vultures over their prey. There is also the idea of accompanying. The picture is that of the Jewish leaders flocking or herding together around Jesus, of being called to accompany one another to their respective seats, ready to pounce on Jesus. There is no question about the evil of their hearts. They *were* ready to pounce on and eliminate Him.

The court was stacked against Jesus. The leaders, both lay and religious, had already *determined* to reject and oppose Him. He was a threat to both their nation and their personal security and position. They feared the loss of both, so they were set on killing Him. (For a discussion of the reasons for their opposition, see notes—Mt.12:1-8; note and DEEPER STUDY # 1—12:10; note—15:1-20; DEEPER STUDY # 2—15:6-9; DEEPER STUDY # 3—16:12.)

> **Thought 1.** The religionists rejected and opposed Christ for two primary reasons, the same two reasons that men reject and oppose Him today.
> 1) Men are unwilling to deny self, to surrender all they are and have to Christ. They fear the loss of something—some security, money, position, power, or pleasure. They love the world and self more than they are willing to love God.

2) Men are unwilling to deny their institutional religion: their religious practices that are *man-made*, *man-conceived*, *man-honoring*.

**Thought 2.** Men do *flock together* to oppose Christ. It is easier to oppose Him in the presence of others.

> "Beloved, follow not that which is evil, but that which is good. He that doeth good is of God: but he that doeth evil hath not seen God" (3 Jn.11).
> "Therefore to him that knoweth to do good, and doeth it not, to him it is sin" (Jas.4:17).

---

**DEEPER STUDY # 1**

(22:66-71) **Jesus, Trials of**: there were at least six trials.
1.     An informal trial during the night before Annas (Jn.18:12-14, 19-23).
2.     An informal trial by night before Caiaphas and some Sanhedrin officials to find a charge against Jesus (Mt.26:57-68; Mk.14:53-65; Lk.22:54, 63-65).
3.     An early morning formal trial before a quickly assembled Sanhedrin to secure the verdict of the full Sanhedrin and to formulate the charge against Jesus (Mt.27:1; Mk.15:1; Lk.22:66-71).
4.     A preliminary questioning by Pilate (Mt.27:2, 11-14; Mk.15:1-5; Lk.23:1-5; Jn.18:28-38).
5.     A preliminary questioning by Herod (Lk.23:6-12).
6.     The formal Roman trial before Pilate (Mt.27:15-26; Mk.15:6-15; Lk.23:13-25; Jn.18:39-40).

The other events following Jesus' arrest seem to be:
1.     Peter's denial (Mt.26:58, 69-75; Mk.14:54, 66-72; Lk.22:54-62; Jn.18:15-18, 25-27).
2.     Judas' suicide (Mt.27:3-10; Acts 1:18-19). Both of these events took place between the first and second trial.
3.     Jesus crowned with thorns and severely beaten by the Roman soldiers (Mt.27:27-30; Mk.15:16-19; Jn.19:1-3).
4.     Simon's carrying Jesus' cross (Mt.27:31-32; Mk.15:20-21; Lk.23:26).
5.     Jesus' warning the women of the coming judgment upon Jerusalem (Lk.23:27-31). (See note—Mt.26:57; 26:59.)

---

**2**     (22:67-68) **Jesus Christ, Claims**: Jesus claimed to be the Messiah. The council did not come right out and accuse Jesus. They wanted Him to incriminate Himself; therefore, they questioned Him: "Art thou the Christ [Messiah]? Tell us." But Jesus could not answer, not directly. Note two facts.
1.     They did not understand the true Messiahship of God. God's Messiahship is spiritual and eternal, not physical and material (see note—Eph.1:3). Jesus had come to save men spiritually, not materially. Therefore if He told them, they would not believe; and if He asked them questions which would lead them to the truth, they would not answer. He had done this often (Lk.20:7, 26, 40).
2.     Jesus did not deny His Messiahship. The way He answered the council was an affirmation. Note His exact words, "If I *tell you*, ye will not believe." It was as though He said, "I am, but if I tell you, declare it vocally, you will not believe it." (See notes—Mt.1:1; DEEPER STUDY # 2—1:18; note—Lk.19:36-38 cp. Mk.11:1-11 for concepts of Messiah.)

> "The woman saith unto him, I know that Messias cometh, which is called Christ: when he is come, he will tell us all things. Jesus saith unto her, I that speak unto thee am he" (Jn.4:25-26).
> "Then said Jesus unto them, When ye have lifted up the Son of man, then shall ye know that I am he, and that I do nothing of myself; but as my Father hath taught me, I speak these things. And he that sent me is with me: the Father hath not left me alone; for I do always those things that please him" (Jn.8:28-29).

**3**     (22:69) **Jesus Christ, Claims**: Jesus claimed to be the Son of Man who will be exalted. Jesus was really making three claims.
1.     That He is the Son of Man (see notes—Lk.4:20-21; Jn.1:51; DEEPER STUDY # 3—Mt.8:20. Cp. Dan.7:13-14.)
2.     That He will not remain dead even if they kill Him. He will be raised into God's presence.
3.     That He will be exalted to sit on the right hand of the power of God.

> "And declared to be the Son of God with power, according to the spirit of holiness, by the resurrection from the dead" (Ro.1:4).
> "This Jesus hath God raised up, whereof we all are witnesses. Therefore being by the right hand of God exalted, and having received of the Father the promise of the Holy Ghost, he hath shed forth this, which ye now see and hear. For David is not ascended into the heavens: but he saith himself, The LORD said unto my Lord, Sit thou on my right hand, until I make thy foes thy footstool. Therefore let all the house of Israel know assuredly, that God hath made that same Jesus, whom ye have crucified, both Lord and Christ (Acts 2:32-36).
> "And what is the exceeding greatness of his power to usward who believe, according to the working of his mighty power, which he wrought in Christ, when he raised him from the dead, and set him at his own right hand in the heavenly places, far above all principality, and power, and might, and dominion, and every name that is named, not only in this world, but also in that which is to come" (Eph.1:19-21).
> "Wherefore God also hath highly exalted him, and given him a name which is above every name: that at the name of Jesus every knee should bow, of things in heaven, and things in earth,

and things under the earth; and that every tongue should confess that Jesus Christ is Lord, to the glory of God the Father" (Ph.2:9-11).

**4** (22:70) **Jesus Christ, Claims**: Jesus claimed to be the Son of God. Note several facts.

1.   "They all" now questioned Jesus. The picture is that of an outroar, voices reacting to His claim to be the Son of Man, voices bursting forth together shouting: "Art thou then the Son of God?"

2.   The definite article "*the*" is important. They were not asking if He were *a* son of God like many men claim. They asked if He were "*the* Son of God."

3.   Jesus unquestionably claimed to be "*the* Son of God." (See note—Mk.14:62 for more discussion.)

> "Then they that were in the ship came and worshipped him, saying, Of a truth thou art the Son of God" (Mt.14:33).
>
> "The beginning of the gospel of Jesus Christ, the Son of God" (Mk.1:1).
>
> "And I [John the Baptist] saw, and bare record that this is the Son of God" (Jn.1:34).
>
> "For God so loved the world, that he gave his only begotten Son, that whosoever believeth in him should not perish, but have everlasting life. For God sent not his Son into the world to condemn the world; but that the world through him might be saved. He that believeth on him is not condemned: but he that believeth not is condemned already, because he hath not believed in the name of the only begotten Son of God" (Jn.3:16-18).
>
> "Jesus heard that they had cast him out; and when he had found him, he said unto him, Dost thou believe on the Son of God? He answered and said, Who is he, Lord, that I might believe on him? And Jesus said unto him, Thou hast both seen him, and it is he that talketh with thee" (Jn.9:35-37).
>
> "Say ye of him, whom the Father hath sanctified, and sent into the world, Thou blasphemest; because I said, I am the Son of God?" (Jn.10:36).
>
> "Jesus said unto her, I am the resurrection, and the life: he that believeth in me, though he were dead, yet shall he live: and whosoever liveth and believeth in me shall never die. Believest thou this? She saith unto him, Yea, Lord: I believe that thou art the Christ, the Son of God, which should come into the world" (Jn.11:25-27).
>
> "Of how much sorer punishment, suppose ye, shall he be thought worthy, who hath trodden under foot the Son of God, and hath counted the blood of the covenant, wherewith he was sanctified, an unholy thing, and hath done despite unto the Spirit of grace?" (Heb.10:29).
>
> "Whosoever shall confess that Jesus is the Son of God, God dwelleth in him, and he in God" (1 Jn.4:15).

**5** (22:71) **Jesus Christ, Claims**: the claim of Jesus was understood, but the leaders rejected His claim. Jesus had both accepted and claimed the charge being made against Him. He was...

- The Messiah.
- The Son of God.
- The Son of Man.

They had heard enough. In their obstinate unbelief, they condemned Him to death—condemned the Man who had come to save the world from its terrible plight of sin and death, from its desperate need for health and love and for salvation and life.

> "Even as the Son of man came not to be ministered unto, but to minister, and to give his life a ransom for many" (Mt.20:28).
>
> "For the Son of man is come to seek and to save that which was lost" (Lk.19:10).

## CHAPTER 23

**E. Jesus' First Trial Before Pilate & Herod: The Shirking of Duty & Personal Concern, 23:1-12**
(Mt.27:11-14; Mk.15: 1-5; Jn.18:28-38)

| | | | |
|---|---|---|---|
| **1 The Sanhedrin dragged Jesus to Pilate**DS1 | And the whole multitude of them arose, and led him unto Pilate. | 6 When Pilate heard of Galilee, he asked whether the man were a Galilaean. | e. The attempt to escape one's duty |
| **2 The trial before Pilate: Shirking duty**DS2 | 2 And they began to accuse him, saying, We found this fellow perverting the nation, | 7 And as soon as he knew that he belonged unto Herod's jurisdiction, he sent him to Herod, who himself also was at Jerusalem at that time. | |
| a. The charges DS2 | and forbidding to give tribute to Caesar, saying that he | 8 And when Herod saw Jesus, he was exceeding glad: | **3 The questioning before Herod: Shirking concern** |
| 1) He is a revolutionary | himself is Christ a King. | for he was desirous to see | |
| 2) He opposes taxes | 3 And Pilate asked him, | him of a long season, because | |
| 3) He claims to be a King | saying, Art thou the King of | he had heard many things of | a. He sought the spectacular |
| b. The questioning of Pilate & the claim of Jesus | the Jews? And he answered and said, Thou sayest it. | him; and he hoped to have seen some miracle done by him. | |
| | 4 Then said Pilate to the chief priests and to the people, I find no fault in this | 9 Then he questioned with him in many words; but he answered him nothing. | b. He was the only man Jesus never answered |
| c. The verdict by Pilate: Jesus was innocent | man. | 10 And the chief priests and scribes stood and vehemently accused him. | c. He listened to false charges by religionists |
| | 5 And they were the more fierce, saying, He stirreth up | 11 And Herod with his men of war set him at nought, and mocked him, and arrayed | d. He did not take the Jews seriously: Joked contemptuously |
| d. The bitter protest & enlarged charge | the people, teaching throughout all Jewry, beginning from Galilee to this place. | him in a gorgeous robe, and sent him again to Pilate. | |
| | | 12 And the same day Pilate and Herod were made friends together: for before they were at enmity between themselves. | **4 Conclusion: Pilate & Herod were brought together in their opposition to Jesus** |

# DIVISION XI

## THE SON OF MAN'S SUFFERINGS: HIS AGONY, TRIALS, AND CRUCIFIXION, 22:39-23:56

**E.     Jesus' First Trial Before Pilate and Herod: The Shirking of Duty and Personal Concern, 23:1-12**

(23:1-12) **Introduction**: this passage is a clear portrait of two men who shirked duty and personal concern.
1.     The Sanhedrin dragged Jesus to Pilate (v.1).
2.     The trial before Pilate: shirking duty (v.2-7).
3.     The questioning before Herod: shirking concern (v.8-11).
4.     Conclusion: Pilate and Herod were brought together in their opposition to Jesus (v.12).

[1]  (23:1) **Religionists**: the Sanhedrin dragged Jesus to Pilate. Feelings ran deep. The depth of their obstinate unbelief is seen in the fact that "the *whole multitude* of them arose and led Him to Pilate." Just picture the scene. All members present (seventy one when a full body was present) marched Him to Pilate. They were so opposed to Him that they wanted the full weight of their position and their comrades standing against Him.

**Thought 1.** Observe obstinate unbelievers. They try to convince and secure as much support as possible against Christ and His followers. Why? To protect their worldly desires and security, their position and authority and wealth.

---
**DEEPER STUDY # 1**
(23:1-7) **Pilate**: see DEEPER STUDY # 1—Lk.23:13.
---

[2]  (23:2-7) **Jesus Christ, Trials—Pilate**: the trial before Pilate, a picture of *shirking duty*. Note five points.
1.     The political charges against Jesus were three (see DEEPER STUDY # 2—Lk.23:2).
2.     The questioning of Pilate and the claim of Jesus. This was one of the charges brought against Jesus, and in the eyes of Rome it would be the most serious. Pilate, somewhat surprised by the charge, scornfully asked Jesus, "Art thou the King of the Jews?" Jesus strongly claimed that He was: "Thou sayest it." However, as John points out, Jesus clearly stated that His kingdom was not of this world. His kingdom was spiritual (Jn.18:36-37).

**Thought 1.** Jesus is not a political revolutionary, not a threat to any civil government. He is the King of man's spirit and of heaven, of the spiritual dimension of being, not of earth. He came to rule and reign in the hearts and lives of men, in the realm of the spiritual and eternal, not in the realm of the physical and temporal (see note—Eph.1:3).

3.      The verdict of Pilate: Jesus was innocent. Note: this is a public verdict. Pilate actually pronounced Jesus innocent to the leaders and the people. However, as shall be seen and as is the case with so many, he lacked the *inner strength* to stand by his convictions. He gave in to the world, going along with their wish.

4.      The bitter protest and enlarged charge. The unbelievers, fitfully aroused, accused Jesus. They were closeminded: obstinate, bitter, spiteful. They said He was guilty of leading a revolution throughout all Israel, from Galilee to Jerusalem.

It should be noted that Jesus' purpose was not to defend Himself nor to escape death. His purpose was to surrender to the *sinful behavior* of men. The *sinful behavior* to which He submitted was...

- the very depth of sin itself.
- the ultimate demonstration of sin.
- the greatest sin that could be committed.

The act of sin to which He subjected Himself was the rejection and killing of the Son of God. Standing there before His accusers, He said nothing, enduring their awful indignities. He endured because He was purposed to die for the sins of men.

Note that Pilate actually declared Jesus innocent four different times (Lk.23:4, 14, 15, 22; cp. Jn.18:38; 19:4, 6).

5.      The attempt to escape one's duty (Pilate). Pilate wished to release Jesus, for he knew the Lord was innocent. However, he had to guard against upsetting the leaders of the Jewish nation. He was in a dilemma. When he heard Galilee mentioned, he saw a way out of his dilemma. Herod, who was ruler of Galilee, was in town for the Passover. He could send Jesus over to Herod and let him pass judgment. As a Galilaean, Jesus belonged under the jurisdiction of Herod.

The point to note is this: Pilate lacked the courage to do what was right. He knew Jesus was innocent, yet he sought to *escape his duty* to declare the truth. He made four attempts to shirk his duty. (1) He tried to get the Jews to handle the matter themselves (Lk.18:31). (2) He sent Jesus to Herod (Lk.23:7). (3) He tried to get the Jews to accept Jesus as the prisoner to be released at the Passover (Lk.23:17-19; Mk.15:6). (4) He suggested flogging Jesus and then letting Him go (Lk.23:16).

**Thought 1.** A man who seeks to escape his duty is an unworthy leader. He is not worthy of the responsibility (position, call, or duty).

"A double minded man is unstable in all his ways" (Jas.1:8).
"Draw nigh to God, and he will draw nigh to you. Cleanse your hands, ye sinners; and purify your hearts, ye double minded" (Jas.4:8).
"No servant can serve two masters: for either he will hate the one, and love the other; or else he will hold to the one, and despise the other. Ye cannot serve God and mammon" (Lk.16:13).
"Their heart is divided; now shall they be found faulty" (Hos.10:2).

---

**DEEPER STUDY # 2**

(23:2) **Jesus Christ, Charges Against**: three political charges were levelled against Jesus.

1.      He was charged with perverting the nation, that is, of treason, of being a revolutionary and committing sedition against Rome. The charge, of course, was false. Jesus was not out to pervert people from an earthly nation; He was out to convert people to a heavenly world, to God and His kingdom which were not of this earth (Jn.19:36).

2.      He was charged with disobeying the laws of the nation, in particular for not paying taxes. Of course this charge was also false. Jesus had taught that obedience to earthly government was absolutely essential for the believer. (See outline and notes—Lk.20:19-26.)

3.      He was charged with claiming to be King, with being a rival to Caesar. Again, this charge was false.
   a.   The very reason the Jewish leaders were not accepting Him (so they claimed) was because He had come in the meekness and love of God, not in the armed might of God, liberating their nation from the Roman conquerors (see Deeper Study # 2—Mt.1:18).
   b.   Jesus had actually refused to let the people set Him up as King (Jn.6:15).

---

**3** (23:8-11) **Herod's Hardened Heart**: the questioning before Herod, a picture of shirking personal concern. Herod showed no concern whatsoever for the truth, nor for his own soul. The possibility that the true Messiah might actually be standing before Him never crossed his mind. (See note, pt.3—Lk.3:1. Also see Deeper Study # 1,2, *Herod*—Mt.14:1-14 for more discussion.)

1.      Herod sought only the spectacular. He had heard many things about Jesus, the amazing power and miracles He had manifested. As a ruler, a very special person, Herod wanted and felt he deserved...

- the privilege of some sign.
- the privilege of gazing.
- the privilege of some spectacle.

Jesus' power, of course, was not to be used for the spectacular, not for the purpose of satisfying an unbeliever's curiosity. (See notes—Lk.4:9-12; 11:20 for more discussion.)

2.      Herod was the only man Jesus never answered. Herod's own household had been penetrated with the gospel. Chuza, Herod's personal steward (Lk.8:3), and Manaen, Herod's foster brother (Acts 13:1), were believers. The noble-

man or court official mentioned in the story shared by Jesus was also probably of Herod's court (Jn.4:46). Apparently, the gospel as lived by these persons had little effect upon Herod. Their sharing was but religious foolishness to him. He treated their reports with disdain, perhaps with some abuse. Jesus, knowing the hopelessness of his unresponsive heart, wasted no time and no words upon him. Jesus said nothing to him at all.

3.    Herod listened to false charges by the religionists. He had failed to listen to John the Baptist (Lk.9:7-9) and to the witnesses in his own household. He had heard "many things of Christ" (v.8), yet he had refused to listen, to truly hear and heed. But now, with Jesus standing before him, he listened to the false charges of those who opposed Jesus.

4.    Herod set Jesus at nought, treated Him as unimportant. The word "nought" (exouthenesas) means to count as nothing, to make nothing of, to think something is unimportant, to count as zero—therefore, to treat with utter contempt.

Note the contrast in the verse. Herod sat there as King "with his men of war" surrounding him, and Jesus stood there beaten and battered in torn, ragged clothes. Herod, judging by appearance, counted the Man who claimed to be the Son of God as nothing. This Man and His claim did not matter, not to Herod.

> **Thought 1.** Many count Christ as unimportant. They think He does not matter—that He can be excluded from life, that He and His claim are meaningless. Such people go about counting their own lives and worldly ways dear unto themselves. (Cp. Lk.9:24; 17:33.)
>
> > "Whosoever shall seek to save his life shall lose it; and whosoever shall lose his life shall preserve it" (Lk.17:33).
> >
> > "And take heed to yourselves, lest at any time your hearts be overcharged with surfeiting, and drunkenness, and cares of this life, and so that day come upon you unawares" (Lk.21:34).
> >
> > "He that believeth on the Son hath everlasting life: and he that believeth not the Son shall not see life; but the wrath of God abideth on him" (Jn.3:36).
> >
> > "I said therefore unto you, that ye shall die in your sins: for if ye believe not that I am he, ye shall die in your sins" (Jn.8:24).
> >
> > "Take heed, brethren, lest there be in any of you an evil heart of unbelief, in departing from the living God" (Heb.3:12).

**4** (23:12) **World, Rejection of Jesus**: Pilate and Herod became friends; the worldly are brought together in their opposition against Christ.

**F. Jesus' Second Trial Before Pilate: The Tragedy of a Compromising Man, 23:13-25**
(Mt.27:15-25; Mk.15: 6-15; Jn.18:39-19:16)

**1 Pilate tried to protect himself, selfishly**[DS1]
a. A man who knew the truth
b. A man who tried to appease out of fear
**2 Pilate tried to compromise truth & clear evidence**

13 And Pilate, when he had called together the chief priests and the rulers and the people,
14 Said unto them, Ye have brought this man unto me, as one that perverteth the people: and, behold, I, having examined him before you, have found no fault in this man touching those things whereof ye accuse him:
15 No, nor yet Herod: for I sent you to him; and, lo, nothing worthy of death is done unto him.
16 I will therefore chastise him, and release him.
17 (For of necessity he must release one unto them at the feast.)
18 And they cried out all at once, saying, Away with this man, and release unto us Barabbas.
19 (Who for a certain sedition made in the city, and for murder, was cast into prison.)
20 Pilate therefore, willing to release Jesus, spake again to them.
21 But they cried, saying, Crucify him, crucify him.
22 And he said unto them the third time, Why, what evil hath he done? I have found no cause of death in him: I will therefore chastise him, and let him go.
23 And they were instant with loud voices, requiring that he might be crucified. And the voices of them and of the chief priests prevailed.
24 And Pilate gave sentence that it should be as they required.
25 And he released unto them him that for sedition and murder was cast into prison, whom they had desired; but he delivered Jesus to their will.

**3 Pilate gave in to worldly pressure**
a. He knew the truth: Jesus was innocent
b. He faced loud voices against Jesus
c. He compromised—gave in to the worldly cries
d. He allowed injustice & wrong & sin to be done

# DIVISION XI

## THE SON OF MAN'S SUFFERINGS: HIS AGONY, TRIALS, AND CRUCIFIXION, 22:39-23:56

## F. Jesus' Second Trial Before Pilate: The Tragedy of a Compromising Man, 23:13-25

(23:13-25) **Introduction**: compromising with the world is sin. Compromise always leads to trouble and tragedy. Pilate is the picture of a man whose compromise led to the greatest tragedy in human history.

1. Pilate tried to protect himself, selfishly (v.13-16).
2. He tried to compromise truth and clear evidence (v.17-21).
3. He gave in to worldly pressure (v.22-25).

**1** (23:13-16) **Compromise—Appeasement—Injustice**: Pilate tried to protect himself, selfishly. He called the court back into session. A decision had been made; he was now ready to give his verdict.

⇒ He had examined Jesus and found no fault in Him: Jesus was innocent.
⇒ He had sent Jesus to Herod for a verdict, and Herod found Jesus innocent.
⇒ No crime worthy of death had been committed by Jesus. Pilate had decided, therefore, that he would chastise Jesus and release Him.

Note that Pilate was trying to appease the Jews. He knew the truth: Jesus was innocent. Jesus should be released and the Jews' behavior rebuked, but Pilate feared displeasing and inflaming the Jews. He was afraid they might cause trouble for him, reporting him to Rome and causing him to lose his position and rule (see DEEPER STUDY # 1—Lk.23:13). Throughout the whole scene Pilate's primary interest was himself, not truth and justice.

**Thought 1.** A compromising man is self-centered. He seeks to protect himself even at the expense of the truth and justice. He fears losing…

- position
- power
- influence
- job
- security
- image
- acceptance
- friends

**"Ye shall do no unrighteousness in judgment; thou shalt not respect the person of the poor, nor honour the person of the mighty: but in righteousness shalt thou judge thy neighbour" (Lev.19:15).**

**"How long will ye judge unjustly, and accept the persons of the wicked?" (Ps.82:2).**

"And moreover I saw under the sun the place of judgment, that wickedness was there; and the place of righteousness, that iniquity was there" (Eccl.3:16).

"Therefore have I also made you contemptible and base before all the people, according as ye have not kept my ways, but have been partial in the law" (Mal.2:9).

"I charge thee before God, and the Lord Jesus Christ, and the elect angels, that thou observe these things without preferring one before another, doing nothing by partiality" (1 Tim.5:21).

"I call heaven and earth to record this day against you, that I have set before you life and death, blessing and cursing: therefore choose life, that both thou and thy seed may live" (Dt.30:19).

---

**DEEPER STUDY # 1**

(23:13) **Pilate**: the procurator of Judea. He was directly responsible to the Emperor for the administrative and financial management of the country. A man had to work himself up through the political and military ranks to become a procurator. Pilate was, therefore, an able man, experienced in the affairs of politics and government as well as the military. He held office for ten years which shows that he was highly trusted by the Roman government. However, the Jews despised Pilate, and Pilate despised the Jews for their intense practice of religion. When Pilate became procurator of Judea, he did two things that aroused the people's bitter hatred against him forever. First, on his state visits to Jerusalem, he and his military guard rode their stallions into the city with the Roman standard, an eagle sitting atop a pole. All previous governors had removed the standard because of the Jews' opposition to idols. Second, Pilate launched the construction of a new water supply for Jerusalem. To finance the project, he took the money out of the temple treasury. The Jews never forgot or forgave this act. They bitterly opposed Pilate all through his reign, and he treated them with equal contempt (see DEEPER STUDY # 1—Mk.15:1-15). On several occasions, Jewish leaders threatened to exercise their right to report Pilate to the emperor. This, of course, disturbed Pilate to no end and caused him to become even more bitter and contemptuous toward the Jews.

---

**2** (23:17-21) **Compromise**: Pilate tried to compromise the truth despite clear evidence. He saw the evidence: Jesus was innocent, and the religionists were only envious of Jesus, feeling He was a threat to their security. Pilate wanted to declare Jesus innocent, but he felt he had to satisfy the cries of these religious worldlings as well. Therefore, he conceived a compromise. It was a long time custom for Rome to release a popular prisoner to the Jews at the Passover Feast in order to humor and secure more cooperation from the population. Within the prison was a notorious criminal, Barabbas. Pilate had him brought before the people along with Jesus and shouted out that the people could choose which one was to be released.

Pilate felt sure that by pitting Barabbas against Jesus, the people would choose Jesus, the One who had ministered and helped so many of them. How wrong the man of compromise was. (The world will always cry out against Jesus to get rid of Him.)

The point to note is the moral weakness of Pilate. He knew Jesus was innocent. He knew the Jews sought to kill Jesus because they envied Him. Jesus should have been released immediately, but Pilate attempted a compromise instead of standing up for the truth.

**Thought 1.** Note a crucial point: when the truth is known, it should be proclaimed, not compromised. Compromise results in three tragedies.
1) Compromise weakens character and testimony.
2) Compromise means that the truth is not being done or lived. A person is agreeing to do something less than what he should be doing.
3) Compromise weakens principle, position, and life.

**Thought 2.** God accepts no compromise concerning His Son, Jesus Christ. A man either stands for Christ or against Christ. There is no neutral ground. Christ is innocent and sinless; He is the Ideal Man, the Son of God in whom all men are to place their trust.

"He that is not with me is against me: and he that gathereth not with me scattereth" (Lk.11:23).

"All men should honour the Son, even as they honour the Father. He that honoureth not the Son honoureth not the Father which hath sent him. Verily, verily, I say unto you, He that heareth my word, and believeth on him that sent me, hath everlasting life, and shall not come into condemnation; but is passed from death unto life" (Jn.5:23-24).

"And this is the record, that God hath given to us eternal life, and this life is in his Son. He that hath the Son hath life; and he that hath not the Son of God hath not life" (1 Jn.5:11-12).

"Submit yourselves therefore to God. Resist the devil, and he will flee from you. Draw nigh to God, and he will draw nigh to you. Cleanse your hands, ye sinners; and purify your hearts, ye double minded. Be afflicted, and mourn, and weep: let your laughter be turned to mourning, and your joy to heaviness. Humble yourselves in the sight of the Lord, and he shall lift you up" (Jas.4:7-10).

**3** (23:22-25) **Worldliness—Compromise**: he gave in to worldly pressure. The scene was dramatic, but tragic. The scene can be simply stated. Pilate...
- knew Jesus was innocent (v.22).
- faced loud voices against Jesus (v.23).
- compromised and gave in to the worldly cries (v.24).
- allowed injustice and wrong and sin to be done (v.25).

The point is this: Pilate, the compromising man, was *morally weak*.
- He was not strong enough to do what he knew was right.
- He lacked the moral strength to stand up for Jesus.
- He was too weak to declare the truth.

**Thought 1.** The pressure of the world to do evil is great. Indecision and compromise are not the way to face the world: decisive dedication to Christ and separation from the world alone can conquer the world.

> "I beseech you therefore, brethren, by the mercies of God, that ye present your bodies a living sacrifice, holy, acceptable unto God, which is your reasonable service. And be not conformed to this world: but be ye transformed by the renewing of your mind, that ye may prove what is that good, and acceptable, and perfect, will unto God" (Ro.12:1-2).
> "Wherefore come out from among them, and be ye separate, saith the Lord, and touch not the unclean thing; and I will receive you, and will be a Father unto you, and ye shall be my sons and daughters, saith the Lord Almighty" (2 Cor.6:17-18).
> "Love not the world, neither the things that are in the world. If any man love the world, the love of the Father is not in him. For all that is in the world, the lust of the flesh, and the lust of the eyes, and the pride of life, is not of the Father, but is of the world" (1 Jn.2:15-16).

**Thought 2.** Most men prefer the company of evil, sinful men to that of the Prince of Life. Note: even worldly religionists choose the world over the Prince of Life.

**Thought 3.** Note a crucial point. It is when we are indecisive or willing to compromise that the pressure to do evil gets to us. Hesitating and being indecisive will cause us to give in to the pressure of sin.

> "By faith Moses, when he was come to years, refused to be called the son of Pharaoh's daughter; choosing rather to suffer affliction with the people of God, than to enjoy the pleasures of sin for a season" (Heb.11:24-25).
> "Ye therefore, beloved, seeing ye know these things before, beware lest ye also, being led away with the error of the wicked, fall from your own stedfastness" (2 Pt.3:17).

## G. Jesus' Crucifixion and Its Events,[DS1] 23:26-49
(Mt.27:26-56; Mk.15:16-41; Jn.19:16-37)

1 **The man who bore His cross: A picture of conversion**

2 **The great crowd of mourners: A picture of hearts that feel for Jesus**

3 **The prediction of Jerusalem's doom: A picture of coming judgment**
  a. So terrible, people should weep over
  b. So terrible, people will wish to be childless

  c. So terrible, people will wish to be buried alive

  d. Judgment is inevitable

4 **The identification with criminals: Being numbered with sinners**
5 **The crucifixion: The summit of sin & love**
  a. At Mount Calvary
  b. Between two criminals

6 **The prayer for His enemies: Forgiveness**
7 **The gambling for His clothes: Being stripped by greed**
8 **The mocking: Misunderstanding His salvation**
  a. By the people & religionists
    1) His claim to save
    2) His claim to be Messiah
  b. By the soldiers

26 And as they led him away, they laid hold upon one Simon, A Cyrenian, coming out of the country, and on him they laid the cross, that he might bear it after Jesus.
27 And there followed him a great company of people, and of women, which also bewailed and lamented him.
28 But Jesus turning unto them said, Daughters of Jerusalem, weep not for me, but weep for yourselves, and for your children.
29 For, behold, the days are coming, in the which they shall say, Blessed are the barren, and the wombs that never bare, and the paps which never gave suck.
30 Then shall they begin to say to the mountains, Fall on us; and to the hills, Cover us.
31 For if they do these things in a green tree, what shall be done in the dry?
32 And there were also two other, malefactors, led with him to be put to death.
33 And when they were come to the place, which is called Calvary, there they crucified him, and the malefactors, one on the right hand, and the other on the left.
34 Then said Jesus, Father, forgive them; for they know not what they do. And they parted his raiment, and cast lots.
35 And the people stood beholding. And the rulers also with them derided him, saying, He saved others; let him save himself, if he be Christ, the chosen of God.
36 And the soldiers also

mocked him, coming to him, and offering him vinegar,
37 And saying, If thou be the king of the Jews, save thyself.
38 And a superscription also was written over him in letters of Greek, and Latin, and Hebrew, THIS IS THE KING OF THE JEWS.
39 And one of the malefactors which were hanged railed on him, saying, If thou be Christ, save thyself and us.
40 But the other answering rebuked him, saying, Dost not thou fear God, seeing thou art in the same condemnation?
41 And we indeed justly; for we receive the due reward of our deeds: but this man hath done nothing amiss.
42 And he said unto Jesus, Lord, remember me when thou comest into thy kingdom.
43 And Jesus said unto him, Verily I say unto thee, To day shalt thou be with me in paradise.
44 And it was about the sixth hour, and there was a darkness over all the earth until the ninth hour.
45 And the sun was darkened, and the veil of the temple was rent in the midst.
46 And when Jesus had cried with a loud voice, He said, Father, into thy hands I commend my spirit: and having said thus, he gave up the ghost.
47 Now when the centurion saw what was done, he glorified God, saying, Certainly this was a righteous man.
48 And all the people that came together to that sight, beholding the things which were done, smote their breasts, and returned.
49 And all his acquaintance, and the women that followed him from Galilee, stood afar off, beholding these things.

  1) Offering Him vinegar[DS2]
  2) His claim to be King

9 **The inscription on the cross: A misunderstood charge**

10 **The unrepentant thief: A picture of hardness even in death**

11 **The repentant thief: A picture of true repentance**
  a. Fearing God

  b. Declaring Jesus' righteousness

  c. Asking Jesus for a place in His kingdom

12 **The awesome darkness: A symbol of separation & loneliness**

13 **The torn veil of the temple: A symbol of open access into God's presence**
14 **The great cry of trust: A picture of glorious triumph**

15 **The centurion's declaration: Jesus' righteousness—a confession to be made by many**
16 **The people's grief: A picture of stricken conscience**

17 **The followers of Jesus: A proof that Jesus lived & served well**

# DIVISION XI

## THE SON OF MAN'S SUFFERINGS: HIS AGONY, TRIALS, AND CRUCIFIXION, 22:39-23:56

## G.     Jesus' Crucifixion and Its Events, 23:26-49

(23:26-49) **Introduction**: the crucifixion of Jesus Christ is both the most shocking event and the most wonderful event of human history. It is the most shocking event in that it is the creature murdering the Creator. It is the most wonderful event in that it is the Creator saving the creature. (Glance at the outline above for the *seventeen events* of the crucifixion as covered by Luke.)

**DEEPER STUDY # 1**
(23:26-49) **Crucifixion, The**: see outline, note, and DEEPER STUDY # 1—Mt.27:26-44 for more discussion.

**1** (23:26) **Conversion—Simon of Cyrene**: the man who bore His cross, a picture of conversion. Note several things.

1. God's plan or providence. Nothing happens by chance, not to the Christian believer. God oversees the life of His people. Thus, Simon's being pressed into carrying the cross for Jesus was in the plan of God.

2. Simon was apparently a pilgrim coming to celebrate the Passover. He was standing along the roadway watching the armed procession make its way through the streets. Apparently there was some expression of concern and sympathy for Jesus, something within his heart that was touched and that reached out to Jesus. God knew this, and directed the soldiers to enlist his help in carrying the Lord's cross.

3. Simon was "the father of Alexander and Rufus" (Mk.15:21). The comment by Mark is interesting. Evidently they were known believers (cp. Acts 13:1; Ro.16:13). The indication is that Simon or at least his two sons were eventually converted.

> **Thought 1.** The man who takes up the cross of Christ will be converted.
>
> > **"And he said to them all, If any man will come after me, let him deny himself, and take up his cross daily, and follow me" (Lk.9:23).**

**2** (23:27) **Godly Sorrow—Sympathy**: there was the great crowd of mourners—a picture of hearts that felt for Jesus. A great crowd of people followed and felt for Jesus, especially women. The word "bewailed" (ekoptonto) means to cut, strike, smite, beat. They were cut to the core of their hearts, actually feeling pain for Jesus. The word "lamented" (ethrenoun) means to cry out loud, to mourn, groan. They were crying out, unable to hold back the pain cutting their hearts. Some of the people, of course, had been followers of Jesus for a long time and were feeling the depth of their Lord's sufferings; whereas other onlookers, as in any crowd witnessing severe suffering, felt only a natural tenderness and lament over one's suffering so much.

> **Thought 1.** A natural response to the Lord's sufferings is not enough. A person must *understand* why Christ suffered and must feel a *godly sorrow* over Christ's having to bear the sins of the world (see DEEPER STUDY # 1— 2 Cor.7:10).
>
> > **"For godly sorrow worketh repentance to salvation not to be repented of: but the sorrow of the world worketh death" (2 Cor.7:10).**
> > **"Remember them that are in bonds, as bound with them; and them which suffer adversity, as being yourselves also in the body" (Heb.13:3).**

**3** (23:28-31) **Jerusalem, Prophecy of**: there was the prediction of Jerusalem's doom—a picture of coming judgment. The significant point to note is what was upon Jesus' mind: judgment. The people had rejected God's Messiah and salvation, choosing to go the way of the world, and the way of the world was doom and destruction. The destruction coming would be so terrible, people...

- would weep for themselves.
- would wish to be childless.
- would wish to be buried alive.

Verse 31 is a proverbial saying: if the world (Rome) treats a green tree like this (Him, a tree with its full provision of sap), how will it treat a dry tree like Israel, a tree with little if any provision of sap, a tree of no use, with no life left, ready to be cut down and destroyed?

> **Thought 1.** Jerusalem rejected the invitation of God time and again. However, God was patient and demonstrated His patience for generations, but the rejection and killing of His Son were too great to leave unpunished. As soon as Christianity could get a solid foothold in the world, Jerusalem was to be judged and doomed. (See outline and notes—Lk.20:13-18.)
>
> God is patient with every man. But continued rejection of His Son brings judgment and eternal doom.
>
> > **"For God so loved the world, that he gave his only begotten Son, that whosoever believeth in him should not perish, but have everlasting life. For God sent not his Son into the world to condemn the world; but that the world through him might be saved. He that believeth on him is not condemned: but he that believeth not is condemned already, because he hath not believed in the name of the only begotten Son of God" (Jn.3:16-18).**
> > **"And as it is appointed unto men once to die, but after this the judgment" (Heb.9:27).**

**4** (23:32) **Jesus Christ, Identified with Sinners**: there was the identification with criminals—a picture of being numbered with sinners. Why was Jesus crucified with criminals? Scripture does not say, but perhaps this was a day set aside for execution, or perhaps the Jewish leaders pressed Pilate to execute Jesus with other criminals. By this, they hoped to add weight to their position that He was no more than a mere man, an imposter who deserved to die just as other criminals. Whatever the reason, the fact that the Son of God was executed right along with other criminals adds to the shame and reproach He bore. This event had been prophesied just as many others had (Is.53:12).

**Thought 1.** Christ was counted as a sinner that He might bear the sin of many.

> "He was numbered with the transgressors; and he bare the sin of many, and made intercession for the transgressors" (Is.53:12).

**5** (23:33) **Crucifixion, The**: the crucifixion was the summit of sin and love. The crucifixion itself was the most horrible of deaths. There was the pain of the driven spikes forced through the flesh of Jesus' hands and feet or ankles. There was the weight of His body jolting and pulling against the spikes as the cross was lifted and rocked into place. There was the scorching sun and the unquenchable thirst gnawing away at His dry mouth and throat. There was the blood oozing from His scourged back, His thorn crowned brow, His stick beaten head. In addition, just imagine the aggravation of flies, gnats, and other insects. And for Jesus, there was the piercing pain of the spear thrust into His side. On and on the sufferings could be described. There has never been a more cruel form of execution than crucifixion upon a cross.

The crucifixion took place on a hill called "*the skull*" (in Latin, calvaria). We get the name Calvary from the Latin word. (See note, pt.11—Mt.27:26-38.)

**Thought 1.** In the simplest of terms, Christ was crucified for our sins in order to bring us to God.

> "Who his own self bare our sins in his own body on the tree, that we, being dead to sins, should live unto righteousness: by whose stripes ye were healed" (1 Pt.2:24).
> "For Christ also hath once suffered for sins, the just for the unjust, that he might bring us to God, being put to death in the flesh, but quickened by the Spirit" (1 Pt.3:18).

Note that two criminals were crucified with Him. He was dying because of them and because of all other men. Why? Because all men are criminals against God, rebelling against Him and breaking His commandments.

> "For all have sinned, and come short of the glory of God" (Ro.3:23).
> "This is a faithful saying, and worthy of all acceptation, that Christ Jesus came into the world to save sinners; of whom I am chief" (1 Tim.1:15).
> "For Christ also hath once suffered for sins, the just for the unjust, that he might bring us to God, being put to death in the flesh, but quickened by the Spirit" (1 Pt.3:18).

**6** (23:34) **Forgiveness—Salvation**: there was the prayer for His enemies—a picture of love and forgiveness to the end. The picture is of Jesus the Mediator. He had come for this very purpose, to stand as the Mediator between God and sinful man. Therefore upon the cross, He prayed for those who stood below crucifying Him. Note several things.

1. It had been predicted that Christ would pray for transgressors (Is.53:12).
2. He prayed for God to forgive those who were crucifying Him. The very purpose for His coming was to make provision for forgiveness of sins. Because of His death, God would be able to forgive the sins of men, even those who were now crucifying Him.
3. The men crucifying Him did not know what they were doing. They did not know who He was.

> "None of the princes of this world knew: for had they known it, they would not have crucified the Lord of glory" (1 Cor.2:8).

**Thought 1.** The most wonderful truth in all the world is this: God will hold no sin against any man if that man will personally trust His Son. If God forgives the men who killed His only Son, God will forgive any man for any sin—if that man will just ask.

> "The God of our fathers raised up Jesus, whom ye slew and hanged on a tree. Him hath God exalted with his right hand to be a Prince and a Saviour, for to give repentance to Israel, and forgiveness of sins" (Acts 5:30-31).
> "Repent therefore of this thy wickedness, and pray God, if perhaps the thought of thine heart may be forgiven thee" (Acts 8:22).
> "Be it known unto you therefore, men and brethren, that through this man is preached unto you the forgiveness of sins: and by him all that believe are justified from all things, from which ye could not be justified by the law of Moses" (Acts 13:38-39).
> "In whom we have redemption through his blood, even the forgiveness of sins" (Col.1:14; cp. Col.2:13).

**7** (23:34) **Mortality—Immortality**: there was the gambling for His clothes—a picture of being stripped by the selfishness, greed, and sin of men. Note two points.

1. The custom seems to have been for the executing soldiers to claim whatever they wished of the clothes of crucified criminals. The soldiers stripped Jesus, dividing His clothes among themselves. However, His coat was valuable: it was seamless, one piece of cloth, woven from top to bottom just as the High Priest's coat or cloak was. The soldiers, therefore, decided to gamble by casting lots for it (Jn.19:23-24). This event was foretold in Ps.22:18.
2. Jesus was stripped by the soldiers, stripped of His mortal clothes. There is symbolism in this act: He allowed all His mortality to be stripped so that He might abolish death and bring life and immortality to light.

"But [God's grace] is now made manifest by the appearing of our Savior Jesus Christ, who hath abolished death, and hath brought life and immortality to light through the gospel" (2 Tim.1:10).

**8** (23:35-37) **Salvation**: there was the mockery, the misunderstanding of His salvation. Note those who mocked and taunted Him.

1. The people and religionists mocked His claim to be the Savior and Messiah. They totally misunderstood God's Messiahship. Both the people and the religionists should have been above this kind of behavior. In addition, they had every opportunity to believe, for He had not hid Himself or His message of salvation. But being part of a sinful crowd and their own unbelief, they led each other to do shameful things.

"...Christ [Messiah] Jesus who gave himself a ransom for all, to be testified in due time" (1 Tim.2:5-6).

"This is a faithful saying, and worthy of all acceptation, that Christ [Messiah] Jesus came into the world to save sinners" (1 Tim.1:15).

**Thought 1.** Leaders, civil and religious, are still men. It is not the position or profession that makes a man, but the heart. A heart of unbelief and enmity, a heart willing to become a participant with the sinful crowd, will stoop to do shameful things, no matter the position or profession.

"Behold, your house is left unto you desolate" (Mt.23:38).

2. The soldiers mocked and taunted Him. In particular they mocked His claim to be King, but they did not understand His claim (Jn.18:36. Cp. Jn.18:33-37; Mt.27:11.)

---

**DEEPER STUDY # 2**
(23:36) **Vinegar**: Jesus was offered drugged wine at the beginning of the crucifixion, but He refused it (Mt.27:34; Mk.15:23). He was also offered vinegar just before His death (Jn.19:29), and here the soldiers use vinegar in some form of mockery with Him.

---

**9** (23:38) **Jesus Christ, King**: there was the inscription on the cross—a misunderstood charge. The sign placed above His head, "The King of the Jews," was intended to mock the Jewish authorities and to reproach His claim. However, God overruled and used the sign to proclaim the truth to the whole world (Lk.23:38). The very charges against Jesus proclaimed His deity and honor.

"He humbled himself, and became obedient unto death, even the death of the cross. Wherefore God also hath highly exalted him, and given him a name which is above every name: that at the name of Jesus every knee should bow, of things in heaven, and things in earth, and things under the earth; and that every tongue should confess that Jesus Christ is Lord, to the glory of God the Father" (Ph.2:8-11).

"Our Lord Jesus Christ: which in his times he shall show, who is the blessed and only Potentate, the King of kings, and Lord of lords; who only hath immortality, dwelling in the light which no man can approach unto; whom no man hath seen, nor can see: to whom be honour and power everlasting. Amen" (1 Tim.6:14-16).

**10** (23:39) **Unbelief**: there was the unrepentant thief—a picture of hardness even in death. The thieves heard the crowd mock Jesus about being the Messiah, the Savior of the world. Hanging there as criminals, guilty before God and men, they should have been searching to see if there were any chance that Jesus could have been who He claimed. They needed to be saved and forgiven. One criminal showed enormous hardness of heart. He mocked the very thought that Jesus was the Christ.

"For God so loved the world, that he gave his only begotten Son, that whosoever believeth in him should not perish, but have everlasting life. For God sent not his Son into the world to condemn the world; but that the world through him might be saved. He that believeth on Him is not condemned: but he that believeth not is condemned already, because he hath not believed in the name of the only begotten Son of God" (Jn.3:16-18).

**11** (23:40-43) **Salvation—Repentance**: there was the repentant thief—a picture of true repentance. The second thief demonstrated the steps to salvation and true repentance.
⇒ He feared God (v.40).
⇒ He declared that Jesus was righteous (v.41).
⇒ He asked for Jesus to remember him (v.42).

Note that Jesus promised him eternal life; the repentant man was to be with Christ in paradise *that very day*. (See DEEPER STUDY # 3, *Paradise*—Lk.16:23.)

"Father, I will that they also, whom thou hast given me, be with me where I am; that they may behold my glory, which thou hast given me: for thou lovedst me before the foundation of the world" (Jn.17:24).

"We are confident, I say, and willing rather to be absent from the body, and to be present with the Lord" (2 Cor.5:8).

"For I am in a strait betwixt two, having a desire to depart, and to be with Christ; which is far better" (Ph.1:23).

"If any man serve me, let him follow me; and where I am, there shall also my servant be: if any man serve me, him will my Father honour" (Jn.12:26).

**12** (23:44) **Judgment—Man, State of**: there was the awesome darkness—a symbol of separation and loneliness. The darkness told man something (see note—Mt.27:45 for detailed discussion).
1.  Man was separated from the light.

"And this is the condemnation, that light is come into the world, and men loved darkness rather than light, because their deeds were evil. For every one that doeth evil hateth the light, neither cometh to the light, lest his deeds should be reproved" (Jn.3:19-20).

2.  Man stood all alone. He could not see in the dark, not well. He was, so to speak, standing in the world all alone, responsible for his own behavior; and he must face God someday all alone to give an account for his behavior.

"And it is appointed unto men once to die, but after this the judgment" (Heb.9:27).

**13** (23:45) **Access—Jesus Christ, Blood**: there was the torn veil of the temple—a symbol of open access into the very presence of God. Note four facts.
1.  The veil (curtain) which was torn was the inner veil (katapetasma), the curtain which separated the Holy of Holies from the Holy Place. There was another veil, an outer curtain (kalumma), which separated the Holy Place from the outer court of the temple.
The Holy of Holies was the most sacred part of the temple. It was the place where the very presence of God was symbolized as dwelling in a very, very special way. It was closed *forever* to everyone except the High Priest. Even he could enter the Holy of Holies only once a year, on the Day of Atonement (Ex.26:33).
2.  At the very hour that Jesus died, the High Priest would be rolling back the outer curtain in order to expose the Holy Place to the people who had gathered to worship in the surrounding court. As he rolled back the outer curtain exposing the Holy Place for worship, both he and the worshippers would stand in amazement. Why? Because they would see the inner veil rent from the top to the bottom. There they would stand, experiencing and witnessing the Holy of Holies, the very special place where the presence of God Himself was supposed to dwell—a sight that the people had never seen before.
3.  The veil was torn from top to bottom. This symbolized that it was torn by an act of God Himself. It symbolized God's giving direct access into His presence (Heb.6:19; 9:3-12, 24; 10:19-23). Now, through the body of Christ, any man can enter the presence of God anytime, anyplace.

"By the which will we are sanctified through the offering of the body of Jesus Christ once for all" (Heb.10:10).

4.  The torn veil symbolized that all men could now draw near God by the blood of Christ.

"But now in Christ Jesus ye who sometimes were far off are made nigh by the blood of Christ. For he is our peace, who hath made both one, and hath broken down the middle wall of partition between us" (Eph.2:13-14).

**14** (23:46) **Jesus Christ, Work—Purpose**: there was the great cry of trust—a picture of glorious triumph. What Jesus cried out was one word in the Greek, *Tetelestai*, "It is finished" (Jn.19:30). It was a cry of purpose, a shout of triumph. He was dying for a specific purpose and that purpose was now fulfilled (see note—Mt.27:50 for detailed discussion).

"I am the door: by me if any man enter in, he shall be saved, and shall go in and out, and find pasture....I am the good shepherd: the good shepherd giveth his life for the sheep....As the Father knoweth me, even so know I the Father: and I lay down my life for the sheep....Therefore doth my Father love me, because I lay down my life, that I might take it again. No man taketh it from me, but I lay it down of myself. I have power to lay it down, and I have power to take it again. This commandment have I received of my Father" (Jn.10:9, 11, 15, 17-18).

**15** (23:47) **Confession**: there was the centurion's declaration—Jesus' righteousness, a picture of the confession to be made by many.
1.  The centurion was bound to be a thoughtful and honest man. He was in charge of the crucifixion, which means he was responsible for overseeing all that took place. As the events unfolded upon the cross, he was stricken more and more with the claim of Jesus and the way in which the events were happening. When Jesus shouted out that His purpose was finished, that His death was the climax of His purpose upon earth, the centurion was convinced. The very fact that Jesus'

death was purposeful was the clincher. God quickened to the soldier's heart the glorious truth: "Certainly this was a righteous man."

2.    The centurion was a Gentile. He symbolized all who were to confess Christ in coming generations.

> **"That if thou shalt confess with thy mouth the Lord Jesus, and shalt believe in thine heart that God hath raised him from the dead, thou shalt be saved. For with the heart man believeth unto righteousness; and with the mouth confession is made unto salvation" (Ro.10:9-10).**

**16** (23:48) **Preparation—Conscience:** there was the people's grief—a picture of stricken consciences. The people had come for entertainment, but they went away with saddened, grieving hearts. God, being the Sovereign Lord of the universe, saw to it that they were stricken in conscience. They were being prepared for the preaching to come after Pentecost.

> **"How much more shall the blood of Christ, who through the eternal Spirit offered himself without spot to God, purge your conscience from dead works to serve the living God?" (Heb.9:14).**

**17** (23:49) **Self-Denial:** there were the followers of Jesus—a proof that Jesus lived and served well. Note that the women were at the cross despite the danger. They were off, some distance away, but they were there nevertheless. They still loved and cared, no matter what. They symbolized that Jesus' life was not in vain.

> **"For whosoever will save his life shall lose it; but whosoever shall lose his life for my sake and the gospel's, the same shall save it" (Mk.8:35).**

| | H. Jesus' Burial: A Secret Disciple Stirred to Step Forth, 23:50-56 (Mt.27:57-61; Mk.15:42-47; Jn.19:38-42) | Jesus. 53 And he took it down, and wrapped it in linen, and laid it in a sepulchre that was hewn in stone, wherein never man before was laid. 54 And that day was the preparation, and the sabbath drew on. | f. A man who cared deeply for Jesus 1) He took care of Jesus' body 2) He acted quickly |
|---|---|---|---|
| 1 The secret believer stirred to step forward for Jesus a. A counsellor b. A good & just man c. A man who had feared to stand up for Jesus sometime before d. A man who looked for the Messiah—for God's K. e. A man who was changed by the death of Jesus | 50 And, behold, there was a man named Joseph, a counsellor; and he was a good man, and a just: 51 (The same had not consented to the counsel and deed of them;) he was of Arimathaea, a city of the Jews: who also himself waited for the kingdom of God. 52 This man went unto Pilate, and begged the body of | 55 And the women also, which came with him from Galilee, followed after, and beheld the sepulchre, and how his body was laid. 56 And they returned, and prepared spices and ointments; and rested the sabbath day according to the commandment. | 2 The women stirred to loyalty & affection a. Showed a fearless loyalty b. Showed deep affection c. Showed an ignorance of the resurrection |

# DIVISION XI

## THE SON OF MAN'S SUFFERINGS: HIS AGONY, TRIALS, AND CRUCIFIXION, 22:39-23:56

**H.    Jesus' Burial: A Secret Disciple Stirred to Step Forth, 23:50-56**

(23:50-56) **Introduction**: a secret believer is a tragedy. In a sense he is the tragedy of tragedies, for he fails to confess Jesus publicly. He ignores the fact of what Jesus said: all persons are lost (Mt.10:32-33). Joseph of Arimathaea was such a man: a secret believer until the death of Jesus. But the death of Jesus changed him.
1.    The secret believer stirred to step forward for Jesus (v.50-54).
2.    The women stirred to loyalty and affection (v.55-56).

[1]    (23:50-54) **Discipleship, Secret—Profession—Believer—Jesus Christ, Death**: the secret believer, Joseph of Arimathaea, was stirred to step forward for Jesus. A revealing description is given about Joseph.
1.    He was a counselor, a senator, a member of the Sanhedrin, the ruling body of Israel. Apparently he was …
*   highly educated
*   highly esteemed
*   well liked
*   very responsible
*   capable of leadership
2.    He was a "good and just" man. He was a man…
*   of good quality
*   of high morals
*   of feelings
*   of compassion
*   of justice
*   of decision
*   of truth
*   of law
3.    He was a man looking for the Messiah and the Kingdom of God (see notes—Lk.2:25-27; DEEPER STUDY # 3—Mt.19:23-24).
4.    He was, however, a man who feared to stand up for Jesus. John says he was "a disciple of Jesus, but secretly for fear of the Jews" (Jn.19:38). Joseph probably had met Jesus and arranged private meetings with Him when the Lord had visited Jerusalem, but he feared making a public profession. His position and prestige were at stake. His peers, the other rulers, opposed Jesus. He believed in Jesus, but out of fear he kept his discipleship a secret. Note: when the vote was taken to put Jesus to death, Joseph did abstain from voting, but he did not stand up for Jesus. He did not participate; he simply remained silent.

**Thought 1.** How many persons are like Joseph? They are believers and good and just people; however they fear what their friends and fellow workers will say. They fear the loss of position, prestige, promotion, acceptance, popularity, friends, job, income, livelihood.

"For whosoever shall be ashamed of me and of my words, of him shall the Son of man be ashamed, when he shall come in his own glory, and in his Father's, and of the holy angels" (Lk.9:26).
"And I say unto you my friends, Be not afraid of them that kill the body, and after that have no more that they can do. But I will forewarn you whom ye shall fear: Fear him, which after he hath killed hath power to cast into hell; yea, I say unto you, Fear not" (Lk.12:4-5).
"For God hath not given us the spirit of fear; but of power, and of love, and of a sound mind" (2 Tim.1:7).
"The fear of man bringeth a snare: but whoso putteth his trust in the LORD shall be safe" (Pr.29:25).

"I, even I, am he that comforteth you: who art thou, that thou shouldest be afraid of a man that shall die, and of the son of which shall be made as grass" (Is.51:12).

5. He was a man changed by the death of Jesus. This is seen in two facts.

   a. Joseph actually went to Pilate and begged for the body of Jesus. This was a tremendous act of courage. The Romans either dumped the bodies of crucified criminals in the trash heaps or left the bodies hanging upon the cross for the vultures and animals to consume. The latter served as an example of criminal punishment to the public. Joseph also braved the threat of Pilate's reaction. Pilate was fed up with the *Jesus matter*. Jesus had proven to be very bothersome to him. He could have reacted severely against Joseph.

   b. Joseph risked the disfavor and discipline of the Sanhedrin. They were the ruling body who had instigated and condemned Jesus, and Joseph was a member of the council. There was no question—he would face some harsh reaction from some of his fellow Sanhedrin members and from some of his closest friends.

The thing that turned Joseph from being a secret disciple to a bold disciple seems to be the cross, the phenomenal events surrounding the cross (the behavior and words of Jesus, the darkness, the earthquake, the torn veil, and other events). When Joseph witnessed all this, his mind connected the claims of Jesus with the Old Testament prophecies of the Messiah. Joseph saw the prophecies fulfilled in Jesus. He stepped forward braving all risks and took his stand for Jesus. A remarkable courage! A courage stirred by the death of Jesus.

**Thought 1.** Every secret believer needs to study the cross of Christ. Really seeing the cross will turn any secret believer into a bold witness for Christ.

**Thought 2.** Joseph courageously asked to take care of the physical body of Christ. Today, the body of Christ is the church. We are to boldly step forward and take care of the church. There are special times of need within the church when special courage is needed to step forward and show care. In those times a fresh look at the cross will be helpful and can be used by God to stir us.

"For I determined not to know any thing among you, save Jesus Christ, and him crucified" (2 Cor.2:1).

"Knowing that he which raised up the Lord Jesus shall raise up us also by Jesus, and shall present us with you. For all things are for your sakes, that the abundant grace might through the thanksgiving of many redound to the glory of God" (2 Cor.4:14-15).

"And that he died for all, that they which live should not henceforth live unto themselves, but unto him which died for them, and rose again" (2 Cor.5:15).

6. He was a man who cared deeply for Jesus. The words and acts of these two verses express care and tenderness, love and affection, as well as courage and boldness. Joseph...

   • took the Lord's body down from the cross.
   • wrapped the body in linen.
   • laid the body in a tomb, a tomb wherein no man had ever been laid.
   • acted quickly, before the Sabbath began. Jesus died at 3 p.m. Friday afternoon which was the day of preparation for the Sabbath (cp. Mk.15:33-34, 37). Work was forbidden on the Sabbath, so if anything was to be done with Jesus' body, it had to be done immediately. Only three hours remained for work. (See note—Mk.15:42 for more discussion.)

This act alone would leave no doubt about the effect of the cross upon Joseph. The cross changed his life. He was no longer a secret believer; he now demonstrated a public stand for Jesus.

**Thought 1.** Position, power, wealth, fame—none of these can make us bold for Christ. Only true affection for Christ will make us bold, and only as we see the cross of Christ will affection for Christ be aroused.

**Thought 2.** Christ identified with men perfectly.
   ⇒ He lived as a man—but perfectly.
   ⇒ He died as a man—but perfectly (as the Ideal Man).
   ⇒ He was buried as a man—but perfectly.

"And he made his grave with the wicked, and with the rich in his death; because he had done no violence, neither was any deceit in his mouth" (Is.53:9).

"Wherefore in all things it behoved him to be made like unto his brethren, that he might be a merciful and faithful high priest in things pertaining to God, to make reconciliation for the sins of the people" (Heb.2:17).

**Thought 3.** God's own Son possessed nothing when He was on earth; therefore when He died, He had to be buried in a borrowed tomb. Note two things.
   ⇒ Christ is the Savior of the poorest. He was born in a stable. He had no place of His own to lay His head (Mt.8:20; Lk.9:58). His tomb was a borrowed tomb.
   ⇒ Yet the rich can serve Him just as Joseph of Arimathaea did.

"And Jesus said unto him, Foxes have holes, and birds of the air have nests; but the Son of man hath not where to lay his head" (Lk.9:58).

"Sell that ye have, and give alms; provide yourselves bags which wax not old, a treasure in the heavens that faileth not, where no thief approacheth, neither moth corrupteth" (Lk.12:33).

"I have showed you all things, how that so labouring ye ought to support the weak, and to remember the words of the Lord Jesus, how he said, It is more blessed to give than to receive" (Acts 20:35).

"For ye know the grace of our Lord Jesus Christ, that, though he was rich, yet for your sakes he became poor, that ye through his poverty might be rich" (2 Cor.8:9).

"Hereby preceive we the love of God, because he laid down his life for us: and we ought to lay down our lives for the brethren" (1 Jn.3:16).

**2** (23:55-56) **Jesus Christ, Love for—Eternal Life**: the women believers were stirred to loyalty and affection. Note three facts.

1. The women demonstrated a fearless loyalty despite all danger. At the cross the men forsook Jesus, but not the women (Mt.26:56, 69-75; cp. Mt.27:55-56, 61; Mk.15:41).

2. The women demonstrated a deep affection for Jesus. They took their own money to buy spices and ointments to embalm Jesus. This they did because they loved Him (Lk.23:56; cp. Mt.27:61; Mk.16:1).

3. The women did not yet understand the resurrection of Jesus. They were preparing His body to lie and eventually to decay in the tomb. The true meaning of *living forever—the human body being remade, recreated, and becoming incorruptible*—had not yet been grasped by them (Jn.5:24-29; cp. 1 Cor.15:42f. Cp. 1 Cor.15:1-58.)

**Thought 1.** The testimony of these women should stir men to stand up for Christ. Too often it is the women who take the lead in standing forth for Christ. This should not be the case. Men...

- should be loyal to Christ, no matter how grave the danger.
- should love Christ to such an extent that they give all they *are and have* to Christ.
- should seek to understand and grasp the resurrection of Christ in all its fullness.

"Be not thou therefore ashamed of the testimony of our Lord" (2 Tim.1:8).

"For I am not ashamed of the gospel of Christ: for it is the power of God unto salvation to every one that believeth; to the Jew first, and also to the Greek" (Ro.1:16).

| | CHAPTER 24 | them, Why seek ye the living among the dead? | |
|---|---|---|---|
| | XII. THE SON OF MAN'S GLORY: HIS RES-URRECTION AND ASCENSION, 24:1-53 | 6 He is not here, but is risen: remember how he spake unto you when he was yet in Galilee, | c. Their proclamation<br>d. Their reminder of Jesus' prophecy |
| | A. Jesus' Empty Tomb: Its Discovery, 24:1-12 (cp. Mt.28:1-15; Mk.16: 1-11; Jn.20:1-18) | 7 Saying, The Son of man must be delivered into the hands of sinful men, and be crucified, and the third day rise again.<br>8 And they remembered his words. | |
| 1 The first day of the week<br>2 The first witness of the resurrection | Now upon the first day of the week, very early in the morning, they came unto the sepulchre, bringing the spices which they had prepared, and certain others with them. | 9 And returned from the sepulchre, and told all these things unto the eleven, and to all the rest. | 6 The immediate unbelief of the apostles |
| 3 The great stone rolled away | 2 And they found the stone rolled away from the sepul-chre. | 10 It was Mary Magdalene, and Joanna, and Mary the mother of James, and other women that were with them, which told these things unto the apostles. | a. The message of the resurrection is carried by women—initially |
| 4 The body's missing from the tomb | 3 And they entered in, and found not the body of the Lord Jesus. | 11 And their words seemed to them as idle tales, and they believed them not. | b. The message of the resurrection is accepted as nonsense |
| 5 The two angels & their unbelievable message<br>a. Their dazzling garments<br><br>b. Their question | 4 And it came to pass, as they were much perplexed thereabout, behold, two men stood by them in shining garments:<br>5 And as they were afraid, and bowed down their faces to the earth, they said unto | 12 Then arose Peter, and ran unto the sepulchre; and stooping down, he beheld the linen clothes laid by them-selves, and departed, wonder-ing in himself at that which was come to pass. | 7 The continued unbelief of Peter<br>a. He ran to see—hopefully<br>b. He saw evidence: Linen clothes folded & off to the side<br>c. He wondered |

# DIVISION XII

## THE SON OF MAN'S GLORY: HIS RESURRECTION AND ASCENSION, 24:1-53

### A. Jesus' Empty Tomb: Its Discovery, 24:1-12

(24:1-12) **Introduction**: the tomb was empty. Discovering the empty tomb was the greatest discovery in human history. However, the great tragedy is that most people either are not aware that Jesus arose or do not believe that He arose. Every man has to discover the fact for himself. The empty tomb and the risen Lord have to become a personal discovery for every man.

1. The first day of the week (v.1).
2. The first witnesses of the resurrection (v.1).
3. The great stone rolled away (v.2).
4. The body's missing from the tomb (v.3).
5. The two angels and their unbelievable message (v.4-8).
6. The immediate unbelief of the apostles (v.9-11).
7. The continued unbelief of Peter (v.12).

[1] (24:1) **Jesus Christ, Resurrection**: the first day of the week, Sunday, was the day upon which Jesus arose, the day after the Jewish Sabbath (Saturday). Note three facts.

1. Luke clearly spells out when Jesus arose: "Upon the first day of the week, very early in the morning." Jesus arose before dawn, before the sun arose on Sunday morning. This was significant to the early Christian believers, so significant that they broke away from the common day for worship during the week, the Sabbath or Saturday. They began to worship on Sunday, the day of the resurrection of their Lord (cp. Acts 20:7; 1 Cor.16:2).

2. Jesus arose on the first day of the week, on Sunday morning. This means that He had been in the grave for three days just as He had said (Mt.12:40; 16:21; 17:23; 20:19; Mk.9:31; 10:34; Lk.9:22; 18:33; 24:7, 46). His resurrection from the dead was a triumph, a conquest over death. Death reigns no more—its rule has been broken (1 Cor.15:55-56; 2 Cor.1:9-10; 2 Tim.1:10; Heb.2:9, 14-15).

3. Again, Jesus arose on the first day of the week, Sunday morning. He was in the grave on the Sabbath, unable to observe the laws governing the great season of the Passover and the Sabbath. He was dead; therefore, the law and its ob-servances had no authority over Him. This is symbolic of the *identification* believers gain in Christ. When a man believes in Jesus Christ, God identifies the man with Christ, in particular with the death of Christ. God counts the man as having

died with Christ. Very simply, *in Christ's death* believers become dead to the law (see notes—Ro.7:4; Mt.5:17-18 for more discussion).

**2**  (24:1) **Jesus Christ, Resurrection**: the first witnesses of the resurrection provide strong evidence of the resurrection.

1.  They were actual witnesses of Jesus' *death and burial*. They knew He was dead, and they knew where He had been laid. They had followed along behind the procession to the tomb (Mt.15:40-41, 47; cp. Mt.27:55-56, 61; Lk.23:55-56). There was no question whatsoever in their mind about His being dead and buried.

2.  They had purchased spices and had *come to anoint* Jesus' body. Apparently they had bought the spices Saturday evening after 6 p.m. when the Sabbath ended. Note: they arose "very early in the morning, the first day of the week [Sunday]" to go and embalm Him. Again, they knew He was dead, and they cared; so they wanted to take care of His body just as loved ones care for the bodies of their deceased.

3.  They were religionists who *strictly obeyed the law*. They were strict in the observance of the Sabbath. Imagine—their loved one was dead, yet they would not break the Sabbath law even to take care of Him (cp. Lk.23:56). The women were obedient to the commandments of God. They were *moral and truthful* and would never think, much less consider, lying about the death and resurrection of Jesus.

**3**  (24:2) **Jesus Christ, Resurrection**: there was the great stone rolled away from the entrance (see DEEPER STUDY # 1, *Stone*—Mt.27:65-66). The rolled away stone perplexed the women (v.4). However, the stone had not been rolled back for the benefit of Jesus, but for the witnesses to the resurrection. When Jesus arose, He was in His resurrection body, the heavenly body of the spiritual dimension; and the spiritual dimension has no physical bounds. But the witnesses needed to enter the tomb and see the truth (see outline and notes—Jn.20:1-10).

**4**  (24:3) **Jesus Christ, Resurrection**: there was the body's missing from the tomb. The account is simple, yet striking: "They entered in, and found not the body of the Lord Jesus." They "beheld," saw, contemplated that Jesus was not there (Mk.16:6). They saw the slab upon which He had been laid, and *He was not there*.

> **"And being fully persuaded that, what he had promised, he was able also to perform" (Ro.4:21).**
> **"For all the promises of God in him are yea, and in him Amen, unto the glory of God by us" (2 Cor.1:20).**
> **"If we believe not, yet he abideth faithful: he cannot deny himself" (2 Tim.2:13).**
> **"Whereby are given unto us exceeding great and precious promises: that by these ye might be partakers of the divine nature, having escaped the corruption that is in the world through lust" (2 Pt.1:4).**

**5**  (24:4-8) **Angels—Jesus Christ, Resurrection**: there were the two angels and their message. Note four significant points about the angels.

1.  The angels were radiant, dazzling figures. Their garments shone (Mt.28:3)...
    *   "like lightning" (visible, quick, startling, striking, frightening, brilliant).
    *   "white as snow" (pure, glistening).
Note the women feared and fell down, bowing in reverence.

2.  The angels asked a pointed question: "Why seek ye the living among the dead?" There was a rebuke in the question. They were seeking to honor a dead Savior, a Savior who was as all other men are, frail and powerless to do anything about life and eternity. Their whole being—their thoughts, feelings, and behavior—were focused upon a dead Savior.

They were living just as the world lives—"strangers from the covenants of promise, having no hope, and without God in the world" (Eph.2:12).

3.  The angels proclaimed the glorious news: "He is not here, but is risen." Note two points.
    a.  "He is not here": the women could see and did see the fact. The fact was clearly evident: Jesus was not in the tomb. He had been there, for the women had seen Him put there. They had witnessed His death and burial, but He was no longer in the tomb (see note—Lk.23:55-56).
    b.  "He is risen." Startling, unbelievable words...
        *   yet, heaven "witnessed that He liveth" (Heb.7:8).
        *   yet, Scripture witnesses that He arose (Ro.1:4; Eph.1:19-20).
        *   yet, He had foretold that He would arise (Lk.9:22; 13:32; 17:25; 18:31-34).

> **"And declared to be the Son of God with power, according to the spirit of holiness, by the resurrection from the dead" (Ro.1:4).**
> **"And what is the exceeding greatness of his power to usward who believe, according to the working of his mighty power, which he wrought in Christ, when he raised him from the dead, and set him at his own right hand in the heavenly places" (Eph.1:19-20).**

4.  The angels reminded the women that Jesus had foretold His death and resurrection (see outline and notes—Lk.18:31-34). Note the words, "And they remembered His words." The followers of Jesus had always been confused about the prophecy of His death and resurrection. They *would not* accept his words literally, refusing to take His predictions at face value. They symbolized His statements; therefore, they never understood His death and resurrection (see note—Lk.18:34).

But note what happened now. They knew they had been wrong. Conviction struck them, and they became the very first witnesses to the resurrection.

"But Jesus beheld them, and said unto them, With men this is impossible; but with God all things are possible" (Mt.19:26).

"For with God nothing shall be impossible" (Lk.1:37).

"God is faithful, by whom ye were called unto the fellowship of his Son Jesus Christ our Lord" (1 Cor.1:9).

"If we believe not, yet he abideth faithful: he cannot deny himself" (2 Tim.2:13).

"Let us hold fast the profession of our faith without wavering; (for he is faithful that promised)" (Heb.10:23).

**6** (24:9-11) **Unbelief—Disciples**: the immediate unbelief of the disciples. The women rushed to the disciples to share the glorious news. But the news "seemed to them as idle tales (hos leros): nonsense, ridiculous talk, wild imagination. "They believed them not." The Greek word is *disbelieved* (epistoun) and is in the imperfect active tense which means they "*kept on disbelieving*," kept on putting no trust or confidence in what the women were claiming. They were *gripped* with a skeptical, unbelieving spirit.

**Thought 1.** The disciples were without excuse. Christ had spent month after month drilling His death and resurrection into His disciples. (See notes—Mt.16:21-28; 17:1-13; 17:22; 17:24-27 for more discussion.)

"Afterward he appeared unto the eleven as they sat at meat, and upbraided them with their unbelief and hardness of heart, because they believed not them which had seen him after he was risen" (Mk.16:14).

"He that believeth on him is not condemned: but he that believeth not is condemned already, because he hath not believed in the name of the only begotten Son of God" (Jn.3:18).

"Take heed, brethren, lest there be in any of you an evil heart of unbelief, in departing from the living God" (Heb.3:12).

"Let us labour therefore to enter into that rest, lest any man fall after the same example of unbelief" (Heb.4:11).

**7** (24:12) **Unbelief—Peter**: the continued unbelief of Peter. Peter's heart was still drawn to the Lord despite his enormous failure. Hearing that the body of Jesus was no longer in the tomb, he rushed to the tomb with his thoughts flying, wondering what had happened to the Lord.

Note a crucial point. Peter stooped down and saw the evidence: the linen clothes were lying off to the side by themselves. However, Peter did not grasp the significance of the evidence. John said he had rushed to the tomb with Peter and did believe, based upon the evidence of the linen clothes. He also verifies that Peter did not grasp the significance at this point (see note—Jn.20:1-10 for a discussion of this significant point). Peter just "departed," wondering within himself what had really happened.

**Thought 1.** It is dangerous not to understand the Lord's Word, not to take His Word at face value. Spiritualizing His words, unless the words are clearly symbolic, often leads to serious unbelief and problems.

**Thought 2.** A person has to be open to the evidence of the resurrection. The tomb is empty; He is risen—and the honest and seeking man will be convinced by the Spirit of God. What is needed is to do as Peter did: run to the tomb to see what really did happen.

"Then he said unto them, O fools, and slow of heart to believe all that the prophets have spoken" (Lk.24:25).

"And he said unto them, Why are ye so fearful? how is it that ye have no faith?" (Mk.4:40).

"He that believeth on the Son hath everlasting life: and he that believeth not the Son shall not see life; but the wrath of God abideth on him" (Jn.3:36).

"I said therefore unto you, that ye shall die in your sins: for if ye believe not that I am he, ye shall die in your sins" (Jn.8:24).

**B. Jesus' Appearance to Two Believers on the Road to Emmaus: An Immortal Journey, 24:13-35**
(Mk.16:12-13)

**1 Scene 1: Taking a lonely but thoughtful walk**[DS1]
a. They had heard about the resurrection: "That same day"
b. They thought about & discussed the events

**2 Scene 2: Considering three critical questions**
a. Jesus drew near, but He was unrevealed

b. Question 1: What are you talking about?
1) A gloomy look

2) Answer: The things that have happened

c. Question 2: What events?
1) Jesus' death
a) He was a great prophet

b) He was crucified

c) He was thought to be the Messiah
2) Jesus' prophecy of three days

3) Jesus' empty tomb & perplexing reports

13 And, behold, two of them went that same day to a village called Emmaus, which was from Jerusalem about threescore furlongs.
14 And they talked together of all these things which had happened.
15 And it came to pass, that, while they communed together and reasoned, Jesus himself drew near, and went with them.
16 But their eyes were holden that they should not know him.
17 And he said unto them, What manner of communications are these that ye have one to another, as ye walk, and are sad?
18 And the one of them, whose name was Cleopas, answering said unto him, Art thou only a stranger in Jerusalem, and hast not known the things which are come to pass there in these days?
19 And he said unto them, What things? And they said unto him, Concerning Jesus of Nazareth, which was a prophet mighty in deed and word before God and all the people:
20 And how the chief priests and our rulers delivered him to be condemned to death, and have crucified him.
21 But we trusted that it had been he which should have redeemed Israel: and beside all this, to day is the third day since these things were done.
22 Yea, and certain women also of our company made us astonished, which were early at the sepulchre;

23 And when they found not his body, they came, saying, that they had also seen a vision of angels, which said that he was alive.
24 And certain of them which were with us went to the sepulchre, and found it even so as the women had said: but him they saw not.
25 Then he said unto them, O fools, and slow of heart to believe all that the prophets have spoken:
26 Ought not Christ to have suffered these things, and to enter into his glory?
27 And beginning at Moses and all the prophets, he expounded unto them in all the scriptures the things concerning himself.
28 And they drew nigh unto the village, whither they went: and he made as though he would have gone further.
29 But they constrained him, saying, Abide with us: for it is toward evening, and the day is far spent. And he went in to tarry with them.
30 And it came to pass, as he sat at meat with them, he took bread, and blessed it, and brake, and gave to them.
31 And their eyes were opened, and they knew him; and he vanished out of their sight.
32 And they said one to another, Did not our heart burn within us, while he talked with us by the way, and while he opened to us the scriptures?
33 And they rose up the same hour, and returned to Jerusalem, and found the eleven gathered together, and them that were with them,
34 Saying, The Lord is risen indeed, and hath appeared to Simon.
35 And they told what things were done in the way, and how he was known of them in breaking of bread.

a) Reports of visions
b) Reports of Jesus' being alive

c) Reports confirmed

d. Question 3: Did not the Prophets predict the Messiah's death & resurrection?
1) A mild rebuke
2) His death & resurrection were necessary
3) He explains the Scripture

**3 Scene 3: Experiencing the burning truth—Jesus is risen; He is alive**

a. The two sought to hear more: Invited Him to abide with them
1) He accepted the invitation
2) He blessed the food

b. God opened their eyes: They knew the Lord

c. They had experienced conviction: A burning within their hearts

**4 Scene 4: Proclaiming the immortal witness**
a. The two rushed to the disciples
b. The exciting meeting, the immortal witness: Christ is risen
1) Had been seen by Simon
2) Had been seen by the two from Emmaus

# DIVISION XII

## THE SON OF MAN'S GLORY: HIS RESURRECTION AND ASCENSION, 24:1-53

**B.** **Jesus' Appearance to Two Believers on the Road to Emmaus: An Immortal Journey, 24:13-35**

**(24:13-35) Introduction**: this is one of the most beloved accounts of the resurrection story. It is an account of Jesus' helping two ordinary persons who had lost hope and fallen into the pit of sadness and despair. Their experience was an immortal journey.

1. Scene 1: taking a lonely but thoughtful walk (v.13-14).
2. Scene 2: considering three critical questions (v.15-27).
3. Scene 3: experiencing the burning truth—Jesus is risen; He is alive (v.28-32).
4. Scene 4: proclaiming the immortal witness (v.33-35).

**1** (24:13-14) **Hopelessness—Despair—Devastation**: the first scene was that of a lonely walk by two persons—two persons who were sad, despairing, and very thoughtful.

The day is important: it was "that same day" that the women discovered the empty tomb and reported it to the disciples (the resurrection day, Easter Sunday). The news had been received with skepticism, as utter nonsense. These two, Cleopas and his companion, had either been present or else had heard the news from some other source. As they made their way to Emmaus they were sad, gripped by a spirit of despair over the Lord's crucifixion. Their hope that Jesus was the promised Messiah had been devastated, dashed against the rocks of death. But in their despair, their thoughts were rushing wildly about, entangled, wondering about the report of the women concerning the empty tomb and the angels. What did it mean?

The point to note is their emotions and thoughts, their...
- sadness and despair (over the Lord's death).
- devastated hope (He is not the Messiah).
- rushing and entangled thoughts (over the reports of an empty tomb and angels).

**Thought 1.** The scene is a symbol of the despair that grips so many in life. Their hopes are devastated, hopes for...
- family
- school
- meaning and purpose
- profession
- acceptance

In their sadness and despair, somewhere, they hear reports of the empty tomb and of the living Lord; but they do not know what the reports mean, not personally.

"My soul is weary of my life; I will leave my complaint upon myself; I will speak in the bitterness of my soul" (Job 10:1).
"For my life is spent with grief, and my years with sighing: my strength faileth because of mine iniquity, and my bones are consumed" (Ps.31:10).
"O my God, my soul is cast down within me" (Ps.42:6).
"I sink in deep mire, where there is no standing: I am come into deep waters, where the floods overflow me" (Ps.69:2).
"But as for me, my feet were almost gone; my steps had well-nigh slipped" (Ps.73:2).
"When I thought to know this, it was too painful for me" (Ps.73:16).
"By the rivers of Babylon, there we sat down, yea, we wept, when we remembered Zion" (Ps.137:1).
"The LORD hath forsaken me, and my Lord hath forgotten me" (Is.49:14).
"Withhold thy foot from being unshod, and thy throat from thirst: but thou saidst, There is no hope: no; for I have loved strangers, and after them will I go" (Jer.2:25).
"But I would not have you to be ignorant, brethren, concerning them which are asleep [dead], that ye sorrow not, even as others which have no hope" (1 Th.4:13).
"That at that time ye were without Christ...having no hope, and without God in the world" (Eph.2:12).

---

**DEEPER STUDY # 1**
(24:13) **Emmaus**: the city and location are unknown. It was about seven miles out of Jerusalem, which would take somewhere around two hours to travel by foot.

---

**2** (24:15-27) **Jesus Christ, Death—Misconception—Puzzlement—Questioning—Perplexity**: the second scene was consideration of three questions. Note the exact words as Cleopas and his companion walked along: "*While they communed together and reasoned, Jesus Himself drew near, and went with them*" (suneporeueto, imperfect tense). The idea is that they were so absorbed in their despair and talk that Jesus *was already* walking along with them when they noticed Him. But note: they did not know Him. His resurrected body differed enough that He was not recognized as Jesus without close observation (see DEEPER STUDY # 1—Jn.21:1). In this particular instance, the Lord "held" (restrained, kept) their eyes from recognizing Him as well. Apparently He wanted them to more freely discuss the events with Him.

1. The first question: What are you talking about; what is it that is causing you to look so sad (skuthropoi)? The Greek word means gloomy, dejected, despondent, sullen, overcast. Jesus could see sadness and despair written all over their faces.

Cleopas was surprised that the stranger did not know. "How could anyone be in Jerusalem and not know why we are sad and despairing?" he asked. Terrible things had happened.

**Thought 1.** These two were seeking to understand the death and empty tomb of Christ. Christ was the subject of their conversation. They were seeking the truth; therefore, Christ drew near them.

> "Ask, and it shall be given you; seek, and ye shall find; knock, and it shall be opened unto you: for every one that asketh receiveth; and he that seeketh findeth; and to him that knocketh it shall be opened" (Mt.7:7-8).
>
> "Then said Jesus to those Jews which believed on him, If ye continue in my word, then are ye my disciples indeed; and ye shall know the truth, and the truth shall make you free" (Jn.8:31-32).

2. The second question: "What events? What circumstances could possibly cause such sadness and despair?" (v.19-24). Cleopas answered, covering three subjects.
    a. Jesus' death.
        ⇒ He was a great prophet.
        ⇒ The rulers crucified him. (Note the whole world is implicated. The Jews delivered Him, and the Gentile Romans condemned and crucified Him.)
        ⇒ We had trusted (elpizomen, hoped) that He was the Messiah, the One who was to save Israel.
    b. Jesus' prophecy of three days. There is significance in the term "three days." Cleopas was sharing how their *dead Master* had told them...
        • to watch for the third day, for some unusual event.
        • that He had spoken of "rising again on the third day," whatever that meant.
        • that they thought the words meant that His triumph would take place on the third day. (See outline and notes—Lk.18:31-34 for more discussion.)
    c. Jesus' empty tomb and perplexing reports from certain women, reports...
        • of an empty tomb
        • of a vision of angels
        • of Jesus' being alive
        • that had been confirmed
        • that Jesus was not seen

**Thought 1.** World events and the terrible things that happen in life often make a person sad and despairing—such things as...

| | | |
|---|---|---|
| • being misunderstood | • helplessness | • loss |
| • being opposed | • death | • fear |
| • being deserted | • hopelessness | • injustice |
| • being betrayed | • divisiveness | |

Christ is concerned. He wants to know what it is that causes so much sadness and despair. He wants us to share our problems with Him.

**Thought 2.** The problem with the two from Emmaus, as it is with so many today, was their *shortsightedness* and *unbelief.*

**Thought 3.** There is one major reason why men refuse to accept a risen Lord. A risen Lord means that a man must subject himself to the Lord and obey and serve Him.

> "Therefore let all the house of Israel know assuredly, that God hath made that same Jesus, whom ye have crucified, both Lord and Christ" (Acts 2:36).
>
> "Him hath God exalted with his right hand to be a Prince and a Saviour, for to give repentance to Israel, and forgiveness of sins. And we are his witnesses of these things; and so is also the Holy Ghost, whom God hath given to them that obey him" (Acts 5:31-32).
>
> "Wherefore God also hath highly exalted him, and given him a name which is above every name" (Ph.2:9).

**Thought 4.** Every man should be engrossed in the death of Christ, but he should also believe and be engrossed in the resurrection of the Lord.

> "Who was delivered for our offences, and was raised again for our justification" (Ro.4:25).
>
> "Who is he that condemneth? It is Christ that died, yea rather, that is risen again, who is even at the right hand of God, who also maketh intercession for us" (Ro.8:34).
>
> "Wherefore he is able also to save them to the uttermost that come unto God my him, seeing he ever liveth to make intercession for them" (Heb.7:25).

3. The third question: "Did not the prophets predict Messiah's death and resurrection?" (v.25-27). Note several facts.

    a. Jesus rebuked the two disciples for being dull and slow to believe. He called them "fools" (anoetoi), which means that they were dull and slow to believe. More was expected of them; they should have known more than they were indicating. They were without excuse, for their minds and hearts were capable of more. Therefore, Jesus rebuked them for being...
        • *slow to believe.*
        • slow to believe *all* the prophets had spoken.

b. Jesus shared that the death and resurrection of the Messiah was a necessity. The words "ought not" (ouchi edei) are strong. They mean there was a constraint, an imperative, a necessity laid upon the Messiah to die and arise. He had no choice. His death and resurrection had been planned and willed by God through all eternity. Therefore, He had to fulfill the will of God, for God had ordained...

- that the Messiah suffer these things.
- that the Messiah enter into His glory. God's plan was not defeated. He conquered through the death of His Son, the Messiah.

c. Jesus explained the Scripture to the two disciples, taught them book by book, showing them the things concerning the Messiah in each book. Note the words "all the scriptures." Prophecies of Christ are found in all the Scripture; therefore, Jesus carried the two disciples through the Scripture in a systematic way, book by book, showing them how God's purpose was fulfilled in the death of the Messiah. The two disciples could now be saved eternally, not just during an earthly reign of an earthly Messiah.

**Thought 1.** The two disciples were feeling hopeless and perplexed, full of sadness and despair for one very simple reason: unbelief. They had *symbolized* or *spiritualized* the Scripture and the clear predictions which Jesus had given his disciples before His death. Therefore, they could not see *beyond* Jesus' death. They were willing to accept and admire a *dead Savior*, a great prophet who had been martyred, but they had great difficulty in accepting a risen Lord. They would not believe the reports of the women, the glorious news of the living Lord.

"And their words seemed to them as idle tales, and they believed them not" (Lk.24:11).
"Let us labour therefore to enter into that rest, lest any man fall after the same example of unbelief" (Heb.4:11).
"For consider him that endured such contradiction of sinners against himself, lest ye be wearied and faint in your minds" (Heb.12:3).

**3** (24:28-32) **Conviction—Conversion**: the third scene was experiencing the burning truth—Jesus is risen and alive forevermore. Note three important points.

1. The two disciples *sought* to hear more. They invited Jesus to abide with them. The words "made as though" do not mean Jesus was play-acting. He never pretends. He would have gone on, for He never enters a life or a home without a personal invitation. The two were seeking the truth, so they wanted Jesus to enter their home and to share more with them. (How unlike so many today!)
Jesus did enter, and He sat down to have dinner with them. He was also asked to give thanks for the meal.
2. God opened the eyes of the two disciples. They immediately knew the Lord. But note why: they had invited Jesus into their home. If they had let Him pass on, the likelihood is that they would never have known it was the Lord.
3. The two disciples had experienced a burning conviction within their hearts.
a. The Word of God being proclaimed is what had stirred the conviction and the burning.

"Wherefore thus saith the LORD God of hosts, Because ye speak this word, behold, I will make my words in thy mouth fire, and this people wood, and it shall devour them" (Jer.5:14).
"Is not my word like as a fire? saith the LORD; and like a hammer that breaketh the rock in pieces?" (Jer.23:29).

b. Their response to the conviction—inviting Christ into their home—led to their coming to know Him personally.

"Behold, I stand at the door, and knock: if any man hear my voice, and open the door, I will come in to him, and will sup with him, and he with me" (Rev.3:20).
"God is faithful, by whom ye were called unto the fellowship of his Son Jesus Christ our Lord" (1 Cor.1:9).
"For where two or three are gathered together in my name, there am I in the midst of them" (Mt.18:20).

**Thought 1.** The two had heard the Scripture explained, and they had heard much. But they had to respond, to invite the Lord into their home before God could open their eyes and bring them to a knowledge of Christ.

**4** (24:33-35) **Jesus Christ, Resurrection**: the fourth scene was proclaiming the immortal witness. The scene was dramatic. It was night, but the two rushed back to the apostles. When they arrived, they found the apostles and some other disciples already gathered together.
They were all bursting with excitement. To the shock of the two from Emmaus, the group had the same immortal witness to share: "The Lord is risen. He has appeared to Simon." As they listened to Simon's experience, they were bursting at the seams, hardly able to contain themselves, waiting to share their own experience.
Finally, their time came to share their experience and the very same immortal witness: "The Lord is risen indeed."

"And ye also shall bear witness, because ye have been with me from the beginning" (Jn.15:27).
"Thou shall be his witness unto all men of what thou hast seen and heard" (Acts 22:15).
"And we are witnesses of all things which he did both in the land of the Jews, and in Jerusalem; whom they slew and hanged on a tree: Him God raised up the third day, and showed him openly" (Acts 10:39-40).

| | | | |
|---|---|---|---|
| | **C. Jesus' Appearance to the Disciples: The Great Statements of the Christian Faith, 24:36-49** (Mk.16:14; Jn.20:19-23; 20:26-21:25) | an honeycomb.<br>43 And he took it, and did eat before them.<br>44 And he said unto them, These are the words which I spake unto you, while I was yet with you, that all things must be fulfilled, which were written in the law of Moses, and in the prophets, and in the psalms, concerning me. | **2 Statement 2: All Scripture must be fulfilled**<br>a. The forewarning<br>b. The utter necessity |
| **1 Statement 1: Jesus is risen**<br><br>a. Jesus' first words: Peace | 36 And as they thus spake, Jesus himself stood in the midst of them, and saith unto them, Peace be unto you. | | |
| b. Jesus' impact<br>1) The disciples were terrified & frightened<br>2) The disciples were troubled & questioning | 37 But they were terrified and affrighted, and supposed that they had seen a spirit.<br>38 And he said unto them, Why are ye troubled? and why do thoughts arise in your hearts? | 45 Then opened he their understanding, that they might understand the scriptures, | c. The spiritual insight needed |
| c. Jesus' proof *DS1*<br>1) He is flesh & bones | 39 Behold my hands and my feet, that it is I myself: handle me, and see; for a spirit hath not flesh and bones, as ye see me have. | 46 And said unto them, Thus it is written, and thus it behoved Christ to suffer, and to rise from the dead the third day: | d. The particular prophecies<br>1) Christ must suffer & arise |
| 2) He shows them his wounds | 40 And when he had thus spoken, he showed them his hands and his feet. | 47 And that repentance and remission of sins should be preached in his name among all nations, beginning at Jerusalem. | 2) Repentance & forgiveness must be preached |
| 3) He talks | 41 And while they yet believed not for joy, and wondered, he said unto them, Have ye here any meat?<br>42 And they gave him a piece of a broiled fish, and of | 48 And ye are witnesses of these things.<br>49 And, behold, I send the promise of my Father upon you: but tarry ye in the city of Jerusalem, until ye be endued with power from on high. | 3) The Holy Spirit and power must be sent |

# DIVISION XII

## THE SON OF MAN'S GLORY: HIS RESURRECTION AND ASCENSION, 24:1-53

**C. Jesus' Appearance to the Disciples: The Great Statements of the Christian Faith, 24:36-49**

(24:36-49) **Introduction**: this was the first appearance of Jesus to *all the disciples at once*. He shared the two great statements (explanations) of the Christian faith.
1. Statement 1: Jesus is risen (v.36-43).
2. Statement 2: all Scripture must be fulfilled (v.44-49).

(24:36-49) **Another Outline**: The Great Statements of the Christian Faith.
1. Statement 1: Jesus is risen (v.36-43).
2. Statement 2: All prophetic Scripture must be fulfilled (v.44-46).
   a. The whole Old Testament.
   b. The death and resurrection of Christ.
3. Statement 3: Repentance and forgiveness of sin are imperative (v.47-48).
   a. The place: Among all nations.
   b. The witnesses: You—disciples.
4. Statement 4: Power is to come upon you (v.49).
   a. The power is the Holy Spirit
   b. The power is given by tarrying (praying).

**1** (24:36-43) **Jesus Christ, Resurrection; Impact of; World Response to**: statement one is that Jesus is risen. The scene took place at night—the night of the very day of the Lord's resurrection. It was a dramatic scene. The Lord had already made at least four appearances. The four appearances named were to...
- Mary Magdalene (Jn.20:14f).
- the women visiting the tomb (Mt.28:1f; Mk.16:1f).
- the two walking to Emmaus (Lk.24:1f).
- Simon Peter (Lk.24:34; 1 Cor.15:5).

The apostles (minus Thomas) and some other disciples had rushed to the known meeting place. The very air was electric. Excitement beat in the chest of every one, and minds were grasping for understanding. Wonder was beginning to overcome sadness and despair, and hope was beginning to stir great anticipation. Reports of appearances were being buzzed about and argued about. Then all of a sudden out of nowhere, into the very midst of all this, *"Christ Himself stood."* Note three things:

1.   The very first words Jesus spoke to the disciples after His death: "Peace be unto you." This was the regular greeting of the Jews of that day, but it had a very special significance now. The disciples needed peace, the peace that only He could give. And He had now risen from the dead to give that peace to them. (See note, *Peace*—Jn.14:27.)

> **"But now in Christ Jesus ye who sometimes were far off are made nigh by the blood of Christ. For he is our peace, who hath made both one, and hath broken down the middle wall of partition between us"** (Eph.2:13-14).
> **"Peace I leave with you, my peace I give unto you: not as the world giveth, give I unto you. Let not your heart be troubled, neither let it be afraid"** (Jn.14:27).
> **"These things I have spoken unto you, that in me ye might have peace. In the world ye shall have tribulation: but be of good cheer; I have overcome the world"** (Jn.16:33).

2.   The impact of Christ's resurrection. The disciples interpreted His sudden appearance in their midst just as they had always interpreted His words—spiritually. When He suddenly appeared, the immediate thought flashing across their minds was that a spirit was appearing to them. They were...
*   terrified, frightened, and troubled.
*   questioning.

**Thought 1.** Unbelievers respond to the resurrection in five ways.
1)   They are terrified, frightened, and troubled by the resurrection. Why? Because it means they must obey and serve Christ. If He is the *living Lord*, then man is His subject.
2)   They question the resurrection, the truth of it. The idea that a man could arise from the dead is beyond their acceptance.
3)   They ignore the resurrection, pay no attention to it, and count it as being meaningless.
4)   They respond to the resurrection, accepting Jesus Christ as their Savior and Lord.
5)   They react to the resurrection—react all the way from mild opposition and cursing to the persecution of any who bear witness to the resurrection.

3.   The proof of Christ's resurrection, that He had risen bodily. The outline of the Scripture above shows the four things Christ did to prove that it really was He and not a spirit who stood before the disciples (see DEEPER STUDY # 1—Lk.24:39-43 for discussion).

---

**DEEPER STUDY # 1**

(24:39-43) **Jesus Christ, Resurrection—Resurrection, Body of**: the risen Christ was not a spirit (v.39); not a vision, a phantom, an hallucination, or any other figment of man's imagination. He was the risen Lord—bodily—not someone else nor some other spirit. His body was none other than that of Jesus, the carpenter from Nazareth. He had physically risen from the dead and His body was real. It differed, yes, but it was His body. It was perfected and no longer subject to the limitations and frailties of the physical universe and its laws; it was now glorified by the power and spoken Word of God (cp. Ro.1:3-4).

How did the Lord's resurrected body differ from His earthly body? Some idea can be gleaned by looking at His resurrected body and the glorified body promised to the believer.
1.   The resurrected body of the Lord was His body, but it was radically changed. It had all the appearance of a physical body, but it was not bound by the physical world and its material substance.
   a.   It was the same body, not some other body. We know this because His resurrected body bore the marks of the nails in His hands and feet (Jn.20:20, 27), and the disciples could recognize Him after close observation.
   b.   It was a body that could travel and appear anyplace, at will and by thought—a body unhampered by space, time, material, or substance. When He appeared it was suddenly, even behind locked doors (Lk.24:36; Jn.20:19).
   c.   It was a body that differed enough that it was not clearly recognized at first, not until it was closely observed.
      ⇒   Mary Magdalene thought He was the gardener (Jn.20:15).
      ⇒   The two disciples walking toward Emmaus thought He was a traveller (Lk.24:31).
      ⇒   The disciples who were fishing did not recognize Him standing on the seashore (Jn.21:4).
   However, after close observation, the Lord was recognized in all these instances.
2.   The resurrected, glorified body that is promised to the believer gives some additional insight into the kind of body Christ has. One of the most wonderful promises ever made to man is given in the words:

> **"Who shall change our vile body, that it may be fashioned like unto his glorious body, according to the working whereby he is able even to subdue all things unto himself"** (Ph.3:21; cp. Mt.13:43; Ro.8:17; Col.3:4; Rev.22:5).
> **"[We shall be] conformed to the image of His Son"** (Ro.8:29; cp. 1 Cor.15:49; 2 Cor.3:18).
> **"Beloved, now are we the sons of God, and it doth not yet appear what we shall be: but we know that, when he shall appear, we shall be like him; for we shall see him as he is"** (1 Jn.3:2).

The body of the believer will undergo a radical change just as the Lord's body was radically changed. Several changes are promised the believer.

a. The believer shall receive a spiritual body.

> **"There is a natural body [soma psuchikon] and there is a spiritual body [som a pneu-matikon]" (1 Cor.15:44).**

Note: the spiritual body (soma) still retains the qualities of the earthly body (soma). The same Greek word is used for both bodies. The difference lies in that it will not be a natural (soulish) body but will be a spiritual body. What does this mean? In essence, the body will be perfected; no longer subject to pain, tears, death, sorrow, or crying (Rev.14:4).
- ⇒ "It is sown in corruption; it is raised in incorruption."
- ⇒ "It is sown in dishonor; it is raised in glory."
- ⇒ "It is sown in weakness; it is raised in power."
- ⇒ "It is sown a natural body; it is raised a spiritual body."

Note that the body is the same body on earth that it will be in heaven. The body just undergoes a radical change of nature. The believer will be the same person in heaven that he is on earth, differing only in that he is perfected. Also note the strong, emphatic declaration: *"There is* a natural body, and *there is* a spiritual body" (1 Cor.15:42-44).

b. The believer shall receive a body that is not "flesh and blood." Flesh and blood are corruptible; they age, deteriorate, die and decay.

> **"Flesh and blood cannot inherit the kingdom of God; neither doth corruption inherit incorruption" (1 Cor.15:50).**

c. The believer shall receive a body that shall be radically changed.

> **"In a moment, in the twinkling of an eye, at the last trump: for the trumpet shall sound, and the dead shall be raised incorruptible, and we shall be changed. For this corruptible must put on incorruption, and this mortal must put on immortality" (1 Cor.15:52-53).**

d. The believer shall be given a body that will not need reproduction for continuing the (redeemed) human race.

> **"In the resurrection they neither marry, nor are given in marriage, but are as the angels of God in heaven" (Mt.22:30).**

**2** (24:44-49) **Prophecy, Fulfilled—Jesus Christ, Death**: statement two is that all Scripture must be fulfilled. Note four points:

1. The forewarning Jesus had given in His predictions. His death and resurrection—the literal events happening just as He had said they would—should not have been a surprise. He had foretold the events and forewarned His followers. (See outline and notes—Lk.18:31-34.)

**Thought 1.** Scripture predicts much that is to happen in the future. However...
- some still will not accept and believe.
- some still spiritualize the predictions.

The greatest of all tragedies is that some still do not accept and believe the Lord's death and resurrection despite the irrefutable evidence.

2. The utter necessity that Christ die and arise. The word "must" (dei) means that His death was an imperative, a necessity, a constraint.

> **"Till heaven and earth pass, one jot or one tittle shall in no wise pass from the law, till all be fulfilled" (Mt.5:18).**
> **"Him, being delivered by the determinate counsel and foreknowledge of God, ye have taken, and by wicked hands have crucified and slain: whom God hath raised up, having loosed the pains of death: because it was not possible that he should be holden of it" (Acts 2:23-24).**
> **"And Paul, as his manner was, went in unto them, and three sabbath days reasoned with them out of the scriptures, opening and alleging, that Christ must needs have suffered, and risen again from the dead; and that this Jesus, whom I preach unto you, is Christ" (Acts 17:2-3).**

Note that Christ gave the three divisions of the Old Testament: the law, the prophets, and the psalms. The whole Old Testament prophesied of His coming and His salvation.

3. The spiritual insight needed to understand the Scriptures. Christ opened the disciples' eyes so they could understand.

> **"But the natural man receiveth not the things of the Spirit of God: for they are foolishness unto him: neither can he know them, because they are spiritually discerned" (1 Cor.2:14; cp. 1 Cor.2:9-14).**

4. The particular prophesies were threefold.
   a. Christ must suffer and arise (see outline and note—Lk.18:31-34).
   b. Repentance and forgiveness must be preached (see notes and Deeper Study # 1—Acts 17:29-30; Deeper Study # 4—Mt.26:28).
   c. The Holy Spirit and power must be sent. As the disciples went forth witnessing, they were to be given the *wonderful* promise (the Holy Spirit) and power of the Father. (See outline and notes, *Holy Spirit*—Jn.14:15-26; 16:7-15 for a discussion of the prophecies concerning the Holy Spirit which Christ had given to the disciples.) Note two points.
      1) The believer was to be equipped for witnessing.
         ⇒ He was to receive the promise of the Father (the Holy Spirit).
         ⇒ He was to receive power, being clothed (endusesthe) with power.
      2) The source of the spirit and power was God.
         ⇒ Christ was to send the promise.
         ⇒ The promise was "of the Father." God gave the promise.
         ⇒ Believers had to tarry, that is, wait upon the Lord and pray for the promise.
         ⇒ The promise was to come from "on high." God Himself was the Source of power for all evangelism.

> "But ye shall receive power, after that the Holy Ghost is come upon you: and ye shall be witnesses unto me both in Jerusalem, and in all Judaea, and in Samaria, and unto the uttermost part of the earth" (Acts 1:8).
>
> "And when he is come, he will reprove the world of sin, and of righteousness, and of judgment" (Jn.16:8).
>
> "Now unto him that is able to do exceeding abundantly above all that we ask or think, according to the power that worketh in us" (Eph.3:20).

| | D. Jesus' Last Appearance: The Ascension,[DS1] 24:50-53 (Mk.16:19-20; Acts 1:9-11) |
|---|---|
| **1 The purpose of the ascension** <br> a. To bless <br><br> b. To provide a witness & give great assurance <br><br> **2 The disciples' response to the ascension** <br> a. Worshipped Him <br> b. Were filled with joy <br> c. Worshipped in the temple—continually | 50 And he led them out as far as to Bethany, and he lifted up his hands, and blessed them. <br> 51 And it came to pass, while he blessed them, he was parted from them, and carried up into heaven. <br> 52 And they worshipped him, and returned to Jerusalem with great joy: <br> 53 And were continually in the temple, praising and blessing God. Amen. |

# DIVISION XII

## THE SON OF MAN'S GLORY: HIS RESURRECTION AND ASCENSION, 24:1-53

## D. Jesus' Last Appearance: The Ascension, 24:50-53

(24:50-53) **Introduction**: Luke closes his gospel with the ascension of Christ and begins Acts with the ascension of Christ (Acts 1:9-11). The ascension closes the Lord's earthly ministry, His mission to save the world. Therefore, the ascension can be said to be the final chapter, the close, the consummation of His journey upon earth. On the other hand, the ascension opens the Lord's heavenly ministry, His mission of intercession for the world and His mission of bearing witness through the lives of believers. Therefore, the ascension can be said to be the first chapter, the opening, the beginning of His journey into heaven as the Risen Lord. In heaven, Jesus Christ is the risen Lord who is the propitiation "for the sins of the whole world" (1 Jn.2:1-2).

1. The purpose of the ascension (v.50-51).
2. The disciples' response to the ascension (v.52-53).

---

**DEEPER STUDY # 1**

(24:50-53) **Jesus Christ, Ascension**: the Lord ascended to the right hand of God, that is, to the position of sovereignty and power (cp. Mk.16:19; Lk.22:69; Acts 1:9-11; 2:36; 5:31; Eph.1:20; Ph.2:9-11; Rev.5:12). The ascension assures (proves, confirms) that seven things are absolutely certain.

1. The ascension assures that God *is*, that He is alive and does exist. The fact that Christ was raised up from the dead and "carried up into heaven" (Lk.24:51) proves that God is. Only God could do such a thing (1 Cor.6:14; 2 Cor.4:14; cp. Jn.3:16. Cp. Acts 2:24, 32; 3:15, 26; 4:14; 5:30; 10:40; 13:30, 33-34; 17:31.)

2. The ascension assures that Christ is God's Son. The very fact that God raised up Christ and "received [Him] up into heaven" proves that Christ is God's Son (Ro.1:3-4; Ph.2:5-11).

3. The ascension assures that heaven is real (Ph.3:20-31).

4. The ascension assures that the gospel is true. When God raised up Christ and received Him into heaven, God validated the message of Christ. What Christ proclaimed and revealed was true: man faces a critical problem, the problem of sin and death and a future of condemnation and separation from God. However, man can be saved by the cross of Christ (Mk.16:16; 1 Pt.2:24).

5. The ascension assures that the Great Commission is the call and mission of believers. Two things show this. First, Christ has ascended into heaven; therefore, He is gone, no longer on earth. If the gospel is to be carried to the ends of the earth, believers have to do it. They are the ones left on earth to do it. Second, it is the risen and ascended Lord who gave the Great Commission. *As the ascended Lord*, He demands that His commission be fulfilled (Mk.16:15; cp. Mt.28:19-20).

6. The ascension assures that power is available to carry out the Great Commission (Mt.28:18; cp. Mk.16:20).

7. The ascension assures that we have a very special Helper in heaven, One who really loves and cares for us. He is One who is "touched with the feeling of our infirmities, [the One who was] in all points tempted like as we are, yet without sin" (Heb.4:15). Therefore, He is ever ready to forgive and to look after us through all of life.

---

**1** (24:50-51) **Jesus Christ, Ascension**: the purpose of the ascension. Two general purposes are given by Luke (see note, *Ascension*—Acts 1:9).

1. The first general purpose of the ascension was to bless the disciples. This was His final blessing, and note: it was the last thing He did on earth. His last gesture and act was to bless His disciples. This showed several things.

    a. It showed that He was the High Priest who had the power to make the sin-offering for them and to bless them with the gift of peace with God. (Cp. Aaron, Lev.9:22.)

> "And Aaron lifted up his hand toward the people, and blessed them, and came down from offering of the sin offering, and the burnt offering, and peace offerings" (Lev.9:22).

b.   It showed that His blessing was the blessing coming from the ascended Lord who was *in heaven* exalted to the right hand of God.

> "And what is the exceeding greatness of his power to us-ward who believe, according to the working of his mighty power, which he wrought in Christ, when he raised him from the dead, and set him at his own right hand in the heavenly places, far above all principality, and power, and might, and dominion, and every name that is named, not only in this world, but also in that which is to come" (Eph.1:19-21).
> "Now unto him that is able to do exceeding abundantly above all that we ask or think, according to the power that worketh in us" (Eph.3:20).

c.   It showed that His blessing was forever, without end, even to the end of the world.

> "Teaching them to observe all things whatsoever I have commanded you: and, lo, I am with you away, even unto the end of the world" (Mt.28:20).

d.   It showed that His blessing was unlimited, from their ascended and *eternal Lord*.

> "And he is before all things, and by him all things consist" (Col.1:17).
> "I am Alpha and Omega, the beginning and the end, the first and the last" (Rev.22:13).

e.   It showed that His blessing was upon them as they went forth as His representatives, witnessing for Him.

> "Go ye therefore, and teach all nations, baptizing them in the name of the Father, and of the Son, and of the Holy Ghost: teaching them to observe all things whatsoever I have commanded you: and, lo, I am with you away, even unto the end of the world" (Mt.28:19-20).

2.   The second general purpose of the ascension was to provide a witness and give great assurance (see DEEPER STUDY # 1—Lk.24:50-53).

[2]   (24:52-53) **Ascension, Results**: the disciples' response to the ascension was threefold.

1.   The disciples worshipped Christ. The ascension stirred worship. Why? The disciples now knew beyond question that He was the true Messiah, the Son of God Himself. He had ascended to the right hand of God; therefore, He was due all the homage, adoration, and praise due God.

> "Philip saith unto him, Lord, show us the Father, and it sufficeth us. Jesus saith unto him, Have I been so long time with you, and yet hast thou not known me, Philip? he that hath seen me hath seen the Father; and how sayest thou then, Show us the Father? Believest thou not that I am in the Father, and the Father in me?" (Jn.14:8-11).
> "And being found in fashion as a man, he humbled himself, and became obedient unto death, even the death of the cross. Wherefore God also hath highly exalted him, and given him a name which is above every name: that at the name of Jesus every knee should bow, of things in heaven, and things in earth, and things under the earth; and that every tongue should confess that Jesus Christ is Lord, to the glory of God the Father" (Ph.2:8-11).

2.   The disciples were filled with joy.
  a.   They were filled with joy because their Lord was now exalted and privileged to take His rightful place: sitting at the right hand of God and being worshipped eternally. They were filled with joy and rejoicing *for Him*.
  b.   They were filled with joy because they now knew that His presence would always be with them. When on earth physically, He could only be in one place and with only a few people at a time. But now, since ascending, He could send His Spirit to dwell with believers everywhere (Omnipresent). Nothing would ever again be able to *separate* their Lord from them.

> "Nevertheless I tell you the truth; It is expedient for you that I go away: for if I go not away, the Comforter will not come unto you; but if I depart, I will send him unto you" (Jn.16:7).
> "Who shall separate us from the love of Christ? shall tribulation, or distress, or persecution, or famine, or nakedness, or peril, or sword?...For I am persuaded, that neither death, nor life, nor angels, nor principalities, nor powers, nor things present, nor things to come, nor height, nor depth, nor any other creature, shall be able to separate us from the love of God, which is in Christ Jesus our Lord" (Ro.8:35, 38-39).

3.    The disciples were in the temple continually. The temple was the focus of God's presence and worship, and it was the center of teaching, the place where the people were instructed in the Scriptures. The disciples were bound to focus their lives in the temple or church...

- because Christ had taught that the temple was His "Father's house" and "the house of prayer."

> **"Saying unto them, It is written, My house is the house of prayer: but ye have made it a den of thieves" (Lk.19:46).**
> **"And said unto them that sold doves, Take these things hence; make not my Father's house an house of merchandise" (Jn.2:16).**

- because they wished to praise God for sending the Messiah and to bear public testimony of Him.
- because the temple was the chosen place of God to manifest His presence among His people (see note— 1 Cor.3:16).

> **"Go, stand and speak in the temple to the people all the words of this life" (Acts 5:20).**
> **"Not forsaking the assembling of ourselves together, as the manner of some is; but exhorting one another: and so much the more, as ye see the day approaching" (Heb.10:25).**

# THE

# OUTLINE & SUBJECT INDEX

REMEMBER: When you look up a subject and turn to the Scripture reference, you have not only the Scripture, you have an outline and a discussion (commentary) of the Scripture and subject.

This is one of the GREAT VALUES of **The Preacher's Outline & Sermon Bible**™. Once you have all the volumes, you will have not only what all other Bible indexes give you, that is, a list of all the subjects and their Scripture references, BUT you will also have...

- An outline of every Scripture and subject in the Bible.
- A discussion (commentary) on every Scripture and subject.
- Every subject supported by other Scriptures or cross references.

DISCOVER THE GREAT VALUE for yourself. Quickly glance below to the very first subject of the Index of Luke. It is:

ABASE - ABASED
Caused by. Selfishness & godless independence.                          Lk.15:14-16

Turn to the reference. Glance at the Scripture and outline of the Scripture, then read the commentary. You will immediately see the GREAT VALUE of the INDEX of **The Preacher's Outline & Sermon Bible**™.

## OUTLINE & SUBJECT INDEX

# INDEX

# INDEX

Position.
- God's Son. — Lk.15:30
- Not above Master, but treated same as the Master. — Lk.6:40

Privileges of.
- Avenged by God. — Lk.18:6-8
- Discussed. — Lk.10:21-24
- Known by God. — Lk.16:19-21
- Trusted by Christ. — Lk.8:23
- Truth revealed to. — Lk.10:21

Secret b. Stirred to step forth by the cross. — Lk.23:50-56

## BENEDICTUS
Song of Zacharias. — Lk.1:67-80

## BETHLEHEM
City of Jesus' birth. Prophesied. — Lk.2:3

## BETHPHAGE
Discussed. — Lk.19:29

## BETROTHED
Engagement before marriage. — Lk.1:27

## BIRDS
Fed by God. — Lk.12:24

## BLASPHEMY
Against the Holy Spirit. — Lk.12:4-12

## BLESSINGS
Misconceptions of. Sign of God's b. — Lk.16:14-15

## BLIND - BLINDNESS, SPIRITUAL
- Caused by. Spiritual dullness. — Lk.9:44-45
- Parable of. Blind leading the blind. — Lk.6:39
- Results. Causes others to be blind (followers, children). — Lk.6:39

## BOASTING
Caused by. Self-sufficiency. — Lk.10:21

## BODY
- Deformed. How to keep from worrying about. — Lk.12:25
- Duty. Not to be anxious about the b. even if deformed. — Lk.12:22-28; 12:25
- Indulgence of. (See INDULGENCE)

## BOLDNESS
Results. Stirs one to step forward for Christ. — Lk.23:50-56

## BONDAGE
- List of. Several things. — Lk.9:47
- What enslaves. Sin, worldliness. — Lk.15:14-16

## BOOK OF LIFE
Duty. To rejoice that one's name is written in. — Lk.10:20

## BORROW - BORROWING (See LENDING)

## BOTTLES
New vs. old b. New life & joy. Purpose of Jesus. — Lk.5:36-39, esp. 37-38

## BRIDEGROOM
Symbolizes. Jesus death. Mission of dying. — Lk.5:35

## BROKEN-HEARTED (See CONTRITION; SORROW, GODLY)
- Healed by Jesus. — Lk.4:17-19
- Touches Christ. — Lk.7:12-13

# INDEX

# INDEX

# INDEX

# INDEX

# INDEX

# INDEX

# INDEX

# INDEX

# INDEX

# INDEX

# INDEX

# INDEX

MARY, MOTHER OF JESUS
    Acknowledged that she needed a Savior.        Lk.1:47-48
    An event for all generations.        Lk.1:47-48
    Discussed. Character of.        Lk.10:38-39
    Humility of.        Lk.1:47-48
    Magnificent song describing God.        Lk.1:46-56
    Proclaimed to be blessed. Reasons.        Lk.1:45
    Submission to God's will.        Lk.1:26-38
    Virgin. Proof.        Lk.1:27
    Visited Elizabeth, John the Baptist's mother.        Lk.1:39-45

MASTER
    Fact. Cannot serve two masters.        Lk.16:13
    Title of Jesus (epistata). Meaning.        Lk.17:11-14

MATERIALISM (See MONEY; RICHES; WEALTH)
    Caused by - Source. Distraction.        Lk.10:40
    Discussed.        Lk.9:23-27; 12:13-21
        Sin of.        Lk.16:19-21
        The man of wealth.        Lk.12:13-21
        Worldly are more dedicated to m. than believers are to
            their pursuits.        Lk.16:8
    Duty.
        Christian & m. Parable of Unjust Steward.        Lk.16:1-13
        Not to be anxious about.        Lk.12:22-34
        Not to seek m., but to trust God.        Lk.12:29-30
        To know that all belongs to God. Man is a steward of.        Lk.16:12
        To use for good by helping others.        Lk.16:9
    Judgment of. Nine reasons listed.        Lk.9:26
    Misconception - Misunderstanding. One of three great m.        Lk.16:14-15
    Results.
        Causes one to lose self.        Lk.9:23-27
        Chokes the Word.        Lk.8:7, 14
        Determines eternal responsibility.        Lk.16:10-12
        Distracts from the essential.        Lk.10:40
        Perils of. Discussed.        Lk.6:20-26
        Used as an excuse for rejecting Jesus.        Lk.14:18-20
    Vs. being spiritually minded.
        Discussed.        Lk.12:13-21
        Seeking m.        Lk.9:46
    Vs. Christ.
        Cannot serve two masters.        Lk.16:13
        Ct. Christ.        Lk.16:14-15
        Preferred over salvation & Jesus.        Lk.8:35-37
    Warning against.
        Craving for more and more.        Lk.21:34-35
        Discussed.        Lk.9:23-27

MATTHEW - LEVI, THE APOSTLE
    Call of.        Lk.5:27-32

MATURITY (See GROWTH, SPIRITUAL)

MEDITATE - MEDITATION
    Verses. List of.        Lk.9:36; 10:41-42

MERCY
    Duty. To cry for m.        Lk.17:12-14; 18:36-38
    Meaning.        Lk.18:13
    Neglect of. Causes a man to lose his soul.        Lk.16:19-21

MESSAGE (See PREACHING)
    Content.
        Peace.        Lk.10:5-6
        Social justice.        Lk.3:10-14
        The kingdom of God.        Lk.4:43-44; 8:1; 9:59-60; 10:8-9

# INDEX

# INDEX

# INDEX

# INDEX

POWERLESSNESS
    Caused by. Lack of faith & a wayward heart.      Lk.9:37-45; 9:42-43

PRAISE
    Discussed.      Lk.14:7-14

PRAY - PRAYER - PRAYING (See DEVOTION)
    Answers - Answered.
        Assured.      Lk.11:11-13
        Reason God delays answer.      Lk.18:6-8
        Why God does not always answer.      Lk.11:5-10
    Discussed.      Lk.11:1-13; 18:1-8; 18:9-14
        Great subject of p.      Lk.11:1-13
        Model p. of Jesus      Lk.11:2-4
    Duty.
        To p. all through life.      Lk.3:21
        To p. constantly.      Lk.2:37; 3:21
        To p. seeking to be re-strengthened.      Lk.4:42
        To p. while being baptized.      Lk.3:21
        To watch & p. for end time.      Lk.21:34-36
    Essential.
        For teaching, discipling, quickening.      Lk.9:18; 9:28
        In facing trials.      Lk.9:28
        To persevere in p.      Lk.18:1
    For what. Great things, even healing.      Lk.18:39
    For whom. Laborers.      Lk.10:2
    Hindrances.
        P. to oneself only.      Lk.18:11-12
        Self-righteousness.      Lk.18:11-12
    How to p.
        Disciples ask how.      Lk.11:1-13
        Man's part & God's part.      Lk.11:5-10
        Spirit needed for p.      Lk.18:9-14
    Kinds.
        Fellowship vs. concentrated p.      Lk.6:12
        Self-righteous vs. humble. Of Pharisee & Publican.      Lk.18:10-14
    Perseverance in.
        Discussed.      Lk.11:5-10
        Secret of prayer.      Lk.18:1-8
        Verses. List of.      Lk.9:28; 11:5-10; 11:11-13
        Why Jesus demands. Two reasons.      Lk.17:11-14
    Prayer life of Christ. (See JESUS CHRIST, Prayer Life)
    Results - Assurance.
        Protects against temptation.      Lk.22:40, 46
    When to p. Three significant times.      Lk.9:18-19

PREACHING
    Call to. Primary c.      Lk.8:1
    Discussed.      Lk.8:1
    Duty.
        To p. peace.      Lk.10:5-6
        To p. social justice.      Lk.3:10-14
        To p. the kingdom of God.      Lk.9:59-60; 10:8-9
    Meaning.      Lk.8:1
    Message of. Kingdom of God.      Lk.4:43-44; 8:1; 9:59-60; 10:8-9
    Mission.
        Of Christ.      Lk.4:17-19
        Of John the Baptist. Eight points.      Lk.3:7-20
    Response to.
        Fourfold.      Lk.8:4-15
        Refuse to hear.      Lk.6:27-31

PREJUDICE
    Broken down - Abolished.
        By compassion.      Lk.10:29-37
        By Jesus' ministry.      Lk.17:15-19
    Caused by. Listed.      Lk.9:49-50
    Results. Prevents compassion.      Lk.10:29-37

# INDEX

# INDEX

# INDEX

Acts - Behavior of.
    Looking back. — Lk.9:61-62
    Misleading others. — Lk.11:44; 17:1-2
    Neglect. — Lk.16:19-21
    Omitting justice & love. — Lk.11:42
    Omission. Determines reward. — Lk.19:15-23
    Perverse. — Lk.9:41
    Powerlessness. — Lk.9:37-40
    Putting heritage before present need. — Lk.11:47-51
    Reluctant obedience. — Lk.9:57-62
    Scandalous s. Public s. — Lk.18:11-12
    Seeking position. — Lk.11:43
    Seeking titles. — Lk.11:43
    Self-indulgence. — Lk.16:19-21
    Self-righteousness. — Lk.18:9
    Self-trust. — Lk.18:9
    Taking away the key of knowledge about God. — Lk.11:52
    Turning back. — Lk.17:31-33
    Wayward heart. — Lk.9:41
Against Christ. Terrible. Four s. — Lk.22:47-53
And suffering. Thought to be the cause of suffering. — Lk.13:1-9
Deliverance from.
    Forgiven because of friends' perseverance. — Lk.5:18-20
    Forgiveness of. Discussed. — Lk.5:21-26
Described. As insanity. — Lk.15:17-19
Duty.
    To confess sin. (See CONFESSION)
    To preach against. — Lk.3:7-20
    To rebuke sin in high places. — Lk.3:19-20
Exposed. (See JUDGMENT)
    Known by Christ. — Lk.12:1-3
    Verses. List of. — Lk.8:17; 12:1-3
Facts about. Inevitable. No place is perfect. (See FORGIVENESS) — Lk.17:1-2
Judgment of. (See JUDGMENT)
Meaning.
    Big "I." — Lk.12:16-19
    Selfishness. — Lk.12:16-19
Results.
    Emptiness. — Lk.15:11-16
    Enslaves. — Lk.15:14-16
    Humiliation. — Lk.15:15
    Judgment. — Lk.17:1-2
    Truth about. — Lk.13:1-9
    Unpardonable s. — Lk.12:10
Secret (See SIN, Exposed)
    Results. Misleads others. — Lk.11:44
    To be exposed. — Lk.12:1-3
Symbol - Type of. Leprosy. — Lk.5:12-16
Unpardonable s. Blasphemy against the Holy Spirit. — Lk.12:10

SIN AND SUFFERING
    Not because of sin. — Lk.13:1-9


SINNER - SINNERS
    And Christ.
        Jesus associates with. — Lk.5:27-32
        Jesus came to save. — Lk.5:27-32
    Deliverance.
        Attitude necessary. — Lk.18:13
        Must repent. — Lk.5:30-32
        Prayer necessary. — Lk.18:13-14
        S. saved. — Lk.7:36-50
    Fact. All men are s. — Lk.13:1-9

SLEEPINESS (See SLOTHFUL)

# INDEX

# INDEX

# PURPOSE STATEMENT

## LEADERSHIP MINISTRIES WORLDWIDE

exists to equip ministers, teachers, and laymen in their
understanding, preaching, and teaching of God's Word
by publishing and distributing worldwide
*The Preacher's Outline & Sermon Bible*®
and related *Outline* Bible materials,
to reach & disciple men, women, boys, and girls for Jesus Christ.

# •MISSION STATEMENT•

1. To make the Bible so understandable - its truth so clear and plain - that men
   and women everywhere, whether teacher or student, preacher or hearer,
   can grasp its Message and receive Jesus Christ as Savior; and...
2. To place the Bible in the hands of all who will preach and teach God's Holy
   Word, verse by verse, precept by precept, regardless of the individual's
   ability to purchase it.

The *Outline* Bible materials have been given to LMW for printing and especially
distribution worldwide at/below cost, by those who remain anonymous. One fact,
however, is as true today as it was in the time of Christ:

**• The Gospel is free, but the cost of taking it is not •**

LMW depends on the generous gifts of Believers with a heart for Him and a love and
burden for the lost. They help pay for the printing, translating, and placing *Outline*
Bible materials in the hands and hearts of those worldwide who will present God's
message with clarity, authority and understanding beyond their own.

LMW was incorporated in the state of Tennessee in July 1992 and received IRS 501(c) 3 nonprofit status in March 1994. LMW is an international, nondenominational mission organization.
All proceeds from USA sales, along with donations from donor partners, go 100% into under-
writing our translation and distribution projects of *Outline* Bible materials to preachers,
church & lay leaders, and Bible students around the world.

9/98

Box 21310 - Chattanooga, TN 37424 • (423) 855-2181 • FAX (423) 855-8616
• E-Mail - outlinebible@compuserve.com — www.outlinebible.org •

# *Equipping God's Servants Worldwide*

1. **PAYMENT PLANS**. Convenient and affordable ways to get/use your FullSet with easy payments.

2. **NEW TESTAMENT**. In 14 volumes. Deluxe version 3-ring binders. Also: SoftBound Set, 3 volume set, and NIV edition. All on 1 CD-ROM disc.

3. **OLD TESTAMENT**. In process; 1 volume releases about every 6-8 months, in sequence.

4. **THE MINISTERS HANDBOOK**. Acclaimed as a "must-have" for every minister or Christian worker. Outlines more than 400 verses into topics like Power, Victory, Encouragement, Security, Restoration, etc. Discount for quantities.

5. **THE TEACHER'S OUTLINE & STUDY BIBLE™**. Verse-by-verse study & teaching; 45 minute lesson or session. Ideal for study, small groups, classes, even home schooling. Each book also offers a STUDENT JOURNAL for study members.

6. **OUTLINE BIBLE CD-ROM.** Includes all current volumes and books; Preacher, Teacher, and Minister Handbook. 1 disc. WORDsearch STEP format. Also 50+ Bible study tools unlockable on same disc.
**FREE Downloads - www.outlinebible.org**

7. THE **OUTLINE**. Quarterly newsletter to all users and owners of *POSB*. Complimentary.

8. **LMW AGENT PLAN**. An exciting way any user sells *OUTLINE* materials & earns a second income.

9. **DISTRIBUTION**. Our ultimate mission is to provide *POSB* volumes & materials to preachers, pastors, national church leaders around the world. This is especially for those unable to purchase at U.S. price. USA sales gain goes 100% to provide volumes at affordable prices within the local economy.

10. **TRANSLATIONS**. Korean, Russian, & Spanish are shipping first volumes — Others in-process: Hindi, Tamil, Telugu, Chinese, French, German, Finnish.

11. **FUNDING PARTNERS**. To cover the cost of all the translations, plus print, publish, and distribute around the world is a multi million dollar project.

    **Church-to-Church** Partners send *Outline* Bible books to their missionaries, overseas church leaders, Bible Institues and seminaries...at special prices.

12. **REFERRALS**. Literally thousands (perhaps even you!) first heard of *POSB* from a friend. Now Referral Credit pays $16.00 for each new person who orders from a customer's Referral.

13. **CURRICULUM & COPYRIGHT**. Permission may be given to copy specific portions of *POSB* for special group situations. Write/FAX for details.

9/98

**For Information about any of the above, kindly FAX, E-Mail, Call, or Write**

# Please PRAY 1 Minute/Day for LMW!

PO Box 21310, Chattanooga, TN 37424 • (423) 855-2181 • FAX (423) 855-8616
• E-Mail - outlinebible@compuserve.com — www.outlinebible.org •

# Sharing

The OUTLINED BIBLE

# With the World!

ISBN 1-57407-004-5

90000

9 781574 070040